CONTEMPORARY'S COMPLETE GED

Coordinating Editor
Patricia Mulcrone, Ed.D.
Professor Emerita
Adult Educational Development
William Rainey Harper College
Palatine, Illinois

Contributing Authors

Critical Thinking Skills—Patricia Mulcrone

Language Arts, Writing—Linda W. Nelson, Associate Professor/Co-Chair

Social Studies—Kathleen D. Millin and Suzanne E. Rausch, Instructors

Science—Suzanne E. Rausch and Kathleen D. Millin

Language Arts, Reading—Patricia Mulcrone and Linda W. Nelson

Mathematics—Janice S. Phillips, Associate Professor

McGraw Hill Wright Group

Special thanks to: LeRoy T. Mulcrone, Schaumburg, IL, consultant for Language Arts, Reading and Social Studies; Anthony A. Nelson, Rolling Meadows, IL, consultant for Language Arts, Writing.

Reviewers

Elaine Bartell, Kathy Brown, Don Dutton, Rick Sousa, Gladys Uri—GED Instructors
Grossmont Adult School, La Mesa, CA

Barbara Daley, Rebecca Bohlen, Bevan Gibson, Patricia Teutrine, Joan Gregery, Colleen Potter—GED Instructors
Southern Illinois Professional Development Center, Edwardsville, IL

Gerald B. Fox, Donald H. Mitchell, Albert L. Geer, Oscar Lynch—Correctional Education Program Teachers
Arizona Department of Corrections

Senior Editor: Paula Eacott
Executive Editor: Linda Kwil
Creative Director: Michael E. Kelly
Marketing Manager: Sean Klunder
Production Manager: Genevieve Kelley
Manager of Editorial Services: Sylvia Bace
Interior Design by Think Design Group LLC

McGraw Hill Wright Group

ISBN: 0-8092-9469-9

Send all inquiries to:

Wright Group/McGraw Hill
130 East Randolph Street, Suite 400
Chicago, IL 60601

Printed in the United States of America.

8 9 10 CUS CUS 07 06 05

The McGraw·Hill Companies

Table of Contents

SOCIAL STUDIES

LANGUAGE ARTS, READING

MATHEMATICS

POSTTESTS

PRACTICE TESTS

Acknowledgments

The editors have made every effort to trace the ownership of all copyrighted material, and necessary permissions have been secured in most cases. Upon notification of any oversight, proper acknowledgment will be made in future editions.

Excerpt on page 4 is adapted from "Select batteries according to how they will be used," Reprinted from the (November 26, 2000) issue by permission of the *Daily Herald*, Arlington Heights, Illinois

Excerpt on page 14 is from "I Have a Dream" speech by Martin Luther King, Jr. Reprinted by arrangement with The Heirs to the Estate of Martin Luther King Jr., c/o Writers House as agent for the proprietor. Copyright 1963 Martin Luther King Jr., renewed 1991 by Coretta Scott King.

Chart on page 17 "Europeans not stingy with holidays, vacation," is from *Chicago Tribune*, August 7, 2000. Copyrighted 2000, Chicago Tribune Company. All rights reserved. Used with permission.

Excerpt on page 19 is from From *Indian Oratory: Famous Speeches by Noted Indian Chieftains* by W. C. Vanderwerth. Copyright © 1971 by the University of Oklahoma Press. Reprinted by permission.

Photo caption on page 22 is from *Chronicle of America* (Dorling Kindersley), copyright © 1997 Dorling Kindersley Ltd. Reprinted by permission of Dorling Kindersley Ltd.

Graphic and text on page 31 is from "How Cells divide," as appeared in *The Daily Herald*, March 31, 2000. Reprinted with permission of AP/Wide World Photos.

Photo and caption on page 35 are reprinted from *How in the World?* copyright © 1990 The Reader's Digest Association Limited. Used by permission of The Reader's Digest Association, Inc., Pleasantville, NY, www.rd.com.

Excerpt on page 40 is from *Message in a Bottle* by Nicholas Sparks. Copyright © 1998 by Nicholas Sparks. By permission of Little, Brown and Company (Inc.).

Excerpt on page 44 is from *Saint Joan* by George Bernard Shaw. Reprinted by permission of The Society of Authors on behalf of the Bernard Shaw Estate.

Excerpts on page 46 are from Anne Frank, *The Diary of A Young Girl by Anne Frank*, copyright 1952 by Otto H. Frank. Used by permission of Doubleday, a division of Random House, Inc.

Standards on page 191 are permission granted from GEDTS (General Educational Development Testing Service) A program of ACE (American Council on Education).

Essays and scores on pages 193–195 and 209–210 are permission granted from GEDTS (General Educational Development Testing Service) A program of ACE (American Council on Education).

Excerpt on page 238 from "Stem Cells Opening Path to Brain Repair," *Chicago Tribune*, June 27, 1999. Copyrighted 1999, Chicago Tribune Company. All rights reserved. Used with permission.

Excerpt on page 239 from "Living With the Myth" by Evan Thomas. From *Newsweek*, July 26, 1999. © 1999 Newsweek, Inc. All rights reserved. Reprinted by permission.

Excerpt on page 244 is from "When you need help climbing out of debt," by Jean Sherman Chatzky as appeared in *USA Weekend*, Feb. 18–20, 2000. Reprinted by permission of Jane Sherman Chatzky, contributing editor, *USA Weekend*.

Excerpt on page 245 adapted from Gloria Steinem, *Revolution From Within*, (New York: Little Brown and Company, 1992), p. 66.

Excerpt on page 247 is from "Don't Cut it Out" by Jon Van and Ronald Kotulak, Chicago Tribune, October 31, 1999. Copyrighted 1999, Chicago Tribune Company. All rights reserved. Used with permission.

Excerpt on page 249 from "The Legacy of Leontis," from *Collected Stories*, Lake View Press, Chicago, IL 1986, copyright by Harry Mark Petrakis. Reprinted by permission.

Excerpts on page 252 are from "Latin American Tall Tree Canopies Not Only Get Conservationists' Nod, but Sellers Say Brew Tastes Richer," as appeared in *The Daily Herald*, December 26, 1998. Reprinted with permission of The Associated Press and from "Coffee is Made in the Shade," as appeared in The Daily Herald, December 26, 1998. Reprinted with permission of The Associated Press.

Excerpt on page 267 is abridged from *7 Habits 11 years later* by Stephen Covey as appeared in *USA Weekend*, July 7-9, 2000. Used with permission. All rights reserved. www.franklincovey.com

Excerpt on page 269 is from "Business," by Steven L. Kent from *Sky* Magazine, April 2000. Reprinted by permission of Steven L. Kent.

Table on page 276 is from Table 1 Average Fixed Costs for Undergraduates, 2000–2001, "Trends in College Pricing, 2000," page 4. Copyright © 2000 by College Entrance Examination Board. Reprinted with permission. All rights reserved. www.collegeboard.com

Excerpt on page 331 is from *We Americans: A Volume in the Story of Man Library.* NGS BOOKS/NGS Image Collection

Excerpt on page 373 is adapted from *How the United States Government Works* by Nancy Gendron Hofmann, Ziff-Davis Press, 1995. Reprinted by permission.

Figure on page 408 is from *Consumer Economics in Action*, 1st edition, by Miller/Stafford, © 1993. Reprinted with permission of South-Western Educational Publishing a division of Thomson Learning. Fax 800 730-2215.

Graph on page 410 "Unemployment Continues Decline," is from the *Chicago Tribune*, October 7, 2000. Copyrighted 2000, Chicago Tribune Company. All rights reserved. Used with permission.

Graph on page 412 "Bringing the Market Home," is from *Chicago Tribune*, September 28, 2000. Copyrighted 2000, Chicago Tribune Company. All rights reserved. Used with permission.

Chart on page 420 is from "Stats," *Chicago Tribune*, October 1, 2000. Copyrighted 2000, Chicago Tribune Company. All rights reserved. Used with permission.

Chart on page 421 is from Forrester Research, Inc., September, 2000. Reprinted by permission.

Table on page 442 is from *World Population: Challenges for the 21st Century* by Leon F. Bouvier and Jane T. Bertrand. © 1999 by Leon F. Bouvier and Jane T. Bertrand. Reprinted by permission of Seven Locks Press.

Figure on page 472 is from "A Brave, New World Emerging at Biopharms," *Chicago Tribune*, February 8, 1998. Copyrighted 1998, Chicago Tribune Company. All rights reserved. Used with permission.

Figures and captions on page 563 are from *College Physics, Fourth Edition* by Raymond A. Serway and Jerry S. Faughn, copyright © 1995 by Raymond A. Serway, reproduced by permission of the publisher.

Excerpt on page 591 is from Eudora Welty, *A Curtain of Green and Other Stories*, (Orlando: Harcourt Brace and Company,1941).

Excerpt on page 594 is from *Winter Dreams.* Reprinted with permission of Scribner, a Division of Simon & Schuster, from *The Short Stories of F. Scott Fitzgerald*, edited by Matthew J. Bruccoli (New York: Scribner, 1989).

Excerpt on page 598 is from Robert James Waller, *The Bridges of Madison County* (New York: Warner Books, Inc., 1992), p. 31.

Excerpt on page 604 reprinted with permission of Scribner, a Division of Simon & Schuster, from *The Old Man And The Sea* by Ernest Hemingway. Copyright © 1952 by Ernest Hemingway. Copyright renewed © 1980 by Mary Hemingway.

Excerpt on pages 605–606 is from Kurt Haberl, *The Newman Assignment*. (Los Altos Hills: May Davenport, Publishers, 1996)

Excerpt on pages 608–609 is from "A Canary for One." Reprinted with permission of Scribner, a Division of Simon & Schuster, from *Men Without Women* by Ernest Hemingway. Copyright 1927 by Charles Scribner's Sons. Copyright renewed 1955 by Ernest Hemingway.

Excerpt on page 610 is from *The Quiet Man and Other Stories* by Maurice Walsh, Appletree Press, 1992. Copyright © the estate of Maurice Walsh, 1935. Reprinted by permission.

Excerpt on page 610 is from Zora Neale Hurston, *Their Eyes Were Watching God* (Philadelphia: J.B. Lippincott Company, 1937), p. 2.

Excerpt on page 611 is from Susan Hill, The Woman in Black, New York: Vintage, 1998.

Excerpt on page 611 is from Jessamyn West, Cress Delahanty, Orlando: Harcourt, Brace and Company.

Excerpt on page 612 is from Joyce Carol Oates, *Upon the Sweeping Flood and Other Stories* (New York: Random House, 1966), p. 100.

Poem on page 617 is from *The Collected Poems of Langston Hughes* by Langston Hughes, copyright © 1994 by The Estate of Langston Hughes. Used by permission of Alfred A. Knopf, a division of Random House, Inc.

Poem on page 618 "Child of the Americas" is from *Getting Home Alive*, Aurora Levins Morales, Firebrand Books, Ithaca, New York. © Copyright 1986 by Aurora Levins Morales. Used by permission.

Poem on page 620 "Dawn Over the Mountains" by Kenneth Rexroth, is from *One Hundred Poems from the Chinese*, copyright © 1971 by Kenneth Rexroth. Reprinted by permission of New Directions Publishing Corp.

Excerpt on page 620 is from "Chicago" in *Chicago Poems* by Carl Sandburg, copyright 1916 by Holt, Rinehart and Winston and renewed 1944 by Carl Sandburg, reprinted by permission of Harcourt, Inc.

Excerpt on page 621 is from "Memory," from *Cats* by Andrew Lloyd Webber, incorporating lines from 'Rhapsody on a Windy Night' from Collected Poems 1909–1962 by T. S. Eliot. Reprinted by permission of Faber and Faber Ltd.

Poem on page 621 is "Poem in Three Parts" by Robert Bly. Reprinted from *Silence in the Snowy Fields*, Wesleyan University Press, Middletown, CT., 1962. Copyright 1962 Robert Bly. Reprinted with his permission.

Poem on page 622 is "Hope" by Emily Dickinson. Reprinted by permission of the publishers and the Trustees of Amherst College from *The Poems of Emily Dickinson*, Thomas H. Johnson, ed., Cambridge, Mass.: The Belknap Press of Harvard University Press, Copyright © 1951, 1955, 1979 by the President and Fellows of Harvard College.

Poem on pages 622–623 is "Barter" by Sara Teasdale. Reprinted with the permission of Scribner, a Division of Simon & Schuster, Inc., from *Collected Poems of Sara Teasdale* by Sara Teasdale. (New York: Macmillan, 1937)

Excerpt on page 626 is from "Memory," from *Cats* by Andrew Lloyd Webber, incorporating lines from 'Rhapsody on a Windy Night' from Collected Poems 1909–1962 by T. S. Eliot. Reprinted by permission of Faber and Faber Ltd.

Poem on page 627 is "Storm Windows" by Howard Nemerov. Reprinted by permission of Margaret Nemerov.

Poem on page 630 is "Richard Cory," by Edwin Arlington Robinson. Reprinted with the permission of Scribner, a Division of Simon & Schuster, Inc., from *Collected Poems of Edwin Arlington Robinson* by Edwin Arlington Robinson. (New York: Macmillan, 1937)

Poem on page 634 is "Leisure" by W. H. Davies, permission provided by Dee & Griffin of Gloucester for the literary trustee. The Trustees of Mrs. H. M. Davies Will Trust.

Footnotes on page 638 are from "Hamlet" from *The Complete Works of Shakespeare* 4th ed. by David Bevington. Copyright © 1992 by HarperCollins Publishers. Reprinted by permission of Pearson Education, Inc.

Excerpt on pages 644–645 is from *West Side Story* by Arthur Laurents, Stephen Sondheim, and Leonard Bernstein, copyright © 1956, 1958 by Arthur Laurents, Leonard Bernstein, Stephen Sondheim and Jerome Robbins. Used by permission of Random House, Inc.

Excerpt on pages 647–648 is from *Born Yesterday* by Garson Kanin. Reprint Permission Granted by Estate of Garson Kanin. Copyright renewed 1973 Garson Kanin.

Excerpt on page 650 is from *I Never Sang for My Father* by Robert Anderson. Reprinted by permission of International Creative Management, Inc. Copyright © 1994 by Robert Anderson.

Excerpt on pages 652–653 is from *A Raisin in the Sun* by Lorraine Hansberry, copyright © 1958 by Robert Nemiroff, as an unpublished work. Copyright © 1959, 1966, 1984 by Robert Nemiroff. Used by permission of Random House, Inc.

Excerpt on page 655 is from John Gray, Ph.D., *Men Are From Mars, Women Are From Venus* (New York: HarperCollins Publishers, 1992), p.10.

Excerpt on page 658 is from "Look Who's Talking-With Their Hands," by Diane Brady. Reprinted from the August 14, 2000 issue of *Business Week* by special permission, copyright © 2000 by The McGraw-Hill Companies, Inc.

Excerpt on page 660 is from "Brady Law still makes sense." Reprinted from the (August 7, 2000) issue by permission of the *Daily Herald*, Arlington Heights, Illinois.

Excerpt on page 664 is from, "Karen Blixen" (Isak Dinesen) in *Writer's Houses* by Francesca Premoli-Droulers, 1995. Reprinted by permission of Editions du Chene, Paris.

Excerpt on page 665 is from Tom Brokaw, *The Greatest Generation*. (New York: Random House, 1998), pp. 165, 169.

Excerpt on page 668 is from *The Good War* by Studs Terkel. Copyright 1984 by Studs Terkel. Reprinted by permission of Donadio & Olson, Inc.

Excerpt on page 670 is from Geraldine A. Ferraro and Linda Bird Francke, *Ferraro: My Story* (New York: Bantam Books, 1985), p 42 & 43.

Excerpt on page 671 is from "Parents Shouldn't Be On Call All the Time" by Nicole Wise. From *Newsweek*, August 7, 2000. © 2000 Newsweek, Inc. All rights reserved. Reprinted by permission.

Excerpt on page 674 is from "Should We Extend the School Year," by Adam Urbanski and Bill Gooding, *Speaking Out* May/June 2000. Copyright 2000, American Federation of Teachers. Reprinted with permission.

Painting on page 680 is Grant Wood, American, 1891-1942, American Gothic, 1930, oil on beaverboard, 74.3 x 62.4 cm, Friends of American Art Collection, All rights reserved by The Art Institute of Chicago and VAGA, New York, NY, 1930.934. Photograph courtesy of The Art Institute of Chicago.

Excerpt on page 680 is from "On Grant Wood, American Gothic, 1930" from *The Geography of the Imagination* by Guy Davenport. Reprinted by permission of David R. Godine, Publisher, Inc. Copyright ©1981 by Guy Davenport.

Excerpt on page 946 is adapted from *The Complete Guide to America's National Parks. Tenth Edition.* Fodor's Travel Publications, Inc. 1998. Copyright National Park Foundation

Excerpt on page 948 is adapted from "Driving Skills and Strategies" from *Colorado/Utah tour book*. © AAA, Reproduced by permission.

Excerpt on page 955 is adapted from "Homework: Fighting insects in the kitchen," *Chicago Tribune*, April 2, 2000. Copyrighted 2000, Chicago Tribune Company. All rights reserved. Used with permission.

Excerpt on page 665 is from Tom Brokaw, *The Greatest Generation*. (New York: Random House, 1998), pp. 165, 169.

Chart on page 1002 is from "Most Common Symptoms of Lupus," Lupus Foundation of America, Inc. Reprinted with permission. Copyright 2001.

Chart on page 1004 is from *American Medical Association Family Medical Guide* by American Medical Association, copyright © 1982 by The American Medical Association. Used by permission of Random House, Inc.

Figure and excerpt on page 1005 are from *Scientific American*, December 2000. Reprinted by permission of Bryan Christie and Scientific American.

Table on page 1006 is used with permission from *Chemistry in the Community, 2nd ed.*, © American Chemical Society, 1993.

Graphic on page 1008 is from *American Medical Association Family Medical Guide* by American Medical Association, copyright © 1982 by The American Medical Association. Used by permission of Random House, Inc. Also, used by permission of American Medical Association, Family Medical Guide, copyright 1994.

Chart on page 1009 "How Much Sleep do we Need?" is by William Dement, *Hope Health Letter*, April 2000. Reprinted by permission of William Dement.

Excerpt on page 1016 is from *Inherit the Wind* by Jerome Lawrence and Robert Edwin Lee, copyright as an unpublished work, 1951 by Jerome Lawrence & Robert Edwin Lee. Copyright © 1955 and renewed 1983 by Jerome Lawrence and Robert Edwin Lee. Used by permission of Random House, Inc.

Excerpt on page 1018 is from "Chapter 14", from *The Grapes of Wrath* by John Steinbeck, copyright 1939, renewed © 1967 by John Steinbeck. Used by permission of Viking Penguin, a division of Penguin Putnam Inc.

Poem on page 1019 "The Truly Great" is from *Collected Poems 1928-1985* by Stephen Spender, copyright 1934 and renewed 1962 by Stephen Spender. Used by permission of Random House, Inc.

Excerpt on page 1022 is from *The Postman* by Antonio Skarmeta (*Il Postino*) translated by Katherine Silver, Pantheon Books, 1987. Reprinted by permission.

Excerpt on page 1024 is from *Crossing America* by Alison Kahn. Alison Kahn/NGS Image Collection

Excerpt on page 1054 is adapted from "Cleaning house can reduce impact of allergens in the air." as appeared in Daily Herald, Oct. 29, 2000. Reprinted by permission of the Carpet and Rug Institute.

Chart on page 1094 is adapted from *American Medical Association Family Medical Guide* by American Medical Association, copyright © 1982 by The American Medical Association. Used by permission of Random House, Inc. Also, used by permission of American Medical Association, Family Medical Guide, copyright 1994.

Figures and captions on page 1097 are from *American Medical Association Family Medical Guide* by American Medical Association, copyright © 1982 by The American Medical Association. Used by permission of Random House, Inc. Also, used by permission of American Medical Association, Family Medical Guide, copyright 1994.

Caption on page 1109 is from *American Medical Association Family Medical Guide* 3e by American Medical Association, copyright © 1982 by The American Medical Association. Used by permission of Random House, Inc. Also, used by permission of American Medical Association, Family Medical Guide, copyright 1994.

Excerpt on page 1111 is from "Whence this Prairie in My Yard? A Short History of Prairie Landscaping in the US" by Neil Diboll. Reprinted by permission of Neil Diboll, Prairie Nursery, Westfield, WI.

Excerpt on page 1120 is from *Arsenic and Old Lace* by Joseph Kesselring, copyright 1941 and renewed 1969 by Charlotte Kesselring. Used by permission of Random House

Excerpt on page 1122 is from *Being There*, copyright © 1970 by Jerzy Kosinski, reprinted by permission of Harcourt, Inc.

Excerpt on page 1124 is from *Divine Secrets of Ya-Ya Sisterhood* by Rebecca Wells. Copyright © 1996 by Rebecca Wells. Reprinted by permission of HarperCollins Publishers, Inc.

Excerpt on page 1126 is from *Don't Sweat the Small Stuff at Work* by Richard Carlson, Ph.D. Copyright © 1998 Dr. Richard Carlson. Reprinted by permission of Hyperion.

Excerpt on pages 1127–1128 is from "A Century at the Movies." From *Newsweek Extra 2000*, Special Issue, Summer, 1998. © 1998 Newsweek, Inc. All rights reserved. Reprinted by permission.

To the Student

If you're studying to pass the GED Tests, you're in good company. In 1999, the most recent year for which figures are available, the American Council on Education GED Testing Service reported that over 750,700 adults took the GED Test battery worldwide. Of this number, more than 526,400 (70 percent) actually received their certificates. One in seven (14 percent) of those who have high school credentials has a GED diploma. One in twenty students (5 percent) in their first year of college study is a GED graduate.

The average age of GED test-takers in the United States was over 24 (and over 30 in Canada) in 1999, but nearly three quarters (70 percent) of GED test-takers were 19 years of age or older. Two out of three GED test-takers report having completed the tenth grade or higher, and more than a third report having completed the eleventh grade before leaving high school.

Why do so many people choose to take the GED Tests? What difference does passing the GED make? Some do so to get a job, to advance in a present job, to go to college, or to qualify for military service. Some have been home schooled and use the GED to document their learning and qualify for college scholarships and financial aid. More than two out of every three GED graduates work toward college degrees or further trade, technical, or business schools. A study in Colorado showed that some GED graduates reported the following: improvements in educational and employment status and in personal finances; greater participation in the community or in cultural activities; and increased awareness of psychological benefits and health strategies.

The GED diploma has been recognized throughout North America by employers and colleges, and more than 14 million adults earned the GED diploma between 1942 and 1999. You probably recognize some of these famous GED graduates: country music singers Waylon Jennings and John Michael Montgomery, comedian Bill Cosby, Olympic gold medalist Mary Lou Retton, former New Jersey Governor James J. Florio, Delaware Lieutenant Governor Ruth Ann Minner, U.S. Senator Ben Nighthorse Campbell, Wendy's founder Dave Thomas, movie actor Kelly McGillis, Famous Amos Cookies creator Wally Amos, and Triple Crown winner jockey Ron Turcotte.

What does GED stand for?

GED stands for the Tests of **General Educational Development.** The GED Test battery is a national examination developed by the GED Testing Service of the American Council on Education. The credential (certificate) earned for passing the test is widely recognized by colleges, training schools, and employers as equivalent to a high school diploma. The American Council reports that almost all (more than 95 percent) of employers in the nation employ GED graduates and offer them the same salaries and opportunities for advancement as high school graduates.

The GED Test reflects the major and lasting outcomes normally acquired in a four-year high school program. Since the passing rate for the GED is normed (based) on the performance of graduating high school seniors, you can rest assured that your skills are comparable. In fact, those who pass the GED Test actually do better than one-third of those graduating seniors. Throughout the test, your skills in communication (both reading and viewing text), information processing, critical thinking, and problem solving are keys to success. There is also special emphasis in the questions on preparation for entering the workplace or entering higher education. Much that you have learned informally or through other types of training can help you pass the test.

What is the test like overall?

THE GED TESTS

Tests	Minutes	Questions	Content/Percentages
Language Arts, Writing			Organization 15% Sentence Structure 30% Usage 30% Mechanics 25%
Part I (65%) (Editing)	75	50	
Part II (35%) (Essay)	45	1 topic: approximately 250 words	
Social Studies	70	50	World History 15% U.S. History 25% Civics and Government 25% Economics 20% Geography 15%
Science	80	50	Life Science 45% Earth and Space Science 20% Physical Science 35% (Physics and Chemistry)
Language Arts, Reading	65	40	Literary Text (75%) Poetry [15%] Drama [15%] Fiction [45%] Nonfiction Prose (25%) Informational Text Literary Nonfiction Viewing Component Business Documents
Mathematics	90		Number Operations and Numbers Sense 20–30% Measurement and Geometry 20–30% Data Analysis, Statistics, and Probability 20–30% Algebra, Functions, and Patterns 20–30%
Booklet One: Calculator		25	
Booklet Two: No Calculator		25	
Totals:	425 minutes (about 7 hours)	240 questions + Essay	

On all five tests, you can expect subject matter to be *interdisciplinary.* All five subjects will be interrelated. For example, a mathematics question might include a social studies chart. A science question might require the use of mathematics computation skills. You are expected to demonstrate the ability to think about many issues.

Special editions of the GED Test include the Canadian French-language, Spanish-language, Braille, large print, and audiocassette formats. Many adult education programs or test centers can assist you if you need accommodations such as special reading or marking devices.

What should I know to pass the test?

You are tested on knowledge and skills you have acquired from life experiences, work experiences, television, radio, books, magazines, newspapers, consumer products, and advertising. Many questions will involve the roles that adults play: citizen and community member, worker, and/or family member. Many documents will be "how to" documents especially found in business settings.

In particular, keep these facts in mind about the specific tests:

A. Part I of the **Language Arts, Writing Test** requires you to recognize or correct errors, revise sentences or passages, or shift constructions in the four areas of organization, sentence structure, usage, and mechanics (capitalization, punctuation, and spelling). The types of letters and memos you would normally write are likely to be included. Informational texts from business-related documents will be used.

In Part II you will have to write a well-developed essay on a topic familiar to most adults. You will be asked to have an *audience* and a *purpose* in mind for the essay. You will write in a *real life context* and *adopt a role.* You will be asked to generate (produce) ideas, express them clearly, organize the ideas, and connect them appropriately.

B. Three of the five tests—Social Studies, Science, and Language Arts, Reading—require that you answer questions based on reading passages or interpret graphs, charts, maps, cartoons, or diagrams. Developing strong reading and thinking skills is the key to succeeding on these tests.

The **Social Studies Test** looks at history in terms of critical points in time and clusters (groups) of historical periods. Psychology, the science of behavior, is not a separate content area, but it is included in other social studies areas. More emphasis is placed on U.S. and world history and civics and government.

The **Science Test** is based on the National Science Education Standards (NSES). It emphasizes scientific understandings and places special emphasis on the environment and on health questions. Science education focuses on the activities or ways in which people use science in their daily lives.

As expected, the **Language Arts, Reading Test** asks you to read literary text and to show that you can comprehend, apply, analyze, synthesize, and evaluate concepts. In addition, the test asks you to read and comprehend nonfiction prose including informational texts (such as job benefits or letters to the editor typical in daily living), literary nonfiction, texts based on viewing components, and business documents.

The **Mathematics Test** consists mainly of word problems to be solved. Therefore, you must be able to combine your ability to perform computations with problem-solving skills. Fifty percent of the problems will require the use of a calculator provided at the test site, and fifty percent of the questions will not permit the use of a calculator. Alternate formats are especially important on this test.

The calculator use is intended to eliminate the tediousness of making complex calculations in realistic, everyday settings. Thus, two separate booklets are used. Booklet One, Mathematical Understanding and Application, permits the use of the calculator provided by the GED Testing Service. Booklet Two, Estimation and Mental Math, does not permit calculator use. Twenty percent (20%) of the questions will include alternate formats of bubble-in grids or graphs (coordinate plane graphs with number lines).

This book has been designed to help you, too, succeed on the test. It will provide you with instruction in the skills you need to pass, background information on key concepts in the five subject areas of language arts/writing, social studies, science, language arts/reading, and mathematics. The book will provide you with plenty of practice through pretests, exercises in each instructional section, posttests, and practice tests in all areas.

Who may take the tests?

Some 3,500 GED Testing Centers are available in all fifty United States, the District of Columbia, eleven Canadian provinces and territories, U.S. and overseas military bases, correctional institutions, Veterans Administration hospitals, and certain learning centers. People who have not graduated from high school and who meet specific eligibility requirements (age, residency, etc.) may take the tests. Since eligibility requirements vary, it would be useful to contact your local GED testing center or the director of adult education in your state, province, or territory for specific information.

May I retake the test?

You are allowed to retake some or all of the tests. Again, the regulations governing the number of times that you may retake the tests and the time you must wait before retaking them are set by your state, province, or territory. Some states require you to take a review class or to study on your own for a certain amount of time before taking the test again.

How can I best prepare for the test?

Many community colleges, public schools, adult education centers, libraries, churches, community-based organizations, and other institutions offer GED preparation classes. While your state may not require you to take part in a preparation program, it's a good idea if you've been out of school for some time, if you had academic difficulty when you were in school, or if you left before completing the eleventh grade. Some television stations broadcast classes to prepare people for the test. If you cannot find a GED preparation class locally, contact the director of adult education in your state, province, or territory.

If I study on my own, how much time should I allow?

The amount of time you should allow for studying depends on your readiness in each of the five subject areas; however, you should probably allow three to six months to do the following:

1. Read the introductory section of the book.
2. Take and score the five Pretests. Decide which areas you need to focus on the most. Use the Countdown Checklist on pages xxv–xxvi to help you plan your study program.
3. Complete the Critical Thinking Skills for the GED Test section of the book.
4. Read and complete the exercises in those areas on which you decided to focus.
5. Take the Posttests to determine how much improvement you've made.
6. Take the Practice Tests to determine whether you're ready for the actual Test.
7. Review the test-taking tips on the following page.
8. Contact the GED administrator of your preparation program or the director of adult education in your state, province, or territory and arrange to take the GED.

What are some test-taking tips?

1. **Prepare physically.** Get plenty of rest and eat a well-balanced meal before the test so that you will have energy and will be able to think clearly. Intense studying at the last minute probably will not help as much as having a relaxed and rested mind.

2. **Arrive early.** Be at the testing center at least 15 to 20 minutes before the starting time. Make sure you have time to find the room and to get situated. Keep in mind that many testing centers refuse to admit those who come once the Test has started. Some testing centers operate on a first come, first served basis; so you want to be sure that there is an available slot for you on the day that you're ready to test.

3. **Think positively.** Tell yourself you will do well. If you have studied and prepared for the test, you should succeed.

4. **Relax during the test.** Take half a minute several times during the test to stretch and breathe deeply, especially if you are feeling anxious or confused.

5. **Read the test directions carefully.** Be sure you understand how to answer the questions. If you have any questions about the test or about filling in the answer form, ask before the test begins.

6. **Know the time limit for each test.** Some testing centers allow extra time, while others do not. You may be able to find out the policy of your testing center before you take the test, but always work according to the official time limit. If you have extra time, go back and check your answers.

7. **Have a strategy for answering questions.** You should read through the reading passages or look over the materials once and then answer the questions that follow. Read each question two or three times to make sure you understand it. It is best to refer back to the passage or graphic in order to confirm your answer choice. Don't try to depend on your memory of what you have just read or seen. Some people like to guide their reading by skimming the questions before reading a passage. Use the method that works best for you.

8. **Don't spend a lot of time on difficult questions.** If you're not sure of an answer, go on to the next question. Answer easier questions first and then go back to the harder questions. However, when you skip a question, be sure that you have skipped the same number on your answer sheet. Although skipping difficult questions is a good strategy for making the most of your time, it is very easy to get confused and throw off your whole answer key.

Lightly mark the margin of your answer sheet next to the numbers of the questions you did not answer so that you know what to go back to. To prevent confusion when your test is graded, be sure to erase these marks completely after you answer the questions.

9. **Answer every question on the test.** If you're not sure of an answer, take an educated guess. When you leave a question unanswered, you will always lose points, but you can possibly gain points if you make a correct guess.

   If you must guess, try to eliminate one or more answers that you are sure are not correct. Then choose from the remaining answers. Remember that you greatly increase your chances if you can eliminate one or two answers before guessing. Of course, guessing should be used only when all else has failed.

10. **Clearly fill in the circle for each answer choice.** If you erase something, erase it completely. Be sure that you give only one answer per question; otherwise, no answer will count.

11. **Practice test-taking.** Use the exercises, reviews, and especially the Posttests and Practice Tests in this book to better understand your test-taking habits and weaknesses. Use them to practice different strategies such as skimming questions first or skipping hard questions until the end. Knowing your own personal test-taking style is important to your success on the GED Test.

How do I use this book?

1. You do not have to work through all of the five sections in this book. In some areas you are likely to have stronger skills than in others. However, before you begin this book you should take the Pretests. These will give you a preview of what the five tests include, but more important, they will help you to identify which areas you need to concentrate on most. Use the **Evaluation Charts** at the end of the Pretests to pinpoint the types of questions you answered incorrectly and to determine the skills in which you need extra work.

2. Complete the sections of the book that the Pretests indicate you need to review. However, to prepare yourself best for the test, work through the entire book.

3. After you have worked through the subject areas that needed strengthening as indicated by the Pretest scores, you should take the full-length Posttests and Practice Tests at the end of this book. These tests will help you determine whether you are ready for the actual GED Test and, if not, what areas of the book you need to review. The Evaluation Charts are especially helpful in making this decision.

4. If you determine that you need still more practice at the GED level in answering the kinds of questions to be found on the GED Test, we recommend that you work through McGraw-Hill/Contemporary's satellite series, available for each of the five GED subject areas:

   Language Arts, Writing
   Social Studies
   Science
   Language Arts, Reading
   Mathematics

   Additional titles that McGraw-Hill/Contemporary offers for effective test preparation in mathematics and writing include *The GED Math Problem Solver* and *The GED Essay.*

5. This book has a number of features designed to help make the task of preparing for the actual GED Test easier as well as effective and enjoyable:

   - A special essay section helps to prepare you for the Part II of the Language Arts, Writing portion of the GED Test.
   - A critical thinking skills section that explains all six levels of thinking skills and provides practice in using the skills of the five levels represented on the test—comprehension, application, analysis, synthesis, and evaluation. This section also provides practice in interpreting graphs, charts, maps, and cartoons. (These make up at least one-half of the Science and Social Studies Tests and a good portion of the Mathematics Test.)
   - Skill builders, hints, and tips help you increase your proficiency in all sections.
   - A variety of exercise types including multiple-choice, fill-in-the-blank, true-false, matching, and short essay questions help to maintain interest.
   - Interdisciplinary writing activities in book sections other than in Language Arts, Writing help you practice the skills introduced earlier in the section.
   - Full-length Posttests and Practice Tests that are simulated GED Tests present questions in the format, level of difficulty, and percentages you will find on the actual tests.
   - Answer keys (coded by skill level) for each section explain the correct answers for the exercises.
   - Evaluation charts for the Pretests, Posttests, and Practice Tests help pinpoint weaknesses and refer you to specific pages for review.
   - Hundreds of questions are provided to strengthen your reading, writing, and thinking skills.

McGraw-Hill/Contemporary prints a wide range of materials to help you prepare for the tests. These books are designed for home study or classroom use. Our GED preparation books are available through schools and bookstores and directly from the publisher. For the visually impaired, a large-print version is available. For further information, call Library Reproduction Service (LRS) at 1-800-255-5002.

COUNTDOWN CHECKLIST

This checklist will assist those who are studying on their own in planning their course of preparation for the GED examination. It will also be helpful as a guide in GED review classes. It is designed to help students spread out their study, pace themselves wisely, and be prepared for the GED Test. Each item should be checked off as it is completed.

Step 1

Begin your review by taking and checking the Pretests on pages 1–60. Take one Pretest at a time. Read as much as you can in your spare time.

Step 2

- Read and study the Critical Thinking Skills for the GED section, pages 211–294. In addition, do as much extra reading as you can.
- If you think you need extra reading help, consider taking a reading test and a reading course at a local school or adult education center.

Step 3

- Go over the Evaluation Charts on the Pretests, circling those areas in which you had the most trouble.
- Divide the instructional material into about ten weeks of work, focusing on those areas in which you need the most time to prepare.
- Below, fill in the pages you plan to complete each week. As you complete each assignment, check it off.

Week 1: pages ____________ Week 6: pages ____________

Week 2: pages ____________ Week 7: pages ____________

Week 3: pages ____________ Week 8: pages ____________

Week 4: pages ____________ Week 9: pages ____________

Week 5: pages ____________ Week 10: pages ____________

Step 4

- Take and check the Posttests and Practice Tests on pages 943–1150.
- Based on where you had trouble, target pages you still need to review. Plan a three-week course to get yourself completely ready to take the GED Test. Divide the pages you still need to review into 3 equal parts. Complete one part each week until you have finished.

Step 5

Take the test.

The night before the test:

- Review the test-taking tips on pages xxii and xxiii.
- Relax. Don't study.
- Get a good night's sleep.

The day of the test:

- Eat a good breakfast, but don't eat heavily.
- Think positively and relax.
- Allow plenty of time to get there; arrive 15–20 minutes early.

Finally, we'd like to hear from you. If our materials have helped you to pass the test or if you feel that we can do a better job preparing you, write to us at the address on the copyright page of this book to let us know. We hope you enjoy studying for the GED Test with our materials and wish you the greatest success.

The Editors

Pretests

How do I use the Pretests?

The Pretests will help you determine what you need to study in this book. They are tests in the *format* and *level of difficulty* of the real GED Test, and four of them are **half-length.** The results of these tests, along with the Countdown Checklist on pages xxv–xxvi will help you map out a plan of study. We recommend the following approach to the Pretests.

1. Take only one Pretest at a time. Don't attempt to do all of the tests at one sitting. Read the directions before you start a test. Except for the essay and the Mathematics Pretest, observe the guidelines for taking the tests in approximately half the time of the full-length Posttests or full-length Practice Tests. While the pretests are not designed to be taken in a strict, timed atmosphere, you should know whether the time you are spending on the Pretests is reasonable. Use the answer sheets at the beginning of each test to mark your choices.

2. Check the answers in the Answer Key and fill in the Evaluation Chart. An Answer Key and an Evaluation Chart follow each test. For all of the questions that you miss, read explanations of the correct answers.

3. Based on the information in the Evaluation Charts, you may choose to do one of two things.

If you miss half or more of the questions in a Pretest, you should work through the entire subject area. If you miss fewer than half of the questions, focus on particular areas of the test that gave you difficulty.

4. For best results you will want to review the section on Critical Thinking Skills for the GED, beginning on page 211. Graphs, charts, maps, tables, and cartoons are included in that section, beginning on page 275.

The order of the Pretests and the time allotted for each is listed below. Only one-half the time of the full-length tests is indicated for all tests except Mathematics. Mathematics is a *skills test* and not timed.

Time Allowed for Each Test

Language Arts, Writing	Part I: Editing	38 minutes
	Part II: Essay	45 minutes (full length)
Social Studies		35 minutes
Science		40 minutes
Language Arts, Reading		33 minutes
Mathematics		not timed

5. Although these are Pretests, you should give them your best effort. If an item seems difficult, mark it and come back later. Always answer every question—even if you have to make an "educated guess." Sometimes you may know more than you give yourself credit for. Also, on the actual GED Tests an item left blank counts as a wrong answer. It's always wise to answer every question as best you can.

Good Luck on the Pretests!

PRETEST

Language Arts, Writing

Part I: Editing

Directions: Part I of the Language Arts, Writing Pretest consists of 25 multiple-choice questions and should take 38 minutes. The questions are based on documents of several paragraphs marked by letters. Each paragraph contains numbered sentences. Most sentences contain errors, but a few may be correct as written. Read the documents, and then answer the questions based on them. For each item, choose the answer that would result in the best rewriting of the sentence or sentences. The best answer must be consistent with the meaning and tone of the rest of the document.

Answer each question as carefully as possible, choosing the best of five answer choices and blackening in the grid. If you find a question too difficult, do not waste time on it. Work ahead and come back to it later when you can think it through carefully.

When you have completed the test, check your work with the answers and explanation at the end of the section.

Use the Evaluation chart on page 11 to determine which areas you need to review most.

Language Arts, Writing Pretest Answer Grid

1	① ② ③ ④ ⑤		10	① ② ③ ④ ⑤		18	① ② ③ ④ ⑤
2	① ② ③ ④ ⑤		11	① ② ③ ④ ⑤		19	① ② ③ ④ ⑤
3	① ② ③ ④ ⑤		12	① ② ③ ④ ⑤		20	① ② ③ ④ ⑤
4	① ② ③ ④ ⑤		13	① ② ③ ④ ⑤		21	① ② ③ ④ ⑤
5	① ② ③ ④ ⑤		14	① ② ③ ④ ⑤		22	① ② ③ ④ ⑤
6	① ② ③ ④ ⑤		15	① ② ③ ④ ⑤		23	① ② ③ ④ ⑤
7	① ② ③ ④ ⑤		16	① ② ③ ④ ⑤		24	① ② ③ ④ ⑤
8	① ② ③ ④ ⑤		17	① ② ③ ④ ⑤		25	① ② ③ ④ ⑤
9	① ② ③ ④ ⑤						

PRETEST

Directions: Choose the *best* answer to each question that follows.

Questions 1–8 refer to the following document.

Batteries

(A)

(1) Many of the gadgets we use regularly which require batteries to power them. **(2)** Flashlights, smoke alarms, toys, and portable CD players are only a few examples from a long list of possibilities. **(3)** When replacing the batteries that these devices require, we should understand the differences between the types of batteries that are available.

(B)

(4) First of all some batteries are rechargeable, and some are not. **(5)** Rechargeable batteries are not good choices for devices that are seldom used. **(6)** Rechargeable batteries are best for high-drain devices. **(7)** Which are used fairly regularly. **(8)** There is a disadvantage to these batteries due to the fact that they require frequent recharging.

(C)

(9) Three kinds of primary-cell batteries are general-purpose, heavy-duty, or alkaline. **(10)** General-purpose batteries are low priced but usually won't last very long. **(11)** Heavy-duty batteries cost more and represent a good choice for low to medium drain devices. **(12)** These batteries are very good choices for smoke, alarms or flashlights.

(D)

(13) Lastly, alkaline batteries work best for high-drain devices that are used often, such as a CD player. **(14)** These batteries are the most expensive of the three primary-cell batteries.

(E)

(15) Knowing the choices of batteries that are available help us save money and frustration. **(16)** In this case, education can truly translate into power.

Source: *Daily Herald.* "Select batteries according to how they will be used" Sunday, November 26, 2000.

1. Sentence 1: **Many of the gadgets we use <u>regularly which require batteries</u> to power them.**

   Which is the best way to write the underlined portion of the text? If the original is the best way, choose option (1).

   (1) regularly which require batteries
   (2) regularly that require batteries
   (3) regularly require batteries
   (4) batteries for which
   (5) require regular batteries which

2. Sentence 4: **First of all some batteries are rechargeable, and some are not.**

   What correction should be made to sentence 4?

   (1) insert a comma after <u>First</u>
   (2) remove the word <u>all</u>
   (3) insert a comma after <u>all</u>
   (4) change <u>rechargeable</u> to <u>Rechargeable</u>
   (5) replace <u>and</u> with <u>so</u>

3. Sentences 6 and 7: **Rechargeable batteries are best for high-drain <u>devices. Which</u> are used fairly regularly.**

   Which is the best way to write the underlined portion of the text? If the original is the best way, choose option (1).

   (1) devices. Which
   (2) devices, and which
   (3) devices. That
   (4) devices those which
   (5) devices that

PRETEST

4. Sentence 8: **There is a disadvantage to these batteries due to the fact that they require frequent recharging.**

If you rewrote sentence 8 beginning with

One disadvantage to these batteries is

the next words should be

(1) recharging due
(2) that they
(3) besides the fact
(4) even though they
(5) resulting in

5. Which sentence below would be most effective at the beginning of paragraph C?

(1) We use batteries very often in household devices.
(2) The disposal of batteries can be a problem.
(3) Batteries in cars keep rising in cost.
(4) Not all batteries are rechargeable as explained earlier.
(5) Batteries that are not rechargeable are called primary cells.

6. Sentence 12: **These batteries are very good choices for smoke, alarms or flashlights.**

What correction should be made to sentence 12?

(1) change are to were
(2) change very to vary
(3) change for to fore
(4) remove the comma after smoke
(5) insert a comma after alarms

7. Which revision would make the document "Batteries" more effective?

(1) move sentence 2 to follow sentence 3
(2) remove sentence 3
(3) move sentence 10 to follow sentence 11
(4) combine paragraphs C and D
(5) combine paragraphs D and E

8. Sentence 15: **Knowing the choices of batteries that are available help us save money and frustration.**

What correction should be made to sentence 15?

(1) change are to is
(2) change help to helps
(3) change us to them
(4) change save to saving
(5) insert a comma after money

PRETEST

Questions 9–16 refer to the following document.

Memo To: All Employees
From: Gregory Bolsho, Human Resources
Subject: Direct Deposit

(A)

(1) I am pleased to announce that beginning March 1, all employees will have the option of using direct deposit. **(2)** Direct deposit provides for the automatic deposit of salary into the financial institution of you're choice. **(3)** Many financial institutions also offer credit cards.
(4) Using direct deposit should reduce the incidence of lost or stolen payroll checks.

(B)

(5) Several steps will have to be followed if you sign up for this option. **(6)** First, you will need to contact your financial institution to confirm that it participates in the direct deposit plan. **(7)** Attached to this memo, you will need to complete a form. **(8)** Be sure that you have signed the form. **(9)** After the form is completed, return them to the business office. **(10)** Direct deposit will go into effect at the end of the pay period after which the form is returned. **(11)** Direct deposit may be an option that you elect for as your choice at any time during the next six months. **(12)** If you chose to use direct deposit, a record of the deposit and copy of your deductions will continue to be issued to you each week on Friday.

(C)

(13) Our company hopes that offering this option will benefit you by providing greater convenience. **(14)** If they have any questions in this matter, you may call the business office.

9. Sentence 2: **Direct deposit provides for the automatic deposit of salary into the financial institution of you're choice.**

What correction should be made to sentence 2?

(1) insert a comma after <u>deposit</u>
(2) change <u>provides</u> to <u>provide</u>
(3) change <u>financial</u> to <u>Financial</u>
(4) change <u>you're</u> to <u>your</u>
(5) no correction is necessary

10. Sentence 3: **Many financial institutions also offer credit cards.**

Which revision should be made to sentence 3?

(1) move sentence 3 to follow sentence 5
(2) move sentence 3 to the end of paragraph B
(3) move sentence 3 to the end of paragraph C
(4) remove sentence 3
(5) no revision is necessary

PRETEST

11. Sentence 5: **Several steps will have to be followed if you sign up for this option.**

The most effective revision of sentence 5 would include which group of words?

(1) you will need to follow
(2) since there are several steps
(3) you have no option
(4) even though this is an option
(5) whether you sign up

12. Sentence 7: **Attached to this memo, you will need to complete a form.**

Which is the best way to write the underlined portion of the text? If the original is the best way, choose option (1).

(1) you will need to complete a form.
(2) is a form to complete.
(3) a complete form is required.
(4) a form is to be completed.
(5) you complete the given form.

13. Sentence 9: **After the form is completed, return them to the business office.**

Which is the best way to write the underlined portion of the text? If the original is the best way, choose option (1).

(1) is completed, return them
(2) was completed, return them
(3) is completing, return them
(4) is completed, returned them
(5) is completed, return it

14. Sentence 11: **Direct deposit may be an option that you elect for as your choice at any time during the next six months.**

The most effective revision of sentence 11 would begin with which group of words?

(1) You having the next six months
(2) To elect direct deposit because
(3) Six months of direct deposit
(4) You may elect to change
(5) For as long as six months later

15. Sentence 12: **If you chose to use direct deposit, a record of the deposit and copy of your deductions will continue to be issued to you each week on Friday.**

What correction should be made to sentence 12?

(1) change chose to choose
(2) insert a comma after record
(3) change deductions to deduction's
(4) change Friday to friday
(5) no correction is necessary

16. Sentence 14: **If they have any questions in this matter, you may call the business office.**

Which is the best way to write the underlined portion of the text? If the original is the best way, choose option (1).

(1) If they have any
(2) If you have any
(3) If they are any
(4) If they had any
(5) If you could have

PRETEST

Questions 17–25 refer to the following document.

Fire Safety

(A)

(1) Most fire-related deaths result from fires in the home, fire is a frightening event. **(2)** Smoke from a fire is especially deadly because it reduces visibility and can impair breathing within minutes. **(3)** To help guard against fire, every person should have a working smoke alarm and fire extinguisher in the home.

(B)

(4) Smoke detectors serve to warn the resident's of a home of fire. **(5)** Change the batteries of smoke alarms once a year or more to ensure that their in working order. **(6)** In most cases when a fire has started or with the smoke alarm sounding, everyone should evacuate a home. **(7)** Be sure to have a plan of evacuation prepared, and be sure that every member of the household knows that plan. **(8)** The establishment of a meeting place that is outside the home where all members of the household will meet is also important. **(9)** Someone outside the home should call the fire department. **(10)** In some instances, when a fire is very limited and immediately located, a fire extinguisher can actually help people fight fires. **(11)** Several kinds of fire extinguishers are available, and each is suitable for a particular type of fire. **(12)** These extinguishers generally come with instructions. **(13)** Training in the use and operation of extinguishers by fire departments may be offered to people in various areas of the country. **(14)** Keeping the extinguisher in an easily accessible location is extremely important.

(C)

(15) Smoke alarms and fire extinguishers served as important tools for protection against fire. **(16)** The cost of these tools is minimal compared to their value.

17. Sentence 1: **Most fire-related deaths result from fires in the <u>home, fire</u> is a frightening event.**

Which is the best way to write the underlined portion of the text? If the original is the best way, choose option (1).

(1) home, fire is
(2) home, or fire is
(3) home fire is
(4) home, and fire is
(5) home so, fire is

18. Sentence 4: **Smoke detectors serve to warn the resident's of a home of fire.**

What correction should be made to sentence 4?

(1) insert a comma after <u>detectors</u>
(2) change <u>serve</u> to <u>serving</u>
(3) change <u>resident's</u> to <u>residents'</u>
(4) change <u>resident's</u> to <u>residents</u>
(5) replace <u>home</u> with <u>dwelling</u>

19. Sentence 5: **Change the batteries of smoke alarms once a year or more to ensure that their in working order.**

What correction should be made to sentence 5?

(1) change <u>batteries</u> to <u>batteries'</u>
(2) replace <u>once a</u> with <u>every</u>
(3) insert a comma after <u>year</u>
(4) change <u>their</u> to <u>they're</u>
(5) no correction is necessary

20. Sentence 6: **In most cases when a fire has started or <u>with the smoke alarm sounding</u>, everyone should evacuate a home.**

Which is the best way to write the underlined portion of the text? If the original is the best way, choose option (1).

(1) with the smoke alarm sounding
(2) alarms sound from the smoke alarm
(3) the sounding of the smoke alarm
(4) there is an alarm sounded that you hear
(5) the smoke alarm sounds

PRETEST

21. Sentence 8: **The establishment of a meeting place that is outside the home where all members of the household will meet is also important.**

The most effective revision of sentence 8 would begin with which group of words?

(1) It is important if meeting
(2) Establish a designated meeting
(3) As a result of establishing
(4) Some of the household will meet
(5) Outside the home establishment

22. Sentence 10: **In some instances, when a fire is very limited and immediately located, a fire extinguisher can actually help people fight fires.**

Which revision to sentence 10 would make the document more effective?

(1) begin a new paragraph with sentence 10
(2) move sentence 10 to follow sentence 3
(3) remove sentence 10
(4) move sentence 10 to follow sentence 15
(5) no revision is necessary

23. Sentence 11: **Several kinds of fire extinguishers are available, and each is suitable for a particular type of fire.**

Which is the best way to write the underlined portion of the text? If the original is the best way, choose option (1).

(1) each is suitable
(2) each are suitable
(3) each being suitable
(4) only some is suitable
(5) each of them are

24. Sentence 13: **Training in the use and operation of extinguishers by fire departments may be offered to people in various areas of the country.**

The most effective revision of sentence 13 would include which group of words?

(1) offers for fire extinguishers
(2) people training because of
(3) extinguishers from fire departments
(4) various use and operation of
(5) fire departments may offer

25. Sentence 15: **Smoke alarms and fire extinguishers served as important tools for protection against fire.**

Which is the best way to write the underlined portion of the text? If the original is the best way, choose option (1).

(1) served as important
(2) serving as important
(3) serves as important
(4) serve as important
(5) has been serving as important

Part II: The Essay

Directions: This part of the test is designed to find out how well you write. The test has one question that asks you to present an opinion and explain your ideas. Your essay should be long enough to develop the topic adequately. In preparing your essay, you should take the following steps:

1. Read the directions and topic carefully.
2. Think about your ideas and plan your essay before you write.
3. Use scratch paper to make notes of your ideas.
4. Write your essay in ink on two other pages of paper.
5. After finishing your writing, read your paper carefully and make appropriate changes.

TOPIC

What is one day that you will always remember?

In your essay, identify the day and the events that occurred. Explain the reasons that the day is so memorable for you.

Information on evaluating your essay is on page 12.

PRETEST

Language Arts, Writing Answer Key

PART I: EDITING

1. (3) The original sentence is a fragment. The sentence can be made complete by adding something at the end or by removing the word *which*.

2. (3) A comma is needed after the introductory expression *First of all* so that the meaning is clear to the reader.

3. (5) Sentence 7 is a fragment that should be attached to sentence 6.

4. (2) The sentence is improved by omitting unnecessary words: *One disadvantage to these batteries is that they require frequent recharging.*

5. (5) The paragraph needs a topic sentence to provide a focus.

6. (4) *Smoke alarms* are one kind of gadget, not two separate items. The comma should not separate *smoke* from *alarms.*

7. (4) Paragraphs C and D should be combined into one paragraph because both explain the three kinds of primary-cell batteries.

8. (2) The subject of the sentence *knowing* requires the verb *helps* for appropriate agreement between subject and verb.

9. (4) The possessive pronoun *your* is needed for the appropriate meaning of the sentence.

10. (4) The sentence is irrelevant and does not belong in the paragraph.

11. (1) Using the active voice rather than the passive voice improves the sentence.

12. (2) In the original sentence, the modifier is misplaced so that *you* rather than *a form* appears attached to this memo.

13. (5) The pronoun *them* should be changed to *it* to agree in number with the noun form.

14. (4) Improve the original sentence by reducing wordiness: *You may elect to change to direct deposit at any time in the next six months.*

15. (1) Change the verb to the correct form, using the present tense to complete the conditional *if.*

16. (2) The pronoun *they* is an incorrect reference. *You* should be used to be consistent with the sentence and passage.

17. (4) Two independent sentences cannot be joined with only a comma.

18. (4) *Residents* is plural and not possessive, so no apostrophe is needed.

19. (4) The meaning of *their* indicates ownership, but the sentence requires *they're* with the meaning *they are.*

20. (5) The sentence needs a parallel construction so that *a fire has started* matches *the smoke alarm sounds.*

21. (2) The sentence is improved by reducing wordiness: *Establish a designated meeting place outside the home for all members of the household.*

22. (1) A new idea about fire extinguishers is begun with sentence 10, so a new paragraph should be started.

23. (1) No correction is needed.

24. (5) Using the active voice rather than the passive voice improves the sentence.

25. (4) The verb *serve* must agree with the subject *smoke alarms and fire extinguishers,* and the verb must appear in the present tense to fit the meaning of the passage.

Evaluation Chart

Use the answer key on page 10 to check your answers to the Pretest. Then find the item number of each question you missed and circle it on the chart below to determine the writing content areas in which you need more practice. Pay particular attention to areas where you missed half or more of the questions. The page numbers for the content areas are listed on the chart below. For those questions that you missed, review the skill pages indicated.

CONTENT AREA	ITEM NUMBER	REVIEW PAGES
Nouns	18	69–73, 102–104
Verbs	15	73–86, 102–104
Subject/Verb Agreement	8, 25	87–91, 102–104
Pronoun Use	13, 16	91–95, 102–104
Sentence Fragments	1, 3	105–108, 131–134
Run-ons, Comma Splices, Sentence Combining	17	108–115, 131–134
Independent/Dependent Clauses, Effective Sentence Structure	4, 11, 14, 21, 24	116–125, 131–134
Dangling or Misplaced Modifiers	12	126–128, 131–134
Parallel Structure	20	129–134
Capitalization, Punctuation	2, 6	135–144, 150–152
Spelling	9, 19	147–149, 150–152
Paragraph Composition	5	153–157, 165–168
Text Division	7, 22	157–160, 165–168
Paragraph Unity and Coherence	10	160–165, 165–168
No correction	23	95–98, 165–168

PRETEST

Part II: The Essay

If possible, give your essay to an instructor to evaluate. That person's opinion of your writing will be useful in deciding what further work you need to do to write a good essay.

If, however, you are unable to show your work to someone else, you can try to evaluate your own essay. Use the five questions in the Essay Evaluation Checklist to help evaluate your writing. The more questions you can answer with a strong yes, the better your chances are for achieving a passing or high score.

Essay Evaluation Checklist

YES	NO	
		1. Does the essay answer the question asked?
		2. Does the main point of the essay stand out clearly?
		3. Does each paragraph contain specific examples and details that develop and explain the main point?
		4. Are the ideas organized clearly into paragraphs and complete sentences?
		5. Is the essay easy to read, or do problems in grammar, usage, punctuation, spelling or word choice interfere?

Important Note

On the actual GED Language Arts, Writing Test, you will be given one score, which is a composite of your scores from Part I and Part II of the test. This score is determined by grading your essay holistically, giving it a score, and then combining this score with your score from Part I in a proportion determined by the GED Testing Service.

Because you are not able to score your essay holistically, it is not possible for you to determine a valid composite score for your performance on this Language Arts, Writing Test. Instead, it is best to look at your performance on each part of the test separately. In this way, you will be able to determine whether you need additional work in one part of the test or the other. Remember that you must take both parts of the Language Arts, Writing Test for your score to count.

Social Studies

This Social Studies Pretest will give you an introduction to the GED Social Studies Test. This test is half the length of the actual GED Test and contains 25 questions. Some of the questions are based on short reading passages, and some of them require you to interpret a graph, chart or table, map, or an editorial cartoon.

You should take approximately 35 minutes to complete this test. At the end of 35 minutes, stop and mark your place. Then finish the test. This will give you an idea of whether you are reading at a pace whereby you can finish the actual GED Test in the time allotted. Try to answer as many questions as you can. Blanks will count as wrong answers, so make a reasonable guess for the answers to questions of which you are not sure.

Use the Answer Key on pages 23–25 to check your answers to the Social Studies Pretest. Then find the item number of each question you missed and circle it on the Evaluation Chart on page 26 to determine the skills and content areas in which you need more practice. Pay particular attention to areas where you missed half or more of the questions. The numbers in **boldface** are questions based on graphics. The page numbers for the content areas and the critical thinking skills are listed on the chart. For those questions that you missed, review the pages indicated.

Social Studies Pretest Answer Grid

1	①	②	③	④	⑤	10	①	②	③	④	⑤	18	①	②	③	④	⑤
2	①	②	③	④	⑤	11	①	②	③	④	⑤	19	①	②	③	④	⑤
3	①	②	③	④	⑤	12	①	②	③	④	⑤	20	①	②	③	④	⑤
4	①	②	③	④	⑤	13	①	②	③	④	⑤	21	①	②	③	④	⑤
5	①	②	③	④	⑤	14	①	②	③	④	⑤	22	①	②	③	④	⑤
6	①	②	③	④	⑤	15	①	②	③	④	⑤	23	①	②	③	④	⑤
7	①	②	③	④	⑤	16	①	②	③	④	⑤	24	①	②	③	④	⑤
8	①	②	③	④	⑤	17	①	②	③	④	⑤	25	①	②	③	④	⑤
9	①	②	③	④	⑤												

PRETEST

Questions 1 and 2 are based upon the following passage.

I Have a Dream

Delivered on the steps at the Lincoln Memorial in Washington, D.C., on August 28, 1963

Five score years ago, a great American, in whose symbolic shadow we stand signed the Emancipation Proclamation. This momentous decree came as a great beacon light of hope to millions of Negro slaves who had been seared in the flames of withering injustice. It came as a joyous daybreak to end the long night of captivity.

But one hundred years later, we must face the tragic fact that the Negro is still not free. One hundred years later, the life of the Negro is still sadly crippled by the manacles of segregation and the chains of discrimination. One hundred years later, the Negro lives on a lonely island of poverty in the midst of a vast ocean of material prosperity. One hundred years later, the Negro is still languishing in the corners of American society and finds himself an exile in his own land. So we have come here today to dramatize an appalling condition.

In a sense we have come to our nation's capital to cash a check. When the architects of our republic wrote the magnificent words of the Constitution and the Declaration of Independence, they were signing a promissory note to which every American was to fall heir. This note was a promise that all men would be guaranteed the inalienable rights of life, liberty, and the pursuit of happiness.

—Martin Luther King, Jr.

1. A year after Dr. King's speech in Washington, D.C., Congress passed the Civil Rights Act in 1964. Which of the following is reasonable to extrapolate?

(1) All Americans supported the Civil Rights Act.
(2) Dr. King believed in Congress, the president, and the American people.
(3) This Act supported only African American citizens.
(4) Dr. King was responsible for drafting the Civil Rights Act.
(5) This act passed unanimously in the House of Representatives and the Senate.

2. What position does Dr. Martin Luther King, Jr., hold in his speech, *I Have a Dream*?

(1) The constitution of the United States gives too little power to the states.
(2) The Declaration of Independence was completely ineffective in freeing African Americans from all forms of segregation.
(3) The Emancipation Proclamation was very effective in freeing African Americans from all forms of segregation.
(4) By 1963, African Americans should have been free from all forms of segregation.
(5) By 1963, African Americans were finally free from all forms of segregation.

PRETEST

Questions 3 and 4 are based on the circle graphs below.

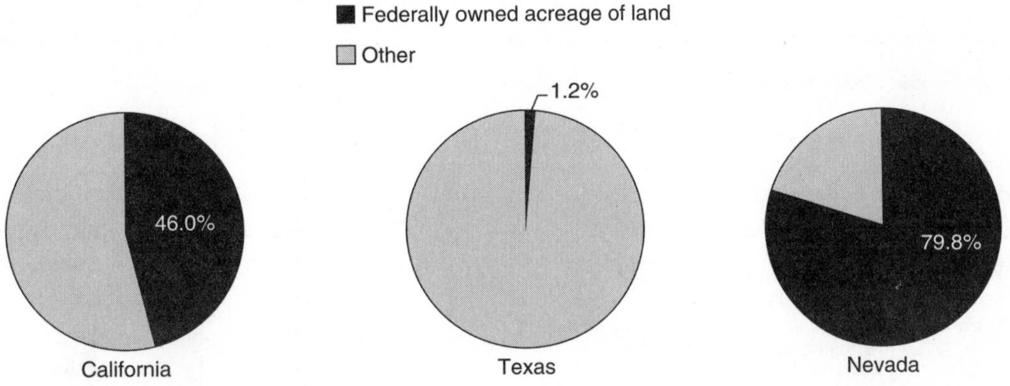

Source: Office of Government-wide Policy, General Services Administration

3. What conclusion can be drawn from the above data on federally owned land acreage by individual states?

(1) California has more acreage than Texas.
(2) Nevada has more national parks than Texas.
(3) The federal government controls the greatest percentage of all land in Nevada.
(4) The percentage of federally owned acreage is similar in Texas and in California.
(5) Nevada has a larger population than California.

4. What type of information is included in the circle graphs?

(1) the names of all fifty states
(2) the percentage of federally owned land
(3) the population of three states
(4) a list of national parks
(5) an explanation of other land ownership

PRETEST

Questions 5 and 6 refer to the following time line.

European and North American Revolutions Time Line 1600-1800

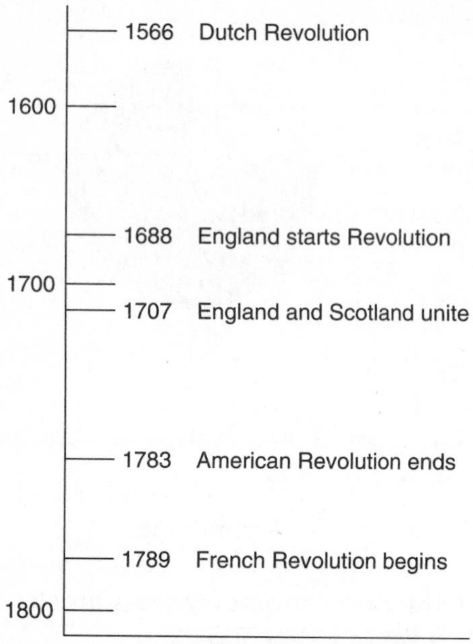

5. Which event on the time line suggests that the American Revolution had a global impact?

(1) the Treaty of Paris
(2) the French Revolution
(3) England and Scotland unite
(4) the Dutch Revolution begins
(5) the Revolution in England starts

6. How many years passed between the revolution in England and the French Revolution?

(1) 50 years
(2) 75 years
(3) 101 years
(4) 30 years
(5) 200 years

Questions 7 and 8 are based on the following graph.

Volume of Water in the Great Lakes

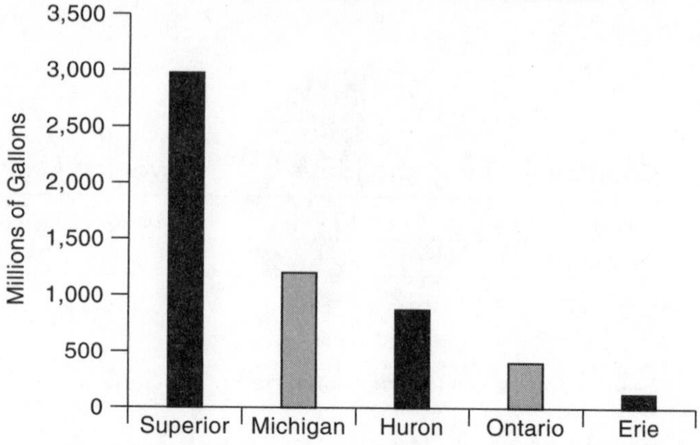

Source: National Ocean Service, U.S. Dept of Commerce

7. Which conclusion can you draw after studying the bar graph?

(1) Lake Superior has the longest shoreline.
(2) Lake Ontario has more water than Lake Erie.
(3) Lake Michigan is deeper than Lake Huron.
(4) Lake Michigan's and Lake Huron's water combined is greater than Lake Superior's.
(5) Lake Superior, with the most water, is the coldest.

8. What type of information is valid based on the graph?

(1) temperature of the water
(2) extent of fish life in the lakes
(3) depth of water in each lake
(4) length of shoreline of each lake
(5) volume of water in five lakes

PRETEST

Question 9 is based on the following chart.

Unlike their U.S. counterparts, workers in Western Europe get generous vacations and holidays.

Country	Public holidays	Vacation time (weeks)
Austria	13	5–6
Belgium	10	4–5
Denmark	9.5	5–6
Finland	12	5–6
France	11	5–6
Germany	9–12*	6
Greece	10	5
Ireland	9	4–5
Italy	12	4–6
Luxembourg	10	5–6
Netherlands	8	4–6
Portugal	14	4–5
Spain	14	4–5
Sweden	11	5–6
UK	8	4–5
United States	7	2–4

*Public holidays in Germany vary from state to state.
Sources: IDS Employment Europe, the European Union as appeared in *The Chicago Tribune*, September, 2000

9. This chart supports which of the following values and beliefs regarding holidays and vacation time around the world?

(1) The French government believes in a thirty-five hour workweek for large companies.
(2) The German government believes in the greatest amount of public leisure time.
(3) The U.S. government assigns a low priority to leisure time.
(4) The Japanese government encourages its citizens in the maximum use of holiday time.
(5) The Italian government considers the number of public holidays a basic right.

Questions 10 and 11 are based on the following chart.

The Relationship between Income and Education for Men, 1997

Level of Education	Median Income
Elementary	
9th grade or less	$19,291
High School (9th - 12th grade)	
no diploma	$24,726
graduate with diploma	$31,215
College	
no degree	$35,945
associate's degree	$38,022
bachelor's degree or higher	$53,450

Source: U.S. Department of Commerce, Bureau of the Census Reports

10. Which of the following conclusions is supported by the chart?

(1) No relationship exists between education level and median income.
(2) Men with an elementary education will earn at least $19,291 per year.
(3) A college education is required to earn over $35,945 per year.
(4) Education is the sole factor that determines a person's income.
(5) Men who have more education are more likely to earn a higher income.

11. On the basis of the data in the chart, what advice might a high school counselor offer a young male client in 1997?

(1) To prepare for the 21st century, you need to major in business at college.
(2) To increase your income, you must get a bachelor's degree from a private university.
(3) To raise your income, you should get your high school diploma.
(4) To make more than $19,000 a year, you must be a lawyer.
(5) To raise your income, you must complete a PhD.

PRETEST

12. American consumers are using a record number of cell phones. As a result, sales of cell phones have been affected. According to the dynamics of supply and demand, what will happen to the price of cell phones?

The price will

(1) increase to make up for the loss in profits
(2) remain the same because the cost to manufacture cell phones stays the same
(3) decrease to encourage consumers to buy cell phones
(4) increase in order for manufacturers to improve the quality of cell phones
(5) remain the same because fewer cell phones will be available for sale

13. Before the Civil War, Virginia was united; however, in 1863 West Virginia chose to become independent. Which is the most reasonable cause of West Virginia's secession from the rest of the state?

(1) Virginia and West Virginia together were too large for only one legislature.
(2) West Virginia was defeated by the North early in the Civil War.
(3) Richmond, Virginia, became the capital of the Confederacy.
(4) West Virginia did not allow ownership of slaves.
(5) Eastern and Western Virginia had religious differences.

Questions 14–16 are based on the following passage.

The great rule of conduct for us in regard to foreign nations is, in extending our commercial relations, to have with them as little political connection as possible. So far as we have already formed engagements, let them be fulfilled with perfect good faith. Here let us stop.

Europe has a set of primary interests which to us have none or a very remote relation. Hence she must be engaged in frequent controversies, the causes of which are essentially foreign to our concerns. Hence, therefore, it must be unwise in us to implicate ourselves by artificial ties in the ordinary vicissitudes (changes) of her politics or the ordinary combinations and collisions of her friendships or enmities . . .

It is our true policy to steer clear of permanent alliances with any portion of the foreign world . . .

—Excerpted from George Washington's Farewell Address

14. Which one of the following statements reflects George Washington's attitude as expressed in this address?

The United States should

(1) offer its assistance wherever needed in the world
(2) avoid becoming involved in world political affairs
(3) withdraw from European affairs while assisting other areas of the world
(4) become as politically connected with Europe as possible
(5) support policies that would increase the territory under its control

PRETEST

15. Based on this quote, how may Washington be best described?

(1) a controversialist
(2) an imperialist
(3) an isolationist
(4) a colonialist
(5) an expansionist

16. Based on his address, what would George Washington think of America's position today as a world power?

He would think that the United States

(1) has been successful in leaving other nations alone
(2) has achieved its primary goal of being a world power
(3) has continued to control the other nations of the world
(4) has become too involved in other nations' affairs
(5) has not changed much from the time when he was president

Question 17 is based on the following passage.

"We Preferred Our Own Way of Living"

My friend, I do not blame you for this. Had I listened to you this trouble would not have happened to me. I was not hostile to the white men. Sometimes my young men would attack the Indians who were their enemies and took their ponies. They did it in return.

We had buffalo for food, and their hides for clothing and for our teepees. We preferred hunting to a life of idleness on the reservation, where we were driven against our will. At times we did not get enough to eat, and we were not allowed to leave the reservation to hunt.

We preferred our own way of living. We were no expense to the government. All we wanted was peace and to be left alone. Soldiers were sent out in the winter, who destroyed our villages. . .

—Excerpted from "Crazy Horse," *Indian Oratory: Famous Speeches by Noted Indian Chieftains* by W. C. Vanderwerth

17. Crazy Horse, chief of the Sioux Indians in the 1870s, said, "We preferred our own way of living." What is he suggesting by this statement?

(1) The Sioux way of life was better than how the white men wanted them to live.
(2) The Sioux were content with their new lifestyle.
(3) The Sioux were happier on the reservation.
(4) The white men's way of life was far superior to that of the Sioux.
(5) The Sioux wished to remain at war with the white men.

PRETEST

Questions 18 and 19 are based on the following graph and passage.

Percentage of Married Women Who Hold Full-Time Jobs and Have Children Under 18 and Husbands Who Work

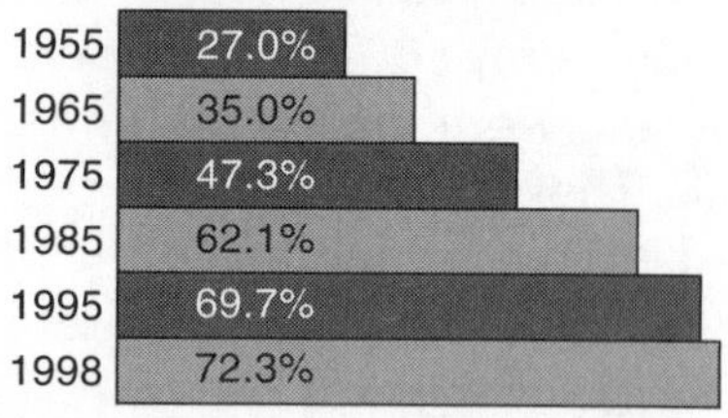

Source: U.S. Department of Labor, Bureau of Labor Statistics

The way a male or female acts or is expected to act in society is called a *role*. In the past the traditional role in the American family for the husband was as breadwinner while the wife's role was homemaker. According to the bar graph above, however, family roles are changing.

18. Which of the following is *least likely* to be considered a cause of the changing role of married women in the family?

(1) additional expenses requiring second incomes in many families
(2) increased numbers of women with careers and families
(3) no respect for the role of homemaker
(4) greater availability of child care options
(5) more opportunities for women

19. According to the bar graph, during which time period was there the greatest increase in the percentage of married women in the work force?

(1) 1955–1965
(2) 1965–1975
(3) 1975–1985
(4) 1985–1995
(5) 1995–1998

20. Between 1935 and 1957, a period that included World War II, the birth rate rose from 16.9 to 25 per 1000 people. What was the most likely cause of this "baby boom"?

(1) the return of young American soldiers from war
(2) the growth of the urban/suburban areas after World War II
(3) the mobility of the American family of the 1950s
(4) the expansion of the middle class and its new wealth
(5) the change in view toward artificial birth control methods

21. Increased personal income lets people purchase more goods and services. For example, spending for houses and cars increases as people feel comfortable in making long-term investments. What is one thing businesses would likely do in such a climate?

(1) increase production to provide greater quantities of goods
(2) lower the prices on the products
(3) spend less money on new equipment and machinery
(4) sell the products to foreign nations
(5) distribute the products equally throughout the country

PRETEST

Questions 22 and 23 are based on the following cartoon.

James Grasdal–Edmonton Journal

22. Which of the following conclusions about the baby boomer generation does this cartoon not support?

(1) Some baby boomers may not have saved enough for retirement.
(2) The children of baby boomers may have to support their parents.
(3) The baby boomer generation has sufficient living funds.
(4) The baby boomer generation needs to worry about financial security.
(5) Children of baby boomers may be worried about the financial security of their parents.

23. Which plan would *best* guarantee a strong financial future for a baby boomer?

(1) investing in high-risk stocks
(2) graduating from a business college
(3) participating in a company savings plan
(4) creating one's own business
(5) opening multiple credit accounts

PRETEST

Questions 24 and 25 are based on the following photograph and caption.

Stock Market Crash

© Bettman/CORBIS

As the day wears on and panic grips the floor of the New York Stock Exchange, wild rumors spread through the financial district. Ambulances race to buildings where bankrupt investors are reportedly killing themselves. Whether these stories are true or not, the very spectacle of a market gone mad has drawn a crowd of thousands to the exchange building and 20 mounted officers have been rushed in to reinforce an overwhelmed police contingent. Among the desperate investors waiting to learn the fate of their life's savings, women, many of them stenographers on Wall Street, make up a sizable part of the multitude. . .

—Excerpted from "Black Tuesday! Wall St. in Chaos as Stocks Crash" in *Chronicle of America*, edited by Clifton Daniel

24. What was one consequence of the sudden fall in stock prices?

(1) Confident bankers bought more stock.
(2) Indifferent shareholders ignored the collapse of the market.
(3) Worried investors frantically sold stock shares.
(4) Pleased factory workers experienced wage increases.
(5) Concerned shareholders bought more stock.

25. Which one of the following expressions best illustrates a value that played a role in the stock market crash of 1929?

(1) "A penny saved is a penny earned."
(2) "Honesty is the best policy."
(3) "Health is everything."
(4) "You can never be too rich. . . ."
(5) "The early bird catches the worm."

PRETEST

Social Studies Answer Key

1. **Comprehension (2)** Not all Americans supported the Civil Rights Act. The Civil Rights Act was to protect the rights of any minority group. Congress drafted the Civil Rights Act which was passed in both the House and the Senate but was not a unanimous decision.

2. **Evaluation (4)** The phrase from Dr. King's speech, "I Have a Dream . . ." told the listeners that even though the Emancipation Proclamation had been in effect for a long time, in practice it was still a dream, not a reality. The Constitution and the Declaration of Independence did not directly address the issue of slavery and equality of minority groups.

3. **Analysis (3)** The United States government owns 79.8% of all the land in Nevada. Much of this land is used for military testing. This testing could include target bombing by the Air Force as well as bomb detonation, including underground nuclear weapons testing.

4. **Comprehension (2)** The circle graphs give information about federally owned acreage in only three states. No information is given about the population of any states. No information is specific to the use of the land in any of these states.

5. **Analysis (2)** This is the only option available that could have been affected by the earlier incident. The other options happened prior to the end of the American Revolution.

6. **Comprehension (3)** The time lapse from 1688 to 1789 is 101 years.

7. **Analysis (2)** The information given is only about the volume of water in the Great Lakes. There is no information about the temperature of the water or the depth of the lakes or the amount of shoreline.

8. **Comprehension (5)** The graph title indicates that the information given is about the volume of water in the Great Lakes.

9. **Evaluation (3)** The chart shows that United States has the lowest number of public holidays compared to the majority of European countries. The European countries are, therefore, considered to assign a greater priority to allowing their citizens leisure time.

10. **Analysis (5)** Although there is no educational requirement to earn larger incomes, studies show that those with a college education have a greater likelihood of earning a higher salary. Many companies will financially assist their workforce in gaining higher education degrees.

11. **Evaluation (3)** High school counselors often cite the statistics concerning career success and the earning of a high school diploma. Often, those that did not finish high school seek the diploma through local school districts, community colleges, adult education centers, and other means.

12. **Analysis (3)** The dynamics of supply and demand recognizes that as a product becomes popular, the manufacturers produce more to meet the demand. This increase of availability allows the market to become competitive (prices decrease) so that more potential buyers are tempted to purchase the product. This does not necessarily mean the quality of the product is changed in any way. A decrease of availability brings greater demand for a product and can drive the prices higher.

13. **Analysis (4)** As the country became divided over the issue of slavery, some states had internal conflicts with the morality of owning slaves as a cheap workforce. The southern states relied more heavily on the plantation system to create a workforce to do the hard fieldwork in raising cotton and tobacco. The northern states had a more industrialized economy, and were able to hire a workforce. West Virginia was more economically and morally aligned with the philosophy of the North. This caused Virginia to divide into the

two states, and they have remained separate since this decision prior to the Civil War.

14. Evaluation (2) George Washington states in his farewell address that the European nations have a different set of priorities and interests. He suggests it would be unwise to complicate our own priorities and get caught up with the ever-changing conflicts that arise in Europe.

15. Application (3) Isolationism involves a philosophy of keeping the country's involvement with internal matters alone and advises against international alliances. Colonists and expansionists, (choices 4 and 5), both seek participation outside the boundaries of their own country. Imperialism (choice 2) has more of an emphasis on an emperor who might have interests in expanding the country's borders.

16. Application (4) America has developed a sense of responsibility for other nations that are in a struggle with foreign powers. Often these struggles are over issues that Americans feel a moral need to support. These issues include democratic principles and human rights. This type of assistance is possible due in part to the large size (land and population) and power (financial and military) that the United States has achieved. Many times the foreign country in the struggle will ask for help from the United States.

17. Analysis (1) Crazy Horse states that the reservation created idleness in the tribe's members. He wanted the Indians to be allowed to live off the land without interference from the white settlers and military.

18. Analysis (3) Although many women have voiced a concern that the choice of a career as a homemaker does not have the same level of respect as it did throughout history, studies show that most women in the workforce believe they are working for financial reasons. Career women have often mentioned that the selection of day care options and larger choices of career opportunities also increase the attraction in participating in the workforce outside the home.

19. Comprehension (3) The difference between 1975 and 1985 is more than a 14 percent increase. All the other time periods show less than a 13 percent gain.

20. Analysis (1) After World War II many young men returned to the United States as heroes. The government encouraged the return to civilian life by giving some financial incentives to get an education and a job. The large number of men that returned to domestic living in the United States got married and started families. This, in turn, had other effects on the growth of our country. Soon the expansion of suburban areas was needed to house the new families. Many families became more mobile in their attempt to increase job opportunities and advancement.

21. Application (1) Industry tries to stay one step ahead of the consumer. Often industry analysts read the economy in an attempt to forecast how much the consumer will purchase in the future. When consumers demonstrate a faith in the economy and are willing to make large investment purchases like houses and cars, industry creates a larger supply to take advantage of the economic growth. This might cause businesses to increase their own investment in their machinery. The government also benefits by the increased spending because of the increase in revenue from sales tax.

22. Analysis (3) Children of the baby boomer generation are finding for the first time in history that they are not necessarily going to improve their living conditions compared to their parents. As the population ages and medical technology allows for greater life spans, the concern is that the children of baby boomers will have to assist in the retirement living of their parents. No longer is the issue simply about providing for one's own retirement; now there is concern that one has to save additional funds for other family members.

23. Application (3) While some people have had success in investing in the stock market, analysts always stress that a savings plan is the best way to ensure financial security. College degrees may allow someone to get a job that pays better than a job that does not require a degree. These higher paying jobs, however, do not necessarily ensure a saving plan. Those who open their own businesses are at financial risk that the businesses may fail.

24. Analysis (3) The crash of the stock market has been blamed on financial panic. With so much of the nation's money held in investments, there was not enough money in the banks to hand to the people who wanted to withdraw their cash. This, in turn, caused many banks to fail. As Americans lost confidence in the economic strength of our nation, the stock market experienced record losses. This had a devastating effect throughout the world, casting many nations as well as the United States into a deep financial depression.

25. Evaluation (4) At the time of the crash of the stock market, many Americans were interested in making a lot of money in a short time through investments. If people had a more conservative attitude, they might not have overextended the lending of money to make more profits for their banks.

SOCIAL STUDIES PRETEST

Evaluation Chart

Use the answer key on pages 23–25 to check your answers to the Pretest. Then find the item number of each question you missed and circle it on the chart below to determine the Social Studies content areas in which you need more practice. Pay particular attention to areas where you missed half or more of the questions. Boldface numbers indicate questions based on graphics. The page numbers for the content areas are listed on the chart below. For those questions that you missed, review the skill pages indicated.

SKILL AREA/ CONTENT AREA	**COMPREHENSION (pages 217–230)**	**APPLICATION (pages 231–236)**	**ANALYSIS (pages 237–262)**	**EVALUATION (pages 271–274)**
World History (pages 297–326)	**6**		**5, 24**	**25**
U.S. History (pages 327–366)	1		13, 17, 20	2
Civics and Government (pages 367–398)	**19**	15, 16	**18**	**9**, 14
Economics (pages 399–426)		21, **23**	**10**, 12, **22**	**11**
Geography (pages 427–443)	**4, 8**		**3, 7**	

PRETEST

Science

The Science Pretest consists of 25 multiple-choice questions. You should take approximately 40 minutes to complete this test. Some of the questions are based on graphs, maps, tables, diagrams, editorial cartoons, and reading passages. Answer each question as carefully as possible, choosing the best of five answer choices and blackening in the grid. If you find a question too difficult, do not waste time on it. Work ahead and come back to it later when you can think it through carefully.

When you have completed the test, check your work with the answers and explanations at the end of the section. Use the Evaluation Chart on page 38 to determine which areas you need to review most.

Science Pretest Answer Grid

1	1	2	3	4	5	10	1	2	3	4	5	18	1	2	3	4	5
2	1	2	3	4	5	11	1	2	3	4	5	19	1	2	3	4	5
3	1	2	3	4	5	12	1	2	3	4	5	20	1	2	3	4	5
4	1	2	3	4	5	13	1	2	3	4	5	21	1	2	3	4	5
5	1	2	3	4	5	14	1	2	3	4	5	22	1	2	3	4	5
6	1	2	3	4	5	15	1	2	3	4	5	23	1	2	3	4	5
7	1	2	3	4	5	16	1	2	3	4	5	24	1	2	3	4	5
8	1	2	3	4	5	17	1	2	3	4	5	25	1	2	3	4	5
9	1	2	3	4	5												

PRETEST

Choose the best answer to each question that follows.

Question 1 is based upon the following cartoon.

Steve Kelley/San Diego Union-Tribune/Copley News Service

1. **Which of these statements provides the *best* support for the opinion of this cartoonist?**

   (1) The cost of a pack of cigarettes is too high and should be lowered.
   (2) Mothers who smoke during pregnancy could have children who suffer learning disabilities.
   (3) As many as 53,000 nonsmoking Americans die annually from inhaling second-hand smoke.
   (4) Adolescents who do not smoke before age 20 are not likely to ever start smoking.
   (5) Smoking is the number one preventable cause of death in America today.

2. **Physicians say that chewing on an aspirin (acetylsalicylic acid) thins the blood and helps prevent the blood from clotting. What is one positive application of this knowledge?**

   Aspirin may be used to

   (1) relieve muscle pain
   (2) reduce inflammation
   (3) lessen the possibility of heart attack
   (4) act as a stimulant
   (5) stop heavy bleeding

Question 3 is based on the following information.

Tsunamis are seismic sea waves that may be produced by earthquakes, volcanic eruptions, or submarine landslides. In the open ocean, they travel at speeds from 500 to 800 kilometers per hour and may be only 30 to 60 centimeters in height. As they approach land, however, they are compressed and may reach 30 meters in height.

3. **Tsunamis could be very dangerous to humans because of the potential for causing what phenomena?**

   (1) earthquakes
   (2) severe flooding
   (3) submarine landslides
   (4) fault lines
   (5) volcanic eruptions

Questions 4 and 5 are based on the chart below.

Transfusion Relationship

Blood type	Can receive blood from	Acts as donor to
O	O	O, A, B, AB
A	O, A	A, AB
B	B, O	B, AB
AB	O, A, B, AB	AB

4. **If a person with blood type AB wishes to donate blood, those with which blood type(s) may receive the blood?**

   (1) only type O
   (2) only types O and B
   (3) only types B and AB
   (4) only type AB
   (5) all types of blood

PRETEST

5. Which of the following blood types can be regarded as a universal donor?

(1) O
(2) A
(3) B
(4) AB
(5) all blood types

Question 6 is based on the following information.

The most common organic acids are *formic acid* and *acetic acid*. Formic acid occurs naturally in red ants and in pine needles. In concentrated form it can burn the skin; however, diluted formic acid is used for its germicidal properties. Acetic acid is responsible for the sour taste of pickles and sharp odors that can burn the nostrils. Cider vinegar contains 3 to 6 percent acetic acid and is made by the natural oxidation of apple cider.

6. Which of the following organic acids is most dangerous in high concentrations of exposure to humans?

(1) citric acid found in citrus fruits
(2) lactic acid found in milk products
(3) hydrochloric acid found in the stomach's gastric juices
(4) oxalic acid found in rhubarb leaves
(5) folic acid, a form of vitamin B used to treat anemia

Question 7 is based on the following illustration.

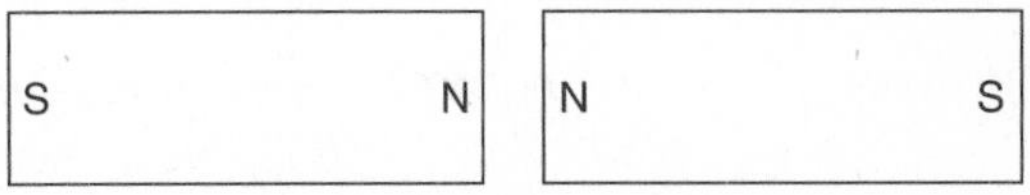

7. If the two bar magnets above were brought closer together, what do you predict would happen?

(1) They would attract each other.
(2) They would repel each other.
(3) They would cancel out each other's magnetic field.
(4) They would create an alternating current.
(5) There would not be any reaction.

Question 8 is based on the following information.

Dave worked in a new energy efficient building where the windows were sealed shut and the air was recirculated. A week before the building was opened, the company installed new carpet and painted the walls. After two months, Dave and his co-workers began to complain about fatigue, headaches, and sore throats. Upon going home at night, their symptoms disappeared. Dave's employer hired a team of air pollution experts to test the working environment of his employees. It was later determined that all of the workers were suffering from "sick building syndrome." This syndrome is a situation in which building occupants experience severe health problems without having specific illnesses. In this particular case, the workers were suffering from problems caused by air pollutants inside the building.

8. Which of the following factors would be most likely to cause "sick building syndrome"?

(1) inadequate temperatures
(2) poor lighting
(3) resins from construction materials
(4) worker stress
(5) humidity

PRETEST

Question 9 is based on the following weather map.

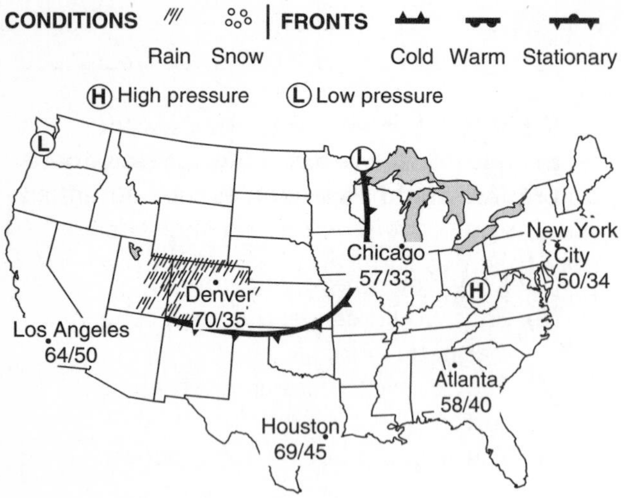

9. Which of the following generalizations would be made by a weather forecaster given the information on this weather map?

(1) Most of the nation is experiencing a drought.
(2) No state should encounter temperatures below 50°.
(3) Denver, Colorado, will probably have a record amount of snow.
(4) Travelers on vacation in Florida should not have to worry about rain.
(5) Laredo, Texas, continues to battle high winds and severe weather.

Question 10 is based on the following information.

The leaf is a flat organ composed of two layers of photosynthetic cells sandwiched between the epidermal, or outer, layers. An epidermal layer is coated with a waxy covering called the *cuticle,* which prevents the loss of gas and water. Tiny holes, called *stomata,* provide openings for the entry of carbon dioxide and the exit of oxygen.

10. Based on the information above, what does the leaf "breathe" through?

(1) its photosynthetic cells
(2) its veins
(3) its cuticle
(4) its epidermal layers
(5) its stomata

Question 11 is based on the following information.

Our blood consists of a liquid, the straw-colored *plasma,* in which are suspended red blood cells, white blood cells, and *platelets.* Red blood cells are used to transport oxygen throughout the body. White blood cells are used to fight infections. Platelets are important in blood clotting.

11. Based on the passage about blood, which of the following blood components are used to repair an open wound?

(1) plasma and white blood cells
(2) red blood cells
(3) white blood cells
(4) platelets
(5) white blood cells and platelets

PRETEST

Question 12 is based on the following diagram.

How Cells Divide

A new study suggests that aging may be caused by mistakes in the transfer of genes and chromosomes during cell division. Here is an illustration of how cells divide.

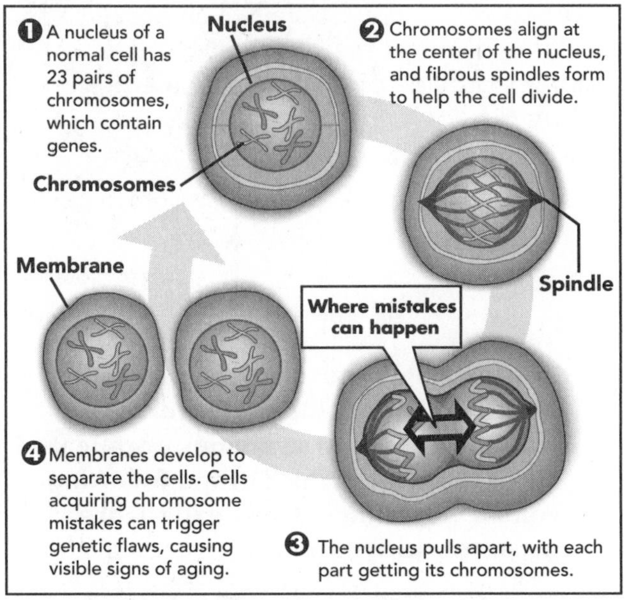

1 A nucleus of a normal cell has 23 pairs of chromosomes, which contain genes.
Nucleus
Chromosomes
2 Chromosomes align at the center of the nucleus, and fibrous spindles form to help the cell divide.
Spindle
Membrane
Where mistakes can happen
4 Membranes develop to separate the cells. Cells acquiring chromosome mistakes can trigger genetic flaws, causing visible signs of aging.
3 The nucleus pulls apart, with each part getting its chromosomes.

Source: Associated Press article in the *Daily Herald*, March 31, 2000

12. According to this study, aging may be the effect of cells losing their capacity to reproduce properly. Which of the following conditions would probably *not* be the result of cellular degeneration or mutation?

(1) arthritis – a chronic disorder that affects the joints and muscles
(2) Alzheimer's disease – a degenerative disease of the central nervous system
(3) osteoporosis – the deterioration of bone
(4) kidney stone – a solid object that is usually caused by an excessive amount of calcium in the urine
(5) cancer – a malignant tumor that tends to spread uncontrollably in the body

Questions 13 and 14 are based on the following passage.

There is, perhaps, no part of the world where the early geological periods can be studied with so much ease and precision as in the United States. Along the northern border between Canada and the United States, there runs a low line of hills known as the Laurentian Hills. Insignificant in height, nowhere rising more than two thousand feet above the level of the sea, these are nevertheless the first mountains that broke the uniform level of Earth's surface and lifted themselves above the waters. Their low stature, as compared with that of other, loftier mountain ranges, is in accordance with an invariable rule by which the relative age of mountains may be estimated. The oldest mountains are the lowest, while the younger and more recent ones tower above their elders and are usually more jagged and dislocated.

13. In the United States, where can early geological periods be studied?

(1) only along the country's northern border
(2) only in the Rocky Mountains
(3) throughout the country easily and precisely
(4) only in swampy Florida
(5) only in the Appalachian Mountains

14. The Appalachian Mountains are lower than the Rocky Mountains. What conclusion can you draw from this?

The Appalachian Mountains are

(1) younger than the Rocky Mountains
(2) older than the Rocky Mountains
(3) the same age as the Rocky Mountains
(4) more scenic than the Rocky Mountains
(5) more torn and dislocated than the Rocky Mountains

PRETEST

Question 15 is based on the following information.

Dentistry Predictions for the Twenty-first Century

- "smart fillings" that prevent further tooth decay
- toothpastes that restore tooth minerals and strengthen teeth
- chewing gums and mouthwashes that reverse early tooth decay
- gene transfer and tissue engineering used for repair of damaged or diseased tissues
- tooth regeneration technology

Source: *Newsweek* October 2000

15. Many people are reluctant to visit the dentist. How do you think the average dental patient will be affected by these predictions for the twenty-first century?

The patient will experience

(1) no need to practice oral hygiene
(2) less pain and more natural results
(3) fewer visits to the dentist for fillings
(4) an increase in cavities
(5) more approved dental plans by HMOs

Question 16 is based on the following illustration.

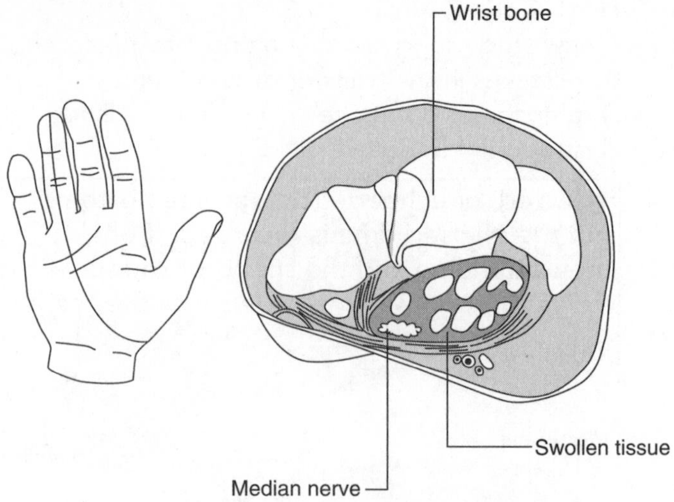

16. Carpal tunnel syndrome is a painful condition that affects many workers whose jobs require strenuous or repeated use of the wrist. Which of the following women would most likely experience carpal tunnel syndrome?

(1) Patti, an interior decorator who works from the home
(2) Lisa, a full-time computer data entry operator
(3) Martha, a child psychologist who works in a large city hospital
(4) Sheri, a first-grade teacher of twenty-two years
(5) Cathie, a part-time corporate travel agent

PRETEST

Question 17 is based on the following information.

The Fathometer is a device used for determining ocean depths. It operates by sending sound waves under water. A sudden pulse of sound is transmitted by a ship and then picked up again after it has been reflected, or echoed, from the sea bottom, and the elapsed time is recorded. If one knows the time and the speed of sound waves through water, the depth of the sea at any point may be computed, often to the nearest foot.

17. Which point would be most relevant to the central idea of this passage?

(1) The depth of the ocean is already known and doesn't require further studying.
(2) The speed at which underwater sound waves travel from the ocean's surface to the bottom remains constant.
(3) Fathometers show only approximate depths and are extremely reliable.
(4) Fathometers work best in shallow waters and shouldn't be used to determine the depth of the ocean.
(5) Fathometers should operate on scientific and not mathematical principles.

Question 18 is based on the information and table below.

Heat is able to pass from one molecule to another through *heat conduction*. In the table that follows, the numbers (called coefficients) indicate the relative rates of heat transfer in the materials listed. For example, water is a better heat conductor than wood.

Heat Conduction Coefficients

Material	Coefficient
silver	100
copper	92
aluminum	50
iron	11
glass	0.20
water	0.12
wood	0.03
air	0.006
perfect vacuum	0

18. According to the information in the table, which are the best conductors?

(1) gases
(2) natural materials
(3) metals
(4) liquids

PRETEST

Question 19 is based on the following information.

The International Space Station is planned as the largest collaborative scientific project in history. Sixteen nations are making plans to take part: United States, Russia, Canada, Belgium, Denmark, France, Germany, Italy, Netherlands, Norway, Spain, Sweden, Switzerland, United Kingdom, Japan, and Brazil. The station will be made up of six laboratories with enough living space for up to seven people. Scientists have planned to conduct research on the growth of living cells and the effects on the human body in an environment with reduced or zero gravity. They will also examine the long-term changes in the earth's environment by observing earth from orbit. The projected completion date for the International Space Station project is 2004.

19. According to the passage, which of the studies below would be best conducted in the International Space Station?

(1) analysis of fossil fuel samples
(2) development of new surgical procedures
(3) examination of tree samples from a rain forest
(4) measurement of greenhouse gasses in the atmosphere
(5) exploration of occupational hazards in the twenty-first century

Question 20 is based on the diagram below.

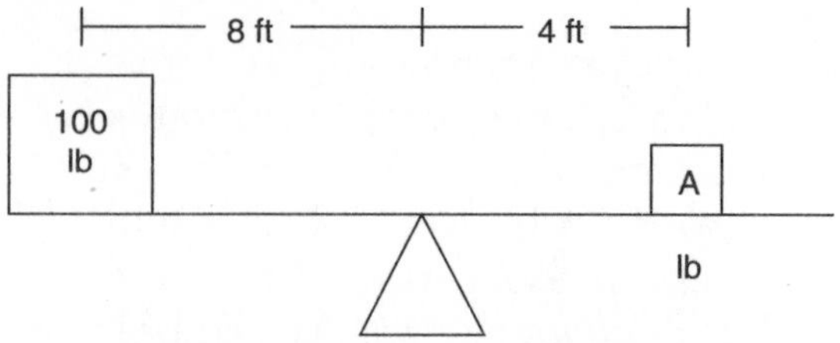

20. In order to balance the lever in the diagram above, how much must object A weigh?

(1) 50 pounds
(2) 100 pounds
(3) 200 pounds
(4) 500 pounds
(5) 1,000 pounds

Question 21 is based on the following information.

Many organizations are exploring the need for alternative fuels and automobiles. One alternative vehicle is the *hybrid car.* It combines the power system of the electric motor and the gasoline engine. Computers adjust the power system needed for different types of driving and braking. When the driver is idling, the engine quits. This cuts back on harmful emissions (substances discharged into the air) and saves gasoline.

21. Based on the information in this passage, which of the following groups of citizens would be most interested in the development of the hybrid car?

(1) consumers hoping to purchase a quality car for less money
(2) environmentalists concerned about the greenhouse effect
(3) automakers reluctant to create a gasoline-electric car
(4) owners of gas stations across the United States
(5) manufacturers of battery-electric vehicles

PRETEST

Question 22 is based on the following information.

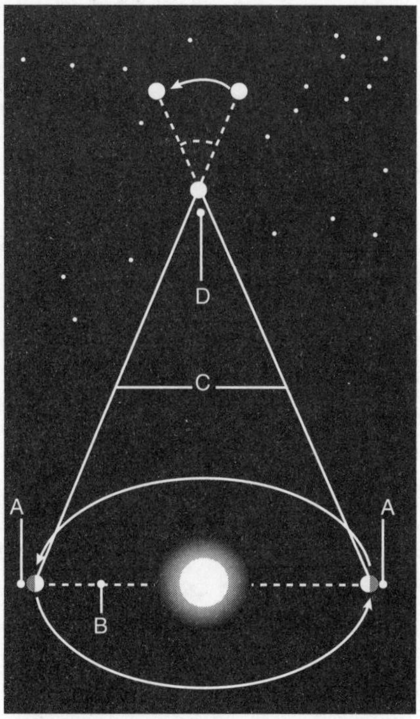

Reprinted from *How in the World?* ©1990 The Reader's Digest Association Limited. Used by permission of The Reader's Digest Association, Inc., Pleasantville, NY, www.rd.com

Determining Distance by Parallax

Since astronomers cannot use radar to work out the distance of a star, they use the parallax method. Photographs are taken of the sky from the same position on Earth all through the year, and these reveal that some stars remain 'fixed', whereas others seem to 'move'. Those stars that show visible movement are closer to the Earth than those which do not. To find the distance of a star which 'moves,' astronomers look at two photographs taken six months apart, from the same observatory (A). (It takes six months for the Earth to reach the far points in its orbit.) Using the diameter of the Earth's orbit around the sun (B) as a baseline, two lines are drawn from each end of the baseline to the star, one to each shifted position (C). Where the two lines intersect, they form the apparent angle of motion (D). Knowing the diameter of the Earth's orbit and the size of the angle of motion, astronomers can calculate the distance to the star.

—Excerpted from *Readers Digest* How in the World?

22. Which component would not be important to an astronomer when calculating the distance of a star?

(1) the exact diameter of Earth's orbit
(2) an observatory outfitted with modern technology
(3) the size of the angle of motion
(4) a clear and accurate photograph of the sky
(5) measurements of the gravitational pull

PRETEST

Questions 23 and 24 are based on the table below.

Energy Expenditure

ACTIVITY	CALORIES PER HOUR
sitting at rest	15
walking	130–200
running	500–900
bicycling	240
swimming	200–700
writing	20

23. According to the table above, which of the people listed below would need to consume 720 calories to maintain body weight after three hours of his or her chosen activity?

(1) a long distance runner
(2) a cyclist
(3) an office worker
(4) an author
(5) a recreational walker

24. For a person concerned with weight loss and without a lot of time to exercise, which activity would be the most efficient choice?

(1) bicycling
(2) swimming
(3) walking
(4) writing
(5) running

Question 25 is based on the following information.

25. Pediatrics professor Samuel Katz said, "Immunization is the single intervention that has most dramatically reduced childhood morbidity and mortality." Which of the following arguments would professor Katz include in support of his theory on immunizations?

(1) Vaccines could cause severe side effects in inoculated children.
(2) Smallpox has been eliminated, and many other life-threatening diseases are seldom found.
(3) The Food and Drug Administration should continue to monitor results of inoculations and complications resulting from them.
(4) Parents should question the need for vaccinations for their infants and toddlers.
(5) The government needs to be involved in policies regarding vaccinations.

PRETEST

Science Answer Key

1. **Evaluation (3)** The author is expressing an opinion about second-hand smoke. The other choices do not address this concern about smoking.

2. **Application (3)** A common cause of a heart attack is a blood clot, which restricts the blood supply to the heart. According to the passage, an aspirin can thin the blood and reduce clotting.

3. **Application (2)** Tsunamis can become giant waves of water. They could create severe flooding and damage in populated coastal areas.

4. **Analysis (4)** The table indicates that a person with blood type AB can act as a donor only to a person with blood type AB.

5. **Analysis (1)** A person with blood type O can donate blood to people of all blood types and, thus, is known as a universal donor.

6. **Analysis (3)** Diluted hydrochloric acid is found in the stomach's gastric juices, but undiluted hydrochloric acid is harmful when humans are exposed to it.

7. **Application (2)** Like charges repel; unlike charges attract. The north poles of each magnet are alike, so they would repel each other.

8. **Analysis (3)** "Sick building syndrome" is caused by environmental factors in the air. Stress, lighting, and humidity are not direct causes of this syndrome.

9. **Evaluation (4)** There is no rain in the forecast for Florida. The other choices are not true based on the information provided.

10. **Analysis (5)** According to the passage, the only opening in the leaf is the *stomata*. This must be the "mouth" through which a plant breathes.

11. **Comprehension (5)** The passage says that white blood cells fight infections and that platelets are important in clotting of blood. Fighting infections and blood clotting are two processes needed to repair a wound.

12. **Application (4)** Kidney stones are the only condition that is not caused by a problem in cellular division.

13. **Comprehension (3)** The passage says that the early geological periods can be studied with ease and precision.

14. **Comprehension (2)** The Appalachian Mountains are lower than the Rocky Mountains; therefore, the Appalachian Mountains are older.

15. **Analysis (2)** The predictions for dental protection will hopefully prevent cavities and gum disease; therefore, fewer painful procedures will be needed.

16. **Application (2)** While all the jobs involve hand motion, Lisa's job involves more repetitive motion of her hands and wrist, which could lead to strain or carpal tunnel syndrome.

17. **Evaluation (2)** Sound waves must travel at a constant speed through the sea in order for the principle under which a Fathometer works to be valid.

18. **Comprehension (3)** The metals silver, copper, aluminum, and iron have the highest heat conduction coefficients; therefore, they are the best conductors among the materials listed.

19. **Application (4)** One of the goals of the International Space Station involves the study of Earth's environment, which would include atmospheric conditions. The other choices would not need to be studied in the station.

20. **Application (3)** If object A is half as far away from the middle of the lever as the 100-pound weight, to balance it must weigh twice as much (200 pounds).

21. **Application (2)** A hybrid car is healthier for the environment; therefore, environmentalists would be very supportive of this development.

22. **Application (5)** The gravitational pull is not important in the study of the distance of stars according to the passage.

23. **Application (2)** A bicyclist would consume approximately 720 calories in three hours ($240 \times 3 = 720$).

24. **Evaluation (5)** Running consumes the most calories per hour, so it is the most efficient weight loss activity among those listed.

25. **Evaluation (2)** Professor Samuel Katz would probably include the positive results such as the elimination of smallpox and the reduction of other serious diseases.

SCIENCE PRETEST

Evaluation Chart

Use the answer key on pages 37–38 to check your answers to the Pretest. Then find the item number of each question you missed and circle it on the chart below to determine the Science content areas in which you need more practice. Pay particular attention to areas where you missed half or more of the questions. The page numbers for the content areas are listed on the chart below. For those questions that you missed, review the skill pages indicated.

SKILL AREA/ CONTENT AREA	COMPREHENSION (pages 217–230)	APPLICATION (pages 231–236)	ANALYSIS (pages 237–262)	EVALUATION (pages 271–274)
Life Sciences (Biology) (pages 459–496)	11	12, 16, 23	4, 5, 8, 10, 15	1, 24, 25
Earth & Space Science (pages 497–532)	13, 14	3, 19, 22		9
Physical Sciences (Chemistry and Physics) (pages 533–577)	18	2, 7, 20, 21	6	17

PRETEST

Language Arts, Reading

The Language Arts, Reading Pretest will give you an introduction to the GED Language Arts, Reading Test. This test is slightly longer than half-length and contains 23 questions. Questions are based on four excerpts: one selection each from **fiction** (a novel), **poetry, drama,** and **nonfiction prose** (a diary). You should take approximately **33 minutes** to complete this test.

At the end of 33 minutes, stop and mark your place. Then finish the test. This will give you an idea of whether or not you can finish the real GED Test in the time allotted. Try to answer as many questions as you can. A blank will count as a wrong answer, so make a reasonable guess for answers to questions of which you are not sure.

When you are finished with the test, check your answers and turn to the Evaluation Chart on page 50. Use the chart to evaluate whether or not you are ready to take the actual GED Test and, if not, in what areas you need more work.

Language Arts, Reading Pretest Answer Grid

1	①	②	③	④	⑤	9	①	②	③	④	⑤	17	①	②	③	④	⑤
2	①	②	③	④	⑤	10	①	②	③	④	⑤	18	①	②	③	④	⑤
3	①	②	③	④	⑤	11	①	②	③	④	⑤	19	①	②	③	④	⑤
4	①	②	③	④	⑤	12	①	②	③	④	⑤	20	①	②	③	④	⑤
5	①	②	③	④	⑤	13	①	②	③	④	⑤	21	①	②	③	④	⑤
6	①	②	③	④	⑤	14	①	②	③	④	⑤	22	①	②	③	④	⑤
7	①	②	③	④	⑤	15	①	②	③	④	⑤	23	①	②	③	④	⑤
8	①	②	③	④	⑤	16	①	②	③	④	⑤						

PRETEST

Questions 1–6 deal with the following passage.

WHAT CONFLICTS DOES THERESA FEEL AS SHE DECIDES WHETHER TO LOOK INTO THE SOURCE OF THE MESSAGE IN THE BOTTLE?

Deanna leaned across the table. "Just what I said—I think we should run this letter in your column this week. I'm sure other people would love to read it.

"We don't even know who they are. Don't you think we should get their permission first?"

"That's just the point. We can't. I can talk to the attorney at the paper, but I'm sure it's legal.

"I know it's probably legal, but I'm not sure if it's right. I mean this is a very personal letter. I'm not sure it should be spread around so that everyone can read it."

"It's a human interest story, Theresa. People love those sorts of things. Besides, there's nothing in there that might be embarrassing to someone. This is a beautiful letter. And remember, this Garrett person sent it in a *bottle* in the *ocean.* He had to know that it would wash up somewhere."

Theresa shook her head. "I don't know, Deanna. . . "

"Well, think about it. Sleep on it if you have to. I think it's a great idea."

Theresa did think about the letter. . . She found herself wondering about the man who wrote it—Garrett, if that was his real name. And who, if anyone, was Catherine? His lover or his wife, obviously, but she wasn't around anymore. Was she dead, she wondered, or did something else happen that forced them apart? And why was it sealed in a bottle and set adrift? The whole thing was strange. Her reporter's instincts took over then, and she suddenly thought that the message might not mean anything. It could be someone who wanted to write a love letter but didn't have anyone to send it to. It could even have been sent by someone who got some sort of vicarious thrill by making lonely women cry on distant beaches. But as the words rolled through her head again, she realized that those possibilities were unlikely. The letter obviously came from the heart. And to think that a man wrote it! In all her years, she had never received a letter even close to that. Touching sentiments sent her way had always been emblazoned with Hallmark greeting card logos. David had never been much of a writer, nor had anyone else she had dated. What would such a man be like? She wondered. Would he be as caring in person as the letter seemed to imply?

—Excerpted from *Message in a Bottle* by Nicholas Sparks

1. Which statement is *not* supporting evidence for the inference that Theresa works for a newspaper?

(1) We should run this letter in your column this week.
(2) I can talk to the attorney at the paper.
(3) This is a beautiful, very personal letter.
(4) Her reporter's instincts took over then.
(5) It's a human interest story, Theresa.

2. Based on Theresa's thoughts about the letter, what are her next actions likely to be?

(1) She will expose the writer of the love letter in her column.
(2) She will discover why the writer made lonely women cry.
(3) She will determine whether she could care for the writer.
(4) She will bring a lawsuit against Garrett for plagiarism.
(5) She will offer Garrett a job working for the newspaper.

PRETEST

3. Based on the passage, what mental comparison does Theresa make in terms of writing ability?

(1) between Deanna and herself
(2) between Catherine and herself
(3) between Garrett and Catherine
(4) between Hallmark and David
(5) between Garrett and David

4. What techniques are most in contrast in the passage?

(1) dialogue versus mental questions
(2) facts versus opinions
(3) hypotheses versus conclusions
(4) chronological events versus flashback
(5) narrator versus author comments

5. What is the overall tone of the language of the passage?

(1) businesslike and formal
(2) romantic and nostalgic
(3) light and humorous
(4) sad and unhappy
(5) factual and legalistic

6. What is the likely overall purpose or intent of the passage?

(1) to give Theresa a reason to determine the identity of the man who wrote the letter
(2) to provide Theresa with an excuse to take a trip to the ocean to look for other bottles
(3) to enable Theresa to have a chance to get a scoop for her column at the newspaper
(4) to allow Theresa to make up her mind about whether to marry David after all
(5) to help Theresa decide whether she would prefer writing Hallmark greeting cards

PRETEST

Questions 7–12 refer to the following poem.

WHERE IS THE SPEAKER OF THE POEM?

The Road Not Taken

Two roads diverged in a yellow wood,
And sorry I could not travel both
And be one traveler, long I stood
And looked down one as far as I could
To where it bent in the undergrowth;

Then took the other, as just as fair,
And having perhaps the better claim,
Because it was grassy and wanted wear;
Though as for that the passing there
Had worn them really about the same,

And both that morning equally lay
In leaves no step had trodden black.
Oh, I kept the first for another day!
Yet knowing how way leads on to way,
I doubted if I should ever come back

I shall be telling this with a sigh
Somewhere ages and ages hence:
Two roads diverged in a wood, and I-
I took the one less traveled by,
And that has made all the difference.

—by Robert Frost

7. Which of the following lines best demonstrates that the speaker feels regret?

(1) Then took the other, as just as fair (line 6)
(2) And having perhaps the better claim (line 7)
(3) And both that morning equally lay (line 11)
(4) Oh, I kept the first for another day! (line 13)
(5) I shall be telling this with a sigh (line 16)

8. Who would be most likely to share the attitude expressed by the speaker of the poem?

(1) a child who received the two toys she most wanted
(2) a farmer who planted whatever crops he wished
(3) a job applicant who received two great job offers
(4) a U.S. resident who paid income taxes each year
(5) a soldier who gladly followed the orders he was given

9. What do the lines *"long I stood/And looked down one as far as I could"* (lines 3-4) reveal about the speaker's feelings?

(1) uncertainty about a decision
(2) confidence in what lies ahead
(3) distaste for what must be done
(4) sorrow about the future
(5) excitement over the unknown

10. What is suggested about the speaker's character in lines 18 and 19?

The speaker

(1) has a difficult time making decisions
(2) sometimes prefers to be different from others
(3) seldom makes appropriate decisions
(4) has problems with self-confidence and esteem
(5) is extremely unrealistic about things in life

PRETEST

11. Which statement best expresses the overall theme of the poem?

(1) Life prepares individuals for any new situation.
(2) Life confuses individuals with threatening circumstances.
(3) Life offers different possibilities but rarely second chances.
(4) Life prevents creative exploration or discovery.
(5) Life requires change for the sake of change.

12. Robert Graves, in his introduction to the Selected Poems of Robert Frost, claims that *"The four natural objects most proper to poems are, by common consent, the moon, water, hills and trees."*

How does *The Road Not Taken* relate to this statement?

The poem

(1) provides a contrast to Graves's claim
(2) contains all four necessary natural objects
(3) serves as ridicule to this statement
(4) meets the requirements for a proper poem
(5) sets a standard for all poetry

PRETEST

Questions 13–18 refer to the following excerpt.

WHAT DOES DUNOIS BELIEVE ABOUT JOAN?

Scene 5

Dunois. Come, Joan! you have had enough praying. After that fit of crying you will catch a chill if you stay here any longer. It is all over: the cathedral is empty; and the streets are full. They are calling for The Maid. We have told them you are staying here alone to pray; but they want to see you again.

Joan. No: let the king have all the glory.

Dunois. He only spoils the show, poor devil. No Joan: you have crowned him; and you must go through with it.

Joan. [shakes her head reluctantly].

Dunois. [raising her] Come come! It will be over in a couple of hours. It's better than the bridge at Orleans: eh?

Joan. Oh, dear Dunois, how I wish it were the bridge at Orleans again! We lived at that bridge.

Dunois. Yes, faith, and died too: some of us.

Joan. Isn't it strange, Jack? I am such a coward: I am frightened beyond words before a battle; but it is so dull afterwards when there is no danger: oh, so dull! dull! dull!

Dunois. You must learn to be abstemious in war, just as you are in your food and drink, my little saint.

Joan. Dear Jack: I think you like me as a soldier likes his comrade.

Dunois. You need it, poor innocent child of God. You have not many friends at court.

Joan. Why do all these courtiers and knights and churchmen hate me? What have I done to them? I have asked nothing for myself except that my village shall not be taxed; for we cannot afford war taxes. I have brought them luck and victory: I have set them right when they were doing all sorts of stupid things: I have crowned Charles and made him a real king; and all the honors he is handing out have gone to them. Then why do they not love me?

Dunois. [rallying her] Sim-ple-ton! Do you expect stupid people to love you for shewing them up? Do blundering old military dug-outs love the successful young captains who supersede them? Do ambitious politicians love the climbers who take the front seats from them? Do archbishops enjoy being played off their own altars, even by saints? Why, I should be jealous of you myself if I were ambitious enough.

—Excerpted from *Saint Joan* by George Bernard Shaw

13. According to lines 15–21, what happened at the bridge of Orleans?

(1) a flood
(2) a coronation
(3) a church service
(4) a battle
(5) a marriage

PRETEST

14. In which activity would Joan be most likely to choose to participate?

(1) a celebration to honor her
(2) a grand ball at the castle
(3) a plot of treason against the king
(4) a rebellion against the church
(5) a fight to protect the king

15. What conflicting feelings about war does Joan reveal in lines 22–26?

(1) fear and excitement
(2) despair and pride
(3) worry and confidence
(4) joy and envy
(5) sorrow and pleasure

16. What effect is produced by the series of questions Dunois asks in lines 49–59?

They serve as comparisons to illustrate the relationship between

(1) Joan and the king's court
(2) Joan and Dunois
(3) Dunois and the king
(4) the king and the people
(5) the king and the church

17. What is the overall effect of this scene?

It reveals

(1) the cruelty of Dunois
(2) the lack of Joan's political understanding
(3) the passionate love of Dunois for Joan
(4) the secret ambition of Joan
(5) the disgust the people feel toward Joan

18. During the time period in which the play is set, the role of women in military service or government leadership was very limited.

How does this information relate to the portrayal of Joan in this passage?

(1) Joan appears more criminal and devious.
(2) It makes the play seem quite absurd and strange.
(3) The king appears very open-minded.
(4) Joan seems even more extraordinary.
(5) Joan appears very representative of her time.

PRETEST

Questions 19–23 refer to the following excerpts.

WHO IS THE YOUNG AUTHOR ANNE FRANK, AND WHY DOES SHE FEEL COMPELLED TO KEEP A DIARY IN THE "SECRET ANNEXE" OF AN OLD OFFICE BUILDING FOR THREE YEARS DURING WORLD WAR II?

Passage One
Friday, 9 October, 1942

Dear Kitty,

I've only got dismal and depressing news for you today. Our many Jewish friends are being taken away by the dozen. These people are treated by the Gestapo without a shred of decency, being loaded into cattle trucks and sent to Westerbork, the big Jewish camp in Drente. Westerbork sounds terrible: only one washing cubicle for a hundred people and not nearly enough lavatories. There is no separate accommodation. Men, women, and children all sleep together. . . .

Passage Two
Friday, 23 July, 1943

Dear Kitty,

Just for fun I'm going to tell you each person's first wish, when we are allowed to go outside again. Margot and Mr. Van Daan long more than anything for a hot bath filled to overflowing and want to stay in it for half an hour. Mrs. Van Daan wants most to go and eat cream cakes immediately. Dussel thinks of nothing but seeing Lotje, his wife; Mummy of her cup of coffee; Daddy is going to visit Mr. Vossen first; Peter the town and a cinema, while I should find it so blissful, I shouldn't know where to start! But most of all, I long for a home of our own, to be able to move freely and to have some help with my work again at last, in other words—school.

Passage Three
Tuesday, 7 March, 1944

Dear Kitty,

If I think now of my life in 1942, it all seems so unreal. It was quite a different Anne who enjoyed that heavenly existence from the Anne who has grown wise within these walls. Yes, it was a heavenly life. Boy friends at every turn, about twenty friends and acquaintances of my own age, the darling of nearly all the teachers, spoiled from top to toe by Mummy and Daddy, lots of sweets, enough pocket money, what more could one want?

—Excerpted from *Anne Frank: The Diary of a Young Girl*

PRETEST

19. In the diary entry selected from October 9, 1942, Anne Frank explains what is happening in Holland during the early years of World War II. The events as paraphrased in relation to the Jewish community would include which of the following emotions?

(1) oppression
(2) celebration
(3) ceremony
(4) glorification
(5) toleration

20. Anne Frank was a real teenager who maintained her spirit and optimism and displayed her talents through her diary. Had she lived to adulthood, what might the reader have expected her to become?

(1) a world-famous athlete
(2) a prize-winning journalist
(3) the leader of a commune
(4) a five-star hotel chef
(5) a children's camp director

21. From Passage Two, what does the reader conclude from the details of the first wishes of the persons who are hiding (from the Nazis)?

(1) They have learned to manipulate others.
(2) They have become greedy and selfish.
(3) They have longed for simple pleasures.
(4) They have become clinically depressed.
(5) They have become foolishly optimistic.

22. *Time* magazine included Anne Frank in its series of the 100 most influential people of the twentieth century and said that Anne "became the most memorable figure to emerge from World War II—besides Hitler." Using this information along with the passages quoted helps to explain all of the following *except*

(1) the contrast of an innocent child with an oppressive dictator
(2) the true and documented effects of war on real people
(3) the reason for movies, plays, and biographies about Anne
(4) the nature of the jealousy between Anne and her sister
(5) the reality of Nazi treatment of people of Jewish descent

23. In the introduction to the book, former First Lady Eleanor Roosevelt wrote, "Anne herself . . . matured very rapidly in these two years, the crucial years from thirteen to fifteen in which change is so swift and so difficult for every young girl." What evidence in Passage Three supports the idea of Anne's growing maturity?

(1) Anne's continuing interest in boyfriends
(2) Anne's ability to get along with her teachers
(3) Anne's being spoiled by both her parents
(4) Anne's continuing supply of sweets and money
(5) Anne's realization of her life in 1942 as different

PRETEST

Language Arts, Reading Answer Key

Message in a Bottle

1. **Comprehension (3)** A personal letter could relate to any home or business, so this is not evidence of a newspaper job. The references to a column as in choice 1, the paper as in choice 2, reporter's instincts choice 4, and human interest story choice 5 are all language related to a newspaper.

2. **Application (3)** Theresa is very taken with the sentiments in the letter and compares the writer to David and others she had dated. There is no evidence that she plans any punitive action such as exposing the writer (choice 1), that Garrett copied someone else's work (choice 4), or that the paper is trying to hire him (choice 5). As a reporter she very briefly thinks of other possibilities such as making lonely women cry (choice 2).

3. **Analysis (5)** Theresa thinks to herself, "David had never been much of a writer, nor had anyone else she had dated." She does not compare the writing ability of Deanna (choice 1), Catherine (choices 2 and 3), or any Hallmark writers (choice 4).

4. **Analysis (1)** Approximately half the passage is dialogue between Deanna and Theresa, and the other half are Theresa's private thoughts revealed by the author. There is no evidence of fact and opinion (choice 2), formal hypotheses and conclusions (choice 3), or time order—chronology (choice 4). There is no mention of a narrator (choice 5).

5. **Synthesis (2)** A number of clues to the tone of the passage as romantic and nostalgic include the ocean, a very personal love letter, some personal relationship between Garrett and Catherine, and touching sentiments. The tone is not businesslike or formal (choice 1) or factual and legalistic (choice 5) because of the dialogue and obviously personal thoughts. There is nothing light and humorous (choice 3) about a separation between Garrett and Catherine or Catherine's possible death. While there may be some sadness (choice 4) in thinking of Garrett and Catherine, Theresa doesn't know exactly what happened, so that isn't the *overall* tone.

6. **Synthesis (1)** Theresa muses at length about the man who wrote the letter, and she obviously wants to meet him. She doesn't really care to search for other bottles (choice 2). If she really wanted a scoop for her paper (choice 3), she wouldn't have to think so long about finding the man. David (choice 4) is only mentioned in passing in terms of his lack of writing ability, and she is not seriously deciding between working at her current job or working for Hallmark (choice 5).

"The Road Not Taken"

7. **Comprehension (5)** To be telling something *"with a sigh"* indicates that the speaker feels regret.

8. **Application (3)** A job applicant who received two great job offers must also make a choice like the speaker in the poem. The job applicant might wonder what might have happened if the unaccepted position had been chosen just as the speaker in the poem wonders about the road not taken.

9. **Analysis (1)** The speaker cannot instantly decide as evidenced by *"long I stood,"* showing uncertainty about the decision.

10. **Analysis (2)** The speaker in choosing the road *"less traveled by,"* indicates a preference for taking a way that fewer people take. He demonstrates a desire to differ from others sometimes.

11. **Synthesis (3)** In the poem, the two roads that confront the speaker represent a choice in life. The speaker must choose one way to go knowing that another interesting possibility exists. Nevertheless, the speaker in the line *"I doubted if I should ever come back"* acknowledges that the chance of returning is

unlikely. The theme of the poem suggests that life offers possibilities but rarely second chances.

12. Synthesis (4) The poem is set in the woods, implying that there are trees. As stated by Graves, this setting includes at least one of the four natural objects most proper to poems.

Saint Joan

13. Comprehension (4) Joan's statement "*We lived at that bridge*" and the reply of Dunois that [we] "*died too; some of us*" indicate a battle.

14. Application (5) Joan states in line 10 "*let the king have all the glory*" and indicates that she does not want the honor. She has fought to crown the king and is loyal to him. She wishes to be in battle as she states when she says "*I wish it were the bridge at Orleans again.* " Her choice, thus, would be a fight to protect the king.

15. Analysis (1) Joan admits that she is "*frightened beyond words before,*" but she finds that life after a battle is "*so dull.*"

16. Analysis (1) Joan's relationship with the king's court is compared. She has shown up the court advisers by successfully helping the king attain power when the advisors were unable to do so. Her success does not make them fond of her.

17. Synthesis (2) Joan's lack of political understanding is revealed when she asks, "*Why do all these courtiers and knights and churchmen hate me?*" She doesn't understand that they do not appreciate her making them appear wrong and inadequate while she succeeds at what she does.

18. Synthesis (4) For anyone to win enough power to crown a king is amazing. For a woman to do so through military means during the play's time setting is even more extraordinary.

Anne Frank: The Diary of a Young Girl

19. Comprehension (1) The clues to oppression are the fact that "many Jewish friends are being taken away by the dozen," being treated. . . without a shred of decency," "not nearly enough lavatories [bathrooms]," and "no separate accommodation." Choices 2, 3, and 4 are incorrect because they depict positive treatment. Choice 5 is less positive than the other three choices but still not harsh enough.

20. Application (2) Anne Frank displayed her skills of observation and her talent for writing in her diary as young as thirteen to fifteen years of age; with this evidence her most likely occupation (had she lived) would have been as a journalist. There is no evidence for the other occupations.

21. Analysis (3) The evidence for simple pleasures includes taking a hot bath, eating cream cakes, seeing a man's wife Lotje, having coffee, paying a visit to Mr. Vossen, seeing the town and cinema, having a home, and going to school. There is no support for the other choices.

22. Synthesis (4) While there may have been some typical jealousy between sisters, this would not have earned Anne Frank a place in history and a designation of one of the most 100 influential people by *Time*. All the other statements are true.

23. Synthesis (5) The items mentioned in choices 1, 2, 3, and 4 (boy friends, teachers, parents, and sweets and money) are not necessarily a sign of maturity *or* lack of maturity. Choice 5 shows a growth in maturity because the life she enjoyed in 1942 was "unreal" *in comparison to* the life she knew two years later in 1944. She says, "It was quite a different Anne who enjoyed that heavenly existence from the Anne who has grown wise within these walls."

Evaluation Chart

Use the answer key on pages 48–49 to check your answers to the Pretest. Then find the item number of each question you missed and circle it on the chart below to determine the reading content areas in which you need more practice. Pay particular attention to areas where you missed half or more of the questions. The page numbers for the content areas are listed on the chart below. For those questions that you missed, review the skill pages indicated.

	COMPREHENSION (pages 217–230)	**APPLICATION (pages 231–236)**	**ANALYSIS (pages 237–262)**	**SYNTHESIS (pages 263–270)**
Fiction (pages 589–614)	1	2	3, 4	5, 6
Poetry (pages 615–636)	7	8	9, 10	11, 12
Drama (pages 637–654)	13	14	15, 16	17, 18
Nonfiction Prose (pages 655–684)	19	20	21	22, 23

PRETEST

Mathematics

The Mathematics Pretest consists of 44 items. It offers you the opportunity to test both your computational and problem-solving skills. These are not multiple-choice items, so you will have to work as accurately and carefully as possible. Try the test without using a calculator. Later, go back and try it again using the calculator when necessary. Be sure to use any diagrams or charts that are provided with the problems. Use the formula page as needed.

When you have finished the Pretest, use the Evaluation Chart on page 60 to determine which areas you need to review most.

Mathematics Pretest Answer Grid

1 ________	12 ________	23 ________	34 ________
2 ________	13 ________	24 ________	35 ________
3 ________	14 ________	25 ________	36 ________
4 ________	15 ________	26 ________	37 ________
5 ________	16 ________	27 ________	38 ________
6 ________	17 ________	28 ________	39 ________
7 ________	18 ________	29 ________	40 ________
8 ________	19 ________	30 ________	41 ________
9 ________	20 ________	31 ________	42 ________
10 ________	21 ________	32 ________	43 ________
11 ________	22 ________	33 ________	44

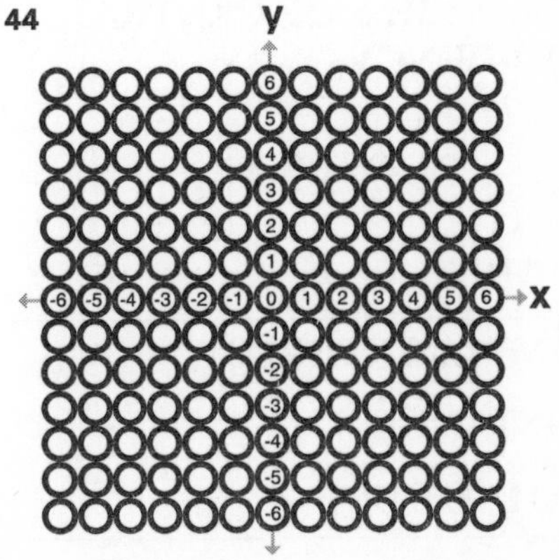

FORMULAS

AREA of a:	
square	Area = side^2
rectangle	Area = length × width
parallelogram	Area = base × height
triangle	Area = $\frac{1}{2}$ × base × height
trapezoid	Area = $\frac{1}{2} \times (\text{base}_1 + \text{base}_2) \times$ height
circle	Area = $\pi \times \text{radius}^2$; π is approximately equal to 3.14.
PERIMETER of a:	
square	Perimeter = 4 × side
rectangle	Perimeter = 2 × length + 2 × width
triangle	Perimeter = $\text{side}_1 + \text{side}_2 + \text{side}_3$
CIRCUMFERENCE of a circle	Circumference = π × diameter; π is approximately equal to 3.14.
VOLUME of a:	
cube	Volume = edge^3
rectangular solid	Volume = length × width × height
square pyramid	Volume = $\frac{1}{3} \times (\text{base edge})^2 \times$ height
cylinder	Volume = $\pi \times \text{radius}^2 \times$ height; π is approximately equal to 3.14.
cone	Volume = $\frac{1}{3} \times \pi \times \text{radius}^2 \times$ height; π is approximately equal to 3.14.
COORDINATE GEOMETRY	distance between points = $\sqrt{(x_2 - x_1)^2 + (y_2 - y_1)^2}$; (x_1, y_1) and (x_2, y_2) are two points in a plane. slope of a line = $\frac{y_2 - y_1}{x_2 - x_1}$; (x_1, y_1) and (x_2, y_2) are two points on the line.
PYTHAGOREAN RELATIONSHIP	$a^2 + b^2 = c^2$; a and b are legs and c the hypotenuse of a right triangle.
MEASURES OF CENTRAL TENDENCY	**mean** = $\frac{x_1 + x_2 + \ldots + x_n}{n}$, where the xs are the values for which a mean is desired, and n is the total number of values for x. **median** = the middle value of an odd number of *ordered* scores, and halfway between the two middle values of an even number of *ordered* scores.
SIMPLE INTEREST	interest = principal × rate × time
DISTANCE	distance = rate × time
TOTAL COST	total cost = (number of units) × (price per unit)

PRETEST

Directions: Solve each problem.

1. Subtract 386 from 72,000.

2. Divide 5310 by 9.

3. In a recent village election six precincts recorded the following voter turnout. What was the average number of voters per precinct?

Precinct	Number of Voters
#26	168
#15	240
#10	195
#7	180
#21	312
#25	87

4. Find 1.43 plus .5.

5. What is .38 divided by .4?

6. Corey needs $120 to buy a new coat. She has saved the money she received from four dividend checks of $16.75 each. How much more money must she add to those savings to pay for the coat?

7. $1\frac{1}{4} - \frac{3}{4} =$

8. $4\frac{1}{5} \times \frac{1}{2} =$

Questions 9 and 10 are based on the chart below, which compares the growth of four local companies.

Company	2001 Sales	2005 Sales
Magic, Inc.	$323,000	$904,400
Futures, Ltd.	$630,000	$925,000
Action Co.	$264,000	$1,497,000
Billings, Int.	$2,000,000	$6,000,000

9. What is the percent of increase for Billings, Int. sales from 2001 to 2005?

10. If Magic, Inc. continues to have approximately the same rate of growth for the next 4 years until 2009, what will be the projected sales in 2009 (to the nearest $500,000)?

11. Martha had $12\frac{2}{3}$ yards of drapery material. She used $\frac{3}{4}$ of it to make the drapes for her family room. How much does she have left to make matching throw pillows?

12. On the first day of their vacation, the Morales family drove 312 miles in 6 hours. At that rate, how far will they travel the next day if they drive for 8 hours?

13. During the last winter carnival, the local college students built a 30-foot snowman out of 100 tons of snow. How much snow will be needed to build a 36-foot snowman this year?

14. Find 72% of $350.

PRETEST

15. Find the length of the diagonal brace used to reinforce the barn door.

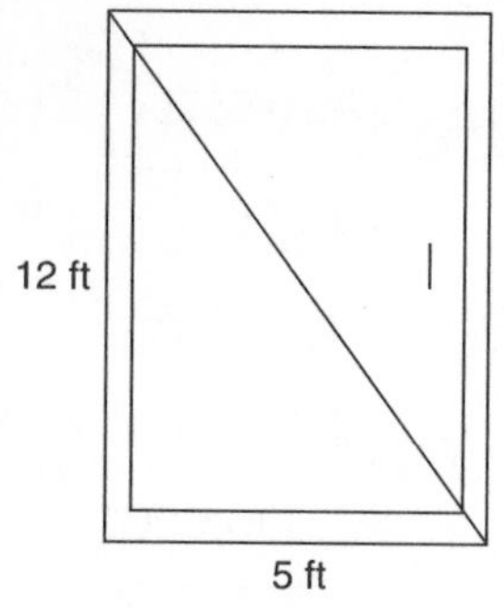

16. Nick's time card shows his hours for one week. If he works 8 hours per day before earning overtime, find Nick's gross pay before deductions for the week of July 8–12.

Phillips Corporation
Time Card

Name: Nick Acino		**SS#: 002-00-0021**
Date	**From**	**To**
7/8	8:30 A.M.	4:30 P.M.
7/9	8:30 A.M.	5:15 P.M.
7/10	8:00 A.M.	4:30 P.M.
7/11	8:30 A.M.	6:00 P.M.
7/12	8:30 A.M.	4:45 P.M.

Regular Hours @ $10.40/hour

Overtime Hours @ $15.60/hour over 40

17. The diameter (d) of a circle is twice as long as the radius (r). If $r = 3$ m and π is equal to approximately 3.14, write the expression that could be used to find the circumference of the circle.

18. Write 173,000 in scientific notation.

19. There were many increases in gasohol sales over a nine-year period. What is the percent of increase from year 3 to year 5?

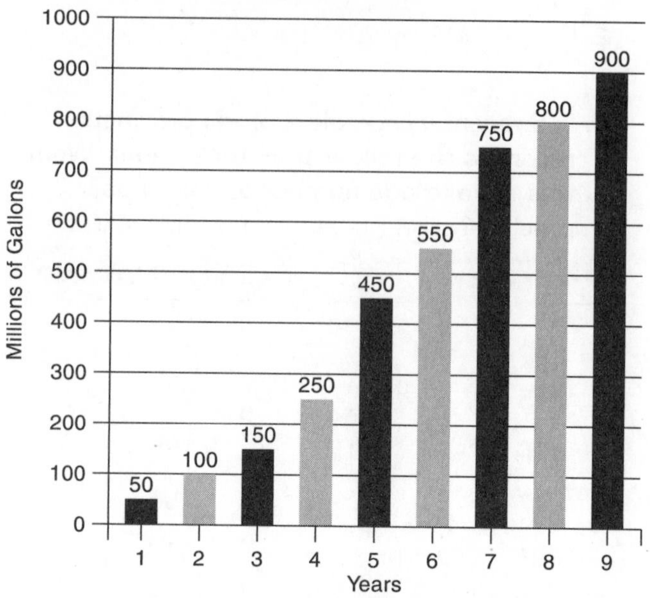

20. Find the number of square *yards* of sod needed to cover the circular putting green shown below. (Hint: 9 sq ft = 1 sq yd)

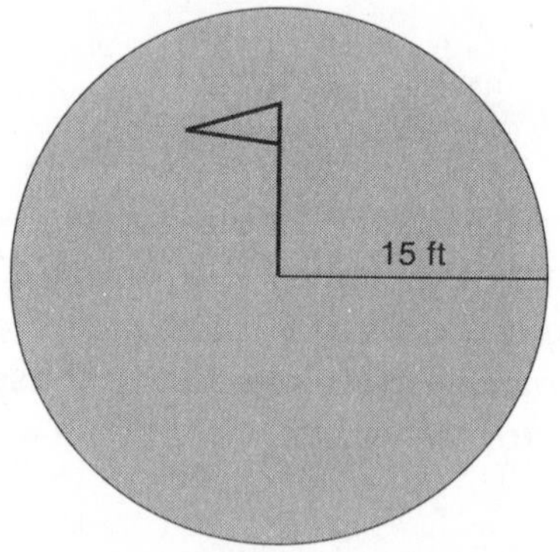

21. Margaret wants to put a wallpaper border around her bedroom walls. The room is a rectangle 15 feet by 20 feet. How many complete *yards* of the wallpaper border must she buy?

22. How much sand is needed to fill a sandbox 8 feet by 6 feet to a depth of 18 inches?

PRETEST

23. Find the measure of angle x in the illustration below.

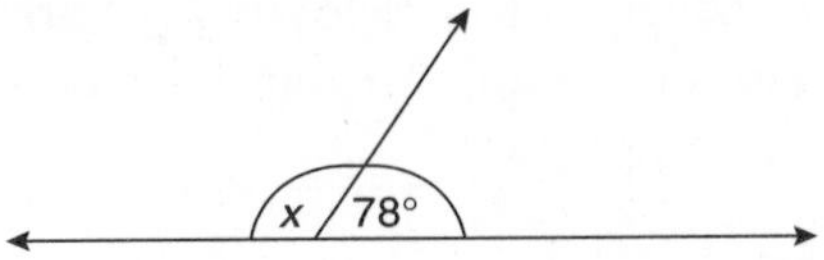

24. Main Street and Union Avenue are parallel roads as shown below. The railroad tracks cut across both streets. What is the angle measure of the land on which the station rests, based on the information given in the diagram?

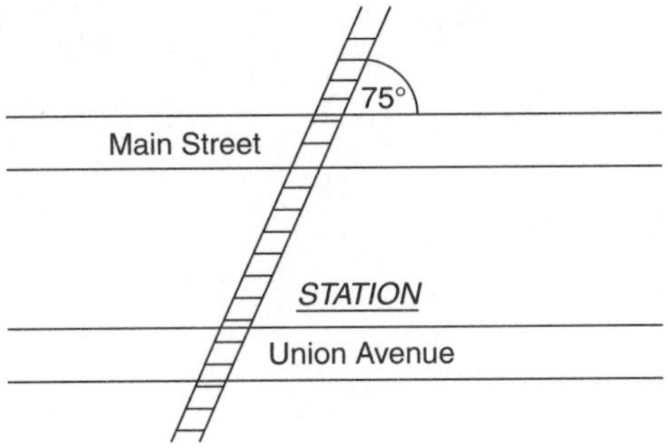

25. Solve for x: $14 = \frac{x}{5}$.

26. Solve for x: $4x - 9 = 7$.

27. Solve for x: $3(x - 2) - 3 = x + 5$.

28. Evaluate $-4 + (-3) - (-2)$.

29. Find the average temperature of most of Illinois for the frigid day reported on this weather map.

30. If $x = -2$ and $y = 5$, find the value of the expression $5y - 3x^2$.

31. Miguel has fourteen coins in his pocket. He has one more dime than quarters and three more nickels than dimes. How many of each coin does he have?

32. Using the diagram below, find the measure of angle A.

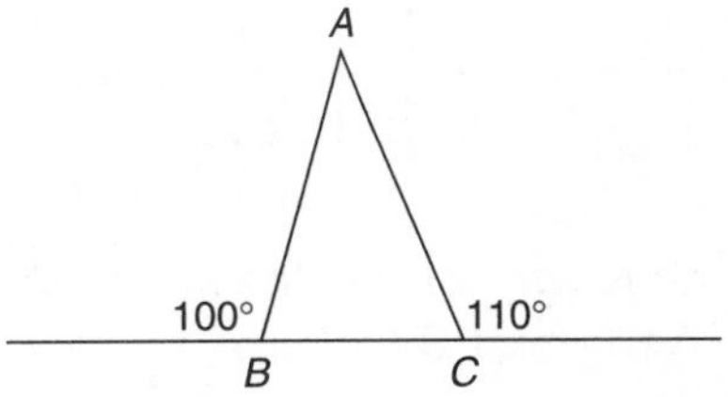

33. If 6 inches of decorative ribbon cost $3.25, how much does a yard cost?

34. If one kilogram = 2.2 pounds, does a 3-kilogram roast beef weigh more or less than a 6-pound roast?

35. To find the height of the evergreen in his backyard, Doug sketched the information shown below. He placed a yardstick parallel to the tree and compared its shadow on the ground with the length of the shadow of the tree. How tall is the tree?

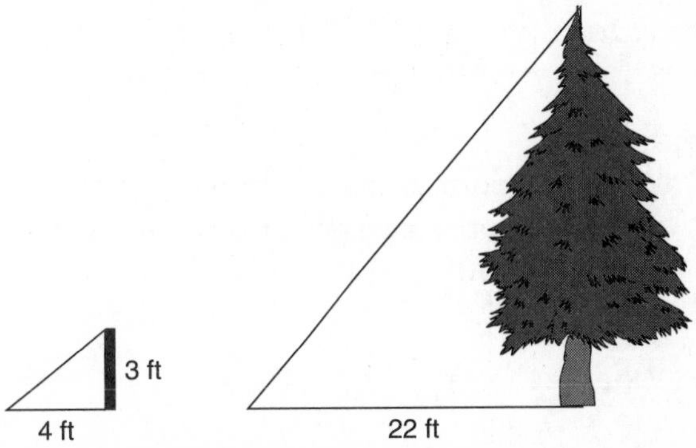

PRETEST

Questions 36 and 37 are based on this drawing.

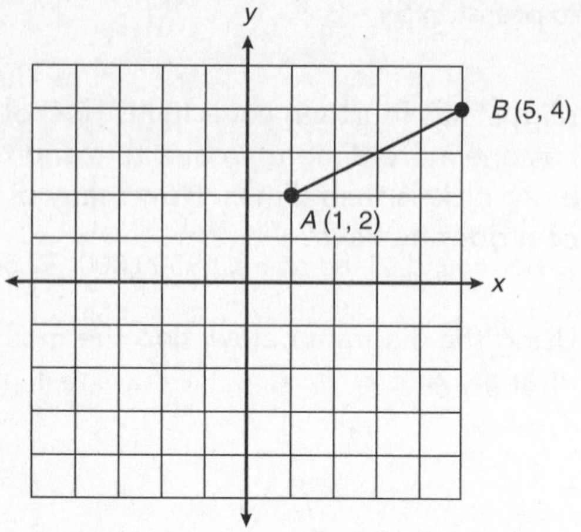

36. Find the length of the line segment from point *A* to point *B*.

37. Find the slope of the line *AB*.

38. In a standard deck of 52 playing cards, what is the probability of drawing an ace on the first draw?

39. Evaluate $\sqrt{25} + (4 \times 3)^2 - (5 \times 2)$.

40. Look at the triangle below. What is the measure of $\angle b$?

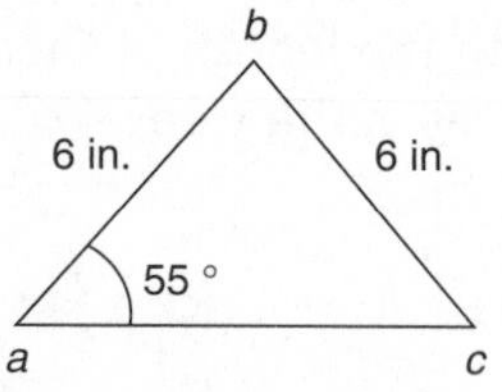

41. With a senior discount, a movie ticket costs \$6. What is the percent of discount if the full price is \$7.50?

42. What is the ratio of 8 ounces to 2 pounds?

43. The store Everything's a Dollar sells each item for one dollar no matter how much it costs. Which of the following graphs represents the relationship between cost and selling price?

(1)

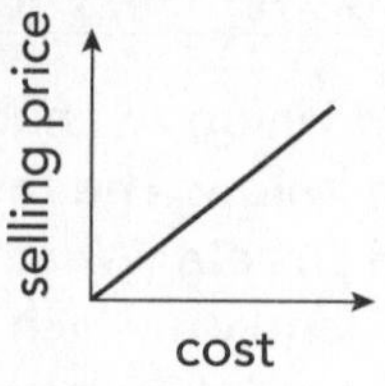

(2)

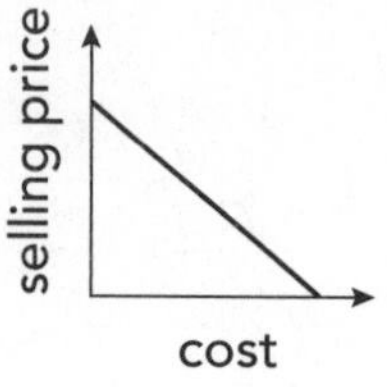

(3)

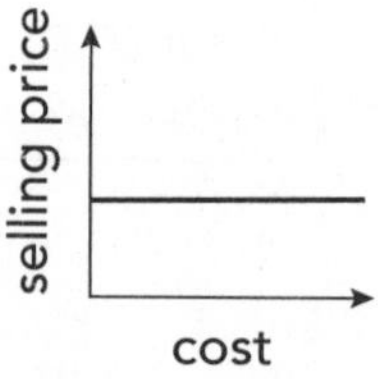

(4)

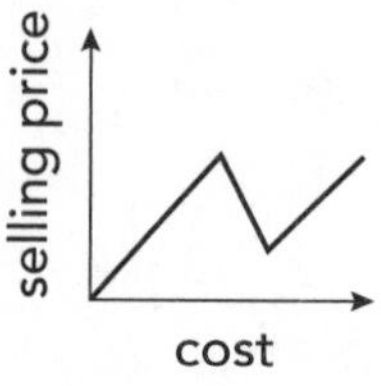

(5)

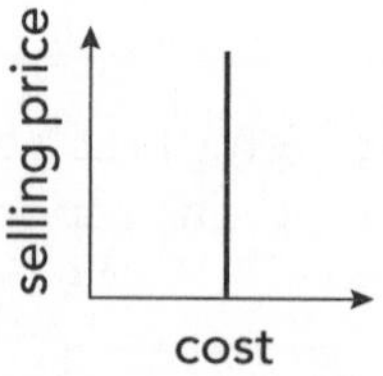

44. Plot the point (–2, 3) on the coordinate plane grid.

Answers are on page 57.

Mathematics Answer Key

1. 71,614

$$\begin{array}{r} 72{,}000 \\ \underline{-\ 386} \\ 71{,}614 \end{array}$$

2. 590

$$\begin{array}{r} 590 \\ 9\overline{)5310} \\ \underline{-45} \\ 81 \\ \underline{81} \\ 00 \end{array}$$

3. 197 voters

Find the total.

$168 + 240 + 195 + 180 + 312 + 87 = 1182$

Find the average. $1182 \div 6 = 197$

4. 1.93

$$\begin{array}{r} 1.43 \\ \underline{+.5\ \ } \\ 1.93 \end{array}$$

5. .95

$$\begin{array}{r} .95 \\ .4\overline{).380} \\ \underline{-36} \\ 20 \\ \underline{20} \\ 0 \end{array}$$

6. $53

First find the total in checks.

$\$16.75 \times 4 = \$67$

Then find the difference.

$\$120 - \$67 = \$53$

7. $\frac{1}{2}$

$$\begin{array}{r} 1\frac{1}{4} = \frac{5}{4} \\ -\ \frac{3}{4} = \frac{3}{4} \\ \hline \frac{2}{4} = \frac{1}{2} \end{array}$$

8. $2\frac{1}{10}$

$4\frac{1}{5} \times \frac{1}{2} = \frac{21}{5} \times \frac{1}{2} = \frac{21}{10} = 2\frac{1}{10}$

9. 200%

Subtract to find the amount of increase.

$$\begin{array}{r} 6 \text{ million} \\ \underline{-\ 2 \text{ million}} \\ 4 \text{ million} \end{array}$$

Write a proportion.

$\frac{\$4 \text{ million}}{\$2 \text{ million}} = \frac{N\%}{100\%}$

$N = \frac{4 \times 100}{2} = \frac{400}{2} = 200$

10. $2,500,000

First compare 2005 to 2001.

$\frac{\$904{,}400}{\$323{,}000} = 2.8$

Then multiply 2005 sales by 2.8 to find the 2009 projection.

$\$904{,}400 \times 2.8 = \$2{,}532{,}320$

Then round to the nearest $500,000: $2,500,000.

11. $3\frac{1}{6}$ yards

If she used $\frac{3}{4}$ of the material, then she has $\frac{1}{4}$ of it left. So

$\frac{1}{4} \times 12\frac{2}{3} = \frac{1}{4} \times \frac{38}{3} = \frac{38}{12} = 3\frac{2}{12} = 3\frac{1}{6}$ yd

12. 416 miles

$\frac{312 \text{ miles}}{6 \text{ hours}} = \frac{x}{8 \text{ hours}}$

$x = \frac{312 \times 8}{6} = \frac{2496}{6} = 416$

13. 120 tons

$\frac{30 \text{ feet}}{100 \text{ tons}} = \frac{36 \text{ feet}}{x}$

$x = \frac{36 \times 100}{30} = \frac{3600}{30} = 120$

14. $252

$\frac{x}{\$350} = \frac{72}{100}$

$x = \frac{\$350 \times 72}{100} = \frac{\$25{,}200}{100} = \$252$

or $\$350 \times .72 = \$252$

15. 13 feet

$a^2 + b^2 = c^2$

$12^2 + 5^2 = c^2$

$144 + 25 = c^2$

$169 = c^2$

$\sqrt{169} = c$

$13 = c$

16. $462.80

Find Nick's hours, including overtime.

$8 + 8\frac{3}{4} + 8\frac{1}{2} + 9\frac{1}{2} + 8\frac{1}{4} = 43$

This is 40 hours regular and 3 hours overtime.

Find Nick's total pay.

$$\begin{array}{r} 40 \times \$10.40 = \$416.00 \\ \underline{+\ 3 \times \$15.60 = \$\ \ 46.80} \\ \$462.80 \end{array}$$

17. 3.14(6)

The formula for circumference is

$C = \pi d.$

$d = 2 \times \text{radius} = 2 \times 3 = 6$

$C = \pi d = 3.14(6)$

18. 1.73×10^5

19. 200% increase

Year 5 – Year 3 = 450 – 150 = 300

$\frac{300 \text{ increase}}{150 \text{ year } 3} = \frac{N\%}{100\%}$

$N = \frac{100 \times 300}{150} = \frac{30000}{150} = 200$

20. 78.5 sq yd

$A = \pi \times \text{radius}^2 = 3.14 \times 15^2$

$= 3.14 \times 225 = 706.5$ sq ft

$= 706.5$ sq ft $\div$ 9 sq ft

$= 78.5$ sq yd

21. 24 yd

$P = 2 \times \text{length} + 2 \times \text{width}$

$= 2 \times 20 + 2 \times 15$

$= 40 + 30 = 70$ ft

Since 1 yd = 3 ft,

$P = 70$ ft $\div 3 = 23\frac{1}{3}$ yards needed, so she must buy 24 yards.

22. 72 cu ft

$V = \text{length} \times \text{width} \times \text{height}$

$= 8 \times 6 \times 1\frac{1}{2}$ (18 in. = $1\frac{1}{2}$ ft)

$= 72$ cu ft

23. 102°

$180° - 78° = 102°$

24. 75°

Since the two angles are corresponding angles, they are equal.

25. x = 70

$14 = \frac{x}{5}$

$5 \cdot 14 = \frac{x}{\cancel{5}_1} \cdot \cancel{5}_1$

$70 = x$

26. x = 4

$4x - 9 = 7$

$4x - 9 + 9 = 7 + 9$

$4x = 16$

$\frac{4x}{4} = \frac{16}{4}$

$x = 4$

27. x = 7

$3(x - 2) - 3 = x + 5$

$3x - 6 - 3 = x + 5$

$3x - 9 = x + 5$

$3x - x - 9 = x - x + 5$

$2x - 9 + 9 = 5 + 9$

$2x = 14$

$x = 7$

28. –5

$-4 + (-3) - (-2)$

$-4 - 3 + 2$

$-7 + 2 = -5$

29. –13°

Find the total.

$-19 - 12 - 18 - 10 - 13 - 12 - 7 = -91$

$-91 \div 7 = -13°$

30. 13

$5y - 3x^2 = 5(5) - 3(-2)^2$

$= 25 - 3(4)$

$= 25 - 12 = 13$

31. 3 quarters, 4 dimes, 7 nickels

Let x = quarters, $x + 1$ = dimes, and $x + 1 + 3$ = nickels. Then

$x + x + 1 + x + 1 + 3 = 14$

$3x + 5 = 14$

$3x + 5 - 5 = 14 - 5$

$3x = 9$

$x = 3$

$x = 3$ quarters, $x + 1 = 4$ dimes, and $x + 1 + 3 = 7$ nickels

32. 30°

$\angle C = 180° - 110° = 70°$

$\angle B = 180° - 100° = 80°$

$\angle A = 180° - (80° + 70°) = 30°$

33. $19.50

Since 6 inches cost $3.25, then double the cost for 1 foot of ribbon.

$2 \times \$3.25 = \$6.50$

Since 1 yard equals 3 feet, multiply by 3.

$3 \times \$6.50 = \$19.50$.

34. more

$\frac{1 \text{ kg}}{2.2 \text{ lb}} = \frac{3 \text{ kg}}{x \text{ lb}}$

$x = \frac{3 \times 2.2}{1} = 6.6 \text{ lb}$

35. $16\frac{1}{2}$ ft

$\frac{3}{4} = \frac{x}{22}$

$x = \frac{3 \times 22}{4} = \frac{66}{4} = 16\frac{1}{2}$

36. about 4.5 or $2\sqrt{5}$

$d = \sqrt{(x_2 - x_1)^2 + (y_2 - y_1)^2}$

$d = \sqrt{(5 - 1)^2 + (4 - 2)^2}$

$d = \sqrt{4^2 + 2^2} = \sqrt{16 + 4} = \sqrt{20} =$

$\sqrt{4 \times 5} = 2\sqrt{5} =$ about 4.5

(Use your calculator to find the square root.)

37. $\frac{1}{2}$

$\frac{y_2 - y_1}{x_2 - x_1} = \frac{4 - 2}{5 - 1} = \frac{2}{4} = \frac{1}{2}$

38. $\frac{1}{13}$

$\frac{4 \text{ aces}}{52 \text{ cards}} = \frac{1}{13}$

39. 139

$\sqrt{25} + (4 \times 3)^2 - (5 \times 2)$

$= 5 + 12^2 - 10 = 5 + 144 - 10$

$= 149 - 10 = 139$

40. 70°

Because side *ab* and side *bc* are each 6 inches, the triangle is isosceles. Then the measure of $\angle c$ is 55°, like $\angle a$. To find $\angle b$, $180° - 2(55°) = 180° - 110° = 70°$.

41. 20%

$\frac{1.50}{7.50} = \frac{N}{100}$

$N = \frac{1.50 \times 100}{7.50} = 20$

42. $\frac{1}{4}$

Since there are 32 ounces in 2 pounds, the ratio is $\frac{8 \text{ ounces}}{32 \text{ ounces}} = \frac{1}{4}$.

43. (3) the selling price always stays at $1. Any variation in cost does not change selling price.

44.

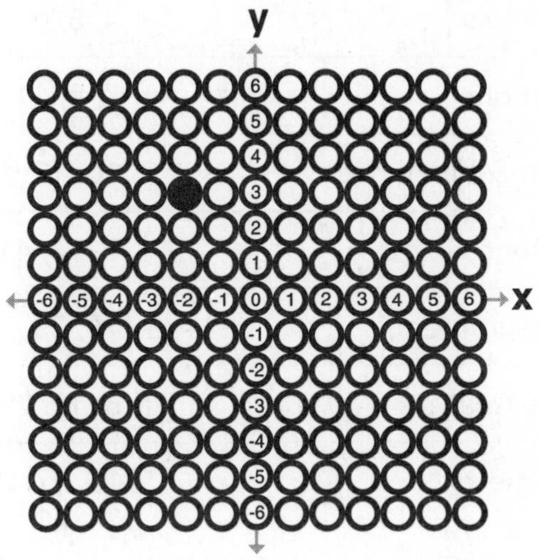

MATHEMATICS PRETEST

Evaluation Chart

After you have used the answer key to check the Pretest, find the item number of each question you missed and circle it on the chart below. These are the mathematics content areas in which you need more practice. Pay particular attention to areas where you missed half or more of the questions. The page numbers for the content areas are listed on the chart. For those questions that you missed, review the skill pages indicated.

SKILL AREA/CONTENT AREA	ITEM NUMBER	REVIEW PAGES
Number Sense	1, 2, 18, 39	711–724
Decimals	4, 5, 6	725–746
Fractions	7, 8, 11	747–774
Ratio & Proportion	10, 12, 13, 42	785–792
Percent	9, 14, 41	793–808
Measurement	16, 33, 34	873–892
Data Analysis	3, 19, 29, 38, 43	815–834
Geometry	15, 17, 20, 21, 22, 23, 24, 32, 35, 40	893–921
Algebra	25, 26, 27, 28, 30, 31, 36, 37, 44	835–872

Language Arts, Writing

The GED Language Arts, Writing Test consists of two parts. You must take both Parts I and II at the same time, but you may work back and forth between the two parts. The total time for both parts is 120 minutes.

What does Part I of the Test contain?

Part I: Editing (65% of the test)

Part I contains 50 multiple-choice questions that require the skill of **application.** You will have 75 minutes to answer these questions. In this part several documents of 200 to 300 words each will be followed by questions about the sentences within the documents. Some questions will ask you to edit or correct errors in the document while other questions may ask you to restate an idea in different words. The questions will test your knowledge of *sentence structure, usage, mechanics* (capitalization and punctuation), and *spelling* (possessives, contractions, and homonyms).

Mastering your editing skills is important so that you can demonstrate the ability to **proofread** and to correct writing in a realistic setting. There will be up to ten errors per document.

What are the content areas of Part I?

Part I of the Test can be broken down into the following **content areas.** The percentages are approximate.

Organization 15%	(7 questions)
Sentence Structure 30%	(15 questions)
Usage 30%	(15 questions)
Mechanics 25%	(13 questions)

What types of documents are used on the test?

Most (80%) of the documents used on the test are *instructional* (how-to) or *informational* texts. Instructional documents consist of instructions or directions using technology, utilizing leisure, increasing personal effectiveness, improving family life, or preparing for the business world. The remainder (20%) of the documents are business documents including memos, letters, notices, editorials, reports, executive summaries, applications, or meeting notes.

What types of questions are on the test?

Three types of questions will appear on the Language Arts, Writing Test:

Correction 45%	(22–23 questions)
Revision 35%	(17–18 questions)
Construction Shift 20%	(10 questions)

In the *correction* type you'll see a sentence followed by a question, "What correction should be made to this sentence?" The five answer choices will focus on different parts of the sentence and test your knowledge on any of the four content areas.

Example Sentence 1: **Time flies quickly during the day, when you're enjoying your job.**

What correction should be made to this sentence?

(1) replace flies with flys
(2) remove the comma after day
(3) replace you're with your
(4) insert a comma after enjoying
(5) no correction is necessary

Note that Sentence 1 tests your understanding of spelling, comma rules, possessives, and contractions. The correct answer is (2) remove the comma after *day.*

In the *sentence revision* type, you may be asked to correct one sentence, a number of sentences, a paragraph, the text as a whole, or a heading. A sentence from the passage will be given with a part underlined. You will need to choose the best way to correct that underlined portion. The first answer choice in this question type is always the original version of the sentence, and this version is sometimes the correct answer!

Example Sentence 2: **Receiving praise is something we all value, the question is how to handle it gracefully.**

Which of the following is the best way to write the underlined portion of this sentence? If you think the original is the best way to write the sentence, choose option (1).

(1) value, the
(2) value the
(3) value and the
(4) value. The
(5) value however the

Sentence 2 tests your understanding of sentence structure and combining. Choice (4) is the best way to rewrite this sentence. The other choices create incorrect sentence structures.

In the *construction shift* type you are asked to choose the best way to rewrite a sentence or combine two sentences. In this type of question, *the original sentences contain no error.* Your job is to understand how the ideas are related in a sentence and which of the answer choices has the same meaning as the original sentence.

> Example Sentence 3: **Although the independent candidate ran a good race, not enough votes were received by him to win.**
>
> If you rewrote sentence 3 beginning with
> *The independent candidate ran a good race,*
> the next word should be
>
> **(1)** and
> **(2)** which
> **(3)** but
> **(4)** so
> **(5)** to

As you can see, the original sentence has no error. To answer this question, you must notice the contrasting relationship between the two ideas of the sentence, then choose (3) *but,* the word that correctly shows this contrast.

Part II: The Essay (35% of the test)

You will be given 45 minutes to complete Part II of the Language Arts, Writing Test. In this part you will be given a topic and asked to write a well-developed essay. You will not be given a choice of topics, but you will not need any special information or knowledge in order to write the essay. The topic will draw on your general knowledge and ask you to explain something about a common issue or problem. In this part of the Language Arts, Writing Test, you should be able to plan, organize your thinking, and communicate your thoughts clearly on paper.

CHAPTER 1

Basic English Usage

What is standard English?

We often communicate without using a single word. Our facial expressions, body posture, gestures, or tone of voice can express our feelings and thoughts to others. Using words, however, increases our ability to explain our ideas more fully and better enables us to achieve our purposes.

As we use the words of a language, grammar and structure become important. For example, which of the choices below would more people choose as the most acceptable?

I smart.

I am very smart.

Smart me am.

Although all three choices express a similar meaning, *I am very smart* is the choice that follows standard English rules of grammar and structure. Have you ever wondered who makes these rules? In the United States, no government agency dictates laws regarding the use of standard English. Rather, the faculty at large, prestigious universities identify and develop usage rules. Knowledge of standard English indicates education. This knowledge is a tool that can be helpful not only in school, but in business as well. It may not be important if you're having a conversation with your mother or best friend, but knowledge of standard English rules may be quite beneficial in getting a better job or furthering your education. Certainly, you must know standard English in order to pass the GED Language Arts, Writing Test.

Writing in Complete Sentences

One major difference between spoken and written English is that we do not always speak in complete sentences. For example, in a conversation you might mix complete sentences with **fragments,** groups of words that are not complete sentences. In the following conversation the fragments are in bold type.

Grocery Cashier:	How are you?
Customer:	**Just fine.**
Grocery Cashier:	Will this be cash or charge?
Customer:	**Cash.**
Grocery Cashier:	Do you have any coupons?
Customer:	I don't have any today. What do I owe you?
Grocery Cashier:	**$83.21.**

Characteristics of a Complete Sentence

1. A complete sentence must have a **subject** that tells whom or what the sentence is about.

   S

2. A complete sentence must have a **predicate** that tells what the subject is or does.

   P

3. A complete sentence contains a **complete thought.** It does not leave the reader hanging and waiting for more.

   C T

Look at the following sentences. The subjects and predicates are labeled for you. Compare these sentences with the characteristics of a complete sentence listed above.

Subject	**Predicate**
I	am just fine.
I	will pay cash.
Your total	is $83.21.

Although we often speak in incomplete sentences without subjects or predicates, generally we must use complete sentences when we write. This is because in writing we cannot use facial expressions, gestures, or tone of voice to communicate our meaning. When writing, use sentences that contain both subjects and predicates. Complete sentences are a feature of standard written English that will be important on the Language Arts, Writing Test and the Essay.

For practice in working with subjects and predicates, try matching a subject from the left column with a predicate from the right. Notice that you are connecting *whom* or *what* the sentence is about with what this subject is or does.

Subject	Predicate
The leaves of the rhubarb plant	is 186,282 miles per second.
The cartoon character Donald Duck	is made up of water.
About 70% of Earth's surface	was born in 1934.
The speed of light	visit the Grand Canyon each year.
Thousands of tourists	are poisonous if eaten.

EXERCISE 1

Subjects and Predicates

Directions: The following trivia quiz is based on classic stories and tales. Match the following subjects (Column 1) with their predicates (Column 2). Notice that you are connecting a noun or noun phrase with what it is or did.

Column 1	Column 2
1. *Star Wars*	**(a)** had the strength of 100 men.
2. Romeo and Juliet	**(b)** sat at a round table in Camelot.
3. The Greek hero Hercules	**(c)** was beaten by the tortoise in a race.
4. The hare	**(d)** told the story of the Force against the Dark Side.
5. King Arthur	**(e)** fell in love and killed themselves.
6. Robin Hood	**(f)** stole from the rich to give to the poor.
7. Ichabod Crane	**(g)** vowed revenge against his uncle for the murder of his father.
8. Hamlet	**(h)** was chased by a headless horseman.

Answers are on page 197.

Parts of Speech

Subjects and predicates are built from the **parts of speech.** You will not have to define or explain these terms on the Language Arts, Writing Test, but knowledge of these major parts of speech and their functions will help you understand how standard English sentences are built. You will be studying the following parts of speech closely.

Basic Parts of Speech

Part of Speech	Function	Examples
noun	names person, place, thing, or idea	**Tony** went to a **bookstore** to buy a **book** on **politics.**
pronoun	replaces a noun	**Someone** recommended a book to **him,** so **he** bought **it.**
verb	shows action or state of being (is, are, was, were, being, be, been)	Elizabeth **plays** cello and piano. She **enjoys** music very much. She **is** very talented.
conjunction	joins words and groups of words	Sasha is a cute dog, **but** she sometimes gets into trouble. The garden **and** deck look nice.
adjective	describes nouns and tells what kind or how many	Bill, who is a **good** fisherman, caught **five** fish in Canada.
adverb	describes verbs, adjectives, or adverbs	Debbie cooks **well** and **often** prepares wonderful crab legs.

What is a noun?

A **noun** names a person, place, thing, or idea. You may not realize it, but you are very familiar with nouns. Complete the lists of nouns by answering the question under each of the following headings.

People

Who talks to you during the week?

a. ___Mother___
b. ______________
c. ______________

Places

Where do you go fairly often?

a. ___work___
b. ______________
c. ______________

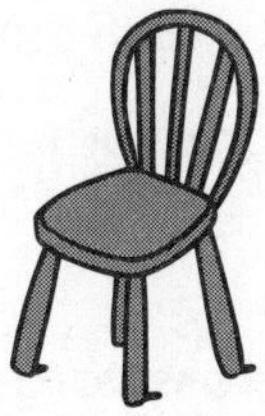

Things

What do you see in your home?

a. ___chair___
b. ______________
c. ______________

Ideas

What qualities do you value in a friend?

a. ___kindness___
b. ______________
c. ______________

Nouns that describe people, places, and things usually are easy to identify. Sometimes, however, ideas are a little harder to recognize as nouns. Read the following words carefully to get a better sense of the category of nouns that describes ideas: *truth, hope, freedom, creativity, success.*

Noun as a Subject

A noun can be the **subject** of a sentence. Think of the subject as the main noun or the *actor* in the sentence. To find the subject of a sentence, ask yourself: Who or what is doing something or being described in this sentence?

The following sentence contains several nouns, but only one is the subject. Which one?

A sign warned drivers about falling rocks along the road.

All of the nouns in the sentence are underlined. If you ask yourself, "What is this sentence about?" you might answer, "falling rocks." But if you ask, "Who or what is doing something?" your answer will be "sign." The noun *sign* is the subject of the sentence.

EXERCISE 2

Nouns and Subjects

Directions: Underline all of the nouns in each of these sentences; then label the subject of each sentence with an **S.**

Example: My neighbor returned three books about health to the library.
S

1. Agnes likes doing crossword puzzles for enjoyment when she has some free time.
2. Sometimes a dictionary provides an answer she needs, but usually she comes up with the word herself after giving the question some thought.
3. On her last birthday her granddaughter gave her a new book and a box of chocolates.
4. All the members of the family ate some of the candy even though they had just eaten cake and ice cream.
5. Agnes was happy to share her gift with other people because she is a very generous person.

Answers are on page 197.

Singular and Plural Nouns: Spelling Tips

Singular means "one" (single). **Plural** means "more than one."

Rules for forming plurals often depend on combinations of **vowels** and **consonants** at the ends of words. You may know that each letter of the alphabet fits into one of these two groups. The vowels are *a, e, i, o,* and *u* (and sometimes *y*). All the other letters are consonants.

The most common rule to form a plural noun is to add -*s* (book-books). Other rules for forming plurals involve the vowels *(a, e, i, o, u,* and sometimes *y*) and consonants (all the other letters of the alphabet).

Rules for Forming Plural Nouns

1. **Add -*es* to words ending with *s, sh, ch, x* and *z.***

   bus → buses — business → businesses

   brush → brushes — watch → watches

   box → boxes — waltz → waltzes

2. **Change the *y* to *i* and add -*es* to a word ending in *y* if a *consonant* comes before the *y.***

   try → tries — puppy → puppies

   secretary → secretaries — baby→ babies

3. **Change the *f* to *v* and add -*es* to some words ending in one *f* or *fe.***

   cliff → cliffs — wife → wives

   leaf → leaves — life → lives

4. **A few nouns have irregular plural forms and must be memorized.**

   woman → women — tooth → teeth

   deer → deer — ox → oxen

5. **Some nouns are always considered singular and can not be made plural.**

   homework — air

   furniture — music

These rules cover some plural forms. If you're not sure how to form a plural, look up the singular word in the dictionary. The plural will sometimes be listed there.

Possessive Nouns

Many people confuse possessive nouns and plural nouns. Look at *friends* and *friend's* in the following sentences. Which shows ownership or possession?

His **friends** came for a visit Saturday.

His **friend's** mother called on Friday.

In the second sentence *friend's* shows possession—the friend has a mother. Notice the possessive ending: *'s*.

Study the following rules for forming possessive nouns.

Rules for Forming Possessive Nouns

1. **Add *'s* to form most singular possessive nouns.**

   benefits of the company → the company's benefits

   computer of my brother → my brother's computer

   music of the orchestra → the orchestra's music

2. **Add *s'* to plural nouns to form most plural possessive nouns.**

   team of several employees → several employees' team

   books of all the students → all the students' books

   nest of wasps → wasps' nest

3. **Add *'s* to plural nouns that do not end in *s*.**

   health care for women → women's health care

   wool of the sheep → sheep's wool

Be careful not to use *'s* to form plurals.

INCORRECT: I planted many *daffodil's* along the house.

CORRECT: I planted many *daffodils* along the house.

EXERCISE 3

Possessive Nouns

Directions: Insert apostrophes wherever they belong in the following sentences. Remember, not all nouns ending in -s are possessive.

Example: Animals have always played a big part in people's lives and history all over the world.

1. Long ago in Egypt, when a cat died, the cats owner would shave off his own eyebrows to show respect for the dead cat.
2. Years ago Australians bought weasels to hunt rabbits, but instead the weasels attacked the Australians chickens.
3. Four hundred years ago explorers sometimes took hogs on ships because they believed that if the hogs were thrown overboard, they would swim to the nearest land.
4. Today in the United States animals such as dogs, birds, and cats are popular childrens pets.
5. Japans scientists have been investigating to see if cows and worms can predict earthquakes.
6. Gardeners know bees are important to gardens, and although a common bee may sting a gardener, a queen bee doesn't sting anything other than another queen bee.

Answers are on page 197.

What is a verb?

Our world is interested in action. We tell our friends what we've been doing. We tell potential employers what we can do. We turn on news to learn what is happening. **Verbs** are the words that show action. Which of these verbs describe actions that do you do everyday?

breathe	eat	talk
cook	hope	think
daydream	sleep	work
drive	study	

Every sentence in English must contain a predicate, and every predicate must have a verb. Sometimes, however, we communicate an idea that does not involve action. When an idea does not involve action, we use another kind of verb—the **linking verb.** Linking verbs link the subject to words that describe the subject. They work much like an equal sign does in mathematics. No action is shown in the following sentences, but the subjects, *name* and *chair,* are connected to words that describe them, *Buddy* and *blue.*

His name is Buddy.	His name = Buddy.
The chair is blue.	The chair = blue.

Is and *are* are forms of the most common linking verb, *to be.* Forms of *to be,* as well as some other common linking verbs, are shown in the box below.

COMMON LINKING VERBS
to be: is, am, are, was, were, be, being, been
other linking verbs: appear, seem, become

Fill in the blanks in the sentences below for practice. Use forms of the linking verbs in the box.

Inge ______________________ an excellent gardener.

Every summer the garden ______________________ beautiful.

Roland ______________________ a person who is always working on a project.

The projects he completes ______________________ usually very impressive.

Function of Verbs

Verbs can tell about the action or what is true. They can explain what has already happened, is happening now, or will happen in the future. We can learn about the time of an event as well as the action of an event from verbs. The tense of a verb changes in order to specify *when* something happens. Information about the time of an event is given through the tense of a verb. To form different tenses, verbs must be changed using one word or several words.

Past:	Yesterday we **hoped** for the best.
Present:	Today we **hope** for the best.
Future:	Tomorrow we **will hope** for the best.

Some verb tenses are formed using a single word, such as *hope.* Other tenses require a verb phrase, such as *will hope.* In the verb phrase *will hope, hope* is the **base verb** and *will* is a **helping verb.** To form all verb tenses, you need the base verb. For some you also need to use helping verbs, as you will see as you review the verb tenses.

Regular Verbs

Knowing how to form different verb tenses correctly is very important for the Language Arts, Writing Test. **Regular verbs** are verbs that form the simple past tense and the **past participle** (used to form the perfect tenses) by adding *-ed* to the base verb. The tenses of regular verbs are the easiest to master. However, knowing some spelling rules for regular verbs is helpful. As you study verb forms, take careful note of when they are used.

Spelling Regular Verb Forms

So far you have been writing different forms of verbs by adding *-ed* or *-ing* to the base verb. However, not all verbs change form so simply. Following are three rules for adding *-ed* and *-ing* that cover regular verbs. Study each rule.

1. **If the base verb ends in -y preceded by a consonant, change the *y* to *i* when adding *-ed,* but keep the *y* when adding *-ing*.**

   apply → applied, applying

   try → tried, trying

2. **If the base verb ends with a silent *e,* drop the *e* before adding *-ed* or *-ing.***

   love → loved, loving

   receive → received, receiving

3. **If the base verb ends in a single vowel and a single consonant other than *h, w,* or *x,* and if the accent falls on the last (or only) syllable of the verb, double the final consonant of the base verb when adding *-ed* or *-ing.* Otherwise, keep the normal spelling.**

   prefer → preferred, preferring

   allow → allowed, allowing

Irregular Verbs

English would be a much easier language to write if all verbs shifted to different tenses according to the patterns of regular verbs. However, many English verbs are irregular—they do not change according to these regular patterns. When you study irregular verbs, you need to learn the simple present, the simple past, and the past participle, which is used to form the perfect tenses.

Have, Do, and Be

Make sure you know the three most common irregular verbs: *have, do,* and *be.* If you are not sure of the forms of these verbs in the following boxes, you should memorize them.

	Present	**Simple Past**	**Past Participle**
I, you, we, they (friends)**	have	had	had
He, she, it (dog)*	has	had	had
I, you, we, they (coworkers)**	do	did	done
He, she, it (horse)*	does	did	done
I	am	was	been
He, she, it (train)*	is	was	been
You, we, they (airplanes)**	are	were	been

*or any singular noun
**or any plural noun

The most common mistake people make with irregular verbs is confusing the past participle with the simple past tense. Remember, the past participle is used to form the perfect tenses, so a helping verb *(has, have,* or *had)* must always be used with a past participle.

INCORRECT: She done her work.
CORRECT: She did her work.
CORRECT: She has done her work.

Other Common Irregular Verbs

A list of the simple present, simple past, and past participle forms of common irregular verbs appears on the following pages. Verbs that follow similar patterns are grouped together. You may already use most of these verbs correctly. Study this list by following these steps:

1. Cover the second and third columns of the list.
2. Read the simple present form in a short sentence using *I* as the subject. *I go.*
3. Test to see if you know the simple past form by putting the sentence in the past tense. *I went.*
4. Test to see if you know the past participle by putting the sentence in the present perfect. *I have gone.*
5. Check your answers against the forms listed in the second and third columns.
6. Study the forms you missed by repeating the sentences over and over in each tense until you have memorized them.

Simple Present	Simple Past	Past Participle*
cost	cost	cost
put	put	put
read	read	read
set	set	set
bring	brought	brought
buy	bought	bought
think	thought	thought
catch	caught	caught
teach	taught	taught
lay (put or place)	laid	laid
pay	paid	paid
say	said	said
send	sent	sent
feel	felt	felt
keep	kept	kept
leave	left	left
mean	meant	meant

Simple Present	Simple Past	Past Participle*
meet	met	met
sleep	slept	slept
get	got	got, gotten
lose	lost	lost
find	found	found
feed	fed	fed
hold	held	held
hear	heard	heard
sell	sold	sold
tell	told	told
understand	understood	understood
make	made	made
fall	fell	fallen
speak	spoke	spoken
take	took	taken
drive	drove	driven
eat	ate	eaten
give	gave	given
ride	rode	ridden
write	wrote	written
begin	began	begun
drink	drank	drunk
sing	sang	sung
draw	drew	drawn
grow	grew	grown
know	knew	known
become	became	become
come	came	come
run	ran	run
see	saw	seen
go	went	gone
lie	lay	lain

*Use the past participle most often with *have*, *has*, or *had*.

There are many more irregular verbs than the ones on this list. Whenever you are unsure of the simple past or past participle of an irregular verb, look up the base verb in the dictionary. The forms of the verb will be listed there.

The Simple Tenses

The **simple present** tense is used for something that happens regularly or something that is always true. The simple present tense is sometimes used for something that is happening now, especially when explaining what a writer or speaker thinks, feels, or believes. The base form of the verb forms the simple present tense unless the subject is *he, she, it,* or a singular noun. For these subjects add *-s* (or *-es* if the verb ends in *s, sh, ch, x* and *z*).

The moon **is** full tonight.

I **drink** orange juice every day.

Samuel **feels** sick.

The **simple past** tense shows action that occurred in the past. To form the simple past of any regular verb, add *-ed* to the base verb. To form the past tense of any irregular verb, consult a dictionary or the chart on pages 77–78.

The driver **stopped** for gas a while ago.

Judy **took** a cruise last month.

The **simple future** tense shows action that will happen in the future. Form the simple future for any subject by using *will* with the base verb.

Next January a new year **will begin.**

EXERCISE 4

The Simple Tenses

Directions: Fill in the correct simple tense form of the verb indicated in the parentheses. Time clues such as yesterday, today, and tomorrow in the sentences will help you decide whether to use the past, present, or future tense.

Example: (prepare) A few days ago Les and Brenda *prepared* a budget for the month.

1. (drink) Every morning Barb ________________ two cups of coffee.

2. (move) In two weeks our neighbors ________________ to Florida.

3. (see) They ________________ that movie twice last week.

4. (try) He ________________ to use the computer for the first time a few hours ago.

5. (vote) I ________________ in the next presidential election.

Answers are on page 197.

The Continuous Tenses

The **continuous tenses** show action continuing in the past, present, or future, as in the following examples.

PAST: Columbus **was looking** for a passage to India when he discovered America.

PRESENT: He can't come to the phone right now because he **is taking** a shower.

FUTURE: We **will be discussing** the essay in the next section of this book.

As you can see, the continuous tenses are formed by combining helping verbs with the base form of the verb plus *-ing*. The following chart shows how to form all the continuous tenses.

	Present Continuous	**Past Continuous**	**Future Continuous**
I	am thinking	was thinking	will be thinking
he, she, it (the computer)*	is thinking	was thinking	will be thinking
we, you, they (students)**	are thinking	were thinking	will be thinking

*or any singular noun
**or any plural noun

EXERCISE 5

The Continuous Tenses

Directions: Fill in the correct continuing tense form of the verb indicated in parentheses. Time clues such as *yesterday, today,* and *tomorrow* in the sentences will help you decide whether to use the past, present, or future tense.

Example: (study) Those students ___*are studying*___ together now to pass the GED Test.

1. (walk) We ______________ out the door when Latisha became sick yesterday.

2. (sleep) At the moment, the baby ______________ very peacefully.

3. (begin) One week from today I ______________ a new job in another state.

4. (shine) The sun ______________ right now, but the weather forecast calls for rain.

5. (retire) Lee ______________ at the end of next spring.

Answers are on page 197.

The Perfect Tenses

The **perfect tenses** show action completed before or continuing to a specific time. These tenses are used to show more specific time relationships than the simple or continuous tenses. Certain words or expressions often serve as clue words for the perfect tenses. These include *since, already, yet, up to now, so far* and *for.*

The **present perfect** tense shows that an action started in the past and either continues into the present or has just been completed.

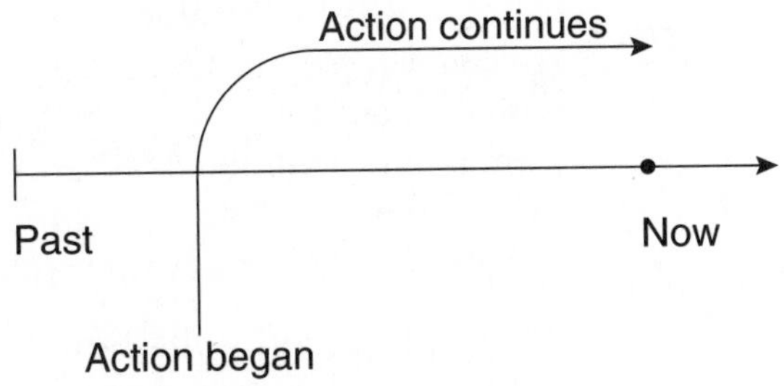

They **have lived** there since 1998.

Surfing the Internet **has grown** increasingly popular.

The **past perfect** tense shows that an action was completed before a specific time in the past.

Up until yesterday, he **had** never **seen** a camel.

The **future perfect** tense shows that an action will be completed by a specific time in the future.

By next month, all the leaves **will have fallen** from those trees.

	Present Perfect	Past Perfect	Future Perfect
I, you, we, they (the parents)**	have thought	had thought	will have thought
he, she, it (a repairman) *	has thought	had thought	will have thought

*or any singular noun

**or any plural noun

EXERCISE 6

The Perfect Tenses

Directions: Fill in the correct perfect tense form of the verb indicated in parentheses. Pay careful attention to the meaning of each sentence before you decide whether to use the past, present, or future perfect.

Example: (start) My car ___*has started*___ every morning up until now.

1. (leave) By 6:00 A.M. tomorrow morning, Juan ______________ for Texas already.
2. (close) The restaurant ______________ by the time we arrived.
3. (save) So far Gwendolyn ______________ enough money for the down payment on a new car.
4. (have) The Johnsons ______________ no chance to meet their new neighbors yet.
5. (run) By the time the traffic clears, we ______________ out of gas.
6. (perform) Up until the development of anesthetics, doctors ______________ surgery with the patient awake.

Answers are on page 197.

EXERCISE 7

Verb Tense Review

Directions: This exercise tests your understanding of simple, continuous, and perfect tenses. Fill in the blank in each sentence with the correct form of the base verb indicated. Be sure to spell all the verb forms correctly. Read each sentence carefully for clues to the correct tense.

1. (achieve) By next summer Pat ____________________ her goal of living in Wyoming and working as a park ranger.

2. (go) Twenty years ago Pat and her husband Greg ____________________ to Wyoming and saw the mountains and parks.

3. (love) Ever since that day they both ____________________ that wilderness area.

4. (return) Every time they have the opportunity, they ____________________ to Wyoming and enjoy the natural beauty of the outdoors.

5. (buy) Last year they ____________________ a home near the parks and made plans to move to Wyoming.

6. (enter) Before they bought the home last year, they ____________________ a contest to try to win a log cabin dream home near Jackson.

7. (lose) Pat had submitted more than five hundred entries, but unfortunately she ____________________ anyway.

8. (be) Chances of winning a contest or lottery usually ____________________ not very good.

9. (feel) The fact is, however, that Pat and Greg still ____________________ very excited about their plans.

10. (study) Right now they ____________________ about wildlife and buying furniture for their new home.

11. (miss) Once they have moved so far away, their friends certainly ____________________ them.

12. (hire) The U.S. Park Service ____________________ some talented and enthusiastic help for its programs every year.

Answers are on page 198.

Using the Correct Verb Tense in a Passage

On the Language Arts,Writing Test, you will have to be able to correct verb tense in the context of a whole passage. Not every sentence in a passage will contain clues such as *a few nights ago* or *tomorrow* to tell you what tense to use. Read the following paragraph and cross out the two incorrect verbs. Write the correct form in the margin.

> Anthony had an embarrassing experience a few years ago. He steps outside briefly to put out some garbage. To his dismay, the door closed behind him. He tried to open the door, but it was locked. Unluckily, he was dressed only in his pajamas. He did not have a key to unlock the door, and no one else is home. He felt very unhappy about the situation.

Did you change *steps* to *stepped* (in the first sentence) and *is* to *was* (in the sixth sentence)? The passage as a whole is written in the past tense. Notice the words *a few years ago* in the first sentence.

In the following GED practice exercise make sure that you choose consistent verb tenses to correct the passage. First, identify verbs. Then, identify the tenses used in the paragraph. Pay attention to any clue words that help clarify the time. Next, determine which verb tense is needed and make any required changes.

GED PRACTICE

EXERCISE 8

Verbs

Directions: Read the following passage and answer the questions. Be sure that all verb tenses are correct and that verb forms are spelled correctly.

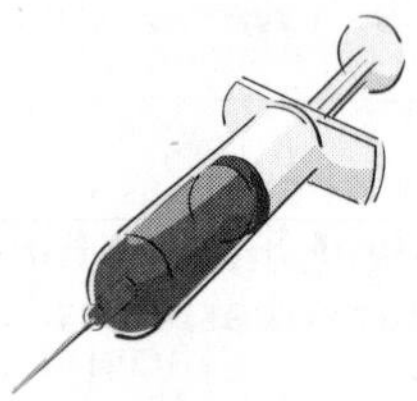

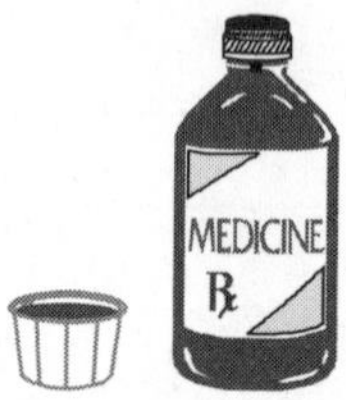

(1) Penicillin is an antibiotic drug that will be used widely today in medical treatments. **(2)** However, in 1942, Anne Sheafe Miller makes medical history as the first patient to be saved by penicillin. **(3)** She was near death as a result of an infection and temperature of almost 107 degrees. **(4)** Before doctors gave her the experimental drug, they should try sulfa drugs, blood transfusions, and surgery. **(5)** Once Anne Sheafe Miller has received penicillin, her temperature dropped overnight. **(6)** She begun to recover and lived more than fifty years longer. **(7)** Since that first successful use of penicillin, we have called antibiotics our miracle drugs. **(8)** We hope these antibiotic drugs are continuing to be effective against disease in the future.

1. Sentence 1: **Penicillin is an antibiotic drug that <u>will be used</u> widely today in medical treatments.**

   Which of the following is the best way to write the underlined portion of this sentence? If you think the original is the best way to write the sentence, choose option (1).

   (1) will be used
   (2) is using
   (3) had been used
   (4) is used
   (5) was used

2. Sentence 2: **However, in 1942, Anne Sheafe Miller <u>makes</u> medical history as the first patient to be saved by penicillin.**

   Which of the following is the best way to write the underlined portion of this sentence? If you think the original is the best way to write the sentence, choose option (1).

   (1) makes
   (2) made
   (3) has made
   (4) will make
   (5) is making

3. Sentence 4: **Before doctors gave her the experimental drug, they <u>should try</u> sulfa drugs, blood transfusions, and surgery.**

   Which of the following is the best way to write the underlined portion of this sentence? If you think the original is the best way to write the sentence, choose option (1).

   (1) should try
   (2) had tried
   (3) are trying
   (4) try
   (5) will be trying

4. Sentence 5: **Once Anne Sheafe Miller <u>has received</u> penicillin, her temperature dropped overnight.**

   Which of the following is the best way to write the underlined portion of this sentence? If you think the original is the best way to write the sentence, choose option (1).

   (1) has received
   (2) will receive
   (3) receives
   (4) is receiving
   (5) received

5. Sentence 6: **She <u>begun</u> to recover and lived more than fifty years longer.**

Which of the following is the best way to write the underlined portion of this sentence? If you think the original is the best way to write the sentence, choose option (1).

(1) begun
(2) began
(3) will begin
(4) has begun
(5) had began

6. Sentence 7: **Since that first successful use of penicillin, we <u>have called</u> antibiotics our miracle drugs.**

Which of the following is the best way to write the underlined portion of this sentence? If you think the original is the best way to write the sentence, choose option (1).

(1) have called
(2) had called
(3) are calling
(4) will have called
(5) will be calling

7. Sentence 8: **We hope these antibiotic drugs <u>are continuing</u> to be effective against disease in the future.**

Which of the following is the best way to write the underlined portion of this sentence? If you think the original is the best way to write the sentence, choose option (1).

(1) are continuing
(2) may be continuing
(3) could have continued
(4) will continue
(5) continued

Answers are on page 198.

Subject-Verb Agreement

Agreement makes the English language easier to understand. **Subject-verb agreement** means that you have chosen the correct verb form to match the number and person of the subject.

If you get dressed one morning and put a tan gym shoe on your right foot and a tan sandal on your left, you're likely to hear some strange comments from people. Yes, the shoes are the same color, but they are different types (or styles) of shoes. In grammar, the subject and verb of a sentence are like a right and left shoe. We expect them to match. Language is easier for everyone to understand when the grammar follows what is expected.

When you are writing, it is important to make subjects match, or agree, with verbs. In this section, you will learn how to make sure you have this agreement.

The Basic Pattern

If the subject of a present-tense verb is *he, she, it,* or any singular noun, the verb must end in *-s* or *-es*. Verbs ending in *s, sh, ch, x,* and *z* require *-es* as an ending.

Notice that even the forms of irregular verbs also end in *-s* or *-es* when the subject is *he, she,* or *it.*

In the following examples, identify each subject. Fill in the correct form of the verb *fall* to agree with each subject.

Snow ____________________ silently on the earth every winter.

Snowflakes ____________________ silently on the earth every winter.

You should have written *falls* in the first sentence because the subject, *snow,* is a singular noun. The subject of the second sentence, *snowflakes,* is a plural noun, so the correct verb is *fall.*

Subject-Verb Agreement Problems

Subject-verb agreement is only a problem in the present tense, with one exception. In the past tense the irregular verb *be* changes form for different subjects. (See page 76).

Keep subject-verb agreement in mind when you see contractions. If you have trouble figuring out the correct form, take the contraction apart. For example, *doesn't* means *does not,* and *don't* means *do not.*

INCORRECT: He don't (do not) want any more.

CORRECT: He doesn't (does not) want any more.

Compound Subjects

S + **S**

The following rules apply to compound subjects and verbs.

If the parts of a compound subject are connected by *and,* the subject is usually plural and the verb does not end in *-s.*

The rolls and the bread **seem** very fresh.

If the parts of a compound subject are connected by *or* or *nor,* the verb agrees with the part of the subject closer to it.

Neither the rolls nor the bread (seems, seem) very fresh.

Neither the bread nor the rolls (seems, seem) very fresh.

In the first sentence the verb must agree with *bread.* You should have chosen *seems.* In the second sentence the verb must agree with *rolls.* You should have chosen *seem.*

Inverted Order

V + **S**

In three common types of sentences the verb comes before the subject. Underline the subject of each of the following sentences; then circle the correct verb.

(Is, Are) my keys on the table?

There (goes, go) Pat and Jan before anyone else.

Over the fireplace (hangs, hang) two pictures.

If you have trouble finding the subject of these sentences, mentally rearrange the word order:

My keys (is, are) on the table.

Pat and Jan (goes, go) there before anyone else.

Two pictures (hangs, hang) over the fireplace.

You should have chosen *keys are* for the first example, *Pat and Jan go* for the second, and *pictures hang* for the third.

EXERCISE 9

Subject-Verb Agreement

Directions: Underline the subject; then circle the correct verb in parentheses.

1. The employees and the boss (was, were) busy yesterday.
2. Neither the employees nor the boss (was, were) busy on Tuesday.
3. The bread or the crackers (comes, come) with the soup.
4. In the drawer (is, are) a serving spoon and butter knife.
5. There (seem, seems) to be many problems with this plan.
6. (Has, Have) the mail arrived yet?
7. (Doesn't, Don't) time seem to go by quickly?

Answers are on page 198.

Interrupting Phrases

The subject and verb of a sentence often are separated by **prepositional phrases** and phrases that add information to the subject. Neither type of phrase affects agreement between subject and verb.

Some of the most common prepositions are *of, in, for, to, from, with, on,* and *by.* The prepositional phrases in the following example sentences are in **bold type.** They are not part of the subject. Underline the subject and then underline the correct verb.

Every player **in the Olympic Games** (trains, train) very hard.

A deck of **cards** (has, have) fifty-two cards.

You should have chosen *player trains* and *deck has.*

Other **interrupting phrases** may seem to make the subject plural, but they do not. They do not change the main subject of the sentence. They often start with words such as *as well as, in addition to,* and *like.* These phrases are set off by commas. Underline the subject and then underline the verb in the following examples.

That roller coaster, like all the others, (is are) very scary.

Chuck, unlike his friends, (likes, like) all roller coasters.

You should have chosen *roller coaster is* and *Chuck likes.*

Indefinite Pronouns as Subjects

Indefinite pronouns are pronouns that do not specify a distinct noun. There are three groups of **indefinite pronouns.** Sometimes these are used as subjects in sentences. Some indefinite pronouns are always singular, some are always plural, and some can be either singular or plural, depending on their antecedents (see page 95). Singular indefinite pronouns almost always end in *-one* or *-body.*

Singular		Plural	Singular or Plural (depending upon their use)
everyone	everybody	both	some
someone	somebody	few	any
no one	nobody	many	more
anyone	anybody	several	most
one	each (one)		all
either (one)	neither (one)		none

Underline the indefinite pronoun in the following sentences and then underline the correct verb. Remember to think about the meaning and make the grammar match appropriately.

One of the rooms (seems, seem) empty.

Some of this room (is, are) white.

Some of those rooms (is, are) white.

You should have chosen *One seems, Some is,* and *Some are.* Don't let the interrupting phrase *of the rooms* confuse you in the first sentence. Think about the meaning. The sentence is about only one of the rooms and *One* is the subject to which you must match the verb. In the second sentence *Some* refers to the singular noun *room,* making the indefinite pronoun singular. However, in the third sentence, *Some* refers to the plural noun *rooms,* making the indefinite pronoun plural. For more information about pronoun reference, see the section on antecedents beginning on page 95.

EXERCISE 10

More Subject-Verb Agreement

Directions: Underline the subject; then underline the correct verb in parentheses for each sentence.

1. LaVerne, as well as Anna and Marina, (looks, look) forward to passing the GED Test.
2. Everybody (wants, want) to pass because having educational credentials is very helpful in life.
3. Each of the sections on the GED (is, are) timed.
4. Most of the questions (is, are) multiple choice.
5. The tests on math and writing (has, have) some parts that are not multiple choice.
6. Determination, along with study, (helps, help) a student to pass.

Answers are on page 198.

What is a pronoun?

A **pronoun** is a word that replaces and refers to a noun. Using a pronoun allows us to avoid repeating the same words over and over again. Notice how repetitious the passage below is because of the lack of pronouns.

> My brother went to visit Grandmother Gwendolyn. Grandmother Gwendolyn lives far away, so my brother doesn't often get to see Grandmother Gwendolyn although my brother is quite fond of Grandmother Gwendolyn. Grandmother Gwendolyn gave my brother a piece of Grandmother Gwendolyn's wonderful cherry pie, for which Grandmother Gwendolyn is famous.

Now read the passage again and note the underlined pronouns.

> My brother went to visit Grandmother Gwendolyn. <u>She</u> lives far away, so <u>he</u> doesn't often get to see <u>her</u> although <u>he</u> is quite fond of <u>her</u>. <u>She</u> gave <u>him</u> a piece of <u>her</u> wonderful cherry pie, for which <u>she</u> is famous.

Personal Pronouns

Personal pronouns are divided into three groups, or cases. Each group has different functions.

	Subjective Case (These pronouns act as subjects. They often *do* the action.)		**Objective Case (These pronouns do not act as subjects. They often *get* the action.)**		**Possessive Case (These pronouns show ownership. They do not need an apostrophe to do that.)**	
First Person (might be used when you're writing a diary or journal).	I	we	me	us	my* our*	mine ours
Second Person (might be used when you're writing advice to somebody else).	you	you	you	you	your*	yours
Third Person (might be used when you're writing about the actions of somebody else).	he she it	they	him her it	them	his* her* its* their	his hers its theirs
Relative	who		whom		whose	

Note that the starred * possessive pronouns are used with another noun, as in *my car.* The possessive pronouns without stars are used alone: *The car is mine.*

Subject and Object Pronouns

The following hints will help you decide when to use subject and object pronouns.

Hint 1: *Is the pronoun the subject of a verb, or is the pronoun getting the action?*

In the following sentence what is the verb? Will the pronoun be the subject of that verb?

A bee stung (he, him) on the arm.

In the sentence above, the verb is *stung*. The subject of *stung* is *bee, so* the pronoun will not be the subject. The object pronoun *him* is correct.

Hint 2: *Cross out any nouns connected to the pronoun with and. Then look at the pronoun alone to see if it is the subject of a verb.*

Which pronoun is correct in the following example?

(She, Her) and Peter will be here soon.

Cross out *and Peter.* Will the pronoun be the subject of the verb *will be?* Which is correct, *She will be here soon* or *Her will be here soon?* The correct pronoun is *She.*

EXERCISE 11

Pronoun Forms

Directions: Replace the words in bold type in each sentence with the correct pronoun. Read the sentence carefully to determine whether to use a subject, object or possessive pronoun. Remember that there are two types of possessive pronouns.

Example: **Robert and I** found **Karen's** earring in the parking lot.

We found **her** earring in the parking lot.

1. **Juan** drove to work with **Kevin and Kelly.**
2. **The men's** shirts cost the same as **Sharon's** hat.
3. The invitation said that children were invited, so I brought **my children.**
4. Give the check to **my husband and me.**
5. Yesterday Mike and **Mike's** family left to go camping.

Answers are on page 198.

Possessives and Contractions

To show ownership, we might use possessive nouns such as *Jay's* or *Mary Kim's.* Notice that we use an apostrophe to form the possessive of nouns. However, if we use possessive pronouns such as *his* or *hers* to show ownership, we do not use an apostrophe. It is easy to confuse some possessive pronouns with **contractions.** The meaning is the key to knowing whether an apostrophe is needed. Look at the two sentences below and note the difference in meaning and punctuation.

The car lost **its** muffler. *(ownership)*

She is glad that **it's** snowing. *(contraction)*

Possessive Pronoun	**Sound-alike Contraction**
its	**it's (it is)**
theirs	**there's (there is)**
their	**they're (they are)**
your	**you're (you are)**
whose	**who's (who is)**

When you're deciding whether to use a contraction in a sentence, substitute the two words for which the contraction stands.

They told us that (their, they're) leaving on Saturday.

Test the sentence with *they are,* the two words that the contraction *they're* stands for: *They told us that they are leaving on Saturday.* The sentence makes sense, so the contraction *they're* is the correct choice.

Do you know (whose, who's) jacket this is?

Test the sentence with *who is: Do you know who is jacket this is?* The sentence makes no sense when the words of the contraction are used, so the possessive pronoun *whose* is the correct choice.

EXERCISE 12

Possessive Pronouns and Contractions

Directions: Underline the correct word to complete each sentence.

1. (There's, Theirs) so much ice in the world, if we melted it all, the earth would flood enough to cover twenty stories of the Empire State Building.
2. The earth is mostly water, so only about 30% of (it's, its) surface is land.
3. Seven of the planets in our solar system have moons, and all (they're, their) moons have names.

4. If you think (you're, your) uncomfortable on a hot day in summer, just consider that the temperature in the center of the sun is about 27,000,000 degrees Farenheit.
5. Stephen Hawking, (who's, whose) contributions to science include knowledge about black holes and the evolution of the universe, may be one of the greatest physicists of the twentieth century.
6. If someone is driving at the speed of light, which is 186,282 miles per second, (it's, its) likely he will get a ticket.

Answers are on page 198.

Identifying Antecedents

The noun that a pronoun replaces and refers to is called its **antecedent.** The relationship between a pronoun and its antecedent must be clear so that the reader can comprehend the meaning. There are several specific pronoun problems that you are likely to find on the Language Arts, Writing Test. To begin with, practice identifying the antecedents of pronouns in correctly-written sentences.

Draw an arrow from the pronoun in this sentence to its antecedent.

William Shakespeare became famous for the plays he wrote.

Did you draw the arrow from *he* to *William Shakespeare*? The pronoun *he* replaces and refers to the noun *William Shakespeare.*

Pronouns often refer to antecedents in other sentences. In the following paragraph, draw arrows from *He* in the second sentence and *they* in the third sentence to their antecedents.

John F. Kennedy was president during the sixties. He gave a famous speech to Americans. He told them they should ask what they could do for their country, not what their country could do for them.

Did you choose *John F. Kennedy* as the antecedent for *He* and *Americans* for *they*?

EXERCISE 13

Identifying Antecedents

Directions: In the following paragraph, the pronouns are numbered. Fill in the correct antecedent for each pronoun. The first two are done for you.

When people read the newspaper one morning, **they** (1) found that **it** (2) contained a story about a farmer in Elburn, Illinois. The farmer had received a bill from ComEd for $544,450.11, and **he** (3) was quite stunned. **His** (4) average monthly electric bill was normally about $120 to $130. The highest electric bill **that** (5) the farmer ever received was $1,500. A ComEd spokesperson **who** (6) spoke to reporters claimed that the bill was a mistake, and **she** (7) said **it** (8) should never have been sent. Many people feel **their** (9) electric bills are too high, but few people receive bills **that** (10) cost half a million dollars in a month.

Pronoun	**Antecedent**
1. they	people
2. it	newspaper
3. he	______
4. his	______
5. that	______
6. who	______
7. she	______
8. it	______
9. their	______
10. that	______

Answers are on page 198.

Agreement in Number

Pronouns and antecedents must agree in number. The pronoun *they* is used in the sentence below because its antecedent, *plants,* is plural.

> Tiny plants called phytoplankton make the food they need from sunlight and minerals from water.

Is *it* used correctly in the following sentence? Decide whether *it* agrees in number with its antecedent.

> These tiny plants live in the sea where it may be eaten by fish.

The pronoun *it* in this sentence has been used incorrectly to refer to plants. The plural pronoun *they* should be used to match the plural noun *plants.*

As you check for pronoun agreement errors on the Language Arts, Writing Test, keep in mind that the antecedent of a pronoun is not always in the same sentence as the pronoun. In the following passage, find the pronoun that does not agree in number with the rest of the passage and correct it.

> Today tomatoes are popular and used in many dishes. Years ago, however, no one ate tomatoes because they were believed to be poisonous. The first person to cultivate tomato plants in North America was Thomas Jefferson. He grew it hundreds of years ago in his garden. Today people know tomatoes are safe to eat although their leaves are toxic.

Did you find the singular pronoun *it*? The rest of the pronouns in the passage are plural—*they* and *their* are used to refer to tomatoes. Therefore, *it* should be replaced with *them.*

Compound Antecedents

The antecedent of a pronoun is not always a single noun. Sometimes the antecedent is made up of two nouns connected by *and, or,* or *nor.* In this example, the two nouns in the antecedent are connected by *and.* The pronoun is plural.

> **Tony and Elizabeth** watched **their** favorite show on Sunday nights.

And makes a **compound antecedent** (an antecedent of more than one noun) plural. Use a plural pronoun to refer to a compound antecedent joined by *and.*

When a compound antecedent is joined by *or* or *nor,* the rule is different. *Or* and *nor* separate the nouns in a compound antecedent. The pronoun must agree with the closest noun in the antecedent.

> Either **Lisa or the kids** will share **their** fruit.
>
> Either **the kids or Lisa** will share **her** fruit.

In the first example above *the kids* is closest to the pronoun, so the pronoun is plural, *their.* In the second example *Lisa* is closest to the pronoun, so the pronoun is singular, *her.*

EXERCISE 14

Agreement in Number

Part A **Directions:** Underline the antecedent of the pronoun; then underline the singular or plural pronoun in parentheses that agrees with it.

Example: American <u>colonists</u> in 1773 rebelled against (its, <u>their</u>) king when taxes were imposed on tea.

1. In 1906 the hot dog was given (its, their) name by a Chicago cartoonist named Thomas Dorgan.
2. I'll give this money to Lance or Mark, and the one who gets it can spend it as (he, they) would like.
3. Neither expensive fertilizers nor expensive machinery will increase (its, their) contribution to food production enough to offset the problem of soil erosion.
4. During the 18th century, neither the King of France nor the American Indians had hamburgers as entrees for (his, their) dinners, since hamburgers were not created until about 1900 in New Haven, Connecticut.
5. The English words *beef, pork,* and *poultry* have (its, their) origins in the French words *boeuf, porc,* and *poularde,* which were brought to England by the Normans in 1066.

Part B **Directions:** Cross out incorrect pronouns in this passage and write in correct ones, making sure the pronouns agree in number.

Each company has certain expectations of their employees. Its expectations often include work practices, dress code, and safety procedures that workers need to follow during their employment. Employees, in turn, have certain expectations about a company and their treatment of personnel. Their expectations often include salary schedules, benefit provisions, and working conditions.

Answers are on page 199.

More than One Antecedent

The meaning of a pronoun is unclear if the pronoun can refer to more than one antecedent. Remember that the reader should not have to guess at the intended meaning. In the following example what was damaged?

> When the car crashed into the wall, it was damaged.

Since two things are mentioned in the same sentence, the pronoun *it* is confusing. Here is one way in which the sentence could be corrected.

> When the car crashed into the wall, the car was damaged.

Sometimes replacing a noun with a pronoun is not the best way to keep the meaning clear. Now look at another example. What has been dropped?

> I was holding the eggs in one hand and the tomatoes in the other when I stumbled and dropped them.

Am I left with broken eggs, bruised tomatoes, or possibly both broken eggs and bruised tomatoes? A better revision of this sentence follows:

> I was holding the eggs in one hand and the tomatoes in the other when I stumbled and dropped everything I was holding.

No Antecedent

Some pronouns are used without any antecedent at all. The pronouns *it, this,* and *they* commonly appear without an antecedent. Here's an example:

> VAGUE: When she registered to take the test, she learned they required two pieces of identification.
>
> CLEAR: When she registered to take the test, she learned that the testing service required two pieces of identification.

The following sentences contain a very common example of a pronoun with no antecedent. Circle the vague pronoun. On a piece of scratch paper, rewrite the sentence it appears in to make the meaning clear.

> Maria has been attending classes after work to increase her job skills. It is something that will help her to obtain a promotion in her company.

Did you circle *It*? You might have revised the previous sentence in several ways. One possibility would be *Increasing her job skills is something that will help her obtain a promotion in her company.*

EXERCISE 15

Clarifying Antecedents

Directions: Read the following sentences carefully, looking for confusing pronoun references. If a sentence or group of sentences is written clearly and does not need to be revised, write **C** in the blank. If revision is needed, write **X** in the blank and revise on a separate sheet of paper.

Example: __X__ The pet stores had rabbits and hamsters for sale, and they were very cute.

The pet store had rabbits and hamsters for sale, and all were very cute.

1. ______ Wendy gave Bonnie her car keys.

2. ______ The man followed Mr. Reynolds in his new car.

3. ______ When Al lost his wallet, it created a problem.

4. ______ We heard on the news that they are trying to find a cure for diabetes.

5. ______ Would you put those dishes next to those glasses after you dry them?

6. ______ Obesity and malnutrition are growing concerns in the United States. This continues to be a threat to the health of many people.

7. ______ The game was supposed to have begun at 2 P.M., but it was cancelled because of rain.

8. ______ Children need to be raised with love and patience. This child-rearing advice is very well-known.

9. ______ The Phillipses met the Mulcrones for dinner, and they paid the check.

Possible answers are on page 199.

Keeping Track of Person

To enable a reader to comprehend clearly what you write, you need to be consistent in the way you use pronouns. Read this paragraph and try to keep track of the pronouns.

> If a person wants to increase your earning power, you might want to consider increasing his education. One report from the U.S. Department of Education showed that male high school or GED graduates between ages 25 and 34 earned 41 percent more than those males who had no high school credentials. For females, the difference was 58 percent higher. Very often a person can get a better-paying job if you have greater education.

The pronouns in this paragraph are mixed between *he* and *you*. All of the pronouns in the paragraph are singular, so they agree in number, but they shift in **person** (from *you* to *he* and back again). Within a passage, the pronouns should not shift from one person to another.

First person: I, me, my, mine, we, us, our, ours

Second person: you, your, yours

Third person: he, she, it, him, her, his, hers, its, them, they, theirs

Here is one way to correct the paragraph:

> If you want to increase your earning power, you might want to consider increasing your education. One report from the U.S. Department of Education showed that male high school or GED graduates between ages 25 and 34 earned 41 percent more than those males who had no high school credentials. For females the difference was 58 percent higher. Very often you can get a better-paying job if you have greater education.

EXERCISE 16

Agreement in Person

Directions: Find which of the pronouns in bold type need to be corrected in the following passage.

One survey report states that 66 percent of **us** just want some time for ourselves. In general, **we** are working more than ever, so **you** have less and less free time. Two strategies **you** can use to save some of that valuable time are helpful. **We** need to learn to combine **your** errands, and **we** need to buy time rather than things.

Answers are on page 199.

GED PRACTICE

EXERCISE 17

Usage

Directions: The following items are based on paragraphs that contain numbered sentences. Some of the sentences may contain errors in usage. A few sentences, however, may be correct as written. Read the passage and then answer the items based on it. For each item, choose the answer that would result in the most effective writing of the sentence or sentences. The best answer must be consistent with the meaning and tone of the rest of the passage.

(A)

(1) The modern world offers many opportunities for living happy and meaningful lives. **(2)** However, it's not a world without conflict. **(3)** Work disputes, social disagreements, and family problems sometimes causes feelings of confusion or helplessness. **(4)** Fortunately, when a conflict arises between you and another person, there are some useful tips that can help.

(B)

(5) First of all, it is important to recognize your own point of view, including whatever biases and judgments we may have. **(6)** Next, you should try to consider the other person's point of view. **(7)** As you talked with the other person, use sentences that begin with the word "I" to explain your feelings. **(8)** At the same time, avoid using sentences such as "You never," or "You always," **(9)** When the other person will talk, listen and try not to interrupt. **(10)** It is important for real communication. **(11)** Also, don't hesitate to give an apology when they are appropriate.

(C)

(12) Perhaps most meaningfully, a code of civility and respect are important to follow. **(13)** Treat others with respect, and in turn, others have respected you. **(14)** The philosopher William James once said, "I will act as if what I do makes a difference."

1. Sentence 2: **However, it's not a world without conflict.**

   What correction should be made to sentence 2?

   (1) replace <u>it's</u> with <u>there's</u>
   (2) replace <u>it's</u> with <u>theirs</u>
   (3) replace <u>it's</u> with <u>its</u>
   (4) replace <u>it's</u> with <u>it was</u>
   (5) no correction is necessary

2. Sentence 3: **Work disputes, social disagreements, and family problems sometimes causes feelings of confusion or helplessness.**

What correction should be made to sentence 3?

(1) change causes to caused
(2) change causes to cause
(3) change causes to will cause
(4) replace of with or
(5) no correction is necessary

3. Sentence 5: **First of all, it is important to recognize your own point of view, including whatever biases and judgments we may have.**

What correction should be made to sentence 5?

(1) replace we with you
(2) replace it is with its
(3) replace your with you're
(4) change is to will be
(5) change is to was

4. Sentence 6: **Next, you should try to consider the other person's point of view.**

What correction should be made to sentence 6?

(1) replace you with I
(2) replace should with must
(3) replace you with he
(4) change try to have tried
(5) no correction is necessary

5. Sentence 7: **As you talked with the other person, use sentences that begin with the word "I" to explain your feelings.**

What correction should be made to sentence 7?

(1) replace you with I
(2) replace your with his
(3) change talked to talk
(4) change begin to begins
(5) change begin to began

6. Sentence 9: **When the other person will talk, listen and try not to interrupt.**

Which is the best way to write the underlined portion of the text? If the original is the best way, choose option (1).

(1) will talk, listen and try
(2) will talk, listen and tried
(3) talk, listen and try
(4) was talking, listen and try
(5) is talking, listen and try

7. Sentence 10: **It is important for real communication.**

   Which is the best way to write the underlined portion of the text? If the original is the best way, choose option (1).

   (1) It is
   (2) There is
   (3) Listening is
   (4) It's
   (5) It will be

8. Sentence 11: **Also, don't hesitate to give an apology when they are appropriate.**

   Which is the best way to write the underlined portion of the text? If the original is the best way, choose option (1).

   (1) when they are
   (2) when their
   (3) when its
   (4) when one is
   (5) if they are

9. Sentence 12: **Perhaps most meaningfully, a code of civility and respect are important to follow.**

   What correction should be made to sentence 12?

   (1) change are to were
   (2) change are to has been
   (3) change are to is
   (4) replace respect with honor
   (5) change are to being

10. Sentence 13: **Treat others with respect, and in turn, others have respected you.**

    Which is the best way to write the underlined portion of the text? If the original is the best way, choose option (1).

    (1) have respected you.
    (2) respected you.
    (3) respected them.
    (4) respects you.
    (5) will respect you.

Answers are on page 199.

Go to **www.GEDWriting.com** for additional practice and instruction!

CHAPTER 2

Sentence Structure

Sense make to rules certain follow must, sentence the in words the as well as, sentence the of structure and order word the, understood be to going is sentence a if.

In other words,

If a sentence is going to be understood, the word order and structure of the sentence, as well as the words in the sentence, must follow certain rules to make sense.

As you can see from this example of a backward sentence, **word order** and **structure** are vital for comprehension. In the first chapter you learned a lot about English grammar. For example, you know what a verb is and how to use it. Learning appropriate usage of the parts of speech helps you communicate in standard English sentences.

In this chapter you will examine the uses and purposes of a complete sentence. You will also study a variety of ways to write and combine sentences. These skills will help you to recognize and correct errors on the multiple-choice part of the Language Arts, Writing Test and to write well on the GED Essay.

Three Characteristics of a Sentence

One of the first topics you reviewed was the characteristics of a complete sentence: a subject and a predicate. Together the subject and predicate must express a complete thought. A group of words that does not meet these requirements is a fragment. Can you identify the fragments in the following joke?

(1) *Two strangers in an art gallery looking at a painting.*

(2) Woman:	This painting is the most horrible thing that I have ever seen!
(3) Man:	Horrible? What do you mean by "horrible"?
(4) Woman:	I mean that it looks more ridiculous than any other painting here. Someone should recommend taking this painting away and putting up another painting that is more interesting than this junk.
(5) Man:	Well, I'm sorry, but I don't agree with you.
(6) Woman:	You don't? Well, you just don't know anything about art. This painting has bad composition. Poor color. No line. Who are you anyway?
(7) Man:	I'm the artist who painted the picture.

The fragments are found in lines (1), (3), and (6). The first fragment is missing part of the verb. It could be corrected to read: *Two strangers in an art gallery <u>are looking</u> at a painting.* The fragment in line (3) is the word *Horrible.* This fragment simply repeats the thought from the previous sentence, *This painting is the most horrible thing that I have ever seen!* The last two fragments in part (6) are *Poor color. No line.* These fragments should have been attached to the previous sentence so that the sentence would read as follows: *This painting has bad composition, poor color, and no line.*

Fragments often occur in speech because a speaker has additional ways, such as facial expressions, gestures, or tone of voice, to communicate his or her meaning more fully. In written communication these additional means are unavailable. Complete sentences become more necessary for clear understanding. It is true that a writer such as a novelist may use fragments to imitate speech, as in the example above, or to create an effect. However, general communication, such as business documents, instructions, or letters, will be more understandable when written in complete sentences. Remember that a complete sentence in English should tell clearly who or what did something or who or what something is.

In a certain type of sentence the subject is clearly understood, but it may not be printed in the sentence. In the following sentences, who is supposed to do the action?

Study hard for the GED Test.

Enjoy your success once you've passed.

The person who is supposed to study is *you.* The person who should enjoy success is also *you.* In a command or instruction the subject of the sentence is understood to be *you.*

In addition to having a subject and predicate, a sentence must express a complete thought. Of course, no sentence will ever tell all the information that you can think to ask. However, if the sentence expresses a complete thought, you should not be left waiting for something more. What is the problem with the following sentence?

When spring comes in May.

In the sentence above the thought is not complete. What will happen when spring comes? You could correct the sentence by writing *When spring comes in May, the rains will begin.*

In the graphic below one part is broken off from the whole. Similarly, a sentence fragment may occur because a writer has failed to attach it to the previous sentence where the fragment actually belongs. Sometimes a fragment occurs because it has been separated from the sentence that follows it. When proofreading for fragments, read slowly enough to consider whether each sentence is truly complete.

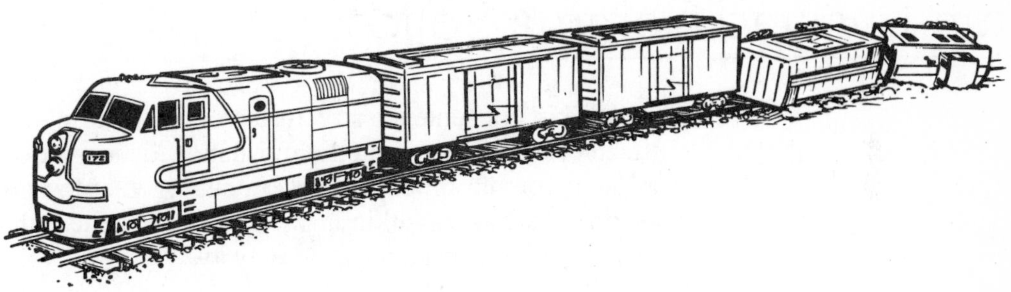

EXERCISE 1

Rewriting Fragments

Part A **Directions:** Write **S** in front of complete sentences and **F** in front of fragments. Rewrite each fragment as a complete sentence on a separate sheet or paper, making sure each has a subject and a predicate and expresses a complete thought.

Examples: F Just a moment.

Wait just a moment, please.

S She read the paper slowly.

1. ______ A million dollars.
2. ______ What time does the meeting begin?
3. ______ A car stopping at the traffic light.
4. ______ Lost in the woods.
5. ______ Have a nice day.

Part B **Directions:** Rewrite the following paragraph, fixing all of the sentence fragments. You can fix these fragments by adding a missing subject or predicate, or by joining two fragments.

The most successful people often are those who are willing to experience failure. Without letting it stop them. One such person was Abraham Lincoln. Lincoln failed in business, failed to get into law school in 1832, and failed to win in more than six elections. He also suffered severe hardship in his life. For example, the deaths of his mother and fiancée. Nevertheless, he became president of the United States and still is respected for many of his efforts.

Answers are on page 200.

Run-ons and Comma Splices

Another kind of sentence structure problem is a run-on or a comma splice. Instead of not having enough information, as is the trouble with a fragment, a run-on or comma splice attempts to put together too much information. A **run-on** actually has within it two or more sentences that should be separated or combined in a more appropriate way.

RUN-ON: The Appalachian Trail, or AT, is over 2,000 miles long it runs through woods from Georgia to Maine.

If you let punctuation be your clue, you can count only one sentence in the example above. *The* begins with a capital letter, and a period follows *Maine.* However, the run-on above comprises two sentences. The first sentence ends with the word *long.* When two or more sentences are joined without correct punctuation or conjunctions, the result is a run-on.

Another type of error, a **comma splice,** results when two complete sentences are joined only by a comma. If you use only a comma to try to correct the run-on above, you will create a comma splice.

COMMA SPLICE: The Appalachian Trail or AT is over 2,000 miles long, it runs through woods from Georgia to Maine.

If you want to correct a run-on using only a punctuation mark and without using any connecting word, then do not use a comma.

Two punctuation marks that will work alone to correct run-ons are given in the examples below.

The Appalachian Trail, or AT, is over 2,000 miles long. It runs through woods from Georgia to Maine.

Notice that a period is used to end the first sentence. The second sentence must begin with a capital letter.

The Appalachian Trail, or AT, is over 2,000 miles long; it runs through woods from Georgia to Maine.

Notice that a semicolon is used to connect the first sentence to the second. No capital letter is used to begin the second sentence.

EXERCISE 2

Run-Ons and Comma Splices

Directions: Some of the following sentences are run-ons or comma splices. If a sentence is correct as written, write **C** in the space. In each run-on or comma splice underline the word that should begin another sentence.

1. ______ If you punch holes in the lid of a small jar and fill it with baking soda, you can reduce odors in your closet.

2. ______ A paste made from meat tenderizer can help the pain from insect bites, this method works well on bee stings.

3. ______ Wet moss can be extremely slippery it can be easily scraped off with a small knife.

4. ______ If your home doesn't look like those in the magazines, it's because real people live there.

5. ______ A short nap of 15 to 20 minutes can improve alertness and sharpen memory.

6. ______ A good remedy against cockroaches is boric acid, it causes the cockroach's stomach to explode.

7. ______ Every year lightning strikes thousands of people it kills about 150 people in the United States each year.

8. ______ The state of New Mexico has more lightning strikes than any other state in the United States.

9. ______ Color can influence the way people feel, for example, the color red can be very stimulating.

10. ______ Children under the age of thirteen are especially good at learning language researchers are still doing studies on language learning and age.

Answers are on page 200.

Sentence Combining

Run-ons or comma splices can also be revised effectively by using connecting words to combine sentences. To make one sentence out of the two sentences below, what common connecting word would you use?

The left front tire of the car is flat.
The car window has a hole in it.

The most common way to combine sentences like these is to use the joining word *and.* In the combined sentence that follows, notice that a comma is necessary before the connecting word—where the period was in the first sentence. The wording of the two original sentences is unchanged.

The left front tire of the car is flat, and the car window has a hole in it.

The combined sentences you have just seen are made up of two independent clauses joined by a comma plus *and.* A **clause** is a group of words that contains a subject and a verb. An **independent clause** can stand on its own as a complete sentence: it has a subject and a predicate, and it expresses a complete thought.

The following joining words, or **coordinating conjunctions,** are used with a comma to combine independent clauses: *and, but, or, nor, for, so, yet.* Notice that the joining words have different meanings. As a writer, you should select the most appropriate connective to explain to the reader the relationship between the two ideas that you are combining. It is the responsibility of the writer to specify the meaning; it is not the responsibility of the reader to guess.

The following chart shows the different coordinating conjunctions and their meanings in a sentence.

Coordinating Conjunction	Meaning
and	adds information
but	shows contrast
or	provides alternative
nor	rejects both alternatives
for	gives reason
so	shows result
yet	shows contrast

EXERCISE 3

Conjunctions

Directions: Choose a logical conjunction from the chart to connect each pair of sentences. Then, on a separate sheet of paper, rewrite each pair as one sentence. Be sure to punctuate each new sentence correctly.

Example: I can't imagine how people wrapped gifts without cellophane tape.

I can't imagine how people watered a garden without a rubber hose.

I can't imagine how people wrapped gifts without cellophane tape, nor can I imagine how people watered a garden without a rubber hose.

1. The first compact microwave ovens were sold in the 1960s. They didn't become widely used until the 1980s.
2. People ate with their hands for centuries. A big change finally occurred in the 1100s when people used forks, knives, and spoons.
3. It seems silly to say we will dial a telephone number. Push button phones are used everywhere.
4. In 1972 you could play table tennis on a large table with a net, paddles, and ball. You could play a computerized version on one of the first home video games.
5. Doing laundry used to take a whole day. When automatic washers became available in the 1940s, people were happy.

Answers are on page 200.

Clues about Commas

Don't use a comma every time you see a coordinating conjunction such as *and* or *but.* So far, you have learned that a comma is needed when two complete sentences are joined. If a coordinating conjunction does not connect two complete sentences, do not use a comma.

NO COMMA NEEDED:

Our family and friends (S) celebrated (V) Thanksgiving together.

We (S) ate (V) everything but the dessert.

My sister-in-law or my daughter (S) always helps (V) with the cooking.

COMMA NEEDED:
(two complete sentences)

Our family celebrated Thanksgiving, and
S V
our friends joined us.
S V

We ate everything, but we didn't eat any
S V S V
dessert.

My sister-in-law helps with the cooking, or
S V
my daughter helps me cook everything.
S V

EXERCISE 4

Using Commas Correctly

Directions: Place commas where they are needed in the following sentences, according to the rule you have just learned. Some of the sentences are correct as written.

1. On Saturday Elizabeth and Jessica were playing a game.
2. Jessica won the first game and Elizabeth asked for a rematch.
3. They started a second game but were interrupted by the doorbell.
4. They started a third game but they were interrupted by the doorbell.
5. Games are popular to play for a number of reasons.
6. Games are inexpensive and entertaining so they are popular to play.
7. A game such as chess has been played for hundreds of years so it is very well known in the world.
8. There is so much to learn about chess.

Answers are on page 201.

EXERCISE 5

Run-Ons and Comma Splices

Directions: The following paragraph contains some run-ons and comma splices. Read each sentence carefully to determine if it is written correctly. On a separate sheet of paper, rewrite the paragraph, correcting all the run-ons and comma splices. Either separate the incorrect sentences into two sentences, or combine them using a comma with *and, but, or, for, nor, so,* or *yet.*

We tend to take our feet for granted, they are actually quite remarkable. Our feet have 52 bones, one quarter of all the bones in the body. Each foot has 33 joints, 107 ligaments, and 19 muscles. Every year approximately 19 percent of people in the United States suffer from foot problems including corns, calluses, fallen arches, fungal infections, and injuries. Women suffer from foot problems about four times as often as men do some of those problems are directly related to the wearing of high heels. We do need to care for our feet, they will be used to carry us thousands and thousands of miles during our lifetimes.

Source: "10 Facts about Feet" *Chicago Tribune,* April 11, 1999

Answers are on page 201.

GED PRACTICE

EXERCISE 6

Sentence Structure

Directions: The following paragraphs may contain any type of usage or sentence structure error you have studied so far. Make sure each sentence is complete and correct.

(A)

(1) During the Cold War, the United States wanted a secure communication system that would work even during nuclear war. **(2)** The U. S. military developed an electronic communication system, this system worked across the world. **(3)** The communication lines stretched across the world like a net, the system became known as the Internet. **(4)** Scientists and researchers throughout the world beginning to use the Internet to share information with one another.

(B)

(5) As computers developed and became more popular, thousands of people began using the Internet as a source of information. **(6)** Today, millions of people use the Internet to communicate, and many others use them to learn information. **(7)** One of the parts of the Internet is the World Wide Web, which provides many sites with information. **(8)** Each site has an address that begins with the letters WWW that stands for World Wide Web. **(9)** No government controls the Internet and be careful about what you read there. **(10)** The information may not be true or honest.

1. Sentence 2: **The U.S. military developed an electronic communication <u>system this system worked</u> across the world.**

   Which of the following is the best way to write the underlined portion of this sentence? If the original is the best way, choose option (1).

   (1) system this system worked
   (2) system, this system worked
   (3) system. This system worked
   (4) system this system has worked
   (5) system this system works

2. Sentence 3: **The communication lines stretched across the world like a <u>net, the system</u> became known as the Internet.**

   Which of the following is the best way to write the underlined portion of this sentence? If the original is the best way, choose option (1).

   (1) net, the system
   (2) net, this
   (3) net, it
   (4) net it
   (5) net. The system

3. Sentence 4: **Scientists and researchers throughout the world beginning to use the Internet to share information with one another.**

   What correction should be made to sentence 4?

   (1) change <u>beginning</u> to <u>begins</u>
   (2) change <u>beginning</u> to <u>began</u>
   (3) change <u>use</u> to <u>using</u>
   (4) insert a comma after <u>scientists</u>
   (5) insert a comma after <u>and</u>

4. Sentence 6: **Today, millions of people use the Internet to communicate, and many others use them to learn information.**

   What correction should be made to sentence 6?

   (1) remove the comma after communicate
   (2) replace and with so
   (3) insert comma after and
   (4) replace them with it
   (5) no correction is necessary

5. Sentence 7: **One of the parts of the Internet is the World Wide Web which provides many sites with information.**

   What correction should be made to sentence 7?

   (1) change is to are
   (2) change provides to provide
   (3) replace which with it
   (4) change is to was
   (5) no correction is necessary

6. Sentence 8: **Each site has an address that begins with the three letters WWW that stands for World Wide Web.**

   Which of the following is the best way to write the underlined portion of this sentence? If the original is the best way, choose option (1).

   (1) WWW that stands
   (2) WWW it stands
   (3) WWW they stands
   (4) WWW and stands
   (5) WWW that stand

7. Sentence 9: **No government controls the Internet and be careful about what you read there.**

   Which of the following is the best way to write the underlined portion of this sentence? If the original is the best way, choose option (1).

   (1) Internet and be
   (2) Internet. So be
   (3) Internet, but be
   (4) Internet, so be
   (5) Internet, be

Answers are on page 201.

Joining Dependent and Independent Clauses

So far you have practiced combining independent clauses with coordinating conjunctions. A second type of conjunction makes one clause "dependent" on the other and shows the relationship between the two clauses. Look at the two short sentences and the combined sentence in the following example. Notice that the wording of the original sentences has not changed.

Sally is a vegetarian. She doesn't eat meat.

Since Sally is a vegetarian, she doesn't eat meat.

The **dependent clause** is *Since Sally is a vegetarian.* This clause is dependent because it is not a complete thought on its own—it needs the independent clause that follows it. The conjunction *since* makes the clause dependent and shows the relationship between the two ideas.

The meanings of conjunctions such as *since* are very important. Below is a list of some common **subordinating conjunctions,** grouped according to meaning.

Subordinating Conjunction	Meaning
before after while when whenever until	shows time relationship
because since so that	shows cause or effect
if unless	shows the condition under which something will happen
though although even though	shows a contrast
as though as if	shows similarity
where wherever	shows place

The clauses in a sentence using one of these conjunctions can be moved around. When the dependent clause comes first, a comma separates the two clauses. When the independent clause comes first, no comma is needed.

When all applications have been reviewed, three applicants will be brought in for interviews.

Three applicants will be brought in for interviews when all applications have been reviewed.

Take care to choose a conjunction that logically relates the two ideas you want to combine. In the first of the following sentences the conjunction *as if* makes the sentence very confusing. In the second sentence *after* shows the order of the actions.

NONSENSE: As if Eric took hundreds of photographs on his trip through Asia, he sent the film to be developed.

MAKES SENSE: After Eric took hundreds of photographs on his trip through Asia, he sent the film to be developed.

EXERCISE 7

Dependent Clauses

__**Part A**__ **Directions:** Using the list of subordinating conjunctions on page 116, fill in the blank with an appropriate word. There are several possible answers in each case. Choose one that makes sense to you.

1. Books were made more cheaply and quickly ____________________ Gutenberg invented moveable type to use in printing in 1450.

2. ____________________ the invention of a process to produce paper in China, the Chinese used clay or wood blocks to make books in the 10th century.

3. In early Egypt scribes would write needed documents on scrolls in a library ____________________ the documents were stored in jars.

4. ____________________ information is stored electronically in the modern world, a lot of paper is still used.

5. The modern age has been called the Information Age ____________________ of the resources available for accessing information.

Possible answers are on page 201.

Part B **Directions:** Complete each sentence below using the subordinating conjunction given. Add another sentence that makes sense. Be sure to place a comma after introductory dependent clauses.

Examples: (if) My wish would be stated in the longest run-on sentence in this book.

My wish would be stated in the longest run-on sentence in this book **if I had only one wish.**

OR

If I had only one wish, my wish would be stated in the longest run-on sentence in this book.

1. (although) love is important in life
2. (unless) I'd like to be given $100,000
3. (when) I'll really feel very happy
4. (because) Honesty usually is the best policy
5. (until) Learning in life continues

Answers are on page 201.

Part C **Directions:** Combine each pair of sentences by changing one of them into a dependent clause. Use one of the subordinating conjunctions listed on page 116. Be sure to place a comma after introductory dependent clauses.

Example: Time really flies. You are having fun.

Time really flies when you are having fun.

1. The hourglass was an early type of clock. It didn't work well if the weather was damp.
2. Clock towers were popular in towns. The clock towers were so tall that an entire village could see the time easily.
3. Hands on a clock were no longer needed. Digital clocks became popular.
4. I have to get up early in the morning. I set an alarm clock.
5. The hours dragged by slowly. The long day would never end.

Answers are on page 202.

Effective Sentence Structure: Using Active and Passive Voice

The **voice** of a sentence is determined by the relationship between the subject and verb. When the subject does the action, the sentence is in the **active voice**. When the subject receives the action, the sentence is in the **passive voice.**

S
Active Voice: The man **drove** to work.

S
Passive Voice: The man **was driven** to work.

In the first example above the man *does* the driving. He does the action. In the second example someone else drives the man. The man *receives* the action.

Usually the active voice is more effective in writing because the active voice is stronger, more emphatic, and less wordy. The passive voice may be used if the agent who does the action is unknown or if the person who is acted upon is more important than the one doing the action.

S
Example: Their house **was robbed.** (by someone)

This sentence is in passive voice because the agent who did the action is unknown.

S
Abraham Lincoln **was elected** president. (by the people)

This sentence is in passive voice because *the people* belong to a vague group which is less important to the author than Abraham Lincoln.

EXERCISE 8

Passive or Active Voice

Directions: Read each sentence below. Mark the sentence as **P** for passive voice or **A** for active voice.

1. ______ The man was bitten by the dog.
2. ______ The dog bit the man.
3. ______ People watch too much TV.
4. ______ Too much TV is watched by people.
5. ______ Last week the driver was given a ticket.
6. ______ Last week a police officer gave the driver a ticket.

Answers are on page 202.

In addition to using the active voice rather than the passive voice to make sentences more effective, you should also avoid wordiness. One definition of good writing calls for the most meaning in the fewest words. Empty or repetitious words that add little to the meaning do not create effective sentences. Read the two example sentences below.

Poor Sentence: Dinner was eaten with a lot of hunger and talking was done with a great deal of cheerfulness by all the various, different members of the family on Friday.

Improved Version: All the family ate hungrily and talked cheerfully at dinner on Friday.

Notice that the improved version contains fewer words and uses the active voice.

EXERCISE 9

Recognizing Effective Sentences

Directions: Read each pair of sentences below. Choose the one that is more effectively written.

1. (a) After the lottery had been lost by me for the tenth week in a row, I made a vow that I would never again play in that lottery anymore.

(b) After I lost the lottery for the tenth week in a row, I vowed never to play again.

2. (a) The storm caused thousands of homes to lose power for several hours.
(b) There were thousands of homes that were affected for several hours by the loss of power that was caused by the storm.

3. (a) In the event of rain, it will be necessary to utilize an umbrella as the need arises.
(b) If it rains, use an umbrella.

4. (a) Applications for various sorts of different types of jobs were submitted by the man looking for work.
(b) The man looking for work applied for various jobs.

5. (a) Thunder and lightning during winter are unusual.
(b) It is unusual that there would be thunder and lightning during winter.

Answers are on page 202.

Sentence Structure and Types of Questions on the GED Test

One kind of question on the Language Arts, Writing Test will require you to change the structure of a sentence or to combine two sentences without changing the meaning. This type of question is called a *construction shift question.* Approximately 15 percent of the questions on the test will be this type. Some information that will help you understand these questions is summarized in the box below.

WHAT YOU NEED TO REMEMBER ABOUT CONSTRUCTION SHIFT QUESTIONS

1. The original sentence or sentences are not wrong but could use improvement.
2. The meaning of the original should not be changed.
3. The wording of the original can change in two ways:

   First: Some of the words will be replaced with *synonyms* (words with similar meanings).

   Second: The structure of the sentence will change.

The original sentence or sentences will contain no error. You will have to figure out which of the answer choices will result in a new sentence that has the same meaning as the original.

There are two types of these questions. Read through the following examples and explanations carefully to become familiar with each. Think about the answers to the two questions below as you read the example below and try to answer the question.

What ideas from the original sentence are given already?

What ideas from the original sentence does this answer still have to supply?

Example Sentence 1: **Many years ago, for the purpose of helping to preserve some natural regions of the United States, lands were declared to be national parks by Teddy Roosevelt.**

If you rewrote Sentence 1 beginning with

Teddy Roosevelt declared some lands to be national parks

the next words should be

(1) in order to (help preserve some natural regions many years ago).
(2) on the other hand (help preserve some natural regions many years ago).
(3) as though (help preserve some natural regions many years ago).
(4) for instance (help preserve some natural regions many years ago).
(5) as soon as (help preserve some natural regions many years ago).

Notice that the *only* choice that provides the same meaning as the original sentence is (1) *in order to.* On the GED Test the choices would not be followed by the part of each answer in parentheses. You must supply the rest of the sentence mentally so that you can choose the right answer. Try another example.

Example Sentence 2: **His family had spaghetti every Wednesday night because of the fact that spaghetti was tasty and inexpensive.**

If you rewrote Sentence 2 beginning with

Spaghetti was tasty and inexpensive,

the next word should be

(1) but
(2) or
(3) his
(4) if
(5) so

To choose the right answer, you should have mentally continued each choice with the words *his family had spaghetti every Wednesday night.* The only answer that provides correct sentence structure, punctuation, and meaning is (5) *so.*

Another variation of the construction shift question could appear in the following way.

Example Sentence 3: **Despite the fact that we do not find any possibility of accommodating you at the present time, in the future, there is every hope that such a possibility will exist.**

The most effective revision of sentence 3 would include which group of words?

(1) there is no future possibility
(2) we hope to accommodate
(3) your request is a matter of fact
(4) a past possibility that
(5) because of the hope

The general meaning of Sentence 3 is this: **Although we cannot help you now, we hope to accommodate you in the future.**

The only answer choice that provides for this meaning is (2) *we hope to accommodate.* Notice the word *include* in the question. Sometimes the question will ask which words begin a sentence or which words combine sentences. Always read the question carefully.

GED PRACTICE

EXERCISE 10

Structure and Usage

Directions: Read the following paragraphs and look for errors in sentence structure and usage. The questions that follow will require you to correct errors as well as choose correct ways of rewriting portions of the paragraph.

(A)

(1) How important is the ability to read for an individual today in American society? **(2)** It is a belief of most people that in our contemporary times, reading skills are very necessary. **(3)** Nevertheless, according to the U.S. Department of Education, illiteracy continued to rise in the U.S. **(4)** Indeed one study estimated that one out of every four adults in the U.S. are functionally illiterate. **(5)** There is another estimate that is disturbing which made the claim that the level of reading of more than one third of elementary and high school students is below grade level.

(B)

(6) Some constructive advice to counter this problem suggests that a family can read together to succeed together. **(7)** Parents should read to their children, parents also need to read themselves. **(8)** An example will be set for children by parents who read themselves and underscore the value of the activity. **(9)** Any kind of reading material is helpful. **(10)** A variety of different kinds of newspapers, magazines, and books can all serve the purpose of the building of skills and the establishment of the habit of reading.

(C)

(11) Modern life is inundated with media. **(12)** Including TV, CD, DVD, and the Internet. **(13)** To encourage reading, parents should fill a home with books and other reading selections. **(14)** An individual will have an easier time in our complex society if that individual has developed good reading skills.

Source: "Want your child to be a reader?" *Chicago Tribune*. February 27, 2000

1. Sentence 2: **It is a belief of most people that in our contemporary times, reading skills are very necessary.**

   The most effective revision of sentence 2 would begin with which group of words?

   (1) Most people agree
   (2) Believed by most people
   (3) It is a fact that
   (4) Most reading skills
   (5) Although contemporary times

2. Sentence 4: **Indeed, one study estimated that one out of every four adults in the United States are functionally illiterate.**

   What correction should be made to sentence 4?

   (1) change estimated to will estimate
   (2) change are to is
   (3) change are to have been
   (4) replace every with each
   (5) no correction is necessary

3. Sentence 5: **There is another estimate that is disturbing which made the claim that the level of reading of more than one third of elementary and high school students is below grade level.**

   If you rewrote sentence 5 beginning with

   Another disturbing estimate

   the next word should be

   (1) since
   (2) reading
   (3) than
   (4) claimed
   (5) so

4. Sentence 7: **Parents should read to their children, parents also need to read themselves.**

Which of the following is the best way to write the underlined portion of this sentence? If the original is the best way, choose option (1).

(1) children, parents
(2) children parents
(3) children so parents
(4) children but, parents
(5) children, but parents

5. Sentence 8: **An example will be set for children by parents who read themselves and underscore the value of the activity.**

The most effective revision of sentence 8 would include which group of words?

(1) children who are an example
(2) parents set an example for children
(3) the value of children themselves
(4) even though parents read
(5) for instance children reading

6. Sentence 10: **A variety of different kinds of newspapers, magazines, and books can all serve the purpose of the building of skills and the establishment of the habit of reading.**

The most effective revision of sentence 10 would begin with which group of words?

(1) Newspapers, magazines, and books help build
(2) In order to serve the habit of reading
(3) The establishment of newspapers, magazines, and books
(4) Because reading is an established habit
(5) As soon as different newspapers, magazines, and books

7. Sentences 11 and 12: **Modern life is inundated with media. Including TV, CD, DVD, and the Internet.**

Which of the following is the best way to write the underlined portion of this sentence? If the original is the best way, choose option (1).

(1) media. Including
(2) media, and including
(3) media, including
(4) media, for including
(5) media, this includes

Answers are on page 202.

Dangling and Misplaced Modifiers

Another way to combine sentences is to use **modifying phrases**—phrases that describe or add information. A correct sentence will always make clear exactly what a modifying phrase modifies and place the modifying phrase as close as possible to the word it modifies. Remember that a writer needs to be sure that the meaning a reader understands from a sentence is the meaning that the writer intends. A reader should not have to guess at the meaning.

Look at the two combinations of the following pair of sentences. What is the difference between the correct and incorrect examples?

The woman took out the frozen turkey from the freezer. She was planning to cook the turkey.

INCORRECT: The woman took out the frozen turkey from the freezer that she was planning to cook.

CORRECT: The woman took out from the freezer the frozen turkey that she was planning to cook.

Look at the two sentences below. How is the meaning changed by the placement of the modifying phrases?

1. We gave a gift with a bright red bow to the girl.
2. We gave a gift to the girl with a bright red bow.

Notice that in sentence 1 the gift has the bright red bow. In sentence 2 the girl is wearing the bright red bow. The placement of the modifying phrase can make a significant difference.

In addition to being misplaced, modifiers also may "dangle." A sentence with a **dangling modifier** contains no word for the modifier to modify. What is the difference between the correct and incorrect examples below?

INCORRECT: Eating the buttery popcorn, my hands became greasy.

CORRECT: As I was eating the buttery popcorn, my hands became greasy.

The incorrect sentence contains a dangling modifier, *Eating the buttery popcorn.* The sentence does not tell you *who* was eating the popcorn. In the correct sentence, the dangling modifier has been changed to a dependent clause containing the subject *I.*

On a piece of paper rewrite the following sentence containing a dangling modifier. Make sure that your new sentence includes a word for the dangler to modify.

Seeing a squirrel dash onto the road, my foot hit the brake.

The dangler is *Seeing a squirrel dash onto the road.* Here are two possible corrections to this sentence:

After I saw a squirrel dash onto the road, my foot hit the brake.

My foot hit the brake after I saw a squirrel dash onto the road.

EXERCISE 11

Dangling and Misplaced Modifiers

Directions: Underline the modifying phrase in each of the following sentences. Rewrite each sentence that contains a dangling or misplaced modifier. Some of the sentences may be correct.

Example: Her cousin sent them an engraved invitation to the party <u>with gold lettering.</u>

Her cousin sent them an engraved invitation with gold lettering to the party.

1. The Martins bought a house on a nearby street that was constructed with vinyl siding.
2. Slowly sinking beneath the horizon, we watched the sunset.
3. Pleased with the effect of the color change, the woman smiled with satisfaction.
4. Upon blowing out the candles, the cake was sliced into pieces for the guests at the birthday party.
5. He bought an instruction book from the bookstore for training dogs on Saturday.
6. A cold drink tasted refreshing after working outside in the heat for several hours.
7. After listening to the music for an hour, the radio program was interrupted by a weather bulletin.
8. The dentist began work on the root canal for the tooth of the patient that had been cracked.
9. Before doing anything drastic, you should consider the options.
10. Our neighbors took their dog to the groomer with fleas.

Answers are on page 202.

Parallel Structure

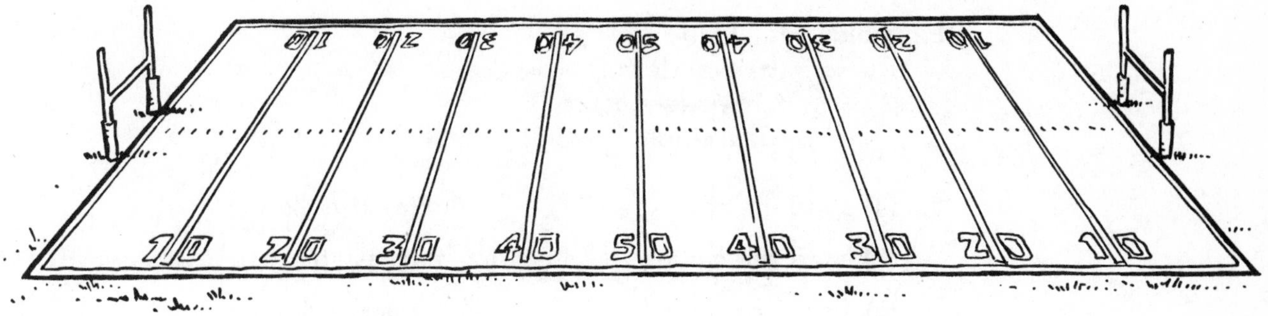

In geometry *parallel* lines are lines that are the same form. They are always the same distance apart, and they go in the same direction. In sentences, two or more elements that have the same function must be written in the same form to have **parallel structure.**

NOT PARALLEL: They enjoy hiking, swimming, and to fish.

PARALLEL: They enjoy hiking, swimming, and fishing.

Do you see the difference? Underline the three parallel parts in the second sentence above. In the first sentence *to fish* is not the same form as the two *-ing* words that make up the series. To make the form parallel, change *to fish* to *fishing.*

Underline the incorrect part of the following sentence. Rewrite the sentence using parallel structure.

She said that she wanted to be beautiful, happy, and have a lot of money.

The corrected sentence should read:

She said that she wanted to be beautiful, happy, and rich.

EXERCISE 12

Parallel Structure

Part A **Directions:** Cross out the word or phrase that is not parallel to the others. Replace it with an appropriate word or phrase.

Example: **(a)** kind
(b) wonderful
(c) ~~wisdom~~ *nice*
(d) friendly

1. **(a)** feed the cat
   (b) start the car
   (c) find a job
   (d) a trip that is taken
2. **(a)** on the table
   (b) the tree has it close by
   (c) in the drawer
   (d) around the corner
3. **(a)** loving grandma
   (b) pretty girl
   (c) funny man
   (d) boy with a smile
4. **(a)** to talk
   (b) singing
   (c) dancing
   (d) studying
5. **(a)** person who is helpful
   (b) music that is relaxing
   (c) a really beautiful place
   (d) book which is enjoyable

Part B **Directions:** Circle the letter of the correct sentence from each pair.

1. **(a)** To be loved, respected, and appreciated were three goals she hoped to attain.
   (b) To be loved, respected, and the appreciation of others were three goals she hoped to attain.
2. **(a)** Thomas Alva Edison invented the light bulb, a doll that could talk, and the musical phonograph.
   (b) Thomas Alva Edison invented the light bulb, a talking doll, and the musical phonograph.
3. **(a)** Time pressure, boring work, and when there is too much work are factors that can affect health.
   (b) Time pressure, boring work, and too much work are factors that can affect health.

4. **(a)** People using computers have complained of eye irritation, difficulty focusing, and eye strain.
(b) People using computers have complained of eye irritation, that they had difficulty focusing, and eye strain.

5. **(a)** He drank some black coffee, ate a quick breakfast, and brushed his teeth.
(b) He drank some black coffee, ate a quick breakfast, and with a toothbrush was cleaning his teeth.

Answers are on page 203.

GED PRACTICE

EXERCISE 13

Structure and Usage

Directions: Read the following paragraphs, checking for errors in misplaced or dangling modification, parallel structure, sentence structure, and usage. Choose an answer that effectively corrects or improves the selected sentences.

(A)

(1) Self-esteem enables us to achieve success in many aspects of life. **(2)** People who have high self-esteem like and respect themselves, they expect others to do the same. **(3)** Self-esteem should not be confused with arrogance, however. **(4)** Exaggerating their accomplishments, arrogant people's egos are inflated. **(5)** Arrogance or conceit are not the same as self-esteem. **(6)** It is believed by many that, in actuality, one sign of low self-esteem is arrogance.

(B)

(7) To build self-esteem, you can draw upon a variety of strategies. **(8)** First, devote some time each day to some activity that you can be very good at doing. **(9)** By accomplishing even small tasks, confidence will grow. **(10)** Second, make a connection with other people they admire. **(11)** Other people's acceptance and that people have supported us are very valuable to us. **(12)** Third, act with integrity. **(13)** If you live according to your values, rather than to compromising to gain money or power, you'll feel better about yourself. **(14)** Perhaps most important of all, treat yourself kindly, and remember that everyone makes mistakes.

1. Sentence 2: **People who have high self-esteem like and respect themselves, they expect others to do the same.**

   Which of the following is the best way to write the underlined portion of this sentence? If the original is the best way, choose option (1).

   (1) themselves, they
   (2) themselves, but they
   (3) themselves, and they
   (4) themselves they
   (5) themselves who

2. Sentence 4: **Exaggerating their accomplishments, arrogant people's egos are inflated.**

   Which of the following is the best way to write the underlined portion of this sentence? If the original is the best way, choose option (1).

   (1) people's egos are inflated
   (2) people's egos that are inflated
   (3) the egos of people are inflated
   (4) inflation of the egos of people
   (5) people inflate their egos

3. Sentence 5: **Arrogance or conceit are not the same as self-esteem.**

   What correction should be made to sentence 5?

   (1) change are to is
   (2) change are to was
   (3) change are to being
   (4) insert a comma after arrogance
   (5) no correction is necessary

4. Sentence 6: **It is believed by many that, in actuality, one sign of low self-esteem is arrogance.**

The most effective revision of sentence 6 would begin with which group of words?

(1) The arrogant signs are
(2) A belief of low self-esteem can
(3) Arrogance is generally
(4) Even though a sign of arrogance
(5) Many who arrogantly believe

5. Sentence 8: **First, devote some time each day to some activity that you can be very good at doing.**

The most effective revision of sentence 8 would include which group of words?

(1) spend some time each day
(2) because each day can be
(3) activities which take some time
(4) doing first things first each day
(5) you cannot do any activity

6. Sentence 9: **<u>By accomplishing</u> even small tasks, confidence will grow.**

Which of the following is the best way to write the underlined portion of this sentence? If the original is the best way, choose option (1).

(1) By accomplishing
(2) If I accomplish
(3) Having accomplished
(4) As you accomplish
(5) The accomplishment of

7. Sentence 10: **Second, make a connection with other people they admire.**

   What correction should be made to sentence 10?

   (1) change <u>admire</u> to <u>admired</u>
   (2) change <u>make</u> to <u>making</u>
   (3) replace <u>they</u> with <u>you</u>
   (4) replace <u>people</u> with <u>persons</u>
   (5) no correction is necessary

8. Sentence 11: **Other people's acceptance and <u>that people have supported us</u> are very valuable to us.**

   Which of the following is the best way to write the underlined portion of this sentence? If the original is the best way, choose option (1).

   (1) that people have supported us
   (2) what people support
   (3) how other people will support
   (4) supporting and caring
   (5) their continuing support

9. Sentence 13: **If you live according to your values, rather than <u>to compromising</u> to gain money or power, you'll feel better about yourself.**

   Which of the following is the best way to write the underlined portion of this sentence? If the original is the best way, choose option (1).

   (1) to compromising
   (2) compromise
   (3) compromised
   (4) your compromise
   (5) for a compromise

Answers are on page 203.

Go to **www.GEDWriting.com** for additional practice and instruction!

CHAPTER 3

Mechanics

If you were going to buy a car, you would check it out carefully to make sure that you got what you wanted. You'd want parts that were usable and a decent body structure that wasn't malformed or bent. You'd also be concerned about the mechanics. You would want to be sure the car could take you where you want to go.

The English language can be compared to a car. Parts that fit and work together on a car are like the grammar and usage of English. The design or the body structure of a car is like the sentence structure of language. Language also has mechanics that help it operate. Capitalization, punctuation, and spelling make up the mechanics of English. When we read, we rely on the signals of capitalization and punctuation to help us understand the writing. We also must be able to recognize the words by accurate spelling. We have all read, or tried to read, writing that contains so many mistakes that it fails in its purpose to communicate.

In this chapter you will review skills that help make writing easier to read—capitalization, punctuation, and spelling. These skills will be tested in multiple-choice questions on Part I of the Language Arts, Writing Test, and they also will help you write your essay correctly for Part II. There are other rules for capitalization and punctuation that are not covered in this book. The material in this chapter focuses on those issues that may appear on the GED Test.

Capitalization

Always capitalize **proper nouns,** or names. The naming process is similar for all nouns. If we get a pet, we might use the common nouns *dog* or *cat* to tell people what it is. Once we give the pet a name such as *Buddy* or *Sasha,* we've used a proper noun and need a capital letter. We name our children, our boats, our artwork, and our businesses. All these particular people, places, and things have names that need capital letters. A good question to ask yourself when you are deciding whether to capitalize is "Am I naming someone or something?"

In each blank write a proper noun and be sure to capitalize it.

Common Nouns (General)	Proper Nouns (Specific)
author	Mark Twain
month	______________
river	______________
person	______________
city	______________
language	______________
school	______________
store	______________

The chart above asks you to think of specific names. Although the following rules explain in more detail some of the types of nouns that are capitalized, they still fall under the basic rule, "If it's a name, capitalize it."

Other Capitalization Rules

1. **Capitalize a word used as a person's title.**

   I would like you to meet **Professor** Thompson.

   She was scheduled to see **Doctor** Garvey on Saturday.

   Don't capitalize these words when they are used as occupations.

   The **judge** ruled on the case in traffic court.

   The **doctor** gave some good advice.

2. **Capitalize the names of specific places. Also capitalize words derived from the names of specific places.**

   They enjoyed **English** more than science.

   Mesa Verde is an ancient site of the Anasazi Indians.

Don't capitalize general geographical terms.

The **desert** is beautiful at night.

They hiked **west** on the trail.

The **city** never sleeps.

3. **Capitalize names of holidays, months, and days of the week.**

   Flowers and candy are popular on **Valentine's Day.**

   We are planning to leave on **Friday, October 17.**

   Don't capitalize the names of seasons unless they are part of the name of a specific event or place.

   If **winter** is here, **spring** cannot be far behind.

   She went to **summer** school last year.

4. **Capitalize the names of historic events and documents.**

   Abraham Lincoln issued the **Emancipation Proclamation** in 1863.

   During the **Industrial Revolution,** people moved from the countryside to the cities.

If you're not sure whether to capitalize something, the dictionary can help. For example, use your dictionary to look up *civil war.* You'll find a definition for the general term, using no capital letters. You may also find an entry for the specific war fought in the United States between the Union and the Confederacy in the 1860s—the Civil War—using capital letters.

EXERCISE 1

Capitalization Rules

Directions: Rewrite the following sentences, putting in capital letters where they belong and taking out those capitals that are incorrect. The number of errors in each sentence is in parentheses.

1. The german composer beethoven produced his most famous work after he was deaf. *(2 errors)*
2. Our friends went to a Concert last monday on Labor day and listened to music from an opera called *The Magic flute* by mozart. *(5 errors)*
3. Not only did Thomas Jefferson write the declaration of independence for the Country, but he also served as a Governor of Virginia. *(4 errors)*
4. On may 30, 1431, when Joan of Arc was burned at the stake after helping to lead french armies against the english, she was only nineteen years old. *(3 errors)*
5. If you take interstate 80 and travel West, you will see many National Parks such as yellowstone or Grand Teton, that have been preserved because of the efforts of John Muir and John Rockefeller. *(5 errors)*
6. One of shakespeare's darkest Tragedies, which was written about 400 years ago, is the story of king Lear and his three daughters. *(3 errors)*
7. The ceiling of the sistine chapel in rome contains a painting 133 feet long and 45 feet wide that was painted by michelangelo for pope Paul III. *(5 errors)*
8. In medicine, Elizabeth Blackwell was one of the first women to become a Doctor, and Florence nightingale received an award for helping to make nursing an honored profession. *(2 errors)*

Answers are on page 203.

Punctuation

As you know from all your work in writing, every sentence ends with a **period** [.], a **question mark** [?], or an **exclamation point** [!]. Watch out for end punctuation that is missing or incorrect. As you learned in the sections about sentence fragments, the fact that a group of words ends with a period or a question mark does not mean it is a complete sentence.

INCORRECT: In a minute.

CORRECT: Elmo will quiet down in a minute.

INCORRECT: What time?

CORRECT: What time is it?

The Comma

A **comma** instructs a reader to pause when reading. It is used to separate units of meaning in language. As a writer, you need to understand the uses of the comma so that you can give appropriate instructions to the reader. Commas are used for specific reasons, some of which you learned about in Chapter 2, Sentence Structure. Remember that *extra* commas, which interrupt reading comprehension, are just as incorrect as missing ones.

Comma Rules

1. **Use a comma with a coordinating conjunction to join two independent clauses.**

   Kate wanted to dive into the pool, but her dog Charlie wanted her to throw his ball.

   Remember that an independent clause is a complete thought. If the second part of the sentence is not a complete thought, do *not* separate it from the first part with a comma.

   INCORRECT: Chrissy finished lunch, and ate a chocolate brownie.

   CORRECT: Chrissy finished lunch and ate a chocolate brownie.

2. **Put a comma after an introductory dependent clause.**

   While Joan was lying by the pool, Tim was at work.

   Remember that if the dependent clause follows the independent clause, no comma is needed.

   INCORRECT: They put on some sunscreen, because the day was very sunny.

   CORRECT: They put on some sunscreen because the day was very sunny.

Now practice Rules 1 and 2. Insert commas wherever they are needed in the following sentences.

Ruth would like a Florida vacation but she needs more money.

The museum opened a new exhibit and featured a collection of Egyptian art.

We like to have garlic bread whenever we have lasagna.

When the moon is full the police are busier than usual.

You should have placed a comma after *vacation* in the first sentence and another comma after *full* in the fourth sentence. No commas are needed in the second and third sentences.

3. Use commas to set off transitional or parenthetical expressions.

Transitional expressions provide a smooth movement from one idea to another. Many expressions such as *however, therefore, furthermore,* or *for example* work this way. You will learn more about transitional expressions on page 163.

Parenthetical expressions add comments, explanations, or interruptions to the sentence. Expressions such as *of course, quite honestly, amazingly,* or *unfortunately* are examples of parenthetical expressions. Because both transitional and parenthetical expressions interrupt or introduce the main sentence, these expressions must be set off with commas.

My child**, on the other hand,** is an angel.

Indeed, what we do comes back to us.

Chicken soup**, as you probably know,** is good for a cold.

The phrases in **bold type** above introduce or interrupt the main flow of the sentence. Notice that these phrases *never* contain the subject or verb of a sentence. They simply add an extra thought to the sentence.

4. Use commas to set off modifying phrases.

William Rainey Harper College, **a community college in the Midwest,** is an excellent school.

Tired and hot, the man sat down under the shady tree to rest a moment.

The hostess served an appetizer with mushrooms, **the one food to which I am allergic.**

Notice that each of the above phrases in bold type describes or modifies another word in the sentence.

Now practice Rules 3 and 4. Place commas wherever they are needed in the following sentences and cross out the commas that are not needed. Be sure to place commas both before and after phrases that interrupt a sentence.

A statue of the sphinx a creature with a human's head and lion's body stands in the desert in Egypt.

The ancient Greek Hippocrates created the Hippocratic Oath a two-part code of conduct still pledged by many doctors today.

Cape Hatteras, has been called "the graveyard of the Atlantic" because of many shipwrecks.

Her plan therefore required that she get a raise.

However her boss wouldn't give her a raise.

Bamboo amazingly can grow 15 inches a day.

Passing directly from a solid to a vapor state dry ice sublimes and does not melt.

In the first sentence commas are needed after *sphinx* and after *body.* You should have placed a comma after *Oath* in the second sentence. The comma after *Hatteras* in the third sentence should be crossed out. In the fourth sentence put in commas before and after *therefore.* In the fifth sentence a comma should be placed after *However.* The sixth sentence requires commas before and after *amazingly.* Finally, in the last sentence put a comma after *state.*

5. **Use commas to separate items in a *series* (a list of three or more items, actions, or descriptions).** Notice that each of the following series is in **parallel structure.**

   Underground hot springs in Iceland supply hot water to public buildings, swimming pools, and hothouse gardens.

   Chinese, English, and Spanish are spoken by more people than any other languages today.

   Ducks can swim, run, and feed themselves a few hours after leaving their eggs.

No comma comes before the first item in a series or after the last item.

INCORRECT: The path looked, silent, dark, and forbidding.

CORRECT: The path looked silent, dark, and forbidding.

Do not use commas to separate only two items.

INCORRECT: Liz reads mysteries, and writes textbooks.

CORRECT: Liz reads mysteries and writes textbooks.

Now practice Rule 5. Place commas wherever they are needed in the following sentences.

> Katherine took Zach Miryam and Sarah to the park.
>
> A bat flew into the center scared three women and disappeared out the window.
>
> Lydia often shares the carrots and celery sticks Greg prepares for her.
>
> The garden was filled with daisies marigolds nasturtiums and weeds.

In the first sentence commas are needed after *Zach* and *Miryam.* The second sentence needs a comma after *center* and a comma after *women.* The third sentence does not need any commas. In the fourth sentence put commas after *daisies, marigolds,* and *nasturtiums.*

EXERCISE 2

Using Commas

Directions: Insert commas wherever they are needed in the body of the following memo. (You should insert a total of nine commas.)

To:	All Employees
From:	Personnel
Date:	March 16, 2002
Subject:	Insurance

The new insurance plan will go into effect in the next month so all company employees need to attend an information session. After hearing the information each employee must of course select a plan option. In addition each employee will need to indicate whether family members are to be covered. An employee may opt for coverage for a spouse dependents or just the employee. Registration for an information session can be completed by dialing extension 608. Six sessions have been scheduled and each will last approximately one hour. If there are any immediate questions please call the director of personnel at extension 442.

Answers are on page 204.

The Apostrophe

1. **Use an apostrophe to show possession.**

   add 's to all singular nouns

   to all plural nouns not ending in s

   add ' to plural nouns ending in s

   Some of Sharon's talents include fundraising and needlepoint.

   Judy maintains three labs' computers very carefully.

   The men's golf game was disrupted by rain.

2. **Use an apostrophe to replace missing letters in contractions.**

   Erinn was wearing hot pink pants that we hadn't seen before.

   Kim and Mark were pleased that they'd finished the basement.

To review the use of the apostrophe, turn back to the section on possessive nouns in Chapter 1, page 72.

Other Punctuation Marks

The punctuation marks in the box below will not be explicitly tested on the multiple-choice section of the Language Arts, Writing Test. However, you may wish to use some of these marks as you write your essay. Additionally, knowledge of these punctuation marks can enhance your reading comprehension. For reference, the most common uses of these marks are provided for you.

Semicolon	;	used to join two complete sentences that are related in meaning
Colon	:	used to introduce a list or concluding explanation, used in time and ratio
Quotation Marks	" "	used to indicate the exact words someone has said
Dash	—	used to interrupt a thought with a shift in tone or idea
Hyphen	-	used to separate syllables or some compound adjectives
Parentheses	( )	used to include examples, explanation, or facts that may be useful or interesting but not necessary to the meaning
Ellipsis	. . .	used to indicate that some of the text has been left out
Brackets	[ ]	used to indicate a comment or change that an author wishes to make in the middle of quoting material by someone else

EXERCISE 3

Punctuation Review

Directions: Each sentence below contains *one* error in punctuation. Find and correct each error.

1. We can learn a lot from other peoples experiences and ideas.
2. Charles Kingsley, said that people shouldn't ever go to sleep at night without having added to another person's happiness that day.
3. If you look in the library you will find many great writers' books.
4. Words and ideas can inspire men's thoughts but music and art can touch their souls.
5. Many famous artists masterpieces hang in the Louvre in Paris.

Answers are on page 204.

GED PRACTICE

EXERCISE 4

Structure, Usage, and Mechanics

Directions: Read the following paragraph and answer the questions. Watch for all the types of errors you've studied so far.

Assembling a First-Aid Kit

(A)

(1) Everyone should have a well-equipped first-aid kit, and some experts recommend having another first-aid kit in the car. **(2)** You could of course purchase a preassembled first-aid kit if you wished. **(3)** The fact of the matter is, however, that it is less expensive most of the time for you to make one up yourself.

(B)

(4) Many items, are needed for a kit to be effective. **(5)** Bandages, sterile gauze pads, adhesive tape, scissors, and safety pins are all required. **(6)** You will also need peroxide for the cleansing of wounds, antihistamine for the relief of itching, and to control fevers acetaminophen will help. **(7)** A spray for burns and an antiseptic ointment for cuts is also important. **(8)** Other items should be included as well. **(9)** For example, tweezers, a thermometer, cotton swabs, and medical gloves are useful.

(C)

(10) These items will provide the basics for a first-aid kit. **(11)** However, you will want one other item because they are extremely helpful to have. **(12)** A first-aid manual will provide valuable information and instruction in the event of an emergency. **(13)** Until you can see a Doctor or get medical treatment, you need to know what to do.

1. Sentence 2: **You *could of course* purchase a preassembled first-aid kit if you wished.**

   Which of the following is the best way to write the underlined portion of the text? If the original is the best way, choose option (1).

   (1) could of course
   (2) could, of course
   (3) ,could of course
   (4) could, of course,
   (5) could of course,

2. Sentence 3: **The fact of the matter is, however, that it is less expensive most of the time for you to make one up yourself.**

   If you rewrote sentence 3 beginning with

   On the other hand, it is

   the next words should be

   (1) one which you make
   (2) generally less expensive
   (3) quite matter of fact
   (4) less time-consuming generally
   (5) expensive to make yourself

3. Sentence 4: **Many items, are needed for a kit to be effective.**

   What correction should be made to sentence 4?

   (1) change are to were
   (2) insert a comma after needed
   (3) remove the comma after items
   (4) insert a comma after kit
   (5) replace are with being

4. Sentence 6: **You will also need peroxide for the cleansing of wounds, antihistamine for the relief of itching, and to control fevers acetaminophen will help.**

   Which of the following is the best way to write the underlined portion of the text? If the original is the best way, choose option (1).

   (1) to control fevers acetaminophen will help
   (2) controlling fevers will be helped by acetaminophen
   (3) when treating fevers acetaminophen is good
   (4) acetaminophen for the control of fevers
   (5) treat fevers with acetaminophen

5. Sentence 7: **A spray for burns and an antiseptic ointment for cuts is also important.**

   What correction should be made to sentence 7?

   (1) change <u>is</u> to <u>are</u>
   (2) insert a comma after <u>burns</u>
   (3) change <u>antiseptic</u> to <u>Antiseptic</u>
   (4) change <u>is</u> to <u>were</u>
   (5) no correction is necessary

6. Sentences 8 and 9: **Other items should be included as well. For example, tweezers, a thermometer, cotton swabs, and medical gloves are useful.**

   The most effective combination of sentences 8 and 9 would include which group of words?

   (1) useful items include
   (2) however useful
   (3) if all goes well
   (4) rather than include
   (5) tweezers for gloves

7. Sentence 11: **However, you will want one other item <u>because they are</u> extremely helpful to have.**

   Which of the following is the best way to write the underlined portion of the text? If the original is the best way, choose option (1).

   (1) because they are
   (2) , because they are
   (3) because its
   (4) because it is
   (5) although they are

8. Sentence 13: **Until you can see a Doctor or get medical treatment, you need to know what to do.**

   What correction should be made to sentence 13?

   (1) remove the comma after <u>treatment</u>
   (2) replace <u>can</u> with <u>will</u>
   (3) insert a comma after <u>Doctor</u>
   (4) replace <u>Until</u> with <u>When</u>
   (5) change <u>Doctor</u> to <u>doctor</u>

Answers are on page 204.

Spelling

The multiple-choice section of the Language Arts, Writing Test will test the spelling of possessives (see Chapter 1) and the spelling of sound-alike words. On the essay portion of the test, spelling will be one of several factors that may affect your score. Some suggestions for improving your spelling will be given in the chapter on the essay.

Sound-alike Words

Sound-alike words are also called **homonyms** or **homophones.** These are words that sound the same but have different meanings and different spellings. Consider the differences in the sentences below.

My shoes are arranged carefully in the closet.

I place them together in *pears.*

I place them together in *pairs.*

Notice the differences in meaning and spelling. Exercise 5 lists more pairs and groups of sound-alike words. Many of them sound exactly alike, such as *to, too,* and *two.* Others should not sound alike if you pronounce them carefully, such as *conscious* and *conscience.*

EXERCISE 5

Spelling Sound-alike Words

Directions: Read the explanations of the differences between the sound-alikes; then practice by filling in the blanks with the correct words.

accept (receive)
except (excluding; leaving out)

1. That store will ____________________ any type of payment ____________________ checks.

affect (act upon)
effect (result)

2. Color can ____________________ us. Its ____________________ can be soothing or energizing.

already (previously)
all ready (completely prepared)

3. Fortunately, they were ____________________ to go because we were ____________________ late.

capital (city that is the official seat of a government)
capitol (building in which a state legislature works)

4. The ____________________ building is located in our state ____________________ .

coarse (rough)
course (plan of action; part of a meal; class)

5. During the art ____________________, she worked with some ____________________ materials to show different textures.

desert (abandon; pronounced duh-ZERT)
dessert (last course of a meal)

6. After dinner I want to go out for ____________________, but I don't want to ____________________ my friends.

its (ownership)
it's (contraction for *it is*)

7. ____________________ true that my car lost ____________________ muffler on the way here.

know (be aware of)
no (negative)

8. You may ____________________ the expression that ____________________ man is an island.

knew (was aware of)
new (not old)

9. The governor ____________________ a ____________________ policy was needed.

passed (went beyond; succeeded)
past (time long ago; by)

10. Once they were ____________________ the town, they ____________________ the truck ahead of them.

their (ownership)
there (place, pointing out something)
they're (contraction for *they are*)

11. ____________________ about to leave, so get ____________________ coats from over ____________________.

to (preposition; word before a verb)
too (more than enough, very; also)
two (number)

12. It costs ____________________ much ____________________ spend ____________________ weeks in Europe.

Answers are on page 204.

EXERCISE 6

Sound-alike Words

Directions: Circle the error in each sentence; then write the correct word in the blank.

Example: I don't (except) offers that seem too good to be true.
accept

1. We are becoming increasingly conscience of the need to preserve our environment. ______________

2. The waitress brought there order very quickly.
____

3. Does Bob no that the hours they are open have changed?
____

4. It's passed that child's bedtime, and he is getting very crabby.
____

5. Sometimes Carol Anne goes camping with her family for almost a weak. ______________

Answers are on page 205.

EXERCISE 7

Structure, Usage, Spelling, and Mechanics

Directions: Read the following paragraphs, looking for errors in capitalization, punctuation, spelling, structure, and usage. Then answer the questions that follow.

Freezing Food

(A)

(1) The modern method of freezing food for preservation can actually be attributed to Clarence Birdseye. **(2)** In the early 1920s Birdseye traveled North and served as a naturalist for the U.S. government on an expedition to Labrador. **(3)** He found that Labrador's whether was very severe. **(4)** Freezing conditions and bitter cold was the norm.

(B)

(5) There was an observation that was made by Birdseye one day, and it led to a useful discovery. **(6)** While watching some men fishing, fish froze almost immediately after they were caught. **(7)** When these fish were cooked, and eaten later, they tasted quite fresh. **(8)** Birdseye realized that the effect of immediate freezing was that it tasted fresh. **(9)** The key to using freezing for food preservation was in the speed of the freezing process. **(10)** Birdseye later returned to the United States. **(11)** Then he developed a process called multiple-plate freezing. **(12)** Basically the same one used today.

(C)

(13) As a result of this method of freezing food and other methods of food preservation, we have increased the availability and quality of food. **(14)** As the world's population continues to grow, the supply of food became more and more of a concern. **(15)** Additional techniques and technologies still need to be developed.

Source: Birdseye Company History from www.birdseye.com

1. Sentence 2: **In the early 1920s Birdseye traveled North and served as a naturalist for the U.S. government on an expedition to Labrador.**

   What correction should be made to sentence 2?

   (1) change served to serves
   (2) change North to north
   (3) change naturalist to Naturalist
   (4) insert a comma after North
   (5) no correction is necessary

2. Sentence 3: **He found that Labrador's whether was very severe.**

Which of the following is the best way to write the underlined portion of the text? If the original is the best way, choose option (1).

(1) Labrador's whether
(2) Labradors' whether
(3) Labradors whether
(4) Labradors' weather
(5) Labrador's weather

3. Sentence 4: **Freezing conditions and bitter cold was the norm.**

What correction should be made to sentence 4?

(1) change was to were
(2) insert a comma after conditions
(3) replace was with have been
(4) replace bitter with intense
(5) change conditions to conditions'

4. Sentence 5: **There was an observation that was made by Birdseye one day, and it led to a useful discovery.**

If you rewrote sentence 5 beginning with

An observation one day

the next words should be

(1) about Birdseye there
(2) discovered it
(3) in spite of Birdseye
(4) will make a discovery
(5) led Birdseye

5. Sentence 6: **While watching some men fishing, fish froze almost immediately after they were caught.**

Which of the following is the best way to write the underlined portion of the text? If the original is the best way, choose option (1).

(1) While watching some men fishing, fish
(2) While watching some men fishing, he saw that fish
(3) While they were watching some men fishing, fish
(4) While they were watching some men fishing, he saw that fish
(5) While they were watching some men fishing, he seeing fish

6. Sentence 7: **When these fish were cooked, and eaten later, they tasted quite fresh.**

What correction should be made to sentence 7?

(1) remove the comma after later
(2) replace they with it
(3) replace eaten with ate
(4) remove the comma after cooked
(5) change were to was

7. Sentence 8: **Birdseye realized that the effect of immediate freezing was that it tasted fresh.**

What correction should be made to sentence 8?

(1) replace <u>it</u> with <u>food</u>
(2) change <u>realized</u> to <u>has realized</u>
(3) change <u>effect</u> to <u>affect</u>
(4) replace <u>it</u> with <u>they</u>
(5) no correction is necessary

8. Sentence 9: **The key to using freezing for food preservation was in the speed of the freezing process.**

The most effective revision of sentence 9 would begin with which group of words?

(1) Without preserving food at all
(2) Another key example of food
(3) Despite the speed of the process
(4) Freezing food quickly was
(5) When using key foods

9. Sentences 11 and 12: **Then he developed a process called <u>multiple-plate freezing. Basically</u> the same one used today.**

Which of the following is the best way to write the underlined portion of the text? If the original is the best way, choose option **(1).**

(1) multiple-plate freezing. Basically
(2) multiple-plate freezing, and basically
(3) multiple-plate freezing. The
(4) multiple-plate freezing, which is basically
(5) multiple-plate freezing, this is

10. Sentence 14: **As the world's population continues to grow, the supply of food became more and more of a concern.**

What correction should be made to sentence 14?

(1) change <u>world's</u> to <u>worlds'</u>
(2) change <u>became</u> to <u>becomes</u>
(3) change <u>continues</u> to <u>continued</u>
(4) insert a comma after <u>more</u>
(5) no correction is necessary

Answers are on page 205.

Go to **www.GEDWriting.com** for additional practice and instruction!

CHAPTER 4

Organization

If you have a closet at home, and you only put one jacket into the closet, you shouldn't have much trouble finding that jacket when you look inside. Whether you've hung the jacket to the left, to the right, or in the center won't make much difference. It won't matter if you've placed the jacket on a shelf or even laid it on the floor. On the other hand, the situation changes if you add the following items: four more jackets, eight sweaters, seven shirts, six pairs of pants, nine pairs of shoes, three caps, six belts, one robe, five pairs of shorts, ten shirts, and an umbrella. How you arrange all of these items greatly affects your ability to find something. The more items you put into the closet, the more important it is to organize them.

The same can be said about writing. Once you begin writing text that is more than one sentence long, you need to organize the writing so that a reader can find the meaning easily and understand your ideas.

In this chapter you will learn how to organize writing successfully. Skills such as composing paragraphs, organizing sentences into paragraphs, dividing text into paragraphs, and maintaining unified, coherent ideas will all be tested in the editing section of the Language Arts, Writing Test. In addition, these same skills will be helpful to you on the essay portion of the test.

Paragraph Composition

Writing is generally organized into paragraphs. A **paragraph** consists of several related, unified sentences that develop an idea. Paragraphs can be short or lengthy, depending on their purposes. Generally, a paragraph requires at least four to six sentences to develop an idea. Of those sentences, the **topic sentence** should include the **topic** and a **controlling idea** to limit the topic.

Topic Sentence = topic + controlling idea

Example: Training a puppy takes patience and repetition.
topic *controlling idea*

In the example topic sentence above, the topic you can expect to read about is *Training a puppy.* The controlling idea that narrows the topic is *patience and repetition.* Notice that the controlling idea narrows the general topic to more specific content. You would not expect to read about the expense and equipment needed for puppy training in this paragraph.

Example: The bird that was once the most abundant bird in the world became extinct in 1914.

In this second example, the topic is *The bird that was once the most abundant bird in the world,* and the controlling idea is *extinct.* (In case you are wondering, that bird was the passenger pigeon.)

EXERCISE 1

Topic Sentences

Directions: Underline the topic and circle the controlling idea in each of the topic sentences below.

1. Benjamin Franklin was a creative inventor.
2. A linguist is more interested in describing how language is used rather than in prescribing how it should be used.
3. The movie we saw last weekend was the worst we had seen in years.
4. Some studies suggest that belief in a treatment or medicine may be more important than previously thought.
5. After living half my life, I have finally learned what really matters.

Answers are on page 205.

A good topic sentence has a clear focus and is neither wordy nor vague. Compare the two examples below.

A. There are a couple of different reasons that were the rationale for our decision about why we chose the car that we bought.

B. We bought the car because of its cost and reliability record.

Sentence A is very repetitious and vague. Sentence B provides a definite focus and prepares the reader for the explanation to come.

EXERCISE 2

Effective Topic Sentences

Directions: Read the topic sentences below. Circle the letter of the more effective one in each pair.

1. **(a)** One positive thing about music is that it can be good to listen to.
   (b) Classical sonatas are relaxing after a stressful day at work.
2. **(a)** The U.S. government comprises the executive branch, the legislative branch, and the judicial branch.
   (b) There are three different segments that make up the government of the United States.
3. **(a)** The leaves of some ordinary garden-variety plants are actually quite toxic.
   (b) Various plants found all over in the world and environment around us can be extremely bad.
4. **(a)** One of the things that I enjoy doing when I have time to do something is gardening.
   (b) Gardening is very enjoyable.
5. **(a)** There are several things about smoking that are negatives.
   (b) The health risks, the costs, and the smell make smoking undesirable.

Answers are on page 205.

Placement of Topic Sentences

Most of the time, a topic sentence is placed at the beginning of the paragraph. However, a topic sentence can also appear at the end, at both the beginning and end of a paragraph, or even in the middle. In certain limited instances, such as in a description, the topic sentence may be implied. In other words, you will not be able to identify any one sentence that states the central idea in the text. Instead, the main idea of the paragraph will have to be inferred by the reader. Remember that the primary purpose of a topic sentence is to help organize the writing by providing a focused central idea on which other sentences build.

Read the paragraph below. Which sentence serves as the topic sentence? Remember that the rest of the sentences in the paragraph should support the main idea expressed in that topic sentence.

> Perfectionism can be a serious problem because it sets up expectations that people must never make mistakes. People around a perfectionist will actually be prevented from doing their best because of the perfectionist's criticism and constant scrutiny of detail. Additionally, perfectionist tendencies hinder the individual as well. The perfectionist is sometimes unable to perform because he or she is so afraid of mistakes. Striving for the best is a positive characteristic that differs greatly from perfectionism.

You should have chosen the first sentence: *Perfectionism can be a serious problem because it sets up expectations that people must never make mistakes.* As in the majority of paragraphs, the topic sentence is first. Notice that the other sentences in the paragraph support the main idea by explaining how perfectionism is a problem.

EXERCISE 3

Topic Sentences in Paragraphs

Directions: Read the paragraphs below. Underline the topic sentence in each one. If the topic sentence is implied, write a sentence giving the main idea that you have inferred from the paragraph.

1. Although working today may be tiring and hard sometimes, working conditions in the past were much worse. Small children under the age of ten often worked in dangerous factories and were not given any medical care for injuries. People were forced to work 12 to 15 hours every day for seven days each week. Early labor movements to force change sometimes resulted in violence as labor unions clashed with company policemen. Today's improved working conditions have come about only through dedicated efforts to change those past conditions. Every September, Labor Day serves as an appropriate time to celebrate those changes.

2. I walk through the two automatic doors to enter the immense, fluorescent-lit store, reaching for one of the steel carts jammed into the area on my left. Loudly colored posters glare at me, hanging over my head as I make my way through the crowded aisles of cans, bottles, and boxes. From the shelves, as I approach, metallic boxes flash out at me and shoot slick rectangles of paper, screaming in thin electronic voices, "Fifty cents off." Clerks behind demonstration counters thrust foam cups of food samples at me, cajoling me to taste and buy. Overhead, somewhere through a scratchy PA system, a tinny recording urges customers to gather quickly at the head of aisle 12. I pause for a moment and take a deep breath.

3. As she entered the dimly lit room, a soft squish that seemed to come from underfoot made her pause. Carefully, she reached out for the light switch, flipping it on and looking about the room. Outside, the wind had subsided, and she knew that finally the storm that had brought strong winds and a violent downpour of rain had ended. As she moved away from the light switch, she heard the noise again. Her heart sank in dismay. She realized upon hearing the noise that she had a problem; water had flooded the basement.

4. The creature was the ugliest thing I had ever seen. Alternating patches of greasy hair and scaly white bumps covered its greasy head. It had three red eyes, one of which appeared to be completely covered by a thin mucus. The mouth was beak-like, flapping open and shut at mindless intervals. The body of the creature was small but muscular, and what appeared to be arms were kept close to the body trunk. Long, spindly legs led down to heavy feet, where, on one foot, a long nail hooked upward into a black curl.

Answers are on page 205.

Text Division

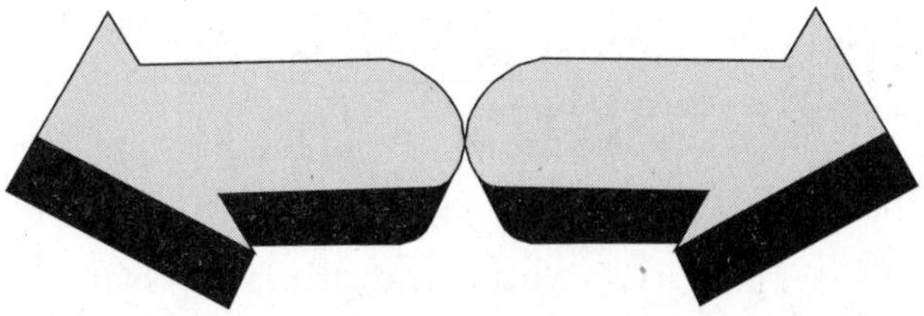

Once you understand what the composition of a paragraph should be, you will be better prepared to divide text into effective paragraphs. You will need to divide text into paragraphs as you write your essay for the Language Arts, Writing Test, but you will also be tested on paragraph division in the editing section. Although three solid pages of unbroken text might alert you that some text division is needed, length alone is not the determining factor in paragraphing. You will want to identify each topic sentence and the relevant sentences that support it. Then, create a new paragraph each time a new idea with another topic sentence and supporting sentences appears. The standard method of beginning a new paragraph requires indenting the first sentence in the paragraph about five spaces from the left margin. In some documents leaving several lines between the paragraphs in a text indicates paragraph division.

The passage below is an example of text that should be divided into two paragraphs. Where do you think the passage should be divided? What idea is presented in the first paragraph? What idea is discussed in the second paragraph?

> Getting organized is sometimes a matter of simplifying life. One way to simplify your life involves setting limits. To begin with, don't buy more than you need or keep items in the hope that someday they will be valuable. Get rid of possessions that you don't need rather than add new space. When you travel, don't bring back lots of souvenirs. Forget the spoon rests and t-shirts and come back with good memories. Another way to simplify your life involves changing your habits. Slow down and don't rush. You'll lose more time if something isn't done right and you have to do it over again. Next, learn to schedule tasks and follow through on what you plan. Also, give your kids the responsibility of organizing themselves. Serve as a good example to them, and you will all benefit.

Source: "Getting Started" *Chicago Tribune*, April 7, 2000

The text should be divided so that the second paragraph begins with this sentence: *Another way to simplify your life involves changing your habits.* Note the way the ideas change. The first paragraph in this text discusses setting limits as a way to simplify life. The second paragraph discusses changing habits as a way to simplify life. Additionally, the wording serves as a signal for a change of ideas. The topic sentence of the second paragraph begins with the expression *Another way* in contrast to the first paragraph, which used the expression *One way.* Good writers try to provide textual devices and transitional expressions that prepare readers for a change of ideas. More explanation of textual devices and transitional expressions will be given on page 163.

EXERCISE 4

Text Division

Directions: Read the passages below and divide them into effective paragraphs. Not all passages need to be divided.

1. Who is the greatest writer in English? In answer to that question, many people would name William Shakespeare. Shakespeare lived in England from 1564 to 1616. He was an actor and playwright in London, but he also wrote poems about nature, love, and change. His plays are divided into three categories: comedies, tragedies, and histories. Probably his greatest play is the tragedy *Hamlet,* but many of his other plays are well-known and appreciated. Before Shakespeare, the most famous writer of English literature was Geoffrey Chaucer. Chaucer lived from 1340 to 1400. He was a military man and later a member of the king's court. He was very influenced by Italian writers. Like Shakespeare, Chaucer also wrote poems, but his poems were much longer. His greatest work is the *Canterbury Tales,* which was never finished.

2. Many great scientific advances occurred in the 20th century. In the early 1900s Albert Einstein proposed his famous theories of relativity and strongly impacted the field of physics. In the 1930s blood banking began because of the initiative of Dr. Bernard Francis. Approximately twenty years later Watson and Crick discovered the double-helix structure of DNA. In 1977 the world's last naturally occurring case of smallpox was recorded, and the disease was finally vanquished. Many notable scientific achievements occurred before the 20th century as well. In the early 1500s the Polish astronomer Copernicus suggested that the planets moved around the sun. Later, in 1543 Vesalius described human anatomy in one of the most significant medical books ever written. The laws of gravity, motion, and optics that Sir Isaac Newton developed at the end of the 17th century influenced the world for more than 200 years.

3. Earthquakes cannot be predicted by catfish. After studying catfish for sixteen years, Japanese researchers concluded that catfish could not serve as indicators of approaching earthquakes. The study, which cost $923,000, was done to determine if there was any truth to an ancient belief that ordinary catfish have the ability to predict earthquakes. Researchers learned that catfish do become more active before an earthquake. That information was not enough to provide reliable data, however. Catfish activity simply did not enable scientists to predict earthquakes accurately enough. As a result, funding for the study was stopped.

Answers are on page 206.

Sometimes, instead of having too much . . .

we have too little.

Text divided into too many paragraphs is just as confusing as text that has not been divided enough. Once again, length is not the sole determining factor in paragraph construction. The paragraph needs to express a main idea and its support, which should be organized properly. Read the paragraphs below. What is the most effective way to reorganize them?

> Offers that seem to be too good to be true usually are. Each year smooth operators, who seemingly offer a good deal, cheat hundreds of people in scams. The U.S. government attempts to investigate and prosecute con artists and frauds, but a consumer needs to act with a little smart caution as well.
>
> Don't hesitate to check into the background of a person or organization before sending money. Read all contracts carefully, checking the terms. Be especially careful about believing everything you read on the Web. Remember, an unbelievably good deal is often a deal you should not believe.

The two paragraphs should be combined into one. The main idea of the paragraph is stated in the first sentence, *Offers that seem to be too good to be true usually are.* The last sentence restates the topic sentence: *Remember, an unbelievably good deal is often a deal you should not believe.* All the other sentences provide explanation and advice about avoiding fraud.

EXERCISE 5

Organizing Text

Directions: Read the seven paragraphs below. On a separate piece of paper, organize and combine the sentences into more effective paragraphs.

(1) It's important to store food carefully to maintain the quality and safety. Improperly stored food can cause health problems.

(2) Furthermore, food that is not stored properly will not taste very good. Eggs are very perishable and require careful storage practices. Buy refrigerated grade A or AA eggs with uncracked, clean shells and keep them refrigerated at 40 degrees or lower.

(3) Do not store eggs in the door of the refrigerator. Egg dishes can be left at room temperature for a maximum of two hours. These guidelines for egg storage will help ensure safety and quality.

(4) Ice cream is another example of a food that benefits from proper storage.

(5) Keep ice cream stored at 0 degrees or lower. Once a carton of ice cream has been opened and used, put plastic wrap over the surface of the remaining ice cream before replacing the carton's lid and storing in the freezer.

(6) The plastic wrap will help prevent a skin from forming and help control the formation of ice crystals.

(7) Be careful to wrap other foods in the freezer tightly so that the odors do not taint the ice cream. A little effort can ensure some good results.

Source: "Top Ten Egg Safety Tips" *Chicago Tribune*, January 12, 2000

Answers are on page 207.

Paragraph Unity

Imagine having a conversation with a friend, and imagine that you are describing your experience of getting soaked in a rainstorm the night before. Suddenly, another person who has been listening to you interrupts your conversation with this announcement: *In Spain the rain falls mainly on the plain.* What would you do? You could stop describing your experience to try to find out what the comment has to do with your story, or you could simply ignore the comment and try to pick up where you left off with your conversation. You may, however, have lost your train of thought. Either way, your story is disrupted.

Written communication, even more so than speech, obligates the author to stay on the subject. Effective **paragraph unity** requires that all the sentences in the paragraph develop the central idea. Sentences that are unnecessary or irrelevant can cause a reader to lose interest or confidence.

Read the letter below. Which sentences are irrelevant?

Alex Robertson, Supervisor
Stanton Corporation
3535 Belvidere Blvd.
Los Angeles, CA 90217

Dear Mr. Robertson:

I have been employed by Stanton Corporation for eighteen months now. During that time, I have been evaluated in my position of technical assistant twice, and both times I received very high ratings in all categories. I showed my wife one of those evaluations. Since I began this position more than a year ago, my knowledge and experience in the job have increased substantially. As a result, I would like to request a raise in my salary because I believe that my contribution to the company has grown. I have not received a raise since I began. Two of my friends got raises last week at the companies where they work, and I would like one as well. Would you please review my personnel record and consider my request?

Sincerely,

Vincent Lowes

Two sentences in this letter are irrelevant: *I showed my wife one of those evaluations,* and *Two of my friends got raises last week at the companies where they work, and I would like one as well.* This information would not matter to a supervisor, and including those sentences weakens the persuasive appeal of the letter.

EXERCISE 6

Irrelevant Sentences

Directions: Read the paragraph below. Cross out the sentences that are irrelevant.

It sometimes takes a lot of courage to make a change for the better in our world. One example of that kind of courage is found in the story of a priest named Damien and his attempt to help the sick. Many years ago, a disease known as leprosy caused people to develop terrible sores on their bodies and eventually die. That was even before the development of computers. The disease was highly contagious, so people were extremely afraid of contracting leprosy. People were also afraid of other diseases as well. In Hawaii those people who became afflicted with leprosy were taken to an island and left there without any medical care. Damien learned of the situation and went to the island to tend the sick. Not only did he tend the sick, but he also drew world attention to the suffering caused by this illness. His efforts inspired research that ultimately led to treatment and a cure. Unfortunately, Father Damien contracted the disease himself and died from it. He should be remembered as a courageous man.

Answers are on page 207.

Paragraph Coherence

Paragraph unity and paragraph coherence are comparable to a jigsaw puzzle. **Paragraph unity** means that all the right pieces for the puzzle are here, with none missing and none accidentally thrown in from some other puzzle box. **Paragraph coherence** means that the puzzle pieces are assembled with all of them smoothly fitting together to create the puzzle picture.

For paragraph coherence, first check the placement of sentences in the paragraph. Second, make sure to provide smooth movement from one thought or sentence to the next. The three methods listed on page 163 can help you achieve that smooth movement.

1. **Use effective grammar, especially pronoun reference.**

   Example: Language is always changing. **It** is a product of the culture. (see Chapter 1)

2. **Repeat words or sentence patterns such as parallel structures.**

   Example: **Not all men** like sports. **Not all women** like shopping. (see Chapter 2)

3. **Use appropriate transitional expressions.** (see below)

   Example: A tomato is technically a fruit. **However,** most people think it is a vegetable.

Transitional Words and Expressions

Certain words and expressions prepare a reader for the information that is coming up. A good reader anticipates what is coming as he or she reads. A good writer will help the reader anticipate correctly and comprehend more clearly. **Transitional expressions** clarify the relationships that exist between ideas; as a result, the reader's understanding of a text improves. Smooth coherence increases comprehension.

The chart below categorizes several of the most common transitional expressions. Notice that expressions in the same group do not always have identical meaning.

To Contrast	To Compare	To Provide Example or Emphasis
however, nevertheless, although, even though, on the other hand, in spite of, despite, on the contrary, yet, regardless, though	in the same way, likewise, similarly, also, just as, like	for example, that is, or instance, indeed, in fact, specifically, of course

To Add to an Idea	To Show Result or Cause	To Show Order or Time
additionally, besides, furthermore, also, moreover, in addition	therefore, as a result, consequently, thus, hence, because, since	meanwhile, so far, at last, then, first, lastly, when, next

EXERCISE 7

Transitional Expressions

Part A **Directions:** Read the sentences below. Choose words to complete the sentences appropriately. If needed, review the chart on page 163. More than one choice is possible.

1. Mexico City is a very large city. ____________________, it is the largest city in the world.

2. Life today is better in some ways than it was in the past. ____________________, in the past, people always had fleas all over themselves.

3. Modern doctors scrub and sterilize their equipment and hands. ____________________, fewer people die from infections after operations.

4. My neighbor was a careless driver who was always in a hurry. ____________________, one day he received a ticket.

5. We were really hoping to visit our family yesterday. ____________________, we didn't have enough time to do so.

Part B **Directions:** Complete the second sentence in each pair so that the sentences make sense.

1. Judy ate a cheeseburger, salad, baked potato, taco, and ice cream cone for lunch. As a result, ____

2. As we get older, we grow more experienced. Furthermore, ________ ____

3. We would love to travel to many places in the world. For example, ____

4. Medical science has proven that smoking is very dangerous to health. Nevertheless, ____

5. Our water has grown increasingly polluted. At the same time, ______ ____

Part C **Directions:** Insert appropriate transitional expressions into the blank spaces in the paragraph below.

The largest living thing on earth is a tree growing in Sequoia National Park in California. The sequoia also happens to be 2,300 to 2,700 years old. It is named the General Sherman Tree after a Civil War general, and its trunk weighs 1,385 tons. The height of the tree above the base is 274.9 feet. ____________________, the General Sherman Tree is not the tallest tree in the world. Another tree, which is almost 100 feet taller, is a redwood on the California coast. ________________, a montezuma cypress in Mexico may be bigger in diameter than the General Sherman. The height and weight of the General Sherman, ____________________, make it the largest living thing in the world.

Source: Sequoia National History Association, Inc.

Answers are on pages 207–208.

GED PRACTICE

EXERCISE 8

Writing Errors

Directions: Read the following paragraphs. Answer the multiple-choice questions, correcting errors in paragraphing, sentence structure, usage, and mechanics.

Coins

(A)

(1) Collecting coins has been a popular hobby for years, but the U.S. Mint's program to honor each of the 50 states with its own quarter has increased interest in coin collecting. **(2)** Stamp collecting is another popular hobby in the United States. **(3)** It is a fact that the first state quarters were issued by the mint in the year 1999. **(4)** The quarters are minted and issued according to the order in which states ratified the Constitution or were admitted into the United States. **(5)** On the front of each quarter being the silhouette of George Washington. **(6)** On the back of each quarter is a unique design for each state.

(B)

(7) In addition to minting the state quarters, the responsibility is the mint's for production of all other U.S. coins. **(8)** All coins minted for general circulation are made in Denver and Philadelphia.
(9) Commemorative coins and regular proof sets are made in San Francisco.

(C)

(10) Some commemorative coins are produced at West Point. **(11)** The location of the actual headquarters of the U.S. Mint that oversees all of the various sites is in Washington, D.C.

(D)

(12) To begin with Thomas Jefferson was the person who suggested the decimal coinage system that the United States uses. **(13)** In 1916 the quarter showed Lady Liberty with an exposed breast. **(14)** In 1917 she was covered up with a coat of mail. **(15)** In 1932 after more than 115 years, she was replaced by George Washington. **(16)** Once in circulation, the average coin lasts for about 25 years. **(17)** However, the amount of time they will last in your pocket will undoubtedly be much less.

1. Sentence 1: **Collecting coins has been a popular hobby for years, but the U.S. Mint's program to honor each of the 50 states with its own quarter has increased interest in coin collecting.**

   What is the best way to write the underlined portion of the text? If the original is the best way, choose option (1).

   (1) years, but
   (2) years but
   (3) years but,
   (4) year's, but
   (5) years', but

2. Sentence 2: **Stamp collecting is another popular hobby in the United States.**

   Which revision should be made to Sentence 2 to make Paragraph A more effective?

   (1) move sentence 2 to follow sentence 6
   (2) move sentence 2 to follow sentence 11
   (3) remove sentence 2
   (4) begin a new paragraph with sentence 2
   (5) no revision is necessary

3. Sentence 3: **It is a fact that the first state quarters were issued by the mint in the year 1999.**

   The most effective revision of sentence 3 would include which group of words?

   (1) despite the mint issuing
   (2) although the state quarters
   (3) the very first quarters because
   (4) quarters before 1999
   (5) the mint began issuing the first

4. Sentence 5: **On the front of each quarter being the silhouette of George Washington.**

   What correction should be made to sentence 5?

   (1) insert a comma after quarter
   (2) replace each with every
   (3) change being to is
   (4) insert side after front
   (5) replace silhouette with head

5. Sentence 7: **In addition to minting the state quarters, the responsibility is the mint's for production of all other U.S. coins.**

   What is the best way to write the underlined portion of the text? If the original is the best way, choose option **(1).**

   (1) the responsibility is the mint's
   (2) the responsibility of the mint's
   (3) the mint having responsibility
   (4) the mint is responsible
   (5) the mint and the responsibility

6. **Which revision would make the document "Coins" more effective?**

   (1) remove sentence 4
   (2) combine paragraphs B and C
   (3) remove sentence 8
   (4) move sentence 11 to the end of paragraph D
   (5) no revision is necessary

7. Sentence 12: **To begin with Thomas Jefferson was the person who suggested the decimal coinage system that the United States uses.**

What correction should be made to sentence 12?

(1) insert a comma after with
(2) change suggested to suggests
(3) insert a comma after system
(4) replace who with he
(5) replace To with Too

8. **Which sentence below would be most effective at the beginning of Paragraph D?**

(1) Famous people are often placed on coins.
(2) There are various different things to know about coins.
(3) In the past coins were different from the way they are today.
(4) All coins are not the same.
(5) A brief look at the history of coins reveals some surprising information.

9. Sentence 17: **However, the amount of time they will last in your pocket will undoubtedly be much less.**

What is the best way to write the underlined portion of the text? If the original is the best way, choose option (1).

(1) they will last
(2) they should last
(3) they last
(4) it will last
(5) it last

Answers are on page 208.

Go to **www.GEDWriting.com** for additional practice and instruction!

CHAPTER 5

Preparing for the GED Essay

If every comma is perfectly placed, if every verb tense is correctly chosen, if every paragraph is effectively divided, will that be enough to make the writing good?

Not necessarily.

Knowing the **form** that writing should follow is certainly helpful. However, writing involves **content** as well as form. Your opinions, explanations, stories, and observations provide the content for your writing. Developing writing that is meaningful to read involves some careful thought, but the way you think differs from the way you need to write. You may think with pictures, images, fragmented sentences, or even feelings. Thus, it takes some work to transform thoughts and ideas into written communication that will be understood by someone else. Writing consists not only of a **product** but also a **process** by which that product is created.

The Writing Process

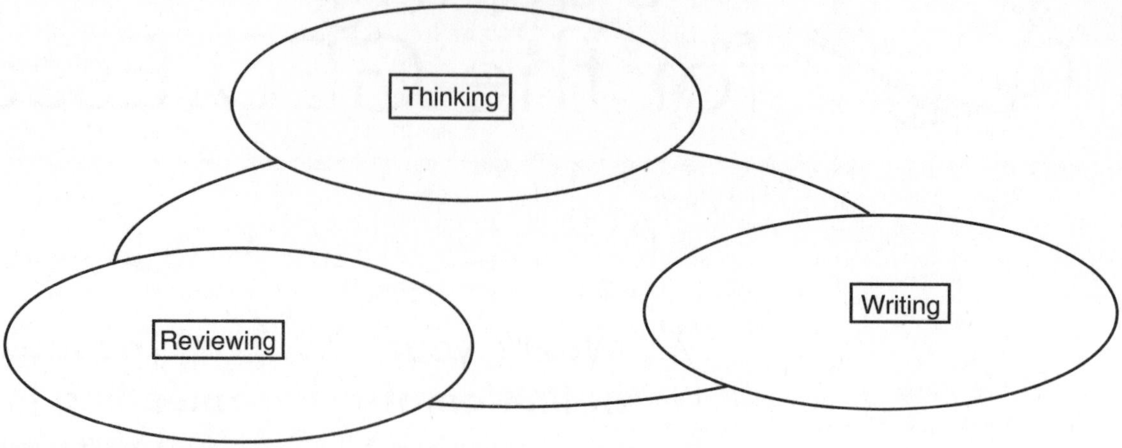

The Writing Process

EXERCISE 1

Making a List

Directions: Choose one of the options below and make a list. Remember to think about what should be on your list. After writing the list, review it to see whether you have forgotten anything or wish to change anything.

1. List of Things to Do for the week
2. List of your goals for the next year
3. List of the features you really want on your next car
4. List of what you have learned so far for the GED Test and what you still have questions about

Answers will vary.

Topic, Purpose, and Audience

The first stage of the writing process is thinking. As you begin thinking and before you start to write, you need to consider the **topic, purpose,** and **audience** for your writing.

The **topic** is the subject of your writing—what you are writing about. If you write a letter to a landlord, the topic may be high rent or faulty air conditioning. If you write an essay about stress on individuals today, the topic may be causes of stress on individuals today or ways to cope with stress today.

Once you have a topic, you need to identify your **purpose.** Why are you writing? What point do you wish to make? Are you writing to tell a story, to voice a complaint, to describe an accident, or to persuade an employer to hire you? When you have determined your purpose, you can consider the best strategies for achieving that purpose.

To best achieve your purpose, you also need to consider the **audience** – who will be reading what you write. Sometimes you're writing for a private audience, perhaps in a journal intended for your eyes alone. More often, however, you are writing to communicate with other people. It's useful to decide whether the writing is aimed at a general group of people or a specific group or person. Just think about the difference in the way you would summarize your life experiences to a potential employer compared to the way you would explain them to your best friend.

On the Language Arts Writing Test, Part II, you will be writing an essay on a topic that has been already selected for you. Although you do not have a choice of topics, you will have some choice regarding the approach to the topic. You will also need to determine the purpose of your writing. In an essay, you are stating your opinion, but what about it? Do you wish to inform others about something, entertain them with your wit, persuade them to make a change, or just complain about a situation? Usually on an essay test such as the GED, you should assume that your audience is general readership.

EXERCISE 2

Practice with Topic, Purpose, and Audience

Directions: Write a short letter on one of the four choices given.

Topic	Purpose	Audience
1. An issue you feel government should address	You want a change.	a government leader
2. A kind act by someone who helped you	You want to express your thanks.	a friend or family member
3. The qualities you really like in someone	You wish to express your admiration.	a famous writer, athlete, star, or leader
4. A problem or inconvenience you've encountered	You would like a refund or restitution.	customer service department of a company

Answers will vary.

Thinking and Generating Ideas for Writing: Stage One

Identifying the topic, purpose, and audience is a good way to begin, but you still need to spend some time thinking about what you will write. As you are thinking about the possibilities, you will find it helpful to make notes.

Writing down ideas as you are thinking is called **brainstorming.** Brainstorming is especially valuable for two main reasons. First of all, by writing down ideas as they come to you, you will reduce the possibility of forgetting them. As adults, we have a lot of things on our mind: family issues, work responsibilities, car problems, and many more. It's easy to forget when there is so much competition for attention. For example, what was the last sentence on the previous page? Only a few minutes ago you saw it, read, it, and understood it, yet you probably cannot recall it unless you turn back to look. Writing down your ideas as you think of them helps prevent their being lost.

Second, when you have brainstormed and written down some ideas, you can easily organize them. Once you have developed a list of ideas, you can select those that seem best, and you can organize them to provide a basic framework from which you can develop your writing.

Seven Steps for Highly Effective Brainstorming

Step 1: Adopt an attitude. Give yourself permission to be silly, stupid, obvious. Don't judge yourself.

Step 2: Consider the topic carefully.

Step 3: List some ideas on the topic.

Step 4: Make choices.

Step 5: Develop associations.

Step 6: Use the five W's (who, what, where, when, why) and organize.

Step 7: Write a main idea sentence.

Now let's apply these steps to a sample topic.

TOPIC: A Place I'll Never Forget

Step 1: **Adopt an attitude.** Give yourself permission to put down any idea that comes to mind without worrying about whether it is silly, stupid, or obvious. You can help prevent writer's block by turning off the voice in your head that criticizes your ideas before you have even written them down. Remember that some of the greatest and most creative inventions have sprung from ideas that were originally labeled ridiculous.

Example: OK, I've got it! As Shakespeare said: The readiness is all! I'm ready to try Step 2.

Step 2: **Consider the topic carefully.** Be sure you understand what you should write about. If the topic is not in question form, turn it into a question that you can address.

Example: What is a place I'll never forget? Why does this place hold such a strong memory for me? What would I like my readers to understand about this place?

Step 3: **List some ideas on the topic.**

Example:

Kauai	Lake in the Woods	My Backyard
wonderful—I'd write to make readers wish they could go there	miserable—I'd write to make readers hope they **never** go there	special—I'd write to share my memories and evoke the reader's sense of home

Step 4: **Make choices.** Select one idea to develop.

Example: the lake in the woods

Step 5: **Develop associations.** Write down any words or phrases that come into your mind as you are thinking.

Example: The Lake in the Woods

childhood—long ago
cold water—leeches
clouds of mosquitoes
grandparents
green water
matches———
ticks
parents
slimy mud
poison ivy
uncle
trails through trees
rooster
brother
uphill
itching
mean
chased me

Step 6: **Use the five W's and organize.** Use the five question words, *who, what, where, when,* and *why* to make questions appropriate to the topic; then answer them.

Example: The Lake in the Woods

Who was there?	**What** happened?	**Where** was the place?
grandparents	**What** was true?	in the country
parents	biting insects	rural area
uncle	nasty plants	north woods
brother	frightening leeches	lake retreat

When did this happen?	**Why** will I never forget?
15 years ago	made me very miserable
in childhood	made me itch and ache
one week visit	made me distrustful of woods

Step 7: **Write a main idea sentence.** In a paragraph, the sentence that states the main idea is called the topic sentence (see Chapter 4.) A topic sentence should contain a topic and a controlling idea.

Example: A place I will never forget is the lake in the woods where one long week of misery created a memory that has lasted more than 15 years.

EXERCISE 3

Brainstorming Practice

Directions: Select one of the topics below. Develop the topic by applying the seven steps for brainstorming. Keep your notes. You will need them to do Exercise 4.

1. A place I'll never forget
2. A person I'll never forget
3. An object that has meaning for me
4. An ideal vacation
5. An embarrassing experience

Answers will vary.

Writing a Draft: Stage Two

Once you've done some thinking, you'll be ready to write a **draft.** This is a first version of writing that you will change later. As you are writing, which of the following should you do?

1. Pause to think carefully about the rules for commas, apostrophes, and grammar so that everything is correct.	**Yes**	**No**
2. Stop often to check your spelling.	**Yes**	**No**
3. Start over every time you make a mistake.	**Yes**	**No**
4. Focus on transforming your notes and thoughts into developed, extended written form.	**Yes**	**No**

The only statement that you should have answered *yes* to is number four, the last one. The most important thing to do when writing a draft is to focus on putting your ideas into written form. Use the ideas that you have generated during brainstorming to help keep the writing on track. Don't interrupt the flow of writing to agonize over corrections. If you're aware that something isn't quite right, *underline* the text in question. You can make changes and improvements later.

EXERCISE 4

Writing a Draft

Directions: Use your notes on the topic you chose for Exercise 3. Write a draft on the ideas you have developed. Save the draft to use in Exercise 5.

Answers will vary.

Reviewing and Editing: Stage Three

The third stage of the writing process involves reviewing what you've written. It's a good idea to review your writing at least twice. At the first reading, consider the content you have written. Are all the ideas you wanted to include actually there? Use the checklist below to help you with any major editing.

Checklist for Revision

1. Is there a sentence that clearly states the main idea?
2. Does the rest of the writing support the main idea?
3. Are enough details and examples included?
4. Has the writing been organized effectively? Should any sentences be moved or removed?
5. Does the writing appear unified and coherent? How smooth is the transition between sentences and paragraphs?
6. Does the writing have a satisfactory conclusion?

After you have reviewed your text and made one set of revisions, read it again. In this second reading you can concentrate on proofing the writing for mechanical, usage, and structural errors. This is the time to think back to the usage rules and practices you have learned.

Proofreading Checklist

1. Does the sentence structure need editing? Are there any fragments or run-ons? Is there any problem in parallelism or modification?
2. Is the grammar correct? Check verb tenses, subject-verb agreement, and pronoun use.
3. Are there any spelling, punctuation, or capitalization errors to be corrected?
4. Is the vocabulary effective and appropriate? Has the same word been used too many times?
5. Does the writing all make sense?

EXERCISE 5

Reviewing and Editing a Draft

Directions: Read the draft you wrote for Exercise 4. Review and edit the draft, using the checklists given above.

Answers will vary.

Types of Writing

Depending on your purpose and your topic, you may use a particular type of writing or a combination of different types. These are the four most commonly used types of writing:

Type of Writing	Purpose
Narrative	tell a story or experience
Descriptive	create a picture or show something
Informative	instruct or explain facts
Persuasive	influence or convince the reader to agree

Whatever type of writing you use, it will still need to be organized and unified. Remember to organize your writing into paragraphs that contain topic sentences that give the main idea. You also need supporting sentences that develop those main ideas. To review paragraph organization, see Chapter 4.

EXERCISE 6

Types of Writing

Directions: Read the start of the story below. What two types of writing can you find?

Everything happened so quickly that now it's almost a blur in my mind. I will tell you, to the best of my abilities, what happened on those fateful days, when King Tutankhamen, still alive and unaware he was destined to die, paid a visit to the House of Life, where I worked as an apprentice scribe.

It was a boiling hot day. Egypt's blazing sun beat down upon the broiling earth without mercy. Even the shade of the palm trees couldn't provide relief from the scorching heat. All was quiet, except for the cries and shouts of the poor boys, happily playing in the cool waters of the Nile. I paused for a moment, stopping my writing in mid-sentence, to gaze longingly at the cheerful sight in the river. That's why I didn't notice . . .

Selection used with permission of Elizabeth Nelson

Answers are on page 208.

Narrative Writing

The purpose of **narrative writing** is to tell a story or relate an experience. Very often, the writing is organized by time order. For this reason the sequencing of events, as well as the verb tenses, is very important. Read the following paragraph. What problem has occurred in the writing?

> The clock outside the depot told him he was late before he even entered the station. As he rushed over to the window to buy a ticket, he saw the train pulling in. He reached into his jacket pocket to take out his wallet. To his great dismay, the pocket was empty. At once he remembers the man bumping into him on the crowded street. He curses inwardly. Then he heard the whistle of the train.

The problem is that the verb tense is not consistent with the time order of the story. Most stories are told in the past tense. This story begins in the past tense, but the writer slips into the present tense with the verbs *remembers* and *curses.* Those verbs should have been *remembered* and *cursed* to remain consistent with the time span used in the narrative.

Notice also that certain transitional words such as *before, At once,* and *Then* in the paragraph help order the events. Below are some transitional words that may be helpful in narrative writing because they indicate time order.

after	before	then
during	finally	when
first	second	later
next	now	meanwhile
simultaneously	at last	at the same time
while	prior to	in the end
at once	eventually	before too long
as soon as	for some time	again

EXERCISE 7

Narrative Writing

Directions: Choose one of the following topics to write a narrative.

1. Tell about the events that happened on a day you will never forget.
2. Tell the story of a time when you lost something or found something.
3. Relate an experience from which you learned something.
4. Write out the story of a good movie you have seen.
5. Write a short story in which you are the hero or heroine.

Answers will vary.

Descriptive Writing

Writing that creates a picture in a reader's mind is **descriptive writing.** Good descriptive writing draws not only on what we see, but also on our other senses, describing how something smells, feels, tastes, and sounds. Including specific details in descriptive writing enables a reader to picture what the writer is trying to show.

When you read the paragraph below, why doesn't it seem to be very effective as a description?

> The forest seemed very big as we drove through it. It was filled with all different things everywhere. There were various plants and things growing near the sides of the road. We drove slowly along, gazing at everything in our path, wishing we had the time to stop.

This paragraph is too general and too vague. The vocabulary isn't very specific. The writing hasn't supplied enough details to create a picture. To visualize the forest a reader would have to make up his or her own picture, but that might not be the one the writer intended to portray.

Now compare the paragraph below to the one you just read. Notice the differences in the vocabulary. Does the description appeal to more than one of the senses?

> The green forest seemed immense as we drove the old, red Chevy through the deserted woods. The woods were filled with tall oaks, graceful beeches, and fragrant pine. Rays of warm sun, welcome in the cool air, caught the leaves of the trees and turned them gold. Purple and white flowers grew in low clusters along the roadside. We heard the crunch of leaves under the tires and the chirping of red-winged blackbirds nearby. Slowly we drove along, gazing in wonder at this evidence of nature's beauty, wishing we had the time to stop.

In the paragraph above details of sight, smell, touch, and sound are described. Did you note the words *red, fragrant, warm,* and *crunch,* for instance?

EXERCISE 8

Descriptive Writing

Directions: Choose one of the following topics to develop into an effective description. Be sure to add appropriate detail.

1. A shopping mall
2. Your favorite room in your home
3. Someone you know well
4. A toy that you remember
5. The most beautiful view you have ever seen

Answers will vary.

Informative Writing

Informative writing is often used to instruct or present facts. The writer's opinion should not be included. A factual story from the newspaper is supposed to be informative. Other common examples of informative writing are recipes and instructions on how to do something.

Informative writing requires clear explanation in order for a reader to follow directions or comprehend the content. Some transitional expressions that help when comparing and contrasting points of information include the following:

Transitional Expressions

For Comparison	For Contrast
not only, but also	however
in the same way	nevertheless
similarly	on the other hand
just as	while
both	whereas
likewise	still

Read the informative paragraph below. What transitional expressions are used to clarify the comparison and contrast that is made?

A garden may consist of annuals, perennials, or a combination of both. Annuals are plants that only live for one season. Perennials, on the other hand, last for many years. Flowers of annuals stay in bloom for the entire season they live. However, perennials only flower for a short time each year. While annuals require replanting every spring, perennials need division or replanting only after several years. Both annuals and perennials contribute beauty and color in their different ways.

You should have found *on the other hand, However, While, Both,* and *different.*

EXERCISE 9

Informative Writing

Directions: Select one of the topics below to write an informative passage.

1. Explain how to prepare a recipe you have.
2. Explain the process of writing an essay.
3. Explain how the three branches of U.S. Government function (see Social Studies Chapter 3, Civics and Government).
4. Explain how to put gas into a car.
5. Explain the order of operations in math (see Math Chapter 2, page 714).

Answers will vary.

Persuasive Writing

Persuasive writing expresses an opinion. The writer wants to influence the reader to accept the validity of a point of view. A persuasive writer must be able to state an opinion, then focus on clear, logical reasons that support that opinion. In other words, as a persuasive writer, you must be prepared to tell what you think and why you think that.

EXERCISE 10

Identifying Supporting Reasons

Directions: Read the statements below. Which ones are persuasive? Which ones do not give real reasons to support the statement?

1. People should exercise regularly because exercise is something everybody should be doing.
2. Prolonged exposure to sun should be avoided in order to prevent sunburn and the risk of skin cancer.
3. At the end of October, the clocks are turned back since that is the time of year when we do this.
4. Winter is the most unpopular season of the year because people just don't like it.
5. Summer is very popular because people can participate in more outdoor activities and enjoy the green lushness of nature.

Answers are on page 208.

An example of a persuasive paragraph is given below. Notice that the topic sentence states the writer's opinion. The rest of the paragraph attempts to persuade the reader of the validity of that opinion by providing reasons and examples.

> Every person in American society today needs to become educated on the use of computers. The widespread introduction of computers during the last two decades has greatly affected American life. The computer has become an integral part of every aspect of society—business, home, community, and even recreation. Some immediate examples of the prevalence of computers are obvious from my own daily life. When I go to work five days a week, I spend several hours working on a computer using information that others have obtained through computers. When I go to the grocery store to buy my family's food, my check has to be cleared through a computer. When I take my car to be repaired, the mechanic hooks it up to a computer. Even when I take a vacation, my plane tickets and reservations are made through a computer. What does this mean? It means that I and others have to keep educated and learn about computers. Thus, we all have to change some of the ways we do things in order to keep up with this change in the world.

Sometimes when you are giving reasons for your opinion, you may be citing the causes or the effects of a situation. Certain transitional expressions help identify those relationships.

Cause-and-Effect Transitional Expressions

as a result	because	consequently
therefore	for this reason	if . . . then
thus	hence	for
then	since	

EXERCISE 11

Persuasive Writing

Directions: Choose one of the following topics to write a persuasive paragraph. Be sure to state your position in a clear topic sentence and to provide supporting sentences that give reasons for your opinion.

1. Should the U.S. government take a greater role in controlling businesses and individuals in our society?
2. Is lying always wrong?
3. Does a man need an education more than a woman?
4. Are the rights of one individual more important or less important than the welfare of a whole society?
5. Should every American be guaranteed by law three weeks of paid vacation every year?
6. Has technology made life better or worse for you?

Answers will vary.

Review of the Writing Process

Examine the topic, brainstorm, and write down some ideas.

State a sentence that gives your main idea on the topic.

Structure your paper into three parts: introduction, body, and conclusion.

Add detail, examples, and support in the body.

You're finished after you read over your work and edit it.

The Written Product

A look at the product created through this writing process shows an essay organized into three major parts: introduction, body, and conclusion.

The Introduction

An **introduction** to an essay has two main functions. First, it introduces the topic and attempts to interest the reader in the text. Second, and even more important for an essay test, the introduction generally includes a **thesis statement,** a sentence that gives the main idea for the whole essay.

Do	Don't
Interest the reader	Apologize
Ask a question	Be too general
State a statistic or fact	Be too wordy
Tell a short story	
Disagree with accepted wisdom	
Give a quotation	
State a thesis	

A good thesis statement is more than just the topic. Many writers will write about the same topic, yet each writer will have a different approach and different focus on the topic. A thesis statement should be more specific than the topic, and it should provide a focus that the rest of the paper supports. Look at the example thesis statements given below.

WEAK: There are several different things I do if I feel stressed out by something.

STRONGER: In order to cope with stress, I read a good book, talk to a friend, or listen to music.

This thesis statement has been improved by preparing the reader for the content of the paper by identifying the three methods the writer uses. The essay should then explain how each method helps the writer cope with stress.

EXERCISE 12

Thesis Statements

Directions: Read the pairs of statements below. Which one makes the better thesis statement for an essay?

1. **(a)** In my opinion, I think something should be done to help people get some kind of medical care that they can afford.
   (b) A universal health care plan is needed in the U.S.
2. **(a)** The best things in life are not free; they are earned.
   (b) It isn't true that the best things in life are free.
3. **(a)** The purpose of this essay is to discuss three major events in my life.
   (b) Three major events that influenced my life were moving to another state, marrying the one I loved, and becoming a parent.

Answers are on page 208.

The Body

The **body** of an essay contains the support for the thesis statement. This is the part where you should be explaining why you think what you do. To develop that explanation well, give examples, cite reasons, retell an experience, or give facts and figures.

Do	Don't
Include details	Assume the reader knows what you mean
Give examples, description, reasons	Keep repeating the opinion that you stated in the introduction
Keep focused	Wander off the thesis

EXERCISE 13

Development and Support for an Essay

Directions: Read the essay that has been started below. Note that the thesis statement is in bold type and prepares for a discussion of three issues. The first issue, *destruction of the environment,* has been developed with reasons and examples for support. Complete the essay by writing two more paragraphs so that each of the remaining two problems stated in the thesis has a paragraph of support.

Be Happy, But Be Concerned

Although I generally agree with advice telling us, "Don't worry. Be happy," I do have some concerns about American life today. **Specifically, the destruction of the environment, the continuing increase of crime, and the lack of affordable medical care for all are problems that we as a country need to address.**

The destruction of our environment continues as we pollute the air, water, and land. Pollution to the atmosphere from car exhaust, manufacturing, and chemical use has caused the death of thousands of plants and animals all over the earth. A well-known example is that of frogs, which are vanishing from the earth. Biologists have suggested that their disappearance may be due to pollution. Furthermore, a study conducted by the United Nations predicted that the threat of global warming brought on from pollution will most likely be even worse than earlier believed. An astounding increase in cases of asthma and allergies has also been linked to environmental pollution. Although we have taken some measures to protect the environment, these are still inadequate, and we need to do more.

The increase in crime is another . . .

Answers will vary.

The Conclusion

The **conclusion** for an essay on an exam can be brief. Most important, you want to end the essay so that there is a sense of closure. The writing should not just stop. To close an essay, you could simply restate or emphasize the thesis statement. Other strategies for concluding include calling for some action, giving a quotation, or answering a question that you raised in the introduction.

Do	Don't
Restate or emphasize your opinion	Disagree with what you have already written
Create a sense of closure	Throw in something you have not discussed
	Use *In conclusion*

EXERCISE 14

Essay Analysis

Directions: Read the essay below. This essay has two major problems. What are they?

Stress is a problem for many of us today. Life is full of lots of changes, and even good change causes stress. When I feel very stressed out, I often go for a walk through the park near my home. Sometimes I just call a friend to talk for awhile. A long, hot bath is another way in which I relax.

At other times, I just eat a box of chocolate candy with lots of toffee and chocolate-covered nuts. I might just retreat for a time and sit in the garden to watch birds and butterflies. In the winter that doesn't work, so I might deal with my stress by exercising and working it off. Sometimes I go shopping, and sometimes I go to a movie. Another good way to deal with stress is to listen to music. Just doing nothing is good too.

Stress is not something anyone seeks out, but like it or not, we have to cope with stress as a part of life.

Answers are on page 209.

Example Essay

Let's look at a sample essay that developed from a topic similar to one that could be used on the GED Essay Test.

Topic: What is one goal that you have? Describe the goal that you identify. Explain why it is important to you.

EXERCISE 15

Developing the Topic

Directions: Think about the topic above and develop ideas by using the seven brainstorming steps presented earlier.

Answers will vary.

Example of Brainstorming Steps

Steps 1, 2, and 3: Adopt an attitude. Consider the topic. List some ideas.

Establishing a healthy living plan | Getting my GED | Taking a trip to Florida

Steps 4 and 5: Make choices. Develop by associating.

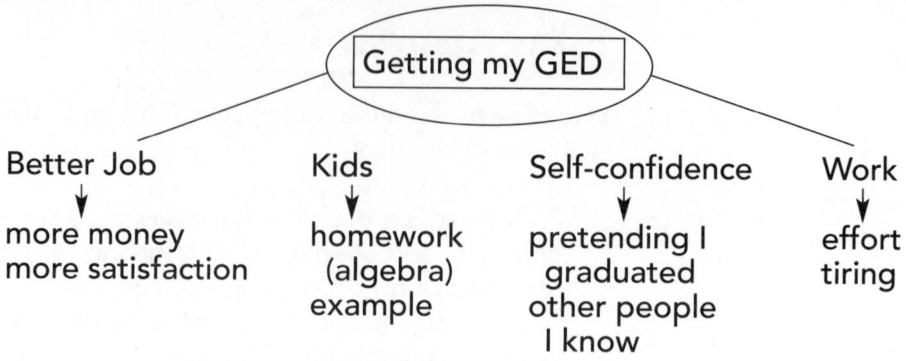

Step 6: Use the five W's and organize.

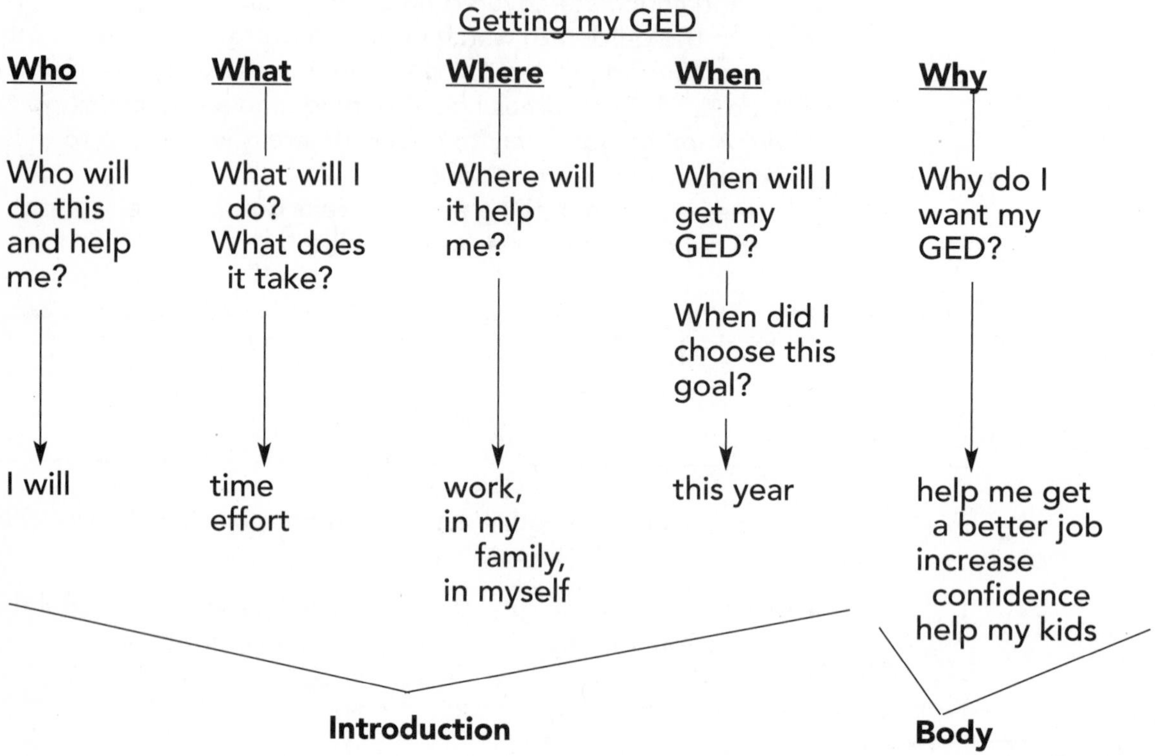

Step 7: Write a main idea sentence (Thesis Statement).

Getting my GED is an important goal for me because I believe it will help me attain a better job, increase my self-confidence, and enable me to help my children.

EXERCISE 16

Drafting an Essay

Directions: Write an essay on the topic and brainstorming notes you developed in Exercise 15.

Answers will vary.

Sample Essay

A Goal That Matters

Looking back now, I can't say exactly when I made my decision. Small wisps of feelings and nagging whispers of thought had been floating through my mind for months. However, one day when I woke up, I had a goal I was ready to work towards. My goal is to get my GED, so I can get a better job, increase my self-confidence, and help my children.

Note that the thesis statement identifies three reasons for the chosen goal.

With a GED, my chances of getting a better job improve. Promotion to a better position generally requires more education. Additionally, more and more companies want a high school diploma just as a condition of employment. Since I have no rich relatives and winning a million dollars is extremely unlikely, I'd better do what I can to get a good job.

The first paragraph in the body explains the first reason.

A second reason I want my GED is that I believe this achievement will help increase my self-confidence. At times, I've lied about having graduated from high school because I haven't wanted to admit that I dropped out. Passing the GED Test and acquiring that diploma will give me a feeling of success. Increasing my knowledge and skills will add to my self-esteem. Success builds confidence, and confidence will help me gain more success.

The second paragraph in the body explains the second reason.

Last, getting my GED should enable me to help my kids. I want to be able to help them with their homework, so I need to learn more myself. Also, I want them to see that I do believe school is important. By studying and furthering my education, I won't just be someone who says, "Do as I say, not as I do."

The third paragraph in the body develops the third reason stated in the thesis.

For these reasons I wish to get my GED. Getting my GED is not just a goal I have. It is also one which I will achieve.

The conclusion restates the main idea of the thesis and calls for action on the part of the writer.

EXERCISE 17

Editing Your Essay

Directions: Read the essay that you have written. Edit it carefully, using the editing checklists from page 176.

Answers will vary.

What You Should Know about the GED Test Essay

Some Common Questions

1. How much time will I have? How long should the essay be? Tell me the specifics.

In Part II of the Language Arts, Writing Test, you will be given 45 minutes to write a well-developed essay. Keep in mind that the development of your idea is very important to the quality of your essay. You will be given scratch paper for prewriting and brainstorming as well as two pages of lined paper on which to write your essay. Only the two pages will be scored.

Your paper must be written in ink, and your handwriting is not judged unless it makes your paper illegible. The directions for the essay will remind you to plan, make notes, draft, and edit.

If you complete your essay in less than 45 minutes, you may return to Part I of the Language Arts, Writing Test.

2. What is the essay topic like?

You will be asked to write an opinion or explanation on a single topic that you will be given at the test. The topic will be general and appropriate for adults. No specialized knowledge will be necessary in order to write on the topic. The topic will be broad enough to allow for many approaches, and no one will be judging your opinion. Rather, you will be evaluated on how well you have presented the opinion you state.

3. How will the essays be scored?

Readers using a process called holistic scoring will read and score your essay on a scale of 1–4. For more information about this scale, see pages 191–192. Each of two readers scores the essay. The scores are then added and divided by 2. To pass the essay test, you must have an essay score that is 2 or higher. If the essay test score is under 2, you must retake the entire Language Arts, Writing Test, no matter what score you may have received on the multiple-choice section.

A reader evaluates an essay on its overall effectiveness rather than by checking for each error. To score well, you should be able plan an essay that effectively supports a focused idea. A paper can contain some errors and still receive a high score. However, the more errors in a paper, the more the reading and comprehension of a reader becomes affected. The greater the interference in the comprehension of a reader, the lower the score will be.

4. What are the standards for the scores?

Here are descriptions of essays at each level of the scoring guide.

Level 4 writing is **effective** because the writer presents a clearly focused main idea that addresses the prompt (the topic) while controlling both the language and sentence structure. The response establishes a clear and logical organization and achieves coherent development with specific and relevant details and examples. Word choice is varied and precise, and there is consistent control of Edited American English (EAE), although a few minor errors may be present. As a result of these combined characteristics, the reader understands and easily follows the expression of ideas in the response.

Level 3 writing is **adequate** because the writer uses the prompt to establish the main idea and generally controls both language and sentence structure. There is an identifiable organizational plan. The writer incorporates specific focused detail, but the development may be uneven. Word choice is appropriate, and the conventions of EAE are generally correct; the errors that are present do not interfere with comprehension. The reader of the 3 response understands the writer's ideas.

Level 2 writing is **marginal** because the writer addresses the prompt but may lose focus or provide few specific details. The response shows some evidence of an organizational plan and has some development, but it may be limited to a listing, repetitions, or generalizations. There is a narrow range of word choice, sometimes including inappropriate selections, and control of sentence structure or the conventions of EAE may be inconsistent. As a result of these combined characteristics, the reader occasionally has difficulty understanding or following the expression of ideas.

Level 1 writing is **inadequate** because the writer has little or no success in establishing and developing a focus, though there may be an attempt to address the prompt. The writer fails to organize ideas or provides little development; the response usually lacks details or examples or presents irrelevant information. There may be minimal, if any, control of sentence structure and the conventions of EAE, or word choice may be ineffective and often inappropriate. The reader of the 1 response has difficulty identifying or following the writer's ideas.

Source: GED Testing Service

Language Arts, Writing, Part II
Essay Scoring Guide

	1	2	3	4
	Inadequate	**Marginal**	**Adequate**	**Effective**
	Reader has difficulty identifying or following the writer's ideas.	**Reader occasionally has difficulty understanding or following the writer's ideas.**	**Reader understands writer's ideas.**	**Reader understands and easily follows the writer's expression of ideas.**
Response to the Prompt	Attempts to address prompt but with little or no success in establishing a focus.	Addresses the prompt, though the focus may shift.	Uses the writing prompt to establish a main idea.	Presents a clearly focused main idea that addresses the prompt.
Organization	Fails to organize ideas.	Shows some evidence of an organizational plan.	Uses an identifiable organizational plan.	Establishes a clear and logical organization.
Development and Details	Demonstrates little or no development; usually lacks details or examples or presents irrelevant information.	Has some development but lacks specific details; may be limited to a listing, repetitions, or generalizations.	Has focused but occasionally uneven development; incorporates some specific detail.	Achieves coherent development with specific and relevant details and examples.
Conventions of EAE	Exhibits minimal or no control of sentence structure and the conventions of (Edited American English) EAE.	Demonstrates inconsistent control of sentence structure and the conventions of EAE.	Generally controls sentence structure and the conventions of EAE.	Consistently controls sentence structure and the conventions of EAE.
Word Choice	Exhibits weak and/or inappropriate words.	Exhibits a narrow range of word choice, often including inappropriate selections.	Exhibits appropriate word choice.	Exhibits varied and precise word choice.

EXERCISE 18

Scoring and Evaluating Essays

Directions: Below you will find a topic and four essays that were written on it. The essays come directly from the GED Testing Service. Read each essay and assign a score. Remember that a score of 4 is high and a score of 1 is low. The answers will reveal how the GED Testing Service actually scored each paper.

Topic: If you could make one positive change to your daily life, what would that change be? In your essay, identify the change you would make. Explain the reasons for your choice.

Essay A

If I could make one positive change in my life, I would be a better communicator. I believe that communication affects our world greatly and that all people should make an extra effort to develop our communication skills. The two major communication skills I wish to improve are listening and speaking.

Listening is one of the most important listening skills. If I could be a better listener, I think I would get more accomplished. By not only hearing but listening to people, I would understand their ideas better. If I would be able to listen to others better, I would have less misunderstandings

Speaking is another communication skill I would like to improve. If my speaking skills were more enhanced, I believe that I could make others understand my meaning clearer and faster. Speaking would also help me to deal with any misunderstandings that might come up in my life.

Speaking and listening are two important communication skills; I would like to improve in my daily life. I feel that these skills would help me to get more accomplished and eliminate many misunderstandings.

In conclusion, I feel that by improving my communication skills I could change my life for the better. By improving my communication skills, I think that I would not just affect my present but my future.

Score _______

Essay B

If I could change on thing in my regular daily life it would be to obtain maximum opportunity. By doing this I mean to achieve my highest goals step by step until I have reached the goals set. One obstacle I would like to overcome day-by-day would be to obtain any knowlegde, whatsoever it may be, every day; in other words learning something new.

Score _______

Essay C

If I could make one positive change in my life, the change would be in my attitude. I would change my attitude toward people and life. My attitude toward certain people I think is outrageous, those certain people are those people who think they're god's gift to the world and I would also change my attitude toward people who are of my age but, act so child like. I would change my attitude toward these people because in the future I may need some of these people that I've treated so negatively. If I continued to treat these people badly, I may not amount to anything in the future. My attitude toward life would also have to change I think because I'm doing so well at this point in my life. Life I think is just a game that everyone has to play in order to survive. I'm not playing to survive I playing only to get by. I feel if my attitude doesn't change at this point, I will never be able to survive the game. The above things about my attitude have to be my positive change in my daily life.

Score _______

Essay D

If I could make one positive change in my life it would be to stop being such a procrastinator. I will put things off until when the angels in heaven above start biting their nails! Putting things off until the next day or when I have more time has really become a problem in the past few years. Recently in my senior English class, I turned in my final research paper of my high school career. It looked really good. All of the words were spelled correctly and form was perfect. I expect an A paper. But what few people knew is that I just barely finished that paper, which was assigned two and a half months prior, at 5:30 that morning. I came to school worn-out and grumpy because I had not had any sleep and because as usual I waited until the last minute to work on my paper. The effect of my procrastination was felt all through the day by my teachers and friends who had to suffer through my sour attitude.

The funny thing about my procrastination is that I can't figure out where I could have possibly picked up such a bad habit. My mother and sister always get their work done on time without running themselves ragged and most of my friends start on long term assignments weeks before the due date.

Lately, I have really been bothered by my lack of attention to time because I will start college in the fall. No one will be there to make me get started on my projects. I want to learn before I leave home how to pace myself and how to force myself to make time for long term projects. If I can't learn the basic steps of time management in the next few months, I can't be sure of what the future holds for me. I'm not sure I could handle the stress of last minute work anymore.

Still, I know that any changes in my daily habits must be made by me. I realize that I must begin with the small things, such as cleaning my room on a scheduled basis rather than putting it off until the weekend or an even later date. I believe even that small of a change would help me with my school, church, and community projects.

I know that my life is in my hands and what I make of it depends on how I spend my time. A procrastinator holds himself back and I must move forward. The only way I can do that is to get up and "Just Do It."

Score _______

Source: GED Testing Service

Answers are on pages 209–210.

Making the Most of Your Time

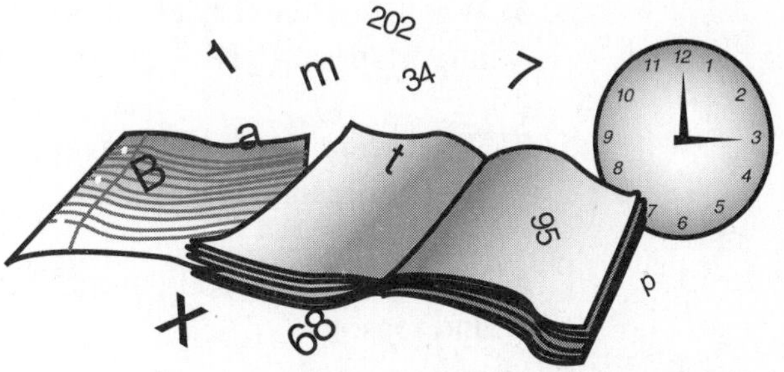

One of the steps you should take in preparing for the GED essay is learning to adapt the writing process to the testing situation. You have practiced all the steps in the writing process before, but you need to have a strategy for using your time well when you take the test. Study the following description of how you might approach the essay. Think about how you could adapt this strategy to suit your own writing style.

Prewrite (5–10 minutes): Study the topic and think about the choices you have. Write down some ideas, make a choice, then jot down some notes. Write a main idea sentence to use as a thesis statement. Be sure you have a clear plan of how your ideas will be organized before you begin drafting your essay.

Draft (25–30 minutes): Neatly write a rough copy of your essay in ink, keeping in mind that you won't have time to recopy the paper. Leave wide margins so that you can go back to add ideas and make corrections. As you write, be sure to refer to the overall organizational plan that you have prepared.

Revise and edit (5–10 Minutes): Read over your essay. Look for changes you can make that will improve the writing and clarify the ideas. Check the structure of the sentences, paragraphs, and whole essay. Make sure you have included a clear thesis statement in your introduction and provided some detailed development for your opinion. Correct any problems in grammar, mechanics, or wording.

Sample Topics for Practice

The best way to study for the essay section of the Language Arts, Writing Test is to practice writing. Here are some essay topics that are similar to ones that may be used on the test. Practice using the skills that you have learned. Time yourself to grow accustomed to writing under a time constraint. Remember that you should spend about 45 minutes on an essay.

1. What do you do to keep healthy? In your essay describe what you do and how it helps you.

2. If anything were possible, what is one wish you would make? Explain the reasons for your choice.

3. Who is someone you admire? Explain the reasons why you admire that person.

4. What should every child be taught? Identify the qualities that you feel are important and give examples of why they are important.

5. What were three major events in your life? Describe each one and explain its significance to you.

6. What makes a good parent? Support your opinion with specific examples and reasons.

7. What are three qualities that you value in a friend? Be specific and use examples to support your views.

8. What is one way in which life has become better today, and what is one way in which life has become worse? Explain your opinion with specific examples.

9. What can be done to help with the problem of road rage? Give suggestions and examples that support your opinion.

10. If you could have any three jobs during your lifetime, what three jobs would you want? Explain why you would want each one.

Go to **www.GEDWriting.com** for additional practice and instruction!

Answer Key

CHAPTER 1
BASIC ENGLISH USAGE

Exercise 1: Subjects and Predicates (page 67)

1. (d) *Star Wars* told the story of the Force against the Dark Side.
2. (e) Romeo and Juliet fell in love and killed themselves.
3. (a) The Greek hero Hercules had the strength of 100 men.
4. (c) The hare was beaten by the tortoise in a race.
5. (b) King Arthur sat at a round table in Camelot.
6. (f) Robin Hood stole from the rich to give to the poor.
7. (h) Ichabod Crane was chased by a headless horseman.
8. (g) Hamlet vowed revenge against his uncle for the murder of his father.

Exercise 2: Nouns and Subjects (page 70)
The nouns are listed below and the subject of the sentence is in **bold type.** If you are confused about the subject in the following sentences, remember to ask yourself: Who or what is doing something or is being described in this sentence?

1. **Agnes,** puzzles, enjoyment, time
2. **dictionary,** answer, word, question, thought
3. birthday, **granddaughter,** book, box, chocolates
4. **members,** family, candy, cake, ice cream
5. **Agnes,** gift, people, person

Exercise 3: Possessive Nouns (page 73)
Corrections are in **bold type.**

1. Long ago in Egypt, when a cat died, the **cat's** owner would shave off his own eyebrows to show respect for the dead cat.
2. Years ago, Australians bought weasels to hunt rabbits, but instead the weasels attacked the **Australians'** chickens.
3. Four hundred years ago, explorers sometimes took hogs on ships because they believed that if the hogs were thrown overboard, they would swim to the nearest land. (no correction needed)
4. Today in the United States, animals such as dogs, birds, and cats are popular **children's** pets.
5. **Japan's** scientists have been investigating to see if cows and worms can predict earthquakes.
6. Gardeners know bees are important to gardens, and although a common bee may sting a gardener, a queen bee doesn't sting anything other than another queen bee. (no correction needed)

Exercise 4: The Simple Tenses (page 80)

	Verb	*Time Clue*
1.	drinks	Every morning
2.	will move	In two weeks
3.	saw	last week
4.	tried	a few hours ago
5.	will vote	next presidential election

Exercise 5: The Continuous Tenses (page 81)

	Verb	*Time Clue*
1.	were walking	yesterday
2.	is sleeping	At the moment
3.	will be beginning	One week from today
4.	is shining	right now
5.	will be retiring	next spring

Exercise 6: The Perfect Tenses (page 82)

	Verb	*Time Clue*
1.	will have left	By 6:00 A.M. tomorrow morning
2.	had closed	by the time we arrived
3.	has saved	So far
4.	have had	yet
5.	will have run	By the time
6.	had performed	Up until the development

Exercise 7: Verb Tense Review (page 83)

	Verb	*Time Clue*
1.	will have achieved	By next summer
2.	went	Twenty years ago
3.	have loved	Ever since that day
4.	return	Every time
5.	bought	Last year
6.	had entered	Before they bought the home last year
7.	lost	Pat had submitted
8.	are	usually
9.	feel	The fact is
10.	are studying	Right now
11.	will miss	Once they have moved
12.	hires	every year

GED Practice Exercise 8: Verbs (page 84)

1. **(4)** The verb needs to be in present tense to match the time clue *today.*
2. **(2)** The verb needs to be in past tense to match the time clue *in 1942.*
3. **(2)** The verb should be past perfect because the action occurred before another past action.
4. **(5)** The verb should be in past tense because the action was completed in the past.
5. **(2)** The verb should be in the past tense because the action was completed in the past.
6. **(1)** The verb should be in present perfect because the action began in the past but is still continuing into the present.
7. **(4)** The verb should be in future tense to match the time clue *in the future.*

Exercise 9: Subject-Verb Agreement (page 89)

	Subject	*Verb*
1.	employees and the boss	were
2.	boss	was
3.	crackers	come
4.	a serving spoon and butter knife	are
5.	problems	seem
6.	mail	Has
7.	time	Doesn't

Exercise 10: More Subject-Verb Agreement (page 91)

	Subject	*Verb*
1.	LaVerne	looks
2.	Everybody	wants
3.	Each	is
4.	Most (questions)	are
5.	tests	have
6.	Determination	helps

Exercise 11: Pronoun Forms (page 93)

1. **He** drove to work with **them.**
2. **Their** shirts cost the same as **her** hat.
3. The invitation said that children were invited, so I brought **mine.**
4. Give the check to **us.**
5. Yesterday Mike and **his** family left to go camping.

Exercise 12: Possessive Pronouns and Contractions (page 94)

1. **There's** so much ice in the world, that if we melted it all, the earth would flood enough to cover twenty stories of the Empire State Building
2. The earth is mostly water so only about 30% of **its** surface is land.
3. Seven of the planets in our solar system have moons, and all **their** moons have names.
4. If you think **you're** uncomfortable on a hot day in summer, just consider that the temperature in the center of the sun is about 27,000,000 degrees F.
5. Stephen Hawking, **whose** contributions to science include knowledge about black holes and the evolution of the universe, may be one of the greatest physicists of the twentieth century.
6. If someone is driving at the speed of light, which is 186,282 miles per second, **it's** likely he will get a ticket.

Exercise 13: Identifying Antecedents (page 96)

	Pronouns	*Antecedent*
3.	he	farmer
4.	His	farmer
5.	that	bill
6.	who	spokesperson
7.	she	spokesperson
8.	it	bill
9.	their	people
10.	that	bills

Exercise 14: Agreement in Number (page 98)
Part A

	Antecedent	*Pronoun*
1.	hot dog	its
2.	one (Mark)	he
3.	machinery	its
4.	Indians	their
5.	beef, pork, and poultry	their

Part B (page 98)
Corrections are in **bold type.**

Each company has certain expectations of **its** employees. Its expectations often include work practices, dress code, and safety procedures that workers need to follow during their employment. Employees, in turn, have certain expectations about a company and **its** treatment of personnel. Their expectations often include salary schedules, benefit provisions, and working conditions.

Exercise 15: Clarifying Antecedents (page 100)
The following sentences are *possible* revisions. The words in bold type replace the confusing pronoun or pronouns. Remember that your sentences can be different from those given here and still be correct. When checking your work, be sure that you have replaced all vague pronouns.

1. Wendy gave Bonnie the keys to **Wendy's** car.
2. The man followed Mr. Reynolds in **the man's** new car.
3. When Al lost his wallet, **losing the wallet** created a problem.
4. We heard on the news that **medical researchers** are trying to find a cure for diabetes.
5. Would you put those dishes next to those glasses after you dry **the dishes**?
6. Obesity and malnutrition are growing concerns in the United States. **These conditions** continue to be a threat to the health of many people.
7. C
8. C
9. The Phillipses met the Mulcrones for dinner, and **the Mulcrones** paid the check.

Exercise 16: Agreement in Person (page 101)
Corrections are in **bold type.**

One survey report states that 66 percent of us just want some time for ourselves. In general, we are working more than ever, so **we** have less and less free time. Two strategies **we** can use to save some of that valuable time are helpful. We need to learn to combine **our** errands, and we need to buy time rather than things.

GED Practice Exercise 17: Usage (page 102)

1. **(5)** no correction is necessary
2. **(2)** The verb must agree with the compound subject *work disputes, social disagreements, and family problems.*
3. **(1)** Pronouns should not shift in a passage. The voice should be consistent. The writer is speaking directly to the reader.
4. **(5)** no correction is necessary
5. **(3)** The verb *talk* must be used in present tense to be consistent with the rest of the sentence.
6. **(5)** The verb tense must be consistent. The sentence states advice and fact and requires present or present continuous tense.
7. **(3)** The pronoun *it* is a vague reference. What is important must be stated.
8. **(4)** The pronoun needs to agree with the antecedent *apology.*
9. **(3)** The verb must agree with the singular subject *code.*
10. **(5)** The verb tense must be consistent with the meaning. Future tense is used to give a prediction.

CHAPTER 2

SENTENCE STRUCTURE

Exercise 1: Rewriting Fragments (page 107)
Part A.
The following are *possible* revisions of these fragments. Remember, your answers can be different and still be correct. When checking your answers, be sure your revised sentences contain a subject and predicate and express a complete thought.

1. F A million dollars is more money than I have.
2. S
3. F A car stopped at the traffic light.
4. F They were lost in the woods.
5. S

Part B (page 108)
Corrected sentences are in **bold type.** Remember, your revised sentences can be different and still be correct.

The most successful people are often those who are willing to experience failure **without letting it stop them.** One such person was Abraham Lincoln. Lincoln failed in business, failed to get into law school in 1832, and failed to win in more than six elections. He also suffered severe hardship in his life. **For example, the deaths of his mother and fiancée were very difficult for him.** Nevertheless, he became president of the United States and still is respected for many of his efforts.

Exercise 2: Run-ons and Comma Splices (page 109)

1. C
2. A paste made from meat tenderizer can help the pain from insect bites. This method works well on bee stings.
   OR
   A paste made from meat tenderizer can help the pain from insect bites; this method works well on bee stings.
3. Wet moss can be extremely slippery. It can be easily scraped off with a small knife.
   OR
   Wet moss can be extremely slippery; it can be easily scraped off with a small knife.
4. C
5. C
6. A good remedy against cockroaches is boric acid. It causes the cockroach's stomach to explode.
   OR
   A good remedy against cockroaches is boric acid; boric acid causes the cockroach's stomach to explode.
7. Every year lightning strikes thousands of people. It kills about 150 people in the United States each year.
   OR
   Every year lightning strikes thousands of people; it kills about 150 people in the United States each year.
8. C
9. Color can influence the way people feel. For example, the color red can be very stimulating.
   OR
   Color can influence the way people feel; for example, the color red can be very stimulating.
10. Children under the age of thirteen are especially good at learning language. Researchers are still doing studies on language learning and age.
    OR
    Children under the age of thirteen are especially good at learning language; researchers are still doing studies on language learning and age.

Exercise 3: Conjunctions (page 111)
The correct conjunction and punctuation are in **bold type.** More than one conjunction may be correct in some sentences.

1. The first compact microwave ovens came out in the 1960s**, but** they didn't become widely used until the 1980s.
2. People ate with their hands for centuries**, but** a big change finally occurred in the 1100s when people used forks, knives, and spoons.
3. It seems silly to say we will dial a telephone number**, for** push button phones are used everywhere.

4. In 1972, you could play table tennis on a large table with a net, paddles, and ball**, or** you could play a computerized version on one of the first home video games.
5. Doing laundry used to take a whole day**, so** when automatic washers became available in the 1940s, people were happy.

Exercise 4: Using Commas Correctly (page 112)
Remember, a comma is needed when two complete sentences are joined by a coordinating conjunction such as *and* or *but.* If you use a comma, make sure the sentences you join have both a subject and a predicate.

1. On Saturday Elizabeth and Jessica were playing a game. (no correction needed)
2. Jessica won the first game, and Elizabeth asked for a rematch.
3. They started a second game but were interrupted by the doorbell. (no correction needed)
4. They started a third game, but they were interrupted by the doorbell.
5. Games are popular to play for a number of reasons. (no correction needed)
6. Games are inexpensive and entertaining, so they are popular to play.
7. A game such as chess has been played for hundreds of years, so it is very well known in the world.
8. There is so much to learn about chess. (no correction needed)

Exercise 5: Run-ons and Comma Splices (page 113)
The sentences in **bold type** show possible ways to correct the run-ons and comma splices in this paragraph. They have been separated into two sentences or combined using a comma with *and, but, or, for, nor, so,* or *yet.*

We tend to take our feet for granted, but they are actually quite remarkable. Our feet have 52 bones, one quarter of all the bones in the body. Each foot has 33 joints, 107 ligaments, and 19 muscles. Every year approximately 19 percent of people in the United States suffer from foot problems including corns, calluses, fallen arches, fungal infections, and injuries. **Women suffer from foot problems about four times as often as men do. Some of those problems are directly related to the wearing of high heels. We do need to care for our feet, for they will be used to carry us thousands of miles during our lifetimes.**

GED Practice Exercise 6: Sentence Structure (page 113)

1. **(3)** This sentence is a run-on but can be corrected by separating the two independent sentences.
2. **(5)** The original sentence is a comma splice and can be corrected by separating the two independent sentences.
3. **(2)** The past tense verb *began* is consistent with the time and tense of the rest of the passage.
4. **(4)** The pronoun *it* is needed to refer to the singular noun *Internet.*
5. **(5)** No correction is necessary.
6. **(5)** The verb *stand* needs to agree with the subject *each.*
7. **(4)** A comma and the conjunction *so* provide logical coordination for two ideas.

Exercise 7: Dependent Clauses (page 117)
Remember, your answers can be different from those in **bold type** and still be correct.
Part A

1. Books were made more cheaply and quickly **after** Gutenberg invented moveable type to use in printing in 1450.
2. **Before** the invention of a process to produce paper in China, the Chinese used clay or wood blocks to make books in the 10th century.
3. In early Egypt, scribes would write needed documents on scrolls in a library **where** the documents were stored in jars.
4. **Although** information is stored electronically in the modern world, a lot of paper is still used.
5. The modern age has been called the Information Age **because** of the resources available for accessing information.

Part B (page 118)
The dependent clause in each of the following sentences is in **bold type.**

1. **Although it can make us miserable,** love is important in life.

2. I'd like to be given $100,000 **unless there are strings attached.**
3. **When I'm done with this,** I'll really feel very happy.
4. Honesty is usually the best policy **because honesty builds trust and self-respect.**
5. Learning in life continues **until life ends.**

Part C (page 118)

The subordinating conjunction in each sentence is in **bold type.**

1. The hourglass was an early type of clock **though** it didn't work well if the weather was damp.
2. Clock towers were popular in towns **because** the clock towers were so tall that an entire village could see the time easily.
3. Hands on a clock were no longer needed **after** digital clocks became popular.
4. **Since** I have to get up early in the morning, I set an alarm clock.
5. The hours dragged by slowly **as though** the long day would never end.

Exercise 8: Passive or Active Voice (page 120)

1. P The man was bitten by the dog.
2. A The dog bit the man.
3. A People watch TV too much.
4. P TV is watched too much by people.
5. P Last week the driver was given a ticket.
6. A Last week a police officer gave the driver a ticket.

Exercise 9: Recognizing Effective Sentences (page 120)

1. **(b)** After I lost the lottery for the tenth week in a row, I vowed never to play again.
2. **(a)** The storm caused thousands of homes to lose power for several hours.
3. **(b)** If it rains, use an umbrella.
4. **(b)** The man looking for work applied for various jobs.
5. **(a)** Thunder and lightning during winter are unusual.

GED Practice Exercise 10: Structure and Usage (page 123)

1. **(1)** The wordiness of the original can be improved and the meaning more clearly presented by revising the sentence to *Most people agree that reading skills are necessary in our contemporary times.*
2. **(2)** The verb *is* must agree with the subject of the sentence *one.*
3. **(4)** The meaning of the original can be preserved, and the sentence can be improved on by changing the passive voice to the active voice: *Another disturbing estimate claimed that more than one third of elementary and high school students read below grade level.*
4. **(5)** The sentences are most effectively combined using a comma and the conjunction *but.*
5. **(2)** The meaning of the original can be preserved and the sentence can be improved on by changing the passive voice to the active voice: *By reading themselves, parents set an example for children, underscoring the value of the activity.*
6. **(1)** The meaning of the original can be preserved, and the sentence can be improved on by omitting useless words: *Newspapers, magazines, and books help build skills and establish the habit of reading.*
7. **(3)** Sentence 12 is a fragment that is best corrected by adding it to sentence 11.

Exercise 11: Dangling and Misplaced Modifiers (page 128)

The modifying phrase in each of the following sentences is in **bold type** and is in the correct place—nearest to the word it modifies.

1. The Martins bought a house **that was constructed with vinyl siding** on a nearby street.
2. **As the sun slowly sank beneath the horizon,** we watched the sunset.
3. **Pleased with the effect of the color change,** the woman smiled with satisfaction. (no correction needed)

4. **Upon blowing out the candles,** he sliced the cake into pieces for the guests at the birthday party.
5. On Saturday at the bookstore, he bought an instruction book **for training dogs.**
6. A cold drink tasted refreshing **after she had been working outside in the heat for several hours.**
7. **After we had been listening to the music for an hour,** the radio program was interrupted by a weather bulletin.
8. The dentist began work on the root canal for the patient's tooth **that had been cracked.**
9. **Before doing anything drastic,** you should consider the options. (no correction needed)
10. Our neighbors took their dog **that had fleas** to the groomer.

Exercise 12: Parallel Structure (page 130)

Part A

1. **(d)** take a trip
2. **(b)** near the tree
3. **(d)** smiling boy
4. **(a)** talking
5. **(c)** place that is beautiful

Part B (page 130)

1. **(a)**
2. **(b)**
3. **(b)**
4. **(a)**
5. **(a)**

GED Practice Exercise 13: Structure and Usage (page 131)

1. **(3)** Correct the original run-on sentence by combining the two sentences with a comma and the coordinating conjunction *and.*
2. **(5)** Correct the dangling modification by placing *people* right after the modifying phrase.
3. **(1)** Subject/ verb agreement requires that the verb *is* be matched with the subject *conceit.*
4. **(3)** The meaning of the original can be preserved, and the sentence can be improved by changing the passive voice to the active voice: *Arrogance is generally a sign of low self-esteem.*
5. **(1)** The wordiness of the original can be improved and the meaning more clearly presented by revising the sentence to *First, spend some time each day doing something you do well.*
6. **(4)** The dangling modifier *By accomplishing* should be corrected by adding a subject.
7. **(3)** Avoid a shift in pronoun use and be consistent with the rest of the paragraph by using *you.*
8. **(5)** The compound subject should be made of parallel structures.
9. **(2)** The phrase *rather than* requires a structure that will be parallel to *live.*

CHAPTER 3

MECHANICS

Exercise 1: Capitalization Rules (page 138)

The corrected words in each of the following sentences are in **bold type.**

1. The **German** composer **Beethoven** produced his most famous work after he was deaf.
2. Our friends went to a **concert** last **Monday** on Labor **Day** and listened to music from an opera called The Magic **Flute** by **Mozart.**
3. Not only did Thomas Jefferson write the **Declaration** of **Independence** for the **country,** but he also served as a **governor** of Virginia.
4. On **May** 30, 1431, when Joan of Arc was burned at the stake after helping to lead **French** armies against the **English,** she was only 19 years old.
5. If you take **Interstate** 80 and travel **west,** you will see many **national parks** such as **Yellowstone** or Great Teton which have been preserved because of the efforts of John Rockefeller.
6. One of **Shakespeare's** darkest **tragedies** which was written about 400 years ago is the story of **King** Lear and his three daughters.
7. The ceiling of the **Sistine Chapel** in **Rome** contains a painting 133 feet long and 45 feet wide that was painted by **Michelangelo** for **Pope** Paul III.

8. In medicine, Elizabeth Blackwell was one of the first women to become a **doctor,** and Florence **Nightingale** received an award for helping to make nursing an honored profession.

Exercise 2: Using Commas (page 142)

To: All Employees
From: Personnel
Date: March 16, 2002
Subject: Insurance

The new insurance plan will go into effect in the next **month,** so all company employees need to attend an information session. After hearing the **information,** each employee **must,** of **course,** select a plan option. **In addition,** each employee will need to indicate whether family members are to be covered. An employee may opt for coverage for a **spouse, dependents,** or just the employee. Registration for an information session can be completed by dialing extension 608. Six sessions have **been scheduled,** and each will last approximately one hour. If there are any immediate **questions,** please call the director of personnel at extension 442.

Exercise 3: Punctuation Review (page 144)

1. We can learn a lot from other people's experiences and ideas.
2. Charles Kingsley said that people shouldn't ever go to sleep at night without having added to another person's happiness that day.
3. If you look in the library, you will find many great writers' books.
4. Words and ideas can inspire men's thoughts, but music and art can touch their souls.
5. Many famous artists' masterpieces hang in the Louvre in Paris.

GED Practice Exercise 4: Structure, Usage, and Mechanics (page 144)

1. **(4)** Use commas to set off parenthetical expressions in a sentence.
2. **(2)** The sentence expresses the appropriate meaning and is less wordy with this revision: *On the other hand, it is generally less expensive to make one up yourself.*
3. **(3)** Do not separate the subject and verb with a comma.
4. **(4)** The series should be revised so the sentence has parallel structure.
5. **(1)** The verb *are* must agree with the compound subject *A spray and an ointment.*
6. **(1)** The sentences should be revised to retain the appropriate meaning: *Other useful items include tweezers, a thermometer, cotton swabs, and medical gloves.*
7. **(4)** The noun *item* requires the use of *it is* for agreement in number.
8. **(5)** Don't capitalize occupations.

Exercise 5: Spelling Sound-alike Words (page 147)

1. That store will **accept** any type of payment **except** checks.
2. Color can **affect** us. Its **effect** can be soothing or energizing.
3. Fortunately, they were **all ready** to go because we were **already** late.
4. The **capitol** building is located in our state **capital.**
5. During the art **course,** she worked with some **coarse** materials to show different textures.
6. After dinner I want to go out for **dessert,** but I don't want to **desert** my friends.
7. **It's** true that my car lost **its** muffler on the way here.
8. You may **know** the expression that **no** man is an island.
9. The governor **knew** a **new** policy was needed.
10. Once they were **past** the town, they **passed** the truck ahead of them.
11. **They're** about to leave, so get **their** coats from over **there.**
12. It costs **too** much **to** spend **two** weeks in Europe.

Exercise 6: Sound-alike Words (page 149)
The corrected word in each of the following sentences is in **bold type.**

1. We are becoming increasingly **conscious** of the need to preserve our environment.
2. The waitress brought **their** order very quickly.
3. Does Bob **know** that the hours that they are open have changed?
4. It's **past** that child's bedtime, and he is getting very crabby.
5. Sometimes Carol Anne goes camping with her family for almost a **week.**

GED Practice Exercise 7: Structure, Usage, Spelling, and Mechanics (page 150)

1. **(2)** Do not capitalize general geographic areas such as directions.
2. **(5)** The spelling should be changed to *weather* to provide the appropriate meaning.
3. **(1)** The verb must agree with the compound subject *conditions and cold.*
4. **(5)** The most effective revision avoids the passive voice and wordiness: *An observation one day led Birdseye to a useful discovery.*
5. **(2)** The modification must be structured to describe *he.*
6. **(4)** Do not put commas between the parts of a compound verb.
7. **(1)** The vague reference of the pronoun *it* needs clarification.
8. **(4)** The revision must keep the appropriate meaning: *Freezing food quickly was the key to food preservation.*
9. **(4)** Sentence 12 is a fragment that needs to be attached to sentence 11.
10. **(2)** Use the present tense to state a fact and be consistent with the meaning of the paragraph.

CHAPTER 4

ORGANIZATION

Exercise 1: Topic Sentences (page 154)
The topic is underlined, and the controlling idea is in **boldface.**

1. Benjamin Franklin was a **creative inventor.**
2. A linguist is **more interested in describing how language is used rather than in prescribing how it should be used.**
3. The movie we saw last weekend was the **worst** we had seen in years.
4. Some studies suggest that belief in a treatment or medicine may be **more important than previously believed.**
5. After living half my life, I have finally learned **what really matters.**

Exercise 2: Effective Topic Sentences (page 155)

1. **(b)** Classical sonatas are relaxing after a stressful day at work.
2. **(a)** The U.S. Government comprises the executive branch, the legislative branch, and the judicial branch.
3. **(a)** The leaves of some ordinary garden-variety plants are actually quite toxic.
4. **(b)** Gardening is very enjoyable.
5. **(b)** The health risks, the costs, and the smell make smoking undesirable.

Exercise 3: Topic Sentences in Paragraphs (page 156)
The topic sentence for each paragraph is underlined.

1. Although working today may be tiring and hard sometimes, working conditions in the past were much worse. Small children under the age of ten often worked in dangerous factories and were not given any medical care for injuries. People were forced to work twelve to fifteen hours everyday for seven days each week. Early labor movements to force change sometimes resulted in violence as labor unions clashed against company policemen. Today's improved working conditions have only come about through dedicated efforts to change those past conditions. Every September, Labor Day serves as an appropriate time to celebrate those changes.

2. **The topic sentence is implied.** It would be something like this: *Shopping at the store seems very unpleasant to me.* I walk through the two automatic doors to enter the immense, fluorescent-lit store, reaching for one of the steel carts jammed into the area on my left. Loudly colored posters glare at me, hanging over my head as I make my way through the crowded aisles of cans, bottles and boxes. From the shelves, as I approach, metallic boxes flash out at me and shoot slick rectangles of paper, screaming in thin electronic voices, "Fifty cents off." Clerks behind demonstration counters thrust foam cups of food samples at me, cajoling me to taste and buy. Overhead somewhere through a scratchy PA system, a tinny recording urges customers to gather quickly at the head of aisle 12. I pause for a moment and take a deep breath.
3. As she entered the dimly lit room, a soft squish that seemed to come from underfoot made her pause. Carefully, she reached out for the light switch, flipping it on and looking about the room. Outside, the wind had subsided, and she knew that finally the storm that had brought strong winds and a violent downpour of rain had ended. As she moved away from the light switch, she heard the noise again. Her heart sank in dismay. She realized upon hearing that noise that she had a problem; water had flooded the basement.
4. The creature was the ugliest thing I had ever seen. Alternating patches of greasy hair and scaly white bumps covered its greasy head. It had three red eyes, one of which appeared to be completely covered by a thin mucus. The mouth was beak-like, flapping open and shut at mindless intervals. The body of the creature was small, but muscular, and what appeared to be arms were kept close to the body trunk. Long, spindly legs led down to heavy feet, where, on one foot, a long nail hooked upward into a black curl.

Exercise 4: Text Division (page 158)
The text for each passage is organized into paragraphs below.

1. Who is the greatest writer in English? In answer to that question, may people would name William Shakespeare. Shakespeare lived in England from 1564 to 1616. He was an actor and playwright in London, but he also wrote poems about nature, love, and change. His plays are divided into three categories: comedies, tragedies, and histories. Probably his greatest play is the tragedy *Hamlet*, but many of his other plays are well-known and appreciated.

   Before Shakespeare, the most famous writer of English literature was Geoffrey Chaucer. Chaucer lived from 1340 to 1400. He was a military man and later a member of the king's court. He was very influenced by Italian writers. Like Shakespeare, Chaucer also wrote poems, but his poems were much longer. His greatest work is the *Canterbury Tales*, which was never finished.
2. Many great scientific advances occurred in the 20th century. In the early 1900s Albert Einstein proposed his famous theories of relativity and strongly impacted the field of physics. In the 1930s, blood banking began because of the initiative of Dr. Bernard Francis. Approximately twenty years later Watson and Crick discovered the double helix structure of DNA. In 1977 the world's last naturally occurring case of smallpox was recorded, and the disease was finally vanquished.

   Many notable scientific achievements occurred before the 20th century as well. In the early 1500s the Polish astronomer Copernicus suggested that the planets moved around the sun. Later in 1543 Vesalius described human anatomy in one of the most significant medical books ever written. The laws of gravity, motion, and optics that Sir Isaac Newton developed at the end of the 17th century influenced the world for over 200 years.

3. Earthquakes can not be predicted by catfish. After studying catfish for sixteen years, Japanese researchers concluded that catfish could not serve as indicators of approaching earthquakes. The study, which cost $923,000, was done to determine if there was any truth to an ancient belief that ordinary catfish have the ability to predict earthquakes. Researchers learned that catfish do become more active before an earthquake. That information was not enough to provide reliable data, however. Catfish activity simply did not enable scientists to predict earthquakes accurately enough. As a result, funding for the study was stopped.

(No division is needed for this paragraph.)

Exercise 5: Organizing Text (page 160)
The text should be organized into three paragraphs.

It's important to store food carefully to maintain the quality and safety. Improperly stored food can cause health problems. Furthermore, food that is not stored properly will not taste very good.

Eggs are very perishable and require careful storage practices. Buy refrigerated grade A or AA eggs with uncracked, clean shells, and keep them refrigerated at 40 degrees or lower. Do not store eggs in the door of the refrigerator. Egg dishes can be left at room temperature for a maximum of two hours. These guidelines for egg storage will help ensure safety and quality.

Ice cream is another example of a food that benefits from proper storage. Keep ice cream stored at 0 degrees or lower. Once a carton of ice cream has been opened and used, put plastic wrap over the surface of the remaining ice cream before putting the carton's lid on and storing in the freezer. The plastic wrap will help prevent a skin from forming and help control the formation of ice crystals. Be careful to wrap other foods in the freezer tightly so that the odors do not taint the ice cream. A little effort can ensure some good results.

Exercise 6: Irrelevant Sentences (page 162)
The irrelevant sentences are in **bold type.**

It sometimes takes a lot of courage to make a change for the better in our world. One example of that kind of courage is found in the story of a priest named Damien and his attempt to help the sick. Many years ago, a disease known as leprosy caused people to develop terrible sores on their bodies and eventually die. **That was even before the development of computers.** The disease was highly contagious, so people were extremely afraid of contracting leprosy. **People were also afraid of other diseases as well.** In Hawaii those people who became afflicted with leprosy were taken to an island and left there without any medical care. Damien learned of the situation and went to the island to tend the sick. Not only did he tend the sick, but he also drew world attention to the suffering caused by this illness. His efforts inspired research which ultimately led to treatment and a cure. Unfortunately, Father Damien contracted the disease himself and died from it. He should be remembered as a courageous man.

Exercise 7: Transitional Expressions
Part A (page 164)
Some suggested answers are given in **bold type.** More than one choice is possible.

1. Mexico City is a very large city. **In fact,** it is the largest city in the world.
2. Life today is better in some ways than it was in the past. **For example,** in the past, people always had fleas all over themselves.
3. Modern doctors scrub and sterilize their equipment and hands. **Thus,** fewer people die from infections after operations.
4. My neighbor was a careless driver who was always in a hurry. **As a result,** one day he received a ticket.
5. We were really hoping to visit our family yesterday. **However,** we didn't have enough time to do so.

Part B (page 164)
The sentences may be completed in various ways. A possible answer in **bold type** is given for each.

1. Judy ate a cheeseburger, salad, baked potato, taco, and ice cream cone for lunch. As a result, **she didn't want any dinner.**
2. As we get older, we grow more experienced. Furthermore, **we become more patient.**

3. We would love to travel to many places in the world. For example, **we really wish we could go to Europe.**
4. Medical science has proven that smoking is very dangerous to health. Nevertheless, **many people continue to smoke.**
5. Our water has grown increasingly polluted. At the same time, **our air has become more polluted as well.**

Part C (page 165)
Answers may vary. Some suggested answers are in **bold type.**

The largest living thing on earth is a tree growing in Sequoia National Park in California. The sequoia also happens to be 2,300 to 2,700 years old. It is named the General Sherman Tree after a Civil War general, and its trunk weighs 1,385 tons. The height of the tree above the base is 274.9 feet. **Nevertheless,** the General Sherman Tree is not the tallest tree in the world. A taller tree, which is almost 100 feet taller, is a redwood on the California coast. **Furthermore,** a montezuma cypress in Mexico may be bigger in diameter than the General Sherman. The height and weight of the General Sherman, **however,** make it the largest living thing in the world.

GED Practice Exercise 8: Writing Errors (page 165)

1. **(1)** correct
2. **(3)** The sentence is irrelevant and does not support the paragraph's main idea.
3. **(5)** The meaning of the original can be preserved, and the sentence can be improved by omitting unnecessary words and using the active voice: *In 1999, the mint began issuing the first state quarters.*
4. **(3)** Correct the fragment by replacing *being* with the verb *is*.
5. **(4)** Correct the dangling modification by placing *the mint* after the modifying phrase *In addition to minting the state quarters.*
6. **(2)** Combine paragraphs B and C because both support the same topic sentence.
7. **(1)** Place a comma after an introductory phrase to a sentence.
8. **(5)** A topic sentence is needed to unify the paragraph: *A brief look at the history of coins reveals some surprising information.*
9. **(4)** Correct the pronoun reference error by using *it* to refer to *coin*.

CHAPTER 5
PREPARING FOR THE ESSAY

Exercises 1–5 (pages 170–176)
Answers will vary. Use the checklists provided to review each step of the process.

Exercise 6: Types of Writing (page 177)
The two types of writing used in the passage are description and narration.

Exercises 7–9 (pages 178–180)
Student writing will vary.

Exercise 10: Identifying Supporting Reasons (page 181)

1. no reason given
2. reason given
3. no reason given
4. no reason given
5. reason given

Exercise 11: Persuasive Writing (page 182)
Student writing will vary.

Exercise 12: Thesis Statements (page 185)

1. **(b)** A universal health care plan is needed in the US.
2. **(a)** The best things in life are not free; they are earned.
3. **(b)** Three major events that influenced my life were moving to another state, marrying the one I loved, and becoming a parent.

Exercise 13: Development and Support for an Essay (page 186)
Student writing will vary.

Exercise 14: Essay Analysis (page 187)

The first problem is that the essay does not have a clear focus or thesis statement. The second problem is that the essay rambles and lists ideas rather than developing them. The writer should have selected two or three strategies for dealing with stress and developed each with supporting examples and reasons.

A possible thesis statement for this essay might read: *In order to cope with stress, I read, walk, or talk with a friend.* Then the essay could develop those three strategies: *read, walk, talk.*

Exercises 15–17 (pages 187–190)

Answers and student writing will vary. Use the checklists to review the process at each step.

Exercise 18: Scoring and Evaluating Essays (page 193)

The scores below were assigned by the GED Testing Service. Each score is accompanied by an explanation and evaluation of the essay.

Essay A: **Score 3.** This essay is understandable and is plainly organized around a main idea based on the prompt—the desire to improve communication as a change in the writer's life. The central idea is given two strands of development—listening and speaking. Although each of these strands is discussed in a direct, understandable paragraph, the reader uses vague generalizations and restatements of the author's ideas rather than progressive development with specific details; for example, *Speaking and listening are two important communication skills* and *Listening is one of the most important listening skills.* Word choice is appropriate but somewhat monotonous. Sentence structure is under control, although there are usage errors such as *I would have less misunderstandings.* and *I could make others understand my meaning clearer and faster.* The conventions of Edited American English are generally controlled.

Essay B: **Score 1.** This essay is one brief paragraph of three sentences, and the reader at times has difficulty following the writer's ideas. While attempting to address the prompt, the writer fails to organize ideas, and the central theme expressed—"to obtain maximum opportunity"—is not developed with either examples or details. Although the writer generally adheres to the conventions of Edited American English in the first two sentences, weak word choice and faulty sentence structure in the last sentence reduce the essay's effectiveness.

Essay C: **Score 2.** In this essay, the prompt is addressed and a main idea immediately established. However, the long single paragraph reads as transcribed thought rather than planned writing and makes it difficult for a reader to follow the writer's ideas. The writer's focus on changing his or her attitude toward other people and life shifts at one point toward a discussion of life as a game. Other than the game metaphor, idea development is limited to insistent repetition of the need to change attitudes. Sentences that run together make reading difficult, and noticeable phrase repetition detracts from the essay. There are few errors in Edited American English, but the absence of appropriate commas impairs readability. Word choices are frequently inappropriate, marked by an intrusion of slang into an otherwise conventional voice.

Essay D: **Score 4.** In a clearly focused discussion, the writer focuses on the need to "stop being such a procrastinator." The reader moves smoothly and logically through a sequence of well-structured sentences describing parts of the psychological puzzle of procrastination. In a clearly organized plan, each paragraph grows progressively more intent on self-discipline so that the reader can appreciate the emotional growth sought by the writer. Ideas are developed with specific relevant examples and some humorous asides—"the angels in heaven above start biting their nails." The writer's choice of words is precise, varied, analytical, and intimate. The essay exhibits consistent control of the conventions of Edited American English throughout.

Source: GED Testing Service

Critical Thinking Skills for the GED

Developing strong reading and thinking (reasoning) skills is key to your success on the GED. This section focuses on skills you will use in taking all of the GED Tests, particularly the writing, reading, and social studies tests. **Knowledge** is the basis for reading and thinking skills. The skills you will develop to build on knowledge include **comprehension, application, analysis, synthesis,** and **evaluation.**

If these sound unfamiliar to you, don't be concerned. The purpose of this section is to provide practice in these six skill areas.

Why is it important for you to develop these skills? Perhaps you remember taking tests in school that required you to memorize and then recall facts. The GED Tests, however, do not test your memory. Instead, you will have to work with the information that you read and that you hold in your memory. In answering questions on the GED, you will comprehend, apply, analyze, synthesize, and evaluate what you read.

You can picture thinking skills as layers of a pyramid. Each higher-level skill rests on the skill that precedes it. That is, each skill is a stepping-stone to one at the next level. The pyramid of thinking skills is shown below.

Pyramid of Thinking Skills

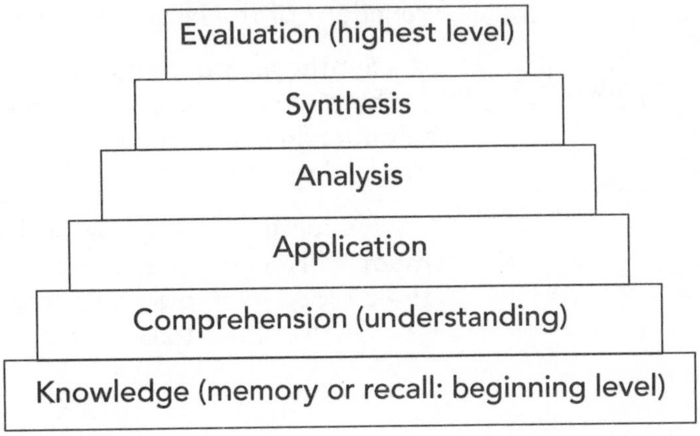

For the GED Test each level of the pyramid is just as important as any other. Mastery of higher-level thinking skills depends upon how well you can perform the lower-level skills. For example, if you don't know very many basic concepts in biology, it is unlikely that you will be able to comprehend information about human biology, apply biological concepts to another branch of science, analyze common problems in human biological systems, synthesize new results from a breeding experiment, or evaluate the impact of environmental changes on a certain species. You can use this example to help you remember what each of the thinking skills means.

Knowledge: also known as *concepts* or *memory* or *recall.* You gain knowledge through words, numbers, objects, and so on. You acquire basic concepts and use memory techniques. In the biology example this would mean memorizing the major systems of the human body.

Comprehension: show your understanding by interpreting or explaining in your own words what something means. In the biology example you might demonstrate comprehension of the major systems of the human body by paraphrasing or restating in your own words how the digestive system works.

Application: transfer your understanding of concepts or principles from one context to another. In the biology example you might apply what you know about cardiovascular systems to designing an exercise program for someone who needs to build endurance.

Analysis: examine the pieces to understand better what makes up the whole, and clarify the relationships among ideas or elements. In the biology example, you might compare and contrast the functions of the large and small intestines.

Synthesis: put many elements together to form something new. In the biology example you might use the scientific method to conduct an experiment breeding fruit flies, then write a paper describing your findings.

Evaluation: judge how well or how poorly an idea or object meets certain criteria, which can be either objective or subjective. In the biology example you might read about cloning theory and use your own criteria to decide if it should be explored.

LEVEL ONE

Knowledge

Forming, Attaining, or Recalling Concepts

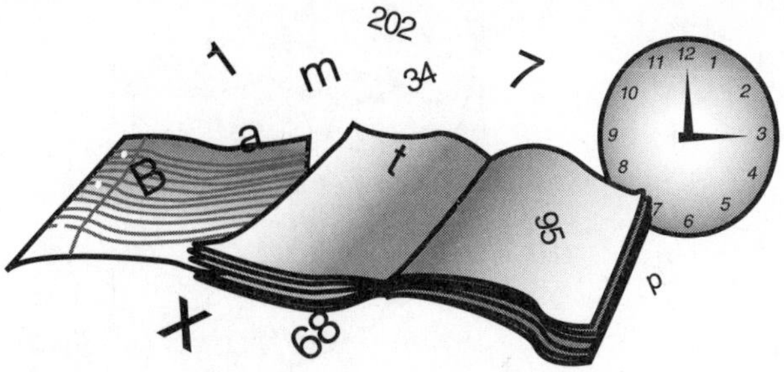

What is knowledge?

Knowledge, sometimes referred to as *concepts* or *memory* or *recall,* is the foundation of the thinking pyramid. You gain knowledge through words, numbers, objects, and so on. At the knowledge level—the base of the thinking pyramid—you *form and attain basic concepts* and use *memory techniques.*

When you form concepts, you notice names, patterns, categories, examples or instances, attributes (characteristics), values, or rules (definitions or statements). To illustrate, let's take a quick trip to the zoo to visit some of the inhabitants.

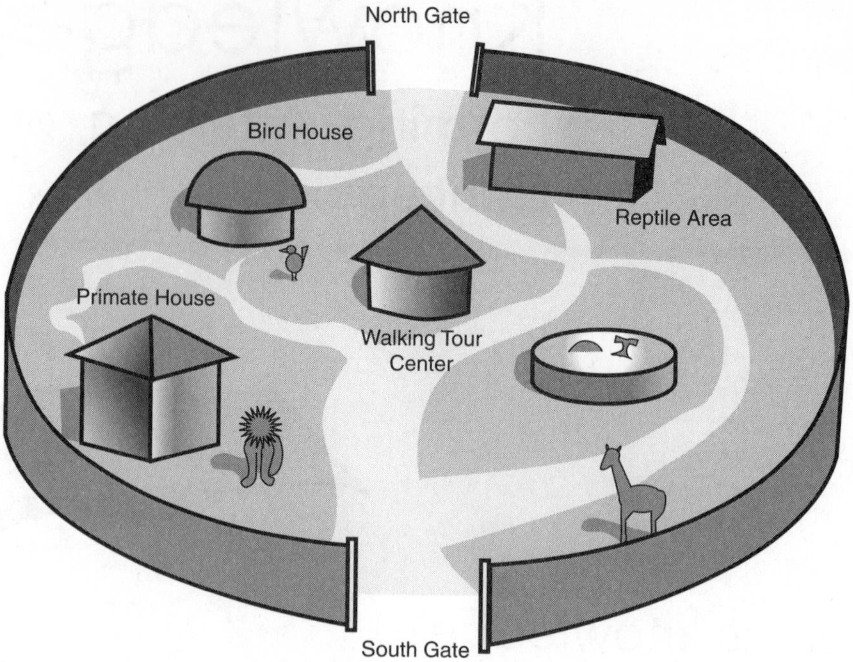

- Names: Ramar, Melouprey, Labybird
- Patterns

  Animal enclosures: males only, females and young, males/females

  Locations: North Gate, South Gate; East Mall, West Mall; Walking Tour Center, Tram/Train Center

  Restaurants: restaurant, lodge, hut, café, garden, patio, cucina (Italian kitchen)
- Categories

  Primates, birds, reptiles

  Countries of origin: Australia, South Africa, India

  Habitats: land, sea, air

  Exhibit houses: Pachyderm House, Perching Bird House, Reptile House

  Reviews: leisure stroll, special exhibits (white crocodile), planned shows (dolphin)
- Examples or instances

  Silver-back gorilla, white-checked gibbon, Guam kingfisher
- Attributes (characteristics)

  Wild-born, no offspring, swing with arms from limb to limb

  Bonds by digging a nest out of a log

  Adult females return to same beach and nesting place; know how to pick algae from rocks.

- Values

  Concern for all living things

  Respect for all safety barriers

  Harmony with nature

- Rules (definitions or statements)

  All buildings at the zoo must be smoke-free.

  For the safety of animals and guests, bicycles and skates are not allowed.

Memory helps you answer the questions *who, what, when, where,* and *how.*

You use memory or recall techniques through:

- Developing awareness

  Underlining

  Midwest Zoo is home to over <u>2,700 animals</u> and over <u>400 different species.</u>

  Listing

  Some of these include *antelope, giraffes, penguins, seals,* and *walruses.*

  Reflecting

  More than thirty animals (lions, elephants, baboons, zebras, etc.) represent the **favorites** for most people.

- Developing associations

  Key words

  living kingdom, fragile kingdom, coast, desert, woods, world, oasis

  Substitute words

  endangered species, planned protection

  Links to other words or ideas

  multizoo breeding, cooperative programs

- Expanding sensory images

  ray of hope, fight for survival

- Recognizing ideas

  Zoo parent programs contribute animal maintenance funds.

  Zoo research studies investigate behaviors, habitats, breeding successes.

- Practicing recall

  Endangered species: **A** is for alligator; **L** is for leopard; **T** is for tiger; **W** is for wolf.

Practice Assignment

Take a trip to your local zoo, or take a trip to the botanical gardens, a museum of natural history, or anywhere else where there is obvious organization. Make notes of the names, patterns, categories, examples, attributes, values, or rules you find there. Form your own concepts. Then practice recall techniques using the approach described in the zoo example on pages 214–215.

Notes

Level One—Knowledge: Key Concepts

LEVEL TWO

Comprehension

Understanding What You Read

What is comprehension?

Comprehension is the second level of the thinking pyramid. Light bulbs are a symbol for understanding because many people associate comprehension or understanding with "a light going on" or an "Aha!" expression. You achieve comprehension by translating words into meaning, interpreting meaning, or extrapolating meaning. You show your understanding by interpreting or explaining in your own words what something means.

When you **translate words into meaning,** you follow directions, read literally (that is, word-for-word), reword a message, translate expressions from one language to another, or convert a message into other forms of communication.

When you **interpret meaning,** you explain clearly what the text means or you paraphrase ideas. You think about the importance of ideas and how the ideas relate. You make inferences on your own from unstated main ideas or assumptions. (The ideas or assumptions are not stated directly, so you are really **reading between the lines.**) You also make generalizations or produce summaries.

When you **extrapolate meaning,** you try to understand general trends, tendencies, or conditions in given information. Then you apply your understanding to make estimates or predictions.

Translating Words into Meaning

Putting a Message into Other Words

In order to translate words into meaning, you may have to express a message in simpler words so that someone else can understand it. When a particular group uses language that is unfamiliar to someone outside the group, it would be of no help to repeat the message word for word. Instead, you would give the intended meaning. Consider the following example in which a "techie" (someone very good with technology) speaks to someone who knows very little about computers.

Techie: Antivirus software helps guard against infections.

Unfamiliar literal translation: Anti-illness soft clothing helps guard against diseases.

Intended meaning: Programs that can be added to the computer help guard against computer malfunctions. (Malfunctions include shutdowns and information loss.)

A word-for-word, literal repetition of the techie's statement would not communicate the meaning. You would have to translate (explain in other words) what the computer expert intended to express. Only by giving such an explanation could you show that you comprehended, or understood, what the techie said.

Using Idiomatic Expressions

Putting a message into other terms sometimes involves using different forms of the same language. **Idiomatic expressions** are a different form of a language. Idiomatic expressions, like slang, do not follow the rules of grammar, so it is difficult to translate them. We use them every day, however, and they add color and interest to the English language.

Common examples of idiomatic expressions are *go for broke* (do whatever it takes), *run it up the flagpole* (seek higher-level approval), *out of the blue* (unexpected), *clear the air* (discuss a misunderstanding), and *push the envelope* (stretch the limits). To understand how the meaning of an idiomatic expression involves word associations, consider the expression *out of the blue.* We associate the color blue with the sky. *Out of the blue* suggests that something drops out of the sky unexpectedly. Thus, the idiomatic expression is understood to mean "unexpected" or "sudden."

EXERCISE 1

Understanding Idiomatic Expressions

Directions: Read the following paragraph and put the numbered words or phrases into other terms by writing the intended meaning for each. The first one is done for you.

Last year Pam and Rob had planned, then decided against, a trip to Australia. This time they decided (1) to go one better. They were (2) up to their necks with settling in a new house and trying to housetrain a new puppy. They planned a five-week trip (3) across the "Big Pond." Pam (4) brushed up on her French and Rob on his Spanish in order (5) to get by. They arranged for train, ship, and car transportation. They couldn't bear, however, to put their dog (6) under lock and key. Instead of sending Molly to stay with the veterinarian, two sets of puppy grandparents (7) came to the rescue. The four would take turns taking care of Molly, knowing they would have (8) to keep their eyes peeled. At the end of five weeks, Molly was (9) none the worse for wear. Her owners were surprised that she even (10) tipped the scales five pounds higher.

1. to outdo or surpass ______ 6. ______

2. ______ 7. ______

3. ______ 8. ______

4. ______ 9. ______

5. ______ 10. ______

Answers are on page 288.

Interpreting Meaning

Explaining Implications of Text

In order to explain what the text means, you must first think about the meaning of words, phrases, and sentences that make up the text. You can ask yourself any of the *who, what, when, where, why,* and *how* questions that are relevant. This helps you to understand the context and arrive at an overall impression and explanation of the text. You show your understanding by being able to explain the text in written, verbal, or graphic form.

Example:

When the Wright brothers finally realized their vision of powered human flight in 1903 at Kitty Hawk, N.C., they made the world a forever smaller place.

Who was involved? the Wright brothers

What did they do? finally realized their vision of powered human flight [finally invented the airplane]

When? in 1903

Where did it take place? Kitty Hawk, N.C. [North Carolina]

Why was this important? They made the world a forever smaller place. [They made it possible for people to travel by airplane all over the world, thereby "shrinking" the world forever.]

EXERCISE 2

Explaining Implications of Text

Directions: Read the following statements and explain the implications of the text.

Statement 1:

After 1905 a psychology professor at Stanford named Lewis Terman believed IQ tests should be used to conduct a great sorting out of the population so that young people would be assigned on the basis of their scores to particular levels in the school system, which would lead to corresponding socioeconomic destinations in adult life.

Who is the subject of the paragraph?

___

When did he state his beliefs?

___

Where did he do his work?

___

What did he believe?

___

Then **what** would result?

___

What are the long-term results of these beliefs and practices?

___

Statement 2:

Just by thinking about it, Albert Einstein discovered the essential structure of the cosmos. The scientific touchstones of our age—the Bomb, space travel, electronics—all bear his fingerprints.

Who? ___

What did he do? ___

How did he do it? ___

What did it lead to? ___

___

Answers are on page 288.

Paraphrasing or Restating Ideas

On the GED Tests you may be required to show how well you comprehend the text by recognizing a restatement of a phrase, a sentence, or an idea. When you paraphrase (restate) information, you use different words and phrases to express the same idea. The following are two examples of restated information.

1. Original

That author's enlightening new book gives deep insights into the nature of human relationships.

Restatement

There is a lot to learn about how people get along from the author's new book.

2. Original

During the last four decades, family life has become more complicated, less locked in to traditional roles.

Restatement

In the last forty years, family life has become harder to define.

EXERCISE 3

Paraphrasing or Restating Ideas

Directions: Rewrite the following sentences in your own words.

1. *This distinctive learning environment in small classes allows me to interact personally with each of my students and ensure their thorough understanding of demanding coursework.*

—David Macaulay, chemistry professor, in the *Daily Herald,* December 6, 1998

Restatement ______________________________

____

2. *The major stumbling block is guaranteeing safeguards against fraud. Critics say a voter's identity cannot be verified over the Internet.*

—John F. Kennedy, Jr., *USA Weekend,* June 11–13, 1999

Restatement ______________________________

____

3. *"Becky Thatcher," actually Laura Hawkins, was Sam Clemens's [Mark Twain's] childhood sweetheart immortalized in print in* Tom Sawyer.

—1999 Visitor's Guide: Hannibal, Missouri, and Mark Twain Lake

Restatement ______________________________

____

Answers are on page 288.

Making Inferences from Unstated Main Ideas

Read the following biographical family sketch and compose a main idea from the information given.

A Family Portrait

The mother was born in the United States, but was taken to Sicily at a young age; she lived half her life there and had all but the last two of eight children there. As an American citizen she was able to emigrate to the United States, taking one daughter with her. Later, other family members came to the United States a few at a time between 1947 and 1949 and settled in Chicago. On a rare day in 1952, all ten family members were home at the same time when a photographer came to the door. He was going door to door and asking whether families wanted to pose for portraits. Someone rounded up everyone in the family and lined them up. The father and the oldest boy found suits to wear. All six daughters wore rather ordinary clothes, but someone arranged bows in the hair of the three youngest girls to help them "dress up." The strap was missing on the shoe of the eight-year-old, but she beamed anyway. Little did they know that this impromptu portrait would be the *only* complete family portrait they would ever take.

Hint: *Think about the past, present, and future.*

Your expression of the main idea is: ________________________________

____

The main idea could be: *Take advantage of the present because the future is unknown.* The reader must infer this from the details provided: *she [the mother]; was able to emigrate to the United States; On a rare day in 1952, all ten family members were home; a photographer came to the door, this impromptu portrait would be the only complete family portrait . . . ever.*

The next exercise provides practice reading between the lines to determine the main idea.

GED PRACTICE

EXERCISE 4

Making Inferences (Reading between the Lines)

Directions: Read the passage and answer the questions that follow on page 224.

In Search of Reality

A news feature told a story that very likely happened during a war. It could have been about any war, but the specifics named the Korean Conflict. It could have been about any soldiers, but it involved American GIs. It could have been about any "enemy," but it identified civilians in South Korea in the summer of 1950. The United States government denies any factual knowledge of the incident.

Korean witnesses of the incident insist that over fifty years ago hundreds of refugees were killed beneath a bridge in a hamlet. These witnesses sought redress and compensation from the U.S. military and the South Korean government, but their claims were rejected. Later some twelve surviving ex-Gis confirmed some of the allegations of the peasants. The ex-GIs said Americans thought North Korean soldiers might be disguised wearing "peasant white" clothes like the South Koreans. The Americans were said to be under orders to let no one through, not soldiers, not civilians.

Source: "Massacre Under the Bridge," by Sang-Hun Choe and Martha Mendoza. *Associated Press*, September 3, 1999

1. **What does the writer imply with the line, "It could have been about any war, but the specifics named the Korean Conflict"?**
   (1) The incident involving the Korean Conflict was the worst possible war occurrence.
   (2) The specific details of any war are impossible to verify because of so much action.
   (3) Incidents such as the one relating to the Korean Conflict might have happened before.
   (4) Specific incidents of war usually are forgotten in the overall outcome.
   (5) There was doubt as to whether this incident happened during the Korean Conflict.

2. **What inference can you draw from the line, "The Americans were said to be under orders to let no one through, not soldiers, not civilians"?**
   (1) Americans had the right to judge the correctness of military orders.
   (2) Americans were not paid to interpret the orders given.
   (3) Americans were confused as to the real intent of the orders given.
   (4) Americans were outraged by the nature of their orders.
   (5) Americans apparently placed high value on obeying orders.

3. **What is the unstated main idea of the passage?**
   (1) Acts committed during time of war are not subject to punishment.
   (2) Truth, especially as it relates to war, is difficult to determine.
   (3) During the Korean Conflict, the United States was protecting democracy.
   (4) North Koreans cannot be distinguished easily from South Koreans.
   (5) The American military needs to review its methods of training.

4. **Which of the following details is *not* stated in the passage?**
   (1) The incident could have happened with any soldiers in any war.
   (2) The U.S. government denies any factual knowledge of the incident.
   (3) Some twelve surviving ex-GIs confirmed some of the allegations.
   (4) The story identified civilians in South Korea in the summer of 1950.
   (5) North Korean soldiers would never be disguised in peasant clothes.

Answers are on page 288.

Producing Summaries

Does this happen to you? You answer the phone at work for another coworker, and the caller gives you a long story about the reason for the call. You generally won't write down every word the caller says. You summarize the message, writing down the key thought or purpose of the call. Another time you might jot down key words or summarize main ideas is when you take class notes.

Here's an example of a message one teacher took for another teacher.

Summarized message:

> To: Mike
>
> From: Lee
>
> Mrs. Kim called. Daughter Anita. Upset about book report grade. Computer down. Quoted department policy. Call mother at work: 555-5555.

Full message represented by the summary:

> To: Mike
>
> From: Lee
>
> Mrs. Kim is very upset that her daughter, a sophomore in high school, received a grade of "0" on her book report. She said that her daughter Anita's book report was late because the computer crashed in the middle of typing the report and she couldn't turn it in on Monday. I asked her how long her daughter had been given to do the assignment, and she said three weeks. I asked why Anita had waited so long to do the assignment and why she hadn't just done the assignment longhand. I reminded Mrs. Kim that department policy does not permit late papers unless there are extenuating circumstances. Please call her at work to reiterate this policy.

SKILL BUILDER

Summarizing the Main Idea

1. Circle key words in a sentence. Which words are absolutely necessary to get the message across?
2. Identify key ideas (groups of key words) contained in a paragraph. List what these ideas have in common. This is the main idea.
3. Notice headlines and titles; they usually contain key ideas.

EXERCISE 5

Summarizing the Main Idea

Directions: Practice summarizing the following message. Use page 227 to write your summary.

Full message (to Christopher from his roommate at college):

Christopher, your mother called from Paris! She said you can't use your family credit cards. She was very upset, but everyone is all right. She lost her wallet while getting on a subway train. She thinks that a young boy and girl who bumped her reached into her purse and stole her wallet. Then they jumped off the train just before the train pulled away. Your mom and dad and aunt and uncle got off at the next stop and immediately went back to the same train stop. The kids were gone, so your mom and the others went to ask the clerk at the station for help. Your aunt did the best she could to try to speak French to the clerk to say what happened. The clerk advised them to to report it to the police.

They had a hard time asking people on the street for directions to the police station. They found it about 45 minutes later and found a very sympathetic English-speaking police officer who took their report. The officer says this happens all the time, and he let your mom use the phone to call the international credit card bureau. She can't get her French francs back, but she reported her credit cards as stolen. The credit card companies closed those accounts immediately, but the young thieves (probably working with their parents) managed to charge over $800 in drapery fabric (of all things) in the time it took to get to the station. Your family is not liable for unauthorized charges, but it will be a few days before cards with new numbers are issued and sent to all of you. Chris, in the meantime, if you need to buy something, I'll put it on my credit card and you can pay me back later.

Possible answers are on page 289.

Extrapolating or Interpolating Meaning

You've already translated words into meaning and interpreted the meaning and intent of words and ideas. A third way to improve your comprehension is to extrapolate or interpolate ideas. To **extrapolate** is to predict from past experience or known data. To **interpolate** is to insert words or values between known text or values.

To extrapolate or interpolate meaning, you try to understand general **trends, tendencies,** or **conditions** in information that you have already. Sometimes you have to make **estimates** or **predictions** when the information is not complete.

Consider the following example. A young couple, Jeff and Jennifer, decided to move with Maggie, their chocolate Labrador Retriever dog, from an apartment in one city to a house in another. How can they decide the method of moving? What arrangements would you make if you were to move?

What information is given?

- who is to be relocated
    - family members
    - pets

What information is extrapolated?

- the 750-mile distance between cities
- the time of year
- what is to be relocated
    - cars or other vehicles
    - furniture, appliances, and so on
    - household goods

EXERCISE 6

Extrapolating or Interpolating Meaning

Directions: Help Jeff and Jennifer consider the method of moving they will use. Finish the statements from the information given.

Trend A: You do some research and learn that a trend in long-distance moving involves three types of contracts. What are the *implications* or *consequences* of each type?

Option 1: A company offers a "nonbinding estimate" of $1,800; based on the weight of your household goods and furniture. You don't know, however, how much your beds, dressers, and other heavy pieces of furniture really weigh.

Implications: Why is this method difficult to budget?

Option 2: A company offers a "binding" (or set) price of $2,200. The fair price may be above or below that.

Implications: What is the disadvantage of this method, even though it allows you to budget moving expenses exactly?

Option 3: A company offers a "not to exceed" price of $2,400. The price could go down but not up.

Implications: What about the judgment of the estimator? What about the top price?

Trend B: Your research also tells you that delivery time generally is two to six days.

Implications: Can everything that is to be moved be put on the truck? What do you need while you wait for your furniture to arrive?

What estimates or predictions can you make about the movers for Jeff and Jennifer?

1. Price: ______________________________

____

2. Fairness versus uncertainty: ______________________________

____

3. Flexibility: ______________________________

____

Possible answers are on page 289.

Notes

Level Two—Comprehension: Key Concepts

LEVEL THREE

Application

Applying What You Read

What is application?

One of the most important outcomes of education is the ability to apply what you have learned. Our symbol for application is a "leap" (a mental one) because the figure above seems to be leaping from one situation to another. Using the skill of **application,** you show that you can transfer your understanding of concepts or principles from the reading passage to a new context or situation. For example, apprentice painters must be able to apply principles of color and texture before they can be awarded their journeymen status and actually work on homes. Likewise, paralegal assistants must be able to apply knowledge learned in a certificate program before they can earn their certificates and work in law offices.

In solving problems on the GED Tests, you will have to apply knowledge that you have gained. You may be given information in the form of a definition, theory, or principle. You will encounter application questions primarily in the areas of science and social studies; however, the Language Arts, Reading Test will include some application questions as well.

GED PRACTICE

EXERCISE 7

Applying Appropriate Definitions or Principles

Directions: To practice your skill in applying definitions, read the following passage about forms of drama and answer the questions that follow.

The major forms of drama are the comedy and the tragedy. Comedies generally are light and amusing. They usually begin in humorously difficult situations and always end happily. Not all comedies are funny and lighthearted, although the majority are. One type of comedy is slapstick, a form of physical comedy that includes pratfalls (embarrassing mishaps) and pie-in-the-face acts. Farce is another type of comedy that features exaggerated circumstances, improbable plots, and foolish action and dialogue.

In contrast to comedies, tragedies often begin happily but always end in disaster. The main character is usually good, but loses to an opponent in a conflict and is either ruined or killed. The major reason for the main character's failure is his or her tragic flaw—the human weakness that has made the tragic hero or heroine vulnerable.

Somewhere between comedy and tragedy lies melodrama, a type of drama that emphasizes the plot and provides thrilling action.

1. Which of the following best classifies the highly physical humor featured by classic comedians such as the Three Stooges or Chevy Chase in the *Vacation* movies?

(1) comedy
(2) slapstick
(3) farce
(4) tragedy
(5) melodrama

2. In the 1990s *Friends* was a popular television program. It portrayed the activities of six young women and men who lived across the hall from each other. What is the best description for this humorous, easygoing look at friendships?

(1) comedy
(2) slapstick
(3) farce
(4) tragedy
(5) melodrama

3. *NYPD Blue* is a popular television police story about serious situations and thrilling action on the streets of New York City. What is this series an example of?

(1) comedy
(2) slapstick
(3) farce
(4) tragedy
(5) melodrama

4. The movie *Titanic* and the book *A Night to Remember* were based on the sinking of a passenger ship. The ship was on its first voyage, and many lives were lost. What is this an example of?

(1) comedy
(2) slapstick
(3) farce
(4) tragedy
(5) melodrama

5. *Third Rock from the Sun* is a comedy whose main characters are aliens who try to have relationships with humans. What is this an example of?

(1) comedy
(2) slapstick
(3) farce
(4) tragedy
(5) melodrama

Answers are on page 289.

GED PRACTICE

EXERCISE 8

Using Application in Science

Directions: Read the definitions below and apply the information to answer the following questions.

The human body is composed of several systems that keep it functioning. Though each system may be viewed separately, it is closely related to the others in the body. A problem in one system invariably affects another. Defined below are five of at least ten systems that make up the human body.

excretory system—the system that excretes or expels water and salts from the body; it includes the urinary system, in which the kidneys, ureters, urethra, and bladder play vital roles

endocrine system—the system made up of glands such as the pituitary, thyroid, and adrenal, which secrete body fluids, stimulating cells and regulating the body's development

lymphatic system—the system that circulates lymph (a pale fluid) to the body's tissues, bathing the cells; lymphocytes found in the system produce antibodies that help fight bacterial infections

digestive system—the system that processes and distributes nutrients from food; composed chiefly of the esophagus, stomach, liver, and large and small intestines

muscular system—the system composed of the three types of tissue that enable the body and its parts to move

1. **AIDS (acquired immunodeficiency syndrome) is a disease that inhibits the body's ability to fight off infections. AIDS would interfere mainly with the proper functioning of which system?**

   (1) excretory
   (2) endocrine
   (3) lymphatic
   (4) digestive
   (5) muscular

2. **The skin (the body's largest organ) may be defined loosely as belonging to this system since, through perspiration, wastes are removed from the body.**

   (1) excretory
   (2) endocrine
   (3) lymphatic
   (4) digestive
   (5) muscular

3. Enlargement of the thyroid gland in the neck, increased appetite, and weight loss are possible symptoms of an overactive thyroid (hyperthyroidism). This is a disease of which system?

(1) excretory
(2) endocrine
(3) lymphatic
(4) digestive
(5) muscular

4. A new "super aspirin" pain reliever (Cox-2 inhibitor), available only by prescription, is said to work especially well with inflammation of joints and muscles. This drug would help with pain in which system?

(1) excretory
(2) endocrine
(3) lymphatic
(4) digestive
(5) muscular

5. A number of foods including apples, berries, broccoli, fish, nuts, brown rice, and tomatoes are said to inhibit the growth of cancerous tumors. The processing of foods in the body is through which system?

(1) excretory
(2) endocrine
(3) lymphatic
(4) digestive
(5) muscular

Answers are on page 289.

Notes

Level Three—Application: Key Concepts

LEVEL FOUR

Analysis

Examining What You Read

What is analysis?

When you analyze something, you take it apart. You examine the content to understand better what makes up the whole. A symbol for analysis can be the magnifying glass because in **analysis** you look closely at individual elements when you examine content. When you analyze, you do one of several things. You identify, classify, or distinguish elements. You make explicit (fully clear) the relationships among ideas or elements. Lastly, you recognize organizational or structural patterns.

On the GED Tests you will be expected to analyze complete passages in the areas of social studies, science, and reading. You will look at specific ideas and pieces of information to understand better the point being made by a writer, graphic artist, or cartoonist.

Recognizing the Main Idea

One way to show that you can analyze material is to recognize the main idea(s). The **main idea** sums up what the writer is saying. In a paragraph the main idea often is stated first. **Details** (or subordinate ideas) that support the main idea are included in the sentences that follow.

Hint: *Sometimes articles that appear as a passage (several paragraphs) in a newspaper or magazine are really one cohesive paragraph.*

Read the following paragraph to identify the main idea. Where is the main idea stated in the paragraph?

New research is overturning old notions about how the brain works. Once thought to be unchangeable, unrepairable, and constantly losing neurons, the brain is now seen to be always changing, eminently repairable, and constantly making new cells. One of the new findings, which has enormous implications, involves brain stem cells, a newly discovered cell that has the almost magical ability to make every other type of brain cell, including more of itself. Preliminary experiments in animals suggest it may be possible to inject brain stem cells into patients with a wide range of mental disorders to cure diseases such as Alzheimer's disease and multiple sclerosis.

—Excerpted from "Stem cells opening path to brain repair," *Chicago Tribune*, June 27, 1999

Which of the following sentences states the main idea of this passage?

(1) The older one gets, the more brain cells are lost.
(2) Research is changing ideas about brain repair.
(3) The brain remains unchangeable and unrepairable.
(4) Animal experiments involving brain cells are promising.
(5) Stem cells cannot cure mental disorders such as Alzheimer's.

The correct answer is (2). The main idea of the passage is stated in the introductory sentence: *New research is overturning old notions about how the brain works.* The passage goes on to explain how the brain can change, repair itself, and make new cells. Choice (1) is not expressed in the passage. Choice (3) is contradicted by the statement *the brain is now seen to be always changing. . . .* Choice (4) agrees with the statement, *Preliminary experiments in animals suggest it may be possible . . . to cure diseases. . . ,* but does not tell what the whole paragraph is about. Choice (5) agrees with the last sentence in the paragraph which once again states *it may be possible to inject brain stem cells. . . ,* but the whole paragraph is not about stem cells.

Read the passage below. Where is the main idea placed in the paragraph?

In 1932 the Museum of Modern Art conducted an exhibit that introduced American architects to European "modernism," with emphasis on glass and steel. In 1966 architect Robert Venturi affirmed the right of designers to use "ornament" in their buildings. Both events emphasized that ideas definitely influence the buildings that influence our lives. It was in 1909, however, that Frank Lloyd Wright introduced the "modernist" Robie House, while Daniel Burnham and Edward Bennett set up the "classical" Plan of Chicago. These two strands capture opposite trends that continue to this day. Thus, 1909 is thought of as the top year for architecture in the twentieth century.

Source: "The Best Years of the Century," *Chicago Tribune*, September 26, 1999

The main idea is stated in the last sentence of the paragraph: *Thus, 1909 is thought of as the top year for architecture in the twentieth century.* The main idea is stated only after supporting details have built a case for it: *In 1932 the Museum of Modern Art, In 1966 architect Robert Venturi, In 1909 . . . Frank Lloyd Wright, . . . Daniel Burnham and Edward Bennett . . .*

If the main idea is not the first sentence in the paragraph, it will most likely be the last sentence in the paragraph.

Read the passage below. Where is the main idea placed in the paragraph?

> JFK, Jr. did not earn his freedom by playing cautiously. "Men are not made for safe havens," lectured his Uncle Bobby. Taking physical risks is a Kennedy family tradition. During World War II, the oldest son Joe Jr., chose the riskiest service branch, naval aviation, and died on a virtual suicide mission in a plane rigged out as a giant bomb. Jack Kennedy chose PT boats, rickety crafts whose crews boasted that "they were expendable." Bobby Kennedy's children always seemed to be falling out of trees. "Aren't you worried about them?" friends asked Ethel Kennedy. "No," she said. She was following the example of Rose and Joe Kennedy, who believed that their kids needed to endure bumps and bruises and breaks. Far worse, the Kennedys believed, was to grow up afraid.
>
> —Excerpted from "Living with the Myth," Special Report by Evan Thomas
> *Newsweek*, July 26, 1999

As you saw in the passage above, occasionally writers put the main idea in the middle of a paragraph. Then the author must ensure that enough supporting details are included before or after to "add up" to the main point the writer is trying to make: *Taking physical risks is a Kennedy family tradition.* Can you see how the sentences before it and the sentences that follow it all add up to the main idea? Most of the details support the *Taking physical risks is a Kennedy family tradition* idea in the middle of the paragraph.

Sometimes the last sentence also serves as a transition to the next paragraph. Note that the last sentence in the example paragraph serves two functions. First, it sums up the details in the paragraph by stating that it was *Far worse . . . to grow up afraid.* That same sentence provides a transition by introducing the main idea in the next paragraph. In the paragraph that follows, the main idea is stated first: *Kennedys extol* [praise] *bravery.*

Relevant and Extraneous Material

As you analyze material, sometimes you have to determine whether the material is **relevant.** This means that the material belongs with or is applicable to the idea(s) in the selection. You may determine that the material is **extraneous**—that it has no relevance or is not vital to the idea(s) in the selection. One way to determine relevance is to be able to recognize propaganda. **Propaganda** is information provided in such a way as to influence or slant the opinion or feelings of the audience that receives the message. When you recognize propaganda, you lessen the power of others to influence you.

Listed below are five techniques used by propagandists.

1. **name-calling**—attaching an unfavorable name to an idea, a person, or a group so as to influence the attitude of the audience against the idea or position

2. **glittering generalities**—high-sounding, but general and vague terms used to influence positively the feelings of the audience toward a subject

3. **bandwagoning**—advising people to do something because "everyone" does it, because it is popular, or because it is the "in" thing to do

4. **transferring**—associating the respect, prestige, or power of one person or object with another person or product so that the audience is influenced favorably

5. **card-stacking**—choosing only specific, favorable points that support a cause and ignoring the unfavorable points

EXERCISE 9

Recognizing Propaganda Techniques

Directions: Look at the following statements and determine the method of propaganda used.

1. **A prominent female psychologist who had appeared on television was hired by a national real estate company to help counsel families enduring the stresses of buying and selling homes. Using the name and reputation of the doctor is an example of which technique?**

   (1) name-calling
   (2) glittering generalities
   (3) bandwagoning
   (4) transferring
   (5) card-stacking

2. **An advertisement promoted the use of natural herbs such as ginkgo biloba (for memory loss) or St. John's Wort (for mild depression). If the advertisement were not to mention possible side effects such as photosensitivity or blood thinning, it is using which technique?**

   (1) name-calling
   (2) glittering generalities
   (3) bandwagoning
   (4) transferring
   (5) card-stacking

3. In preparation for the turn of the century and the new millennium, many people convinced others that they should prepare for the "Y2K [Year 2000] problem" by stocking up on canned food, water, cash, etc. If people did this just because so many others were doing it, what technique was involved?

(1) name-calling
(2) glittering generalities
(3) bandwagoning
(4) transferring
(5) card-stacking

4. In response to teenage violence in the schools in recent years, many school boards have adopted a "zero tolerance" policy toward student threats or actual violence. A well-known political activist who labelled certain school boards as "racist" was using which technique?

(1) name-calling
(2) glittering generalities
(3) bandwagoning
(4) transferring
(5) card-stacking

5. In an effort to attract adult students, colleges and universities have advertised with slogans such as "college of the future," "21st-century learning environment," or "virtual university." These slogans are examples of which technique?

(1) name-calling
(2) glittering generalities
(3) bandwagoning
(4) transferring
(5) card-stacking

6. The local public school board is asked to consider a proposal from a group of parents to start up a separate "charter school." The parents have sought and won approval from the State Board of Education. The teachers in the school district are not in favor of the proposal and appeal to the school board to disapprove the proposal, arguing that their national teachers' association opposes it. What propaganda technique is illustrated here?

(1) name-calling
(2) glittering generalities
(3) bandwagoning
(4) transferring
(5) card-stacking

Answers are on page 289.

Distinguishing Facts from Opinions and Hypotheses

Some of the material you will read on the GED Tests will be based on facts, opinions, or hypotheses. **Facts** can be proved by using one or more of the five senses. Newspapers and magazine articles are based largely on facts.

Opinions are beliefs that may or may not be supported by facts. Opinions express feelings or ideas and are influenced greatly by one's background, values, and outlook on life. For example, editorials and columns in newspapers generally present a writer's opinions along with the facts.

Hypotheses are educated guesses that are made to explain a phenomenon or an event. Hypotheses may be proved or disproved by the passage of time or the acquiring of additional information. The statements below show how facts, opinions, and hypotheses differ.

EXERCISE 10

Recognizing Facts, Opinions, and Hypotheses

Directions: Read each group of statements below. Write *F* for the statements that express a fact, *O* for those that express an opinion, and *H* for those that express a hypothesis.

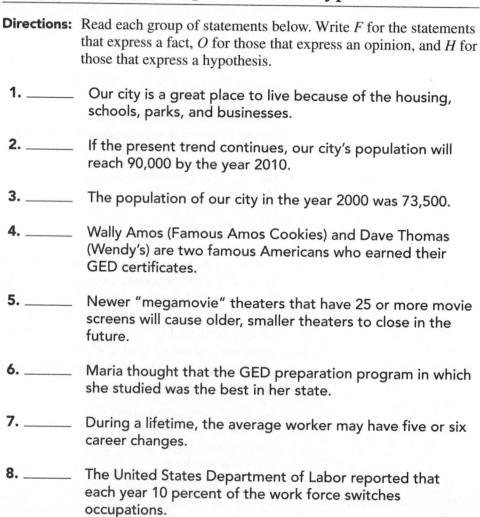

1. ______ Our city is a great place to live because of the housing, schools, parks, and businesses.

2. ______ If the present trend continues, our city's population will reach 90,000 by the year 2010.

3. ______ The population of our city in the year 2000 was 73,500.

4. ______ Wally Amos (Famous Amos Cookies) and Dave Thomas (Wendy's) are two famous Americans who earned their GED certificates.

5. ______ Newer "megamovie" theaters that have 25 or more movie screens will cause older, smaller theaters to close in the future.

6. ______ Maria thought that the GED preparation program in which she studied was the best in her state.

7. ______ During a lifetime, the average worker may have five or six career changes.

8. ______ The United States Department of Labor reported that each year 10 percent of the work force switches occupations.

Answers are on page 289.

Adequacy of Facts

Before you reach a decision or draw a conclusion, you need to evaluate the information that is available. Is there enough information to make this decision? Is this decision supported adequately by the facts?

When you don't have all the facts, you can't make an informed decision. Suppose you were interested in an issue in your community, such as "Should a new community center be built to provide services for lower-income residents?" To be able to judge how you feel about the issue, you need to know all the facts. You need to know the following:

1. How many people could be served at the center (each day, week, month, or year)?
2. Which agencies, groups, or institutions will provide services?
3. What will the services be (adult education classes, medical services, counseling, recreation, child care, and so on)?
4. Will the services be free to residents, on sliding scale, or at full charge?
5. Who will pay for the construction project? Will local taxes be increased to support the center?
6. Where will people park? What will be the impact on the neighboring businesses?

Knowing these facts (and others) will help you decide where you stand on the community center issue.

Similarly, when you answer questions on the GED Tests, you may need to determine whether there is enough information to support the writer's conclusion or point of view.

EXERCISE 11

Determining Adequacy of Facts

Directions: Read the passage from *MoneySmart* by weekend magazine columnist Jean Sherman Chatzky. The passage is a commentary about serious debt reduction. Put **F** next to the charges that the commentator has supported with facts, **CS** next to those supported with credible sources, and **N** next to comments for which the author has not cited any evidence.

Is counseling right for you? If you're far behind on payments, look into joining a program, says Gerri Detweiler, co-author of *Slash Your Debt* (Financial Literacy Center, $10.95). If you're just having trouble making ends meet, you probably don't need a formal program. Instead, talk to a financial planner or take a course in debt management. Either way, you'll have to learn to live on less than you earn. (Your credit cards may not be the problem, says Steve Rhode, co-founder of Debt Counselors of America: Look at things like premium cable, advanced phone services, or your car lease.) You also can try to negotiate with creditors yourself; explain why you're having trouble and ask for a lower interest rate. Many will work with you.

It should take six to seven years, at most, to get out of debt if you're in a counseling program (typically, it takes four to six years). If that looks out of reach, bankruptcy might make more sense for you than counseling. But because counseling services get a "fair share" rebate from your creditors (8–12% of what you pay on your debts), you can't count on them to tell you this.

—Exerpted from "When you need help climbing out of debt,"
USA Weekend, February 18–20, 2000

1. ______ Is counseling right for you? If you're far behind on payments, look into joining a program, says Gerri Detweiler, co-author of *Slash Your Debt* (Financial Literacy Center, $10.95).

2. ______ (Your credit cards may not be the problem, says Steve Rhode, co-founder of Debt Counselors of America: Look at things like premium cable, advanced phone services, or your car lease.)

3. ______ It should take six to seven years, at most, to get out of debt if you're in a counseling program (typically, it takes four to six years).

4. ______ But because counseling services get a "fair share" rebate from your creditors (8–12% of what you pay on your debts), you can't count on them to tell you this.

Answers are on page 290.

Distinguishing Conclusions from Supporting Statements

A conclusion is something you arrive at after considering the statements that are offered in support as "evidence." If the statements are given first, it is a natural progression to lead into the conclusion. As you read the conclusion, think about the number and strength of the supporting statements that came before the conclusion. Decide whether you are convinced and, indeed, whether you accept the conclusion. If the conclusion comes first in the paragraph, you need to withhold judgment until you have read the supporting statements.

The author of a passage usually gives clues that point to the conclusion. Consider the following example.

GED PRACTICE

EXERCISE 12

Distinguishing Conclusions from Supporting Statements

Directions: Read the passage below. Then determine whether the numbered sentences (or parts of sentences) are supporting statements or conclusions.

(1) As infants and small children, we cannot possibly earn our welcome in the world; **(2)** yet we sense very soon whether we are in fact welcome. **(3)** The comfort of having someone respond to our cries and needs, **(4)** the sensuousness of being cuddled and held, **(5)** the reassurance of seeing ourselves intensely "mirrored" in the faces of caregivers, **(6)** the sheer pleasure of hearing sounds and, a little later, **(7)** words of love and encouragement—**(8)** all these things confirm (or their absence denies) our welcome. **(9)** Perhaps that's why the most child-loving cultures, **(10)** and those childrearing practices that seem to produce the most secure children, share a belief: **(11)** it is not possible to "spoil" a child before the age of two or three. **(12)** Total dependence on the world creates a corresponding right to feel that it is totally dependable, **(13)** and that we are the center of it.

—Source: "It's Never Too Late for a Happy Childhood" in *Revolution from Within* by Gloria Steinem

1. Which sentence (or part of a sentence) suggests the strongest, most definite belief (the conclusion)?

(1) sentence 1: As infants and small children, we cannot possibly earn our welcome in the world;
(2) sentence 5: the reassurance of seeing ourselves intensely "mirrored" in the faces of caregivers,
(3) sentence 7: words of love and encouragement—
(4) sentence 8: all these things confirm (or their absence denies) our welcome.
(5) sentence 11: it is not possible to "spoil" a child before the age of two or three.

2. Which of the following sentences is a <u>secondary conclusion</u> rather than a supporting statement?

(1) sentence 2: yet we sense very soon whether we are in fact welcome.
(2) sentence 3: The comfort of having someone respond to our cries and needs,
(3) sentence 6: the sheer pleasure of hearing sounds
(4) sentence 10: and those childrearing practices that seem to produce the most secure children,
(5) sentence 13: and that we are the center of it.

3. Which of the following groups of words is the strongest clue that points to a conclusion to follow?

(1) yet we sense (sentence 2)
(2) and, a little later (sentence 6)
(3) all these things confirm (sentence 8)
(4) (or their absence denies) (sentence 8)
(5) share a belief: (sentence 10)

4. What is the purpose of the words *a corresponding right* in Sentence 12?

(1) a link between <u>dependence on the world</u> and <u>it is totally dependable</u>
(2) an explanation of the author's feeling about childhood
(3) a statement of the childhood "bill of rights" document
(4) a contrast between childhood and adulthood views
(5) a summary of different means to spoil a young child

Answers are on page 290.

Drawing Conclusions through Inductive and Deductive Reasoning

The **scientific method** is based on logical reasoning. When you draw conclusions that support evidence gathered in an investigation, you are following logic. Two methods of reasoning that are involved in logic are inductive reasoning and deductive reasoning.

Inductive reasoning involves drawing a conclusion by moving from the specific to the general. In following induction, you observe the behavior or characteristics of members of a class or group and then apply this information to the unobserved members of the group. In other words, you **generalize** about the other members of the group.

EXERCISE 13

Drawing Conclusions through Inductive Reasoning

Directions: To see how a doctor follows inductive reasoning, read the following passage; then answer the questions that follow on a separate piece of paper.

Don't cut it out. It may be time to stop most of the adenoidectomies and adenotonsillectomies that more than 425,000 children under the age of 15 undergo each year.

A study of 461 children with persistent middle ear infections, the most common reason for these operations, found that those who had their adenoids removed or who had both adenoids and tonsils removed fared little better than those who did not undergo surgery, said Dr. Jack L. Paradise of the Children's Hospital of Pittsburgh.

The average number of ear infections in children who had an adenotonsillectomy was 1.4 per year compared to 2.1 per year for children who did not have surgery, he reported in the *Journal of the American Medical Association.*

"Given that we found both operations to have limited efficacy, and in view of their not inconsiderable risks, morbidity, and costs, we believe that neither operation ordinarily should be considered as an initial intervention in such children," Paradise said. Medical treatment followed by ear tubes should be tried first, he added.

—Excerpted from Discoveries: "Don't Cut It Out," *Chicago Tribune*, October 31, 1999

1. Which population was studied?
2. What groups were studied?
3. What were the finding(s) of the study?
4. What conclusion was drawn from the study?
5. What generalization can be made as a result of this study?

Answers are on page 290.

Deductive reasoning involves drawing a conclusion by applying a generalization to a specific example or case. For a valid conclusion to be drawn, the generalization must be known, accepted, and true. In the case on page 247, medical researchers will use their generalizations (arrived at through inductive means) to treat future cases. If a generalization is faulty, however, it cannot be applied to a specific example.

EXERCISE 14

Drawing Conclusions through Deductive Reasoning

Directions: Read the generalization. Then write **yes** for each conclusion that is valid based on the generalization and **no** for each conclusion that is not valid.

Generalization: A stroke is a condition in which there is lessening or loss of consciousness, sensation, and motion caused by the rupture or obstruction of an artery of the brain.

1. ______ A cerebral hemorrhage occurs when a defective brain artery bursts; therefore, a cerebral hemorrhage often can lead to a stroke.

2. ______ An embolism is the sudden blockage of a blood vessel by a mass or an air bubble in the blood; therefore, an embolism in the brain can lead to a stroke.

3. ______ A tumor is a mass of tissue that does not swell and that rises from tissue that already exists; therefore, brain tumors generally lead to a stroke.

4. ______ An aneurysm is a permanent, abnormal, blood-filled swelling of a vessel; therefore, the rupture of an aneurysm can cause a stroke.

5. ______ Phlebitis is the inflammation of a vein; varicose veins are abnormally swollen or dilated veins; therefore, phlebitis and varicose veins can lead to a stroke.

Answers are on page 290.

Analysis in Literature

Style is the writer's way of using language to express an idea, and it varies considerably among individual writers. Style is established by the writer's choice of words and helps to create **tone,** the attitude an author conveys toward the subject and reader. An example of how tone is used is shown in the following dialogue from *The Woman in Black:* "'I am sorry to disappoint you,' I said. 'But I have no story to tell!'" The author Susan Hill gives you a clue that the narrator is unhappy (perhaps exasperated) by use of the exclamation point (!). To make sure, the author adds that the narrator then "went quickly from the room, and from the house."

GED PRACTICE

EXERCISE 15

Recognizing Style and Tone

Directions: Read the passage and answer the questions that follow.

Leontis Marnas married Angeliki when he was fifty-eight years old. She was twenty-four. She had been in the United States only a little over two years. All that time she spent working from dawn to dark in the house of an older brother who had paid her passage from Greece. Her days were endured scrubbing floors and caring for his children. In addition, the unhappy girl did not get along with her brother's wife, who was a sullen and unfriendly woman.

Leontis was not aware at that time of how desperately Angeliki wished for liberation from her bondage. When he visited the house in the evening to play cards with her brother, she released upon him all the smoldering embers of her despair. He would have been ashamed to admit that he mistook her attention for affection and her desperation for passion. He was bewildered and yet wished ardently to believe that a young and comely woman could find him attractive. He could not help being flattered and soon imagined that he was madly in love.

In the twenty-eight years since Leontis emigrated from Greece to the United States, he had made a number of attempts to marry. Several times he almost reached the altar, but in the end these efforts were always unsuccessful. Even when he was a young man the bold girls had frightened him, and the shy sweet girls to whom he was attracted lacked the aggressiveness to encourage him. He was without sufficient confidence to make the first move, and as a result always lost his chance.

—Excerpted from "The Legacy of Leontis" in *A Petrakis Reader* by Harry Mark Petrakis

1. How does the author portray the character Leontis Marnas?

(1) harsh and bitter
(2) foolish and unrealistic
(3) sympathetic and likable
(4) confirmed in his bachelor ways
(5) determined and overly confident

2. How does the author portray the character Angeliki?

(1) lazy and uncaring
(2) shy and sweet
(3) sullen and unfriendly
(4) unhappy and desperate
(5) passionate and aggressive

3. Which of the following is not used by the author to create sympathy for the character Angeliki?

(1) her young age of twenty-four
(2) her being in the United States only two years
(3) her hard work caring for her brother's children
(4) her desperation to be liberated
(5) her desire to marry for wealth

4. Describe the overall tone of the excerpt.

(1) nostalgic
(2) mocking
(3) tragic
(4) angry
(5) sentimental

5. Which of the following does the author's style include?

(1) sympathy for Leontis but not for Angeliki
(2) comparison and contrast of Leontis and Angeliki
(3) focus on chronological sequence of events
(4) cause and effect to explain Leontis's misfortune
(5) use of exaggeration for humorous effect

Answers are on page 290.

Analysis in Science: The Scientific Method

The **scientific method** is a system of investigation on which all scientific inquiry is based. Most science courses offer at least a basic summary of the procedure. It can be reduced to six steps:

1. Identify and state the problem.

2. Collect information.

3. Make a hypothesis.

4. Make a prediction on the basis of the hypothesis.

5. Make observations and perform experiments to test the hypothesis.

6. Draw a conclusion.

In step 1, the scientist identifies a problem that needs to be solved or a question that must be answered. Step 2 requires that the scientist gather as much information about the problem as possible. At step 3, the scientist makes an educated guess that might explain the reason for the problem or answer the question. Formulating a hypothesis is an important step in the scientific method. At step 4 the scientist predicts what the outcome of the experiment or observation will be if the hypothesis is correct. During step 5, the scientist observes or experiments to test the hypothesis. According to step 6, if the results confirm [agree with] the scientist's prediction, the hypothesis is correct. If the results do not confirm the prediction, the hypothesis must be changed or discarded.

When following the scientific method, a scientist must be objective. The results of the experiment must not be influenced in any way by the scientist's hunches or beliefs. The results of the experiment must speak for themselves. For this reason, experiments involving the scientific method require the use of controls so that the outcome is not biased by the experimenter's expectations. When the results of an experiment or observation can be explained by a hypothesis, a **theory** is formed. When a theory has few exceptions, it is called a **law.**

Let's look at a situation to which we might apply the scientific method to solve a problem.

EXERCISE 16

Analysis in Science: The Scientific Method

Directions: Read the passage below. Then fill in the steps of the scientific method with the correct information from the passage.

The National Audubon Society, the Smithsonian Institution, and other conservative groups are putting their stamp on shade-grown coffee such as Café Audubon, which they hope will save the tall trees in Latin America where U.S. and Canadian migratory birds seek refuge from the cold.

Scientists are not sure why certain species are dwindling, but they know the decline parallels the felling over the last 20 years of the canopies protecting coffee plantations from the equatorial sun. Birds seek refuge there since so much of the rain forest has been lost in wintering grounds that stretch from Mexico to Colombia.

Until 1996, agriculture experts encouraged large coffee plantations to cut down trees shielding the sun-shy plants and grow high-yield, sun-tolerant hybrids that need high doses of pesticides and chemical fertilizers.

Changes in coffee growing harmful to environment

Traditionally, coffee beans were grown in rain forest. Today, trees are being cut down and replaced with fields that are easier and more efficient to harvest. Chemical pesticides are needed to help the beans develop outside of the protective canopy. These chemicals are poisoning the water and pose a health threat to the farmers. Here is a look at how coffee bean growing has changed and what it means to the environment.

In the 1970s, coffee farmers began cutting through the shade canopy to ward off coffee leaf fungus and to produce larger yields. Consider the growing technique:

1. The sun and rain beat down on the coffee plants, hampering growth.
2. Chemical pesticides and fertilizers are used to feed and protect the vulnerable plants.
3. The soil becomes soaked with the harmful chemicals.
4. Without the roots of the trees to hold it firm, the contaminated soil is washed into streams, causing a great health risk to people.

—Excerpted from "Coffee is Made in the Shade," and "Latin American Tall Tree Canopies Not Only Get Conservationists' Nod, But Sellers Say Brew Tastes Richer" As Appeared in *The Daily Herald*, December 26, 1998

1. **Problems:**
   a. Certain species of birds have been dwindling in the last 20 years.
   b. ____________________

2. **Information (observable facts):**
   a. U.S. and Canadian migratory birds seek refuge from the cold in tall trees in Latin America.
   b. Today trees are being cut down and ____________________
   c. ____________________

3. **Hypothesis:** In the 1970s farmers cut through shade canopy to ____
   ____

   Reducing the shade canopy resulted in ____________________
   ____

4. **Prediction:** The new way of growing coffee will be ____________________
   ____

5. **Observation(s) (perform experiment):**
   (a.) The sun and rain beat down on the coffee plants, hampering growth.
   (b.) Chemical pesticides and fertilizers are used to feed and protect the vulnerable plants.
   (c.) ____________________
   (d.) ____________________
   ____

6. **Conclusion(s):** ____________________
   result from the new way of growing coffee. We need to return to
   ____

Answers are on page 290.

Recognizing Organizational Patterns

Writings in social studies and science are organized according to certain patterns. Likewise, literary works such as novels, short stories, plays, and forms of nonfiction also are based on organizational patterns. Three common patterns used in writing are sequence or time order, comparison and contrast, and cause and effect. These organizational patterns can be the framework for a single paragraph or entire books. There may be a mixing of these three patterns within both single paragraphs and longer selections. Generally, however, you can see a predominant pattern within paragraphs of longer selections.

Recognizing Sequence

Often writers organize their works on the basis of **sequence,** sometimes known as **time order.** With this pattern of organization, events follow a series. Sequence is an organizational pattern that is especially common in social studies for describing historical events. It also is used widely in science writing to outline the steps in an experiment. Sequence is used as a pattern of organization in literature as well. In novels, short stories, and plays, plot events must follow a sequence.

SKILL BUILDER

Recognizing Sequence in a Passage

Some words and phrases that signal sequence include *on* (a certain date—e.g., January 1), *not long after, now, before, next, then, when, first, second,* and *third.*

EXERCISE 17

Recognizing Sequence

Directions: Read the following summary of a famous play. Then write **1** for the event that occurs first, **2** for the event that occurs second, and so on.

Romeo and Juliet is a famous play written by William Shakespeare. Like its more modern-day counterpart, *West Side Story,* it is the story of two young people. Romeo and Juliet come from two different, powerful families that are enemies. Romeo sees Juliet one day and falls in love with her. Juliet falls in love with Romeo as well, and they marry secretly.

Not knowing that Juliet already is married, Juliet's father insists that she must marry someone else. She doesn't know what to do and turns to a local priest for help. The priest gives her a drug that makes her look as if she is dead. Her grieving family believes that she is dead. The priest is supposed to find Romeo to tell him the truth. Unfortunately, the priest does not find Romeo.

Meanwhile, Romeo believes that Juliet is dead. Overcome with sorrow, he kills himself. Juliet awakens from the effect of the drug and sees the truly dead Romeo. The tragedy is complete when Juliet takes her own life.

Sequence of Events

a. ______ Thinking Juliet is dead, Romeo kills himself.

b. ______ The priest tries to find Romeo but does not.

c. ______ Romeo's and Juliet's powerful families came to be enemies.

d. ______ Finding Romeo is dead, Juliet kills herself.

e. ______ Romeo meets Juliet and falls in love with her.

f. ______ The priest gives Juliet a drug that makes Juliet appear to be dead.

g. ______ Romeo and Juliet marry secretly because their families are enemies.

h. ______ Juliet's father insists that she marry someone other than Romeo.

i. ______ Juliet turns to a local priest for help.

j. ______ Juliet awakens from the drug-induced sleep.

Answers are on page 291.

Using Comparison and Contrast

A writer uses the comparison/contrast pattern of organization to explain or show the similarities and differences among ideas, people, or things. A writer who points out how two or more ideas, things, or people are alike is making a **comparison.** Likewise, a writer who points out how they are different is using **contrast.**

Let's think of an example that applies to people. Think about the people with whom you have lived or worked. Some live or work better with others who have similar habits or work styles. Others are motivated by working with those who are different from them. When you describe how people are similar, you are using comparison. When you describe how people are different, you are using contrast. Frequently, these techniques are used together in writing.

Comparisons and contrasts are made with words, phrases, sentences, paragraphs, or whole passages. Now let's look at comparison and contrast patterns.

SKILL BUILDER

Identifying Comparison and Contrast Patterns

Words and phrases that signal comparisons include *like, likewise, also, similarly, on the one hand, in the same way* or *fashion,* and *compared to.* Words and phrases that signal contrasts include *however, but, on the other hand, differently, on the contrary, while, although, yet, conversely, on the other side of the coin, versus, in contrast to,* and *either . . . or.*

EXERCISE 18

Identifying Comparison and Contrast Patterns

Directions: Read the following passage in which the writer compares and contrasts major interests of our first ladies since the 1960s. Then fill in the blanks with the appropriate comparison and contrast phrases or names.

Hint: In this exercise, comparison words have been indicated in underlined type and contrast words have been indicated in **boldface type.**

In the history of the United States there had been forty-three first ladies up until the end of the previous century. All the first ladies were (by definition) wives, and all also were mothers. In that time period, of course, some were married to Democratic presidents **while** others were married to Republican presidents. Since the

1960s, Democratic first ladies included Jacqueline Lee Bouvier Kennedy, Claudia Taylor Johnson, Rosalynn Smith Carter, and Hillary Rodham Clinton; **conversely,** Republican first ladies included Patricia Ryan Nixon, Elizabeth Bloomer Ford, Nancy Davis Reagan, and Barbara Pierce Bush. Several first ladies were known to the nation by nicknames: "Jackie" Kennedy, "Lady Bird" Johnson, "Pat" Nixon, and "Betty" Ford.

Each of the nation's first ladies has been identified with particular special interests, causes, or projects. On the one hand, some first ladies concentrated their efforts on causes that developed during the time their husbands were governors of various states. **On the other hand,** other first ladies pursued personal interests. **In contrast to** those who pursued personal interests and those who followed their husbands' agendas, some first ladies pursued both types of programs.

Both Pat Nixon and Barbara Bush promoted volunteer service. Pat Nixon, Rosalynn Carter, and Hillary Clinton all encouraged support for the performing arts. Betty Ford and Nancy Reagan similarly supported the campaign against alcohol and drug dependency.

Some causes were **different** with each first lady. Lady Bird Johnson worked for the environment and beautification and for the "War on Poverty." Pat Nixon worked to increase the White House art collection. Betty Ford's special cause was support for women's rights and the Equal Rights Amendment (ERA). Rosalynn Carter devoted efforts toward peace and human rights and better mental health care. Nancy Reagan helped charitable groups and renovated the White House. Barbara Bush showed great interest in literacy and established a literacy foundation. Finally, Hillary Clinton concentrated her efforts on children and families and on health care reform.

The nation owes a debt of gratitude to all the first ladies. They supported their husbands as presidents; likewise, they helped pursue the presidents' agendas. Sometimes, **however,** they earned our respect by working toward national causes of their own.

Source: A Glimpse into the Past, the National First Ladies' Library, the White House

Comparative Words and Phrases (Similarities)

Which first ladies belonged to the Democratic Party?

1. ______________________________

2. ______________________________

3. ______________________________

4. ______________________________

Which first ladies belonged to the Republican Party?

1. ______________________________

2. ______________________________

3. ______________________________

4. ______________________________

Compare the causes that were similar and identify the first ladies associated with those causes.

Volunteer Service

1. ______________________________

2. ______________________________

Promotion of the Performing Arts

1. ______________________________

2. ______________________________

3. ______________________________

Campaign Against Alcohol or Drug Dependency

1. ______________________________

2. ______________________________

Contrasting Words and Phrases (Differences)

Contrast the causes that were different by naming the first lady associated with each cause.

1. White House art collection ______________________________

2. Peace and human rights ______________________________

3. Mental health care ______________________________

4. Literacy ______________________________

5. Equal Rights Amendment ______________________________

6. War on poverty ______________________________

7. Renovation of the White House ______________________________

8. Health care reform ______________________________

Answers are on page 291.

Identifying Cause-and-Effect Relationships

The **cause and effect** pattern of organization shows a relationship between events. We connect causes with effects every day. Sometimes the cause is listed first, and it is easy to see the effect that results. Other times the effect is stated first, and you have to trace back to its cause. Several effects can come from a single cause, or a number of causes can result in a single effect.

SKILL BUILDER

Recognizing Cause-and-Effect Relationships

The cause-and-effect relationship is frequently signaled by key words such as *because, since, therefore, as a result, consequently, accordingly, if . . . then, led to, brought about, the outcome was, the result was,* and *was responsible for.*

First, let's practice recognizing causes and effects by noticing some of the **signal words** listed.

Example 1:

The *Journal of the American Medical Association* was cited in a study of some people who have mild to moderate asthma and rheumatoid arthritis. Some of these people wrote essays about traumatic (very stressful) experiences in their lives. The outcome was that the patients had better health four months later, according to their doctors.

The signal words The outcome was are underlined above.

The **cause:** People wrote essays about their traumatic experiences.

The **effect:** Those people had better health four months later.

Example 2:

The National Fire Protection Association reports that the top five causes of fatal home fires are smoking, arson, heaters, electrical systems, and children's playing with lighters, matches, or candles.

What are the *signal words* used above?
causes . . . are

What are the five **causes** mentioned above?

1) smoking, 2) arson, 3) heaters, 4) electrical systems, 5) children's playing with lighters, matches, or candles

What is the **effect** of those causes?
fatal home fires

Now, let's work with a longer passage.

EXERCISE 19

Identifying Cause-and-Effect Relationships

Directions: Read the passage below, noting cause-and-effect signal words. Write each **effect** that resulted from the stated **cause.** Or, trace each **cause** from the stated **effect.** The first one is done for you.

A home builder specializing in retirement housing nationwide was very successful in designing homes for seniors aged fifty-five years of age and older in the Southwest and Southeast parts of the United States. The builder promoted a particular community lifestyle that included an emphasis on recreation. Accordingly, the corporation researched a colder, Midwestern climate and believed it would be successful there as well. The builder decided to build a similar community with thousands of homes. In order to find enough land, it chose a location some 45 miles from a major city.

Many seniors took advantage of the development because they could have the community lifestyle without moving away from their families and lifelong friends. The construction of thousands of new homes brought about the need for a number of community services. The closest hospital was fifteen miles away; consequently, there was an increase in the demand for emergency health services. Other outcomes included the need for additional grocery stores, pharmacies, movie theaters, restaurants, and other facilities.

The building of stores, pharmacies, theatres, and restaurants led to general development of the whole town, and other age groups were attracted to the area. Many young families moved in, and this led to the need for more schools and more taxes to support the schools. The younger families, especially, supported the schools because they had children in the school system, but many seniors did not want their taxes to be raised for the schools. The result was a division between the two groups. At last word, local governmental leaders still were trying to resolve the issue.

Example:
Cause: The builder promoted a particular community lifestyle that included an emphasis on recreation.

Effect: A home builder specializing in retirement housing nationwide was very successful in designing homes for seniors aged fifty-five years of age and older in the Southwest and Southeast parts of the United States.

1. **Cause:** ____

   ____

   Effect: The builder decided to build a similar community with thousands of homes.

2. **Cause:** Seniors could have the community lifestyle without moving away from their families and lifelong friends.

   Effect: ____

   ____

3. **Cause:** ____

   ____

   Effect #1: This brought about the need for a number of community services.

   Effect #2: Other outcomes included the need for additional grocery stores, pharmacies, movie theatres, restaurants, and other facilities.

4. **Cause:** The closest hospital was fifteen miles away.

   Effect: ____

   ____

5. **Cause:** ____

   ____

   Effect #1: This led to general development of the whole town.

   Effect #2: Other age groups were attracted to the area.

6. **Cause:** Many young families moved in.

   Effect: ____

Answers are on page 291.

Notes

Level Four—Analysis: Key Concepts

LEVEL FIVE

Synthesis

Putting Elements Together to Form a New Whole

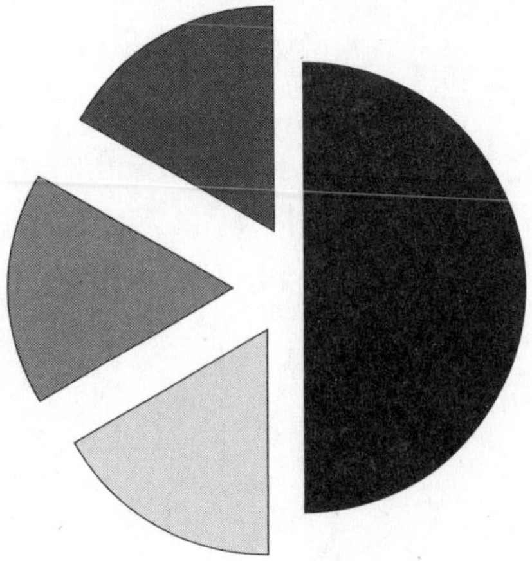

What is synthesis?

The symbol for synthesis above shows the separate parts of a circle chart that make up a whole circle when they are fit together. **Synthesis** involves putting many elements together to form one new whole. This is what you do when you write an essay based on facts from various sources or based on your personal knowledge and experience. Synthesis can involve drawing inferences from multiple parts of a single text, such as when you read an entire literary selection in poetry, prose (fiction or nonfiction), or drama (plays).

You encounter synthesis-level critical thinking skills in the Language Arts, Writing section of this book. Synthesis in writing involves putting elements together to create a whole piece of writing. In Part II of the Language Arts, Writing Test, you will be asked to write an expository essay that includes an introduction, body, and conclusion. You will be asked to think about the audience to which you are writing and the purpose of your essay. You write your essay in a real-life context and adopt a role.

As you would expect, there are many writing activities in the Language Arts, Writing section of the book. It is said that clear writing is clear thinking, so additional writing activities are included in three other sections: Science; Social Studies; and Language Arts, Reading. By writing paragraphs to answer the variety of questions asked, you strengthen your synthesis skills.

Let's practice using synthesis. For example, let's say that four relatives decide to take a four-day trip for a long week-end in a major city. To share the experience with family members who didn't go, the four agree that each one will take notes for one aspect of the trip. They decide that the major categories are:

- Getting there (transportation)
- Seeing the sights (attractions)
- Eating out (restaurants)
- Adapting to local ways (customs)

Thus, they will be able to answer the expected questions comparing the city visited with their home city. They will be able to form an overall impression of the trip.

Here are the four relatives' notes:

Getting there:

Airport smaller than one at home

Sometimes walked ten blocks to get around

Took cabs when distance was greater than ten blocks

Cab drivers very diverse but not always knowledgeable

Sometimes needed to show cab drivers maps to find attractions

Can't save a seat on a ferry if someone gets up to look over the side

Looked at buses and subways but didn't take any

Gridlock in traffic in downtown

Seeing the sights:

Wide range of plays available in the theatre district

Could stand in line after 3:00 to try to get half-price tickets

Famous department store featured in an old movie had great merchandise, but store itself is old

Television network tours were advertised as available every hour, but couldn't get tickets

Went to historic islands to see a famous monument and trace immigrants

Eating out:

Many delicatessens

Many ethnic restaurants (Italian, Jewish, etc.)

Hotel breakfast buffet good way to start day

Loved free beverage machine in hotel lobby (mocha, decaf/regular, hot chocolate, etc.)

Found famous restaurant from television chef

Got autographs in books: "Spaghetti is truth" and "Spaghetti is love"

Local patterns:

Most people assertive; had to get more assertive ourselves

Got wrong answers in asking for directions

People seem to dress in a wide variety of clothing styles from jeans to formal

Points for traffic violations could lead to license suspension

Tipping expected, but maybe at lower rate based on reactions of cabdrivers and wait staff

Writing Activity

Based on the information above, practice synthesis by writing an essay about one or more aspects of the city that the relatives visited. You could choose to work with three others to write a longer essay. If so, someone from the group will have to write an introductory paragraph to introduce the subject and a concluding paragraph to tie the elements together at the end. Good luck!

Another skill of synthesis involves the study of two or more pieces of writing that are related in terms of subject matter. You may read two or more articles, essays, speeches, biographies, or other texts on the same subject. You may study one piece in prose form, and another in poetry or drama form. You may derive additional information on the same subject from another form such as a graph, map, table or chart, or cartoon. You may combine information from written text and from some other visual component such as a painting, film, photograph, computer image, or other visual means.

Classics—that is, works that have withstood the test of time—invite a variety of opinions and interpretations of the original works. Even works that are not considered classics but have attracted a good deal of attention are often analyzed by many writers. Sometimes the original writer will "revisit" his own work and talk about it later. Your task as the reader is to read two or more versions of or opinions about the original work and form your own opinions. Again, synthesis involves studying two or more sources to form a new whole—a *new understanding* of the text.

Let's practice this skill with two sources, one from a well-known author and one from another writer. *The 7 Habits of Highly Successful People* by Stephen Covey was published in 1989, and it was included on *The New York Times* Bestsellers List for more than a decade.

EXERCISE 20

Using Synthesis

Directions: Read the passage below and answer the following questions.

What Is the Author Saying about His Original Work?

IN MY BOOK *The 7 Habits of Highly Effective People,* I laid out what I believe are the seven basic principles of effective living, based on such immutable [unchangeable] qualities as responsibility, integrity, respect, mutual understanding, patience and purpose. These principles are as true today as they were in 1989, when *7 Habits* was published.

But technology has changed our world profoundly. Today we are under even more pressure in our professional and personal lives than we were a decade ago. I attribute this in part to technology, because it often has served to quicken the pace, and to separate us rather than bring us closer together.

Technology can be a great tool to help us become more effective—in our work and our relationships. Remember this and you are already a step ahead: Technology is a good servant but a bad master.

Now for the seven habits, revisited here to reflect the new challenges of life in a technological world:

1 BE PROACTIVE.® Ask yourself, "Are my actions based on self-chosen values or on my moods, feelings and circumstances?"

2 BEGIN WITH THE END IN MIND.® Ask yourself, "What would I want written on my tombstone? Have I written a personal mission statement that provides meaning, purpose and direction to my life? Do my actions flow from my mission?"

3 PUT FIRST THINGS FIRST.® Ask yourself, "Am I able to say no to the unimportant, no matter how urgent, and yes to the important?"

4 THINK WIN-WIN.® "Do I seek mutual benefit in all of my relationships?"

5 SEEK FIRST TO UNDERSTAND, THEN TO BE UNDERSTOOD.® Ask yourself, "Do I avoid talking initially about my concerns and instead express my understanding of the other person and his or her point of view?

6 SYNERGIZE.® Ask yourself, "Do I seek and value opinions, viewpoints and perspectives from others to create solutions that are better than I would have created on my own?"

7 SHARPEN THE SAW.® Ask yourself, "Am I continually improving the physical, mental, spiritual and social dimensions of my life?"

—Excerpted from "*7 Habits* 11 years later" by Stephen Covey in *USA Weekend*, July 7–9, 2000. Used with permission.

Part A **Directions:** Read the following statements about ways in which a person could choose to live. Next to each statement, put the number of the author's seven habits with which it agrees.

a. ______ Do your most important or creative work in the first two hours of the day.

b. ______ Have a family mission statement that agrees with your personal mission statement. Use technology to help write the statement with relatives who are far away.

c. ______ You decide when to do routine things such as return phone or e-mail messages.

d. ______ For high-quality relationships, have "face-to-face interaction first," if possible, and think about benefits to others as well as yourself.

e. ______ Ignore interruptions, especially during "family time"; organize life activities and commitments.

f. ______ Keep promises, be kind and courteous, make your expectations clear, make apologies, accept feedback, and remain loyal to others.

g. ______ Work with family or others to arrive together at solutions to problems.

h. ______ Listen effectively to other persons, carrying on relationships through technology if necessary.

i. ______ Take a long walk, learn a new software program, or send an inspirational message to friends.

Answers are on page 291.

Part B **Directions:** Now read a second passage and answer the following questions.

What Perspective Does a Second Author Provide?

TEN YEARS LATER, COVEY'S BOOK—STILL ON *THE NEW YORK TIMES* BESTSELLERS LIST AND PUBLISHED by Simon & Schuster—has become an icon of a generation obsessed with self-help. Covey was already a highly sought-after speaker when he published *The 7 Habits;* he has gone on to become a counselor to political leaders, chief executives and ordinary people the world over and the vice chairman of Franklin Covey, a global professional-services company and publishers of the Franklin Planner products.

Although his seven habits are now recognized as a tried-and-true short course in leadership, Covey is as self-effacing as ever. "I shouldn't get credit for creating any of the principles," he says. "I just packaged and sequenced timeless principles that transcend culture and never change."

Covey did not write *The 7 Habits* by sitting at a computer and typing out the pages. He created the book by organizing the material that he presents in his lectures. He uses speaking engagements as opportunities to refine his messages. "I have the core of the speech, and then I start adding, because I find that if I have a dynamic happening with the audience, the material changes to fit that dynamic," he explains.

In fact, Covey wants to make sure people focus on the seven habits and not on him. Sometimes he worries about having become, in effect, a guru.

—Excerpted from "Business" by Steven L. Kent, *Sky*, April 2000

1. The first passage is written in the first person ("I") because the author is writing about his work. In what person is the second passage written by Steven L. Kent?

____

2. What information does Kent reveal about what Covey has become in the decade since *The 7 Habits* was published?

____

3. Kent explains how Covey wrote *The 7 Habits.* What was the other activity in which Covey was engaging when he wrote the book?

____

____

4. What attitude do you think Kent has about Covey and his book?

____

Possible answers are on page 292.

Notes

Level Five—Synthesis: Key Concepts

LEVEL SIX

Evaluation

Judging What You Read

Judging Information against Criteria

When you **evaluate** something, you make a judgment. The scales of justice are a good symbol for evaluation because you "weigh" how well or how poorly an idea or object meets certain standards. For example, when you evaluate a movie, you judge it according to the quality of its acting, directing, cinematography, sound track, and other standards. Standards used in making a judgment are called **criteria.**

Criteria may be either subjective or objective. **Objective** criteria are standards that are not affected by an individual's personal tastes, beliefs, or opinions. In contrast, **subjective** criteria are standards that are affected by an individual's personal tastes, beliefs, or opinions.

The following situation illustrates the difference between objective and subjective criteria. In 2000, a great deal of attention was given to taking and reporting the results of the national census, which is done every ten years.

EXERCISE 21

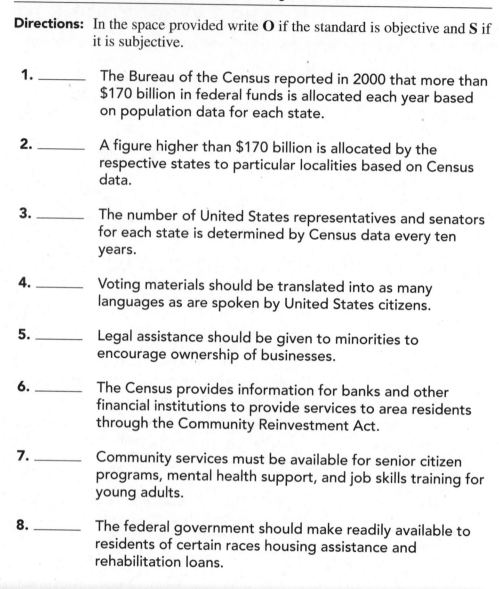

Evaluating Objective and Subjective Criteria

Directions: In the space provided write **O** if the standard is objective and **S** if it is subjective.

1. ______ The Bureau of the Census reported in 2000 that more than $170 billion in federal funds is allocated each year based on population data for each state.

2. ______ A figure higher than $170 billion is allocated by the respective states to particular localities based on Census data.

3. ______ The number of United States representatives and senators for each state is determined by Census data every ten years.

4. ______ Voting materials should be translated into as many languages as are spoken by United States citizens.

5. ______ Legal assistance should be given to minorities to encourage ownership of businesses.

6. ______ The Census provides information for banks and other financial institutions to provide services to area residents through the Community Reinvestment Act.

7. ______ Community services must be available for senior citizen programs, mental health support, and job skills training for young adults.

8. ______ The federal government should make readily available to residents of certain races housing assistance and rehabilitation loans.

Answers are on page 292.

The Roles of Values and Beliefs

When people make decisions, they are, in part, influenced by facts. But we all have deeply held values and personal beliefs that also influence our decision-making. Some of the literature selections that you read on the GED Tests will consist of commentaries—writers' opinions of various literary and artistic works. These commentaries are based on the writers' own values. In social studies and science-related issues, you will see that personal values have a big impact on decision making.

EXERCISE 22

Understanding the Role of Values and Beliefs

Directions: Here is a summary of a real case reported in the media (including accounts from *Time, Newsweek,* and many newspapers) at the end of the previous century. Read the passage and identify the value or belief represented by each statement listed.

The Rope Became Longer and Longer

At first it seemed extraordinarily simple. A mother had bound her only child to an inner tube when the sea was swallowing her boatmates one by one. In the end, only the six-year-old boy survived the attempt to reach the promised land of freedom. Some reasoned that the boy should stay in the country his mother had so desperately tried to reach. The mother had perished in the attempt, but the boy should have freedom as his mother's last will and testament.

The boy's natural father, however, disagreed. The father lived in a dictatorship and supported its ideals. Though he was divorced from the boy's mother, back home in his country he was, by all accounts, a loving father. He even passed the Immigration and Naturalization Service (INS) "test" showing a right to custody. He knew his son's shoe size, his teachers, his friends. With the death of the boy's mother, the father insisted on his parental right to raise his son.

On one side of the rope was freedom (and a bicycle, toys, Disney World, Barney at Universal Studios, and birthday parties). Congress moved toward offering him "honorary citizenship" so he wouldn't be an "alien,"and presidential candidates argued that the boy should be allowed to stay in the United States to avoid communist oppression.

On the other side of the rope was dictatorship (and a loving father, a stepmother, a baby half-brother, and two sets of loving grandparents). The INS ruled that the boy should be returned to his father, and the President and Attorney General said he should go back to his father. Presidential candidates campaigned that child custody cases should be settled by the courts.

The human tug of war continued. And the rope became longer and longer.

1. **Statement:** "In the end, only the six-year-old survived the desperate attempt to reach the promised land of freedom."

   Value: ______________________________

2. **Statement:** "The father lived in a dictatorship and supported its ideals."

   Value: ______________________________

3. **Statement:** "He even passed the Immigration and Naturalization Service (INS) 'test' showing a right to custody. He knew his son's shoe size, his teachers, his friends."

   Value: ______________________________

4. **Statement:** "the father insisted on his parental right to raise his son."

   Value: ______________________________

5. **Statement:** "and a bicycle, toys, Disney World, Barney at Universal Studios, and birthday parties . . ."

   Value: ______________________________

6. **Statement:** "and a loving father, a stepmother, a baby half-brother, and two sets of loving grandparents . . ."

   Value: ______________________________

7. **Statement:** "The INS ruled that the boy should be returned to his father, and the President and Attorney General said he should go back to his father."

   Value: ______________________________

Answers are on page 292.

Interpreting Graphs and Illustrations

About half of the questions on the GED Science, Social Studies, and Mathematics Tests will be based on graphics. You will need to understand how a writer uses pictorial information to support a point. The types of graphics that will appear on the tests include graphs, maps, tables or charts, and editorial cartoons.

To read and interpret graphic materials, you must pay close attention to all of the information that is given, including both pictures and words. This means that you must look at how the material is labeled and the figures and numbers that are used. You may be asked to use a graph, map, or table to locate a particular number or fact, or you may be required to make an interpretation such as stating the main idea, reading between the lines, or drawing a conclusion.

Interpreting Graphs

A graph is a way of presenting facts. Text passages that include a lot of figures can be difficult to understand, so writers often include graphs to help you, the reader, see the information in a way that can help you to understand it better. The types of graphs that are used to present information visually are pictographs, line graphs, bar graphs, and circle or pie graphs.

Pictographs

Pictographs are the simplest form of graphs. **Pictographs** use symbols to show how certain quantities of a thing compare. Symbols in pictographs commonly are used to represent people, cars, houses, and dollars. Whole symbols and partial symbols may be used in a pictograph. Like all graphs, pictographs have a title that gives the main idea. A **key** showing the amount that each symbol stands for always is provided to help the reader interpret the graph.

Information can be shown graphically in a variety of ways. For example, we can obtain information on average college costs from the Internet web site "News from the College Board" (http://www.collegeboard.org).

Average Fixed Charges for Undergradutes, 2000–2001 (weighted)

	Tuition Fees			Room and Board		
Sector	**1999–2000**	**2000–2001**	**% Change**	**1999–2000**	**2000–2001**	**% Change**
Two-Year Public	1,649	1,705	3.4%	*	*	*
Two-Year Private	6,968	7,458	7.0%	4,541	4,736	4.3%
Four-Year Public	3,362	3,510	4.4%	4,718	4,960	5.1%
Four-Year Private	15,518	16,332	5.2%	5,957	6,209	4.2%

*Sample too small to provide meaningful information

Thse are enrollment-weighted averages, intended to reflect the average costs that students face in various types of institutions.

Source: Annual Survey of Colleges,

We can use the information from the chart above to create a pictograph in which every $1,000 in tuition and fees cost is represented by the [$] symbol and every $1,000 in room and board cost is represented by the [🔑] symbol.

EXERCISE 23

Reading a Pictograph

Directions: Look at the pictograph entitled ***Average Fixed College Costs 2000–2001.*** Answer the following questions.

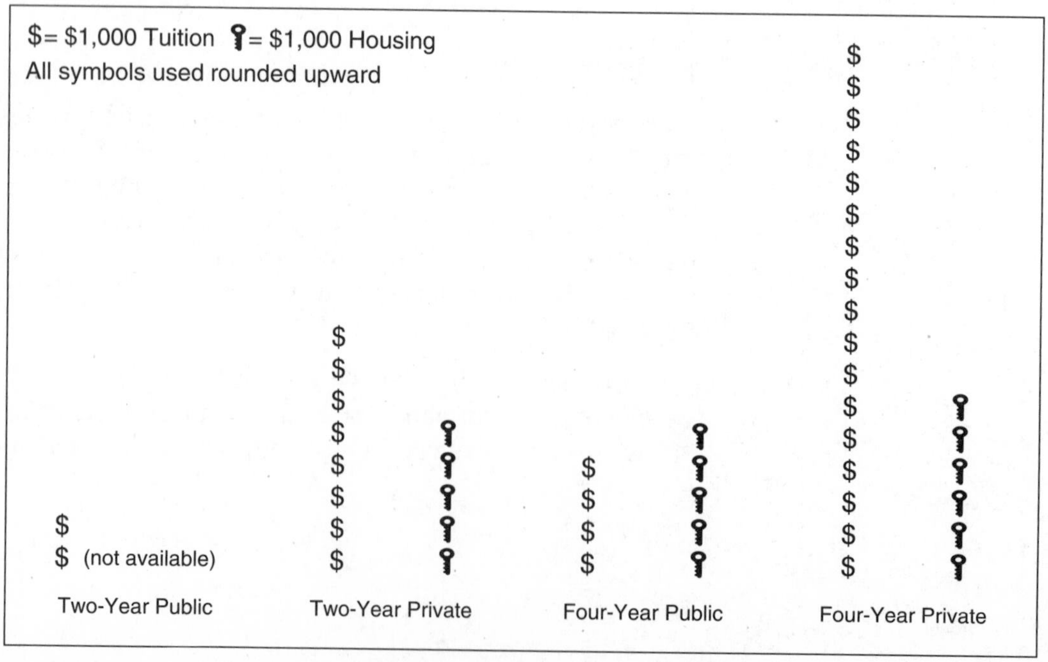

1. What information does the *title* of the pictograph tell us about the following?

   (1) ________________ and ________________ college costs

   (2) for the years ________________ and ________________

2. What are the four types of colleges included in the graph?

   (1) ________________________________

   (2) ________________________________

   (3) ________________________________

   (4) ________________________________

3. What is the *range* of college costs for tuition and fees (rounded in $1,000s)? from ________________ to ________________

4. What is the *range* of college costs for room and board (rounded in $1,000s)? from ________________ to ________________

5. Which of the two types of colleges appear to have similar costs for room and board? ________________ and ________________

6. Assuming a college student lived at home (and had no additional costs for room and board), what are the *least average costs* shown?

   $________________ for ________________

7. What are the total average costs at a four-year private college?

   $________________ for tuition and fees plus

   $________________ for room and board equals

   $________________ total

Answers are on page 293.

Line Graphs

Line graphs are used to show a relationship among two or more things. They may show a change in the quantity of something in relation to dates, years, or fixed amounts. Line graphs are especially useful for illustrating trends.

EXERCISE 24

Reading a Line Graph

Directions: Look at the line graph below, and answer the following questions.

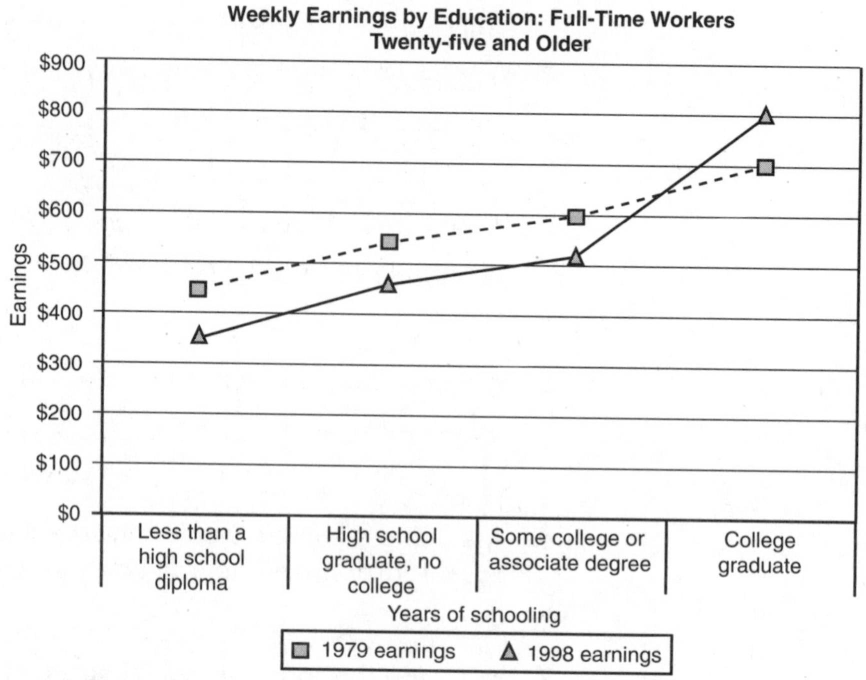

Source: U.S. Dept. of Labor

1. What information does the *title* of the graph tell us about the following?

   ________________ earnings by ________________

   for ________________ workers

   who are ________________ and older

2. What is the *range* of earnings shown on the vertical axis?

   from ________________ to ________________

3. What are the *categories* of education shown on the horizontal axis?

less than ____________________

____________________ graduate, no ____________________

some ____________________ or ____________________

____

4. What year does the *solid line* represent? ____________________

5. What year does the *dotted line* represent? ____________________

6. What were the weekly earnings of a high school graduate in 1979?

____

7. Did the weekly earnings of a high school graduate increase or decrease between 1979 and 1998? ____________________

8. Were the weekly earnings of a college graduate greater in 1979 or in 1998? ____________________

9. For which categories of worker were the weekly earnings better in 1979 than in 1998?

____

____

____

Answers are on page 293.

Bar Graphs

Bar graphs are used to show comparisons among sizes or quantities of similar items at different times. You should read a bar graph in the same way you would read a line graph: read the title, look at the vertical axis, and look at the horizontal axis. Instead of lines, a bar graph uses rectangular blocks or bars running either vertically or horizontally. Sometimes a bar graph includes a key when two or more sets of information are being compared.

EXERCISE 25

Reading a Bar Graph

Directions: Look at the bar graph below, and answer the following questions.

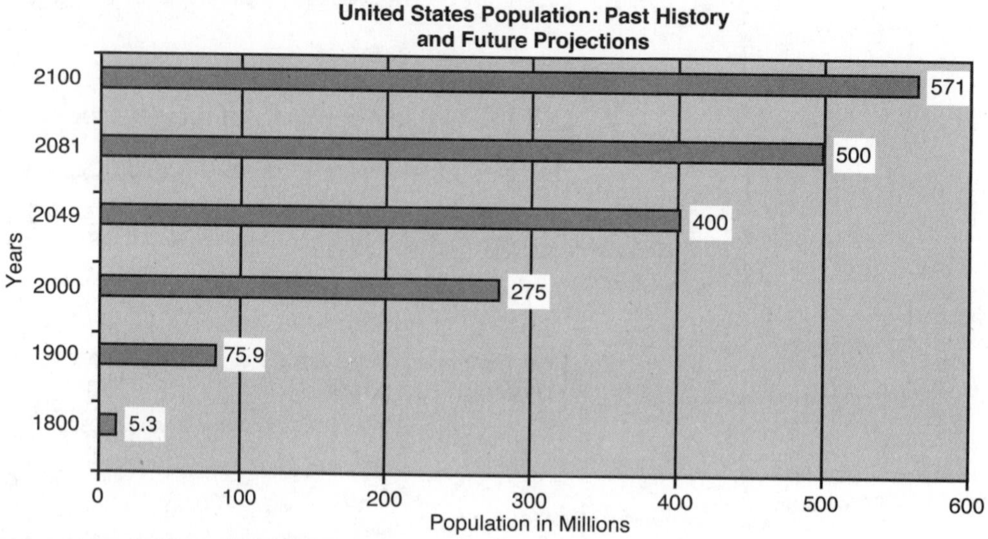

Source: U.S. Census Bureau

1. In which year shown on the graph did the United States have its smallest population? ______________

2. Between which years was there the greatest increase in U.S. population?

   ______________ and ______________

3. Between which years is a U.S. population increase of 100 million expected?

   between ______________ and ______________

4. What is the range (in millions) of U.S. population represented on the *horizontal axis*? ______________ to ______________

5. What is the range of years represented on the *vertical axis*?

   ______________ to ______________

Answers are on page 293.

Circle Graphs

Circle graphs, or **pie graphs,** show information as parts of a whole. Each "slice" is labeled and represents a percentage (part) of the whole. All of the slices must add up to 100 percent. A knowledge of basic arithmetic is necessary to answer questions based on a circle graph. As with the line and bar graphs discussed previously, a circle graph has a title that describes the main topic. Like some bar graphs, some circle graphs also provide a key to help the reader understand the information shown.

EXERCISE 26

Reading Circle Graphs

Directions: Look at the circle graphs below and answer the questions that follow.

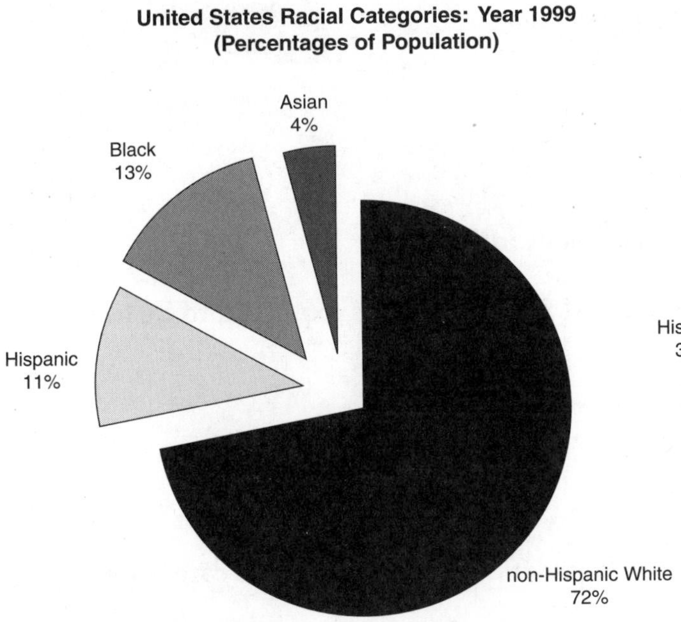

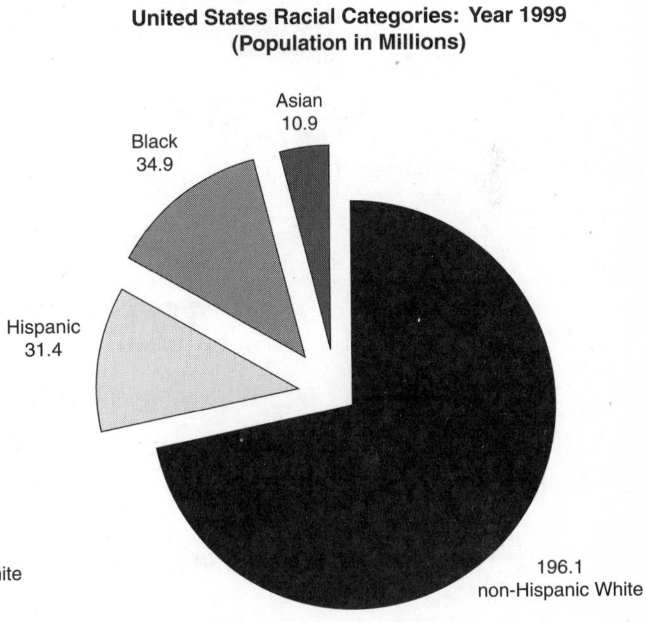

Source: U.S. Census Bureau

Study the circle graphs for 1999.

1. What percentage of the U.S. population was in each of these categories?

non-Hispanic White ______________%

Hispanic ______________% Black ______________%

Asian ______________%

2. In 1999 what was the U.S. population in each of these categories?

non-Hispanic White ______________

Hispanic ______________ Black ______________

Asian ______________

United States Racial Categories: Estimated 2050
(Population in Millions)

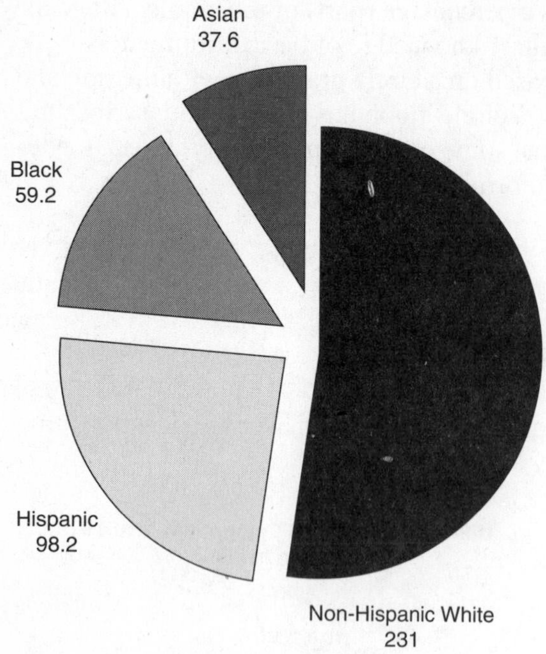

United States Racial Categories: Estimated 2050
(Percentages of Population)

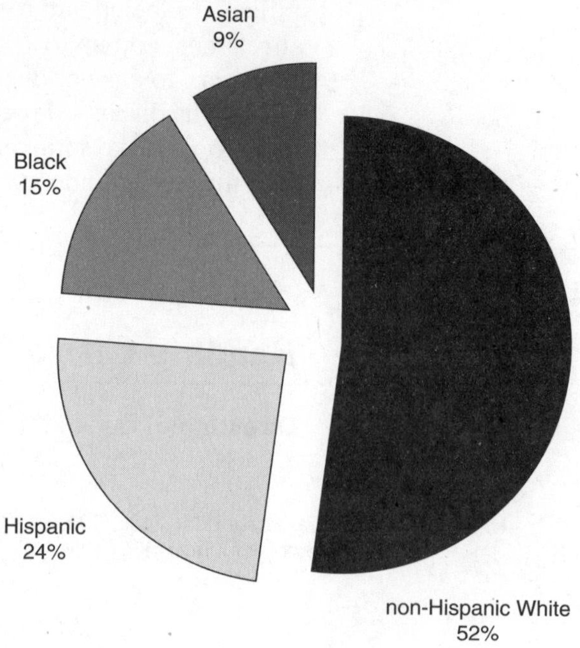

Source: U.S. Census Bureau

Study the circle graphs estimated for 2050.

3. What percentage of the U.S. population is expected to be in these categories?

non-Hispanic White ________________%

Hispanic ________________% Black ________________%

Asian ________________%

4. What is the estimated population for each of these categories?

non-Hispanic White ________________

Hispanic ________________ Black ________________

Asian ________________

Answers are on page 293.

Interpreting Maps

Like graphs, maps are another way of presenting pictorial information. Maps can provide a variety of information about a place. For example, a **demographic map** shows the distribution of a certain segment of a population. The percentage change of the United States population in each state between 1990 and 2000 as determined by the 2000 census can be displayed on a map.

A **regional road map** shows the location of towns, special points of interest, metric conversion (miles to kilometers), highway markers (interstate, United States, and state), and types of highways (controlled access, toll, major, or principal thoroughfares). **Topographical maps** (often in color) usually show mountains and bodies of water (oceans, gulfs, lakes, rivers, and so on).

A **key,** or **legend,** explains the symbols on the map. Some maps also include a scale of miles that you can use as a guide to find the distance from a given location to a destination.

For example, the legend for the Houston, Texas, area map shows that every $\frac{3}{4}$ inch equals 4 miles or just over 6 kilometers. To find the distance from West University Place to Bellaire, use a ruler to measure the distance (a little less than $\frac{1}{2}$ inch). Then use the legend to convert $\frac{1}{2}$ inch to miles (about 2 miles).

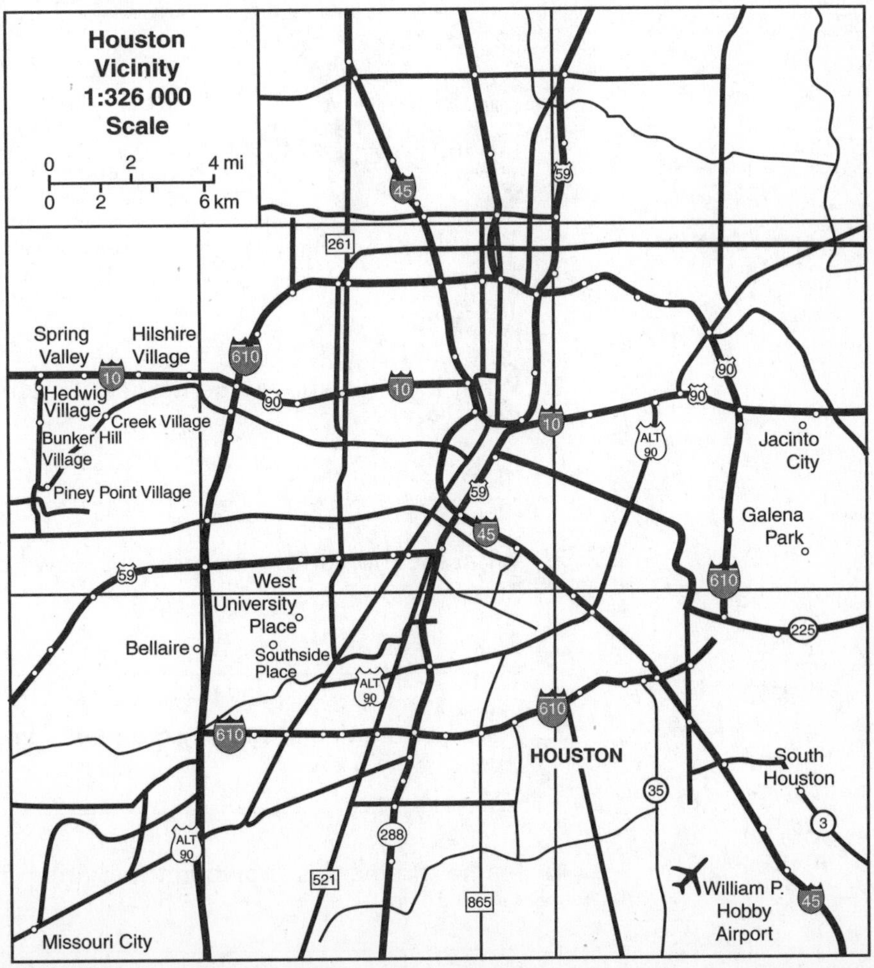

From reading the newspaper or watching television, you probably are familiar with a **weather map** which shows high and low temperatures for the day; weather conditions (rain, snow, clouds, high- or low-pressure systems); fronts (cold, warm, and stationary), and degree of severe weather risk (slight, moderate, or high). Let's look at an example in the next exercise.

EXERCISE 27

Reading a Weather Map

Directions: Look at a weather map for March 4 and answer the following questions.

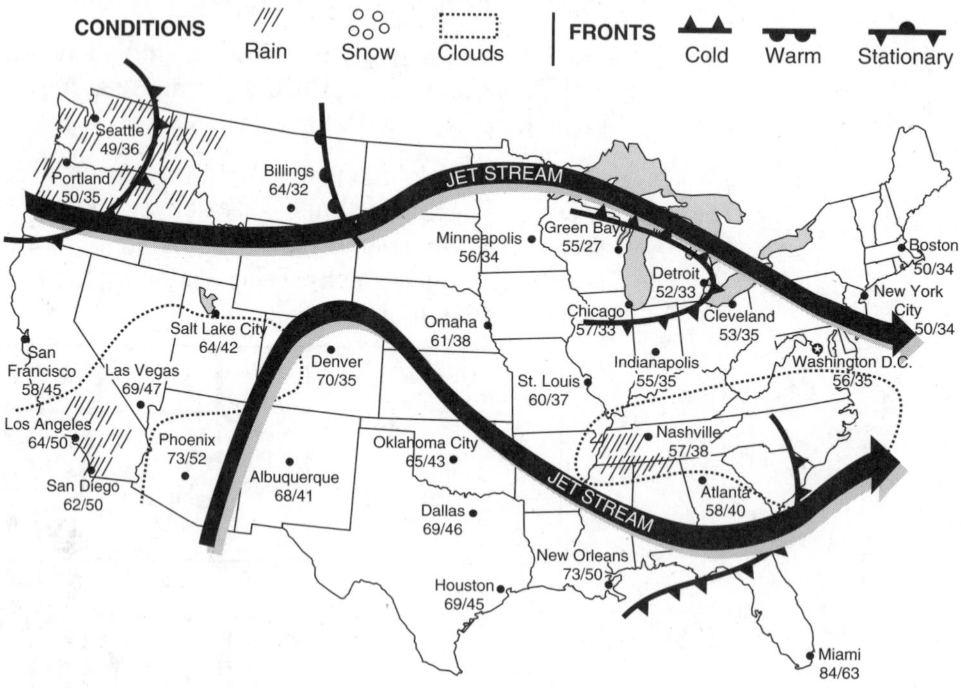

1. What location shows the highest "high" temperature in the United States?

____

2. What location shows the lowest "low" temperature in the United States?

____

3. Name two cities in which cold fronts appear.

____

4. Name three cities shown in the direct path of the southern jet stream.

____

Answers are on page 293.

Interpreting Tables

A **table,** sometimes called a **chart,** is a way to organize many facts into a small space. Tables are used to keep scores in games, list train schedules, assign work tasks, compare weather reports, and so on. A table has a title at the top. The separate columns and rows within a table are labeled so that the reader will know how the information is organized in the table.

In a special issue of *National Geographic Traveler* (October 1999), editors chose "50 Places of a Lifetime." Characteristics of some of these places are compared in a table, including location, population, size, and climate.

Favorite Places to Visit

Place	Continent	Population	Size in Square Miles	Climate (Fahrenheit) Summer	Winter
New York City, USA	North America	7,420,000	301		
Barcelona, Spain	Europe	1,600,000	38	high 70s	40s/50s
Australian Outback	Australia	60,000	2,500,000		90s/40s
London, England	Europe	7,000,000	625	75	40
Venice, Italy	Europe				
(historic center)		67,369	3	90s	40s
(mainlands/islands)		211,204			
Danang-Hue, Vietnam	Asia	78,000,000	100 miles long	90s	70s
San Francisco, USA	North America	735,315	46.7	80s	55–75
Antarctic Peninsula	Antarctic			26.5	–32
(summer research stations)		10,000	51,000		
(ice shelves)		1,000	5,500,000		
Hawaiian Islands		1,193,000	6,450	88	57
Vermont, USA	North America	588,658	9,614	80s	below 32
England's Lake District	Europe	40,000	880	60	40
Amazon Forest	South America	20,000,000	2,700,000	80s	80s
Canadian Maritimes	North America	1,800,000	51,000	70s	24
Paris, France	Europe	2,100,000	40	65	40
Sahara Desert	Africa	2,000,000	3,500,000	130	
Tuscany (West Central Italy)	Europe	4,000,000	8,875	high 80s	60s

Source: information from *National Geographic Traveler*

EXERCISE 28

Reading a Table

Directions: The table on page 285 compares information about sixteen favorite places. Identify the place or places with the following characteristics.

1. Smallest population ______________________

2. Largest population ______________________

3. Population in a range of 2 million ______________________

4. Population ten times greater in summer than winter ______________________

5. Population of about 7 million ______________________

6. Smallest in size (square miles) ______________________

7. Largest in size (square miles) ______________________

8. Warmest in summer ______________________

9. Warmest in winter ______________________

10. Coldest in winter ______________________

Answers are on page 293.

Interpreting Editorial Cartoons

An **editorial cartoon** expresses the opinion of the cartoonist about a political or social issue. Editorial cartoons often caricature (depict in cartoon figures) politicians or public administrators. The caricatures exaggerate a feature of the person being illustrated.

Political symbols often appear in editorial cartoons as well. For example, the donkey represents the Democratic party, the elephant represents the Republican party, a bearded man dressed in stars and stripes (Uncle Sam) represents the United States, a dove represents peace, and a hawk represents war. Cartoonists use humor or satire to express their opinions on important issues affecting our country and world.

EXERCISE 29

Interpreting an Editorial Cartoon

Directions: Look at the political cartoon featuring the Supreme Court justices. Answer the following questions.

Permission of the Fort Worth Star - Telegram

1. What occupation does the figure at the podium represent?

____

2. For what issue (case) is the figure pleading? _______________

3. Who is hearing the case? _______________

4. What is *ironic* about the question the attorney asks? (*Ironic* means the opposite of the actual meaning.) _______________

5. What general message do you think the attorney is stating about our being careful not to offend others? _______________

____

Answers are on page 294.

Answer Key

Exercise 1: Understanding Idiomatic Expressions (page 218)

1. to outdo or surpass
2. very, very busy
3. across a major body of water [such as the Atlantic Ocean]
4. reviewed
5. communicate reasonably well
6. in a kennel
7. helped out
8. to remain very alert
9. fine
10. weighed

Exercise 2: Explaining Implications of Text (page 220)

Statement 1:
Who? Lewis Terman
When? after 1905
Where? Stanford University
What? "IQ tests should be used to conduct a great sorting out of the population so that young people would be assigned on the basis of their scores to particular levels in the school system." [This means students would be "tracked" into ability levels such as remedial, regular, and accelerated.]
Then what? This would lead to corresponding socioeconomic destinations in adult life. [This means the "sorting" or tracking of students would continue throughout life.]
What are the long-term results? We can speculate that the tracking could involve college entrance and placement in particular programs, would limit future jobs, would segregate housing, and so on.
Statement 2:
Who? Albert Einstein
What did he do? "discovered the essential structure of the cosmos"
How? "just by thinking about it" [presumably by the power of his own mind]
What did it lead to? "The scientific touchstones of our age—the Bomb, space travel, electronics—all bear his fingerprints." ["Bear his fingerprints" means his theories helped to lead to their development. "The Bomb" refers to the atomic bomb. "Space travel" includes manned and unmanned travel to the moon and beyond. "Electronics" includes radio, television, computer, and the Internet.]

Exercise 3: Paraphrasing or Restating Ideas (page 221)

1. The set-up in small classes allows me to work one-on-one with students and make sure they understand difficult work in classes.
2. The major problem is cheating. You can't tell who a voter is on the Internet.
3. Sam Clemens remembered his childhood sweetheart Laura Hawkins with the character Becky Thatcher in *Tom Sawyer.*

GED Practice Exercise 4: Making Inferences (Reading Between the Lines) (page 223)

1. **(3)** The comment that "it could have been about any war" suggests that this was not the first time such an incident occurred.
2. **(5)** There is no evidence in the statement that Americans could judge or interpret their orders. There is no evidence that Americans were confused or outraged. The fact that the Americans obeyed the orders, regardless of the nature of the orders, suggests their placing high value on obeying.
3. **(2)** The clues that suggest that truth is difficult to determine include the following: the United States government's denial of any factual knowledge; the insistence of Korean witnesses; the rejection of claims; confirmation of allegations by surviving ex-GIs; and possible "peasant white" clothing disguise.
4. **(5)** The passage states that "*North Korean soldiers might be disguised . . .*"

Exercise 5: Summarizing the Main Idea (page 226)
Possible summary of message is as follows: Christopher, Mom called from Paris! Very upset but everyone's OK. Can't use your credit cards. Lost wallet on train—a young boy and girl stole and jumped off. All four went back but kids gone. Went to clerk for help. Went to report it to the police—hard to find. Nice officer took report. Lost French francs but reported credit cards stolen. Closed those accounts but thieves changed over $800. Your family not liable. A few days before new cards issued and sent. Need something, use my card. Pay me later.

Exercise 6: Extrapolating or Interpolating Meaning (page 229)

Trend A:

Option (1)

Implications: This method is difficult to budget because you don't know what the price really will be when movers load up the truck. You could end up paying more.

Option (2)

Implications: This allows you to budget exactly for the move, but you don't know whether you will "make" or "lose" money on the deal.

Option (3)

Implications: You have to trust the judgment (and honesty) of the estimator. There is a question of whether the top price is fair.

Trend B:

You need to have certain essential belongings available to you, so they can't be packed on the truck. You need interim arrangements or another place to stay until your furniture arrives.

Estimates or predictions:

1. Price can vary widely among moving companies. Jeff and Jennifer may need to consider other factors.
2. Fairness and exactness of price may be sacrificed to avoid uncertainty. Those who need to know the exact cost in advance need to take the binding price. The fairest way may be to actually wait to weigh the goods, but this also is the most uncertain method.
3. Flexibility of pick-up and delivery time may be as important as price.

GED Practice Exercise 7: Applying Appropriate Definitions or Principles (page 232)

1. **(2)** The passage describes physical humor and comedians such as "Stooges."
2. **(1)** The passage describes an easygoing look at friends and friendships.
3. **(5)** The passage describes serious situations and thrilling action. ["NYPD" stands for New York Police Department.]
4. **(4)** The passage describes the sinking of a ship and loss of lives.
5. **(3)** The passage describes an improbable plot.

GED Practice Exercise 8: Using Application in Science (page 234)

1. **(3)** The passage states that the lymphatic system helps fight infection.
2. **(1)** The passage states that the excretory system expels water and salts from the body.
3. **(2)** The passage states that the endocrine system is made up of glands such as the thyroid.
4. **(5)** According to the passage, muscles belong to the muscular system.
5. **(4)** The passage states that the digestive system processes and distributes nutrients from food.

Exercise 9: Recognizing Propaganda Techniques (page 240)

1. **(4)** transferring
2. **(5)** card-stacking
3. **(3)** bandwagoning
4. **(1)** name-calling
5. **(2)** glittering generalities
6. **(4)** transferring

Exercise 10: Recognizing Facts, Opinions, and Hypotheses (page 242)

1. O
2. H
3. F
4. F
5. H
6. O
7. H
8. F

Exercise 11: Determining Adequacy of Facts (page 244)

1. CS (Credible Source)
2. CS (Credible Source)
3. NS (No Support)
4. F (Fact)

GED Practice Exercise 12: Distinguishing Conclusions from Supporting Statements (page 245)

1. **Choice (5)** contains the conclusion from Sentence 11 that despite the comfort, reassurance, cuddling, and words of encouragement that are given to infants and small children, *it is not possible to "spoil" a child before the age of two or three.*
2. **Choice (4)** is a secondary conclusion because it arrives at the conclusion of *practices that seem to produce the most secure children.*
3. **Choice (5)** contains the strongest clue in the word *belief* and the *colon (:),* which serves as a marker that a conclusion is to follow.
4. **Choice (1)** includes the link between the word *dependence* and a derivation of the same word: *dependable.*

Exercise 13: Drawing Conclusions through Inductive Reasoning (page 247)

1. A study was conducted of 461 children with persistent middle ear infections.
2. The study looked at those who had had surgery (adenoids and tonsils out) and those who had not.
3. Ear infections were reduced to an average of 1.4 per year for those who had surgery from 2.1 per year for those who did not have surgery.
4. Children who had adenoids and/or tonsils out did not do much better than those who had not had surgery.
5. Medical treatment followed by ear tubes should be tried first before resorting to surgery.

Exercise 14: Drawing Conclusions through Deductive Reasoning (page 248)

1. *Yes.* A cerebral hemorrhage results from the bursting (rupture) of a brain artery.
2. *Yes.* An embolism results from the blockage (obstruction) of a blood vessel; if the embolism is found in an artery of the brain, it can lead to a stroke.
3. *No.* A tumor is not a rupture or an obstruction of an artery of the brain.
4. *Yes.* An aneurysm is a blood-filled swelling of a vessel (artery). The rupture of an aneurysm can lead to a stroke.
5. *No.* Phlebitis results from the swelling of a vein, not an artery of the brain.

Exercise 15: Recognizing Style and Tone (page 249)

1. **(3)** The author creates sympathy for Leontis because he is an older man, he is bewildered, and he has not been successful with women.
2. **(4)** Angeliki is unhappy and desperate because she is only twenty-four years of age, she works hard from "dawn to dusk," she does not get along with her brother's wife, and because she "wished liberation from her bondage."
3. **(5)** There is evidence in the passage for all statements except for Angeliki's desiring to marry for wealth.
4. **(5)** The sentimental tone in the passage comes from dealing with the plight (difficult circumstances) of the characters.
5. **(4)** Leontis's misfortune can be explained by his past lack of success with attracting women, his bewilderment and self-flattery at Angeliki's attention, and his imagining that "he was madly in love." The first statement is false because the author creates sympathy for *both* characters. The second statement is not accurate because both characters are described but not in relation to each other. The third statement is not accurate because ages are mentioned and the fact that Angeliki has been in the country two years; however there is no focus on time order. The fifth statement is incorrect because there is no exaggeration or humor in the passage.

Exercise 16: Analysis in Science: The Scientific Method (page 252)

1. **b.** Changes in coffee growing are harmful to the environment.

2. b. Today trees are being cut down and replaced with fields that are easier and more efficient to harvest.

c. Chemical pesticides are needed to help the beans develop outside of the protective canopy.

3. In the 1970s farmers cut through shade canopy to combat fungus to produce high coffee yields.
Reducing the shade canopy resulted in the reduction in the number of species of migratory birds.

4. The new way of growing coffee will be harmful to the environment and to people.

5. c. The soil becomes soaked with the harmful chemicals.

d. Without the roots of the trees to hold it firm, the contaminated soil is washed into streams, causing a great health risk to people.

6. Greater health risks result from the new way of growing coffee. We need to return to the shade method of growing coffee.

Exercise 17: Recognizing Sequence (page 255)

a. 8
b. 7
c. 1
d. 10
e. 2
f. 6
g. 3
h. 4
i. 5
j. 9

Exercise 18: Identifying Comparison and Contrast Patterns (page 256)

Which first ladies belonged to the Democratic Party?

1. Jacqueline Lee Bouvier Kennedy
2. Claudia Taylor Johnson
3. Rosalynn Smith Carter
4. Hillary Rodham Clinton

Which first ladies belonged to the Republican Party?

1. Patricia Ryan Nixon
2. Elizabeth Bloomer Ford
3. Nancy Davis Reagan
4. Barbara Pierce Bush

Volunteer Service

1. Pat Nixon
2. Barbara Bush

Promotion of the Performing Arts

1. Pat Nixon
2. Rosalynn Carter
3. Hillary Clinton

Campaign Against Alcohol or Drug Dependency

1. Betty Ford
2. Nancy Reagan

Contrast the causes that were different by naming the first lady associated with each cause.

1. Pat Nixon
2. Rosalynn Carter
3. Rosalynn Carter
4. Barbara Bush
5. Betty Ford
6. Lady Bird Johnson
7. Nancy Reagan
8. Hillary Clinton

Exercise 19: Identifying Cause-and-Effect Relationships (page 260)

1. *Cause:* The corporation researched a colder, Midwestern climate and believed it would be successful there as well.
2. *Effect:* Many seniors took advantage of the development.
3. *Cause:* the construction of thousands of new homes
4. *Effect:* There was an increase in the demand for emergency health services.
5. *Cause:* building of stores, pharmacies, theaters, restaurants, and so on
6. *Effect:* need for more schools and more taxes to support the schools

Exercise 20: Using Synthesis (page 267)

Part A

a. 1
b. 2
c. 1
d. 4
e. 3
f. 4
g. 6
h. 5
i. 7

Part B (page 269)

1. The second passage written by Steven L. Kent is written in the third person ("he" or "Covey").
2. Kent reveals that Covey "has gone on to become a counselor to political leaders, chief executives and ordinary people the world over" and that Covey has become vice chairman of "a global professional-services company and publishers of the Franklin Planner products."
3. Kent explains that Covey wrote *The 7 Habits* "by organizing the material that he presents in his lectures." Covey did not write the book by simply sitting at a computer without the experience of interacting with audiences.
4. Kent apparently admires Covey and his book. Kent says "Covey is as self-effacing as ever." He also says that Covey "worries about having become, in effect, a guru." In other words, Kent recognizes that Covey is an established authority on the subject of "highly effective people" but that Covey does not seek the acclaim or status of a "guru."

Exercise 21: Evaluating Objective and Subjective Criteria (page 272)

1. Objective
2. Objective
3. Objective
4. Subjective: note the use of the word *should*
5. Subjective: note the use of the word *should*
6. Objective
7. Subjective: note the use of the word *must*
8. Subjective: note the use of the word *should*

Exercise 22: Understanding the Roles of Values and Beliefs (page 273)

1. promised land of freedom
2. dictatorship (or communism)
3. closeness or involvement with a child
4. parental right or authority to raise a child
5. material things, fun
6. family or family relationships
7. government or law or rulings

Answer Key

Exercise 23: Reading a Pictograph (page 276)

1. **(1)** Public, Private
   (2) 2000, 2001
2. **(1)** Two-Year Public
   (2) Two-Year Private
   (3) Four-Year Public
   (4) Four-Year Private
3. $2,000 to $15,000
4. $5,000 to $6,000
5. Two-Year Private and Four-Year Public
6. $2,000 for tuition and fees
7. $17,000 plus $6,000 equals $23,000

Exercise 24: Reading a Line Graph (page 278)

1. weekly; education; full-time; 25 years of age and older
2. $0 to $900
3. less than a high school diploma; high school graduate, no college; some college or associate degree; college graduate
4. 1998
5. 1979
6. about $550
7. decreased (from $548 to $479)
8. 1998
9. less than a high school diploma; high school graduate, no college; and some college or associate degree

Exercise 25: Reading a Bar Graph (page 280)

1. 1800
2. between 1900 and 2000
3. between 2049 and 2081
4. 0 and 600 (million)
5. 1800 to 2100

Exercise 26: Reading Circle Graphs (page 281)

1. non-Hispanic White 72%; Hispanic 11%; Black 13%; Asian 4%
2. non-Hispanic White 196.1 million; Hispanic 31.4 million; Black 34.9 million; Asian 10.9 million
3. non-Hispanic White 52%; Hispanic 24%; Black 15%; Asian 9%
4. non-Hispanic White 213 million; Hispanic 98.2 million; Black 59.2 million; Asian 37.6 million

Exercise 27: Reading a Weather Map (page 284)

1. Miami: 84 degrees
2. Green Bay [Wisconsin]: 27 degrees
3. Green Bay, Chicago, Detroit
   Portland or Seattle
4. Denver, Oklahoma City, and New Orleans

Exercise 28: Reading a Table (page 286)

1. Antarctic Peninsula: 10,000 (summer research); 1,000 (ice shelves)
2. Danang-Hue, Vietnam: 78,000,000
3. Paris, France: 2,100,000 or Sahara Desert: 2,000,000
4. Antarctic Peninsula: 10,000 in summer; 1,000 in winter
5. New York City, USA: 7,420,000 or London, England: 7,000,000
6. Venice, Italy (historic center): 3 square miles
7. Antarctic Peninsula (ice shelves): 5,500,000 square miles
8. Sahara Desert: 130 degrees
9. Australian Outback: 90s
10. Antarctic Peninsula: –32 degrees

Exercise 29: Interpreting a Political Cartoon (page 287)

1. a lawyer (an attorney)
2. free speech
3. the justices of the Supreme Court of the United States
4. The issue is free speech, yet the attorney is giving the Supreme Court the choice to hear "just the parts that don't offend anyone." That's not free speech.
5. The general message is that being so careful not to offend anyone can result in the violation of our freedom of speech [protected by the First Amendment to the United States Constitution].

Social Studies

What is the GED Social Studies Test like overall?

The GED Social Studies Test requires you to know some of the basic social studies concepts that will be covered in this book. You will not have to recall facts, but you will have to draw upon your *prior knowledge* of important social studies concepts, principles, events, and skills. The test includes clusters of historical time periods and critical historical points.

The context of the test is that of daily life settings that show you as an individual, as an acquirer, organizer, and user of information. It depicts common roles of adults, including that of citizen, family member, worker, and consumer. The test studies relationships between science, technology, and society and acknowledges local and global problems, issues, and events. You might say that the test has a world view. The test integrates research, communications, and the workplace and shows the diverse population of the United States.

Some of the skills you will need to demonstrate include information processing and technical skills, problem solving skills, interpersonal and social participation skills, and critical and creative thinking skills. To answer successfully, you will need to be able to show that you can comprehend (understand) what you read, apply information to a new situation, analyze relationships among ideas or concepts, and make judgments about the material presented.

How many questions are on the test?

There are 50 multiple-choice questions, and you will be given 70 minutes to complete the test.

- Approximately 40% of the questions will be based on reading passages of up to 250 words each.
- Approximately 40% will be based on visuals—graphs, maps, charts, photos, pictures, diagrams, advertisements, political cartoons, or practical documents.

  Some examples of practical documents are voters' handbooks or registration forms, tax forms, driver's manuals, insurance forms, bank statements, workplace benefits packages or contracts, almanacs, atlases, political speeches, and local, state, or national budgets.
- The remaining 20% of the questions will be reading passages and visuals together.

What's on the test?

The GED Social Studies Test can be broken down into these content areas:

National History (United States or Canadian)	25%
World History	15%
Geography	15%
Civics and Government	25%
Economics	20%

These essential social studies concepts are covered in Chapters 1–5 of this section. However, keep in mind that a given question may draw from a number of these subjects. In discussing society or people, it is natural to touch on a number of topics. For example, a question on the U.S. Constitution may draw from material covered in both political science and history. The test acknowledges the **interdisciplinary** nature of social studies.

Some particular documents that are helpful for you to study are fundamental U.S. or Canadian documents: excerpts from the *Declaration of Independence, U.S. Constitution, Federalist Papers, Bill of Rights,* Supreme Court landmark cases, (*Charter of Rights and Freedoms* in Canada). Don't forget to review newspapers and magazines.

What themes are represented by the Social Studies content?

There are ten themes reflected in the content:

<u>Culture</u> (anthropology and sociology)
<u>Time, continuity, and change</u> (history)
<u>People, places, and environments</u> (geography)
<u>Individual development and identity</u> (behavioral sciences)
<u>Individuals, groups, and institutions</u> (behavioral sciences)
<u>Power, authority, and governance</u> (civics and government)
<u>Production, distribution, and consumption</u> (economics)
<u>Science, technology, and society</u> (applications of social science)
<u>Global connections</u> (history, geography, and economics)
<u>Civic ideals and practice</u> (history, civics, and government)

What are the thinking skills needed for the test?

Thinking skills that you will be tested on include

Understanding Ideas	20%
Applying Ideas	30%
Analyzing Ideas	30%
Evaluating Ideas	20%

Of the thinking skills listed above, the skill of **analysis** is especially important. Questions of this type might involve looking for main ideas, drawing conclusions, identifying supporting details, comparing and contrasting views, or tracing causes or effects of events.

CHAPTER 1
World History

To study world history is to read about the origins of the human race and its cultural development from primitive times to ancient civilizations to the present. The world's social, religious, industrial, agricultural, political, and economic traditions can all be traced to early humanity.

Early Humanity

The study of the earliest humans is considered prehistory because there is no written account of their lifestyles. From archeologists' discoveries of primitive dwellings, cave drawings, skeletal remains, and artifacts, we know where the earliest human communities existed. **Anthropologists** have examined these artifacts—items such as tools, weapons, and pottery—and have intensely researched bone fragments and **fossil** remains to uncover evidence about different periods of human development.

The earliest stage of cultural development has been classified as the **Stone Age** because of the evidence that early humans used stone tools. Stones were shaped to use as knives and spear points for hunting and defense and as tools, such as hammers, axes, and scrapers. Later, people made stone and bone tools like needles, harpoons, fishhooks, and arrowheads. These early people were **nomadic**—they had no permanent shelters and followed the herds of animals that they hunted for survival.

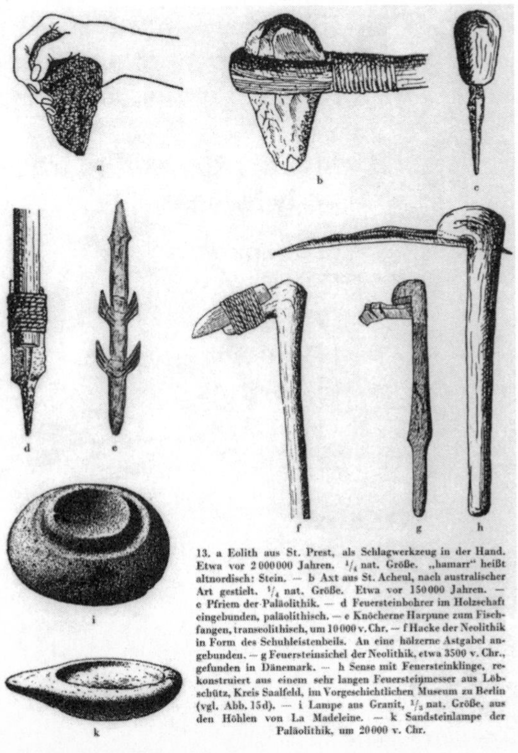

a
b
c
d
e
f
g
h
i
k
13. a Eolith aus St. Prest, als Schlagwerkzeug in der Hand. Etwa vor 2 000 000 Jahren. 1/4 nat. Größe. „hamarr" heißt altnordisch: Stein. — b Axt aus St. Acheul, nach australischer Art gestielt. 1/4 nat. Größe. Etwa vor 150 000 Jahren. — c Pfriem der Paläolithik. — d Feuersteinbohrer im Holzschaft eingebunden, paläolithisch. — e Knöcherne Harpune zum Fischfangen, transeolithisch, um 10 000 v. Chr. — f Hacke der Neolithik in Form des Schuhleistenbeils. An eine hölzerne Astgabel angebunden. — g Feuersteinsichel der Neolithik, etwa 3500 v. Chr., gefunden in Dänemark. — h Sense mit Feuersteinklinge, rekonstruiert aus einem sehr langen Feuersteinmesser aus Löbschütz, Kreis Saalfeld, im Vorgeschichtlichen Museum zu Berlin (vgl. Abb. 15d). — i Lampe aus Granit, 1/3 nat. Größe, aus den Höhlen von La Madeleine. — k Sandsteinlampe der Paläolithik, um 20 000 v. Chr.

© Bettmann/Corbis

What might have been the uses of the artifacts pictured here?

Over time many groups of early humans ceased their nomadic lifestyle to become hunters and gatherers in areas of abundant game, fresh water, and fertile soil. Scientific study of these sites has shown that these early farmers were able to determine which crops would grow best for their soil and climate. With such developing knowledge of agriculture, these people learned to work the land and to domesticate animals. Many of these early groups built more permanent shelters. Gradually communities developed, and societal organization became necessary for survival.

Within these newly formed communities, some individuals practiced special skills or trades. Commerce developed through **bartering** goods (e.g., food, cloth, or pottery) or services (e.g., medicinal, labor). As the basic communities grew, a need for rules and organization also grew; so the early forms of government were created. A unifying factor in these early settlements was fear and lack of knowledge about the surrounding world. The ways early humans explained these natural phenomena led to the early forms of religion and to the development of traditions and beliefs.

GED PRACTICE

EXERCISE 1

Early Humanity

Directions: Select the *best* answer to each question based on what you learned from the passage.

1. Which of the following would be considered a fossil?

(1) a clay pot used for cooking
(2) a club used for defense
(3) the ancient remains of a bird
(4) the spear of a hunter
(5) a basket made for gathering food

2. Identify the skill or trade that did not have its beginnings with early humans.

(1) banker
(2) tailor
(3) farmer
(4) doctor
(5) carpenter

Answers are on page 444.

Early Civilization

Evidence of much of humanity's early technological advancement has been found in ancient Egyptian civilization. Beginning about 5000 B.C., the Nile River Valley in northeast Africa provided the agricultural conditions for many permanent settlements to develop. The abundance of good harvests allowed for thriving communities that continued to expand. With the support and influence of the rulers and religious leaders, cultural advancement took place in art, music, entertainment, technology, and science.

The ancient **Egyptians** are considered one of the most advanced of the early civilizations. Evidence of their contributions to the world can be seen in the magnificent statues of their gods, in pottery and jewelry, in the ruins of their colossal pyramids and tombs, within their written language known as hieroglyphics, and in their perfection of the mummification process.

Egyptian religion promoted the existence of an afterlife. Rulers, wealthy citizens, and religious leaders believed in preservation of the body after death by means of embalming with chemicals to prevent decomposition. The dead were then wrapped and placed into coffins that had been decorated to resemble their appearance. These rituals assisted the deceased in maintaining their status while crossing into the world of the dead.

Ordinary citizens and slaves did not have such a burial. In fact, servants were often sealed into the grave with their dead masters so that they could serve them when they reached the other side. The rulers of Egypt, the **pharaohs**, were thought to be gods among men. This status entitled them to have pyramids or tombs erected for their eventual placement after death. Their earthly treasures of jewelry, statues, weapons, and furniture were buried with them to insure their wealth in the hereafter. Although many of these precious artifacts were stolen or destroyed over the centuries, researchers have been able to learn valuable information about this early civilization through the treasures that remained.

We learned much about the early Egyptian culture after we were able to translate the symbols and pictures found on the walls of the tombs. This symbolic picture writing, called **hieroglyphics,** presented accounts of the tomb's occupant and the society he or she lived in. In the early 1800s a French scholar, Jean Champollion, deciphered a slab of black stone. Now known as the **Rosetta Stone**, it has two hieroglyphic scripts and one ancient Greek script written on it. By 1822 Champollion was able to translate from the Greek back through the two sets of hieroglyphic scripts. Since that discovery, archaeologists and scholars have been able to translate the written language of ancient Egypt.

© Bettmann/Corbis

The Rosetta Stone is on display at the British Museum in London, England.

GED PRACTICE

EXERCISE 2

Early Civilization

Directions: Read the following questions and select the *best* response.

1. Which of the following statements is true based on the information about the early Egyptians?

(1) The Egyptians had an advanced language with a lettered alphabet.
(2) The Egyptians did not understand written language.
(3) The Egyptians recorded their history with a symbolic language.
(4) The Egyptians did not record their early history.
(5) The Egyptians had only a few people who could write.

2. Which of the following descriptions of the Egyptian culture is not true?

(1) The Egyptians were a strong civilization that conquered many other tribes.
(2) Art and music were very important in the Egyptian culture.
(3) Wealthy Egyptians were preserved after their deaths.
(4) The Egyptians were successful farmers because of the fertile Nile Valley.
(5) Treasures and servants were often buried with the Egyptian dead.

Answers are on page 444.

Civilizations Begin to Interact

The Fertile Crescent

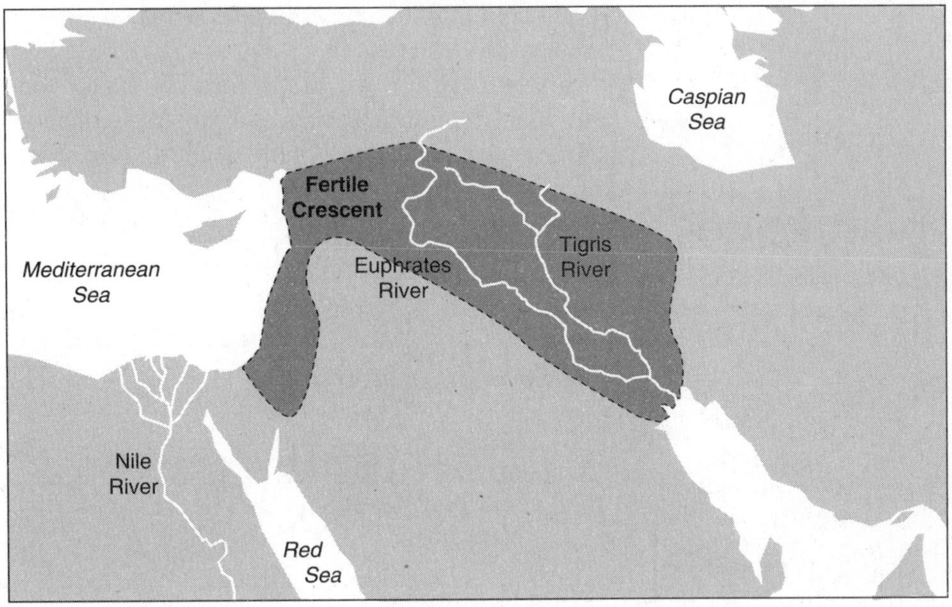

The Middle East and the coastal regions of the Mediterranean Sea, as well as the Nile Delta, were the locations for the beginnings of many early civilizations, including Babylonian, Sumerian, Phoenician, Persian, and Greek. This close proximity allowed for trade and also created competition for land and resources. This competition led to many conflicts and wars between rival groups. The interaction among various cultures created changes in and exchanges of traditions and technology. Some civilizations developed vast empires, which expanded their land holdings at the cost of extinguishing smaller cultural groups.

The classical civilizations that had the largest impact on the world's cultural development are the **Greek** and **Roman empires**. Greek civilization continued the Egyptian priorities of art, literature, music, theater, architecture, and the sciences. The first major citizen participation in government occurred in ancient **Athens**, a powerful Greek city-state. All male citizens participated in the assembly, which determined laws and policies.

During the golden age of ancient Greece (500 B.C. to 300 B.C.), many great philosophers and educators such as **Socrates, Plato,** and **Aristotle** shared their wisdom with the world. For the first time, the improvement of the mind and the body was viewed as an important priority for society. The challenge of improved physical fitness was the reason the **Olympic Games** were begun in ancient Greece. The Olympics as we know them today were revived more than a hundred years ago, in 1896, in Athens, Greece.

Eventually, the Romans conquered the Greeks, copying their architecture, art forms, poetry, and even some of their mythological gods. Both the Greeks and the Romans had maintained early people's practice of using myth to explain natural phenomenon like seasonal changes, flooding and severe weather, and success in agriculture. To make the myths easier to understand and appreciate, the Greeks and Romans both had gods with human attributes. Greek and Roman mythology has continued to exist even after our understanding of the universe has outgrown the need for story-like explanations.

Greek Name	Roman Name	Occupation
Zeus	Jupiter	Chief of the gods
Poseidon	Neptune	God of the sea
Hades	Pluto	God of the underworld
Hera	Juno	Goddess of Marriage/wife of the chief
Hestia	Vesta	Goddess of hearth and home
Ares	Mars	God of war
Athena	Minerva	Goddess of science and education
Apollo	Apollo/Sol/Phoebus	God of the sun
Artemis	Diana	Goddess of the moon and the hunt
Aphrodite	Venus	Goddess of love and beauty
Hermes	Mercury	God of commerce and speed
Hephaestus	Vulcan	God of fire and the forge
Eros	Cupid	God of love
Persephone	Proserpina	Goddess of spring/wife of the god of the underworld
Dionysis	Bacchus	God of wine and revelry

Notice that many of the planets were named for Roman Gods. Do you recognize any of the names?

While the Greeks believed in the fitness of the mind and the body, the Romans were more interested in military strength and acquiring land for the empire. Thus, athletic competition and training for combat as a form of entertainment developed in Rome. The Roman government differed from the Athenian model as well. One, two, or sometimes three consuls were chosen by the Roman senate, a group of the wealthiest landholders, or patricians. The vast majority of the citizens were plebeians—the small farmers, tradesmen, artisans, and merchants.

Wealth and connections among family members thus determined position in the social classes within Roman culture. This status determined if a member of the society was considered worthy of having a vote. This system of government was called a **republic.** The lower class of slaves and the common class of farmers and tradesmen were limited in their rights of marriage partners and land ownership.

One lasting contribution of the Romans was the calendar introduced by **Julius Caesar** in 46 B.C. The old calendar had become out of step with the seasons, so Caesar made the months of unequal days and added leap years to make the reckoning more equal to an actual year. This Julian calendar, with some modifications, is still in use today.

GED PRACTICE

EXERCISE 3

Civilizations Begin to Interact

Directions: Read the following questions and choose the *best* response.

1. **Which of the following is a feature *only* of the Roman civilization and not the Greek civilization?**

   (1) athletic competition and training
   (2) military strength to fight off invaders
   (3) interest in art and music as entertainment
   (4) citizen participation in government
   (5) creation of an accurate calendar

2. **Which of the following activities would *not* be an example of the Greek philosophy of improvement of mind and body?**

   (1) going to an educational movie
   (2) taking a yoga stretching class
   (3) playing a computer strategy game
   (4) watching a football game
   (5) enrolling in a math class

Answers are on page 444.

Writing Activity 1

Write a paragraph about an activity you participate in that could be an example of the Greek philosophy of self-improvement.

Civilizations Develop Religions

At the time of the expansion of the Roman Empire in the first century B.C., the belief systems of the Egyptians, Greeks, and Romans still centered on a group of gods. The tribes in what is now Israel practiced **Judaism** and believed in one God. With the birth of **Jesus Christ** in the Palestinian town of Bethlehem, the religious practices and beliefs of the Western world would soon be affected by a new religion called **Christianity.** This new religion was founded on the belief that Jesus was the Messiah that Jewish law had prophesied.

After Jesus' death, Christian ideas and beliefs were spread by a small group of men called disciples. Eventually, because Rome was the center of western civilization at that time, it became the center of the Church. The leader of the new church was given the title of *Pope.* The regional leaders, called bishops, expanded Christianity throughout Europe in a variety of methods, including religious war.

Beginning in A.D. 1095, European kings organized the **Crusades** to fight the enemies of the Roman Catholic Church. Christian knights and soldiers battled for ownership of the Holy Land (in current day Israel and Palestine) against the Muslims. The Muslim Arabs followed the religion of **Islam,** founded by the prophet **Mohammed** in A.D. 612. They held Palestine until Islamic Turks took it and began preventing Christians from making safe pilgrimages to the Holy Land. The Crusades were fought in an attempt to restore Christian access to the Holy Land and to reconnect the two branches of Christianity (Roman Catholic and Eastern Orthodox) that had been separated since the fall of Rome.

Religions developed in the Far East as well. **Hinduism** is a long-established religion practiced by millions. This religion is based on a belief that all people are born into a particular **caste**, or class, and must do what is expected within that caste. Like Hinduism, **Buddhism** is practiced by millions. It began in the sixth century B.C. in India, and teaches that one's soul will attain *Nirvana,* a divine state free of earthly ills, through self-denial and correct living.

The Chinese philosopher **Confucius** was a contemporary of Buddha. Confucian teachings stressed social harmony and challenged everyone to live under high moral codes of conduct. Unlike Buddhism and Hinduism, however, **Confucianism** is not a religion but a philosophy, whose goal is harmony on earth.

Writing Activity 2

All the major religions (Buddhism, Christianity, Hinduism, Islam, Judaism) have a few basic beliefs in common. For example, followers of each of these religions believe that people should not steal or lie. In two or three paragraphs, explain why you think the different religions have these common beliefs.

Chinese Dynasties

Even before the Roman Empire, **Chinese dynasties** had been flourishing in Asia for centuries. Confucius lived during the Chou dynasty, a time of warfare among land-owning feudal lords. The first emperor of China founded the **Ch'in Dynasty** (221 B.C.–206 B.C.). Historians have traced the origin of the name *China* back to this word. Ch'in centralized the monarchy, organized the country into regions called provinces and appointed officials to carry out imperial rule. One of the longest lasting contributions of this dynasty was the construction of the Great Wall to serve as a protective border against invaders.

The next dynasty in China was the **Han Dynasty** (206 B.C.–A.D. 220). The Han ruler was responsible for successfully driving back the nomadic warriors that threatened to take over the north and west sides of China. He also reestablished the importance of education and Confucian thought.

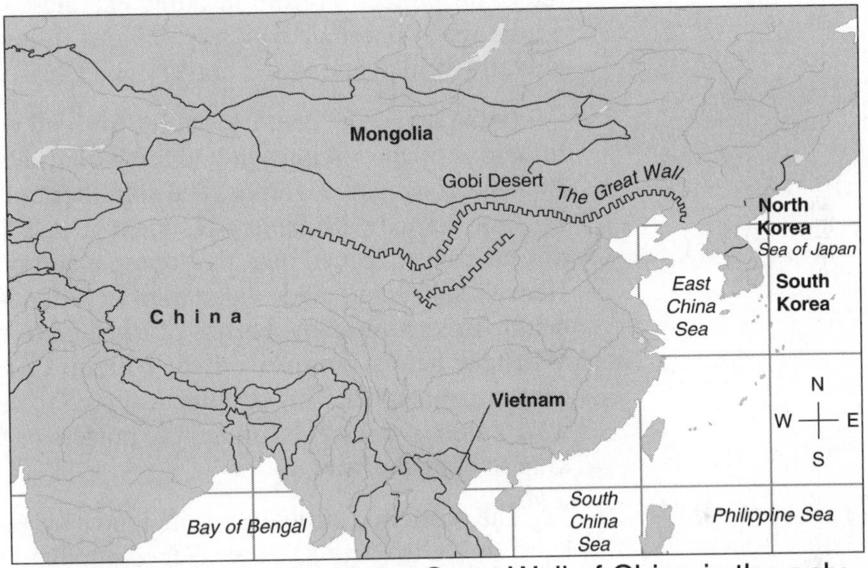

It has been reported that the Great Wall of China is the only man-made structure on Earth that is visible from space.

EXERCISE 4

Chinese Dynasties

Directions: Read the following questions and select the *best* answer.

Based on the information regarding the Chinese dynasties, label the statements as fact (F) or opinion (O).

_______ The Great Wall of China is still a good defense system.

_______ The Han Dynasty was the most successful dynasty.

_______ Confucius lived during the Chou Dynasty.

_______ The name *China* originated from the Ch'in dynasty.

Answers are on page 444.

The Middle Ages and the Feudal System

With the fall of the Roman Empire in A.D. 476, western Europe was thrown into chaos. Tribal chiefs and kings of small regions took control for local protection. Most of the population, except for royalty and clergy, was illiterate. It was a time when art and literature and architecture no longer flourished. This period was called the **Dark Ages.**

During the Dark Ages in Europe, a social order known as the **feudal system** was instituted. This was a well-defined system of classes or levels within society. It was based on the belief that if everyone had a place in society, there would be less conflict. The feudal system had top-ranking nobles: the king, the lords, the lesser lords, and the knights. The peasants and the townspeople made up 90 percent of the population. The lord was responsible to the king and managed the estate that the peasants worked in return for protection from invading enemies. To keep them from taking advantage of unarmed peasants, knights followed a code of honor called **chivalry,** which combined bravery and Christian values.

In the early 13th century, battles for land were being fought in England. Invasions by the Vikings and ongoing conflicts with the Roman Church kept England constantly fighting. The split that finally divided the church in England started with **Henry II**, when he and **Thomas Becket**, the Archbishop of Canterbury, argued over the supreme authority of the king and the church. Henry's son, John, made an attempt to settle the conflict after his father's death. This required the barons of England to pay heavy taxes to the church. When the barons complained, the **Magna Carta** was written in 1215 to protect their rights. This document served to establish rights of even those who were not nobles. It limited the powers of the monarchy, forcing even the king to obey the laws.

The economic structure of the feudal system was very weak. Poor harvests led to famines. A weakened population was not able to fight off infectious diseases, which had spread throughout the trade routes. During the 14th century, a terrifying plague hit Europe. Infected fleas carried by rats through the towns transmitted the **bubonic plague,** also known as the **Black Death**. The villages and early cities had inadequate sewage systems, which contributed greatly to the spread of the plague. This plague is said to have killed one-third of all Europeans; no class, from peasants to royalty, escaped. Towns and farms were completely abandoned. Without farming, trading, and craft working, the economy collapsed even further. Western Europe took more than 100 years to recover.

GED PRACTICE

EXERCISE 5

The Middle Ages and the Feudal System

Directions: Choose the *best* response to each of the following questions.

1. **What was the main idea of Feudalism in the Middle Ages?**

   (1) protection of the lower classes
   (2) transition of wealth
   (3) education of the nobles
   (4) preservation of the middle class
   (5) suppression of the peasants

2. The *Magna Carta* states:

   In the first place we have granted to God, and by this our present charter confirmed for us and our heirs forever that the English church shall be free, and shall have her rights entire, and her liberties inviolate; and we will that it be thus observed; which is apparent from this that the freedom of elections, which is reckoned most important and very essential to the English church. . .

   What is the main idea of this section of the *Magna Carta*?

   (1) Liberties are only granted by the Pope.
   (2) The church in England will be free from the king's rule.
   (3) Elections should not be free so that a king will always be in power.
   (4) God created the *Magna Carta* because the people deserved it.
   (5) Church members only have freedom in England.

Answers are on page 444.

The Hundred Years' War

In addition to the plague, a war of great duration also weakened the European economy during this time. In 1337, England held some of northern France as the result of a royal marriage. Conflict grew because of economic rivalries between the two countries. Finally, when King Edward III of England tried to claim the French throne, the **Hundred Years' War** broke out.

After English victories, the winning commanders allowed their soldiers to pillage the French countryside. Further financial pressure was put on the French people by their king in order to pay debts. The peasants revolted under the stress of war, famine, and taxes. A peasant girl named **Joan of Arc** inspired them to fight with her against the English and to show loyalty for France. Her faith and patriotism helped lead the French troops to successfully beat back the enemy. Joan was eventually captured by the English and burned at the stake for heresy because she claimed she was instructed by heavenly voices.

EXERCISE 6

The Hundred Years' War

Directions: Identify the following statements as **true (T)** or **false (F)** based on the above passage.

1. ______ France controlled some of England as a result of royal marriage.

2. ______ The French were not able to prevent pillaging by the English.

3. ______ Joan of Arc was a French war heroine who died in battle.

4. ______ The French were very supportive of their government.

Answers are on page 445.

The Renaissance

Periods in world history shift between times of great warfare and times of intellectual development. In the late Middle Ages, about A.D. 1400, Western Europe was becoming more stable, both politically and economically. Many wealthy Europeans were in positions of power. These wealthy nobles and merchants were able to fund cultural pursuits such as music, art, and literature. This period of time is known as the **Renaissance,** from a French word meaning "rebirth." Not since the fall of the Roman Empire had there been such a revitalized interest in and support of arts, crafts, and architecture. The depression of the past several hundred years had ended. This was a time when wealthy patrons supported great French and Italian artists. **Michelangelo** created the sculpture of David; and other artists, such as Donatello, **Leonardo da Vinci,** and Raphael Sanzio completed their timeless masterpieces during the golden years of the fifteenth and early sixteenth centuries. Great poets, writers, and inventors also flourished at this time.

One invention that greatly advanced culture in Europe and eventually the world was the **printing press.** In the1440s a German engraver, **Johannes Gutenberg,** created the first printing press that used movable pieces of type. Because the teachings in the Bible were a major influence upon most of Europe, it was only fitting that Gutenberg's first published book was the Bible. His invention started a revolution in printing, which made books available to all classes of people.

The Gutenberg Press

© Underwood & Underwood/Corbis

GED PRACTICE

EXERCISE 7

The Renaissance

Directions: Read the following questions and select the *best* answer based on the passage on page 309.

1. Which of the following statements about the Renaissance is opinion?

(1) The arts were a significant aspect of the Renaissance.
(2) Wealthy patrons supported many French and Italian artists.
(3) Many wealthy Europeans were in powerful positions during the Renaissance.
(4) The best poetry was created during the Renaissance.
(5) The Gutenberg Bible is a historical literary work.

2. Which was the most important factor in beginning the Renaissance?

(1) French and Italian artists were creating masterpieces.
(2) Gutenberg invented the printing press.
(3) Western Europe had stabilized.
(4) Poets and other writers flourished during this time.
(5) Michelangelo sculpted his David.

Answers are on page 445.

America is Discovered

In 1492, while Spain was under the rule of King Ferdinand and Queen Isabella, the Italian navigator **Christopher Columbus** received permission and support to find a faster trade route to China and the East Indies. He believed that by sailing directly west, instead of south around the Cape of Good Hope as other explorers had done, he would discover a more direct route. It is because of this historic journey, during which he landed in an unknown hemisphere, that we celebrate the discovery of America.

Explorers of the New World

YEAR	EXPLORER	REGION
1000	Leif Ericson	Newfoundland
1492	Christopher Columbus	the Caribbean
1497	John Cabot	the east coast of Canada
1497	Amerigo Vespucci	the northeast coast of South America
1513	Juan Ponce de Leon	Florida and Mexico

Writing Activity 3

Was Columbus the discoverer of America? Some argue that he was simply wrong in his calculations and stumbled onto the new continent by mistake. Others point to evidence that earlier explorers from other countries came to the new continent first. Write a paragraph or more on how you feel about all of the possible discoverers of the New World.

The Reformation Divides Christianity

The Catholic Church suffered a great upheaval in 1517, when a German monk named **Martin Luther** made a list of complaints against the church. These 95 complaints sparked another split in Christianity. The new group was called **Protestants**; their split from the Catholic Church started a reformation period throughout Europe. The **Reformation** gave local noblemen the chance to stop the payment of taxes to Rome and to seize local Roman Catholic land for themselves.

The royal family of England also had quarrels with the Roman Catholic Church. **King Henry VIII** wanted to annul his marriage to Catherine of Aragon, since after 18 years of marriage she had not produced a son to be the next heir to the English throne. The Pope refused to give the king an annulment of this marriage so he would be free to marry Anne Boleyn. In 1529, Henry VIII took control of the church in England, and by 1534 the Act of Supremacy had given the king power over the English church.

After Henry VIII's death, his first daughter, **Mary Tudor**, inherited the throne. She was raised as a Catholic and attempted to return England to Catholicism. Because of her persecutions of those who did not follow her lead back to the Roman church, she was given the nickname Bloody Mary. When Mary died, her Protestant half-sister, **Elizabeth I**, became queen.

The Ruling Monarchs from the House of Tudor, England

Henry VII	Henry VIII	Edward VI	Lady Jane Grey*	Mary I	Elizabeth I
1485—1509	1509—1547	1547—1553	1553	1553—1558	1558—1603

*Proclaimed Queen for nine days and beheaded for treason

In the 1500s, **Philip II** of Spain attempted to centralize power over all Europe. The Netherlands in northern Europe had long been establishing itself as a center of trade and banking. Philip II sent many troops to reassert Catholic theology over the Dutch who, with the help of **Calvinist** preachers, were becoming increasingly Protestant. The Dutch revolt won their independence in 1581 with some support from the English, who did not want to see Catholic rule spread to their own shores. The Spanish sent a fleet of ships called an *armada* to England, only to have them sink in a terrible storm as they approached the English Channel.

GED PRACTICE

EXERCISE 8

The Reformation Divides Christianity

Directions: Select the *best* answer based on the information provided.

1. **What conclusion can you draw about the Reformation?**

   The Reformation was about

   (1) a variety of religious freedoms
   (2) the beginning of Protestantism
   (3) European economic expansion
   (4) the combining of many religions
   (5) additional taxation of noblemen

2. **Which of the following people encouraged Catholicism during the Reformation?**

   (1) Elizabeth I
   (2) Mary I
   (3) Calvinist preachers
   (4) Catherine of Aragon
   (5) Henry VIII

Answers are on page 445.

Writing Activity 4

Write a paragraph on how the United States might be different if the Spanish Armada had successfully conquered England.

The Enlightenment

As the Renaissance was a period of focus on the arts, the period known as the **Enlightenment** saw a new focus on science and technology. From the late 1500s and into the 1600s, scholars and early scientists began questioning humanity's place in nature as taught by the Roman Catholic Church. It was at this time that **Copernicus, Galileo,** and **Sir Isaac Newton** proposed new ideas about astronomy and physics. Medical science rose to a new level of prominence, in part because **Anton van Leeuwenhoek** and his microscope gave new understanding of microbes and diseases. **William Harvey** discovered and demonstrated the circulation of blood.

Later, in the late seventeenth and eighteenth centuries, philosophers and statesmen began questioning people's role in society in addition to the study of the physical world. **John Locke** became a very influential author who wrote about the role that the individual played in society. Others, such as the writers **Voltaire** and **Jean-Jacques Rousseau,** argued that common sense, tolerance, and a natural belief that human beings were good were needed to make a great society work.

"I GUESS YOU CAN SAY THAT SINCE LEEUWENHOEK OUR FAMILY HAS BEEN IN SHOW BUSINESS."

GED PRACTICE

EXERCISE 9

The Enlightenment

Directions: Read the following questions and select the *best* answer.

1. **What is one consequence of the Enlightenment?**

   (1) Doctors could cure all diseases in people.
   (2) Influential authors changed how people understood diseases.
   (3) The church supported scientific discoveries.
   (4) New discoveries made scientists wealthy.
   (5) The microscope helped to identify causes of diseases.

2. **Which of the following is a true statement about the Enlightenment?**

   (1) Doctors became less important.
   (2) It was proven that man is naturally good.
   (3) Copernicus promoted new ideas about astronomy.
   (4) No one understood blood circulation.
   (5) The arts were made available to everyone.

Answers are on page 445.

Control of Eastern Europe

While religious and political changes took place in western Europe during the 1600s, there were other battles for power in eastern Europe. Russia had many leaders that would be given the title **czar**, or supreme ruler. In 1613, after competing factions had murdered many new czars, **Michael Romanov** was elected. The Romanov family quickly increased the power of the monarchy. They gave the nobles power over the peasants in order to gain the nobles' support for their new policies. The peasants were treated like slaves, causing continued uprisings.

In 1682 **Peter the Great** became czar of Russia. He pushed for technological development of the nation by bringing in various technical specialists from western Europe. This opened the doors to international trade and economic growth. Many leaders at that time foresaw the need to improve their technology so that they would not be left behind in the new global levels of commerce. Through Peter the Great's efforts in this area, Russia became a European power.

EXERCISE 10

Control of Eastern Europe

Directions: Number the following list of events in chronological order.

______ Russia became a European power.

______ Competing factions murdered new czars.

______ Treating peasants like slaves caused uprisings.

______ Michael Romanov became czar of Russia.

______ Peter the Great became czar of Russia.

Answers are on page 445.

The French Revolution and Napoleon

In late-eighteenth-century France, social unrest existed between the aristocracy and the impoverished citizenry. The citizens were angry and frustrated at the excessive lifestyle of **King Louis XVI** and his wife, **Marie Antoinette,** while much of the country was poverty-stricken. The people were also being exposed to the openness of thought expressed by Voltaire and Rousseau. The Americans had successfully rebelled against the British monarchy to win their independence, proving that monarchies could be resisted.

Because of the national uneasiness in France, in 1788 the king called for a meeting of the Estates-General, an assembly that had not been called for nearly 175 years. Three hundred of the deputies represented the monarchy, 300 represented the church, and the other 600 represented the masses. The last group called for a vote by head and created the National Assembly, which voted to limit the powers of both the monarchy and the church.

Ongoing struggles between the National Assembly and the French king led to some people challenging the king's loyalty to France. The king and his family were caught on occasion moving to secret locations because they feared for their safety. Eventually the French peasants revolted in 1789, beginning with the storming of the **Bastille**, a Paris prison that symbolized oppression to the people. Both the king and the queen, as well as hundreds of aristocrats, were later beheaded.

Years of unrest continued because France lacked effective leadership. The people required a strong leader because the new governing body, the Directorate, was weak and disorganized. The people were eager to follow **Napoleon Bonaparte**, whom they considered a war hero. He was an artillery lieutenant who gained recognition for his daring victories over the British, defeated Austria, and fought in Syria and Egypt. With the support of the armies and the people, he easily overthrew the Directorate. He established a new government, later known as the First Empire. Napoleon introduced a new system of laws that became known as the **Napoleonic Code.** The code recognized that all male citizens were equal under the law. It also allowed the people of France to participate in the religion of their choice and to work in the occupation of their choice.

That same year Napoleon declared himself emperor of France. He wanted to conquer Europe, and his armies engaged the British in the west and in the Mediterranean, in addition to the Austrians, Prussians, and Russians in the east. His downfall came in 1815 at the hands of the British and their allies at the **Battle of Waterloo,** near Brussels, Belgium. Following this disastrous defeat, the British banished Napoleon to the island of St. Helena, where he died in 1821.

Writing Activity 5

The common expression "met his Waterloo" refers to Napoleon's last battle. Based on what you have just read about Napoleon, what do you think is the significance of this statement as it applies to anyone? Write your opinion in two or three paragraphs.

Central America

Shortly after the American Revolution and the French Revolution, Mexico won its independence from Spain in 1821. Following this lead, independence was declared in Nicaragua, Costa Rica, El Salvador, Honduras, and Guatemala. They formed the short-lived Federation of Central American States, which dissolved in 1838. Unfortunately, many of those countries suffered through a series of failed governments. Only Costa Rica built a tradition of democracy similar to that of the United States. It would be well into the 20th century before the other Central American nations stabilized.

GED PRACTICE

EXERCISE 11

Central America

Directions: Read the question and select the *best* answer.

What consequences might there be for a country that has many sudden changes in its leadership, whether from coup or revolt?

(1) suspicion of an unstable and unreliable current government
(2) rapid population decrease as people flee
(3) change in currency making commerce weak
(4) food shortages caused by of lack of regulation
(5) loss of land and established borders

Answer is on page 445.

The Industrial Revolution

In nineteenth-century Europe and the United States, changes continued to occur in technology and the social order. This period is referred to as the **Industrial Revolution.** Factories were built in the larger cities, with mechanized assembly lines for mass production of goods. For the first time, a new working class was earning wages in factory jobs.

As the people in the United States and throughout most of Europe had achieved independence from foreign rulers, each nation now had to face its own economic problems and deal with the changes caused by the Industrial Revolution. Populations moved from a mostly rural existence to crowded cities where workers formed a large part of the community. The telegraph and telephone provided means of long distance communication, which brought people and communities closer together.

While the business leaders gained great wealth, they often did so at the expense of poorly paid factory workers. German author **Karl Marx** wrote about the terrible working conditions of the period and the flaws he saw in the capitalist system that created them. He believed that capitalism would drag more workers into poverty.

Marx explained his ideas in a book called ***The Communist Manifesto,*** which influenced Vladimir Lenin and helped bring about the overthow of the Russian czar in 1917 (see page 320).

EXERCISE 12

The Industrial Revolution

Directions: Label each statement as **true (T)** or **false (F).**

1. ______ Everyone got rich during the Industrial Revolution.
2. ______ The telegraph and the telephone were not important inventions.
3. ______ Many people moved to the cities to get jobs in factories.
4. ______ The middle class had always worked for wages in factories.
5. ______ Marx thought that the factories were a good idea.

Answers are on page 445.

The World Enters World War I

After the **Napoleonic Wars**, many European nations formed alliances for mutual protection and economic reasons. Rulers of several nations were also related by blood or marriage. Members of one family, the **Hapsburgs,** sat on many of the European thrones. Some Central European nations had been formed as a result of previous wars and still felt the domination of certain powers. This consolidation of power in the monarchies was seen by some as an organized effort to take freedoms away from the new working class.

In the Balkans, various national alliances engaged in warfare for economic reasons. Austria had created the new state of Albania to keep Serbia from becoming too powerful. Many people in the Austrian province of Bosnia felt aligned to Serbia and wanted to be free from Austrian control. When **Archduke Francis Ferdinand,** the heir to the Austrian throne, and his wife, Sophie, visited Sarajevo, Bosnia, in June 1914, the couple was assassinated.

This attack caused the **Austro-Hungarian Empire** to declare war on Serbia, which looked to its Russian allies to provide aid. Germany, allied to Austria-Hungary, insisted that Russia cease its mobilization of troops. When Russia refused, Germany declared war on both Russia and its ally France. In order to get a first-strike position on France, Germany moved its forces through the neutral country of Belgium.

This act of aggression brought Great Britain into the war as it acted to defend Belgium. Eventually, in 1918, a weakened Germany agreed to an armistice. The **Treaty of Versailles** ended the war and required Germany to dissolve its standing army.

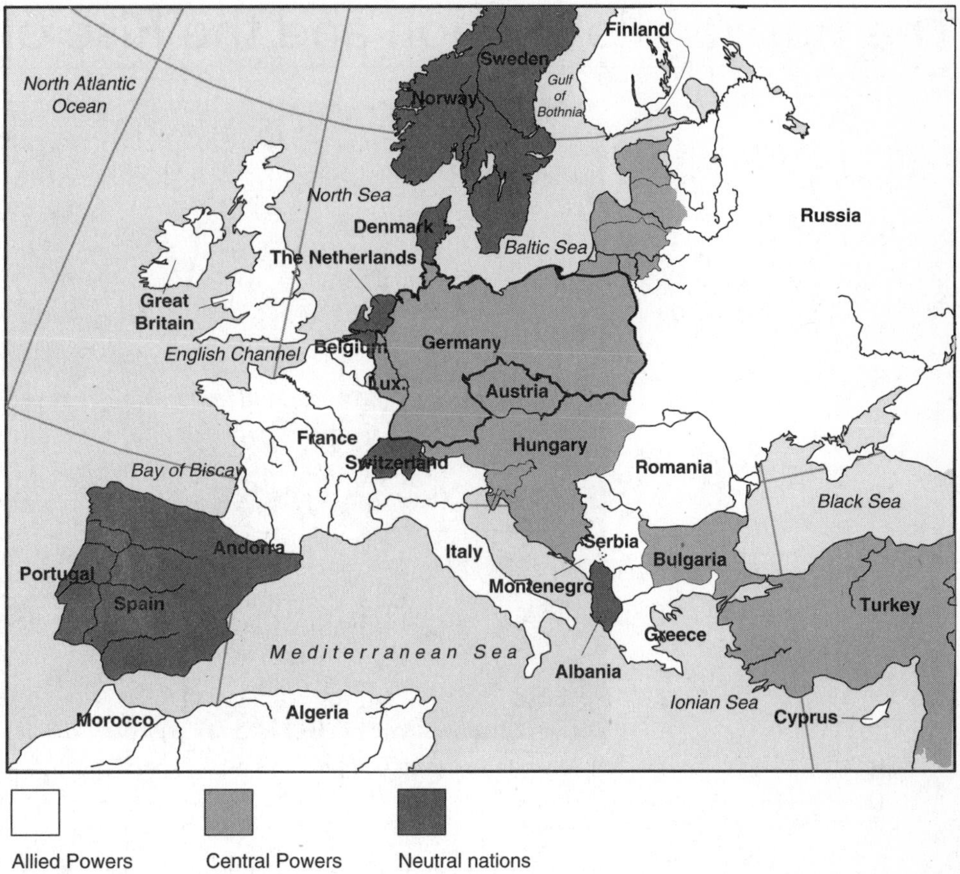

EXERCISE 13

World War I

Directions: Place an **X** next to the countries that were allies of Germany in World War I according to the map.

1. ______ France

2. ______ Russia

3. ______ England

4. ______ Belgium

5. ______ Austria-Hungary

Answers are on page 445.

The Russian Revolution and the Rise of Communism

© Austrian Archives/Corbis

In 1917, one year before the end of World War I, Russia's resources had been depleted. The working class was in poverty, food shortages existed, and the people no longer believed in the rule of **Czar Nicholas II** of the Romanov Dynasty. New leaders were able to generate support from the desperate citizens. At this time, **Vladimir Lenin** led the **Bolsheviks** into a position of power. Czar Nicholas was forced to give up the throne, and he and his family were killed.

Lenin followed the beliefs presented earlier by Karl Marx in *The Communist Manifesto,* forming a **Communist** government and a classless society, the **Soviet Union**. Lenin and his followers killed anyone who disagreed with their policies, giving the leadership of the Communist Party total control of the government. In March 1918 the Soviet Union signed a treaty with Germany, taking itself out of the war and dissolving the Soviet army. After Lenin's death in 1924, another Bolshevik, **Josef Stalin,** and his supporters climbed to power to try to industrialize the poverty-stricken nation. Stalin continued Lenin's policies and became sole dictator of the Soviet Union, taking the titles of Marshal and Premier. He and his immediate supporters had absolute control in this **totalitarian** government until his death in 1953.

EXERCISE 14

The Russian Revolution and the Rise of Communism

Directions: Read the following questions and select the *best* answer.

1. Based on the information on the Russian Revolution, which of the following is a likely assumption as to why the Communist Party rose to power?

(1) The citizens resisted the Industrial Revolution.
(2) Russia signed a treaty with Germany.
(3) Czar Nicholas II and his family were executed.
(4) The working class lost faith in their ruler.
(5) The totalitarian government had absolute control.

2. Match the leader with what he is best known for.

______	Czar Nicholas	**a.** wrote *The Communist Manifesto*
______	Vladimir Lenin	**b.** gave up the throne and was killed
______	Josef Stalin	**c.** brought industrialization
______	Karl Marx	**d.** gave the Communist Party total control

Answers are on page 446.

World War II

The treaty ending World War I dealt harshly with Germany, throwing the country into financial chaos. Without a strong leader to guide the rebuilding of Germany, **Adolf Hitler** did not have trouble focusing the nation's attention on national pride and economic recovery through conquest. The **Nazi Party**'s strength increased as it provided Germany with scapegoats, blaming the poor economic conditions mainly on the Jews. In addition to this propaganda campaign, the Nazi intimidation tactics forced other Germans to focus hatred against those selected by the Nazi Party as traitors. The genocide of millions of Europeans at the direction of Hitler, or the **Holocaust** as it is now known, was not entirely understood until after World War II.

World War II brought an alliance among Italy, Germany, and Japan. Each of these nations sought expansion of its territories. In the 1920s **Benito Mussolini** became dictator of Italy, and in 1936 he invaded Ethiopia. In the 1930s Hitler had gained control of Germany, annexed Austria, and invaded Czechoslovakia. He then signed a nonaggression treaty with Russia. Great Britain entered the war when Germany invaded Poland, but it could not stop Hitler from occupying both Poland and France.

By 1940 Britain was the last holdout against the Nazis until Germany attacked the Soviet Union in 1941. The Soviets then entered the war in support of the British. During this time the United States had been providing medical and military supplies to Britain and the Soviet Union, known as the **Allies**, but had stayed out of the fighting. On December 7, 1941, Japan bombed **Pearl Harbor,** a major U.S. naval base in Hawaii. Within three days of this attack, Germany and Italy declared war on the United States. Now the United States was fighting on two fronts: Europe and the Pacific.

The United States and the Allied forces, mainly Britain and the Soviet Union, broke all German resistance. In May of 1945, Germany surrendered. It wasn't until August 1945, after the United States dropped atomic bombs on **Hiroshima** and **Nagasaki,** that the war with Japan ended. At the end of the war in Europe, the Soviet Union, under Stalin, gained control of the same middle European countries that Hitler had invaded. This Soviet dominance began a period of time known as the **Cold War**, during which major world powers attempted to maintain military strength to ward off invasion.

EXERCISE 15

World War II

Directions: Fill in the blank with a word that would correctly complete the sentence.

1. ____________________ is a campaign of giving false or biased information to influence the attitudes of groups of people.

2. The Holocaust is considered an act of ____________________ because millions of people were killed because they were not accepted as valuable citizens.

3. World War II brought an alliance among Italy, ____________________, and ____________________.

4. The United States dropped atomic bombs on ____________________ and ____________________, bringing an end to the war.

5. A period of time called the ____________________ ____________________ began, during which countries built up their armies to ward off invasions.

Answers are on page 446.

India is Divided

Since the eighteenth century, **India** had been part of the **British Empire**. It was predominantly a land of Hindus and Muslims. Conflicts between these two groups were commonplace, and occasionally violent. During the years between the two world wars, Great Britain attempted to mediate differences between the two groups while still retaining political and economic control. At the end of World War II, Great Britain negotiated with both Hindu and Muslim leaders of India to create two independent nations. Since the conflicts between the two different religions could not be resolved, the Hindu nation of India and the Muslim nation of **Pakistan** were created.

Among the leaders of India's Congress, **Mohandas Gandhi** had long advocated Indian independence from Britain. He was an advocate of **civil disobedience,** and led many people to peacefully protest British rule. While Gandhi got the British out of India, he objected to the division of the nation. He was concerned that the formation of two separate countries would lead to years of civil warfare within each country; those of the majority religion fighting the members of the minority religion. Only five months after the independence of India and Pakistan, Gandhi was assassinated by a Hindu militant.

After Gandhi's death, the first leader of the new government of India, **Jawaharlal Nehru,** focused efforts on improving industry and the economy of the newly independent nation. A major concern of the government was India's continued struggle with its population problem. The **Green Revolution** of the 1970s saw the development of stronger strains of rice. In order to try to feed India's huge population, larger yields of crops were produced with greater resistance to disease. The government's control incentives were unable to bring the population excesses under control, and the new crops produced by the Green Revolution could not alleviate the huge population's hunger. These issues are still of great concern in India.

Nehru and Gandhi

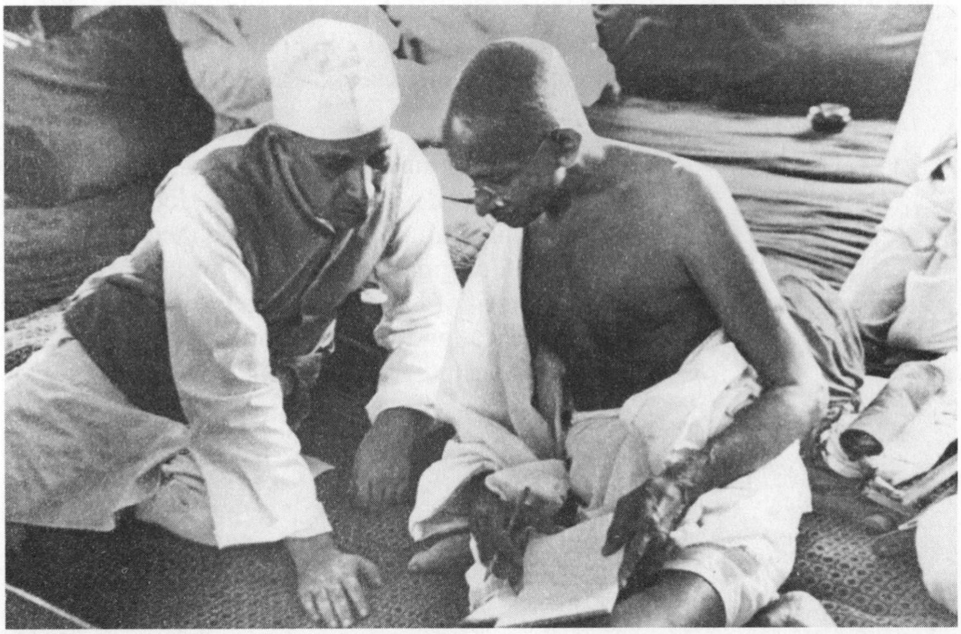

EXERCISE 16

India is Divided

Directions: Match the following causes and effects in India's history.

1. ______	creation of India and Pakistan	**a.** attempt to curb overpopulation
2. ______	assassination of Gandhi	**b.** two religions could not compromise
3. ______	technological advancement of India	**c.** Green Revolution
4. ______	creation of stronger strains of rice	**d.** Hindu militant
5. ______	population control incentives	**e.** Jawaharlal Nehru

Answers are on page 446.

Technology as a Future

Since World War II, world history has been deeply connected to advancements in science and technology. Space exploration, such as the Soviet launching of **Sputnik** (1957), followed by the NASA program that put Americans on the moon in 1969, has led technological development. One obvious benefit of the technology that has dominated world history is the beginning of the computer age. Computers have allowed the space program to have remote control of a vehicle in orbit around the earth or in deep space, and to make calculations quickly and accurately. Gradually, this technology has been made available to the civilian population and heavily used in communication, research, and commerce.

Technology has come to determine wealth and power. No longer is the acquisition of land the determining factor for power among nations. The world has seen a shift in focus to global commerce. Tiny countries such as Japan and South Korea are major factors in the electronic marketplace. The **Internet**, originally intended to be a computer network for the U.S. Department of Defense, has developed into a global research, commerce, and communication tool. It and other forms of instant electronic communication have connected every part of the world into a global economy.

EXERCISE 17

Technology as a Future

Directions: Complete the following paragraph using information given on page 324.

Recent history has been greatly influenced by developments in ____________________ and ____________________. The Soviet launching of ____________________ began space exploration, which advanced technological ____________________ greatly. The ________________ ____________________ is one obvious benefit. Computers are also used in ____________________, ____________________, and ____________________.

Technology has come to determine ____________________ and ____________________. The Internet and other ____________________ forms of communication have made a ____________________ economy.

Answers are on page 446.

Writing Activity 6

Some people feel that the technology available today makes society move too fast, encouraging a deterioration in tradition and a lack of curiosity about the past. Do you agree or disagree with this opinion? Support your answer by writing at least two or three paragraphs.

Go to **www.GEDSocialStudies.com** for additional practice and instruction!

CHAPTER 2

U.S. History

We study the past because each of us is a result of those who came before. By understanding past triumphs and failures, we can better understand events that take place in our society today and better prepare ourselves for the future. This chapter will highlight some of the most important events in U.S. history from the discovery of North America to the present. You will not only learn *what* happened but will be better able to understand *why* it happened.

A New Nation is Born

Although it is commonly assumed that **Christopher Columbus** discovered the Americas, many argue that they were really discovered by **Leif Ericson.** Few recognize that the Norwegian Vikings traveled to the New World, but 400 years before Columbus set sail, the Vikings landed on North America's shores at what is now Newfoundland. They were actually the first Europeans to reach North America.

Columbus Day, celebrated each year on the second Monday in October, honors a hero's "mistake." When Columbus sailed from Spain in 1492, he was searching for a shorter route to the treasures of the East. The "shortcut" Columbus took by sailing west landed him on a small island in what is now the Bahamas. Thinking he was in India, he called the native Americans "Indians," a name that remains today. Columbus died in 1506, never knowing that he had actually landed in North America.

Columbus's error, however, opened the doors for later exploration of the New World. A partial listing of explorers demonstrates the multicultural influences on the foundation of the United States: Italian explorer **Amerigo Vespucci**, for whom the Americas are named; **Hernando de Soto** (Spain), who discovered the Mississippi River; **Francisco Vasquez de Coronado** (Spain), who explored what would become the southwestern United States; as well as **John Cabot** (England) and **Henry Hudson** (The Netherlands). As Spain grew in wealth and power because of settlements in what is now Central and South America, the French ventured north to Canada. The English settled on the coastland between the areas claimed by Spain and France.

GED PRACTICE

EXERCISE 1

A New Nation is Born

Directions: Using the map, choose the *best* answer for each question below.

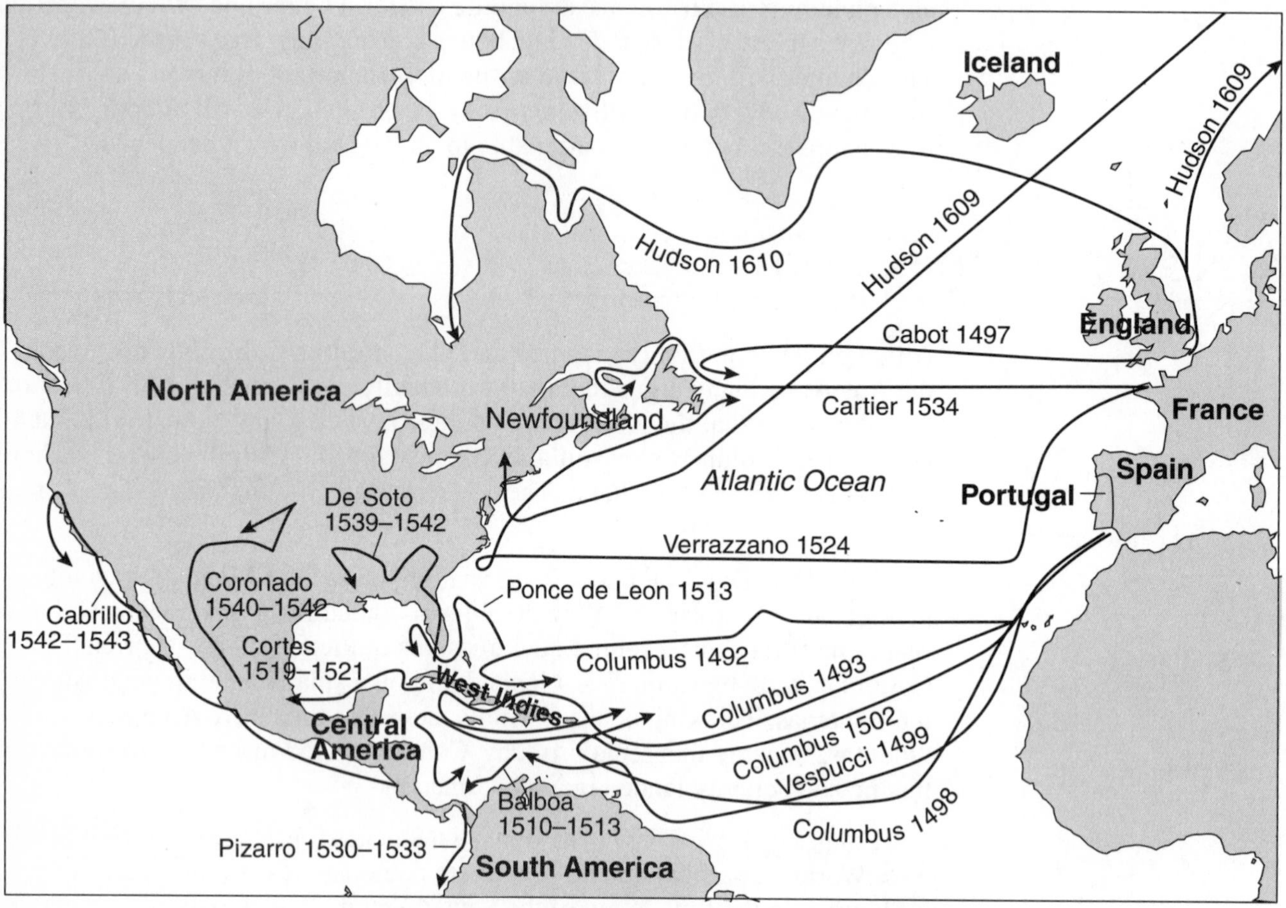

1. From the map of European explorations in the Americas, which of the following conclusions can be drawn?

(1) Most explorers were from France.
(2) Columbus was the only explorer from Spain.
(3) John Cabot explored the east coast of America.
(4) Many countries sent explorers to the New World.
(5) Henry Hudson explored the Gulf of Mexico.

2. What is the purpose of this map?

(1) show resources in the New World
(2) compare the financing of each exploration
(3) highlight slave routes to America
(4) distinguish African and Asian explorers
(5) illustrate the routes taken by explorers

Answers are on page 446.

The Original Thirteen Colonies

As the English colonies became more and more crowded with newcomers, some people looked to settle in the land beyond the Appalachian Mountains, which had been claimed by France. In the mid-1700s, England and France fought over the land in the northern and central parts of North America. This became known as the **French and Indian War**. England won the war in 1763. The Treaty of Paris gave England total control over the land from the east coast of North America all the way to the Mississippi River. The land from Georgia to Maine became known as **the thirteen colonies**. (See the map on page 330.)

A council or governor appointed by the king of England governed each of the thirteen colonies. These leaders were to control the colonies in the name of the king. Because colonists came from many areas, they brought with them different customs, religious beliefs, and dialects. This diversity of people made each colony unique and difficult to govern.

Coming to a strange land and trying to make a new start was difficult for the colonists. The people who came to the colonies were often poor, and they had to begin life there using only what they could bring with them on the ships from England. However, the **Pilgrims** at Plymouth Colony (Massachusetts) survived the first difficult year with help from the local native American population. The natives taught the settlers how to plant and care for indigenous crops such as corn. In the fall of 1621, the Pilgrims and local native Americans celebrated a good harvest and observed the first **Thanksgiving.** The Pilgrims gave thanks for new opportunities and new freedoms.

One of the reasons the English settlers came to the colonies was the chance to own land. New economic opportunities opened up because of the vast expanse of land available for farming. In the northern colonies, the abundance of natural resources permitted the development of trades such as shipbuilding and iron mining. Fur trading and fishing also played a significant role in the colonial economy. Though individual ambition and effort were rewarded, the king ruled supreme and taxed the colonists for what he believed was his rightful share of their earnings.

GED PRACTICE

EXERCISE 2

The Original Thirteen Colonies

Directions: Using the map, choose the *best* answer for the following questions.

Colonial America In 1763

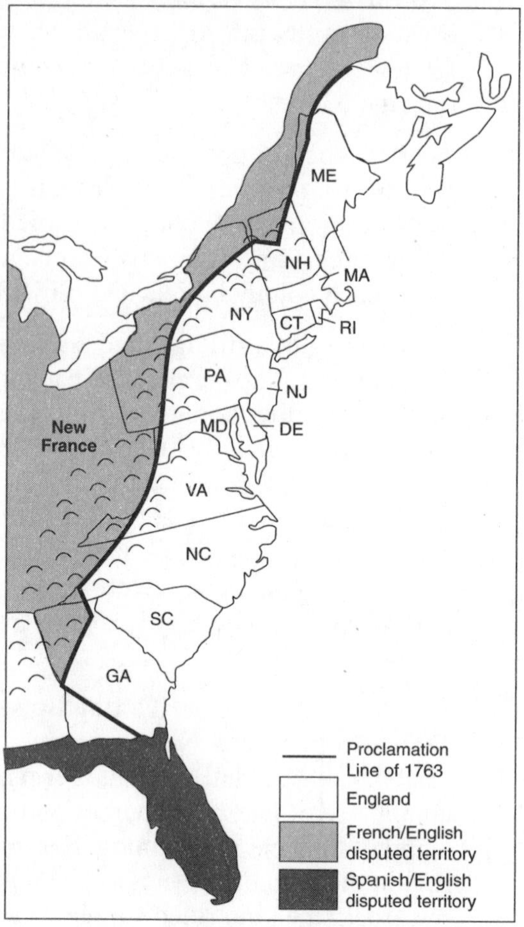

1. From the details in the map, what can we tell about the New England state of Maine?

(1) It was not discovered by the English.
(2) It was owned and controlled by the French.
(3) It was governed and subdivided by Spain.
(4) It was considered a part of Canada.
(5) It was originally part of Massachusetts.

2. Which of the following can be proved by the map to be false?

(1) Georgia was the last colony to become a state.
(2) Pennsylvania was the most powerful colony.
(3) In the 1700s, France gave up all interest in the New World.
(4) England controlled much of the eastern seaboard.
(5) The first colonists in New York were Dutch.

Answers are on page 446.

© Bettmann/CORBIS

Although the colonists retained much of their cultural traditions and customs, they were forced to make changes as they adapted to a new environment. The richness of the soil proved a source of wonder to early settlers, many of whom had left farmlands that were exhausted by overuse. One 7th-century visitor pointed out, "if men be neither industrious nor provident, they may starve in the best place of the world."

—Excerpted from *WE AMERICANS: A Volume in the Story of Man Library,* the National Geographic Society

Writing Activity 1

Write two or three paragraphs to answer one of the following questions.

A. Do you think it would be more difficult to govern the United States now, when there are so many more ethnic groups and a larger population, or in the 1700s, when the colonies were just getting established?

B. How do you think a new arrival to the colonies felt? Do you think that new arrivals to the United States feel the same today? Why?

The Declaration of Independence

After the **French and Indian War,** England needed to finance a huge war debt. **King George III** decided that the colonists would pay for the war because they were the ones who benefited from the victory. As a result, the king and the English Parliament passed the Stamp Act of 1765 and the Townshend Acts of 1767. The **Stamp Act** required all official documents in the colonies to bear a British stamp paid for with a new tax. The **Townshend Acts** placed large import taxes on glass, lead, and tea. The colonists were outraged by these taxes and protested them by dumping tea into Boston Harbor. This incident is usually referred to as **the Boston Tea Party.** The English Parliament punished the colonies for these protests by passing laws known as the **Intolerable Acts,** which sought to further establish the authority of the King.

The colonists were quick to respond. In September 1774, at the **First Continental Congress,** representatives from all thirteen colonies demanded that the Intolerable Acts be repealed. Moreover, the colonists demanded to be treated fairly and given the same rights as all other English citizens. However, the king and Parliament refused.

Battles between British soldiers and colonists had already taken place by May 1775, when the **Second Continental Congress** began. Inspired by colonist **Thomas Paine**'s pamphlet "Common Sense," in which he explained why separation from England was necessary, **Thomas Jefferson** drafted the **Declaration of Independence.** This important document justified the need for a revolution by listing grievances that the colonists had against King George III. The Second Continental Congress approved the declaration on July 4, 1776.

An Excerpt from the Declaration of Independence

When in the Course of human events, it becomes necessary for one people to dissolve the political bands which have connected them with another, and to assume among the Powers of the earth, the separate and equal station to which the Laws of Nature and of Nature's God entitle them, a decent respect to the opinions of mankind requires that they should declare the causes which impel them to the separation.

We hold these truths to be self-evident, that all men are created equal, that they are endowed by their Creator with certain unalienable Rights, that among these are Life, Liberty, and the pursuit of Happiness.

GED PRACTICE

EXERCISE 3

The Declaration of Independence

Directions: Use information from the passage and the excerpt from the Declaration of Independence to answer the following questions.

1. Which of the following led directly to the Boston Tea Party?

(1) the French and Indian War
(2) the Stamp Act
(3) the Townshend Acts
(4) the Intolerable Acts
(5) the Declaration of Independence

2. What was the main idea of the excerpt from the Declaration of Independence?

(1) Colonists wanted to pay less in taxes to England.
(2) All men are created equal and have inalienable rights.
(3) The king needs to reside in the colonies to govern.
(4) A member of Parliament should be from the colonies.
(5) The colonies demanded stronger ties to England.

Answers are on page 446.

The Revolutionary War

Patriotism does not come without sacrifice. The Revolutionary War was a long and costly conflict for both sides. The fighting ended in 1781 when the British army under General Charles Cornwallis was surrounded by American troops and their ally, the French fleet, at Yorktown. Finally, in 1783, the Treaty of Paris was signed. In addition to granting U.S. independence, the treaty gave the new nation all the land that England had won in the French and Indian War: west to the Mississippi River, north to the Great Lakes, and south to Florida.

EXERCISE 4

The Revolutionary War

Directions: Complete the cause-and-effect chart using information from the passages.

Causes	Effects
1. The Townshend Acts	**a.** Boston Tea Party
2. ____________________	**b.** First Continental Congress
3. The Declaration of Independence	**c.** ____________________
4. King's refusal to compromise	**d.** Declaration of Independence
5. ____________________	**e.** Signing of the Treaty of Paris

Answers are on page 447.

The Beginnings of American Government

The first U.S. central government, under the **Articles of Confederation,** was deliberately made weak in order to prevent the abuses the colonies suffered under the King. Within the framework of this new system of government, each of the 13 states was determined to maintain its sovereignty. This posed a serious problem for the new nation because it limited the powers of the central government in dealing with major issues, such as trade regulation, currency, and national defense.

Government leaders realized that the country might collapse if something was not done to address these issues. To correct the problem, they called a convention to amend the Articles of Confederation in Philadelphia in May 1787. This convention eventually created the **Constitution**—the document by which the United States has been governed for more than 200 years.

The Beginnings of American Government

Powers of the States	Powers of the Central Government
The thirteen states had the power to • levy taxes • regulate business and commerce • decide whether to support the decisions of the central government	The central government had the power to • make treaties with other nations • govern Indian affairs • declare war • develop a postal service

Weaknesses of the *Articles of Confederation*

The *Articles of Confederation* limited the powers of
- trade regulation
- currency
- defense of new nation

GED PRACTICE

EXERCISE 5

The Beginnings of American Government

Directions: Read the following questions and select the *best* answer based on the passage on page 334.

1. Why would the states want to maintain their sovereignty under the Articles of Confederation?

(1) They wanted to remain independent from the other states.
(2) Some states wanted to be English colonies again.
(3) They wanted the country to collapse.
(4) Some states wanted to have their own armies.
(5) They were concerned about central government abuses.

2. Which was not a consideration in creating the new Constitution?

(1) There was no specific outline for the powers of the central government.
(2) The Articles of Confederation allowed the king to have power in the colonies.
(3) The new government could not issue powers to the individual states.
(4) With the Constitution, there would be no army to defend the nation.
(5) It was illegal for the nation to print money without states' approval.

Answers are on page 447.

The U.S. Constitution and Federalism

The challenge facing the Constitutional Convention was to develop a written document that would give the central government more power while allowing the states to retain their sovereignty. To accomplish this, the Constitution was written to create a federal system of government. Under **federalism,** a union is formed by the states. A central government is given final authority over certain clearly defined areas, such as national defense and the ability to regulate trade. All other powers are left to the individual states.

Although the Constitution established the framework for American democracy, its acceptance was no easy accomplishment. Several disputes arose between the **Federalists,** who wanted a strong central government with authoritative control over the states, and the **Anti-Federalists,** who feared that the individual states would lose their freedom under a strong central government.

The Federalists were largely members of the merchant class who favored commercial and industrial expansion. The Anti-Federalists were largely farmers who favored individual liberties and did not believe strongly in territorial expansion. Two historical figures whose policies reflected these opposing positions were **Alexander Hamilton** (a Federalist) and Thomas Jefferson (an Anti-Federalist).

The disputes that arose out of the Constitutional Convention and their compromises are illustrated in the following chart.

Dispute	Compromise:
Should the states be governed by a strong central government (Federalists' view) or should the new government be based on the sovereignty of the states (anti-Federalists' view)?	1. The President was to be elected by electoral college; the Senate, by the state legislatures (this was later changed by the Seventeenth Amendment, adopted in 1913); and House of Representatives, by the people. 2. The Bill of Rights—the first ten amendments—was added to the Constitution later to guarantee individual rights.
Should the makeup of Congress be based on each state's population (large states' view) or should all states have equal representation (small states' view)?	Bicameral legislature (two houses in Congress) 1. Members of the House of Representatives were based on each state's population. 2. Senate would have two delegates from each state. (This was called the **"Great Compromise."**)
Should slaves be counted in the population (southern states' view) or should slaves be excluded from the population count (northern states' view)?	1. Slave importation would be allowed until at least 1808. 2. Slaves would be counted as three-fifths of a person only for purposes of representation and for assessing taxes; however, they were not permitted to vote.

GED PRACTICE

EXERCISE 6

The U.S. Constitution and Federalism

Directions: Based on the preceding chart, choose the *best* answer for each of the following questions.

1. **Why was counting slaves as only three-fifths of a person favorable to the northern states?**

   (1) It limited the number of senators representing the South.
   (2) It limited the South's number of seats in the House of Representatives.
   (3) It was based on the amount of property for taxing purposes.
   (4) It kept slavery from spreading from the South to the North.
   (5) It equalized the number of representatives for the North and the South.

2. **Today, many Southern conservatives—Democrats and Republicans alike—are strong supporters of states' rights. Which philosophy would these Americans likely have supported in the 1780s?**

   (1) antifederalism
   (2) federalism
   (3) colonialism
   (4) democracy
   (5) monarchy

Answers are on page 447.

Writing Activity 2

Frederick Douglass, a slave and abolitionist leader, is quoted as having said, "If there is no struggle there is no progress." Write two or three paragraphs about a situation in your life that might demonstrate an application of Douglass's quote.

Early Domestic and Foreign Policy

The years between 1791 and 1803 saw the United States expand geographically. Between 1791 and 1796, Vermont, Kentucky, and Tennessee were admitted to the Union under the administration of **George Washington**, the first U.S. president. In 1803, under President Thomas Jefferson, Ohio was admitted to the Union, but the largest acquisition of land for the United States occurred with the **Louisiana Purchase** in 1803. By paying France $15 million for the territory, Jefferson doubled the size of the country. He subsequently appointed **Lewis and Clark** to explore the acquired territory.

The United States in 1803

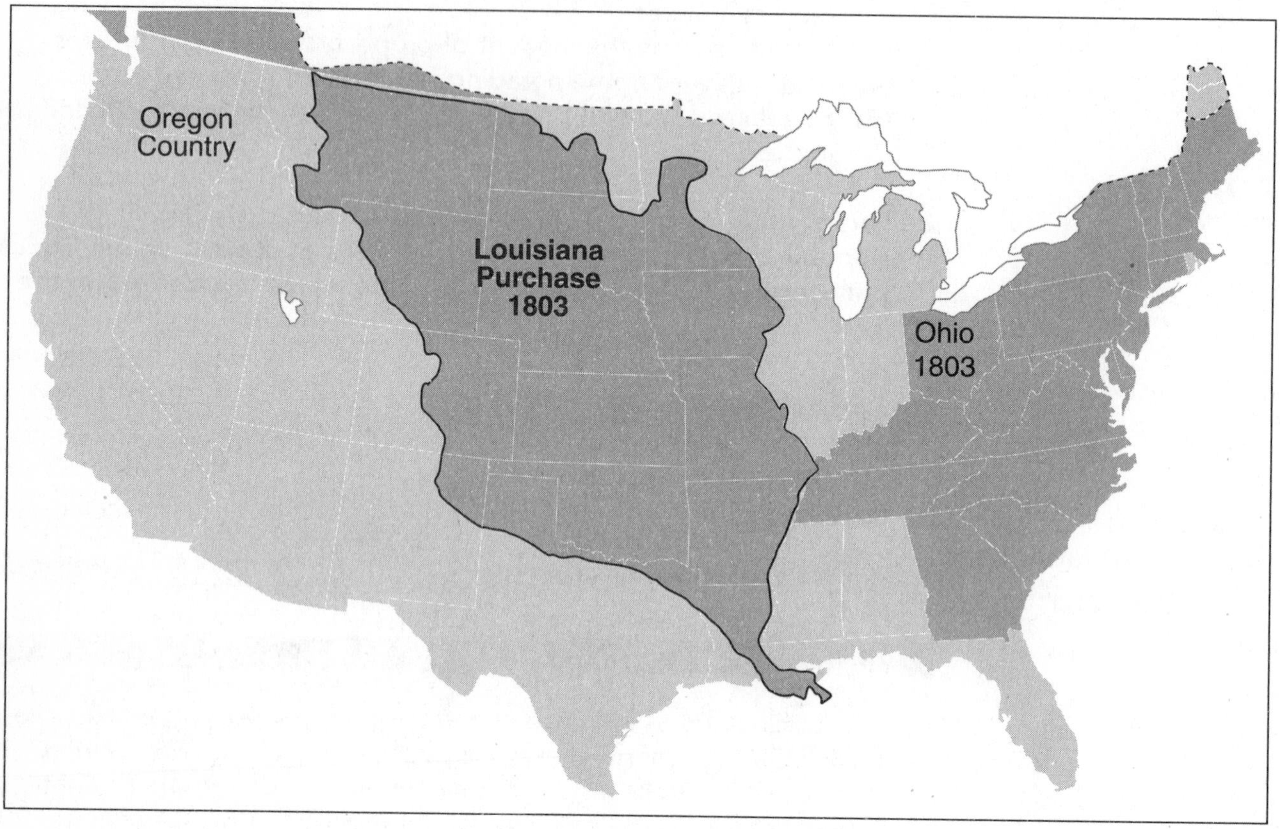

The War of 1812

In 1812, the United States declared war against Great Britain. President **James Madison** favored the war in part because England allegedly interfered with U.S. trade with other European nations and because it aided the Indians in their uprisings in the West. As part of its strategy to cripple the U.S. economy, Britain imposed a blockade of U.S. ships going to France and forced U.S. seamen to join its navy. Despite successful military campaigns, the United States did not win the unpopular war. Both sides ended the war in 1814 with the signing of the **Treaty of Ghent**. The Federalists, who had been pro-British in foreign affairs, lost political strength and declined as an important voice in U.S. politics.

Because of the shortages created by the British blockade during the war, the United States began to manufacture its own goods. A new sense of nationalism developed as the United States turned its focus inward.

GED PRACTICE

EXERCISE 7

The War of 1812

Directions: Choose the *best* answer for each of the following questions.

1. Which of the following could explain why the Federalists were pro-British and, therefore, did not support "Mr. Madison's War"?

(1) The Federalists did not vote for President Madison and had a personal vendetta against him.
(2) Madison declared war against Great Britain without consulting with the U.S. Congress.
(3) The Federalists were mainly merchants and shipowners who feared that their trade with other European nations would suffer.
(4) The Federalists did not believe that the United States had a navy strong enough to challenge the British.
(5) The Federalists were against the higher taxes that would have to be raised to support a war.

2. Which of the following causes contributed to the sense of nationalism in the United States after the War of 1812?

(1) The Federalists were required to trade only with Indians.
(2) The United States needed to manufacture its own goods.
(3) The Federalists, considered traitors, were used as scapegoats.
(4) The Treaty of Ghent focused attention on the United States.
(5) The U.S. military demonstrated superior battle tactics.

Answers are on page 447.

The Monroe Doctrine

The strong sense of nationalism that developed after the War of 1812 bolstered the Era of Good Feelings during the presidency of **James Monroe**. For the first time the United States could afford to look inward and pay less attention to European affairs. As a result, U.S. westward expansion continued, with victories over several native American tribes.

In 1823, President Monroe proclaimed to the world that European powers would no longer be allowed to colonize the Americas. He indicated that the United States would remain neutral in European conflicts as long as the European powers left the emerging republics in North and South America alone. Known as the **Monroe Doctrine,** this foreign policy statement marked the appearance of the United States on the world political stage.

Writing Activity 3

In two or three paragraphs, discuss a current world situation that best represents an attempt to enforce the principles of the Monroe Doctrine.

Jacksonian Democracy and the Mexican War

The Era of Good Feelings did not survive Monroe's term. After Monroe left office, sectionalism became a problem for the United States. **Sectionalism** refers to the political, cultural, and economic differences among regions of the country—in this case the agricultural South and West and the industrial Northeast. The conflicting demands that each section put upon the government caused great political turmoil.

The first U.S. president elected to office as a result of these factional differences was **Andrew Jackson** in 1828. A Southerner and hero in the War of 1812, Jackson was considered to be a **populist,** a man who represented the interests of the common people. He believed that all people, not just the propertied few, should have a voice in deciding how the government should be run.

As the champion of the common people, Jackson opposed the establishment of a national bank because he believed that it would only benefit the wealthy and because he feared the Eastern merchants and industrialists would control it. Under Jacksonian democracy, farmers and craftspeople gained a louder voice in government than they had had under previous administrations. Despite pressure to annex Texas during his second term, Jackson refused, fearing a war with Mexico.

President **James Polk**, Jackson's successor, had no such fear. Congress, agreeing to the demands of the Texans, annexed the Texas Republic in 1845. Thus, the expansionist fervor in the United States was renewed. **Manifest Destiny—**the drive to extend the U.S. borders to the Pacific Ocean—became a rallying cry. When President Polk was unable to purchase the territory that included New Mexico and California, the United States declared war on Mexico in 1846 as a result of a territorial dispute between the two countries.

The **Treaty of Guadalupe Hidalgo** that ended the war resulted in the **Mexican Cession** in 1848. The Mexican government gave to the United States the land that would later become California, Utah, Nevada, and parts of Colorado, New Mexico, Arizona, and Wyoming. Thus, the United States had set its continental boundaries. The following map shows the boundaries of the United States by 1853.

Expansion of the United States, 1783–1853

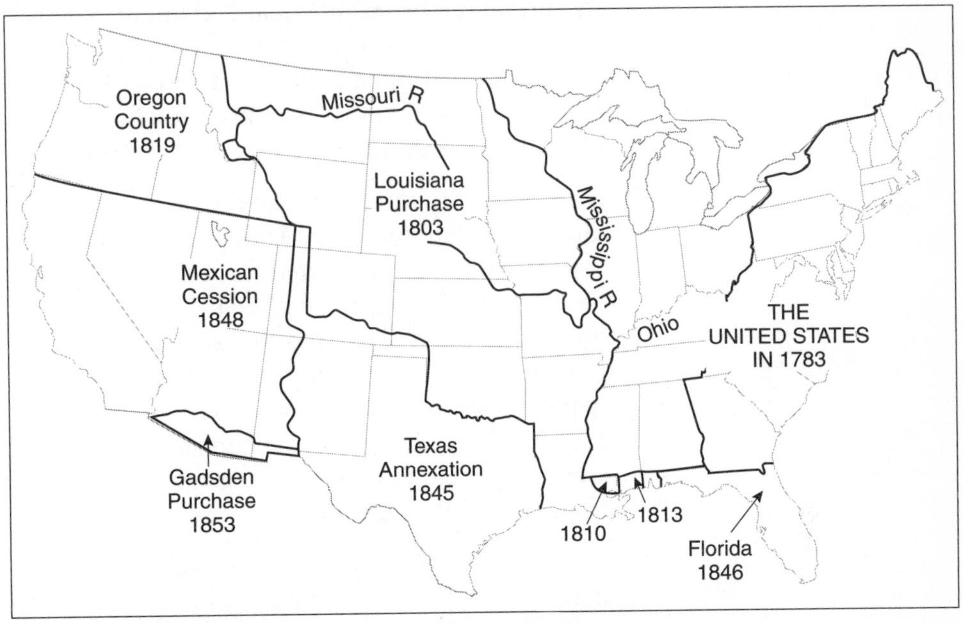

GED PRACTICE

EXERCISE 8

Jacksonian Democracy and the Mexican War

Directions: Choose the *best* answer for each of the following questions.

1. **Which word below best describes Jackson's attitude toward the people of the United States?**

   (1) racist
   (2) populist
   (3) colonialist
   (4) sectionalist
   (5) federalist

2. **What does the above map of the expansion of the United States illustrate?**

   (1) the boundaries of the newest colonies
   (2) the population centers in the new territories
   (3) the agricultural and industrial centers in the territories
   (4) the boundaries of the new expansion territories
   (5) the regions of war that allowed the expansion of territories

Answers are on page 447.

Prelude to War

By the 1850s, all the land that makes up today's continental United States was under the control of the federal government. Sectionalism persisted, however, as citizens seemed more loyal to their own region than to the Union as a whole. **Tariffs** (taxes imposed on goods imported into a country) were viewed by certain regions as unequal and unfair. The people of the South and West thought the tariffs were harder on them than on the North because of the South's lack of manufacturing. Expansion laws were also seen by different sections of the country as unjust; however, it was the issue of slavery that ultimately pitted one region against the other.

One central question that the country had to answer was whether new territories admitted to the Union would become free states or slave states. Some Americans supported the concept of **popular sovereignty,** which meant that the people who were affected should determine what was best for their own state. Others believed that slavery should not be permitted in the new territories and states, but they did not advocate banning slavery from regions where it already existed. **Abolitionists,** however, believed that slavery was evil and demanded that it be banned throughout the country. Compromises were attempted to resolve the problem, but none resulted in a lasting solution to the question of slavery.

The **Dred Scott decision** of 1857 only worsened the strained relations between the North and the South. The case involved Dred Scott, a slave who sued for his freedom because his master had taken him to a free territory. The Supreme Court ruled that a slave was property and could not sue in federal court. The South applauded the court's decision, but the North opposed it bitterly. The division between the regions became more evident and more hostile; war became inevitable.

GED PRACTICE

EXERCISE 9

Prelude to War

Directions: Choose the *best* answer for each question.

1. A *referendum* is a political procedure that allows voters to approve or disapprove a measure proposed by the voters themselves or by the legislature. This method is most similar to which of the following proposed solutions to the issue of slavery?

(1) abolitionism
(2) compromise
(3) popular sovereignty
(4) secession
(5) territorial balance

2. The passage cites the Dred Scott decision as a decisive event leading to the Civil War. Which value was upheld by the Supreme Court's decision?

(1) Slavery was inhuman.
(2) States had more rights than people.
(3) New states could permit slavery.
(4) Slavery could only be maintained in the South.
(5) Human beings could be treated as property.

Answers are on page 447.

Secession

When **Abraham Lincoln** was elected president in 1860, he promised to restrict slavery to the states where it already existed. The Southern states, feeling that they were being treated unfairly, feared that the North would eventually dominate them. They voted to secede from the United States and to form their own government—the **Confederate States of America**.

South Carolina was first to secede in 1860; by February 1861 Georgia, Florida, Alabama, Mississippi, Louisiana, and Texas had seceded. **Jefferson Davis** was elected president of the Confederacy. In response, President Lincoln determined that the only way to preserve the Union was through the use of force. The South was disobeying the laws of the land. Lincoln believed that if the South did not follow the law, any state that chose to disagree with a national decision would feel that it could simply ignore the law. The Confederacy's firing on **Fort Sumter** in April 1861 opened the bloodiest war in the nation's history.

EXERCISE 10

Secession

Directions: Based on the following map, match the state in the left column with its description in the right column.

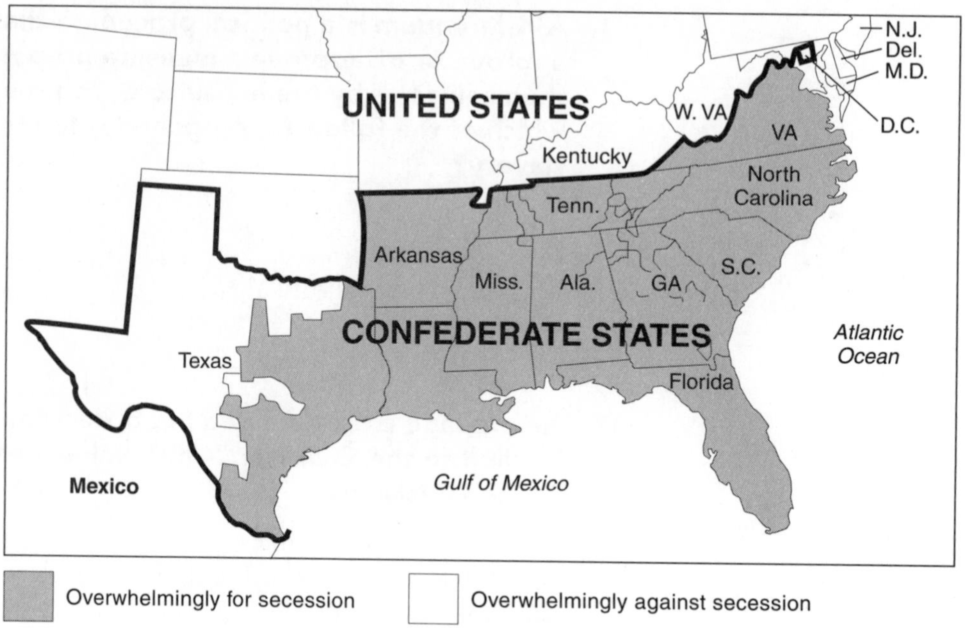

1. ______ Virginia
2. ______ Texas
3. ______ Kentucky
4. ______ Mississippi

a. As a "border state," it remained in the Union despite being a slave state.

b. As a solid Southern slave state, it voted overwhelmingly to secede from the Union.

c. This state split in two over the issue of secession, with the western part loyal to the Union.

d. The entire state seceded from the Union even though only its eastern part voted to do so.

Answers are on page 448.

The Civil War

The nation could not exist half slave and half free, and the war that settled the question lasted four years. Most of the war was fought in the South. The North had the advantage of a larger army because of its greater population, an ability to manufacture goods needed for the war effort because of its mechanization, an excellent transportation system, and an abundance of natural resources. The South, on the other hand, had the advantage of a greater familiarity with battle sites, as the war was fought on its soil, and great confidence in its outstanding military leaders.

In 1862, President Lincoln issued the **Emancipation Proclamation.** The document ordered the freeing of slaves in those slave states that were in rebellion against the Union. As a result, the Union army's ranks grew by 180,000 former slaves who then fought against the South.

A Proclamation
(excerpt)

"That on the first day of January, A.D. 1863, all persons held as slaves within any State or designated part of a State the people whereof shall then be in rebellion against the United States shall be then, thenceforward, and forever free; and the executive government of the United States, including the military and naval authority thereof, will recognize and maintain the freedom of such persons and will do no act or acts to repress such persons, or any of them, in any efforts they may make for their actual freedom."

The war ended on April 9, 1865, when the Confederate general **Robert E. Lee** surrendered. However, the task ahead for President Lincoln and the citizens of the Union was enormous. The division between the North and the South had to be mended, and the devastated South had to be rebuilt. The South's readmission to the Union would prove to be difficult.

GED PRACTICE

EXERCISE 11

The Civil War

Directions: Choose the *best* answer for each of the following questions.

1. **Which of the following supports the main idea of the excerpt from the Emancipation Proclamation?**
   (1) All slaves in all states were freed.
   (2) The military would capture freed slaves.
   (3) Only slaves in the Confederate states were freed.
   (4) The proclamation was effective in 1862.
   (5) The federal government would not support freed slaves.

2. **What effect did the Emancipation Proclamation have on the outcome of the war?**
   (1) The South was more determined to win the war, winning most of the battles following the Proclamation.
   (2) The South gained a reliable source of soldiers in the freed slaves.
   (3) It officially ended the war since slavery was no longer an issue.
   (4) It made President Lincoln one of the most popular presidents in American history.
   (5) It gave the Union army additional troops because many former slaves fought on the side of the North.

Answers are on page 448.

Reconstruction

Lincoln's plan for reuniting the nation included allowing the South to regain citizenship rights and statehood. However, he did not live to see the plan, known as **Reconstruction**, carried out. While attending a play five days after the war was over, Abraham Lincoln was assassinated by a Confederate sympathizer.

Lincoln was succeeded by a Tennesseean, **Andrew Johnson**. During his presidency, the passage of the **Thirteenth Amendment** in December 1865 abolished slavery in the United States.

Though he supported the Union, Johnson was mistrusted by Congress as being pro-South. This mistrust contributed to Johnson's becoming the first U.S. president to be impeached—charged with official misconduct. However, the Senate failed by one vote to convict Johnson; therefore, he was not removed from office.

By 1870, the **Fourteenth Amendment** was ratified, guaranteeing citizenship to blacks, and the **Fifteenth Amendment**, passed the same year, gave blacks the right to vote. Despite these gains, racial issues and their resulting problems would plague the South for years.

Writing Activity 4

Write two or three paragraphs about one of the following options.

A. a situation during which you felt especially grateful toward a public or government official

B. a situation during which you felt mistrust for a public or government official

The Industrial Revolution

The **Industrial Revolution** was the change in the economy's character from a manual means of production to a mechanical one. Goods were mass-produced by machinery rather than crafted by hand. Because of this change in production methods, more goods could be produced at lower costs.

Great Britain is generally credited as the place of origin of the Industrial Revolution. By the late 19th century, the United States, with its abundant natural resources and growing population, had become the world's industrial leader, further cementing its position as a world power.

The number of factories in the United States grew, attracting people from rural areas who could earn more money working in urban factories than on farms. As a result, the population of the cities grew. With increased earnings, people could buy more goods and improve the quality of their lives. This consumer demand encouraged existing businesses to expand, new products to be created, and new industries to be developed.

EXERCISE 12

The Industrial Revolution

Directions: Identify the following facts as **true (T)** or **false (F)** based on the above information.

1. ______ Industry attracted people from rural areas to the cities.

2. ______ Consumer demand encouraged business growth.

3. ______ Increased earnings did nothing to improve the quality of life.

4. ______ The Industrial Revolution began in the United States.

5. ______ The Industrial Revolution increased the population in rural areas.

Answers are on page 448.

Growth of Big Business and Urbanization

Rapid and widespread industrialization led directly to the development of big business. As one company bought another related company, large corporations began to control the marketplace. This was true especially in the steel, railroad, and oil industries. Working conditions for employees deteriorated as businesses ran unchecked by the government, and power became concentrated in the hands of a few powerful industrialists. The government practice of noninterference in the affairs of business is termed ***laissez-faire*** business policy.

Urbanization is the shift of the population away from rural areas and to cities where people could be close to jobs. Before industrialization, only one out of every six Americans lived in the cities. By 1890, one-third of the population lived in the cities. Cities such as New York, Chicago, and Philadelphia had populations of more than one million people. These cities were railway centers that provided transportation for people, supplies, and manufactured goods.

Businesses and factories found an abundant labor supply in the cities. The tremendous number of immigrants who entered the United States from 1870 to 1900 flooded the job market. People from Ireland, Germany, Italy, Russia and the Scandinavian countries fled poverty at home and came to the United States in search of a better life. Their willingness to work long hours for little money forced other workers to accept the same conditions. Immigrants were often prevented from living in certain areas or from applying for certain jobs. Signs reading "Help Wanted—No Irish Need Apply" were a common sight in cities such as Boston and New York. Yet people continued to come to the cities, bringing with them different cultures and backgrounds. Thus, cities became true melting pots of American society.

Writing Activity 5

Do Americans accept immigrants more readily today than in the nineteenth century? Write two or three paragraphs explaining your position. Be sure to include examples to support your point of view.

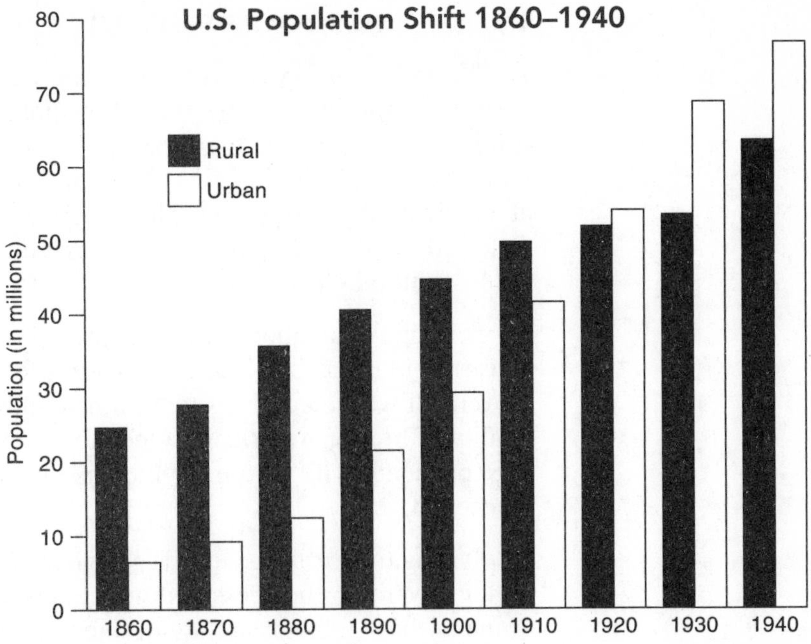

Source: U.S. Census Bureau

GED PRACTICE

EXERCISE 13

Growth of Big Business and Urbanization

Directions: Choose the answer that *best* completes the statements below.

1. **The 2000 census estimated the U.S. population at more than 275 million. Figures in the bar graph support the fact that the United States reached *nearly half* this population by what year?**

   (1) 1900
   (2) 1910
   (3) 1920
   (4) 1930
   (5) 1940

2. **The urban population increased dramatically from 1860 to 1930. What happened to the rural population?**

   (1) It stayed the same.
   (2) It increased rapidly.
   (3) It increased slowly.
   (4) It decreased rapidly.
   (5) It first increased, then decreased.

Answers are on page 448.

Labor and Progressivism

Health, safety, and comfort for laborers were largely ignored during the period of rapid industrialization. In response to these conditions, **labor unions** were organized to represent the needs of the workers when dealing with employers. The Knights of Labor, formed in 1869, was the first attempt at a nationwide labor union. The American Federation of Labor (AFL) followed in 1881. By 1904, more than a million laborers had joined the AFL, led by **Samuel Gompers**.

In addition to labor, other groups and individuals emerged to fight the abuses of industrialization. The **Progressive Era** arose out of a reform movement whose goal was to eliminate political corruption and improve the quality of life for Americans. One great supporter of **Progressivism** was the U.S. president with whom the movement was closely associated—**Theodore Roosevelt**.

During the Progressive Era, the government abandoned its hands-off policy toward big business and initiated reforms that affect Americans today. Some of these reforms are highlighted in the following chart.

Progressive Reforms
Sherman Anti-Trust Act—outlawed monopolies
Hepburn Act—gave Interstate Commerce Commission increased authority to regulate the nation's railroads
Pure Food and Drug Act—set standards for production and sale of food and drugs
United States Department of Agriculture (USDA)—began inspecting meat
Child Labor Laws—prohibited child labor
Minimum wage and worker's compensation laws—improved working conditions and wages

GED PRACTICE

EXERCISE 14

Progressivism

Directions: Read the passage below and choose the *best* answer to each of the questions that follow.

The Sherman Anti-Trust Act outlawed price-fixing (the agreement between companies to set their prices), underproduction of goods, market sharing, and any other form of monopolizing among producers of a similar product. However, public utilities such as gas, electric power, and water companies are exempted from these restraints. These government-sanctioned monopolies are permitted to exist so that essential services are not duplicated and natural resources are not wasted.

1. According to the Sherman Anti-Trust Act, which of the following is an example of an illegal monopoly?

(1) the existence of only one power company in a city, giving consumers no choice of service provider
(2) a large commercial bank that has branches located throughout the city in direct competition with other banks
(3) a hamburger chain's restaurants, all of which belong to the same system of franchises
(4) oil manufacturers in a state that agree on a minimum price to set for gasoline
(5) a local telephone company that sets minimum and maximum rates for customers in a particular service area

2. Why did the Sherman Anti-Trust Act allow government-sanctioned monopolies?

(1) to give consumers a choice of service provider
(2) to promote competition
(3) to conserve resources
(4) to set prices for goods and services
(5) to allow new businesses to grow

Answers are on page 448.

The United States as a World Power

From the time it achieved its independence from England, the United States stayed out of the affairs of other countries. This policy of **isolationism** prevented the United States from forming alliances.

In 1867, the secretary of state for the United States (**William Henry Seward**) bought the territory of Alaska from Russia against the wishes of most Americans. The purchase turned out to be a good investment, however, because of Alaska's many natural resources. Also, because Alaska was the first land acquired that was outside the boundaries of the continental United States, the purchase marked the beginning of a new foreign policy. The United States was no longer an isolationist country.

Another motive for the United States to become less isolationist was the need to develop more markets for its manufactured goods. U.S. ships sailed the Pacific Ocean carrying goods to Japan and China. These ships often docked in the many island ports along the way to buy supplies and to make repairs. By the late 1890s, the U.S. government had taken possession of a number of Pacific islands for their convenient locations and available resources. This marked America's emergence as an **imperialist** country—a nation that controls other territories or nations.

The Spanish-American War

The emergence of America on the world scene was strengthened by the **Spanish-American War**. The United States supported rebels in Cuba who revolted against Spain. The battleship ***Maine*** was sent to Cuba to protect American citizens there. It exploded, killing 260 American sailors, and Spain was held responsible. The United States declared war against Spain in 1898 and won the war in four months. Under the terms of the peace treaty, the United States gained control of Guam, Puerto Rico, and the Philippines. These new territories and the islands in the Pacific increased the number of territories under American control.

GED PRACTICE

EXERCISE 15

The United States as a World Power

Directions: Choose the *best* answer to each of the following questions.

1. **Which of the following current foreign policy actions is a direct result of early American imperialist policy?**

   (1) America's military support of Israel in the Middle East
   (2) the support of Taiwan's status as independent from China
   (3) America's establishment of military bases in the Philippines' Subic Bay
   (4) the stationing of American troops in western Germany
   (5) America's patrolling of waters off the Libyan coast

2. **From the end of the American Civil War until the Spanish-American War in 1898, most Americans were isolationists. Which is the most likely cause of such widespread desire for withdrawal from international concerns?**

   (1) the lack of information about events taking place in foreign lands
   (2) the desire to expand U.S. boundaries farther across the continent into Canada and Mexico
   (3) the disillusionment with foreign allies who had refused to take sides during the Civil War
   (4) the nation's preoccupation with reconstruction and industrialization after the Civil War
   (5) the resentment toward the new immigrants flooding the country

Answers are on page 448.

Source: Library of Congress

During the Spanish-American War, Teddy Roosevelt was lieutenant colonel of the Rough Riders regiment, which he led on a charge at the Battle of San Juan Hill. He was one of the most conspicuous heroes of the war and went on to become the 26th president of the United States in 1900. Isolationists loathed Roosevelt for his interventionist policies. Here he is depicted as the world's policeman, carrying his "big stick."

World War I

In the 1910s, conflicts over boundary lines and power struggles among European countries resulted in a war that, by its end, involved twenty-seven nations. For this reason, it was called a world war. The nations divided themselves into two rival groups—the **Central Powers** and the **Allied Powers**. The Central Powers included Germany, Austria-Hungary, Bulgaria, and Turkey. The Allied Powers included Great Britain, France, Russia, Belgium, and Italy.

The United States tried to remain neutral during the early years of the war, which had begun in 1914. In 1917, however, in response to German attacks on ships carrying American citizens, the United States declared war. The war resulted in many changes in the United States. Factories shifted their production to the manufacture of needed military weapons and supplies. Women and older children replaced draftees as factory workers. Shipyards built only naval vessels. To conserve food for the soldiers, the U.S. government asked that the consumption of meat and bread be restricted to particular days.

Strengthened by the United States' entrance in the war on their side, the Allies drove the Central Powers back to their own boundaries. When the Allies broke through the German lines, the Germans conceded defeat.

The **Treaty of Versailles,** signed in early 1919, officially ended the war. One condition of the treaty was that the **League of Nations** be established to maintain peace throughout the world. Although the idea of the League of Nations was conceived by U.S. president **Woodrow Wilson**, Congress did not want the United States to become involved in European affairs again, so the country did not join the League of Nations. This was a major factor in the organization's decline. After the war, the United States returned to a policy of isolationism, and domestic issues became the focus of the postwar period.

The Suffrage Movement

Both before and after the war, women's participation in politics was highly controversial. Social and cultural traditions of the late 19th century dictated that a woman's "true" place was in the home. This was in contrast to the high numbers of middle-class women who held jobs, particularly during World War I. Women were encouraged to take on social or community service but participation in politics or public meetings was deemed "unladylike."

Women in many parts of the United States were not allowed to own property or to have a will. Change in these restrictions was difficult because women did not enjoy **suffrage,** or the right to vote. Despite not being able to vote in many states, women played an important role in many of the reform movements in the 19th and early 20th centuries. In fact, many historians credit women's vocal support of the temperence movement with the delay in their getting the national right to vote. The alcohol lobbyists managed to convince enough men that if women were allowed to vote, alcohol would be declared illegal.

In the early 20th century, women banded together to force the government to add a constitutional amendment guaranteeing women's right to vote. This amendment, the **Nineteenth**, was ratified in 1920. The **Eighteenth Amendment** outlawing alcohol, commonly referred to as **Prohibition,** had already been ratified in 1919.

Writing Activity 6

In many parts of the world women still do not have a voice in government. In two or three paragraphs, explain why you think women don't have the same level of participation in society as men in these places.

From the Roaring Twenties to the Stock Market Crash

During the 1920s, the Immigration Acts of 1921 and 1924 were enacted to preserve jobs for American workers. These acts strictly limited the number of immigrants who could enter the United States. The government at this time enacted few regulations and lowered taxes to the individual. As a result, the people had more money to spend, and businesses were able to expand. This period in U.S. history was called the **Roaring Twenties** because of the prosperity the nation enjoyed. The period was characterized by speculation (taking unwise risks in investments hoping to increase gains), bootlegging (the manufacture and purchase of illegal liquor, the sale of which was banned by the Eighteenth Amendment), and an emphasis on materialism.

Unfortunately, by the end of the decade, the Roaring Twenties became quiet, as the stock market fell in 1929. Businesses failed and the unemployment rate soared. The government maintained that if businesses were left alone, the country would quickly recover from the economic depression. By 1932, however, the number of unemployed workers reached 11 million, nearly 10 percent of the nation's 123 million people. The U.S. economy required drastic measures in order to recover.

© Eric Smith, Capital-Gazette

Writing Activity 7

According to this cartoonist, why did the Wall Street investors not want the American public to panic about losses? Had Americans not panicked, the banks would have been able to adjust to overlending and would have recovered. What do you think the government could have done to prevent the panic? Write one or two paragraphs about an idea that might have prevented the stock market crash.

The New Deal

In 1932, the voters overwhelmingly elected Democrat **Franklin D. Roosevelt** president on his campaign promise to give Americans a "New Deal." The goals of the **New Deal** were to bring relief to people who were in need, to direct the recovery of the economic system, and to establish reforms that would prevent another depression from occurring.

Roosevelt's programs radically changed governmental policy. Within his first 100 days in office, he persuaded Congress to approve an unprecedented number of bills to address the nation's economic crisis. Many of the agencies created during the New Deal remain today. Most notable are the Social Security system and the Federal Housing Administration. The Federal Deposit Insurance Corporation ensured that bank deposits up to $100,000 would be insured by the government if the banks failed, and the Agricultural Adjustment Act paid farmers to cut back on crops so that food prices would remain stable.

Roosevelt instituted the National Industrial Recovery Act, which provided unlimited workers for public projects, and the Civilian Conservation Corps, a program that recruited young unmarried men to work in U.S. forests and national parks.

Roosevelt's actions reversed the economic and emotional climate of the country. Voters reelected him by the largest margin (up to that time) in U.S. history.

EXERCISE 16

The New Deal

Directions: Match the group in the left column with the New Deal legislation it would have most likely supported in the right column.

1. ______	sharecroppers	**a.** National Industrial Recovery Act
2. ______	unemployed laborers	**b.** Federal Deposit Insurance Corporation
3. ______	the elderly	**c.** Civilian Conservation Corps
4. ______	environmentalists	**d.** Agricultural Adjustment Act
5. ______	bankers	**e.** Social Security Act

Answers are on page 449.

World War II

Beginning of World War II

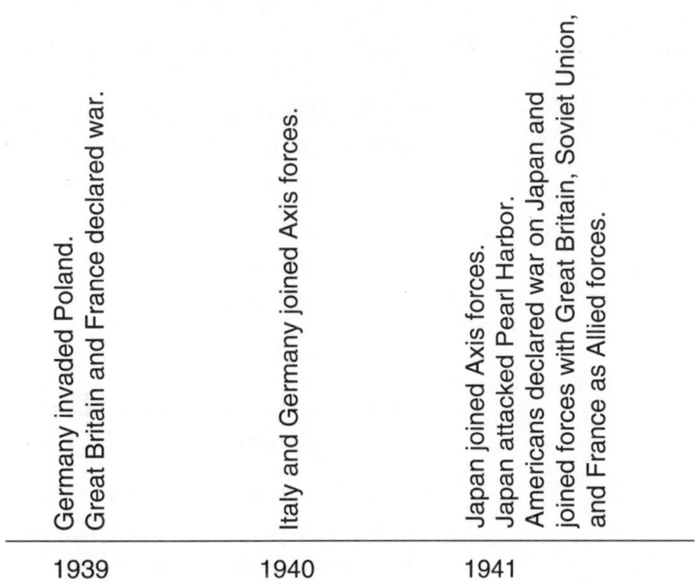
Germany invaded Poland.
Great Britain and France declared war.
Italy and Germany joined Axis forces.
Japan joined Axis forces.
Japan attacked Pearl Harbor.
Americans declared war on Japan and joined forces with Great Britain, Soviet Union, and France as Allied forces.
1939
1940
1941

Although World War II began in Europe in 1939, the United States did not officially join the fighting for more than two years. On December 7, 1941, the Japanese Air Force attacked **Pearl Harbor**, an American naval base on the island of Hawaii. After the attack, the United States declared war on Japan and its **Axis** allies, Germany and Italy. The United States joined Great Britain, the Soviet Union, France, and others as the **Allied Forces.**

World War II was truly a global war. Battles were fought in Europe, North Africa, Asia, and on many Pacific Ocean islands. During the six years of the war, millions of lives were lost and millions of dollars were spent. Although the Axis powers (see Social Studies Chapter 1 page 321) won the early battles, the Allied invasion at Normandy on June 6, 1944, turned the tide of the war in favor of the United States and the Allies.

In February 1945 President Roosevelt, Great Britain's **Winston Churchill**, and the Soviet Union's Josef Stalin met in the Soviet city of **Yalta** to prepare for the Axis surrender. Under the Yalta agreement, Germany was divided into four zones, each under the control of one of the major Allied powers.

In April of that year, one month before massive Allied military efforts forced Germany to surrender, President Roosevelt died. Vice President **Harry Truman** succeeded him. Truman was determined to end the war with Japan. The dropping of atomic bombs on **Hiroshima** and **Nagasaki** brought a quick surrender from Japan on September 2, 1945. Soon after, the **United Nations** was established as an organization to maintain world peace.

Although the war ended many years ago, its scars remain. In addition to the death of thousands of people and the radioactive fallout from the dropping of the atomic bombs in Japan, the Nazi extermination of six million Jews—now known as the Holocaust—is a continual reminder of the war's atrocities.

GED PRACTICE

EXERCISE 17

World War II

Directions: Read the following questions and select the *best* answer.

1. **World War II was the first technical war. Which of the following military items does *not* support that statement?**

   (1) amphibious airplanes
   (2) aircraft carriers
   (3) the atomic bomb
   (4) fuel-efficient aircrafts
   (5) dark green army fatigues

2. **Which of the following conclusions can you draw based on the information about World War II?**

   (1) The formation of the United Nations ended the war.
   (2) Italy was the last country to join the Allied forces.
   (3) Japan caused the United States to enter the war in 1941.
   (4) Adolf Hitler wanted an alliance with the United States.
   (5) President Roosevelt welcomed troops after the war was over.

Answers are on page 449.

Writing Activity 8

About 32,000 World War II veterans die every month. Most are in their seventies or eighties. In two or three paragraphs, discuss how you think this generation of Americans was affected by the war.

The Korean Conflict

At the end of World War II, the Soviet Union and the United States (who were allies at the time) agreed that the nation of Korea should be free from Japanese control. To protect this freedom, the Soviet Union occupied the northern half, while the United States occupied the southern half.

By 1950, however, a "cold war" had developed between the United States and the Soviet Union. There was no direct aggression, but the two nations tried hard to influence other countries. Each feared that the other would try to take control of Korea.

South Korea held public elections to determine its leadership, while a Communist government was established in North Korea. Armies representing the North and the South were stationed along the border. When a North Korean army crossed the border into the South, President Truman committed U.S. troops and asked for troop support from the United Nations.

President Truman claimed that the **Korean Conflict** was a "UN" action and never asked Congress for a formal declaration of war. Despite this, the United States suffered 137,000 casualties; the UN's losses were 263,000. It was not until 1953, under newly-elected president **Dwight D. Eisenhower**, that a treaty was signed, maintaining the separation of North and South Korea at the **38th parallel**. However, tensions between the two countries still exist today.

The end of the Korean Conflict marked only the end of armed conflict. The United States and the Soviet Union did not trust each other. Each increased its military forces, and both developed the hydrogen bomb. This nuclear weapon was far more powerful than the atomic bomb. The mistrust between the two superpowers continued the **Cold War**—a war of words and beliefs—the Soviet Union pushing communism and the United States spreading its capitalist influence.

GED PRACTICE

EXERCISE 18

The Korean Conflict

Directions: Choose the *best* answer for each of the following questions.

1. Which of the following is an opinion about the Korean Conflict?

(1) Dwight Eisenhower finally ended American military action in Korea.
(2) The Soviet Union and the United States mistrusted each other's intentions in Korea.
(3) The Korean conflict was an extension of American policy to contain communism.
(4) Our government has no right to make soldiers fight in an undeclared war.
(5) After the war, the boundary between the two countries was reinstated.

2. Which of the following is a direct cause of the Korean Conflict?

(1) different customs in North and South Korea
(2) the alliance of the Soviet Union and the United States in World War II
(3) public elections in South Korea
(4) United Nations troops in North Korea
(5) North Korean troops crossing the border

Answers are on page 449.

Writing Activity 9

The following quote is from Dwight D. Eisenhower's *State of the Union address* from January 9, 1959.

"We seek victory—not over any nation or people—but over ignorance, poverty, disease, and human degradation wherever they may be found."

In two or three paragraphs, explain how this relates to the United States' position with respect to the Korean Conflict.

The Eisenhower Years

In the 1950s, during Dwight D. Eisenhower's first term as president, **Senator Joseph McCarthy** used the country's hatred and fear of communism to his political advantage. He accused hundreds of government officials, prominent businesspeople, and entertainers of being part of a Communist plot to take over the country. Although his charges were never proven, they ruined many people. However, his reputation was so badly damaged that he soon lost his influence and power.

President Eisenhower's second term was marked by economic development and social change. Important technological advances encouraged America's involvement in the exploration of space. In 1957, the launching of the first artificial satellite (**Sputnik**) by the Soviet Union precipitated the entry of the United States into the space race.

Also during the Eisenhower administration, the modern civil rights movement began as a direct result of the famous U.S. Supreme Court decision ***Brown* v. *Topeka Board of Education***. In the case, the court ruled that "separate educational facilities are inherently unequal." This ruling was resisted in many school districts throughout the South. The most celebrated case occurred in Little Rock, Arkansas, when black students were refused entry to all-white Central High School. President Eisenhower sent federal troops to ensure the students' safety. Later, the **Civil Rights Act of 1957** established the Civil Rights Commission to investigate illegal voting requirements based on race, national origin, or religion.

GED PRACTICE

EXERCISE 19

The Eisenhower Years

Directions: Choose the *best* answer to the following questions.

1. McCarthyism has often been compared to the Salem witch trials in colonial Massachusetts. What did the two events have in common?

(1) People were burned at the stake.
(2) Accusations were made with little evidence.
(3) Congress held hearings.
(4) Federal troops were used.
(5) Mostly women were convicted.

2. Why is the *Brown* v. *Topeka Board of Education* decision significant today?

(1) It sanctioned schools segregated on the basis of race.
(2) It allowed Eisenhower to set a precedent by sending out federal troops.
(3) It served as the legal basis for school busing to achieve desegregation.
(4) It permitted blacks to attend private schools.
(5) It helped to increase Eisenhower's personal popularity.

Answers are on page 449.

The Kennedy Administration

John F. Kennedy, the first Catholic and the youngest man to be elected president, brought great promise to the office. Kennedy's challenge to America is encapsulated in the quote below, delivered at his inauguration on January 20, 1961.

> And so, my fellow Americans: ask not what your country can do for you—ask what you can do for your country. My fellow citizens of the world: ask not what America will do for you, but together what we can do for the freedom of man. Finally, whether you are citizens of America or citizens of the world, ask of us here the same high standards of strength and sacrifice which we ask of you. With a good conscience our only sure reward, with history the final judge of our deeds, let us go forth to lead the land we love, asking His blessing and His help, but knowing that here on earth God's work must truly be our own.

Youth rallied to his call when Kennedy established the **Peace Corps** to share America's wealth and knowledge with developing nations.

The U.S. space program helped symbolize Kennedy's vision of a "new frontier" as the Mercury 7 astronauts ushered in the era of U.S. manned space flights. In 1961, the Soviet Union began supplying nuclear missiles to pro-Soviet **Cuba**, located some 90 miles off the Florida coast. President Kennedy established a naval blockade to prevent any Soviet ships from reaching Cuba. He demanded that the missile site already established be dismantled and the missiles be removed. Soviet Premier **Nikita Khrushchev,** not wanting to risk war, agreed to withdraw all of the missiles from Cuba.

On the domestic front, Kennedy continued Eisenhower's policy of guaranteeing civil rights to the nation's black minority. In 1963, a civil rights commission found that voting rights of blacks were still being denied. Also that year, the **Reverend Martin Luther King, Jr.,** led a series of nonviolent protests throughout the South, culminating in a historic march on Washington that August.

President Kennedy's death by an assassin's bullet in November 1963 prevented many of his social programs from becoming realities. In 1964, his successor, **Lyndon B. Johnson** pushed through Congress the most significant achievement of his career—**the Civil Rights Act.** The law forbade racial discrimination in circumstances where federal funds were used.

GED PRACTICE

EXERCISE 20

The Kennedy Administration

Directions: Choose the statement that *best* answers each question below.

1. The Soviet Union's attempt to establish a missile base in Cuba may be interpreted as a direct violation of which important policy?

(1) the Declaration of Independence
(2) the Truman Doctrine
(3) the Monroe Doctrine
(4) the Treaty of Paris
(5) the U.S. Constitution

2. Based on the information in the passage, what can you conclude?

(1) The Soviet Union sought to control Cuba.
(2) The Soviet Union planned an attack on the United States from Cuba.
(3) Cuba and the United States enjoyed friendly relations.
(4) Cuba, a Communist country, was an ally of the Soviet Union.
(5) Cuba planned to attack the United States.

Answers are on page 449.

The Vietnam War

Despite President Johnson's domestic achievements in the area of civil rights, his foreign policy—particularly with regard to the **Vietnam War**—proved to be his undoing. Under Johnson, the Vietnam War was escalated in 1965. The number of American soldiers fighting in the undeclared war grew from approximately 25,000 in 1963 to more than 500,000 by 1968. In the United States, public controversy over the war painfully divided the country. Supporters maintained that the war was necessary to contain communism and protect democracy in the Far East. Critics maintained that the war was essentially a civil war in which outsiders did not belong.

Antiwar protests occurred on college campuses across the nation. Draft resisters fled to Canada to avoid having to serve in the war. President Johnson continued to seek a military end to the war, but because of the division within the country, he chose not to seek reelection to the presidency in 1968. His decision not to run opened the door to new leadership and a new direction for the American people.

Détente and Watergate

Richard M. Nixon was elected president in 1968. He continued Johnson's earlier bombing strategy to force surrender in Vietnam. He ordered troops into Cambodia, a military move that was unpopular with the American people. Nixon did, however, gradually withdraw troops, and negotiate a pullout by March 1973. The agreement to end the war included a cease-fire, U.S. withdrawal of all military troops, and a release of all prisoners captured during the war.

His policy of **détente** (the easing of tensions between nations) helped to establish the first **SALT** (Strategic Arms Limitation Talks) agreement. The United States and the Soviet Union agreed to limit the number of missiles each could have. Nixon was the first American president ever to visit the People's Republic of China, to which he traveled in 1972.

Overshadowing all of these achievements in Nixon's career, however, was his involvement in the **Watergate** scandal that began in June 1972, during his reelection campaign. The scandal involved a break-in at the Democratic Committee Headquarters, whose offices were located in the Watergate apartment and office complex in Washington, D.C. Nixon's part in the attempted cover-up led to his resignation in 1974. To spare the country the difficulties of impeachment proceedings, he became the first U.S. president ever to resign from office.

EXERCISE 21

Détente and Watergate

Directions: Label each statement below as **fact (F)** or **opinion (O).**

1. ______ Nixon's involvement in Watergate ruined his presidency.
2. ______ Nixon's strategy in Vietnam would have worked if he had had more time.
3. ______ Nixon wanted the United States to be involved with China.
4. ______ The SALT treaty limited the number of missiles the United States could have.
5. ______ The agreement to end the Vietnam War included complete U.S. withdrawal.

Answers are on page 449.

Ending the Twentieth Century

Significant Events in Presidential Administrations

President	Term	Party	Significant Events in Administation
Jimmy Carter	1977-1981	Democrat	• encouragement of peace treaty between Egypt and Israel • establishment of full diplomatic relations with China • signing of second SALT (Strategic Arms Limitation Talks) treaty with Soviet Union • return of Panama Canal to Panama • takeover of American Embassy in Teheran, Iran in which more than sixty Americans were held hostage
Ronald Reagan	1981-1989	Republican	• supporting hard-line defense policies • joining with France and Italy to maintain peacekeeping force in Beirut, Lebanon • holding of four summit meetings with Mikhail Gorbachev • development of Iran Contra Scandal • elimination of short-and-medium range missiles from Europe

President	Term	Party	Significant Events in Administation
George Bush	1989-1993	Republican	• collapse of communism in Eastern Europe • invasion of Kuwait by U.S. forces resulting in a quick victory • end of "Cold War" • U.S. economy going into recession
Bill Clinton	1993-2000	Democrat	• approval of North American Free Trade Agreement (NAFTA) • impeachment of a second President of the United States on issues of perjury and obstruction of justice • joining of United States North Atlantic Treaty Organization (NATO) nations in aerial bombing campaign • strength of economy • military intervention in Bosnian Civil War

GED PRACTICE

EXERCISE 22

Ending the Twentieth Century

Directions: Use the chart to answer the following questions.

1. **Considering the events that occurred between 1977 and 2000, which of the following was not a challenge for one of the presidents?**
   (1) hostage situations
   (2) moral character issues
   (3) foreign affairs
   (4) an economic depression
   (5) military defense issues

2. **During which years did the United States witness the disbanding of the Soviet Union?**
   (1) 1977–1981
   (2) 1981–1989
   (3) 1989–1993
   (4) 1993–1999
   (5) 1999–2001

Answers are on page 449.

Writing Activity 10

Choose one of the presidents from the chart on pages 364–365. Analyze the significant events from his administration and discuss whether or not you think he was a successful president. Write at least two or three paragraphs supporting your opinion.

Go to **www.GEDSocialStudies.com** for additional practice and instruction!

CHAPTER 3

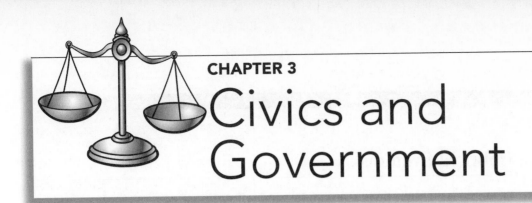

Civics and Government

To maintain order in a society, governments with rules and laws are established to meet the needs of the individuals who make up the society. The main goals of local, state, and federal governments in the United States are to maintain order, provide necessary services, and protect basic freedoms and liberties. In turn, U.S. citizens have the responsibility to get involved and participate in their government through voting and other methods. Citizen participation is an essential ingredient in the U.S. system of government.

Types of Political Systems

Several types of political systems exist in the world. The differences among political systems chiefly concern the way the government acquires and uses its authority.

Types of Political Systems

Democracy	Dictatorship	Monarchy	Oligarchy
• head of government is chosen by the people to be governed • *pure democracy* allows the people to make decisions directly • *representative democracy* includes election of representatives by the people	• one leader completely controls the political, social, and economic aspects of life in a country • official is not elected by the people	• power to rule is held by a royal family • power is passed within the family from generation to generation	• government by a few leaders who form a group, usually from upper classes • officials are *not* elected by the people

GED PRACTICE

EXERCISE 1

Political Systems

Directions: Listed below are applications of political systems in the world. Choose the appropriate response for each question.

1. **Adolf Hitler's rise to power in Germany is an example of what type of political system?**
   (1) pure democracy
   (2) monarchy
   (3) dictatorship
   (4) representative democracy
   (5) oligarchy

2. **What type of political system is headed by Queen Elizabeth II of England?**
   (1) dictatorship
   (2) oligarchy
   (3) pure democracy
   (4) representative democracy
   (5) monarchy

3. **The president of the United States is elected by the electoral college. What type of system is this?**
   (1) dictatorship
   (2) monarchy
   (3) pure democracy
   (4) oligarchy
   (5) representative democracy

4. **In ancient Athens (Greece) tribes and generals took turns at power. This is an example of what type of political system?**
   (1) dictatorship
   (2) monarchy
   (3) pure democracy
   (4) oligarchy
   (5) representative democracy

Answers are on page 450.

GED PRACTICE

EXERCISE 2

Methods of Obtaining Power

Directions: Listed in this chart are five ways by which government leaders may assume power. Read the definitions and apply them to the questions that follow.

ancestry	leader comes from a family that has led the country for many generations
divine right	leader claims to have been placed in his or her position by God
conquest	leader acquires territory through military domination
revolution	leader comes to power as a result of an overthrow of an earlier political system
popular vote	leader is chosen by the vote of the people to be governed

1. The French, inspired in part by the revolt of the thirteen colonies against England, replaced their monarchy with a republic through force. How did their new leader come to power?

(1) ancestry
(2) divine right
(3) conquest
(4) revolution
(5) popular vote

2. Austria maintained its independence from Hitler's Germany until Nazi troops occupied the small nation and forced it to join the Third Reich. How did Hitler acquire power over Austria?

(1) ancestry
(2) divine right
(3) conquest
(4) revolution
(5) popular vote

3. President Corazon Aquino of the Philippines outpolled former president Ferdinand Marcos in the election of 1986. How did Aquino win the presidency?

(1) ancestry
(2) divine right
(3) conquest
(4) revolution
(5) popular vote

Answers are on page 450.

The U.S. Federal Government

The U.S. Constitution is based on the idea of federalism. Under **federalism,** the authority of the government is divided between the states and a central government. The central government is further divided into three branches: the **legislative,** which makes the laws; the **executive,** which carries out the laws; and the **judicial,** which interprets the laws. Under this separation of powers, no one part of government is able to dominate another. Each branch of government is able to exert its authority to prevent another branch from becoming too powerful. The government of the United States cannot operate effectively without the support and participation of its citizens, and there must be communication among the three branches of government.

The Legislative Branch: Maker of Laws

The legislative branch of the government is outlined in Article One of the Constitution. The U.S. legislature, called the **U.S. Congress**, is made up of two houses—the House of Representatives and the Senate. The **House of Representatives** is called the lower house, and the **Senate** is called the upper house. Each of the houses has equal power in Congress.

In the House of Representatives, each state's number of representatives is based on its population in relationship to the population of the entire country. Smaller states have fewer representatives than larger states have. To determine the correct number of representatives for each state, a **census**, or counting of the population, occurs every 10 years. In the Senate, states are equally represented, with two senators each.

Representatives are chosen by popular election and serve for two years. Senators are also chosen by popular election, although under the original Constitution they were chosen by the state legislatures. Senators serve six-year terms. The number of terms that members of the Congress may serve is not limited by the Constitution.

GED PRACTICE

EXERCISE 3

Legislative Representation

Directions: Choose the *best* answer for each of the questions below.

1. Although New Jersey is smaller in area than Wyoming or Nevada, it has a larger number of representatives. Based on this fact, which of the following can you infer to be true?

(1) New Jersey has a dwindling population.
(2) New Jersey is primarily an urban, industrial state.
(3) New Jersey is a densely populated state.
(4) New Jersey is an urban state with a dwindling population.
(5) New Jersey is densely populated but dwindling in population.

2. Arizona, one of the fastest-growing Sunbelt states, is attracting residents from the industrial Northeast. Based on this fact, which of the following hypotheses could be true?

(1) The number of senators for Arizona will need to be increased.
(2) The number of representatives for Arizona will need to be adjusted.
(3) The number of representatives for the Northeast states that are losing residents will need to be adjusted.
(4) Both (1) and (2)
(5) Both (2) and (3)

3. Which of the following conclusions can you draw about the legislative branch of government?

The members of Congress

(1) are elected to serve the needs of the people
(2) do not need to cooperate with the president of the United States
(3) are required to serve at least two terms
(4) are not allowed to participate in specialized committees
(5) are chosen by the president and his staff of advisors

Answers are on page 450.

The U.S. Congress has the power to

- levy and collect taxes
- approve treaties (Senate only)
- borrow money
- impeach the president (House only)
- regulate commerce
- introduce bills other than tax bills
- coin money
- introduce a revenue or tax bill (House only)
- declare war
- approve presidential appointments (Senate only)
- provide and maintain an army and navy
- admit new states to the Union

These powers are called **enumerated** powers because they are listed in Article One of the U.S. Constitution. In addition to enumerated powers, the Constitution provides for powers that are not listed. The **elastic clause** enables the legislative branch to "stretch" its authority to meet the needs of specific situations that the founding fathers could not foresee.

EXERCISE 4

The Legislative Branch

Directions: Write **C** in the space if the action listed is an example of a power stated in the U.S. Constitution and listed in the table above. Write **E** in the space if it is an example of an application of the elastic clause, which allows Congress to stretch its authority to meet needs not mentioned in the Constitution.

1. ______ Congress approved economic sanctions against Iraq following the Gulf War.

2. ______ Congress approved the North American Free Trade Agreement (NAFTA) in 1993.

3. ______ Congress admitted Hawaii as the 50th state of the Union.

4. ______ The Senate approved President Clinton's appointment of Ruth Bader Ginsburg to the U.S. Supreme Court.

5. ______ Congress passed the Immigration Act in 1990.

Answers are on page 450.

Writing Activity 1

Thomas Jefferson, third president of the United States, said, "The government is the strongest of which every man feels himself a part." In two or three paragraphs, discuss your interpretation of this quotation.

The Executive Branch: Enforcer of the Laws

Article Two of the U.S. Constitution outlines the powers of the executive branch of the U.S. government. The executive branch consists of the president, the vice president, and the agencies and departments that are necessary to administer and enforce the laws of the country. The president serves for four years and is limited to serving a maximum of two terms. The vice president serves if the president becomes disabled or dies in office before completing the term.

As described in Article Two of the U.S. Constitution, the president has the following responsibilities:

- serves as commander in chief of the armed forces
- grants reprieves and pardons for offenses against the United States
- appoints judges to the U.S. Supreme Court and ambassadors, with the approval of the Senate
- nominates and appoints major executive officers
- vetoes (refuses to approve) some bills sent by Congress

> The President serves as both our symbolic and political leader. In many countries this dual leadership role is held by separate individuals. The power of office, combined with the considerable economic, political, and military might of the United States, makes our President one of the world's most visible and powerful leaders.

Source: *How the United States Government Works* by Nancy Gendron Hofmann

EXERCISE 5

Presidential Powers

Directions: Place an **X** next to the four specific powers of the president as defined in the U.S. Constitution and explain why you feel that the framers of the Constitution reserved these powers for the president.

1. ______ collects taxes

2. ______ serves as commander in chief

3. ______ grants reprieves and pardons

4. ______ appoints Supreme Court judges

5. ______ declares war

6. ______ nominates major executive officers

Answers are on page 450.

GED PRACTICE

EXERCISE 6

The Executive Branch

Directions: Choose the *best* answer for the question below.

The Twenty-second Amendment to the Constitution limits a president to serving no more than two full terms. Which of the following could be a result of this decision?

(1) creation of a third party
(2) unconstrained presidential power
(3) institution of new policy ideas
(4) reduction of the president's pension
(5) weakened image of the president

Answer is on page 450.

Writing Activity 2

Write two or three paragraphs about your ideal U.S. president. What kind of person would you select? What specific policies would he or she promote? Use real examples of past administrations if you can.

The Judicial Branch: Interpreter of the Laws

Article Three of the U.S. Constitution describes the Supreme Court of the United States. The purpose of the **Supreme Court** is to rule on the constitutionality of certain laws passed by Congress, the president, and the states themselves. The authority to decide whether or not a law is in keeping with the spirit of the Constitution is called **judicial review.**

The Supreme Court is composed of nine justices appointed for life by the president. The head of the court is called the **chief justice.** The judicial branch of the federal government consists of the U.S. Supreme Court, the 11 circuit courts of appeals distributed throughout the country, and approximately 90 federal district courts. The Supreme Court is the most powerful court in the United States.

The Supreme Court has the powers to rule on

- cases involving a state and citizens of another state
- controversies among two or more states
- cases between citizens of different states
- conflicts over patents and copyrights

In Supreme Court rulings, a decision is reached when a majority of the justices agree. When all nine justices are present and vote, a majority decision requires at least five votes.

GED PRACTICE

EXERCISE 7

The Judicial Branch

Directions: Choose the *best* answer to complete each of the following statements.

1. Chief Justice Charles Evans Hughes wrote in 1907, "The Constitution is what the Judges say it is." Which Supreme Court power does this quotation best define?

(1) checks and balances
(2) ignoring legislative decisions
(3) being "above the law"
(4) judicial review
(5) judicial restraint

2. What is the purpose of the statement in Question 1?

(1) define the role of the Supreme Court
(2) show that the Supreme Court is the final authority
(3) show the attitude of Chief Justice Hughes
(4) both (1) and (2)
(5) (1), (2), and (3)

Answers are on page 450.

Throughout the history of the U.S. Supreme Court, the court has had to decide whether or not it should preserve and uphold the federal system (which included supporting the authority of each state) or uphold the rights of the individual. Supreme Court justices who lean toward upholding the rights of the states are described as exercising **judicial restraint.**

EXERCISE 8

States' v. Individuals' Rights

Directions: For each of these landmark cases, write **I** if it is a victory for the rights of the individual.

1. ______ the case of *Plessy* v. *Ferguson* (1896), in which the Supreme Court upheld a lower-court decision that ruled that separate but equal facilities for blacks and whites were correct and legal

2. ______ the case of *Korematsu* v. *United States* (1944) in which the Supreme Court upheld a lower-court decision that ruled that it was legal for the government to relocate the Japanese-American population during World War II

3. ______ the case of *Dred Scott* v. *Sanford* (1857), in which the Supreme Court agreed with a lower court that freeing Dred Scott would be depriving his owner of personal property without due process of law

4. ______ the case of *Miranda* v. *Arizona* (1966), in which the Supreme Court ruled that a person accused of a crime must be informed of his or her rights or any resulting confession would be invalid

5. ______ the case of *Brown* v. *Topeka Board of Education* (1954), in which the Supreme Court ruled that separate facilities for the races were not equal and, therefore, were unconstitutional

Answers are on page 451.

On June 13, 1967, Thurgood Marshall became the first African American to sit on the U.S. Supreme Court. In addition to his many years as a civil rights lawyer, Marshall served on the U.S. Court of Appeals and as a solicitor general, the attorney who represents the government before the Supreme Court.

Source: *Civics for Democracy*

System of Checks and Balances

The framers of the Constitution understood that the powers of the three branches of the federal government had to be balanced so that no one center of power dominated the other two. To prevent any one branch from imposing its will on the others, the U.S. Constitution allows for certain actions by one branch to restrain the activities of another. One such restraint is the ability of the president to refuse approval of **(veto)** a bill sent from Congress.

However, Congress could still pass the bill into law by a two-thirds majority vote of its members. This procedure is called **overriding a veto.** Finally, if the issue is brought to the Supreme Court, the Court can still declare the law unconstitutional. This happens if the justices conclude that the law contradicts the principles of the Constitution. Compromises within the three branches of government assure citizens of the United States that changes in laws will occur with great consideration among the lawmakers.

EXERCISE 9

System of Checks and Balances

Directions: In column I, write the branch of government that exercises the power described on the left. In column II, write the branch of government that is checked by the use of that power. The first one is done for you.

Power	I Who exercises power?	II Who is checked?
1. to appoint federal judges	**(a)** *executive*	**(b)** *judicial*
2. to impeach the president	**(a)** ______	**(b)** ______
3. to approve appointment of judges	**(a)** ______	**(b)** ______
4. to override a veto	**(a)** ______	**(b)** ______
5. to rule a law unconstitutional	**(a)** ______	**(b)** ______
6. to veto a bill	**(a)** ______	**(b)** ______

Answers are on page 451.

The Enactment of a Law

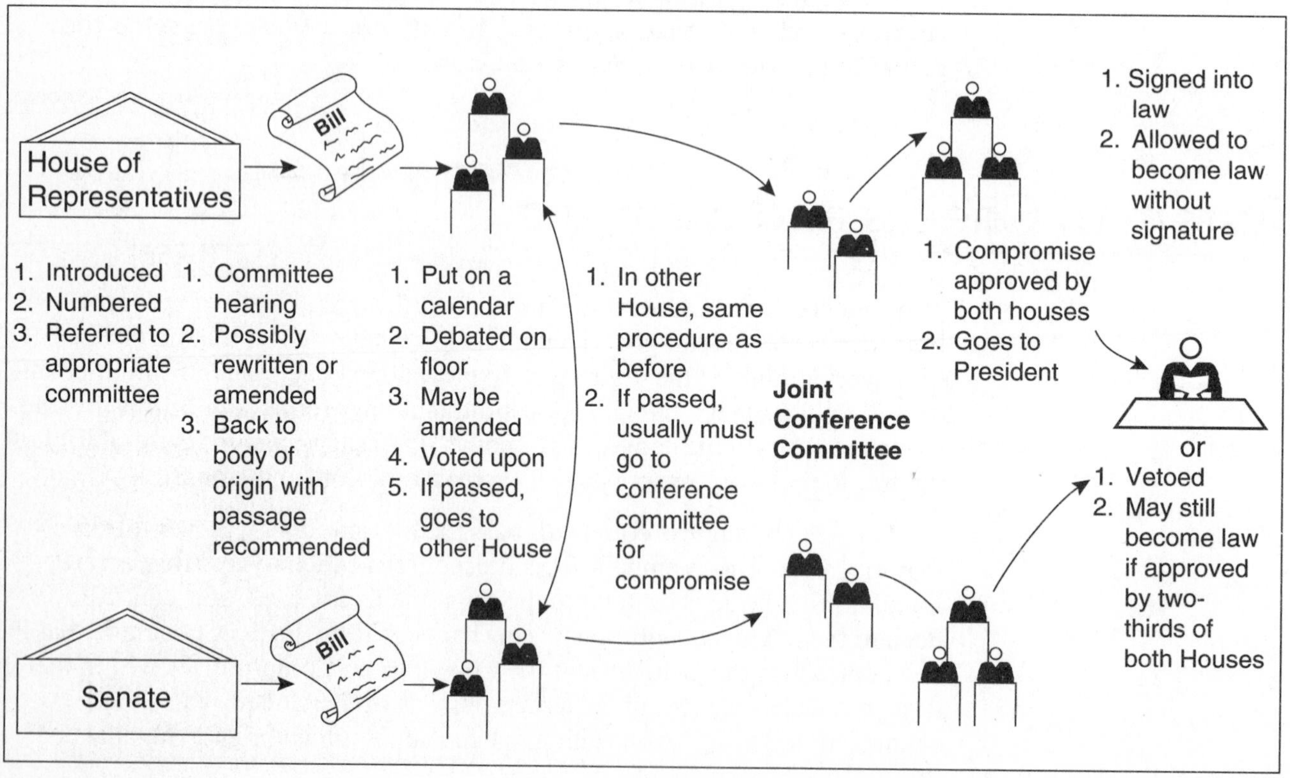
House of Representatives
Bill
Senate
Bill
1. Introduced
2. Numbered
3. Referred to appropriate committee
1. Committee hearing
2. Possibly rewritten or amended
3. Back to body of origin with passage recommended
1. Put on a calendar
2. Debated on floor
3. May be amended
4. Voted upon
5. If passed, goes to other House
1. In other House, same procedure as before
2. If passed, usually must go to conference committee for compromise
Joint Conference Committee
1. Compromise approved by both houses
2. Goes to President
1. Signed into law
2. Allowed to become law without signature
or
1. Vetoed
2. May still become law if approved by two-thirds of both Houses

GED PRACTICE

EXERCISE 10

The Enactment of a Law

Directions: Choose the *best* answer for each of the following questions.

1. **Which statement is best supported by the preceding chart?**
   (1) Bills justified by the elastic clause in the Constitution must be introduced directly by the president.
   (2) Before being sent to the president, a bill must be approved in identical form by both houses of Congress.
   (3) A filibuster on certain bills may not take place in either house.
   (4) A bill introduced in the Senate may be changed by the House, but not vice versa.
   (5) The president must sign all bills for them to become law.

2. **Which of the following is *not* true according to the preceding chart?**
   (1) Vetoed bills cannot become law.
   (2) Bills passed in the Senate go to the House.
   (3) Bills can become law without the president's signature.
   (4) Bills can be amended after they come out of committee.
   (5) All bills are debated on the floor of the House and Senate.

Answers are on page 451.

Amending the Constitution

There have been only 27 changes to the Constitution since it was written in 1787. A change to the Constitution is called an **amendment.**

The first ten amendments to the Constitution are called the **Bill of Rights.** It was only after the inclusion of these guarantees of personal freedoms for citizens that some states would ratify the Constitution. Consider the first five amendments stated below and summarize the main idea of each in your own words.

First Amendment	The establishment of a specific, government-approved religion is prohibited. Freedom of speech, freedom of the press, right to assemble, and right to petition the government to address grievances.
Second Amendment	right to keep and bear arms
Third Amendment	restriction of quartering soldiers in private homes only allowed under specific conditions
Fourth Amendment	protection from unreasonable search and seizure
Fifth Amendment	provisions concerning prosecution and due process of law double jeopardy restriction. private property not to be taken without compensation

Writing Activity 3

Under each picture, write two or three complete sentences explaining how one of the first five amendments applies to the rights of a U.S. citizen.

____

____

____

____

____

____

____

____

____

State and Local Governments

State Government

Article Four of the U.S. Constitution defines the role of state governments. The structure of the state government resembles that of the federal government. The executive authority of the state is the governor. Like the president, the governor has veto power.

The legislative branch, which makes the laws, is composed of two houses in 49 of the 50 states. In 1937, Nebraska changed to a single-house system to cut costs. Each state has its own court system, which includes trial courts, appellate courts, and a state supreme court.

Each state has its own written constitution, mostly based on the federal model. These state constitutions outline the powers and duties of the various state officials and agencies. Like the federal governmental system on which they are based, the 50 state governments have a system of checks and balances among the three branches of government. In addition, the state constitutions cannot conflict with the U.S. Constitution.

Most criminal codes and civil laws, such as a legal drinking age, are established by state law. The state also establishes laws for contracts, business charters, and marriage and divorce. Another responsibility of state government is to charter local governments. The powers of municipalities—villages, towns, and cities—are outlined and defined in charters approved by the state.

EXERCISE 11

Powers of State Government

Directions: In the spaces provided, write **S** if the power belongs to the states, **F** if it belongs to the federal government, and **B** if it belongs to both.

1. ______ vetoing a bill by the chief executive
2. ______ passing laws that provide for the welfare of its citizens
3. ______ declaring war against a foreign country
4. ______ setting import quotas and duties
5. ______ establishing a legal age for drinking alcoholic beverages
6. ______ setting up guidelines for chartering a business

Answers are on page 451.

Local Government

While the structure and organization of the federal and state governments are similar, local governments can be quite different. Local governments are usually one of three types: mayor-council, council-manager, and commission. Local governments are created by the state legislatures.

Under the **mayor-council** form of municipal government, the mayor is the executive and is elected by the voters. The council is the legislature; each council member is elected by voters in a ward or district established by legal boundaries.

Under the **council-manager** form of government, members of the council are elected by the people. The duties of the council are to make policies, set goals, and provide leadership. The council hires a manager to oversee the day-to-day operations of the government and carry out the policies set by the council. The council-manager form of government is the most common.

Under the **commission** form of government, commissioners are elected by the people. Their job is to make policies and to run a specific department of the city or county. For example, one commissioner may be in charge of public safety (fire, police, civil defense), while another commissioner may be in charge of public works (water, sewers, roads).

All municipalities receive most of the money to operate from local taxes, fees, and service charges. When local governments need large amounts of money for projects, they generally borrow money by issuing bonds. The graphs in Exercise 12 show the sources of income for cities and how they are allocated.

EXERCISE 12

City Income and Expenditures

Directions: Read the two graphs and fill in the blanks in the following sentences.

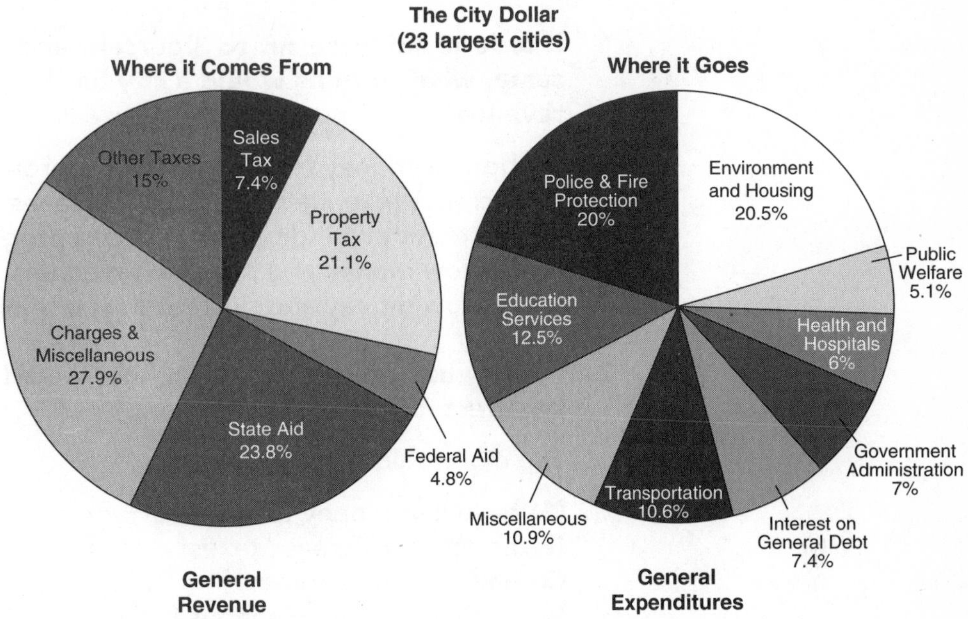

1. The income that a government receives is called ________________, and the money it spends is called ________________.
2. In the graph, the largest source of income for the city is ________________.
3. The largest percentage of the city dollar goes to ________________.

Answers are on page 451.

GED PRACTICE

EXERCISE 13

City Budgeting

Directions: Choose the *best* answer for the following questions.

1. If federal aid were cut to 3 percent and state aid remained the same, what options would a city have to make up for the loss in revenue?

(1) borrow money from a more prosperous state
(2) increase revenue by raising local taxes or fees
(3) decrease expenditures by cutting programs
(4) borrow money and increase revenue
(5) borrow money and decrease expenditures

2. If a city had no general debt, how would the rest of its budget be affected?

The city would

(1) have less money to spend
(2) be able to increase taxes
(3) have to cut programs
(4) have more miscellaneous funds
(5) have to lend money

Answers are on page 451.

Civic Involvement in Local Government

There are many opportunities for citizens to become involved in their local government. Most effective changes in local government are generated by groups of concerned people, but citizens can initiate projects independently by writing letters, sending electronic messages, making telephone calls, and attending public meetings. Examples of a few successful topics for projects instituted by citizens in their communities are drinking-water safety, hazardous waste cleanup, pesticide spraying, noise pollution, homelessness assistance, and child care programs.

GED PRACTICE

EXERCISE 14

Civic Involvement

Directions: Choose the *best* answer for each of the following questions based on the information provided.

1. Which of the following is probably *not* a reason why people hesitate to participate in the affairs of their community?

(1) lack of knowledge about the issues
(2) fear of jeopardizing their jobs
(3) shortage of free time to devote to a project
(4) concern of harassment by other citizens
(5) absence of community need

2. Based on what you know about how local governments operate, which of the following people would be most likely to respond to an individual's complaint?

(1) the mayor
(2) a state senator
(3) a city councilman
(4) a city manager
(5) the governor

Answers are on page 451.

Writing Activity 4

A good citizen tries to be informed and is eager to help when possible in the community. Consider a need in your community. Write two or three paragraphs about how citizens and the local government could improve the situation.

The U.S. Political System

The voting public has been viewed as holding a range of positions on political issues. These political positions can be illustrated as occupying one of five segments of a spectrum. The segments are generally referred to as ***political labels***. To win an election, each political party must obtain a majority of the votes cast. Since most U.S. voters occupy the middle three parts of the spectrum, both political parties must appeal to this group of voters to win.

The following illustration shows the five political positions.

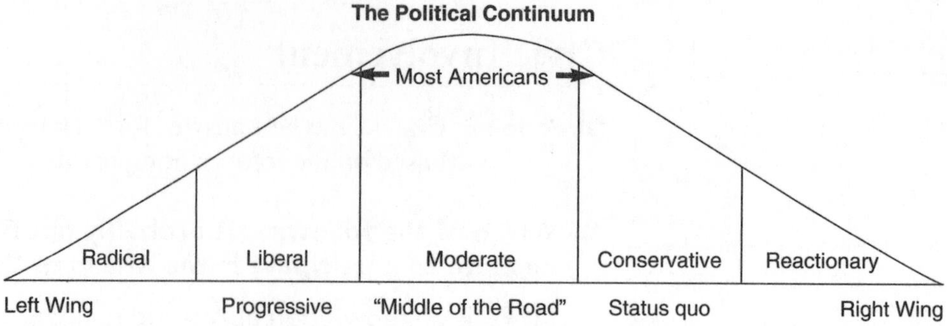

radical: one who advocates sweeping changes in laws and methods of government with little delay

liberal: one who advocates political change in the name of progress, especially social improvement through governmental action

moderate: one who believes in avoiding extreme changes and measures in laws and government

conservative: one who advocates maintaining the existing social order and believes that change, if any, should be gradual

reactionary: one who resists change and usually advocates a return to an earlier social order or policy

EXERCISE 15

The Political Spectrum

Directions: Read the passage below and use the definitions above to identify the political position of each speaker represented in the five quotations that follow the passage.

An issue in life in the United States that has generated many positions and has divided the population is bilingualism. Many Americans are concerned that we are quickly becoming a bilingual country—the primary and secondary languages being English and Spanish. Americans have varying opinions about the increasing concessions made to our Spanish-speaking minority.

1. **"We might as well accept the fact that Hispanic-Americans are here to stay and are significant contributors to our American way of life. Instead of criticizing them for speaking in their native tongue, the government should improve bilingual programs to make it easier for Hispanics to learn English."**
   What type of opinion is the speaker expressing?

   (1) radical **(2)** liberal **(3)** moderate **(4)** conservative **(5)** reactionary

2. **"Let's not lose our heads. We don't need harsher laws, nor do we need to spend more money. The current strategies to bring Hispanics into the mainstream of American society by helping them to overcome language barriers are sufficient. We just need to work harder at them."**
   What type of opinion is the speaker expressing?

   (1) radical **(2)** liberal **(3)** moderate **(4)** conservative **(5)** reactionary

3. **"I'm tired of seeing my tax dollars spent to make it easier for people too lazy to learn the language. Every public sign written in Spanish should be taken down—my Italian parents didn't have it that easy back in the thirties. Then these people would have to learn English—they'd have to sink or swim."**
   What type of opinion is the speaker expressing?

   (1) radical **(2)** liberal **(3)** moderate **(4)** conservative **(5)** reactionary

4. **"English has been the primary language here and always will be. I suggest that before Hispanics are granted citizenship or are given jobs, they should be made to pass a test on standard English."**
   What type of opinion is the speaker expressing?

   (1) radical **(2)** liberal **(3)** moderate **(4)** conservative **(5)** reactionary

5. **"Unless the laws that treat Mexicans as second-class citizens because of their inability to speak the language are changed immediately, starting tomorrow, Mexicans should stop picking lettuce, washing dishes, and sweeping floors—doing the dirty work at low pay that other Americans think they are above doing."**
   What type of opinion is the speaker expressing?

   (1) radical **(2)** liberal **(3)** moderate **(4)** conservative **(5)** reactionary

Answers are on page 451.

Political Parties

A **political party** is a group whose goal is to influence public policy by getting its candidates elected to office. Although the U.S. Constitution makes no provision for political parties, they serve a useful function in our democracy. Political parties

- define the issues and propose possible solutions for governmental problems
- act as another check in our governmental system of checks and balances by monitoring the policies of the party in power
- enable citizens to become involved in the governmental apparatus
- help to keep the number of candidates running for public office manageable

For more than a century, there have been two *major* political parties in the United States: the Democrats and the Republicans.

The differences between the Democratic and Republican parties tend to center on domestic, economic, and social issues as well as foreign policy. Most fundamentally, however, the two parties differ in their views of the role of government in solving problems.

In general, the **Democratic Party** favors a strong federal government at the expense of the sovereign rights of the states. This party advocates government regulation of business, endorses labor unions, and champions federal programs for the disadvantaged and minorities.

The **Republican Party,** on the other hand, favors stronger state authority at the expense of the federal government. This party advocates individual free enterprise, supports a strong national defense, and believes in keeping any government social programs to a minimum.

There are exceptions to these generalizations, of course; sometimes the distinctions between the two parties become increasingly blurred.

EXERCISE 16

Political Parties

Directions: Write **D** in the space provided if the statement generally applies to the Democratic Party philosophy and **R** if it generally applies to the Republican Party philosophy.

1. ______ favors having state and local governments solve their own problems

2. ______ supports labor unions and the right of their members to strike

3. ______ represents the interests of individual entrepreneurs and investors

4. ______ advocates spending large amounts of money for welfare and other social services

5. ______ often supports "guns" (defense spending) over "butter" (domestic spending)

Answers are on page 452.

Writing Activity 5

Are you a Republican, a Democrat, or an independent? Write two or three paragraphs describing your party affiliation or why you have none. List reasons why you are loyal to that party or political orientation.

Interest Groups

Once public officials are elected, they are under constant pressure exerted by individuals, businesses, governmental agencies, community organizations, and others who make up their constituency. **Interest groups** are organized groups, not associated with a political party, who actively seek to influence public opinion, policies, and actions. The attempt to influence legislation is called **lobbying**. Lobbyists constantly watch for bills that may affect the group or groups they represent. For example, when the automobile emission-control law was being proposed, lobbyists for the automobile manufacturers worked hard to ensure that the law would be reasonable, not too costly, and not disruptive to automobile production.

Political Action Committees, known as PACs, seek to influence public officials directly. PACs contribute to legislators' campaign funds in the hope of obtaining favorable votes on legislation important to the committees.

GED PRACTICE

EXERCISE 17

Interest Groups

Directions: Choose the correct answer for each question below based on the information provided about interest groups.

1. Which of the following conclusions can be drawn about interest groups?

Interest groups in the United States

(1) do not contribute to campaign costs
(2) influence citizens and legislators
(3) select the vice presidential candidate
(4) are usually made up of more Democrats than Republicans
(5) form the electoral college during election years

2. Some advocates of campaign finance reform would like to abolish all lobbying efforts at the national level. What is one possible effect of this ban?

(1) Campaign costs will decrease.
(2) Legislators will have more contact with their constituents.
(3) Fewer opinions will be heard by the legislators.
(4) More people will run for office.
(5) The government will run out of money.

Answers are on page 452.

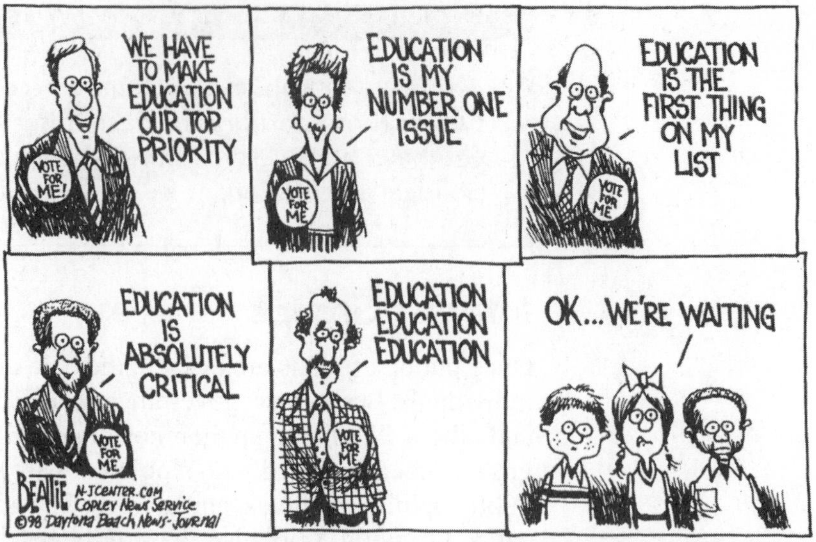

© Bruce Beattie/Copley News Service

Writing Activity 6

How do you think a member of the interest group the National Education Association would evaluate the message in this cartoon? Discuss your answer in about two or three paragraphs.

The Electoral Process and Voting

Both the Democratic and Republican parties maintain national party headquarters and staffs. Every four years, each party holds a national convention to nominate a presidential candidate who must have won a majority of delegates in the primaries that precede the nominating convention. A political **primary** enables members of a party to express their preference for a candidate to run in the general election. In most primary elections, the candidate must receive a **plurality** (more votes than any other candidate) to win. Primaries may be open or closed. In an **open primary** voters need not declare their party affiliations. In a **closed primary** voters must declare a party affiliation.

At the nominating convention, each state sends a designated number of delegates, who are local and state party representatives, to help select the party's nominee. At the end of a forum in which the issues are discussed and speeches are delivered, the delegates vote to choose the party's nominee and to approve the party's platform. The **platform** is a formal declaration of the principles on which the party stands.

After the candidates from each party campaign for office, the general election is held. In the general election, the winner must receive a **majority** of the votes cast in each state to earn that state's electoral votes. The president and vice president are chosen by popular vote within each state, but the electoral college later officially elects the president based on the winner of the popular vote in each state. The number of electoral votes for each state is equal to the number of U.S. representatives from that state plus its two senators.

Once elected, public officials are responsible to a **constituency**—the people who elected them to office. The elected official is obligated to faithfully serve this group of people. For the president of the United States, of course, the constituency is the entire U.S. population.

EXERCISE 18

The Electoral Process and Voting

Directions: Match each definition on the right with the correct term on the left.

1. ______ plurality

2. ______ primary

3. ______ platform

4. ______ majority

5. ______ constituency

a. declaration of a party's stand on the issues

b. the people a public official represents

c. more than half of the votes cast in an election

d. a party election to select a candidate to run in the general election

e. more votes than any other candidate (but not more than half)

Answers are on page 452.

The Electoral College

The **electoral college** consists of a group of electors from each state who cast votes for the president and vice president according to who won the popular vote in their state. To be officially elected president, a candidate must receive 270 electoral votes. The electoral college was originally established to serve as a check and balance against an unsound decision made by the voters and to preserve the voice of the less populated states. Recently, however, the electoral college has been the target of great criticism.

Critics of the electoral college were very vocal during the presidential election of 2000. For the first time since the election of 1888, a candidate was elected president without receiving the majority of the popular vote. Candidate Albert Gore narrowly won the **popular vote** but still lost the presidency to George W. Bush because of the electoral college. After the election, it took some 36 days to declare the winner. Of the 538 possible electoral votes, 271 were pledged to Bush and 267 were pledged to Gore, as shown in the map below. In the aftermath of the election, the American people learned of great numbers of disputed ballots and of the need to update election technology, increase training of poll workers, and further educate voters. Some politicians and other citizens have come to believe that the electoral college institution has outlived its usefulness and should be abolished.

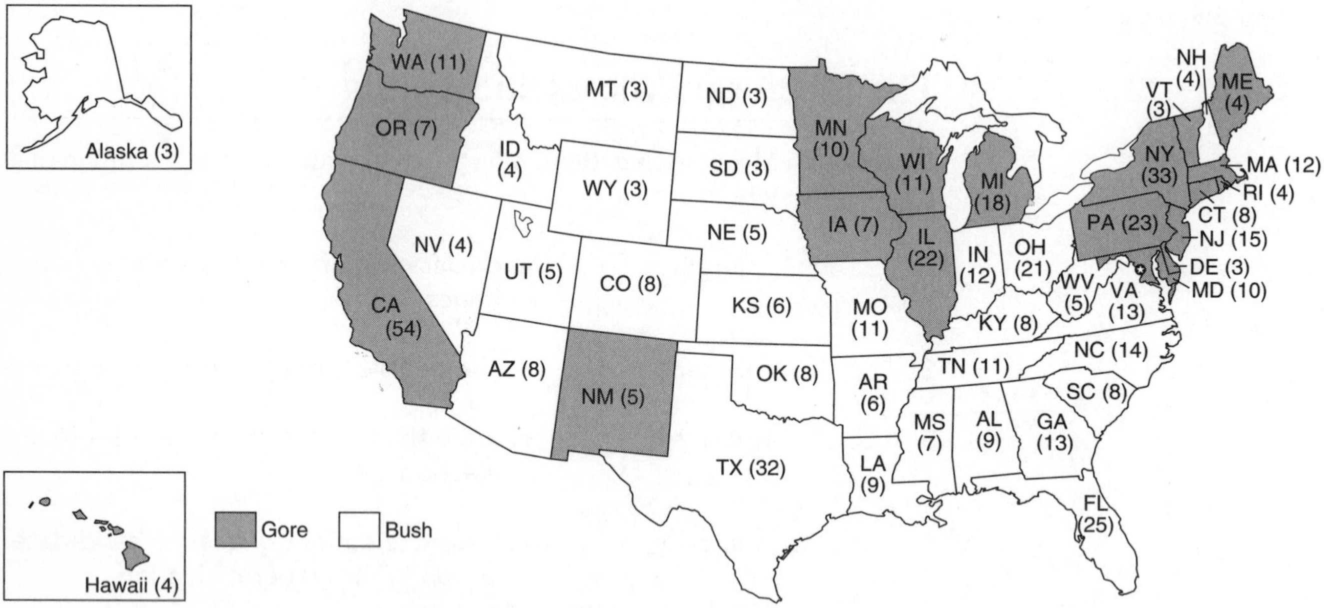

GED PRACTICE

EXERCISE 19

The Electoral College

Directions: Choose the correct answer based on the information provided in the map above.

Based on the electoral map above, which of the following statements is true?

(1) Gore won more states than Bush.
(2) Each candidate won an equal number of states.
(3) Bush won California.
(4) Gore won the states with the largest urban populations.
(5) Gore won his home state of Tennessee.

Answer is on page 452.

Voter Registration Application

For U.S. Citizens

	You can use this form to: ■ register to vote ■ report that your name or address has changed ■ register with a party Please print in blue or black ink	This space for office use only.				
1	Mr. Mrs. Miss Ms. Last Name	First Name		Middle Name(s)		(Circle one) Jr Sr II III IV
2	Address (see instructions)— Street (or route and box number)	Apt. or Lot #	City/Town	State	Zip Code	
3	Address Where You Get Your Mail If Different From Above (see instructions)		City/Town	State	Zip Code	
4	Date of Birth ___/___/___ Month Day Year	5 Telephone Number (optional)		6 ID Number (see item 6 in the instructions for your State)		
7	Choice of Party (see item 7 in the instructions for your State)			8 Race or Ethnic Group (see item 8 in the instructions for your State)		
9	I swear/affirm that: ■ I am a United States citizen ■ I meet the eligibility requirements of my state and subscribe to any oath required. (See item 9 in the instructions for your state before you sign.) ■ The information I have provided is true to the best of my knowledge under penalty of perjury. If I have provided false information, I may be fined, imprisoned, or (if not a U.S. citizen) deported from or refused entry to the United States.			Please sign full name (or put mark) Date: ___/___/___ Month Day Year		
10	If the applicant is unable to sign, who helped the applicant fill out this application? Give name, address and phone number (phone number optional).					

GED PRACTICE

EXERCISE 20

Registering to Vote

Directions: Choose the best answer for the following question.

Which of the following conclusions can be drawn from this voter Registration Application?

(1) Non-citizens can vote in elections in the United States.

(2) Only registered voters may cast a ballot.

(3) Voters do not need to re-register if they move to another state.

(4) Assistance in filling out the application is not acceptable.

(5) All states have the same eligibility requirements.

Answer is on page 452.

EXERCISE 21

Voter Rules

Directions: Write **fact (F)** or **opinion (O)** for each of the following statements about voting in the United States.

1. ______ The most serious offense a citizen can commit is voter fraud.
2. ______ The Voting Rights Act of 1965 abolished literacy tests.
3. ______ All states should have one-time lifetime registration.
4. ______ The Twenty-sixth Amendment gave 18-year-olds the right to vote.
5. ______ Non-citizens should be allowed to vote in elections.

Answer is on page 452.

The Impact of the Media

Another significant force in the modern U.S. political process is the **media**. Television, radio, newspapers, magazines, and the Internet are all part of the media. By far, television has the greatest influence on the U.S. voter, as evidenced by the huge sums of campaign money spent on television. Close elections may be won or lost on the basis of a candidate's media campaign.

Some political observers believe that television is undermining the U.S. democratic process since only those who have the money to finance huge publicity campaigns are able to run for office. This makes it nearly impossible for candidates who are not wealthy to run for office.

GED PRACTICE

EXERCISE 22

The Impact of the Media

Directions: Choose the *best* answer for each of the following questions.

©1997 Jimmy Margulies, The Record New Jersey. Reprinted by permission.

1. What is the main idea conveyed by the author of this cartoon?

(1) There does not need to be a limit on campaign spending.
(2) Campaign spending does not affect the federal government.
(3) Congress may ignore citizens' concerns over campaign spending.
(4) Campaign contributions should only be received by interest groups.
(5) The public does not need disclosure of campaign spending.

2. In the cartoon, to whom does the author think the congressman is listening?

(1) the public.
(2) special interest groups
(3) other congressmen
(4) state legislators
(5) no one

Answers are on page 452.

Becoming a Citizen of the United States

© Dean Wong/Corbis

Immigrants to this country have many reasons for wanting to become U.S. citizens. Benefits of **U.S. citizenship** include the right to vote in elections and traveling outside the country for an extended time with a U.S. passport. (Non-citizens may not be allowed to return to the United States if absent for more than six months.) Once permanent residents become citizens, they can experience all of the benefits of living in the United States.

In order to become a citizen of the United States, a person has to apply for citizenship. The process is overseen by the **Immigration and Naturalization Service (INS)**, a division of the Justice Department in the executive branch.

A few requirements for an applicant are:

- be at least 18 years of age
- be a resident in the United States for five years after applying for permanent residence
- be a person of good moral character
- demonstrate an understanding of the English language
- demonstrate a knowledge and understanding of fundamentals of history and principles of government

U.S. Department of Justice
Immigration and Naturalization Service

START HERE - Please Type or Print

Part 1. Information about you.

Family Name	Given Name	Middle Initial

U.S. Mailing Address - Care of

Street Number and Name	Apt. #
City	Country
State	Zip Code

Date of Birth (month/day/year)	Country of Birth
Social Security #	A #

Part 2. Basis for Eligibility (*check one*)

a. ☐ I have been a permanent resident for at least five (5) years
b. ☐ I have been a permanent resident for at least three (3) years and have been married to a United States Citizen for those three years
c. ☐ I am a permanent resident child of United States citizen parent(s)
d. ☐ I am applying on the basis of qualifying military service in the Armed Forces of the U.S. and have attached completed Forms N-426 and G-325B
e. ☐ Other. (Please specify section of law) ____________

GED PRACTICE

EXERCISE 23

Becoming a Citizen of the United States

Directions: Read the information on the form and answer the following questions.

1. Which of the following applicants could be denied citizenship according to the naturalization form?

(1) a deserter from the armed forces
(2) a child of naturalized parents
(3) a wife of a U.S. citizen
(4) a permanent resident of ten years
(5) a sergeant in the U.S. Army

2. Which of the following statements is incorrect regarding becoming a citizen of the United States?

In order to become a citizen, an applicant must

(1) not have committed any serious crimes
(2) pass a history and government exam
(3) fill out a naturalization application
(4) understand the English language
(5) have a full-time job

Answers are on page 452.

Writing Activity 7

What does being a citizen of the United States mean to you? In two or three paragraphs, discuss the advantages or disadvantages of being a citizen in this country.

Go to **www.GEDSocialStudies.com** for additional practice and instruction!

CHAPTER 4

Economics

"Whoever we are—professionals or homemakers, farmers or college students—we need to understand the basics of the world economy if we are to be effective citizens and consumers." This quote by Randy Charles Epping from *A Beginners Guide to the World Economy* clearly stresses the importance of understanding today's global **economy**.

Economists study how a society meets its unlimited material needs with its limited resources. The fact that resources are limited requires people to make choices about what needs to satisfy.

Factors of Production

Every society must answer three basic questions when determining the type of economic system under which it will operate. These questions are:

- **What should be produced?** What do members of a society need and want?
- **How should it be produced?** Should each person make his or her own goods, or should businesses or the government manufacture them for the entire society?
- **How should the products be distributed?** Should the products be given to everyone equally or only to those who can afford to buy them?

To answer these questions, each government must first identify its goals and values and then determine what resources are available to produce what the society needs.

The following chart identifies three vital **factors of production: natural resources, capital,** and **labor.**

Factors of Production	Definition	Examples
1. natural resources	• raw materials	• ore to make steel • trees
2. capital	• equipment, factories, or machines • money invested in enterprises	• sewing machines used to manufacture clothes • lumber to build a building
3. labor	• people who do the work	• seamstresses who cut and sew • construction workers to build buildings

Despite careful and efficient management, the factors of production (natural resources, capital, and labor) remain limited. The demands society makes upon them, however, are continually increasing. All countries are concerned about environmental protection and awareness, but natural resources such as coal, air, water, and virgin timber are in great demand around the world. A continued supply of natural resources depends on reasonable economic growth and cooperation among all nations.

EXERCISE 1

Factors of Production

Directions: In each example, write **N** if the factor of production refers to natural resources, **C** if it refers to capital, and **L** if it refers to labor.

1. ______ gemstones imported by the United States from India
2. ______ computers and printers used in a publishing firm
3. ______ trees harvested from the forests of Maine
4. ______ carpenters who help build new shopping malls
5. ______ silicon chips used in hand-held computers

Answers are on page 452.

Writing Activity 1

In two or three paragraphs, discuss how industrial growth in your community has affected its natural resources.

Economics and Government

A nation's system of government often determines the type of economic system under which the nation will operate. Recent history has shown that changing economic systems often brings political changes as well. Political leaders around the world assemble to exchange views and examine economic issues in order to keep the world economy as stable as possible.

Capitalism

Capitalism is an economic system based on the private ownership of the resources of production. Investment decisions are made by the individual or corporation rather than by the government. The production, distribution, and prices of goods and services are determined by competition in a free market. The government intervenes only when necessary to protect the public interest. The U.S. system of government is founded on the principle of individual freedom. Capitalism is the predominant economic system under which the American economy operates.

Other governments place the importance of the collective (all the people) above the individual. This emphasis on the collective permitted the emergence of economic systems that are alternatives to capitalism. Two such types are socialism and communism.

Socialism

Under **socialism,** the most important industries and services are publicly and cooperatively owned. These industries, which may include steel production, banking and finance, public transportation, or healthcare, are controlled by the government with the intent of providing equal opportunity for all.

In socialist economies, ownership of private property is permitted; however, owners of businesses together with the government decide what goods and services are produced, how they are produced, and who should get them. The economy of Sweden is a socialist economy.

Communism

A third economic order does not permit private ownership of property and the means of production at all. Under **communism,** the government, described as the community, owns the property and distributes the society's merchandise in accordance with the "common good." The government decides what goods and services are produced and who should get them. The economies of the People's Republic of China and Cuba operate under the principles of communism, as did the economy of the former Soviet Union.

None of these three economic systems exists in pure form. That is, no completely capitalist, socialist, or communist economy exists in the modern world. In its operation, each of the economic systems incorporates some aspect of another.

The term **mixed economy** is used to describe the U.S. economy since some government regulation of private enterprise exists. For example, the Food and Drug Administration ensures that any new medicine or drug that is marketed in the United States has been properly tested before it is sold to the public. The U.S. government becomes involved in situations in which there could be harm to the health and safety of its citizens.

GED PRACTICE

EXERCISE 2

Economic Systems

Directions: Choose the *best* answer for each question below.

1. Which economic system is best described by the quotation "From each according to his ability, to each according to his needs" ?

(1) capitalism
(2) socialism
(3) communism
(4) mixed economy
(5) none of the above

2. The quotation "In the area of economics, the government that governs least governs best" best describes which type of economic system?

(1) capitalism
(2) socialism
(3) communism
(4) mixed economy
(5) none of the above

Answers are on page 452.

GED PRACTICE

EXERCISE 3

Economic Systems and Governments

Directions: The diagram below shows the continuum of economic systems. Look at the diagram and answer the questions that follow it.

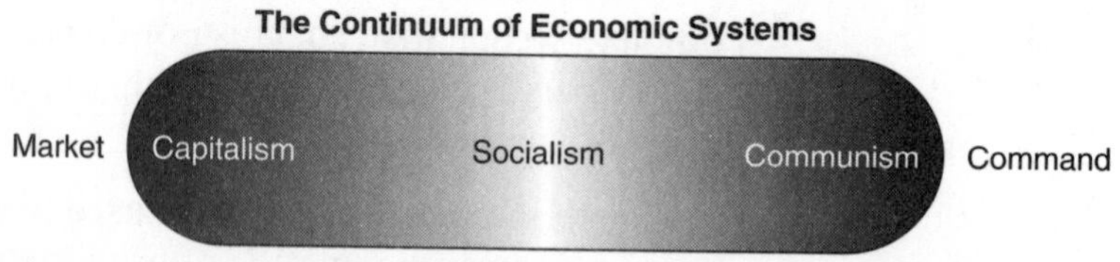

1. According to the continuum of economic systems, which of the following conclusions may be drawn?

(1) Communism is the best example of the market system.
(2) Capitalism is the best example of the command system.
(3) Socialism is the opposite of capitalism.
(4) Capitalism is the opposite of communism.
(5) Capitalism is better than any other system represented.

2. Which of the following situations best supports the statement "Each of the economic systems incorporates some aspect of the other"?

(1) In socialist Sweden, SAAB, the automobile manufacturer, is owned and run by the government.
(2) In Cuba, the government-controlled media schedules the broadcasting for all television and radio programs.
(3) In the United States, a dairy manufacturer is told by a government agency the percentages of milk and cream a product sold as ice cream must contain.
(4) In the People's Republic of China, all of the nation's farms are nationalized, and young people are forced to work them.
(5) In the United States, major air carriers engage in "price wars" to attract passengers during the vacation seasons.

Answers are on page 453.

Writing Activity 2

Some Americans believe that the government should pay for health insurance for everyone. Others think that people can do a better job than the government of taking care of themselves. What do you think? Discuss your opinion in at least two paragraphs.

Supply and Demand

The foundation of American capitalism is supply and demand. **Supply** is the quantity of goods and services available for sale at all possible prices. **Demand** is the desire to buy the product or service and the ability to pay for it.

Producers or suppliers are in business to make a profit; therefore, they supply goods and services at a price. They must charge prices high enough to cover their costs for production and earn a profit for themselves. Consumers who are willing and able to buy these goods and services create demand.

The amount of production (supply) of an item and its price depend on the cost of production and the demand in the marketplace. In general, producers seek the highest possible prices to maximize their profits. Consumers seek the lowest possible prices to keep money in their pockets. These opposing goals of producers and consumers significantly affect prices.

In general, the higher the price, the greater the number of companies that wish to supply a product or service. A high-priced item or service that yields a large profit will attract many producers, who will compete with one another for a share of the market. This applies chiefly to manufactured goods and to services. Precious minerals and metals such as diamonds and gold, which are scarce, command higher prices than more common minerals and metals.

A good example of the relationship between price and supply is the running shoes phenomenon. When they were introduced to the buying public, running shoes bearing the trademarks of such companies as Nike and Reebok created great demand. Consumers—adults and teens—paid higher prices for the labels than they ordinarily might have for other brands. As a result, several competitors entered the market (increasing the supply) seeking to make money on the product. Each running shoe manufacturer fought to capture a share of the market.

When too many producers compete in the marketplace, however, supply exceeds demand because buyers cannot or will not buy all of the goods offered for sale. As a result, a surplus occurs and prices fall. Producers no longer reap the profits necessary for them to compete successfully. Some businesses streamline their operations, and others are forced out of business.

From the consumer's viewpoint, the higher the price, the lower the demand; the lower the price, the greater the demand. If prices for running shoes became too high, consumers might stop buying them and revert to wearing off-brands. On the other hand, when prices for an item fall too low and consumer demand exceeds the producer's ability to provide the product, a shortage in supply occurs. As a result, prices rise higher, and in extreme cases, the product is rationed. Under **rationing**, the quantity of the item sold is restricted.

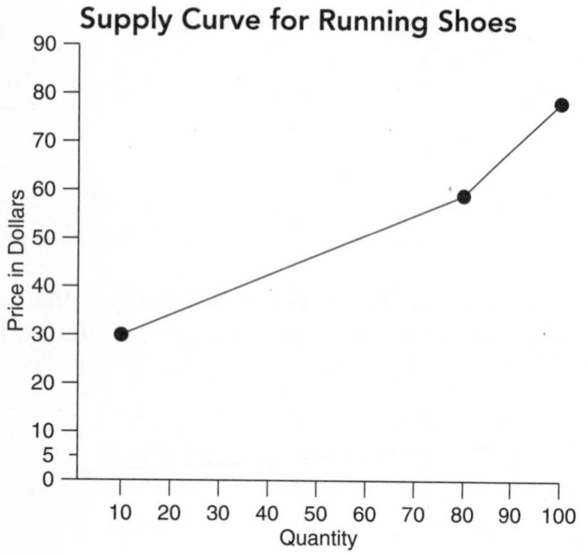

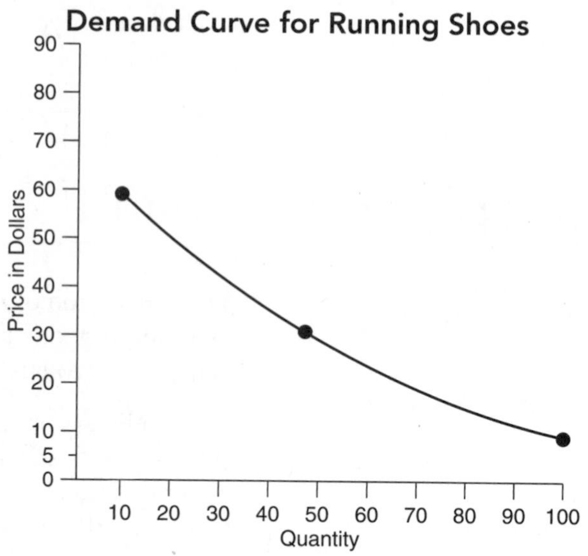

As shown in the graph on the left, as the price of running shoes goes up, the quantity supplied increases. In this graph, producers cannot supply running shoes at a price of $5. However, as the price increases to $30, about ten pairs of running shoes are available for purchase. According to this graph, what would happen to the supply if the price were $60?

You're right if you said that there would be about 80 pairs of running shoes available for purchase.

As shown in the graph on page 404, as the price of running shoes goes down, the quantity demanded rises. At $60 each, the demand would be for ten pairs. If the price were lowered to $30, the demand would increase to about 45 pairs. According to this graph, if the price rose to $70 per pair, would demand increase or decrease?

Since the graph shows no values for $70 per pair, you can infer that there is no demand for running shoes at this price.

Supply and Equilibrium

To produce exactly the amount that consumers are willing to buy, producers must determine at what point supply equals demand. Economists call this point the **equilibrium.** Equilibrium occurs when the supply and demand curves intersect. This establishes the market price for a product or service.

When the price is greater than the equilibrium, demand falls and there is more of a product or service than people want to buy. This is called a **surplus.** When the price falls below the equilibrium, demand increases, exceeding supply, and a **shortage** in the product or service occurs.

The following graph illustrates equilibrium.

Equilibrium for Running Shoes

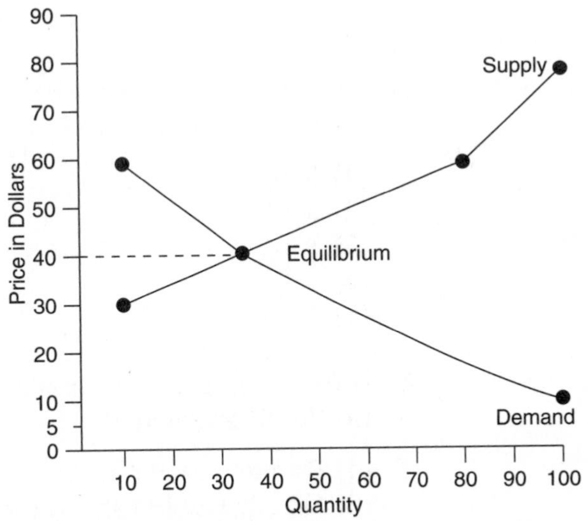

What is the price at which the supply of running shoes equals demand? The equilibrium point on the graph indicates that this is about $40.

GED PRACTICE

EXERCISE 4

Supply, Demand, and Equilibrium

Directions: Study the graph and answer the following questions.

Supply, Demand, and Equilibrium
Digital Cameras

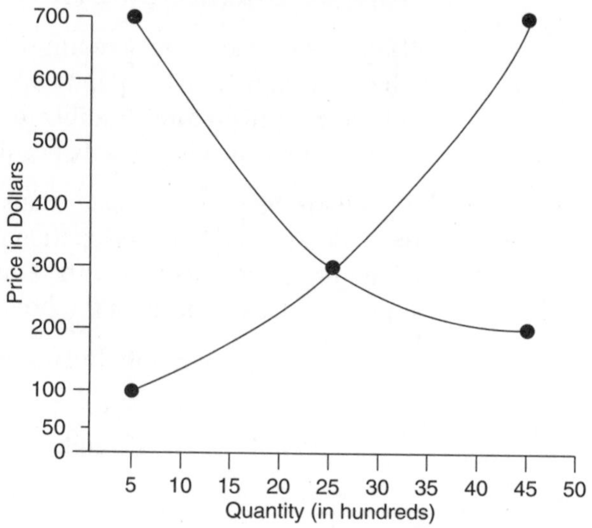

1. According to the graph, what is the approximate market price of these digital cameras?

(1) $500
(2) $400
(3) $300
(4) $200
(5) $100

2. If the market price for digital cameras fell to $150, what would be the likely result?

(1) Demand would decrease.
(2) Supply would remain the same.
(3) Demand would increase.
(4) Producers would not be able to satisfy demand.
(5) The item would become scarce.

3. In recent years, the Asian economies have developed the technology to manufacture and export to the United States electronic equipment such as digital cameras. If demand for digital cameras were low, what impact would Asia's entrance into the market have on the sale of digital cameras in the United States?

(1) Prices for digital cameras would increase because the supply would be greater.
(2) Prices for digital cameras would decrease because the supply would be lesser.
(3) A surplus of digital cameras might occur as a result of lower prices.
(4) Stores would cease ordering and stocking digital cameras.
(5) Prices for digital cameras would not be affected.

Answers are on page 453.

Imports and Exports

Our interconnected global economy allows consumers to purchase quality products at the most affordable prices. By opening the trading markets across the globe, businesses are able to produce and export products and import items from all over the world.

© Brian Kelley Courtesy The Signal—Santa Clara, CA

Writing Activity 3

According to this cartoon, the United States is consuming foreign goods and services in excess of its own exports. How do you feel this situation impacts the U.S. worker? Discuss your answer in two or three paragraphs.

Economic Growth

Economic growth is a major goal of an economic system. In a growing economy, there is an increasing capacity to produce more goods and services. During periods of great economic growth, consumers are increasingly able to buy these goods and services. However, the best type of growth is steady and controllable.

The world economy must grow evenly, or problems will occur. There have been several periods in our country's history when the economy has increased rapidly. During those periods, citizens experience positive economic times and many new businesses are created. When the rate of growth slows down, workers can be laid off and businesses are closed.

The Business Cycle

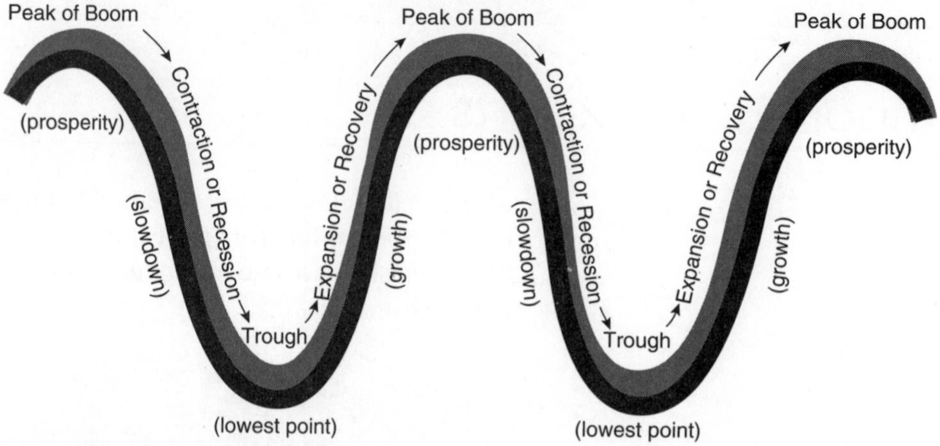

Source: *Consumer Economics in Action* by Roger LeRoy Miller and Alan D. Stafford

GED PRACTICE

EXERCISE 5

Economic Growth

Directions: Study the graph and answer the following questions.

1. **According to the graph, which of the following is not a stage in the business cycle?**

   (1) peak
   (2) depression
   (3) unemployment
   (4) recession
   (5) recovery

2. During which of the following business cycle stages would you assume that the economy is functioning poorly and the most people are suffering economically?

(1) peak
(2) depression
(3) unemployment
(4) recession
(5) recovery

Answers are on page 453.

Inflation and Its Effects

When too much money and credit are available and too few goods are available to satisfy demand, the dollar loses its value and the prices of goods increase. The country begins a period of **inflation.**

For consumers to be able to keep pace with the rise in the cost of goods, their wages must increase. For producers to pay the increased wages, they must produce more goods and charge higher prices for them. This circular pattern in which wage increases feed on price increases is called an **inflationary spiral.** An "inflation psychology" sets in as consumers rush to make major purchases because they believe that prices will only increase.

For inflation to fall, demand must be decreased and credit restricted. However, one result of curbing high inflation is an economic recession. From 1990 through 2000, U.S. Federal Reserve chairman Alan Greenspan skillfully guided and adjusted financial instruments that led the United States out of a period of inflation and through a period of economic stability.

Deflation and Its Effects

When too little money and credit are available, and more goods are available than necessary to satisfy demand, the dollar gains value and the prices of goods decrease. Under these circumstances, the economy enters a period of **deflation.** Because goods remain unsold, producers' profits fall. Falling profits lead to layoffs. Unless the situation is corrected, a recession occurs; if the recession is prolonged, a depression can result. Although the United States has not experienced a depression since the 1930s, the U.S. economy has been affected by varying levels of economic challenges in Mexico, Brazil, and Asian countries throughout the 20th century and into the 21st century.

GED PRACTICE

EXERCISE 6

Economic Growth

Directions: Read the graph on U.S. unemployment rates and answer the following questions.

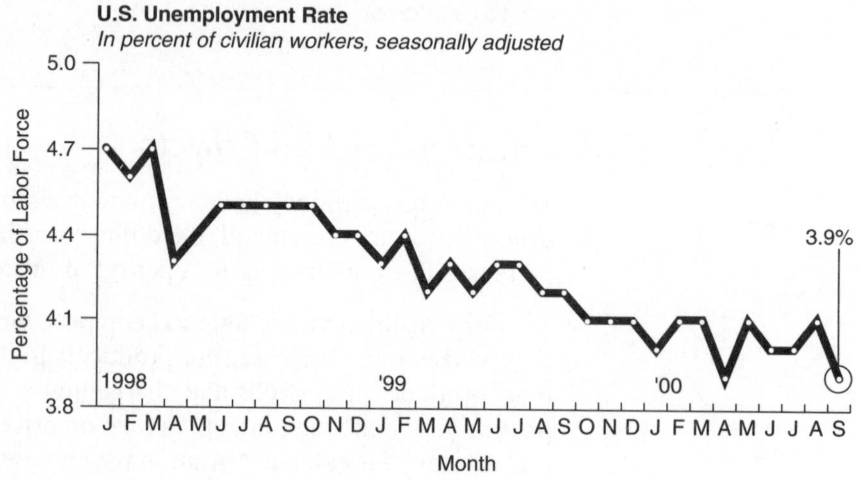

Source: U.S. Dept. of Labor

1. **According to the graph, which of the following is true?**
   (1) Every U.S. citizen was experiencing economic growth and job satisfaction.
   (2) All Americans were employed and enjoying new purchases.
   (3) The unemployment rate had declined from 1998 to 2000.
   (4) The unemployment rate in 2000 was the lowest in the history of the United States.
   (5) The unemployment rate was at a thirty-year low in every country around the world.

2. **Which of the following assumptions can be made about the information presented on the U.S. unemployment rate?**
   (1) There had been an increase in hiring in all jobs.
   (2) The unemployment rate was usually at its lowest point in February.
   (3) All workers received a cost of living increase in 1998.
   (4) The unemployment rate will continue to decline until it is at zero percent.
   (5) Only certain jobs showed an increase in hiring.

Answers are on page 453.

Writing Activity 4

How has inflation or deflation affected your spending patterns or those of your parents? Write two or three paragraphs describing the effect of inflation or deflation.

Measurement of Economic Growth

Econometrics is the use of statistical methods to study economic and financial data. These data are then interpreted by economic experts to show how the economy is performing. Among the more commonly used economic statistics are stock market trading, unemployment percentages, number of housing starts, and the gross domestic product (**GDP**).

The GDP represents the total amount of all goods and services produced in one year within a country's borders. The gross national product (**GNP**) measures international activities and is more of a global measure of economic enterprises.

Top 5 Countries with the Highest Gross Domestic Product

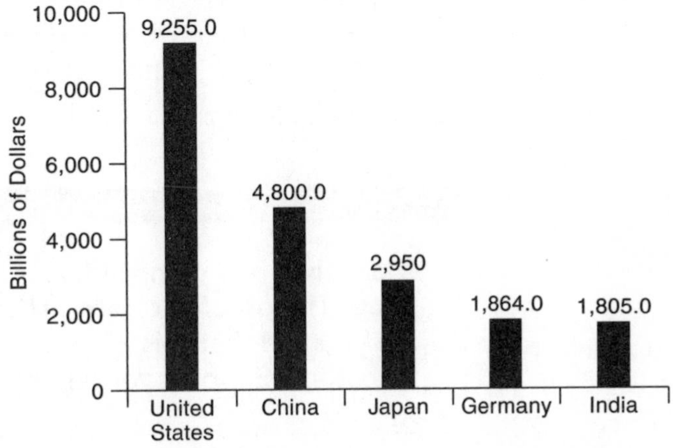

Source: Central Intelligence Agency, *The World Factbook 2000*

EXERCISE 7

Measurement of Economic Growth

Directions: Determine whether each of the following is **fact (F)** or **opinion (O)** based on the information provided on economic growth.

______ GDP and GNP are both statistical methods used to measure economic activity.

______ A carpenter selling cabinetry he or she has produced contributes to the country's GDP.

______ Financial statistics of stock market trading can only be interpreted by economists.

______ The United States produced more goods and services than Germany in 1998.

______ All countries should soon be able to match the GDP of the United States.

Answers are on page 453.

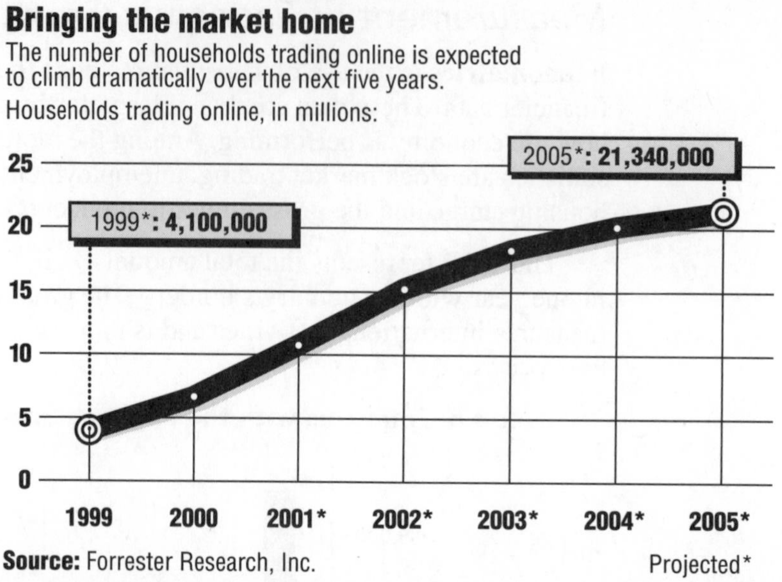

Writing Activity 5

More than half of individual investors were trading on-line in 2000. The graph indicates an increase over the next five years. Do you feel that this is a positive or negative opportunity for investors? Support your opinion with two or three paragraphs.

The Consumer Price Index

The **Consumer Price Index (CPI)** is the measure of change in prices of a group of goods or services that an average consumer would purchase. As stated in the graph below, the CPI in the United States has increased steadily since World War II.

Consumer Price Index 1915–1999

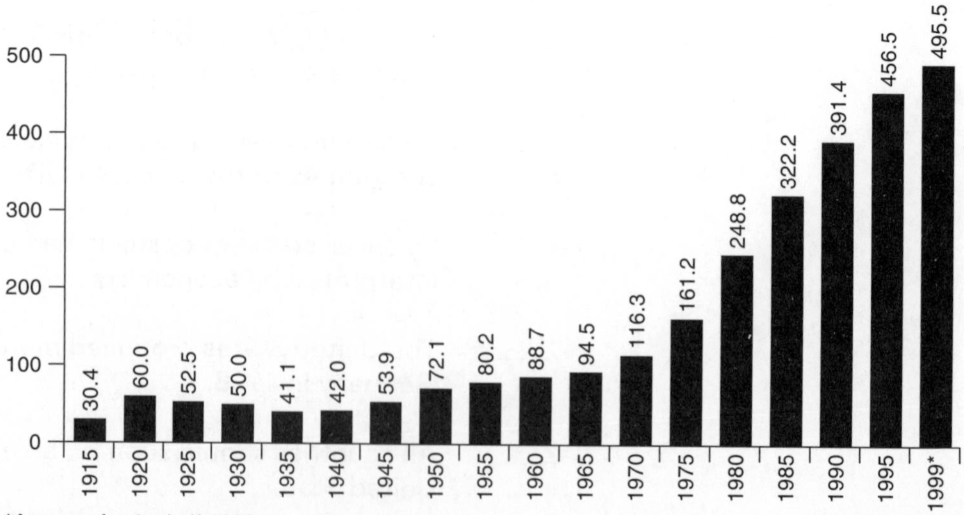

*Average for 1st half 1999.

EXERCISE 8

Consumer Price Index

According to the CPI graph on page 412, how much did something that cost one dollar in 1967

cost in 1970? _________

in 1990? ___________

What do you predict will happen in 2010? ____________________________

Answers are on page 453.

Money and Monetary Policy

Money is the medium of exchange accepted by a society in payment for goods and services. A nation's money supply consists mainly of coins, bills, and checking and savings deposits.

The increased power of computers and the other advancements in technology has led to increased use of "electronic money" or digital representation of currency in the United States. By 2002, eleven European nations were expected to launch the *euro* as their shared currency. The *euro* could make it easier to transfer funds from country to country.

Selection of Major World Currencies
November 29, 2000

Country	Currency	Value (in units per dollar)
Austria	schilling	16.0570
France	franc	7.6546
Germany	mark	2.2823
Great Britain	pound	0.7028
Greece	drachma	397.1700
Japan	yen	111.1800
Italy	lira	2,259.4900
Mexico	peso	9.3890

Source: *The New York Times*

The U.S. **Federal Reserve Board** is responsible for setting the nation's monetary policy—the regulation of the nation's supply of money and credit in order to keep the economy in balance. Through the national banking system, the Federal Reserve Board controls the availability of credit to consumers in two ways—by determining the reserve ratio and setting the discount rate.

EXERCISE 9

Money and Monetary Policy

Directions: Using the information provided on money, decide whether each of the following statements is a **fact (F)** or an **opinion (O).**

1. ______ The dollar is the most widely used unit of money.
2. ______ Money makes trade among countries convenient.
3. ______ All countries should use the dollar as their unit of money.
4. ______ The peso is a unit used in many Latin American countries.
5. ______ Personal checks are easier to use than money.

Answers are on page 453.

The Reserve Ratio

Every lending institution—banks and savings and loan associations—must hold on to a certain amount of its deposits. This amount that cannot be lent out is called the **reserve ratio.** Most banks are members of the nation's Federal Reserve System (the Fed). By controlling the reserve ratio, the Fed determines the amount of money banks are able to lend.

Suppose, for example, Kathy wants to borrow $10,000 to buy a new car, and John wants to borrow $6,000 for a new roof. They go to the same bank and apply for a loan. The bank uses money from depositors to lend to customers such as Kathy and John.

Suppose further that the bank has $20,000 in deposits and the Fed has established the reserve ratio at 10 percent. That means that the bank must keep $2,000 in reserve (10 percent of $20,000). This leaves the bank $18,000 to lend. The bank has enough money to cover Kathy's loan and John's loan. Kathy now has $10,000 more in purchasing power, so she can buy a car. John now has $6,000 more in purchasing power, so he can replace his roof.

But what if the economy is in a period of inflation? The Fed might raise the reserve ratio to 25 percent. Now the bank must keep on deposit $5,000, leaving only $15,000 to lend. The bank can no longer loan money to both Kathy and John. The bank must make a decision. No matter who gets the loan, the other person's purchasing power will not increase. Thus, consumer demand has been lowered indirectly. When this process is implemented nationwide, the impact on the economy is significant, chiefly because less money is available to lend.

The Discount Rate

A second way in which the Fed influences the nation's economy is through the discount rate. The **discount rate** is the rate of interest the Fed charges member banks to borrow money.

Banks make money by charging a higher interest rate on loans than they pay to those who deposit money into checking and savings accounts. Suppose, for example, that Suzanne deposits $1,000 in the bank at a 5 percent interest rate. If she leaves the funds on deposit for one year, she can collect $1,050 from the bank. This includes her $1,000 deposit plus the $50 in interest the bank owes her. During this time, however, the bank lends $1,000 to Samantha for a year. The bank charges her 15 percent interest. After one year, Samantha owes the bank $1,150. The bank then gives Suzanne her $1,050. The profit to the bank is $100. Obviously, the more money a bank has to lend, the more profit it can make.

To have more money to meet demand, banks often borrow from the Federal Reserve System. The bank then lends the money to its customers (borrowers) at a higher rate.

The Fed adjusts the discount rate to affect the supply of money. For example, if the discount rate is 5 percent, consumer banks might lend money out for 10 percent. If the discount rate were raised to 15 percent, consumer banks might charge 20 percent. Thus, you can see the impact a changing discount rate has on the availability of credit in the U.S. economy.

EXERCISE 10

The Discount Rate

Directions: For each statement, write **T** if it is true or **F** if it is false.

1. ______ The role of the Fed is to serve as a clearinghouse for all banks in one region.

2. ______ Two ways in which the Federal Reserve influences the money supply are coining money and setting the prime rate.

3. ______ Purchasing power is increased through the banking system by banks lending funds from deposited money after first setting aside required reserves.

4. ______ Most banks belong to the Federal Reserve System.

5. ______ The prime rate is the interest rate the Fed charges member banks to borrow money.

Answers are on page 453.

Government and Fiscal Policy

While the U.S. Federal Reserve Board directly influences the supply of money and credit in the economy, the government, through its fiscal policy, also indirectly affects the nation's economic condition.

In establishing **fiscal policy,** the president proposes an annual budget to the Congress. As Congress determines what programs are needed, it must also consider how these programs will be funded. Raising taxes is the simplest and most common answer.

Consumers and businesses pay these taxes to the government. The government, in turn, spends the money on programs designed to benefit the citizens and the country, such as education, interstate highways, and the military.

By deciding whether to raise or lower taxes and whether to increase or decrease spending, the government is controlling a major part of the money supply. For example, during inflationary times, the government might exercise fiscal policy by taking money out of the pockets of consumers by increasing taxes. During periods of deflation, the government might put more money in the hands of consumers by cutting spending and lowering taxes.

If the government spends less than it collects in taxes, a **budget surplus** results. If the government spends more than it collects, the condition is called **deficit spending.** A **balanced budget** results when the income from taxes equals the money spent on programs.

EXERCISE 11

Government and Fiscal Policy

Directions: Circle the correct answer choice in parentheses for each statement.

1. During a recession, to put more money in circulation, the president and Congress should (increase/decrease) domestic spending while (raising/lowering) taxes.
2. During an inflationary period, the Fed should (increase/decrease) the money in circulation by (raising/lowering) the discount rate while (increasing/decreasing) the reserve ratio.
3. When the government spends more money than it receives in taxes, there is a (budget surplus/budget deficit).

Answers are on page 453.

The American Consumer

Throughout this chapter on economics, you have studied how people's needs are met. Responsible consumers need a basic understanding of the economic system and how it affects their lives as workers and family members.

GED PRACTICE

EXERCISE 12

The American Consumer

Directions: Study the cartoon and answer the following questions.

Gary Huck, © UE/Huck-Konopacki

1. **How does the author of the cartoon feel about the American Dream?**

   The American Dream

   (1) is easily attained by all Americans
   (2) can never be achieved by Americans
   (3) is becoming more difficult to obtain
   (4) will only be realized by baby boomers
   (5) means owning valued material possessions

2. **According to this cartoon, what is " the American Rude Awakening"?**

   (1) losing material possessions
   (2) never getting a good job
   (3) not going to school
   (4) having less money than your neighbor
   (5) realizing that money does not buy happiness

Answers are on page 454.

Spending Money

The typical U.S. consumer is advised to develop a financial plan. In many families both spouses work full time in order to meet a budget that reflects their goals and values. A budget is a plan for spending and saving one's income.

A **fixed expense** is an expense over which a consumer has little control. A **flexible expense** varies, and a **luxury expense** is one that a consumer could live without.

Average Budget for Typical American Home

The chart below shows average spending by families in different income brackets. A family unit consists of a wage earner aged 47.1 years with 2.5 persons living together.

	Middle Income	Percent of Budget	Higher Income	Percent of Budget	Highest Income	Percent of Budget
TOTAL BUDGET	26,496	100	37,574	100	64,236	100
Taxes	1,822	6.9	3,327	8.9	8,825	13.7
Food	3,859	14.6	5,256	14.0	7,127	11.1
Beverages	281	1.0	385	1.0	554	.8
Housing	7,616	28.7	9,910	26.4	16,619	25.9
Apparel and Services	1,335	5.0	1,958	5.2	3,391	5.3
Transportation	4,610	17.4	6,463	17.2	9,624	15.0
Health Care	1,409	5.3	1,560	4.2	2,080	3.2
Entertainment	1,116	4.2	1,816	4.8	3,074	4.8
Personal Care	332	1.3	463	1.2	661	1.0
Reading	142	.5	191	.5	292	.5
Education	255	1.0	307	.8	904	1.4
Tobacco and Supplies	301	1.1	332	.9	291	.5
Miscellaneous	606	2.3	876	2.3	1,210	1.9
Cash Contributions	758	2.9	935	2.5	2,045	3.2
Personal Insurance and Pensions	2,054	7.8	3,795	10.1	7,539	11.7
TOTAL BUDGET	26,496	100	37,574	100	64,236	100

Source: U.S. Bureau of Labor Statistics

EXERCISE 13

Spending Money

Directions: Label each of the categories below according to which consumer group in the table on page 418 (middle, higher, highest) spends the highest percentage of its income on those things.

1. ____________________ apparel (clothing)

2. ____________________ entertainment

3. ____________________ taxes

4. ____________________ tobacco

5. ____________________ housing

Answers are on page 454.

Not only are more adult American consumers using credit cards, but in many households young adults are carrying credit cards as well.

Young Adults and Credit Cards

- Forty-one percent of students in that age group (18-22) work full time while school is in session.
- Thirty percent of the students say their parents rarely or never discuss saving or investing with them.
- Only 21 percent of students have had a personal finance course through school.
- Among reasons college students list for carrying a credit card: establishing a good credit history (63 percent), handling emergencies (43 percent), and protecting themselves from the dangers of carrying cash (19 percent).
- About 430 American colleges and universities have banned credit card marketing on campus.
- Less than half of college students balance their checkbooks monthly. Ten percent of students leave all their finances up to their parents.
- College seniors estimate that they will have a debt of more than $16,000 upon graduation, including student loans.
- About half of students have bounced a check during college.

Source: *Chicago Tribune*, October 1, 2000

Writing Activity 6

What impact do you think that the increased use of credit cards has on young consumers? Discuss your answer in about two or three paragraphs.

Technology and the Consumer

E-commerce consists mainly of buying and selling over the Internet. In 2000 many consumers shopped on-line. The Forrester Research report predicted that by 2005, U.S. on-line sales would total $269 billion. That is 11 percent of all retail sales in the United States.

GED PRACTICE

EXERCISE 14

Technology and the Consumer

Directions: Read the information about shopping on-line and answer the questions below.

Why Consumers Shop On-line

Reason	Percent
Convenience	84%
Product depth	41
Better experience	36
Rich content	31
Value	26
Brand	20
Customer service	11
Interactive tools	7
Novelty	4

Source: September 2000 Forrester Research, Inc.

1. What do you infer to be the main reason that American consumers shop on-line?

(1) best prices
(2) more choices
(3) comfort and accessibility
(4) fun and interest
(5) helpful customer service

2. By the year 2005, what do you predict will be the main reason American consumers shop on-line?

(1) best prices
(2) more choices
(3) comfort and accessibility
(4) fun and interest
(5) helpful customer service

Answers are on page 454.

Technology and the Worker

The workplace for many Americans is the office. As a result of increased technology, many workers **telecommute.** They are able to work out of their homes with personal computers and fax machines. According to the Bureau of Labor Statistics, in 1997 more than 25 million American workers had flexible work schedules, largely due to technology and worker demand.

Businesses utilize mobile communications to assist employees with time management and efficiency.

Wireless Subscribership: June 1985–June 2000

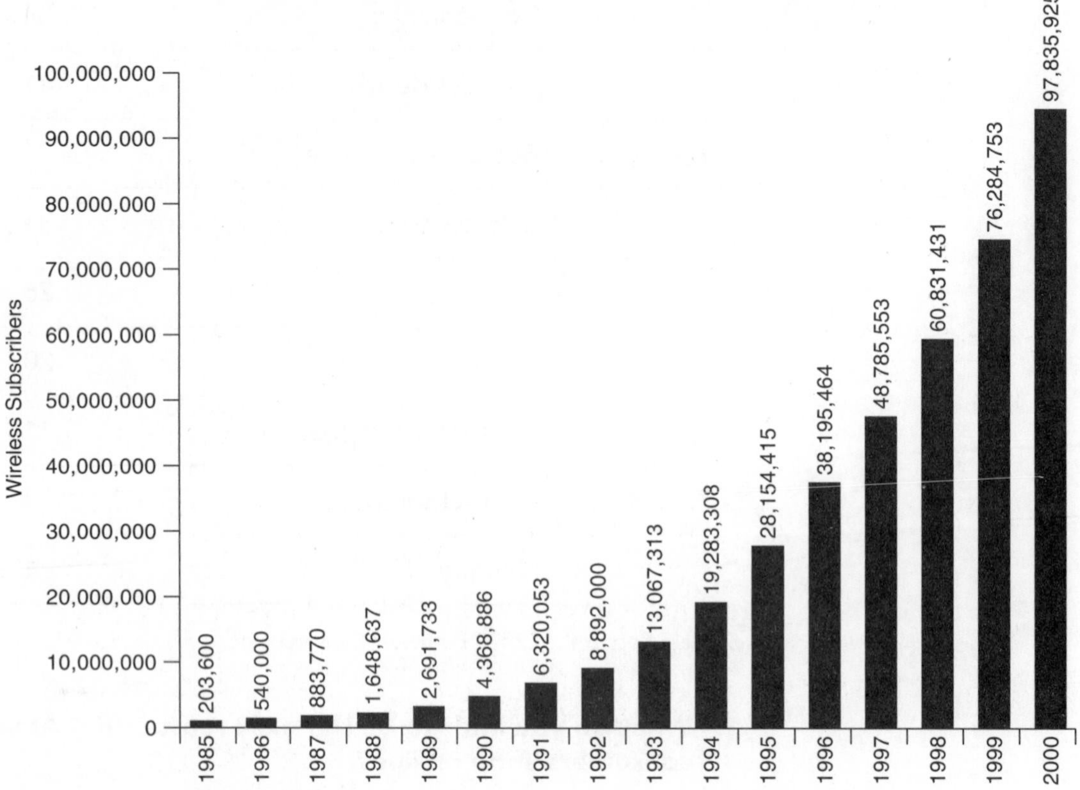

The CTIA Semi-Annual Wireless Industry Survey. Used with permission of CTIA

The advancement of technology allows workers to communicate with companies in different countries. Managers from every country are required to deal effectively with employees of many nationalities. In *The Evolving Global Economy* Kenichi Ohmae states, "Today's global economy is genuinely borderless. Information, capital, and innovation flow all over the world at top speed, enabled by technology and fueled by consumers' desires for access to the best and least expensive products."

The Technology Revolution, like the Industrial Revolution, has transformed the U.S. workplace. At the close of the 20th century, there had been an elimination of 42 million jobs and the creation of 67 million jobs. Many jobs were eliminated as quickly as new jobs were created. As jobs became more technical, more workers went back to school in order to be competitive in the workplace. The trend for higher education increased; however, so did the costs for college tuition.

GED PRACTICE

EXERCISE 15

Technology and the Worker

Directions: Read the graph on education trends and answer the question below.

U.S. Higher Education Trends: Bachelor's Degrees Conferred

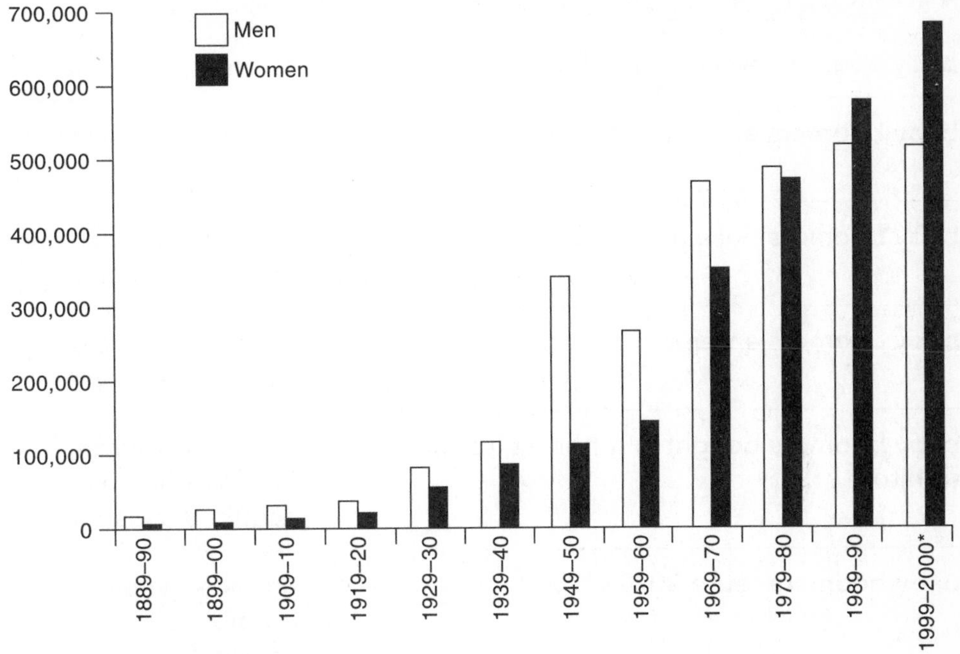

Source: National Center for Education Statistics, U.S. Department of Education
*Figures for 1999–2000 are projected.

Which of the following assumptions could be made based on the graph?

(1) In 1999–2000 more women attended college than ever before.
(2) More men attended college than did women.
(3) Americans in pursuit of higher education decreased in 1950.
(4) Higher education has always been a priority in the United States.
(5) The cost of higher education has decreased since 1980.

Answer is on page 454.

The Baby Boom Generation

American citizens born between 1946 and 1964 are called **baby boomers**. These 76 million people have unmistakably affected the economy of the United States, and economists predict that they will continue to affect the economy through 2030.

Cause	Effect
baby boomers were born 1946–1964	• strong sales of baby food
baby boomers entered school	• increase in elementary-school construction • shortage of teachers
baby boomers became teenagers	• national focus on parenting techniques and family values
baby boomers entered job market	• overcrowded job market • depressed wages
baby boomers bought first homes, cars, furniture	• real estate surge • prices of homes at new heights • acquired substantial debt from loans
baby boomers retire 2010–2030	• possible employment opportunities • possible exhaustion of Social Security and strain on Medicare
baby boomers downsize homes and liquidate investments	• possible fall in housing prices • possible market decline

Source: *Boomeromics* by William Sterling and Stephen Waite

GED PRACTICE

EXERCISE 16

The Baby Boom Generation

Directions: Considering the chart on the causes and effects of the baby boom generation, answer the questions below.

1. According to the chart, which of the following is true about the future for the baby boom generation?

In 2030, most baby boomers will

(1) buy their first car
(2) earn depressed wages
(3) acquire substantial debt from loans
(4) be deceased
(5) downsize their homes

2. Which of the predictions about the children of baby boomers is unlikely based on the cause-and-effect chart?

The children of the baby boom generation may

(1) receive increases in Social Security benefits
(2) be eligible for promotions because of job openings
(3) experience a loss of value in their home
(4) have to provide physical care for aging parents
(5) need to contribute to their parents' financial needs

Answers are on page 454.

Writing Activity 7

Economist Horace Brock said, "The nation that fixed the most hired the most." Do you think that this quote describes the United States at the end of the 20th century? Support your answer with at least two or three paragraphs.

Go to **www.GEDSocialStudies.com** for additional practice and instruction!

CHAPTER 5

Geography

Geography is the study of the landform features of the surface layer of the earth. The physical features of the land's surface have been studied and recorded by many specially trained experts. **Geologists** study the rock layers and composition of the earth, **cartographers** make maps to represent the landform features, and **geophysicists** explain the forces that create those landforms.

Mapping

Mapping of the earth's surface can be difficult because of the earth's spherical shape. When flat maps are created, sizes and shapes of the continents are distorted. The mapping of a sphere is called a **map projection.** There are several map projection types that try to correct for this distortion. Some examples are

- **Mercator** (which is accurate for the equatorial areas but distorts at the poles)
- **Gnomic** (which identifies a single area on the globe but distorts around the edges)
- **Conic** (which maps a small triangular section, but not much of the planet at a time)

Maps are also created to identify specific features of the earth. These topics include

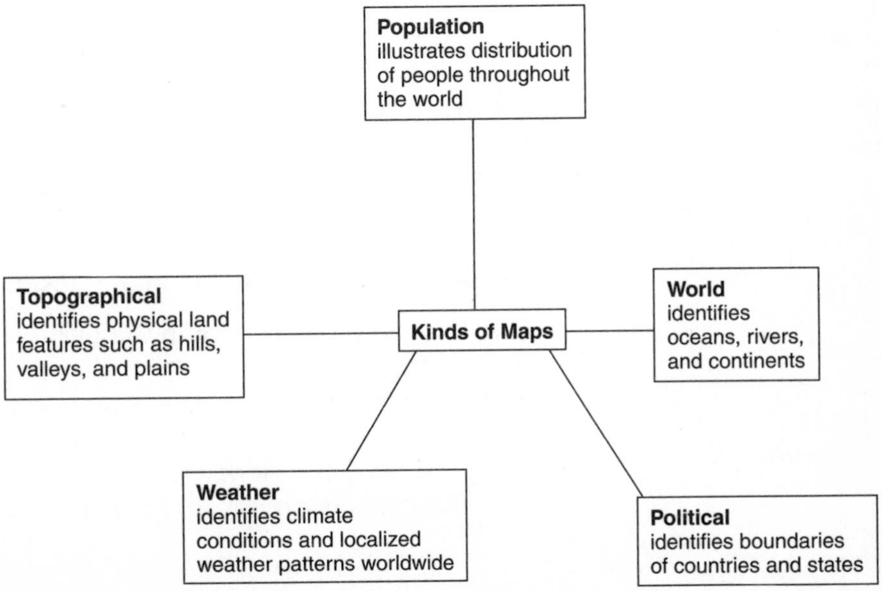

A very common type of map is a **topographical map.** These maps show relief features, or surface configurations, of an area. Traditionally, these maps were made by physically measuring an area; this is called surveying. More recently, mapmakers are relying on aerial photographs to assist in creating maps that give true accuracy of ground detail. These views especially help in creating urban maps that are designed to show roadways and direction. When these aerial pictures are taken by infrared photography, environmentalists can determine areas in the world that may contain deposits of coal or oil by the heat that these resources produce.

© Bettmann/Corbis

GED PRACTICE

EXERCISE 1

Styles of Maps

Directions: Complete the following statements about the different types of maps.

1. What assumption can be made about mapping the earth?

(1) It is not difficult to map the earth accurately using the *Mercator* method.
(2) Mapping any spherical shape is impossible.
(3) Aerial maps can only be used to map urban areas.
(4) A three-dimensional sphere always gets distorted on a flat map.
(5) Mapmakers do not try to correct for the distortion of a sphere.

2. **Which of the following is the *best* map to show the boundaries for the 50 states in the United States?**

   (1) topographical map
   (2) population map
   (3) world map
   (4) political map
   (5) weather map

3. **Which type of map would show the highest elevation of the Cascade Mountains?**

   (1) topographical map
   (2) population map
   (3) world map
   (4) political map
   (5) aerial map

Answers are on page 454.

Map Symbols

In making maps, mapmakers provide symbols to show important features of the area being mapped. A **legend** or **key** tells what the symbols mean.

For example, on a political map, a star usually indicates a state or nation's capital. On a population map, the number of people that live in a given city is indicated by the size of the dot that locates the city. Larger dots indicate cities with large populations, while smaller dots indicate cities with smaller populations.

On road maps, a scale of miles is often provided in the legend. A scale of miles is most commonly shown in inches. For example, the legend on a map scale might read "one inch equals 50 miles." An example of a scale is shown on the map on page 430. Maps are also drawn to align with compass point directions. The compass point will indicate which direction is north, usually toward the top of the page or screen.

You can measure distance with a ruler or with a strip of paper that has a straight edge. Lay a strip of paper against the map to make a straight line between the two points you are measuring for distance. Mark off the two points on the paper's edge, and lay the paper strip against the scale of miles. The distance between the two points will be the number of miles from one place to another.

EXERCISE 2

Measuring Distances

Directions: Study the map and answer the questions that follow.

1. According the map shown here, approximately how far is Denver from San Francisco? ______

2. Which of the following cities shows the greatest population: Los Angeles, Seattle, or Denver? ______

3. In what direction would you travel if you were heading to California from Colorado? ______

Answers are on page 455.

Latitude and Longitude

The **equator,** an imaginary line that circles the earth's center, divides the earth into two **hemispheres,** or halves. The land and the water above the equator lie in the **Northern Hemisphere;** the area land and water below the equator is known as the **Southern Hemisphere.** Canada, the United States, and Mexico, as well as Europe, Russia, and Asia are all in the Northern Hemisphere. Most of South America and Africa, as well as all of Australia, are in the Southern Hemisphere.

The distance from the equator is measured on maps and globes by degrees of latitude. Lines of **latitude** are parallel lines that measure distance north and south of the equator in degrees. These lines are often marked on maps and globes in 20-degree increments. The equator is located at 0 degrees latitude, the North Pole at 90 degrees north latitude, and the South Pole at 90 degrees south latitude. Most of the continental United States lies between 25 and 50 degrees north latitude. Hawaii is at about 21 degrees north latitude, and Alaska is between 61 and 72 degrees north latitude.

Lines of **longitude** are lines that measure distances in degrees east and west of the **prime meridian,** an imaginary line running through Greenwich, England. Lines of longitude divide the world into the Eastern and Western Hemispheres. The prime meridian is located at 0 degrees longitude. There are 180 degrees east of the prime meridian and 180 degrees west of it, for a total of 360 degrees around the earth. Most of the United States, including Alaska and Hawaii, lies between 65 and 125 degrees west longitude.

The lines of latitude and longitude cross each other to form what is called a grid. To locate a particular place on a globe or map, you must find the point where two lines intersect. The number of degrees latitude and longitude indicate the location. For example, in the grid diagram on page 432, the island of Madagascar, located off the southeast coast of Africa, is located at approximately 20 degrees south latitude and 45 degrees east longitude.

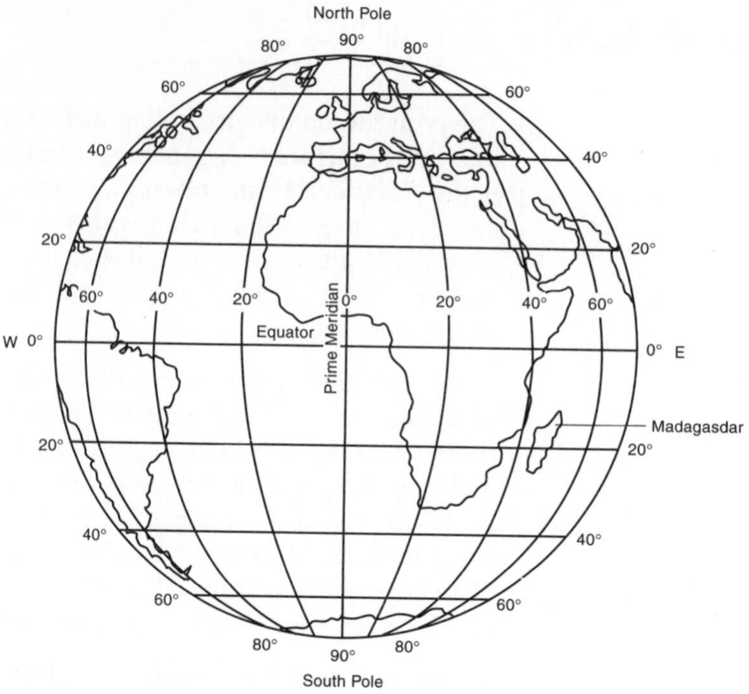

Based on the grid, which continent is found at 50 degrees north latitude and 0 degrees longitude?

If you answered *Europe,* you would be correct. The point where the 50-degree-north line of latitude meets the 0-degree line of longitude is on the continent of Europe.

GED PRACTICE

EXERCISE 3

Latitude and Longitude

Directions: Choose the *best* answer for each of the following questions, which are based on the information in the grid.

1. Which of the following is at 15 degrees north latitude and 20 degrees east longitude?

(1) northern Europe
(2) eastern South America
(3) western Africa
(4) southern Asia
(5) central Africa

2. What country is located nearest 30 degrees south latitude and 20 degrees east longitude?

(1) Italy
(2) Chile
(3) Egypt
(4) South Africa
(5) England

Answers are on page 455.

Time Zones

There are 24 standard time zones, divided according to lines of longitude. The earth rotates 15 degrees in one hour, so each time zone covers 15 degrees of latitude. The 24 time zones equal 360 degrees of latitude, or one complete rotation of the earth.

In the continental United States, there are four **time zones:** eastern, central, mountain, and pacific. As people travel west, they move into an earlier time zone for every 15 degrees of latitude they travel. For example, people completing a journey west through the Eastern time zone at 5:00 P.M. would have to change their watches to 4:00 P.M. as they entered the next time zone (central). The four time zones for the continental United States are shown on the following map.

Time Zones Across North America

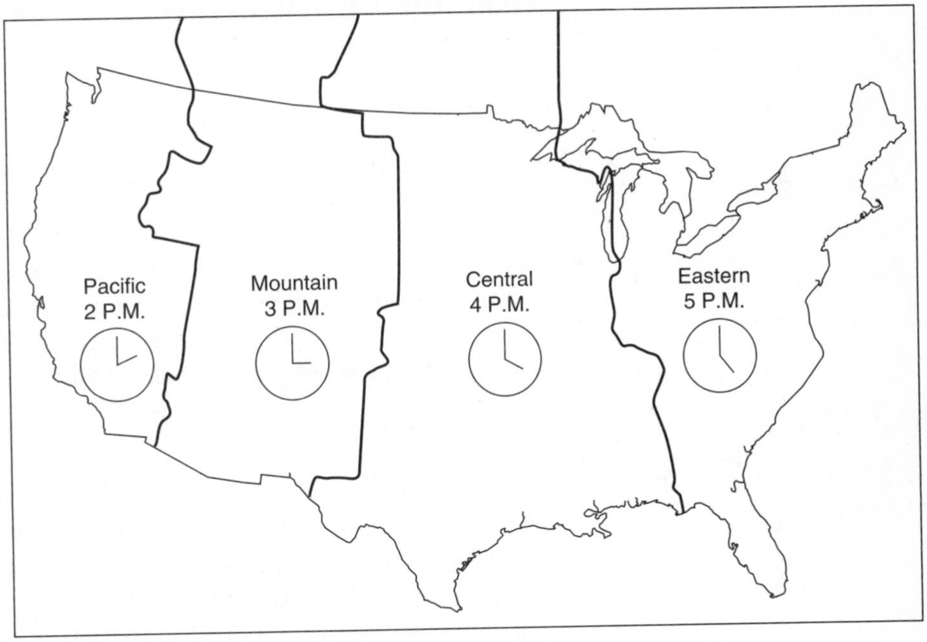

GED PRACTICE

EXERCISE 4

Time Zones

Directions: Use the map on page 433 to choose the *best* answer for each question.

1. According to the map, what time is it in Los Angeles when it is midnight in Philadelphia?

(1) 9:00 A.M.
(2) 9:00 P.M.
(3) 3:00 P.M.
(4) 3:00 A.M.
(5) 2:00 A.M.

2. What time is it in Denver when it is noon in Milwaukee?

(1) 10:00 A.M.
(2) 12:00 P.M.
(3) 11:00 A.M.
(4) 1:00 P.M.
(5) 9:00 A.M.

3. The lines marking the four time zones are irregular. All of Indiana (except a tiny section of northwest Indiana) lies in the eastern time zone. Which of the following is the most reasonable explanation for why northwest Indiana lies in a central time zone?

(1) The people in northwest Indiana voted to be included in the central time zone.
(2) The time zone must be evenly divided; in order to obtain an even division, part of Indiana was put in the central time zone.
(3) Since part of Kentucky was in the central time zone, Indiana had to have its borders stay in line with the state directly to the south.
(4) Northwest Indiana was once part of Illinois but kept the same time after becoming part of Indiana.
(5) Northwest Indiana is connected to the Chicago area for economic and business reasons, so it makes sense to be on the same time.

4. Which group would likely benefit the most from northwest Indiana's falling within the central time zone?

(1) the people who work in and travel frequently to and from Chicago
(2) the children who go to school in Northwest Indiana
(3) the businesspeople in Northwest Indiana
(4) the international travelers on vacation in the Midwest
(5) the bankers who do online trading with the Chicago Board of Trade

Answers are on page 455.

Topography

Topographical maps can show land features anywhere in the world because in spite of regional differences, there are a few standard features that appear everywhere. Generally, geographers divide the earth into flatlands (plains) and highlands (hills, plateaus, and mountains).

Plains are typically areas with little or no land elevation and few trees. **Hills** are elevations of less than 1000 feet that have sides sloping up to flat or rounded tops. **Plateaus** rise sharply above the level of the neighboring areas and have elevations less than 500 feet and broad, flat tops**. Mountains** are elevations of over 1000 feet, usually with steep, rocky inclines on all sides and pointed or rounded tops.

Mapmakers illustrate the varying heights and shapes of landmasses by using **contour lines,** lines that connect points of the same elevation in feet or meters. The closer together the contour lines, the steeper the incline. The base line for determining the height of the highland elevations is **sea level.** The following is an example of a contour map.

Contour Map

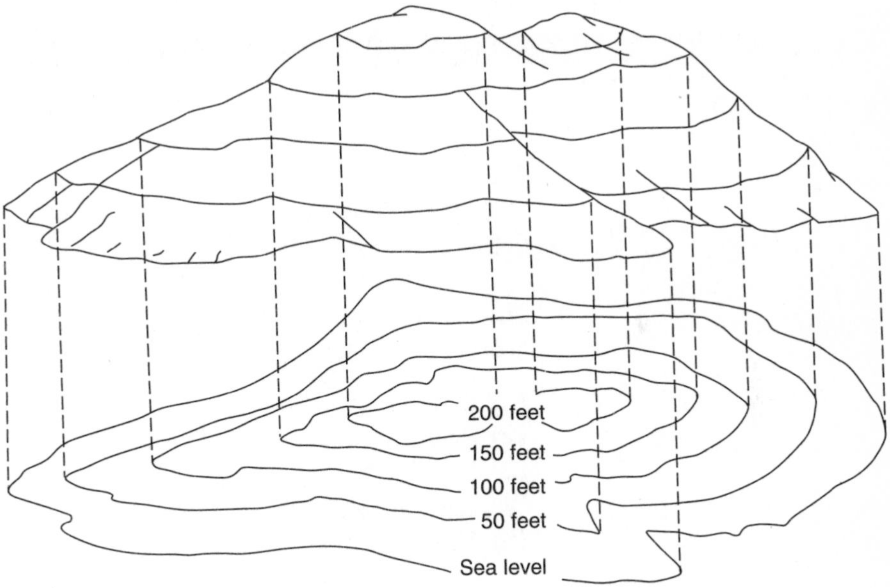

What would this land form be classified as—a plain, a hill, a plateau or a mountain? ________________

Because the landmass is lower than 1000 feet and has a rounded top, it would be classified as a *hill.*

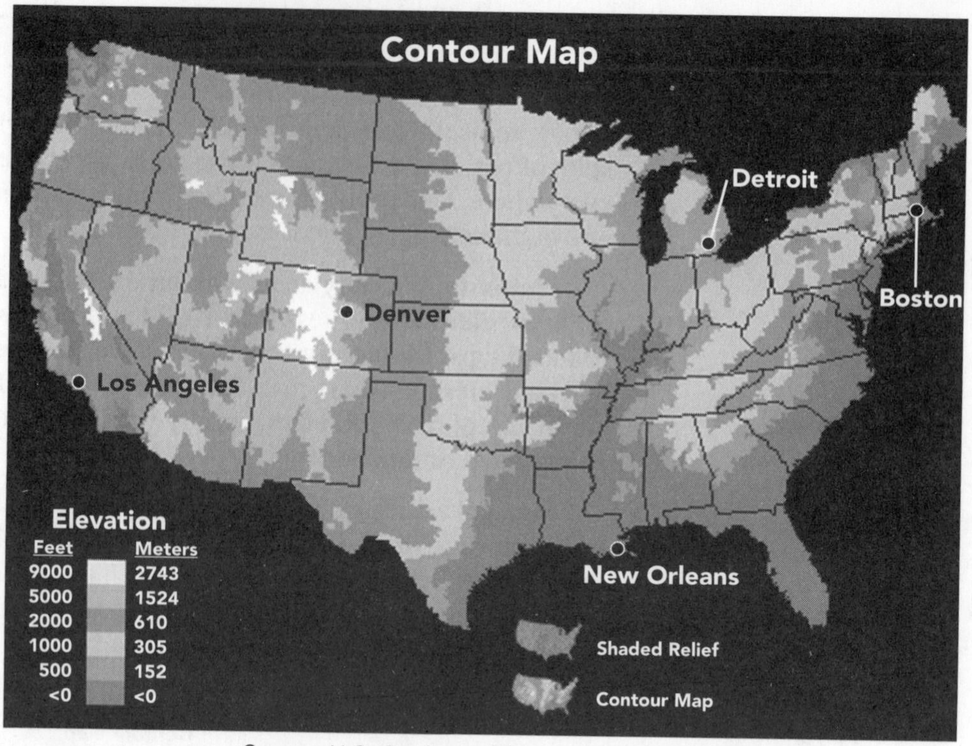

Source: U.S. Geological Survey, National Atlas of the United States

GED PRACTICE

EXERCISE 5

U.S. Topography

Directions: Choose the *best* answer for each question below.

1. **Based on its location, which of the following cities in the United States is at the highest altitude?**

   (1) Detroit
   (2) Boston
   (3) Denver
   (4) Los Angeles
   (5) New Orleans

2. **Low-lying land is often subject to flooding. Land that lies below sea level acts as a bowl that collects water. As a result, an effective pumping system is needed to handle the flooding. Which of the following cities best meets this description?**

   (1) Detroit
   (2) Boston
   (3) Denver
   (4) Los Angeles
   (5) New Orleans

Answers are on page 455.

Climate

The physical features of the earth can also affect a region's climate. Climatologists, scientists who study weather patterns and conditions, are also geographers because of the close cause-and-effect relationship between landforms and weather patterns.

Plains regions have a uniform climate characterized by hot, dry weather during the summer and very cold temperatures during the winter. Because plains are frequently treeless, there are no barriers against the cold air that sweeps across them during the winter. Hills and plateaus generally share the same climate characteristics of the plains near which they are located. Mountains often act as boundaries between different climate regions. The lower slopes of the mountains usually share the climate of the surrounding area, but the higher elevations have colder temperatures. Also, mountains are often snowcapped because the colder air is unable to hold moisture. This moisture falls to earth as snow.

GED PRACTICE

EXERCISE 6

Climate

Directions: Choose the *best* answer for each question below.

1. Based on the information in the passage, what conclusion can you draw?

During the winter it is likely to be colder in the

(1) mountains than the plains
(2) plains than the hills
(3) plateaus than the mountains
(4) hills than the mountains
(5) plains than the plateaus

2. According to the passage, colder air is unable to hold moisture. Based on this information, what conclusion can you draw?

In summer,

(1) the mountains have less precipitation than the plains
(2) the mountains have more precipitation than the plains
(3) the mountains and plains have the same amount of precipitation
(4) the mountains and the hills have the same amount of precipitation
(5) the mountains have less precipitation than the hills

Answers are on page 455.

GED PRACTICE

EXERCISE 7

Mount Everest

Directions: Study the illustration of Mt. Everest and answer the question based on the picture and caption.

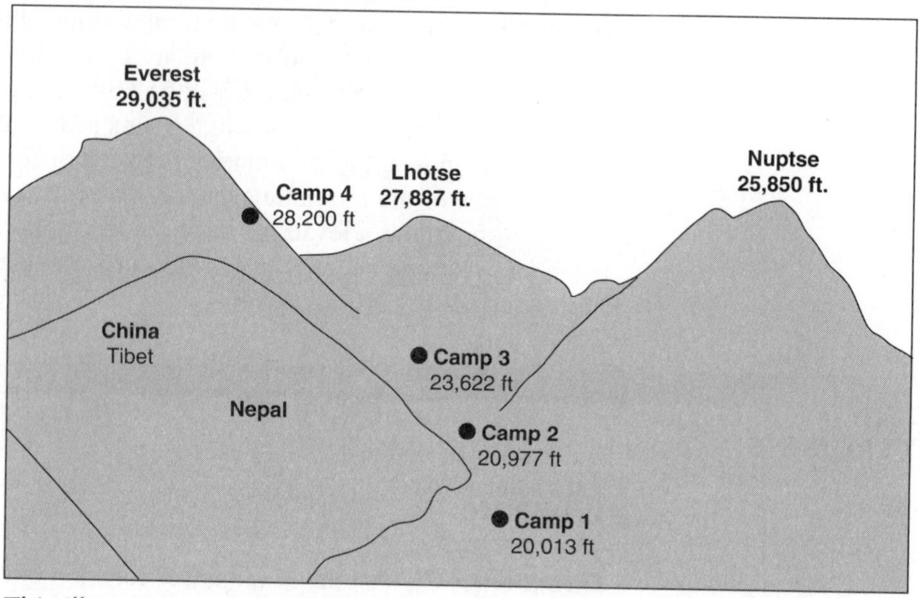

This illustration of the tallest mountain on Earth, Mount Everest, indicates camps at various elevations along the ascent. Mountain climbers must stay for several days at each camp while adjusting to the thinning air.

What conclusion is supported by the information above?

(1) It would take four days to climb to the top of Mount Everest.
(2) It would take less than one week to climb to the top of Mount Everest.
(3) It would take at least two weeks to climb to the top of Mount Everest.
(4) It would take at least one month to climb to the top of Mount Everest.
(5) It would be impossible to climb to the top of Mount Everest.

Answer is on page 455.

GED PRACTICE

EXERCISE 8

The Indian Peninsula

Directions: Study the map and answer the questions that follow.

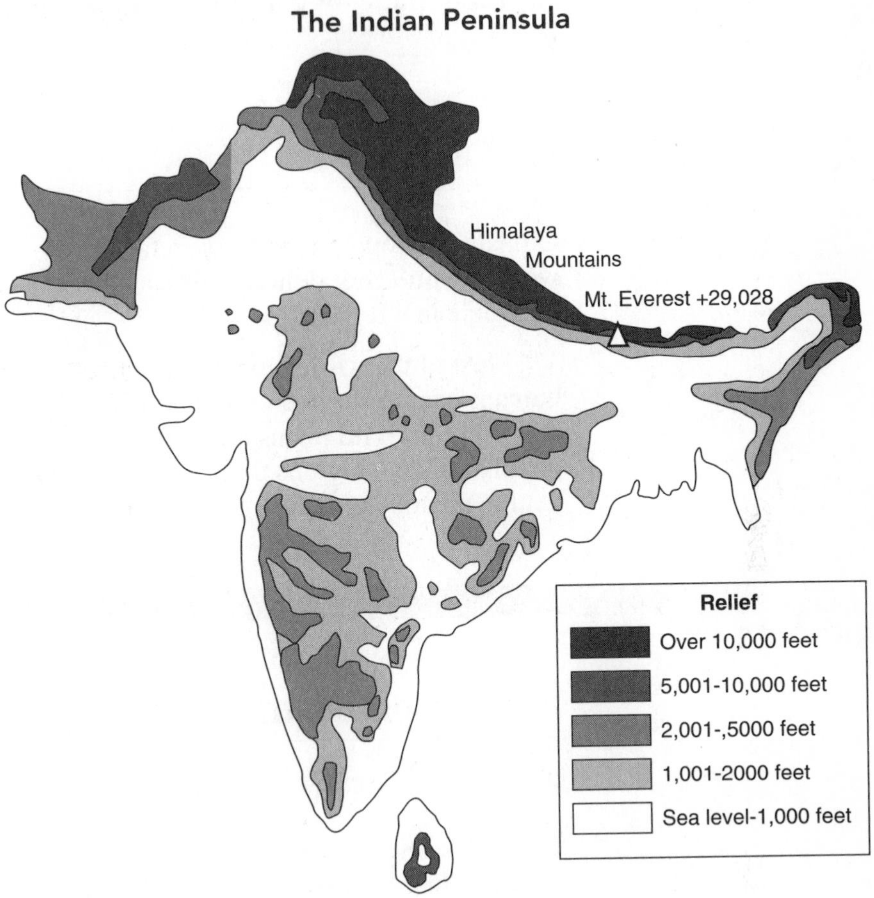

1. **What is the highest point in the Himalaya Mountains?**
   (1) 6,000 feet
   (2) 10,300 feet
   (3) 19,861 feet
   (4) 29,028 feet
   (5) 33,411 feet

2. **The majority of the land shown on the map may be generally described as being at what elevation?**
   (1) over 10,000 feet
   (2) between 5,000 and 10,000 feet
   (3) between 2,000 and 5,000 feet
   (4) between 1,000 and 2,000 feet
   (5) between sea level and 1,000 feet

Answers are on page 455.

Writing Activity 1

In one or two paragraphs, describe the topography of the area in which you live. Compare the topography to that of another location where you would like to live. Do you live near mountains, hills, plains, or plateaus? Would you prefer a location with greater elevation or more mountains? Describe how the topography of your region affects the climate and agriculture.

Population Distribution

Climate and topography are two factors that affect where people live in the world. **Population demographics** is the study of the numbers and locations of people in a region.

Most of the world's population lives in the temperate zones because humans cannot survive very long in regions with extreme cold or intense heat. Also, regions with plains allow for a greater and more even distribution of population than regions that are mountainous. In mountainous regions, people tend to inhabit the land at the foot of the mountains or in the valleys.

GED PRACTICE

EXERCISE 9

Population Distribution

Directions: Choose the *best* answer for each question below.

1. According to the passage, which of the following factors would not affect population distribution?

(1) high elevations
(2) cultivated plains
(3) grassy valleys
(4) subzero temperatures
(5) rapid waterways

2. Of the following states, which would most likely have the least even distribution of population because of its land features?

(1) the farm fields of Georgia
(2) the rolling hills of New Jersey
(3) the grassy plains of Kansas
(4) the mountains of West Virginia
(5) the small lakes of Minnesota

Answers are on page 455.

GED PRACTICE

EXERCISE 10

Other Factors Affecting Population Distribution

Directions: Use the chart below to choose the best answer to the following question.

Other Factors Affecting Population Distribution

Causes	Effects
• Job location	• Agricultural areas used to be major population centers because of farming. • After the Industrial Revolution, cities with factories became major population centers.
• Quality of life that a region provides	• Many Americans left cities to move to the suburbs looking for safety, clean air, better schools, and open spaces.
• Ethnicity	• Nearly all-white towns circled large minority-dominated cities.

According to the chart, which of the following can be connected to the quality of life that a region provides?

(1) Americans left the cities because houses were cheaper in the suburbs.
(2) Most Americans no longer farm and have moved to the cities for recreation.
(3) Many Americans left the cities to move to cleaner and safer suburbs.
(4) Residents of the cities have become used to pollution and crowding.
(5) People move to be close to other people of the same financial background.

Answer is on page 456.

Population Growth

A serious problem facing the human race in the twenty-first century is population growth. Currently 95 million people are added to the world population every year. By the middle of the twenty-first century, the world population could exceed nine billion people! Two factors that contribute to population growth are an increase in fertility (live births) and a decline in mortality (death) rates.

Selected Country Populations (in thousands)

Country	1960	1995	2000	2010	2025	2050
France	45,684	58,104	59,061	59,944	60,393	59,883
Germany	72,673	81,594	82,688	82,483	80,877	73,303
Italy	50,200	57,204	57,194	55,828	53,237	41,197
United Kingdom	52,372	58,079	58,336	58,727	59,535	56,667
United States	180,671	267,115	277,325	298,885	332,481	349,318
Canada	17,909	29,402	30,678	33,010	36,385	42,311
Japan	94,096	125,068	126,428	127,044	121,348	104,921
Australia	10,315	17,866	18,838	20,853	23,931	25,761
Algeria	10,800	28,109	31,599	38,636	47,322	57,731
Nigeria	42,305	111,721	128,786	168,369	238,397	244,311
Pakistan	49,955	136,257	156,007	200,621	268,904	345,484
Philippines	27,561	67,839	75,037	88,813	105,194	130,893
Turkey	27,509	60,838	65,732	74,624	85,791	100,664
Haiti	3,804	7,124	7,817	9,416	12,513	15,174
Mexico	36,530	91,145	98,881	112,891	130,196	146,645

Source: United Nations, *World Population Prospects: The 1996 Revision*; for 2050, United Nations, *The 1998 Revision*

EXERCISE 11

Population Growth

Directions: Write **fact (F)** or **opinion (O)** for each of the following statements regarding population growth in the selected countries in the chart on page 442.

_______ Not all countries will experience a population growth by 2050.

_______ Population growth is the most important issue facing all world countries.

_______ The U.S. population in 2050 will be nearly twice as large as in 1960.

_______ Populations in Japan and western Europe will decline because no one wants to work there.

_______ Population growth in the poorer countries will still be high in 2050.

Answers are on page 456.

Writing Activity 2

What challenges do you feel an increasing world population will cause? Support your answer in two or three paragraphs.

Go to **www.GEDSocialStudies.com** for additional practice and instruction!

SOCIAL STUDIES

Answer Key

CHAPTER 1

WORLD HISTORY

GED Practice Exercise 1: Early Humanity (page 298)

Application

1. **(3)** Fossil remains are not made by humans. All of the other choices are items that are made by people and are, therefore, artifacts.

Application

2. **(1)** Currency and members of society that were called money lenders were not established until a much later time. The other choices have a connection to the roles that early man started in the first societies.

GED Practice Exercise 2: Early Civilization (page 300)

Analysis

1. **(3)** Even though the Egyptians did not have an alphabet of letters as languages have today, the symbols they used did allow for them to record events and conditions of their society.

Analysis

2. **(1)** There has not been any information that the Egyptians were a warring group. They did enslave the lower classes and trade in slavery, but the growth of their civilization came more from successes in farming and commerce. There is no recorded history of the Egyptians declaring war on neighboring tribes. All the other choices are supported in the text.

GED Practice Exercise 3: Civilizations Begin to Interact (page 303)

Comprehension

1. **(2)** The Romans were far more interested in aggressive military strength. It was this military priority that allowed the Romans to conquer the Greeks.

Application

2. **(4)** Aggressive contact sports would more likely be an activity that exemplifies Roman ideology. The other choices could be activities that improve the mind or the body.

Exercise 4: Chinese Dynasties (page 305)

Analysis

Fact and Opinion

Opinion: The value of the Great Wall as a defensive structure is opinion because you cannot gather data to prove or disprove the opinion as a fact.

Opinion: It is not possible to determine the quality of success for a dynasty. There are too many factors that would enter into an evaluation to determine the success of a governing body.

Fact: A date of birth is a factual piece of information that can be matched to a time frame.

Fact: Historical information that has been recorded can give origination of a word.

GED Practice Exercise 5: The Middle Ages and the Feudal System (page 307)

Comprehension

1. **(5)** The nobles wanted the peasants to work their land and pay taxes. The peasants were led to believe that it was in their best interest to be protected by the lord, but in reality there was not much the nobles could do other than keep in good standing with the ruler to ask for assistance if there was an invasion.

Analysis

2. **(2)** The *Magna Carta* was a charter to confirm the freedom the Church of England had from the King's rule.

Exercise 6: The Hundred Years' War (page 308)

Comprehension

1. False England held some of France's northern territories because of a royal marriage.
2. True The French were not able to protect the outer areas. The war had left France financially ruined and with a weakened army.
3. False Joan of Arc was executed by the British for heresy.
4. False The French people were in revolt because of war, famine, and taxes.

GED Practice Exercise 7: The Renaissance (page 310)

Analysis

1. **(4)** The reference to the best poetry is an opinion statement. Many scholars of poetry would argue that each period had its own poetry style, which added to the variety of poetic verse, but it is a personal opinion as to which style a reader prefers.

Analysis

2. **(3)** Western Europe had to stabilize politically and economically before painting, literature, and sculpture could flourish.

GED Practice Exercise 8: The Reformation Divides Christianity (page 312)

Analysis

1. **(2)** The *Reformation* is the name of the period of time when Martin Luther brought up criticisms about the Roman Catholic Church, which led to the new Christian belief system called Protestantism (from its protest against the Catholic Church).

Comprehension

2. **(2)** Mary I ordered the deaths of many people who would not accept the Catholic Church.

GED Practice Exercise 9: The Enlightenment (page 313)

Analysis

1. **(5)** The invention of the microscope allowed scientists to see bacteria and microbes that caused diseases.

Comprehension

2. **(3)** The enlightenment period focused on science. Copernicus is the only choice specifically mentioned in the text.

Exercise 10: Control of Eastern Europe (page 314)

Events are 5, 1, 3, 2, and 4.

GED Practice Exercise 11: Central America (page 316)

Analysis

(1) One consequence of many changes in any country's government is instability. The people inside the country as well as those who deal with the country from the outside have no faith that the current leadership will remain in power.

Exercise 12: The Industrial Revolution (page 317)

1. **(F)** Only the industrialists got rich; the workers were poorly paid.
2. **(F)** The telegraph and telephone allowed long-distance communication.
3. **(T)**
4. **(F)** The middle class was working in factories for the first time.
5. **(F)** Marx thought that the industrialists were forcing workers to be poor.

Exercise 13: World War I (page 319)

Comprehension

1. France was not allied to Germany; it was allied to Russia.
2. Russia was not allied to Germany; it was allied to France.
3. England was not allied to Germany; it joined the war to protect Belgium.
4. Belgium was not allied to Germany; it tried to remain neutral but was invaded by Germany as the German army advanced on France.
5. Hungary was allied to Germany. At the time the Austria-Hungarian Empire also included modern day Slovakia and the Czech Republic. Italy also supported Germany.

Exercise 14: The Russian Revolution and the Rise of Communism (page 321)

1. **(4)** With the desperation caused by meager resources, poverty, food shortages, and other poor conditions, the people lost faith in the rule of the czars and accepted communism.
2. **(1) b (2) d (3) c (4) a**

Exercise 15: World War II (page 322)
Comprehension

1. Propaganda
2. genocide
3. Germany; Japan
4. Hiroshima; Nagasaki (Japan)
5. Cold War

Exercise 16: India Is Divided (page 324)
Analysis

1. **(b)** Hindus occupied India, and Muslims occupied Pakistan.
2. **(d)** A militant Hindu assassinated Gandhi because he was against the passive attitude that Gandhi encouraged.
3. **(e)** Jawaharlal Nehru led the Indian people into improving their technological position in world commerce.
4. **(c)** The Green Revolution brought a genetically superior rice to areas in the world that had difficulty feeding their populations.
5. **(a)** Even though incentive programs were started, the nation was still unable to prevent continued overpopulation.

Exercise 17: Technology as a Future (page 325)
Comprehension

Recent history has been greatly influenced by developments in **science** and **technology.** The Russian launching of **Sputnik** began space exploration, which advanced technological **development** greatly. The **computer age** is one obvious benefit. Computers are also used in **communication, research,** and **commerce.** Technology has come to determine **wealth** and **power.** The Internet and other **electronic** forms of communication have made a **global** economy.

CHAPTER 2
U.S. HISTORY

GED Practice Exercise 1: A New Nation is Born (page 328)
Analysis

1. **(4)** The map shows the country from which each of the explorers started his journey. It shows that representatives from many nations visited America.

Comprehension

2. **(5)** The map shows the paths each explorer took and the area of North America where each explorer landed.

GED Practice Exercise 2: The Original Thirteen English Colonies (page 330)
Comprehension

1. **(5)** Two places on the map are labeled MA (Massachusetts), but one has ME (Maine) written in it. This indicates that Maine was originally a part of Massachusetts.

Evaluation

2. **(3)** The map shows the area west of the thirteen colonies to be disputed by France and Britain. Therefore, the map indicates that France still had interest in the New World. The other choices, whether true or untrue, cannot be supported by the information in the map.

GED Practice Exercise 3: The Declaration of Independence (page 333)
Comprehension

1. **(3)** The passage states that the colonists were outraged by the taxes imposed by the Townshend Acts, and protested them by dumping tea into Boston Harbor.

Analysis

2. **(2)** The main idea of the *Declaration of Independence* was to state that people had rights and freedoms referred to as inalienable. This means that the people of the colonies wanted to exercise this freedom to govern themselves and not be governed by a king across the Atlantic Ocean.

Exercise 4: The Revolutionary War (page 334)
Analysis
2. The Intolerable Acts sought to further establish the authority of the King.
3. The document explained why separation from England was necessary.
5. The British Army was defeated.

GED Practice Exercise 5: The Beginnings of American Government (page 335)
Analysis
1. (5) The founding fathers made the central government weak on purpose to avoid repeating the abuses the colonies had suffered under the king. Maintaining state sovereignty was one way to do this.

Comprehension
2. (1) The founding fathers needed to review and change the *Articles of Confederation* because they had not specified enough of the responsibilities for the federal government.

GED Practice Exercise 6: The U.S. Constitution and Federalism (page 337)
Analysis
1. (2) The population determines how many people represent that region in the House of Representatives. If the slave population was counted as full individuals, then the House of Representatives would have had more Southerners, and they would have had a majority vote. The South did not want to give slaves full rights because they would challenge the white governments in the South.

Application
2. (1) According to the passage, Anti-Federalists were largely farmers who favored individual liberties and feared authoritative control by a central government.

GED Practice Exercise 7: The War of 1812 (page 339)
Comprehension
1. (3) The federalists, who were merchants and shipowners, feared that the war would interrupt their trade with other European nations.

Analysis
2. (2) The British blockades of United States ships required America to start manufacturing its own goods.

GED Practice Exercise 8: Jacksonian Democracy and the Mexican War (page 341)
Analysis
1. (2) Because he believed that all people, not just those with property, should have a voice in government, Jackson's attitude can be described as *populist.*

Comprehension
2. (4) The map shows the boundaries of the newest land acquisitions. In some cases the land was purchased, acquired by deed, or annexed.

GED Practice Exercise 9: Prelude to War (page 343)
Application
1. (3) Popular sovereignty permitted the people to approve or disapprove of a legislative action; therefore, of the choices given popular sovereignty is the most similar to a referendum.

Evaluation
2. (5) When the Supreme Court ruled that Dred Scott could be returned to his master, it was upholding the practice of treating slaves as personal property.

Exercise 10: Secession (page 344)
Comprehension

1. **c** Virginia split in two over the issue of secession, with the western part (now known as West Virginia) loyal to the Union.
2. **d** Texas seceded from the Union despite the fact that only the eastern part of the state voted to do so.
3. **a** Kentucky was a border state that remained with the Union despite being a slave state.
4. **b** Mississippi was a solidly Southern state that voted overwhelmingly to secede from the Union.

GED Practice Exercise 11: The Civil War (page 346)
Analysis

1. **(3)** The Proclamation was to free all slaves in territories currently rebelling against the Union. Slave states loyal to the Union (such as Kentucky) were not affected.

Analysis

2. **(5)** The passage says, "As a result, the Union army's ranks grew by 180,000 former slaves who fought against the South." This was a considerable contribution to the Union's forces.

Exercise 12: The Industrial Revolution (page 347)
Comprehension

1. **(True)** People left the rural areas to get jobs in the factories that were based in the cities.
2. **(True)** Any time that consumers demand more of a product, the manufacturer will create more of the product to sell to make more profit.
3. **(False)** Increased earnings allow a consumer to buy more products and may allow for more recreation.
4. **(False)** Great Britain is credited with beginning the Industrial Revolution.
5. **(False)** People moved from rural areas to the cities in search of jobs.

GED Practice Exercise 13: Growth of Big Business and Urbanization (page 349)
Comprehension

1. **(5)** Half of the 2000 U.S. Census population of 275 million is 137.5 million. In 1940 the U.S reached 131 million (57 million rural and 74 million urban population); this is close to 137.5 million.

Comprehension

2. **(3)** The chart shows a slow but steady increase in rural population until 1930.

GED Practice Exercise 14: Progressivism (page 350)
Application

1. **(4)** Agreement by oil companies on a minimum price to set for gasoline is an example of price-fixing, an act outlawed by the Sherman Anti-Trust Act.

Comprehension

2. **(3)** The passage says that government-sanctioned monopolies like public utilities are allowed to exist in order to save resources.

GED Practice Exercise 15: The United States as a World Power (page 352)
Analysis

1. **(3)** The Philippines were ceded to the United States under the terms of the treaty that ended the Spanish-American War; therefore, the U.S. establishment of military bases there is a result of the policy of expanding American control over other areas.

Analysis

2. **(4)** The most likely explanation for America's isolationist position from the end of the Civil War until the Spanish-American War is that the country was preoccupied with healing its wounds and rebuilding the South after the Civil War.

Exercise 16: The New Deal (page 356)

Application

1. d
2. a
3. e
4. c
5. b

GED Practice Exercise 17: World War II (page 358)

Application

1. **(5)** Dark green military fatigues are not an example of technology. The clothing chosen in any war is designed to camouflage the soldier to make him blend into the natural surroundings.

Analysis

2. **(3)** The passage says that World War II began in Europe in 1939, but the United States did not join the war until after Japan attacked Pearl Harbor.

GED Practice Exercise 18: The Korean Conflict (page 359)

Analysis

1. **(4)** The belief that the U.S. government should not commit soldiers to an undeclared war represents opinion and not a fact.

Comprehension

2. **(5)** The passage states that when North Korean troops crossed the border, President Truman committed U.S. troops, effectively beginning the war.

GED Practice Exercise 19: The Eisenhower Years (page 361)

Application

1. **(2)** At both the Salem witch trials and the McCarthy hearings, accusations were made with almost no evidence, but simply being accused was enough to make people think someone was guilty.

Analysis

2. **(3)** The *Brown v. Topeka Board of Education* decision is significant today because it ruled that "separate but equal" educational facilities could no longer exist. This serves as the legal basis for school busing to achieve desegregation.

GED Practice Exercise 20: The Kennedy Administration (page 362)

Application

1. **(3)** The Soviet attempt to establish a missile base in Cuba may be interpreted as a direct violation of the principles of the Monroe Doctrine, which opposed foreign interference in the affairs of the Western Hemisphere.

Analysis

2. **(4)** From reading the passage, it may be assumed that Cuba, a Communist nation, was an ally of the Soviet Union.

Exercise 21: Détente and Watergate (page 364)

Comprehension

1. Opinion
2. Opinion
3. Opinion
4. Fact
5. Fact

GED Practice Exercise 22: Ending the Twentieth Century (page 365)

Comprehension

1. **(4)** None of the presidents listed had to deal with an economic depression.

Comprehension

2. **(3)** From 1989 through 1993 many of the Soviet Union countries reestablished themselves as independent nations.

CHAPTER 3

CIVICS AND GOVERNMENT

GED Practice Exercise 1: Political Systems (page 368)

Application

1. **(3)** Hitler had absolute authority to govern his country.
2. **(5)** Queen Elizabeth II inherited her position of government in England.
3. **(5)** The president of the United States is elected by the people through a system of representation by electors from each state.
4. **(4)** Since tribes and generals took turns, you can assume that there was not an election. It was "government by a few."

GED Practice Exercise 2: Methods of Obtaining Power (page 369)

Application

1. **(4)** France's overthrow of the monarchy in favor of a republican form of government is an example of a revolution.
2. **(3)** Because Hitler overpowered Austria militarily, the method used to gain power is conquest.
3. **(5)** The election of Corazon Aquino as President of the Philippines is an example of a leader coming to power through popular vote.

GED Practice Exercise 3: Legislative Representation (page 371)

Analysis

1. **(3)** Since the number of representatives a state has is based on its population, you can infer that New Jersey, in spite of its small size, is densely populated.
2. **(5)** Because the number of a state's representatives is based on its population, and because Arizona is gaining residents at the expense of states in the Northeast, the number of representatives for both Arizona and northeastern states will need to be adjusted.
3. **(1)** The members of Congress are chosen by popular election, and their duties include making laws for the American people.

Exercise 4: The Legislative Branch (page 372)

Application

1. **E** The power to impose economic sanctions is not stated in the Constitution; therefore, the elastic clause applies.
2. **C** The power to approve treaties is stated in the Constitution.
3. **C** The power to admit a state is stated in the Constitution.
4. **C** The power to approve presidential appointments is stated in the Constitution.
5. **C** The power to introduce legislation is stated in the Constitution.

Exercise 5: Presidential Powers (page 374)

Evaluation

Answers marked should be *serves as commander in chief, grants reprieves and pardons, appoints Supreme Court Judges,* and *nominates major executive officers.* Explanations will vary for each power according to the reader's opinion.

GED Practice Exercise 6: The Executive Branch (page 374)

Analysis

(3) If the years an individual president can serve are limited, new policy ideas can be instituted because of a change in political party and/or candidate.

GED Practice Exercise 7: The Judicial Branch (page 375)

Comprehension

1. **(4)** The practice of deciding on the constitutionality of a law (which the Supreme Court does) is called the power of judicial review.
2. **(4)** The quotation both defines the role of the Supreme Court and affirms that the Court is the final authority on the Constitution's meaning.

Exercise 8: States' vs. Individuals' Rights (page 376)

Application

Cases 1, 2, and 3, represent victories of the state over the individual.

4. I In ruling that an accused must be informed of his or her rights, the Supreme Court supported the rights of the individual.

5. I In ruling that separate facilities for the races were not equal, the Supreme Court upheld the rights of the individual.

Exercise 9: System of Checks and Balances (page 378)

Comprehension

1. (a) executive	**(b)** judicial
2. (a) legislative	**(b)** executive
3. (a) legislative	**(b)** executive
4. (a) legislative	**(b)** executive
5. (a) judicial	**(b)** legislative
6. (a) executive	**(b)** legislative

GED Practice Exercise 10: The Enactment of a Law (page 379)

Evaluation

1. (2) This choice is supported by the part of the chart that shows that a bill must go to a conference committee for compromise.

2. (1) In the chart, specific procedures are outlined for allowing a vetoed bill to become law.

Exercise 11: Powers of State Government (page 381)

Application

1. B **2.** B **3.** F **4.** F **5.** S **6.** S

Exercise 12: City Income and Expenditures (page 383)

Comprehension

1. revenue; expenditures

2. charges and miscellaneous

3. environment and housing

GED Practice Exercise 13: City Budgeting (page 384)

Analysis

1. (5) The only ways for a city to make up for lost revenue are to raise taxes or fees and to decrease expenditures. Borrowing from a more prosperous state is not a plausible alternative.

Analysis

2. (4) If a city had the same income with no general debt to finance, it would have more money to spend.

GED Practice Exercise 14: Civic Involvement (page 385)

Analysis

1. (5) All of the choices are possible reasons as to why a citizen would be hesitant to get involved in community affairs. Because *every* community has many needs at many levels, this choice would be the only logical answer.

Application

2. (3) Based on the passage, the city council member would be most likely to respond to a complaint, because he or she has the smallest constituency.

Exercise 15: The Political Spectrum (page 386)

Application

1. (2) Because the speaker advocates social improvement through government action, the speaker may be classified as a liberal.

2. (3) Because the speaker believes in avoiding extreme changes in laws and government, he may be classified as moderate.

3. (5) Because the speaker advocates a return to an earlier policy, he may be classified as a reactionary.

4. (4) Because the speaker advocates maintaining the social order, he may be classified as a conservative.

5. (1) Because the speaker advocates swift, sweeping changes in laws, the speaker may be classified as a radical.

Exercise 16: Political Parties (page 388)
Application
1. **R** **Republicans** generally favor stronger state and local authority.
2. **D** **Democrats** generally endorse the efforts of labor unions.
3. **R** **Republicans** advocate free enterprise.
4. **D** **Democrats** support government expenditures for the disadvantaged and minorities.
5. **R** **Republicans** tend to favor defense spending at the expense of domestic spending.

GED Practice Exercise 17: Interest Groups (page 389)
Analysis
1. **(2)** The main goal of an interest group is to influence citizens and legislators.
2. **(3)** If lobbying is banned, Congressmen and Senators may not receive as much input as they did before.

Exercise 18: The Electoral Process and Voting (page 391)
Comprehension
1. e **2.** d **3.** a **4.** c **5.** b

GED Practice Exercise 19: The Electoral College (page 392)
Analysis
1. **(4)** The map supports Gore winning in states with large urban populations such as New York and Illinois. None of the other statements is supported by the map.

GED Practice Exercise 20: Registering to Vote (page 393)
Analysis
(2) In order to vote in the United States, you need to be a registered voter.

Exercise 21: Voter Rules (page 394)
Analysis
1. opinion **2.** fact **3.** opinion **4.** fact **5.** opinion

GED Practice Exercise 22: The Impact of the Media (page 395)
Analysis
1. **(3)** The money stuffed in the ears of the congressman prevents him from hearing the needs of the citizens.
2. **(2)** The money represents campaign contributions by special interest groups.

GED Practice Exercise 23: Becoming a Citizen of the United States (page 397)
Application
1. **(1)** According to the information provided on citizenship, an applicant would need to disclose if he ever had legal action taken against him regarding military service. This would put him at a great risk of being denied citizenship.
2. **(5)** Having a full-time job is the only choice given that is not a requirement based on the information provided about becoming a citizen.

CHAPTER 4
ECONOMICS

Exercise 1: Factors of Production (page 400)
Application
1. **N** Gemstones are found in nature.
2. **C** Computers and printers are equipment used to provide a service.
3. **N** Trees are raw materials found in nature.
4. **L** Carpenters who build shopping malls are laborers.
5. **C** Silicon chips are used in the production of computers.

GED Practice Exercise 2: Economic Systems (page 402)
Comprehension
1. **(3)** This quotation reflects the communist goal of working together to provide equal opportunity for all.
2. **(1)** This quotation reflects the capitalist feature of government noninterference in business.

GED Practice Exercise 3: Economic Systems and Governments (page 402)

Comprehension

1. (4) Because capitalism and communism occupy the extremes of the continuum, you can conclude that they are opposites.

2. (3) An aspect of a U.S. dairy manufacturer's operations (capitalist system) is dictated by a government agency's requirement (a feature of a socialist system).

GED Practice Exercise 4: Supply, Demand, and Equilibrium (page 406)

Comprehension

1. (3) The point where the line intersects is at $300.

Analysis

2. (3) As the price decreases, the demand increases.

Analysis

3. (3) With a greater supply brought about by the entrance of Asian economies into the market and a low demand for digital cameras, the supply would exceed demand, resulting in a surplus.

GED Practice Exercise 5: Economic Growth (page 408)

Comprehension

1. (3) Unemployment is a factor that may lead to a recession or depression; it is not a stage in the business cycle.

Analysis

2. (2) A depression is a severe decline in business, which usually affects the majority of citizens in a country.

GED Practice Exercise 6: Economic Growth (page 410)

Analysis

1. (3) The unemployment rate decreased from 4.7% in 1998 to fewer than 4.1% in 2000.

Analysis

2. (5) According to the Bureau of Labor Statistics, there was a decline of 66,000 manufacturing jobs.

Exercise 7: Measurement of Economic Growth (page 411)

1. Fact
2. Fact
3. Opinion
4. Fact
5. Opinion

Exercise 8: Consumer Price Index (page 413)

1967 = $1.16 1990 = $3.91 2010 = answers will vary (prediction)

Exercise 9: Money and Monetary Policy (page 414)

1. Fact
2. Opinion
3. Opinion
4. Fact
5. Opinion

Exercise 10: The Discount Rate (page 415)

Comprehension

1. F According to the passage, the role of the Fed is to regulate the nation's supply of money and credit.

2. F The two primary ways in which the Federal Reserve influences the money supply are by setting the reserve ratio and the discount rate.

3. T

4. T

5. F The discount rate is the interest rates the Fed charges member banks to borrow; the prime rate, not mentioned in the passage, is the rate banks charge to their best customers.

Exercise 11: Government and Fiscal Policy (page 416)

Comprehension

1. decrease; lowering To stimulate the economy during a recession, the government should increase domestic spending while lowering taxes. The actions put more money into circulation and into the hands of consumers.

2. **decrease; raising; increasing** Inflation is an increase in the amount of money in circulation. To reduce inflation, the Fed reduces the amount of money in circulation by raising the discount rate. This makes it more costly for banks to borrow from the Fed. By increasing the reserve ratio, the Fed reduces the amount of money a bank can lend.
3. **budget deficit** When operating at a budget deficit, the government is spending more money than it takes in.

GED Practice Exercise 12: The American Consumer (page 417)

Analysis

1. **(3)** The opinion of the cartoonist is that some Americans are experiencing loss of jobs, homes, and material possessions instead of meeting the goals necessary to achieve the "American Dream."
2. **(2)** The "American Rude Awakening" is unemployment, foreclosure, and reposession.

Exercise 13: Spending Money (page 419)

1. Highest Income
2. Higher and Highest Income (tie)
3. Highest Income
4. Middle Income
5. Middle Income

GED Practice Exercise 14: Technology and the Consumer (page 421)

Comprehension

1. **(3)** The chart claims that 84% of consumers shop on-line because of convenience.
2. **(3)** Because 84% of customers shop on-line for convenience, you can assume that this will continue to be important.

GED Practice Exercise 15: Technology and the Worker (page 423)

Analysis

(1) The graph indicates that in 1999–2000, more than 650,000 women attended college and received bachelor's degrees. This figure was the highest in history for both men and women.

GED Practice Exercise 16: The Baby Boom Generation (page 425)

Analysis

1. **(5)** According to the predictions made in the chart, most baby boomers will be between the ages of sixty-six and eighty-four in the year 2030. It would be incorrect to assume that they will *all* be deceased, and they will have done all the other choices before that time. At that age, they will probably be downsizing their homes because their children will have grown up.

Analysis

2. **(1)** The data in the chart indicates that social security may be exhausted by the year 2030. If this prediction is correct, the children of the baby boom generation will not receive an increase in benefits. All of the other predictions would be likely according to the chart.

CHAPTER 5

GEOGRAPHY

GED Practice Exercise 1: Styles of Maps (page 428)

Analysis

1. **(4)** When a spherical shape is flattened, as on a map, the surface will be stretched or distorted in some places.

Comprehension

2. **(4)** Political maps show boundaries of political areas like countries or states or provinces.

Comprehension

3. **(1)** Topographical maps have contour lines that indicate elevation. Many lines show a dramatic increase of elevation that would indicate a mountain.

Exercise 2: Measuring Distances (page 430)
Comprehension
1. The student needs to measure and calculate based on scale. (approximately 900 miles)
2. Los Angeles has a much larger dot; therefore, it has a larger population.
3. To go from Colorado to California you would travel west.

GED Practice Exercise 3: Latitude and Longitude (page 432)
Comprehension
1. **(5)** Central Africa

Comprehension
2. **(4)** South Africa

GED Practice Exercise 4: Time Zones (page 434)
Application
1. **(2)** Los Angeles falls within the pacific time zone, which is three hours earlier than the eastern time zone in which Philadelphia falls.

Application
2. **(3)** Denver falls within the mountain time zone, which is one hour earlier than the central Time zone in which Milwaukee falls.

Analysis
3. **(5)** Northwest Indiana is economically tied to the Chicago metropolitan area; therefore, for economic reasons Northwest Indiana is in the same time zone as Chicago.

Analysis
4. **(1)** People who travel and work in the Chicago area would benefit mostly from the placement of the Northwest corner of Indiana in the central time zone.

GED Practice Exercise 5: U.S. Topography (page 436)
Analysis
1. **(3)** Denver has the highest elevation of those cities listed. It is nicknamed the mile-high city because its elevation is close to one mile above sea level.

Analysis
2. **(3)** New Orleans is the only city among the choices given that lies largely below sea level. Since New Orleans is built on low-lying land, it experiences frequent flooding.

GED Practice Exercise 6: Climate (page 437)
Analysis
1. **(1)** The passage states that the higher elevations usually have lower temperatures.

Application
2. **(2)** Air is colder at higher elevations, so there is more likely to be precipitation in the mountains than the plains.

GED Practice Exercise 7: Mount Everest (page 438)
Evaluation
1. **(3)** Since climbing up to high elevations requires stays of several days at each of four camps at the various altitudes to adjust to the reduced oxygen, it generally takes at least two weeks to get to the top of Mount Everest.

GED Practice Exercise 8: The Indian Peninsula (page 439)
Comprehension
1. **(4)** Mount Everest, the highest mountain in the world, is also the highest point in the Himalayan Mountains at 29,028 feet. This is about five miles above sea level.

Comprehension
2. **(5)** The Indian Peninsula is mainly between sea level and 1,000 feet above sea level.

GED Practice Exercise 9: Population Distribution (page 440)
Analysis
1. **(5)** Rapid waterways do not affect the population of the area. Waterways have often been a source of transportation, but the speed of flow is not important. Cold temperatures and high elevations would prevent a large population from settling in that area. Grassy valleys and cultivated plains would draw a larger population.

Application

2. **(4)** The mountains of West Virginia would not allow for an even distribution of population.

GED Practice Exercise 10: Other Factors Affecting Population Distribution (page 441)

Analysis

(3) The quality of our living conditions can dramatically change the population distribution. Many people move to areas that provide a cleaner, safer environment.

Exercise 11: Population Growth (page 443)

Analysis

1. **(Fact)** Not all countries have demonstrated a population growth in the last part of the twentieth century.
2. **(Opinion)** Many countries have large population issues such as starvation. Many countries have a steady population and may have other major issues to deal with like unemployment.
3. **(Fact)** Based on the fact that the U.S. population has shown an increase in the 1960, 1995, and 2000 columns, you can predict that the population will increase steadily and double that of 1960.
4. **(Opinion)** The phrase "because no one wants to work there" makes this statement an opinion because it's too broad a generalization. We have no way of knowing what every person in Japan and Western Europe thinks.
5. **(Opinion)** Any future forecast is made from predictions based on current facts, which may be inconclusive. Many factors could change current population trends in a country.

Science

What is the GED Science Test like overall?

The GED Science Test requires you to know some of the basic science concepts that will be covered in this book. You will not have to recall specific facts or formulas, but you will have to draw upon your prior science knowledge. You will need the skill of distinguishing a science fact, name, or term from a principle, concept, or law.

The context of the Science Test is that of daily living or workplace settings and shows you as an individual acquirer, organizer, and user of information in a lifelong process. It depicts your common roles as an adult, including that of citizen, family member, worker, or consumer. The test includes studies of relationships between science and technology, research, communications, and society. The test acknowledges local and global problems, issues, and events, and frequently, the test requires problem-solving skills.

You will need to be able to show that you can comprehend (understand) what you read, apply information to a new situation, analyze relationships between ideas or concepts, and synthesize information from two or more sources. In order to answer the questions successfully, you will need to demonstrate that you have the general reading competency of a high school graduate.

What's on the test?

The GED Science Test is based on the National Science Education Standards *(NSES)* Scientific Understanding Strands and is divided into these content areas:

- Life Science (Biology) 45%
- Earth and Space Science 20%
- Physical Science 35%
  - Chemistry
  - Physics

How many and what type of questions are on the test?

There are 50 multiple-choice questions, and you will be given 80 minutes to complete the test.

Passage sets versus stand-alone questions

- Approximately 25% (12–13) of the questions are based on passage sets. This means that two or more questions are based on the same passage or the same graphic.
- Approximately 75% (37–38) of the questions will be single, stand-alone questions. This type of question could, for example, state the scientific theory and then ask a question based on using the theory in a real-life situation.

Reading text versus graphics

- Approximately 50% (25) of the questions will be based on text material.
- Approximately 50% (25) of the questions will be based on visuals—graphs, maps, charts or tables, photos, pictures, diagrams, advertisements, or political cartoons.

What themes are represented by the Science content?

Six themes are reflected in the content:

- The theme "Fundamental Understandings" comprises the majority with 60% (or 30) of the test questions.
- "Science in Personal and Social Perspectives" is the next largest category, with 17% (or 8) of the test questions. As you prepare for this theme, you should pay particular attention to issues relating to the environment and health.
- The remaining 12 questions are made up of these four themes: "Unifying Concepts and Processes," "Science as Inquiry," "Science and Technology," and "History and Nature of Science."

What else do I need to know to prepare?

Essential science concepts are covered in Chapters 1–4 of this section. However, keep in mind that a given question may draw from a number of these subjects. In discussing science as it affects people, it is natural to touch on a number of topics. We say that the test acknowledges the *interdisciplinary* nature of science. For example, a question could involve a daily living situation of moving furniture, could use the physics principle of the lever (a simple machine) and could draw on the skill of multiplication from mathematics in order to arrive at pounds of force necessary.

Besides reading the science material and answering the questions, you can also prepare by reviewing the health sections of newspapers and magazines or health newsletters provided by some employers. Also, you need to prepare in mathematics because the test assumes that you have proficiency through beginning algebra.

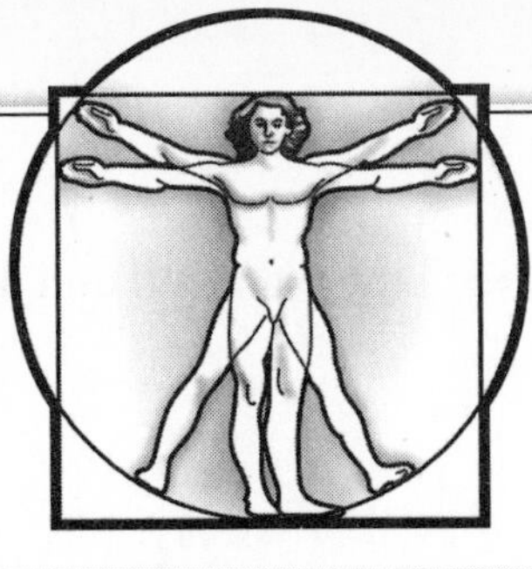

CHAPTER 1

Life Science

Biology—The Study of Living Things

Biology is the scientific study of all life forms. Biologists are interested in how living things grow, how they change over time, and how they interact with one another and with their environment. Of particular interest are the characteristics that all living things have in common. All living things react to stimuli, take in food and use it to grow, eliminate wastes, and reproduce. The starting point for any systematic study of biology is an examination of the basic unit of life, the cell.

The Cell, the Basic Unit of Life

The **cell** is the smallest unit of living material capable of carrying on the activities of life. Like the bricks of a building, cells are the "building blocks" of an organism. Cells were first observed in 1665 by Robert Hooke with the aid of a crudely made microscope.

Cells vary widely in size and appearance. It is the number of cells in an organism, however, and not the size of cells, that determines the size of an organism. The cells of a human being and a whale are of equal size. The whale is larger because its genetic pattern dictates that a larger number of cells be produced.

Types of Cells

Two kinds of cells are known to exist—**plant cells** and **animal cells**. Cells are responsible for the exchange of food and wastes within the organism. Inside of all cells are the structures that provide the specific jobs needed for these exchanges. One difference between the two is that a plant cell has a cell wall that protects it and an animal cell does not. Also, plant cells contain **chloroplasts,** structures active in the food-making process, while animal cells do not.

Both plant and animal cells are surrounded by a delicate boundary, the **cell membrane.** The cell membrane

- preserves the cell by acting as a barrier between it and the outside environment
- helps the cell maintain its shape
- regulates molecular traffic passing into and out of the cell

The following illustration shows the differences between the plant cell and the animal cell:

Cell Structure

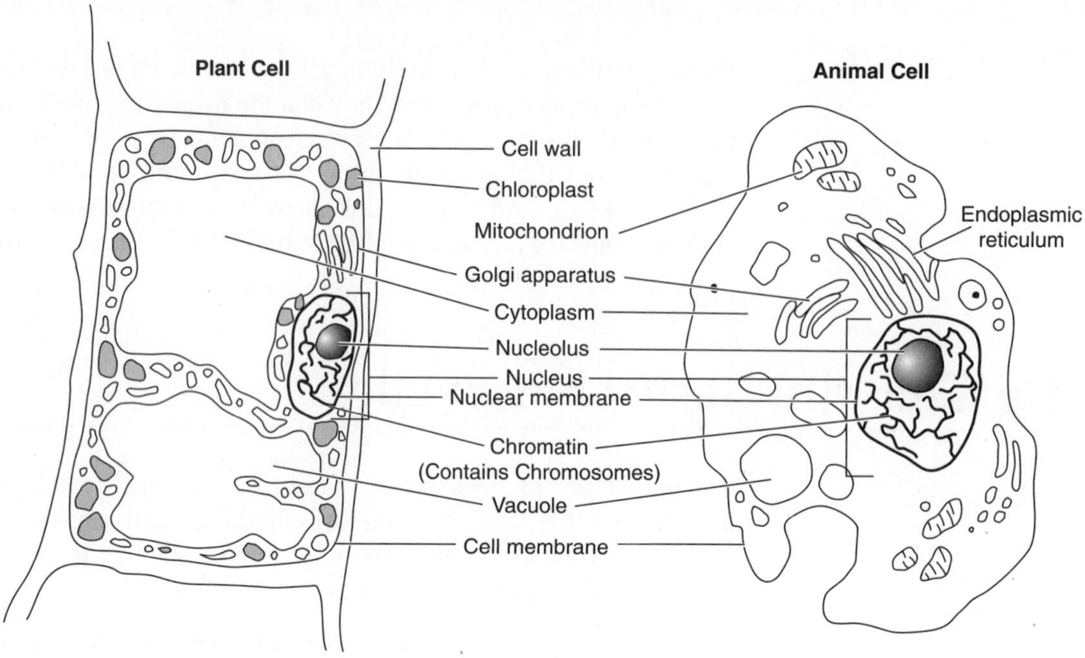

A highly specialized and complex structure, the cell has its own control center, transportation system, power plants, factories for making needed materials, and even a reproductive blueprint, or chemical recipe.

Cytoplasm	protoplasm found between the nuclear membrane and the cell membrane
Endoplasmic reticulum	a tubular transport system within the cell or to the outside
Mitochondrion	power plant inside cell which produces energy for cellular function; plural is mitochondria

Golgi apparatus	the packaging plant, which gathers proteins and carbohydrates in membraneous sacs; in gland cells it releases hormones to the rest of the body
Nucleus	the control center for the cell, surrounded by a double nuclear membrane; it contains the chromosome or genetic blueprint for the cell
Chromosome	the genetic blueprint found in the nucleus; it contains DNA that makes up the genes, which are the genetic code for the cells, organs, and structure of the body
Nucleolus	the holding tank for RNA, the essential acid for the chemical activity of the cell and the chromosome information that permits the manufacture of protein

EXERCISE 1

Cell Structure

Directions: Match each term on the right with the mechanical function it performs on the left. Write the letter of the correct term in the space provided.

1. ______	regulator of traffic passing into and out of the cell	**a.** nucleus
2. ______	control center for the cell	**b.** endoplasmic reticulum
3. ______	means of transportation for material within the cell	**c.** cell membrane
4. ______	factory in which RNA ingredients are assembled and stored	**d.** nucleolus

Answers are on page 578.

EXERCISE 2

Cells

Directions: Choose the *best* answer for each of the following questions.

1. What is the main idea of the informational text?

(1) All living things are made of cells.
(2) The nucleus is the control center of the cell.
(3) There are differences between plant and animal cells.
(4) The cell is an organized structure with subsystems.
(5) The Golgi apparatus functions as a packaging plant in the cell.

2. In plant cells, chloroplasts are active in the chemical processes required to make food. Animal cells have no chloroplasts. On this basis, what can we conclude?

(1) Plant cells are more complex than animal cells.
(2) Plant cells and not animal cells generate chemical reactions.
(3) Animal cells prey upon plant cells as a food source.
(4) Animal cells are more complex than plant cells.
(5) Animals must obtain food from outside sources.

3. According to the text, mitochondria are the power plants that produce energy for important life processes in the animal cell and are responsible for cellular respiration. What part of a plant cell serves a similar function?

(1) the cell wall
(2) the nucleus
(3) the nucleolus
(4) the chromosome
(5) the chloroplast

Answers are on page 578.

Cells and Active Transport

Every cell has a membrane that selectively permits the passage of certain molecules in and out of the cell. The movement of molecules through the cell membrane without any effort on the cell's part is achieved by diffusion. **Diffusion** is the movement of molecules from an area of high concentration to an area of low concentration. Vibrating molecules are propelled away from one another after they collide. It is through this process that odors can fill a large room in a short period of time. Diffusion is important in higher organisms. In the human body, for example, oxygen moves from the air sacs in the lungs through cell membranes and into the blood through diffusion.

A cell's cytoplasm contains many substances in varying degrees of concentration. These concentrations differ sharply from those in the fluid surrounding the cell. Such differences are so essential that the cell can die if the differences are not maintained. Given the opportunity, diffusion would quickly eliminate these critical differences. Therefore, the cell must be able to negate, and sometimes even reverse, the process of diffusion. This is accomplished by active transport. During **active transport,** the cell moves materials from an area of low concentration to an area of high concentration. This work requires energy.

EXERCISE 3

Cells and Active Transport

Directions: In the blank spaces below, write the words that correctly complete each of the following statements.

1. Diffusion is the movement of molecules from an area of ________ concentration to an area of ________ concentration.

2. In active transport, materials are moved from an area of ________ concentration to an area of ________ concentration.

Answers are on page 578.

GED PRACTICE

EXERCISE 4

Diffusion and Osmosis

Directions: Choose the best answer for each of the following questions.

1. **How does the process of diffusion function in the human body?**

   (1) It allows for concentrations of materials, where needed, in the body, through stockpiling.
   (2) It regulates blood flow between organs through veins and arteries.
   (3) It allows an even distribution of substances throughout all cells of the body.
   (4) It comes into play in times of extreme illness and stress.
   (5) It plays an insignificant role in the body's functioning.

2. **Osmosis may be described as a process through which water in a solution is able to move through the cell membrane from a *higher* concentration to a *lower* one in order to maintain balance on either side of the membrane. If the salt solution in blood plasma surrounding red blood cells is higher than the solution inside the cells, which is most likely to occur?**

   (1) Water will leave the cell and pass into the blood plasma.
   (2) Water will leave the blood plasma and pass into the cell.
   (3) The cell will expand because of a gain in water.
   (4) The cell will carry on respiration at a slower rate.
   (5) Cellular division starts to try to save the cell.

Answers are on page 578.

Mitosis—Cell Division

Active cell transport requires energy. Energy is also needed for the growth of an organism. As a cell grows, its cell membrane becomes less able to provide oxygen and nutrients for the interior of the cell, and wastes become unable to leave the cell. In addition, a nucleus can control only so much cytoplasm. Therefore, when a cell reaches its limit in size, it must divide or undergo a process called mitosis.

Mitosis is the process through which cells reproduce themselves by division. In a multicellular organism mitosis leads to tissue growth and maintenance. In a single-celled organism mitosis results in two new genetically identical independent organisms. Mitosis can be divided into four stages or phases, as shown in the diagrams.

Stage 1: Prophase

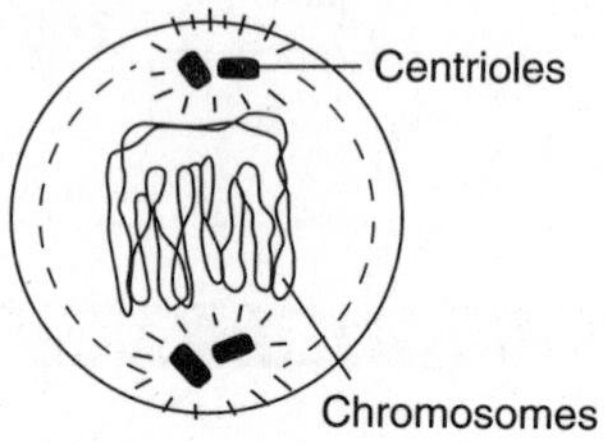

Stage 2: Metaphase

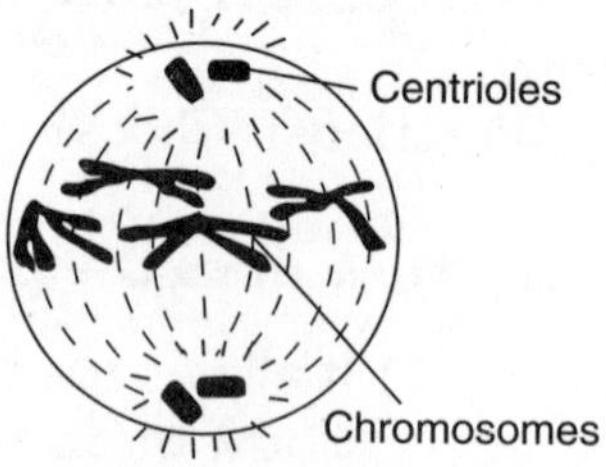

Stage 3: Anaphase

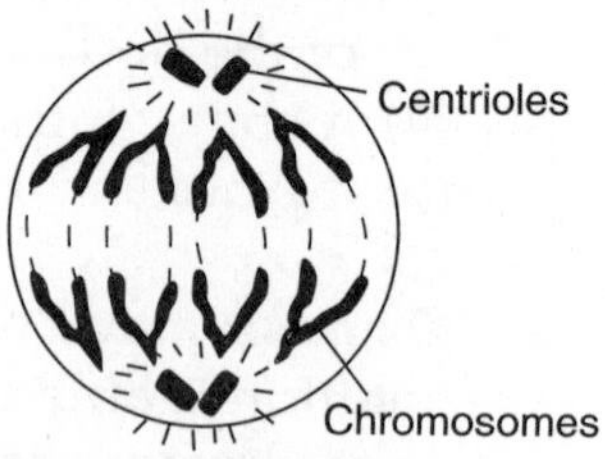

Stage 4: Telophase

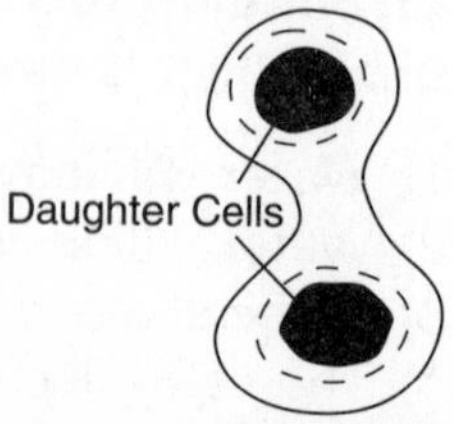

(Animal Cell)

Stage 1: Prophase Just before prophase begins, genetic material in the nucleus is duplicated (doubled). Then the nuclear membrane and nucleolus disappear. The chromosomes (genetic material) shorten, visible centrioles appear at opposite ends of the cells, and small fibers start to form between them.

Stage 2: Metaphase During metaphase the spindle fibers attach themselves to the center of the chromosomes (centromeres). The chromosomes are now quite thick and visible. They begin to line up at the equator of the cell.

Stage 3: Anaphase During anaphase, the centromeres divide, and the duplicate pairs of chromosomes separate. The separate pairs then move toward the poles of the cell.

Stage 4: Telophase When the chromosomes arrive at the poles, telophase begins. The nuclei re-form, the chromosomes gradually become less visible, and the cell separates to form two new cells. The daughter cells are genetically and physically identical to the parent cell except for size.

In single-cell organisms cell division results in the creation of two new individuals. In complex organisms (made of more than one cell) the new daughter cells form a subsystem of the parent cell. In many organisms cell reproduction is at its peak while the organism grows. As the organism ages, the process is limited to the replacement of old and damaged cells.

EXERCISE 5

Mitosis

Directions: Match each phase of mitosis on the left with its description on the right.

1. ______ Prophase

2. ______ Metaphase

3. ______ Anaphase

4. ______ Telophase

(a) The chromosomes become easily visible.

(b) The chromosomal material lines up at the center of the cell.

(c) The cell divides to form two new cells.

(d) The pairs of chromosomes move to opposite poles.

Answers are on page 578.

Meiosis—Reproductive Cell Division

While mitosis involves general cell division, a special type of cell division for reproductive purposes is called meiosis. **Meiosis** is a process in which a parent cell undergoes two special types of cell division that result in the production of four **gametes** (reproductive cells).

Each gamete has half the number of chromosomes of the original parent cell. Each organism has a chromosome number that is characteristic of that organism. For example, all of the cells in the human body contain 46 chromosomes except for the gametes (the reproductive cells). The reproductive cells (sperm and egg) cannot carry the same number of chromosomes as those of other parts of the body. If they did, the offspring that would result from the union of the egg and sperm would have twice the normal amount of genetic material after cell division. In animals this doubling would result in the termination of the embryo early in development. To prevent termination, the sex cells undergo meiosis, a special division process.

The following illustrations show the two stages of meiosis.

Meiosis I

Prophase 1 Metaphase 1 Anaphase 1 Telophase 1

As the preceding diagram shows, the chromosome pairs come together to exchange genes. This process is called crossing over. **Crossing over** ensures a recombination of genetic material. Later the pairs separate, and one chromosome of each pair moves to a new cell. During telophase 1, the cytoplasm divides, and two daughter cells are formed. Each daughter cell is called a **haploid** cell, a cell that contains half the number of chromosomes of the original parent cell.

Meiosis II

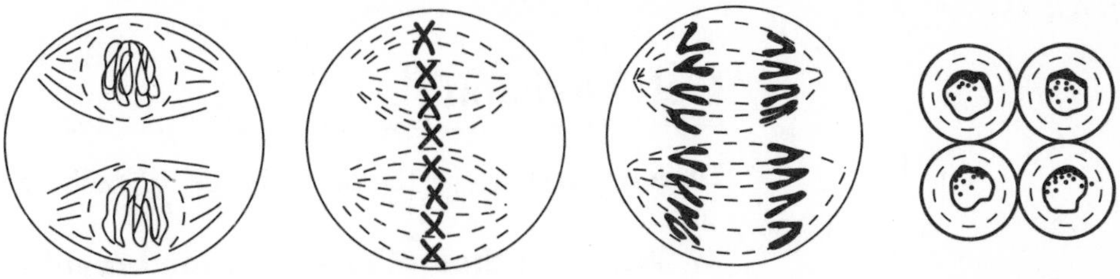

(*Note:* Only one daughter cell from Meiosis I is shown here.)

In Meiosis II the chromosomal material combines, separates, and moves to new cells, resulting in four reproductive cells. In human beings, when two haploid cells (a sperm and an egg, each containing 23 chromosomes) unite in fertilization, they form a **diploid** cell, a cell containing 46 chromosomes. The fertilized cell contains 46 chromosomes, or 23 pairs—half from the mother and half from the father.

EXERCISE 6

Meiosis

Directions: Number the steps in meiosis in the order in which they occur.

_______ Two new cells divide, resulting in four reproductive cells.

_______ Chromosomes come together in pairs.

_______ Chromosome pairs separate, and each chromosome moves to a new cell.

_______ Chromosomes exchange genes.

Answers are on page 578.

GED PRACTICE

EXERCISE 7

Cell Division

Directions: Choose the *best* answer for each of the following questions.

1. Which method of reproduction provides for the most variety in offspring?

(1) asexual (nonsexual) reproduction: genetic information from a single parent to offspring
(2) mutative reproduction: occasional mutation of a cell changing the organism's appearance
(3) sexual reproduction: exchange of genetic information from two parents
(4) cloning: duplication of genetic information of a single organism
(5) cellular reproduction: cell division into two cells

2. Cancer is a condition in which cells that serve no function in the body invade healthy ones. On this basis, what can we conclude about malignant cancer cells?

(1) They do not reproduce by mitosis.
(2) They divide by meiosis.
(3) They divide more unpredictably than normal cells.
(4) They divide less frequently than benign cells.
(5) They are parasites and do not reproduce by division at all.

Answers are on page 578.

Genetics and Heredity

Heredity is the term used to describe the passing of traits from parents to children. Every species has its own set of traits that it transmits to its offspring. **Genetics** is the study of how traits are passed on. **Geneticists,** the scientists who study heredity, have found that hereditary information of an organism is carried by the chromosomes of the cell nucleus.

Genes determine all of our inherited traits. Every human being receives two genes for each trait—one from the mother and one from the father. Genes may be **dominant** or **recessive.** The dominant gene, if present, will always appear in an offspring. For example, because brown eye color is a dominant trait, 90 percent of human beings have brown eyes. If two dominant genes are inherited, the resulting trait will be a combination of the two inherited characteristics.

Sexual reproduction ensures that the offspring has genetic material from both parents. This genetic material is thoroughly remixed with every fertilization so that, with the exception of identical twins, no two offspring of the same parents are exactly alike genetically.

Sex and Mutations

Whether a mother gives birth to a boy or girl is determined by the X and Y chromosomes. A person receives two sex chromosomes—one from the father's **sperm cell** and one from the mother's **egg cell**. Egg cells contain a single X chromosome. Male sperm cells may contain either an X or a Y chromosome. If two X chromosomes unite, a female will be created. If the sperm reaching the egg has a Y chromosome, a male will be produced. The sperm cells, then, carry the chromosome that determines the **sex** of offspring.

Sometimes a mistake occurs in the genetic makeup of a chromosome during cell duplication. This change in the genes, called a **mutation,** may be passed on to offspring. Two mutations in humans are **Down's Syndrome**, which results in brain damage, and **muscular dystrophy**, a disease that causes muscles to waste away.

GED PRACTICE

EXERCISE 8

Genetics and Heredity

Directions: Study the diagram and choose the *best* answer for the questions that follow.

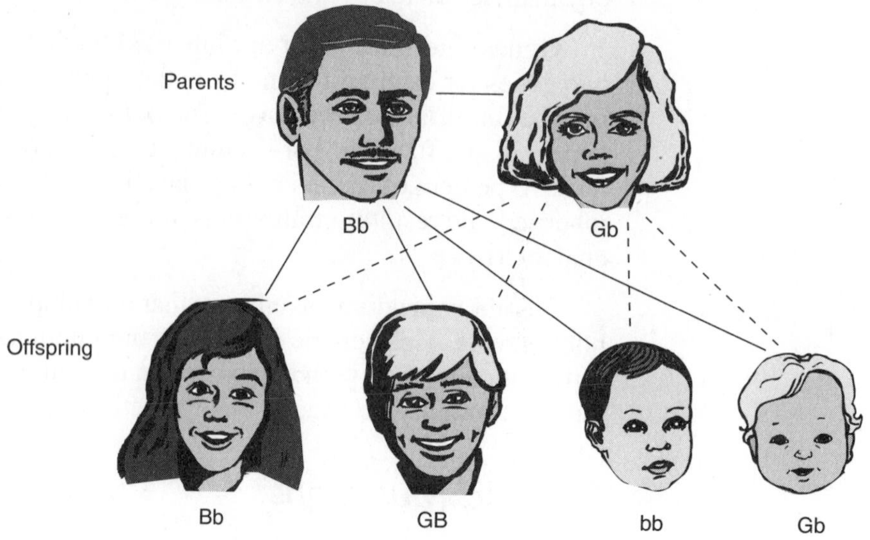

How Eye Color is Inherited

G = Dominant Green Eye Gene

B = Dominant Brown Eye Gene

b = Recessive Blue Eye Gene

1. **According to the diagram, what percentage of this couple's children might have blue eyes?**
   (1) 75 percent
   (2) 50 percent
   (3) 0 percent
   (4) 25 percent
   (5) 100 percent

   The following question is *not* based on the preceding diagram.

2. **The Jones family has had four children, all girls. Their fifth child is a boy. Why did this change occur?**
   (1) the conception classes taken by the parents
   (2) the timing of the fertility cycles
   (3) the father's contribution of a Y chromosome
   (4) the mother's contribution of a Y chromosome
   (5) the "law of averages" finally catching up

Answers are on page 578.

Cloning

Bob Englehart/The Hartford Courant

Until the mid-1990s, reproduction involved the contribution of genetic material from two parent organisms. In 1996 in Scotland, a sheep named Dolly was created by a process that is called **cloning.** The egg cell (whose nucleus had been removed) from an adult sheep was "fertilized" with the nucleus of a mature female mammary cell. The developing embryo had the full genetic information from a single adult and was considered a clone of the adult from which the mammary nucleus had come. Cloning human individuals has many moral and ethical issues regarding whether it is right or wrong to "interfere" with the natural reproductive process. These issues have prevented researchers from pursuing experiments dealing with people.

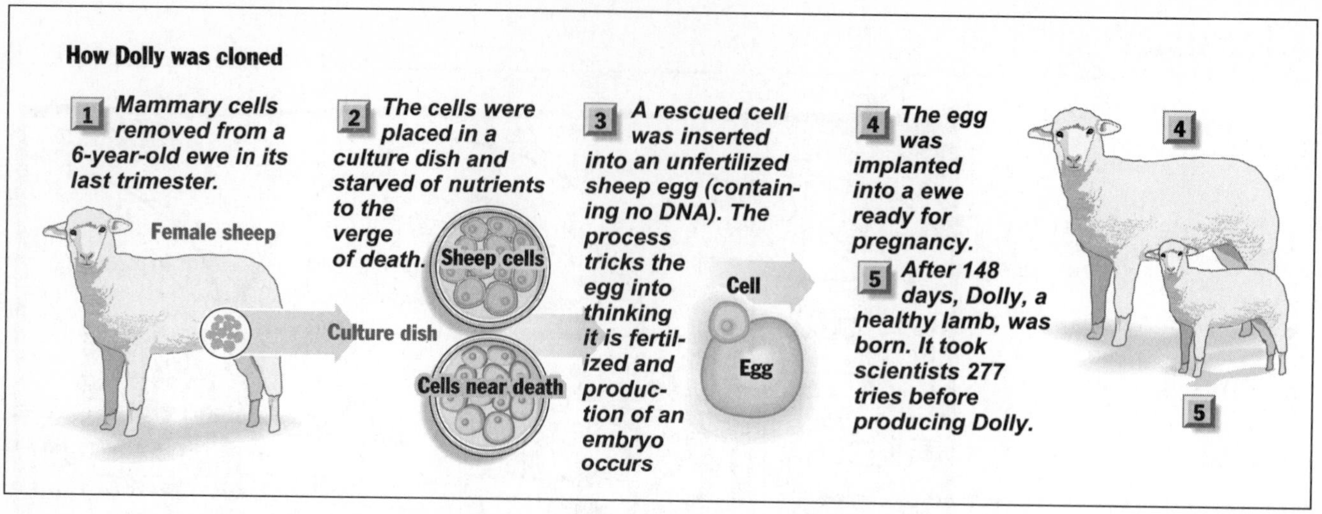
How Dolly was cloned
1 Mammary cells removed from a 6-year-old ewe in its last trimester.
Female sheep
2 The cells were placed in a culture dish and starved of nutrients to the verge of death.
Sheep cells
Culture dish
Cells near death
3 A rescued cell was inserted into an unfertilized sheep egg (containing no DNA). The process tricks the egg into thinking it is fertilized and production of an embryo occurs
Cell
Egg
4 The egg was implanted into a ewe ready for pregnancy.
5 After 148 days, Dolly, a healthy lamb, was born. It took scientists 277 tries before producing Dolly.
4
5

Source: Lara Weber and Rick Tuma, Chicago Tribune, February 8, 1998.

EXERCISE 9

Cloning

Directions: Mark the following statements about cloning as being true **(T)** or false **(F)**.

1. ______ Scientists are working on ways to clone a deceased child.
2. ______ A clone has two parents but looks like only one of them.
3. ______ The first sheep to be cloned was created in the United States.
4. ______ A cloned organism still must go through the development of an embryo.
5. ______ The egg cell that is used for a clone must have the original nucleus removed.

Answers are on page 578.

Organ Systems

Once an organism has successfully completed the reproductive process, the newly developing offspring's cells begin specializing into what will become the variety of internal organs. The human body is made up of several **organ systems** that specialize in functions that are necessary for an organism to thrive. The nervous system is made up of the brain, the spinal cord, and nerve cells. The circulatory system is in charge of circulating the blood from the heart through a series of arteries, veins, and capillaries (small connecting vessels).

The circulatory system works very closely with the respiratory system, using blood cells to exchange oxygen and carbon dioxide through the lungs. Nutrients are distributed and wastes are removed from the human body by the digestive and excretory systems. All of these systems are able to maintain their form and position in the human body because of the skeletal and muscular systems.

EXERCISE 10

Organ Systems

Directions: Match each health concern on the left with the correct system on the right.

1. ______	ulcer	**a.** nervous system
2. ______	cough	**b.** circulatory system
3. ______	broken arm	**c.** muscular system
4. ______	heart attack	**d.** digestive system
5. ______	migraine headache	**e.** respiratory system
6. ______	muscle cramp	**f.** skeletal system

Answers are on page 578.

The Nervous System

The **nervous system** is the means of communication of the body and contains the brain, the spinal cord, and specialized neurons. The brain is divided into two hemispheres, each of which is responsible for different but overlapping functions. If a portion of the brain is injured in an accident, another region can often be trained to compensate for the nonfunctioning area.

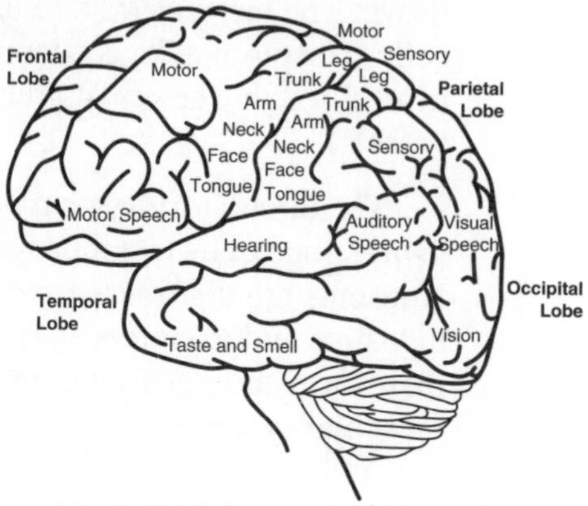

Speech, Sight, and Visual Memory

People who have had strokes or severe concussions may lose the ability to use the speech center in the brain located in the area called the **temporal lobe,** found near the temples. Another lobe is called the **occipital.** This lobe is located in the back of the brain and is in charge of sight. If you hit the back of your head the stimulus to this section of the brain is responsible for your "seeing stars." The **optic nerve** in the eye connects to the occipital lobe of the brain, where images projected on the **retina** (the back wall of the eye ball) are recorded and evaluated. This part of the brain also is in charge of visual memory.

If you were to be asked how many windows are on the front of your home or the total number of windows you had in your home, you would count the windows by visualizing them in your mind. This ability to visualize is also called **photographic memory.**

Voluntary and Involuntary Functions

The brain has both voluntary and involuntary levels of function. The portion of the brain that controls voluntary functions is referred to as the **cerebrum.** It controls all motor coordination and intrepretation of sensory information from inside and outside the body. If the temperature outside the body is cold, the brain receives the information from the sensory neurons in the skin. The message is relayed to the brain, which acts on the information. You might react to this message by adding more clothing or moving to a warmer area.

The message to move comes from the cerebrum, but the **cerebellum** is the large part of the brain that coordinates the actual movements of the muscles. The cerebellum is in charge of involuntary muscle action, so a new skill or newly learned sport involves teaching the cerebellum how to coordinate the aquired movements. This is also the region that is responsible for personality and for decision making. If the cerebellum is injured, the personality of the victim may be dramatically altered. Passive or shy people have been known to become very hostile and verbal, while people with outgoing personalities have become withdrawn and introverted. One such documented case involved a railway worker, Phineaus Gage. While supervising at a site he was struck with a metal spike that went through his cheek and up and out of his cerebellum. Suprisingly, the injuries were not fatal, but he became very aggressive and short-tempered and was no longer able to be in a position of authority.

Another subconcious portion of the brain is the **medulla oblongata,** located in the back of the brain. It governs involuntary body functions like breathing and digestion. The neurons are located everywhere throughout the body and are responsible for taking messages to and from the brain to the organs and the muscles. The motion of your diaphragm, which draws in air, and the **peristalsis** or movement of food through the digestive tract are both examples of how the medulla regulates involuntary systems.

The Nervous System

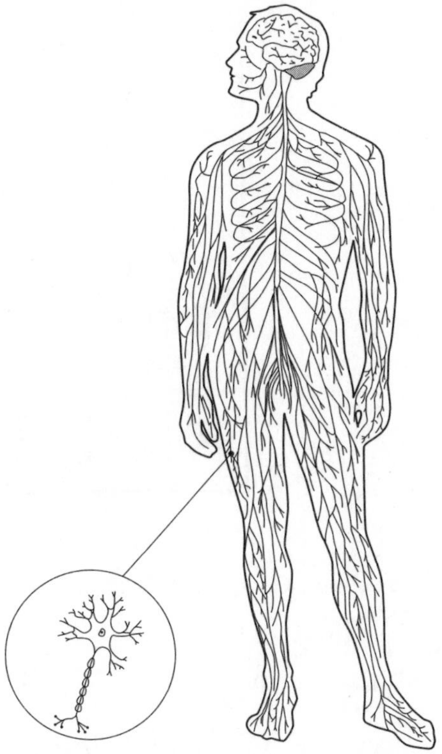

Spinal Cord and Message Transport

The **spinal cord** is the long system of nerves that travels down the spine from the brain. At times the spinal cord acts as a body defense system that prevents injury by immediately acting on an emergency nerve-cell message. This immediate response, called a **reflex,** is used when the message going to the brain and out to the trauma area would take too long. An example is your hand coming into contact with a hot material. Your reflex response is to remove the hand before the brain has even had time to register and evaluate the situation. Blinking is another example of how a reflex helps protect sensitive areas, such as the eyes.

In the case of spinal injury, the messages relayed from the brain might not be able to travel the spinal cord to the muscle site. This injury is referred to as **paralysis.** The muscles do not act if they cannot receive the message from the brain. As a person ages, the bones lose strength. In the case of the spinal column, the individual vertebrae may move and pinch the spinal cord. This action can be very painful and may cause temporary paralysis. Doctors may advise surgery for the patient to fuse vertebrae together to prevent slippage.

It is recommended that we maintain calcium in our diets to keep bones strong. As we age, we are also advised to exercise to strengthen the back muscles in order to relieve stress on the spinal vertebrae. (We are also reminded to use our leg muscles to help us lift objects.)

"Whoa! *That* was a good one! Try it, Hobbs—just poke his brain right where my finger is."

EXERCISE 11

The Nervous System

Directions: Answer the following questions based on what you have learned about the nervous system.

1. **Which region of the brain would be in control of the following activities in the human body?**

   a. ______________________ muscle coordination and skill in playing sports

   b. ______________________ a reflex to put hands up to block an object from hitting the face

   c. ______________________ automatic increased heart rate while doing exercises

   d. ______________________ thinking of what tasks need to be done at work

2. **Identify the following statements as true or false.**

   _______ The cerebrum controls reflex response.

   _______ Photographic memory relies on memory in the occipital lobe.

   _______ Voluntary functions such as walking are controlled by the cerebrum.

   _______ There are four hemispheres in the brain.

Answers are on page 578.

Writing Activity 1

Sometimes the functioning of the brain is negatively affected by injury or drug use. Some conditions of brain disfunction have a possible genetic component like Alzheimer's disorder. Write about someone you know who has had a condition where the brain was not fully functioning. What was the treatment given to that patient? If you do not know of anyone who has suffered with any of these conditions, can you imagine how your life might change if something like this happened to you or a family member?

The Circulatory and Respiratory Systems

The **circulatory system** has the job of transporting nutrients to the cells and removing the cell's waste. It does this by means of a system of vessels called arteries, veins, and capillaries. These vessels provide the pathway for the carriers of the nutrients and waste: the blood cells. When the blood cells are pumped out of the heart through **arteries,** they are rich with oxygen, having just returned from the lungs. These blood cells are squeezed tightly in single file through the **capillaries** where the actual exchange of gases into and out of the cells occurs. The route back to the heart takes the blood cells by way of the **veins.**

When in the heart, the blood receives an extra push to get it to the lungs, where it releases the carbon dioxide from the cell and receives new oxygen. The heart is the main pump for this flow of cells. There are four chambers in the heart. The two smaller chambers that receive blood are called the **atria.** The two lower chambers are called the **ventricles.** The pulse from these lower chambers is responsible for sending the blood to the next location. The heart has a complex series of valves at the opening of each chamber in the heart. These valves are one-way doors to prevent blood from flowing backwards into the previous chamber. The heart itself has many small capillaries that feed its own muscular walls.

Depending on a person's diet and lifestyle, these small vessels may become clogged with a material called **plaque.** The plaque attaches to the walls of the capillary and to clumps of plaque that already exist. When the capillaries cannot make the exchange of gases or feed the heart muscle, a section of the heart starves, undergoing damage that could cause a heart attack. Doctors recommend that people be aware of how easily their bodies might create plaque using cholesterol found in their diet. Treatments can include medication, change in exercise and diet, expansion of the clogged vessel with a balloon device (an *angioplasty* procedure), or bypass or replacement surgery.

The Circulatory System

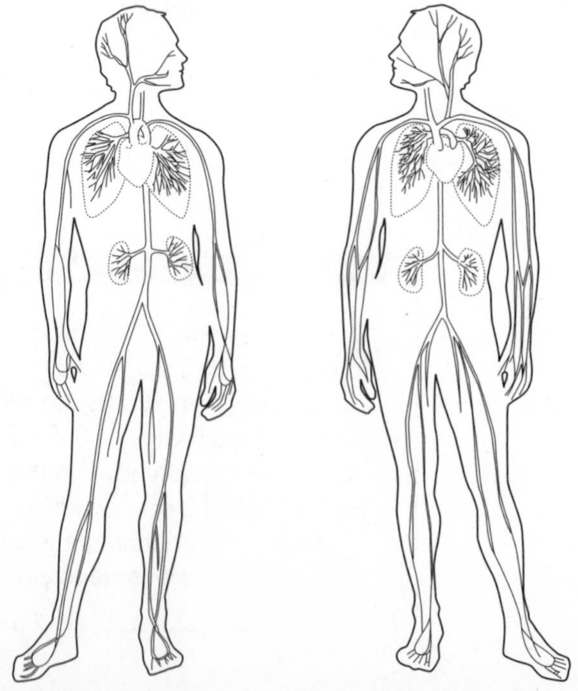

Respiratory System

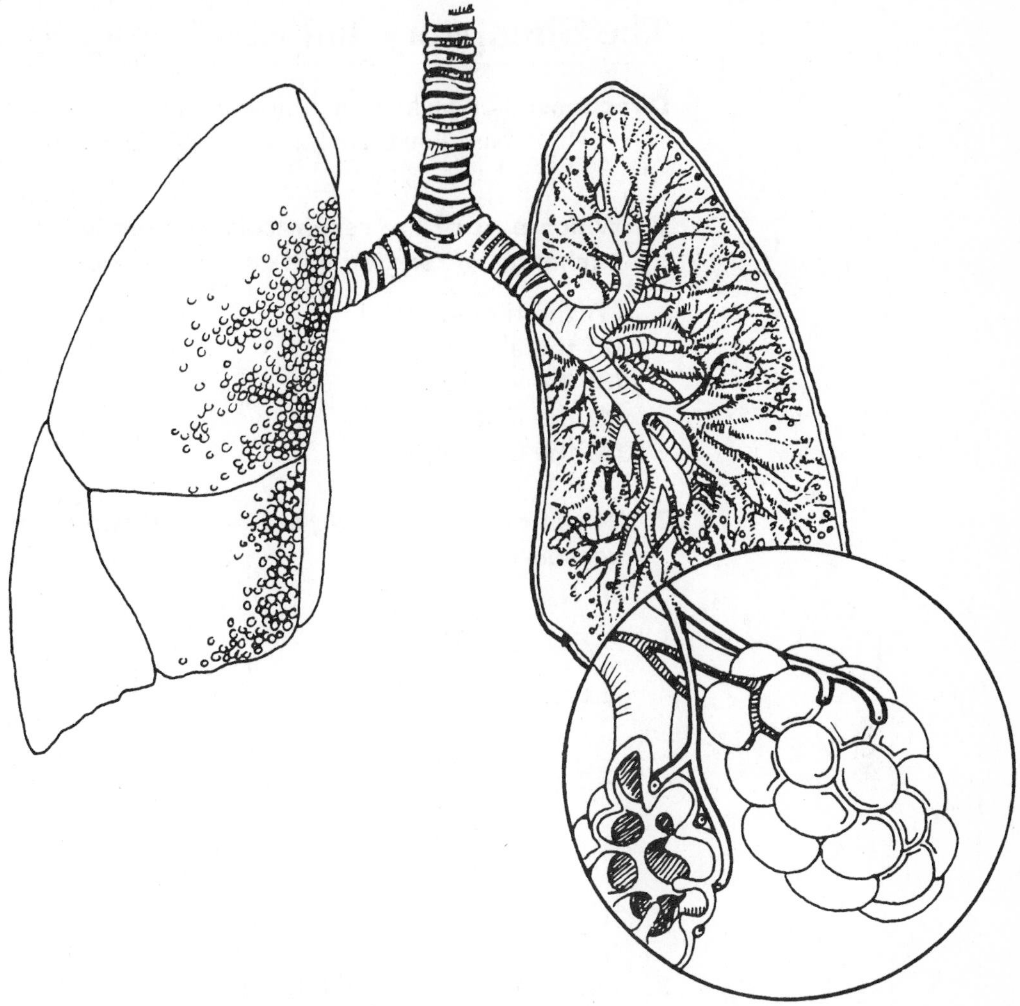

The **respiratory system** involves the exchange of the outgoing carbon dioxide from the cells with the incoming air. This exchange takes place in the lungs, which are able to exchange gases through small spongelike sacs called **alveoli.** Carbon dioxide and oxygen diffuse in and out of the cells to the alveoli and are transported inside and outside the body through the branchlike system of **bronchiole.** The bronchiole connect to the **trachea** or wind pipe and release breath through the mouth and nose.

In those people who smoke, the particles of tar that are inhaled become trapped in these small sacs. This condition or irritation in the lung makes the lungs much less soft and flexible than those of nonsmokers. The lung tissue loses the flexibility necessary when breathing needs to be accelerated (such as during exercise or when fighting off infections such as pneumonia).

EXERCISE 12

The Circulatory and Respiratory Systems

Directions: For each of the following questions, choose the *best* answer based on the information on pages 478–479.

1. Which part of the respiratory system is responsible for the actual exchange of oxygen and carbon dioxide?

(1) the trachea
(2) the alveoli
(3) the windpipe
(4) the lungs
(5) the bronchiole

2. Which of the following are parts of the heart (H) and which are vessels (V)?

_______ atria

_______ capillaries

_______ veins

_______ ventricles

_______ arteries

3. Which of the following behaviors would be beneficial for the circulatory and respiratory systems?

(1) smoking cigarettes
(2) eating fried foods
(3) exercising strenuously
(4) painting in unventilated areas
(5) exercising moderately daily

Answers are on page 579.

The Digestive and Excretory Systems

Digestion is the breakdown of food into simple molecules so it can be absorbed into the cells. Digestion begins when food enters the mouth. The action of chewing the food while it is being mixed with saliva starts the breakdown. The stomach continues the chemical breakdown using gastric acids. The food then travels to the **small intestine,** which is in charge of absorbing the digested nutrients. The **pancreas,** the **gall bladder** and the **liver** each focus its digestive enzyme on specific food chemicals. The small intestine connects the stomach to the **large intestine** (also called the **colon).** The large intestine is next in line with the job of absorbing water that is remaining in the digested food. It also stores the waste material until it is expelled from the body.

The Digestive and Excretory System

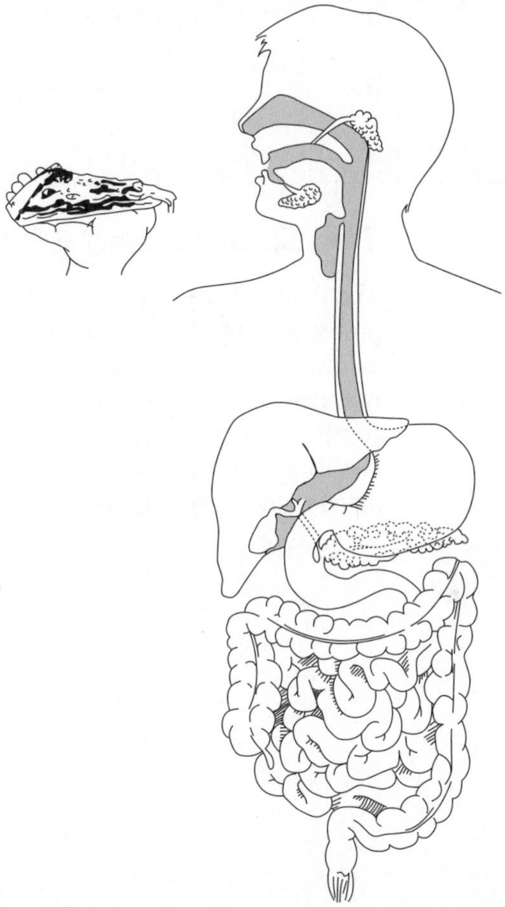

The digestive system uses **enzymes** which are chemically very acidic. These acids are produced when a stimulus (such as food) is present or can be produced in response to stress. When they are produced in the stomach and there is no food for them to digest, acids may have a digestive effect on the stomach's protective mucous lining. The area that has been damaged by the acids is called an **ulcer.** Several common regions in the digestive tract may be susceptible to this condition. Acids can also churn at the connection from the stomach to the **esophagus** (the tube from the mouth to the stomach). This is a sensitive area that is not used to having contact with digestive acids. A person with this condition is said to be suffering from **acid reflux**. The sharp pain in the chest area may be confused with the symptoms of a heart attack.

EXERCISE 13

The Digestive and Excretory Systems

Directions: Match the definitions on the left with the correct terms on the right from the reading.

1. ______	acidic chemicals used to digest	**a.** large intestine
2. ______	tube from mouth to stomach	**b.** enzymes
3. ______	portion of digestive path that absorbs nutrients	**c.** ulcer
4. ______	also known as the colon	**d.** esophagus
5. ______	damaged section of stomach lining	**e.** small intestine

Answers are on page 579.

The Skeletal and Muscular Systems

The human body depends on the **skeletal** and **muscular systems** for motion and protection. The human skeleton contains 206 bones, made mostly of the minerals calcium and phosphorus. The inner section of a bone has soft tissue called **marrow,** where blood cells are created. Bones are connected at places called **joints.** Some joints, such as the plates of the skull, are fixed. Some, such as the vertebrae, are slightly movable, and some are quite movable such as the elbow or the shoulder. **Ligaments** are attached to bones and help hold them together.

Human Skeleton

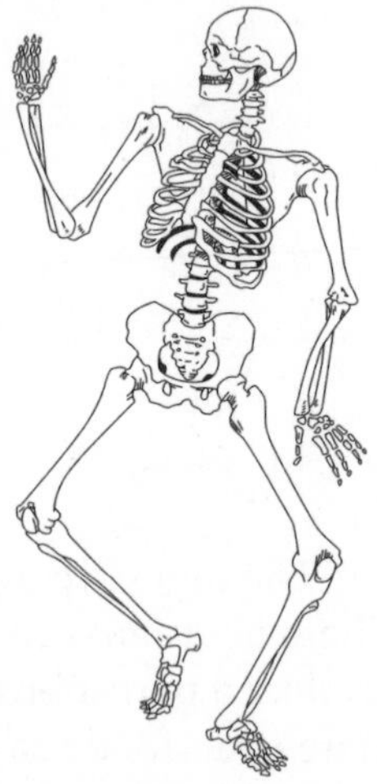

In order for bones to remain strong, calcium needs to be present in the diet. Warnings are given to women, especially as they advance in age, to take calcium supplements to maintain bone strength or density. If the bones lose density, they become brittle and break easily. This condition is referred to as **osteoporosis.**

The muscular system includes three types of muscles—skeletal, smooth, and cardiac muscles—which allow the skeleton of the human body to move and support itself. **Skeletal muscles** are responsible for voluntary movement. As these muscles contract, the attachment to the bone causes movement. **Smooth muscles** are found in the organs. Their contractions move food along the digestive tract and help blood move through the vessels. The **cardiac muscles** are found only in the heart; when they contract, the heart is said to "beat." This beating is the rhythm that pumps blood through the heart to the lungs and then out through the body.

Skeletal Muscle of Arm

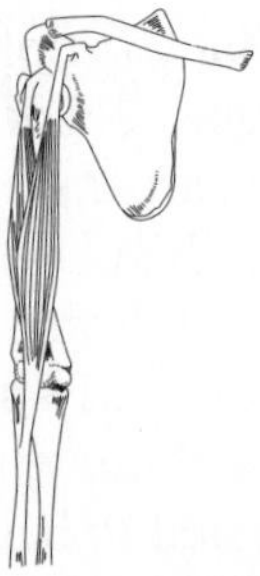

Weight lifters who are interested in adding to the bulk of their muscles often combine protein additives to their diet along with the weight training. For some, use of questionable muscle bulk stimulators has become popular. These chemicals are not without side effects, however. Studies show that those who use steroids have much greater health risk factors in major organs, and some steroids even have a negative effect on fertility and facial and body acne.

EXERCISE 14

The Skeletal and Muscular Systems

Directions: Based on the reading, fill in the blanks below.

1. There are three types of muscles: ____________________, ____________________, and ____________________.
2. The medical condition for having very brittle bones is called ____________________.
3. ____________________ may help build muscle bulk, but they also have negative side effects.
4. Blood cells are actually created in the ____________________ of the long bones.
5. The complete adult human body has ____________________ bones that make up the skeleton.
6. ____________________ are attached to bones to help hold them together.

Answers are on page 579.

Transplantation

Organs that have been damaged by disease or injury need to be replaced. This replacement procedure is called **transplantation.** Once a doctor has determined that an organ needs to be replaced, the patient is placed on a waiting list for an organ to become available. Organs are donated by the next of kin of someone who has died with organs still in good condition. The organ donors are matched by tissue type and blood type to decrease the chance of organ rejection by the immune system of the organ recipient. The types of organs and tissues that are transplanted include the heart, liver, kidneys, lungs, cornea, bone marrow, and skin.

Many people are apprehensive about transplantation. Some believe that they will feel different after organ transplantation. This is especially the case with heart-transplant recipients. Many psychologists warn that this reaction is normal because of the long association of emotions and personality traits with the heart. Some common expressions of this are: "I love you with all my heart" or "My heart belongs to you." Usually psychological counseling can help with the emotional acceptance of any organ transplant. Those who are interested in being organ donors are asked to fill out donor cards and sign the backs of their driver's licenses. The medical community also advises potential organ donors to communicate their wishes to family members because organ donations are not permitted without consent from the next of kin.

EXERCISE 15

Transplantation

Directions: Identify the following comments as opinion **(O)** or fact **(F)** according to the reading.

1. ______ If you have a heart transplant, you will feel uncomfortable knowing it was another person's organ.

2. ______ The immune system may try to reject a new organ.

3. ______ The next of kin is responsible for legally donating organs of the deceased.

4. ______ If the donor is an artist, the organ recipient will become more artistic.

5. ______ Organ donation is wrong because people should accept their "time" to die.

Answers are on page 579.

Writing Activity 2

Write two or three paragraphs about a situation in which you had a special concern with any of the organ systems described. What was the situation, and how did you deal with it?

Growth, Energy, and Living Things

Thus far, we have covered systems that are at work for the growth and development of animals, specifically humans. Some of the characteristics that distinguish living things from nonliving things are the capacities for growth, food consumption, and release of energy for cellular work. It is also important to look at the systems at work for growth and development of other living things, such as plants. Important biological processes involved in these functions for plants are the *nitrogen cycle, photosynthesis,* and *cellular respiration.*

The Nitrogen Cycle

Nitrogen, which makes up nearly 80 percent of Earth's atmosphere, is an essential ingredient for living tissues. Human beings and other animals depend on plants as a source of nitrogen. Plants cannot manufacture nitrogen themselves, so to obtain it they must depend on other organisms.

Free nitrogen, however, cannot be used by organisms, so it must combine with other elements to form **nitrates** that can be used. Plants absorb these nitrates to manufacture **amino acids,** which are essential components of protein needed by living cells. Amino acids are used to manufacture both proteins and nucleic acids that are absorbed by human beings and other animals.

The conversion of free nitrogen into a combined form is called **nitrogen fixing.** This is best achieved by certain bacteria—microorganisms and decomposers—that live in the soil. These microorganisms live in special sacs, called **nodules,** on the roots of legumes—plants such as alfalfa, peas, and beans. The microorganisms produce **nitrogenase,** an enzyme that is essential to nitrogen fixing.

Scientists believe that all of the nitrogen in Earth's atmosphere has been fixed and liberated many times. At any one time probably only a few pounds of nitrogenase exist on our planet. This small amount, however, is enough to sustain all life on Earth.

GED PRACTICE

EXERCISE 16

The Nitrogen Cycle

Directions: Choose the *best* answer for each of the following questions.

1. **Symbiosis describes the relationship between two organisms that are different but that live together for their mutual benefit. The microorganisms that live in the nodules attached to legumes may be described as symbiotic. What would be another example of a symbiotic relationship?**

   (1) bacteria that can live only in the stomachs of hoofed animals and that help the animals digest food
   (2) bees that make their hives in caves, thereby providing a ready source of food for bears
   (3) soldier ants that live and work together in colonies
   (4) tapeworms that live in the intestines of human beings
   (5) scavengers such as vultures that feed on the carcasses of dead animals

2. **Which of the following farming procedures best illustrates the process of increasing soil nutrients by assisting in nitrogen fixing?**

   (1) rotating a crop of cotton one year with a crop of beets
   (2) irrigating the land with more modern methods
   (3) using more advanced equipment to plow the land
   (4) rotating planting in alternating years with crops of soybeans or peas
   (5) using airplanes to spray the crops with insecticides

Answers are on page 579.

Photosynthesis

Plants provide the oxygen we need to breathe and the nutrients we need to thrive. Green plants are self-sufficient because they are able to make their own food, whereas human beings and lower animals must obtain their food to live. **Photosynthesis** is the food-making process by which green plants convert the light from the sun into usable chemical energy. The process of photosynthesis involves several steps.

The first step is the capture of energy by the plant. In most plants the process of photosynthesis takes place within the **chloroplasts,** where chlorophyll molecules absorb light. **Chlorophyll** is the substance that gives plants their green color. Using the energy that chlorophyll releases from sunlight, the plant splits water into its two components—oxygen and hydrogen. The oxygen is released to the atmosphere, and the hydrogen recombines with carbon dioxide to produce carbohydrate molecules (a form of starch) in the plant.

Two other chemicals inside the leaves do the same job as chlorophyll. **Xanthophyll** and **carotene** appear as yellow- and orange-colored pigments that are masked during the summer by the chlorophyll. Eventually the shorter daylight hours of fall cause the plant to stop the production of chorophyll, allowing us to see the other pigments.

The food that is created by photosynthesis is transported through the plant by the **phloem.** This cellular transport system carries the newly created food down the stem of the plant to the storage center called the root. Many roots (such as the carrot or the radish) are used by people as a food source. Water is transported by a similar system called the **xylem.** This cellular system allows the roots to take in water from the soil and transport it up to the leaves through the stem for the process of photosynthesis.

EXERCISE 17

Photosynthesis

Directions: Choose the *best* answer for each of the following questions.

1. Indicate whether the following statements are true (T) or false (F) about plants and the process of photosynthesis.

a. ______ Plants that do not possess chlorophyll must use a process other than photosynthesis to produce the energy they need.

b. ______ Photosynthesis is used by flowering plants to make energy by converting the sun's energy.

c. ______ Plants that do not use the process of photosynthesis must obtain food from another source.

Question 2 is based on the information in the following passage.

The leaves of certain plants have some areas that lack chlorophyll and some ares containing chlorophyll. A coleus plant, with its brightly colored leaves, is one example. In an experiment in which the pigment (color) of the coleus leaf is removed, an iodine solution will identify places where starch is present by turning that part of the leaf brown.

2. Which of the following would you predict to happen to a coleus leaf in such an experiment?

(1) The areas that were green originally would turn brown.
(2) The leaf would not turn brown at all.
(3) The leaf would turn yellow and red.
(4) The entire leaf would turn brown.
(5) Only half the leaf would turn brown.

Answers are on page 579.

Cellular Respiration

Cellular respiration is the complex series of chemical reactions through which a cell releases the energy trapped inside glucose molecules. **Glucose,** a form of sugar, is the end product of the process of photosynthesis. The process of cellular respiration, then, is the reverse of photosynthesis. During cellular respiration, cells (plant or animal) break down the glucose so that energy is released for cellular work. Because it cannot float freely in the cell, the energy is repackaged and stored.

Cellular respiration occurs in three stages, beginning with the breakdown of a molecule of glucose and ending with the energy needed for the cell to perform its work. Energy that is not used is released in the form of heat.

GED PRACTICE

EXERCISE 18

Cellular Respiration

Directions: Choose the *best* answer for each of the following questions.

1. **From the information about cellular respiration, what can we infer?**

   (1) Photosynthesis in plants must always precede cellular respiration.
   (2) No relationship exists between photosynthesis and cellular respiration.
   (3) Photosynthesis and respiration share many processes.
   (4) Cellular respiration occurs only in animal cells.
   (5) Plants do not perform cellular work.

2. **The rate of cellular respiration in humans can be measured by the amount of carbon dioxide exhaled. Which of the following would you expect to be true about the rate of cellular respiration for a group of students who are the same age, height, and weight?**

   (1) Africans would have a higher rate of cellular respiration than Asians.
   (2) Boys would have a higher rate of cellular respiration than girls.
   (3) Girls would have higher rates of cellular respiration than boys.
   (4) Physically active people would have higher rates of cellular respiration than nonphysically active people.
   (5) Nonathletes would have higher rates of cellular respiration than athletes.

3. **Which of the following procedures would be *most effective* in proving your hypothesis in the preceding example?**

   (1) measuring the amounts of carbon dioxide exhaled by the students immediately after they woke up
   (2) measuring the amounts of carbon dioxide exhaled by every student after vigorous exercise
   (3) measuring the amounts of carbon dioxide exhaled by one student at rest and another student after vigorous exercise
   (4) measuring the amounts of carbon dioxide exhaled by half the students at rest and half the students after vigorous exercise
   (5) taking a reading of all of the students' blood pressures over a week's time

4. **Gas exchange that occurs in the large forested areas on our planet helps keep the balance with all the carbon dioxide produced in human processes. In some areas large tracts of forests are being cut down by the logging industry. These areas are necessary to maintain the balance between the carbon dioxide and oxygen cycles. Which of the following suggestions would contribute most to maintaining these large forests?**

   (1) Pump out large amounts of oxygen to make up for the missing gas.
   (2) Have loggers replace the quantity of trees logged with new trees.
   (3) Make machines that would absorb the extra carbon dioxide.
   (4) Stop all logging all over the planet and stop using wood products.
   (5) Remove residents from populated areas and start new forests.

Answers are on page 579.

Classification of Organisms

Not only do we study internal organ systems, but we also relate and group organisms by similarities. The classification system for living things moves from the general to the specific. Each downward step in the classification system provides more details about the organism that is classified. The **kingdom** is the broadest grouping. Within each kingdom the organisms with the greatest similarities are grouped further into a **phylum,** followed by a **class.** The class is followed by an **order,** a **family,** a **genus,** and a **species.** The human classification (Homo sapiens) is illustrated in the following chart.

TAXONOMY OF HUMAN CLASSIFICATION

Category	Taxon	Characteristics
Kingdom	Animalia	Is multicellular, cannot make its own food, is able to move
Phylum	Chordata	Has a notochord (skeletal rod) and hollow nerve cord
Class	Mammalia	Has hair or fur, female secretes milk to nourish young
Order	Primate	Has flattened fingers for grasping, keen vision, poor sense of smell
Family	Hominidae	Walks on two feet, has flat face, eyes facing forward, color vision
Genus	Homo	Has long childhood, large brain, speech ability
Species	Sapiens	Has reduced body hair, high forehead, prominent chin

GED PRACTICE

EXERCISE 19

Classification of Organisms

Directions: Read the definitions of the five kingdoms, from lowest to highest, into which all living organisms are classified. Then choose the *best* answer for each of the questions that follow.

KINGDOMS OF LIVING ORGANISMS	
kingdom monera	simple one-celled, mobile organisms lacking organelles, some of which can produce their own food (Example: bacteria)
kingdom protista	single-celled, mobile organisms having a more complex cell structure than monera (Example: paramecia)
kingdom fungi	multicellular, lacks chlorophyll, cannot move, obtains food from other organisms (Example: mushroom)
kingdom plantae	multicellular, has chlorophyll, produces its own food, has no mobility (Example: moss)
kingdom animalia	multicellular, capable of moving and obtaining its own food (Example: bird)

1. **Streptococcus is a single-celled organism that has no organelles and that occurs in a sequence of chains. It causes strep throat when it invades that area. In which kingdom would it be classified?**

   (1) monera
   (2) protista
   (3) fungi
   (4) plantae
   (5) animalia

2. **Mold is a parasite that grows on bread, cheese, or other foods. It lacks chlorophyll and obtains nutrients from the host. In which kingdom would it be classified?**

   (1) monera
   (2) protista
   (3) fungi
   (4) plantae
   (5) animalia

Answers are on page 579.

Evolution and Natural Selection

Organisms are assigned classifications, but very often their characteristics are altered over generations. Organisms that go through such change are said to evolve. One explanation for these changes that has scientific support is the **theory of evolution.** Proposed in 1859 by **Charles Darwin** in his book *On the Origin of Species,* the theory holds that all forms of life developed gradually (over 600 million years) from different and often much simpler ancestors. With weaker or less adaptable strains dying out, these forms of life adapted over the years to meet the demands of their environment. Thus, all lines of descent can be traced back to a common ancestral organism.

As offspring differed from their parents, generations with characteristics that were less and less alike resulted. Ultimately, new species were formed from the diverse offspring because these new characteristics were inheritable.

The new characteristics of the offspring are explained by a process called natural selection. According to the theory of **natural selection,** the species that are best adapted to their living conditions survive, and those that do not adapt die out. This theory is also known as the "survival of the fittest." The **creationist theory** holds that all species have been created and remained unchanged since the beginning of time. Darwin demonstrated that evolution is an ongoing process whose final outcome has not yet been determined.

The studies of the theory of evolution began when Darwin was undergoing a natural history survey on his ship the *H.M.S. Beagle* in the Galapagos Islands. While on the islands, Darwin studied populations of finches. These small birds had been isolated on the islands for many generations, and several groups of these birds showed specific beak adaptations that allowed them to be successful in certain niches. Some of the birds had short beaks that could break nuts, and others had long beaks that let them feed off fish from the ocean. These adaptations or successful mutations allowed the varieties of finches to live together on the small islands without competing for food.

Great moments in evolution

GED PRACTICE

EXERCISE 20

Evolution and Natural Selection

Directions: Choose the *best* answer for each question below.

1. An unusual member of the animal kingdom is the duckbill platypus—an animal that has many characteristics of birds, mammals, and reptiles. The animal, found in Australia and Tasmania, has a ducklike bill, has webbed and clawed feet, is covered with thick fur, and reproduces by laying eggs. Which of the following hypotheses related to Darwin's theory of evolution could be applied to the platypus?

(1) The platypus is the result of the interbreeding of three distinct animal classes.
(2) The platypus is the earliest living member of the mammalian family.
(3) The platypus developed independently in a closed environment during the early history of mammals.
(4) The platypus was not subject to the influences described in Darwin's theory.
(5) Mammal life originated in Australia and Tasmania hundreds of millions of years ago.

Question 2 refers to the following passage.

Mammals are classified in two groups—**placental** (having a placenta that nourishes the fetus) and **marsupial** (having a pouch in which the young are nourished and carried). Most of the world's marsupials are found on the continent of Australia and the islands nearby, where few placental mammals lived during the early history of the continents.

2. What can we infer based on the preceding information about how marsupials differ from placental mammals?

(1) Marsupials are less biologically advanced than placental mammals.
(2) Placental mammals are more primitive than marsupials.
(3) Marsupials cannot survive in areas other than Australia and North America.
(4) Marsupials are the oldest forms of life on Earth.
(5) Marsupials descended from the reptiles.

3. Which of the following mammals does not exhibit a physical adaptation to environmental conditions?

(1) a bird's migration south
(2) an eagle's keen eyesight
(3) a mouse's sensitive ears
(4) a seal's flippers
(5) a bear's dense fur

Answers are on page 580.

Writing Activity 3

There has been a great deal of controversy about teaching the theory of evolution as science. In two paragraphs explain why it might be difficult for a science teacher to present the creationist argument in science class.

Ecology and Ecosystems

The science of **ecology** involves the interrelationship of a living organism with its nonliving environment. Ecology is the study of how we live on the planet Earth. The ecologist studies the relationships among the component organisms and their environments. A self-supporting environment is called an **ecosystem.** The photosynthetic producers, the consumers, the decomposers, and their environment constitute an ecosystem.

In a typical ecosystem the **primary producers** are the green plants that derive their energy from the sun. A **primary consumer** would be a rabbit that feeds on the leaves of the green plant. A **secondary consumer** in this ecosystem would be a fox that preys on the rabbit. A **tertiary,** or **third-level, consumer** would be the buzzard that feeds on the carcass that the fox leaves behind. Finally, **decomposers**—the bacteria and fungi that feed on the scraps left by the buzzard—provide the nitrates necessary for the green plants, the first link in this chain.

As environmentalists study the natural cycles, they begin to understand the impact of human intervention. Yellowstone (the first U.S. National Park), located in the northwest corner of Wyoming, was once the home to the gray wolf. Local ranchers were concerned that the wolf was a threat to their herds. They eliminated the population of wolves to protect their interests. Studies have shown that the natural food web that existed in that area kept a balance in the numbers and healthy qualities of the herds of hooved animals such as deer. The numbers of herbivores increased because there was no predator to limit their population. These herbivores challenged the natural area by overgrazing. This lack of available food made the remaining deer weaker and unable to fight off disease. The government has stepped in and started a reintroduction program for the gray wolf. The wolf pairs (male and female) have come from the Northern Rockies in Canada. The government has also guaranteed the local ranchers that they will be financially reimbursed for any animals killed by wolves.

The ecological balance of a community is delicate. The removal of one key element can destroy a system, sometimes permanently.

EXERCISE 21

Ecology and Ecosystems

Directions: The following passage describes an imbalance in a particular ecosystem. Read the passage and fill in the blanks below with the correct element in the ecosystem.

At the turn of the century, ranchers moved onto the grassy Kaibab Plateau in northern Arizona. They were attracted by the fine grazing areas and large numbers of deer for hunting. Fearing that the mountain lion, another inhabitant of the region, would prey on the cattle and deer, the ranchers waged a campaign to eliminate the cat from the plateau. They were successful in their effort, and mountain lions disappeared within a few years.

Their success produced terrible ecological results, however. Increased numbers of deer, along with herds of grazing cattle, stripped the land of all grasses. Soon, heavy rains caused major erosion, and the land was reduced to a fraction of its usefulness. This problem has occurred repeatedly where humans have changed an ecosystem without considering the possible consequences.

1. primary producer ____________________
2. primary consumers ________________ and ________________
3. tertiary consumer ____________________
4. The destruction of the ____________________ led to the increase of grazing by ____________________ and ____________________, which led to ____ of the land and its eventual ____________________ by heavy rains.

Answers are on page 580.

Go to **www.GEDScience.com** for additional practice and instruction!

CHAPTER 2

Earth and Space Science

Earth science is the study of the planet Earth—its origin and the forces at work that are constantly changing the surface of the planet. Earth science differs from the life sciences in that it focuses on nonliving rather than living things. Earth science is a very broad field that covers the subjects of astronomy, geology, meteorology, paleontology, and oceanography.

Astronomy: The Study of Space

One of the oldest fields of study in science deals with how Earth was created and how this planet fits into the design of the universe. **Astronomy** is the study of the size, movements, and composition of the planets, stars, and other deep-space objects. By observing the stars, planets, comets, and other objects in space, astronomers hope to understand how our planet was created and how it evolved. A number of important theories have been advanced to explain the beginning of Earth and the universe in which it lies. One such theory, which astronomers use to explain how the universe began and how the planets and the stars started their formation, is illustrated below.

The Beginning of the Universe

The leading theory to explain the origin of the universe is the **big bang theory**. According to this theory, a "cosmic egg," made up of dust and gas containing all the matter in the universe, exploded. This explosion occurred 15 to 20 billion years ago, creating the basic atoms of our lightest gases from which the stars formed. The big bang theory is widely accepted because it accounts for the measured expansion of the universe and the background radiation found in all directions in outer space. Scientists theorize, according to the **open universe theory,** that the universe will either continue the expansion indefinitely or begin a collapse. If enough mass can be identified in the universe, calculations show that the universe will gravitationally collapse at some point in the distant future; this is referred to as the **closed universe theory.** This collapse, also referred to as the *big crunch,* predicts that the total mass of the universe is large enough to gather up all matter into a concentrated central point.

The most distant objects detected by science are known as **quasars** (quasi-stellar radio sources). These objects are so far away that astronomers have no way of knowing what they are at this time. The light and energy that has arrived from these objects is about 16 billion years old. It is likely that the energy that we receive now came from these objects during their formation. Every time science investigates deep-space objects, scientists must remember that information we receive now took time to get to Earth. Even the light from the sun takes eight minutes to reach Earth. We will not know what is happening now on the sun for another eight minutes. The nearest star to the sun is Alpha Centauri, which is more than four light years away. We will not know the current condition of this star for another four years.

Stars and Galaxies

The big bang theory also explains how stars are formed. According to supporters of the theory, the energy from the bang was so powerful that matter lighter than air remained suspended in space (just as the energy from an explosion releases particles that remain in the atmosphere). Eventually, the force of gravity exerted itself, and the matter was drawn, along with helium and hydrogen gases, into dark, cloudlike formations called **nebulae.** The gaseous matter became compressed, and the colliding of the compressed particles produced heat. A star developed when the temperature reached 15 million degrees centigrade—the temperature at which the nuclear reaction called **fusion** begins.

The lifetime of a star ranges from a few hundred thousand years to billions of years. Most stars eventually use up their supply of hydrogen, which ends the fusion reaction and leaves only gravity. The compaction without the energy source at the center forces the outer layers to swell as they become cooler. This is said to be the **red giant stage,** which marks the beginning of the death of a star. The outer layers are cast off in a process called a **nova** (with the explosive release of these outer layers called a **supernova**).

The explosion results in clouds of dust and gas, referred to as a **nebula,** with the core of the star's being left after the release of the outer layers. The core collapses under remaining gravity into a **dwarf star.** If the collapse is more significant (from a more massive star), a very dense star called a **neutron star** will be created. These stars spin at a very fast rate and are nicknamed **pulsars** as a result of energy released from their poles as they spin. The most massive stars, which are said to be **black holes**—remains of the giant stars that have gravitational fields so strong that not even light escapes from them—contract indefinitely.

Stars exist within a very large formation called a **galaxy.** Hundreds of millions of galaxies are believed to exist in the universe. They are also grouped together. The universe is a very organized system of grouped objects separated by great expanses of space. Our galaxy, **the Milky Way**, is a spiral galaxy. The other galaxy shapes include barred spirals, ellipticals, and irregulars. The Milky Way is composed of at least 100 billion stars and enough matter, in the form of dust and gas, to create millions of additional suns. The following illustration shows the heart of the Milky Way galaxy.

THE MILKY WAY GALAXY

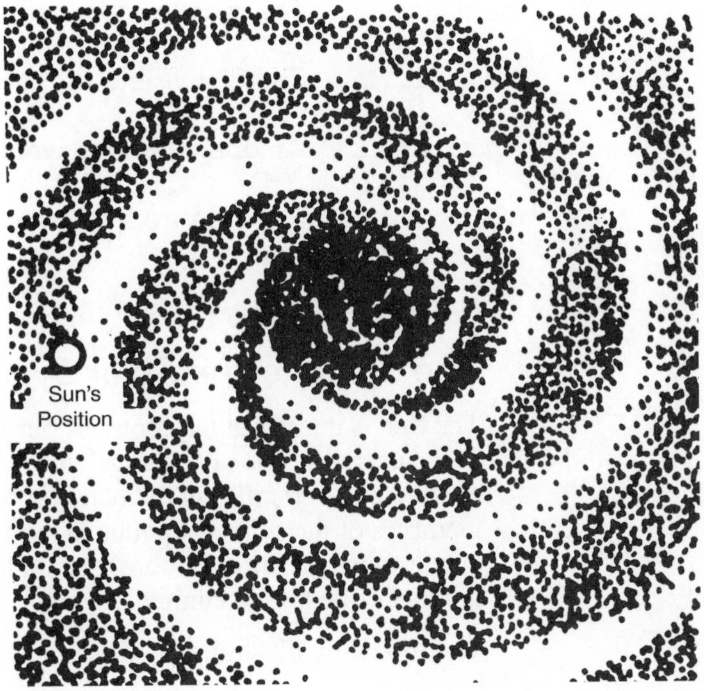

EXERCISE 1

Stars and Galaxies

Directions: Answer the following questions based on the information in the reading.

1. Number the steps in star formation in the correct sequence.

_____ Heat is produced by the colliding of molecules.

_____ Fifteen million degrees centigrade is reached, and visible light is emitted.

_____ Dust and gas move throughout the universe.

_____ Gas and dust become compressed because of gravitational forces.

2. Identify the following statements as either true (T) or false (F).

_____ The most massive stars become pulsars.

_____ The first visible sign of a star's death is a red giant.

_____ An open universe would expand until gravity stops it.

_____ The light from all stars takes eight minutes to reach Earth.

Answers are on page 580.

The Sun and the Solar System

The Sun is the star at the center of our **solar system**. Compared to other stars in the universe, it is of "average" mass and age. The Sun is 4 to 5 billion years old and 860,000 miles in diameter (about 100 times Earth's diameter). Other members of the solar system include the nine **planets,** seven of which have one or more **satellites** (moons), 1,600 large **asteroids,** and an ever increasing number of identified **comets.**

The following illustration shows our solar system.

Our Solar System

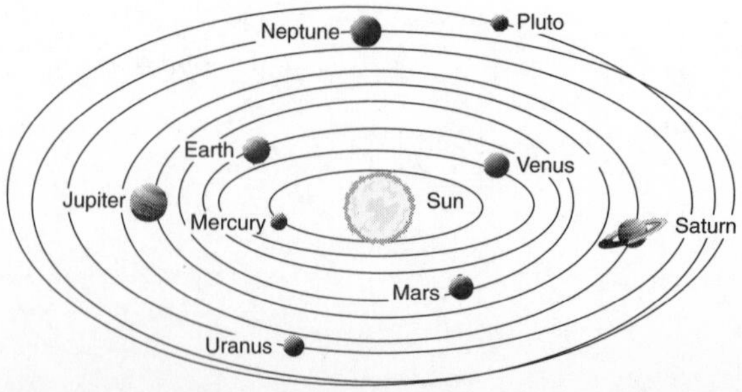

The inner planets (**Mercury, Venus, Earth,** and **Mars**) are small, with high densities and few satellites. At first, Venus was nicknamed our twin or sister planet because its diameter and distance to the Sun are close to those of Earth. We have since sent probes to the surface of Venus and have found it to be a remarkably hostile world. The cloud cover blocked any long-range views of the surface, and some scientists made the assumption that it was likely a tropical or jungle planet. The Russians sent probes called *venera* to the surface. Before these probes melted and were no longer able to transmit information, they were able to send photographs of the surface as well as climate readings. The surface is dry, and it is far too hot for water to exist. Moisture that does occur in the heavy cloud cover is sulfuric acid. The cloud cover is also mainly carbon dioxide, the greenhouse gas. The runaway greenhouse effect on the surface makes the temperature hot enough to melt metal on the surface. The atmosphere is so dense that it makes the atmospheric pressure one hundred times greater than it is on Earth.

Mars is more likely to be a place that people may explore. Early probes have determined that there is water in a permafrost form under the martian soil. Early views of Mars led people to believe that Mars had civilization that had created water canals or an irrigation system. Closer views reveal that the surface has evidence of stream beds that contained water when the planet was warmer. U.S. probes have sent back photos and information about the surface features and climate conditions.

Two distinct landform features include *Mons Olympus* (the highest mountain in the solar system at three times the height of Mt. Everest) and *Vallis Marineris* (a canyon that would stretch from New York to Los Angeles). Colonization of Mars would depend on our ability to terreform the surface of the planet. Terreforming is climatic changing of a planet to fit the needs of the life forms creating the change.

The outer planets (**Jupiter, Saturn, Uranus,** and **Neptune**) are large gas giants and have many moons. **Pluto,** the most remote of all the distant planets, is so far from the Sun that it is an icy world that sees our sun as only a faint star. Galileo observed some of these gas giants. He was the first to see the four large moons that orbit Jupiter. We now refer to these as the Galilean moons, and they are visible as small points of light near Jupiter through binoculars or a telescope. We have discovered that the colorful bands on Jupiter's gaseous surface travel in opposite directions. These wind belts also cause great hurricane-like storms on the surface. One such storm, the Great Red Spot, has been observed for more than 300 years.

Saturn is known for its extensive ring system. All the outer gaseous planets have some ring system, but the small moons around Saturn actually keep the rings distinct by clearing up any loose particles. The density of Saturn is less than that of water, and it has been joked that it would float in a large bathtub but would leave a "ring"!

The planets are believed to have begun as clumps of matter within the dust cloud that formed the Sun. They were too small to achieve the conditions needed to become stars. Instead, they cooled and became the planets as we know them. Our space probes have reached all except the most distant outer planets, and it appears that Earth is the only inhabited body in our solar system.

EXERCISE 2

The Sun and the Solar System

Directions: Choose the *best* answer for each of the following items.

1. **The "Goldilocks problem" in astronomy (in which one of the eight planets other than Earth is too hot to support life and the other too cold to support life) applies to which two planets?**

   (1) Pluto and Neptune
   (2) Mars and Saturn
   (3) Mercury and Venus
   (4) Venus and Mars
   (5) Jupiter and Uranus

2. **Match each planet on the left with the correct characteristic on the right.**

   _____ Jupiter **a.** most extensive ring system

   _____ Mars **b.** Galilean Moons

   _____ Saturn **c.** hottest surface temperature

   _____ Venus **d.** highest mountain

3. **Identify which of the following planetary facts are true (T) and which are false (F).**

   _____ Jupiter has huge dust storms on the surface.

   _____ Early views of Mars led us to believe there were irrigation canals.

   _____ Jupiter has bands of winds that blow in opposite directions.

   _____ The sun is between four and five billion years old.

   _____ Venus has a thick cloud that produces rain every day.

Answers are on page 580.

EXERCISE 3

Space Travel

Directions: Read the following passage and choose the *best* answers for the item that follows.

People have pursued travel into space in order to collect information without the use of probes. Space capsules built to support human life during space travel started with the NASA (National Aeronautics and Space Administration) flights to the moon in the 1960s. Those craft were engineered for one, two, or three-person flight missions. The next generation of spacecraft started the concept of space stations (such as Skylab and the Russian station Mir) to test the long-term effects of space and microgravity.

Currently, the United States has a small fleet of space shuttle-craft called **orbiters**. These ships were created to reenter the atmosphere and land like an airplane. After servicing, the shuttles are relaunched into space. These shuttles are also part of the construction and maintenance of the new International Space Station. This station is a mutual construction and research effort from many countries interested in advancing knowledge about the future of humanity in space.

1. **Number the following spacecraft in order of their creation.**

   ______ international space station

   ______ probes

   ______ orbiters

   ______ capsules

   ______ space station (skylab)

2. **Finish the following sentences based on information provided in the above reading.**

   1. Orbiter space crafts are made to re-enter the atmosphere and ____________________.
   2. The Space Station is being constructed by ____________________.
   3. The two previous space stations were called ____________________ and ____________________.
   4. N.A.S.A. stands for ____________________.

Answers are on page 580.

EXERCISE 4

The Planets

Directions: Use the information in the table to complete each of the statements that follow. Write the name of the correct planet in the blank.

Planet	Length of Year	Rotates on Its Axis Every	Number of Satellites	Distance from Sun (miles)
Mercury	88 days	58 days	0	36 million
Venus	225 days	243 days	0	67 million
Earth	365.26 days	23.9 hours	1	93 million
Mars	686.98 days	24.6 hours	2	142 million

1. The length of the day is approximately the same on ____________________ and ____________________.

2. Of the planets listed, based on Earth years, you would age at the fastest rate on ____________________.

3. Mars takes a little more than three times longer to revolve around the Sun than does ____________________.

Answers are on page 580.

Writing Activity 1

Space has always intrigued us. Deep space is so vast that we can understand and study only a small part of it. This allows us to imagine possible realities of other worlds and other intelligent life-forms. Have you ever seen a movie or read a book about space travel? In two or three paragraphs, explain how the film or book described the life-forms or other worlds that might exist. Do you think that their description is possible?

Geology: The Forces that Shape Our Earth

Planetary surface conditions identify each planet as a unique world. No planet has the same surface conditions as our own Earth. Historically, the Earth's crust has been referred to as rock solid. It was only recently that geologists have been able to measure and record the motion of the crust. The surface is constantly changing because of forces such as volcanoes and earthquakes. **Geology** is the study of the features of Earth and how they affect its development. In the last century alone, geologists made significant discoveries that revolutionized the entire field of earth science. Probably the most significant of all findings made in recent history has been the formulation of the **Plate Tectonics Theory,** which explains the development of mountains and ocean trenches and the occurrence of earthquakes and volcanic eruptions.

Continental Drift and Plate Tectonics

Scientists have long observed that accurately drawn maps of Africa and South America suggest that the two continents once fit together. Using this observation, called the **jigsaw fit,** geologists formulated the **Theory of Continental Drift.** According to the theory all seven continents formed a supercontinent millions of years ago called **Pangaea.** It broke apart and split into the land masses that are recognized today as the seven continents.

Despite the fact that the continents appear to interlock like pieces of a puzzle, scientists could not explain why the continents drifted apart. The **Plate Tectonics Theory**, advanced in the 1960s, provided an explanation of the phenomenon. According to the theory, Earth is made up of the crust, mantle, outer core, and inner core, as depicted in the following illustration:

Earth's Structure

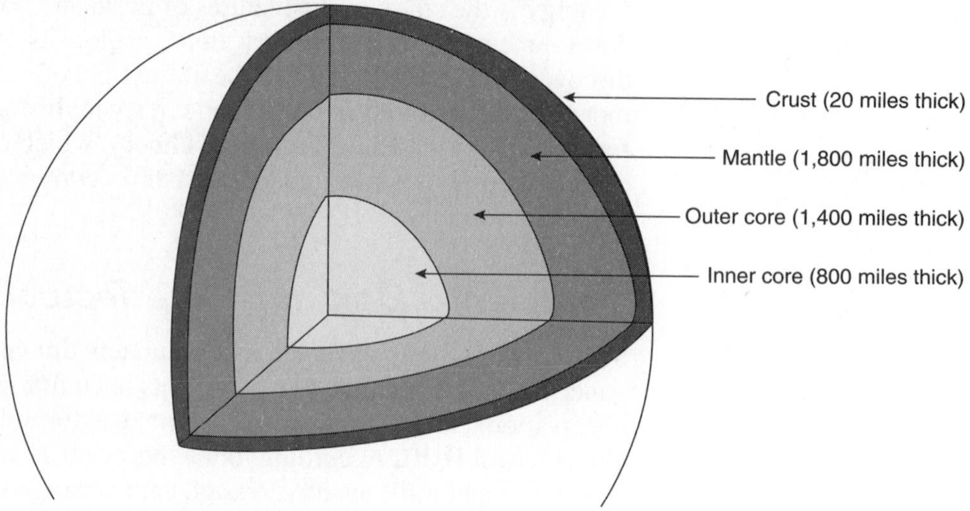

The crust and upper mantle are made up of about twenty plates. These plates may be likened to plates floating on the surface of water in a vast sink. They move very slowly—approximately one-half inch to four inches per year. Attached to the surface of these plates are the continents and the ocean floor. As the plates slowly move, they carry the continents with them. Geologists explain that the plates move because currents of partially-molten rock in the mantle carry them.

This motion can be demonstrated when a saucepan of liquid, such as soup or spaghetti sauce, is placed on a burner of the stove. As the liquid near the bottom of the pan gets hot, it rises to the surface and moves out of the way for the newer, hotter material that is rising right behind it. Earth's mantle is like liquid, heated by the core. As it rises to the surface (the crust), it moves over to make room for the newer, hotter mantle rising right behind it. The older cooler material is denser and, therefore, sinks back to near the core, where it is heated again. This circulation pattern is called a **convection current,** and it is responsible for the motion experienced at the crust.

GED PRACTICE

EXERCISE 5

Plate Tectonics

Directions: Choose the *best* answer for each of the following questions.

1. **According to the passage, the Theory of Plate Tectonics helps explain which of the following?**

   (1) Earth's gravitational pull
   (2) earthquakes, volcanoes, and mountains
   (3) the theory of continental drift
   (4) seasonal changes
   (5) magnetic north and south poles

2. **Which of the following *could not* be the result of plate tectonics as described in the reading above?**

   (1) mid-oceanic ridges where the seafloor is splitting open
   (2) large volcanic mountain ranges along crustal boundaries
   (3) the movement of the western portion of California in a northern direction
   (4) a deep glacier valley region found in mountain ranges of the far North
   (5) earthquakes that occur near moutain boundary regions as in South America

Answers are on page 580.

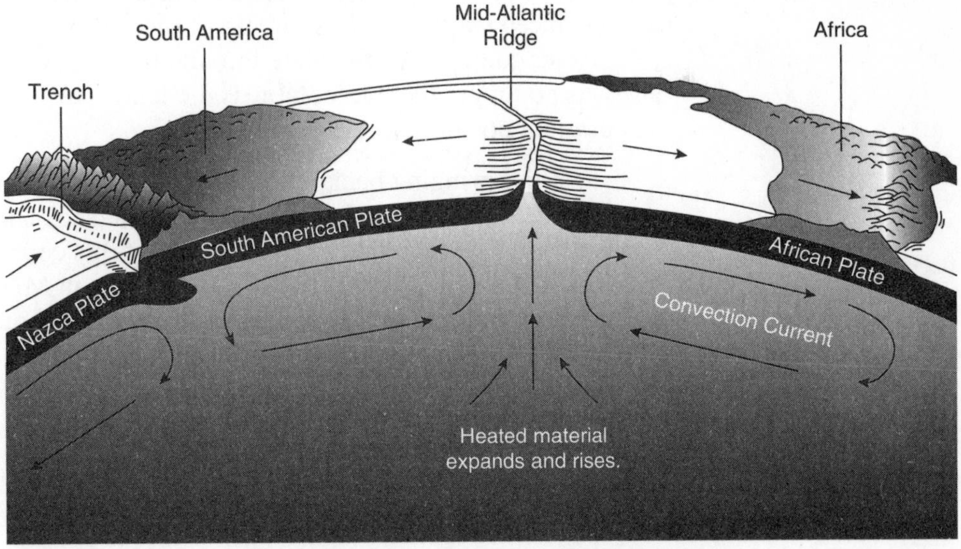

Mountain Formation and Earthquakes

This motion of the plates appears to explain the formation of mountains and ocean trenches and the occurrence of earthquakes and volcanoes. For example, when two plates collide, one plate piles atop another, forming a mountain. This action is known as **buckling.** Some mountains that have been created in this manner are the Himalayas of Tibet and the Alps in southern Europe, near Italy.

When one plate is forced down into the mantle of another, a **trench** is created. A **volcano** occurs when the heat beneath the surface of Earth melts the plate material that was forced into the trench and sends the molten rock to the surface. This type of plate boundary action, called **subduction,** occurs all along the North and South American continents. The Cascade Mountains in Oregon and Washington are a volcanic chain created by subduction. The Andes of Peru are also volcanic as a result of the Pacific Plate's being melted under the South American Plate. Islands called *island arcs* are also created in this manner. Japan and the Philippines, as well as the Aleutian Islands off Alaska's coast, have frequent volcanic eruptions as a result of their origins by subduction.

An **earthquake** is formed by the shifting and breaking of the surface rocks when two plates slide past each other. This plate boundary action is called **translocation** or **transform faulting.** The best example of two plate boundaries that are slowly grinding past each other occurs in the San Andreas Fault in California. The San Andreas system passes through San Francisco and travels southward past San Diego out through the Gulf of California. The Pacific Plate is slowly moving in a northwesterly direction. This movement will eventually carry the coast of California north to the Alaskan shore.

The vibrations caused by the slippage of plates are called **seismic waves.** The strength of these waves is measured by a device called a **seismograph** and then rated on the **Richter Scale.** Earthquakes measuring more than 4.5 on the Richter Scale are considered potentially dangerous.

Some of the strongest earthquakes are felt not along plate boundaries but in the central regions of the continents. One such location is the midwestern United States. At one point in its geologic history, this region was covered with a mile-high block of ice. During the last ice age, one such block of ice advanced south to almost the tip of the state of Illinois. The weight of this glacier compressed the plate into the mantle. After the ice melted, the weight was no longer there to compress the land. The land began to spring back to its original position on the mantle.

This springing back up of the land, called **elastic rebounding,** continues until the crustal plate in this area is in balance. The balance point is known as **isostasy.** The fault that exists because of this compression and springing up is called the New Madrid fault, after the town in Missouri that is found where the fault follows the Mississippi River. In 1911, one of the largest earthquakes in the history of the United States occurred along the New Madrid faultline. Geologists predict that another large-scale earthquake will occur at the same location sometime in the future.

GED PRACTICE

EXERCISE 6

Earthquakes

Directions: Choose the *best* answer, according to the map below, for the questions that follow.

U.S. Earthquake Zones and Seismic Risk

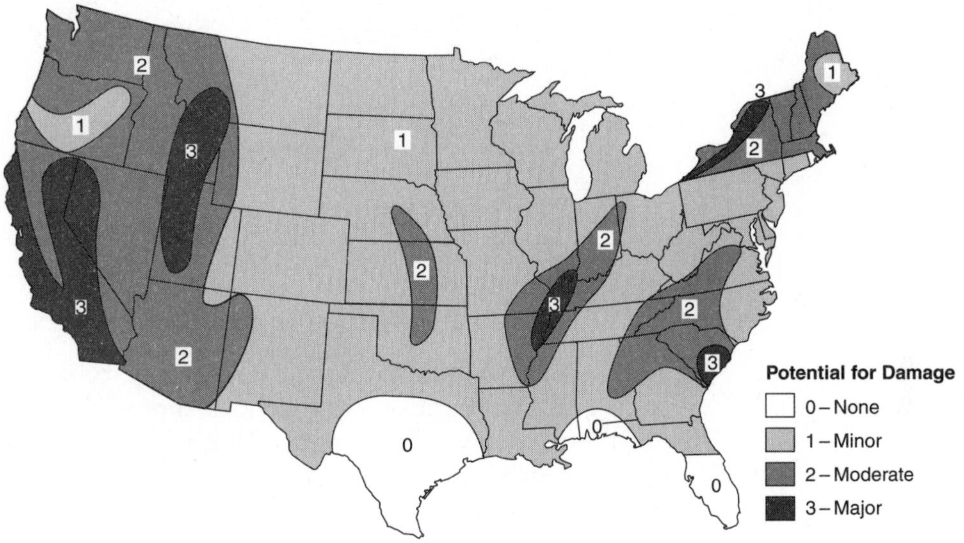

1. Which of the following statements about earthquakes is supported by the map?

(1) California is the only state in which residents might expect major earthquake damage.
(2) Texas and Florida are the only states that do not have to worry about earthquakes.
(3) The greatest potential for moderate to major earthquake damage is in the Western United States.
(4) Most of the continental United States is not affected by earthquakes.
(5) Earthquakes are the most dangerous phenomenon on Earth.

2. Identify which of the following statements are true (T) and which are false (F).

_______ Seismic waves can also be called vibrations.

_______ The springing back up of the land is called isostasy.

_______ All earthquakes occur along plate boundaries.

_______ One plate forced under another plate is called subduction.

Answers are on page 581.

Writing Activity 2

Earthquakes are common in some locations around the Earth. California has the edge of one active plate that causes periodic earthquakes to hit from San Fransico to Los Angeles. In one or two paragraphs, describe how you think the government should prepare for the fact that their region is in an active geologic center. Do you think that they should have regulations about building codes and emergency plans that would not be necessary for other regions? What might be some reasons that people would choose to live in a high risk area?

EXERCISE 7

The Pacific Northwest

Directions: Use the information in the passage below to identify the following statements as opinion **(O)** or fact **(F)**.

The Cascade Mountain Range in northwestern United States has seen volcanic eruptions throughout time. Scientists explain that the Northwest Pacific Coast of the United States is part of the Ring of Fire that surrounds the Pacific Ocean. The Pacific Ocean basin is being dragged under surrounding continental plates and melted by the hot magma deep inside the crust. When this additional buildup of magma creates pressure on the softer crustal layers above, a volcano is created. The volcanos of the Cascade Range will, therefore, be active while the Pacific Basin continues to be melted under the region.

1. ______ If you move to the Pacific Northwest, you will be killed by a volcanic eruption.

2. ______ The Cascade Mountains will never erupt again and are considered extinct.

3. ______ The states of California, Oregon, and Washington are on the Ring of Fire.

4. ______ It is much more dangerous to live on the West Coast than on the East Coast.

Answers are on page 581.

GED PRACTICE

EXERCISE 8

Continental Drift

Directions: Read the passage below and choose the *best* answer for the question that follows.

Ascension Island is a small volcanic island located in the South Atlantic halfway between Africa and South America. It is a famous breeding ground for sea turtles. Giant green turtles each year swim more than 2,000 miles from the coast of South America to lay their eggs on Ascension Island. This phenomenon has puzzled scientists for years.

Which of the following geological hypotheses best explains the behavior of the giant sea turtles?

(1) Ascension Island is the only place in the world where turtle eggs can survive.
(2) Predators, such as alligators that live on the coast of South America, eat turtle eggs, forcing the sea turtles to migrate.
(3) The turtles laid their eggs on Ascension Island millions of years ago before the continents of Africa and South America became separated.
(4) The turtles have found that the climate on Ascension Island is the best for turtle eggs.
(5) Ascension Island authorities have passed laws to protect the turtles by creating a nature sanctuary.

Answer is on page 581.

Geologic Time

The drifting of continents and the formation of mountains are very gradual events that occur over a long period of time (possibly millions of years!). What is a long period of time to you? You might consider 50 years a long time. In geology, however, 50 years is not very long, because **geologic time** extends back nearly five billion years, when geologists believe Earth was formed. We owe our concept of **absolute time**—time not influenced by man's arbitrary reference points—to geology. Geologists are able to fix periods of time by studying the rocks found in Earth's crust. These rocks serve as records of time.

The rocks found in Earth's crust are of three types, described according to their origins. These rocks are igneous, metamorphic, and sedimentary. **Igneous rocks** are formed when molten rock (**magma**) hardens. **Metamorphic rocks** are those that have been changed by high pressure and temperature within the crust. **Sedimentary rocks** are made of pieces or sediments that were weathered or broken up, then cemented and compacted together. In sedimentary rock, the oldest layers are on the bottom and the youngest are on the top.

The Rock Cycle

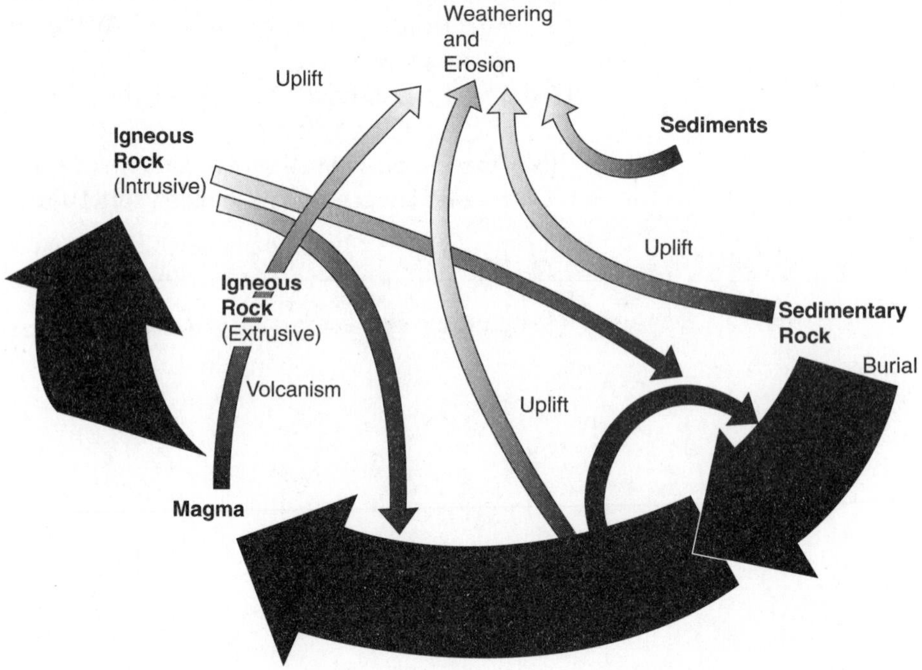

Instruments for Measuring Time

We have determined which rocks are older than others, but how do we find out how old that is? Radiometric measurement is one tool that scientists use to measure absolute time. In **radiometric measurement,** geologists measure the rate of radioactive decay in the minerals found in the rock. Over the last century, scientists have learned that radioactive substances will change, or decay, into nonradioactive substances over a period of time. This method is valid for matter up to 50,000 years old. Radiometric dating works well with samples of igneous and sedimentary rocks because it measures the radioactivity of minerals created when the rocks were formed. For metamorphic rock, however, the age of the original rock and the age of metamorphism are difficult to pinpoint.

Geologists also can examine the types of animal fossils found in layers of sedimentary rock so as to give an estimation of the rock's age. Igneous and metamorphic rock rarely contain fossils. Scientists have found that certain layers of sedimentary rock contain certain kinds of fossils, no matter where in the world the rock is located. Moreover, scientists have found that certain fossils are always found at lower layers than others, indicating that a sequence exists to the evolution of organisms.

GED PRACTICE

EXERCISE 9

Measuring Geologic Time

Directions: Choose the *best* answer for each of the following questions.

1. According to the information in the preceding passage, which correctly describes the placement of the three types of rocks?

(1) Igneous rock is located at the surface, metamorphic in the middle, and sedimentary on the bottom.
(2) Sedimentary rock is located at the surface, metamorphic in the middle, and igneous at the bottom.
(3) Metamorphic rock is located at the surface, sedimentary in the middle, and igneous at the bottom.
(4) Igneous rock is located at the surface, sedimentary in the middle, and metamorphic at the bottom.
(5) Sedimentary rock is located at the surface, igneous in the middle, and metamorphic at the bottom.

2. Trilobite fossils are found at a depth of 18 meters in a rock bed, and coral fossils are found at 14 meters. Which of the following is likely to be true about each organism?

(1) Coral is older than trilobites.
(2) Coral and trilobites are the same age.
(3) Coral and trilobites share a common ancestry.
(4) Trilobites are more advanced than corals.
(5) Trilobites are older than corals.

Answers are on page 581.

Minerals and Rocks

Minerals are the building blocks of rocks. A **mineral** is a natural, inorganic solid with a specific composition and structure. All specimens of a given mineral share certain physical properties. Some physical properties of minerals are crystalline form, hardness, color, and cleavage (the way they break). More than 95 percent of Earth's crust is made up of the minerals formed from the elements oxygen and silicon. The following chart shows the eight main elements, including the percentage of the crust's weight and volume that they occupy.

Element	Percentage of Crust's Mass (weight)	Percentage of Crust's Volume (space)
Oxygen	46.71	94.24
Silicon	27.69	0.51
Aluminum	8.07	0.44
Iron	5.05	0.37
Calcium	3.65	1.04
Sodium	2.75	1.21
Potassium	2.58	1.85
Magnesium	2.08	0.27

GED PRACTICE

EXERCISE 10

Minerals and Rocks

Directions: Choose the *best* answer for each of the following questions.

1. According to the information in the table, which element represents less of the crust's weight but occupies more than three times the space of silicon, a major component of the crust?

(1) sodium
(2) calcium
(3) potassium
(4) magnesium
(5) iron

2. Which of the following *best* explains why oxygen, a gas, is the largest component of Earth's crust?

(1) Oxygen gives Earth's crust its lightness.
(2) Oxygen is the most abundant element in the world.
(3) Oxygen is found in plants, which occupy significant parts of Earth's crust.
(4) Oxygen is needed to sustain all life on Earth.
(5) Oxygen is capable of combining with most of the elements in Earth's crust.

Answers are on page 581.

Writing Activity 3

Many people have a special interest in minerals that have certain qualities. Some of these qualities are said to be curative, warding off disease or changing moods. Some of these qualities are known as gemstone values. Jewelry is often sold with gemstones said to be birthstones for particular months. In one or two paragraphs, write about your birthstone (if you know what it is) or write about your favorite mineral or gemstone.

The Changing Earth

Erosion is the transportation of weathered pieces of bedrock through the agents of wind, water (rivers and ice), and gravity. As mountains are built up by tectonic forces, they are also broken down and carried away by weathering and erosion.

The pull of **gravity** makes surface material move downward. Downslope movements may be rapid or very slow. They may involve only the surface material, or they may involve the bedrock underneath. Houses built on hills can contribute to soil movements because the weight of the homes may add to the gravitational force. Wind contributes to the erosional process by carrying surface material from one location to another. **Glaciers,** huge sheets of ice that can move slowly over land, pick up and carry rocks and soil with them. When they pass through river valleys, the glaciers deepen those valleys. Mountain glaciers, coupled with the downward force of gravity, create avalanches that can cause great erosional damage.

Of all the erosional agents, running water is the most powerful. Rivers, working with the force of gravity, have a devastating erosional impact. The action of rivers flowing against the land has formed gorges as large as the Grand Canyon. As rivers erode land, they carry deposits with them. **Deltas** are formed at the mouths of rivers that empty into a lake or an ocean. The soil that is carried along a river and deposited at its mouth is the richest and most fertile of all soils. The Nile and Mississippi Rivers have formed deltas that are noted for their rich soil, making these regions highly desirable for agriculture.

Soil Conservation

Erosion has proven to be one of farmers' worst fears. In the 1930s many farmers of the central plains of the United States overused their land; this meant that the nutrient content had no time to recover. The crops grown in such soil were weak; thus, when an extended drought struck crops quickly died. With no plant roots to hold the soil, high winds blew much of the topsoil away from this farming region, which became known as the **Dust Bowl.** The devastation took place at a very sensitive time in the United States economy. Many of the farming families could not make the payments on their farms and lost the land in foreclosure by banks.

The U.S. government realized that the health of the nation depended on strong agriculture. The government started programs to assist farmers financially and to teach soil conservation techniques that would prevent this crisis from happening in the future. Some techniques used to prevent erosion include planting trees for windbreak barricades, using contour plowing so the wind and water cannot pick up speed to carry soil away, or terracing or making flat fields along hillsides to create more growing land. Other techniques are resting and revitalizing soil with nutrients from plants (such as beans) or fertilizers or letting the land have some resting time to recover.

Much of the fear of losing the soil so necessary for successful farming comes from the realization of how long it takes for natural processes to create even an inch of topsoil. The process begins with the breakdown of the bedrock material. This action is called **weathering.** Eventually the bedrock is broken down into small particles and mixed with water and minerals to form the new layer called **subsoil.** Subsoil does not have the organic material necessary to provide nutrients to assist with growing plants. This organic material comes from the decomposition and decay of dead plant and animal tissue with organic material referred to as **humus.** Humus is a necessary part of any fully developed soil layer called **topsoil.** This creation of layers takes hundreds of years to finish what is called a mature soil profile.

EXERCISE 11

The Changing Earth

Directions: Choose the *best* answer for each of the following items.

1. Name the agent of erosion most likely responsible for the following landform features.

______________________ large boulders that tumble down the slope of a hill or cliff

______________________ sand dunes that move and change location in the desert

______________________ a wide valley that used to be as narrow as the river that cut the valley

______________________ a flood plain area that has the top soil layer removed during heavy rains

2. Which of the following procedures followed by a farmer is *not* related directly to preventing erosion?

(1) planting grass in gullies to act as a filler
(2) planting crops in alternate rows (strip farming)
(3) contour plowing around a hill
(4) planting new trees to replace those that die
(5) planting more seeds than are necessary to yield a bountiful crop

3. Determine and label the following statements as either fact (F) or opinion (O).

a. _______ Many farmers of the Midwest had no choice but to overfarm in the 1930s.

b. _______ The United States government should not tell farmers how to grow crops.

c. _______ Soil conservation techniques are necessary to avoid another Dust Bowl.

d. _______ The Dust Bowl occurred in the central plains of America in the 1930s.

Answers are on page 581.

Paleontology: The Study of Past Life

Paleontology is the study of the evidence of Earth's past. Rock layers hold fossils that can be identified and connected to a long history of life-form changes for planet Earth. Some of the fossil remains are of large dinosaurs that once roamed the land. These dinosaurs are extinct now; and only a few distant descendants, such as the alligator and the crocodile, remain. Scientists study how the conditions of the Earth might have changed to have had quite an impact on extremely successful organisms such as the dinosaurs. By understanding the conditions of Earth and examining the changes, we hope to learn and prevent future changes that might affect human existence.

© The Field Museum Neg #GN89714-2C

Sue, the most complete skeleton of a Tyrannosaurus Rex ever found, is on display at the Field Museum in Chicago.

Paleontologists have had great success in studying the past through rock layers in the Grand Canyon. Nature has provided a very easy way of examining the layers of the Earth without having to drill down through the crust. The Colorado River created the way for us over the millions of years that it has cut throught the sedimentary layers. These layers are nicely ordered and hold information about the changes of climate and weather conditions that have affected Earth.

A specialized field within paleontology is **archaeology,** the study of historic and prehistoric peoples and their cultures. Archaeologists study past civilizations by examining the remaining artifacts (tools and pottery), structures (monuments and dwellings), and recorded inscriptions (writing and drawings).

Writing Activity 4

Choose one of the following questions and write a paragraph about what you think might be the answer.

1. What might be a reason that someone is attracted to the field of paleontology?
2. Why do you think it is valuable to study the fossil history of the world?
3. Why do people find dinosaurs so interesting?

Oceanography: The Study of Earth's Oceans

Earth's surface is 71 percent covered by oceans. The study of large bodies of water is called **oceanography.** From their studies of the oceans, oceanographers have made many discoveries that help them to understand and explain phenomena they observe on Earth. For example, the theory of plate tectonics was further substantiated by the finding that a ridge encircling the globe lies under the ocean—the **oceanic ridge.**

This ridge circles the globe like the seam of a baseball. Numerous openings have been photographed along the crest of this ridge. Evidence from the pictures provided the basis for the theory that magma forces itself up from the ridges, pushes the ocean plates apart, cools, and forms new rock that becomes part of the ocean plate. Inventions such as **sonar** (an underwater ranging device), deep-diving submarines, and remote-control cameras have aided in our exploration of the oceans.

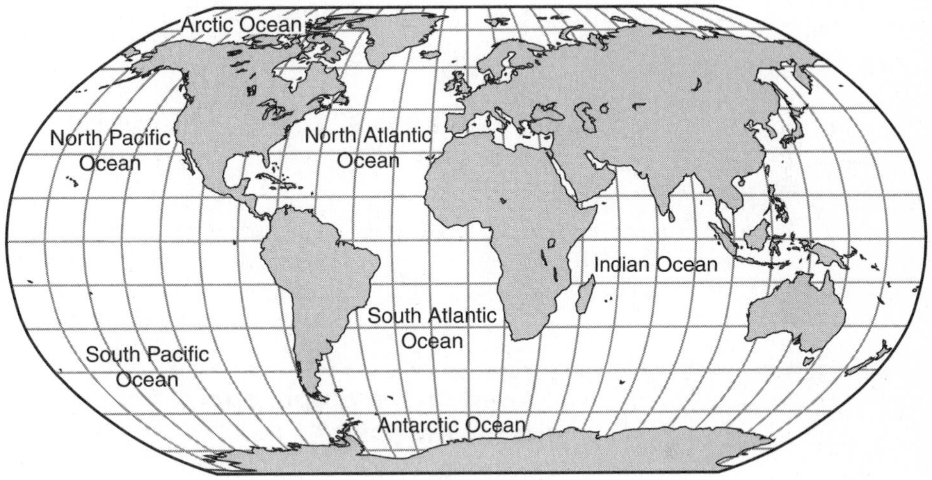

The Beginning of the Oceans

Oceanographers are not sure how Earth's oceans began. Many believe that the oceans were formed by the release of gases (hydrogen and oxygen) trapped in the magma in the Earth's interior. These gases were released, cooled, and condensed into the water that covers most of our planet's surface.

Although scientists are not certain about the beginning of Earth's oceans, they do know that the volume of water covering Earth is affected by the formation of glaciers and the melting of huge blocks of ice covering Earth's surface. The graph on page 520 illustrates the change in sea level during the past 20,000 years. (Glaciers covered much of Earth 20,000 years ago.)

GED PRACTICE

EXERCISE 12

Change in Sea Level

Directions: Choose the *best* answer for each of the following questions.

CHANGE IN SEA LEVEL
DURING THE PAST 20,000 YEARS

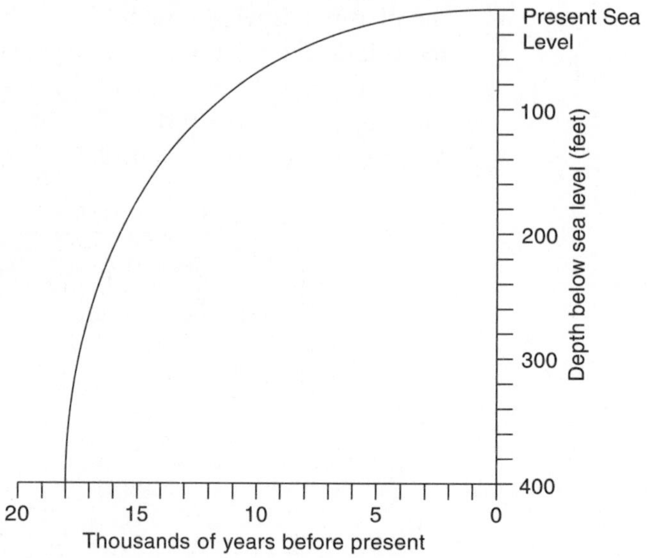

1. Based on the graph, approximately when was Earth's sea level at its lowest point?

(1) 1,000 years ago
(2) 5,000 years ago
(3) 10,000 years ago
(4) 15,000 years ago
(5) 18,000 years ago

2. Which of the following explanations best describes why the oceans have a seafloor ridge?

(1) The weight of the water makes the seafloor buckle.
(2) Magma from below forces the seafloor to split.
(3) Over time, Earth's crust ages and ridges appear.
(4) Sonar sends sound waves to the seafloor, disrupting the crust.
(5) Gravity pulling from the moon and the sun causes the seafloor to rupture.

Answers are on page 581.

GED PRACTICE

EXERCISE 13

The Beginning of the Oceans

Directions: Choose the *best* answer for each of the following questions.

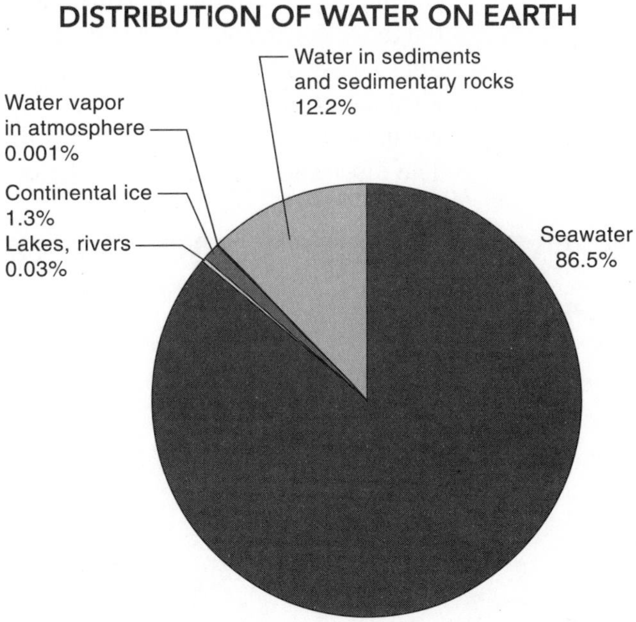

1. **Which of the following sources yields the smallest amount of water throughout Earth?**

   (1) seawater
   (2) lakes and rivers
   (3) continental ice
   (4) water vapor in the atmosphere
   (5) water in sediments and sedimentary rocks

2. **To which theory does the presence of 12 percent of water in sediments and in sedimentary rocks lend support?**

   (1) continental drift
   (2) plate tectonics
   (3) the rise of Earth's sea level over time
   (4) the origin of the oceans
   (5) evolution

3. **What percent of the water on Earth is available for us as drinking water?**

   (1) 12.2 percent
   (2) .001 percent
   (3) 1.3 percent
   (4) .03 percent
   (5) 86.5 percent

Answers are on page 581.

Ocean Tides

One phenomenon of oceans that can be easily observed is the occurrence of tides. **Tides** result from the rising and falling of the ocean's surface caused by the gravitational pull of the Sun and the Moon on Earth. The Moon is the dominant factor in causing tides because of its closeness to Earth.

When the Moon is directly overhead, the ocean beneath it tends to bulge up, causing a tide. On the opposite side of Earth, the oceans experience a lesser bulge. As Earth rotates once every twenty-four hours, it experiences two high tides and two low tides. The position of the Moon in relation to the Sun and Earth determines the period and height of the tides. **Spring tides** are tides of greater-than-average range. **Neap tides** are tides of smaller-than-average range. The illustration in the exercise below shows a spring tide and a neap tide.

GED PRACTICE

EXERCISE 14

Ocean Tides

Directions: Choose the *best* answer for each of the following questions.

SPRING AND NEAP TIDES

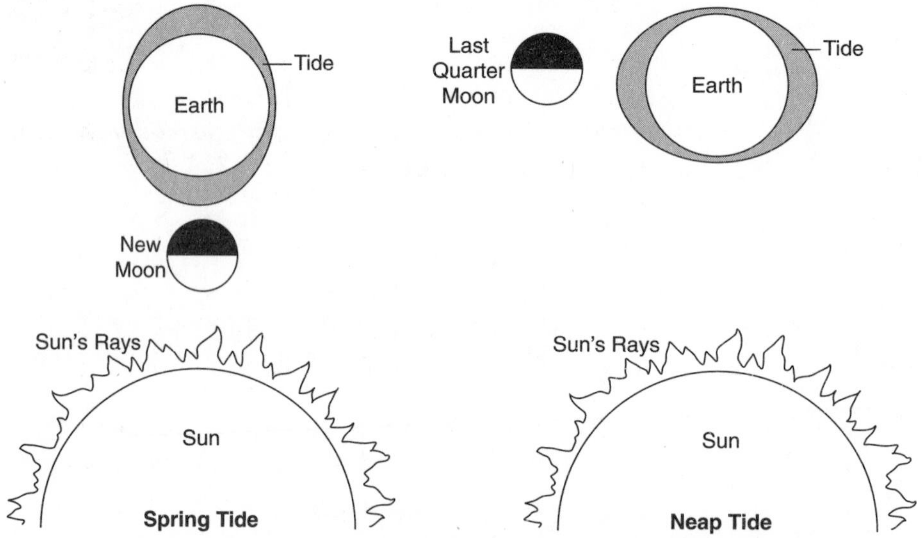

1. Spring tides are tides of greater-than-average range. During which phase of the Moon is the gravitational pull of the Moon together with that of the Sun likely to be greatest, causing a spring tide?

(1) first quarter—when the Moon is to the right side of Earth
(2) full moon—when Earth is between the Sun and the Moon
(3) last quarter—when the Moon is to the left side of Earth, as shown
(4) new moon—when the Moon is between Earth and the Sun
(5) crescent moon—-when the moon is between new and first quarter

Question 2 is based on the following explanation.

Syzygy (siz'-e-je) is a rare alignment of the Sun, the Moon, and Earth that causes extraordinarily high tides. This phenomenon occurred during the period from December 30, 1986, to January 4, 1987. It aggravated the severe storms that occurred along the U.S. Atlantic Coast. Three coinciding events occurred during this five-day period.

A. The Moon's orbit was closest to Earth—about 223,000 miles instead of 240,000 miles.

B. The Moon was directly between Earth and the Sun, causing a new moon.

C. Earth's orbit was the closest to the Sun—91 million miles, instead of the normal 93 million miles.

2. Imagine these conditions: the Moon's orbit is farthest from Earth, Earth is between the Sun and Moon, and Earth's orbit is farthest from the Sun. These conditions would likely result in which of the following situations?

(1) the same effect as syzygy
(2) the least effect on tide levels
(3) higher high tides
(4) spring tides
(5) unusually low tides

Answers are on page 581.

Meteorology—The Study of Earth's Atmosphere

The **atmosphere** is the invisible layer of air that envelops Earth. Scientists believe that it is primarily because of our atmosphere that life exists on Earth and not on neighboring planets such as Mars and Venus.

Meteorology is the study of Earth's atmosphere to understand and predict the weather. The atmosphere is not one distinct air mass that surrounds Earth; it is composed of several layers of air that begin at specific altitude ranges. Meteorologists have identified four layers of Earth's atmosphere. In ascending order (from lowest to highest) they are the troposphere, stratosphere, ionosphere, and exosphere.

Atmosphere Layer	Altitude	Conditions
Troposphere	Earth's surface to seven to ten miles	Earth weather-occurrence cloud formation
(Tropopause is the area between the Troposphere and the Stratosphere.)		
Stratosphere	begins at seven to ten miles; extends to 30 miles	little vertical air motion airplane travel
Ionosphere	30 to 300 miles	thin air with electrified particles radio-wave transmission
Exosphere	over 300 miles	the highest layer extreme heat from the sun during the day extreme cold at night without the sun's rays

GED PRACTICE

EXERCISE 15

Layers of Earth's Atmosphere

Directions: Read the following passage and study the diagram below. Then choose the *best* answer for each of the following questions.

At different altitudes of Earth's atmosphere, we are able to observe different phenomena. Also, scientists are able to use different technologies to explore and understand Earth and the regions in outer space.

Atmospheric Phenomena and Observation Tools

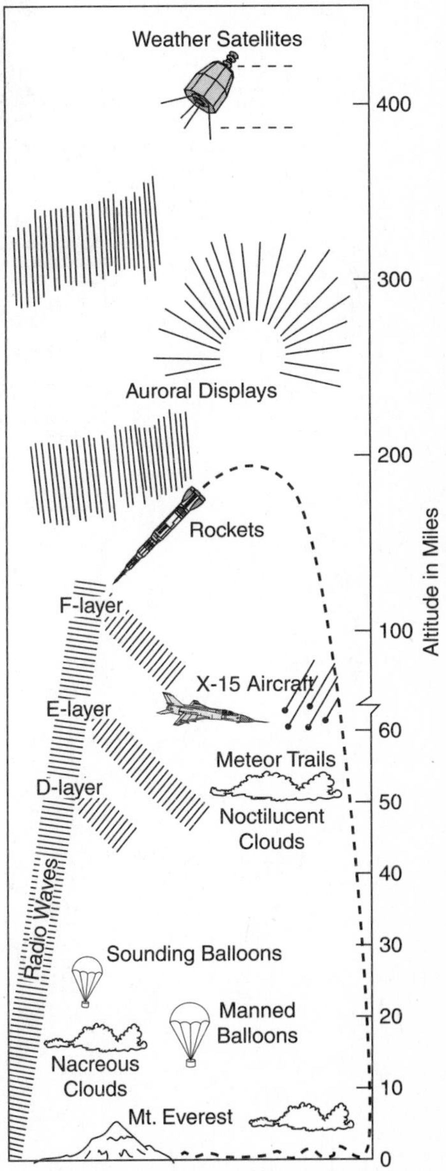

1. *Noctilucent* clouds, spectacular clouds that can be seen only at dusk, appear shortly after sunset. At which atmospheric level are these clouds visible?

(1) the exosphere
(2) the troposphere
(3) the stratosphere
(4) the ionosphere
(5) the tropopause

2. At what layer may "D" layer radio waves that are transmitted around the world be found?

(1) the lower range of the stratosphere
(2) the upper range of the stratosphere
(3) the lower range of the ionosphere
(4) the upper range of the ionosphere
(5) the upper range of the troposphere

3. What does the illustration suggest about the peak of Mt. Everest?

(1) It is at times hidden by clouds.
(2) It extends beyond the tropopause.
(3) It lies in the troposphere.
(4) It touches the stratosphere.
(5) It is not high enough to touch these layers.

Answers are on page 582.

Steve Sack. Reprinted by permission of the Star Tribune.

Writing Activity 5

Explain how the cartoonist is trying to educate the reader about the seriousness of the global warming issue. Do you know which of your activities, daily or annual, might affect the amount of greenhouse gases or carbon dioxide? For example: Do you drive a car or use public transportation?

GED PRACTICE

EXERCISE 16

Ozone in the Atmosphere

Directions: Read the following passage and choose the *best* answer for the question that follows.

Ozone, chemically O_3 and a toxic gas, occurs in the atmosphere when the Sun's ultraviolet rays cause ionization in oxygen atoms. Ozone is beneficial to us because it absorbs ultraviolet rays, preventing these lethal wavelengths from reaching Earth's surface. At lower levels in Earth's atmosphere, however, especially in large urban areas, ozone can be created from a chemical reaction involving solar heat and the exhaust from cars. The chief ingredient of smog, this form of ozone is harmful to human beings and can cause difficulty in breathing.

Where is the harmful form of ozone that can be seen as smog formed?

(1) in the exosphere
(2) in the troposphere
(3) in the stratosphere
(4) in the ionosphere
(5) in the tropopause

Answers are on page 582.

The Water Cycle

In predicting the weather, meteorologists must consider not just the air surrounding us but also how it interacts with the water that covers Earth's surface. The atmosphere and the **hydrosphere** (the watery portion of Earth) create the **water cycle.** This cycle helps to explain precipitation, an important element in our weather.

The Sun is a key link in the chain of events that makes up the water cycle. The Sun radiates heat, which daily **evaporates** millions of tons of water from Earth's oceans, lakes, rivers, and streams into the air. As moist air rises, it slowly cools. Finally, it cools so much that the humidity (the amount of water vapor the air is holding) reaches 100 percent. At this point the water vapor **condenses,** and clouds form. Depending on the temperature and other conditions, either rain or snow falls as **precipitation** when the clouds cannot hold all of the water. The rain or melted snow eventually flows to the ocean, and the cycle is completed again. The illustration that follows shows the water cycle.

THE WATER CYCLE

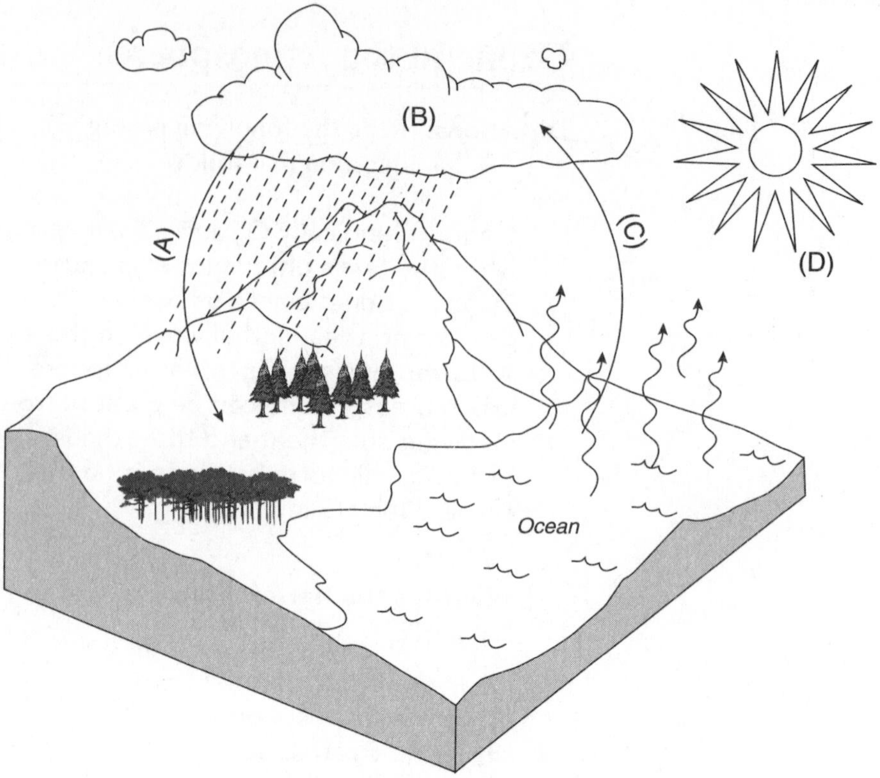

EXERCISE 17

The Water Cycle

Directions: Identify the letters in the illustration that correspond to each process below.

1. ______ Condensation occurs, forming clouds.
2. ______ The Sun radiates heat.
3. ______ Precipitation in the form of rain or snow falls.
4. ______ Water evaporates into the atmosphere.

Answers are on page 582.

GED PRACTICE

EXERCISE 18

Humidity

Directions: Read the following passage and answer the questions below.

Humidity is the amount of water vapor in the air at a given time. At warm temperatures, air can hold more moisture than it can at cold temperatures. **Relative humidity** is the amount of vapor the air is holding expressed as a percentage of the amount the air is capable of holding. For example, at 86 degrees Fahrenheit, air can hold a maximum of 30.4 grams of water per cubic meter. If the air at the same temperature is holding only 15.2 grams of water, the relative humidity is 50 percent. At the point at which the air becomes saturated (exceeds the level of water vapor it can hold), it releases water vapor in the form of dew or condensation.

1. **If the air at 75 degrees is holding the maximum amount of moisture that it can, and the temperature suddenly drops to 60 degrees, what is likely to be the result?**

   (1) The humidity will remain unchanged.
   (2) The relative humidity will decrease.
   (3) Precipitation will be released in the form of rain.
   (4) Precipitation will be released in the form of hail.
   (5) Precipitation will be released in the form of snow.

2. **During subfreezing days in many parts of the country, the indoor relative humidity decreases when homes are heated. Furniture and skin dry out, and static electricity increases. For health reasons, doctors recommend the use of humidifiers. Which of the following best explains the lack of humidity in the air indoors?**

   (1) The amount of water vapor in the air goes down.
   (2) The water vapor in the air evaporates.
   (3) The humidity in winter is lower.
   (4) The cold temperatures prevent humidity.
   (5) Dry air can only occur in warm air.

Answers are on page 582.

Warm and Cold Air Masses

Humidity is a characteristic of air as is temperature. These characteristics affect how an air mass or body of air interacts in the atmosphere. Air masses are created when a body of air takes on the characteristics from the land or water over which it forms. The central region of Canada usually creates cold and dry air masses. Air masses that form over the Gulf of Mexico are warm and have high humidity. The Pacific Northwest creates air masses that are cool but also humid. The air masses that begin over the southwestern region of the United States are often dry but warm. Meteorologists track these air masses to help them make weather forcasts. The air masses that move across the United States from west to east help meteorologists predict the weather.

Cold air masses tend to be unstable and turbulent and move faster than warm air masses. When a cold air mass comes into contact with a warm air mass, it forces the warmer air upwards. This forces any moisture in that air to condense quickly. The clouds that are formed by quick vertical air movements are **cumulus clouds**—puffy, cottonlike clouds. If the air is holding a great deal of moisture, the instant vertical draft creates a **cumulonimbus** or thunderhead. These are the storm clouds that drop a heavy load of precipitation quickly. Very often the quick rush of moist air will create a separation of electric charges within the cloud. This is how **lightning** is created. The release of the charged particles through the air superheats the individual air particles. They expand so fast that small sonic booms, or **thunder,** are heard.

Warm air masses are usually stable, and the wind that accompanies them is steady. Clouds that are formed by warm air masses are **stratus clouds**—low-lying, level clouds that in warm weather bring precipitation in the form of drizzle. As the warm air continues over the cooler air mass, the cloud formation becomes higher and thinner. The highest wispy clouds are **cirrus clouds,** and do not contain enough moisture to bring precipitation.

Air Masses Cause Fronts

A **front** occurs when two air masses collide and a boundary between the two masses forms. The weather for the land below is affected. Fronts may be either weak or strong. Strong fronts generally bring precipitation.

When cold air acts like a plow and pushes warm air back, a **cold front** forms. If the cold air retreats, and the warm air pushes it away, a **warm front** occurs. Sometimes, the boundary between the two air masses does not move, and the front becomes stationary. **Stationary fronts** bring conditions similar to those brought by warm fronts. The precipitation that results, however, is usally milder and lasts longer.

More commonly, these collisions of fronts take place at the change of seasons. In the central part of the United States, spring means collisions of the newly arriving warm, moist air from the Gulf of Mexico with the retreating dry and cold air from central Canada. This annual springtime tradition generates the conditions that cause tornadoes. **Tornadoes** are the result of a very isolated strong updraft of warm, moist air. The rotation of the planet puts the circulation pattern of a counterclockwise spin into the updraft. (This is known as the **Coriolis Effect** and is demonstrated by all wind and water currents in both hemispheres. It is the reason the trade vessels in the Atlantic Ocean coming from Europe to North America must travel south to the equator instead of straight across the Atlantic.) Tornadoes may have wind speeds of up to 300 miles per hour, and they travel across the ground at around 30 miles per hour. Most tornadoes are produced in a region known as Tornado Alley: an area starting in the northern sections of Texas, through Oklahoma, Kansas, Missouri, and parts of Iowa and Illinois.

Hurricanes are also seasonal storms. As the energy from the sun leaves the northern hemisphere in the late summer, the oceans near the equator develop air mass and water-current low pressure systems. Hurricane season is August through October, when the conditions are right for the start of these large circulation patterns that are fueled by the warm ocean waters near the equator.

EXERCISE 19

Air Masses, Fronts, and Weather

Directions: Choose the *best* answer for the following questions.

1. **Which of the following changes in the weather can occur when a strong warm air mass displaces a cold air mass?**
   (1) Cumulus clouds may form, winds may become gusty, and thunderstorms may result.
   (2) Stratus clouds may form, winds may become steady, and drizzling may occur.
   (3) Stratus clouds may form, winds may become turbulent, and thunderstorms may result.
   (4) Cumulus clouds may form, winds may become steady, and thunderstorms may result.
   (5) The sky may remain cloudless, and no winds or precipitation may occur.

2. **Based on the passage, what causes an air mass to form?**
   (1) air taking on the characteristics of the land or water over which it forms
   (2) cold air overcoming weaker warm air over a large area
   (3) the Coriolis Effect from the rotation of the planet
   (4) the stability of the winds that cause weather patterns
   (5) the collision of moist air and dry air that generates storms

3. **Identify the following statements as true for a tornado (T), a hurricane (H), or both (B).**

   a. ______ Wind speeds are sometimes measured at three hundred miles per hour.

   b. ______ Winds spin around a low pressure center in a counterclockwise direction.

   c. ______ The low pressure is fueled by the heat from the ocean waters near the equator.

   d. ______ These storms generally occur during the spring and very often in the Midwest.

Answers are on page 582.

Go to **www.GEDScience.com** for additional practice and instruction!

CHAPTER 3

Physical Science

Chemistry—The Study of Matter

Chemistry is the branch of science that deals with the composition, structure, and properties of matter as well as the changes it undergoes. **Matter** is any substance that occupies space and has mass. Your chair, desk, and table are composed of matter. Even the air you breathe is composed of matter. Matter exists in four states— **solid, liquid, gas,** and **plasma** (an ionized gas of which the Sun is made). The starting point for a systematic study of chemistry generally begins with an examination of the basic unit of matter, the atom.

The Atom, the Basis of Matter

In chemistry, atoms are the building blocks for matter. The **atom** is the smallest particle of an element that has the properties of that element. An **element** is a substance that occurs in nature and that cannot be broken down into a simpler substance. Nearly 100 fundamental substances known as elements are known to occur in nature. A few elements have been produced synthetically by man. Atoms also form molecules. A **molecule** is the smallest part of a compound that can exist by itself. A molecule consists of two or more atoms joined together chemically.

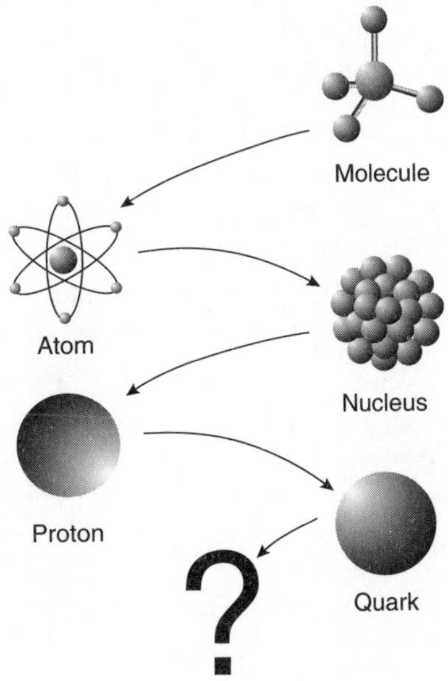

In the early 19th century, only a few elements were known to exist. According to the theory of John Dalton, an atom cannot be made, destroyed, or divided; and atoms of the same element are alike. This concept became known as **atomic theory.** Later physicists discovered that the nucleus of an atom can be split by bombarding it with neutrons, a process known as **nuclear fission.**

A Russian chemist, **Dmitri Mendeleyev**, constructed a table, known as the **periodic table,** by which he calculated the atomic weights of the different elements. The elements are identified by symbols taken largely from Latin names for the elements. Hydrogen is the lightest known element, having only one proton and was, therefore, assigned the atomic number 1. An atom of oxygen, an abundant gas on Earth, has a mass 16 times that of a hydrogen atom; therefore, oxygen was given an atomic mass of 16. Oxygen is the eighth lightest element and is assigned the atomic number 8. Dalton's and Mendeleyev's discoveries were the most significant in the field of chemistry since that of Antoine-Laurent Lavoisier, a French chemist who identified oxygen as the key element that supports combustion. An example of the periodic table appears on page 541.

Atomic Structure

Scientists have learned a great deal about atoms since Dalton's time. For example, an atom is composed of a nucleus with electrons that surround it. The **nucleus**, located in the center of the atom, is made up of protons and neutrons. A **proton** is a positively charged particle. An element's atomic number is determined by the number of protons it has. Because hydrogen has only one proton in its nucleus, it has an atomic number of 1. A **neutron** has a mass nearly equal to that of a proton but has no charge at all. The nucleus has a positive charge, determined by the number of protons it contains. The nucleus provides the mass number for an element.

An **electron** is a negatively charged particle. Electrons occupy an orbit, or shell, that surrounds the nucleus. Each shell can hold only a fixed number of electrons. It is the number of shells that distinguishes one element from another. The greater the number of shells with orbiting electrons that an element has, the greater its atomic number. The illustration on page 535 shows the structure of an atom.

THE HELIUM ATOM

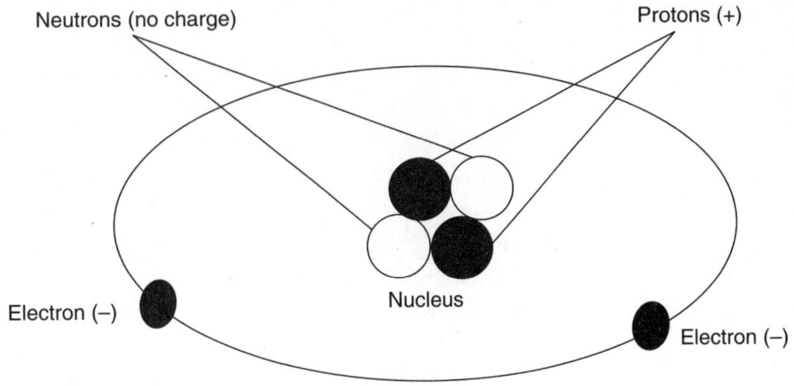

EXERCISE 1

Atomic Structure

Directions: Match each term on the right with the correct description on the left.

1. ______	the second lightest element; contains two protons in its nucleus	**a.** oxygen
2. ______	a negatively charged particle	**b.** neutron
3. ______	the part of an atom that determines an element's mass	**c.** proton
4. ______	a particle that has no charge	**d.** helium
5. ______	a positively charged particle	**e.** electron
6. ______	an element containing eight protons in its nucleus	**f.** nucleus

Answers are on page 583.

Nuclear Energy

The nucleus of every atom contains an almost unimaginable amount of potential energy. The protons that are locked together are all positive and naturally repel each other. It takes the strongest force in the universe, **nuclear force,** to keep those subatomic particles locked together. Science has been able to unlock and capture this energy by splitting larger atoms (those with the greatest number of protons) by firing a neutral neutron at the atom. This process of splitting the larger atoms is **nuclear fission.** The fuel for this reaction is uranium because of the great size of its nucleus and its unstable qualities. When a material is unstable and able to release radiation it is said to be **radioactive.** This radioactive material is made into pellets that are held by fuel rods placed in a heavily shielded nuclear reactor. The process of regulating the release of the nuclear energy requires that the fuel rods remain partially covered with control rods. These control rods prevent free neutrons from splitting too many uranium atoms in an uncontrolled explosion.

Radioactivity and Environmental Protection

One of the dangers of nuclear energy is that such an explosion could release radioactive materials into the environment, causing serious and extensive contamination of radioactivity to any living organisms, plants and animals in the vicinity. One such explosion occurred at a Ukranian nuclear power plant, Chernobyl, in the early 1980s. A combination of poor operator judgment and a tight testing schedule created the conditions that caused too many of the fuel rods to be exposed. The overwhelming heat from the reaction melted through the containment walls, and an explosion sent radioactive particles and gases outside to the nearby forest and town.

To stop the fire and prevent further leakage, the entire reactor was encased in cement, which is now referred to as the *sarcophagus* (a stone coffin). Local animals that were contaminated as well as the entire nearby forest and even construction equipment used during the cleanup had to be buried as well. Evacuation of the residents of the town near the reactor did not allow the packing of personal belongings. The town remains empty to this day, and the objects left behind convey a very eerie "ghost town" effect.

The United States also has experienced the fear of a near disaster. A nuclear power plant at Three Mile Island, located in New Jersey, sprang a leak of cooling water. This leak allowed the reactor to become very hot. The American reactor, however, was equipped with an automatic shut-off system that was activated when the recorded temperature exceeded maximum capacity. There was no leakage of radioactive materials, and nuclear-energy advocates explain that this fact proves that the automatic system keeps nuclear power safe. These advocates still do not have an answer to the biggest concern nuclear-energy opponents have: the safe disposal of radioactive wastes. Currently these wastes are sealed in large barrels and are transported to empty underground mines that are reinforced with a lining to protect the environment.

EXERCISE 2

Nuclear Energy

Directions: Read the passage below and choose the *best* answer for each of the following items. You may need to refer to the periodic table shown on page 541.

Nuclear energy may be released in two ways: by fission and by fusion. Nuclear *fission* involves the splitting of the nucleus of a heavy chemical element by bombardment with neutrons. Nuclear *fusion* involves the uniting of two nuclei of an element at high temperatures and pressure to form the nucleus of a new, heavier, element. In each process, nuclear energy is released.

1. According to the information in the passage and the atomic masses shown in the periodic table, when would energy from nuclear fusion be released?

(1) when uranium nuclei are fused to make plutonium
(2) when hydrogen nuclei are fused to make oxygen
(3) when oxygen nuclei are fused to make helium
(4) when hydrogen nuclei are fused to make helium
(5) when helium nuclei are fused to make hydrogen

2. Energy from nuclear fission would be released in the splitting of the nucleus of which element?

(1) plutonium
(2) hydrogen
(3) oxygen
(4) helium
(5) carbon

3. Identify the following statements about nuclear power as true (T) or false (F).

_______ The Three Mile Island accident contaminated a nearby forest.

_______ Nuclear waste is safe to dispose of in landfills.

_______ The Chernobyl accident could have been prevented.

_______ Fuel rods must also have control rods to control the reaction.

Answers are on page 583.

Radioactivity that is Useful

Not all radioactivity is harmful. Particles of **radioactive carbon** are in the air and inhaled by animals and people every day. It is this radioactive carbon that allows paleontologists to calculate how long an organism has been dead. Once the organism dies, it no longer takes in additional radioactive C_{14}, and the amount of radioactive carbon that is present in the organism starts to decay or lose some of its radioactivity in the form of subatomic particles called alpha or beta particles. The release of alpha and beta particles would contaminate nearby objects with radioactivity. This process of **radiocarbon dating** has given scientists a tool to examine and date fossils from once-living organisms including early man.

Smoke detectors also have a small, safe amount of material that gives off alpha particles. Some smoke detectors contain small amounts of Am_{243} (Americium) that releases a steady stream of alpha particles between two electrodes. When smoke particles interrupt the current between the two electrodes, an alarm sounds.

Radioactive materials are also used in the treatment of some cancers. An entire branch of medicine, called nuclear medicine, researches and uses radioactive materials to treat the human body.

One of the first medical explorers to use radioactivity was Marie Curie. In 1903 she and her husband, Pierre, won the Nobel Prize for their research. Unfortunately, they did not understand the harmful effects of radiation until they had both suffered permanent physical damage from their long exposure to it.

One of the most popular forms of radiology involves the use of Xrays to detect broken bones. While having Xrays at the doctor's or dentist's office, the patient is also given a protective lead cover to prevent overexposure of the other parts of the body. **CAT** (computerized axial tomography) **scans** use computers to monitor the body's reaction to Xrays from a variety of angles. Doctors use CAT scans as well as **MRI** (magnetic resonance imaging) screens to help in diagnosis of internal problems.

EXERCISE 3

Isotopic Elements

Directions: Read the passage below and study the table. Then choose the *best* answer for each of the items on page 539.

Sometimes the number of neutrons in the atom of an element varies. This can affect the mass number of an element. For example, the element carbon has six protons in its nucleus, but it can also have six or seven neutrons in its nucleus. An element whose number of neutrons can vary in its nucleus is described as isotopic. Thus, two isotopes of carbon exist—carbon 12 and carbon 13—and they have different chemical properties. Of the two, carbon 12 is the more common.

Element	Atomic Number	Mass Number
Hydrogen	1	1.01
Helium	2	4.00
Lithium	3	6.94
Beryllium	4	9.01
Boron	5	10.81

1. The only element in the chart that could have an isotope of mass number 6 and whose two nuclei might be fused to form carbon 12 would be which of the following?

(1) hydrogen
(2) helium
(3) lithium
(4) beryllium
(5) boron

2. Deuterium and tritium are two isotopes that have mass numbers of 2 and 3, respectively. Of the two isotopes, tritium is especially radioactive. Based on the preceding chart, to which element would these two isotopes belong, knowing that they both have only one proton?

(1) hydrogen
(2) helium
(3) lithium
(4) beryllium
(5) boron

3. Identify the following statements as either fact (F) or opinion (O).

_______ Radioactivity is very dangerous, and people should not use it.

_______ Radiation can be used to treat certain medical problems.

_______ Lead is used as a screen to protect internal organs when using Xrays.

_______ CAT scans and MRIs are the best ways to diagnose disease.

_______ Radioactive wastes need to be securely protected from contaminating the environment.

Answers are on page 583.

Elements and Periodicity

In the periodic table, elements are organized according to their atomic and physical properties. The table relates the properties of the elements to their atomic numbers. Elements in the same row (across) have the same number of shells containing a varying number of electrons. Elements in the same column (down) have the same number of electrons in their outermost shell.

In classifying elements according to physical properties, scientists consider color, odor, taste, density, boiling point, solubility (ability to dissolve), malleability (capability of being shaped by beating), and hardness. Out of these properties arose the three broad groupings that chemists have used to categorize all of the elements—**metals, nonmetals,** and **metalloids**.

	FEATURES	EXAMPLES
Metals	conduct heat and electricity well melt at high temperatures have high density and brilliant luster	sodium gold aluminum
Nonmetals	melt at low temperatures have low luster are less dense than metals are poor conductors of heat and electricity	carbon sulfur oxygen
Metalloids	have properties of metals and nonmetals	antimony arsenic

According to **periodic law**, as the atomic number increases for elements in a column, similar properties occur regularly and to a greater degree. For example, the metals with the atomic numbers 3, 11, and 19—lithium, sodium, and potassium, respectively—are all chemically active metals. In many cases, the greater the atomic number, the higher the degree of certain physical or chemical properties. Whereas the second member of this group, sodium, is chemically active, the fourth member, rubidium, is so highly active that it bursts into flame upon exposure to air.

The periodic table appears on page 541.

Periodic Table of Elements

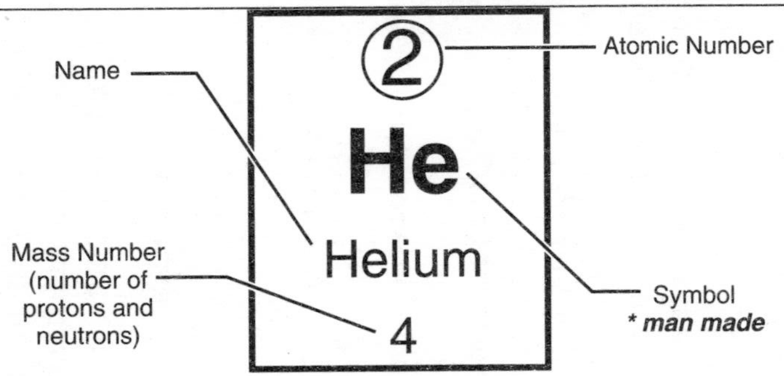

Period																		
1	(1) **H** Hydrogen 1																	(2) **He** Helium 4
2	(3) **Li** Lithium 7	(4) **Be** Beryllium 9											(5) **B** Boron 11	(6) **C** Carbon 12	(7) **N** Nitrogen 14	(8) **O** Oxygen 16	(9) **F** Fluorine 19	(10) **Ne** Neon 20
3	(11) **Na** Sodium 23	(12) **Mg** Magnesium 24											(13) **Al** Aluminum 27	(14) **Si** Silicon 28	(15) **P** Phosphorus 31	(16) **S** Sulfur 32	(17) **Cl** Chlorine 35	(18) **Ar** Argon 40
4	(19) **K** Potassium 39	(20) **Ca** Calcium 40	(21) **Sc** Scandium 45	(22) **Ti** Titanium 48	(23) **V** Vanadium 51	(24) **Cr** Chromium 52	(25) **Mn** Manganese 55	(26) **Fe** Iron 56	(27) **Co** Cobalt 59	(28) **Ni** Nickel 59	(29) **Cu** Copper 64	(30) **Zn** Zinc 65	(31) **Ga** Gallium 70	(32) **Ge** Germanium 73	(33) **As** Arsenic 75	(34) **Se** Selenium 79	(35) **Br** Bromine 80	(36) **Kr** Krypton 84
5	(37) **Rb** Rubidium 85	(38) **Sr** Strontium 88	(39) **Y** Yttrium 89	(40) **Zr** Zirconium 91	(41) **Nb** Niobium 93	(42) **Mo** Molybdenum 96	(43) **Tc*** Technetium 98	(44) **Ru** Ruthenium 101	(45) **Rh** Rhodium 103	(46) **Pd** Palladium 106	(47) **Ag** Silver 108	(48) **Cd** Cadmium 112	(49) **In** Indium 115	(50) **Sn** Tin 119	(51) **Sb** Antimony 122	(52) **Te** Tellurium 128	(53) **I** !odine 127	(54) **Xe** Xenon 131
6	(55) **Cs** Cesium 133	(56) **Ba** Barium 137	(57) **La** Lanthanum 139	(72) **Hf** Hafnium 178	(73) **Ta** Tantalum 181	(74) **W** Tungsten 184	(75) **Re** Rhenium 186	(76) **Os** Osmium 190	(77) **Ir** Iridium 192	(78) **Pt** Platinum 195	(79) **Au** Gold 197	(80) **Hg** Mercury 201	(81) **Tl** Thallium 204	(82) **Pb** Lead 207	(83) **Bi** Bismuth 209	(84) **Po** Polonium 209	(85) **At** Astatine 210	(86) **Rn** Radon 222
7	(87) **Fr** Francium 223	(88) **Ra** Radium 226	(89) **Ac** Actinium 227	(104) **Rf** Rutherfordium 261	(105) **Db** Dubnium 262	(106) **Sg** Seaborgium 263	(107) **Bh** Bohrium 262	(108) **Hs** Hassium 265	(109) **Mt** Meitnerium 266	(110) **Uun*** Unnilennium 269	(111) **Uuu*** Unununium 272	(112) **Uub*** Ununbium 277		(114) **Uuq*** Ununcuadium 285		(116) **Uuh*** Ununhexium 289		(118) **Uuo*** Ununactium 293

Rare Earth Elements

Lanthanide series	(58) **Ce** Cerium 140	(59) **Pr** Praseodymium 141	(60) **Nd** Neodymium 144	(61) **Pm*** Promethium 145	(62) **Sm** Samarium 150	(63) **Eu** Europium 152	(64) **Gd** Gadolinium 157	(65) **Tb** Terbium 159	(66) **Dy** Dysprosium 163	(67) **Ho** Holmium 165	(68) **Er** Erbium 167	(69) **Tm** Thulium 169	(70) **Yb** Ytterbium 173	(71) **Lu** Lutetium 175
Actinide series	(90) **Th** Thorium 232	(91) **Pa** Protactinium 231	(92) **U** Uranium 238	(93) **Np*** Neptunium 237	(94) **Pu*** Plutonium 244	(95) **Am*** Americium 243	(96) **Cm*** Curium 247	(97) **Bk*** Berkelium 247	(98) **Cf*** Californium 251	(99) **Es*** Einsteinium 252	(100) **Fm*** Fermium 257	(101) **Md*** Mendelevium 258	(102) **No*** Nobelium 259	(103) **Lr*** Lawrencium 262

GED PRACTICE

EXERCISE 4

Elements and Periodicity

Directions: Choose the *best* answer for each of the following questions.

1. **The metals copper, silver, and gold are in the same family (column), having atomic numbers of 29, 47, and 79 respectively. According to the principle of periodic law, of the three metals, gold would have the highest degree of which physical property?**

   (1) value
   (2) rarity
   (3) volatility
   (4) malleability
   (5) scarcity

2. **Radon is in the same family as helium, neon, argon, krypton, and xenon. Which of the following facts would help you to determine that radon has a greater density than the other elements in the same family?**

   (1) Radon is found in the ground, whereas other elements are not.
   (2) Radon has a higher atomic number than the other elements in its family.
   (3) Radon poses potential health problems where great concentrations are found in the ground.
   (4) Radon is used in many medical treatments that require chemical reactions in the body.
   (5) Radon is atomically very unstable and is dangerous to use.

Answers are on page 583.

Elements and Chemical Reactions

Each chemical reaction has two components: a reactant and a product. A **reactant** is the substance or substances that enter into the reaction. The **product** is the substance or substances that result from the reaction. A chemical reaction may be either a **combination reaction,** in which two elements or substances are combined, or a **decomposition reaction,** in which an element or substance is broken down.

A chemical reaction is written in a shorthand called a **chemical equation.** A chemical formula uses symbols for elements and shows the number of atoms for each element of a substance. For example, the chemical reaction that produces water would be written this way:

$$2H_2 + O_2 \rightarrow 2H_2O$$

When you read a chemical equation, the large number tells how many **molecules** (structures containing more than one atom) are present. When only a single molecule or atom is present, the number 1 is not written. The smaller subscript number tells how many atoms of an element are present in each molecule.

The equation for water says that two molecules of hydrogen gas (H_2) plus one molecule of oxygen gas (O_2) combine to form two molecules of water (H_2O). Notice that one molecule of hydrogen gas (H_2) contains two atoms of hydrogen, and one molecule of oxygen gas (O_2) contains two atoms of oxygen. Each molecule of water (H_2O) contains two atoms of hydrogen and one atom of oxygen.

The chemical reaction in which one atom of carbon unites with two atoms of oxygen to form carbon dioxide would be written this way:

$$C + O_2 \rightarrow CO_2$$

This equation says that one molecule of carbon plus one molecule of oxygen (two atoms of oxygen) combine to form one molecule of carbon dioxide (CO_2).

All chemical reactions are governed by the **Law of Conservation of Matter.** This law holds that matter can neither be created nor destroyed in a chemical reaction. A chemical equation adheres to this law; it shows the same number of atoms on both sides of the arrow for each element involved in a reaction. For example, the following chemical reaction occurs when methane gas (CH_4) is burned with oxygen:

$$CH_4 + 2O_2 \rightarrow CO_2 + 2H_2O$$

Methane gas burns with oxygen to form carbon dioxide and water vapor; specifically, one molecule of carbon dioxide and two molecules of water. Notice that the reaction begins with one carbon atom (C) and ends with one carbon atom (C). The reaction begins with four hydrogen atoms (H_4) and ends with four hydrogen atoms ($2H_2$ or $2 \times 2 = 4$). The reaction begins with four oxygen atoms ($2O_2 = 2 \times 2 = 4$) and ends with 4 oxygen atoms ($O_2 + 2O = 4$).When the number of atoms of each element is equal on both sides of the equation, we say that the equation is **balanced.**

EXERCISE 5

Balanced Equations

Directions: Identify each of the following equations as either balanced **(B)** or unbalanced **(U).**

1. ______ $N_2 + O_2 \rightarrow 2NO$

2. ______ $Fe + HCl \rightarrow FeCl_3 + H_2$

3. ______ $2H + O \rightarrow H_2O$

4. ______ $2Fe_2O_3 + 3C \rightarrow 2Fe + 3CO_2$

5. ______ $2NaBr + Cl_2 \rightarrow Br_2 + 2NaCl$

Answers are on page 583.

GED PRACTICE

EXERCISE 6

Chemical Reactions

Directions: Choose the *best* answer for each of the following questions.

1. **The chemical reaction that gives soda pop (a carbonated beverage) its fizz results from dissolving a molecule of carbon dioxide into a molecule of water. Which of the following represents the chemical equation for the process?**

   (1) $CO_3 + H_2O \rightarrow H_2CO_4$
   (2) $CO_2 + H_2O \rightarrow H_2CO_3$
   (3) $CO + H_2O \rightarrow H_2CO_2$
   (4) $CO_2 + H_2O \rightarrow H_2CO_2$
   (5) $CO + 2H_2O \rightarrow H_4CO_2$

2. **What is the relation of reactants to products of a chemical reaction?**

   (1) They always double in mass.
   (2) They must always balance.
   (3) They never equal each other in mass.
   (4) They always need a catalyst.
   (5) They must triple themselves to balance.

Question 3 refers to the following passage.

A **physical change** is a change that does not produce a new substance. For example, when you *saw* wood or dissolve salt in water you are not changing the chemical composition of the substances. However, a new substance *is* formed when a **chemical change** takes place. The result is a change in the chemical composition of a substance. Some common chemical changes include the burning of wood and the rusting of metal on a car.

In an experiment concerning physical and chemical changes, you add 10g of copper sulfate to 100 ml of water. You heat the solution over a low flame and stir. After the solution cools, you place a piece of aluminum foil in the copper sulfate solution. After 24 hours, the solution has changed from deep blue to a very light blue, and the aluminum has acquired a deep copper coating.

3. Which of the following pieces of information would you need to see at the end of the experiment to prove that a chemical change or a new substance had occurred?

(1) whether the copper sulfate solution had been heated
(2) whether the solution had been stirred
(3) whether twenty-four hours had passed
(4) whether the aluminum had acquired a copper coat
(5) whether the aluminum was breakable

Answers are on page 583.

Elements in Combination

Compounds are formed when two or more elements combine in a chemical reaction. The resulting product usually has different properties from either of the component elements. Compounds, when formed, can be broken down into simpler substances only by chemical action. For example, water, the most commonly known compound, is composed of two atoms of hydrogen and one atom of oxygen. When water is subjected to extreme temperatures, it can be reduced to its component elements—hydrogen and oxygen—and its liquid characteristic is lost.

Mixtures are substances that are formed when two or more elements or compounds are mixed in different proportions. The resulting product retains the properties of the combining elements. In most mixtures the combining ingredients can be separated easily. For example, gunpowder is a mixture of charcoal (a form of carbon), sulfur, and potassium nitrate (a compound of potassium and nitrogen). When mixed, the three ingredients form gunpowder, a highly explosive substance. These three ingredients can be identified by their different colors in this mixture.

A **solution** is a mixture formed when a solid, liquid, or gaseous substance is dissolved in a liquid. The substance that is dissolved into the liquid is called the **solute**. The liquid in which the substance is dissolved is called the **solvent.** One of the characteristics that distinguishes a solution from a mixture is that a solution is homogeneous—the same throughout. An **aqueous solution** features water as the solvent. A **tincture,** such as the antiseptic tincture of iodine, has alcohol as the solvent. Sometimes a solution is formed when a substance is dissolved in a gas or solid.

When metals are combined in varying proportions, they often form **alloys.** In an alloy, each metal dissolves into the other at high temperatures. Common examples of alloys are brass (copper and zinc), bronze (copper, tin, and other elements), and steel (iron, carbon, and other elements). An **amalgam** is formed when a metal is dissolved into mercury, a liquid metal. Amalgams are used chiefly in making tooth cements and are referred to as silver fillings (although more people today choose the porcelain or tooth-colored fillings).

GED PRACTICE

EXERCISE 7

Elements in Combination

Directions: Read the definitions below of five kinds of substances known to scientists. Then choose the *best* answer to the questions that follow.

compound a substance that is composed of two or more elements, in specific proportions, but has properties different from the combining elements

mixture a substance that is composed of two or more elements or other substances but that keeps the properties of the combining ingredients

solution a homogeneous substance formed by dissolving a solid, liquid, or gas into a liquid

alloy a substance formed by the combination of metals in which one metal dissolves into another at high temperatures

amalgam an alloy that includes mercury and that is usually soft and may be liquid

1. Table salt—sodium chloride, one of the most common substances occurring in nature—is best classified as which of the following?

(1) a compound
(2) a mixture
(3) a solution
(4) an alloy
(5) an amalgam

2. Air is composed of nitrogen (78 percent), oxygen (21 percent), argon (0.93 percent), carbon dioxide (0.03 percent), and other gases (0.04 percent). How may air be *best* described?

(1) a compound
(2) a mixture
(3) a solution
(4) an alloy
(5) an amalgam

Answers are on page 584.

Chemical Bonding

When compounds are made, a bond is formed between two or more elements. A **bond** is a force that holds together two atoms, two ions (electrically charged particles), two molecules, or a combination of these. Bonding may result from either the transfer or the sharing of electrons between atoms.

When electrons are transferred from one atom to another, an **ionic bond** is formed. In the following example, an ionic bond is formed when an electron from a sodium atom is transferred to the outermost shell of a chlorine atom. The result is the common compound table salt.

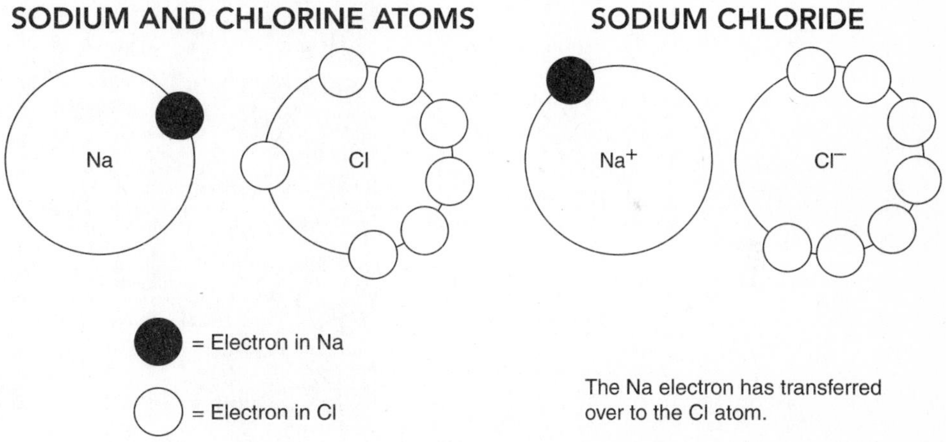

In the preceding example, both sodium and chlorine are electrically neutral (have no charge); however, when the sodium atom loses its electron, it becomes positively charged. Opposite charges attract, forming a bond. Ionic compounds such as salt typically have high melting and boiling points, are flammable, conduct electricity when dissolved in water, and exist as solids at room temperatures.

When two or more atoms of different elements share electrons to form a molecule, a **covalent bond** is formed. In the illustration on page 548, a covalent bond is formed when two atoms of hydrogen are bonded to one atom of oxygen to form the compound water.

WATER MOLECULE

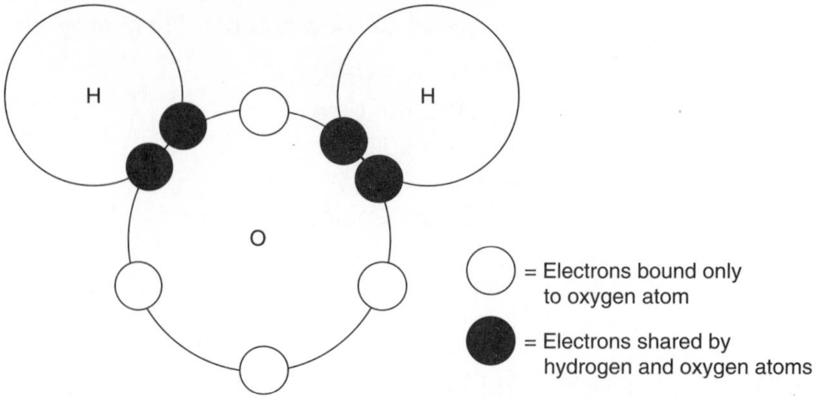

In covalent bonding, the outermost shell of the element with the greatest number of electrons is filled to capacity at eight electrons. Once the combining element achieves eight electrons in its outermost ring, it cannot combine with another element. Covalent compounds such as water typically have low melting and boiling points, are nonflammable, have poor conductivity, and exist as gases and liquids.

© Charles D. Winters/Photo Researchers, Inc.

Polymers have been around since the turn of the 20th century. At that time chemists found that the waste products from organic compounds of phenol and formaldehyde could be treated with heat and high pressure. The resulting material is very hard and is used to make billiard balls and telephones as well as handles on pots and pans. More research with these kinds of organic compounds led to the invention of nylon 66 by two chemists from the Dupont company. Vulcanized rubber that is used to make automobile tires is also the product of experimenting with the bonding of these types of polymer chains.

Another type of synthetic polymer is **polyester** which is used in the making of many types of fabric. Another example of wearable polymers is acrylic. Acrylic feels like wool but is less expensive and can be machine washed. The fabric industry cautions that heat from a fire breaks the bonds, and the fragments react with oxygen to continue the burning reaction, possibly adhering to the skin. Warning labels are put on the garments; some fabrics, especially for sleepwear, are treated with flame-retardant material.

Plastics are another chemical invention of bonding. The variety of chemical bonds allows some plastics, such as PET, to be tough and solvent. This plastic, which has a recycling code of 1, can be found in soda bottles and recycled into new bottles or carpeting or sleeping bags. Another type of plastic (PVC) is a tough, flexible plastic used in pipes or vinyl siding and can be recycled into toys and playground equipment.

Recycling Codes for Plastic Products

Recycling code	Type of plastic	Physical properties	Examples	Uses for recycled products
1	polyethylene terephthalate (PET)	tough, rigid; can be a fiber or a plastic; solvent resistant; sinks in water	soda bottles, clothing, electrical insulation, automobile parts	backpacks, sleeping bags, carpet, new bottles, clothing
2	high density polyethylene (HDPE)	rough surface; stiff plastic; resistant to cracking	milk containers, bleach bottles, toys, grocery bags	furniture, toys, trash cans, picnic tables, park benches, fences
3	polyvinyl chloride (PVC)	elastomer or flexible plastic; tough; poor crystallization; unstable to light or heat; sinks in water	pipe, vinyl siding, automobile parts, clear bottles for cooking oil, blister packaging	toys, playground equipment
4	low density polyethylene (LDPE)	moderately crystalline, flexible plastic; solvent resistant; floats on water	shrink wrapping, trash bags, dry-cleaning bags, frozen-food packaging, meat packaging	trash cans, trash bags, compost containers
5	polypropylene (PP)	rigid, very strong; fiber or flexible plastic; light-weight; heat- and stress-resistant	heatproof containers, rope, appliance parts, outdoor carpet, luggage, diapers, automobile parts	brooms, brushes, ice scrapers, battery cable, insulation, rope
6	polystyrene (P/S, PS)	somewhat brittle, rigid plastic; resistant to acids and bases but not organic solvents; sinks in water, unless it is a foam	fast-food containers, toys, videotape reels, electrical insulation, plastic utensils, disposable drinking cups, CD jewel cases	insulated clothing, egg cartons, thermal insulation

EXERCISE 8

Chemical Bonding

Directions: Choose the *best* answer for each of the following questions.

1. **In ionic bonding, how are atoms are held together?**
   (1) by sharing electrons
   (2) by transferring electrons
   (3) by chemical attraction
   (4) by temperature
   (5) by cohesion

2. **In covalent bonding, how are atoms held together?**
   (1) by sharing electrons
   (2) by transferring electrons
   (3) by chemical attraction
   (4) by temperature
   (5) by cohesion

3. **Use the Recycling Code Chart to identify the correct code from 1 to 6 for the following items.**

   ______ shrink wrap, trash bags, and meat packaging

   ______ milk containers, toys and bleach bottles

   ______ diapers, luggage, and appliance parts

   ______ fast food containers, VCR cassettes and utensils

   ______ pipes, automobile parts, and clear bottles for cooking oil

Answers are on page 584.

Acids, Bases, and Salts

Many compounds that result from ionic and covalent bonding are categorized as acids or bases. An **acid** is a covalent compound that produces hydrogen ions when dissolved in water. Acids have a sour taste. Common acids are acetic acid (the main component of vinegar), citric acid (found in citrus fruits), lactic acid (found in milk), and hydrochloric acid, a component of stomach acid used in digestion.

A **base** is a compound that forms hydroxide ions when dissolved in water. Bases are able to take a proton from an acid or to give up an unshared pair of electrons to an acid. Bases are described as **alkaline** because they dissolve in water and have a slippery feel. Many hydroxides are bases. Household cleaning agents such as ammonia, borax, lye, and detergents are common examples of bases.

When an acid combines with a base, a salt is formed and water released because the metal found in the base replaces the hydrogen contained in the acid. Inorganic acids, bases, and inorganic salts can conduct electricity when dissolved in water. Chemists apply the **litmus test** to a substance to determine whether it is an acid or a base. An acid turns blue litmus paper red, and a base turns red litmus paper blue.

GED PRACTICE

EXERCISE 9

Acids, Bases, and Salts

Directions: Read the the explanation and scale below. Choose the *best* answer for each question that follows.

The designation pH (potential for hydrogen-ion formation) is a value by which certain substances are classified according to acidity or alkalinity. The pH scale ranges from 0 to 14, with the value 7 representing neutrality. The pH scale is illustrated below.

pH SCALE

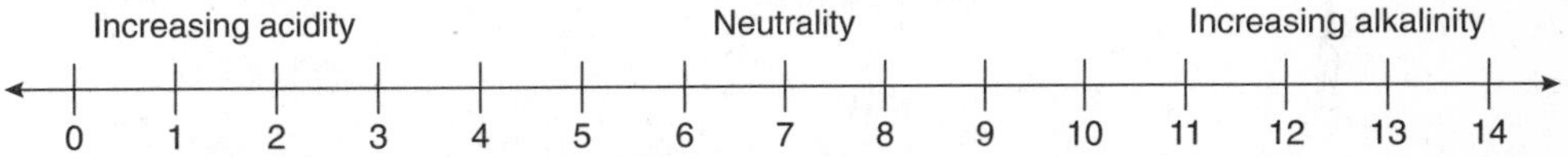

1. According to the pH scale, between which numbers would acetic acid, a very mild acid, most likely be found?

(1) 7 and 8
(2) 0 and 1
(3) 2 and 3
(4) 4 and 5
(5) 10 and 11

2. According to the pH scale, where would ordinary tap water be found?

(1) between 0 and 1
(2) between 3 and 4
(3) exactly at 7
(4) exactly at 1
(5) between 5 and 6

3. Which of the following could be used to prove that a substance is an acid?

(1) The substance has a pH above 7.
(2) The substance has a slippery feel.
(3) It neutralizes a base to form a salt and water.
(4) When mixed with water, a solid would form.
(5) The liquid turns red when mixed with water.

Answers are on page 584.

GED PRACTICE

EXERCISE 10

A Car Battery

Directions: Read the passage below and answer the questions that follow.

Acids, bases, and inorganic salts (salts obtained from nonliving things) are effective conductors of electricity. The common car battery demonstrates an electric current generated by the chemical action between an acid and a metal.

In a car battery pure lead (the negative post) and lead dioxide (the positive post) are submerged in sulfuric acid (the conductor). Distilled water is added periodically to maintain the proper level of sulfuric acid. The pure lead loses two electrons when it reacts with the sulfuric acid—the acid changes the lead to lead dioxide. At the same time, the positive post containing lead dioxide gains two electrons and changes the sulfuric acid in which it is submerged into lead sulfate (a salt) and water. The current that makes the car start results from the flow of electrons from the lead dioxide to the lead through the sulfuric acid to the starter switch, all of which makes a complete circuit. A diagram of a car battery is shown below.

CAR BATTERY

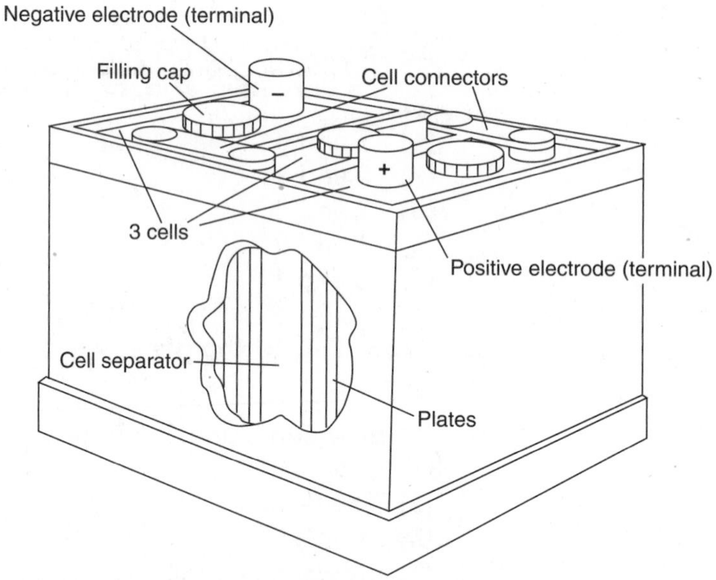

1. **An *electrolyte* is an inorganic compound that will conduct an electric current when dissolved in water. What is an electrolyte in the preceding example?**

   (1) lead dioxide
   (2) sulfuric acid
   (3) distilled water
   (4) carbon particulates
   (5) carbonic acid

2. A substance is oxidized when it loses electrons. In the preceding example, which of the following compounds is oxidized?

(1) lead
(2) lead dioxide
(3) lead sulfate
(4) water
(5) sulfuric acid

3. The substances that oxidize and reduce other substances are called oxidizing agents and reducing agents. According to the reading, in which item are the oxidizing and reducing agents in the correct order?

(1) lead dioxide and water
(2) sulfuric acid and lead dioxide
(3) lead and sulfuric acid
(4) lead sulfate and lead dioxide
(5) sulfuric acid and water

4. Which of the following can you conclude to be true when a battery is discharged and can no longer generate a current?

(1) The sulfuric acid can no longer oxidize the lead.
(2) The lead dioxide can no longer reduce the sulfuric acid.
(3) The battery has run out of sulfuric acid.
(4) The amount of water is too low to generate power.
(5) The metal casing has corroded.

Answers are on page 584.

Acid Rain

A common example of acid's ability to corrode is seen in the increasing acidity of rainwater. As pollutants such as sulfur and carbon from factories enter the water cycle, new compounds are created. Sulfuric acid in weak concentration as well as carbonic acid come down in the form of precipitation. When these acids come into contact with stone statues or metalwork, corrosion occurs. Old gravestones, marble facades on buildings, and inscriptions that can no longer be read exemplify the disintegration that occurs gradually every time it rains.

Acids in the Human Body

A variety of acids is found in the human body. Your body actually does a remarkable job in controlling its own pH balance. Your blood, for example, needs to remain within the range of 7.35 and 7.45. If the pH of your blood is more acidic, you suffer **acidosis.** If the pH is above 7.45, you are said to have **alkalosis.** The body fights the change in pH by natural chemical balancers called **buffers.** A buffer solution has a weak acid and its conjugate base in equal amounts. The liquid portion of blood is an example of a buffer solution. In some cases, the body may generate too much acid. This is often the case when someone experiences heartburn, which can be temporarily relieved by taking an antacid to neutralize the excess stomach acid.

Reaction Rate, Catalysts, and Equilibrium

Chemical reactions occur at different rates determined by the conditions under which the reactions take place. Sugar dissolves more quickly in hot water than in cold. White phosphorus bursts into flame when exposed to the air. Reactions such as these may be speeded up or slowed down when another substance is introduced.

A **catalyst** is a substance that increases the rate of a chemical reaction but itself remains chemically unchanged. Some catalysts have a negative effect. A negative catalyst slows down the chemical reaction. Negative catalysts, such as the chemicals used in undercoating a car to retard the rusting process, are often inhibitors.

A given set of reactants may react to form more than one product. Often, the by-products react to form the original reactants. When the rate of forward reaction balances the rate of reverse reaction, **chemical equilibrium** occurs. For example, the carbon monoxide in car exhaust systems enters the atmosphere and reacts with oxygen to form carbon dioxide. The carbon dioxide is broken down by sunlight into the original reactant—carbon monoxide. This reaction represents chemical equilibrium because the reaction reverses itself. Chemical reactions such as these create a cycle.

GED PRACTICE

EXERCISE 11

Reaction Rate, Catalysts, and Equilibrium

Directions: Choose the *best* answers for the following questions.

1. Lipase is an enzyme produced by the liver that helps in the digestion of fats by speeding up the rate at which lipids (fats) are changed into fatty acids and glycerol. According to this description, what can we conclude that an enzyme is?

(1) a product in a chemical reaction
(2) a negative catalyst
(3) a biological catalyst
(4) a temporary product
(5) a by-product that is unstable

2. Which of the following processes illustrates chemical equilibrium?

(1) bonding
(2) photosynthesis
(3) respiration
(4) oxidation
(5) organic synthesis

Answers are on page 584.

CHAPTER 4

Physical Science

Physics—The Study of How Matter Behaves

Physics is the branch of science that concerns the behavior of matter in our world—the forces that cause matter to behave as it does. Physics helps to explain how cellular molecules can move from a lower concentration in an organism to a higher one, how ocean tides occur, and how matter exists in the states of a solid, liquid, or gas. Many of the properties and behaviors of matter can be explained by force and energy. A **force** shows the presence of energy in an environment. **Energy** is the capacity to do work. The area of physics that deals with forces, energy, and their effect on bodies is **mechanics.**

"*Now* that desk looks better. Everything's squared away, yessir, squaaaaaared away."

Mechanics

The study of **mechanics** was one of the first sciences developed. Ancient Greek philosopher and scientist **Aristotle** theorized that heavy bodies fall faster than light bodies. This theory was proved false in the early 17th century by Italian scientist and mathematician **Galileo**, who dropped items of different weights from the leaning tower of Pisa. The force acting upon the objects was not fully understood, however, until Englishman **Sir Isaac Newton** formulated laws of gravity and motion that explained how different forces act on objects.

The Force of Gravity

Gravity is the most commonly experienced of all forces in nature. The presence of gravity was first proposed by Newton when he observed the motion of an apple falling from a tree. On the basis of this simple observation, he developed the **Law of Universal Gravitation,** which holds that every body having a mass exerts an attractive force on every other body having a mass in the universe. The strength of the force depends on the masses of the objects and the distance between them. (**Mass** is the measure of the amount of matter in an object.) Thus, the apple's falling illustrates the gravitational pull (attraction) of the larger Earth on the smaller apple. The Law of Universal Gravitation also explains how the planets, attracted by the much larger Sun, remain in their orbits as they revolve around it.

NEWTON'S THREE LAWS OF MOTION

The Law of Inertia

A body remains at rest or continues in a state of uniform motion unless a force acts on it. For example, when you drive a car and suddenly jam on the brakes, you continue to move forward. This is because your body's tendency is to remain in the same state of uniform motion (moving forward). The brakes were applied to the car, so its uniform motion was changed.

The Law of Applied Force

A body's change in speed and direction is proportional to the amount of force applied to it. For example, the vanes on a windmill, which move by the force of the wind, will accelerate according to the speed and direction of the wind that drives them.

The Law of Action and Reaction

For every action there is an equal but opposite reaction force. For example, a gun's muzzle kicks backward when a bullet is discharged from it.

EXERCISE 1

Laws of Force and Motion

Directions: Identify the following statements as **(G)** illustrating Newton's Law of Universal Gravitation, **(I)** applying to the Law of Inertia, **(AF)** applying to the Law of Applied Force, or **(AR)** applying to the Law of Action and Reaction.

1. ______ A ball on a pool table rebounds off another ball it just hit.

2. ______ A rocket is propelled upward by the powerful downward discharge of exhaust gases.

3. ______ A bullet fired into the air eventually falls to the ground.

4. ______ A pendulum in a clock, once set in motion, continues to swing, thereby regulating the clock's movement.

5. ______ A jet airplane, upon landing, lowers the flaps on its wings. The flaps create drag, a force that reduces lift and helps the plane to slow down.

Answers are on page 585.

EXERCISE 2

The Force of Gravity

Directions: Read the paragraph below and answer the questions that follow.

An astronaut weighs in before blast-off. He weighs only a fraction of his original weight when he steps on a scale on the moon. Journeying to Jupiter, he finds that his weight has increased several times over his original weight.

1. How may these changes in weight be *best* explained?

(1) the amount of force each planetary body exerts as the astronaut weighs himself
(2) the distance from the Sun of the planetary bodies on which he weighs himself
(3) changes in the atmospheric pressure on the different heavenly bodies
(4) the amount of calories consumed during the flight
(5) the duration of time that elapsed between weigh-ins

2. What do you estimate the weight change for the same astronaut would be if he were to land on Mercury?

Answers are on page 585.

Work, Energy, and Power

According to physics, **work** occurs when a **force** succeeds in moving an object it acts upon. For example, a person who lifts a 50-pound weight one foot off the floor is performing work. For work to be performed, the movement of the object must be in the same direction as the force—in this case vertical. Work may be expressed as any force unit times any distance unit and may be written as follows:

$$W = F \times D$$

The amount of work done is the amount of force multiplied by the distance moved. In the preceding example, 50 foot-pounds of work is done when 50 pounds are lifted one foot:

$$50 \text{ lb} \times 1 \text{ ft} = 50 \text{ ft lb}$$

Energy is required to do work. In the example above, muscular energy is illustrated in the form of a body that is capable of doing work. Energy may be classified as either kinetic or potential energy.

Kinetic energy is energy possessed by a body in motion. The form of energy shown by a moving train is kinetic energy.

Potential energy is energy that is stored or is available for use by a body. For example, coal has potential energy that is released only when it is burned. A boulder positioned on a hilltop has potential energy before it is released. When the boulder is pushed, its potential energy becomes kinetic.

Power is the rate at which work is done. Power is generally measured in horsepower, which is equal to 550 foot-pounds per second or 33,000 foot-pounds per minute.

The Law of Conservation of Energy

The **Law of Conservation of Energy** holds that all of the energy of the universe is conserved. The capacity for energy to do work can be changed from one kind to another, but it cannot be lost. This principle can be illustrated in the following example of energy generated from a waterfall:

Water possesses **potential energy.** When water moves rapidly in a downward motion, drawn by the pull of gravity, the potential energy is changed into **kinetic energy.** Kinetic energy from a waterfall can be harnessed to power a turbine, a rotary engine, creating **rotational energy.** This is sufficient to generate **electrical energy,** which in turn is converted into **light** and **heat energy,** which we use in our homes. The initial potential energy has been changed into five different forms.

EXERCISE 3

Forms of Energy

Directions: Identify the following statements as either demonstrating kinetic energy (**K**) or demonstrating potential energy (**P**).

1. ______ a strong west wind blowing across a region
2. ______ a stick of unlit dynamite
3. ______ a hamburger
4. ______ a waterfall

Answers are on page 585.

GED PRACTICE

EXERCISE 4

Types of Energy

Directions: Read the following definitions of the five types of energy. Then choose the *best* answers for the questions below.

nuclear energy	energy from splitting an atom or fusing atoms
chemical energy	energy from the reaction of two or more substances combining with one another
electrical energy	energy from an electric current
solar energy	energy from the heat of the Sun
steam energy	energy from steam pressure

1. **Which form of energy results from the fission of uranium-235 nuclei that is used to generate electrical power?**

   (1) nuclear energy
   (2) chemical energy
   (3) electrical energy
   (4) solar energy
   (5) steam energy

2. **Which form of energy results from the ignition of a gas and air mixture and powers a car?**

   (1) nuclear energy
   (2) chemical energy
   (3) electrical energy
   (4) solar energy
   (5) steam energy

Answers are on page 585.

Simple Machines

A **machine** is a device that transmits or multiplies force. A machine operates on the principle of a little force as being applied through a great distance and a great resistance being overcome through a short distance.

A **lever** is a simple machine used to perform work by lifting a great weight. A lever is just a bar that is free to pivot on its support (called a **fulcrum**). Through the use of a lever, for example, a 1,000-pound weight can be lifted with relatively little effort (force).

THE LEVER—A SIMPLE MACHINE

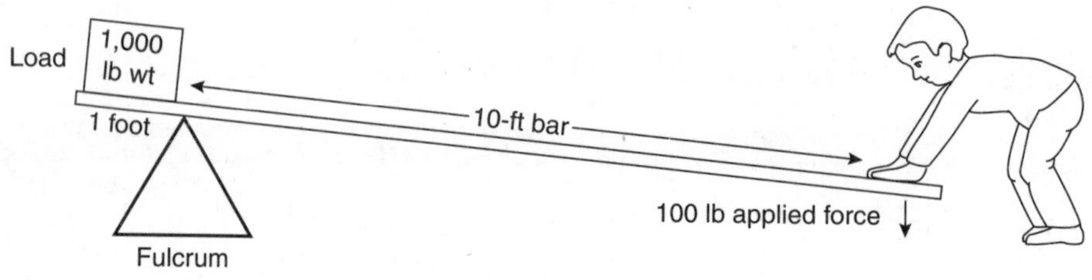

The illustration above shows that it would take 100 pounds of force for a person to lift a 1,000-pound weight positioned 1 foot from the fulcrum when the lever bar is 10 feet long. This may be expressed as follows:

$$1{,}000 \text{ lb} \times 1 \text{ ft} = 100 \text{ lb} \times 10 \text{ ft}$$

In this case a relatively small force (100 lb) applied at a great distance from the object (10 ft) is able to overcome great resistance (1,000 lb). According to this principle the greater the distance between the fulcrum and the applied force, the less force required to perform the work.

The wheelbarrow, the crowbar, the pulley, and the inclined plane are simple machines. Complex machines are made up of more than one simple machine.

EXERCISE 5

Simple Machines

Directions: Choose the *best* answer for each of the following questions.

1. **According to the principle that a little force applied through a great distance can overcome great resistance, which would be most likely to happen if the lever bar in the preceding illustration is increased to 20 feet in length and the weight remained at the end of the bar?**

   (1) The effort to lift the weight would increase to 150 pounds of applied force.
   (2) The effort to lift the weight would remain at 100 pounds of applied force.
   (3) The effort would be decreased by half, to 50 pounds of applied force.
   (4) The resistance of the weight would double.
   (5) The resistance of the weight would triple.

2. **What are some other types of household items that could be considered levers? (Hint: Any tool that makes the job easier is likely a lever.)**

Answers are on page 585.

The Nature of Heat and Energy

Today we know that heat is the result of the random motion of molecules. It is nothing more than energy itself. One theory of physics that has contributed greatly to our understanding of the phenomenon of heat is kinetic theory, a basic theory that explains how different states of matter can exist.

The Kinetic Theory of Matter

According to the **Kinetic Theory of Matter,** matter exists in three states—solid, liquid, or gas. A fourth state, **plasma,** is an ionized gas; the Sun is made up of plasma. The form, or phase, of matter is determined by the motion of the molecules within it.

Solids are composed of atoms or molecules in limited motion. These atoms or molecules are in direct contact with one another, allowing little or no space for random movement. The attractive forces of the particles keep the solid intact and give the solid its definite shape and structure.

In **liquids,** individual atoms or molecules are able to move past one another into new positions, giving this form of matter its fluidity. Cohesive forces hold liquids intact.

Gases are substances in which the individual atoms or molecules are in constant random motion. The motion, or kinetic energy, increases along with an increase in temperature. Molecules are unable to hold together, and this property gives gases the ability to flow or spread out to fill the container in which they are placed.

Heat, Temperature, and the States of Matter

The state of matter depends on its heat content. **Temperature** is a measure of heat intensity. The change from one state of matter to another involves the addition or subtraction of a certain amount of heat per gram of substance. For example, at 32 degrees Fahrenheit, water, a liquid, changes to ice, a solid. When the temperature is raised above 32 degrees Fahrenheit, the ice, a solid, changes to water, a liquid. At temperatures at or above 212 degrees Fahrenheit, the boiling point of water, the water changes to steam, a gaseous state. Impurities in water affect its freezing point.

Certain materials expand when their temperatures are raised and shrink when they are lowered. Liquids expand more noticeably than solids, but gases expand even more. The mercury thermometer employs this principle. Temperature can be measured in degrees centigrade or degrees Fahrenheit. On the **centigrade** (or **Celsius) scale,** 0 degrees represents the freezing point of water, and 100 degrees is the boiling point. On the **Fahrenheit scale,** 32 degrees represents the freezing point of water, and 212 degrees is the boiling point. Temperature is measured in degrees by thermometer, and heat is measured by the calorie or **British Thermal Unit (BTU).** A **calorie** is the amount of heat needed to raise one gram of water one degree centigrade. The BTU is the amount of heat required to raise one pound of water 1 degree Fahrenheit.

Heat is transferred by three methods. The first is called **conduction,** the transfer of heat between objects that are in direct contact. You have experienced this whenever you have picked up a hot item, such as a handle on a heated pan. The second method is **convection.** This method depends on the currents of water and air. When you are adding hot water to one end of the bathtub filled with water, convection transfers the heat to the rest of the water. The third method is **radiation.** You can feel waves of heat by putting your hands near a radiator (used to heat many apartments).

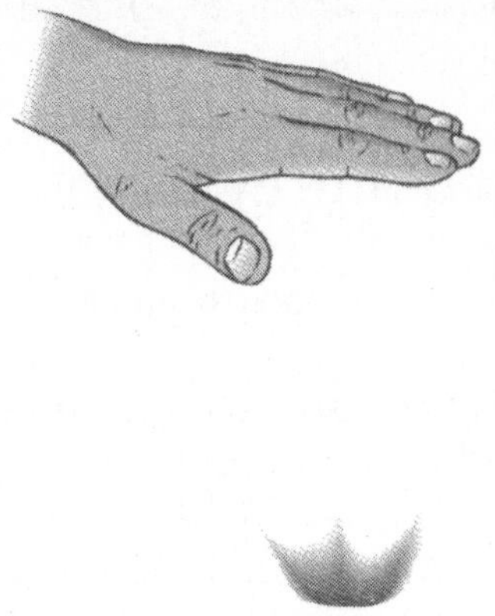

Heating a hand by convection

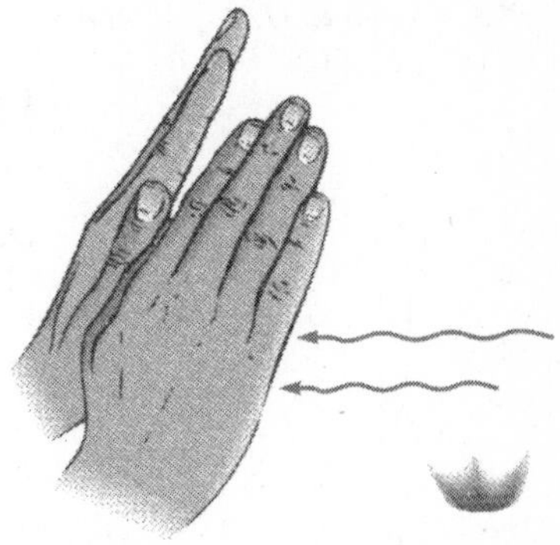

Warming hands by radiation

Source: College Physics, Fourth Edition

EXERCISE 6

Kinetic Theory of Matter

Directions: Identify the following statements as either true **(T)** or false **(F)**.

1. ______ There is more rigid molecular structure in a solid than in a gas.

2. ______ An increase in temperature decreases the molecular motion of a gas.

3. ______ Molecules moving past each other in a liquid give it fluidity.

4. ______ Molecules in a gas are close together and exhibit little motion.

5. ______ Heat is transferred by conduction, convection, or coercion.

Answers are on page 585.

GED PRACTICE

EXERCISE 7

Heat and Temperature

Directions: Read the passage below and answer the questions that follow.

Different materials expand at different degrees of temperature change and in different percentages of their length, volume, or surface. Buckling can occur when a material such as asphalt used for road surfaces reacts to changes in temperature, causing potholes. This is one of the reasons for the widespread use of reinforced concrete (concrete with a steel framework) rather than asphalt on road surfaces and the use of reinforced concrete in high-rise apartment construction.

© Frank Siteman/Stock Boston

1. **What does the widespread use of reinforced concrete in construction suggest?**

   (1) Concrete and steel expand and contract at nearly the same temperatures.
   (2) Reinforced concrete expands at temperatures much higher than ordinary asphalt and does not buckle.
   (3) Reinforced concrete does not expand and contract at all.
   (4) Asphalt can be used only on roadways and never in construction.
   (5) Asphalt is much more expensive and harder to use than concrete.

2. **Which heat transfer method is demonstrated when your hand is positioned directly over the flame of a lighted candle?**

   (1) convection
   (2) conduction
   (3) radiation
   (4) expansion
   (5) coersion

Answers are on page 585.

The Nature of Waves

A **wave** is a periodic or harmonic disturbance in space or through a medium (water, for instance) by which energy is transmitted. Water, sound, and light all travel in waves. The illumination a lamp provides comes from light waves (a form of electromagnetic waves) while the music emanating from a stereo comes from sound waves. The powers to preserve food and warm it come from electromagnetic waves, and the power that transmits signals to a television set comes from radio waves (another form of electromagnetic waves). The energy that gives a waterbed its soothing motion comes from water waves.

Types and Properties of Waves

Waves transmit energy in different ways, and all phases of matter transmit waves. An example of a solid transmitting wave energy is an earthquake that takes place when rocks are under pressure and snap or slide into new positions. Waves that are felt and seen in water are examples of a liquid transmitting wave energy. Gases also transmit wave energy, as in an explosion, when heat, sound, and light waves are generated. Two basic types of waves exist: longitudinal waves and transverse waves.

longitudinal wave Particles of the medium move back and forth in the same direction as the wave itself moves. An example of a longitudinal wave is a sound wave that occurs when a tuning fork is tapped, as shown below.

LONGITUDINAL WAVE

When a tuning fork is tapped, the prongs move from right to left in a rapid periodic motion. A sound wave is produced, and it moves parallel (right and left) to the moving prong.

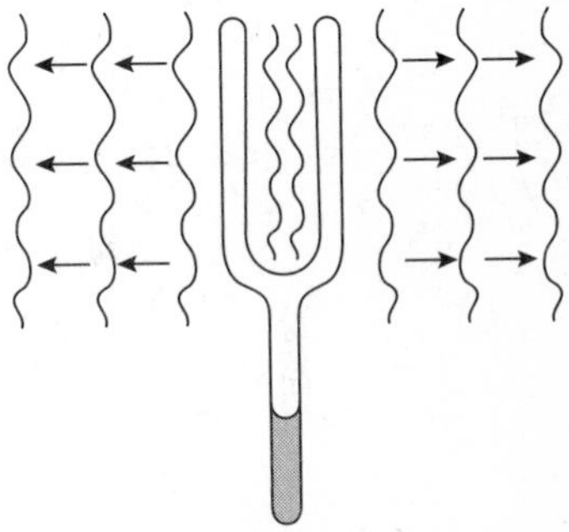

transverse wave Particles of the medium move at right angles to the direction of the wave's movement. An example of a transverse wave is one that occurs when a pebble is tossed into a still pond. Light travels in transverse waves. An example of a transverse wave is shown below.

TRANSVERSE WAVE

When a stone is dropped into a pond, the waves produced appear to move outward. These waves move at right angles to the dropped stone.

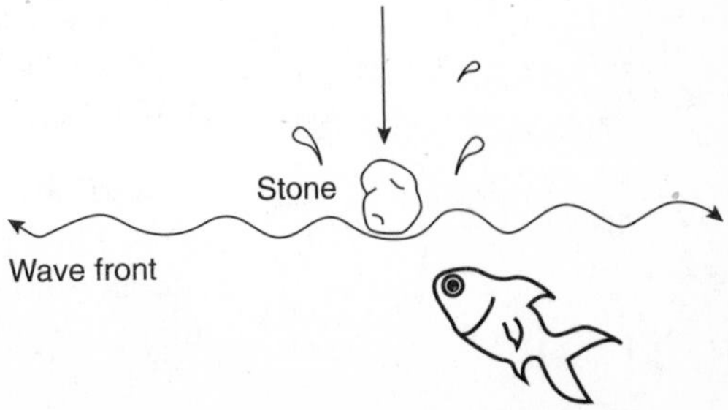

Waves have two components, a crest and a trough. A **crest** is the point of highest displacement in a wave, and the **trough** is the point of lowest displacement. Crests and troughs are easily visible in water waves.

Two specific characteristics of a wave are length and frequency:

- **Wavelength** is defined as the distance between two successive wave crests or two successive wave troughs.
- **Wave frequency** is the number of wave crests that pass a given point per second.

Therefore, the shorter the wavelength, the higher the wave frequency. In fact, a wave's speed equals the wavelength times the wave frequency.

When a source of a wave is in motion, a compression of the wavelength is detected. This can be demonstrated with sound waves. As a train passes you by while you are standing on the platform, you will notice a distinct drop in the pitch or sound quality. This drop in sound pitch is heard by the observers standing on the side during an automotive race such as the Indianapolis 500. Water waves demonstrate the same compression in the direction of motion. The water waves in the front of a boat are squeezed together, while those at the rear of the boat are far apart. This is referred to as the **Doppler Effect.** Scientists use the Doppler Effect to forecast tornadoes and to detect the motions of stars in our galaxy.

SOUND WAVE

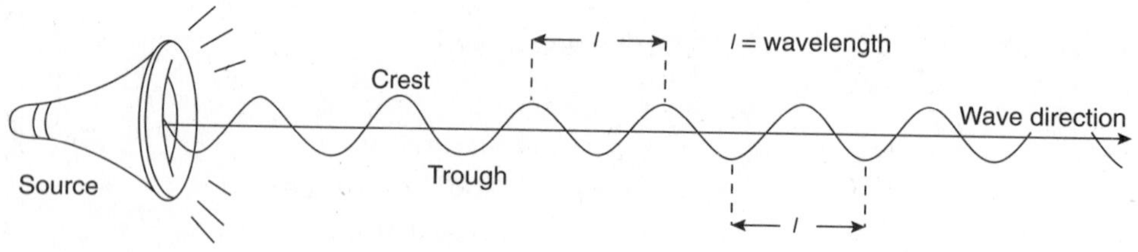

Sound waves, as illustrated above, are longitudinal waves. A musical pitch, or tone, is heard when there is a definite frequency to a wave. The lower the frequency, the lower the tone. For example, the frequency of a bass speaker in a stereo system is lower than a tweeter, or high-frequency speaker, because the low-pitched sound of the bass results from a lower number of vibrations per second.

A sound wave is a wave of compression. It begins at a source—in the case above, a horn speaker. The speaker vibrates, compressing the air in front of it and, like a spring, pushes it away. As the wave passes, the air molecules are forced together. The sensation of hearing results when these waves strike the eardrum.

Sound waves can travel through solids, liquids, and gases. In fact, the human body can be a medium for sound waves. **Ultrasonic waves,** very high-pitched waves, are used in medicine today to detect diseases or to show images of unborn fetuses.

EXERCISE 8

Wave Types

Directions: In the space provided, write **L** if the example is an example of a longitudinal wave and **T** if it is an example of a transverse wave.

1. ______ a wave that can be seen when a loose rope held end to end is jerked at one end
2. ______ the noise caused by the detonation of an atomic bomb
3. ______ the hum created when an arrow is released from a bow
4. ______ waves that appear on the surface of the ocean

Answers are on page 585.

GED PRACTICE

EXERCISE 9

Properties of Waves

Directions: Look at the illustration below and choose the best answers to the questions that follow.

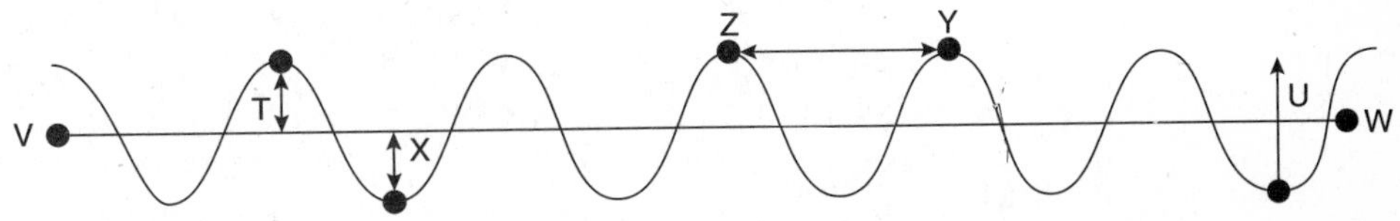

1. **According to the illustration above, which points could be used to measure wavelength?**
   (1) T and Y
   (2) X and Y
   (3) Z and Y
   (4) V and W
   (5) T, X, and U

2. **The Doppler Effect is used for which of the following purposes?**
   (1) to find fish in lakes
   (2) to predict storms and tornadoes
   (3) to test wave frequency
   (4) to reflect images to satellites
   (5) to heighten sound in stereos

Answers are on page 585.

The Nature of Light

Physicists define **light** as a form of electromagnetic energy that stimulates sensitive cells of the retina of the human eye to cause perception of vision. Electromagnetic energy can be expressed in wavelength ranges along a continuum, or spectrum. Light occupies the center of a spectrum that ranges from the low end **(gamma rays)** to the high end **(radio waves).** The other rays that occupy the electromagnetic spectrum are Xrays, ultraviolet rays, and infrared rays. **Ultraviolet** rays are invisible and are chiefly responsible for sunburn and tan. Heat-emitting objects such as the sun or a radiator send out **infrared rays** that can be detected only by certain sensitive instruments.

THE ELECTROMAGNETIC SPECTRUM

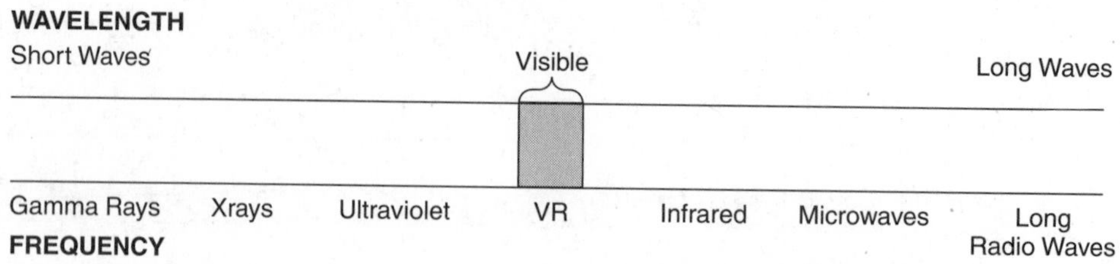

The visible rays of the spectrum are recognized by the human eye as color. In order, these colors are red, orange, yellow, green, blue, indigo (deep blue), and violet. The shortest wavelengths that we can see are those we call violet; the longest ones are those we call red.

Two theories about the nature of light exist: the wave theory and the particle theory. These theories seem to oppose each other but really just focus on different properties of light. According to the **Wave Theory of Light,** light is a luminous energy emitted by a light source and travels through space as a transverse wave. According to the **Particle Theory of Light,** light energy is both radiated (transmitted) and absorbed as tiny packets, or bundles, and not as continuous waves. Atoms and molecules are able to emit or absorb light energy in specific amounts.

GED PRACTICE

EXERCISE 10

The Photoelectric Principle

Directions: Read the passage below and answer the question that follows.

The electric eye, or photoelectric cell, is a mechanism used to open and close a garage door when a beam of light is activated or broken. The principle of the electric eye is based on the photoelectric effect. The photoelectric effect occurs when a beam of light strikes certain metals, causing electrons to be knocked out of the metal, producing an electric current. This is how it happens:

Light falling on the inside of a bulb coated with an active substance causes electrons to be emitted. The electrons are attracted to a positively charged electrode positioned in the center of the bulb as a filament. An electric current results when the electrons (negatively charged particles) are attracted to the positively charged particles of the electrode. It is observed that electrons are knocked loose only when a certain light energy is reached. The current can then be controlled by changes in light intensity. It appears that electrons are able to absorb only a certain amount of light at one time. When light shines on the electric eye, a current is established and the door moves. When the beam of light is broken, the door stops.

How does the principle of the electric eye act?

(1) to support the wave theory of light that light comes only from a luminous source
(2) to dispute the belief that all light exists only as a continuous wave
(3) to support the particle theory of light, which states that light energy is transmitted in packets and bundles and not as waves
(4) to complement the idea that light acts like particles in a wave
(5) to contradict the idea that light is generated only in a star

Answer is on page 585.

PROPERTIES OF LIGHT WAVES	
reflection	the angular return of a light wave that occurs when it strikes a shiny surface *Example:* light bouncing off a mirror
refraction	the apparent bending of light waves as they pass from one medium to another *Example:* drinking straw looking broken in a glass of water
diffraction	the bending of light waves according to their wavelengths as they pass near the edge of an obstacle or through a small opening *Example:* "rainbow" pattern on an old phonograph record held edgewise toward white light
interference	the altering of brightness of light rays that occurs when they interfere with each other, causing reinforcement and cancellation *Example:* holding thumb and finger together and looking through the opening at a bright light
polarization	the restriction of light waves to a particular plane, horizontal or vertical *Example:* sunglasses that minimize glare off shiny surfaces

GED PRACTICE

EXERCISE 11

Properties of Light Waves

Directions: Use the information above to choose the *best* answer for each question below.

1. **A coin lying at the bottom of a pool is located at a different point from where the eye perceives it to be. The light rays from the coin bend as they pass from water to air. This demonstrates**

   (1) reflection
   (2) refraction
   (3) diffraction
   (4) interference
   (5) polarization

2. **Rays of light striking a polished piece of chrome appear to bounce off its surface. This demonstrates**

   (1) reflection
   (2) refraction
   (3) diffraction
   (4) interference
   (5) polarization

Answers are on page 585.

The Nature of Electricity

Electricity is another invisible but vital form of energy that we often take for granted. Without electricity, however, our lives would be paralyzed. The more urbanized we become, the more dependent on electricity we are. Nuclear energy, despite its potential hazards, is an important source for generating the electrical power we need. Physicists define **electricity** as a form of energy that results from the flow of loose electrons— electrons weakly bound to atoms. Electricity is closely related to magnetism; therefore, the attractive force of magnetism must be discussed in order to explain electrical energy.

Magnetism and Electrical Charges

The points of attraction at opposite ends of a magnet are called its **poles.** Magnets have a north and a south pole, also called a positive and a negative pole. The opposite poles of two magnets (a north pole and a south pole) will attract each other. Correspondingly, similar poles (two north or south poles) will repel each other. The space around magnets is called a **magnetic field.** Only a few natural and synthetic materials can be magnetized—iron, steel, nickel, cobalt, and some alloys. A magnet, with its poles and lines of force, is illustrated below.

MAGNET AND LINES OF FORCE

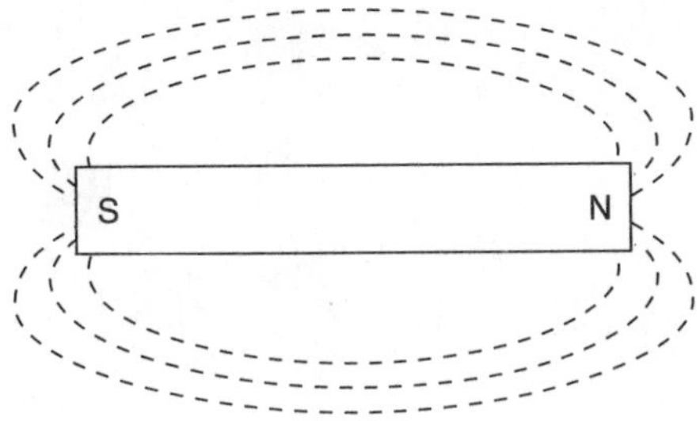

Magnetic Lines of Force

Every magnetic substance contains domains, groups of molecules with attractive forces. Before a substance is magnetized, these domains are arranged randomly so that the field of one domain is canceled out by the field of another. When the substance is magnetized, the domains line up parallel to the lines of force, with all north poles facing in the same direction. This arrangement makes a permanent magnet out of a material in which the domains are too weak to disarrange themselves.

In most elements the atoms possess a slight magnetic field because of their spinning electrons. However, the fields cancel each other out because the atoms rotate and spin in different directions. In a magnet, however, whole groups of atoms line up in one direction and increase one another's magnetic effect rather than cancel it out. These magnetic concentrations are **magnetic domains.**

Static Electricity and Magnetism

Static electricity is a stationary electrical charge caused by the friction of two objects, one positively charged and the other negatively charged. Static electricity operates on the same principle as magnetism. The rubbing of the carpet by your shoes causes your body to become electrified. The shock you feel is caused by your negatively charged body being neutralized by the positive charge of the object you touch. Upon contact your body is no longer charged. Static electricity is stored and does not move. The charged object must be brought into contact with another object that has an opposite charge for electrical shock to occur.

Magnetized and Unmagnetized Iron Atoms

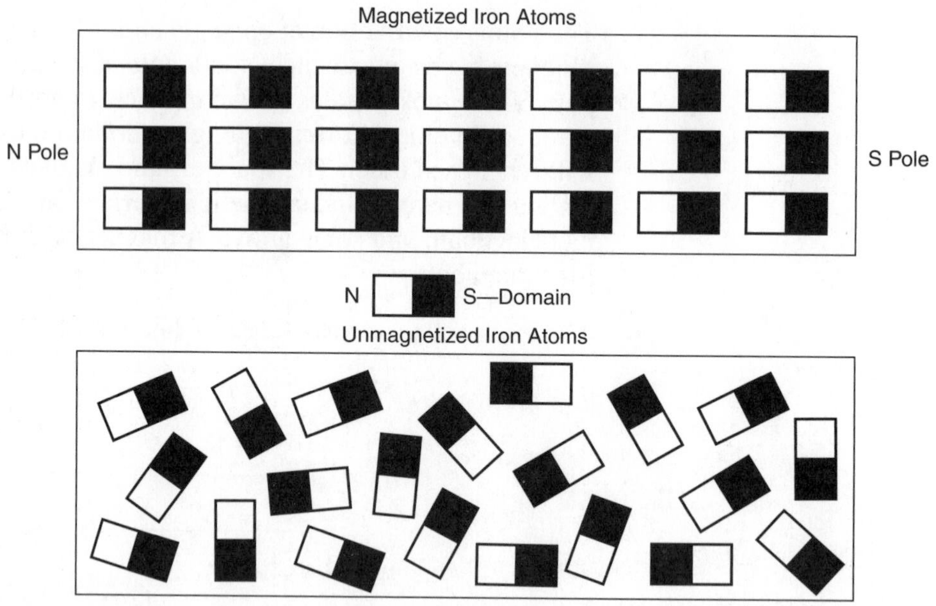

GED PRACTICE

EXERCISE 12

Electricity and Magnetism

Directions: Choose the *best* answer for the questions on page 573. The first question is based on the following paragraph.

Earth itself is surrounded by a magnetic field. This may be because of strong electric currents in Earth's core and the rotation of Earth. The north magnetic pole is located in Canada; the south magnetic pole is in nearly the opposite location. The strong magnetic attraction of these poles tends to align the needle of a compass in a northerly–southerly direction.

1. What makes a compass tell direction?

(1) The whole Earth acts as a magnet.
(2) The Chinese discovered the magnetic poles.
(3) The Greeks discovered the magnetic poles.
(4) Large iron deposits are located in Canada.
(5) The magnetic attraction of Earth is increasing.

2. Which of the following would be attracted to either pole of a magnet?

(1) a piece of aluminum
(2) a piece of brass
(3) a piece of tin
(4) an unmagnetized piece of cobalt
(5) a magnetized piece of cobalt

Answers are on page 586.

Electric Currents

Early scientists who experimented with electric charges found that charges could move easily through certain materials called **conductors.** As you learned in the chemistry section, metal was found to be a good conductor of electricity, as were salt solutions, acids, and hot gases. Other materials such as rubber were found not to conduct charges at all. These materials are called **insulators.**

An **electric current** is created by an electric charge in motion. In a solid conductor, such as wire, the current is a stream of moving electrons. In a liquid or gas, the current may be positively and negatively charged atoms—**ions.** An electric current flowing through a solid conductor can be compared to the flow of water through the pipes in your plumbing system. An electric current moves slowly—about a hundredth of an inch per second. Although our lights come on instantly when a switch is turned on, it is because the wires are always filled with electrons, just as a water pipe is always filled with water.

Electromagnets

An **electromagnet** is a core of soft magnetic material surrounded by a coil of wire. An electric current is passed through the wire to magnetize the core when a switch is flicked or a button is pushed. The device then has the power to attract iron objects. When the switch is turned off, the attraction is broken. Electromagnets are used in radios and in ordinary doorbells.

EXERCISE 13

Conductors and Insulators

Directions: Identify the following terms as either a conductor of electricity (**C**) or an insulator (**I**).

1. ______ leather
2. ______ wood
3. ______ salt water
4. ______ plastic
5. ______ copper

Answers are on page 586.

GED PRACTICE

EXERCISE 14

Electromagnets

Directions: Choose the *best* answer for the following questions.

1. Why would a radio with a strong electromagnet be placed far away from the navigation instruments on a plane or ship?

(1) The radio wouldn't work because of electrical interference.
(2) The radio couldn't be heard clearly because of static.
(3) The accuracy of the compass would be affected by the magnetic field established by the radio's electromagnet.
(4) The radio's electromagnet would cause all the navigation instruments to malfunction.
(5) The radio would draw too much electrical energy, causing the electrical system of the ship or plane to discharge.

2. Identify which of the following are true (T) or false (F).

______ You need an insulator to keep electricity flowing only along wires.

______ Electromagnets are used in doorbells.

______ When the switch is in the off position, electricity still is flowing through the circuit.

Answers are on page 586.

Creating Electricity

Electricity is created by power companies and sent to our homes by high voltage wires through transformers. There are several ways to create electricity. Because there is a concern about the limited quantities of fossil fuels, alternative power supplies for electricity are being used.

One system requires the fission of nuclear energy in nuclear power plants. These plants bombard the nuclei of large unstable uranium atoms with neutrons. The large release of heat is used to heat water, which is used to turn a **turbine,** a wire loop connecting two magnets. When the turbine is forced to turn, the electrons are stolen from the magnets and sent through the wire as electricity. This alternative energy has many drawbacks, including the safe disposal of radioactive nuclear waste left over from the reaction.

© Telegraph Colour Library/FPG

Another alternative is **solar energy.** Scientists have found that pure silicon (found in sand and one of the most common elements in the crust of the Earth) is electrically excited in the presence of light. You may have experienced this if you own a solar calculator, but it may not have performed in a dimly lighted area. The sun's energy excites the electrons, which then flow along wires to provide electricity to the attached appliance.

©Hank Morgan / Rainbow

Other alternative energies are limited to the availabililty of the conditions necessary to generate electricity. One such alternative is **wind power,** which has been successfully captured through the use of windmills throughout the history of civilization. California has wind farms where many large windmills are connected to generate electricity. These new models on the old design limit the number of arms on the mill and make these arms out of durable synthetic materials. Windmills do not need a strong wind; in fact, strong winds can damage the mechanics. The best condition is a steady wind that maintains a continuous motion of the flywheel.

© VCG/FPG

Hydroelectric power is another source that has to be limited to the already established use of the water flow in the region. Many rivers are used as transportation and cannot be dammed to provide the reservoir of water needed to control the flow of water through the turbine system. Yet hydroelectric power, as well as wind and solar powers is a clean, renewable resource. Critics suggest that the reason these systems have not been fully developed is the fear energy companies have in reducing their own incomes.

© Telegraph Colour Library/FPG

EXERCISE 15

Creating Electricity

Directions: Use the information above to fill in the blanks in each statement below.

1. Hydroelectric power is not always possible because sometimes rivers are used for ____________________.

2. Fossil fuels will not be around forever, so we need to explore the use of other energy systems called ____________________.

3. Windmills do not need strong wind, but they do need ____________________ wind.

4. Pure silicon has electrons that are excited into motion by ____________________.

5. A loop or wire that is turned between two magnets and creates electricity is a ____________________.

Answers are on page 586.

Go to **www.GEDScience.com** for additional practice and instruction!

SCIENCE

Answer Key

CHAPTER 1

LIFE SCIENCE: BIOLOGY

Exercise 1: Cell Structure (page 461)
Comprehension
1. c **2.** a **3.** b **4.** d

Exercise 2: Cells (page 462)
1. **Comprehension (4)** The other choices do not identify the main idea. They serve as details to support the main idea that the cell is complex, with organized subsystems.
2. **Comprehension (5)** Chloroplasts are important in the food-making process for plants. Because animal cells cannot make their own food, we can infer that they must obtain nutrients elsewhere.
3. **Application (5)** Because chloroplasts create energy, they can be thought of as the power plant of the plant cell.

Exercise 3: Cells and Active Transport (page 463)
Comprehension
1. high/low **2.** low/high

GED Practice Exercise 4: Diffusion and Osmosis (page 463)
1. **Analysis (3)** Diffusion is the passage of molecules from an area of higher concentration to an area of lower concentration. This process allows for an even distribution of substances throughout the cells of the body.
2. **Analysis (1)** In osmosis, water moves from an area of higher concentration of water to an area of lower concentration of water. The salt water has a lower concentration of water, so the water will leave the cell in an attempt to equalize the percentage of water outside as well as inside the cell. The cell will lose water.

Exercise 5: Mitosis (page 465)
Comprehension
1. a **2.** b **3.** d **4.** c

Exercise 6: Meiosis (page 467)
Comprehension
4, 1, 3, 2

GED Practice Exercise 7: Cell Division (page 468)
1. **Application (3)** Because of the exchange and recombination of chromosomal material, the method of reproduction that allows for the most variety is sexual reproduction.
2. **Analysis (3)** Because cancerous cells spread to invade healthy cells, we can conclude that cancer cells divide more unpredictably than normal cells.

GED Practice Exercise 8: Genetics and Heredity (page 470)
1. **Comprehension (4)** The diagram shows only one child out of four that does not have a dominant green-eye gene or a dominant brown-eye gene. This is the only child that will have blue eyes; therefore, the chances are that 25% of the children will have blue eyes.
2. **Analysis (3)** The Y chromosome that determines a child's sex is carried by the father.

Exercise 9: Cloning (page 472)
Comprehension
1. False 2. False 3. False 4. True 5. True

Exercise 10: Organ Systems (page 473)
Application
1. d **2.** e **3.** f **4.** b **5.** a **6.** c

Exercise 11: The Nervous System (page 477)
Application
1. **a.** cerebellum **b.** spinal cord
   c. medulla oblongata **d.** cerebrum
2. **(False)** The spinal cord is responsible for the reflex condition.
   (True)
   (True)
   (False) There are two hemispheres of the brain.

Exercise 12: The Circulatory and Respiratory Systems (page 480)

1. **Comprehension (2)** The alveoli are the small sacs in the lungs that are responsible for the actual exchange of oxygen and carbon dioxide.
2. **1. H** Heart **2. V** Vessels **3. V** Vessels **4. H** Heart **5. V** Vessels
3. **Application (5)** Moderate daily exercise helps to condition the heart and lungs. Strenuous exercise (choice 3) puts too much pressure on these systems. Smoking (choice 1) is damaging to the respiratory system, and fried foods (choice 2) hurt the circulatory system by promoting the buildup of plaque in the blood vessels. Painting (choice 4) in nonventilated areas allows unfiltered toxins to enter the lungs.

Exercise 13: The Digestive and Excretory Systems (page 482)

Comprehension

1. b **2.** d **3.** e **4.** a **5.** c

Exercise 14: The Skeletal and Muscular Systems (page 483)

Comprehension

1. skeletal, smooth, cardiac
2. osteoporosis
3. Steroids
4. marrow
5. 206
6. Ligaments

Exercise 15: Transplantation (page 484)

Analysis

1. **O** The word *feel* reveals that this is not a fact.
2. **F** Rejection is always a possibility in transplantation.
3. **F** Even if the person has a donor card, the hospital consults the next of kin to avoid legal conflicts and unfavorable publicity.
4. **O** There is no scientific data on how the interests or talents of the donor could ever affect the recipient of the donated organ or tissue.
5. **O** The words *wrong* and *should* reveal that the statement is an opinion.

GED Practice Exercise 16: The Nitrogen Cycle (page 486)

1. **Analysis (1)** The only case that shows a mutually beneficial relationship between two different organisms is that of bacteria that live in the stomachs of hoofed animals and at the same time help the animal to digest food.
2. **Application (4)** Soybeans are legumes that are important in the nitrogen-fixing process. The introduction of soybeans into the crop-rotation process improves the possibility of replenishing the supply of nitrogen.

Exercise 17: Photosynthesis (page 487)

1. **Comprehension**

a. True **b.** False **c.** True

2. **Analysis (1)** Green pigment indicates the presence of chlorophyll. The areas of the coleus leaf that were green originally contained starch, which is produced through photosynthesis. Therefore, the starch turns brown when iodine is applied.

GED Practice Exercise 18: Cellular Respiration (page 488)

1. **Comprehension (1)** Glucose molecules must be present for cellular respiration to occur. Because glucose molecules are the end product of photosynthesis in plants, you can infer that photosynthesis must precede cellular respiration.
2. **Application (4)** The more active a person is, the more energy he or she expends and the more carbon dioxide he or she exhales. Physically active people would have higher rates of cellular respiration than non-physically active people.
3. **Evaluation (4)** The rate of cellular respiration is affected by whether or not a person is at rest or physically active. Choice (4) is best because a larger number of people are being sampled.
4. **Evaluation (2)** The other choices are unrelated.

GED Practice Exercise 19: Classification of Organisms (page 491)

1. **Application (1)** Streptococcus is a single-celled organism of the bacteria family and fits in the kingdom Monera.
2. **Application (3)** Mold lacks chlorophyll and obtains food from another organism. It is classified in the kingdom Fungi.

GED Practice Exercise 20: Evolution and Natural Selection (page 493)

1. **Application (3)** According to the passage, certain forms of life adapted to meet the demands of the environment. The fact that the duckbill platypus is found only in and around Australia supports the hypothesis that the platypus developed independently in a closed environment during the early history of mammals.
2. **Comprehension (1)** This is the best answer because the other choices are not true.
3. **Evaluation (1)** Of the choices listed, the migration pattern of a bird is a behavioral adaptation, not a physical one.

Exercise 21: Ecology and Ecosystems (page 496)
Application

1. grass for grazing
2. cattle, deer
3. mountain lion

Analysis

4. The destruction of the **mountain lion** led to the increase of grazing by **deer** and **cattle,** which led to **stripping the grasses** of the land and its eventual **erosion** by heavy rains.

CHAPTER 2

EARTH AND SPACE SCIENCE

Exercise 1: Stars and Galaxies (page 500)
Comprehension

1. 3, 4, 1, 2
2. **1. False** They would become black holes.
   2. True Red giants are the first visible sign we have of star death.
   3. False An Open universe would mean no stopping of expansion because of lack of gravity.
   4. False The Sun is eight light minutes away; all other stars are much farther away.

Exercise 2: The Sun and the Solar System (page 502)

1. **Application (4)** According to the story of "Goldilocks and the Three Bears," Goldilocks tried the bowls of porridge and found them too hot, too cold, or just right. This would correspond to Venus being too hot, Mars being too cold, and Earth being just right in temperature.

Comprehension

2. **1.** b **2.** d **3.** a **4.** c
3. **(False)** Mars has dust storms, Jupiter has a gaseous surface.
   (True) The canals turned out to be possibly old river beds from earlier, warmer conditions.
   (True) The wind bands travel in the opposite direction, giving the planet a stripped look.
   (True) The sun is thought to be about five billion years old, halfway through its life cycle.
   (False) While the planet is covered in clouds, the vapor in the clouds is sulfuric acid, not rain (H_20).

Exercise 3: Space Travel (page 503)
Analysis

1. 5, 1, 4, 2, 3
2. 1. land like an airplane
   2. mutual efforts from many countries
   3. Skylab and Mir
   4. National Aeronautics and Space Administration

Exercise 4: The Planets (page 504)
Application

1. Earth, Mars
2. Mercury
3. Venus

GED Practice Exercise 5: Plate Tectonics (page 507)
Comprehension

1. **(2)** In the passage, the occurrence of earthquakes, volcanoes, and mountains is explained by the theory of plate tectonics.
2. **(4)** Glaciers carve out glacier valleys and are not caused by plate tectonics.

GED Practice Exercise 6: Earthquakes (page 509)
Evaluation

1. **(3)** The map shows the potential for the occurrence of the most moderate and major earthquake damage as being in the western United States. Choice (5) is an opinion statement.
2. **(True)**
   (False) Springing back up is elastic rebound; isostacy is when the crust is in balance.
   (False) Not all earthquakes occur along the plate boundaries. The New Madrid earthquake zone in Missouri is the middle of the North American Plate.
   (True)

Exercise 7: The Pacific Northwest (page 510)
Analysis

1. Opinion
2. Fact
3. Fact
4. Opinion

GED Practice Exercise 8: Continental Drift (page 511)

Analysis (3) This is the best choice because it takes into account both the theory of plate tectonics and the behavior of sea turtles.

GED Practice Exercise 9: Measuring Geologic Time (page 513)

1. **Comprehension (5)** The text states that sedimentary rocks are deposited near Earth's surface and that metamorphic rock is located just below igneous rock.
2. **Analysis (5)** The trilobite rocks are likely to be older than the coral because the greater the depth at which fossils are found, the older they are likely to be.

GED Practice Exercise 10: Minerals and Rocks (page 514)

1. **Analysis (3)** Potassium, which makes up 1.85 percent of Earth's crust, is the only element that occupies three times more space than does silicon.
2. **Analysis (5)** The fact that oxygen combines with most of Earth's elements explains why it constitutes such a great part of Earth's crust.

Exercise 11: The Changing Earth (page 517)

1. gravity, wind, glaciers, running water
2. **Application (5)** Planting more seeds than necessary is a procedure most farmers follow to increase their chances of a bountiful harvest and has nothing to do with preventing erosion.

Analysis

3. **1.** Opinion **2.** Opinion **3.** Opinion (This is good advice but not fact.) **4.** Fact

GED Practice Exercise 12: Change in Sea Level (page 520)

1. Comprehension (5) According to the graph, nearly 18,000 years ago the depth of the oceans was at almost 400 feet below sea level, its lowest level.
2. (2) Plate tectonics describes the movement of the crustal plates due to the flow of the mantle, which pulls the sea floor open allowing magma to ooze out.

GED Practice Exercise 13: The Beginning of the Oceans (page 521)

1. **Comprehension (4)** At 0.001 percent, water vapor in the atmosphere yields the lowest amount of water on Earth.
2. **Evaluation (4)** According to the text, many scientists believe that oceans were formed by the release of water bound up in Earth's interior.
3. **Comprehension (4)** Drinking water is purified from fresh water lakes and rivers.

GED Practice Exercise 14: Ocean Tides (page 522)

1. **Analysis (4)** According to the illustration, the Moon is in a direct line with the Sun; therefore, Earth receives the combined gravity from the Sun and the Moon. This occurs during the new phase.
2. **Application (2)** The opposite condition of syzygy occurs when the Sun and the Moon are at their farthest distances from Earth. This means the least amount of gravity is affecting the tides, and the tidal difference is the lowest measured.

GED Practice Exercise 15: Layers of Earth's Atmosphere (page 525)

1. **Comprehension (4)** The ionosphere extends from 30 miles to 300 miles in Earth's atmosphere. Noctilucent clouds are found at heights above 50 miles.
2. **Comprehension (3)** "D" radio waves are found at the same level as noctilucent clouds—in the lower ionosphere.
3. **Comprehension (1)** Clouds (located in the troposphere) shown at the same level as Mt. Everest's peak suggest that it may be occasionally hidden by clouds.

GED Practice Exercise 16: Ozone in the Atmosphere (page 527)

Analysis (2) Smog is visible and, therefore, lies in the troposphere, the level that is closest to the surface of Earth.

Exercise 17: The Water Cycle (page 528)

Analysis

1. B **2.** D **3.** A **4.** C

GED Practice Exercise 18: Humidity (page 529)

1. **Analysis (3)** According to the passage, warm air holds more moisture than cold air; therefore, when the temperature drops, the cold air cannot hold the amount of moisture that the warmer air held. At that temperature, the saturation point would be exceeded and the excess humidity would be released as rain.
2. **Analysis (3)** At a given time, water vapor in the air is constant. Cold air can hold less than warm air; and when air is heated, it has a greater capacity to hold moisture. If that moisture is not added to the air, the humidity level goes down.

Exercise 19: Air Masses, Fronts, and Weather (page 532)

1. **Comprehension (2)** According to the passage, warm fronts bring low-lying clouds, steady winds, and drizzling rain.
2. **Comprehension (1)** According to the passage, an air mass is formed when a body of air takes on the characteristics from the land or water over which it forms.
3. **a. T** (tornado) **b. B** (both) **c. H** (hurricane) **d. T** (tornado)

CHAPTER 3
PHYSICAL SCIENCE: CHEMISTRY

Exercise 1: Atomic Structure (page 535)
Comprehension
1. d **2.** e **3.** f **4.** b **5.** c **6.** a

Exercise 2: Nuclear Energy (page 537)
1. **Application (4)** The passage states that fusion involves the uniting of two nuclei of a chemical element at high temperatures and pressures to form a new element. Hydrogen, the lightest element, is the only element listed whose nuclei when fused can form the second lightest element—helium.
2. **Application (1)** The passage states that fission involves the splitting of the nucleus of a heavy element. Plutonium is not a gas and, therefore, is the only heavy element listed.

Analysis
3. **1. False** That occurred at Chernobyl.
   2. False There are risks with any storage.
   3. True This could have been prevented if the priority had been safety and not the test schedule.
   4. True The control rods cover the fuel rods and prevent unchained reaction.

Exercise 3: Isotopic Elements (page 538)
1. **Application (3)** According to the chart, lithium's atomic mass is 6.94. Of all the elements shown, it would be the most likely to have an isotope of 6. If two lithium isotopes are fused, the atomic mass of the new element would be 12—the atomic mass of carbon.
2. **Application (1)** According to the passage, an isotope is a form of an element whose number of neutrons in its nucleus varies. The only element represented that is capable of doubling or tripling its mass to achieve a final mass of 2 or 3 would be hydrogen.

Analysis
3. **1.** Opinion **2.** Fact **3.** Fact
   4. Opinion **5.** Fact

GED Practice Exercise 4: Elements and Periodicity (page 542)
1. **Application (4)** The passage states that as the atomic number increases for elements in a column, similar chemical properties occur regularly and to a greater degree. The only physical property of which gold would have a higher degree is malleability because it is a soft and workable metal.
2. **Analysis (2)** Radon has the greatest atomic number in this group of elements, which are all in the same column, or family, in the periodic table. According to the periodic law, properties of elements in the same family occur to a greater degree as the atomic number increases.

Exercise 5: Balanced Equations (page 544)
Comprehension
1. **B (balanced).** The reaction begins and ends with two atoms of nitrogen (N) and two atoms of oxygen (O).
2. **U (unbalanced).** The reaction begins with one atom of iron (Fe), one atom of hydrogen (H), and one atom of chlorine (Cl). However, it ends with one atom of iron, two atoms of hydrogen, and three atoms of chlorine. Therefore, it is not balanced.
3. **B (balanced).** The reaction begins and ends with two atoms of hydrogen (H) and one atom of oxygen (O).
4. **U (unbalanced).** The Fe (iron) does not balance out. The right side of the equation needs to read: $4Fe+3CO_2$.
5. **B (balanced).** All the elements are balanced at 2.

GED Practice Exercise 6: Chemical Reactions (page 544)
1. **Analysis (2)** None of the others is a balanced equation indicating one molecule of carbon dioxide (CO_2) and one molecule of water (H_2O). Choice (4) started with carbon dioxide and water, but the equation does not balance.
2. **Comprehension (2)** According to the passage, a chemical equation is balanced when it follows the Law of Conservation of Matter, which states that matter can neither be created nor destroyed in a chemical reaction.

GED Practice Exercise 7: Elements in Combination (page 546)

1. **Application (1)** Salt is a compound composed of elements sodium and chlorine and has properties different from each.
2. **Application (2)** Air is a mixture of at least four gases. Each gas retains its own distinct properties.

Exercise 8: Chemical Bonding (page 550)

1. **Comprehension (2)** The passage says that ionic bonding is achieved by the transfer of electrons.
2. **Comprehension (1)** The passage says that a covalent bond is one in which atoms are held together by sharing electrons.

Application

3. 4, 2, 5, 6, 3

GED Practice Exercise 9: Acids, Bases and Salts (page 551)

1. **Analysis (4)** Acetic acid, a mild acid contained in vinegar, would be found at the acidic end of the pH scale closest to neutrality—between the values 4 and 5. Choices (1) and (5) are alkaline, and choices 2 and 3 are strong acids.
2. **Analysis (3)** Water is neither acidic nor alkaline; therefore, it would be neutral on the pH scale.
3. **Evaluation (3)** A substance is an acid if it neutralizes a base to form a salt.

GED Practice Exercise 10: A Car Battery (page 552)

1. **Application (2)** In the example, sulfuric acid, a conductor of electricity, is dissolved in water.
2. **Application (1)** The passage says that the lead loses two electrons when it reacts with sulfuric acid; therefore, lead is oxidized.
3. **Application (2)** Sulfuric acid is an oxidizing agent because it causes the lead in the battery to lose electrons. The lead dioxide is a reducing agent because it causes the sulfuric acid to gain electrons.
4. **Analysis (2)** A battery is completely discharged when the sulfuric acid is no longer capable of oxidizing lead and the lead dioxide is no longer able to reduce the sulfuric acid. The oxidation-reduction process that causes an electric current to flow cannot occur, and the battery is dead.

GED Practice Exercise 11: Reaction Rate, Catalysts, and Equilibrium (page 554)

1. **Analysis (3)** A catalyst is an agent that speeds up a chemical reaction but that is not affected by the reaction itself. Lipase speeds up the rate at which fats are changed into fatty acids. Because lipase is found in the body, it may be described as a biological catalyst.
2. **Application (5)** According to the passage, chemical equilibrium occurs when the rate of forward reaction balances the rate of reverse reaction. In photosynthesis, plants take in water and carbon dioxide from the air to make starch with the light energy from the sun. The by-product of oxygen is released. The reverse of the process is respiration, the taking in of oxygen and combining of it with starch to form carbon dioxide and water, which plants then use for photosynthesis. Thus, the forward reaction of photosynthesis is balanced by the reverse reaction of respiration, resulting in chemical equilibrium.

CHAPTER 4

PHYSICAL SCIENCE: PHYSICS

Exercise 1: Laws of Force and Motion (page 557)
Application

1. AR **2.** AR **3.** G **4.** I **5.** AF

Exercise 2: The Force of Gravity (page 557)

1. **Application (1)** Weight is the function of the attractive force between two objects. According to the passage, the strength of the force depends on the masses of the objects. Since Jupiter is larger than Earth, the attractive force must be greater, so the astronaut would weigh more on Jupiter.
2. **Application** The astronaut's weight would be less on Mercury since that planet has less mass.

Exercise 3: Forms of Energy (page 559)
Application

1. K **2.** P **3.** P **4.** K

GED Practice Exercise 4: Types of Energy (page 559)

1. **Application (1)** Nuclear energy results from the splitting of an atom of a heavy chemical element such as U-235.
2. **Application (2)** Gas and air are mixtures. When they are ignited, the *chemical* process of combustion occurs.

Exercise 5: Simple Machines (page 561)

1. **Analysis (3)** According to the passage, the greater the distance between the fulcrum and the applied force, the less the force required to perform the work. If the distance is increased to 20 feet, then the effort would be halved.
2. **Application** Answers will vary. Examples of simple machines include: screwdriver, can opener, nutcracker, scissors, wrench, and pliers.

Exercise 6: Kinetic Theory of Matter (page 563)
Comprehension

1. True **2.** False **3.** True
4. False **5.** False

GED Practice Exercise 7: Heat and Temperature (page 564)

1. **Analysis (1)** Because concrete and steel both expand at about the same temperatures, they are ideal to use for roadways. Since concrete expands at a higher temperature, choice (2) is false.
2. **Application (1)** Convection is described as heat transferred by currents of gases and liquids. Warm air rising off a candle flame demonstrates convection.

Exercise 8: Wave Types (page 567)
Application

1. T (transverse wave)
2. L (longitudinal wave)
3. L (longitudinal wave)
4. T (transverse wave)

GED Practice Exercise 9: Properties of Waves (page 567)

1. **Comprehension (3)** The passage states that the wavelength is the distance between two successive wave crests or troughs. Points Z and Y are two successive wave crests.
2. **Application (2)** The Doppler Effect has become an important part of forecasting weather, especially when there are circulating wind patterns as you would see with a tornado, hurricane, or any low-pressure center.

GED Practice Exercise 10: The Photoelectric Principle (page 569)

Evaluation (2) The passage states that an active substance emits electrons when light falls on it. Light intensity determines the strength of the current generated by the emission of electrons. This suggests that light energy is transmitted in packets or bundles and disputes the belief that light exists only as a continuous wave.

GED Practice Exercise 11: Properties of Light Waves (page 570)

1. **Application (2)** Refraction is the bending of light waves as they pass from one medium to another—in this case, from water to air.
2. **Application (1)** Reflection is the return of a light wave when it strikes a shiny or very flat surface.

GED Practice Exercise 12: Electricity and Magnetism (page 572)

1. **Analysis (1)** According to the text, the strong magnetic attraction coming from Earth's core tends to align the needle of the compass in a north-south direction.
2. **Application (5)** A magnetized object will attract either end of an unmagnetized object made of iron, steel, nickel, or cobalt but will attract only the opposite pole of another magnetized object. Aluminum, brass, and tin cannot be attracted.

Exercise 13: Conductors and Insulators (page 574)
Application

1. I (insulator) **2.** I (insulator) **3.** C (conductor) **4.** I (insulator) **5.** C (conductor)

GED Practice Exercise 14: Electromagnets (page 574)

1. **Analysis (3)** The radio's electromagnet should not be placed near the compass because it would affect the magnetic reading from the North Pole.
2. **(True)** An insulator prevents the electricity from leaving the wire.
   (True) The electromagnet allows the doorbell to make a circuit when pressed.
   (False) The circuit is broken when the switch is in the off position.

Exercise 15: Creating Electricity (page 577)
Comprehension

1. transportation
2. alternative energies
3. steady
4. light
5. turbine

Language Arts, Reading

The GED Language Arts, Reading Test consists of prose passages of about 200 to 400 words, poetry passages of about eight to twenty-five lines, and drama excerpts. Each passage is followed by four to eight multiple-choice questions. These questions require you to interpret selections from popular literature, classical literature, and commentaries about literature and the arts. To answer successfully, you will need to

- understand what you read
- apply information to a new situation
- analyze elements of style and structure in passages
- synthesize parts of passages into a whole

How many questions are on the test?

There are 40 multiple-choice questions, and you will be given 65 minutes to complete the test. Each passage on the Language Arts, Reading Test is preceded by a **purpose question.** This question is *not* a title for the passage. Rather, it is intended to help you focus your reading of the piece. To get an idea of what the test is like, look at the Posttest at the end of this book. The Posttest is based on the actual GED Test.

What's on the test?

The GED Language Arts, Reading Test can be broken down into the content areas it covers and the skills it tests. The following subjects make up the content of the test:

1. Literary Texts (30 items) 75%

Prose Fiction from three general time periods: (45%)
Before 1920
1920–1960
After 1960
Poetry (15%)
Drama (15%)

2. Nonfiction Texts (10 items) 25%

Informational Text: newspaper or magazine articles, editorials, or speeches
Literary Nonfiction: biographies, autobiographies, essays, diaries, letters, or reviews
Critical reviews of fine or performing arts: commentary about films, television, videotapes, photos, artwork, computer images, or charts
Business Documents

Only seven passages will be included in each test form. Each test will have one commentary work about a visual medium, but there will be no graphics. You will not have to recall or have prior knowledge of the text of specific literary works, including titles, dates, or authors.

Also remember that you will be tested on your ability to think through certain ideas and concepts. You will be asked to do more than just find a statement or quotation that was given in a passage.

What thinking skills are needed for the test?

Thinking skills that you will be tested on include:

Comprehension (Literal and Inferential) 20%

Paraphrasing, summarizing, explaining

Application 15%

Transferring ideas to new situations

Analysis 30–35%

Drawing conclusions; understanding consequences; making inferences; identifying style and structure; making comparisons and contrasts; using cause and effect

Synthesis 30–35%

Drawing on the passage as a whole or on several sources; interpreting organizational structure or overall tone, point of view, style, or purpose; making connections

In the Critical Thinking Skills section of this book, the thinking skills above are explained and demonstrated. See pages 211–294.

CHAPTER 1

Interpreting Prose Fiction

The fiction passages presented on the Language Arts, Reading Test are taken from either novels or short stories. Both novels and short stories usually present imaginary people and events that imitate life. Novels and short stories are written in **prose**—ordinary spoken language—and share common literary devices and techniques. These devices and techniques will be explored in this section.

By reading fiction, you can enjoy stories about interesting people and situations and gain a greater understanding of life. Your understanding of literature will also aid you as a moviegoer or as a viewer of television, videotapes, or DVDs. Many aspects of literature can be applied to films and television programs because the script is the basis for any of these.

Think of the author as a type of artist who works with a palette. On the palette the artist mixes colors, just as the author mixes together **characters, settings,** and **plots.** The artist works with an overall purpose for his subject matter just as the author conveys **themes**. The artist and the author speak through a particular **point of view** which may be direct or indirect. In the finished product the artist and the author each convey an attitude toward his or her work through a particular **style** shown. The artist achieves an overall result through a painting or other work of art; the fiction author achieves an overall result through a novel or short story.

The Novel and the Short Story

Although many elements in fiction are common to both the novel and the short story, there are basic differences between the two forms. The **novel** is a long, book-length story. Often, the novelist writes a story that involves several characters and events in their lives. A skillful novelist brings together characters with their unique personalities, adventures, and struggles; the novelist then combines them into one main plot. The **short story** is also a work that deals with imaginary characters, locations, or events, but the story is much shorter than a novel. Moreover, a short story usually focuses on fewer characters and only one event or action. By narrowing the focus, the short-story writer achieves a single effect.

Edgar Allan Poe, one of America's earliest and best short-story writers, believed that a short story should be read in one sitting. Of course, how long that is depends upon how long you choose to sit and read, but the idea is that you could read a short story in a much briefer time span than a novel—not many hours, days, or even weeks.

A good short-story writer gets to the point and quickly develops believable characters and events. The writer has limited space in which to create a work of art. Think about how the writer presents his or her ideas as well as the meaning behind the ideas themselves.

Although novels and short stories are developed around fictional characters, the events that occur may sometimes be based on fact. This is especially true in historical novels. For example, *The Agony and the Ecstasy,* by Irving Stone, describes events surrounding the life of Italian Renaissance artist and sculptor Michelangelo and his clashes with Pope Julius II. The book is set in the real-life locations of Florence and Rome, Italy, and includes real people of the sixteenth century. Many of the events and the dialogue among characters cannot be known because conversations were not recorded hundreds of years ago.

Two other examples of this historical fiction type are *A Tale of Two Cities,* by Charles Dickens, and *Les Miserables,* by Victor Hugo. The French Revolution is the physical and political setting for both novels; however, the plots and the characters are fiction.

Basic Elements of Fiction

The five basic elements of fiction (setting, characterization, plot, theme, and point of view) are illustrated in the following puzzle. Framing the puzzle is **style,** which includes the author's **language** and **tone.** These elements and other literary terms will be explained in this section. As you progress through this section, this diagram will help you to understand the parts (elements) that make up the whole (novel or short story).

BASIC ELEMENTS OF FICTION
The Novel and the Short Story

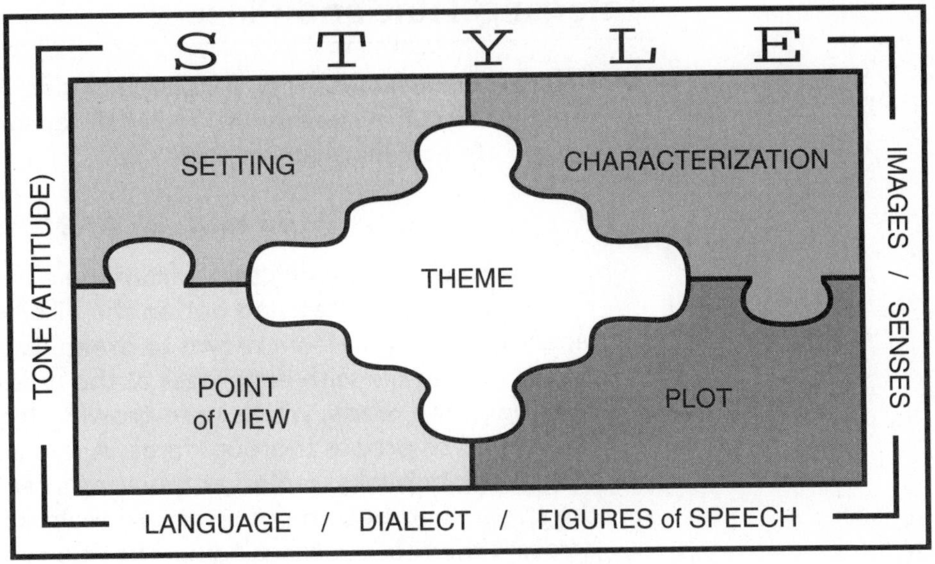

Time and Place as Part of Setting

The **setting** of a short story or novel is the **time** (of day or year), **place** in which the action occurs, and the **atmosphere,** or **mood.** The atmosphere, or mood, includes the weather and conditions of the physical place: dark and dirty if in a dungeon, or colorful and bright if at a carnival. The atmosphere, or mood, also includes the feelings of the characters placed in the setting: discouraged or sad, happy or playful, and so on.

Some authors are very direct about revealing their settings. They state early in a work exactly when and/or where the story is happening:

- "Not long ago there lived in uptown New York, in a small, almost meager room, though crowded with books, Leo Finkle, a rabbinical student in the Yeshivah University."

  —Excerpted from *The Magic Barrel* by Bernard Malamud

- "Every day one summer in Larkin's Hill, it rained a little. The rain was a regular thing, and could come about two o'clock in the afternoon."

  —Excerpted from *A Curtain of Green* by Eudora Welty

- "Miami was hot and muggy and the land wind that blew from the Everglades brought mosquitoes even in the morning."

  —Excerpted from *The Strange Country* by Ernest Hemingway

Inferring Time and Place

In many stories, the time and place are not directly stated. As the reader, you need to read between the lines, or look for clues, to identify a specific time and place. The following exercise will help you practice the skill of inference.

EXERCISE 1

Inferring Time and Place

Directions: Read the following paragraph to infer setting. Underline all the clues that suggest time (when the action happens) and place (where the action happens).

WHAT KIND OF WAR IS THIS?

The cold passed reluctantly from the earth, and the retiring fogs revealed an army stretched out on the hills, resting. As the landscape changed from brown to green, the army awakened, and began to tremble with eagerness at the noise of rumors. It cast its eyes upon the roads, which were growing from long troughs of liquid mud to proper thoroughfares. A river, amber-tinted in the shadow of its banks, purled at the army's feet; and at night, when the stream had become of a sorrowful blackness, one could see across it the red, eyelike gleam of hostile camp fires set in the low brows of distant hills.

Once a certain tall soldier developed virtues and went resolutely to wash a shirt. He came flying back from a brook waving his garment bannerlike. He was swelled with a tale he had heard from a reliable friend, who had heard it from a truthful cavalryman, who had heard it from his trustworthy brother, one of the orderlies at division headquarters. He adopted the important air of a herald in red and gold . . .

To his attentive audience he drew a loud and elaborate plan of a very brilliant campaign. When he had finished, the blue-clothed men scattered into small arguing groups between the rows of squat brown huts.

—Excerpted from *The Red Badge of Courage* by Stephen Crane

1. At what time of day does the action take place?

   What details act as clues?

2. Crane wrote a universal novel, which appeals to all time periods and places, but when does the action more likely take place: in the 1860s or the 1990s?

   What details act as clues?

3. Where does the action take place?

   What details act as clues?

Answers are on page 685.

Atmosphere, or Mood, as Part of Setting

An important part of setting is **atmosphere,** or **mood**—the sensations and emotions associated with details of the physical setting.

For example, if a story opens with a nighttime setting, a thunderstorm, a castle, and a man approaching the door, the author is creating an atmosphere of mystery or suspense. On the other hand, if a story opens with early morning as the setting and children playing happily in a playground, the atmosphere is lighthearted. The exercise below will help you practice the skill of recognizing atmosphere.

EXERCISE 2

Recognizing Atmosphere, or Mood

Directions: Read the passage below and answer the question that follows.

HOW DOES THIS MAN FEEL?

During the whole of a dull, dark, and soundless day in the autumn of the year, when the clouds hung oppressively low in the heavens, I had been passing alone, on horseback, through a singularly dreary tract of country, and at length found myself, as the shades of evening drew on, within view of the melancholy House of Usher. I know not how it was—but, with the first glimpse of the building, a sense of insufferable gloom pervaded my spirit. . . . I looked upon the scene before me—upon the mere house, and the simple landscape features of the domain—upon the bleak walls—upon the vacant eye-like windows—upon a few rank sedges—and upon a few white trunks of decayed trees—with an utter depression of soul. . . .

—Excerpted from "The Fall of the House of Usher" by Edgar Allan Poe

Which descriptive words and phrases does Poe use to create an atmosphere of gloom?

Answers are on page 685.

Writing Activity 1

Pick a favorite restaurant. Visit it at noon and again in the evening. Describe the décor and how the atmosphere changes from lunchtime to dinnertime. How are the patrons dressed at the two times? Is the service different at those two times? Are the meals offered different? Is there music playing? Notice that a real-life setting often is the basis for fiction.

EXERCISE 3

Identifying Parts of Setting

Directions: Read the passage below and answer the questions that follow.

HOW DOES THE SEASON AFFECT THE MOOD?

Some of the caddies were poor as sin and lived in one-room houses with a neurasthenic [exhausted, broken down] cow in the front yard, but Dexter Green's father owned the second best grocery store in Black Bear—the best one was "The Hub," patronized by the wealthy people from Sherry Island—and Dexter caddied only for pocket-money.

In the fall when the days became crisp and gray, and the long Minnesota winter shut down like the white lid of a box, Dexter's skis moved over the snow that hid the fairways of the golf course. At these times the country gave him a feeling of profound melancholy—it offended him that the links should lie in enforced fallowness [inactive period], haunted by ragged sparrows for the long season. It was dreary, too, that on the tees where the gay colors fluttered in summer there were now only the desolate sand-boxes knee-deep in crusted ice. When he crossed the hills the wind blew cold as misery, and if the sun was out he tramped with his eyes squinted up against the hard dimensionless glare.

—Excerpted from "Winter Dreams" in *All the Sad Young Men* by F. Scott Fitzgerald

1. What is the current season (time) of the year?
2. Is the action taking place in the present, the past, or the future? (What verb tense is used?)
3. In the excerpt, where (place) is Dexter and what is he doing? What details act as clues?
4. How does Fitzgerald describe the same setting (place) in fall, in winter, and in summer?
5. What is the effect of the scenery on Dexter? What atmosphere, or mood, does the author convey through his character?

Answers are on page 685.

Characterization: Who is in the Story

Characters are the fictional people in a novel or short story. **Characterization** is the method by which a writer creates fictional people who seem lifelike and believable. Writers may use any of these different methods to create character:

- describing the character and his or her actions
- revealing the character's speech patterns
- revealing what other characters say about the character
- revealing the character's unspoken thoughts

GED PRACTICE

EXERCISE 4

Inferring Characterization

Directions: Read the passage below and answer the questions that follow.

WHAT KIND OF BOY IS HUCK FINN?

You don't know about me, without you have read a book by the name of "The Adventures of Tom Sawyer," but that ain't no matter. That book was made by Mr. Mark Twain, and he told the truth, mainly. There was things which he stretched, but mainly he told the truth. That is nothing. I never seen anybody but lied, one time or another, without it was Aunt Polly, or the widow, or maybe Mary. Aunt Polly—Tom's Aunt Polly, she is—and Mary, and the Widow Douglas, is all told about in that book—which is mostly a true book; with some stretchers, as I said before.

Now the way that the book winds up, is this: Tom and me found the money that the robbers hid in the cave, and it made us rich. We got six thousand dollars apiece—all gold. Well, Judge Thatcher, he took it and put it out at interest, and it fetched us a dollar a day apiece, all the year round—more than a body could tell what to do with. The Widow Douglas, she took me for her son, and allowed she would sivilize [sic] me; but it was rough living in the house all the time, and so when I couldn't stand it no longer, I lit out. I got into my old rags, and my sugar-hogshead again, and was free and satisfied. . . .

—Excerpted from *The Adventures of Huckleberry Finn* by Mark Twain

1. Which description best fits Huck's personality?

(1) the world's biggest liar
(2) an uncaring, uninterested youth
(3) a sad orphan adopted by the Widow
(4) a somewhat uncivilized boy
(5) a very educated future judge

2. In this excerpt, from whom do we primarily learn about Huck's character?

(1) Huck's narrative about himself and others
(2) Aunt Polly, Mary, and the Widow Douglas
(3) Huck's unspoken thoughts
(4) Mark Twain's comments in *Tom Sawyer*
(5) Huck shown in action scenes

3. From what we know about Huck, what kind of character do you think his friend Tom is?

(1) a saintly, caring lad
(2) a highly educated schoolmate
(3) a romantic, adventuresome boy
(4) a uncertain, conflicted boy
(5) a lying, disrespectful youth

Answers are on page 685.

Dialogue as an Element of Characterization

Another way an author reveals character is through dialogue. **Dialogue** is conversation among characters in a story. Quoting what a character says allows authors to reveal a character's attitudes, feelings, and true personality in the character's own words rather than through descriptions alone.

In novels and short stories, quotation marks are placed around each speaker's exact words. Usually an author will provide transitions such as *he said* and *she replied* to indicate when a character is speaking.

The following sentences illustrate the difference between a speaker's exact words and a restatement of a person's words:

Exact words: "You seem to have a 'frozen shoulder,' so I am recommending physical therapy to improve your range of motion," he said.

Restatement: He said I had a "frozen shoulder" and recommended physical therapy to improve my range of motion.

Paragraph indenting and quotation marks indicate a new speaker. In longer conversations, *he said* and *she asked* may not be used in each sentence. Notice that the speakers are identified only once in this passage:

"Are you looking for anything in particular?" inquired the discrete furniture salesperson.

"We're looking for new bedroom furniture to replace our set that is more than thirty years old," Trina replied. "I like the Italian look with marble tops, but Roy likes the American traditional look."

"Well, let's see if we can find a look that appeals to both of you."

EXERCISE 5

Using Dialogue as an Element of Characterization

Directions: Read this passage, in which the speakers are not identified. Who could be the four characters in this dialogue? What seems to be the chief interest of each speaker?

1. "I'm so excited that the four of us are taking this great trip to London and Paris. What a great way to celebrate our wedding anniversaries. I just have to see Buckingham Palace and have "high tea" at Harrod's department store."
2. "Well, I really want to see Westminster Abbey and the artwork at the National Gallery in London. I want to spend more time at the Louvre Museum in Paris where they have the *Mona Lisa*."
3. "I think we ought to start out with the half-day London Tour so we can get an overview of the city. Then we can go back to the Tower of London or anything else we want to see."
4. "I don't care what we see as long as I can spend a whole day at the British Museum. I do want to take that tour of Leeds Castle, Canterbury, and Dover. Oh, and I just realized that we'll see history in action. We're going to be in France on July 14, which is Bastille Day. That's like our Fourth of July."

Speaker Number 1/Chief Interest: ______________________

Speaker Number 2/Chief Interest: ______________________

Speaker Number 3/Chief Interest: ______________________

Speaker Number 4/Chief Interest: ______________________

Possible answers are on page 686.

EXERCISE 6

Identifying Characters through Dialogue

Directions: Read the passage below and answer the questions that follow.

WHAT RELATIONSHIP IS FORMING?

Looking half out the windshield and half into the compartment, he took out a business card and handed it to her. "Robert Kincaid, Writer-Photographer." His address was printed there, along with a phone number.

"I'm out here on assignment for *National Geographic,*" he said. "You familiar with the magazine?"

"Yes." Francesca nodded, thinking, Isn't everybody?

"They're doing a piece on covered bridges, and Madison County, Iowa, apparently has some interesting ones. I've located six of them, but I guess there's at least one more, and it's supposed to be out in this direction."

"It's called Roseman Bridge," said Francesca over the noise of the wind and tires and engine. Her voice sounded strange, as if it belonged to someone else, to a teenage girl leaning out of a window in Naples, looking far down city streets toward the trains or out at the harbor and thinking of distant lovers yet to come. As she spoke, she watched the muscles in his forearm flex when he shifted gears.

—Excerpted from *The Bridges of Madison County* by Robert James Waller

1. How do we know that the two speakers from the excerpt do not know each other?
2. Which character speaks first?
3. Which character is local, and which character is a visitor to the area?
4. Do we know anything of the occupation of either character?
5. How do we know that one character spent part of her youth in a foreign country?
6. What do you think the female speaker is thinking or feeling by the end of the passage?

Answers are on page 686.

Writing Activity 2

Find a place to sit in a shopping mall. Observe the physical appearances of persons who walk by. Note especially the interactions between couples. Describe their expressions as they walk and speak. How are they dressed? What are their hair styles? Are they wearing jewelry? Try to imagine what their personalities are like. Remember that personality is the essence of characterization.

Plot: What Happens in the Story

The events that occur in a story make up the **plot**. The plot events occur in some time order, or sequence.

To see how events might follow a logical sequence, arrange the plot events below in order. Place the number **1** in the blank before the first event, **2** in front of the second event, and so on. Notice the cause-and-effect relationship between events: one event leads to another, which leads to another, and so on.

a. ______ Two sisters wrote an outline for the book with sample chapters.

b. ______ For years, my five sisters and I had discussed writing our own cookbook.

c. ______ I contacted a publisher about printing the book sometime in the future.

d. ______ The publisher wanted the material right away.

e. ______ The cookbook will have to wait to be written when we have more time.

f. ______ Three sisters got promotions in their work positions and became even busier.

Answer: The order of the sentences should be b, a, c, d, f, and e.

Flashback as an Element of Plot

An author may choose to present events out of order. The events begin sometime in the past, then progress in order until, by the end of the story, the characters have returned to the time and place of the opening scene. One such popular technique is called **flashback.** For example, in the 1960 novel *To Kill a Mockingbird,* by Harper Lee, the main character, Scout, starts the narration with "When he was nearly thirteen, my brother Jem got his arm badly broken at the elbow." Then Scout indicates, "When enough years had gone by to enable us to look back on them, we sometimes discussed the events leading to his accident." The story then shifts to years past when their father Atticus practiced law in the fictional town of Maycomb.

Parts of a Plot

The events that make up a fiction plot may be grouped and labeled according to their function in a story. The diagram illustrates the basic parts of a plot: **exposition, conflict, climax,** and **resolution.**

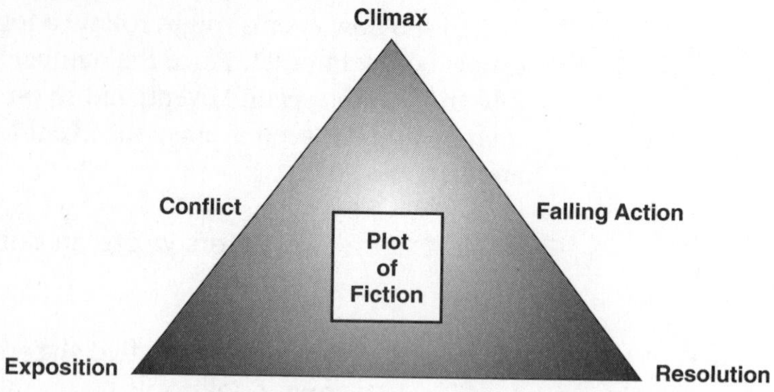

Exposition refers to background information that "sets the stage" for a story. The exposition also introduces setting, characters, and conflict. **Conflict,** or friction between opposing characters or forces, is the basis of every plot. Conflicts are usually stated in this pattern: character or force versus (vs.) character or force.

Most stories and novels are centered around one of the following conflicts:

- individual vs. self—inner struggles characters suffer while trying to decide what to do—change jobs, get divorced, have children, admit the truth about something
- individual vs. another—disagreements between characters
- individual vs. society—struggles against the rules, conventions, or pressures of living with other humans
- individual vs. nature and other forces—struggles against forces beyond a character's control, such as an earthquake or other natural disaster, or an abstraction such as evil

Another element of plot is **climax,** the point of highest intensity in the plot. The climax of a story occurs when the conflict comes to a head. The climax of many westerns occurs when the hero and villain meet face-to-face in a gun duel. An example is the classic 1952 film western *High Noon,* in which the lonely town marshall faces the evil gunman. The climax does not always occur at the very end of the story, but it usually occurs in the last part. All of the events and conflicts involving characters must be evident before they can lead to the climax.

Mystery stories have very obvious climaxes. All of the clues come together to provide the answer to "Whodunit?" Several series are good examples of this type: the Sherlock Holmes detective series by Sir Arthur Conan Doyle; the murder mysteries with Belgian detective M. Hercule Poirot or elderly principal detective Ms. Jane Marple by Agatha Christie; and the Sam Spade detective series by Dashiell Hammett, whose classic work is *The Maltese Falcon.*

Following the climax, all of the loose ends are tied together, and readers learn the **resolution,** or outcome of the conflict. The resolution of the story is usually its ending.

Bear in mind that novels and stories do not have to follow the traditional plot pattern just described. For example, many stories have open endings in which conflicts are not resolved. And many stories include **subplots**—"stories within stories" that involve conflicts of their own. Nevertheless, it is helpful to know the parts of the traditional plot because most stories include some form of exposition, climax, and resolution.

GED PRACTICE

EXERCISE 7

Identifying Details of Plot (and Conflict)

Directions: Read the following passage composed of selected parts of a short story that show details of plot and conflict. Then answer the questions that follow on page 602.

HOW ARE HUSBAND AND WIFE THE "MAGI"?

"Jim, Darling," she cried, "don't look at me that way. I had my hair cut off and sold it because I couldn't have lived through Christmas without giving you a present. It'll grow out again—you won't mind, will you? I just had to do it. . . .

Jim drew a package from his overcoat pocket and threw it on the table. . . .

White fingers and nimble tore at the string and paper. And then an ecstatic scream of joy; and then, alas! A quick feminine change to hysterical tears and wails. . . .

For there lay The Combs—the set of combs, side and back, that Della had worshipped for long in a Broadway window. . . . And now, they were hers, but the tresses that should have adorned the coveted adornments were gone. . . .

Jim had not yet seen his beautiful present. She held it out to him eagerly upon her open palm. The dull precious metal seemed to flash with a reflection of her bright and ardent spirit.

"Isn't it a dandy, Jim? I hunted all over town to find it. You'll have to look at the time a hundred times a day now. Give me your watch. I want to see how it looks on it.

Instead of obeying, Jim tumbled down on the couch and put his hands under the back of his head and smiled.

"Dell," said he, "let's put our Christmas presents away and keep 'em a while. They're too nice to use just at present. I sold the watch to get the money to buy your combs."

—Excerpted from "The Gift of the Magi" by O. Henry

1. **One important plot detail that affects the outcome of the story is that Della has her hair cut off. Why did she do this?**
   (1) She thought her husband would like her new hairstyle better.
   (2) She had a disease that would be better controlled through shorter hair.
   (3) She sold her hair in order to have money to buy Jim a Christmas present.
   (4) She wanted to present a different image for an anticipated new job.
   (5) She was an actress who was preparing for a role that called for short hair.

2. **Another plot detail is that Jim sells his watch. Why does he do that?**
   (1) He sold the watch so that he could buy Della a set of combs.
   (2) He wanted a more modern timepiece that would be more reliable.
   (3) He lost interest in keeping items that were antiques.
   (4) He no longer had any sentimental attachment to the watch.
   (5) He wanted money that he could contribute to Christmas charities.

3. **The author O. Henry is known for ending his short stories ironically, in ways that the reader does not expect. In this case, which of the following details was expected?**
   (1) Della sacrificed her hair to buy Jim a Christmas present.
   (2) Jim sacrificed his watch to buy Della a Christmas present.
   (3) Della did not need the combs after her hair was cut short.
   (4) Jim did not need the watch chain after he sold his watch.
   (5) Della and Jim shopped all over town for the perfect gifts.

Answers are on page 686.

Writing Activity 3

Plan a special event or help someone else who is doing so. The special event could be a birthday party, picnic, school reunion, wedding reception, retirement party, or something else. Arrange the events in the sequence (chronological or time order) as they unfold. After the event is over, note that you can "flash back" to some earlier time in the sequence. The plot of a story can be told in any time order.

Point of View: Who Tells the Story

When you read fiction, ask yourself, "Through whose eyes, or **point of view,** is the story being told?" An author can choose from a variety of ways to tell a story. For example, if you were to write a story about auto racing, you might choose from the following points of view:

- the race car driver wanting to win and picturing the trophy
- the family of the driver expressing concern for his safety
- the other drivers hoping to win and focusing on their own positions
- the track announcer informing the spectators as the race progresses
- the fans or spectators favoring particular drivers and seeking excitement
- the manager or the crew in the pit focusing on mechanical stability and fuel supply
- the sponsor hoping to increase sales through support of the driver
- the television announcer offering commentary about the event

The point of view from which a story is told is important because the reader has to identify with, or "become," the character. For this reason, sometimes authors tell their story through the eyes of the **main character**—the character whom the action affects most. Only the thoughts of the main character are revealed when the author chooses this point of view.

A writer, having decided who is to tell, or **narrate,** the story, may relate the events in first person or third person. In **first-person narration,** the word *I* is used, and the narrator speaks directly to the reader. In his famous novel *The Adventures of Huckleberry Finn* Mark Twain created Huck Finn as the narrator to tell the story. Huck is the main character, and the story is told through his eyes, using the first-person *I* method. Similarly, in *The Catcher in the Rye,* by J. D. Salinger, the first-person narrator is Holden Caulfield.

In **third-person narration,** the story is told by an outsider—someone who is not involved in the action—and the main character is referred to as *he* or *she*. There are several different approaches to the third-person point of view, depending on how much the author wants readers—and the main characters—to know.

In the short story "The Celebrated Jumping Frog of Calaveras County" Mark Twain quotes the character Smiley who talks about his gifted frog Dan'l Webster, who wanted an education. In the short story "The Short Happy Life of Francis Macomber" Ernest Hemingway describes the hunter's activities and the lion's thoughts as the animal is shot. You can tell that the story is told in the third person because Hemingway uses the word *he* to refer to both Macomber and the lion.

Now let's take a closer look. In the novel *The Old Man and the Sea,* by Ernest Hemingway, the old man Santiago hooks the 18-foot marlin with a simple line. Read the passage below and consider: if a fish could think and talk, what would be the marlin's thoughts as it is being reeled in?

EXERCISE 8

Determining Point of View

Directions: Underline each noun or pronoun (*I, me, he, his, himself, you, your,* or *who*) that represents the fisherman. Put brackets [] around each noun or pronoun that refers to the fish. The first paragraph is done for you.

HOW MIGHT THE FISH FEEL?

["Fish,"] the old man said. ["Fish,] [you] are going to have to die anyway. Do [you] have to kill me too?"

That way nothing is accomplished, he thought. His mouth was too dry to speak but he could not reach for the water now. I must get him alongside this time, he thought. I am not good for many more turns. Yes, you are, he told himself. You're good for ever.

On the next turn, he nearly had him. But again the fish righted himself and swam slowly away.

You are killing me, fish, the old man thought. But you have a right to. Never have I seen a greater, or more beautiful, or a calmer or more noble thing than you, brother. Come on and kill me. I do not care who kills who.

Now you are getting confused in the head, he thought. You must keep your head clear. Keep your head clear and know how to suffer like a man. Or a fish, he thought.

"Clear up, head," he said in a voice he could hardly hear. "Clear up."

—Excerpted from *The Old Man and the Sea* by Ernest Hemingway

Answers are on page 686.

Writing Activity 4

Pick a favorite sporting event and watch it on television to its conclusion. (Or better yet, attend the event in person if you can.) Identify at least two points of view from which the event can be described. Write a summary of the event two different ways. Different points of view for real events can be the basis for fictional accounts later.

Theme: What the Story Means

Behind all of the action in a story or movie is the writer's or director's purpose or focus. The creator of a work wants it to have meaning for the audience. The main idea, or **theme,** may be an insight into life, a viewpoint about a social issue, a new view of an old problem, or a positive or negative look into human nature.

In successfully written fiction, as in effective films, the theme is rarely stated directly. Instead, it is implied or suggested. The reader or viewer is expected to interpret the meaning from all elements presented. For example, since the early 1980s, many writers and filmmakers have given us stories about problematic, dysfunctional families. Typically family members no longer understand or support each other. Some examples are *The Bridges of Madison County,* by Robert J. Waller or *American Beauty,* by Alan Ball. Often, the theme is possible reconciliation. Another common theme is the search for true love as is seen in 1990s films such as *Sleepless in Seattle, You've Got Mail,* and *Runaway Bride.*

GED PRACTICE

EXERCISE 9

Inferring Theme

Directions: Read the passage below and choose the *best* answer to each question that follows.

WHAT CONCERNS EDDY, MR. NEWMAN, AND DANNY?

"Eddy, for your courage in facing and breaking your own personal sound barrier, I give you the gift of sound—a collection of tapes for your headphones that represent the best music ever recorded in all styles except disco, which does not qualify as music."

We laughed as he handed Eddy a box about the size of a shoebox. A label was pasted to the lid which listed the songs on each numbered tape. Rhea peeked over Eddy's shoulder and cried with delight, "Oh, all the music in the world."

"Not quite," Mr. Newman said, "but it's a good start. In addition I award you a report card with the 'A' you earned in my course of life, and another well-deserved certificate, a diploma."

He handed Eddy one of the high school's report cards and a diploma, complete with the leather cover and Mrs. Voss's signature. Eddy started to cry. Rhea handed the box of tapes to my Dad, who was closest to her, and hugged Eddy, patting him on the back and saying, "There, there," the way someone had probably taught her in The Home.

Then Mr. Newman turned to me. "Danny, your pain was more than physical, although that was bad enough, and for a few days, we thought we might lose you. Sometimes I wasn't even sure what your assignment was. It didn't really matter because eventually it became a matter of survival. Beyond that, you also graduated. The report cards won't be mailed home until tomorrow; however, I managed to get an early copy printed out by the computer at school. There are quite a few 'D's' here, but I do see one well-earned 'A' in English, no less. At the bottom, a check mark and initials are clearly seen in a space marked 'Requirements completed for graduation.' You already have your diploma. I also have an envelope for you. It contains two reference letters, one by me and one by Mrs. Voss to introduce you to an admissions counselor we both know at the junior college, who can expedite matters for you if you heed our encouragement and look more carefully at your education."

—Excerpted from *The Newman Assignment* by Kurt Haberl

1. Two of the conflicts resolved within this passage involve Eddy, the school custodian, and Danny, a high school senior. Which of the following is not a *probable* conflict?

(1) Eddy overcomes his fear of speaking in front of others.
(2) Danny survives physical injuries from an accident.
(3) Eddy and Danny each pass the Newman assignment.
(4) Eddy and his wife Rhea have marital problems.
(5) Danny overcomes personal and physical difficulties to graduate.

2. The theme of the passage is best stated in which of these ways?

(1) Barriers can be overcome through effort and sacrifice.
(2) The purpose of hard work is to win achievement awards.
(3) Good intentions do not always make up for difficulties.
(4) The truth will always emerge in the proper time and setting.
(5) Mental suffering is the way to build personal character.

Answers are on page 687.

Writing Activity 5

Read the front page of your area newspaper for a few days. Each day identify the major issues represented by the stories. What insights or viewpoints about human nature are represented by the stories? Remember that a theme can be the reason for selection of stories or series of stories and that fictional accounts often follow such events.

Style: Tying All the Elements Together

Style refers to the author's unique use of the language—the choice and arrangement of words. Style includes the author's **tone,** the attitude revealed or displayed toward the subject of the work of fiction or toward the characters. Style is what makes the writing unique. An author's style may contain long, complex sentences, everyday spoken language, dialect, or figures of speech. Style is what holds all the elements together.

Types of Styles

Authors who publish many works often become known and appreciated for their styles as well as their themes and characters. Ernest Hemingway, for example, is known for a terse (short, tight) writing style of few words. On the other hand, Charles Dickens is known for a narrative style characterized by long sentences and vivid descriptions. Edgar Allan Poe often used long, complex sentences, the repetition of words, and many dashes, exclamation points, and italics to add emotion and suspense to his stories. He opens the short story "The Tell-Tale Heart" with: "True!—nervous—very, very dreadfully nervous I had been and am! But why *will* you say that I am mad?" In her 1931 novel *The Good Earth,* Pearl S. Buck uses a vivid, graphic style to describe the China in which she lived for forty years in the early twentieth century.

Tone and Style: The Author's Attitude

When reading, you must infer the author's tone. The **tone** of a novel or short story is the overall attitude that an author conveys toward his or her subject. When listening to a person speak, you can infer the person's attitude by the sound of his or her voice. The tone tells you whether the person means to be sarcastic, bitter, serious, funny, amazed, sympathetic, or something else. The author conveys the intended tone through use of the dialogue among word choice, characters, sentence structure, figures of speech, and punctuation.

An author's choice of words and phrasing reflects his or her attitude. What tone is presented in the paragraphs below? Write a few words that describe the tone of this passage:

Our first-born was a lovely, intelligent girl whose first real sentence at the age of six months was "Me baby." All things on four legs including lions and tigers were "Doggie." She read valentines sent to her by her preschool classmates and invented names for her baby brother including "Little Daddy" and "Oil Can Harry." As she grew, she developed a love for words and started writing her own poems.

Our second (and last)-born was a boy who as a toddler could spend hours arranging his little Matchbox cars or painting houses at a small easel. If the house scene had a fireplace, he would be sure to draw in every brick. Advice from his preschool teacher was to provide him with art materials but not to try to channel (and possibly "kill") his interest in art. It was very predictable that his art later in life turned into a talent for architectural design.

You might have written *nostalgic, light, retrospective, funny,* or *humorous.* The author is a parent looking back on a daughter and a son whose interests and talents were evident at an early age. The author's tone is not sad or resentful, but full of fond, humorous memories.

To determine the tone of a passage, ask yourself the following questions:

- What subject is the author describing?
- How does the author feel about the subject?
- What language or descriptive details reveal the author's attitude?

GED PRACTICE

EXERCISE 10

Detecting Style and Tone

Directions: Read the passage below and answer the questions that follow.

WHAT IS THE AUTHOR'S TONE?

"Americans make the best husbands," the American lady said to my wife. I was getting down the bags. "American men are the only men in the world to marry."

"How long ago did you leave Vevey?" asked my wife.

"Two years ago this fall. It's her, you know, that I'm taking the canary to."

"Was the man your daughter was in love with a Swiss?"

"Yes," said the American lady. "He was from a very good family in Vevey. He was going to be an engineer. They met there in Vevey. They used to go on long walks together."

"I know Vevey," said my wife. "We were there on our honeymoon."

"Were you really? That must have been lovely? . . . Where did you stop there?"

"We stayed at the Trois Couronnes," said my wife.

"It's such a fine old hotel," said the American lady.

"Yes," said my wife. "We had a very fine room and in the fall the country was lovely."

"Were you there in the fall?"

"Yes," said my wife.

We were passing three cars that had been in a wreck. They were splintered open and the roofs sagged in.

"Look," I said. "There's been a wreck."

The American lady looked and saw the last car. "I was afraid of just that all night," she said. "I have terrific presentiments about things sometimes. I'll never travel on a *rapide* again at night. There must be other comfortable trains that don't go so fast."

— Excerpted from "A Canary for One" by Ernest Hemingway

1. If the author read this excerpt, how would his voice sound?

(1) uninterested and mocking
(2) angry and bitter
(3) tragic and depressed
(4) serious and grave
(5) astonished and amazed

2. What is the author's attitude toward the American lady?

She should be

(1) congratulated for her strength
(2) respected for her high ideals
(3) tolerated and sympathized with
(4) imitated for her special graces
(5) exposed for her false values

3. The American lady apparently opposed the marriage of her daughter to a Swiss, but was seemingly taking the canary to her, probably to console her. This probably creates what feeling for the daughter on the part of the reader?

(1) indifference
(2) sympathy
(3) annoyance
(4) gratitude
(5) disbelief

Answers are on page 687.

Dialect as an Element of Style

Dialect is the pattern of speech characteristic to a certain region. From their accents, we can sometimes tell if people are from the Deep South or New England in the United States or perhaps from England or Ireland. Regional expressions, word choices, and pronunciation contribute to dialect.

For example, think about how this expression conveys the lack of integration of people from one part of the country to another: "You can put kittens in the oven, but that doesn't make them biscuits." In other words, kittens will never be biscuits, just as Northerners will never be Southerners. In England, a sign that reads Police Enforcement Cameras means that traffic is being monitored by radar. When a travel official says, "We'll collect you" that means that you will be notified and taken to the appropriate spot (such as a bus stop). "No busking" in the metro stations means you cannot play music for donations.

Writers of fiction may have their characters speak in dialects. Below are two examples of how the dialect of an area and time period are used in novels. The first example is from "Over the Border" from a 1935 collection, *The Quiet Man and Other Stories,* by Irish writer Maurice Walsh.

> "Hould her, you devil, Jureen!" he warned as he sprang up on his own side, but the mare did not even flick an ear.
>
> "Here, lad!" I called, and felt for a shilling.
>
> "Thank you, sir—and God spare you!"
>
> "Hup, mare!"

The next passage is from Zora Neale Hurston's 1937 novel *Their Eyes Were Watching God.* It is written in a dialect that was spoken by some rural southern African Americans of the time.

> "What she doin' coming back here in dem overhalls? Can't she find no dress to put on?—Where's dat blue satin dress she left here in?—Where all dat money her husband took and died and left her?—What dat ole forty year ole 'oman doin' wid her hair swingin' down her bak lak some young gal?—Where she left dat young lad of a boy she went off here wid?"

Figures of Speech as an Element of Style

Figures of speech are not meant to be taken literally. They are expressive ways of describing. You hear figures of speech in spoken English every day. While figures of speech are often particularly associated with poetry and drama, figurative language is used in fiction writing to create vivid pictures and original descriptions.

There are many kinds of figures of speech. In literature, especially in poetry, you can find specific figures of speech called ***similes, metaphors,*** and ***personification.*** A brief explanation of each will help you recognize the use of this type of descriptive language.

A **simile** (sim′-ih-lee) is a comparison that shows a likeness between two unlike things. A simile uses the words *like, than,* or *as.*

The moon came out of the earth like a round flame.

Then his mind blanked like a TV suddenly switched off.

His wife's smile is as pretty as a field of roses in bloom.

The prospector was madder than a caged coyote.

A **metaphor** (met′-uh-for) is a comparison that does not contain *like, than,* or *as.* A metaphor implies that one thing is something else.

Her legs got those dark blue rivers running all over them.

The vision of the two hats, identical, broke upon him with the radiance of a brilliant sunrise.

Personification (per-sahn-ih-fih-kay′-shun) attributes some human activity or quality to an animal or thing.

. . . the ocean has been singing to me, and the song is that of our life together.

For two days, the earth drank the rain, until the earth was full.

See Chapter 2, Interpreting Poetry, and Chapter 3, Interpreting Drama, of the Language Arts, Reading Test for more explanation and examples of figures of speech.

EXERCISE 11

Noticing Figures of Speech

Directions: Read the following fiction passages and underline all the expressions that are figures of speech.

IS THE FOG ALIVE?

Fog was outdoors, hanging over the river, creeping in and out of alleyways and passages, swirling thickly between the bare trees of all the parks and gardens of the city, and indoors, too, seething through cracks and crannies like sour breath, gaining a sly entrance at every opening of a door. It was a yellow fog, a filthy, evil-smelling fog, a fog that choked and blinded, smeared and stained.

—Excerpted from *The Woman in Black* by Susan Hill

WHAT DOES THE TEENAGED GIRL SEE?

No, looking at herself in the plate glass windows she passed, she was very content with what she saw: under the large hat her neck looked slender and reedlike, a blossom's stem; her eyes were shadowed, her entire aspect gentle, and even, she thought, mysterious.

—Excerpted from "Cress Delahanty" by Jessamyn West

Answers are on page 687.

EXERCISE 12

Identifying Images as Part of Overall Style

Directions: Read the passage below. Underline all descriptions and images that appeal to your senses of sight and hearing. (Other senses of smell, taste, and touch are not emphasized in this selection.)

WHAT IMAGES DOES THE WRITER CALL TO MIND?

In agony the brakes cried, held: the scene, dizzy with color, rocked with the car, down a little, back up, giddily, helplessly, while dust exploded up on all sides. "Mommy!" Timmy screamed, fascinated by the violence, yet his wail was oddly still and drawn out, and his eyes never once turned to his mother. The little Mexican boy had disappeared in front of the car. Still the red dust arose, the faces at the bus jerked around together, white eyes, white teeth, faces were propelled toward the windows of the bus, empty a second before. "God, God," Annette murmured; she had not yet released the steering wheel, and on it her fingers began to tighten as if they might tear the wheel off, hold it up to defend her and her child, perhaps even to attack.

A woman in a colorless dress pushed out of the crowd, barefooted in the red clay, pointed her finger at Annette and shouted something gleefully. She shook her fist, grinning, others grinned behind her; the bus driver turned back to his bus. Annette saw now the little boy on the other side of the road, popping up safe in the ditch and jumping frantically—though the sharp weeds must have hurt his feet—laughing, yelling, shouting as if he were insane. The air rang with shouts, with laughter. A good joke. What was the joke? Annette's brain reeled with shock, sucked for air as if drowning.

—Excerpted from "First Views of the Enemy" in *Upon the Sweeping Flood and Other Stories* by Joyce Carol Oates

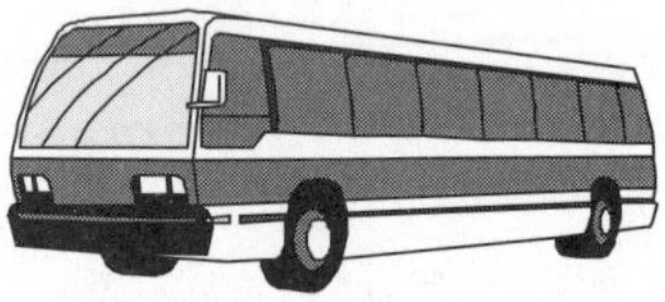

Answers are on page 687.

How to Read Fiction on Your Own

You have learned about the basic elements of fiction illustrated in the puzzle on page 591. In both the novel and the short story, the elements contribute to the whole. While your examination of each element of fiction contributes to your understanding, it is the whole, not its parts, that represents a work of art. Use the tips that follow to guide your reading of literature.

TIPS ON READING FICTION

As you read a short story or novel, ask yourself:

- What is the setting (time and place)?
- What is the atmosphere (or mood)?
- Who are the characters?
- Are they named or described?
- Do the characters use special dialogue?
- What is the plot?
- What is the exposition (or background information)?
- Is flashback used?
- What is the conflict?
- What is the climax?
- What is the resolution?
- Are there subplots?
- From whose point of view is the story told?
- Is there first-person, third-person, or author-third person narration?
- What are clues to the theme?
- What is the author's style like?
- What is the author's tone?
- Are there special elements such as dialect or figures of speech?

Go to **www.GEDReading.com** for additional practice and instruction!

CHAPTER 2

Interpreting Poetry

> Poetry is simply the most beautiful, impressive and widely effective mode of saying things, and hence its importance.
>
> —Matthew Arnold

> All poetry is difficult to read,
> —The sense of it is, anyhow.
>
> —Robert Browning

Do you find that you agree with the Matthew Arnold quotation above or the Robert Browning quotation above? Perhaps you feel that there is truth to each of these. For centuries, poetry has served as a means to provoke thought, honor an individual, express emotion, amuse a reader, commemorate an event, evoke a memory, or plead love. **Poetry** is language that expresses ideas and emotions in a tightly controlled and structured way. Simply put, poetry is the best words in their best order.

Poetry is compressed. **Imagery** (word pictures that appeal to the five senses) and figures of speech enable the poet to convey ideas in just a few words.

Some poems are written in **rhyme,** the repetition of a sound at the end of two or more words, like *say* and *hay.* **Sounds** and **rhythms,** or the "beat," arouse feelings and evoke thoughts. All of these characteristics of poetry make it a distinct form of literature.

On the Language Arts, Reading Test, you will be expected to demonstrate your understanding of a poem's meaning. You should be able to read a poem, spend a few minutes interpreting it, and answer questions about the theme.

Idea and Emotion in Poetry

The following poems are about human relationships. The first poem is a song. The second poem is a sonnet, a 14-line poem that follows a particular form. Both poems express similar emotions and ideas.

GED PRACTICE

EXERCISE 1

Understanding Idea and Emotion in Two Poems

Directions: Read each poem aloud and answer the questions that follow.

WHAT ARE THE POETS SAYING AND HOW ARE THEY SAYING IT?

I know not whether thou hast been absent:
I lie down with thee, I rise up with thee,
In my dreams thou art with me.
If my eardrops tremble in my ears,
I know it is thou moving within my heart.

—Aztec Love Song

Sonnet 43

How do I love thee? Let me count the ways.
I love thee to the depth and breadth and height
My soul can reach, when feeling out of sight
For the ends of Being and ideal Grace.
I love thee to the level of every day's
Most quiet need, by sun and candlelight.
I love thee freely, as men strive for Right;
I love thee purely, as they turn from Praise.
I love thee with the passion put to use
In my old griefs, and with my childhood's faith.
I love thee with a love I seemed to lose
With my lost saints—I love thee with the breath,
Smiles, tears, of all my life!—and, if God choose,
I shall but love thee better after death.

—Elizabeth Barrett Browning

1. **Which theme is found in both poems?**

   (1) separation
   (2) sacrifice
   (3) beauty
   (4) romantic love
   (5) wisdom

2. **On the basis of the emotion expressed in these two poems, which one of the following words would best describe the speakers' feelings?**

   (1) devoted
   (2) proud
   (3) sad
   (4) amused
   (5) scornful

Answers are on page 688.

TIPS ON READING POETRY

- Read the title as a clue to the meaning.
- Read the whole poem to get the general ideas and mood.
- Ask yourself, What is this about? What is the poet saying? What does the poem mean? What is the theme?
- Note the use of any objects or events that might serve as symbols to represent meaning. What feelings and ideas do you associate with those symbols?
- Reread the poem using the punctuation as a guide. (Stop where there's a period or other end mark, not at the end of a line.)
- Notice how lines are grouped together and if lines are repeated. What is the poet stressing by repeating words and lines?
- Notice the language used and unusual word choices, comparisons, imagery, and figures of speech.
- Read the poem aloud so you can hear it, especially if words rhyme.
- To understand the poem's tone and theme summarize in your own words what the poem is saying.

The Shape of Poetry

The structure and form of poetry distinguish it from other types of literature. Many poets choose a highly structured format, in which they shape their ideas using rhyme, rhythm, and stanzas. A **stanza** is a group of lines that work together to express an idea. A new stanza signals that a new idea is being introduced in a poem. Often, stanzas are separated by a blank space.

The following poem contains two stanzas:

Dreams

stanza 1 Hold fast to dreams
For if dreams die
Life is a broken-winged bird
That cannot fly.

stanza 2 Hold fast to dreams
For when dreams go
Life is a barren field
Frozen with snow.

—Langston Hughes

When you sing a song, you may sing a verse, a chorus, the second verse, the same chorus, the third verse, a chorus, and so on. A **verse** is any piece of poetry that is arranged in a pattern. Many songs were poems before they were set to music, and song lyrics often have many of the characteristics of poetry.

The term ***free verse*** refers to verses without a regular rhythmic pattern and usually without rhyme. Much of today's poetry is free verse.

Capitalization and Punctuation

In poetry a comma or a dash means "pause." A period means "stop." If the poem contains capitalization and punctuation, it should be read in sentences, not just one line at a time. Sometimes the reader may have to run two or more lines together. For example, in the poem "Child of the Americas," which follows, lines 4 and 5 are read *I am a U.S. Puerto Rican Jew, a product of the ghettos of New York I have never known.*

The use of capital letters in poetry can vary. Sometimes a poet capitalizes each line. Sometimes a poet capitalizes a word for emphasis.

EXERCISE 2

The Shape of Poetry

Directions: Read aloud the poem below and answer the questions that follow. Notice the capitalization and punctuation as you read.

WHY DOES THE SPEAKER DESCRIBE HERSELF AS A CHILD?

Child of the Americas

I am a child of the Americas,
a light-skinned mestiza of the Caribbean,
a child of many diaspora,* born into this continent at a crossroads.

I am a U.S. Puerto Rican Jew,
a product of the ghettos of New York I have never known.
An immigrant and the daughter and granddaughter of immigrants.
I speak English with passion: It's the tool of my consciousness,
a flashing knife blade of crystal, my tool, my craft.

I am Caribeña, island grown, Spanish is in my flesh,
ripples from my tongue, lodges in my hips:
the language of garlic and mangoes,
the singing in my poetry, the flying gestures of my hands.
I am Latinoamerica, rooted in the history of my continent:
I speak from that body.

I am** not african. Africa is in me, but I cannot return.
I am not taína. Taíno is in me, but there is no way back.
I am not european. Europe lives in me, but I have no home there.

I am new. History made me. My first language was spanglish.
I was born at the crossroads
and I am whole.

**diaspora* means migration or scattering of people
***am* was *an* in the original

—Aurora Levins Morales

1. There are three lines in the first stanza. How many sentences are there? (Notice periods.)

____

2. List at least three details that contribute to the speaker's description of herself as born "at the crossroads" where many ways come to meet together.

   (a) _______________

   (b) _______________

   (c) _______________

3. In which stanza does the speaker announce that she is proud of her heritage? Give the clue word you find.

____

4. To what does she compare English?

____

5. **What do the emotions and ideas expressed in the poem invite a reader to do?**

   (1) study American history
   (2) learn another language
   (3) appreciate multiculturalism
   (4) research family background
   (5) plan a family reunion

Answers are on page 688.

The Language of Poetry

You were introduced to descriptive language in the fiction section of this book. While figures of speech contribute greatly to style in short stories and novels, poetry relies even more heavily on this special language. This is because of the compression of ideas that a poem requires. In this section you will review some of the devices introduced in the fiction section and analyze how they are used in poems to arouse the mind and emotions.

Imagery

A poet relies on readers' abilities to create images, or pictures, in their minds from the words on a page. Images may appeal to any senses, enabling readers to experience the emotions and ideas conveyed. For this reason, the poet must choose the perfect word to convey a thought. When a poem appeals to your senses and enables you to imagine a scene, the poem is rich in **imagery.**

Dawn Over the Mountains

The city is silent,
Sound drains away,
Buildings vanish in the light of dawn,
Cold sunlight comes on the highest peak,
The thick dust of night
Clings to the hills,
The earth opens,
The river boats are vague,
The still sky—
The sound of falling leaves.
A huge doe comes to the garden gate,
Lost from the herd,
Seeking its fellows.

—Tu Fu

Can you "hear" the silence in line 1 and then the *sound of falling leaves* in line 10? Can you "feel" the *cold sunlight* in line 4 and see *a huge doe* . . . at *the garden gate* in line 11?

Personification

Recall that **personification** is a form of imagery in which human activities or qualities are attributed to an animal or a thing. In other words, a nonhuman thing comes "alive" as it is given human abilities.

Carl Sandburg used personification to immortalize a city in his famous poem "Chicago." Notice that he addresses the city as a person. Here are the opening lines:

Chicago

Hog Butcher for the World,
Tool Maker, Stacker of Wheat,
Player with Railroads and the Nation's Freight Handler;
Stormy, husky, brawling,
City of the Big Shoulders:

—Excerpted from "Chicago" by Carl Sandburg

The names Sandburg calls the city in the first three lines refer to the commerce and industry Chicago was known for. Chicago is personified—made human—when the poet calls it by a name normally associated with people.

EXERCISE 3

The Language of Poetry

Directions: Write **imagery** if a line evokes an image or **personification** if it attributes a human quality to an inanimate object.

Line 1: Midnight, not a sound from the pavement. ________________

Line 2: Has the moon lost her memory? ________________

Line 3: She [the moon] is smiling alone. ________________

Line 4: In the lamp light the withered leaves collect at my feet. ________________

Line 5: And the wind begins to moan. ________________

—Excerpted from *Cats: The Book of the Musical* by Trevor Nunn

Answers are on page 688.

Simile and Metaphor

A **simile** is a comparison of two unlike things. You will recall from Chapter 1 that a simile uses words such as *like, than,* or *as* to compare two unlike things. Poet Robert Bly uses similes in the following poem, "Poem in Three Parts." What things are being compared with one another? Underline the three similes.

Poem in Three Parts

I

Oh, on an early morning I think I shall live forever!
I am wrapped in my joyful flesh,
As the grass is wrapped in its clouds of green.

II

Rising from a bed, where I dreamt
Of long rides past castles and hot coals,
The sun lies happily on my knees;
I have suffered and survived the night,
Bathed in dark water, like any blade of grass.

III

The strong eaves of the box-elder tree,
Plunging in the wind, call us to disappear
Into the wilds of the universe,
Where we shall sit at the foot of a plant,
And live forever, like the dust.

—Robert Bly

You should have underlined these similes: *I am wrapped in my joyful flesh,/as the grass is wrapped in its clouds of green.; I have suffered and survived the night,/Bathed in dark water, like any blade of grass.;* and *we shall sit at the foot of a plant,/And live forever, like the dust.*

Recall that a metaphor is an implied or suggested comparison between two things. A metaphor does not contain *like, than,* or *as.* With a metaphor, one thing *is* the second thing to which it is being compared.

The Langston Hughes poem "Dreams," presented on page 617, contains this metaphor:

Life is a barren field/Frozen with snow.

This metaphor presents an image of land that is empty; nothing can grow. Life without dreams is a wasteland.

Note the comparison between hope and a bird in "Hope" by Emily Dickinson. Underline all the words that contribute to the metaphor.

Hope

Hope is the thing with feathers
That perches in the soul,
And sings the tune without the words,
And never stops at all,

And sweetest in the gale is heard;
And sore must be the storm
That could abash the little bird
That kept so many warm.

I've heard it in the chillest land,
And on the strangest sea;
Yet, never, in extremity,
It asked a crumb of me.

—Emily Dickinson

The metaphor of hope as a bird is extended and developed throughout the poem. You should have underlined the following words: *feathers, perches, sings, bird, crumb.*

GED PRACTICE

EXERCISE 4

Review of Figurative Language and Theme

Directions: Read the poem and answer the questions that follow.

HOW DOES THE SPEAKER VALUE BEAUTY?

BARTER

(1) Life has loveliness to sell,
All beautiful and splendid things,
Blue waves whitened on a cliff,
Soaring fire that sways and sings,
(5) And children's faces looking up,
Holding wonder like a cup.

Life has loveliness to sell,
  Music like a curve of gold,
Scent of pine trees in the rain,
  Eyes that love you, arms that hold,
And for your spirit's still delight,
Holy thoughts that star the night.

Spend all you have for liveliness,
  Buy it and never count the cost;
For one white singing hour of peace
  Count many a year of strife well lost,
And for a breath of ecstasy
Give all you have been, or could be.

—Sara Teasdale

1. What idea is suggested by the simile in stanza 1 that compares a child's face to a cup?

(1) Cups and children are both wonderful.
(2) Children's faces are filled with much emotion.
(3) Children are often thirsty.
(4) Faces are shaped like cups.
(5) Children are full of energy.

2. To what does the poet compare music in stanza 2?

(1) the scent of pine trees
(2) the rain
(3) eyes that love
(4) arms that hold
(5) a curve of gold

3. Which word best describes <u>thoughts</u> as they are identified in the metaphor, "Holy thoughts that star the night" in stanza 2?

(1) distant
(2) pointed
(3) late
(4) isolated
(5) bright

Answers are on page 688.

The Sound of Poetry

Poets rely on many devices to communicate their messages to readers. Most poetry is written to be read aloud. As the poet writes the words, he or she is aware of the sound of the poem. Many poets use "sound words" to enhance the imagery and message of their poetry. Three common poetic devices are **rhyme, rhythm,** and **alliteration.**

Nursery rhymes introduce the literature of language to children. **Rhyme** is the repetition, in two or more words, of the stressed vowel sound and of the syllables that follow that sound.

Star light, Star bright, first star I see tonight

Just as word choices produce a desired effect in poetry, so does the beat, or rhythm, of a poem. **Rhythm** is the rise and fall of stressed words and syllables. If the rhythm is regular, or ordered strictly, the poem is said to have **meter.**

The repetition of consonant sounds, usually at the beginning of words, is **alliteration.** *Susie sells seashells down by the seashore* is an example of alliteration. Nursery rhymes contain much alliteration, and advertising slogans and jingles incorporate this technique frequently.

Words that Stand for Sounds

Another device sometimes used in poetry is the choice of a word to imitate a natural sound. **Onomatopoeia** (ahn′-uh-mah′-tuh-pee′-uh) refers to the use of words whose sounds imitate their meanings. Sound-imitating words include *buzz, screech, boom,* and *crash. Whisper* is also a sound word.

EXERCISE 5

The Sound of Poetry

Directions: Read the beginning stanzas from the poem and answer the questions that follow. Notice how the rhyme, the rhythm, and alliteration add to the experience of the poem.

WHAT MIGHT THE RAVEN REPRESENT?

Once upon a midnight dreary, while I pondered weak and weary,
Over many a quaint and curious volume of forgotten lore—
While I nodded, nearly napping, suddenly there came a tapping,
As of someone gently rapping, rapping at my chamber door.
"'Tis some visitor," I muttered, "tapping at my chamber door—
    Only this, and nothing more."

Ah, distinctly I remember it was in the bleak December;
And each separate dying ember wrought its ghost upon the floor.
Eagerly I wished the morrow;—vainly I had sought to borrow
From my books surcease* of sorrow—sorrow for the lost Lenore—
For the rare and radiant maiden whom the angels name Lenore—
    Nameless *here* for evermore.

And the silken sad uncertain rustling of each purple curtain
Thrilled me—filled me with fantastic terrors never felt before;
So that now, to still the beating of my heart, I stood repeating
"'Tis some visitor entreating entrance at my chamber door—
Some late visitor entreating entrance at my chamber door;—
    This it is and nothing more."

**surcease* means an end

—Excerpted from "The Raven" by Edgar Allan Poe

1. List two different examples of alliteration from stanzas one or two:

   a. ______________________________

   b. ______________________________

2. **What effect does the repetition of the word rapping have?**

   (1) It uses sound to develop the image of persistent knocking.
   (2) It adds to the atmosphere of boredom and isolation.
   (3) It creates a bird-like sound through the use of personification.
   (4) It lightens the mood of the poem through sound.
   (5) It creates alliteration with the poem's title.

3. **What word best describes the feeling or atmosphere created in the poem by the language, events, and rhythm?**

   (1) aggressive
   (2) eerie
   (3) bitter
   (4) embarrassed
   (5) inexperienced

Answers are on page 688.

Inferring Mood

Mood is very important in poetry. When a poet creates a poem, the words chosen help present an overall feeling. The mood may be humorous and light, somber and serious, or still something else.

Within a poem, the mood sometimes changes. Read the following song from the musical *Cats.* As you read, identify the mood of each part. Circle the word that most accurately describes the mood of the lines.

Memory

Midnight, not a sound from the pavement.
Has the moon lost her memory?
She is smiling alone.
In the lamp light the withered leaves
collect at my feet
And the wind begins to moan.

1. (a) optimistic
(b) lonely
(c) eager

Memory. All alone in the moonlight
I can smile at the old days.
I was beautiful then.
I remember the time
I knew what happiness was,
Let the memory live again. . . .

2. (a) nostalgic
(b) humorous
(c) afraid

Daylight. I must wait for the sunrise
I must think of a new life
And I mustn't give in.
When the dawn comes tonight will
be a memory, too
And a new day will begin. . . .

3. (a) depressed
(b) sarcastic
(c) hopeful

Touch me. It's so easy to leave me
All alone with the memory
Of my days in the sun.
If you touch me you'll understand what
happiness is.
Look, a new day has begun.

4. (a) regretful
(b) content
(c) confused

—Excerpted from *Cats: The Book of the Musical* by Trevor Nunn

The first part of the song refers to the moon smiling alone and the wind moaning. The word *lonely* (b) most accurately describes the mood. For the second part, you should have chosen (a) *nostalgic* because the cat (narrator) is smiling and remembering. For the third part, *hopeful* (c) describes the cat anticipating daylight and a new day. The last part sounds final. A new day has begun. *Content* (b) describes the mood. You should see four different moods in this song.

GED PRACTICE

EXERCISE 6

Language, Sound, and Mood

Directions: Read the poem and answer the questions.

WHAT IS THE SPEAKER REFLECTING UPON?

Storm Windows

People are putting up storm windows now,
Or were, this morning, until the heavy rain
Drove them indoors. So, coming home at noon,
I saw storm windows lying on the ground,
Frame-full of rain; through the water and glass
I saw the crushed grass, how it seemed to stream
Away in lines like seaweed on the tide
Or blades of wheat leaning under the wind.
The ripple and splash of rain on the blurred glass
Seemed that it briefly said, as I walked by,
Something I should have liked to say to you,
Something . . . the dry grass bent under the pane
Brimful of bouncing water . . . something of
A swaying clarity which blindly echoes
This lonely afternoon of memories
And missed desires, while the wintry rain
(Unspeakable, the distance in the mind!)
Runs on the standing windows and away.

—Howard Nemerov

1. **In lines 6–8, the simile that compares crushed grass to seaweed on the tide and wheat . . . under the wind contributes to which recurring images in the poem?**

   (1) winter and summer
   (2) wind and water
   (3) doors and houses
   (4) earth and sky
   (5) night and darkness

2. **Which word best describes the mood in the poem?**

   (1) fearful
   (2) curious
   (3) foolish
   (4) forgiving
   (5) regretful

Answers are on page 688.

Interpreting and Analyzing Poetry for Meaning

When you interpret a poem, you rephrase it, putting the poem into your own thoughts and words. You may simply change words around to make a statement more understandable to you. You may guess at the poet's main purpose and ask yourself, "Why is the poet using this comparison?" or "Why does the poet say this?"

To understand poetry, seek the stated information from the text of the poem, but also use your own experience and knowledge to derive meaning and a fuller appreciation of what you have read.

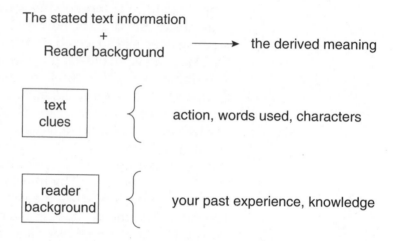

The stated text information
+
Reader background → the derived meaning

text clues { action, words used, characters

reader background { your past experience, knowledge

Read the following stanzas from the poem "My Last Duchess" by Robert Browning. Browning, like most poets, was interested in enabling a reader to see something revealing within a poem. Use the clues from the text, combined with your own assessment of human beings to answer the questions.

That's my last Duchess painted on the wall,
Looking as if she were alive. I call
That piece a wonder, now: Frá Pandolf's hands
worked busily a day, and there she stands,
Will't please you sit and look at her?

She had a heart
A heart—how shall I say?—too soon made glad,
Too easily impressed; she liked whate'er
She looked on, and her looks went everywhere.
Sir, 'twas all one! My favor at her breast,
The dropping of the daylight in the West,
The bough of cherries some officious fool
Broke in the orchard for her, the white mule
She rode with round the terrace—all and each
Would draw from her alike the approving speech,
Or blush, at least. She thanked men,—good! but thanked
My gift of a nine-hundred-years-old name as if she ranked
With anybody's gift.

—and if she let
Herself be lessoned so, nor plainly set
Her wits to yours, forsooth, and made excuse,
—E'en then would be some stooping; and I choose
Never to stoop. Oh sir, she smiled, no doubt,
Whene'er I passed her; but who passed without
Much the same smile? This grew; I gave commands;
Then all smiles stopped together. There she stands
As if alive. Will't please you rise? We'll meet
the company below, then . . .

—Excerpted from "My Last Duchess" by Robert Browning

1. Who is the speaker of the poem?

(1) Frá Pandolf
(2) the Duke
(3) a visitor

2. What kind of person was the Duchess?

(1) foolish and clumsy
(2) vain and envious
(3) kind and friendly

3. What did the speaker dislike about her?

(1) She treated everyone well.
(2) She talked too much.
(3) She blushed frequently.

4. In addition to discussing a portrait of the Duchess, how is the character of the speaker also portrayed in the poem?

(1) through what the speaker says about the Duchess
(2) through what the speaker is wearing
(3) through what the visitor says to the speaker

For question 1, you should have chosen answer (2) because the speaker states *That's **my*** last Duchess. The answer to question 2 is (3) because the poem states *She had a heart . . . too soon made glad* and *all and each would draw from her alike the approving speech* . . . For question 3, the answer is (1). The Duke is resentful that the Duchess appreciated others' gifts as much as his. Lastly, (1) is the answer to question 4. What the Duke says about the Duchess reveals a great deal about him.

GED PRACTICE

EXERCISE 7

Inferring Meaning

Directions: Read the poem below, looking carefully for clues in the text to answer the questions.

WHAT LANGUAGE CONTRIBUTES TO THE IMAGE OF ROYALTY?

Richard Cory

Whenever Richard Cory went down town,
We people on the pavement looked at him:
He was a gentleman from sole to crown,
Clean favored, and imperially slim.

And he was always quietly arrayed,
And he was always human when he talked;
But still he fluttered pulse when he said,
"Good morning," and he glittered when he walked.

And he was rich—yes, richer than a king—
And admirably schooled in every grace:
In fine, we thought that he was everything
To make us wish that we were in his place.

So on we worked, and waited for the light,
And went without the meat, and cursed the bread;
And Richard Cory, one calm summer night,
Went home and put a bullet through his head.

—Edwin Arlington Robinson

1. Who is the speaker of the poem?

(1) Richard Cory
(2) a townsperson
(3) Richard Cory's wife
(4) a nobleman
(5) a small child

2. What word describes the attitude of the townspeople towards Richard Cory?

(1) indifferent
(2) cautious
(3) superior
(4) envious
(5) distrustful

3. From lines 13 and 14, what can be inferred about the lives of the townspeople?

(1) They seldom work.
(2) Their lives are hard.
(3) Their lives are uneventful.
(4) They face many changes.
(5) They lead isolated lives.

4. What is the overall theme of the poem?

(1) Wealth can rarely buy love.
(2) Money is often the root of all evil.
(3) Love and life will find a way to thrive.
(4) The grass is always greener on the other side.
(5) Things are not always what they seem.

Answers are on page 689.

Combining Ideas Together to Develop Meaning

Questions on the Language Arts, Reading Test require you to comprehend, apply, and analyze thoughts in poetry as well as in other literature. Additionally, you will sometimes be asked to consider another source of information in relation to the poem you read. You will be **synthesizing,** combining pieces of information together to arrive at an idea. To do that, you will want to understand the poem you read, think about what makes sense to you in view of your own knowledge and experience, and consider the other additional information you are given.

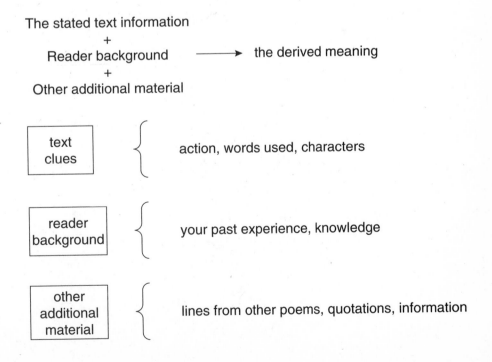

The stated text information
+
Reader background → the derived meaning
+
Other additional material

text clues	action, words used, characters
reader background	your past experience, knowledge
other additional material	lines from other poems, quotations, information

The excerpt that follows comes from a poem written by Alfred, Lord Tennyson. The poem is written about the explorer Ulysses, who has traveled for many years across the ocean in his ship.

Old age hath yet his honor and his toil.
Death closes all; but something ere* the end,
Some work of noble note, may yet be done,
Not unbecoming men that strove with Gods.
The lights begin to twinkle from the rocks;
The long day wanes; the slow moon climbs; the deep
Moans round with many voices. Come, my friends.
'Tis not too late to seek a newer world.
Push off, and sitting well in order smite
The sounding furrows; for my purpose holds
To sail beyond the sunset, and the baths
Of all the western stars, until I die.
It may be that the gulfs will wash us down;
It may be we shall touch the Happy Isles,
And see the great Achilles, whom we knew.
Tho' much is taken, much abides; and tho'
We are not now that strength which in old days
Moved earth and heaven, that which we are, we are,—
One equal temper of heroic hearts,
Made weak by time and fate, but strong in will
To strive,to seek, to find, and not to yield.

**ere* means before

—Excerpted from "Ulysses" by Alfred, Lord Tennyson

Before you try to answer the next two questions:

- Think about the text clues in this excerpt from Tennyson.
- Think about your own knowledge and experience with human beings.
- Think about the meaning of the quotations.

1. Earlier in the poem, the speaker states: "I am a part of all that I have met." In what way is this line consistent with the rest of the poem?

(1) It adds to the image of a sailing ship.
(2) It suggests that each individual is incomplete.
(3) It reminds us of how our experiences shape our lives.
(4) It adds to the tone of suspense.
(5) It emphasizes the uncertainty of the future.

2. The poet T. S. Eliot in his poem, "East Coker," states, "Old men ought to be explorers."

How does this quotation relate to the poem *Ulysses*?

(1) It reaffirms the poem's theme that exploration is lifelong.
(2) It also suggests that a new world is needed.
(3) It recreates the fears and fantasies of people.
(4) It reinforces the idea that youth is wasted on the young.
(5) It predicts that travel opportunities are limited.

For question 1 the answer is (3). To be *a part of all* encountered suggests experience affects one's development. This is similar to the poem's theme of exploration bringing about experience. The answer to question 2 is (1). The speaker of the poem states *Old age hath yet his honor* and *'Tis not too late to seek. . .*, echoing the idea expressed in the quotation from Eliot's poem.

GED PRACTICE

EXERCISE 8

Interpreting a Poem

Directions: Read the poem and answer the questions that follow.

WHAT DOES NATURE HAVE TO OFFER?

Leisure

What is this life if, full of care,
We have no time to stand and stare.

No time to stand beneath the boughs
And stare as long as sheep or cows.

No time to see, when woods we pass,
Where squirrels hide their nuts in grass.

No time to see, in broad daylight,
Streams full of stars, like skies at night.

No time to turn at Beauty's glance,
And watch her feet, how they can dance.

No time to wait till her mouth can
Enrich that smile her eyes began.

A poor life this if, full of care,
We have no time to stand and stare.

—W. H. Davies

1. **If the speaker of the poem were hired for a new job, predict what company benefit would have the greatest appeal.**

(1) profit-sharing
(2) life insurance
(3) child care
(4) overtime work
(5) paid vacation

2. **What effect does line 10, "And watch her feet, how they can dance" have on the poem?**

It reinforces the wonder of

(1) beauty and enjoyment
(2) activity and practice
(3) nature and learning
(4) complexity and design
(5) art and progress

3. **Which piece of advice would the speaker of the poem give, based on the overall attitude the speaker expresses?**

(1) Work hard if you wish to succeed.
(2) Take time to smell the roses.
(3) Laugh and the world laughs with you.
(4) If at first you don't succeed, try again.
(5) Time flies when you're having fun.

Answers are on page 689.

EXERCISE 9

More Practice with Interpretation

Directions: Read the poem and answer the questions that follow.

WHAT IS THE POET SAYING ABOUT DEATH?

Because I Could Not Stop for Death

Because I could not stop for Death,
He kindly stopped for me;
The carriage held but just ourselves
And Immortality.

We slowly drove, he knew no haste,
And I had put away
My labor, and my leisure too,
For his civility.

We passed the school where children played
At wrestling in a ring;
We passed the fields of gazing grain,
We passed the setting sun.

We paused before a house that seemed
A swelling of the ground;
The roof was scarcely visible,
The cornice but a mound.

Since then 'tis centuries; but each
Feels shorter than the day
I first surmised the horses' heads
Were toward eternity.

—Emily Dickinson

1. Match the stanza on the left with the images on the right by writing the correct letter in the space provided.

Stanza 1 ______ **a.** images of a schoolyard, farm, land, dusk

Stanza 2 ______ **b.** the narrator riding in a carriage with two others

Stanza 3 ______ **c.** a slow ride as the narrator accepts her fate

Stanza 4 ______ **d.** the narrator remembering the day of the carriage ride, hundreds of years before

Stanza 5 ______ **e.** the carriage pausing at a gravesite

2. What is the effect of capitalizing the words <u>Death</u> and <u>Immortality</u> in lines 1 and 4?

The words illustrate that

(1) death is a major theme
(2) they are the chief concerns of a person's life
(3) they are characters in the poem
(4) the two words are opponents, one fighting the other
(5) they are two unexplainable concepts that people must face

3. What is revealed about the speaker from lines 17–20 in the last stanza?

The speaker

(1) knows when she is going to die
(2) feels time moves too slowly
(3) never looks back at the past
(4) enjoys carriage rides
(5) believes in eternal life

Answers are on page 689.

Go to **www.GEDReading.com** for additional practice and instruction!

CHAPTER 3

Interpreting Drama

All the world's a stage,

And all the men and women merely players.

—William Shakespeare

What is drama?

Drama is a form of literature that uses action to tell a story. The story is performed by actors who portray various characters who become involved in **conflict,** a struggle between opposing forces in a plot. The main character in a drama is called the **protagonist,** and the conflict with which he or she struggles may be external or internal. We encounter drama, not only with plays, movies, and TV, but also every day in our lives and in the lives of those around us.

The requirements for interpreting drama on the Language Arts, Reading Test are similar to the requirements for interpreting prose fiction and poetry. For example, on the test you may be asked to read an excerpt from a play and interpret the meaning or tone of the characters' speech. You will need to think about the text you read as well as your own knowledge and experience of human behavior.

Reading a play differs from reading a novel or short story in some ways. A play is designed to be performed. It is a set of instructions for a stage production. For example, the instructions tell an actor what to say, a set designer how to prepare the setting, a costume designer which costumes are needed. The people involved in the production of a play will generally collaborate with the playwright or director to create the performance. However, when you are reading a play, you must create the performance by using your imagination to envision the production. It is important to picture the action, characters, and setting in your mind. You need to read carefully to infer setting, characterization, and theme, just as you do when you read prose and poetry.

One of the greatest playwrights of all time is William Shakespeare. An excerpt from his play, *Hamlet*, follows. In the play set several hundred years ago, Hamlet is the Prince of Denmark. Read the dialogue on page 638. Try to visualize the scene and identify the conflict.

WHAT DOES HAMLET LEARN?

Act I, Scene v

GHOST: My hour is almost come
When I to sulphurous and tormenting flames
Must render up myself.

HAMLET: Alas, poor ghost!

GHOST: Pity me not, but lend thy serious hearing
To what I shall unfold.

HAMLET: Speak, I am bound to hear.

GHOST: So art thou to revenge, when thou shall hear.

HAMLET: What?

GHOST: I am thy father's spirit,
Doomed for a certain term to walk the night,
And for the day confined to fast in fires,
Till the foul crimes done in my days of nature
Are burnt and purged away: but that I am forbid
To tell the secrets of my prison house,
I could a tale unfold whose lightest word
Would harrow up thy soul, freeze thy young blood,
Make thy two eyes like stars start from their spheres,
Thy knotted and combined locks to part,
And each particular* hair to stand on end,
Like quills upon the fretful porcupine.
But this eternal blazon* must not be
To ears of flesh and blood. List, list, oh, list!
If thou didst ever thy dear father love—

HAMLET: Oh, God!

GHOST: Revenge his foul and most unnatural murder.

HAMLET: Murder!

GHOST: Murder most foul, . . .

*_particular_ means individual

*_eternal blazon_ means description of eternity

—Excerpted from _Hamlet_ by William Shakespeare

Now we can see the start of the conflict Hamlet faces. What should he do? Should he believe his own eyes and ears? Should he trust the ghost is telling the truth? Should he seek revenge for the death of his father? What would you do in his position? To learn about all the other complications, complexities, and considerations involved, you would have to read on in the play.

EXERCISE 1

Comprehending a Play

Directions: The previous passage from *Hamlet* could be written in the form of narrative fiction. Fill in the blanks below to complete the narrative.

Hamlet was outside when a ______________________________.

The ghost began to ______________________. At first, Hamlet ______________________________ for the ghost. The ghost claimed to be ______________________. The ghost wanted Hamlet to ______________________________. Hamlet felt ______________ ______________________.

Answers are on page 689.

Reading a Play or Script

Dialogue

Drama contains **dialogue,** the exchange of conversation among the characters. Dialogue in a play and the way the lines are said reveal a great deal about the characters. Reading dialogue can sometimes be challenging because a playwright may write the dialogue to imitate speech. The spelling of words may be nonstandard in an attempt to imitate the pronunciation that different people give speech. Some clues are available, however, to help you understand the dialogue that you read.

Clue #1: *The speakers are identified each time one speaks.*

In the scene at the beginning of this section the clues HAMLET and GHOST indicate who is speaking. The names and the use of the colon [:] help to distinguish which character says what.

Clue #2: *Punctuation marks are used to end a character's speech.*

In the Language Arts, Writing section of this book, you reviewed punctuation. Notice the end marks, especially for questions (?) and exclamations (!). Punctuation is used in drama to show volume of voice and emotion. Dashes (—) and ellipses (. . .) are also used to show pauses. Dashes are used to show a break in thought, while ellipses indicate that there is a pause in the action or that one character is being interrupted by another character.

Clue #3: *Line spacing between lines of dialogue indicates who is speaking.*

A more obvious visual clue that indicates when a different speaker is talking is the white space between lines of dialogue.

How Drama Differs from Other Forms of Literature

Although drama has much in common with the two other forms of literature you have studied—poetry and fiction—each of the three forms of literature treats its subject differently. Illustrated below are differences in the way each form of literature treats the same subject—a marriage proposal.

Prose: The young couple, John and Mary, went for a midnight boat ride on the Mississippi River. John gave Mary a diamond ring, and she accepted his proposal of marriage.

Poetry:
Lovers in the moonlight
Aboard the *Delta Miss*
Exchanged a ring and promises
And sealed them with a kiss.

Drama: *[John and Mary board the* Delta Miss *for a midnight cruise.]*

JOHN: *[Embracing Mary]* I love you. *[He gives her a package.]*

MARY: *[Surprised]* What's this?

JOHN: It's a symbol of our future together—if you agree to marry me next month.

MARY: *[Opening the package and seeing a diamond ring]* Oh, John!

JOHN: *[Slipping the ring on her finger]* Don't ever take it off.

MARY: No . . . *[flustered]* I mean yes! I mean *no I* won't take it off . . . Yes, I'll marry you. *[They kiss.]*

EXERCISE 2

Noticing Dialogue and Punctuation

Directions: Read the dialogue below and notice the punctuation. Then complete the sentences that follow.

[The scene begins in a nineteenth-century parlor as Catherine, Edward and Victoria's daughter, enters with tea]

CATHERINE: Would you like some tea and . . .

EDWARD: Not now—Can't you see we're talking?

VICTORIA: *You're* talking—I'm not!

EDWARD: Oh—a little irritable, are we?

VICTORIA: No—just bored—with you. . .

CATHERINE: *[Mumbling]* I'm leaving. *[She exits.]*

1. Catherine interrupts ______________________.
2. ______________________ asks two questions.
3. ______________________ is rude to Catherine.
4. Victoria is upset with ______________________.

Answers are on page 689.

Stage Directions

Stage directions are used to assist the actors and director in interpreting the writer's intentions and purpose and to help the reader follow the imagined actions. In the brief scene in Exercise 2, the stage directions are the introductory words *[The scene begins in a nineteenth-century parlor as Catherine, Edward and Victoria's daughter, enters with tea]* and the directions *[Mumbling]* and *[She exits].*

In this example notice that the playwright has inserted the directions within the dialogue. In the scene above, the stage directions tell the reader who Catherine is and why she leaves. A play excerpt later in this chapter will require you to follow the action as well as the words.

GED PRACTICE

EXERCISE 3

Inferring Mood from Dialogue

Directions: Choose the *best* answer to the questions that follow.

1. **Which of the following words best describes the mood of the scene in Exercise 2?**

   (1) tense
   (2) happy
   (3) suspenseful
   (4) nostalgic
   (5) humorous

2. **What does the use of the dash [—] imply in the dialogue in Exercise 2?**

   (1) fast speech
   (2) a brief pause
   (3) rudeness
   (4) humor
   (5) shyness

Answers are on page 689.

Structure of Drama

A play is composed of **acts**—the major divisions of a dramatic work. Acts are composed of scenes. **Scenes** show an action that occurs in one place among characters.

Shakespeare developed and refined the structure of drama as we know it today. He presented his plots in five acts. These acts are subdivided into numbered scenes. The diagram below shows the relationship between the acts and the corresponding elements of a traditional plot.

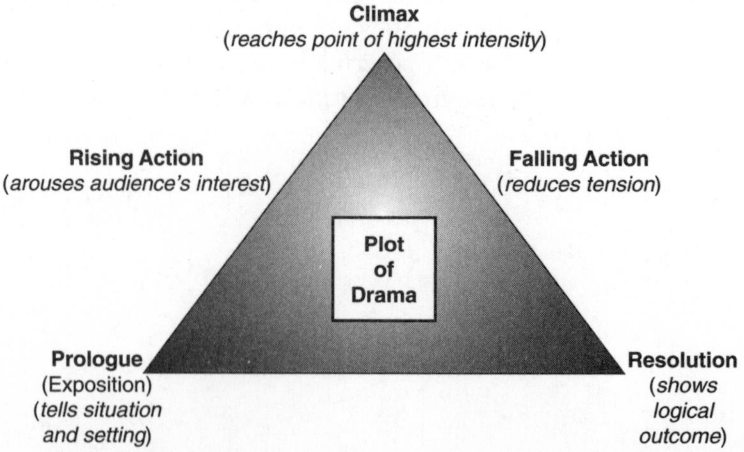

A **prologue** begins classical drama. Because there was no scenery in early drama, the audience needed to know when and where the story was taking place and what circumstances caused the upcoming action. An actor would come on stage and introduce the play by explaining the setting and some of the plot.

The **epilogue** ends classical drama. At the end of the play an actor would come on stage and deliver a summary poem or speech. Although the prologue and epilogue are not as common in drama today, some television dramas and movies use them to help the audience understand the plot.

Elements of Drama

Plot, setting, characterization, and theme are all elements which apply to drama. As you can see from the diagram on page 642, the plot in drama is tightly structured. As in a short story, there is **exposition** that orients the audience to the dramatic situation and setting.

The **rising action** is made up of all of the events that create suspense and arouse the audience's interest. We wonder *What will happen next? What will the main character do?* All of these events and conflicts lead to the **climax,** the point of highest intensity in the play.

The **falling action** may be brief. The conclusion or **resolution** is the logical outcome of the plot. As in fiction, the resolution ties up all of the loose ends of the plot.

Interpreting a Scene

The following scene from *West Side Story* has been included to give you practice in reading plays. The more comfortable you are with following the format of a play, the better your understanding of it will be. Read the following scene and try to imagine the characters, setting, mood, and action.

GED PRACTICE

EXERCISE 4

Interpreting a Scene

Directions: Read the excerpt from a scene in a play. Answer the questions that follow.

TO WHOM DOES MARIA OWE LOYALTY?

Act I, Scene iv

[. . . *It is at this moment that Tony and Maria—at opposite sides of the hall—see each other. They have been cheering on their respective friends, clapping in rhythm. Now as they see each other, their voices die, their smiles fade, their hands slowly go to their sides. The lights fade on the others, who disappear into the haze of the background as a delicate cha-cha begins and Tony and Maria slowly walk forward to meet each other. Slowly, as though in a dream, they drift into the steps of the dance, always looking at each other, completely lost in each other; unaware of anyone, any place, any time, anything but one another.*]

TONY: You're not thinking I'm someone else?

MARIA: I know you are not.

TONY: Or that we have met before?

MARIA: I know we have not.

TONY: I felt, I *knew* something-never-before was going to happen, had to happen. But this is—

MARIA: [*interrupting*] My hands are cold. [*He takes them in his.*] Yours, too. [*He moves her hand to his face.*] So warm. [*She moves his hands to her face.*]

TONY: Yours, too.

MARIA: But of course. They are the same.

TONY: It's so much to believe—you're not joking me?

MARIA: I have not yet learned how to joke that way. I think now I never will.

[*Impulsively, he stops to kiss her hands; then tenderly, innocently, her lips. The music bursts out, the lights flare up, and Bernardo is upon them in an icy rage.*]

BERNARDO: Go home, *"American."*

TONY: Slow down, Bernardo.

BERNARDO: Stay away from my sister!

TONY: . . . Sister?

BERNARDO: [*to Maria*] Couldn't you see he's one of them?

MARIA: No; I saw only him.

BERNARDO: *[as Chino comes up]* I told you: there's only one thing they want from a Puerto Rican girl!

TONY: That's a lie!

RIFF: Cool, boy.

CHINO: [*to Tony*] Get away.

TONY: You keep out, Chino. *[To Maria:]* Don't listen to them!

BERNARDO: She will listen to her brother before—

RIFF: *[overlapping]* If you characters want to settle—

GLAD HAND: Please! Everything was going so well! Do you fellows get pleasure out of making trouble? Now come on—it won't hurt you to have a good time.

—Excerpted from *West Side Story* by Arthur Laurents, Leonard Bernstein, Jerome Robbins, Stephen Sondheim

1. What do we learn about the relationship between Tony and Maria from the dialogue in lines 11–14?

(1) They are very old friends.
(2) They were once married long ago.
(3) They have been finally reunited.
(4) They worked together once.
(5) They are meeting for the first time.

2. What word best describes Tony's reaction when he learns that Maria is Bernardo's sister?

(1) embittered
(2) surprised
(3) resentful
(4) satisfied
(5) grateful

3. How does the mood of this passage change?

(1) from romantic to tense
(2) from romantic to humorous
(3) from informal to formal
(4) from sad to frightening
(5) from nostalgic to suspenseful

Answers are on page 689.

From Idea to Production

The ancient Greeks sat in an outdoor theater on a hillside to watch plays; today we turn on our television sets or attend live productions. We escape for a while as we are entertained by situations that often are more exciting than our own lives.

To appreciate a play or TV drama fully, it helps to know how drama is created and produced. A play is created by a writer (playwright or dramatist). Usually, it is written to be performed, rather than to communicate directly to *readers.* It takes the work of many different people with different talents and skills to put on a performance. Costumers, set designers, makeup artists, and many others contribute.

The following diagram illustrates the process by which a play—an idea in the writer's head—becomes the reality of a live production.

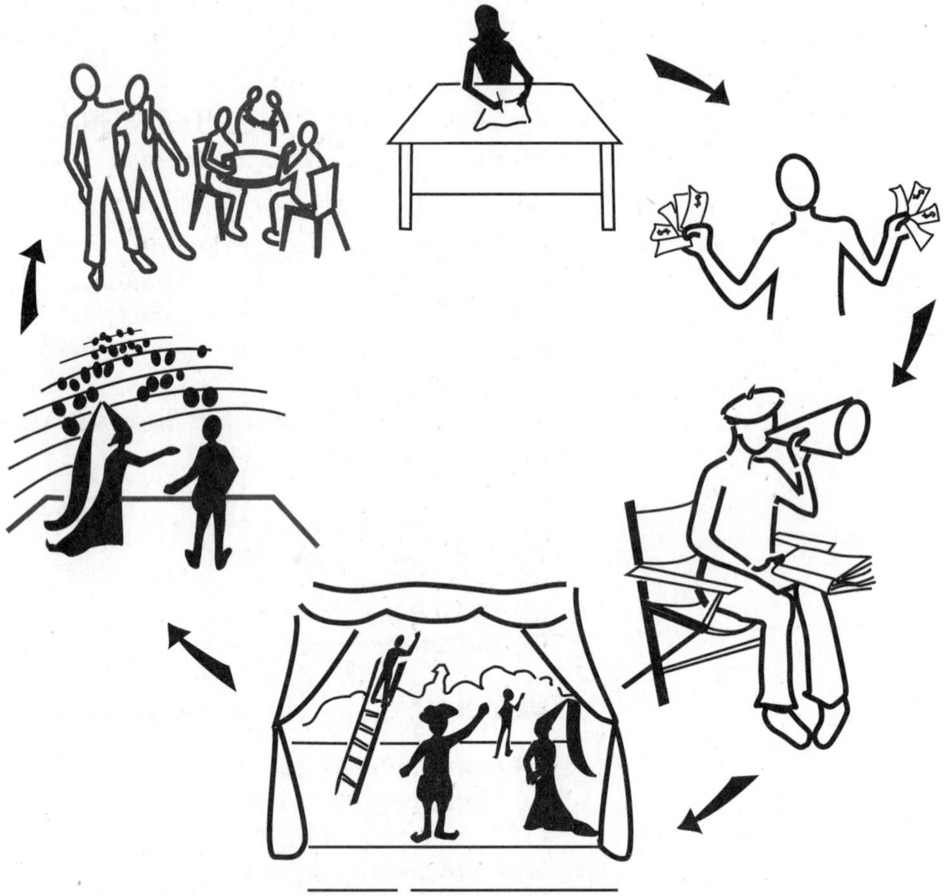

When playwrights or screenplay writers create a script, they visualize their final work as a performance. The producer, who finances the production, chooses a director who will effectively present the raw material—the script. The director casts actors and actresses who fit the characters the writers have created.

Characterization

Characters in plays intended to be brought to life by actors before a live audience are not developed in exactly the same ways as characters in novels and stories. How can you interpret a character? One way is by listening to the character's dialogue and watching his or her facial expressions and mannerisms. Another way to interpret a character is to be aware of the motivation for the character's actions.

Dialogue and Nonverbal Communication

A writer of fiction need not rely solely on dialogue for the reader to understand why characters behave the way they do. The novelist or short story writer can tell us through writing how a character thinks and feels and why the character feels that way.

In drama, however, personalities are revealed by what characters say. Thus, in drama more than in fiction, dialogue carries greater responsibility for getting the author's point across.

Another difference between interpreting character in drama and in prose fiction is that in drama, character is revealed by the actor's **nonverbal communication**—mannerisms, tone of voice, facial expressions, and costumes.

Motivation

In drama, a character's behavior is based on his or her **motivation**—the reasons for the character's actions. You might ask, *Why is a character acting this way?* until you learn the nature of the character. Actors who perform the roles of characters ask themselves, *What is my motivation? What are my character's reasons for acting this way?*

Below is an excerpt from a play about the developing relationship between a man and woman. They are having a discussion in which much is revealed about their personalities and backgrounds.

GED PRACTICE

EXERCISE 5

Understanding Character

Directions: Read the passage below and answer the questions that follow.

WHAT ARE THE CHARACTERS' PERSONALITIES?

BILLIE: Oh, and you know that little thing you gave me about Napoleon?

PAUL: No, what?

BILLIE: By Robert G. Ingersoll?

PAUL: Oh, yes.

BILLIE: Well, I'm not sure if I get that either.

PAUL: No deep meaning there.

BILLIE: There must be. He says about how he goes and looks in Napoleon's tomb.

PAUL: Yuh.

BILLIE: And he thinks of Napoleon's whole sad life.

PAUL: Yuh.

BILLIE: And then in the end he says he himself would have rather been a happy farmer.

PAUL: (*quoting*). "—and I said I would rather have been a French peasant and worn wooden shoes. I would rather have lived in a hut with a vine growing over the door, and the grapes growing purple in the kisses of the autumn sun. I would rather have been that poor peasant, with my loving wife by my side, knitting as the day died out of the sky—with my children upon my knees and their arms about me—I would rather have been that man and gone down to the tongueless silence of the dreamless dust, than to have been that imperial impersonation of force and murder, known as 'Napoleon the Great.'"

BILLIE: (*impressed*). How can you remember all that stuff? (*The music, which has by now become part of the background, suddenly changes. A Debussy record comes to a close and a wild Benny Goodman side replaces it.* PAUL *is startled, so is* BILLIE. *Then* BILLIE *rushes over and turns it off.*)

BILLIE: Once in a while. Just for a change.

(PAUL *laughs.*)

PAUL: Don't try so hard, Billie. Please. You miss the whole point.

BILLIE: Well, I like to like what's better to like.

PAUL: There's room for all sorts of things in you. The idea of learning is to be bigger, not smaller.

BILLIE: You think I'm getting bigger?

PAUL: Yes.

BILLIE: Glad to hear it. (*She sits at the desk again.*) So he would rather be a happy peasant than be Napoleon. So who wouldn't?

PAUL: So Harry wouldn't, for one.

BILLIE: What makes you think not?

PAUL: Ask him.

—Excerpted from *Born Yesterday* by Garson Kanin

1. **What is suggested about Billie's character when the music shifts and she says, "Well, I like to like what's better to like." (line 34)?**

   (1) Billie is content with her own taste.
   (2) Billie likes just about anything.
   (3) Billie is very religious and devout.
   (4) Billie admires what she believes is high culture.
   (5) Billie doesn't know what she likes.

2. **On the basis of Paul's character as revealed in the excerpt, what would he most likely do if Billie said she did not understand an artwork she had seen?**

   (1) Call Billie stupid names.
   (2) Show off his knowledge.
   (3) Ignore Billie altogether.
   (4) Discuss the work with Billie.
   (5) Pretend he did not understand the artwork.

3. **What does Paul mean when he says to Billie, "The idea of learning is to be bigger, not smaller." (lines 35–36)?**

   Learning

   (1) makes a person act in a big-hearted manner
   (2) gives a person a very inflated ego
   (3) fills a person with strange thoughts
   (4) is valuable if it produces money
   (5) enables a person to grow in life

4. **Based on the excerpt, what can be inferred about Paul's feelings toward Harry?**

   (1) Paul does not admire Harry.
   (2) Paul does not know Harry.
   (3) Paul is amused by Harry.
   (4) Paul is indifferent to Harry.
   (5) Paul is protective of Harry.

5. **What purpose do the lines " . . . with a vine growing over the door, and the grapes growing purple in the kisses of the autumn sun." (lines 17–18) have in the passage Paul quotes?**

   (1) They add to the image of the beauty of a simple life.
   (2) They create a sense of wild adventure.
   (3) They compare the sun to Napoleon.
   (4) They create an atmosphere of foolishness.
   (5) They add to a sense of destruction.

Answers are on page 690.

GED PRACTICE

EXERCISE 6

Interpreting a Scene from a Play

Directions: Read the passage below and answer the questions that follow.

WHAT PROBLEM IS BEING DISCUSSED BY ALICE AND GENE?

ALICE: I'm doing a lot for my kids. I don't expect them to pay me back at the other end. *[Gene wanders around, thinking, scuffing the grass.]* I'm sure we could find a full-time housekeeper. He can afford it.

GENE: He'd never agree.

ALICE: It's that or finding a home. *[Gene frowns.]* Sidney's folks like where they are. Also, we might as well face it, his mind's going. Sooner or later, we'll have to think about powers of attorney, perhaps committing him to an institution.

GENE: It's all so ugly.

ALICE: *[smiling]* Yes, my gentle Gene, a lot of life is.

GENE: Now, look, don't go trying to make me out some soft-hearted . . . *[He can't find the word.]* I know life is ugly.

ALICE: Yes, I think you know it. You've lived through a great deal of ugliness. But you work like a Trojan to deny it, to make it not so. *[After a moment, not arguing]* He kicked me out. He said he never wanted to see me again. He broke Mother's heart over that for years. He was mean, unloving. He beat you when you were a kid. . . . You've hated and feared him all your adult life. . . .

GENE: *[cutting in]* Still he's my father, and a man. And what's happening to him appalls me as a man.

ALICE: We have a practical problem here.

GENE: It's not as simple as all that.

ALICE: To me it is. I don't understand this mystical haze you're casting over it. I'm going to talk to him tomorrow, after the session with the lawyer, about a housekeeper. *[Gene reacts but says nothing.]* Just let me handle it. He can visit us, and we can take turns coming to visit him. Now, I'll do the dirty work. Only when he turns to you, don't give in.

GENE: I can't tell you how ashamed I feel . . . not to say with open arms, "Poppa, come live with me . . . I love you, Poppa, and I want to take care of you." . . . I need to love him. I've always wanted to love him. *[He drops his arms and wanders off.]*

—Excerpted from *I Never Sang for My Father* by Robert Anderson

1. What is the relationship between Alice and Gene?

(1) husband and wife
(2) nurse and doctor
(3) sister and brother
(4) close friends
(5) mother and son

2. Alice would agree with which of the following statements?

(1) All children should care for their elderly parents.
(2) Nursing homes are for people who have no children.
(3) The best situation for the elderly is staying in their own houses.
(4) Children should get powers of attorney before placing parents in institutions.
(5) Elderly parents should not expect their children to take care of them.

3. What is last emotion that Gene exhibits?

(1) dismay
(2) relief
(3) disgust
(4) shame
(5) frustration

4. What does Gene's last speech reveal?

(1) acceptance of his father's love
(2) anger with Alice's negative attitude
(3) eagerness to visit his father and offer to care for him
(4) guilt that he doesn't love his father
(5) inability to make decisions that affect his future

Answers are on page 690.

GED PRACTICE

EXERCISE 7

More Practice in Interpreting Drama

Directions: Read the passage below and answer the questions that follow.

WHAT IS ASAGAI'S VIEW OF LIFE?

Act III

ASAGAI: That will be the problem for another time. First we must get there.

BENEATHA: And where does it end?

ASAGAI: End? Who even spoke of an end? To life? To living?

BENEATHA: An end to misery! To stupidity! Don't you see there isn't any real progress, Asagai, there is only one large circle that we march in, around and around, each of us with our own little picture in front of us—our own little mirage that we think is the future.

ASAGAI: That is the mistake.

BENEATHA: What?

ASAGAI: What you just said—about the circle. It isn't a circle—it is simply a long line—as in geometry, you know, one that reaches into infinity. And because we cannot see the end—we also cannot see how it changes. And it is very odd but those who see the changes—who dream, who will not give up—are called idealists. . . and those who see only the circle—we call *them* "realists"!

BENEATHA: Asagai, while I was sleeping in that bed there, people went out and took the future right out of my hands! And nobody asked me, nobody consulted me—they just went out and changed my life!

ASAGAI: Was it your money?

BENEATHA: What?

ASAGAI: Was it your money he gave away?

BENEATHA: It belonged to all of us.

ASAGAI: But did you earn it? Would you have had it at all if your father had not died?

BENEATHA: No.

ASAGAI: Then isn't there something wrong in a house—in a world—where all dreams, good or bad, must depend on the death of a man? I never thought to see *you* like this Alaiyo. You! Your brother made a mistake and you are grateful to him so that now you can give up the ailing human race on account of it! You talk about what good is struggle, and what good is anything! Where are we all going and why are we bothering!

BENEATHA: AND YOU CANNOT ANSWER IT!

ASAGAI: *(shouting over her)*. I LIVE THE ANSWER!

—Adapted from *A Raisin in the Sun* by Lorraine Hansberry

1. According to lines 18–28, What has happened to upset Beneatha?

(1) Money she planned on using was given away.
(2) A thief robbed her home of all valuables.
(3) She lost her job because of sleeping late.
(4) She found saving money impossible.
(5) She earned a lot of money that was spent.

2. Instead of a circle to march in as identified by Beneatha in line 6, what symbol could picture life as she describes it?

(1) a merry-go-round
(2) a willow tree
(3) a set of parallel lines
(4) a vast ocean
(5) an interstate road

3. What feeling does Beneatha display?

(1) patience
(2) anger
(3) courage
(4) worry
(5) boredom

4. What attitude does Asagai display towards the picture of life Beneatha describes?

(1) indifference
(2) fear
(3) acceptance
(4) curiosity
(5) disapproval

Answers are on page 690.

Review of Tips for Reading Drama

- Visualize the scene and action in your mind.
- Think about what a character says about others in the play and think about what that speech may reveal about the character speaking.
- Note the stage directions that indicate the characters' movements and emotions.
- Be alert to the use of punctuation as clues to meaningful pauses, interruptions, and silences.
- Use your own knowledge and experience to assess characters and motivation.
- Consider the implications of both the time and place of the setting.

Go to **www.GEDReading.com** for additional practice and instruction!

CHAPTER 4

Interpreting Prose Nonfiction

If you read a daily or weekly newspaper, you read nonfiction. If you read articles in magazines such as *TV Guide, People, Newsweek, Time, Sports Illustrated,* or *Better Homes and Gardens,* you read nonfiction. If you read articles or books explaining how to garden or cook, buy a car or a house, or take care of a pet, you read nonfiction.

Detecting the Author's Purpose

Nonfiction is literature that is based on fact. The nonfiction author writes about actual people, events, and ideas. The author's purpose may be to record, document, examine, analyze, inform, instruct, entertain, or persuade. In this chapter, we will focus on two key questions, as well as other nonfiction concerns:

- What is the author's purpose for writing the piece?
- What details does the author include to support his or her theories?

For example, look at the following passage.

WHAT IS THE AUTHOR POINTING OUT ABOUT MEN AND WOMEN?

Remembering Our Differences

Without the awareness that we are supposed to be different, men and women are at odds with each other. We usually become angry or frustrated with the opposite sex because we have forgotten this important truth. We expect the opposite sex to be more like ourselves. We desire them to "want what we want" and "feel the way we feel."

We mistakenly assume that if our partners love us they will react and behave in certain ways—the ways we react and behave when we love someone. This attitude sets us up to be disappointed again and again and prevents us from taking the necessary time to communicate lovingly about our differences.

Men mistakenly expect women to think, communicate, and react the way men do; women mistakenly expect men to feel, communicate, and respond the way women do. We have forgotten that men and women are supposed to be different. As a result our relationships are filled with unnecessary friction and conflict.

Clearly recognizing and respecting these differences dramatically reduces confusion when dealing with the opposite sex. When you remember that men are from Mars and women are from Venus, everything can be explained.

—Excerpted from *Men Are from Mars, Women Are from Venus* by John Gray

EXERCISE 1

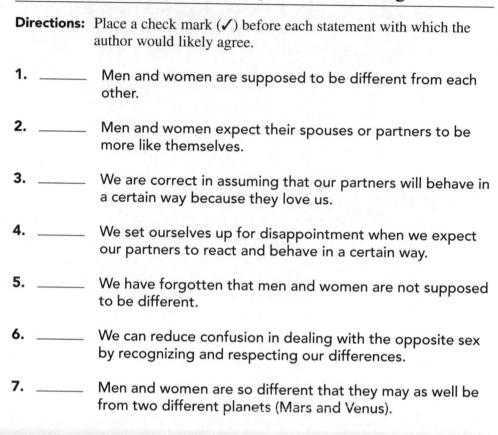

Detecting the Author's Purpose for Writing

Directions: Place a check mark (✓) before each statement with which the author would likely agree.

1. ______ Men and women are supposed to be different from each other.

2. ______ Men and women expect their spouses or partners to be more like themselves.

3. ______ We are correct in assuming that our partners will behave in a certain way because they love us.

4. ______ We set ourselves up for disappointment when we expect our partners to react and behave in a certain way.

5. ______ We have forgotten that men and women are not supposed to be different.

6. ______ We can reduce confusion in dealing with the opposite sex by recognizing and respecting our differences.

7. ______ Men and women are so different that they may as well be from two different planets (Mars and Venus).

Answers are on page 690.

What is the author's purpose in writing the passage? His purpose is clear. Look particularly at the last line, in which he explains the title of the book and introduces the major premise for his book—that men and women are very different. He believes that the way for men and women to learn to get along with each other is to recognize and respect each other's differences.

In this section, you will read a variety of nonfiction excerpts. As in the previous fiction, poetry, and drama sections, you will be asked to understand what you read, apply information to new situations, analyze elements of style and structure, and synthesize parts of passages into new wholes.

Types of Nonfiction

Nonfiction prose appears in many forms and covers every conceivable subject. To organize such a wide range of material, libraries use the Dewey decimal system or the Library of Congress system in categorizing books. Under the Dewey decimal system, broad categories of books and other publications are identified by a three-digit number. For example, nonfiction books that fall within the category of literature are found in the 800s. Under the Library of Congress system, categories of books are given an alphabetical prefix. For example, books that fall within the category of literature are assigned the letter *P.*

Forms of nonfiction prose include the following: **informational text** (newspaper or magazine articles, editorials, or speeches); **literary nonfiction** (biographies, autobiographies, essays, diaries, journals, letters, and reviews); and **viewing components** (review or commentary about fine and performing arts, including films, television, photos, artwork, computer images, or charts). A description and example from each category is represented in this section. One more point to remember before we take a closer look, however, is that sometimes these categories overlap. The longer pieces, such as biographies and autobiographies, very likely can include letters, photos, and so on.

Informational Text

Article—Giving You Just the Facts

An **article** is a short nonfiction piece, often appearing in a newspaper or magazine. An article informs and sometimes entertains readers. The writer presents facts, usually in an objective manner. An article should contain the answers to these questions: *Who, What, Where, When, Why,* and/or *How.* A **feature article** is a special nonfiction piece written on a topic that has high reader interest.

BusinessWeek Los Angeles Times

Newsweek

TIME The New York Times

EXERCISE 2

Reading an Article for Facts

Directions: Read the following article with attention to the questions *Who, What, Where, When, Why,* and/or *How.* Then analyze each statement to determine the questions that are answered in each sentence. The first one is done as a sample.

CAN BABIES SPEAK THROUGH SIGN LANGUAGE?

(1) A growing body of research supports [doctoral student and parent Jennifer] Neale's faith in the power of sign language for babies. **(2)** Once considered useful only for the deaf or hard-of-hearing, sign language is becoming a powerful tool to promote early communication for everyone. **(3)** The reason: Professionals say children can communicate with hand signs much sooner than they can master verbal skills. **(4)** "It's a question of how children mature," says Marilyn Daniels, an associate professor of speech communication at Pennsylvania State University and author of a forthcoming book called *Dancing with Word Signing for Hearing Children's Literacy.*

(5) Daniels is one of numerous researchers who encourage families to learn and use basic signs as early as possible. **(6)** Most suggest using American Sign Language (ASL) because it's easy to learn, standardized, and an official language used by the deaf community. **(7)** But others note that even homemade signs can encourage communication at least six months before most children start to form basic words. **(8)** Signing not only increases the parents' bond and interaction with their babies, it helps reduce a major source of tantrums and stress for infants. **(9)** It also creates a more physically expressive environment.

—Excerpted from "Look Who's Talking with Their Hands" by Diane Brady, *Business Week,* August 14, 2000

Sentence 1: *When:* (not specifically stated, but "A growing body of research" suggests the current time period of August 14, 2000.)

Who: doctoral student and parent Jennifer Neale

What: supports research/power of sign language for communicating with babies

Sentence 2: ______________________________

____

Sentence 3: ______________________________

____

Sentence 4: ______________________________

____

Sentence 5: ____

____

Sentence 6: ____

____

Sentence 7: ____

____

Sentence 8: ____

____

Sentence 9: ____

____

Answers are on page 691.

Writing Activity 1

What is your opinion about trying to communicate with babies before they can speak? Do you think this is a good or bad idea? What are the advantages and disadvantages of communicating with infants earlier? Use your notebook or journal to write your response.

Make Newspaper and Magazine Nonfiction Reading a Habit

A good way to prepare for the GED Test is to make a habit of reading a major daily newspaper regularly. This enables you to practice your reading and critical thinking skills and allows you to enjoy interesting nonfiction. For further practice and information, another good habit is to read a weekly news magazine or the magazine included with many metropolitan newspapers.

As you read your newspaper or magazine, note whether news or feature articles seem sufficiently objective in reporting the facts.

Editorial: Trying to Persuade

An **editorial** is a relatively short piece of nonfiction from a periodical (newspaper or magazine) that is designed to persuade or convince you to believe a certain way or to take a certain action. While an editorial needs to be based on facts, this is the one section of the periodical in which the opinions and views of the publisher are permitted and should be labeled as opinion. While the main editorial for the particular publication is usually in essay form, other editorials may appear as regular **columns** by other publication (or syndicated) staff, **letters to the editor, guest editorials** from readers, or **cartoons.**

EXERCISE 3

Reading an Editorial for Informed Opinion

Directions: In the editorial below, the editor of a metropolitan newspaper comments on a national law. The excerpt includes the first sentence, some background material, and then the concluding sentence of the piece. Answer the questions that follow.

DOES THIS STUDY CHANGE YOUR MIND ABOUT THE BRADY LAW?

Do waiting periods and criminal background checks on prospective handgun buyers deter violent crime?

That question has generated heated debate ever since a federal law requiring both was first proposed more than a decade ago.

A new report published by the *Journal of the American Medical Association* is stoking the controversy again, as authors of the study conclude the Brady Law has failed to significantly decrease handgun homicides since its 1994 enactment.

For one thing, we have never argued that the Brady Law should take sole credit for the declining crime rates of recent years. We concur with the authors of this study on their assertion that many varied factors—including a shift in demographics, aggressive police work, tougher mandatory sentences and a good economy—have contributed.

Factoring those reports into the equation, as well as a separate study linking background checks in California to violent crime reduction in that state, puts Brady's effectiveness in a more positive light. The law's background check requirement remains a reasonable and prudent guard against those who seek handguns with criminal intent.

—Excerpted from "Brady Law Still Makes Sense",
Daily Herald, August 7, 2000

1. What question does the editorial raise?

____

2. What information does the *Journal of the American Medical Association* study provide about the effectiveness of the Brady Law?

____

3. What opinion does the editorial reaffirm in its conclusion?

____

4. Based on the editorial, what action would the newspaper publisher oppose?

____

Answers are on page 691.

Speech: Telling You as It Is

A **speech** is spoken communication about a topic. A speech is similar to an essay in its organization. The speaker should have an interesting introduction, support for the main idea, and a strong conclusion. Among other things, a speech may entertain, inform, instruct, inspire, or persuade.

Notable speeches include Abraham Lincoln's 1863 "Gettysburg Address," John F. Kennedy's 1961 "Inaugural Address," and Martin Luther King, Jr.'s 1963 "I Have a Dream" civil rights speech. Excerpts from two of these speeches appear in this section.

Because speeches are considered to be nonfiction, they can be analyzed by examining tone, style, message, and purpose.

GED PRACTICE

EXERCISE 4

Analyzing a Speech for Purpose

Directions: Read the famous speech below (with sentences numbered) and answer the questions that follow.

WHAT IS THE OVERALL TONE OF LINCOLN'S SPEECH?

Address at the Dedication of the Gettysburg National Cemetery

(1) Four score and seven [87] years ago our fathers brought forth on this continent, a new nation, conceived in liberty, and dedicated to the proposition that all men are created equal.

(2) Now we are engaged in a great civil war; testing whether that nation, or any nation so conceived and so dedicated, can long endure. **(3)** We are met on a great battlefield of that war. **(4)** We have come to dedicate a portion of that field as a final resting-place for those who here gave their lives that this nation might live. **(5)** It is altogether fitting and proper that we should do this.

(6) But in a larger sense, we cannot dedicate—we cannot consecrate—we cannot hallow—this ground. **(7)** The brave men, living and dead, who struggled here have consecrated it, far above our poor power to add or detract. **(8)** The world will little note, nor long remember, what we say here, but it can never forget what they did here. **(9)** It is for the living, rather, to be dedicated here to the unfinished work which they who fought here have thus far so nobly advanced. **(10)** It is rather for us to be here dedicated to the great task remaining before us—that from these honored dead we take increased devotion to that cause for which they gave the last full measure of devotion; that we here highly resolve that these dead shall not have died in vain; that this nation, under God, shall have a new birth of freedom; and that government of the people, by the people, for the people, shall not perish from the earth.

—Abraham Lincoln

1. Which sentence in the speech is a reference to the ability of the nation to last after the American Civil War?

(1) Sentence 1
(2) Sentence 2
(3) Sentence 3
(4) Sentence 4
(5) Sentence 5

2. Which sentence in the speech is a reference to the beginnings of the American democratic nation?

(1) Sentence 1
(2) Sentence 2
(3) Sentence 3
(4) Sentence 4
(5) Sentence 5

3. In sentence 10 what does President Lincoln indicate is the greatest task remaining?

(1) bury the Civil War dead
(2) honor those who have died
(3) change the government
(4) have a new birth of freedom
(5) perish from the earth

4. What is *not* a purpose of the speech?

(1) to dedicate the Gettysburg National Cemetery
(2) to rebuke the South for its Civil War actions
(3) to honor those who gave their lives in battle
(4) to dedicate a portion of the field as a final resting place
(5) to inspire all the American people to persevere

Answers are on page 691.

GED PRACTICE

EXERCISE 5

Interpreting a Speech

Directions: The passage below is from John F. Kennedy's inaugural address. Read the excerpt and answer the questions that follow.

WHAT DOES THE PRESIDENT ASK OF HIS FELLOW CITIZENS?

In your hands, my fellow citizens, more than mine, will rest the final success or failure of our course. Since this country was founded, each generation of Americans has been summoned to give testimony to its national loyalty. The graves of young Americans who answered the call to service surround the globe.

Now the trumpet summons us again—not as a call to bear arms, though arms we need; not as a call to battle, though embattled we are; but a call to bear the burden of a long twilight struggle, year in and year out, "rejoicing in hope, patient in tribulation," a struggle against the common enemies of man: tyranny, poverty, disease, and war itself.

Can we forge against these enemies a grand and global alliance, North and South, East and West, that can assure a more fruitful life for all mankind? Will you join me in this historic effort?

In the long history of the world, only a few generations have been granted the role of defending freedom in its hour of maximum danger. I do not shrink from this responsibility; I welcome it. I do not believe that any of us would exchange places with any other people or any other generation. The energy, the faith, the devotion which we bring to this endeavor will light our country and all who serve it, and the glow from that fire can truly light the world.

And so, my fellow Americans, ask not what your country can do for you; ask what you can do for your country.

My fellow citizens of the world, ask not what America will do for you, but what together we can do for the freedom of man.

—John F. Kennedy

1. Which word best describes the tone of the speech?

(1) sarcastic
(2) light-hearted
(3) angry
(4) uplifting
(5) sad

2. What is one thing the speech motivates listeners to do?

(1) preserve the right to bear arms
(2) enlist in the armed services
(3) serve their country
(4) take national loyalty oaths
(5) prepare themselves for battle

3. In the speech, how does Kennedy describe the United States?

(1) approaching world war
(2) longing to return to the past
(3) defending freedom for all
(4) struggling to survive
(5) becoming weaker by selfishness

4. Which of the following stylistic devices is *not* used in the speech?

(1) a standard, predictable rhythm and the use of rhyme
(2) the use of the personal pronouns we and us
(3) phrases in which subjects and objects are inverted
(4) the repetition of key words such as my fellow
(5) questions that invite readers to answer yes silently

Answers are on page 691.

Literary Nonfiction

Biography: Revealing Details about People

Most people like to read about other people's lives; consequently, biography is a popular form of nonfiction. A **biography** is a factual book or sketch that records the life of an individual. Biographies are written about historical figures, politicians, sports figures, current and past celebrities, and others.

Biographers report major events in a person's life and interpret their meaning. A biography often is meant to entertain as well as to educate; you can certainly learn from the experiences of others. Typically, biographies are written as a tribute after someone's death, but other biographies are written about people who are still alive.

Most major writers and literary figures are subjects of biographies because critics and readers want to know more about the personal lives of writers and how those events relate to their writings. Also, biographies often are written about famous entertainers.

In one instance, a writer wrote about the houses of other writers and the creative process. The passage below is by Francesca Premoli-Droulers, who wrote a biographical sketch of writer Karen Blixen in the context of Blixen's working on her autobiography. Note what Premoli-Droulers says about Blixen's tone.

WHAT DOES A HOUSE SAY ABOUT A WRITER?

In 1935, Karen began work on a book that was to become a kind of autobiography: *Out of Africa.* The tone is restrained, the emotions are under control, and the prose flows with a serene power. Still, from the opening sentences, it is possible to sense the lacerating intensity of her memories: "I had a farm in Africa, at the foot of the Ngong Hills. The Equator runs across these highlands, a hundred miles to the North, and the farm lay at an altitude of over six hundred feet. In the day-time you felt that you had got high up, near to the sun, but the early mornings and evenings were limpid [clear] and restful, and the nights were cold." This narrative, published in the United States in 1937 and then in Denmark, met with considerable success. Fifty-one years later the movie won a clutch of Oscars and made the author posthumously [occurring after death] famous throughout the world.

—Excerpted from "Karen Blixen" (Isak Dinesen) in *Writers' Houses*
by Francesca Premoli-Droulers

Question: What did Premoli-Droulers say about Blixen's writing?

Answer: She said, "The tone is restrained, the emotions are under control, and the prose flows with a serene power." You get the sense that the surroundings of a farm in Africa contributed to the serenity of Blixen's prose: "the early mornings and evenings were limpid and restful."

Many times, nonfiction authors interview their sources, then summarize the interview in their own words. In his 1998 collection of biographical sketches, *The Greatest Generation,* author Tom Brokaw relates the stories of many ordinary as well as famous persons of the World War II generation.

GED PRACTICE

EXERCISE 6

Finding the Notable in a Biography

Directions: Read the biographical sketch below of Magaret Ray Ringenberg and answer the questions that follow.

WHAT CAREER OPTIONS WERE OPEN TO WOMEN IN THE 1940s?

In 1940 she [Margaret Ray Ringenberg] started taking lessons at the local airfield and earned her license by the time she was twenty-one, just in time for the Army Air Force to recruit her for the WASPs [Women's Air Force Service Pilots]. "I was flabbergasted," she remembers. "What an opportunity. My father said, `I didn't get to serve and I don't have any boys, so I guess you'll have to do it.'"

After six months of rigorous training in a wide variety of military aircraft in Sweetwater, Texas, Maggie was sent to Wilmington, Delaware, the 2nd Ferrying Division, assigned to testing and transporting the planes used to train young men for combat flying. . .

In the mid-fifties she discovered a new dimension to her flying: the Powder Puff Derby, a cross-country air race for women pilots. For the next twenty years, she was a competitor in the Derby, later named the Classic Air Race. She won it in 1988 and finished second six times. That was a warm-up for her big race.

In 1994 Margaret Ringenberg, the former farm girl who fell in love with flying at the age of seven and learned in the WASPs that she could hold her own against the best of the best, decided to compete in a race around the world. Twenty-four days in a small, twin-engine plane, a Cessna 340, more than a hundred hours in the air. She was seventy-two years old at the time, the oldest entrant.

—Excerpted from "Margaret Ray Ringenberg" in *The Greatest Generation*
by Tom Brokaw

1. Margaret Ray Ringenberg's father supported his daughter's joining the Army Air Force during World War II. Which of the following was *not* one of his reasons?

(1) Mr. Ray didn't get to serve in the Army himself.
(2) Margaret earned her pilot's license by the age of twenty-one.
(3) Margaret was apparently capable of rigorous training.
(4) Mr. Ray said he was an early proponent of women's liberation.
(5) Margaret saw service in the Army Air Force as an opportunity.

2. What is the *best* evidence in the biographical sketch for the premise that Margaret viewed flying seriously all her life?

(1) In the 1950s she entered the women's Powder Puff Derby, a cross-country race.
(2) She fell in love with flying when she was only seven years of age.
(3) She tested and transported planes for training for combat flying.
(4) She responded to the Army Air Force when it recruited her for the WASPs.
(5) She competed in a race around the world in 1994 at age seventy-two.

3. If Margaret Ray Ringenberg were to speak to elementary school children today, what career advice would she likely give them?

(1) Use the wisdom of your parents to select a future career field.
(2) Follow your mind and heart as to your career interests and choices.
(3) Find role models of the same gender to bolster your confidence.
(4) Follow in traditional career choices so as not to upset parents.
(5) Do not openly show your talents if you expect to be accepted.

Answers are on page 691.

Not all biographical works document the lives of famous or distinguished individuals. In *Slats Grobnik and Some Other Friends,* Chicago journalist Mike Royko reprinted newspaper columns from 1966 to 1973 and told stories about Slats, "a neighborhood truant raised in a second-floor flat above a tavern with the El tracks in back."

Authors may use interviews to record oral histories and to create biographies. In *Hard Times,* Studs Terkel recorded facts and impressions about the lives of many different "common people" who were affected by the Great Depression of the 1930s. Similarly, Studs Terkel produced "an oral history of World War II" in the 1984 biography, *The Good War.* In the example on page 668 Terkel interviews columnist Mike Royko about his recollections of the war years.

GED PRACTICE

EXERCISE 7

Using Oral History to Create Biography

Directions: Read the biographical sketch below and answer the questions that follow.

DO AUTHORS REMEMBER AN EVENT WITH MORE DETAIL?

I was nine years old when the war started. It was a typical Chicago working-class neighborhood. It was predominantly Slavic, Polish. There were some Irish, some Germans. When you're a kid, the borders of the world are the few blocks of two-flats, bungalows, cottages, with a lot of little stores in between. My father had a tavern. In those days they put out extras. I remember the night the newsboys came through the neighborhood. Skid-Row kind of guys, hawking the papers. Germany had invaded Poland: '39. It was the middle of the night, my mother and father waking. People were going out in the streets with their bathrobes to buy the papers. In our neighborhood with a lot of Poles, it was a tremendous story.

Suddenly you had a flagpole. And a marker. Names went on the marker, guys from the neighborhood who were killed. Our neighborhood was decimated. There were only kids, older guys, and women.

Suddenly I saw something I hadn't seen before. My sister became Rosie the Riveter. She put a bandanna on her head every day and went down to this organ company that had been converted to war work. There was my sister in slacks. It became more than work. There was a sense of mission about it. Her husband was Over There. She went bowling once a week. They had a league. I used to have to go with her, because the presence of her little brother would discourage guys from making passes at her.

—Excerpted from "Neighborhood Boys" in *The Good War* by Studs Terkel

1. What is the relative importance of the detail, "My sister became Rosie the Riveter"?

(1) Women started to wear slacks for the first time.
(2) Women could now join weekly bowling leagues.
(3) Women went to work to support the war effort.
(4) Women proved they could handle machinery.
(5) Women no longer had to be wives and mothers.

2. How would you describe the overall reaction of Mike Royko's neighborhood at the outbreak of World War II in 1939?

(1) disbelieving
(2) uninterested
(3) passive
(4) involved
(5) fearful

3. If a neighborhood such as in Mike Royko's boyhood were to be recreated today and there were a national crisis, what would the effect likely be?

(1) Neighbors would not band together, so there would be no apparent effect.
(2) Female and male members of the neighborhood would react separately.
(3) People would work but ignore anything else outside the neighborhood.
(4) Neighbors would form an organized information network with officers.
(5) Neighbors would closely monitor and discuss events through various media.

Answers are on page 692.

Autobiography: Telling about Yourself

Only you can write your autobiography, the story of your own life. An **autobiography** is a self-biography. Many writers of autobiographies are not professional writers but notable individuals telling their own stories. Autobiographies are also known as **memoirs.** An example of a memoir is *Ever the Winds of Chance,* in which well-known American poet Carl Sandburg chronicles his years as a college student and young adult.

Some notable autobiographies include *Life on the Mississippi* by Mark Twain, recounting the author's journey on the river; *The Diary of Anne Frank,* a diary of a young Jewish girl who hid from the Nazis during World War II; *Out of Africa,* the autobiography of Karen Blixen (Isak Dinesen), which was the basis for the film of the same title; and *The Autobiography of Malcolm X* which served as the basis for Spike Lee's film about Malcolm X.

Like authors of fiction, authors of nonfiction exhibit particular styles. Autobiographies, especially, tend to be written in a less formal style because the writers are revealing the personal details of their lives. Here, Geraldine A. Ferraro, the first woman to be nominated as a candidate by a major political party for vice president of the United States, talks about her experience in Congress.

GED PRACTICE

EXERCISE 8

Studying a Noteworthy Autobiography

Directions: Read the passage below and answer the questions that follow.

HOW TOUGH WAS THE JOB OF CONGRESSWOMAN?

I had run on the slogan, "Finally . . . a tough Democrat," but I didn't realize until I got to Washington how true that slogan was.

You had to be tough to be a female member of Congress. Because there were so few of us, still only twenty-four in House and Senate in 1983, we were very visible and therefore ripe targets for criticism. There were traps everywhere, even on the most insignificant details, and I made sure I fell into as few of them as possible. . . .

I felt terribly frustrated by what seemed to be the male indifference to women's issues, especially the economic predicament confronting women of all ages—single or married, homemakers or women who also worked outside the home. Though women represented forty-three percent of the work force, the "feminization of poverty" was growing. For most, their paychecks were essential to support either themselves or their families. Fully two-thirds of the women in the work force were single, widowed, divorced, or married to men who earned less than fifteen thousand dollars a year. . .

—Excerpted from *Ferraro: My Story* by Geraldine A. Ferraro with Linda Bird Francke

1. What was the main idea of the second paragraph?

(1) You had to be tough to be a female member of Congress.
(2) Because there were so few of us. . . we were very visible.
(3) [We were] therefore ripe targets for criticism.
(4) There were traps everywhere, even on the most insignificant details.
(5) I made sure I fell into as few of them as possible.

2. According to the biographical sketch on page 670, which of the following does *not* describe Congresswoman Ferraro?

(1) tough
(2) frustrated
(3) committed
(4) indifferent
(5) concerned

Answers are on page 692.

Essay: Presenting One Person's View

An **essay** is a nonfiction work in which an author presents a personal viewpoint on a subject. Let's look first at a passage by an ordinary person whose essay was published in a national news magazine.

WHAT ARE THE RESPONSIBILITIES OF PARENTS?

You've heard the calls. I've heard the calls. I've taken them, too—which is one reason that my phone isn't on all the time.

But there's another reason, too. I believe we well-meaning parents need to get comfortable with the fact that we cannot and should not orchestrate every moment in our children's lives for them. Partly because the effort turns out to be futile, but more importantly because it prevents our kids from learning life skills they need to succeed in the real world. There are times they need to ad lib. There are times they need to wait. There are even times they need to turn to someone else—another family member, a teacher, a neighbor—and ask for help.

—Excerpted from "My Turn: Parents Shouldn't Be On Call All the Time"
by Nicole Wise, *Newsweek*, August 7, 2000

Writing Activity 2

Elsewhere in the parent's essay the writer gives her views that some phone calls are vital—such as when her daughter called from the hospital—and other calls are routine or unnecessary. Should parents be accessible and available to their children at all times? Answer the question and state your reasons for your beliefs. Your answers will begin to form your personal essay on your philosophy of parenting. Use your notebook or journal for your response.

Traditionally, an essay is a formal piece of writing, an expository piece that exposes and analyzes a subject. Essays embrace a variety of tones, styles, language, and themes. An essay is a *written* communication of an opinion or a point of view.

Following is an excerpt from a well-known formal essay, "On the Duty of Civil Disobedience," by Henry David Thoreau. The essay was written after Thoreau was jailed for refusing to pay a poll tax that he viewed as support for the Mexican War. The essay is personal in that Thoreau uses it to explain his views; it is serious in tone, and the vocabulary is somewhat different from that of today's prose. The ideas put forth in this excerpt of the long essay were shared by civil rights leaders of the 1960s and 1970s, the Nazi-resisters of the 1930s and 1940s, and others.

GED PRACTICE

EXERCISE 9

Interpreting a Formal Essay

Directions: Read the passage below and answer the questions that follow.

WHAT IS THE PURPOSE OF GOVERNMENT?

On the Duty of Civil Disobedience

I heartily accept the motto,—"That government is best which governs least;" and I should like to see it acted up to more rapidly and systematically. Carried out, it finally amounts to this, which also I believe,—"That government is best which governs not at all;" and when men are prepared for it, that will be the kind of government which they will have. Government is at best but an expedient; but most governments are usually, and all governments are sometimes, inexpedient. The objections which have been brought against a standing army, and they are many and weighty, and deserve to prevail, may also at last be brought against a standing government. The standing army is only an arm of the standing government. The government itself, which is only the mode which the people have chosen to execute their will, is equally liable to be abused and perverted before the people can act through it. Witness the present Mexican war, the work of comparatively a few individuals using the standing government as their tool; for, in the outset, the people would not have consented to this measure.

This American government,—what is it but a tradition, though a recent one, endeavoring to transmit itself unimpaired to posterity, but each instant losing some of its integrity? It has not the vitality and force of a single living man; for a single man can bend it to his will. It is a sort of wooden gun to the people themselves; and, if ever they should use it in earnest as a real one against each other, it will surely split. . . .

—Excerpted from "On the Duty of Civil Disobedience" by Henry David Thoreau

1. What does the title of the essay imply?

A citizen

(1) is disloyal for disobeying laws
(2) should serve in the army
(3) should appreciate U.S. citizenship
(4) is obligated to break an unjust law
(5) must vote in all elections

2. "The government itself, which is only the mode which the people have chosen to execute their will." In the previous line, what does the word <u>execute</u> mean?

(1) capital punishment of criminals
(2) kill during a war
(3) carry out; perform
(4) ignore the wishes of
(5) create; originate

3. For what purpose does Thoreau believe that the army exists?

(1) for discretionary use by each individual
(2) for the express wishes of government
(3) as a necessary part of democracy
(4) as the symbol of individual heroism
(5) as an entity independent of government

4. What is Thoreau's interpretation of government?

(1) mode to express the people's will
(2) group of knowledgeable leaders
(3) tool of the standing army
(4) means to give fewer freedoms
(5) way to encourage prosperity

Answers are on page 692.

As you learned in the section on fiction, style includes the author's unique use of language to express ideas. It is the writer's style that distinguishes a formal essay from an informal one.

EXERCISE 10

Comparing and Contrasting Essay Viewpoints

Directions: Read each passage below and answer the questions that follow.

Should We Extend the School Year?

YES

Adam Urbanski, Vice President, American Federation of Teachers

"It's a wise investment in education."

The question of time is directly linked to the success or failure of the standards movement in American education. At last, we are asking *all* students to meet higher standards. But not all of our students are able to do this without additional help from their teachers. Thus, some teachers will need more time to help those students who otherwise would be less likely to attain the higher standards now expected of them. This translates into additional classes, extra tutoring, after-school programs or summer sessions.

NO

Bill Goodling, Member of the U.S. House of Representatives

"Focus on quality, not quantity."

[The] move to adopt year-round teaching . . . is ambitious, and there may be some school districts that will be interested . . . However, I believe the issue is not how much time a teacher spends in the classroom, but the quality of that time. Next to parents, the most important part of a child's education is a well-trained teacher in the classroom. . . . Federally mandating year-round teaching would be a definite step in the wrong direction. Year-round teaching should always be a decision left up to states and, ultimately, school districts.

—Excerpted from "Speak Out" *AFT On Campus*, May/June, 2000

1. What qualifications does each essay writer have to respond to the question about year-round schools?

   ____

   ____

2. Summarize in one or two sentences the position that each essay writer takes on whether American schools should be in session year-round.

   ____

   ____

Possible answers are on page 692.

Writing Activity 3

What is your position on having mandatory year-round schools? Basically, are you for or against the idea? What could be the advantages and disadvantages of year-round schools? How would this affect your job, family schedules, vacations, taxes, and so on? Have a friend or family member answer the same questions. Then look at your answers and your friend's or family member's answers to see how the views are similar (comparison) or different (contrast).

Diaries, Journals, and Letters

Have you ever kept a diary or journal? Both diaries and journals are daily records of personal activities, events, travels, or reflections. You may keep records for yourself or for your children or grandchildren. Should you ever write your autobiography, you may refer to your diaries or journals as sources of material.

In the passage below, an author returns to her birthplace in another country 5,000 miles away some 45 years after she left as a child. Because it's an excerpt from a travel journal, it includes incomplete sentences.

Saturday, July 15
Continued to walk the streets of Alta Villa. Saw old people with nothing else to do but sit outside on chairs. An old nun was delighted to see us. Strangers (to us) greeted and kissed us and remembered my parents. Memories never cease here. Paramount are relationships: "son of," "daughter of," "sister of," "brother of," "cousin of," etc. Had some home-made ice-cream at Teresa's house.

Continued walking and had *deja vu* feeling again. Hills, fig plants, flowers, etc. Felt that I was close to drop-off point. Could this be where I fell down the hill chasing after Jack and Marie? I was told that Dad's farm was in the vicinity and that while the hill didn't lead to the Mediterranean, it once had led to a river, now dry. So I could have been rolling toward the river then. Dad saved me, and I lost one shoe. Could I *really* remember from about age two, or do I remember a story told over and over to me?

Ralph Waldo Emerson referred to his journals as his savings banks in which he deposited his thoughts. Below is an entry from one of his journals. Later, he "withdrew" those thoughts to write some of his famous speeches, essays, and poems.

GED PRACTICE

EXERCISE 11

Interpreting a Diary or Journal

Directions: Read the passage below and answer the questions that follow.

WHAT IS EMERSON'S ATTITUDE TOWARD LIFE?

Society everywhere is in conspiracy against the manhood of every one of its members. . . . The virtue in most request is conformity. Self-reliance is its aversion. It loves not realities and creators, but names and customs.

Whoso would be a man, must be a nonconformist. He who would gather immortal palms must not be hindered by the name of goodness, but must explore if it be goodness. Nothing is at last sacred but the integrity of your own mind.

—Excerpted from "Self-Reliance" by Ralph Waldo Emerson

1. As Emerson looked around the society of his time, he saw that conformity was everywhere. Which of the following concepts would have best described the *opposite* behavior that Emerson advocated?

(1) conspiracy
(2) agreement
(3) authority
(4) fraternity
(5) individuality

2. Based on the passage, with which of the following statements about conformity might Emerson agree?

(1) When in doubt, it is best to follow the crowd.
(2) Leadership is finding a parade and getting in front.
(3) You are the most reliable judge of what's best for you.
(4) It is best to agree with others for the sake of harmony.
(5) Those who don't challenge authority do best.

Answers are on page 693.

Writing Activity 4

Are you going on a trip soon? Is there soon to be a major change in your life? Keep a journal every day for at least a week. Don't worry about writing complete thoughts. Just get your ideas down. Then set your journal aside for a while to let it "cool." That's so you'll have a fresh perspective when you return to your writing. Are there major topics that appear in the thoughts you expressed? You could develop them into essays.

Viewing Component

The **viewing component** of the Language Arts, Reading Test will include critical reviews or published commentary of fine and performing arts, including films, television programs, photography, artwork, computer images, or charts. **Commentary** is a form of nonfiction in which the writer comments about any of the visual forms listed. A person who writes commentary—a **critic**—evaluates a nonfiction form and assesses the work's strengths and weaknesses.

The Style and Language of Commentary

Because a reviewer (or critic) is both describing and analyzing a visual form, the style and language of commentary often is highly descriptive. As the reader of commentary, you must be able to analyze style (including tone) to evaluate the reviewer's judgment about the visual form. A reviewer may write general commentary about nonfiction in a newspaper or magazine column that appears regularly.

A review deals with a specific work. The reviewer reacts to one book, film, or work of art. However, criticism may discuss trends or characteristics of a whole *type of art.* To understand criticism, you must be able to read on two levels. First, you must understand facts about both the visual form and its creator. Then, you have to understand the critic's opinions.

As you read, look for statements of facts and opinion. Remember that most reviews are persuasive essays. The critic's purpose is illustrated with details and examples. Notice the critic's style, including tone and language.

GED PRACTICE

EXERCISE 12

Evaluating a Film or Television Review

Directions: The following television review presents views not only about a specific show but about the nature of TV programming. Read the review and answer the questions that follow.

HOW DOES THE REVIEWER RATE THE "ALL-TIME BEST" SITCOMS?

M*A*S*H

The show *I Love Lucy* created a new comic form for television, and *All in the Family* used social issues for comic purposes. *Cheers* created a television "family" so that strangers could develop close relationships that could continue to be explored. *Seinfeld* was a long-running show about the most routine and often most trivial of matters. But *M*A*S*H* did what only the greatest—the classic—comedies do: mix hilarity and tragedy, often in equal measure.

*M*A*S*H* made us laugh till we cried. And though its anti-war message occasionally got heavy-handed, it was never at the expense of laughter or character. Like all great sitcoms, it succeeded mainly by exploring, indeed celebrating, the chemistry between the characters. The last episode of *M*A*S*H* was the most-watched program in TV history for good reason. M*A*S*H had an underriding urgency to its comedy—it's about life, death, war, and the redeeming grace of humor—that makes it, in our eyes, the best sitcom in history.

1. If you were retitling the review, which of the following titles would you choose?

(1) Keeping It All in the Family
(2) "Lucy" Changing Our Viewing
(3) Watching the Last of the Best
(4) TV Is Getting Better (Worse)
(5) Using Comedy for Social Issues

2. What would the reviewer say that a sitcom that hopes to become the best in history must do?

(1) contain very powerful anti-war messages
(2) have strong relationships among characters
(3) closely follow the comic form of "I Love Lucy"
(4) use "All in the Family" as a writing blueprint
(5) use humor to cover up the tragedy in a story

3. What is the tone of the review?

(1) appreciative
(2) questioning
(3) unfavorable
(4) uncertain
(5) sarcastic

Answers are on page 693.

Tips for Reading Nonfiction Commentary

When you read nonfiction commentary, ask yourself these questions:

1. What facts about the work itself does the critic include?
2. What does the critic say about the author, the author's abilities, and the author's background?
3. What does the critic like about the visual form? What does the critic dislike about the visual form? Look for words that communicate the critic's feelings about the form.
4. What statements are based on facts about the visual form? What statements are based on the critic's opinion or personal reaction to the visual form?
5. Does the critic recommend the visual form? Does the critic recognize the value of the visual form?
6. What is the critic's style? *How* does he or she present the message?

GED PRACTICE

EXERCISE 13

Interpreting Artistic Commentary

Directions: Read the commentary about the famous American painting shown below and answer the questions that follow.

HOW DOES THE AUTHOR FEEL ABOUT THE PAINTING?

—American Gothic by Grant Wood. Photograph courtesy of The Art Institute of Chicago

A geography of the imagination would extend the shores of the Mediterranean all the way to Iowa.

Eldon, Iowa—where in 1929 Grant Wood sketched a farmhouse as the background for a double portrait of his sister Nan and his dentist, Dr. B. H. McKeeby, who donned overalls for the occasion and held a rake. Forces that arose three millennia ago in the Mediterranean changed the rake to a pitchfork, as we shall see.

Let us look at this painting to which we are blinded by familiarity and parody. In the remotest distance against this perfect blue of a fine harvest sky, there is the Gothic spire of a country church, as if to seal the Protestant sobriety and industry of the subjects. Next there are trees, seven of them, as along the porch of Solomon's temple, symbols of prudence and wisdom.

Next, still reading from background to foreground, is the house that gives the primary meaning of the title, *American Gothic,* a style of architecture. It is an example of a revolution in domestic building that made possible the rapid rise of American cities after the Civil War and dotted the prairies with decent, neat farmhouses. It is what was first called in derision a balloon-frame house, so easy to build that a father and his son could put it up. It is an elegant geometry of light timber posts and rafters requiring no deep foundation, and is nailed together. Technically, it is, like the clothes of the farmer and his wife, a mail-order house, as the design comes out of a pattern, this one from those of Alexander Davis and Andrew Downing, the architects who modified details of the Gothic Revival for American farmhouses . . .

—Excerpted from "On Grant Wood, *American Gothic,* 1930" by Guy Davenport in *Transforming Vision,* selected and introduced by Edward Hirsch

1. In the first line reviewer Guy Davenport introduces his commentary regarding the painting with, "A geography of the imagination would extend the shores of the Mediterranean all the way to Iowa."

The effect of this line is to

(1) question whether the painting is American or European (Mediterranean)
(2) establish the influence of Mediterranean art on American art
(3) provide a lesson to compare American and European geography
(4) introduce the subject of soil and ocean shores conservation
(5) show that the shores of Iowa are similar to those of the Mediterranean

2. The reviewer says, "Let us look at this painting to which we are blinded by familiarity and parody." ***Parody*** **means to imitate something for the purposes of comic effect or ridicule. What is the reviewer asking the reader to do?**

(1) find anything and everything to criticize about the painting
(2) compose a literary or a musical comedy of the painting
(3) go beyond our usual or common understanding of the painting
(4) learn so much about the painting that one could describe it blind-folded
(5) look at the painting only under controlled indoor, darker lighting

3. Which of the following words would ***not*** **describe a house built in the tradition of American Gothic?**

(1) easy to build by few workers
(2) supported by a shallow foundation
(3) elegant in simple lines
(4) built by mail-order design
(5) elaborate in rich detail

4. The artist draws the subjects in the painting and the reviewer describes them as having "Protestant sobriety and industry." What conclusion can you reach about what the subjects are like?

(1) rich, exciting, and mysterious
(2) happy, carefree, and irresponsible
(3) educated, professional, and opinionated
(4) loose, careless, and unthinking
(5) serious, steady, and hardworking

Answers are on page 693.

Business Documents

The final type of nonfiction that will be included on the Language Arts, Reading Test is **business documents.** Documents may be contracts or lease agreements, written work requirements or guidelines for conduct (employee handbooks, policy or procedural manuals, pamphlets, or memoranda), or other forms.

Let's focus on documents one could find in the workplace. These include **handbooks** or **procedure manuals, policies** (or rules of conduct), and **programs.** These business documents address the following topics:

- Handbooks or Procedure Manuals: classification levels, work schedules, compensation and salary schedules, benefits programs, payroll deductions, health and safety conduct, travel reimbursement, medical needs, leaves of absence with and without pay, review and evaluation, disciplinary or dismissal measures, grievance, or termination
- Policies: equal opportunity employment, standards of conduct/ethics, attendance and tardiness, communications, vacation and holiday, promotion or transfer, recruitment for employment of other individuals, substance abuse, drug and alcohol testing, smoking, sexual harassment, discounts, or environment
- Programs: orientation or employee development, insurance, educational assistance, employee assistance (counseling), substance abuse prevention, retirement, or recycling

Let's use *office communications* to examine how policies could be stated and interpreted. Means of communication can include verbal or written means: verbal conversations among employees; telephone/voice mail; FAX (short for facsimile, or documents transmitted over phone lines), standard intraoffice or interoffice memoranda or letters; e-mail (electronic mail) sent through personal computers networked together or through an Internet access service provider (such as America Online or Microsoft Network); computer help desks; Web pages authored by individuals or departments and available through World Wide Web servers; video conferencing tools; and probably other means yet to be invented!

In any event, companies have rules and guidelines for the manner in which employees may communicate with each other. Read the following guidelines (which are a composite of those of several companies) regarding usage of computers and electronic mail.

GED PRACTICE

EXERCISE 14

Interpreting Business Documents

Directions: Read the excerpt below representing a company policy manual and answer the questions that follow on page 684.

HOW SHOULD THE READER INTERPRET THIS DOCUMENT?

Computer Usage and Electronic Mail

Ventures, Inc., is committed to providing employees with state-of-the-art equipment and technical support services to assist in the performance of employee job responsibilities in the most efficient manner.

Ventures restricts access to computer rooms and other secured areas to authorized employees and to visitors or vendors who are accompanied by authorized employees. This is to ensure security for and to guard against disclosure of confidential, proprietary information regarding Company products and services.

Only Ventures employees may utilize company hardware and software during regularly scheduled work hours and at other times as approved by the immediate supervisor.

Only software installed by Ventures technical staff is allowed, and copying of software for employee private or home use is prohibited unless expressly approved by the immediate supervisor.

Only work-related documents that relate specifically to employee job function may be produced on equipment provided by Ventures. That includes the work station computer, local area printer, copier, scanner, FAX machine, digital camera, and other designated equipment.

Ventures reserves the right to access, review, and/or monitor employee usage of computers and other equipment for any business purpose. The Company is able to retrieve through its communication systems any computer information or electronic messages received or sent by employees. The Company retains permanent storage of such information files or messages in its permanent archives.

1. What is the stated purpose of the company policy manual on use of computers and electronic mail?

(1) to create an atmosphere of fear so that employees stay on task
(2) to assist employees to perform their jobs in an efficient manner
(3) to enable the human resources department to monitor employee performance
(4) to explain one specific aspect of the annual employee appraisal system
(5) to set up employee requirements for professional development

2. How can the policy of Ventures, Inc., toward general access to computer rooms and other secured areas be summarized?

(1) favorable
(2) cautious
(3) unobstructed
(4) independent
(5) restrictive

3. If the reader were to study another page from the same company's policy manual, the reader could expect what general attitude regarding employee substance abuse?

(1) tolerance
(2) forgiveness
(3) regulation
(4) indifference
(5) understanding

4. What is the overall point of view or perspective from which the policy manual is written?

(1) the management of a company
(2) competing computer companies
(3) a technology association
(4) an employee labor union
(5) departmental employee groups

Answers are on page 694.

Go to **www.GEDReading.com** for additional practice and instruction!

Answer Key

CHAPTER 1
INTERPRETING PROSE FICTION

Exercise 1: Inferring Time and Place (page 592)

1. The action takes place in early morning. Clues are *retiring fogs, an army stretched out . . . resting,* and *the army awakened.*
2. Clues as to the time period are subtle, but you can assume that the action took place in the 1860s because the method of communication seems very informal and "word-of-mouth." There are no official orders and no instruments of technology such as telephones, walkie-talkies, or e-mail. Present are *blue-clothed men,* an indication of soldiers of the Northern Army during the Civil War.
3. The action takes place on a site of a battlefield in the hills. Clues are *army stretched out on the hills, a river, hostile camp fires, distant hills, a brook,* and *rows of squat brown huts.*

Exercise 2: Recognizing Atmosphere or Mood (page 593)

Details that create an atmosphere of gloom include: a description of the day *(dull, dark, and soundless),* the tract of country (*clouds hung oppressively low* and *dreary*), and the House of Usher (*melancholy, bleak walls,* and *decayed trees).* These elements affect the character who had been riding alone on horseback so that *a sense of insufferable gloom pervaded [his] spirit* and who feels *an utter depression of soul.*

Exercise 3: Identifying Parts of Setting (page 594)

1. The current season is fall heading into winter: *In the fall when the days became crisp and gray, and the long Minnesota winter shut down like the white lid of a box . . .*
2. This part of the action takes place in the past because the past tense of verbs is used: *were, owned, patronized, became, moved, gave, offended, haunted, was, crossed, tramped,* and *squinted.*
3. Dexter is walking through the fairways of a golf course that *lie in enforced fallowness* because it is off-season. There are *desolate sandboxes knee-deep in crusted ice.*
4. In fall, *the days became crisp and gray.* In winter, *Dexter's skis moved over the snow that hid the fairways,* the links were *haunted by ragged sparrows for the long season,* and *the wind blew cold as misery.* In summer, there were *tees where the gay colors fluttered.*
5. The scenery *gave him a feeling of profound melancholy [sadness or depression].*

GED Practice Exercise 4: Inferring Characterization (page 595)

1. **(4)** Although Huck misspells the word, he is afraid that the Widow Douglas would *civilize* him. Huck refers to the author Mark Twain as mainly telling the truth (with some "stretchers") in the book *Tom Sawyer,* but Huck is not saying that he himself was a liar. Thus, Choice 1, *the world's biggest liar* is not true. There is no evidence for choices 2, 3, or 5.
2. **(1)** Huck starts out by saying to the reader, *You don't know about me,* then proceeds to relate the narrative about himself and about Tom Sawyer, Aunt Polly, Mary, and the Widow Douglas.
3. **(3)** Huck refers to his adventures with Tom Sawyer and finding money that *robbers hid in the cave.* Huck also talks about leaving when he couldn't stand the Widow Douglas's efforts to civilize him, and then feeling *free and satisfied.* Because Huck so closely relates himself to Tom, we can assume that Tom is also romantic and adventuresome. There is no evidence for the other choices.

Exercise 5: Using Dialogue as an Element of Characterization (page 597)

The clue that there are up to four speakers comes in the first line which indicates *the four of us taking this great trip.* We can't tell which speakers are male and which are female because of the nature of the special interests that each speaker has.

The first speaker leads us to presume that there are two couples since the purpose for the trip is to celebrate wedding anniversaries. This person likes the formal aspects of the trip including royalty and "high tea."

The second speaker likes viewing art.

The third speaker is a typical traveler/sightseer who wants to *get the lay of the land before* getting a closer look at any particular tourist attraction.

The fourth speaker has a particular interest in British history and also probably French history because of the comment about the Bastille Day celebration.

Exercise 6: Identifying Characters through Dialogue (page 598)

1. We know that the two speakers don't know each other and have just met because he reaches for a business card and hands it to her.
2. Robert Kincaid speaks first, telling the other character that he's on assignment for *National Geographic.*
3. Francesca is local because she knows the location of the Roseman Bridge; Robert Kincaid is the visitor since he's looking for the bridges.
4. We know that he is a "Writer-Photographer," but the passage does not reveal her occupation.
5. We know that Francesca recalls being a teenager in Naples, which is in Italy.
6. Francesca seems distracted; *her voice sounded strange, as if it belonged to someone else . . .* The fact that *she watched the muscles in his forearm flex* is a clue that she seems to be developing some interest in him.

GED Practice Exercise 7: Identifying Details of Plot (and Conflict) (page 601)

1. **(3)** She sacrificed by selling her hair in order to have money to buy Jim a Christmas present.
2. **(1)** He sacrificed by selling the watch so that he could buy Della a set of combs.
3. **(5)** It is true that Della shopped all over town for the perfect gift, but Jim bought the combs in the store where Della had previously noticed them. Moreover, this detail does not compare with the irony that each gave up a prized possession in order to buy the other a gift. In so doing, the gift each gave the other was no longer practical.

Exercise 8: Determining Point of View (page 604)

Nouns or pronouns in the passage that refer to the old man are <u>underlined.</u> Nouns or pronouns that refer to the fish are shown in brackets [ ].

["Fish,"] the <u>old man</u> said. ["Fish,] [you] are going to have to die anyway. Do [you] have to kill <u>me</u> too?"

That way nothing is accomplished, <u>he</u> thought. <u>His</u> mouth was too dry to speak but <u>he</u> could not reach for the water now. <u>I</u> must get [him] alongside this time, <u>he</u> thought. <u>I</u> am not good for many more turns. Yes, <u>you</u> are, <u>he</u> told <u>himself.</u> <u>You</u>'re good for ever.

On the next turn, <u>he</u> nearly had [him]. But again the [fish] righted [himself] and swam slowly away.

[You] are killing <u>me,</u> [fish,] the <u>old man</u> thought. But [you] have a right to. Never have <u>I</u> seen a greater, or more beautiful, or a calmer or more noble thing than [you], [brother]. Come on and kill <u>me.</u> <u>I</u> do not care [who] kills <u>who.</u>

Now <u>you</u> are getting confused in the head, <u>he</u> thought. <u>You</u> must keep <u>your</u> head clear. Keep <u>your</u> head clear and know how to suffer like <u>a man.</u> Or a [fish], <u>he</u> thought.

"Clear up, head," <u>he</u> said in a voice <u>he</u> could hardly hear. "Clear up."

In terms of how the fish might feel if it could think or talk, possibly the fish would feel some "kinship" with the man who describes the fish as beautiful, calm, and noble and who calls him "brother." The fish might empathize with the man who is doing what he must do, that is to fish. This may be the case even though for the man to be successful in fishing means that the fish will be caught and die. The fish might also admire the man for his courage and suffering.

GED Practice Exercise 9: Inferring Theme (page 605)

1. **(4)** There is no evidence in the text that Danny and Rhea are having marital problems.
2. **(1)** Both Danny and Eddy overcome barriers through effort and sacrifice. Danny graduates from high school in spite of an assistant principal who always blames him unfairly, a father who is verbally abusive, and other boys who cause the auto accident that nearly kills Danny. Eddy, who lacks general ability and fears speaking, gives an excellent speech at graduation.

GED Practice Exercise 10: Detecting Style and Tone (page 608)

1. **(1)** The author would probably read the lines in an uninterested and mocking *tone* because the American lady's daughter was in love with a Swiss engineer who *was from a very good family* and yet not good enough to marry her daughter. The American was determined that her daughter marry an American because *Americans make the best husbands.*
2. **(5)** A woman such as the American should be exposed for her false values because she was overlooking the fact that her daughter was in love; instead, she made light conversation about train travel, the country, the season of the year, and a hotel.
3. **(2)** The reader feels sympathy for a young woman who cannot marry the man of her choice because of her mother's influence and, perhaps, control.

Exercise 11: Noticing Figures of Speech (page 611)

Fog was outdoors, hanging over the river, creeping in and out [personification] of alleyways and passages, swirling thickly between the bare trees of all the parks and gardens of the city, and indoors, too, seething through cracks and crannies like sour breath [simile], gaining a sly entrance [personification] at every opening of a door. It was a yellow fog, a filthy, evil-smelling fog [personification], a fog that choked and blinded, smeared and stained. . . . [personification]

No, looking at herself in the plate glass windows she passed, she was very content with what she saw: under the large hat her neck looked slender and reedlike, a blossom's stem [metaphor]; her eyes were shadowed [metaphor], her entire aspect gentle, and even, she thought, mysterious.

Exercise 12: Identifying Images as Part of Overall Style (page 612)

This passage is heavy in descriptions and images that appeal to your sense of sight and are underlined; those that appeal to your sense of hearing are in **boldface.** The other senses of taste, touch, or smell are not indicated in this particular passage.

In agony the **brakes cried,** held: the scene, dizzy with color, rocked with the car, down a little, back up, giddily, helplessly, while dust exploded up on all sides. "Mommy!" Timmy **screamed,** fascinated by the violence, yet his **wail** was oddly still and drawn out, and his eyes never once turned to his mother. The little Mexican boy had disappeared in front of the car. Still the red dust arose, the faces at the bus jerked around together, white eyes, white teeth, faces were propelled toward the windows of the bus, empty a second before. "God, God," Annette **murmured;** she had not yet released the steering wheel, and on it her fingers began to tighten as if they might tear the wheel off, hold it up to defend her and her child, perhaps even to attack.

A woman in a colorless dress pushed out of the crowd, barefooted in the red clay, pointed her finger at Annette and **shouted** something gleefully. She shook her fist, grinning, others grinned behind her; the bus driver turned back to his bus. Annette saw now the little boy on the other side of the road, popping up safe in the ditch and jumping frantically—though the sharp weeds must have hurt his feet—**laughing, yelling, shouting** as if he were insane. The air rang with **shouts,** with **laughter.** A good joke. What was the joke? Annette's brain reeled with shock, sucked for air as if drowning.

CHAPTER 2
INTERPRETING POETRY

GED Practice Exercise 1: Understanding Idea and Emotion in Two Poems (page 616)

1. **(4)** Romantic love is mentioned in both poems; it is referred to repeatedly in Sonnet 43.
2. **(1)** The speakers in both poems express love consistently, proclaiming constant devotion toward the loved one.

Exercise 2: The Shape of Poetry (page 618)

1. There is one sentence; a period ends it.
2. The first stanza states the speaker is a *child of the Americas, mestiza of the Caribbean,* and a *child of many diaspora.* In the second stanza, she describes herself as *a U.S. Puerto Rican Jew, a product of the ghettos, an immigrant.* The third stanza states she's *Caribeña Latinoamerican.* In the fourth stanza, she claims *Africa is in me, Taino is in me,* and *Europe lives in me.*
3. In stanza five, she uses the word *whole,* which suggests a positive view of completeness.
4. She compares it to a tool of consciousness, a knife blade.
5. **(3)** The citing of many cultures joining together and the sense of pride and wholeness expressed by the speaker suggest an appreciation of multiculturalism.

Exercise 3: The Language of Poetry (page 621)

Line 1: imagery
Line 2: personification
Line 3: personification
Line 4: imagery
Line 5: personification

GED Practice Exercise 4: Review of Figurative Language and Theme (page 622)

1. **(2)** The lines suggest that children's faces are able to contain feeling in the same way a cup can contain a liquid.
2. **(5)** In line 8 the speaker compares music to a *curve of gold*
3. **(5)** Thoughts are compared to stars that shine bright.

Exercise 5: The Sound of Poetry (page 625)

1. Examples in stanza 1 are *weak and weary, quaint* and *curious, nodded, nearly napping.* Examples in stanza 2 are *surcease of sorrow, lost Lenore,* and *rare and radiant.*
2. **(1)** Repeating the word *rapping* with its short **a** vowel sound is suggestive of knocking.
3. **(2)** The language such as *dreary, bleak,* and *ghost* and events such as a knock at the door at midnight combine with the rhythm to create an eerie feeling.

GED Practice Exercise 6: Language, Sound, and Mood (page 627)

1. **(2)** The images of water and wind created throughout the poem with words such as *rain, stream, swaying,* and *storm* are reinforced in the comparison by the words *on the tide* and *under the wind.*
2. **(5)** The setting of rainy day images such as *crushed grass* and language such as *lonely afternoons of memories* create a sense of regret.

GED Practice Exercise 7: Inferring Meaning (page 630)

1. **(2)** In line 2 the speaker states *We people on the pavement,* identifying himself as one of the townspeople.
2. **(4)** The speaker states in stanza 3 that Richard Cory was rich and that *we* (the townspeople) wished to be in his place.
3. **(2)** The townspeople work and hope for something better, often going without better quality, more expensive food.
4. **(5)** Things are not always what they seem. A man who appears to have everything is so unhappy with his life that he commits suicide.

GED Practice Exercise 8: Interpreting a Poem (page 634)

1. **(5)** The speaker longs for leisure time to enjoy life and consequently would be attracted by vacation time.
2. **(1)** The one dancing is Beauty, and the dancing and the show are appreciated by the speaker.
3. **(2)** Throughout the poem, the speaker emphasizes the joys of stopping to notice animals, woods, streams, and skies—all embodiments of Beauty. Enjoy life while the opportunity exists.

Exercise 9: More Practice with Interpretation (page 635)

1. Stanza 1 (b)
   Stanza 2 (c)
   Stanza 3 (a)
   Stanza 4 (e)
   Stanza 5 (d)
2. **(3)** Death and Immortality are characters who ride in the carriage with the narrator.
1. **(5)** From the last stanza, we can infer that the poet believes that the narrator was taken from earth but lives on.

CHAPTER 3

INTERPRETING DRAMA

Exercise 1: Comprehending a Play (page 639)
(Exact wording may vary)

Hamlet was outside when a ghost appeared. The ghost began to speak. At first, Hamlet felt sorry for the ghost. The ghost claimed to be the spirit of Hamlet's father. The ghost wanted Hamlet to revenge the murder of Hamlet's father. Hamlet felt shocked and horrified.

Exercise 2: Noticing Dialogue and Punctuation (page 641)

1. **Edward and Victoria;** the ellipsis indicate that Catherine interrupts Edward's speech.
2. **Edward;** both of Edward's speeches are questions.
3. **Edward;** Edward is bothered by Catherine's interruption.
4. **Edward;** Victoria's tone and responses to Edward indicate that she is upset with him.

GED Practice Exercise 3: Inferring Mood from Dialogue (page 642)

1. **(1)** The rudeness of Edward toward Catherine, Victoria's responses to Edward, and Catherine's abrupt departure all indicate that the mood of the scene is *tense.*
2. The use of the long dash [—] indicates a brief pause or break in thought: *Not now—; You're talking—;* and *Oh—.*

GED Practice Exercise 4: Interpreting a Scene (page 644)

1. **(5)** In lines 11 and 12 Tony and Maria verify that they have not met before.
2. **(2)** The punctuation is a clue that Tony feels surprise. The ellipses [. . .] indicate a pause and the question mark following *Sister* indicates a surprised reaction.

3. (1) The dialogue and action (Tony kisses Maria) suggest romance. The mood changes with the stage direction *Bernardo is upon them in an icy rage.* The rest of the passage's dialogue builds tension.

GED Practice Exercise 5: Understanding Character (page 647)

1. (4) Billie tries to like what she thinks is high culture.

2. (4) Paul attempts to explain and discuss the significance of the reading passage to Billie. In the same way, he would explain and discuss an artwork with her.

3. (5) The phrase *to be bigger* suggests growth. Learning helps a person grow.

4. (1) Paul is impressed by the writer who attacks Napoleon as *that imperial impersonation of force and murder.* Paul believes that Harry, however, would like to be like Napoleon. The impression Paul makes between Harry and Napoleon suggests Paul does not admire Harry.

5. (1) The lines provide pleasant images and metaphor, recommending the simple life and its beauty.

GED Practice Exercise 6: Interpreting a Scene from a Play (page 650)

1. (3) Alice's second line of dialogue, in which she suggests finding a home for her senile father (as her husband Sidney did for his parents) and the discussion about powers of attorney imply that she and Gene are sister and brother. Another clue to their relationship comes later in the scene: *He broke Mother's heart over that for years.*

2. (5) Alice's first line of dialogue, in which she *says I'm doing a lot for my kids. I don't expect them to pay me back at the other end,* suggests that she believes elderly parents should not expect their children to take care of them.

3. (4) Based on Gene's dialogue, he is not relieved; he is ashamed that he can't ask his father to live with him.

4. (4) Gene's line, *I can't tell you how ashamed I feel . . . not to say with open arms, 'Poppa, come live with me . . . I love you, Poppa, and I want to take care of you,'* indicates that he feels guilty for not loving his father.

GED Practice Exercise 7: More Practice in Interpreting Drama (page 652)

1. (1) Beneatha states that *They just went out and changed my life.* Asagai's question in line *21 Was it your money he gave away?* confirms that someone gave away money Beneatha had counted on.

2. (1) Like the circle comparison Beneatha makes, a merry-go-round would also go around and around without moving anywhere else.

3. (2) Notice the words and exclamation marks in Beneatha's speech *An end to misery! To stupidity!* (line 4). Also she begins shouting, as indicated by the capital letters in line 32.

4. (5) Asagai displays disapproval not only in his disagreement with Beneatha, but also in lines 27 and 28 when he says, *I never thought to see you like this Alaiyo. You!*

CHAPTER 4
INTERPRETING PROSE NONFICTION

Exercise 1: Detecting the Author's Purpose for Writing (page 656)

The author would agree with statements **1, 2, 4, 6,** and **7.**

In statement 3, we are *not* correct in assuming that our partners will behave in a certain way.

In statement 5, we have forgotten that men and women *are* supposed to be different.

Exercise 2: Reading an Article for Facts (page 658)

Sentence 2: *What:* sign language is becoming a powerful tool to promote early communication for everyone

Sentence 3: *Why:* Professionals say children can communicate with hand signs much sooner than they can master verbal skills.

Sentence 4: *How:* "It's a question of how children mature"

Who: Marilyn Daniels, an associate professor of speech communication and author of a forthcoming book . . .

Where: at Pennsylvania State University

Sentence 5: *Who:* Daniels

What: one of numerous researchers who encourage families to learn and use basic signs as early as possible

Sentence 6: *What:* Most suggest using American Sign Language (ASL)

Why: because it's easy to learn, standardized, and an official language used by the deaf community

Sentence 7: *What:* But others note that even homemade signs can encourage communication at least six months before most children start to form basic words.

Sentence 8: *What:* Signing not only increases the parents' bond and interaction with their babies, it helps reduce a major source of tantrums and stress for infants.

Sentence 9: *What:* It also creates a more physically expressive environment.

Exercise 3: Reading an Editorial for Informed Opinion (page 660)

1. The question raised is, "Do waiting periods and criminal background checks on prospective handgun buyers deter violent crime?"
2. The study concludes that *the Brady Law has failed to significantly decrease handgun homicides since its 1994 enactment . . .*
3. The editorial affirms the publisher's belief that *the law's background check requirement remains a reasonable and prudent guard against those who seek handguns with criminal intent.*
4. The newspaper would not favor a repeal (abandonment or recall) of the Brady Law.

GED Practice Exercise 4: Analyzing a Speech for Purpose (page 661)

1. **(2)** Sentence 2: "testing whether that nation . . . can long endure."
2. **(1)** Sentence 1: ". . . a new nation, conceived in Liberty. . . ."
3. **(4)** It is necessary of course to bury the dead (Choice 1) and honor the dead (Choice 2), but the real challenge after the Civil War is for the nation to "have a new birth of freedom." President Lincoln does not say anything about changing the government (Choice 3). He says the government "shall not perish from the earth," so this makes Choice 5 incorrect.
4. **(2)** *Rebuke* means to reprimand, and there was no evidence of criticism of the South in the speech.

GED Practice Exercise 5: Interpreting a Speech (page 662)

1. **(4)** As a first (inaugural) speech of his presidency, Kennedy wants to inspire listeners.
2. **(3)** The most persuasive call to serve the public is in the second to the last paragraph: "ask not what your country can do for you; ask what you can do for your country."
3. **(3)** In paragraph 4, Kennedy says that "only a few generations have been granted the role of defending freedom in its hour of maximum danger."
4. **(1)** The speech does not rhyme or display a standardized rhythmic pattern.

GED Practice Exercise 6: Finding the Notable in a Biography (page 665)

1. **(4)** Statements in Choices 1, 2, 3, and 5 are true. In Choice 4, the key word *said* makes the reason untrue; while Mr. Ray may have actually believed in women's liberation, he did not say it in the passage provided.
2. **(5)** All statements in Choices 1, 2, 3, 4, and 5 are true, but only Choice 5 shows participation in flying at the age of seventy-two. This is the best evidence of a serious interest in flying all her life.

3. (2) As a female pilot in World War II, Ringenberg certainly demonstrated her willingness to enter a nontraditional field. She selected her career herself, so she did follow her own mind and heart.

GED Practice Exercise 7: Using Oral History to Create Biography (page 668)

1. (3) Statements in choices 1, 2, and 4 are true, but significance is not in wearing slacks, joining bowling leagues, or handling machinery. The true significance is that women enthusiastically supported the war effort by going to work at jobs previously done by men. Rosie the Riveter is a symbol for any woman going to work at a man's job while the men were away at war. Choice 5 is untrue because women still were wives and mothers.

2. (4) The best word to describe the overall reaction of the neighborhood is *involved.* Neighbors bought newspapers in their bathrobes; flagpoles went up; women such as Mike Royko's sister went to work at converted factories.

3. (5) There is evidence that such a neighborhood re-created would, once together, monitor and discuss events. Choices 1, 2, and 3 are incorrect because they show neighbors not reacting, reacting separately, or ignoring events outside the neighborhood. Choice 4 is incorrect because there is no evidence that neighbors would react with an organized (rather than an informal) information network.

GED Practice Exercise 8: Studying a Noteworthy Autobiography (page 670)

1. (1) Statements in all five choices are true, but the idea that "You had to be *tough* to be a female member of Congress" is the *main idea* because it is broader than the other statements. Choices 2, 3, 4, and 5 are all details that support the main idea.

2. (4) Congresswoman Ferraro used the word *indifference* [lack of concern] to describe the Congressmen's attitude toward women's issues, but she herself was not indifferent. There is direct evidence for Choices 1 and 2 because she said she had to be tough, and she was frustrated over women's issues. The reader can infer that she was committed (Choice 3) and concerned (Choice 5) because of her response to social issues.

GED Practice 9: Interpreting a Formal Essay (page 672)

1. (4) The word *duty* implies an obligation; therefore, the title suggests that a person is obligated to break an unjust law.

2. (3) The government represents the people and is the means by which a people carry out their desires. The other choices do not help to define government in this sense.

3. (2) The essay includes the statement, "The standing army is only an army of the standing government."

4. (1) The essay states, "the government . . . is only the mode which the people have chosen to execute their will."

Exercise 10: Comparing and Contrasting Essay Viewpoints (page 674)

1. Essay writer Adam Urbanski is vice president of the American Federation of Teachers (AFT). The AFT is a major national labor organization for teachers. You can assume, therefore, that Urbanski is knowledgeable about the American school system and in a position to comment about year-round schools. The other essayist is a U.S. Congressman, so we can assume that he has some national perspective about schools, at least from the standpoint of appropriation of federal funds to schools.

2. Urbanski says that the proposal for year-round schools is "a wise investment in education" whose success or failure is related to the standards movement in education. Goodling does not believe that we should have year-round schools because he thinks it is a question of *quality,* rather than *quantity* of time in the classroom.

GED Practice Exercise 11: Interpreting a Diary or Journal (page 676)

1. **(5)** As is evident by the title "Self-Reliance," Emerson believed in the power of the individual, rather than in the group or in greater society. Choices 1, 2, and 4 do not express Emerson's beliefs because they all involve working with others. Choice 3 does not express his beliefs because the person in authority would be dictating action to the individual.
2. **(3)** Emerson felt that the individual was the most reliable source by saying, *Nothing is at last sacred but the integrity of your own mind.* He would not have agreed with following the crowd (Choice 1), agreeing just for the sake of harmony (Choice 4), not challenging authority (Choice 5). The passage does not deal with the concept of leadership (Choice 2).

GED Practice Exercise 12: Evaluating a Film or Television Review (page 678)

1. **(5)** The reviewer says that "the classic" was able to "mix hilarity and tragedy" and that *M*A*S*H made us laugh until we cried.*
2. **(2)** The reviewer states, "Like all great sitcoms [M*A*S*H] succeeded mainly by exploring, indeed celebrating, the chemistry between the characters."
3. **(1)** The reviewer showed admiration for the sitcoms discussed.

GED Practice Exercise 13: Interpreting Artistic Commentary (page 680)

1. **(2)** In using the metaphor *a geography of the imagination,* the reviewer is asking the reader to make the "journey" in time and history from architecture in the Mediterranean area of Europe to farm country in Iowa. The effect, thus, is to show that this example of American art and architecture was influenced by Europe. Choice 1 is false, and Choices 3, 4, and 5 are too literal in focusing on geography and conservation.
2. **(3)** If we are "blinded by familiarity and parody," we are not looking carefully at the painting because we know it so well and perhaps because the painting has sometimes been criticized as too common in subject. Thus, the reviewer is asking us to take a more careful look at the painting to understand it better. There is no support in the text for the other choices.
3. **(5)** American Gothic is simple in design, so it cannot be "elaborate in rich detail." All the other choices are true descriptions.
4. **(5)** *Sobriety* is a characteristic that means *serious, steady,* and *earnest. Industry* is the characteristic of being hard working (and productive). The other choices are not reasonable conclusions.

GED Practice Exercise 14: Interpreting Business Documents (page 683)

1. **(2)** The Company states the purpose of the policy manual in the first paragraph: ". . . to assist in the performance of employee job responsibilities in the most efficient manner."
2. **(5)** The policy is deemed restrictive according to the statement in the second paragraph: "*Ventures* restricts access to computer rooms and other secured areas to authorized employees and to visitors or vendors who are accompanied by authorized employees."
3. **(3)** Because the use of computers and e-mail is definitely regulated, we have no reason to believe the company would be any more tolerant, forgiving, or understanding (Choices 1, 2, and 5) on the issue of substance abuse. Choice 4 is inaccurate because *indifferent* would mean that the company didn't care enough to enforce policies.
4. **(1)** All paragraphs include the company name, *Ventures, Inc.*, or *Ventures*, or *the Company;* all instructions are directed to employees; references are in the third person form as *employees* (and not the more informal second person *you*).

Mathematics

What kind of test is the GED Mathematics Test?

The GED Mathematics Test consists of questions based on mathematical problems people encounter in everyday life as individuals, family members, workers, and citizens. All of the questions will be based on information presented in words, diagrams, charts, graphs, or pictures. The math problems will test not only your ability to do arithmetic, algebra, and geometry operations, but your ability to apply problem-solving skills. To be successful, you will need to

- understand what the *question* is asking
- organize data and identify information necessary to solve the problem
- select a problem-solving strategy using appropriate mathematical operations
- set up the problem, estimate, and then compute the exact answer
- check the reasonableness of the answer

Actually, you already use these skills when you use math to solve problems at home, at the store, and at work. This section will give you lots of practice in basic math skills as well as these crucial problem-solving areas.

How many questions are on the Test? What does it look like?

The GED Mathematics Test is presented in two separate booklets: Part I permits the use of a calculator; Part II does not. You will have to complete both parts of the Test to earn a score. There are 50 problems, and you will be given 90 minutes to complete the Test. Some of the problems will not require any computation. Instead, on 25% of the Test you will have to identify the correct way to set up a problem to solve it. Some of the questions will appear in item sets. In these problems you will use information from multiple sources such as a circle graph, bar graph, or table and text to answer as many as two or three questions.

The question format may be **multiple-choice** items or **alternate-format** items. On multiple-choice items you will be asked to select from a list of answers. In alternate-format items no possible responses are provided. Alternate formats may include

- entering a number (whole, decimal, or fraction—not mixed) on a standard grid
- entering an ordered pair representing a point on the coordinate plane grid

To get an idea of what the Test is like, look at the Practice Test at the end of this book. This Practice Test is based on the real GED Test.

What's on the Test?

The GED Mathematics Test can be broken down into the content areas it covers and the skills it tests. The Test covers the following content areas:

Number Sense and Operations	20–30%
Data, Statistics, and Probability	20–30%
Algebra, Functions, and Patterns	20–30%
Measurement and Geometry	20–30%

In each of these content areas the problems will test your ability to follow mathematical procedures (15–25% of the test), demonstrate an understanding of concepts (25–35% of the test), and/or apply problem-solving skills (approximately 50% of the test).

Number Sense and Operations problems will ask questions pertaining to estimating, computing, and ordering numbers such as wholes, integers, fractions, decimals, percents, exponents, and scientific notation in a variety of real-world and mathematical problem situations. You will be asked to explain, analyze, and apply mathematical concepts in problems involving ratios, proportions, percents, and square roots.

Data, Statistics, and Probability problems will ask you to interpret data from tables, charts, and graphs. You will evaluate and make inferences from information presented and apply measures of central tendency. You may be asked to find an informal line of best fit, interpret a frequency distribution, and compare/contrast different sets of data based on your analysis.

Algebra, Functions, and Patterns problems may ask you to analyze, represent, and convert between situations involving tables, graphs, verbal descriptions, and equations. You may be asked to create and use algebraic expressions and equations to model and solve problems, to evaluate formulas, to recognize direct and indirect variation, and to analyze relationships among variables.

Measurement and Geometry problems may ask questions pertaining to the concepts of perpendicularity, parallelism, congruence, and similarity of geometric figures, including polygons, 3-D figures, and circles. You may be asked to use the Pythagorean theorem, right triangle trigonometry, and coordinate geometry to model and solve problems. You will be asked to solve and estimate solutions to problems involving length, perimeter, area, volume, angle measurement, capacity, weight, and mass. In these problems you may use metric and customary measures and rates and read scales, meters, and gauges to answer questions.

The chapters in this section will provide you with explanations, examples, and exercises in all of these content areas. Some of the material will be familiar and even seem easy. You will still want to sharpen your skills in those areas. Other areas will be new and challenging and will require concentrated study and repeated practice to learn.

What math resources can I use on the Test?

Calculator

The GED Mathematics Test will be presented in two separate booklets. In Part I a calculator will be provided for your use; in Part II no calculator will be permitted. All testing centers will distribute the same calculator: the Casio *fx*-260 SOLAR. It is important that you become familiar with the calculator and practice using it for problem solving. The calculator icon will be used occasionally throughout the text to remind you to practice using the calculator. Instructions for using the calculator will be attached to the GED Test. A copy of those instructions can be found on page 923.

Formula Page

$a^2+b^2=c^2$

A formula page with a list of common formulas is provided with all Test forms. During the Test you may use this page to help you solve problems. You should become familiar with the formulas on the page, learn how to select the appropriate formula for a problem, and practice evaluating a formula using given values. The formula page is on page 922. The formula page icon will appear occasionally throughout the text to remind you to refer to that page.

Scratch Paper and Pencil

A mathematician's best "friends" are paper and pencil. At the Test, you will be given scratch paper to use. If you organize your work on the paper, you will be able to easily review problems later and find information that might help you with other problems. You should also use scratch paper and pencil as you work through this textbook to take notes and/or practice skills.

What can help me prepare for the Test?

To be successful, you must constantly practice and test each skill as you learn it. Remember that this is a workbook, not just a book to read. Learning mathematics is like learning to play the piano. You can read a book about it or watch someone else do it, but until you actually practice it yourself, you won't know how to play a piano or solve a math problem.

How can I get rid of "math anxiety"?

Many people feel that they are just "not good in math." If this is true of you, listed below are some ideas that will help.

1. Accept the fact that while you have some math anxiety, most other people do too.

2. Math requires logic, but often intuition comes first. Don't be afraid to use the ideas that pop into your mind.

3. You can be creative. It is okay to solve a problem in a way that's different from what is given in the book.

4. Estimating answers is helpful with many problems.

5. Use all the resources at hand—your fingers, paper, pencil, formula page, calculator—whatever works for you.

6. Have confidence in yourself and your ability to learn math concepts and try new approaches.

7. Practice! Practice! Practice!

CHAPTER 1

Whole Numbers and Operations

Basic to solving all math problems is a good, strong foundation in whole number math facts, mainly the addition facts and multiplication tables. If you are unsure of any of these facts, now is the time to review and memorize those that give you trouble. Just as you can remember the phone numbers, addresses, and other important numbers in your life, you can remember these facts. Your ability to work with numbers depends on how quickly and accurately you can do these computations.

Before starting work on problem solving, let's review the basic operations of addition, subtraction, multiplication, and division with whole numbers. The examples below will help refresh your memory about the basics of these operations. An **estimate** for each problem is also shown.

Addition

Example 1 shows how to **regroup** (carry) in some addition problems. Don't forget that numbers can be added in any order without affecting the answer.

Example 1 486 + 39 + 1725 + 89

$$\begin{array}{r} {\scriptstyle 122} \\ 486 \\ 39 \\ 1725 \\ +\ \ 89 \\ \hline 2339 \end{array}$$

← **Regroup to the next column to the left.**

Estimate:

$$\begin{array}{r} 500 \\ 50 \\ 1700 \\ +\ \ 100 \\ \hline 2350 \end{array}$$

Subtraction

Example 2 illustrates **regrouping** (borrowing) in subtraction problems. Remember that the number following the subtraction sign (–) is the number subtracted and placed on the second line.

Example 2 4006 – 957

$$\begin{array}{r} {\scriptstyle 3991} \\ \not{4}\not{0}\not{0}\not{6} \\ -\ 957 \\ \hline 3049 \end{array}$$

← **Regroup from the 400 by reducing it to 399 and adding 10 to the 6 to make 16.**

Estimate:

$$\begin{array}{r} 4000 \\ -1000 \\ \hline 3000 \end{array}$$

Multiplication

Example 3 shows both **regrouping** and **indenting** in multiplication problems. Numbers can be multiplied in any order without affecting the answer.

Example 3 48 × 32

$$\begin{array}{r} {}^{2} \\ {}^{1} \\ 48 \\ \times\, 32 \\ \hline 96 \\ 144 \\ \hline 1536 \end{array}$$

← **Regroup to the next column to the left.**

← **Indent rows one column at a time.**

Estimate: 50 × 30 = 1500

Division

For most people, division is the most complicated operation. Example 4 shows the basic steps. Remember that the number following the division symbol (÷) is the divisor.

Example 4 3049 ÷ 6

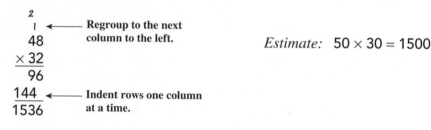

STEP 1 Divide by the number that follows the division sign (÷). Divide into the first number that you can. Since 6 won't divide into 3, divide into 30.

$$6\overline{)3049}\quad\text{quotient: } 5\_$$

Divisor (6) — **Dividend** (3049)

STEP 2 Multiply and subtract. Bring down the next number. If you can't divide into it, write a zero in the answer before you bring down the next number.

$$\begin{array}{r} 50\_ \\ 6\overline{)3049} \\ -30 \\ \hline 04 \end{array}$$

STEP 3 Divide 6 into 49. Multiply. Subtract. Write the **remainder** as a part of your answer.

$$\begin{array}{r} 508 \text{ r1} \\ 6\overline{)3049}\phantom{\text{ r1}} \\ -30\phantom{\text{ r1}} \\ \hline 049\phantom{\text{ r1}} \\ -48\phantom{\text{ r1}} \\ \hline 1\phantom{\text{ r1}} \end{array}$$

Estimate: 3000 ÷ 6 = 500

$$\begin{array}{r} 500 \\ 6\overline{)3000} \end{array}$$

TIP

There is no one correct estimate. Use numbers that are easy to work with when estimating. Estimates will vary.

Your calculator can be used to perform basic whole number operations. Become familiar with the keys on your calculator and how to use them.

Start keys:	ON	*turns the calculator on*
	AC	*clears all numbers and operations, displays 0.*
	C	*clears only the last number or operation entered*
Operation keys:	+	*addition*
	–	*subtraction*
	×	*multiplication*
	÷	*division*
Number keys:	0, 1, 2, 3, 4, 5, 6, 7, 8, 9	
Equals sign:	=	

To Perform an Operation

PROCESS	KEY IN:	DISPLAY	Example: 12 ÷ 3 = 4
Step 1	AC to clear the display	0.	0.
Step 2	first number	first number	12.
Step 3	operation symbol (÷)	first number	12.
Step 4	second number	second number	3.
Step 5	equals sign (=)	answer	4.

Practice using your calculator. Be sure to estimate a reasonable answer to each problem you do. This will be a good way for you to determine whether or not your calculator answer is reasonable. Whether you work with or without a calculator, you are responsible for your answers. It is easy to hit the wrong key or to enter numbers in the wrong order. Your estimate and common sense will help you recognize when this happens.

EXERCISE 1

Whole Number Operations

Directions: Solve each problem using paper and pencil. Find an estimate and an exact answer for each problem. Compare the two answers. Are they close? After you finish each problem, check your answer with your calculator.

1. $\begin{array}{r} 25 \\ +64 \\ \hline \end{array}$

2. $\begin{array}{r} 425 \\ +\ 46 \\ \hline \end{array}$

3. $\begin{array}{r} 7348 \\ +4385 \\ \hline \end{array}$

4. $578 + 36$

5. $356 + 12 + 477$

6. $228{,}347 + 6{,}287$

7. $\begin{array}{r} 574 \\ -362 \\ \hline \end{array}$

8. $\begin{array}{r} 4383 \\ -2225 \\ \hline \end{array}$

9. $\begin{array}{r} 348{,}000 \\ -\ 36{,}549 \\ \hline \end{array}$

10. $2860 - 644$

11. $712 - 99$

12. $5000 - 879$

13. $\begin{array}{r} 43 \\ \times\ 3 \\ \hline \end{array}$

14. $\begin{array}{r} 87 \\ \times 95 \\ \hline \end{array}$

15. $\begin{array}{r} 268 \\ \times\ 47 \\ \hline \end{array}$

16. 4000×30

17. 258×64

18. 4230×16

19. $7\overline{)287}$

20. $9\overline{)5643}$

21. $15\overline{)4050}$

22. $5418 \div 6$

23. $\frac{1200}{60}$

24. $7448 \div 16$

Answers are on page 924.

Problem Solving

In this section, we will discuss five steps you can use to solve word problems. Most of the problems on the Mathematics Test are word problems that you can solve more skillfully if you practice these five steps.

5 STEPS FOR SOLVING WORD PROBLEMS

1. Understand what the question is asking.
2. Organize data and identify information necessary to solve the problem.
3. Select a problem-solving strategy using mathematical operations.
4. Set up the problem, estimate, and then compute the exact answer.
5. Check the reasonableness of the answer.

STEP 1 **Understand what the question is asking.** Read the problem thoroughly and then determine exactly what the question is asking. In the example below the question is in *italic* type.

Example Two pancakes contain 120 calories. *How many calories did Fred consume* if he had a stack of 6 pancakes for breakfast?

STEP 2 **Organize the data and identify information necessary to solve the problem.** Choose only the information needed to solve the problem. As in real life, there is often more information than you need. Once in a while there may not be enough information to solve the problem. Select numbers with their unit labels. In the examples below the question is in *italic* type and the necessary information is underlined.

Example 1 In the precinct, only 700 people are registered voters out of an adult population of 1200. If 300 voters are women, *how many voters are men?*

(In this problem the number 1200 is not needed to solve the problem.)

Example 2 At the 20% off sale, Alan bought 6 ties. *How much did he pay?*

(There is not enough information given to solve the problem because the original price of the ties is not given.)

STEP 3 **Select a problem-solving strategy using appropriate mathematical operations.** After you have determined the question and identified the necessary information, you will select a problem-solving strategy. Each problem will contain key words or concepts that will help you decide what to do. Many times, your intuition will help you determine which arithmetic operation to choose. This intuition comes from both your personal experience and your understanding of math concepts. Remember, there are only four operations from which to choose: addition, subtraction, multiplication, and division. The following chart will help you decide which operation to use.

ADD

1. When *combining* amounts to get a larger number
2. When finding a *total*

The order in which numbers are added makes no difference in addition. For example:

$2 + 4 = 6$ and $4 + 2 = 6$

SUBTRACT

1. When *taking away* an amount to obtain a smaller number
2. When *finding the difference* between two amounts

Keep in mind that the order of the numbers makes a difference in subtraction. The number following the minus sign is the number subtracted. For example:

$6 - 4 = 2$ but $4 - 6 = -2$

MULTIPLY

1. When *given one* unit of something and *asked to find* the total for *several*
2. When asked to *find a fraction of* a quantity
3. When asked to *find a percent of* a quantity

There are three ways to show multiplication.

$2 \times 4 = 8$ $2 \bullet 4 = 8$ $2(4) = 8$

The order in which numbers are multiplied makes no difference in multiplication. For example:

$2 \times 4 = 8$ and $4 \times 2 = 8$

DIVIDE

1. When *given* the amount for *several* equal items and *asked to find* the amount for *one* item
2. When *splitting*, cutting, sharing *into equal* parts
3. When asked *how many times* some quantity goes into another
4. When asked to *find an average*

There are three ways to show division.

$8 \div 4 = 2$ $\frac{8}{4} = 2$ $4\overset{2}{\overline{)8}}$

Remember that the order of the numbers makes a difference in division. The number you are dividing by must be the divisor. For example:

$\frac{8}{4} = 2$ but $\frac{4}{8} = \frac{1}{2}$

Example 1 How *many miles did Luis get per gallon* when he drove 300 miles on 15 gallons of gas? (**Divide** because you are asked to find the number of miles for *one* gallon when you are given the miles for 15 gallons.)

Example 2 Sandy lost 34 pounds on her diet. *What was her original weight,* if her weight is now 123 pounds? (**Add** because you are asked to combine her current weight with the pounds she lost to get her original weight.)

Example 3 Ali's monthly salary is $2500. *What is his yearly salary?* (**Multiply** because you are given one month's salary and asked to find the salary for several months. Notice that you will need to know there are twelve months in a year to solve the problem.)

STEP 4 **Set up the problem, estimate the answer, and then compute the exact answer.** After choosing the operation, set up the problem. (In some problems, you may be asked only to identify the correct setup and not have to proceed any further.) Next, estimate an answer using compatible, rounded numbers. For some problems an estimate can be the final answer, as when a question asks for an approximate or rounded value. At other times, you can use the estimate to check whether you have chosen the right setup and whether your answer makes sense. The estimate is especially important if you are using a calculator; the estimate can help you check to make sure you entered the numbers and symbols correctly on the calculator.

After estimating the answer, solve the problem using the exact information and operations you've set up. Do the computations carefully and accurately.

STEP 5 **Check the reasonableness of the answer.** The final step in solving any problem is to evaluate your answer. Does your solution answer the question? Is your answer a sensible one? Is your calculation close to your estimate?

Let's go through the five problem-solving steps for the next two examples.

Example 1 On the first day of your 750-mile road trip, you drove 448 miles in 7 hours. What was your average rate of speed?

Question:	What was your average speed?
Information:	448 miles; 7 hours
Operation:	*average* means divide
Setup and Estimation:	420 miles ÷ 7 hours = 60 miles per hour *(estimate)*
Computation:	448 miles ÷ 7 hours = **64 miles per hour** *(exact)*
Is the answer reasonable?	Yes, because 64 miles per hour is a reasonable speed on the highway and it is very close to the estimate.

Example 2 A secretary makes \$572 per week. Find the secretary's annual pay.

Question:	What is the secretary's annual pay?
Information:	\$572 per week; 52 weeks in one year (annual)
Operation:	Multiply to find the total for 52 weeks when given one week.
Setup and Estimation:	\$600 × 50 weeks = \$30,000 annually *(estimate)*
Computation:	\$572 × 52 weeks = **\$29,744 annual pay** *(exact)*
Is the answer reasonable?	Yes, because \$29,744 is a reasonable annual salary and is close to the estimate.

Look at Example 2 above. Suppose you had misunderstood the problem and had divided instead of multiplying: \$572 ÷ 52 = \$11. This *wrong* answer tells you that the secretary earned \$11 in a year. Would it make sense for the secretary to earn less in a year than in a week? No. By checking whether your answer makes sense, you may be able to catch a mistake.

EXERCISE 2

Problem Solving

Directions: The following problems will give you a chance to practice the 5-step approach to problem solving. For each problem fill in the chart.

Question:

Information:

Operation:

Setup and Estimation: Estimate:
Computation: Exact answer:

Is the answer reasonable?

1. As you leave for a three-day mini-vacation, the odometer on your car reads 49,752 miles. If you drive 162 miles to get to your destination and the same distance to return home, what will your mileage on the odometer read at the end of the trip?

(1) 324 **(2)** 49,428 **(3)** 49,590 **(4)** 49,914 **(5)** 50,076

2. Michele and her three coworkers shared the winning lottery ticket. How much was each person's share if the ticket was worth $12,000,000?

(1) $2,000,000 **(2)** $3,000,000 **(3)** $4,000,000
(4) $6,000,000 **(5)** Not enough information is given.

3. Approximately how many square miles larger is Canada than the United States? The United States is 3,675,633 square miles, and Canada is 3,851,809 square miles.

(1) 17,000 **(2)** 18,000 **(3)** 170,000 **(4)** 180,000 **(5)** 1,800,000

4. A catalog listed sale prices for three different models of 19-inch TVs: $199, $249, and $189. If the buyer for the motel purchased 97 TVs at the lowest price, what was the total cost?

(1) $286 **(2)** $637 **(3)** $18,333 **(4)** $19,303 **(5)** $24,153

5. Marta is self-employed and pays $2496 quarterly for estimated tax. How much should she put aside for the tax payment each month if a quarter is three months?

(1) $624 **(2)** $832 **(3)** $7488 **(4)** $9984 **(5)** $29,952

6. José makes $2000 a month. He pays $425 for a month's rent and $90 per week for food. How much does he have left each month after paying for rent?

(1) $515 **(2)** $1485 **(3)** $1575 **(4)** $1910 **(5)** $2425

7. If an employer gives each employee a $500 end-of-year bonus, what is the total cost of the bonus program for 25 employees?

(1) $20 **(2)** $475 **(3)** $525 **(4)** $10,000 **(5)** $12,500

Answers are on page 925.

Multistep Problems

Many of the problems you see on the Mathematics Test will take more than one calculation to solve. As with problems you've already done, use the 5-step process, but identify all the steps you need to take.

Example The yearly rainfall for four consecutive years in Rock Falls was 22 inches, 28 inches, 31 inches, and 19 inches. Find the average rainfall over the four-year period.

Question:	What is the average rainfall?
Information:	22 in., 28 in., 31 in., and 19 in.; 4 years
Operations:	Step 1: To get the total rainfall—add Step 2: *average* means divide
Setup and Estimation:	$20 + 30 + 30 + 20 = 100$ inches *(setup)* $100 \div 4 = 25$ inches *(estimate)*
Computation:	$22 + 28 + 31 + 19 = 100$ inches $100 \div 4 =$ **25 inches** *(exact)*
Is the answer reasonable?	Yes, because the average is within the range of 19 to 31 inches. The estimate and the calculation are not only close; they're an exact match!

Tip

With multistep problems, after you have finished your calculations, go back and see if your answer to the question makes sense. If you have forgotten a step, this can help you catch yourself and finish the problem correctly.

Personalizing a Problem

If you have trouble restating a problem, reread it several times. Think about how you might solve a similar problem in your own life. Many of the problems on the GED Test will involve questions about practical, everyday situations.

Example The total cost of a computer system is \$3210. A down payment of \$1500 is made, and the balance is to be paid in 18 equal monthly payments. *Find the monthly payments.*

As you read this problem, recall the times you have purchased something and put down a deposit, planning to pay the rest later. You subtracted the deposit from the purchase price to find out how much you still owe.

$3210 purchase price
–1500 deposit
$1710 amount owed

According to the problem, you can pay the amount owed in 18 equal payments. So you have to divide by 18 to find out how much you will pay each month.

$1710 ÷ 18 = **$95 per month**

Restating the Problem Using Words, Sketches, or Diagrams

It often helps to restate the problem by organizing the information in a way that puts the problem in your own words. You might actually talk to yourself. As you do this, jot down notes, sketches, or diagrams that help you organize your thoughts.

Example 1 To better insulate his house, Miguel had to put new weather stripping around the large window in his family room. The window frame measured 5 feet wide and 4 feet high. *How many feet of weather stripping did he need for that window?*

First sketch the window and label the lengths of the 4 sides. Remember that the opposite sides of the window are the same length and the stripping goes around the entire window.

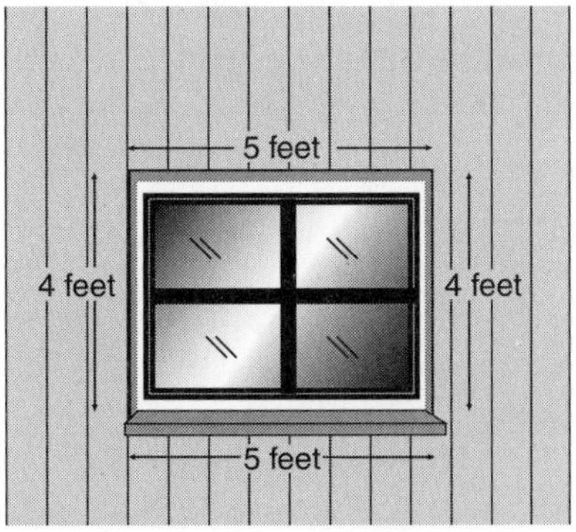

This sketch helps you see that you have to add all the sides.

Miguel will need 18 feet of weather stripping: 5 + 5 + 4 + 4 = **18.**

<u>Example 2</u> John had a checking account balance of $425 before he deposited $187. After he made this deposit, he wrote two checks—one to the grocery for $43 and another to the cleaners for $21. *Find the checkbook balance after he completed these transactions.*

Make a chart to show these transactions.

Amount in Account		Checks Written		Checkbook Balance
$425 +187 $612	−	$43 +21 $64	=	$612 − 64 **$548**

<u>Example 3</u> The math teacher drives 7 miles each way to school. *How many miles does the teacher drive to and from school during a five-day workweek?*

Draw a sketch to show the teacher's route each day. Remind yourself that the teacher does this five times per week.

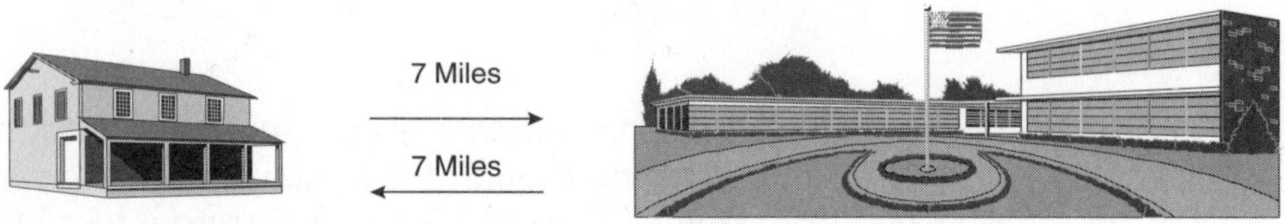

The round trip is 7 + 7 = 14 miles. The teacher makes this roundtrip drive 5 times per week, so the total driving would be 5 × 14 = **70 miles.**

Go to **www.GEDMath.com** for additional practice and instruction!

CHAPTER 2

Number Sense

In mathematics there are rules and procedures that guide every operation. It is essential to become familiar with the rules and the appropriate application of the rules. This is an important part of number sense. There are special rules for the use of symbols—such as parentheses, exponents, and radicals—and for the order of all operations performed. Good problem solving will require you to use your number sense and mathematical knowledge effectively. In this chapter you'll look at these topics and learn how to use this information to evaluate formulas.

Powers

When a number is multiplied by itself, we say that it is **squared.** We show that with a small "2" placed to the upper right of the number. For example, $7^2 = 7 \times 7 = 49$. This means seven squared is 7 times 7, which is 49.

In the expression 7^2, the two is called the **power** or **exponent,** and the seven is called the **base.** It is best to think of the exponent as an instruction. The exponent tells you what to do with the base. When the exponent is two, the base is squared, and we multiply the base by itself.

Examples

$3^2 = 3 \times 3 = 9$

$9^2 = 9 \times 9 = 81$

$10^2 = 10 \times 10 = 100$

$(\frac{1}{3})^2 = \frac{1}{3} \times \frac{1}{3} = \frac{1}{9}$

Sometimes the exponent is a number other than 2. The exponent tells how many times to multiply the base by itself. For example:

$3^4 = 3 \times 3 \times 3 \times 3 = 81$

$5^3 = 5 \times 5 \times 5 = 125$

$10^6 = 10 \times 10 \times 10 \times 10 \times 10 \times 10 = 1{,}000{,}000$

$(\frac{2}{3})^3 = \frac{2}{3} \times \frac{2}{3} \times \frac{2}{3} = \frac{8}{27}$

SPECIAL RULES ABOUT POWERS

1. The number 1 to any power is 1. $1^5 = 1 \times 1 \times 1 \times 1 \times 1 = 1$
2. Any number to the first power is that number. $6^1 = 6$
3. Any number to the zero power is 1. $14^0 = 1$

When you multiply a number by itself, you get a **perfect square.** For instance, $6^2 = 36$; so 36 is a perfect square. Some perfect squares that are helpful to know are listed here.

$1^2 = 1$	$6^2 = 36$	$11^2 = 121$	$20^2 = 400$
$2^2 = 4$	$7^2 = 49$	$12^2 = 144$	$30^2 = 900$
$3^2 = 9$	$8^2 = 64$	$13^2 = 169$	$40^2 = 1600$
$4^2 = 16$	$9^2 = 81$	$14^2 = 196$	$50^2 = 2500$
$5^2 = 25$	$10^2 = 100$	$15^2 = 225$	$100^2 = 10,000$

Square Roots

The operation opposite of squaring a number is finding the **square root** of a number. The symbol for square root is the **radical symbol,** $\sqrt{\ }$**.** For instance, $5^2 = 25$, so $\sqrt{25} = 5$. $\sqrt{25}$ is read, "the square root of 25." Being familiar with perfect squares makes many square roots easy to recall. For instance, $\sqrt{100} = 10$ because $10^2 = 100$.

If you need to find the square root of a number that is not a perfect square, you can do one of three things: simplify the square root, approximate the square root, or use a calculator.

Example 1 Simplify a square root by writing the number as a product of numbers using perfect squares if possible.

$\sqrt{75}$ can be expressed as $= \sqrt{25 \times 3} = \sqrt{25} \times \sqrt{3} = 5\sqrt{3}$. You choose 25 and 3 because 25 is a perfect square and you can find its square root.

Example 2 Approximate the square root of a number by looking at the perfect square closest to the number to make an estimated guess at the answer.

$\sqrt{75}$ is between $\sqrt{64}$ and $\sqrt{81}$ so

$\sqrt{64} = 8$

$\sqrt{75} \approx 8.7$ ← ($\sqrt{75}$ is between 8 and 9 but closer to 9, so we estimate about 8.7.)

$\sqrt{81} = 9$

Your calculator can be used to perform powers and roots. Become familiar with these keys on your calculator and how to use them.

Keys:	x^2	squares the numbers
	x^y	raises the number to the power indicated
	SHIFT	accesses key operations indicated above the key
	$\sqrt{\ }$	finds the square root of the number

To Find Powers and Roots

Process	**Key In:**	**Display**	**Example: $5^2 = 25$**
Step 1	AC to clear the display	0.	0.
Step 2	base	base	5.
Step 3	square symbol (x^2)	answer	25.

Process	**Key In:**	**Display**	**Example: $5^4 = 625$**
Step 1	AC to clear the display	0.	0.
Step 2	base	base	5.
Step 3	power symbol (x^y)	base	5.
Step 4	exponent	power	4.
Step 5	equals sign (=)	answer	625.

Process	**Key In:**	**Display**	**Example: $\sqrt{36} = 6$**
Step 1	AC to clear the display	0.	0.
Step 2	number	number	36.
Step 3	SHIFT	number	36.
Step 4	square root symbol ($\sqrt{\ }$)	answer	6.

EXERCISE 1

Powers and Roots

Directions: Evaluate the powers below. Use your calculator to check your answer.

1. 8^2 **2.** 9^3 **3.** 1^7 **4.** 2^4 **5.** 4^0

6. 10^3 **7.** 0^2 **8.** 3^3 **9.** 12^2 **10.** 5^4

Evaluate the square roots below. When finding the square root of a perfect square, give the exact answer. When finding a square root that is not a perfect square, give either an approximate answer or a simplified answer. Use your calculator to check your answers.

11. $\sqrt{81}$ **12.** $\sqrt{9}$ **13.** $\sqrt{1}$ **14.** $\sqrt{50}$ **15.** $\sqrt{32}$

16. $\sqrt{144}$ **17.** $\sqrt{28}$ **18.** $\sqrt{400}$ **19.** $\sqrt{0}$ **20.** $\sqrt{12}$

Answers are on page 925.

Parentheses

Parentheses are powerful symbols in mathematics problem solving. As you know, parentheses can be used to indicate multiplication. For example, $5(3) = 15$. Parentheses can also be used as a grouping symbol to organize a problem. For instance, $5(3 + 6) = 45$. Before you multiply by 5, you should add 3 and 6 because they are grouped together inside the parentheses. Use parentheses anytime you want to **emphasize an operation** and want that operation **to precede other operations.** As you practice the order of operations described below, you will see how the parentheses impact the answer to a problem.

Order of Operations

Accurate calculations depend on careful use of addition, subtraction, multiplication, and division. These operations must be performed in a certain order when there are two or more operations in the same problem. The rules that describe that order are called the **order of operations.** All operations should be performed moving from the left to the right. Be sure to start at the beginning for every problem. Do not skip a step unless there is no operation to do at that level.

ORDER OF OPERATIONS

First, do all the work grouped inside parentheses or above a fraction bar.

Second, evaluate powers and square roots.

Third, multiply and divide as indicated from left to right.

Last, add and subtract as indicated from left to right.

Example 1 Calculate the expression $5 + 7 \times 3$.

First, notice there are no parentheses in the problem. Then multiply 7×3. $5 + 7 \times 3 =$

Last, add $5 + 21$ to get 26. $5 + 21 = \mathbf{26}$

Example 2 Calculate $3(5 + 7)$.

First, add the numbers inside the parentheses. $3(5 + 7) =$

Then multiply 3×12 to get 36. $3 \times 12 = \mathbf{36}$

Example 3 Calculate $\frac{5+7+6}{3}$.

First, add the numbers grouped above the fraction bar. $\frac{5+7+6}{3} =$

Then divide by 3 to get 6. $\frac{18}{3} = \mathbf{6}$

Example 4 Calculate $3 \times 5 + 2 \times 10$.

First, notice there are no parentheses. Then multiply 3×5 and 2×10. $3 \times 5 + 2 \times 10 =$

Last, add $15 + 20$ to get 35. $15 + 20 = \mathbf{35}$

Example 5 Calculate 4×5^2.

First, notice there are no parentheses. Then raise 5 to the second power. $4 \times 5^2 =$

Last, multiply 4×25 to get 100. $4 \times 25 = \mathbf{100}$

The calculator that you will use on the GED Test has the order of operations programmed in it. If a problem has more than one operation, the calculator will follow the order of operations to arrive at the answer. Be sure to key in the problem correctly.

Keys:	[(	open parentheses
	)]	close parentheses

To evaluate a numerical expression on a calculator, key in the numbers, symbols, and operations as they occur. Use the *open parentheses* and *close parentheses* keys to indicate an operation that is to be calculated first. If a number precedes the parentheses, it indicates that you are to multiply the amount in the parentheses by the number. For example:

$5(3 + 8)$ means $5 \times (3 + 8)$ <u>You must key in the multiplication sign.</u>

EXERCISE 2

Order of Operations

Directions: Evaluate each numerical expression below without using a calculator. Be sure to follow the order of operations rules. Then use a calculator to check your answers.

1. $5 + 9 \times 3$	**2.** $(4 + 9) \times 5$	**3.** $12 - 3 - 2$	**4.** $2 + 6 \times 4 + 8$
5. $12 - (7 + 4)$	**6.** $12 - 7 + 4$	**7.** $\frac{6+9}{3}$	**8.** $\frac{6}{3} + 9$
9. $8 \times 3 + 6 \times 4$	**10.** $4 \times (8 - 3)$	**11.** $4 \times 8 - 3$	**12.** $30 + 5 \times 2$
13. $7 - 5 + 3 - 5$	**14.** $6 + 21 \div 3 - 5$	**15.** $15 - 3 + 2^3$	**16.** $4(5 + 3)^2$

Answers are on page 926.

Setup Problems

Some problems on the GED Test will require you to identify the correct setup to solve them. These setup problems do not require you to perform the calculations. You are being tested on your ability to demonstrate how you can use numbers, operations, and mathematical processes to solve problems.

To set up a problem, represent the mathematical relations using numbers and operation symbols. This relationship is called an **arithmetic expression.** There are rules that must be followed when writing an arithmetic expression involving more than one arithmetic operation.

WRITING ARITHMETIC EXPRESSIONS

1. Write an arithmetic expression using numbers and operation symbols following the rules of operations and identifying the individual steps in the multistep problem.
2. Use parentheses or the fraction bar to separate one part of an arithmetic expression from another.
3. Follow the **order of operations** rules to indicate the order in which the arithmetic expression should be solved.

   First, do the operations grouped inside parentheses or above the fraction bar.

   Second, multiply and divide as indicated from left to right.

   Last, add and subtract as indicated from left to right.

Example If Becky can walk a mile in 20 minutes, how far can she walk in 3 hours?

Question:	How far does she walk in 3 hours?
Information:	One mile in 20 minutes; 3 hours 60 minutes in one hour
Operations:	Step 1: To get the total minutes—multiply 3×60 Step 2: To get the number of miles—divide by 20
Setup and Estimation:	$\frac{3 \times 60}{20}$ This is the arithmetic expression that sets up the problem.
Computation:	$3 \times 60 = 180$, $180/20 =$ **9 miles**
Is the answer reasonable?	Yes, because one mile in 20 minutes would be 3 miles per hour $\times$ 3 hours = 9.

EXERCISE 3

Arithmetic Expressions

Directions: In each of the following problems, select the arithmetic expression that represents the appropriate setup to solve the problem.

1. In 2001 Harper College charged $55 per credit hour. Find the total bill for a student who takes 15 credit hours and pays a $75 activity fee.

(1) $55 + 75 + 15$
(2) $75 + 15 \times 55$
(3) $(75 + 55) \times 15$
(4) $75 \times 55 \times 15$
(5) $55 \times 15 - 75$

2. If Kelly buys a dozen oranges @ 45¢ each and eight apples @ 50¢ each, how much is his total bill?

(1) $12 + .45 + 8 + .50$
(2) $12 \times .45 \times 8 \times .50$
(3) $(12 + 8) \times (.45 + .50)$
(4) $12 \times .45 + 8 \times .50$
(5) $(12 + .45) \times (8 + .50)$

3. Angela used her 75¢-off coupon to buy a roll of film for her camera. If the film was priced at $3.98 and tax was 31¢, how much change did she receive if she paid with a $5 bill?

(1) $5.00 - (3.98 + .31 - .75)$
(2) $5.00 - 3.98 - .31 - .75$
(3) $3.98 + .31 + .75 - 5.00$
(4) $3.98 + .31 - .75 - 5.00$
(5) $5.00 + 3.98 + .31 + .75$

4. As a waiter Jorge was responsible for four tables. If his customers left tips of $5, $7, $3, and $9, what was the average tip per table?

(1) $5 + 7 + 3 + 9$
(2) $4 \times (5 + 7 + 3 + 9)$
(3) $\frac{5 + 7 + 3 + 9}{4}$
(4) $5 + 7 + 3 + 9 \div 4$
(5) $4 \div (5 + 7 + 3 + 9)$

Answers are on page 926.

EXERCISE 4

Word Problems

Directions: Solve each problem. Check your work using your calculator.

1. **You just inherited an apartment building. If your income from apartment rentals is $5160 per month, what is your yearly income?**

   (1) $ 430
   (2) $ 5,160
   (3) $15,480
   (4) $61,920
   (5) Not enough information is given.

2. **There were 395 people who registered for a sightseeing tour. If a tour bus can hold 72 people, how many buses will be needed to accommodate everyone?**

   (1) 5
   (2) 6
   (3) 7
   (4) 10
   (5) 50

3. **A garment factory completed an order for 500 pairs of pants and was paid $5500. If the factory received $9130 for a second order for pants at the same price, how many pairs of pants were in the second order?**

   (1) 363
   (2) 500
   (3) 830
   (4) 913
   (5) 3630

4. **A charity organization collected $348,284 in a recent fund-raising drive. Of the amount collected, some was put aside to pay expenses. The remaining money was divided equally among six local charities. What amount did each charity receive?**

   (1) $ 58,041
   (2) $ 58,047
   (3) $ 58,053
   (4) $348,284
   (5) Not enough information is given.

Questions 5–7 refer to the information in the table below.

The local school district has experienced a recent increase in enrollment. The table compares enrollment figures between 1992 and 2002 for its five schools.

High School Student Enrollment

Year	*Lincoln*	*Mead*	*Sandburg*	*Austin*	*Edison*
1992	1420	1650	1847	1296	1318
2002	1686	1982	2234	1648	1846

5. Which school had the greatest increase in enrollment?

(1) Lincoln
(2) Mead
(3) Sandburg
(4) Austin
(5) Edison

6. What was the total increase in enrollment in the district during the ten-year period?

(1) 1865
(2) 2865
(3) 7531
(4) 9396
(5) Not enough information is given.

7. What was the average increase in enrollment per school in the district?

(1) 373
(2) 1865
(3) 1879
(4) 7531
(5) 9396

8. Four technicians for Transcom must produce 1298 parts in a week's time. The first one produces 350 parts, the second produces 375 parts, and the third produces 417 parts. Which expression shows how many parts remain for the fourth technician to make?

(1) $1298 \div 4$
(2) $350 + 375 + 417$
(3) $1298 - (350 + 375 + 417)$
(4) $(350 + 375 + 417) - 1298$
(5) $(350 + 37 + 417) \div 3$

9. Gary bought a new sport-utility vehicle. The price was \$19,700 including an AM/FM CD/cassette radio and automatic transmission. The car dealer gave him a \$500 rebate for the purchase of the new car, and Gary made a down payment of \$3150. What would be the expression for his monthly payments if he takes 60 months to pay the remaining balance?

(1) $19700 + 3150 + 500 \div 60$
(2) $60 \div (19700 + 3150 + 500)$
(3) $\frac{19700 - (3150 + 500)}{60}$
(4) $\frac{19700 - 3150 + 500}{60}$
(5) $60 \times (19700 + 3150 + 500)$

10. The manager of a men's shop can buy 80 men's suits for \$4800 and a variety of sports coats at \$43 each. If she decides to buy the 80 suits and 25 coats, which expression shows how to find the total cost of the order?

(1) 25×43
(2) $25 + 43 + 4800$
(3) $25 \times 43 \times 4800$
(4) $4800 + 25 \times 43$
(5) $(4800 + 25) \times 43$

Answers are on page 926.

Formulas

Letters of the alphabet often are used to represent numbers that you need to find. For instance, you may remember the distance formula $d = rt$. The letters *d, r,* and *t* are used to represent numbers for distance, rate, and time. Letters used this way are called **unknowns** or **variables.** This use of letters helps us express general relationships about numbers.

$a^2+b^2=c^2$

Formulas are a way of showing these general relationships. Some common formulas that help us are the area of a circle ($A = \pi r^2$), the perimeter of a rectangle ($P = 2l + 2w$), and the Pythagorean theorem ($a^2 + b^2 = c^2$). The GED Mathematics Test will include a formula page that will help you solve some problems on the Test. As you read a particular problem, you will have to decide which formula will help you solve it. You should become familiar with the formula page and practice using it as you solve problems. It is located on page 922.

Evaluating Formulas

When you replace letters with numbers in a formula, you **substitute** numbers for letters. When you perform mathematical operations on the substituted values, you are **evaluating** a formula. When you evaluate a formula, be sure to follow the **order of operations.**

Example 1 The formula for the perimeter of (distance around) a rectangle is $P = 2l + 2w$. Find the perimeter of a rectangle if the length is 6 and the width is 5.

STEP 1 Substitute in the formula. $P = 2l + 2w$
$P = 2(6) + 2(5)$

STEP 2 Multiply first. $P = 12 + 10$

STEP 3 Add. $P =$ **22**

Example 2 Find the volume of a rectangular box whose length is 7 inches, width is 5 inches, and height is 3 inches. Use the formula for volume $V = lwh$ (see the formula on page 922).

STEP 1 Find the formula for volume. $V = lwh$

STEP 2 Substitute the values given. $V = (7)(5)(3)$

STEP 3 Multiply as indicated by the parentheses. $V =$ **105 cubic inches**

EXERCISE 5

Evaluating Formulas

$a^2+b^2=c^2$

Directions: Select the appropriate formula from the formula page. Substitute the values given and evaluate the formula. The units for your answers are given in parentheses following the problem.

1. Find the area of the square at the right. (The answer will be in square inches.)

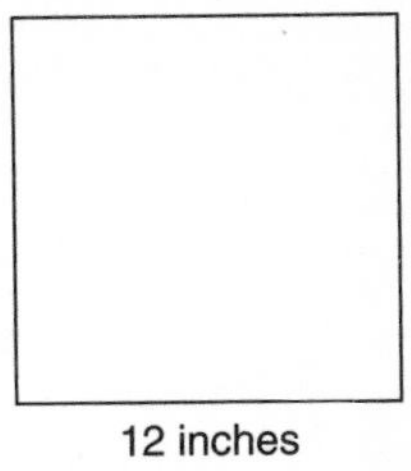

2. Find the perimeter of the square above. (The answer will be in inches.)

3. Find the volume of the cube at the right. (The answer will be in cubic inches.)

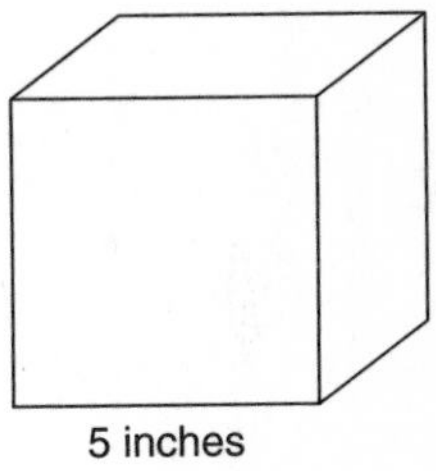

4. Find the distance (*d*) traveled if you are going 38 miles per hour (*r*) for 2 hours (*t*). (The answer will be in miles.)

5. Find the area of a triangle where the base (*b*) is 12 centimeters and the height (*h*) is 9 centimeters. (The answer will be in square centimeters.)

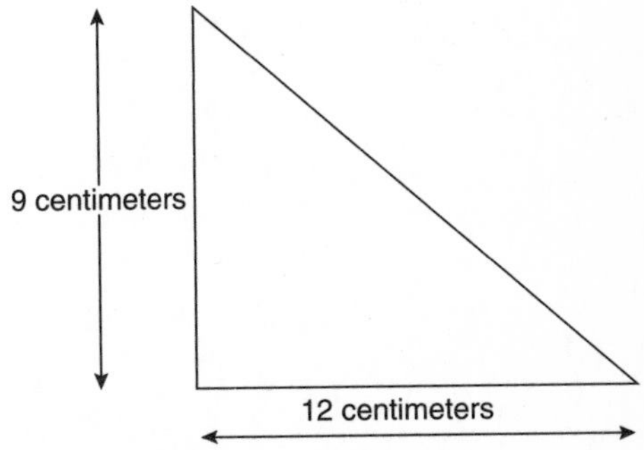

6. Find the total cost of three children's jackets that cost $49.95 each.

7. Find the volume of a cylinder if $\pi \approx 3.14$, the radius (r) is 6 inches, and the height (h) is 10 inches. (The units in the answer will be in cubic inches.)

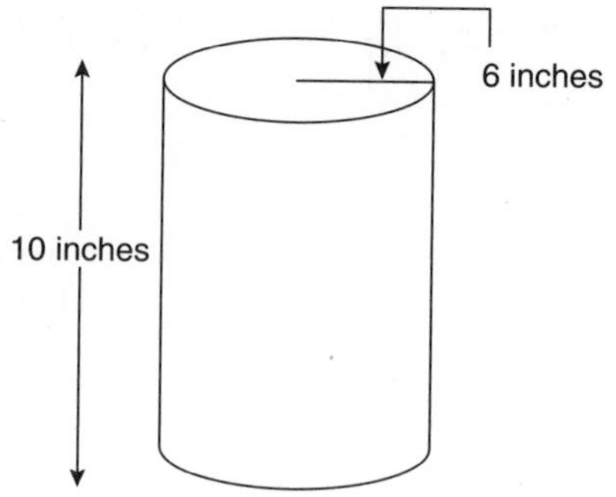

Answers are on page 926.

Go to **www.GEDMath.com** for additional practice and instruction!

CHAPTER 3

Decimal Numbers and Operations

Every day we use familiar decimal numbers. A person's normal temperature is 98.6°. A cup of coffee and bagel with cream cheese is $3.25. The odometer on the car reads 12,356.8 miles. To fully understand and use decimals correctly, in this chapter you will review place values, reading decimals, rounding decimals, comparing and ordering decimals, and performing decimal operations.

Using Decimals

In our number system, you use ten digits (0, 1, 2, 3, 4, 5, 6, 7, 8, 9) to write every number. The place that a digit occupies in a number tells us the value of the digit. This means that each digit has a **place value.**

You can use the place value chart below to read numbers. The whole numbers are to the left of the **decimal point.** The decimals, which are parts of a whole, are to the right of the decimal point. The places to the right of the decimal point are called **decimal places.** Decimal places represent fractional values whose parts are tenths, hundredths, thousandths, and so on. Note that the names of the decimal places end in *th.*

							3	**2**	**6**	**.**	**7**	**5**				
Billions	Hundred Millions	Ten Millions	Millions	Hundred Thousands	Ten Thousands	Thousands	Hundreds	Tens	Ones	**AND**	Tenths	Hundredths	Thousandths	Ten Thousandths	Hundred Thousandths	Millionths

Tip

The decimal point separates the whole-number places from the decimal places. The point is read as "and."

The number 326.75 has two decimal places (tenths and hundredths), but *only* the last decimal place is named when the number is read. The number is read as "326 *and* 75 hundredths."

$326.75 = 326 \text{ and } \frac{75}{100}$

326 *and* 75 hundredths

READING DECIMALS

1. Read the whole part first.
2. Say "and" for the decimal point.
3. Read the decimal part.
4. Say the place value of the last digit.

- **If there is no whole number, start at step 3. For instance, .008 is read as "8 thousandths."**

Zeros in Decimals

The zero is very important in writing and reading decimal numbers. To see how important zeros are, read the names of each of the decimals below.

.5 (5 tenths) .05 (5 hundredths) .005 (5 thousandths)

You can see that the only digits used to write these numbers are 0 and 5. The actual value of the number depends on the place value of each digit. The zeros in the numbers hold the number 5 in a specific decimal place.

EXERCISE 1

Reading and Writing Decimals

Directions: In problems 1–5, select the number that matches the written value. Remember that the word *and* stands for the decimal point.

1. five hundredths

(1) 500 **(2)** .05 **(3)** .5 **(4)** .50 **(5)** .500

2. six and two tenths

(1) 6.2 **(2)** .62 **(3)** 62.0 **(4)** .062 **(5)** .602

3. one hundred and twenty-five thousandths

(1) 125,000 **(2)** 125.000 **(3)** .125 **(4)** 100.025 **(5)** 120.005

4. one thousand thirty-two

(1) 1000.32 **(2)** 1032 **(3)** .1032 **(4)** 1.032 **(5)** 1320

5. four hundred thirty and six thousandths

(1) 436,000 **(2)** .436 **(3)** 430.006 **(4)** 400.036 **(5)** 430.06

In problems 6–8, fill in the grid sections that correspond to your answer. Remember to select the decimal point as necessary. Write the following in number form:

6. seven tenths

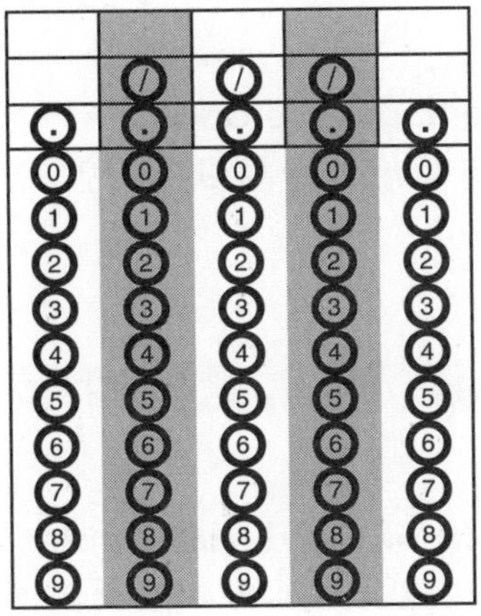

7. six and thirty-two thousandths

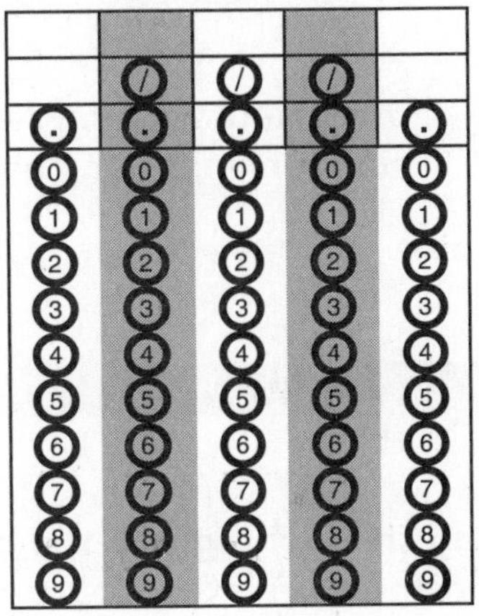

8. sixty-five ten-thousandths

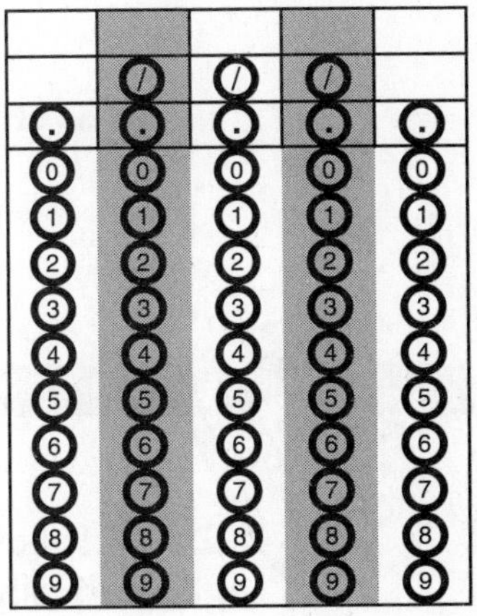

Answers are on page 927.

Comparing and Ordering Decimals

Sometimes you need to compare decimals to see which one is larger. If numbers do not have the same number of decimal places, it can be difficult to compare them. Luckily, decimal numbers can be rewritten with attached zeros to make it easier to compare numbers that have the same number of decimal places.

Attaching zeros to the right of the last decimal digit does not change the value of the number. For example, \$12 can also be written as \$12.00. Likewise, 12.5, 12.50, and 12.500 all have the same value.

To compare .14 and .126, attach a zero to .14 to make it .140. Now both .126 and .140 are expressed in thousandths and have the same number of decimal places.

$$.14 \ = .140$$
$$.126 = .126$$

You can now see that 126 thousandths is smaller than 140 thousandths because 126 is less than 140.

Example Put 4.8, 4.12, 4.2, and 4.1003 in order from the *smallest to the largest.*

STEP 1 Attach zeros so that each number has the same number of decimal places. Then number the mixed decimals in order from the smallest to the largest.

4.8	= 4.8000	4th
4.12	= 4.1200	2nd
4.2	= 4.2000	3rd
4.1003	= 4.1003	1st

STEP 2 Using your ranking system, put the *original numbers* in order from smallest to largest.

1st	4.1003
2nd	4.12
3rd	4.2
4th	4.8

Zeros following the last digit to the right of the decimal point are eliminated automatically on the calculator. You can enter numbers such as 4.50 into a calculator and display will show 4.50. On the other hand, if 4.50 is the answer to a math problem, the calculator will eliminate the zero and display only 4.5. The calculator is programmed to eliminate unnecessary zeros. If 4.5 is the answer to an arithmetic problem referring to money, it will be necessary for you to reattach the zero so that it reads $4.50.

EXERCISE 2

Comparing Decimals

Directions: Solve the following problems.

1. Select the *larger* number in each pair.

   (a) .005; .05 **(b)** 4.1; 4.01 **(c)** .7; .68 **(d)** .5; .51 **(e)** 1.033; 1.03

2. Arrange each set of numbers in order of size with the *largest* number first.

   (a) 1.95; 2.105; 2.15 **(b)** .0035; .0503; .005 **(c)** 6.4; 6; 6.07; 6.607

3. Put these weights in order from the *lightest* to the *heaviest*.

   14.3 lb   14.03 lb   14.003 lb   14.3033 lb

4. Sarah has to pile these crates in order from the *heaviest on the bottom* to the *lightest on the top.* What would be the correct order to pile the crates from bottom to top?

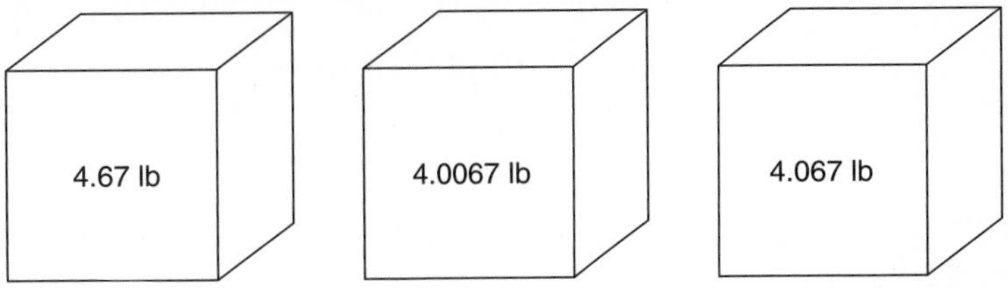

Answers are on page 927.

Rounding Decimals

You might solve a problem involving money and get $25.128 for the answer. Since money is expressed in hundredths and not thousandths, you must round off the answer to dollars and cents. Following are the steps to round off the answer.

Example 1 Round off $25.128 to the nearest cent.

STEP 1 Underline the place value to which you are rounding. — $25.128 (the 2 is underlined)

STEP 2 Identify the digit to the right of the place to which you are rounding. — $25.128 ← **digit to the right**

STEP 3 If the digit to the right of the underlined number
(a) **is 5 or more,** increase the digit in the place to which you are rounding by 1 and drop the digits to the right
(b) **is less than 5,** keep the same digit in the place to which you are rounding and drop the digits to the right

$25.128 ← **5 or more**
+ 1
$25.13

Example 2 Round 10.0239 to the nearest thousandth.

5 or more (points to the 9)

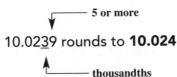

10.0239 rounds to **10.024**

thousandths (points to the underlined 3)

Example 3 A bank computes the interest on Sonya's savings account and finds it to be $37.7034. Round off this interest to the nearest cent.

less than 5

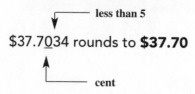

$37.7034 rounds to **$37.70**

cent

EXERCISE 3

Rounding Decimals

Directions: Solve the following problems.

1. A $\frac{3}{16}$-inch drill bit has a diameter of .1875 inches. What is the size of the drill bit to the nearest thousandth inch?
2. On the state income tax form, numbers are rounded to the nearest dollar. Round $1826.53 to the nearest dollar amount.
3. At the gas station, the pump says the gas costs $1.698 per gallon. In dollars and cents, how much will you pay per gallon?
4. The 8% sales tax on an $16.99 item is $1.3592. Round this amount to the nearest cent.
5. The value of π is 3.14159. Round off this value to the nearest hundredth. (This Greek symbol pronounced "pie" is used in geometric measurement.)
6. Juanita's normal temperature is 98.6°. Round her temperature to the nearest degree.

Answers are on page 927.

Scientific Notation

Our number system is based on multiples of ten. **Scientific notation** uses this idea of a base of 10 to give us a shortened method of writing extremely large or extremely small numbers. The notation is used a lot in science, but we are seeing it more often in everyday life as we use calculators and computers.

We can express multiples of 10 using powers of ten. To designate decimal values such as .1, .01, .001, we use negative powers of ten. A negative exponent is used to indicate the **reciprocal** value. The reciprocal of 10 is $\frac{1}{10}$. So $10^{-1} = \frac{1}{10^1} = .1$.

Let's look at some powers of ten using positive and negative exponents.

$10^0 = 1$	$10^{-1} = \frac{1}{10} = .1$
$10^1 = 10$	$10^{-2} = \frac{1}{10^2} = \frac{1}{100} = .01$
$10^2 = 100$	$10^{-3} = \frac{1}{10^3} = \frac{1}{1000} = .001$
$10^3 = 1000$	
$10^4 = 10{,}000$	

WRITING A NUMBER IN SCIENTIFIC NOTATION

1. Represent the number as a number between 1 and 10.
2. Write a multiplication sign and represent the number's value to the correct power of 10.

Use scientific notation to write numbers in shortened form. Simply count the number of positions that the decimal point must be moved to determine which power of 10 to use. The power of 10 is positive for whole numbers and negative for decimals.

Example 1 Express 86,200,000 in scientific notation.

STEP 1 Represent the number as a mixed decimal between 1 and 10. Insert the decimal point between 8 and 62 to get 8.62.

$86{,}200{,}000 = 8.62 \times 10^?$

STEP 2 Count the number of places the decimal point moved to get from 86,200,000 to 8.62. Since the point moved 7 places to the left, the power of 10 is 7.

$86{,}200{,}000 = \mathbf{8.62 \times 10^7}$

← 7 places

Example 2 Express .00098 in scientific notation.

STEP 1 Represent the number as a mixed decimal between 1 and 10. Insert the decimal point between 9 and 8 to get 9.8.

$.00098 = 9.8 \times 10^?$

STEP 2 Count the number of places the decimal point moved to get from .00098 to 9.8. Since the point moved 4 places to the right, the power of 10 is –4.

$.00098 = \mathbf{9.8 \times 10^{-4}}$

→ 4 places

There are times when a number has too many digits to be displayed on the calculator. Then the calculator will automatically display the answer in scientific notation. It will look a little bit unusual because the "× 10" will not be displayed; only the number between 1 and 10 and the exponent are displayed.

Process	Key In:	Display	Example: 526,000 × 1,000,000
Step 1	AC to clear the display	0.	0.
Step 2	first number	first number	526000
Step 3	×	first number	526000
Step 4	second number	second number	1000000
Step 5	=	answer in scientific notation	5.26 ^{11} This represents 526,000,000,000 which has 12 digits. The calculator will display only 10 digits.

Keys: EXP use to enter a number in scientific notation

You can enter a number in scientific notation using the EXP key. This is helpful in a problem when you are entering a number that has more than 10 digits.

Process	Key In:	Display	Example: 250,000,000,000 ÷ 5 which is $2.5 \times 10^{11} \div 5$
Step 1	AC to clear the display	0.	0.
Step 2	number from 1 to 10	number from 1 to 10	2.5
Step 3	EXP	scientific notation	2.5 ^{00}
Step 4	exponent	scientific notation	2.5 ^{11}
Step 5	÷	scientific notation	2.5 ^{11}
Step 6	divisor	divisor	5.
Step 7	=	answer	5. ^{10} which is 50,000,000,000

EXERCISE 4

Scientific Notation

Directions: Express each of the numbers below in scientific notation.

1. .0082

2. 500

3. 38,200

4. .58

Each number below is written in scientific notation. Find the actual value.

5. 1.624×10^3

6. 3.12×10^{-1}

7. 8.24×10^0

8. 7.13×10^3

Answers are on page 927.

Adding and Subtracting Decimals

A cashier who totals your bill is adding decimals. One who makes change for you is subtracting decimals. These are the basic rules to follow.

ADDING AND SUBTRACTING DECIMALS

1. Line up the decimal points.

2. Be sure that the whole numbers are to the left of the decimal point.

3. Add or subtract the numbers.

4. Bring the decimal point straight down in the answer.

Example 1 Add 4.5 and 38.68.

Read this space as a zero. Line up the decimal points.

```
    4.50  ← Attach a zero to help you keep the columns lined up.
 + 38.68
 -------
   43.18
```

Tip

You may attach zeros following the decimal point or following the last digit *after* the decimal point. This will help you keep the place value columns lined up but won't change the value of the numbers.

Example 2 Add 2.1, .48, 38, and .005.

Notice that the whole number is on the left of the decimal.

Fill in zeros to line up the columns.

```
    2.1          2.100
     .48          .480
→ 38             38.000
 +   .005      +   .005
 --------      --------
                 40.585
```

Tip

When you subtract decimals, fill in zeros to get enough decimal places.

Example 3 Subtract .0856 from 12.1.

```
                   0 9 9 1
  12.1           12.~~1000~~  ← Attach zeros.
 -  .0856       -   .0856
 --------       ---------
                  12.0144
```

Example 4 Jake gave the cashier a $20 bill to pay the $7.48 lunch check. How much change did Jake get back?

Remember to attach a decimal point and zeros.

```
                  1 9 9 1
 $20.00          $~~20.00~~
 - 7.48          -  7.48
 ------          -------
                 $12.52
```

EXERCISE 5

Adding and Subtracting Decimals

Directions: Solve each problem. Grid your answers for the problems indicated. Use your calculator to check your answers.

1. Add 12.4 and 2.64.

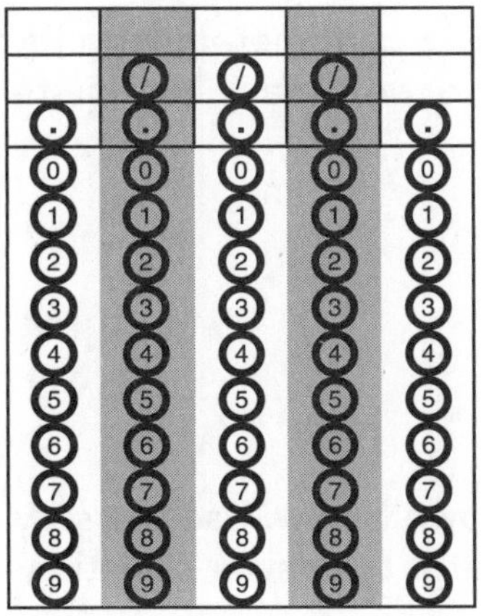

2. Add 5.9, 2.46, 6, 3.07, and .48.

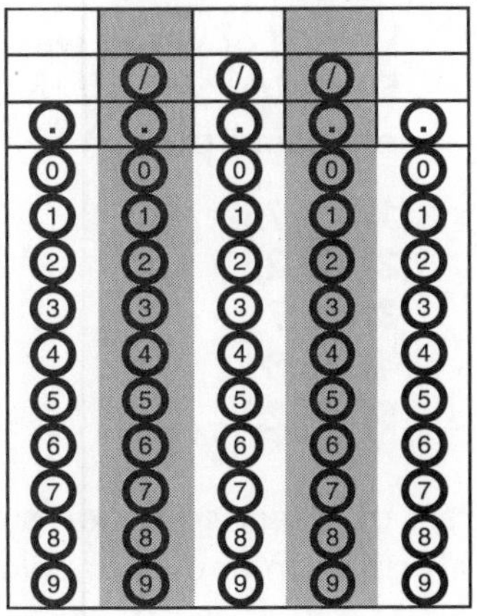

3. Subtract 5.2 from 43.

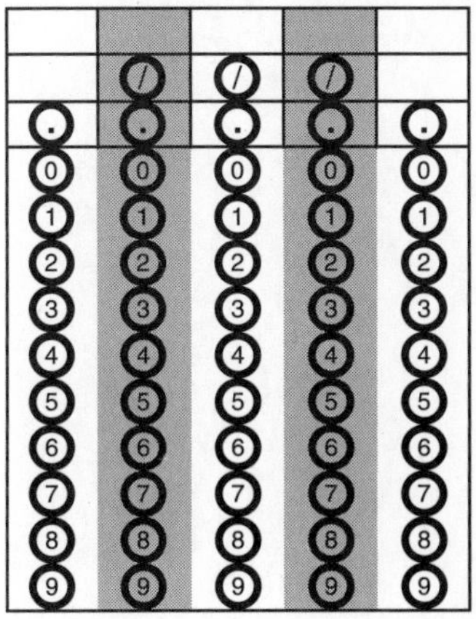

4. Find the difference between 85.2 and 6.9.

5. Find the distance around the field shown. All distances are in meters.

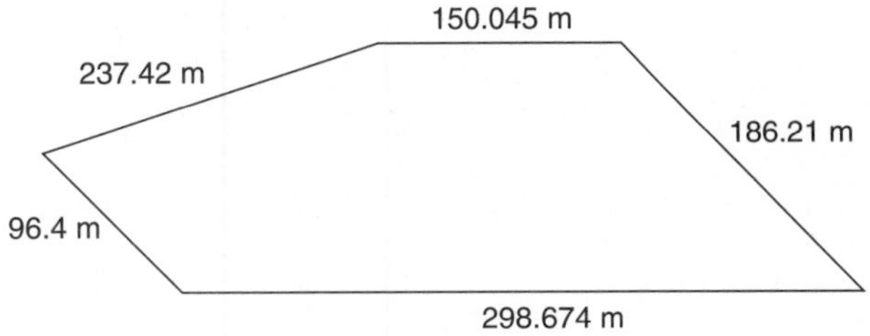

6. Can you balance a checkbook? At the beginning of the week, your balance was $472.24. During the week, you wrote checks for $42.87, $5.93, $20, $17.48, and $38.40. What is your new balance?

7. At the start of a trip, your mileage meter read 25,176.3; at the end of the trip, it read 28,054.1. How far did you travel?

8. Sam bought a sandwich for $4.75, a cup of soup for $1.95, and a can of pop for $.75. How much change did he receive from $10?

(1) $2.55
(2) $3.55
(3) $4.50
(4) $6.70
(5) $7.45

9. Although Jill's temperature is usually 98.6°, it rose to 104.2° when she had a fever. Her medication brought her fever down to 102.8°. By how many degrees did the medication bring it down?

(1) 0.6
(2) 1.4
(3) 1.6
(4) 2.0
(5) 2.2

10. A piece of wood was 46.75 centimeters long. If you trim .5 centimeters off the end, how many centimeters long is the remaining piece?

(1) 41.75
(2) 46.25
(3) 46.7
(4) 46.8
(5) 47.25

Part of a service order is shown below. Use the service order information and your calculator to answer questions 11 and 12.

Lake Marine Service		**DATE: 8/12**		**NAME: Kim Yang**
Qty.	**Part**	**Amount**	**Labor**	**Charge**
1	Gear lube	$17.50	Winterize	$70
1	Grease	4.95	Weld skeg	$90
1	Oil	6.00	Repair ladder	no charge
1	Gas	16.25		
3	Antifreeze	6.75		
	Total Parts		**Total Labor**	$160
			Total Parts	
			Tax	$3.66
			Invoice Total	

11. Find the total cost of the parts.

12. What is the invoice total for Mr. Yang's boat?

Answers are on page 927.

Multiplying Decimals

Decimals are multiplied the same way as whole numbers, and then the decimal point is placed in the answer. These are the rules for multiplying decimals.

MULTIPLYING DECIMALS

1. Multiply the two numbers as whole numbers, ignoring the decimal points.
2. Find the total number of decimal places in the numbers being multiplied.
3. Count the total number of decimal places in the answer. Starting at the right, move to the left the same number of places, and put the decimal point there.

Example 1 Multiply 3.2 and 4.05.

```
  4.05  <------ 2 decimal places
 × 3.2  <------ 1 decimal place
   810
 12 15
12.960     Count and move to the left
  <--      a total of 3 decimal places.
```

The final answer is **12.96** because you can drop the unnecessary zero.

Example 2 28 × .06

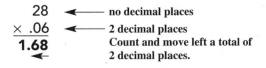

```
   28  <------ no decimal places
 × .06 <------ 2 decimal places
  1.68         Count and move left a total of
  <--          2 decimal places.
```

Tip

Sometimes you have to put zeros at the beginning of the answer to have enough decimal places.

Example 3 $.043 \times .0056$

```
  .0056  <—— 4 decimal places
× .043   <—— 3 decimal places
   168
  224
  2408          You need a total of 7 decimal places.
                Attach 3 zeros at the beginning of the
.0002408        number and then the decimal point.
```

EXERCISE 6

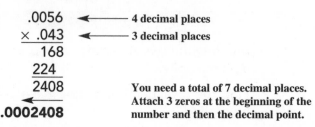

Multiplying Decimals

Directions: Multiply as indicated. Check your answers using your calculator.

1. 0.342×1.5 **2.** $46 \times .00034$ **3.** $0.85 \times .06$

4. $\$6.50 \times .085$ **5.** $\$128 \times .07$ **6.** $\$72.45 \times .3$

7. Monica pays $7.85 each month for newspaper home delivery. Which expression shows how much she pays for the newspaper over a year's time?

(1) $7.85 \times 4 \times 12$
(2) $(7.85 + 4) \times 12$
(3) 7.85×12
(4) 7.85×52
(5) 7.85×365

8. At the store, Dick bought a 3.5 pound package of chicken at $1.69 a pound and 2 gallons of milk at $3.30 per gallon. Which expression shows what Dick paid?

(1) $(3.5 + 1.69) + (2 + 3.30)$
(2) $(3.5 + 2) + (1.69 + 3.30)$
(3) $(3.5 \times 1.69) + (2 \times 3.30)$
(4) $3.5(1.69 + 3.30)$
(5) $2(1.69 + 3.30)$

Answers are on page 928.

Dividing Decimals

Split $45.75 equally among five people. How many $.59 hamburgers can you buy for $8? To solve these problems you have to divide decimals.

There are two basic types of decimal division: (1) division of decimals by whole numbers and (2) division of decimals by decimals. Let's look at examples of each type.

Dividing by a Whole Number

DIVIDING DECIMALS BY WHOLE NUMBERS

1. Divide by the number that follows the division sign (÷).
2. Divide as though both numbers were whole numbers. Keep numbers aligned properly.
3. Place the decimal point in the answer directly above the decimal point in the dividend.

Example 1 Dividing a decimal by a *whole* number: 36.48 ÷ 4

```
   9.12
4)36.48
 - 36
   04
  - 4
    08
   - 8
     0
```

Place the decimal point directly above the decimal point in the dividend.

Example 2 Dividing a whole number by a *larger* whole number, which requires you to attach a decimal point and zeros: 12 ÷ 25

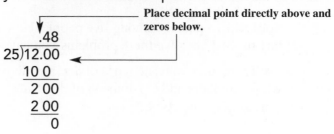

Place decimal point directly above and zeros below.

```
     .48
25)12.00
   10 0
    2 00
    2 00
       0
```

Example 3 Dividing by a whole number that doesn't divide into the first number after the decimal point, requiring you to put in a zero placeholder before continuing your division: .35 ÷ 7

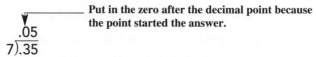

Put in the zero after the decimal point because the point started the answer.

```
  .05
7).35
```

Dividing by a Decimal

DIVIDING DECIMAL NUMBERS BY DECIMAL NUMBERS

1. Move the decimal point in the divisor all the way to the right.
2. Move the decimal point in the dividend the same number of places to the right.
3. Place the decimal point in the answer directly above the decimal point in the dividend.
4. Divide as though both numbers are whole numbers.

Example 1 4.864 ÷ .32

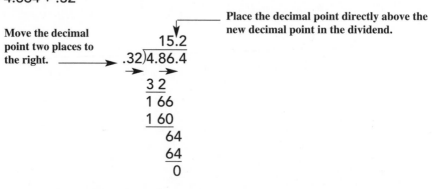

Move the decimal point two places to the right.

Place the decimal point directly above the new decimal point in the dividend.

```
       15.2
.32)4.86.4
    3 2
    1 66
    1 60
       64
       64
        0
```

Tip

Sometimes you will have to add zeros to move the decimal point.

Example 2 25 ÷ .125

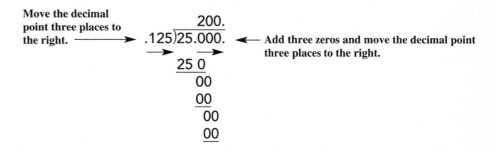

Move the decimal point three places to the right. →

```
         200.
.125)25.000.
     25 0
        00
        00
         00
         00
```

← Add three zeros and move the decimal point three places to the right.

EXERCISE 7

Dividing Decimals

Directions: Solve each division problem. Check your answers using your calculator. (In division problems, be sure to enter the divisor after the division symbol.)

1. Divide 6.005 by .05.   **2.** .012 ÷3   **3.** 2.8 ÷ .04

4. Divide 56 by .08   **5.** 4.75 ÷ 2.5   **6.** 24.36 ÷ 4

7. How many $1.25 items can you buy for $20?

Answers are on page 928.

Multiplying and Dividing by Multiples of 10

The easy way to multiply or divide by multiples of ten (10, 100, 1000, and so on) is simply to move the decimal point. When you multiply, you move the decimal point to the right. When you divide, you move the point to the left. In either case, the decimal point moves as many places as there are zeros in the multiple of ten. (As the examples show, you add zeros when necessary.)

Example 1 .13 × 1000 = 130. → **3 zeros move the decimal point 3 places to the right in multiplication.**

Example 2 9.5 ÷ 100 = .095 ← **2 zeros move the decimal point 2 places to the left in division.**

EXERCISE 8

Multiplying and Dividing Decimals by Multiples of 10

Directions: Use the shortcuts to multiply and divide the decimals below. Use your calculator to check your answers.

1. $.38 \times 10$ **2.** $.472 \times 10{,}000$ **3.** $.0972 \times 100$

4. $.617 \div 10$ **5.** $456.12 \div 100$ **6.** $57 \div 1000$

7. One stamp costs $.34. How much does a roll of 100 stamps cost?

8. How much does each person receive if $25,000 is divided evenly among 100 people?

9. Finishing Touch Decorators can paint 1.5 rooms in an hour. Working 10 hours each day, how many days will it take them to paint a 75-room building?

Answers are on page 928.

Estimating for Problem Solving

Estimation is a handy tool to use in solving decimal problems. If a problem involves decimals, reread the problem and replace the mixed decimals with whole numbers. This will help you see how to solve the problem. After choosing the correct operations to use, work the problem with the original decimal numbers if an exact answer is necessary.

Example 1 What is the cost of 12.8 gallons of gasoline at $1.89 per gallon?

Estimation: What is the cost of 13 gallons of gasoline at $2 per gallon? Using whole numbers helps you see that you should multiply 2×13, which equals 26. Your answer in the original problem should be about **$26.** The exact answer is 24.192, which rounds to $24.19.

Example 2 Approximately how much did Emil spend on his recent shopping spree? This is what he bought: a blazer, \$59.95; slacks, \$34.95; shirt, \$24.99; tie, \$15.75; belt, \$12.25; shoes, \$34.95.

Estimation: To estimate the answer, round off the numbers to easy-to-use numbers that are multiples of 5 and 10.

\$59.95 ≈	\$ 60
\$34.95 ≈	\$ 35
\$24.99 ≈	\$ 25
\$15.75 ≈	\$ 15
\$12.25 ≈	\$ 10
\$34.95 ≈	\$ 35
Total	**\$180**

Emil spent approximately \$180. The exact amount is \$182.84. If Emil wanted to know quickly about how much he was spending, an estimate would give him a close enough answer.

Estimating can help you see how to do a problem, provide you with an approximate answer, allow you to choose a multiple-choice answer, or help you double-check your work.

EXERCISE 9

Estimating

Directions: Estimate the answers to the following problems. Use your calculator to find the exact answers.

1. Dino drove his truck the following distances during the week: Monday, 4.8 miles; Tuesday, 12.3 miles; Wednesday, 74.5 miles; Thursday, 10 miles; and Friday, 8.1 miles. Approximately how far did he travel?

2. Connie had \$50 in her purse. She spent \$24.75 on cosmetics and \$2.50 on a magazine. After these purchases, approximately how much did she have left in her purse?

3. If a bushel of apples costs \$12.95, what will ten bushels cost?

4. How many streamers, each 1.75 feet long, can be cut from a roll of crepe paper 36 feet long?

Answers are on page 928.

EXERCISE 10

Decimal Word Problems

Directions: Use estimation to help you solve the problems. Sometimes you may need to find the exact amount. Check your work with a calculator.

1. You are building a bookcase with shelves that are 3.2 feet long. How many complete shelves can be cut from a 12-foot board?

(1) 2
(2) 3
(1) 4
(1) 5
(5) Not enough information is given.

2. Mr. Stansky earns a part-time salary of $425 every four weeks. During the past four weeks he also received commissions of $485.75, $399.87, $642.15, and $724.52. What was his total income for the past 4-week period?

(1) $ 535.46
(2) $ 669.32
(3) $2252.29
(4) $2256.42
(5) $2677.29

3. On a bicycle road trip, Otis rode 2492 miles in 140 hours. What was his average speed in miles per hour?

(1) 1.78
(2) 17.8
(3) 178
(4) 1780
(5) 34,888

4. The carat is a unit of measure used to weigh precious stones. It equals 3.086 grains. How many grains does a 2.8 carat diamond weigh?

(1) 3.086
(2) 5.886
(3) 8.6408
(4) 86.408
(5) 8640.8

Questions 5 and 6 are based on the table below.

As an assistant accountant for a computer company, you must calculate each employee's gross earnings, total of deductions, and net pay by using the following table.

Employee Number	Regular Pay	Overtime Pay	Gross Earnings	Social Security Tax (FICA)	Federal Income Tax (FIT)	Total of Deductions	Net Pay
247	307.20	69.12		26.34	56.45		
351	368.80	96.81		32.60	83.81		
178	338	114.03		31.64	81.37		

5. Find the net pay for employee 178 after deductions are taken out.

(1) $113.01
(2) $339.02
(3) $452.03
(4) $565.04
(5) Not enough information is given.

6. How much did employee 247 make per hour to earn his regular pay for a 40-hour work week?

(1) $4.44
(2) $7.68
(3) $8.45
(4) $9.22
(5) $9.41

7. A new sedan can be bought for $3500 down and monthly payments of $345.81 for 48 months. To the nearest dollar, what is the total cost of the sedan?

(1) $ 3,846
(2) $13,099
(3) $16,599
(4) $20,099
(5) Not enough information is given.

8. If large eggs are on sale for $.99 per dozen, what is the cost of one egg to the nearest cent?

(1) $.06
(2) $.07
(3) $.08
(4) $.09
(5) $.10

9. The odometer of your sports car read 7353.2 miles at the start of a trip. When you returned, it read 8747.6 miles, and you had used 56.4 gallons of gasoline. How many miles per gallon did you get? (Round your answer to the nearest tenth.)

(1) 2.5
(2) 24.7
(3) 247
(4) 7864.4
(5) 78,644.2

10. One evening, a waiter received the following tips: $7.25, $.80, $5.75, $10, $6, $3.70. $4.90. What was his average tip for the evening?

(1) $ 2.80
(2) $ 3.22
(3) $ 5.49
(4) $22.56
(5) $38.40

Answers are on page 928.

Go to **www.GEDMath.com** for additional practice and instruction!

CHAPTER 4

Fractions and Operations

We encounter fractions in all aspects of life without even thinking about it.

Cut the pie into eight parts, so everyone gets a piece.
Let me borrow half a dollar.
It's a quarter past seven; I'd better hurry, or I'll be late.
I bought $3\frac{7}{8}$ yards of fabric.

Understanding Fractions

Fractions represent parts of a whole that has been divided into equal sections. The top number, called the **numerator,** tells how many parts of the whole you have. The bottom number, called the **denominator,** tells into how many total sections the whole has been divided.

5	numerator—parts of the whole you have
8	denominator—total number of sections in the whole

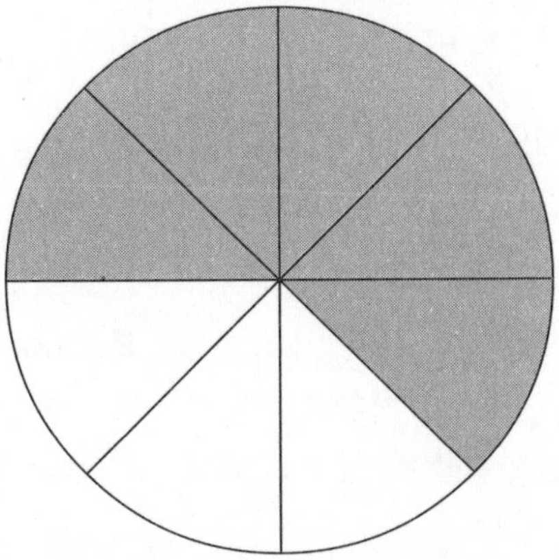

This circle is divided into 8 total parts.

$\frac{5}{8}$ of this circle is shaded.

$\frac{3}{8}$ of this circle is not shaded.

Tip

There are three meanings for fractions. $\frac{5}{8}$ means

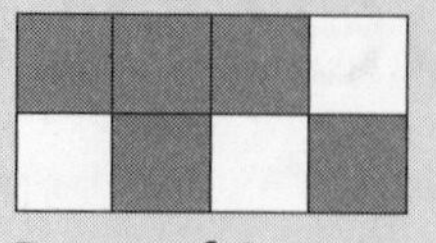

5 out of 8 parts

5 items compared to 8

$5 \div 8 = .625$

$$8\overline{)5.000}\quad .625$$

5 divided by 8

There are many types of fractions that you will use in your work.

Proper fraction: A fraction whose numerator is smaller than the denominator — $\frac{1}{2}, \frac{2}{5}, \frac{1}{7}, \frac{3}{9}$

Improper fraction: A fraction whose numerator is the same as or larger than the denominator — $\frac{5}{5}, \frac{5}{4}, \frac{3}{2}, \frac{7}{3}$

Mixed number: The combination of a whole number and a proper fraction — $2\frac{1}{3}, 3\frac{1}{4}, 6\frac{1}{5}$

A group of fractions may be classified by their denominators.

Like fractions: A group of fractions that has the same denominator — $\frac{1}{8}, \frac{3}{8}, \frac{6}{8}, \frac{9}{8}$

Unlike fractions: A group of fractions that has different denominators — $\frac{1}{4}, \frac{7}{8}, \frac{3}{5}, \frac{9}{2}$

EXERCISE 1

Types of Fractions

Directions: Match the letter from the second column that best describes the following groups of fractions. You may use more than one letter to describe each group.

1. ______	$\frac{2}{3}, \frac{5}{3}, \frac{1}{3}, \frac{7}{3}$	**A.** proper fractions
2. ______	$1\frac{3}{4}, 7\frac{1}{5}, 2\frac{1}{8}$	**B.** improper fractions
3. ______	$\frac{9}{3}, \frac{10}{5}, \frac{4}{2}, \frac{6}{6}$	**C.** like fractions
4. ______	$\frac{1}{5}, \frac{3}{7}, \frac{7}{8}, \frac{1}{3}$	**D.** unlike fractions
5. ______	$\frac{1}{2}, \frac{5}{4}, \frac{2}{5}, \frac{3}{7}$	**E.** mixed numbers

Answers are on page 929.

Raising and Reducing Fractions

To use fractions effectively, you must be able to rename fractions conveniently. In some cases you will want to **raise a fraction to higher terms,** or in other cases to **reduce a fraction to lower terms.** In either case, you are changing both the numerator and the denominator of the fraction to find an **equivalent fraction**—a fraction that has the same value. For example, a half-dollar has the same value as two quarters. As equivalent fractions, these can be written as $\frac{1}{2} = \frac{2}{4}$. This relationship can also be shown in this picture of a rectangle.

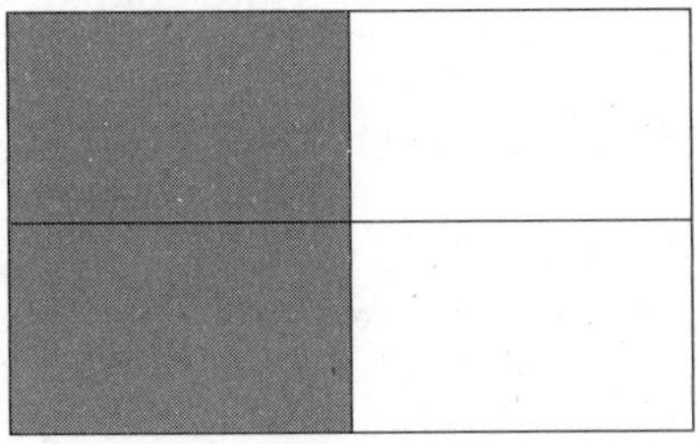

This rectangle has been divided into four equal sections. Two out of the four sections, or $\frac{2}{4}$ of the rectangle, are shaded. Notice that $\frac{2}{4}$ is equivalent to half the rectangle. So we say that

$$\frac{2}{4} = \frac{1}{2}.$$

TO RAISE A FRACTION TO HIGHER TERMS

Multiply both the numerator and the denominator by the same number. You will obtain an equivalent fraction.

Example 1 $\frac{5 \times 2}{8 \times 2} = \mathbf{\frac{10}{16}}$

TO REDUCE A FRACTION TO LOWER TERMS

Divide both the numerator and the denominator by the same number. You will obtain an equivalent fraction.

Hint: *Look for a number that divides evenly into both the numerator and the denominator.*

Example 2 $\frac{10 \div 2}{16 \div 2} = \mathbf{\frac{5}{8}}$

A fraction is in the **lowest terms** if there is no whole number that will divide evenly into both the numerator and denominator. For example, $\frac{3}{8}$ is already in lowest terms because there is not a whole number other than 1 that divides evenly into 3 and 8. Fraction answers should always be reduced to lowest terms.

Tip

All fraction answers for the GED Mathematics Test will be given in lowest terms.

Your calculator can be used to reduce fractions. Become familiar with the following keys on your calculator.

Fraction Keys:	a *b/c*	use to enter and display fractions and mixed numbers
	d/c	reduces fraction and/or changes a mixed number to an improper fraction

NOTE: *Repeated use of the a b/c key will yield the reduced fraction and the decimal equivalent. Repeated use of the SHIFT and d/c key will yield the reduced improper fraction and mixed number.*

To Enter and Reduce Fractions

PROCESS	**KEY IN:**	**DISPLAY**	**Example:** $\frac{5}{10}$
Step 1	AC to clear display	0.	0.
Step 2	numerator	numerator	5.
Step 3	a *b/c* key	numerator and fraction symbol	5⌟.
Step 4	denominator	numerator, fraction symbol, and denominator	5⌟10.
Step 5	=	reduced fraction	1⌟2.
Step 6	a *b/c* key	decimal equivalent	0.5

PROCESS KEY IN:		DISPLAY	Example: $4\frac{6}{8}$
Step 1	AC to clear display	0.	0.
Step 2	whole number	whole number	4.
Step 3	a *b/c* key	number and fraction symbol	4⅃.
Step 4	numerator	number, fraction symbol, and numerator	4⅃6.
Step 5	a *b/c* key	number, fraction symbol, numerator, and fraction symbol	4⅃6⅃.
Step 6	denominator	number, fraction symbol, numerator, fraction symbol, and denominator	4⅃6⅃8.
Step 7	=	reduced mixed number	4⅃3⅃4.
Step 8	SHIFT	mixed number $4\frac{3}{4}$	4⅃3⅃4.
Step 9	*d/c* key	improper fraction in reduced form $\frac{19}{4}$	19⅃4
Step 10	a *b/c* key	decimal equivalent	4.75
Step 11	a *b/c* key	mixed number in reduced form $4\frac{3}{4}$	4⅃3⅃4.
Step 12	SHIFT	mixed number	4⅃3⅃4.
Step 13	*d/c* key	return to improper fraction reduced form	19⅃4

Practice entering, reducing, and switching between fractions and decimals and between mixed numbers, improper fractions, and decimals.

EXERCISE 2

Raising and Reducing Fractions

Directions: Solve each problem.

Raise each fraction to higher terms as indicated by the new denominator. First, decide which number you will use to raise the denominator to the new denominator. Then multiply the numerator by the same number. The first problem is partially solved.

1. $\frac{3 \times 3}{8 \times 3} = \frac{\quad}{24}$ **2.** $\frac{3}{4} = \frac{\quad}{20}$ **3.** $\frac{1}{6} = \frac{\quad}{36}$

4. $\frac{3}{7} = \frac{\quad}{21}$ **5.** $\frac{6}{7} = \frac{\quad}{28}$ **6.** $\frac{2}{5} = \frac{\quad}{30}$

Reduce each fraction to lower terms as indicated by the new denominator. Remember to divide the numerator and the denominator by the same number. The first problem is partially solved for you.

7. $\frac{12 \div 4}{16 \div 4} = \frac{\quad}{4}$ **8.** $\frac{21}{28} = \frac{\quad}{4}$ **9.** $\frac{40}{50} = \frac{\quad}{5}$

10. $\frac{2}{6} = \frac{\quad}{3}$ **11.** $\frac{24}{36} = \frac{\quad}{3}$ **12.** $\frac{30}{42} = \frac{\quad}{7}$

Reduce each fraction to lower terms. Enter the answers to problems 15–18 on the grid provided. Use the / for the fraction bar.

13. $\frac{6}{8}$ **14.** $\frac{15}{20}$

15. $\frac{9}{27}$ **16.** $\frac{4}{12}$

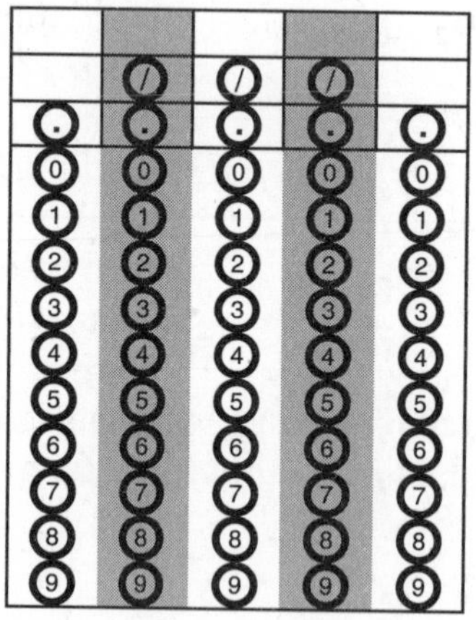

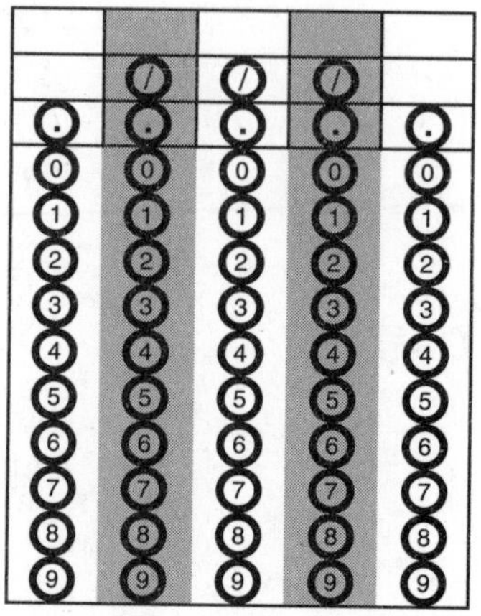

17. $\frac{25}{30}$

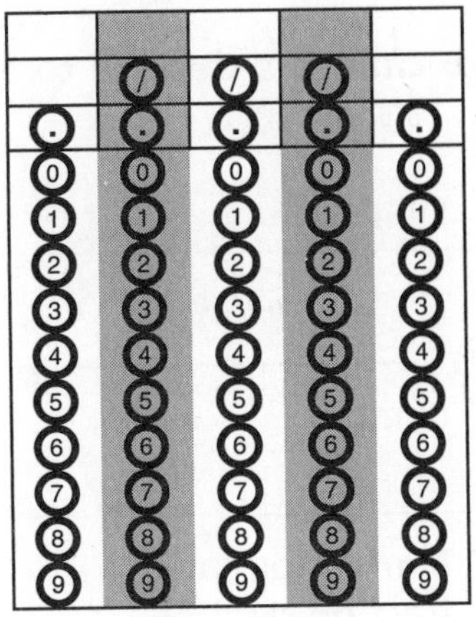

18. $\frac{12}{18}$

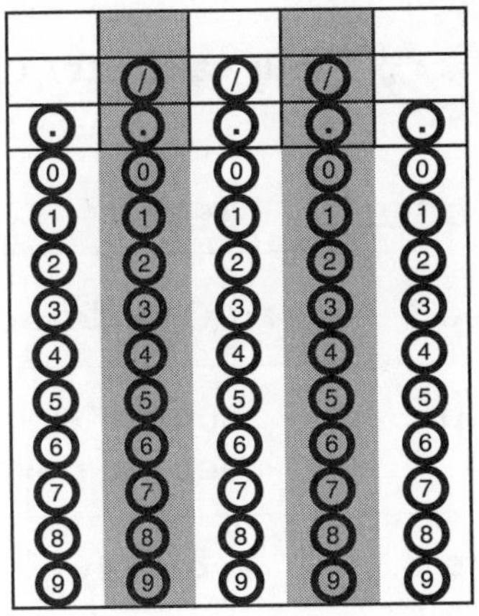

Answers are on page 929.

Relating Fractions and Decimals

In many arithmetic problems, you will work with both fractions and decimals. Each fraction can be expressed as a decimal and vice versa. That's because both decimals and fractions represent parts of a whole.

You can think of decimals as fractions with denominators in multiples of 10: 10, 100, 1000, and so on.

For example:

One decimal place is tenths:	.3 =	$\frac{3}{10}$
Two decimal places is hundredths:	.03 =	$\frac{3}{100}$
Three decimal places is thousandths:	.003 =	$\frac{3}{1000}$

CHANGING A DECIMAL TO A FRACTION

1. Put the number (with the decimal point removed) in the numerator of the fraction.
2. Make the denominator the value of the last place value in the decimal.

Example 1 Change .75 to a fraction.

STEP 1 Write the number 75 without a decimal point as a numerator. $\frac{75}{}$

STEP 2 Write 100, the value of the last decimal place, as a denominator. $\frac{75}{100}$ **This can be reduced to $\frac{3}{4}$.**

Example 2 Change .039 to a fraction.

$.039 = \frac{39}{1000}$ ← **number without decimal point** (39); ← **Three decimal places are thousandths.** (1000)

Your calculator can be used to change a decimal to a fraction in reduced form.

PROCESS	KEY IN:	DISPLAY	Example: .75
Step 1	AC to clear display	0.	0.
Step 2	number without decimal point	number	75.
Step 3	a *b/c* key	numerator and fraction symbol	75⌋.
Step 4	place value of the last digit	numerator, fraction symbol, and denominator	75⌋100.
Step 5	=	reduced fraction $\frac{3}{4}$	3⌋4.
Step 6	a *b/c* key	decimal equivalent	.75

Tip

Repeated use of the a *b/c* key will switch back and forth between the fraction and decimal.

CHANGING A FRACTION TO A DECIMAL

1. Divide the numerator by the denominator to two decimal places.

$$\frac{3}{4} = 4\overline{)3.00}\quad \begin{array}{r} .75 \\ 3.00 \\ \underline{2\,8} \\ 20 \\ \underline{20} \end{array}$$

2. If after two decimal places there is still a remainder, you may do one of two things.

Example 1
Divide again if the divisor will divide evenly.

$$\frac{5}{8} = 8\overline{)5.000}\quad \begin{array}{r} .625 \\ 5.000 \\ \underline{4\,8} \\ 20 \\ \underline{16} \\ 40 \\ \underline{40} \end{array}$$

or

Example 2
Make a fractional remainder.

$$\frac{2}{3} = 3\overline{)2.00}\quad \begin{array}{r} .66\frac{2}{3} \\ 2.00 \\ \underline{1\,8} \\ 20 \\ \underline{18} \\ 2 \end{array}$$

Tip

Example 2 is a repeating decimal. After two decimal places, you can bring up the remainder to be a part of a fraction. If necessary, you can round off decimals; for example, $.66\frac{2}{3} = .67$.

Your calculator can be used to change a fraction to a decimal in two different ways.

PROCESS	KEY IN:	DISPLAY	Example 1: $\frac{5}{8}$
Step 1	AC to clear display	0.	0.
Step 2	numerator	numerator	5.
Step 3	a *b/c* key	numerator and fraction symbol	5⌋.
Step 4	denominator	numerator, fraction symbol, and denominator	5⌋8.
Step 5	=	reduced fraction $\frac{5}{8}$	5⌋8.
Step 6	a *b/c* key	equivalent decimal value	0.625

PROCESS	KEY IN:	DISPLAY	Example 2: $\frac{5}{8}$
Step 1	AC to clear display	0.	0.
Step 2	numerator	numerator	5.
Step 3	÷	numerator	5.
Step 4	denominator	denominator	8.
Step 5	=	equivalent decimal	0.625

Tip

Some fractions are repeating decimals. For example, $\frac{1}{3} =$ 0.3333333 repeating can be rounded off to .33 or changed to $.33\frac{1}{3}$ exactly. (Use long division by hand and bring the remainder up as the numerator over the divisor in fraction form.)

EXERCISE 3

Changing Between Fractions and Decimals

Directions: Solve each problem. Use your calculator to check your work.

Change the following decimals to fractions. Reduce if necessary.

1. .05 **2.** .450 **3.** .07 **4.** .32 **5.** .005 **6.** 3.1

Change the following fractions to decimals. Write a fractional remainder after two decimal places. Check your answers with your calculator.

7. $\frac{3}{8}$ **8.** $\frac{1}{5}$ **9.** $\frac{4}{9}$ **10.** $\frac{5}{4}$ **11.** $\frac{5}{6}$

Answers are on page 929.

Relating Mixed Numbers and Improper Fractions

In your work with fractions, you will have to make another type of change. This involves changing mixed numbers to improper fractions and the reverse operation of changing improper fractions to mixed numbers.

CHANGING A MIXED NUMBER TO AN IMPROPER FRACTION

1. Multiply the whole number by the denominator.
2. Add that value to the numerator of the fraction.
3. Write the sum over the original denominator.

Example 1 Change $3\frac{7}{8}$ to an improper fraction.

STEP 1 Multiply the whole number by the denominator. $3 \times 8 = 24$

STEP 2 Add that value to the numerator of the fraction. $24 + 7 = 31$

STEP 3 Write the sum over the original denominator. $\frac{31}{8}$

So $3\frac{7}{8} = \mathbf{\frac{31}{8}}$.

CHANGING AN IMPROPER FRACTION TO A MIXED NUMBER

1. Divide the numerator by the denominator to get the whole-number part of the answer.
2. Put the remainder over the denominator to get the fractional part of the mixed number.

Example 2 Change $\frac{11}{5}$ to a mixed number.

STEP 1 Divide the numerator by the denominator. $\frac{11}{5} = 5\overline{)11}$ → quotient 2; $11 - 10 = 1$

$$\begin{array}{r} 2 \\ 5\overline{)11} \\ \underline{10} \\ 1 \end{array}$$

STEP 2 Put the remainder over the denominator. The answer is $\mathbf{2\frac{1}{5}}$.

Tip

Refer to the calculator examples for entering fractions (page 751). By using the a *b/c* key, SHIFT, and *d/c* key, you can move back and forth between an improper fraction, mixed number, and equivalent decimal.

EXERCISE 4

Changing Improper Fractions and Mixed Numbers

Directions: Solve each problem. Use your calculator to check your work.

Change the following to improper fractions.

1. $1\frac{5}{9}$ **2.** $12\frac{1}{4}$ **3.** $3\frac{2}{5}$ **4.** $4\frac{1}{8}$ **5.** $2\frac{1}{2}$ **6.** $6\frac{2}{3}$

Change the following to whole or mixed numbers.

7. $\frac{4}{3}$ **8.** $\frac{17}{7}$ **9.** $\frac{9}{9}$ **10.** $\frac{9}{8}$ **11.** $\frac{17}{5}$ **12.** $\frac{3}{2}$

Answers are on page 929.

Comparing Numbers

On the GED Test, you will sometimes have to compare whole numbers, fractions, and decimals. In mathematics you can use a number line to help you "see" the relationships among numbers.

The Number Line

The number line is similar to a ruler except that it has no beginning or end. Indicate this by putting arrows at both ends of the line. You can say that all numbers are represented on this line even though it would be impossible to label all of them.

Note that the numbers get larger as you go to the right on the line. Whole numbers as well as mixed numbers can be represented on the number line.

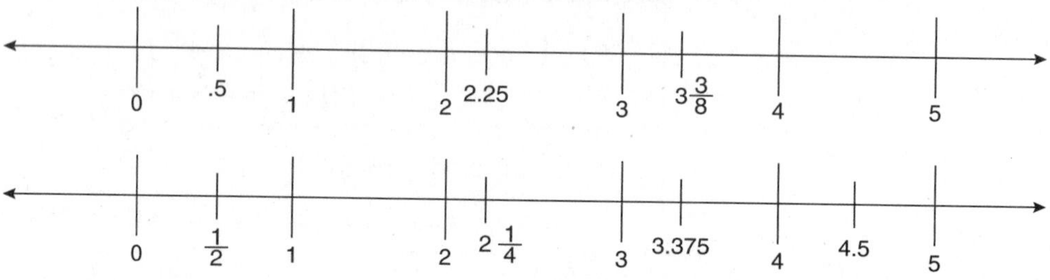

As the illustration shows, the same points can indicate either fractions or decimals. For example, $2\frac{1}{4}$ has the same value as 2.25.

You can use the number line to compare numbers and show their order. If you are given two numbers, then one of three statements must be true.

1. The two numbers are equal.
2. The first is larger than the second.
3. The first is smaller than the second.

There are symbols to indicate these relationships.

Symbol	Meaning	Example
$=$	is equal to	$4 = 4$
$>$	is greater than	$7 > 3$
$<$	is less than	$3 < 7$

Tip

The arrow always points to the smaller number.

Comparing Decimals

When you compare decimals, make sure you have the same number of decimal places in each number. Attach as many zeros as needed after the last number in the decimal. Remember that attaching zeros to the end of a decimal number does not change its value.

Example Compare .064 and .06.

.064 has 3 decimal places. .064
.06 has 2 decimal places. (Attach a zero to get three decimal places.) .060

Now both numbers are expressed in thousandths.

Because 64 > 60, **.064 > .06.**

Comparing Fractions

Sometimes you can compare fractions by using your number sense about fractions. It helps to use one half and one whole as benchmarks.

For instance, to compare $\frac{3}{8}$ and $\frac{5}{6}$ we can say that
$\frac{3}{8}$ is less than $\frac{1}{2}$ (because you know that $\frac{4}{8}$ is $\frac{1}{2}$) and
$\frac{5}{6}$ is almost one whole (because you know that $\frac{6}{6}$ is a whole).
Therefore, $\frac{5}{6} > \frac{3}{8}$.

To compare fractions accurately, both fractions need to have the same denominator. This is called the **common denominator.** For instance, we know that $\frac{11}{16}$ is greater than $\frac{3}{16}$ because 11 is greater than 3. If the fractions that you are comparing have different denominators, you must find a common denominator and raise the fractions to higher terms.

TO FIND A COMMON DENOMINATOR

Consider the larger denominator. Does the other denominator divide into it evenly?

If the answer is *yes*:

1. The larger denominator is the common denominator.
2. Raise the other fraction to higher terms to match the common denominator.

Example

Compare $\frac{1}{4}$ and $\frac{3}{8}$.

8 is the larger denominator.

8 is evenly divisible by 4.

Thus, 8 is the common denominator.

Raise to higher terms: $\frac{1}{4} \times \frac{2}{2} = \frac{2}{8}$

We know that $\frac{2}{8} < \frac{3}{8}$.

So $\frac{1}{4} < \frac{3}{8}$.

If the answer is *no*:

1. Find the multiple of the larger denominator that is evenly divisible by the other denominator.
2. The multiple will be the common denominator.
3. Raise both fractions to higher terms to match the common denominator.

Example

Compare $\frac{2}{3}$ and $\frac{3}{4}$.

4 is the larger denominator.

4 is *not* evenly divisible by 3.

The multiples of 4 are 4, 8, 12, 16, and so on. 12 is the multiple that is evenly divisible by 3.

Raise both fractions to 12ths.

$\frac{2}{3} \times \frac{4}{4} = \frac{8}{12}$ $\quad$ $\frac{3}{4} \times \frac{3}{3} = \frac{9}{12}$

We know that $\frac{8}{12} < \frac{9}{12}$.

So $\frac{2}{3} < \frac{3}{4}$.

Comparing Fractions and Decimals

We can compare fractions and decimals by first changing the decimal to a fraction or the fraction to a decimal. The calculator can help you quickly change a fraction to a decimal by dividing the denominator into the numerator.

Example	Compare $\frac{7}{8}$ and .75.	
STEP 1	Change $\frac{7}{8}$ to a decimal.	$\frac{7}{8} = 8\overline{)7.000}$ = .875
STEP 2	Write .75 with 3 decimal places.	$.75 = .750$
STEP 3	Compare .875 and .750.	$.875 > .750$
STEP 4	Conclusion:	$\frac{7}{8} > .75$

EXERCISE 5

Comparing Numbers

Directions: Compare the numbers as indicated. Use your calculator as needed.

Select the larger number in each pair of numbers below.

1. $\frac{7}{8}$ or $\frac{3}{5}$ **2.** $\frac{2}{3}$ or $\frac{4}{9}$ **3.** $\frac{3}{10}$ or $\frac{3}{4}$

Insert the appropriate symbol (< , > , or =) between each pair of numbers below.

4. 3 ☐ 8 **5.** 6 ☐ 0 **6.** $\frac{3}{8}$ ☐ $\frac{1}{8}$ **7.** $\frac{3}{10}$ ☐ $\frac{4}{5}$

8. $2\frac{3}{8}$ ☐ $\frac{5}{2}$ **9.** $\frac{5}{6}$ ☐ $\frac{8}{9}$ **10.** .3 ☐ $\frac{1}{4}$ **11.** $\frac{1}{2}$ ☐ $\frac{6}{12}$

12. $\frac{9}{9}$ ☐ $\frac{2}{2}$ **13.** .07 ☐ .0873 **14.** .4 ☐ .27 **15.** $\frac{3}{5}$ ☐ .6

Answers are on page 929.

Operations with Fractions

Adding and Subtracting Fractions

When you are asked to add or subtract fractions or mixed numbers, you must be sure that the fractions have common denominators. If they don't, rewrite the fractions with common denominators before adding or subtracting.

TO ADD FRACTIONS

1. Be sure all fractions have common denominators.
2. Add the numerators.
3. Put the total over the common denominator.
4. Reduce the answer to the lowest terms.

Example 1 Add $\frac{3}{8}$ and $\frac{1}{8}$.

STEP 1 Since the denominators are the same, add the numerators.

STEP 2 Reduce the answer.

$$\frac{3}{8} + \frac{1}{8} = \frac{4 \div 4}{8 \div 4} = \mathbf{\frac{1}{2}}$$

Example 2 Add $\frac{1}{10}$ and $\frac{3}{5}$.

STEP 1 Find the common denominator and equivalent fractions.

STEP 2 Add the numerators.

$$\frac{1}{10} = \frac{1}{10}$$
$$+\frac{3 \times 2}{5 \times 2} = \frac{6}{10}$$
$$\mathbf{\frac{7}{10}}$$

Example 3 $\frac{2}{3} + \frac{1}{6} + \frac{3}{4}$

STEP 1 Find the common denominator for all numbers.

STEP 2 Add the numerators and put them over the denominator.

STEP 3 Change the improper fraction to a mixed number.

$$\frac{2}{3} = \frac{8}{12}$$
$$\frac{1}{6} = \frac{2}{12}$$
$$+\frac{3}{4} = \frac{9}{12}$$
$$\frac{19}{12} = \mathbf{1\frac{7}{12}}$$

Check your work by adding the fractions on your calculator. When you add three or more fractions, enter the first fraction, then the plus sign, then the second fraction, then another plus sign, then the last fraction, followed by the equal sign. The calculator keeps a running sum and always reduces the final answer.

You follow the same method for adding mixed numbers. Add the fractions first, in case you need to combine your fraction total with the whole numbers.

TO ADD MIXED NUMBERS

1. Be sure fractional parts have common denominators.
2. Add the fractional parts. Simplify to a mixed number, if necessary.
3. Add the whole numbers.
4. Be sure your answer is in lowest terms.

<u>**Example 4**</u> Alfonso bought $1\frac{3}{4}$ pounds of chicken and $6\frac{2}{3}$ pounds of ground beef for the picnic. How much did he buy altogether?

STEP 1 Find the common denominator: 12.

STEP 2 Add the fractions.

STEP 3 Simplify the improper fraction $\frac{17}{12}$ to the mixed number $1\frac{5}{12}$.

STEP 4 Add the whole numbers.

STEP 5 Add $1\frac{5}{12}$ to 7 to get $8\frac{5}{12}$.

$$\begin{array}{rl} 1\frac{3}{4} & = 1\frac{9}{12} \\ +\ 6\frac{2}{3} & = 6\frac{8}{12} \\ \hline & 7\frac{17}{12} = 7 + 1\frac{5}{12} = \mathbf{8\frac{5}{12}} \end{array}$$

The process of subtracting fractions is similar to adding fractions.

TO SUBTRACT FRACTIONS

1. Be sure the fractions have common denominators.
2. Subtract the numerators.
3. Put the difference over the common denominator.
4. Be sure your answer is in lowest terms.

Example 5 $\frac{7}{16} - \frac{3}{16}$

$$\begin{array}{r} \frac{7}{16} \\ -\frac{3}{16} \\ \hline \frac{4}{16} = \mathbf{\frac{1}{4}} \end{array}$$

Example 6 $\frac{11}{12} - \frac{3}{8}$

$$\begin{array}{rcr} \frac{11}{12} & = & \frac{22}{24} \\ -\frac{3}{8} & = & \frac{9}{24} \\ \hline & & \mathbf{\frac{13}{24}} \end{array}$$

Sometimes there is an extra step when you subtract mixed numbers. You may have to regroup a whole number to a fraction before you can subtract a fraction that is too large.

Tip

To rewrite 1 borrowed from the whole number when you regroup, use the denominator of the fraction subtracted.

Example 7 $1 - \frac{3}{8}$

(Replace the 1 with $\frac{8}{8}$.)

$$\begin{array}{rcr} 1 & = & \frac{8}{8} \\ -\frac{3}{8} & = & -\frac{3}{8} \\ \hline & & \mathbf{\frac{5}{8}} \end{array}$$

Example 8 $1 - \frac{5}{6}$

(Replace the 1 with $\frac{6}{6}$.)

$$\begin{array}{rcr} 1 & = & \frac{6}{6} \\ -\frac{5}{6} & = & -\frac{5}{6} \\ \hline & & \mathbf{\frac{1}{6}} \end{array}$$

TO SUBTRACT MIXED NUMBERS

1. Be sure the fractions have common denominators.
2. Subtract the numerators. If you have to regroup 1 borrowed from a whole number, convert it to an improper fraction with the same denominator and add it to the original fraction if there is one.
3. Subtract the whole numbers.

Example 9 The jockey needs to lose $9\frac{1}{4}$ pounds. He has already lost $5\frac{3}{4}$ pounds. How much does he have left to lose?

STEP 1 Notice that you can't take $\frac{3}{4}$ from $\frac{1}{4}$.

STEP 2 Subtract 1 whole from 9, leaving 8.

STEP 3 Regroup 1 whole as $\frac{4}{4}$ and add that to $\frac{1}{4}$ to get $\frac{5}{4}$.

STEP 4 Subtract the fractions and whole numbers.

STEP 5 Reduce the fraction.

$$9\frac{1}{4} = 8\frac{4}{4} + \frac{1}{4} = 8\frac{5}{4}$$
$$-5\frac{3}{4} = \qquad -5\frac{3}{4}$$
$$3\frac{2}{4} = \mathbf{3\frac{1}{2}\ pounds}$$

EXERCISE 6

Adding and Subtracting Fractions

Directions: Solve each problem. Check each answer with your calculator.

1. $\frac{1}{10} + \frac{7}{10}$	**2.** $\frac{2}{3} + \frac{1}{4}$	**3.** $\frac{3}{8} + \frac{1}{12}$	**4.** $\frac{5}{6} + \frac{1}{6}$
5. $1\frac{5}{12} + 6\frac{4}{12}$	**6.** $4\frac{1}{5} + 3\frac{2}{7}$	**7.** $4\frac{2}{9} + 5\frac{1}{9}$	**8.** $3\frac{7}{8} + 2\frac{5}{6} + 3\frac{1}{3}$
9. $\frac{9}{10} - \frac{3}{10}$	**10.** $\frac{5}{8} - \frac{1}{2}$	**11.** $\frac{4}{5} - \frac{1}{2}$	**12.** $\frac{11}{16} - \frac{5}{16}$
13. $4\frac{3}{4} - 2\frac{5}{8}$	**14.** $25\frac{1}{6} - 11\frac{1}{2}$	**15.** $10 - 4\frac{2}{3}$	**16.** $20 - \frac{4}{5}$

Answers are on page 929.

Multiplying Fractions

Unlike adding and subtracting fractions, there is no need for common denominators when you multiply and divide. You will multiply straight across, multiplying numerator by numerator and denominator by denominator. You can reduce before you multiply.

TO MULTIPLY FRACTIONS

1. Reduce numerators and denominators by canceling before you multiply.
2. Multiply straight across.
3. Be sure your answer is reduced to lowest terms.

Example 1 $\frac{3}{4} \times \frac{1}{2}$

In this example there is no reducing. Multiply straight across. $\frac{3}{4} \times \frac{1}{2} = \mathbf{\frac{3}{8}}$

Example 2 $\frac{6}{15} \times \frac{5}{12}$

STEP 1 The 15 and 5 can be divided by 5. $\frac{6}{{}_3\cancel{15}} \times \frac{\cancel{5}^1}{12}$

STEP 2 The 6 and 12 can be divided by 6. $\frac{{}^1\cancel{6}}{{}_3\cancel{15}} \times \frac{\cancel{5}^1}{\cancel{12}_2}$

STEP 3 Multiply straight across. $\frac{1}{3} \times \frac{1}{2} = \mathbf{\frac{1}{6}}$

You can also cancel with three fractions. Sometimes you have to "jump" over the middle number.

Example 3 $\frac{3}{8} \times \frac{4}{7} \times \frac{5}{9}$

STEP 1 Divide both the 3 and 9 by 3.
Divide both the 4 and 8 by 4. $\frac{{}^1\cancel{3}}{{}_2\cancel{8}} \times \frac{\cancel{4}^1}{7} \times \frac{5}{\cancel{9}_3}$

STEP 2 Multiply straight across. $\frac{1}{2} \times \frac{1}{7} \times \frac{5}{3} = \mathbf{\frac{5}{42}}$

TO MULTIPLY MIXED NUMBERS

1. Change mixed numbers to improper fractions.
2. Reduce numerators and denominators divisible by the same number.
3. Multiply straight across.
4. Be sure your answer is reduced to lowest terms.

Example 4 shows multiplying mixed numbers.

Example 4 Holly usually jogs $2\frac{1}{3}$ miles daily. She jogged the full distance on 3 days and $\frac{1}{2}$ the distance on another day. How many miles did she jog in all?

STEP 1 Change all mixed numbers to improper fractions. $2\frac{1}{3} \times 3\frac{1}{2} = \frac{7}{3} \times \frac{7}{2}$

STEP 2 Multiply and change the improper fraction back to mixed numbers. $\frac{7}{3} \times \frac{7}{2} = \frac{49}{6} = \mathbf{8\frac{1}{6}}$

Tip

Sometimes you may have to multiply a whole number by a fraction or a mixed number. Rewrite the whole number over 1 and then multiply as usual.

For example, 4 can be written as $\frac{4}{1}$, so

$$\frac{1}{2} \times 4 = \frac{1}{\cancel{2}_1} \times \frac{\cancel{4}^2}{1} = \frac{2}{1} = 2.$$

EXERCISE 7

Multiplying Fractions

Directions: Solve each problem. Check your answers using the calculator. Grid the answers to problems 1–2. Use / for the fraction bar.

1. $\frac{6}{15} \times \frac{5}{12}$

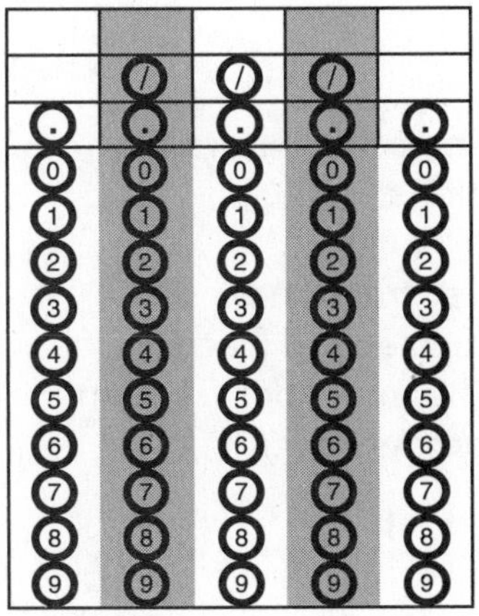

2. $\frac{3}{8} \times \frac{2}{15} \times \frac{6}{7}$

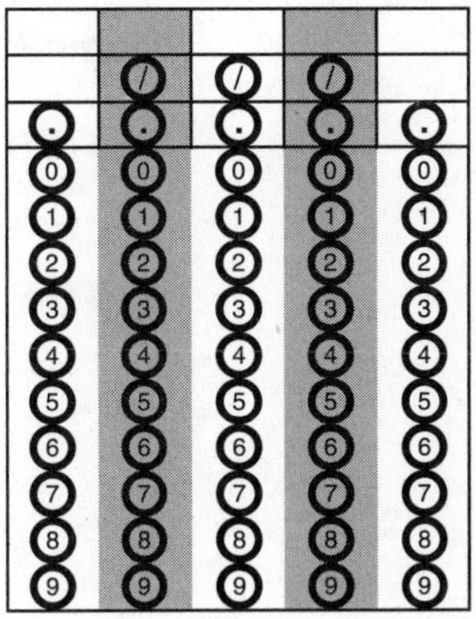

3. $8\frac{1}{6} \times 4$

4. $\frac{5}{9} \times \frac{2}{5} \times \frac{3}{8}$

5. $2\frac{1}{2} \times 2\frac{1}{3}$

6. $2\frac{3}{4} \times \frac{6}{7}$

7. $1\frac{3}{10} \times 5$

8. $3\frac{3}{8} \times 1\frac{3}{9}$

Answers are on page 930.

Dividing Fractions

Division is the opposite operation of multiplication. For instance, when we divide a number by 2, we are actually multiplying by $\frac{1}{2}$.

The fraction $\frac{1}{2}$ is called the **reciprocal** of 2. Two numbers whose product is 1 are reciprocals. Because $5 \times \frac{1}{5} = 1$, the numbers 5 and $\frac{1}{5}$ are reciprocals. To find the reciprocal of a number, you invert it, which means you exchange the numerator and denominator.

TO DIVIDE FRACTIONS OR MIXED NUMBERS

1. Change mixed numbers to improper fractions.
2. Multiply the first fraction by the reciprocal of the second.
3. Change any improper fractions back to mixed numbers.

To divide a fraction, follow the method shown below.

Example 1 Divide $\frac{7}{8}$ by $\frac{3}{4}$.

STEP 1 Multiply the first fraction by the reciprocal of the second. $\frac{7}{8} \div \frac{3}{4} = \frac{7}{8} \times \frac{4}{3}$

STEP 2 Multiply across and change the improper fraction to a mixed number. $\frac{7}{\cancel{8}_2} \times \frac{\cancel{4}^1}{3} = \frac{7}{6} = \mathbf{1\frac{1}{6}}$

To divide a mixed number, first change any mixed numbers to improper fractions.

Example 2 $4\frac{2}{3} \div 1\frac{1}{2}$

STEP 1 Change both mixed numbers to improper fractions. $4\frac{2}{3} \div 1\frac{1}{2} = \frac{14}{3} \div \frac{3}{2}$

STEP 2 Multiply the first fraction by the reciprocal of the second fraction. Then change the improper fraction back to a mixed number. $\frac{14}{3} \times \frac{2}{3} = \frac{28}{9} = \mathbf{3\frac{1}{9}}$

EXERCISE 8

Dividing Fractions

Directions: Solve each problem. Check your work using the calculator.

1. $\frac{4}{10} \div \frac{2}{3}$

2. $\frac{3}{7} \div \frac{6}{35}$

3. $1\frac{3}{8} \div 11$

4. $\frac{2}{5} \div 4$

5. $3\frac{2}{3} \div 1\frac{1}{2}$

6. $9 \div 2\frac{1}{2}$

Answers are on page 930.

Simplifying Fraction Problems

The best way to simplify fraction word problems is to **restate** the problem using whole numbers. Many times the fractions are intimidating and make it difficult to figure out what to do in the problem. Let's look at a few examples of restating fraction problems.

Example 1 An upholstery cleaner schedules $1\frac{1}{2}$-hour appointments for each couch to be cleaned. How many couches can he clean in a $7\frac{1}{2}$-hour work day?

Restated: An upholstery cleaner schedules 2-hour appointments for each couch to be cleaned. How many couches can he clean in an 8-hour workday?

Solution: After restating the problem it seems even more obvious that it is a division problem to see how many 2-hour segments are in an 8-hour day. Therefore, solve the problem using the original numbers.

$$7\frac{1}{2} \div 1\frac{1}{2} = \frac{15}{2} \div \frac{3}{2} = \frac{\overset{5}{\cancel{15}}}{\underset{1}{\cancel{2}}} \times \frac{\overset{1}{\cancel{2}}}{\underset{1}{\cancel{3}}} = 5$$

Be sure that the number following the division symbol is the number that represents the type of segments you are dividing by. In this example you are dividing by $1\frac{1}{2}$-hour segments.

The cleaner will clean **5 couches.**

Tip

You can always look for key words or basic concepts that indicate the operation to use. A frequently used key word in fraction problems is "of." **This always indicates multiplication.**

For example, a problem may ask you to find $\frac{3}{4}$ *of* \$24.

Multiply: $24 \times \frac{3}{4} = \frac{\overset{6}{\cancel{24}}}{1} \times \frac{3}{\underset{1}{\cancel{4}}} = 18.$

So $\frac{3}{4}$ *of* \$24 is **\$18.**

Item Sets

Some problems on the Mathematics Test will be presented as item sets. An **item set** refers to information given in a paragraph or two or in an illustration. Then several questions based on that information (usually 3 to 5 questions) will follow.

Tip

The key to solving questions based on item sets is choosing only the information needed to answer that particular question.

The next group of problems follows the item set format. These problems require you to use your skills with whole numbers, decimals, and fractions.

EXERCISE 9

Item Sets

Directions: Solve each problem. Use your calculator to check each answer.

Questions 1–3 are based on the information below.

Fidel wants to build bookshelves in his den. He needs 8 shelves, each $5\frac{1}{4}$ feet long. He must buy the lumber for the shelves in 6-foot lengths and then cut the $5\frac{1}{4}$-foot pieces from those lengths. The cost of the lumber is 98 cents per linear foot.

1. How much will the lumber cost for all of the shelves?

(1) \$5.88 **(2)** \$7.84 **(3)** \$47.04 **(4)** \$252 **(5)** \$470.40

2. How many linear feet of lumber will he waste by cutting?

(1) $\frac{3}{4}$ **(2)** $4\frac{1}{2}$ **(3)** 6 **(4)** 8 **(5)** 10

3. The cost of varnishing all of the shelves will amount to an additional \$12. Fidel can buy pre-varnished $5\frac{1}{4}$-foot length shelves for \$13.95 each. How much will he save if he does the cutting and varnishing himself?

(1) \$52.56 **(2)** \$59.04 **(3)** \$73.24 **(4)** \$83.70 **(5)** \$111.60

Questions 4–6 are based on the diagram below.

The owner of a campground is planning to add two new roads, Birch Trail and Pine Way. The campground area is $\frac{7}{8}$ miles deep and $\frac{3}{4}$ mile wide.

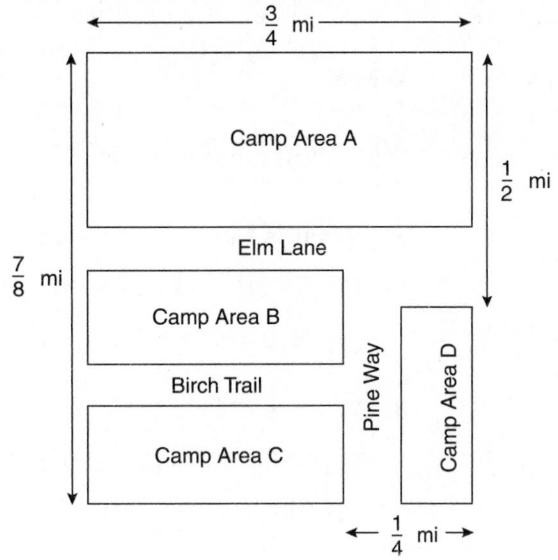

4. What is the length of Pine Way?

(1) $\frac{1}{8}$ mile **(2)** $\frac{3}{8}$ mile **(3)** $\frac{3}{4}$ mile **(4)** $1\frac{3}{8}$ miles

(5) Not enough information is given.

5. What is the total length of the two new roads?

(1) $\frac{1}{8}$ mile **(2)** $\frac{5}{12}$ mile **(3)** $\frac{7}{8}$ mile **(4)** $1\frac{1}{4}$ miles **(5)** $1\frac{5}{8}$ miles

6. How wide is Elm Lane?

(1) $\frac{1}{16}$ mile **(2)** $\frac{1}{8}$ mile **(3)** $\frac{3}{16}$ mile **(4)** $\frac{1}{4}$ mile

(5) Not enough information is given.

Questions 7–9 are based on the information below.

Mike Maloney gets paid an hourly wage for the first 40 hours he works. He gets $1\frac{1}{2}$ times his hourly wage for any overtime hours past the original 40 hours. The chart below shows his time sheet for the second week in April.

WEEK	NAME	EMPLOYEE #	HOURLY RATE	HOURS
4/8 – 4/14	Mike Maloney	08395	$12.72	$43\frac{1}{4}$

7. What is Mike's hourly wage per hour of overtime?

(1) $6.36 **(2)** $15.90 **(3)** $19.08 **(4)** $25.44

(5) Not enough information is given.

8. What is Mike's total pay for the third week in April?

(1) $508.80 **(2)** $550.14 **(3)** $570.81 **(4)** $825.21

(5) Not enough information is given.

9. Which expression represents Mike's total pay for the second week in April?

(1) $(40 \times 12.72) + (3\frac{1}{4} \times 12.72)$ **(2)** $40 \times 1\frac{1}{2} \times 3\frac{1}{4} \times 12.72$

(3) $(12.72 \times 40) + (1\frac{1}{2} \times 12.72 \times 3\frac{1}{4})$ **(4)** $12.72 \times 1\frac{1}{2} \times 43\frac{1}{4}$

(5) Not enough information is given.

Answers are on page 930.

EXERCISE 10

Fraction Review

Directions: Solve each problem. Use your calculator to check your work.

1. An 8-foot post was set $2\frac{3}{4}$ feet into the ground. What is the exact length of the post above ground?

(1) $5\frac{1}{4}$ ft **(2)** $5\frac{3}{4}$ ft **(3)** $6\frac{3}{4}$ ft **(4)** $10\frac{3}{4}$ ft
(5) Not enough information is given.

2. If sales tax is $8\frac{1}{2}$ cents per dollar, how much tax would you pay on a $6 item?

(1) 12¢ **(2)** 48¢ **(3)** $48\frac{1}{2}$¢ **(4)** 51¢ **(5)** 54¢

3. Using the diagram below, find the total distance traveled on a trek from school to library to gas station to home.

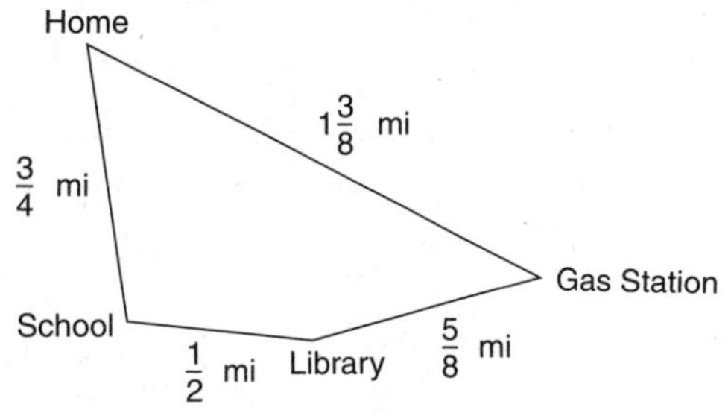

(1) $1\frac{12}{22}$ mi **(2)** $2\frac{1}{2}$ mi **(3)** $2\frac{4}{6}$ mi **(4)** $3\frac{1}{4}$ mi **(5)** 4 mi

4. A dosage of medicine is $1\frac{1}{2}$ milliliters. How many dosages can be given from a bottle containing 30 milliliters?

(1) 5 **(2)** 10 **(3)** 15 **(4)** 20 **(5)** 30

5. Find the total weight of 2 cartons of potatoes, including the weight of the cartons as well as the weight of the contents of the cartons. Each carton contains $16\frac{3}{4}$ pounds of potatoes.

(1) $8\frac{3}{8}$ lb **(2)** $16\frac{3}{4}$ lb **(3)** $33\frac{1}{2}$ lb **(4)** $18\frac{3}{4}$ lb
(5) Not enough information is given.

6. Find the missing length *l* in the drawing below.

(1) $4\frac{3}{4}$ in.

(2) $5\frac{3}{4}$ in.

(3) 6 in.

(4) $8\frac{1}{8}$ in.

(5) Not enough information is given.

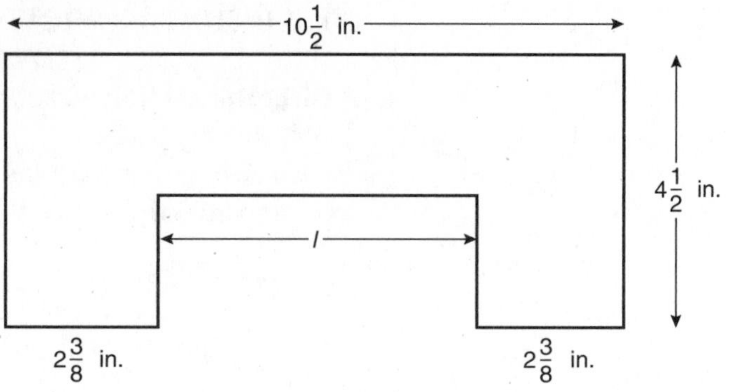

7. The price of round-trip airfare to Dallas is \$285. How much will it cost a family of four if the husband pays full fare, the wife pays $\frac{2}{3}$ of full fare, and the two children each pay $\frac{1}{2}$ of the regular price?

(1) \$475 **(2)** \$570 **(3)** \$617.50 **(4)** \$760 **(5)** \$1140

8. Mr. Cortez owns a $10\frac{1}{2}$-acre tract of land, and he plans to subdivide this tract into $\frac{1}{4}$-acre lots. He must first set aside $\frac{1}{6}$ of the total land for roads. Which of the following expressions shows how many lots this tract will yield?

(1) $10\frac{1}{2} \div \frac{1}{4} - \frac{1}{6}$ **(2)** $(10\frac{1}{2} - \frac{1}{6}) \div \frac{1}{4}$ **(3)** $[10\frac{1}{2} - (10\frac{1}{2} \times \frac{1}{6})] \div \frac{1}{4}$

(4) $10\frac{1}{2} \times \frac{1}{4} - \frac{1}{6}$ **(5)** Not enough information is given.

9. A carpenter wanted three pieces of wood each $1\frac{5}{8}$ feet long. If he planned to cut them from a 6-foot piece of wood, how much of the piece would be left?

(1) $1\frac{1}{8}$ ft **(2)** 3 ft **(3)** $4\frac{3}{8}$ ft **(4)** $4\frac{7}{8}$ ft

(5) Not enough information is given.

10. A politician wants to get her message to $\frac{2}{3}$ of the population of 48,000 in Springfield. However, her advertising campaign reaches $\frac{3}{4}$ of the number she intended. How many people does she actually reach?

(1) 16,000 **(2)** 24,000 **(3)** 36,000 **(4)** 68,000 **(5)** 72,000

Go to **www.GEDMath.com** for additional practice and instruction!

CHAPTER 5

Number Relationships

In previous sections you have considered whole numbers, decimals, fractions, and their relationships. In this section you will expand your understanding of number relationships by looking at **signed numbers,** which include all positive numbers, zero, and all negative numbers.

Number Line

The **number line** shown below represents all of the real numbers that you use. You use **negative numbers** (numbers less than zero), **zero,** and **positive numbers** (numbers greater than zero).

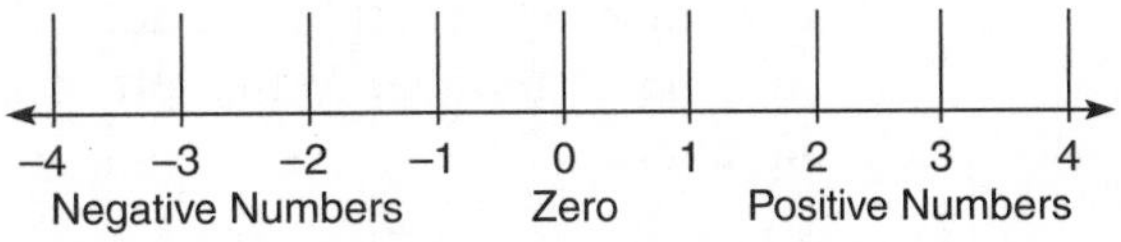

Positive numbers may have a plus sign in front of them, like +7, or no sign in front, like 7. Negative numbers have a minus sign in front of them, like –2 (read as "negative 2"). The graph of a signed number is a dot on the number line. On the number line below, you see the graph of –3.5, –1, and 3.

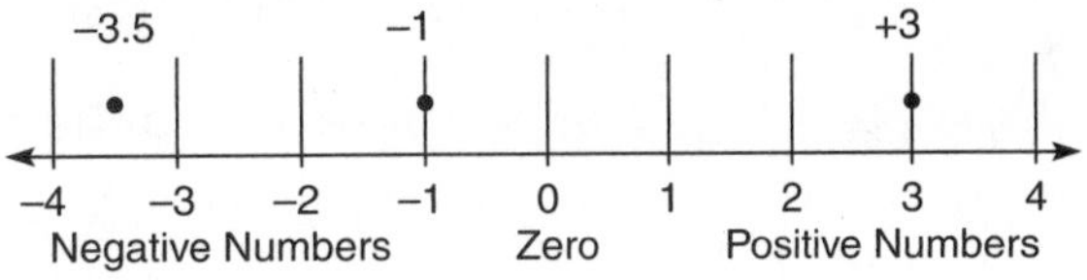

You can enter both positive and negative numbers on your calculator. To enter a positive number, you simply enter the digits. You do not need to enter the + sign. To enter a negative number, you first enter the digits and then use the +/– key to make the number negative.

Key: +/– indicates a negative number

PROCESS	KEY IN:	DISPLAY	Example: –5
Step 1	AC to clear the display	0.	0.
Step 2	digits	digits	5.
Step 3	negative symbol	negative number	–5.

You can use the number line to show the relationship among signed numbers. A number to the right of another number **is greater than** (>) the other number. A number to the left of another number **is less than** (<) the other number.

Tip

Remember that the symbols > and < always point to the smaller number.

Example 1 1 > –3 because 1 is to the right of –3.

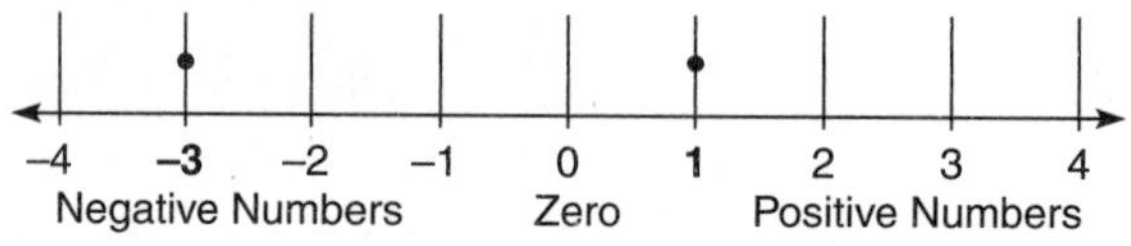

Example 2 –2.5 > – 4 because –2.5 is to the right of –4.

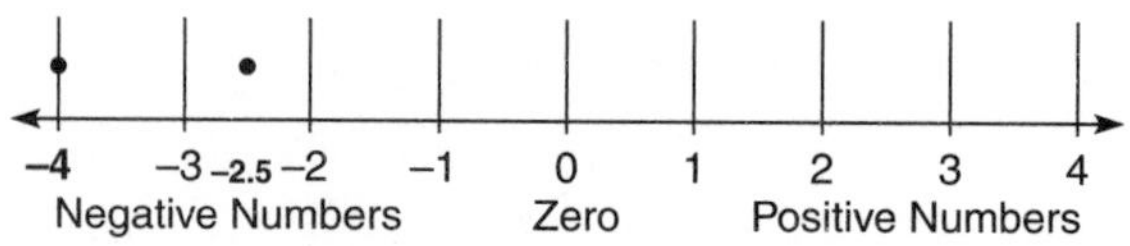

Example 3 $-3\frac{1}{2} < -\frac{1}{2}$ because $-3\frac{1}{2}$ is to the left of $-\frac{1}{2}$.

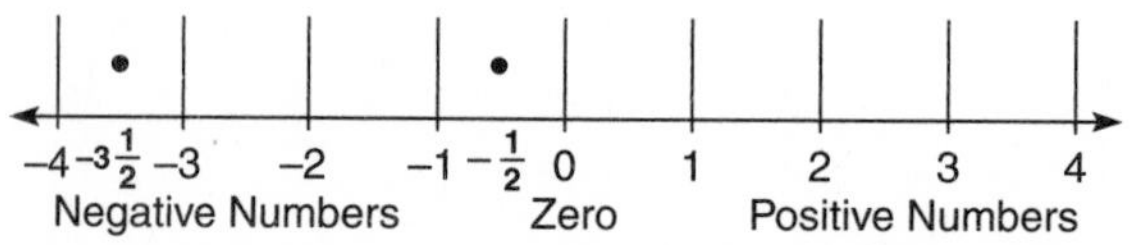

EXERCISE 1

Number Line

Directions: Use the > and < symbols to identify the relationships between the numbers graphed below.

1.

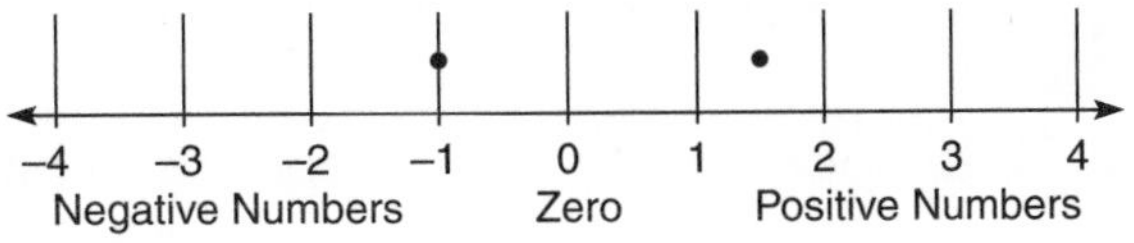

2.

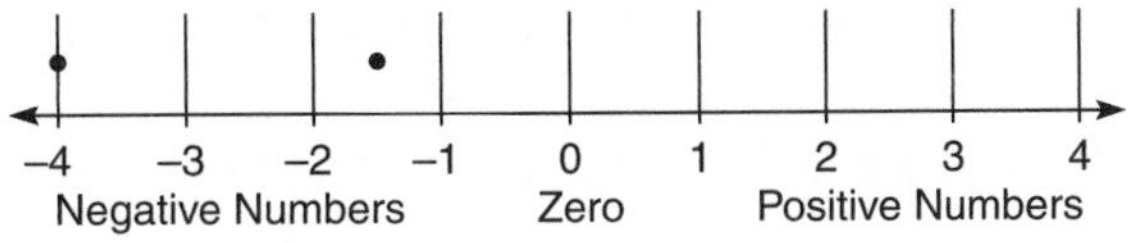

3.

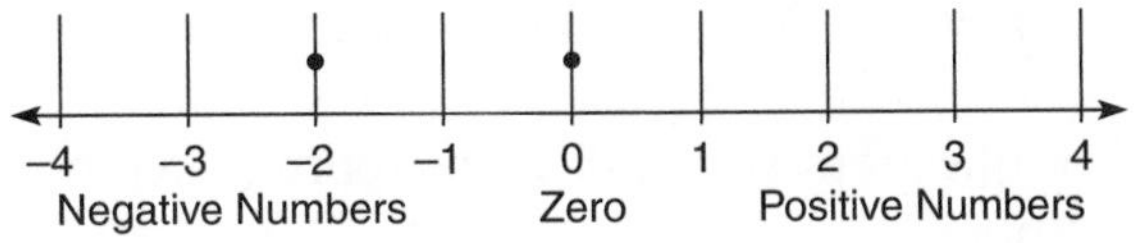

4.

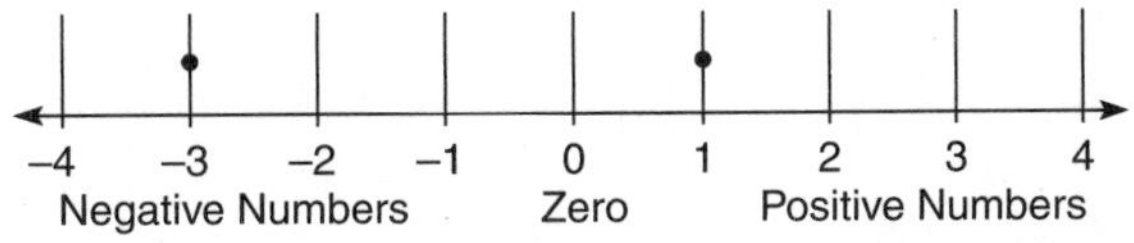

Answers are on page 930.

Absolute Value

The **absolute value** is the distance on the number line between zero and the number. Since distance is always a positive value, the absolute value of a number is always positive or zero. The symbol for absolute value is | |.

$|7| = 7$ **The absolute value of 7 is 7.**

$|-7| = 7$ **The absolute value of –7 is 7.**

Tip

The absolute value of a positive number is the same positive number. The absolute value of a negative number is the same number without the negative sign. The absolute value of zero is zero.

EXERCISE 2

Signed Numbers

Directions: Solve each problem. For questions 1–5, represent the quantities with either positive or negative numbers.

1. a loss of $12
2. a temperature 15° below zero Fahrenheit
3. a three-yard loss on the second down of a football game
4. a credit of $75 on your credit card
5. a stock rise of 4.5 points

For questions 6–11, place the correct symbol, < or >, between the pairs of numbers.

6. 7   11   **7.** –9   –4   **8.** –3   1

9. 0   –4   **10.** –6   2.4   **11.** $-\frac{1}{4}$ $-\frac{1}{2}$

For questions 12–15, find the absolute values.

12. $|9|$ **13.** $|-\frac{1}{2}|$ **14.** $|2\frac{3}{4}|$ **15.** $|-3|$

Answers are on page 930.

Operations with Signed Numbers

Signed numbers can be added, subtracted, multiplied, and divided. Let's use a personal financial situation to understand these operations with signed numbers.

Todd has a part-time job while attending the technical institute. In the month of April, he earns $132, $120, $180, $49, $68, and $75. (These are all positive values.) His total earnings are $624. When you combine all the positive numbers, you get a larger positive number.

During the month of April, Todd pays the following bills: car insurance, $105; gas, $88; lunches, $100; and rent, $290. (These are all negative values.) His total expenses are $583. When you combine all his bills, you get a larger negative number, which can be written –$583.

To find out how much money Todd has left at the end of April, you have to find the difference between his income (the positive total) and his expenses (the negative total). If his income is larger, he'll have a positive amount left (profit). If his expenses are larger than his income, he'll be in a negative situation. (He'll owe money.) The difference between +624 and –583 is +41. Todd has a profit of $41.

Combining Signed Numbers

The first two rules about combining signed numbers are the same ones that you just used to understand Todd's financial situation.

COMBINING SIGNED NUMBERS

1. If the numbers being combined are all positive or all negative, ADD THE NUMBERS AND KEEP THE SAME SIGN.

Example 1 $8 + 7 = 15$ (both positive and the result is positive)

Example 2 $-8 - 7 = -15$ (both negative and the result is negative)

2. If the numbers being combined are opposite in sign, SUBTRACT THE NUMBERS AND USE THE SIGN FROM THE NUMBER WITH THE LARGER ABSOLUTE VALUE.

Example 3

$-8 + 7 = -1$

sign of larger number

Example 4

$-7 + 8 = +1$ (or just 1)

sign of larger number

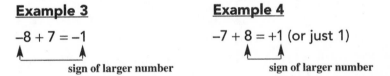

The next problem contains some positive and some negative numbers. Use both rules to come up with the answer.

Example $-6 + 1 + 14 - 2 - 8 + 6 - 9$

STEP 1 Combine the positive numbers. $1 + 14 + 6 = 21$

STEP 2 Combine the negative numbers. $-6 - 2 - 8 - 9 = -25$

STEP 3 Find the difference between 21 and 25, which is four. $25 - 21 = 4$

STEP 4 Take the negative sign because $|-25| > |21|$. $-25 + 21 = -4$

Tip

Notice that –25 indicates that there are more negatives than the 21 positives, so the answer has to be negative.

EXERCISE 3

Combining Signed Numbers

Directions: Solve each problem. Check your answers with a calculator.

1. 7 + 8 **2.** 6 – 8 **3.** –3 + 2 **4.** –9 – 8

5. –3 – 2 **6.** –127 + 94 **7.** 140 – 236 **8.** –12 + 6 + 3

9. 16 + 23 – 4 **10.** –5 – 7 – 1 – 6 **11.** 5.2 – 6.7 + 5.3 **12.** –4.5 – 3.2

Answers are on page 930.

Eliminating Double Signs

Sometimes you encounter a number that has two signs in front of it. You always want to **eliminate** double signs. There are two rules for doing this.

ELIMINATING DOUBLE SIGNS

1. If the double signs are the same, replace them with a + sign.

Example 1 +(+3) = +3

Example 2 – (–8) = + 8

Example 3 – 4 – (–12) = – 4 + 12 = +8

Same double signs Replace with + sign

(Note: a double negative changes the following number to a positive.)

2. If the double signs are opposite, replace them with a – sign.

Example 4 +(– 4) = – 4

Example 5 –(+2) = – 2

Example 6 5 + (–7) = 5 – 7 = –2

Opposite double signs Replace with – sign

EXERCISE 4

Eliminating Double Signs

Directions: Solve each problem. Check your answers using a calculator.

1. $-6 - (-2)$ **2.** $-6 + (-2) - (-9)$ **3.** $3 - (+8)$

4. A running back on a football team makes the following yardage on six plays: +23, –4, +8, +3, –6, and –2. What is his total gain or loss?

5. What is the drop in temperature if the thermometer goes from 12°F to –7°F?

6. At Arlington Park Racetrack, Larry had $140 to begin the day. On the first race, he won $56; on the second race, he lost $14; on the third race, he lost $32; on the fourth race, he lost $18; on the fifth race, he won $26. How much money did he have at the end of the 5 races?

Answers are on page 930.

Multiplying and Dividing Signed Numbers

Let's return to Todd and his finances to understand the multiplication and division of signed numbers. If Todd earns $8 per hour and works 7 hours, then he earns 7 × $8, or $56. A positive number $8 times a positive number 7 is a positive number $56.

If Todd had to pay $8 per day to park in the parking lot for the past seven days, how much *more* money did he have seven days *ago*? He had (–7) × (–8) or $56 *more* 7 days ago than he has now. A negative number (–7) times a negative number (–8) equals a positive number (56).

Suppose Todd spends $5 each day for lunch. How much does he spend in 7 days? The money *spent* (–5) times the number of days (7) equals –$35. The rules on the next page for multiplying and dividing signed numbers will help you solve problems such as those related to Todd's financial situation.

MULTIPLYING AND DIVIDING SIGNED NUMBERS

1. When you are multiplying or dividing two numbers with the *same* sign, the answer is *positive.*

Example 1	$8 \times 7 = 56$	Both positive, the answer is positive.
Example 2	$26 \div 2 = 13$	Both positive, the answer is positive.
Example 3	$-8 \times -7 = 56$	Both negative, the answer is positive.
Example 4	$(-26) \div (-2) = 13$	Both negative, the answer is positive.

2. When you are multiplying or dividing two numbers with *opposite* signs, the answer is *negative.*

Example 5	$-7(8) = -56$	Opposite in sign, the answer is negative.
Example 6	$\frac{-48}{12} = -4$	Opposite in sign, the answer is negative.
Example 7	$8(-7) = -56$	Opposite in sign, the answer is negative.
Example 8	$\frac{12}{-48} = -\frac{1}{4}$	Opposite in sign, the answer is negative.

Tip

When multiplying a string of signed numbers, count the number of negative signs to determine whether the answer is positive or negative.

*If there is an *even* number of negative signs, the answer will be *positive.*

*If there is an *odd* number of negative signs, the answer will be *negative.*

Example 1	$(-3)(-2)(-1)(-5) = \mathbf{30}$	(4 negative signs; 4 is even, answer is positive)
Example 2	$(-1)(-5)(-4) = \mathbf{-20}$	(3 negative signs; 3 is odd, answer is negative)

EXERCISE 5

Multiplying and Dividing Signed Numbers

Directions: Solve each problem. Check your answer with a calculator.

1. (8)(5) **2.** 12(–12) **3.** –5(6) **4.** –22(4)

5. –15(–15) **6.** (–9)(–4) **7.** (–6)(–7)(–2) **8.** –8(5)(0)

9. –25 ÷ 5 **10.** $\frac{-48}{-16}$ **11.** $\frac{7}{-14}$ **12.** $\frac{-50}{-10}$

13. The temperature fell $1\frac{1}{2}$° five days in a row. What was the total drop in temperature?

14. A-One Sales bought 9 cell phones at a cost of $246 each. How much does the company owe for the phones? (Express the answer as a negative number.)

Answers are on page 930.

EXERCISE 6

Using Signed Numbers in Problem Solving

Directions: Use your understanding of signed numbers to solve each problem below.

1. On a cold winter morning, the temperature at 3:00 A.M. was –12°, but it went up 25° by 11:00 A.M. By noon it had risen another 7°. What was the temperature at noon?

(1) 13° **(2)** 20° **(3)** 30° **(4)** 32° **(5)** 44°

2. When Heather got her paycheck, she immediately sat down to pay her bills. Her take-home pay was $575. She also received a bonus check from her employer for $125 and a tax refund of $46. Her bills included an insurance payment for $98, cleaning bill for $26, long distance phone charges of $38, and car payment of $310. If she also put $50 in her savings plan, which expression below shows how much spending money she had left?

(1) 575 + 125 – 46 – 98 – 26 – 38 – 310 – 50
(2) 575 + 125 + 46 –98 – 26 – 38 – 310 + 50
(3) 575 – 125 – 46 + 98 + 26 + 38 + 310 – 50
(4) 575 + 125 + 46 – (98 + 26 + 38 + 310 + 50)
(5) Not enough information is given.

For questions 3–5, use the following information.

Foods that Add Calories		Activities that Burn Off Calories	
1 slice of cheesecake	+475 calories	1 set of tennis	–200 calories
1 chocolate sundae	+560 calories	1 hour of swimming	–480 calories
1 soda pop (12 oz)	+105 calories	1 mile of walking	–172 calories
1 orange juice (8 oz)	+96 calories	1 hour of dancing	–264 calories
1 apple (medium)	+70 calories	1 hour cross-country skiing	–430 calories
3 chocolate chip cookies	+160 calories		

3. This afternoon, Mark had a chocolate sundae before playing three sets of tennis. After tennis, he had a glass of orange juice and six cookies. How many calories has he burned or gained during the afternoon?

(1) –40 **(2)** +216 **(3)** +376 **(4)** +616 **(5)** +1416

4. To the nearest tenth, how many miles would you need to walk to work off a slice of cheesecake and two 12-ounce bottles of soda pop?

(1) 2.4 **(2)** 2.8 **(3)** 3.4 **(4)** 4 **(5)** Not enough information is given.

5. How many calories are burned if you dance for 3 hours and swim for $\frac{1}{2}$ hour?

Answers are on page 931.

Go to **www.GEDMath.com** for additional practice and instruction!

CHAPTER 6

Statistics and Data Analysis

Mathematics is the study of number relationships. To set up a relationship, you begin with numerical information called **data.** When the data is collected and organized, it is called **statistics.** You can put the data into mathematical formats. For example, a fraction compares two parts; an operation relationship names a mathematical action such as subtraction; and an equation describes a rule for manipulating numbers. You use these formats and others to analyze data.

In this chapter you will develop skills with **data analysis** formats, including ratio, rate, proportion, percent, and probability. Further, you'll study methods of data analysis such as range, measures of central tendency, and data organization using tables, charts, and graphs.

Ratio and Rate

A **ratio** is a mathematical way of comparing two quantities. Some everyday uses of ratio are "Six out of every eight students in my class watched the World Series," "I drove 55 miles per hour on the expressway, and people were speeding by me," and "The recipe for cookies contained one cup of sugar for every two cups of flour."

If the ratio compares two quantities with different units that cannot be converted to a common unit, it is called a **rate.** For example, 55 *miles* per *hour* is a rate. Whether you call the comparison a ratio or a rate, it can be written as a fraction, as a comparison using the word *to,* or as a comparison using a colon. You can set up a ratio whenever you are comparing two numbers.

Tip

If you write a ratio as a fraction, reduce it but do not change to a mixed number. Improper fractions are acceptable. For instance, $\frac{3}{2}$ is preferred to $1\frac{1}{2}$ and $\frac{5}{1}$ is preferred to 5.

Example 1 Write a ratio for "six out of eight students."

The ratio is **6 to 8** or **6:8** or $\frac{6}{8}$. ($\frac{6}{8}$ can be reduced to $\frac{3}{4}$)

Example 2 Write a rate for "55 miles per hour."

The rate is **55 miles to 1 hour** or **55:1** or $\frac{55}{1}$.

Tip

The word *per* often tells you to set up a ratio. The ratio in Example 2 is a rate because it compares two different units: miles to hours.

Sometimes it is necessary to change the form of one of the numbers to make a comparison.

Example 3 Eggs cost 96 cents per dozen. What is the cost per egg?

First, you have to change one dozen eggs to 12 eggs to write the ratio.

$\frac{96 \text{ cents}}{12 \text{ eggs}} = \frac{8 \text{ cents}}{1 \text{ egg}}$ which means that each egg costs **8 cents.**

EXERCISE 1

Ratio and Rate

Directions: Write each comparison as a ratio or a rate in fraction form. Be sure to reduce each fraction completely. You can use your calculator to reduce the fractions. Remember that improper fractions are preferred to mixed numbers or whole numbers.

1. 3 miles to 12 miles
2. 15 minutes to 1 hour
3. 27 feet to 18 feet
4. 3 pounds of meat for 4 people
5. 88 feet in 8 seconds
6. 300 miles on 15 gallons of gas
7. $56 earned in 7 hours
8. $84 for 12 boards

Answers are on page 931.

Applications of Ratio

The real value of ratio is its application to real-life problem solving. For example, "Which is the better buy?" is a question frequently posed by shoppers. These problems can be solved by using ratios to compare the cost per unit of weight for each item. Many grocery stores post signs that show the cost per unit for each item.

Example There are three sizes of Wow Chow on the grocer's shelves. Which is the best buy?

Wow Chow
$2.79
for
3 pounds

Wow Chow
$4.45
for
5 pounds

Wow Chow
$15.40
for
20 pounds

To find the per-unit cost for each item, calculate the ratio of cost to one unit of weight by reducing the fraction using the denominator as the divisor. You can use your calculator to divide.

This is represented by the ratio $\frac{\text{cost}}{\text{weight}}$.

(1) $\frac{\$2.79}{3 \text{ pounds}} = \frac{\$.93}{1 \text{ pound}} = \$.93$ per pound

(2) $\frac{\$4.45}{5 \text{ pounds}} = \frac{\$.89}{1 \text{ pound}} = \$.89$ per pound

(3) $\frac{\$15.40}{20 \text{ pounds}} = \frac{\$.77}{1 \text{ pound}} = \$.77$ per pound

Notice that each ratio was reduced by the number in the denominator to get a per one unit cost. The 20-pound bag costs 77 cents per pound, the 5-pound bag costs 89 cents per pound, while the 3-pound bag costs 93 cents per pound. The 20-pound bag is the best buy. Now all you would need to decide is how much dog food you *really* want to buy.

EXERCISE 2

Applications of Ratio

Directions: Solve each problem.

Questions 1–3 are based on the information in the table below. Write each ratio as a fraction to compare the expenses.

PAINTER'S WEEKLY WORK EXPENSES

Tools	Supplies	Transportation	Telephone	TOTAL
$25	$120	$40	$15	$200

1. Compare the cost of supplies to total expenses.
2. The total expenses are how many times greater than the expense for transportation?
3. Find the ratio of supplies to tools.
4. A company has assets of $6,800,000 and liabilities of $1,700,000. What is the company's ratio of liabilities to assets?
5. In a tennis club of 750 members, 500 members are men. What is the ratio of female members to total membership?
6. You own 300 shares of Consolidated Technologies stock and receive a dividend of $729. What is the dividend per share?

Questions 7 and 8 are based on the information below.

The Miranda family purchased a 250-pound side of beef and had it packaged. They paid $365 for the side of beef. During the packaging, 75 pounds of beef were discarded as waste.

7. How many pounds of beef were packaged?
8. What was the cost per pound to the nearest penny for the packaged beef?

Answers are on page 931.

Proportion

A **proportion** is a statement that two ratios (fractions) are equal. The statement $\frac{7}{8} = \frac{14}{16}$ is an example of a proportion. In other words, it means "7 is to 8 as 14 is to 16." In a proportion you find that when you multiply the diagonal numbers, the results are equal. You can say that in a proportion the cross products are always equal. This fact can help you solve many math problems involving proportional relationships.

Example 1 $\frac{7}{8} = \frac{14}{16}$

$7 \times 16 = 112$ and $8 \times 14 = 112$ show that the cross products are equal. Notice that if the product 112 is divided by one factor, the result is the other factor. For instance, $112 \div 7 = 16$ because $7 \times 16 = 112$.

A useful type of proportion is one in which one of the ratios is not completely known. The missing quantity is represented by a symbol such as a letter of the alphabet. Example 2 shows how to solve for the missing quantity.

Example 2 If 3 apples cost 75 cents, find the cost of 20 apples.

Set up a proportion to solve the problem. Then solve the proportion for the missing quantity.

STEP 1 Set up the proportion where c represents the unknown cost of the apples. Notice that both fractions have apples in the numerator and money in the denominator.

$$\frac{3 \text{ apples}}{\$.75} = \frac{20 \text{ apples}}{\$c}$$

STEP 2 Set up the solution by multiplying the cross product and dividing by the other given number.

$$c = \frac{20 \times .75}{3}$$

STEP 3 Calculate the answer by multiplying and dividing.

$$c = \frac{20 \times .75}{3} = \frac{\$15.00}{3} = \$5.00$$

$$c = \$5$$

Therefore, **20 apples cost $5.**

Solving a proportion is a two-step multiplication and division problem.

Tip

When setting up a proportion, be sure to set up both fractions in the same order. The relationship between the numerator and the denominator on the left side of the equals sign should be reflected in the same order on the right side of the equals sign. It helps to write unit labels by each number as a reminder to keep both sides of the proportion in the same order.

TO SOLVE A PROPORTION

1. Set up a proportion, making sure that the fraction on the left side of the equal sign is set up in the same order as the fraction on the right side.
2. Set up the method of solution by setting the missing value equal to the cross product of the diagonal of the two given numbers divided by the remaining number.
3. Solve by multiplying the cross product and then dividing.

Example 3 $\frac{5}{6} = \frac{n}{42}$

STEP 1 Set up the proportion. $\frac{5}{6} = \frac{n}{42}$

STEP 2 Set up the solution. $n = \frac{5 \times 42}{6}$

STEP 3 Calculate the answer. $n = \frac{210}{6} = 35$

$n = \mathbf{35}$

EXERCISE 3

Solving Proportions

Directions: Solve the following proportions for the missing element symbol in each.

1. $\frac{2}{5} = \frac{m}{10}$ **2.** $\frac{x}{7} = \frac{3}{21}$ **3.** $\frac{5}{y} = \frac{15}{20}$ **4.** $\frac{6}{4} = \frac{12}{z}$ **5.** $\frac{n}{12} = \frac{30}{24}$

Answers are on page 931.

Application of Proportion

Proportion has a great many applications in problem solving. In this section you will consider problems involving cost, mixtures, rates, ratio, and scale. In later sections, you will continue to use proportion to solve problems involving measurement, percent, and geometric relationships. If a problem sets up a relationship between two quantities and then asks you to extend that same relationship into a new situation, you should consider using a proportion to solve the problem.

Example 1 A 25-acre field yields 350 bushels of wheat. At that rate, how many bushels will a 60-acre field yield?

STEP 1 Set up the proportion. $\frac{25 \text{ acres}}{350 \text{ bushels}} = \frac{60 \text{ acres}}{b}$

STEP 2 Set up the solution. $b = \frac{350 \times 60}{25}$

STEP 3 Calculate the answer. $b = \frac{21000}{25} = 840$

$b =$ **840 bushels of wheat**

The most challenging part of setting up a proportion is putting the numbers in the right part of the proportion. Notice the setup in the example below.

Example 2 A baseball player hits 10 home runs in the first 45 games. If he continues at the same rate, how many home runs can he expect to hit during the 162-game season?

STEP 1 Set up the proportion. Be sure to set up both sides of the equals sign in the same order. $\frac{10 \text{ HRs}}{45 \text{ games}} = \frac{H}{162 \text{ games}}$

STEP 2 Set up the solution. $H = \frac{10 \times 162}{45}$

STEP 3 Calculate the answer. $H = \frac{1620}{45} = 36$

$H =$ **36 home runs in 162 games**

EXERCISE 4

Application of Proportion

Directions: Solve each problem. Choose the best answer for each problem.

1. A car travels 128 miles on 8 gallons of gas. Which choice below will tell you how far the car can travel on a full tank of gas that holds 20 gallons?

(1) $128 \times 8 \times 20$ **(2)** $\frac{128 \times 20}{8}$ **(3)** $\frac{8 \times 20}{128}$ **(4)** $\frac{128 \times 8}{20}$ **(5)** $\frac{128}{8 \times 20}$

2. At Wilkins Department Store the ratio of managers to sales clerks is 2:9. If Wilkins currently has 189 sales clerks, how many managers are there?

(1) 11 **(2)** 42 **(3)** 200 **(4)** 378 **(5)** 1701

3. On the scale drawing at the right, $\frac{1}{8}$ inch = 1 foot. If the length of a room on the scale drawing is $2\frac{1}{4}$ inches, how many feet long is the actual room?

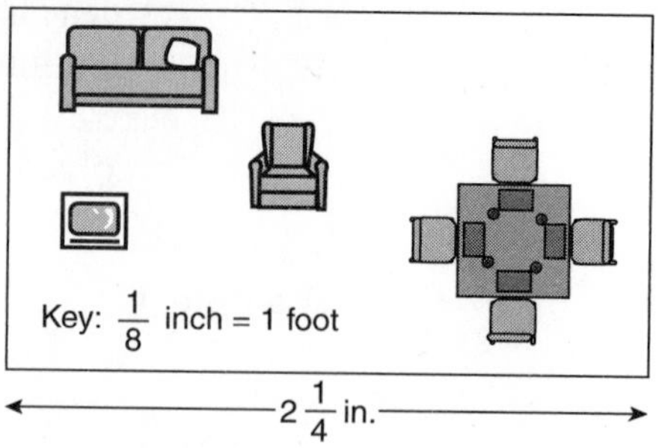

(1) $2\frac{1}{8}$ **(2)** $2\frac{3}{8}$ **(3)** 9 **(4)** $16\frac{1}{4}$ **(5)** 18

4. Two pancakes contain 120 calories. Ellen had a stack of 7 pancakes. How many calories did she have?

(1) 127 **(2)** 240 **(3)** 420 **(4)** 840 **(5)** Not enough information is given.

5. This picture must be enlarged to a width of 10 inches. What will be the height of the enlargement?

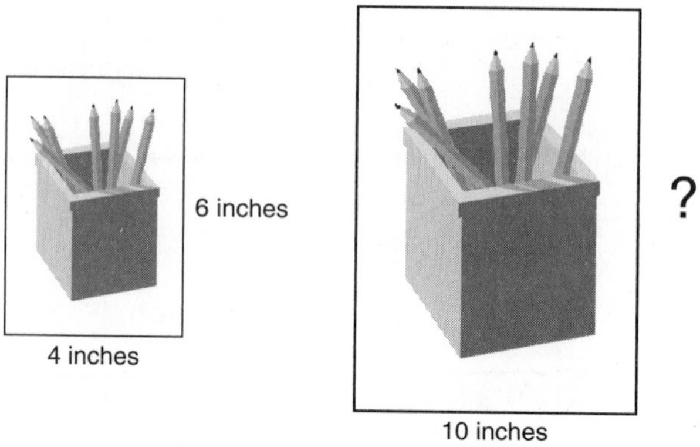

(1) 12 inches **(2)** 14 inches **(3)** 15 inches
(4) 16 inches **(5)** 20 inches

Answers are on page 931.

Go to **www.GEDMath.com** for additional practice and instruction!

CHAPTER 7

Percents

Percents are one of the most common and practical applications of math. You use percents when you buy on installment, pay taxes, get a loan, get discounts on purchases, read major-league baseball standings, or even listen to the weather report.

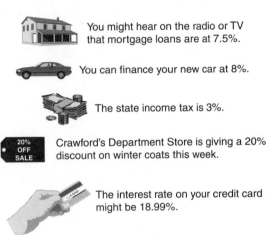

You might hear on the radio or TV that mortgage loans are at 7.5%.

You can finance your new car at 8%.

The state income tax is 3%.

Crawford's Department Store is giving a 20% discount on winter coats this week.

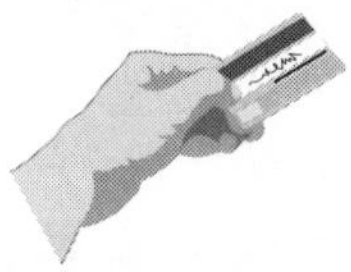

The interest rate on your credit card might be 18.99%.

Percents are everywhere!

What Are Percents?

Percents, like decimals and fractions, are parts of a whole. A percent is a part of a whole that has been divided into 100 equal pieces. **Percent** means "per hundred."

The symbol for percent is %. For example, $50\% = .50 = \frac{50}{100}$.

In problem solving you may need to change percents to equivalent decimals or fractions or vice versa. The following chart shows the relationship among some common percents, fractions, and decimals. You should become familiar with this list because these relationships are used over and over again.

Percent	Fraction	Decimal
1%	$\frac{1}{100}$	.01
5%	$\frac{5}{100} = \frac{1}{20}$	.05
10%	$\frac{10}{100} = \frac{1}{10}$	.10
25%	$\frac{25}{100} = \frac{1}{4}$	.25
$33\frac{1}{3}\%$	$\frac{33\frac{1}{3}}{100} = \frac{1}{3}$	$.33\frac{1}{3}$
50%	$\frac{50}{100} = \frac{1}{2}$	.50
$66\frac{2}{3}\%$	$\frac{66\frac{2}{3}}{100} = \frac{2}{3}$	$.66\frac{2}{3}$
75%	$\frac{75}{100} = \frac{3}{4}$	.75
100%	$\frac{100}{100} = 1$	1.00

Tip

Since 100% is one whole, anything less than 100% is less than one whole. For example, 75% of a quantity is a part of that quantity.

Interchanging Percents, Fractions, and Decimals

Problem solving may require changing back and forth from fractions to decimals to percents. To change a percent to a fraction or decimal, multiply the number by one hundredth.

The % symbol means "$\times \frac{1}{100}$" or "$\times .01$."

CHANGING PERCENTS TO FRACTIONS OR DECIMALS

1. To change a percent to a fraction, multiply the number by $\frac{1}{100}$.

   Example $13\% = 13 \times \frac{1}{100} = \frac{13}{1} \times \frac{1}{100} = \frac{13}{100}$
2. To change a percent to a decimal, multiply the number by .01.

   Example $13\% = 13 \times .01 = .13$

Tip

Multiplying by .01 moves the decimal point 2 places to the left.
13% = 13.% = .13

Example The following percents are changed to an equivalent fraction and to an equivalent decimal. (Be sure to reduce fractions to lowest terms.)

80% *To a fraction:* $80 \times \frac{1}{100} = \frac{\cancel{80}^{4}}{1} \times \frac{1}{\cancel{100}_{5}} = \mathbf{\frac{4}{5}}$

To a decimal: $80 \times .01 = .80 = \mathbf{.8}$

$33\frac{1}{3}\%$ *To a fraction:* $33\frac{1}{3} \times \frac{1}{100} = \frac{\cancel{100}^{1}}{3} \times \frac{1}{\cancel{100}_{1}} = \mathbf{\frac{1}{3}}$

To a decimal: $33\frac{1}{3} \times .01 = \mathbf{.33\frac{1}{3}}$

150% *To a fraction:* $150 \times \frac{1}{100} = \frac{\cancel{150}^{3}}{100} = \frac{1}{\cancel{100}_{2}} = \frac{3}{2} = \mathbf{1\frac{1}{2}}$

To a decimal: $150 \times .01 = 1.50 = \mathbf{1.5}$

.6% *To a fraction:* $.6\% = \frac{6}{10}\% = \frac{\cancel{6}^{3}}{10} \times \frac{1}{\cancel{100}_{50}} = \mathbf{\frac{3}{500}}$

To a decimal: $.6\% = .6 \times .01 = \mathbf{.006}$

Tip

Always read a decimal carefully for its meaning.

100% represents the whole thing. For example, 100% of 25 is 25.

200% is more than one whole. For example, 200% is the same as 2 times a whole. Thus, 200% of 25 is 50. Anything over 100% is more than one whole.

$\frac{3}{4}\%$ and .75% are less than 1%. $\frac{3}{4}\%$ means "three quarters of one percent," and .75% means "seventy-five hundredths of one percent," not 75 percent.

Tip

Any proper fraction or decimal followed by % means "less than 1%."

In some problems you are given a fraction or a decimal, and you need to change it to a percent. You can do this by dividing by one-hundredth.

CHANGING FRACTIONS AND DECIMALS TO PERCENTS

1. To change a fraction to a percent, divide by $\frac{1}{100}$ and attach a % symbol. (Remember dividing by $\frac{1}{100}$ is the same as multiplying by its reciprocal 100.)

   Example 1 Change $\frac{7}{8}$ to a percent.

   $$\frac{7}{8} \div \frac{1}{100} = \frac{7}{\cancel{8}_2} \times \frac{\cancel{100}^{25}}{1} = \frac{175}{2} = 87\frac{1}{2} \qquad \text{So } \frac{7}{8} = 87\frac{1}{2}\%.$$

2. To change a decimal to a percent, divide by .01 and attach a % symbol. (Remember dividing by .01 moves the decimal point two places to the right.)

   Example 2 Change .3 to a percent.

   $$.3 \div .01 = .30 \div .01 = 30 \qquad \text{So } .3 = 30\%.$$

   Example 3 Change 2.04 to an equivalent percent.

   $$2.04 \div .01 = 2.04 \div .01 = 204 \qquad \text{So } 2.04 = 204\%.$$

EXERCISE 1

Interchanging Percents, Fractions, and Decimals

Directions: Change each percent to an equivalent fraction and to an equivalent decimal.

1. 87%	**2.** 40%	**3.** 2%	**4.** $16\frac{2}{3}\%$	**5.** $7\frac{1}{2}\%$
6. 9%	**7.** 300%	**8.** 125%	**9.** .5%	**10.** 9.9%
11. $\frac{1}{2}\%$	**12.** 75%	**13.** $\frac{1}{4}\%$	**14.** 5%	**15.** 50%

Change the following numbers to equivalent percents.

16. $\frac{3}{5}$	**17.** .95	**18.** $\frac{1}{3}$	**19.** .0025	**20.** $\frac{3}{8}$
21. 4.5	**22.** $\frac{9}{10}$	**23.** .625	**24.** $2\frac{1}{4}$	**25.** .4

Answers are on page 931.

Solving Percent Problems

There are three types of questions in percent problems. Let's look at a statement involving percents to determine what kind of questions could be asked.

15 is 25% of 60

From this statement you can see that 15 is a part of 60 and that 60 is the whole amount. 25% means $\frac{25}{100}$ or 25 parts out of the whole, where 100 represents the whole. In a percent problem you will either be looking for the **part** (15 in this example), the **whole** (60 in this example) or the **percent** (25 in this example). 100 will always represent the whole percent.

A percent word problem can be solved by setting up a proportion that shows that the relationship between the part and the whole is the same as the relationship of a percent part to 100%. The proportion below shows how to set up a problem like this.

$$\frac{\text{PART}}{\text{WHOLE}} = \frac{\text{\% PART}}{\text{100 (\%WHOLE)}}$$

In the example above, the proportion would look like this.

Part → 15; Percent Part → 25%

$$\frac{15}{60} = \frac{25\%}{100\%}$$

Whole → 60; Percent Whole (always 100%) → 100%

To solve a percent word problem, you must read the problem carefully and first decide if the number you are looking for is the **part,** the **whole,** or the **percent part.** Remember the percent whole is always 100%. You can always use a proportion to find the missing number.

If you are looking for the part, you may use an alternative method to help you find it. You may multiply the whole by a decimal equivalent of the percent. Examples of both methods will be given on page 798. However, to find the whole or the percent part, it is usually most reliable to use a proportion to solve the problem.

SOLVING A PERCENT PROBLEM

1. Decide if you are looking for the part, the whole, or the percent part. Label the missing value with *N*.
2. If you are looking for the part, you may choose to solve the problem one of two ways:
   (1) Multiply the whole by the decimal equivalent of the percent part. *Or*
   (2) Set up the proportion $\frac{N}{\text{WHOLE}} = \frac{\%\text{PART}}{100\ (\%\text{WHOLE})}$ and solve for *N*.
3. If you are looking for the whole, set up the following proportion and solve for *N*.
$$\frac{\text{PART}}{N} = \frac{\%\text{PART}}{100\ (\%\text{WHOLE})}$$
4. If you are looking for the % part, set up the following proportion and solve for *N*.
$$\frac{\text{PART}}{\text{WHOLE}} = \frac{N}{100\ (\%\text{WHOLE})}$$
5. To solve for *N*, multiply diagonally and divide by the third number.

To illustrate the use of this method in solving percent problems, work through the following three examples.

Example 1 Find 40% of 120.

Solution: You are looking for the **part** of 120.

Method 1

40% of 120 means .40 x 120

Change 40% to .40

Multiply $.40 \times 120 = 48.00 = 48$

So 40% of 120 is **48.**

Method 2

Set up the proportion.

$$\frac{N}{120} = \frac{40}{100}$$

$$N = \frac{40 \times 120}{100} = \frac{4800}{100} = \mathbf{48}$$

So 40% of 120 is 48.

Example 2 18 is what percent of 72?

Solution: You are looking for the **percent part.**

Set up the proportion: $\frac{18}{72} = \frac{N}{100}$

Set up the method of solution for *N*: $N = \frac{18 \times 100}{72} = \frac{1800}{72} = \mathbf{25}$

So 18 is **25%** of 72.

Example 3 60 is 120% of what number?

Solution: You are looking for the **whole.**

Set up the proportion: $\frac{60}{N} = \frac{120}{100}$

Set up the method of solution for *N*: $N = \frac{60 \times 100}{120} = \frac{6000}{120} = \mathbf{50}$

So 60 is 120% of **50.**

Notice that the part (60) is larger than the whole (50). This is because the percent is 120%, which is more than 100%.

You can calculate percentages on your calculator. Because the % symbol is on the case, you must first use the SHIFT key and then the = key to access the % key.

Key: % percent symbol (on the case above the = symbol)

PROCESS	KEY IN:	DISPLAY	Example 1: Find 30% of 50.
Step 1	AC to clear the display	0.	0.
Step 2	whole	whole	50.
Step 3	×	whole	50.
Step 4	percent	percent	30.
Step 5	SHIFT	percent	30.
Step 6	= (% symbol on case)	answer	15.

PROCESS	KEY IN:	DISPLAY	Example 2: 12 is what percent of 15?
Step 1	AC to clear the display	0.	0.
Step 2	part	part	12.
Step 3	÷	part	12.
Step 4	whole	whole	15.
Step 5	SHIFT	whole	15.
Step 6	= (% symbol on case)	answer	80.

EXERCISE 2

Percent Problems

Directions: In each problem decide which you are looking for: part, whole, or percent. Then solve the problem. Use your calculator to check your work.

1. Find 4% of 30.
2. 14 is 7% of what amount?
3. What percent of 56 is 14?
4. What is 200% of 45?
5. 10 is 2.5% of what number?
6. 210 is what percent of 600?
7. What number is .5% of 62?
8. 16% of what number is 18?
9. What percent of $340 is $30.60?
10. 20 is what percent of 5?

Answers are page 932.

Percent Problem Solving

As you know, percents are a part of the math that people do every day—at work, while shopping, or in personal money matters. On the following pages, you will study special types of percent problems such as finding interest, discounts, and repayments of loans. In general, percent word problems are multistep problems. You know that you always multiply and then divide after you have set up the proportion. You may also have to perform some addition or subtraction to get a final answer.

Percent word problems require careful reading to identify what the question is asking. For example, the question might be "What is the final sale price for an item discounted 20%?" To find the final sale price, you will first have to determine 20% of the original price and then subtract that amount from the original price.

You can use your calculator to simplify finding the result when you need to add or subtract the percentage from the original amount.

PROCESS	**KEY IN:**	**DISPLAY**	**Example 1: Find the sale price on a \$35 item discounted 20%.**
Step 1	AC to clear the display	0.	0.
Step 2	whole	whole	35.
Step 3	×	whole	35.
Step 4	percent	percent	20.
Step 5	SHIFT	percent	20.
Step 6	= (% symbol on case)	part	7.
Step 7	–	answer	28.

PROCESS	**KEY IN:**	**DISPLAY**	**Example 2: Find the total cost of a \$4 item with a 7% tax.**
Step 1	AC to clear the display	0.	0.
Step 2	whole	whole	4.
Step 3	×	whole	4.
Step 4	percent	percent	7.
Step 5	SHIFT	percent	7.
Step 6	= (% symbol on case)	part	.28
Step 7	+	answer	4.28

The following examples are typical percent problems.

Example 1 To pass her science test, Amy must get 75% of the problems correct. Out of the 80 questions on the test, how many may she miss and still pass?

STEP 1 Find 75% of 80 problems. $.75 \times 80 = 60$ problems
This means Amy needs to get 60 problems correct to pass the test.

STEP 2 Subtract 60 problems from 80 problems. $80 - 60 =$ **20 problems**
She can miss 20 problems and still pass the test.

Example 2 Find the 15% tip on an $18 tab.

STEP 1 Find 15% of $18. $.15 \times \$18 =$ **$2.70**
The tip is $2.70

In this example, the question asks only for the amount of the tip. If the problem had asked you to find the total cost, you would have added the $18 and $2.70 to get a total of $20.70.

Example 3 A car depreciates 20% the first year it is owned. Elena's car cost $12,480 originally. What was the car worth after the first year?

STEP 1 Find 20% of $12,480. $.20 \times \$12{,}480 = \$2{,}496$
The amount of depreciation is $2,496.

STEP 2 Subtract $2,496 from $12,480. $\$12{,}480 - \$2{,}496 =$ **$9,984**
Depreciation reduces the value of the car from $12,480 to $9,984.

EXERCISE 3

Percent Word Problems

Directions: Solve each problem.

1. On her test Rachel got 8 wrong out of 40 questions. What percent did she get *right*?

2. Mrs. Gawedzinski put 15% down on her new car purchase. If the down payment was $1800, how much did the car cost?

3. Employees at Taylor's Music Mart get a 20% discount on all purchases. If Brandon buys three CDs at $9.99 each, what will he have to pay after his employee discount?

4. A political campaign conducted a poll to determine how the candidates were doing. The results were as shown in the table below. What percent of the voters was undecided?

Gore	Bush	Buchanan	Nader	Undecided
180	140	12	48	120

Questions 5–7 refer to the following information. Enter each answer in the corresponding number grid.

Each month Jesse takes home a $2100 paycheck. He immediately puts 12% of this amount into his savings account. Jesse pays $420 monthly for rent.

5. How much money does Jesse save each month?

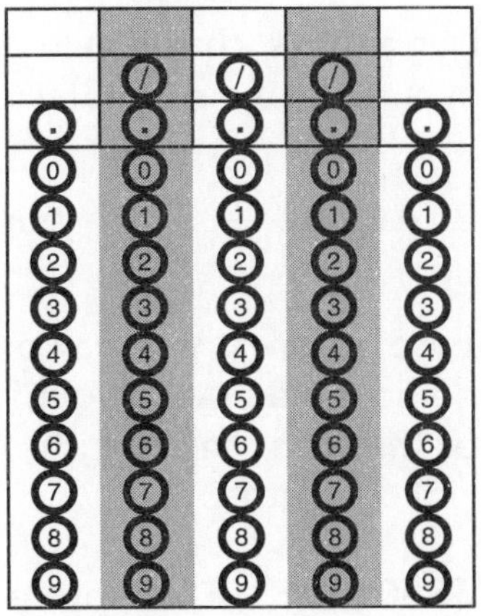

6. Jesse's rent is what percent of his take-home pay?

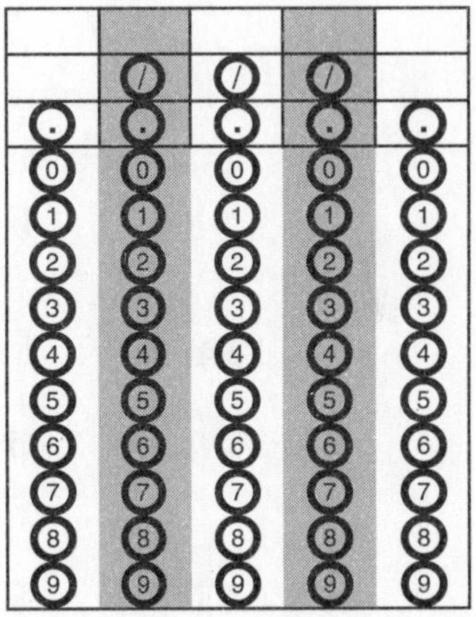

7. Jesse's employer has offered him a 5% raise for next year. At that rate, what will be his annual take-home pay next year?

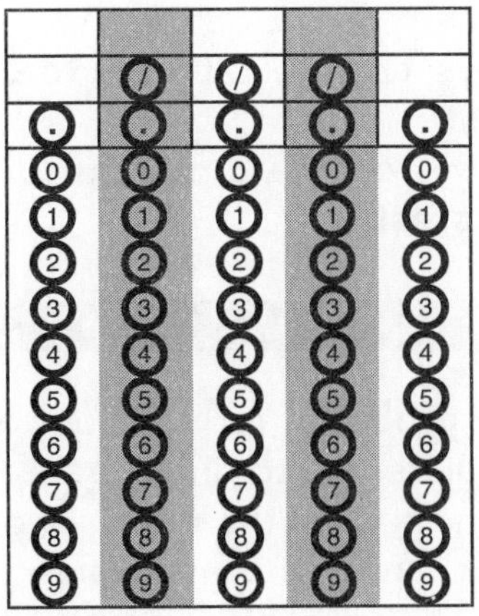

Answers are on page 932.

Interest Problems

Interest is the amount earned on an investment or the cost to be paid for a loan. If you borrow or invest money, you will be dealing with an **interest rate** that is expressed as a percent. The original amount of money that is borrowed or invested is called the **principal.** Interest rates are calculated on an annual basis.

To find interest, multiply the *principal* times the *interest rate* (expressed as a decimal). If a loan is longer or shorter than one year, multiply the amount of interest by the length of time in years or fraction of a year.

The length of **time** of a loan must always be expressed in terms of years. If the time is given in months, change the time to a fraction of a year by comparing the given number of months to 12 months.

For example, 9 months $= \frac{9 \text{ months}}{12 \text{ months}} = \frac{3}{4}$ year.

If the time is given in days, change it to a fraction of a year by comparing the given number of days to 360 (approximately the number of days in a year).

For example, 120 days $= \frac{120 \text{ days}}{360 \text{ days}} = \frac{1}{3}$ year.

Example Find the amount of interest you pay on a $850 credit card balance at 18%. Determine how much you would pay in interest if you carry that balance for the following lengths of time: a) 1 year, b) 2 years, c) 120 days, or d) 6 months.

STEP 1 $850 × 18% = $850 × .18 = $153 interest

STEP 2 Multiply by the time expressed in years or fractions of a year.

a) For 1 year, multiply $153 × 1 year = **$153 per year in interest.**

b) For 2 years, multiply $153 × 2 years = **$306 in interest for the two years.**

c) For 120 days, change 120 days to $\frac{1}{3}$ year. Multiply $153 × $\frac{1}{3}$ = **$51 interest.**

d) For 6 months, change 6 months to $\frac{1}{2}$ year. Multiply $153 × $\frac{1}{2}$ = **$76.50 interest.**

Tip

Some interest problems require you to find only the interest, and others require you to find the total amount of the loan or investment. The total is the principal plus the interest. You must read problems carefully to make sure you understand whether you are being asked for the *interest* or the *principal plus interest.*

SOLVING INTEREST PROBLEMS

1. To find the interest earned on an investment or paid on a loan, multiply the principal times the decimal equivalent of the interest rate times the length of time expressed in years. *interest* = *principal* × *rate* × *time*

   Example 1 Find the interest earned on $250 invested at 5% for 2 years.

   interest = $250 × .05 × 2 = $25
   The interest earned in 2 years is $25.

2. To find the total amount of the loan or investment, add the principal to the interest.

   Example 2 Find the total amount repaid on a $500 loan borrowed at 9% for 3 years.

   interest = $500 × .09 × 3 = $135.
   principal + interest = $500 + $135 = $635
   The total amount repaid is $635.

3. To find the rate of interest for a year, set up a percent proportion and solve the proportion.

   Example 3 The yearly interest paid on a $1500 loan is $120. What is the annual rate of interest?

   $$\frac{\$120\text{ (part/interest)}}{\$1500\text{ (whole/principal)}} = \frac{N\text{ (\%part/rate)}}{100\text{ (\%whole)}} \quad N = \frac{\$120 \times 100}{\$1500} = 8$$

   The annual interest rate is 8%.

4. To find the principal, set up a percent proportion and solve the proportion.

   Example 4 Find the principal investment if 12% interest earned on the investment is $576.

   $$\frac{\$576\text{ (part/interest)}}{N\text{ (whole/principal)}} = \frac{12\text{ (\%part)}}{100\text{ (\%whole)}} \quad N = \frac{\$576 \times 100}{12} = \$4800$$

   The principal invested is $4800.

$a^2+b^2=c^2$

Tip

The formula for interest can be found on formula page 922. The formula is *interest* = *principal* × *rate* × *time*.

EXERCISE 4

Interest Problems

Directions: Solve each problem.

1. Margaret borrowed $18,000 for 90 days at an annual rate of 12% to buy inventory for her gift shop. How much interest did she pay?

   (1) $24 **(2)** $540 **(3)** $1,500 **(4)** $2,160 **(5)** $216,000

2. To take advantage of a close-out sale, a motel owner borrows $31,000 to buy 124 color television sets. The loan is for 90 days at an annual interest of 12.5%. Find the total amount to be repaid.

   (1) $968.75 **(2)** $3,875 **(3)** $31,968.75 **(4)** $34,875

   (5) Not enough information is given.

3. You borrowed $6000 and paid $480 in interest. Which expression shows how to find the percent of interest?

   (1) $\frac{6000 \times 100}{480}$ **(2)** $\frac{480 \times 100}{6000}$ **(3)** $\frac{480 \times 6000}{100}$ **(4)** $\frac{480 - 100}{6000}$ **(5)** $\frac{6000}{480}$

4. Chris borrowed some money for one year at a rate of 8%. If he paid $360 in interest that year, how much did he borrow?

   (1) $28.80 **(2)** $288 **(3)** $2,880 **(4)** $4,500 **(5)** $36,000

Questions 5 and 6 are based on the problem below.

Darryl has saved $25,000, which he plans to use in building a summer cottage by a lake. The lot he wants costs $15,000. The builder estimates that it will cost $65,000 to build the cottage and an extra $5,000 to cover expenses for permits and insurance. Darryl will use his savings and take out a loan for the remaining amount to pay for everything.

5. At 10.5%, how much interest will he owe on the amount he borrows at the end of two years?

   (1) $8,400 **(2)** $8,925 **(3)** $12,600 **(4)** $23,100 **(5)** $682,500

6. Darryl is trying to find a better interest rate for his loan. He wants to compare the amount of interest he will have to pay at a 7% rate with the amount of interest he will have to pay at a 9% rate. Find that difference.

   (1) $1200 **(2)** $1700 **(3)** $4200 **(4)** $5400 **(5)** $9600

Answers are on page 932.

EXERCISE 5

Percent Review

Directions: Solve each problem. Use your calculator to check your work.

1. During a recent shopping spree, Ron and Becky bought some new accessories for their apartment. Becky chose a throw pillow at \$14.95, and Ron purchased a rural landscape painting for \$135. How much did they actually spend if they paid 7% sales tax on their purchases?

(1) \$16.30 **(2)** \$17.44 **(3)** \$139.45 **(4)** \$149.95 **(5)** \$160.45

2. Paint that regularly sells for \$15.90 per gallon is on sale at a 20% discount. Which expression shows how to find the price of the paint after the discount?

(1) \$15.90 × .20(15.90)
(2) \$15.90 + .20(15.90)
(3) \$15.90 – .20(15.90)
(4) \$15.90 ÷ .20(15.90)
(5) \$15.90 – .20

3. Marcie bought a new car for \$18,800. She made a down payment of \$2,500. If she finances the remainder at 8% annually for three years, how much does she actually pay for the car?

(1) \$1,304 **(2)** \$1,504 **(3)** \$20,104 **(4)** \$22,712 **(5)** \$25,740

4. Last year Riley paid \$1,200 in state income tax. If the state tax is calculated at a 3% yearly tax rate, what was Riley's income?

(1) \$4,000 **(2)** \$12,000 **(3)** \$36,000 **(4)** \$40,000 **(5)** \$400,000

5. Pam deducts a $4\frac{1}{2}$% real estate commission when she sells a condominium for her client. How much money will the client then receive for the sale of a \$96,000 condo?

(1) \$4,320 **(2)** \$21,333 **(3)** \$74,667 **(4)** \$91,680 **(5)** \$100,320

Questions 6–11 refer to the information and chart below.

Emile's net earnings (take-home pay) for last year were $24,000. The list below shows his expenses for the year.

EXPENSE	COST	EXPENSE	COST
Rent	$6000	Clothing	$1000
Food	3600	Dues	300
Utilities	2400	Phone	300
Medical	600	Entertainment	1200
Insurance	1500	Savings	2400
Car	3800	Miscellaneous	600

6. What percent of his total net income did Emile spend on rent?

(1) $\frac{1}{4}$ **(2)** 2.5 **(3)** 4 **(4)** 25 **(5)** 40

7. What is the ratio of savings to total income?

(1) $\frac{1}{24}$ **(2)** $\frac{1}{10}$ **(3)** $\frac{10}{1}$ **(4)** $\frac{24}{1}$ **(5)** $\frac{9}{10}$

8. Entertainment and savings account for what percent of Emile's expenditures?

(1) 5 **(2)** 10 **(3)** 15 **(4)** 50 **(5)** 75

9. Assume that insurance costs are expected to rise 12% next year. How much will Emile pay for insurance then?

(1) $12 **(2)** $125 **(3)** $180 **(4)** $1320 **(5)** $1680

10. Emile's property taxes rose 7% last year. How much of his take-home pay went to property taxes?

(1) $42 **(2)** $420 **(3)** $6042 **(4)** $6420 **(5)** Not enough information is given.

11. Emile's net pay is 67% of his gross pay. Which expression below shows how you would find his gross pay?

(1) $\frac{24000 \times 100}{67}$ **(2)** $\frac{24000 \times 67}{100}$ **(3)** $\frac{67 \times 100}{24000}$ **(4)** $\frac{24000}{67 \times 100}$

(5) Not enough information is given.

Answers are on page 932.

Go to **www.GEDMath.com** for additional practice and instruction!

CHAPTER 8

Probability

Probability can be called the language of chance. The weather reporter says there is a 40% chance of rain today, but you still don't know if it's going to rain or not. **Probability** helps us predict the future based on analyzing past performance, but nothing is guaranteed. Probability is a practical mathematical tool used in developing mortality rates for insurance companies, constructing polls to assess public opinion during elections, and evaluating statistical data in scientific experiments.

You can use a game spinner to illustrate probability. Assume that the spinner is perfectly balanced and there is an even chance it will stop on any color. Each spin of the wheel is an **event.** The color it stops at is an **outcome** of the event.

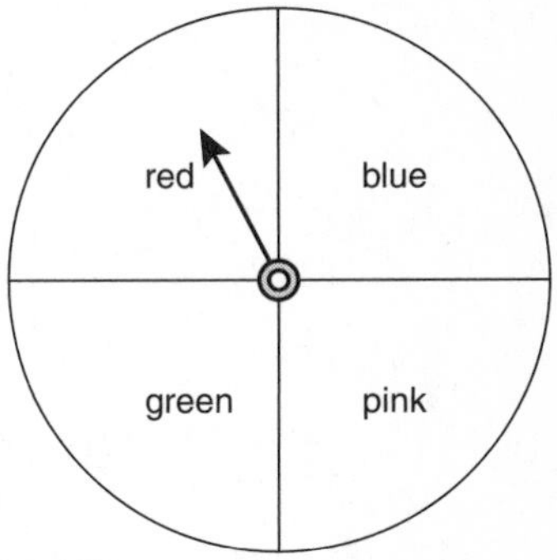

There are four possible outcomes when you spin this wheel: red, blue, green, and pink. A **favorable outcome** occurs when you spin the wheel and get the color you want. The probability a particular event will occur is the ratio of the number of favorable outcomes to the number of possible outcomes of that event.

PROBABILITY OF AN EVENT

$$\text{Probability of an Event} = \frac{\text{Number of Favorable Outcomes}}{\text{Total Number of Possible Outcomes}}$$

Probability can be expressed in ratio, fraction, or a percent form. The probability of an event ranges in value from 0 to 1.

For example: A probability of $\frac{3}{4}$ is a fraction greater than 0 but less than 1. It indicates that there are three favorable outcomes out of four possible outcomes. There is a 75% chance of a favorable outcome.

1. A probability of 0 means there is 0% chance the outcome will be favorable.
2. A probability of 1 means there is 100% chance the outcome will be favorable.
3. The probability of an event will *not* happen is 1 minus the probability the event will happen.

$1 - \frac{3}{4} = \frac{1}{4}$ indicates that there is one outcome out of four that is not favorable. There is a 25% chance of an unfavorable outcome.

Using the spinning wheel, the probability of stopping at red would be $\frac{1}{4}$. There is one favorable outcome (red) out of a total of four possible outcomes (red, blue, green, and pink). Since $\frac{1}{4}$ can also be written as 25%, you can say there is a 25% chance of landing on red.

Using the spinning wheel again, find the probability of landing on *either* red *or* green. Now there are two favorable outcomes out of four possible outcomes. The probability is $\frac{2}{4}$, which reduces to $\frac{1}{2}$. Thus, the probability of landing on red or green is $\frac{1}{2}$, or 50%.

Probability of 0 or 1

A probability of 0 or 0% means an event will not take place. Using the same spinning wheel, the probability of landing on purple is 0 because the number of favorable outcomes of purple on this wheel is 0. So you would have $\frac{0}{4} = 0$. There is 0% chance of landing on purple.

A probability of 1 or 100% means an event is certain to happen. You can use the spinning wheel to find the probability of landing on red, green, blue, or pink. The number of favorable outcomes is 4, and the number of possible outcomes is 4. Now you have $\frac{4}{4} = 1$. There is 100% certainty that the spinner will land on red, green, blue, or pink.

EXERCISE 1

Probability

Directions: Solve each problem. Remember to use your calculator to check your calculations.

Questions 1–4 are based on the following information.

A deck of playing cards has 52 cards divided evenly into 4 suits of 13 cards each. There are two red suits (hearts and diamonds) and two black suits (spades and clubs). Each suit has an ace, king, queen, jack, 10, 9, 8, 7, 6, 5, 4, 3, and 2.

1. If a single card is picked from a deck of playing cards, what is the probability that it is the ace of spades?

2. From the same deck of cards what is the probability of drawing a heart? Give your answer as a percent.

3. In a deck of playing cards what is the probability of drawing a king? Give your answer as a fraction.

4. What is the probability of drawing a ten of diamonds from a deck of playing cards?

For question 5–10, consider the roll of a single die. A single die has six faces as shown.

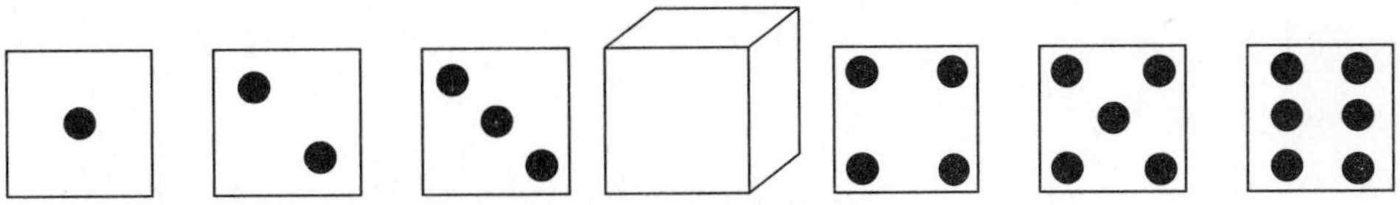

5. What is the probability of *not* rolling a 5?

(1) $\frac{1}{6}$ **(2)** $\frac{1}{5}$ **(3)** $\frac{1}{3}$ **(4)** $\frac{1}{2}$ **(5)** $\frac{5}{6}$

6. What is the probability of rolling either a 3 or a 4?

(1) $16\frac{2}{3}\%$ **(2)** 25% **(3)** 30% **(4)** $33\frac{1}{3}\%$ **(5)** 40%

7. What is the probability of rolling an even number?

(1) $16\frac{2}{3}\%$ **(2)** 20% **(3)** 30% **(4)** $33\frac{1}{3}\%$ **(5)** 50%

8. What is the probability of rolling a number greater than 6?

(1) 0 **(2)** $\frac{1}{6}$ **(3)** $\frac{1}{3}$ **(4)** $\frac{1}{2}$ **(5)** 1

9. What is the probability of rolling a number less than 5?

(1) 0% **(2)** 30% **(3)** $33\frac{1}{3}\%$ **(4)** 40% **(5)** $66\frac{2}{3}\%$

10. What is the probability of rolling a number less than 7?

(1) 0% **(2)** 25% **(3)** 60% **(4)** 70% **(5)** 100%

11. What is the probability that you will read this page in March instead of another month?

(1) $\frac{1}{25}$ **(2)** $\frac{1}{12}$ **(3)** $\frac{1}{4}$ **(4)** $\frac{1}{3}$ **(5)** Not enough information is given.

12. What is the probability that your social security number will end in 8?

(1) $\frac{1}{12}$ **(2)** $\frac{1}{10}$ **(3)** $\frac{1}{8}$ **(4)** $\frac{4}{5}$ **(5)** Not enough information is given.

13. You flip a coin nine times, and each time it lands on heads. What is the probability that it will land on heads the tenth time you flip it?

(1) $\frac{1}{9}$ **(2)** $\frac{1}{10}$ **(3)** $\frac{1}{2}$ **(4)** $\frac{9}{10}$ **(5)** Not enough information is given.

14. In every shipment of clay pots, a number of them will be broken. In a recent shipment, 240 out of 960 were cracked. At the same rate, what is the probability of getting pots that are *not* cracked?

(1) $\frac{1}{24}$ **(2)** $\frac{1}{4}$ **(3)** $\frac{1}{2}$ **(4)** $\frac{3}{4}$ **(5)** Not enough information is given.

Answers are on page 933.

Dependent Probability

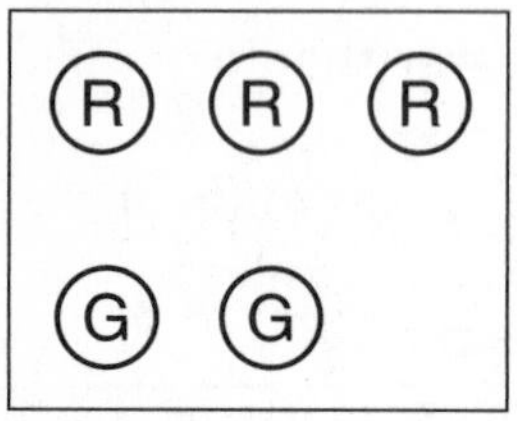

Suppose a box contains two green balls and three red balls. If one ball is drawn from the box, the probability of drawing a green ball is $\frac{2}{5}$ and the probability of drawing a red ball is $\frac{3}{5}$. If you do not replace the ball drawn, there are now only four balls in the box. The probability for the drawing of the next ball now depends on which ball you drew the first time. This situation is called **dependent probability.**

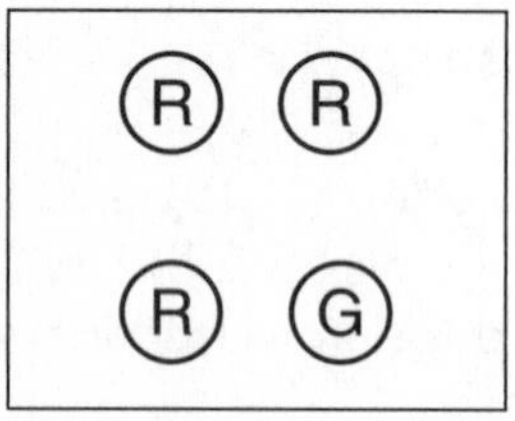

1st Possibility: You drew a green ball.

If you drew a green ball on the first draw, the box now contains one green ball and three red balls. In this situation, the probability of next drawing a green ball is now $\frac{1}{4}$ and the probability of drawing a red ball is $\frac{3}{4}$.

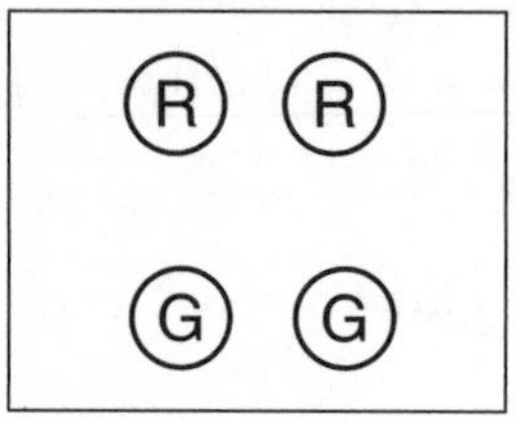

2nd Possibility: You drew a red ball.

If you drew a red ball on the first draw, the box now contains two green balls and two red balls. The probability of drawing a green ball is now $\frac{2}{4} = \frac{1}{2}$, and the probability of drawing a red ball is now $\frac{2}{4} = \frac{1}{2}$.

Tip

A second draw depends on the first draw. If the first draw is not replaced, the total number of possibilities is reduced by one. This is an example of dependent probability.

EXERCISE 2

Dependent Probability

Directions: Solve each problem.

Questions 1–4 are based on the following situation. Express your answers as fractions. Draw a picture if necessary to help you find the probabilities.

Two cards are drawn in succession from a deck of 52 playing cards without the first card being replaced.

1. Find the probability that the first card drawn is an ace.

2. If the first card drawn was an ace, what is the probability that the second draw is also an ace?

3. What is the probability that the second card drawn is an ace if the first card drawn was not an ace?

4. Suppose the first card drawn is a spade and not replaced. What is the probability that the second card drawn is a spade?

Questions 5–7 are based on the following situation. Express your answers as fractions.

A committee is to be chosen at random from a group of seven men and three women. The names of the ten people are placed on slips of paper and put in a hat.

5. What is the probability that the first name drawn from the hat will be a woman's?

6. If the first name drawn is a man's, what is the probability that the second name drawn will also be a man's?

7. What is the probability that the third name drawn will be a woman's if the first two draws were also women's names?

Questions 8–10 are based on the following situation. Express your answers as fractions.

A change purse contains 3 nickels, 4 dimes, and 2 quarters.

8. What is the probability that the first coin taken from the purse will be a quarter?

9. If the first coin taken from the purse was a nickel, what is the probability that the next coin will be a quarter?

10. What is the probability that the third coin taken from the purse will be a nickel if the first two coins were also nickels?

Answers are on page 933.

Go to **www.GEDMath.com** for additional practice and instruction!

CHAPTER 9

Data Analysis

Data is information and **statistics** is the study of the data. You use **data analysis** to describe the data numerically and graphically. To begin, you collect the data from a representative sample or an experiment. Then you organize the data, analyze the data, and draw a conclusion. On the GED Test you will be asked to examine given data and explore the distribution of the data by looking at the spread, the center, and the pattern, if any. The purpose of data analysis is to describe the most important features of a set of data.

One way to describe a set of data is to measure the spread of the data by calculating the **range,** the difference between the largest and smallest values. In a recent discussion in an adult education class, the students were talking about the sizes of their immediate families. They found that the smallest family size was 3 members and the largest family size was 10 members. In this situation the range was 7 (10 – 3 = 7); the family sizes were spread over a range of 7 members. The range clearly defines the spread between the extreme values in the data.

Measures of Central Tendency

There are three common ways of looking at the center of a set of data. These measures of central tendency are called the **mean,** the **median,** and the **mode.** Each measure is a numerical value that can be used to describe the data. It is important to remember that each one of these measures can be influenced by the range of the values, the size of the sample, and other characteristics that might distort or influence the results. Use common sense in addition to the measure of central tendency when you interpret data and draw a conclusion.

The **mean** is the *average* of a set of data. To find the average, you add the data and then divide by the number of items. For instance, Brenda bowled scores of 132, 147, and 108 at the bowling alley last night. To find her mean (average) score, you add 132 + 147 + 108 = 387 and then divide by 3 (the number of scores): 387 ÷ 3 = 129. Therefore, her mean, or average, bowling score is 129.

The **median** of a set of data is found by arranging the numbers from smallest to largest and then choosing the *middle* number in the arrangement. That middle number is the median. You would arrange Brenda's three bowling scores to read in order 108, 132, 147. The middle score is 132, so the median is 132. (If there had been an even number of values in the arrangement, instead of three values, you would find the average of the two numbers in the middle to find the median.)

The **mode** of a set of data is the *most frequent* item in the set. For example, at the bowling alley, Brenda rented size 8 bowling shoes. The clerk said size 8 was the most frequently requested women's shoe size. If you look at the number of requests for each shoe size and size 8 was requested most, then the number of requests for size 8 would be the mode. In some distributions there can be no mode if no one item occurs more frequently than another, or there can be two modes (bimodal), three modes, or more depending upon the frequency of the items.

To Find the Mean

1. Add the numbers.
2. Divide by the number of numbers.

To Find the Median

1. Arrange the numbers in order from lowest to highest.
2. If there is an odd number of numbers, choose the middle number.
3. If there is an even number of numbers, find the average of the two numbers in the middle.

To Find the Mode

1. Select the number that appears most frequently. This is the mode.
2. If no number appears more often than any other, there is no mode.
3. If more than one number appears most frequently, there can be more than one mode.

Tip

Deciding which number represents the *typical value* in a set of data is often based on a critical look at the type of values in the set of data. The median may more likely be the typical value if the set of data contains extreme values. The mode may be the typical value when the same value occurs repeatedly. In general, the mean is most often considered the typical value when the set of data is not a set that contains a few extreme values or has unduly repetitious values.

Example 1 Mr. Williams wants to know the average monthly gas bill for his car and his wife's car. The chart below lists the total gas expenses for both cars for the last six months of the year. What is the *average* monthly gas bill? What is the *median* gas bill?

July	\$148.70
August	385.60
September	195.20
October	208.40
November	186.75
December	220.88

To find the average:
Add all six months; the total is $1345.53.
Then divide by 6 (the number of months) to get $224.255.
Round off the amount to an average of **$224.26.**
Mr. and Mrs. Williams can use this information to help them budget their money each month.

To find the median:	Arrange the bills in order.	Average the middle numbers.
To find Mr. Williams's median gas bill, arrange the amounts in order from smallest to largest. Since there is no middle number, you must find the average of the two middle numbers.	148.70 186.75 195.20 } middle 208.40 220.88 385.60	195.20 + 208.40 403.60 $201.80 2)$403.60

The median is $201.80.

Because you know that the median is $201.80, you know that half the gas bills were lower than $201.80 and half the gas bills were higher than $201.80.

Example 2 To get information on the number of evening diners at his Shamrock Inn, Michael O'Shay accumulated the following information for the first 17 days of March. What is the range in the number of diners? What are the mean, median, and mode of the number of diners? Which measure best represents the most common number of diners daily? How would you describe the business at the Inn?

Friday, March 1	48	Sunday, March 10	30
Saturday, March 2	53	Monday, March 11	21
Sunday, March 3	37	Tuesday, March 12	39
Monday, March 4	21	Wednesday, March 13	21
Tuesday, March 5	32	Thursday, March 14	42
Wednesday, March 6	38	Friday, March 15	46
Thursday, March 7	45	Saturday, March 16	86
Friday, March 8	28	Sunday, March 17	117
Saturday, March 9	44		

The **range** is the difference between the lowest and the highest number: 117 – 21 = 96. The range between the lowest and highest number of diners is **96.**

The **average** is the total divided by the number of dates: 748 ÷ 17 = 44. There is an average of **44 diners per day.**

The **median** is the middle of the numbers arranged from lowest to highest. The median is **39 diners.** Half the dates the number of diners is less than 39, and half the dates the number of diners is more than 39.

The **mode** is the number of diners most frequently repeated. The mode is **21 diners.** On three dates there were 21 diners each night. The pattern suggests that this most often happens on Monday.

As you look at the data, you probably notice that on Sunday, March 17, St. Patrick's Day, there were more diners than usual. In fact, on that particular weekend, there were a large number of diners. This suggests that the average is not a typical value because of a distortion by the large crowds for St. Patrick's Day, and that the median is a more accurate representation of the typical number of daily diners. The median is often used when the mean does not give a true picture because of a few unusually high or low numbers.

EXERCISE 1

Measures of Central Tendency

Directions: Solve each problem. Use your calculator to perform the calculations.

1. Seven salesclerks reported the sales figures below during the week of April 19. To the nearest cent, what was the average of the sales figures?

Walt	$4300
Abelina	$5600
Ben	$1875
Felix	$4250
Sunil	$2876
Elsa	$4108
Desiree	$2983

Questions 2–5 are based on the information below. Round your answer to the nearest whole number.

The scorekeeper for the Three Lakes girls' basketball team recorded the results of the last six games.

Date	Opponent	Three Lakes	Opponent	Win or Loss
12/4	Crandon	48	37	W
12/6	Antigo	45	63	L
12/10	Lakeland	53	42	W
12/12	Northland	72	24	W
12/18	Pines	68	44	W
12/20	Eagle River	74	51	W

2. What is the average points scored by the opponents? What is the average score by Three Lakes?

3. What is the median score of the Three Lakes team?

4. What is the range of scores for Three Lakes?

5. What is the mode of the wins and losses?

Questions 6–10 are based on the information below.

On May 24, 2000, seven of the most widely-held stocks in the stock market were listed with their closing price per share and volume (number of shares traded that day).

Stock	Price per Share	Volume
AT&T	$34.81	16,959,000
Cisco Systems	$50.55	64,840,400
Compaq	$26.50	13,411,500
GE	$49.50	11,384,500
Intel	$109.88	24,695,600
Lucent	$54.56	9,819,900
Microsoft	$63.19	28,274,700

6. What is the range in stock prices for the most widely-held stocks?

7. What is the mean price per share of these stocks? What is the median price per share of these stocks?

8. According to the volume of shares traded this day, what is the mode for the prices per share?

9. If you owned 100 shares of the most expensive stock and 100 shares of the least expensive stock, how much money in total would you have invested in the two stocks? What would be the average price per share of stock that you own?

10. If the price of the GE stock rises $2.25 per share the next day and then falls $1.50 per share the day after that, what is the average value of a share over those three days?

Answers are on page 933.

Charts, Tables, and Schedules

Charts, tables, and schedules are used to organize data. These visual organizers make the information easy to find and use. To use charts, tables, and schedules effectively, here are some strategies you should remember.

- Read the title and headings to clearly understand how the information is organized.
- Survey the rows and columns to gain an overall understanding of the number patterns.
- Read the numbers carefully and notice if they contain fractions, decimals, or percents.
- Notice the labels on the numbers; do they represent money, measures, sizes, or time?

Charts are used to organize and display data for comparison. On the GED Test you may be asked to select information from a chart and then use that information to solve the problem. Some familiar examples of charts you see every day include the food pyramid, survey results, and nutritional food labels.

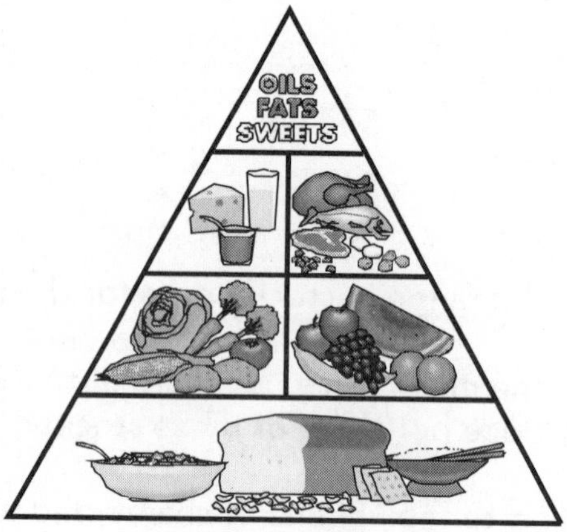

The Food Pyramid

Noodle Soup Nutrition Facts Serving size per can 2	
Fat	2g
Cholesterol	10mg
Sodium	890mg
Carbohydrates	8g
Protein	8g

Nutritional Food Label

Example 1 According to the survey in the chart, approximately how many times greater is an adult's day off to a good start by getting a good night's sleep than by taking a hot shower/bath?

A good night's sleep is 56% and a hot shower/bath is 8%. "How many times greater" indicates division.

$8\overline{)56}$ = 7 **7 times greater**

Off to a Good Start *What starts your day off right?* **Adults polled say:**	
A good night's sleep	56%
Intimacy	11%
Seeing a smiling face	10%
A tasty breakfast	9%
A hot shower/bath	8%
Getting good news	4%

Tables are lists of figures and values in orderly sequences. The numbers presented in **rows** read across and numbers in **columns** read up and down. Examples of tables that you may have used include a multiplication table, an income tax table, or a sales tax table.

1040 EZ Tax Table (in dollars)

If line 5 is at least—	But less than—	Your tax is—
30,000	30,050	5,619
30,050	30,100	5,633
30,100	30,150	5,647
30,150	30,200	5,661
30,200	30,250	5,675
30,250	30,300	5,689
30,300	30,350	5,703
30,350	30,400	5,717
30,400	30,450	5,731
30,450	30,500	5,745
30,500	30,550	5,759
30,550	30,600	5,773
30,600	30,650	5,787
30,650	30,700	5,801
30,700	30,750	5,815
30,750	30,800	5,829

Example 2 Using the 1040 EZ Tax Table, determine how much tax a person who has taxable income of $30,725 will pay.

$\$30{,}700 \le \underline{\$30{,}725} \le \$30{,}750$

Since $30,725 lies between $30,700 and $30,750, find $30,700 in the first column and $30,750 in the second column. Read the tax in the third column: **$5,815.**

Schedules present organized information pertaining to events and time. Schedules can influence your life. You may check a train schedule to plan your transportation to work or read a loan repayment schedule to plan your family budget.

Chicago Planet Watch (9/30/00)

Planet	Rise	Set
Mercury	9:00 A.M.	7:19 P.M.
Venus	9:20 A.M.	7:42 P.M.
Mars	4:17 A.M.	5:32 P.M.
Jupiter	9:28 P.M.	12:16 P.M.
Saturn	8:58 P.M.	11:19 A.M.

Example 3 How much time elapses between the rise and the set of the planet Mars?

Mars rises at 4:17 A.M. and sets at 5:32 P.M. From 4:17 A.M. to 12:17 P.M. is 8 hours. From 12:17 P.M. to 5:17 P.M. is 5 hours. From 5:17 P.M. to 5:32 P.M. is 15 minutes.

8 hours + 5 hours + 15 minutes = **13 hours 15 minutes** total time

EXERCISE 2

Charts, Tables, and Schedules

Directions: Solve each problem.

Questions 1–5 are based on the following chart that compares the U.S. population in 1990 and in 2000.

U.S. Population (times one thousand)

Race	1990 Population	2000 Population	% Change
Caucasian	188,315	196,659	4%
African American	29,304	33,476	14%
Hispanic	22,379	32,440	45%
Asian/Pacific Islander	6,996	10,504	50%
American Indian, Eskimo, Aleutian Islander	1,797	2,050	14%
TOTAL	248,791	275,129	11%

1. How much did the Hispanic population increase from 1990 to 2000?

2. What is the approximate ratio of the African-American population in 2000 to the total population in 2000?

   (1) $\frac{1}{8}$ (2) $\frac{1}{3}$ (3) $\frac{1}{6}$ (4) $\frac{1}{14}$ (5) $\frac{11}{14}$

3. In 1990, what percent of the total population was Caucasian?

   (1) 4% (2) 25% (3) 67% (4) 76% (5) 90%

4. Which group showed the highest percent rate of change?

   (1) Caucasian (2) African American (3) Hispanic
   (4) Asian/Pacific Islander (5) American Indian, Eskimo, Aleutian Islander

5. What was the average yearly rise in the Asian/Pacific Islander population from 1990 to 2000?

   (1) 5 (2) 50 (3) 350.8 (4) 3508 (5) Not enough information is given.

Questions 6–7 are based on the following table of powers and roots.

Number	Square	Square Root	Number	Square	Square Root	Number	Square	Square Root
1	1	1	11	121	3.32	21	441	4.58
2	4	1.41	12	144	3.46	22	484	4.69
3	9	1.73	13	169	3.61	23	529	4.80
4	16	2	14	196	3.74	24	576	4.90
5	25	2.24	15	225	3.87	25	625	5
6	36	2.45	16	256	4	26	676	5.10
7	49	2.65	17	289	4.12	27	729	5.20
8	64	2.83	18	324	4.24	28	784	5.29
9	81	3	19	361	4.36	29	841	5.39
10	100	3.16	20	400	4.47	30	900	5.48

6. Describe the number pattern in the "square" column.

7. What is the ratio of the square root of 25 to the square of 25?

8. What is $8^2 \times 3^2$?

9. What is $\sqrt{9} \times \sqrt{9}$?

10. What is $\sqrt{8} + \sqrt{8}$?

Questions 11–12 are based on the following schedule.

News Radio Hourly Schedule

Local News	National News	Sports News	Weather	Traffic	Business Report	Features
:00	:04	:08	:12	:14	:15	:18
:20	:24	:28	:32	:34	:35	:38
:40	:44	:48	:52	:54	:55	:58

11. According to the schedule, what percent of each hour is dedicated to sports news?

12. What is the ratio of the time spent on weather and traffic to the entire hour?

Answers are on page 933.

Graphs

Graphs are useful tools for organizing and displaying large amounts of information by putting the data in a visually effective format. You can often understand an entire situation with only a quick look at a graph. By organizing data into a graph, you can interpret, compare, and analyze the numbers.

Tables, charts, and schedules generally present exact data. On the other hand, graphs often present data that has been rounded off to simplify the presentation of the information. When you read the graph, you'll estimate the answer based on what you see.

You may have to estimate a value when it is not at the mark for a distinct value. It is called **interpolation** to estimate the value between two given values. It is called **extrapolation** to estimate a value outside the given values. For both interpolation and extrapolation you will need to use ratios to find the answer. For example, consider the enrollment bar graph shown below from which you will first interpolate information in Example 1 and then extrapolate information in Example 2.

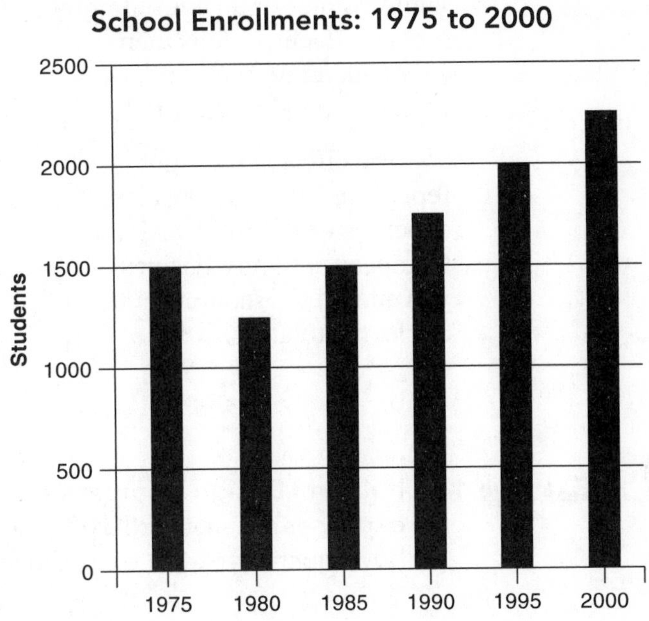

Example 1 What was the approximate enrollment in 1993?

1993 is $\frac{3}{5}$ of the five years between 1990 to 1995. So $\frac{3}{5}$ of the 250 students between 1750 and 2000 is $\frac{3}{5} \times 250 = 150$. Finally, $1750 + 150 = 1900$. By **interpolation,** in 1993 the enrollment was **1900 students.**

Example 2 What do you predict the enrollment will be in 2005?

The graph shows that enrollments have been rising about 250 students every five years since 1980. Without any other information you can predict that the enrollments will continue the same pattern. So by **extrapolation,** you can predict that in 2005 the enrollment will be **2500 students.**

You can draw conclusions based on the data presented. From the School Enrollments graph you could draw the conclusion that the enrollments have risen regularly since 1980. What you cannot say is that enrollments grew because many new homes were built in the area. The graph does not explain why enrollments increased. Be very careful when you analyze graphs to draw conclusions based only on the information given.

Circle Graphs

The circle in a **circle graph** represents a whole quantity. For instance, a circle could represent the whole population of the United States or an entire family income. Each circle is then subdivided into sections that represent parts of the whole.

The circle at the right represents all of the business expenses of Kacimi Design Company, a family business. If you add all the sections in the circle, the total is 100%.

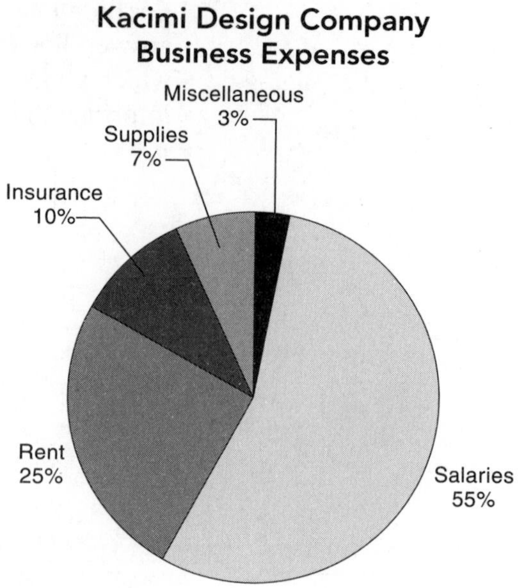

Example 1 If Kacimi Design Company business expenses totaled $250,000 last year, how much were the expenses for rent?

You see from the graph that rent expenses account for 25% of the total. $\frac{n}{250000} = \frac{25}{100}$

Set up and solve a proportion. $n = \frac{250000 \times 25}{100} = \$62{,}500$

The expenses for rent were **$62,500.**

Example 2 What is the ratio of insurance costs to the total budget?

Set up a ratio of insurance to total. $\frac{10\%}{100\%} = \frac{10}{100} = \frac{1}{10}$

The ratio is **1 to 10.**

Another way of saying this is $1 out of every $10 spent is used for insurance.

EXERCISE 3

Circle Graphs

Directions: Solve each problem using the charts and graphs as appropriate.

1. Using the circle graph and the chart, find the average yearly amount spent on salaries in the three years from 1998 to 2000.

Kacimi Design Company

Year	Total Expenses
1998	$92,000
1999	$156,000
2000	$250,000

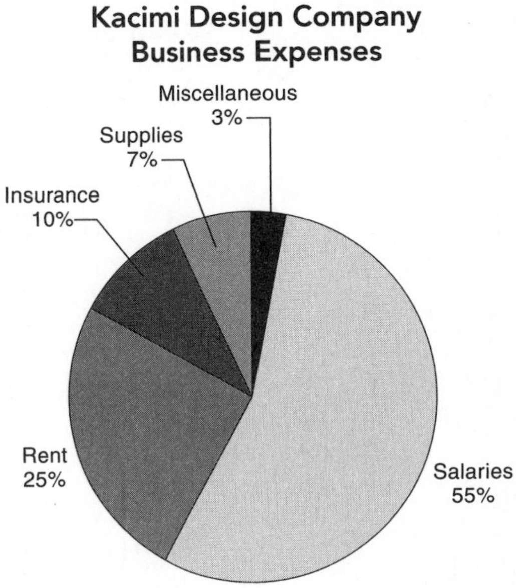

Questions 2–8 are based on the graph below.

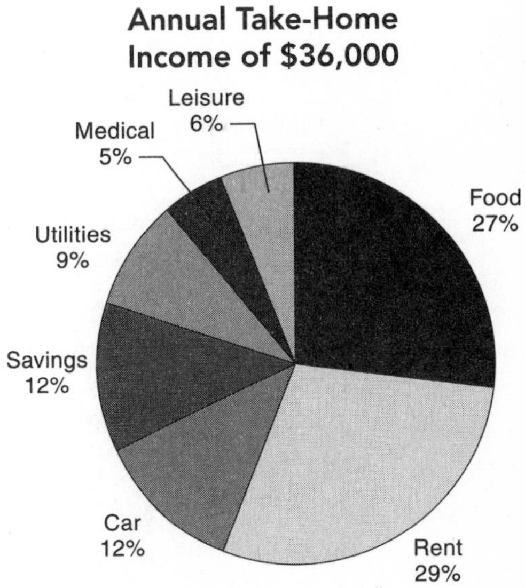

2. How much is spent for car expenses in a year?

3. What is the average *monthly* expense for food?

4. How much is spent on clothing during the year?

5. What is the ratio of rent to entire take-home income?

6. What is the ratio of medical expense to entire take-home income?

7. How much more money is spent on utilities expenses than leisure expenses during the entire year?

8. If savings are decreased to 10% annually, how much less money is saved during the year?

Answers are on page 934.

Bar Graphs

A **bar graph** is an excellent way of comparing amounts. The bars on the graph can run horizontally (across) or vertically (up and down).

The horizontal bar graph below shows the distance five experimental cars traveled on one gallon of gas. You can see that Car Z had the best gas mileage (traveled the farthest on one gallon of gas) and that Car T traveled 30 miles on one gallon of gas.

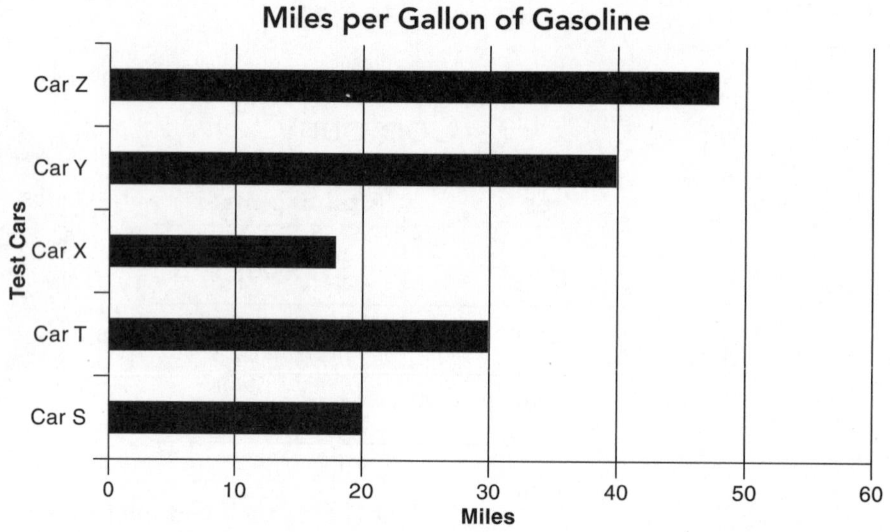

The bar graph shows clearly that Car Z performs better than the other cars by a wide margin. It is also obvious that Car X goes the shortest distance on a gallon of gas.

Notice that you have to estimate the values for Car X and Car Z because the bars do not end on distinct values. If you perform calculations using the estimates, your answers will be approximate. In many cases, the approximate answer will be sufficient.

You can use information from the graph to describe the data presented. The range is the difference between the fewest miles per gallon and the most miles per gallon ($48 - 18 = 30$). The difference between the best performing car and the worst performing car is approximately 30 miles per gallon.

You can also look at the graph and see that the median is 30 miles per gallon. Remember to put the amounts in order before choosing the middle number.

EXERCISE 4

Bar Graphs

Directions: Use the vertical bar graph below to answer the questions.

1. What was Smiths' income in 1998?

Smith Family Income and Expenses: 1998–2001

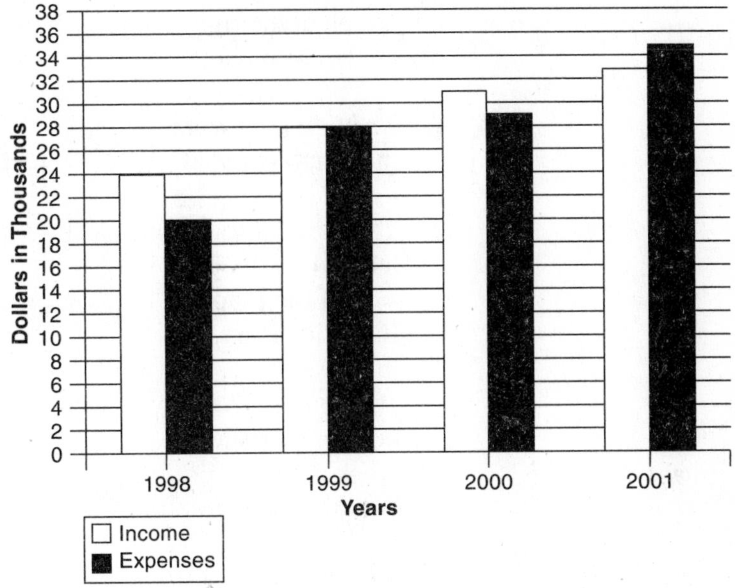

2. What were the average expenses per year for the years 1998 to 2001?

3. In what year did the Smiths' expenses exceed income?

4. In 2000 what was the difference between income and expenses?

5. What was the Smiths' average income per year for the years 1998 to 2001?

6. What is the ratio of expenses to income in 1998?

7. What conclusions can you draw from the information in the bar graph?
   (1) Expenses rose faster than income from 1998 to 2001.
   (2) Income rose faster than expenses from 1998 to 2001.
   (3) Expenses rose because products cost more in 2001 than in 1998.
   (4) Income rose because the Smiths received bigger bonuses in 2001 than they did in 1998.
   (5) If the pattern continues, income will always be higher than expenses.

Answers are on page 934.

Line Graphs

Line graphs are used to show trends or patterns. On a line graph, each point relates two values. One is the value on the vertical (up and down) axis at the left side, and the other is the value on the horizontal (left to right) axis at the bottom.

As you look at the line graph at the right, notice the following:

1. The title tells what the graph is about.

2. The vertical scale is labeled on the left side of the graph. Each line is an increase of 10 degrees. The horizontal scale is labeled on the bottom of the graph. Each line is an increase of 1 hour.

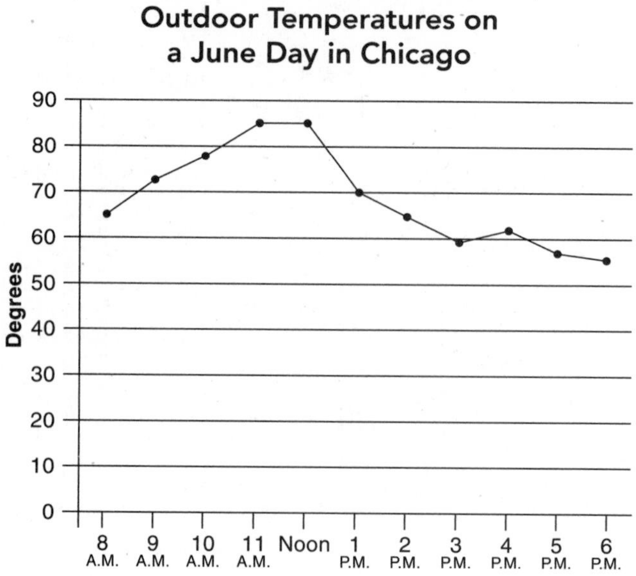

3. The line shows the following trend: the temperature rose until 11:00 A.M. and remained steady until noon. Then the temperature fell.

On some graphs you can use **correlation** to describe the relationship between the values on the horizontal axis and the values on the vertical axis.

The horizontal values and the vertical values can have a **positive correlation** when both values increase or both decrease at the same time. In the graph to the right you can see that as advertising dollars increase, sales also increase. This is a positive correlation between advertising and sales.

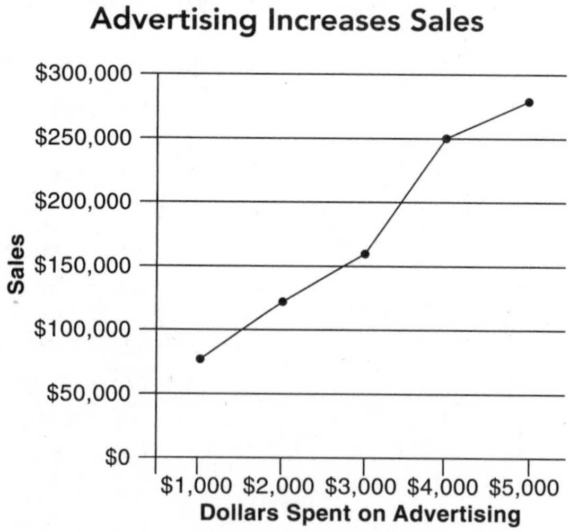

A **negative correlation** exists when one value increases at the same time the other value decreases. As the line graph on the right shows, profits fell as expenses rose. This is a negative correlation between expenses and profits.

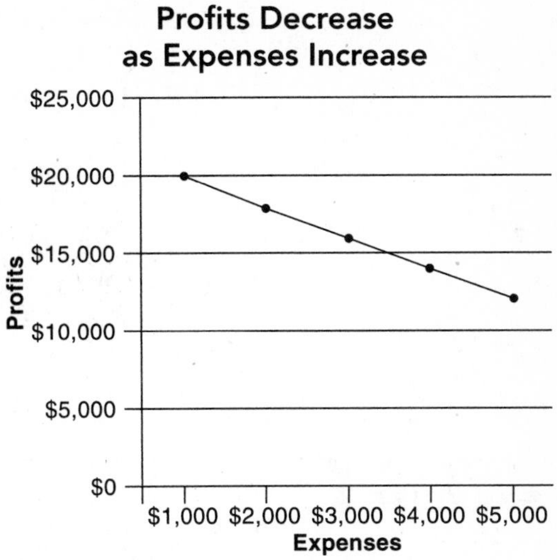

You can also use a line graph to compare two different trends. Below is an example of this. One trend is shown with a line with circles; the other is shown with a line with squares. When a graph uses two or more lines, you can compare information from the lines.

EXERCISE 5

Line Graphs

Directions: Use the graph below to answer the questions.

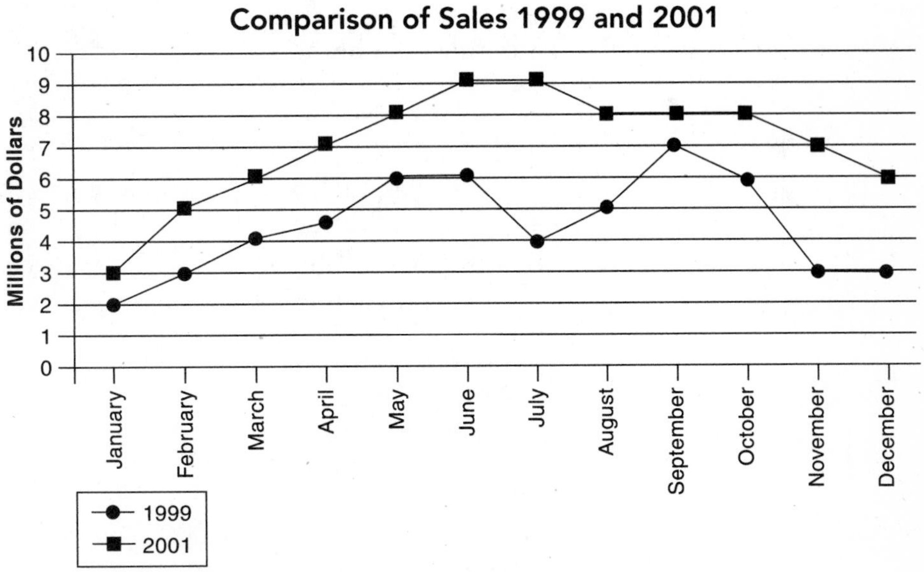

1. The title tells us that the graph compares ______________ in ______________ (year) and ______________ (year).

2. The vertical scale is labeled in ______________ .

3. The horizontal scale is labeled in ______________________.

4. In June of 1999 sales were about ______________________.

5. In June of 2001 sales were about ______________________.

6. The graph shows that both 1999 and 2001 had seasonal highs and lows. In general, 2001 had considerably ______________ sales all year long.

Answers are on page 934.

EXERCISE 6

Mixed Graph Practice

Directions: Solve each problem. Questions 1–5 are based on the circle graph below.

Gross pay represents earnings. Net pay is take-home pay. FICA stands for Federal Insurance Contribution Act, which is Social Security.

Distribution of Gross Pay

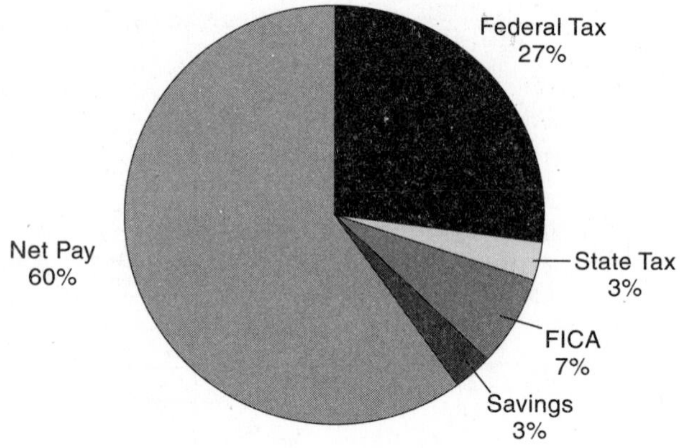

1. What is the ratio of savings to earnings?

2. If you make $18,000 per year, what is your *monthly* take-home pay?

3. If you make $36,000 per year, what is your annual contribution to Social Security?

4. If you wanted to have take-home pay of $24,000, how much would your actual earnings have to be?

5. One year, Bill earned $40,000. The deductions from his paycheck were federal tax, FICA, and state tax. What was his yearly take-home pay?

Questions 6–12 refer to the bar graph below.

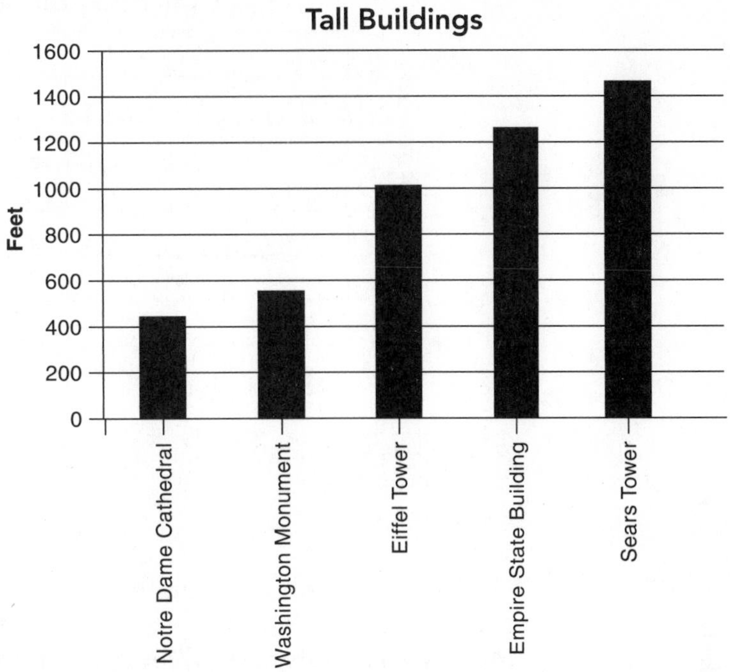

6. What is the difference in height between the Empire State Building and the Sears Tower?

7. If a 107-foot TV antenna were erected at the top of the Sears Tower, what would be the total height of the tower?

8. The Empire State Building is how many times as tall as the Notre Dame Cathedral?

9. The height of Notre Dame Cathedral is approximately what percent of the height of the Sears Tower?

10. What is the average height of these five structures?

11. What is the median height of these five structures?

12. If each floor is about 13 feet tall, about how many floors are in the Sears Tower?

Questions 13–18 refer to the line graph below.

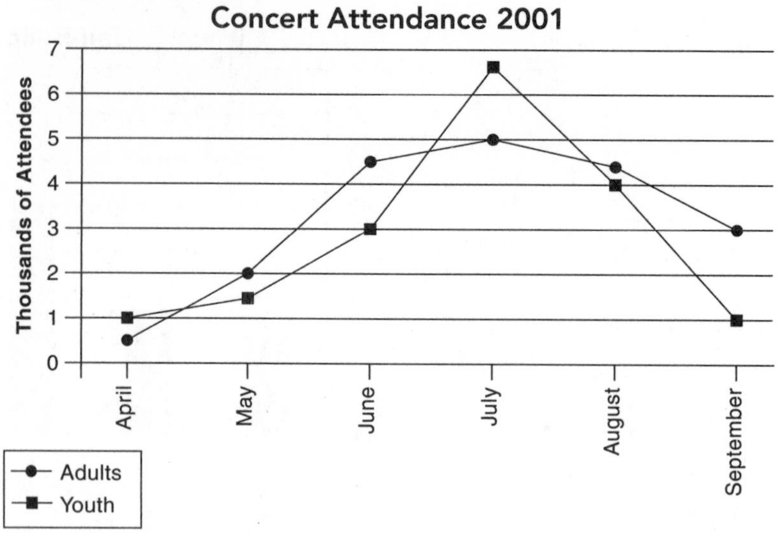

13. How many people attended concerts in June?

14. In which months was youth attendance higher than that for adults?

15. If adult tickets were $12.50 and youth tickets were $8.50, what were the receipts for the concerts held in August?

16. As spring turns to summer, what is the correlation between the time of year and attendance in general?

17. As summer turns to fall, what is the correlation between the time of year and attendance in general?

18. What was the average monthly concert attendance for both adults and youth combined?

Answers are on page 934.

Go to **www.GEDMath.com** for additional practice and instruction!

CHAPTER 10

Algebra

Algebra, an extension of arithmetic, is an organized system of rules that help to solve problems. Think of algebra as a game. When you first sit down to play, you review the rules and try to understand how to apply them.

Every game has its own vocabulary, which is defined in the rules. As you play the game, you find yourself using the vocabulary of the game and following the rules. The more you play the game, the easier it is to remember both the vocabulary and the rules. In this section you will begin your study of algebra with a look at its special vocabulary and the rules of mathematics. You will notice that the rules of algebra are the foundation of the arithmetic you use every day.

The Language of Algebra

Algebra uses letters of the alphabet to represent unknown quantities. These letters are called **variables.** These letters are variable because they change value from problem to problem. The letters can be capital letters, lowercase letters, or even Greek letters. Some examples are x, t, n, B, R, and ϕ. **Constants** are fixed values. The value of a constant is known and does not change from problem to problem. Examples of constants are 8, 75, 0, π, and $\sqrt{3}$.

In algebra you work with the four operations of addition, subtraction, multiplication, and division. The chart below shows the symbols that are used for these four operations.

OPERATION	SYMBOL	EXAMPLE	MEANING
Addition	+	$5 + n$	5 plus *n*
Subtraction	–	$8 - n$ n – 8	8 take away *n* n take away 8
Multiplication	• ( ) *no symbol*	5 • 3 5(4) 5*n*	5 times 3 5 times 4 5 times *n*
Division	÷ fraction bar	$n \div 3$ $\frac{n}{3}$ $3 \div n$ $\frac{3}{n}$	*n* divided by 3 3 divided by *n*

Whenever a number and a variable are multiplied together, the number part is called the **coefficient** of the variable. In the expression $7x$, the coefficient of x is 7. The variable x is multiplied by 7.

Tip

Whenever the variable is written without a number in front of it, the coefficient is understood to be 1. Therefore, x means $1x$, and the coefficient is 1.

Algebraic Expressions

An **algebraic term** can be a constant, a variable, or the multiplication or division of numbers with variables. Some examples of terms are 4, y, $3n$, or $\frac{x}{2}$.

An **algebraic expression** is any combination of numbers, variables, grouping symbols, and operations. In an algebraic expression, terms are separated by + and – signs. The sign before the term belongs to the term. For example, $5 - 3y$, $a + 4$, and $\frac{m}{4} + 2$ are all algebraic expressions.

$5 - 3y$	$a + 4$	$\frac{m}{4} + 2$
1st term 2nd term	1st term 2nd term	1st term 2nd term

$5 - 3y$ is an algebraic expression that has two terms: 5 and $-3y$.

$a + 4$ is an algebraic expression that has two terms: a and $+4$.

$\frac{m}{4} + 2$ is an algebraic expression that has two terms: $\frac{m}{4}$ and $+2$.

EXERCISE 1

Terms

Directions: Name the terms in the following expressions.

1. $8 + n$ **2.** $8x + 7y - 6$ **3.** $2x^2 - \frac{3}{x}$ **4.** $8ab + 12$

Answers are on page 935.

Evaluating Algebraic Expressions

An algebraic expression has no value until the variables in the expression have been replaced with numbers. To **evaluate** an expression, replace every variable with a given value for the variable. Then evaluate the resulting numerical expression. Remember to follow the rules for the order of operations and the rules for signed numbers.

Evaluate the algebraic expressions for the given values of the variables.

Example 1 Evaluate $3x - 4$ when x is 5.
$3x - 4 = 3(5) - 4 = 15 - 4 = \mathbf{11}$

Example 2 Evaluate $t^2 - t + 3$ when t is 4.
$t^2 - t + 3 = (4)^2 - 4 + 3 = 16 - 4 + 3 = \mathbf{15}$

Example 3 Evaluate $7 + 4(8 - x)$ when x is -2.
$7 + 4(8 - x) = 7 + 4(8 - (-2)) = 7 + 4(8 + 2) = 7 + 4(10) = 7 + 40 = \mathbf{47}$

In Example 3 you must do the work inside the parentheses first. $8 - (-2)$ means $8 + 2$ following the rules for signed numbers.

EXERCISE 2

Evaluating Algebraic Expressions

Directions: Evaluate the following expressions for the given values.

1. $12 - 4n$, when n is 2
2. $3y + 9$, when y is -2
3. $x^2 - 3x + 2$, when x is 5
4. The formula for distance is $d = rt$, where r is the rate, t is the time, and d is the distance. Find the distance if the rate is 60 miles per hour and the time is 2.5 hours.
5. The formula for the perimeter of a rectangle is $2(l + w)$ where l is the length and w is the width of the rectangle. Find the perimeter of the rectangle if the length is 15 inches and the width is 7 inches.

Answers are on page 935.

Equations

An **equation** states that one expression is equal to another expression. For example, the equation $x + 7 = 10$ sets the expression $x + 7$ equal to the expression 10. In the equation $x + 3 = 2x - 9$, the expression $x + 3$ is set equal to the expression $2x - 9$.

It is important to recognize the difference between an expression and an equation.

An equation always has an **equal sign.**

Expression	Equation
$x + 7$	$x + 7 = 10$
$2x - 9$	$x + 3 = 2x - 9$

AN EQUATION ALWAYS HAS THREE PARTS		
left-side expression	equal sign	right-side expression

An equation may be true or false depending on the replacement value for the variables. The equation $x + 7 = 10$ says that some number $\boldsymbol{x}$ added to 7 equals 10. Since you know that $3 + 7 = 10$, you know that $x = 3$ is the **solution** of the equation. The solution is the value of the variable that makes the statement true. If you had said that $x = 2$, you would not have found the solution of the equation. You **solve** an equation when you find the solution for the variable. On the GED Mathematics Test, you may have to translate a word problem into an equation. You will also write and interpret your own equations.

Example Solve the equation $2x + 5 = 17$.

This equation means that a number multiplied by 2 and added to 5 equals 17. Do you know what the number is? You're right if you said **6,** because $2(6) + 5 = 17$.

EXERCISE 3

Equations

Directions: Write in words what each equation means. Use the words *a number* for any variable.

1. $5 + 7y = 19$ **2.** $9y = 27$ **3.** $a - 5 = 23$ **4.** $\frac{10}{y} - 5 = 0$ **5.** $\frac{y}{8} = 9$

Answers are on page 935.

Solving One-Step Equations

Among the most important uses of algebra are solving equations and using equations to solve word problems.

Eyeballing the Solution

Solving an equation means finding the value of the variable that makes the equation true. Some equations will be fairly easy to solve because you know your math facts. If you can look at the equation and see the answer, you are "eyeballing" the equation.

For example, $x - 4 = 10$ is an equation. What value of x will make this true? You would choose $x = 14$ because you know $14 - 4 = 10$. Another example is $3x = 15$. What value of x makes this equation true? The answer is 5 because you know $3(5) = 15$.

EXERCISE 4

Eyeballing

Directions: Solve the following equations by "eyeballing" them. Ask yourself, "What number would make this equation true?" Then choose that number to represent the variable shown in the problem.

1. $r - 2 = 0$ **2.** $4 + x = 9$ **3.** $p - 5 = 8$ **4.** $5a = 10$

5. $\frac{x}{5} = 2$ **6.** $t + 3 = 8$ **7.** $3x = 9$ **8.** $\frac{36}{n} = 9$

Answers are on page 935.

Algebraic Solutions

Let's look at algebraic methods of solving one-step equations. Before you start solving equations, you must understand a couple of mathematical ideas.

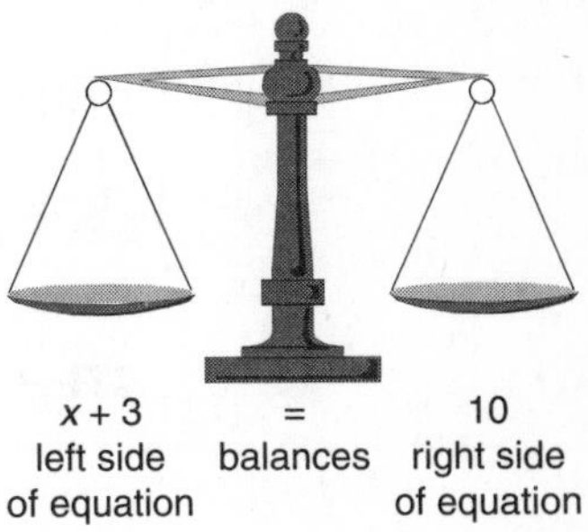

First, an equation is a perfect balance between what is on the left side of the equal sign and what is on the right side of the equal sign. If you make any changes on the left side, you must make the same changes on the right side. For instance, if you add 7 to the left side, you must add 7 to the right side for the two sides to remain equal. Then you know the result will be true.

Second, your goal in solving an equation is to get the variable all by itself on one side of the equation. Concentrate on the variable. In the equation $x + 3 = 10$, concentrate on the x. Notice that the x is being added to 3. This will tell you how to solve the equation.

Tip

Keep the equation in balance and concentrate on the variable.

To solve an equation, perform the opposite operation (called the **inverse operation**). Addition and subtraction are opposites, and multiplication and division are opposites. In the equation $x + 3 = 10$, you see that 3 is being added to x. The opposite of adding three is subtracting three. Subtract three from both sides to get x all by itself.

Example 1 $x + 3 = 10$

STEP 1 Look at x. 3 is added to it. $x + 3 = 10$

STEP 2 Subtract 3 from both sides. $x + 3 - 3 = 10 - 3$
$x + 0 = 7$

STEP 3 Solve the equation. $\mathbf{x = 7}$

SOLVING AN EQUATION

1. Keep the equation in balance.
2. Concentrate on the variable.
3. Perform the opposite operations.
4. Isolate the variable on one side of the equation.

Example 2 $7x = 21$

STEP 1 Look at x. It is multiplied by 7. $7x = 21$

STEP 2 Divide by 7 on both sides of the equation. $\frac{7x}{7} = \frac{21}{7}$

$1x = 3$

STEP 3 Solve the equation. $\mathbf{x = 3}$

Check the answers to each problem by substituting the answer in the original equation. For example, when you solved $7x = 21$, you got $x = 3$. Check that answer by substituting 3 for x in the original problem.

Substitute 3 for x. $7x = 21$
This is a true statement, $7(3) = 21$
so $x = 3$ is the solution for $7x = 21$. $21 = 21$

Example 3 $8 = \frac{x}{5}$

STEP 1	Look at x. It is divided by 5.	$8 = \frac{x}{5}$	
STEP 2	Multiply both sides by 5.	$5 \bullet 8 = \frac{x}{5} \bullet 5$	
STEP 3	Solve the equation.	$\mathbf{40 = x}$	Check: $8 = \frac{40}{5}$ is true.

EXERCISE 5

One-Step Equations

Directions: Solve for *x*. Check your answers.

1. $x + 6 = 15$ **2.** $2x = 6$ **3.** $5x = 75$ **4.** $x - 3 = 12$

5. $\frac{x}{3} = 12$ **6.** $x - 8 = 0$ **7.** $\frac{x}{4} = 16$ **8.** $\frac{1}{2}x = 14$

Answers are on page 935.

Solving Algebra Word Problems

To use algebra to solve mathematical problems, you have to translate the problem into algebraic language. Let a variable represent the unknown quantity. The letters *x*, *y*, and *z* are most often used as variables. A few English phrases are used repeatedly in algebra problems. Become familiar with the phrases and their algebraic expressions in the chart.

English Phrase	Operation	Algebraic Expression
The **sum** of two numbers	add	$x + y$
Five **more than** a number		$x + 5$
A number **increased by** 4	+	$x + 4$
A number **added to another number**		$x + y$
Nine **plus** a number		$9 + x$
The **difference** between two numbers	subtract	$x - y$
Seven **decreased by** a number		$7 - x$
A number **reduced by** 4	–	$x - 4$
Three **less than** a number	Be sure the number	$x - 3$
Six **subtracted** from a number	subtracted follows the	$x - 6$
Six **minus** a number	minus sign.	$6 - x$

English Phrase	Operation	Algebraic Expression
The **product** of two numbers	multiply	
	no symbol	xy
Five **multiplied by** 7	( )	$5(7)$
	•	$5 \bullet 7$
Six **times** a number	no symbol	$6y$
Twice a number *or* **double** a number		$2y$
Two-thirds **of** a number		$\frac{2}{3}x$ or $\frac{2x}{3}$
The **quotient** of two numbers	divide	
	fraction bar	$\frac{x}{y}$ or $x \div y$
	÷	
A number **divided by** three	Be sure the number	$\frac{x}{3}$
	you are dividing by is	
Seven **divided by** a number	below the fraction bar	$\frac{7}{x}$
	or	
Half a number	follows the division	$\frac{x}{2}$ or $\frac{1}{2}x$
	symbol.	
	powers and roots	
A number **squared**	raise to the 2nd power	x^2
A number **cubed**	raise to the 3rd power	x^3
The **square root** of a number	square root	$\sqrt{x}$

TRANSLATING EXPRESSIONS

1. Assign a variable to the unknown quantity.
2. Use that variable to write an expression for any other unknown quantity.
3. Identify the phrases that indicate the mathematical operation.
4. Use the operation to write the expression. (Use parentheses to group an operation with two numbers to be calculated first when a second operation is to be performed on the result.)

Translate: The square of a number decreased by the number.

Let x be the number.
The square of a number is x^2.
Decreased by means to subtract.
Write $x^2 - x$.

Using the chart as a guide to the examples below, translate the following English phrases into algebraic expressions.

Example 1 Four more than a number = $\mathbf{4 + x}$

Example 2 Six decreased by half a number = $\mathbf{6 - \frac{1}{2}x}$

Example 3 Twelve divided by a number squared = $\frac{12}{x^2}$

Example 4 Twice the sum of a number and four = $2(x + 4)$

Example 5 The difference between twice a number and four = $2x - 4$

EXERCISE 6

Translating English to Algebra

Directions: Translate the English phrases to algebraic expressions using x and y to stand for the unknown numbers.

1. five less than a number
2. the product of fourteen and a number
3. the difference between two numbers divided by 3
4. the sum of a number squared and another number squared
5. three fourths of a number
6. seven more than twice a number
7. the square of a number increased by twelve
8. a number cubed divided by 4
9. five times a number divided by twice the same number
10. the sum of half a number and three

Answers are on page 935.

Translating Equations

You can now practice translating an entire sentence into an algebraic equation. Remember, an equation has three parts: left-side expression, equal sign, and right-side expression.

Many key words or phrases indicate *equals.* Become familiar with the list below:

equals	is	the result is
is equal to	are	the answer is
equal to	was	the sum is
the same as	were	the difference is
yields	gives	the quotient is
makes	leaves	the product is

TRANSLATING EQUATIONS

1. Assign a variable to the unknown quantity.
2. Write two expressions for the values.
3. Use an equal sign between the expressions.

Example 1 Three times a number is one more than twice the number.

$3x = 1 + 2x$

Example 2 Four more than a number equals 15.

$4 + x = 15$

Example 3 Twice a number reduced by six is equal to 9.

$2x - 6 = 9$

Tip

To identify the variable in a word problem, isolate the term or element that you don't know. Then assign a variable to that term.

Example 4 To promote holiday sales, a magazine offers one-year subscriptions for $15 and additional gift subscriptions for $12 each. With a one-year subscription, how many gift subscriptions can you get if you have $75 to spend altogether?

Let x represent the number of $12 gift subscriptions. Then 12 times x is the cost of the additional subscriptions. The basic statement is original subscription price plus additional subscription cost is 75.

$15 + 12x = 75$

In Example 4, the variable was identified first. Then algebraic expressions and the operation were written. Finally, these values were translated into an algebraic equation.

EXERCISE 7

Translating Sentences to Equations

Directions: Translate each sentence to an equivalent algebraic equation.

1. One-fourth of a number equals 18.
2. Two less than a number is 40.

3. Three times a number increased by 1 is 25.

4. Nine increased by half a number gives a result of 13.

5. The product of 6 and a number makes 35.

6. The difference between two numbers is 8.

7. Eighteen more than twice a number is 22.

8. A number divided by 4 yields a quotient of 18.

9. Twice a number, reduced by 3, is equal to 5 times the same number increased by 9.

In questions 10–14, select the equation that could be used to find the unknown in the problem.

10. A man has x dollars. After paying a bill of \$48, he has \$75 left.

(1) $x + 48 = 75$ **(2)** $48 - x = 75$ **(3)** $x - 48 = 75$ **(4)** $75 - 48 = x$

11. A golfer has x number of golf balls. After playing eighteen holes of golf, he has lost 5 balls and has 19 left. How many balls did he have before he played the eighteen holes of golf?

(1) $x - 5 = 19$ **(2)** $\frac{x}{5} = 19$ **(3)** $x - 18 = 19$ **(4)** $x + 5 = 19$

12. In a wrestling meet Tito scored 5 points, which represented one-seventh of his team's final score. What was the final score, x?

(1) $x + \frac{1}{7} = 5$ **(2)** $x - 5 = \frac{1}{2}$ **(3)** $x - 5 = 7$ **(4)** $\frac{x}{7} = 5$

13. A plumber charges \$25 for a house call plus \$32 per hour for the time worked. If the charge is \$84, how many hours, h, did he work?

(1) $32 + h + 25 = 84$ **(2)** $32h = 84$ **(3)** $25 + 32h = 84$ **(4)** $\frac{h}{32} + 25 = 84$

14. Inga will not tell her age x. In 6 years, her age will be $\frac{7}{6}$ as much as it is now. How can her age be written?

(1) $x + 6 = \frac{7}{6}x$ **(2)** $x - \frac{7}{6}x = 1$ **(3)** $\frac{x}{6} = \frac{7}{6}x$ **(4)** $\frac{7}{6}x = 6$

Answers are on page 935.

Solving One-Step Algebra Word Problems

This next exercise combines practice in translating, setting up, and solving one-step algebra problems. Look at an example before you begin the exercise.

Example Sue has money, and Tom has $\frac{2}{3}$ as much money as Sue. If Tom has \$48, how much does Sue have?

STEP 1 Translate and set up the equation. Let x represent Sue's money. Then $\frac{2}{3}x$ represents Tom's money. So $\frac{2}{3}x = 48$.

STEP 2 Solve the equation. Multiply both sides by $\frac{3}{2}$.

$\frac{2}{3}x = 48$

$\frac{3}{2} \times \frac{2}{3}x = 48 \times \frac{3}{2}$

$x = 48 \bullet \frac{3}{2} = 72$ So Sue has **\$72.**

EXERCISE 8

Solving One-Step Algebra Word Problems

Directions: Solve each problem.

1. If seven less than a number is 8, find the number.
2. Baseballs cost \$3.25 each. How many baseballs can you buy for \$52?
3. Steve invested $\frac{3}{4}$ of his year-end bonus. If he invested \$1875, how much is his bonus?
4. Amanda sold her stereo set for \$120 less than she paid for it. If she sold the stereo set for \$72, what did she originally pay for it?
5. After $5\frac{1}{2}$ feet were cut off a wooden beam, $6\frac{1}{2}$ feet were left. What was the original length of the beam?
6. After Roy gained 14 pounds, he weighed 172 pounds. What was his original weight?
7. Twelve years from now, Lucille will be 48 years old. How old is she now?
8. By purchasing a fleet of cars for its salespeople, Tower Manufacturing gets a discount of \$1620 on each car purchased. This is 9% of the regular price. Find the regular price.

Answers are on page 935.

Simplifying Algebraic Expressions

Many algebraic expressions contain two or more terms. For instance, $2x - 7$ has two terms, and $3x - 9y + 7x$ has three terms. To simplify an algebraic expression, combine like terms and remove all symbols of grouping such as parentheses ( ) and brackets [ ].

Simplifying by Combining Like Terms

Like terms are terms that contain the same variables to the same power.

Examples of like terms are $4x$ $7x$ $12x$ and $2xy$ xy $17xy$ and $9x^2$ $4x^2$ x^2.

Examples of unlike terms are $3x$ 4y -2 $2xy$ and $3x$ $4y$ $3x^2$.

You can combine like terms to simplify an expression.

<u>**Example 1**</u> $3x + 5x = \mathbf{8x}$ (Just add the coefficients—the numbers.)

<u>**Example 2**</u> $7y^2 - 5y^2 = \mathbf{2y^2}$ (You can also subtract coefficients.)

<u>**Example 3**</u> $3x^2 + 6y + 2x^2 - 4y = \mathbf{5x^2 + 2y}$
(First, combine the x^2 terms and then combine the y terms.)

<u>**Example 4**</u> $2x - 3y - 5y + 2 + 4x - 6 = \mathbf{6x - 8y - 4}$
(Combine the x terms, combine the y terms, and combine the numbers.)

Tip

Remember to use the rules for combining signed numbers when you combine the coefficients. (You can find the rules on page 779.)

EXERCISE 9

Combining Like Terms

Directions: Simplify the following expressions by combining like terms.

1. $3x + 12x$

2. $3x^2 + 14 + 7x + 2x^2 - 5$

3. $7y - 4y$

4. $4a + 3b - 2a - 3b + a$

5. $2x + 3y + 6y + 7x$

6. $x + 2y - y$

7. $7x^2 + 3x + 4x - 2x$

8. $9a^2 + 4a + a + 3a^2$

9. $8x - 3 + 5x$

10. $5xy + 7x - 3y - x + 4xy$

Answers are on page 936.

Removing Grouping Symbols

Some algebraic expressions are grouped together using parentheses or brackets. These symbols draw your attention.

SIMPLIFYING GROUPING SYMBOLS

To simplify an expression containing grouping symbols, use one of the following procedures.

1. Remove the parentheses and distribute the multiplication over every term in the parentheses.

   <u>Example 1</u> $3(2x - 4) = 3(2x) + 3(-4) = \mathbf{6x - 12}$
   <u>Example 2</u> $-3(4x - 1) = -3(4x) + -3(-1) = \mathbf{-12x + 3}$

2. Remove the parentheses and distribute the negative sign over every term in the parentheses, following the rules for double signs.

   <u>Example 3</u> $3x - (6x - 4) = 3x - (6x) - (-4) = \mathbf{3x - 6x + 4}$

   or $-3x + 4$ after combining like terms

3. Remove the parentheses but do not change the signs on any terms if there is a plus sign or no sign in front of the parentheses.

   <u>Example 4</u> $6x + (2x - 7) = \mathbf{6x + 2x - 7}$

   or $8x - 7$ after combining like terms

EXERCISE 10

Simplifying Grouping Symbols

Directions: Simplify the following expressions by removing grouping symbols.

1. $5(3x + 2)$	**2.** $4(7x - 8)$	**3.** $6x + (12x - 7)$
4. $-2(x - 1)$	**5.** $3(2x + 4 - 3y)$	**6.** $-6(5x - 12)$
7. $x - 2(9 + 6x)$	**8.** $2(x - y)$	**9.** $4x - (2 - x)$

Answers are on page 936.

Solving Multistep Equations

You study multistep equations because you will use them to solve some algebra word problems on the GED Mathematics Test. To solve multistep equations, you follow the step-by-step approach shown below. Always plan to start with step 1 and progress through the steps in order, but keep in mind that some equations will not need every step.

SOLVING EQUATIONS STEP BY STEP

1. Simplify expressions on both sides of the equation.
2. Get all the variables on the left side of the equation using addition or subtraction from the right side of the equation.
3. Concentrate on the variable, *undo addition and subtraction* using the opposite operation.
4. To isolate the variable, *undo multiplication and division* using the opposite operation.

Example 1 $3x + 7 = 13$

STEP 1 The expression is already simplified. $3x + 7 = 13$

STEP 2 The variable is already on the left side. $3x + 7 = 13$

STEP 3 Undo addition using the opposite operation.

$$3x + 7 - 7 = 13 - 7$$
$$3x = 6$$

STEP 4 Undo multiplication using the opposite operation.

$$\frac{3x}{3} = \frac{6}{3}$$
$$\mathbf{x = 2}$$

Example 2 $3(x - 2) + 18 = 6 + 2(x + 6)$

STEP 1 Simplify the expressions.

$$3x - 6 + 18 = 6 + 2x + 12$$
$$3x + 12 = 2x + 18$$

STEP 2 Move the variable to the left side.

$$3x - 2x + 12 = 2x - 2x + 18$$
$$x + 12 = 18$$

STEP 3 Undo addition using the opposite operation.

$$x + 12 - 12 = 18 - 12$$
$$\mathbf{x = 6}$$

EXERCISE 11

Solving Multistep Equations

Directions: Solve the following equations.

1. $3x + 9 = 15$ **2.** $2x - 26 = 2$ **3.** $8(x - 4) = 0$

4. $2(5x - 11) + 12x = 0$ **5.** $\frac{4x}{3} - 14 = 14$ **6.** $\frac{x}{3} + 4 = 9$

Answers are on page 936.

Solving Multistep Problems

To set up a multistep problem, you have to translate from English to algebra. Remember to check your answer to see if it satisfies the original problem.

Example Tony worked 35 hours last week and only a few hours this week. He makes $15 per hour, and his paycheck for the two weeks is $795 before deductions. How many hours did he work this week?

STEP 1 Let x be the number of hours he worked this week.

STEP 2 Let $x + 35$ be the total number of hours worked during both weeks. $15(x + 35)$ is the expression that represents the amount of money he is paid for working at $15 per hour.

STEP 3 Write the equation to set up the problem. Since he earned $795, the equation is $15(x + 35) = 795$

STEP 4 Solve the equation.

$$15(x + 35) = 795$$

$$15x + 525 = 795$$

$$15x + 525 - 525 = 795 - 525$$

$$15x = 270$$

$$\frac{15x}{15} = \frac{270}{15}$$

$$\mathbf{x = 18}$$

Tony worked 18 hours this week.

EXERCISE 12

Setting Up and Solving Multistep Equations

Directions: Solve each problem.

Questions 1 and 2 are based on the following information.

Bret went on a 3-day ski trip. His rental equipment cost $32 per day and he paid for a lift ticket each day. His total bill was $180. Find the cost of the daily lift ticket.

1. Which equation best describes the problem? (Let x represent the cost of the daily lift ticket.)

(1) $x + 96 = 180$
(2) $3x + 32 = 180$
(3) $x + 32 = 180$
(4) $3(x + 32) = 180$
(5) Not enough information is given.

2. What is the cost of the daily lift ticket?

(1) $20 **(2)** $28 **(3)** $60 **(4)** $84 **(5)** $148

Questions 3 and 4 are based on the following information.

The distance around a triangle is 56 inches. If one side is 24 inches and the other two sides have the same measure, find the length, *x*, of one of these two sides.

3. Which equation best describes the problem above?

(1) $x + 24 = 56$ **(2)** $2x + 56 = 24$ **(3)** $2x - 24 = 56$
(4) $2x + 24 = 56$ **(5)** $x - 24 = 56$

4. What is the length of one of the two equal sides?

(1) 16 **(2)** 32 **(3)** 40 **(4)** 80 **(5)** 160

Questions 5 and 6 are based on the following information.

Twice as many adult tickets as children's tickets were sold for a soccer game. Also 38 tickets were given free of charge to contest winners. The attendance at the game was 8324 people. How many tickets of each type were sold?

5. Which equation best describes the problem above? Let x be the number of children's tickets sold.

(1) $x + 2x + 38 = 8324$ **(2)** $2x + x = 8324$ **(3)** $2(x + 2) - 38 = 8324$
(4) $2(x - 2) = 8324$ **(5)** Not enough information is given.

6. How many adult tickets were sold?

(1) 2762 **(2)** 2775 **(3)** 4143 **(4)** 4181 **(5)** 5524

Answers are on page 936.

Inequalities

The relationship between two amounts is not always equal, so you cannot always use an equation to solve a problem. If the relationship is not equal, you can use **inequalities** such as **< (is less than)** or **> (is greater than)** to solve the problem.

For example, $x + 3 > 10$ is an algebraic inequality. What value of x would make this a true statement? Several values of x would make this statement true. The letter x could be 8, because $8 + 3 > 10$. The letter x could also be 25, because $25 + 3 > 10$. In fact, x could be any number greater than 7. The solution is $x > 7$.

When you solve any inequality, the set of possible solutions is often infinite. You must be aware of the boundary of the solution. In this case the boundary is 7; x cannot be 7 or less than 7, but it can be any number greater than 7.

Solving Inequalities

The algebraic methods for solving an inequality are much the same as for algebraic equations. There is, however, one major rule you must keep in mind when solving an inequality that you don't need when you solve an equation.

RULE FOR MULTIPLYING AND DIVIDING AN INEQUALITY BY A NEGATIVE

When you multiply or divide both sides of an inequality by a negative number, it changes the direction of the inequality sign.

For example you know that $8 < 12$.	$8 < 12$	
If you multiply both sides by –2, you get 8(–2), which is –16, and 12(–2), which is –24.	$8(-2) > 12(-2)$	Notice that the arrow changed direction from *less than* to *greater than.*
You know that –16 is greater than –24.	$-16 > -24$	

You may see the signs ≤ meaning **is less than or equal to** and ≥ meaning **is greater than or equal to.** So if an answer is $x \geq 3$, this means that the answer is 3 or a number greater than 3. For example, a person's age for a senior discount must usually be greater than or equal to 65, so you could say "age ≥ 65."

SOLVING INEQUALITIES

1. Keep the inequality in balance. Whatever operation you perform on one side of the inequality, perform on the other.
2. Concentrate on the variable. Your goal is to get the variable on one side of the inequality.
3. Perform the opposite operation. First, do addition or subtraction; then do multiplication or division.
4. Remember to change the direction of the inequality sign when you multiply or divide by a negative number.

Example 1 $x + 3 > 10$

Look at x. It is added to 3. Subtract 3 from both sides. The inequality is solved when x is all by itself on the left side of the inequality.

$x + 3 > 10$

$x + 3 - 3 > 10 - 3$

$\mathbf{x > 7}$

Check: Choose any number greater than 7. For instance, if you choose 9, then 9 + 3 is 12 and that is greater than 10. Your answer that $x > 7$ makes sense.

Example 2 $-4x < 12$

Divide both sides by −4. Notice that you are dividing by a negative number, so change the direction of the inequality sign.

$-4x < 12$

$\frac{-4x}{-4} > \frac{12}{-4}$

$\mathbf{x > -3}$

Check: Choose any number greater than −3. For instance, if you choose 0, then −4(0) is 0 and that is greater than −3. Your answer that $x > -3$ makes sense.

EXERCISE 13

One-Step Inequalities

Directions: Choose either (a) or (b) to represent the relationship that makes the most sense for the following situations.

1. If x represents the voting age in the U.S., then **(a)** $x \geq 18$ **(b)** $x \leq 18$
2. If x represents your speed in a school zone, then **(a)** $x \geq 25$ **(b)** $x \leq 25$
3. If x represents the driving age, then **(a)** $x \geq 16$ **(b)** $x \leq 16$
4. If x represents the items in your grocery cart in the express line, then **(a)** $x \geq 10$ **(b)** $x \leq 10$

Solve each of the following inequalities for *x*. Check your answers.

5. $x - 3 > -5$ **6.** $5 + x < 7$ **7.** $-3 + x < -10$ **8.** $\frac{x}{-3} < 12$

9. $x - 5 \geq -1$ **10.** $-4x > 8$ **11.** $x - 7 \leq 0$ **12.** $-5x > -20$

Answers are on page 936.

Coordinate Graphing

In earlier sections you saw how graphs could be used to display data visually. Graphs can also be used to represent an equation. To understand the graph of an equation, you must first learn how points are plotted on a grid. The grid is called a **rectangular coordinate plane.** A horizontal number line called the ***x*-axis** and a vertical number line called the ***y*-axis** intersect at a point called the **origin.**

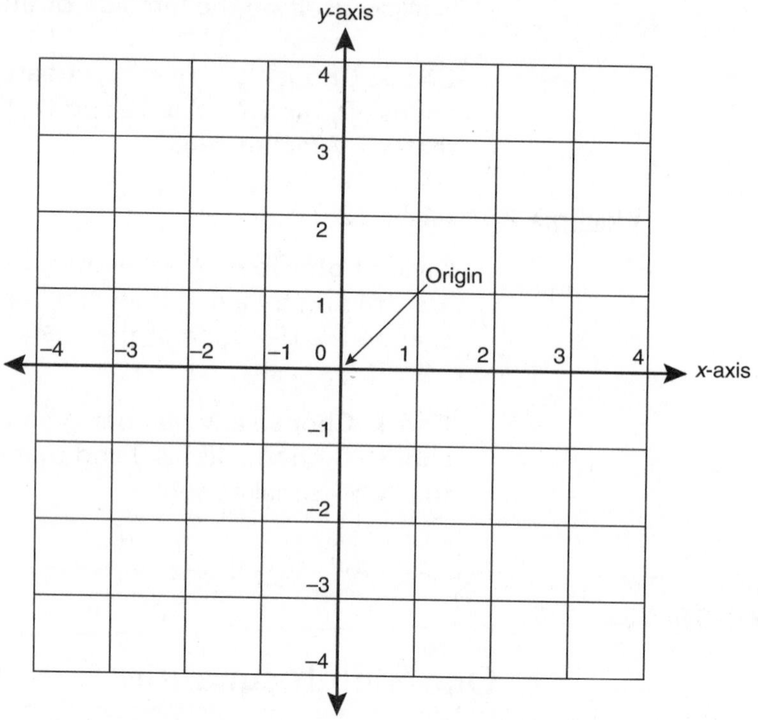

Each point that is graphed is identified by an **ordered pair** of numbers ***(x, y)***. The first number in the ordered pair is called the ***x*-coordinate,** and the second number is called the ***y*-coordinate.** The order of the coordinates is very important. The *x*-coordinate is always given first in the ordered pair, and the *y*-coordinate is always given second.

PLOTTING A POINT WITH THE COORDINATES (X, Y)

1. Start at the origin (0, 0).
2. If x is positive, move x units to the right.
   If x is negative, move x units to the left.
   If x is 0, make no move.
3. If y is positive, move y units upward.
   If y is negative, move y units downward.
   If y is 0, make no move.
4. Place a point at the location and label the ordered pair (x, y).

Example 1 Plot the point (3, 4).

Start at the origin.

x is 3 → move 3 units right.

y is 4 → move 4 units up.

Place a point at that location.

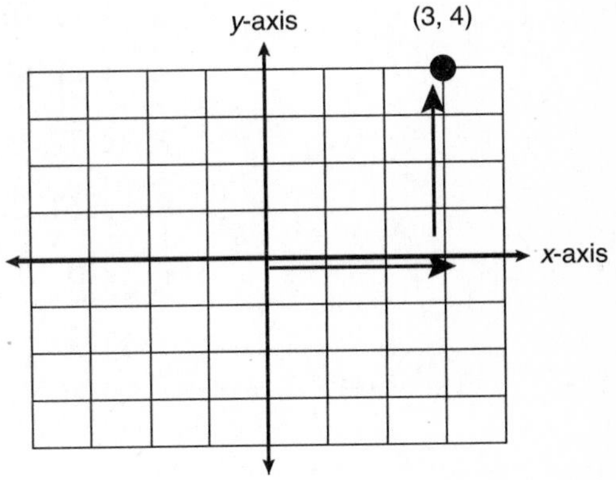

Example 2 Plot the point (–3, 2).

Start at the origin.

x is –3 → move 3 units left.

y is 2 → move 2 units up.

Place a point at that location.

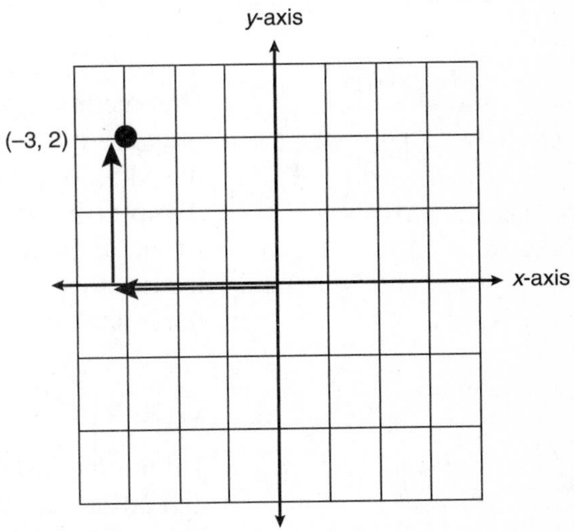

EXERCISE 14

Ordered Pairs

Directions: Plot the following points on the coordinate plane at right. Label each point A, B, C, and so on.

1. A (–3, 4)
2. B (–3, 0)
3. C (–2, –3)
4. D (1, –1)
5. E (3, 0)
6. F (4, 3)
7. G (2, 2)
8. H (0, 3)
9. I (0, 0)

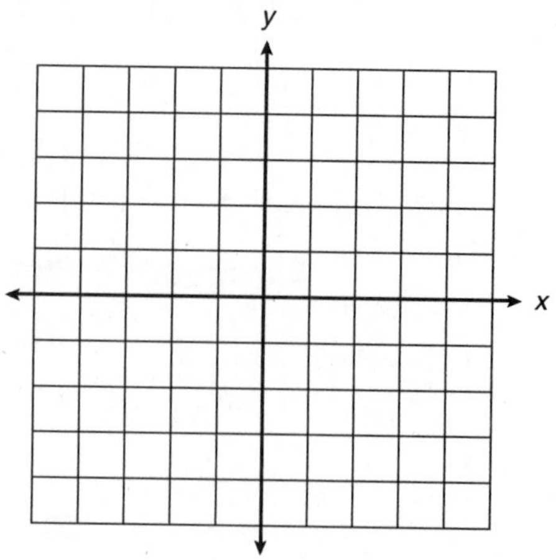

Answers are on page 936.

Distance Between Two Points

$a^2+b^2=c^2$

There are two methods of finding the distance between two points on a graph. One method is to **count the number of units** between the points. You can only use this method when the two points are on the same horizontal line or the same vertical line. The second method is to **use the formula for the distance between two points.** (Note: You do not need to memorize the formula; the formula is on formula page 922.) You can use this method to find the distance between any two points, whether or not they are on the same horizontal or vertical line.

Counting

To find the distance between point *B* and point *A* as shown at right, count the units from *B* to *A*. Since the points are on the same vertical line, the distance is 4 units.

To find the distance between point *B* and point *E* as shown at right, count the units from *B* to *E*. Since the points are on the same horizontal line, the distance is 6 units.

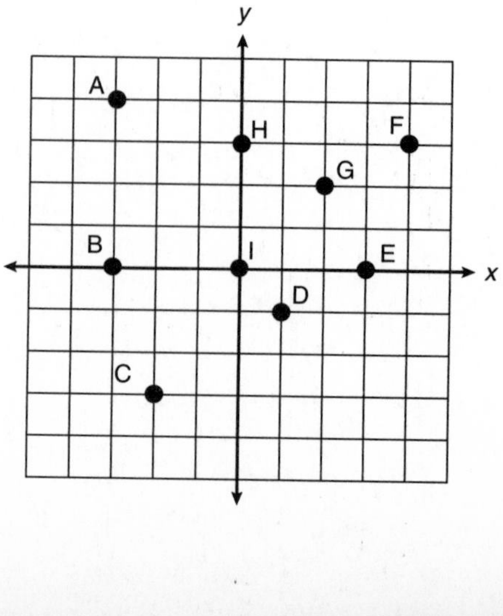

Using a Formula

To find the distance between any two points you can use the **distance formula** $d = \sqrt{(x_2 - x_1)^2 + (y_2 - y_1)^2}$ for the points (x_2, y_2) and (x_1, y_1).

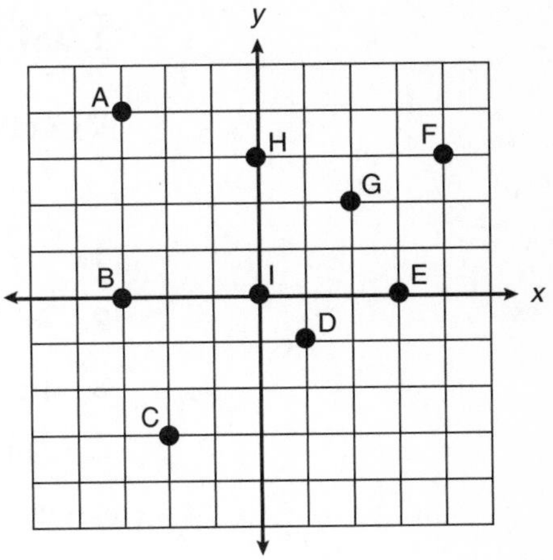

In the formula, x_1 is the x-coordinate of one graphed point and x_2 is the x-coordinate of the other point. Similarly, y_1 is the y-coordinate of the first graphed point and y_2 is the y-coordinate of the other point. For example, in the points (4, 2) and (3, –3), $x_1 = 4$ and $x_2 = 3$, $y_1 = 2$ and $y_2 = -3$.

Using the graph above, look at the next examples. Each uses the distance formula to find the distance between the two given points.

Example 1 Find the distance from point *A* to point *I*.

Let point *A* be $(x_1, y_1) = (-3, 4)$.

Let point *I* be $(x_2, y_2) = (0, 0)$.

So $x_1 = -3$ and $x_2 = 0$; $y_1 = 4$ and $y_2 = 0$.

$d = \sqrt{(x_2 - x_1)^2 + (y_2 - y_1)^2}$

$d = \sqrt{(0 - -3)^2 + (0 - 4)^2}$

$= \sqrt{(3)^2 + (-4)^2}$

$= \sqrt{9 + 16}$

$= \sqrt{25}$

$\mathbf{d = 5}$

Example 2 Find the distance from point *C* to point *F*.

Let point *C* be $(x_1, y_1) = (-2, -3)$.

Let point *F* be $(x_2, y_2) = (4, 3)$.

So $x_1 = -2$ and $x_2 = 4$; $y_1 = -3$ and $y_2 = 3$.

$d = \sqrt{(x_2 - x_1)^2 + (y_2 - y_1)^2}$

$d = \sqrt{(4 - -2)^2 + (3 - -3)^2}$

$= \sqrt{(6)^2 + (6)^2}$

$= \sqrt{36 + 36}$

$= \sqrt{72}$

$\mathbf{d = 8.49}$

(Use your calculator to find the square root.)

Tip

Use the distance formula only if the points are not on a horizontal or vertical line. If the points are on the same horizontal or vertical line, simply count the units between them.

EXERCISE 15

Distance Between Two Points

Directions: Use the graph below to find the distance between the following points. Use either the counting method or the formula method.

1. I to E
2. H to F
3. I to F
4. D to G
5. A to D
6. I to H
7. E to H
8. I to D

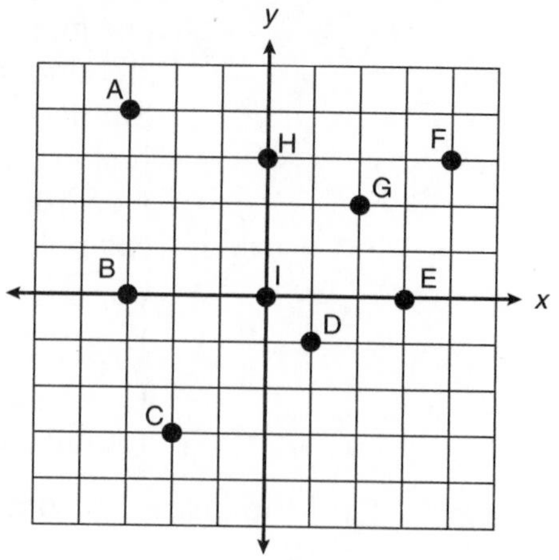

Answers are on page 937.

The Graph of a Line

An equation that shows the relationship between x and y to the first power is called a **linear equation.** The graph of the equation is the set of all points determined by the equation. These points all fall in a straight **line.** Notice the word *linear* contains the word *line.*

For example, $y = x + 4$ is a linear equation. To obtain a set of points that follow the rule of the equation, you must substitute values of x into the equation to get the corresponding values of y. You can arbitrarily select *any* three values for x and substitute them. Suppose you choose 0, 1, and 2 as values to substitute for x.

For $\boldsymbol{x = 0}$, $y = x + 4$ becomes $y = 0 + 4 = 4$. So when $x = 0$, then $y = 4$. This gives you the ordered pair **(0, 4).**

For $\boldsymbol{x = 1}$, $y = x + 4$ becomes $y = 1 + 4 = 5$. So when $x = 1$, then $y = 5$. This gives you the ordered pair **(1, 5).**

For $\boldsymbol{x = 2}$, $y = x + 4$ becomes $y = 2 + 4 = 6$. So when $x = 2$, then $y = 6$. This gives you the ordered pair **(2, 6).**

If we plot the ordered pairs on a coordinate graph and draw the line that connects them, you have the line that represents all ordered pairs that satisfy the equation $y = x + 4$.

The graph to the right shows the points and the line.

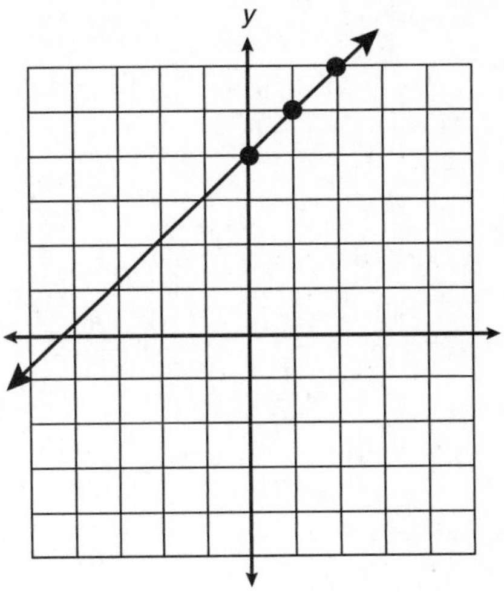

Intercepts

An intercept is a coordinate point located on an axis. A line crosses the y-axis at a point called the **y-intercept** and crosses the x-axis at a point called the **x-intercept.** Look at the example below.

$3y = 2x + 6$

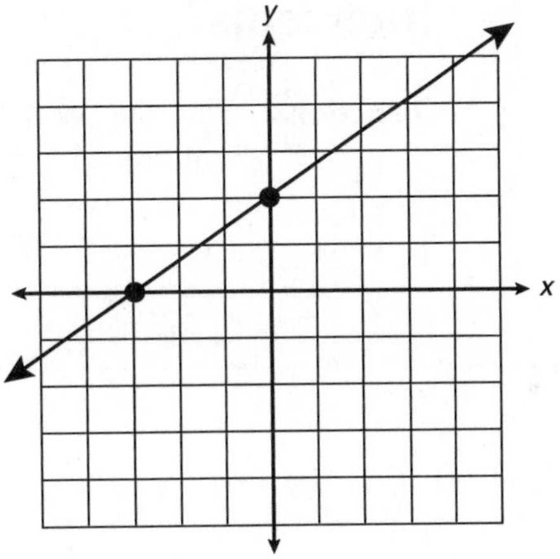

The graph of the line for the equation $3y = 2x + 6$ crosses the x-axis at the x-intercept (–3, 0) and crosses the y-axis at the y-intercept (0, 2).

FINDING INTERCEPTS

1. To find the *x*-intercept of a line, substitute 0 for *y* in the equation and solve for *x*.

   Example In the equation $y = x + 2$
   Substitute 0 for *y*. $0 = x + 2$
   Solve for *x*. $0 - 2 = x + 2 - 2$
   $-2 = x$

   The *x*-intercept is (–2, 0). Notice that *y* in the ordered pair is 0.

2. To find the *y*-intercept of a line, substitute 0 for *x* in the equation and solve for *y*.

   Example In the equation $y = x + 2$
   Substitute 0 for *x*. $y = 0 + 2$
   Solve for *y*. $y = 2$

   The *y*-intercept is (0, 2). Notice that *x* in the ordered pair is 0.

EXERCISE 16

Intercepts

Directions: Find the coordinates of the *x*-intercepts and *y*-intercepts in the equations below.

1. $y = x - 4$ **2.** $y = 2x - 6$ **3.** $y = x + 5$

Answers are on page 937.

The Slope of a Line

$a^2+b^2=c^2$

An equation whose graph is a straight line has a special number associated with the line. This number is called the **slope** of the line. The slope is actually the **ratio** of the change in *y*-values to the change in *x*-values as we go from point to point on the line.

The formula for the slope of a line is given on formula page 922. For two general points (x_2, y_2) and (x_1, y_1), the **slope** is $\frac{y_2 - y_1}{x_2 - x_1}$. This means that the slope is the change in *y*-values over the change in *x*-values.

FINDING THE SLOPE OF A LINE

1. Choose two points on the line.
2. Subtract the *y*-coordinates to find the change in *y*.
3. Subtract the *x*-coordinates to find the change in *x*.
4. Write the slope as the ratio $\frac{\text{change in } y}{\text{change in } x}$.
5. Reduce the ratio.

Example 1 Find the slope of the line that contains the points (2, 1) and (–2, –1).

Subtract the *y*-coordinates to find the change in *y*: $1 - (-1) = 1 + 1 = 2$

Subtract the *x*-coordinates to find the change in *x*: $2 - (-2) = 2 + 2 = 4$

$$\text{Slope} = \frac{\text{change in } y}{\text{change in } x} = \frac{2}{4} = \frac{1}{2}$$

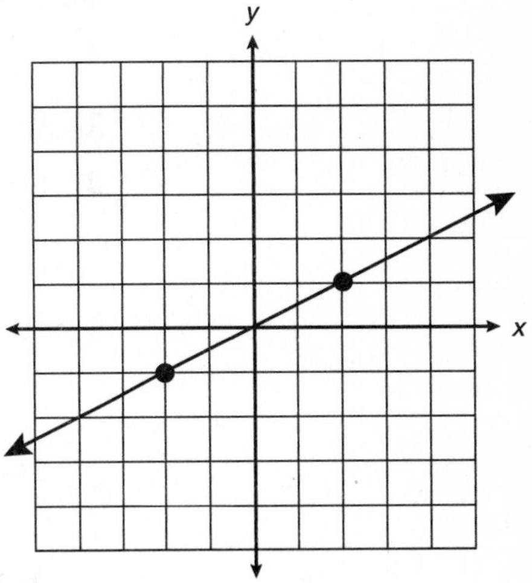

The slope is $\frac{1}{2}$. The line has a positive slope, which means it slants upward. As you move from point to point on the line, you move one unit up for every two units to the right.

Example 2 Find the slope of the line graphed below.

Let $(x_2, y_2) = (0, 4)$ and $(x_1, y_1) = (2, -2)$

$$\text{Slope} = \frac{\text{change in } y}{\text{change in } x} = \frac{4-(-2)}{0-2} =$$

$$\frac{6}{-2} = -\frac{3}{1} = -3$$

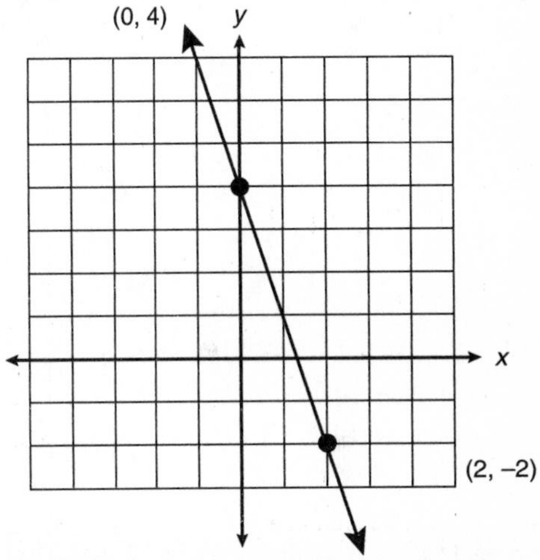

The slope is **–3.** The line has a negative slope, which means it slants downward. As you move from point to point on the line, you move three units down for every one unit to the right.

Tip

- If the slope of a line is a positive number, the line slants upward. If the slope of the line is a negative number, the line slants downward.
- A line that is parallel to the *x*-axis has a slope of zero. A line that is parallel to the *y*-axis has no slope.

EXERCISE 17

The Slope of a Line

Directions: Solve each problem. For questions 1–4, find the value of the slope of the line that contains the two given points.

1. (0, 0) and (3, 4)

2. (–5, –1) and (6, 0)

3. (–9, 3) and (9, 3)

4. (–1, –2) and (–2, –1)

For questions 5–8, find the slope of the graphed lines.

5.

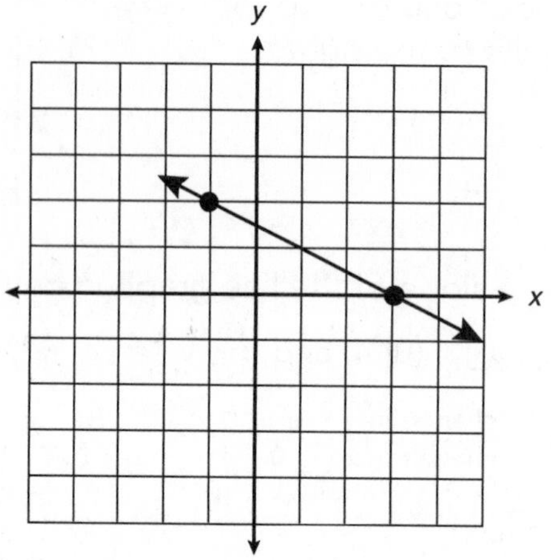

6.

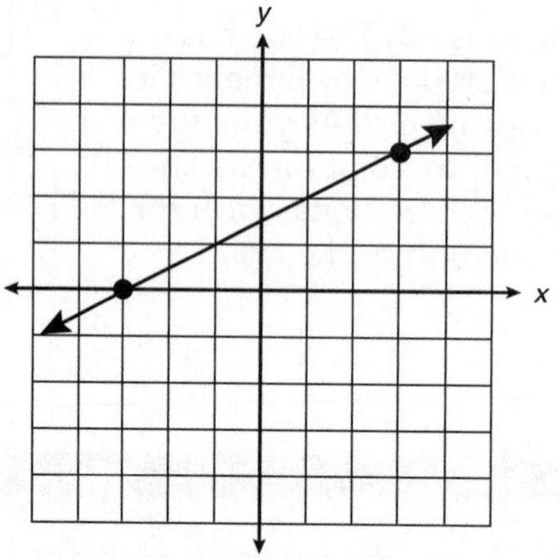

7.

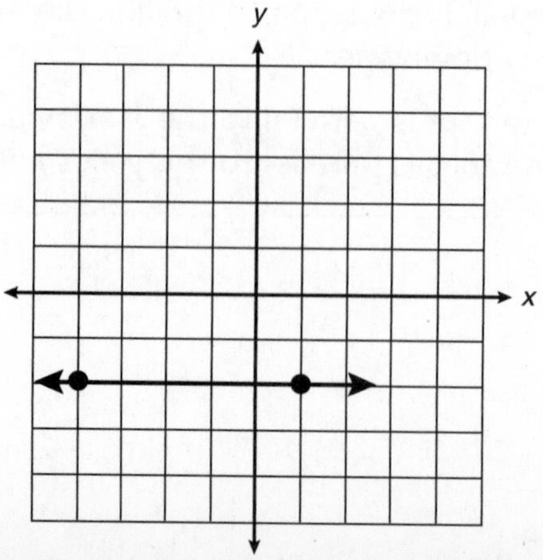

8.

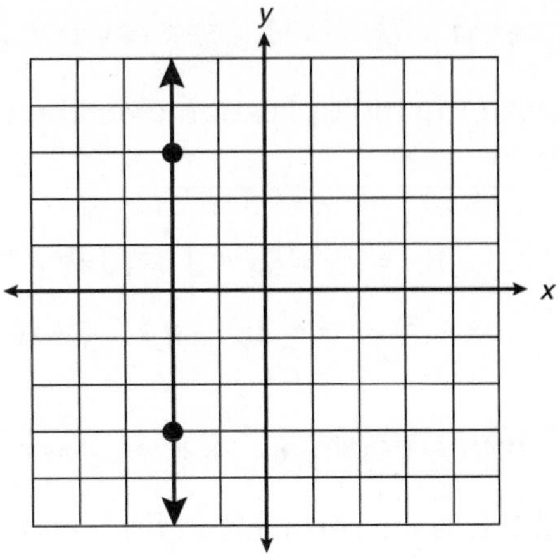

Answers are on page 937.

Multiplying Algebraic Expressions

Algebraic expressions can be multiplied together. An algebraic expression may consist of a number (coefficient), a letter (variable), and/or an exponent. When you multiply variables with exponents, you can add the exponents if the variables are the same. For example, x^2, x^3, and x^5 all have the same base variable, x. So $x^2 \bullet x^3 \bullet x^5 = x^{2+3+5} = x^{10}$. However, since x^2 and y^3 have different bases, you can't add the exponents. Therefore, $x^2 \bullet y^3 = x^2y^3$.

MULTIPLYING VARIABLE WITH EXPONENTS

1. Keep the base.
2. Add the exponents on like bases.

Examples

$x^2 \bullet x^3 = x^{2+3} = \mathbf{x^5}$

$x^2y^3 \bullet x^4y^5 = x^{2+4} \bullet y^{3+5} = \mathbf{x^6y^8}$

$y^4 \bullet y^7 = \mathbf{y^{11}}$

$x \bullet x^3 = x^1 \bullet x^3 = x^{1+3} = \mathbf{x^4}$

Tip

Any variable without an exponent shown is understood to have an exponent of 1. In the last example, x is understood to be x^1.

ONE TERM TIMES ONE TERM

1. Multiply the coefficients.
2. Multiply the variables. Keep the same base and add the exponents.

Examples

$4x \bullet 7x^2 = 4 \bullet 7 \bullet x^1 \bullet x^2 = \mathbf{28x^3}$

$-3y^2 \bullet 5xy = -3 \bullet 5 \bullet x \bullet y^2 \bullet y^1 = \mathbf{-15xy^3}$

ONE TERM TIMES AN EXPRESSION OF TWO OR MORE TERMS

Distribute the multiplication over the expression by multiplying each term.

Examples $5x(2x + 3) = 5x \bullet 2x + 5x \bullet 3 = \mathbf{10x^2 + 15x}$

$-x(2x^2 + 3x - 7) = -x \bullet 2x^2 - x \bullet 3x - x(-7) = \mathbf{-2x^3 - 3x^2 + 7x}$

MULTIPLYING A TWO-TERM EXPRESSION TIMES A TWO-TERM EXPRESSION

1. Multiply each term in the first expression times each term in the second expression.

(This is often called the *FOIL* method—standing for *F*irst term times the first term, *O*uter term times outer term, *I*nner term times inner term, and *L*ast term times last term.)

2. Combine like terms and simplify the result, if possible.

Examples $(x + 4)(x + 3) = x^2 + 3x + 4x + 12 = \mathbf{x^2 + 7x + 12}$

$(x - 8)(x + 2) = x^2 + 2x - 8x - 16 = \mathbf{x^2 - 6x - 16}$

EXERCISE 18

Multiplying Algebraic Expressions

Directions: Multiply as indicated.

1. $8x \bullet 3x^2$ **2.** $7xy(-4x)$ **3.** $(-6ab^2)(3a^2)$ **4.** $(-5x^2y)(3xy^2)$

5. $2x(x^2 + 1)$ **6.** $3y(2y^2 - 4y - 7)$ **7.** $(x + 5)(x + 2)$ **8.** $(x - 4)(x - 1)$

Answers are on page 937.

Factoring

Some problems require factoring algebraic expression. To **factor** means to find and separate numbers that have been multiplied. An example from arithmetic can help to explain factoring. There are two ways to multiply to get the number 15: $3 \times 5 = 15$ and $15 \times 1 = 15$. You can say that 1, 3, 5, and 15 are factors of 15. The factors are the numbers that were multiplied.

Factoring is the process of looking for the factors in a multiplication problem. This process can be used to solve some types of equations and to simplify some expressions. Algebraic expressions can be the answer to a multiplication problem. You must determine what expressions were multiplied to get the given expression.

Finding the Greatest Common Factor

The expression $2x + 10$ has two terms, $2x$ and 10. To factor $2x + 10$, look for the largest number that is a factor of both $2x$ and 10. Since $2x = 2 \bullet x$ and $10 = 2 \bullet 5$, you will notice that 2 is the **greatest common factor** of both terms. You write $2x + 10 = 2(x + 5)$ in **factored form.**

Example 1 Factor $7x^2 + 14x$.

STEP 1 Look for the common factors. 7 and x are common factors in both terms.

$7x^2 + 14x$

$\underline{7} \bullet \underline{x} \bullet x + 2 \bullet \underline{7} \bullet \underline{x}$

STEP 2 Write the common factors in front of the parentheses which contain the rest of the expression.

$\mathbf{7x(x + 2)}$

To check this factored expression, multiply $7x$ by $x + 2$ to be sure the result is $7x^2 + 14x$.

$$7x(x + 2) = 7x \bullet x + 7x \bullet 2 = 7x^2 + 14x$$

Example 2 Factor $65y^3 - 35y^2 + 15y$.

STEP 1 Look for the common factors. 5 and y are common factors in all three terms.

$65y^3 - 35y^2 + 15y$

$\underline{5y} \bullet 13y^2 - \underline{5y} \bullet 7y + \underline{5y} \bullet 3$

STEP 2 Write the common factors in front of the parentheses which contain the rest of the expression.

$\mathbf{5y(13y^2 - 7y + 3)}$

Example 3 Factor $3x^2 + x$.

STEP 1 Look for the common factors. x is the common factor in both terms. Note that 1 is a factor of x; x means $1x$.

$3x^2 + x$

$3 \bullet \underline{x} \bullet x + 1 \bullet \underline{x}$

STEP 2 Write the common factor in front of the parentheses which contain the rest of the expression.

$\mathbf{x(3x + 1)}$

EXERCISE 19

The Greatest Common Factor

Directions: Write each expression in factored form.

1. $21y^3 - 14y^2$ **2.** $100a^4 - 16a^2$ **3.** $121p^5 - 33p^4$ **4.** $8x^2 - 4$

5. $9x^3y^2 + 36x^2y^3$ **6.** $10x^5 - 5x^3 + 10x^2$ **7.** $4x^4 + 25x^3 - 20x^2$

8. $9x^3 - 9x$ **9.** $3x^2 + x$ **10.** $6xy^2 + 12x^2y$

Answers are on page 937.

Factoring by Grouping

In an expression of four or more terms, you can use the method of **factoring by grouping** to factor the expression. You generally separate the four terms of the expression into pairs of terms. Then you factor out the common factor from each pair. If possible, factor the common factor from the results.

FACTORING BY GROUPING

1. Separate the four terms into pairs that have common factors.
2. Factor out the common factor from each pair of terms.
3. Put the common factor in front of the other factors.

__Example 1__ $x^2 + 5x + 2x + 10$

STEP 1 Separate into pairs of terms. $(x^2 + 5x) + (2x + 10)$

STEP 2 Factor each pair. $x(x + 5) + 2(x + 5)$

STEP 3 Put the common factor $(x + 5)$ in front and the remaining parts of the terms in the second parentheses. $\mathbf{(x + 5)(x + 2)}$

__Example 2__ $2y^2 - 8y + 3y - 12$

STEP 1 Separate into pairs of terms. $(2y^2 - 8y) + (3y - 12)$

STEP 2 Factor each pair. $2y(y - 4) + 3(y - 4)$

STEP 3 Put the common factor $(y - 4)$ in front and the remaining parts of the terms in the second parentheses. $\mathbf{(y - 4)(2y + 3)}$

EXERCISE 20

Factoring by Grouping

Directions: Use grouping to factor these expressions with four terms.

1. $x^2 + 4x + 3x + 12$

2. $x^2 - 2x + 5x - 10$

3. $8y^2 + 6yz + 12yz + 9z^2$

4. $2xy^2 - 8y^2 + x - 4$

Answers are on page 937.

Factoring to Reverse FOIL

An expression, which has two or three terms, begins with an x^2 term, and ends with a constant, may be factored by reversing the FOIL method of multiplying. To begin, look at the factors and the sign of the constant term. Choose the factors and appropriate signs that will combine to make the coefficient of the middle x term. Then write the factors in parentheses using x and the factors and appropriate signs. Look at the following examples to better understand this process.

Example 1 $x^2 + 7x + 10$

STEP 1	Note that $x^2 = x \bullet x$.	$x^2 + 7x + 10$
STEP 2	Factor the constant term. Since the coefficient of the middle x term is +7, choose the factors 2 and 5, which combine to 7.	$+10 = 1 \bullet 10$ or $(-1)(-10)$ or $2 \bullet 5$ or $(-2)(-5)$
STEP 3	Write the answer using parentheses beginning with x followed by the numerical factors.	$\mathbf{(x + 2)(x + 5)}$
	To check your answer, you can use the FOIL method to multiply the factors.	$(x + 2)(x + 5) = x^2 + 7x + 10$

Example 2 $x^2 - 11x + 10$

STEP 1	Note that $x^2 = x \bullet x$.	$x^2 - 11x + 10$
STEP 2	Factor the constant term. Since the coefficient of the middle x term is −11, choose the factors −1 and −10, which combine to −11.	$+10 = 1 \bullet 10$ or $(-1)(-10)$ or $2 \bullet 5$ or $(-2)(-5)$
STEP 3	Write the answer using parentheses beginning with x followed by the numerical factors.	$\mathbf{(x - 1)(x - 10)}$
	To check your answer, you can use the FOIL method to multiply the factors.	$(x - 1)(x - 10) = x^2 - 11x + 10$

Example 3 $x^2 + 3x - 10$

STEP 1 Note that $x^2 = x \bullet x$. $x^2 + 3x - 10$

STEP 2 Factor the constant term. Since the coefficient of the middle x term is +3, choose the factors –2 and 5, which combine to +3. $-10 = (-1)(10)$ or $(1)(-10)$ or $(-2)(5)$ or $(2)(-5)$

STEP 3 Write the answer using parentheses beginning with x followed by the numerical factors. $\mathbf{(x - 2)(x + 5)}$

To check your answer, you can use the FOIL method to multiply the factors. $(x - 2)(x + 5) = x^2 + 3x - 10$

Example 4 $x^2 - 9x - 10$

STEP 1 Note that $x^2 = x \bullet x$. $x^2 - 9x - 10$

STEP 2 Factor the constant term. Since the coefficient of the middle x term is –9, choose the factors 1 and –10, which combine to –9. $-10 = (-1)(10)$ or $(1)(-10)$ or $(-2)(5)$ or $(2)(-5)$

STEP 3 Write the answer using parentheses beginning with x followed by the numerical factors. $\mathbf{(x + 1)(x - 10)}$

To check your answer, you can use the FOIL method to multiply the factors. $(x + 1)(x - 10) = x^2 - 9x - 10$

Example 5 $x^2 - 25$

STEP 1 Note that $x^2 = x \bullet x$. $x^2 - 25$

STEP 2 Factor the constant term. Since there is no x term and the middle coefficient is 0, choose the factors 5 and –5, which combine to zero. $-25 = (-1)(25)$ or $(1)(-25)$ or $(5)(-5)$

STEP 3 Write the answer using parentheses beginning with x followed by the numerical factors. $\mathbf{(x + 5)(x - 5)}$

To check your answer, you can use the FOIL method to multiply the factors. $(x + 5)(x - 5) = x^2 - 25$

EXERCISE 21

Factoring to Reverse FOIL

Directions: Factor each expression below.

1. $x^2 - 7x - 8$ **2.** $x^2 - 5x + 4$ **3.** $x^2 + 2x - 15$

4. $x^2 - 16$ **5.** $x^2 - 6x + 8$ **6.** $x^2 - 100$

Answers are on page 937.

EXERCISE 22

Algebra Review

Directions: Solve each problem.

1. If a $1500 computer decreases in value $240 per year, which expression shows the value at the end of *x* years?

(1) $1500 - (240 + x)$ **(2)** $1500 - 240x$ **(3)** $1500 - x$

(4) $1500 + 240x$ **(5)** $1500 + x$

2. Joe spent one-third of his monthly salary and then spent $70 more. At that point, he had spent half of his salary. Choose the equation that represents this information.

(1) $3x + 70 = 2x$ **(2)** $\frac{1}{3}x = 70 \div \frac{1}{2}x$ **(3)** $\frac{1}{3}x - 70 = \frac{1}{2}x$

(4) $\frac{1}{3}x + \frac{1}{2}x = 70$ **(5)** $\frac{1}{3}x + 70 = \frac{1}{2}x$

3. Monty has a board 42 inches long. He wishes to cut it into three pieces so that one piece is six inches longer than the shortest piece and the third piece is twice as long as the shortest piece. How many inches long should the shortest piece be?

(1) $4\frac{2}{3}$ **(2)** $5\frac{1}{4}$ **(3)** 9 **(4)** $11\frac{1}{3}$ **(5)** 12

4. Use the formula $d = rt$ (where *d* is the distance, *r* is the rate, and *t* is the time) to determine the rate of speed of a sprinter who runs 200 yards in 25 seconds.

(1) 8 yards per second
(2) 175 yards per second
(3) 225 yards per second
(4) 5000 yards per second
(5) Not enough information is given.

5. An archer shoots an arrow upward at an initial rate of 100 feet per second. The height *h* of the arrow after *t* seconds is given by the formula $h = 100t - 16t^2$. Determine the height of the arrow in feet after 3 seconds.

(1) 48 **(2)** 134 **(3)** 156 **(4)** 204 **(5)** 252

Use the following table of student test scores to answer questions 6 and 7.

The grade for the course is the average of tests A, B, and C and final exam D that counts as two tests. The formula is

$$\text{average} = \frac{A + B + C + 2D}{5}$$

Student	Test A	Test B	Test C	Final Exam D
Sylvia	88	82	64	70
Gavin	72	78	85	85
Frank	68	76	80	
Juan	90	80	70	60

6. Find the grade Gavin will receive for the course.

7. What score will Frank need on his final exam to get an average of 80?

In problems 8–14, match each sentence with the appropriate algebraic equation using the variable *x* for the missing number.

Sentence	Equation
8. Five less than a number is 10.	________ $\frac{x}{10} = 5$
9. 10 divided by a number is 5.	________ $5 - x = 10$
10. 5 more than a number is 10.	________ $x + 5 = 10$
11. The sum of a number and 5 is 10.	________ $x - 5 = 10$
12. 5 minus a number is 10.	________ $\frac{10}{x} = 5$
13. A number divided by 10 is 5.	________ $5x = 10$
14. The product of 5 and a number is 10.	________ $5 + x = 10$

In problems 15–18, solve each equation for the given variable.

15. $x - 7 = 4$

16. $5x - 4 = 11$

17. $\frac{x}{3} + 6 = 18$

18. $2(x - 1) = 16$

In problems 19 and 20, solve each inequality for the given variable.

19. $x - 6 < -5$

20. $\frac{x}{-2} > 5$

21. If six times a number is subtracted from ten times a number, the result is six less than twice the number. Find the number.

(1) -3 **(2)** $-\frac{4}{3}$ **(3)** -1 **(4)** $\frac{4}{5}$ **(5)** 1

22. On a business trip, Dana traveled to her destination at an average speed of 55 mph. Coming home, her average speed was 45 mph, and the trip took two hours longer. How many hours did she travel altogether?

(1) 9 **(2)** 11 **(3)** 20 **(4)** 405 **(5)** 495

23. Diego's car gets 24 miles per gallon of gasoline. Which expression below best shows how to find how many gallons he needs for a trip of 672 miles?

(1) $\frac{24}{x} = 672$ **(2)** $\frac{x}{24} = 672$ **(3)** $24x = 672$ **(4)** $x + 24 = 672$
(5) $672 - x = 24$

24. Yesterday, you spent twice as much money as you did today. Altogether you spent $48. How much did you spend yesterday?

(1) $12 **(2)** $16 **(3)** $24 **(4)** $32 **(5)** Not enough information is given.

25. After Pauly bought some cotton material, she found that she had only $\frac{3}{4}$ of what she needed. How many more yards does she need to buy?

(1) $\frac{1}{4}$ **(2)** $\frac{3}{4}$ **(3)** 3 **(4)** 4 **(5)** Not enough information is given.

Plot the following points on the coordinate plane below. Label each point with the corresponding letter.

26. A (–3, 4)

27. B (–3, 0)

28. C (–2, –3)

29. D (1, –1)

30. E (3, 0)

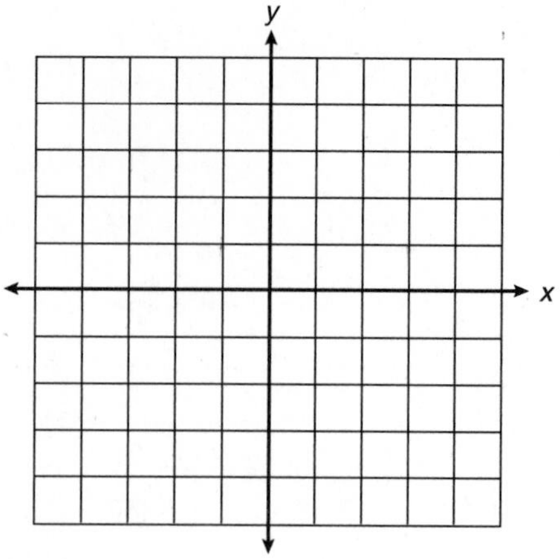

Use the coordinate plane below to answer questions 31–34.

31. Find the distance from point *C* to point *A*.

32. Find the distance from point *A* to point *B*.

33. What is the slope of the line that connects points *A* and *B*?

34. What is the slope of the line that connects points *A* and *C*?

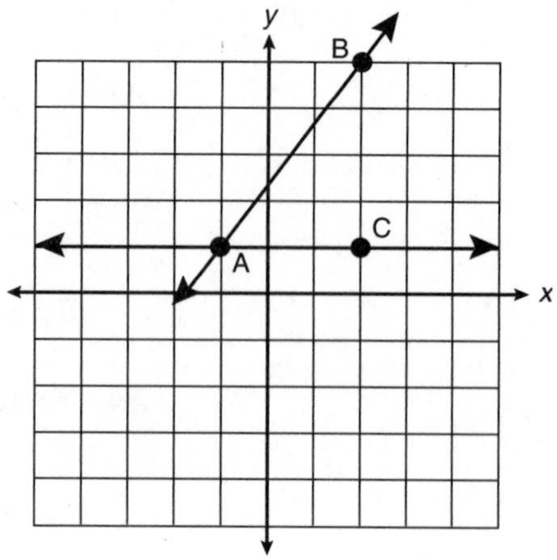

Multiply as indicated in problems 35–38.

35. $7x \bullet 9x^2$

36. $5xy(-2x)$

37. $2y(4y^2 - 3y - 6)$

38. $(x - 3)(x + 6)$

Factor the algebraic expressions in problems 39–42.

39. $12y^3 - 14y^2$

40. $5x^3y^2 + 25x^2y^3$

41. $x^2 - 10x + 16$

42. $x^2 - 81$

Answers are on page 937.

Go to **www.GEDMath.com** for additional practice and instruction!

CHAPTER 11

Measurement

What is measurement? What do you do when you measure the length of a room or the weight of a package? To measure any physical object, you assign both a number and a unit of measurement to it. For instance, a room is 23 feet long, and a package weighs 2 pounds 3 ounces. Units of measurement connect the real world to your number system.

Standard Measurement

The units of measurement below are the **standard units of measure** used most often in the United States.

Units of Length

12 inches (in.) = 1 foot (ft)
3 feet = 36 inches = 1 yard (yd)
5280 feet = 1760 yards = 1 mile (mi)

Units of Capacity

8 ounces (oz) = 1 cup (c)
2 cups = 16 ounces = 1 pint (pt)
2 pints = 4 cups = 32 ounces = 1 quart (qt)
4 quarts = 8 pints = 16 cups = 128 ounces = 1 gallon (gal)

Units of Weight

16 ounces (oz) = 1 pound (lb)
2000 pounds = 1 ton (T)

Units of Time

60 seconds (sec) = 1 minute (min)
60 minutes = 1 hour (hr)
24 hours (hr) = 1 day
7 days = 1 week
52 weeks = 1 year (yr)
12 months = 1 year
365 days = 1 year

Converting Units

When solving measurement problems, it is often convenient to change the units of measure. This is called making a **conversion.** There are two types of conversions. One is a conversion from a large unit to a smaller unit. For example, a weight given in pounds (large unit) might be converted to ounces (smaller unit). The other is a conversion from a small unit to a larger unit, such as changing feet (small unit) to yards (larger unit).

To **convert** from one unit of measure to another unit of measure, you multiply or divide by a **conversion factor.** A conversion factor is the ratio that describes the relationship between the large and small unit. For example, because 12 inches equals 1 foot, the conversion factor is $\frac{12 \text{ inches}}{1 \text{ foot}}$. You would multiply or divide by $\frac{12 \text{ inches}}{1 \text{ foot}}$ to convert between inches and feet.

CONVERTING UNITS OF MEASURE

1. To change a LARGE UNIT to a SMALLER UNIT: multiply by the conversion factor. (This is because it takes <u>more</u> small units to be equivalent.)

$$\text{LARGE UNIT} \underset{\div}{\overset{\times}{\rightleftarrows}} \text{SMALL UNIT}$$

2. To change a SMALL UNIT to a LARGER UNIT: divide by the conversion factor. (This is because it takes <u>fewer</u> large units to be equivalent.)

Example 1 Change 7 feet to inches.

Because you are changing from a large unit (feet) to a smaller unit (inches), multiply. The conversion factor is $\frac{12 \text{ inches}}{1 \text{ foot}}$ because there are 12 inches in a foot. $\frac{12 \text{ inches}}{1 \text{ foot}} \times 7 \text{ feet} = 84 \text{ inches}$. So 7 feet is equivalent to **84 inches.**

Example 2 Change $2\frac{1}{2}$ tons to pounds.

Because you are changing from a large unit (ton) to a smaller unit (pounds), multiply. The conversion factor is $\frac{2000 \text{ pounds}}{1 \text{ ton}}$ because there are 2000 pounds in a ton. $\frac{2000 \text{ pounds}}{1 \text{ ton}} \times 2\frac{1}{2} \text{ tons} = 5000 \text{ pounds}$. So $2\frac{1}{2}$ tons is equivalent to **5000 pounds.**

Example 3 Change 48 ounces to pints.

Because you are changing from a small unit (ounces) to a larger unit (pints), divide. The conversion factor is $\frac{16 \text{ ounces}}{1 \text{ pint}}$ because there are 16 ounces in a pint. $48 \text{ ounces} \div \frac{16 \text{ ounces}}{1 \text{ pint}} = 3 \text{ pints}$. So 48 ounces is equivalent to **3 pints.**

Example 4 Change 20 ounces to pounds.

Because you are changing from a small unit (ounces) to a larger unit (pounds), divide. The conversion factor is $\frac{16 \text{ ounces}}{1 \text{ pound}}$ because there are 16 ounces in a pound. $20 \text{ ounces} \div \frac{16 \text{ ounces}}{1 \text{ pound}} = 1\frac{1}{4} \text{ pounds}$. So 20 ounces is equivalent to $\mathbf{1\frac{1}{4}}$ **pounds.**

NOTE: $1\frac{1}{4}$ pounds can also be expressed as 1 pound 4 ounces.
$\frac{1}{4}$ pound is $\frac{1}{4}$ of 16 ounces $= \frac{1}{4} \times 16$ ounces $= 4$ ounces.

Example 5 A tailor needs 18 inches of seam tape that costs $1.08 per yard. How much does he pay for the material?

Notice that you must first convert from inches to yards because the price is given in yards. To change 18 inches (small unit) to yards (larger unit), divide by the conversion factor $\frac{36\text{ inches}}{1\text{ yard}}$. So 18 inches $\div \frac{36\text{ inches}}{1\text{ yard}} = \frac{1}{2}$ yard = .5 yard. (It may be easier to use a decimal value to perform the calculations needed to solve the problem.)

To calculate how much the tailor must pay for the material, use the cost formula, $c = nr$, where c is the total cost, n is the number of units, and r is the cost per unit.

c = .5 yard × $1.08 per yard = $.540 = **$.54**

Check: If 18 inches is half a yard, it makes sense that the tape costs $.54 which is half of the price of a yard ($1.08).

EXERCISE 1

Conversions

Directions: Convert the measurements in the following problems.

1. 5 yards = ________ feet
2. 40 ounces = ________ pounds
3. 96 hours = ________ days
4. 20 quarts = ________ gallons
5. 2 quarts = ________ ounces
6. 2 days = ________ minutes
7. 3 pints = ________ quarts
8. If Pike's Peak is 14,110 feet high, what is its elevation in miles (to the nearest tenth)?
9. If a half-gallon of milk costs $2.96, what is the cost of 8 ounces of milk?
10. One shrub is to be placed every 15 feet along an expressway. How many shrubs are to be planted along a 2-mile stretch of the expressway?

Answers are on page 938.

Basic Operations with Measurements

You often need to add, subtract, multiply, or divide measurements. Review these skills.

ADDITION WITH MEASUREMENTS

1. Add like units.
2. Write the answer in simplest form.

Example 1 Add 3 pounds 8 ounces to 15 ounces.

$$\begin{array}{r} 3 \text{ lb } 8 \text{ oz} \\ + \quad 15 \text{ oz} \\ \hline 3 \text{ lb } 23 \text{ oz} \end{array}$$

Be sure to add ounces to ounces.

Because 23 ounces is more than 16 ounces (1 pound), simplify by dividing by 16. Then add the 1 pound to the 3 pounds.

$$\begin{array}{r} 1 \text{ r } 7 = 1 \text{ lb } 7 \text{ oz} \\ 16\overline{)23} \\ -16 \\ \hline 7 \end{array}$$

3 pounds 23 ounces = 3 pounds + 1 pound 7 ounces =
4 pounds 7 ounces

SUBTRACTION WITH MEASUREMENTS

1. Subtract like units.
2. Regroup units when necessary.
3. Write the answer in simplest form.

Example 2 Take 5 pounds 7 ounces from 8 pounds 12 ounces.

$$\begin{array}{r} 8 \text{ lb } 12 \text{ oz} \\ -5 \text{ lb } \ \ 7 \text{ oz} \\ \hline \mathbf{3 \text{ lb } \ \ 5 \text{ oz}} \end{array}$$

Subtract ounces from ounces.
Then subtract pounds from pounds.

Example 3 Subtract 2 yards 2 feet from 6 yards 1 foot.

$$\begin{array}{r} \overset{5}{\cancel{6}} \text{ yd } \overset{4}{\cancel{1}} \text{ ft} \\ -\ 2 \text{ yd } 2 \text{ ft} \\ \hline \mathbf{3 \text{ yd } 2 \text{ ft}} \end{array}$$

From 6 yards, regroup 1 yard to 3 feet. Add 3 feet to 1 foot.
Then subtract feet from feet and yards from yards.

MULTIPLICATION WITH MEASUREMENTS

1. Multiply like units if units are involved.
2. Write the answer in simplest form.

Example 4 Multiply 4 feet 8 inches by 3.

```
  4 ft 8 in.      Multiply 8 inches by 3, then multiply 4 feet by 3. Keep the units separate.
×      3
 12 ft 24 in. ←  Since 12 inches = 1 foot, simplify 24 inches to 2 feet.
```

12 feet 24 inches = 12 feet + 2 feet = **14 feet**

In some cases, as in Example 5, you will have to change units to the same form before you can do any calculating.

Example 5 Multiply 8 feet by 2 yards.

First change yards to feet by multiplying by the conversion factor $\frac{3 \text{ ft}}{1 \text{ yd}}$.

$\frac{3 \text{ ft}}{1 \text{ yd}} \times 2 \text{ yds} = 6 \text{ ft}$

Then multiply 8 feet × 6 feet = **48 square feet**
(NOTE: feet × feet = square feet)

DIVISION WITH MEASUREMENTS

1. Divide into the larger unit first.
2. Convert the remainder to the smaller unit.
3. Add the converted remainder to the existing smaller unit, if any.
4. Then divide into the smaller units.
5. Write the answer in simplest form.

Example 6 Divide 2 quarts 5 ounces by 3.

```
     0 qt 23 oz = 1 pt 7 oz
 3)2 qt  5 oz
  − 0 qt
    2 qt = 64 oz ←  3 will not go into 2 quarts. Change 2 quarts to 64 ounces.
           69 oz ←  Add 64 ounces to 5 ounces. Then divide by 3.
          −69 oz
            0
```

EXERCISE 2

Basic Operations with Measurements

Directions: In the following practice problems, add, subtract, multiply, or divide as indicated. Be sure the final answer is in simplest form. For example, an answer of 15 inches should be changed to 1 foot 3 inches.

1. 9 feet 4 inches – 2 feet 9 inches

2. 1 hour 20 minutes + 3 hours

3. 130 pounds – 8 pounds 4 ounces

4. 5.3 inches × 7

5. 22 feet 6 inches ÷ 3

6. 5 hours 20 minutes ÷ 8

7. What is the difference in weight of two boxes of cereal, one weighing 1 pound 4 ounces and the other weighing 13 ounces?

8. If you divide a 6-foot-8-inch board into four equal lengths, how long will each piece be?

9. Each of 45 delegates to the convention will be given a badge made of a 4-inch piece of ribbon. At 65 cents per yard, how much will the ribbon cost to make the badges?

(1) \$1.80 **(2)** \$2.40 **(3)** \$3.25 **(4)** \$3.60 **(5)** \$6.50

10. At a price of \$365 per ounce, which of the following represents the value of 1 pound 3 ounces of gold?

(1) 3(\$365) **(2)** 16(\$365) **(3)** 3 + 16 + \$365 **(4)** 19(\$365) **(5)** $\frac{\$365}{19}$

11. Shane has a part-time job at the local hardware store. He earns \$9 per hour. Last week he worked the following times: Monday, $2\frac{1}{2}$ hours; Wednesday, 3 hours; Friday, 4 hours 45 minutes; Saturday 7 hours 15 minutes; and Sunday, 4 hours. How much was he paid last week?

(1) \$20 **(2)** \$21.50 **(3)** \$180 **(4)** \$193.50 **(5)** Not enough information is given.

Answers are on page 938.

The Metric System

The **metric system** is an international **decimal** measuring system used to simplify trade and commerce among countries. The basic units of measure are

- **Length: meter (m)** A meter is a few inches longer than our standard yard.

  1 meter = a little more than 39 inches

  1 yard = 36 inches

- **Weight: gram (g)** A gram is a very small unit of weight; there are about 30 grams in one ounce.

  1 gram = 1 kernel of unpopped popcorn 

  1 ounce = 30 kernels of unpopped popcorn

- **Liquid Capacity: liter (L)** A liter is a little bit bigger than a quart.

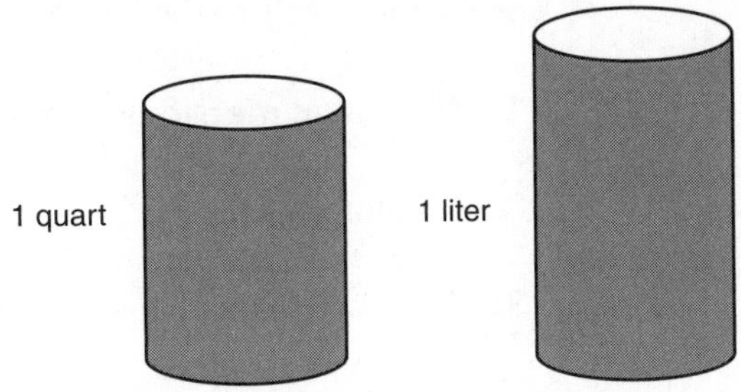

Units of measure are derived from the basic units: meter, gram, and liter. Prefixes are attached to the basic unit to indicate of the amount of each unit.

For example, the prefix *centi* means one-hundredth ($\frac{1}{100}$); therefore, one *centi*meter is one-hundredth of a meter, one *centi*gram is one-hundredth of a gram, and one *centi*liter is one-hundredth of a liter.

The following six prefixes can be used with every unit:

kilo (k)	**hecto (h)**	**deka (dk)**	**UNIT**	**deci (d)**	**centi (c)**	**milli (m)**
1000	100	10		$\frac{1}{10}$	$\frac{1}{100}$	$\frac{1}{1000}$

Examples

1 kilometer = 1 km = 1000 meters
1 centimeter = 1 cm = $\frac{1}{100}$ meter = .01 meter
1 kilogram = 1 kg = 1000 grams
1 milliliter = 1 mL = $\frac{1}{1000}$ liter = .001 liter
5 km = 5000 meters
5 cm = $\frac{5}{100}$ meter = .05 meter
12 kg = 12,000 grams
19 mL = $\frac{19}{1000}$ milliliters = .019 liter

The most common relationships used in metric measures are shown in the chart below.

Length	Weight	Capacity
1 km = 1000 m 1 m = .001 km	1 kg = 1000 g 1 g = .001 kg	1 kL = 1000 L 1 L = .001 kL
1 m = 100 cm 1 cm = .01 m	1 g = 1000 mg 1 mg = .001 g	1 L = 100 cL 1 cL = .01 L
1 m = 1000 mm 1 mm = .001 m		1 L = 1000 mL 1 mL = .001 L

EXERCISE 3

The Metric System

Directions: Fill in the blanks with the word that makes the sentence true.

1. The basic metric unit of measure for weight is the ______________.
2. A millimeter is ______________ meters.
3. The metric measure most closely related to a quart is ______________.
4. If an inch is about 2.5 cm, then 10 inches is about ______________ centimeters.
5. If a dosage of a prescription drug is 20 mg, then that amount is ______________ than a gram.
6. If a mile is 1760 yards, then a kilometer is ______________ than a mile.
7. A 2-liter bottle of pop is ______________ liquid than a half-gallon of milk.
8. If a kilogram is a little more than 2 pounds, then a 150-pound person weighs about ______________ kilograms.
9. The basic metric unit for length is ______________ .
10. The metric system is a decimal system, and that means that the prefixes are multiples of ______________ .

Answers are on page 939.

Conversion in the Metric System

Conversions between units in the metric system move the decimal point to the right or left because the conversion factor is always 10 or a power of 10. As with standard measurement, when you change from a large unit to a smaller unit you multiply, and when you change from a small unit to a larger unit you divide.

Tip

Remember in your work with decimal numbers that when you multiply by a power of ten, you move the decimal point to the right. When you divide by a power of ten, you move the decimal point to the left.

To change from a large unit to a smaller unit,
move the decimal point to the *right*.

→

(*large*) kilo hecto deka UNIT deci centi milli (*small*)

←

To change from a small unit to a larger unit,
move the decimal point to the *left*.

TO CHANGE METRIC UNITS

1. List the prefixes from largest to smallest.
2. Put a mark at the starting prefix.
3. Count the moves from the first prefix right or left to the new prefix.
4. In the number, move the decimal point the same number of places in the same direction.

Example 1 Change 420 meters to kilometers.

STEP 1 Recognize that changing meters to kilometers is going from small units to larger units and that you will move the decimal point to the left.

STEP 2 Beginning at the UNIT (for meters), you will see a move three prefixes to the left.

k h dk unit d c m

STEP 3 Move the decimal point from the end of 420 to the left three places. 420.

Place the decimal point before the 4. .420

Your answer is 420 meters = **.420 kilometers.**

Example 2 Convert 4.2 kilograms to grams.

STEP 1 Kilograms to grams is moving from a large unit to a smaller unit.

STEP 2 k h dk unit d c m

STEP 3 Move three places to the right. 4.2 kilograms = **4200 grams**

Example 3 Convert 4 meters 48 centimeters to centimeters.

STEP 1 Meters to centimeters is moving from a large unit to a smaller unit.

STEP 2 k h dk unit d c m

STEP 3 Move two places to the right. 4.00 meters = 400 centimeters

STEP 4 Add 400 centimeters to the 48 centimeters for a total of **448 centimeters.**

Example 4 On an airplane trip from London to Chicago, you are told that the luggage weight limit is 20 kilograms. There is an extra charge of $2.80 for every kilogram over that limit. If your luggage weights 23,000 grams, what additional charge can you expect to pay?

STEP 1 First change 23,000 grams to kilograms. k h dk unit d c m

STEP 2 Move the decimal point 3 moves left. 23,000 g = 23.000 kg = 23 kg

STEP 3 Subtract to find the over-limit amount. 23 kg – 20 kg = 3 kg

STEP 4 Multiply the extra charge by 3. $2.80 × 3 = **$8.40**

EXERCISE 4

Metric Measurement

Directions: Convert to the units shown.

1. 500 meters to centimeters
2. 7423 milligrams to grams
3. 50.3 centimeters to millimeters
4. .027 kilograms to grams
5. 1 kiloliter 47 liters to liters
6. 642 centimeters to meters
7. Find the length in meters of the gearshaft illustrated below.

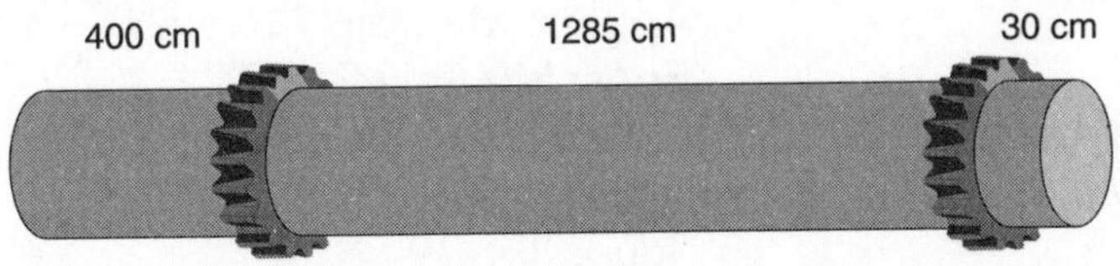

8. The recommended dosage of vitamin C is 857 milligrams per day. How many grams of vitamin C will Max take in one week if he takes the recommended dosage?
9. Terry competed in a 1000-meter speed-skating race; how many kilometers did he skate?
10. The speed limit sign in Canada reads 80 kilometers per hour and the speed limit sign in the United States reads 55 miles per hour. If 1 kilometer = .621 mile, which country allows the motorist to drive at a faster speed?
11. Which expression can be used to find the cost of .75 kilogram of cheese at the price of $6.40 per kilogram?

    (1) $\frac{\$6.40}{.75}$ **(2)** $.75 \times \$6.40$ **(3)** $\frac{\$6.40}{2}$ **(4)** $.75 + \$6.40$ **(5)** $\$6.40 - .75$

12. One yard is approximately .91 meter. A football field is 100 yards long. What is the length of a football field in meters?

    (1) 30 **(2)** 49.5 **(3)** 91 **(4)** 100 **(5)** 109

Answers are on page 939.

Problem Solving with Money

Some of the ways you handle money include paying bills, making purchases, writing a budget, and writing bills and receipts. Look at a few problems that require calculations involving money. To do these calculations, you use the formula $c = nr$.

To find the total cost c, multiply the number of units n by the cost per unit r. For example, you buy 4 tires at \$98 each. To find the total cost of the tires, multiply $4 \times \$98 = \$392$.

Example Margaret bought the following groceries on May 15: $1\frac{1}{2}$ dozen apples at \$2.69 per dozen, 2 dozen eggs at \$.94 per dozen, 2 boxes of bran flakes at \$3.15 each, 1 pound of margarine at \$1.58 per pound, and 3 cans of soup at \$.79 per can. How much change did Margaret receive from a twenty-dollar bill?

STEP 1 Use the formula $c = nr$ to find the total cost of each item.

Apples: Multiply $1.5 \times 2.69 = 4.035$, which rounds to	\$4.04
Eggs: Multiply $2 \times .94$	\$1.88
Bran flakes: 2×3.15	\$6.30
Margarine: 1×1.58	\$1.58
Soup: $3 \times .79$	+ \$2.37

STEP 2 Add to find the total cost of all items. \$16.17

STEP 3 Subtract the total cost from \$20. $\$20.00 - 16.17 = \$\,3.83$

The change Margaret received was **\$3.83.**

Tip

Always round money to the hundredths place. In general, you round upward. For instance, suppose you want one item and the price is 3 items for \$1.24. If you divide \$1.24 by 3, you get about \$.413. The actual price you would pay for one item is \$.42 even though .413 would normally round to .41.

EXERCISE 5

Money Problems

Directions: Solve each problem.

1. Lola works at Corey's Fashions. Her customer made the purchases shown on the sales slip at the right. How much money should Lola collect from this customer?

Qty	Item	Unit Price	Amount
1	Dress	$49.95	
2	Shirts	$14.95	
3	Hosiery	$ 4.95	
		Subtotal	
		Tax (7%)	
		Total	

2. Mr. Barnes stocked his garden supply store with 2 tons of sand in 50-pound bags for $138 per ton. If he sells the entire order of bags of sand for $5.95 per bag, what will be his profit?

   (1) $3.19 **(2)** $69 **(3)** $200 **(4)** $276 **(5)** $470.40

3. You need 78 feet of molding to finish decorating the family room. What is the cost of the molding if each 1-yard length costs $1.98?

   (1) $26 **(2)** $51.48 **(3)** $154.45 **(4)** $234 **(5)** $463.32

4. Better Bran cereal costs $2.79 for a 1-pound 9-ounce box; Wheatos cereal in a 12-ounce box costs $2.49; Friendly Flakes costs $3.19 for a 1-pound 13-ounce box; and Sugar Snaps is $2.39 for 1 pound 4 ounces. Which cereal is the most economical purchase?

   (1) Better Bran **(2)** Wheatos **(3)** Friendly Flakes
   (4) Sugar Snaps **(5)** They are all the same.

5. A prescription for a multisymptom cold reliever costs $8.64 for 36 capsules. The generic equivalent costs $6.48 for 36 capsules. How much money do you save per dose using the generic medicine if each dose is 2 capsules?

   (1) $.06 **(2)** $.12 **(3)** $.18 **(4)** $.24 **(5)** $2.16

6. First-class postage is $.34 for up to 1 ounce and $.28 for each additional ounce. Which of the following represents the cost of sending a 4-ounce envelope by first class?

   (1) $4(.34)$ **(2)** $4(.28)$ **(3)** $(.34 + .28)$ **(4)** $.34 + 3(.28)$ **(5)** $\frac{.34 + .28}{2}$

Answers are on page 939.

Time Problems

Many jobs require you to punch in on a time clock when you arrive at work and punch out when you leave. The time card will record a starting time and an ending time. Using this information, an employer can calculate wages.

A.M. means "hours between midnight and noon."
P.M. means "hours between noon and midnight."

Numbers to the left of the colon are hours. **3:30** **Numbers to the right of the colon are minutes.**

HOW TO CALCULATE TIME

1. Count the number of morning hours.
2. Count the number of afternoon hours.
3. Add the morning and afternoon hours together.
4. Change the number of extra minutes to a fraction of an hour.
5. Simplify your answer.

Tip

60 minutes is one hour. Minutes can be calculated as fractions of an hour. For example, 10 minutes is $\frac{10}{60} = \frac{1}{6}$ of an hour.

Example 1 Tina worked overtime on Thursday. She started at 7:30 A.M. and ended at 6:45 P.M. How long did she work?

1. Count the morning hours. Count from 7:30 to 12:30, which is 5 hours.
2. Count the afternoon hours. Count from 12:30 to 6:30, which is 6 hours.
3. Total hours is $5 + 6 = 11$.
4. Subtract $6{:}45 - 6{:}30 = {:}15 = \frac{15}{60} = \frac{1}{4}$ hour
5. Tina worked **$11\frac{1}{4}$ hours.**

Example 2 Lucy's time card showed a starting time of 8 A.M. and an ending time of 6:30 P.M. If she gets paid \$10 per hour straight time and \$15 per hour overtime (any time more than the straight eight-hour shift), how much did she make that day?

1. Calculate the work hours.

From 8 A.M. to noon is 4 hours.
From noon to 6 P.M. is 6 hours.

$6{:}30 - 6{:}00 = {:}30 = \frac{1}{2}$ hour

Total $= 10\frac{1}{2}$ hours

2. Calculate the overtime hours. $10\frac{1}{2}$ hours $-$ 8 hours $= 2\frac{1}{2}$ hours

3. Calculate the pay.

8 hours at \$10 per hour = $8 \times \$10 = \$\ 80$

$2\frac{1}{2}$ hours at \$15 per hour = $2\frac{1}{2} \times \$15 = \underline{\$\ 37.50}$

\$117.50 total pay

$a^2+b^2=c^2$

Time is an important factor in the calculation of distance. You can use the distance formula $d = rt$ to solve problems. If you know rate and time, you can find the distance d by multiplying the rate r by the time t traveled. This formula is found on formula page 922.

Tip

Time must be in hours or fractions of an hour if the rate is in miles per hour.

For instance, if you travel 6 hours at 55 miles per hour, you can find the distance traveled by using the formula $d = rt$. Let r be 55 and t be 6; then $d = rt = 55 \times 6 = 330$. The distance traveled is **330 miles.**

On the other hand, you often know the distance to be traveled but have to figure out the length of time required for a trip. Suppose you must travel 726 miles and the legal speed limit is 55 mph.

Use the formula $d = rt$. $d = rt$

Let $d = 726$ and $r = 55$. $726 = 55t$

Solve the equation for t. $\frac{726}{55} = \frac{55}{55}t$

The trip will take **$13\frac{1}{5}$ hours.** $13\frac{1}{5} = t$

EXERCISE 6

Time Problems

Directions: Solve each problem.

1. The sign on the parking meter states, "12 minutes for a nickel; maximum deposit 75 cents." How many *hours* can you legally park for the maximum deposit?

   (1) $1\frac{1}{4}$ **(2)** 3 **(3)** $6\frac{1}{4}$ **(4)** $7\frac{1}{2}$ **(5)** 15

2. In his retirement, Roger works part-time at a restaurant during the lunch shift from 10 A.M. to 2:30 P.M. Monday through Friday. He earns $12 per hour. Which expression shows how much he earns in four weeks?

   (1) $4\frac{1}{2} + 12 + 5 + 4$ **(2)** $(4\frac{1}{2} \times 12) + (5 \times 4)$ **(3)** $4\frac{1}{2} \times 12 \times 5 \times 4$

   (4) $4\frac{1}{2}(12 + 5 + 4)$ **(5)** $4\frac{1}{2} \times 12$

3. Sonya and Olaf leave home at 8:30 A.M. to begin their driving tour of Wisconsin. At 3:45 P.M., they decide to stop for the day. If they drove a steady 50 miles per hour, how many miles did they drive that day?

   (1) 362.5 **(2)** 387.5 **(3)** 437.5 **(4)** 426.5 **(5)** 600

Questions 4–6 refer to the time card below.

MARSHALL MANUFACTURING

Name: Mark Musselman			**SS#: 000-45-0000**		
Date	**5/20**	**5/21**	**5/2**	**5/23**	**5/24**
From	8:00 A.M.	8:00 A.M.	8:00 A.M.	8:00 A.M.	8:00 A.M.
To	4:00 P.M.	5:30 P.M.	4:00 P.M.	4:00 P.M.	4:30 P.M.
Total Regular Hours			@ $12.85 per hour		
Overtime Hours *			@ $18.00 per hour		

*(overtime is hours over 40)

4. According to his time card, Mark Musselman worked the week of 5/20 to 5/24. How many overtime hours (any time more than the straight eight-hour shift) did he work that week?

   (1) 0 **(2)** $\frac{1}{2}$ **(3)** $1\frac{1}{2}$ **(4)** 2 **(5)** $2\frac{1}{2}$

5. What is Mark's full pay before deductions? Include regular hours and overtime hours.

(1) \$36 **(2)** \$514 **(3)** \$550 **(4)** \$539.70 **(5)** \$756

6. If state income tax is 3%, federal income tax is 25%, and social security tax (FICA) is 7%, how much will Mark's take-home pay be after these deductions?

(1) \$154.00 **(2)** \$192.50 **(3)** \$375.50 **(4)** \$515 **(5)** \$1925.00

7. An airplane travels 960 miles per hour. Which expression tells how far it travels in 20 minutes?

(1) 960×2 **(2)** $960 \times \frac{1}{3}$ **(3)** $\frac{960}{20}$ **(4)** $\frac{3}{960}$ **(5)** $\frac{1}{3} \div 960$

8. A tornado traveled 75 miles in $2\frac{1}{2}$ hours. Which expression shows how fast the tornado is traveling in miles per hour?

(1) $2\frac{1}{2} \times 75$ **(2)** $75 + 2\frac{1}{2}$ **(3)** $75 - 2\frac{1}{2}$ **(4)** $2\frac{1}{2} \div 75$ **(5)** $75 \div 2\frac{1}{2}$

Answers are on page 939.

Reading and Interpreting Scales and Meters

You often have to read a scale or meter to get information. For instance, a map is a scale drawing you use when you travel. You read a thermometer when you're sick, and you read an electric meter to check your electric bill. On the next few pages, take a look at some scales and meters.

READING SCALES AND METERS

1. Read the labels and keys carefully.
2. If instructions are included, refer to the scale or meter as you read them.
3. Write down the information you get as you read the scale or meter.
4. Ignore extra information that is not needed for the problem.

Scale Drawings

A map is a drawing of land area. When a map is drawn to **scale,** it is drawn in proportion to the land it represents. A **key** is given so you may calculate distances on the map. A key has the information about the ratio for that particular drawing. You can use the scale to set up a proportion to find a distance.

Look at the local map below. Answer the following questions while referring to the map. Notice the scale of miles near the top of the map.

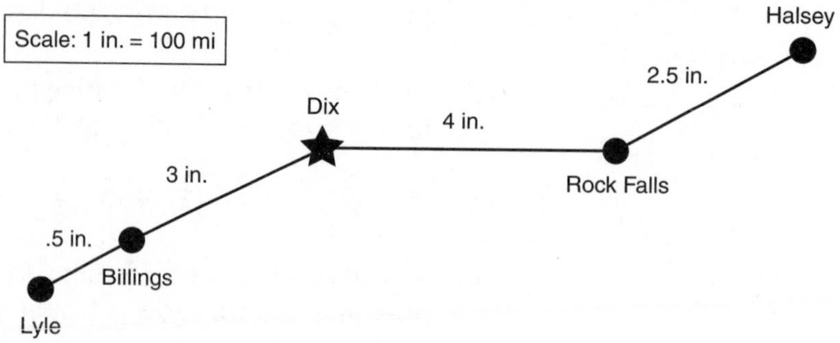

Example 1 If the distance from Halsey to Rock Falls on the map is 2.5 inches, what is the actual distance between Halsey and Rock Falls?

The ratio is 1 inch to 100 miles. If the distance on the map between Halsey and Rock Falls is 2.5 inches, you can set up the following proportion to solve the problem.

$$\frac{1 \text{ in.}}{100 \text{ mi}} = \frac{2.5 \text{ in.}}{n}$$

$$n = \frac{100 \times 2.5}{1} = 250$$

The actual distance between Halsey and Rock Falls is **250 miles.**

Check: This answer makes sense because each inch is 100 miles. Since you have more than 2 inches, there are more than 200 miles.

Example 2 To go by road from Lyle to Halsey, you must go through Billings, Dix, and Rock Falls. How much farther is it from Lyle to Halsey than from Billings to Rock Falls?

STEP 1	Calculate the distance in inches from Lyle to Halsey.	$.5 + 3 + 4 + 2.5 = 10$ inches
STEP 2	Calculate the distance from Billings to Rock Falls.	$3 + 4 = 7$ inches
STEP 3	Subtract to find the difference.	$10 - 7 = 3$ inches
STEP 4	Set up a proportion.	$\frac{1 \text{ in.}}{100 \text{ mi}} = \frac{3 \text{ in.}}{n}$
STEP 5	Solve the proportion.	$n = \frac{3 \times 100}{1} = 300$

It is **300 miles farther** from Lyle to Halsey.

Reading Meters

Meters are devices used to measure time, speed, distance, and energy used. You might recognize some meters such as a speedometer, barometer, or thermometer. Meters give information to solve problems. It's important that you read a meter accurately. Always notice the labels on the meter and read the instructions for use if they are given.

The Electric Meter

Appliances such as refrigerators, fans, TVs, and dishwashers require electricity. The electric meter is the instrument that measures the amount of electricity used in kilowatt-hours (kWh).

The numbers above the dial indicate one complete round around the dial. Notice that the numbers may go in different directions around the dial.

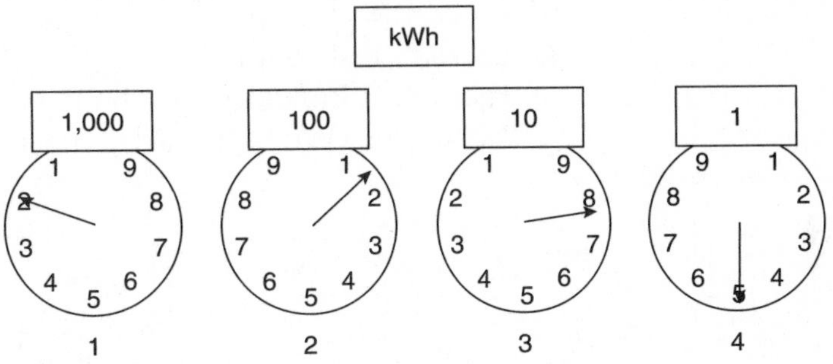

Example How many kilowatt-hours are shown on the meter above?

Start reading the dials with the left dial. If the pointer is between two numbers, read the *smaller* of the two numbers.

Dial (1) is 2, so $2 \times 1000 = 2000$

Dial (2) is 1, so $1 \times 100 = 100$

Dial (3) is 7, so $7 \times 10 = 70$

Dial (4) is 5, so $5 \times 1 = 5$

Total kWh used: $= \mathbf{2175}$

EXERCISE 7

Scales and Meters

Directions: Solve each problem.

1. The scale on a map is 1 inch = 180 miles. How many inches apart on this map are two cities if the distance between them is 450 miles?

   (1) 1 **(2)** $1\frac{1}{2}$ **(3)** 2 **(4)** $2\frac{1}{2}$ **(5)** $3\frac{1}{2}$

2. What is the scale for a map in which 2000 miles is represented by 10 inches?

   (1) 1 in. = 2 mi **(2)** 1 in. = 20 mi **(3)** 1 in. = 200 mi
   (4) 1 in. = $\frac{1}{2}$ mi **(5)** 1 in. = 100 mi

3. Emma's last reading on her electric meter was 3843 kWh. Her new reading is indicated on the meter shown below. If the charge is 12.5¢ per kWh, what is Emma's new electric bill?

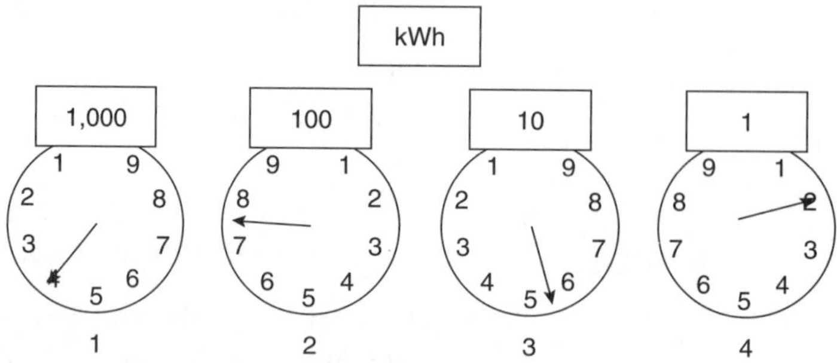

   (1) \$113.63 **(2)** \$909 **(3)** \$2,020 **(4)** \$2,562.50 **(5)** \$11,362.50

4. Scott wanted to check his gas bill shown below. From the information given, find his total current bill.

Account #: 12345678 Meter #: 00386	Meter Readings Current 3380 Previous –3207 Number of 100 cu ft units used = 173
Gas supply charge @$.3065 per 100 cu ft	$
Monthly customer charge	$ 2.00
Distribution charge	$ 19.16
Subtotal	
Utility tax (5%)	
Total current bill	

   (1) \$3.71 **(2)** \$53.02 **(3)** \$74.19 **(4)** \$77.89 **(5)** \$203.87

Go to **www.GEDMath.com** for additional practice and instruction!

Answers are on page 940.

CHAPTER 12

Geometry

Geometry is the study of shapes and the relationships among them. The geometry that you are required to know for the GED Mathematics Test is fundamental and practical. You will not be asked to "prove" theorems. Instead, you will review the basic concepts in geometry and apply them to everyday situations. The study of geometry always begins with a look at basic geometry vocabulary and concepts. Just as numbers are the foundation of arithmetic, points are the foundation of geometry.

A **point** is a location in space. You label points with letters of the alphabet.

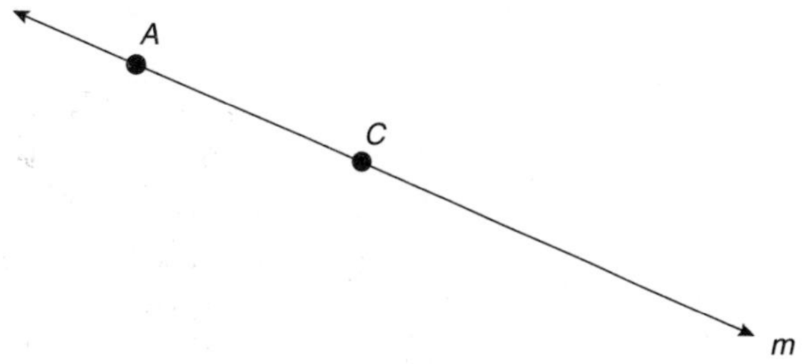

A **line** is an infinite collection of points lined up straight. A line can be identified by naming two points on the line or by using one letter naming the line. The line above can be called line *AC* or line *m*.

You can describe a line in several ways.

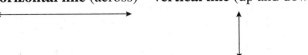

horizontal line (across) **vertical line** (up and down) **diagonal line** (slanted)

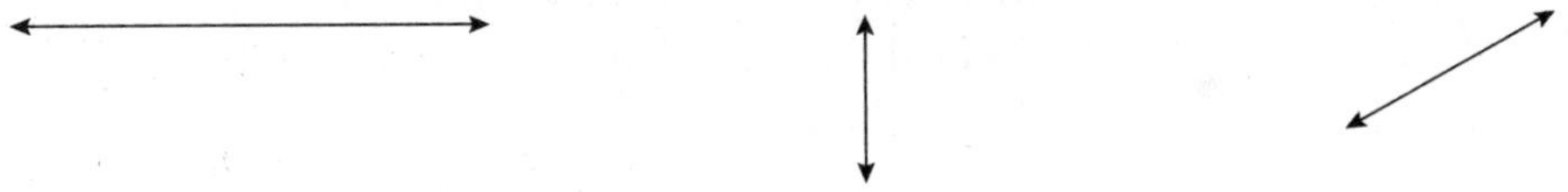

An **angle** is formed when two lines intersect. The point of intersection is called the **vertex** of the angle. In the angle shown at the right, point *S* is the vertex. The two sides are **rays** *ST* and *SR*. Rays continue infinitely. An angle is named with a small angle symbol ∠ and three points, one on each ray with the vertex in the middle: ∠ *RST*. Sometimes, you may name an angle by only its vertex: ∠*S*.

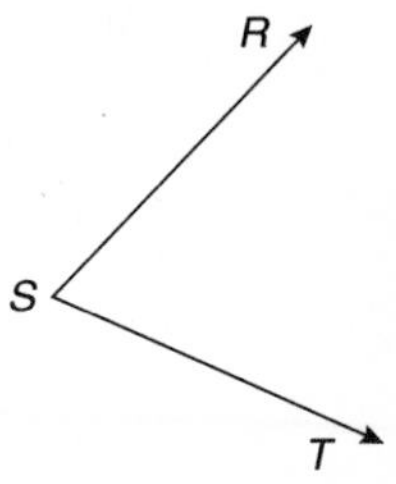

An angle is measured in **degrees.** The symbol for degrees is a familiar one from weather reports, such as 72°. The arc between the sides of the angle is a portion of a full 360° circle. The angle on the circle at right is about 60°.

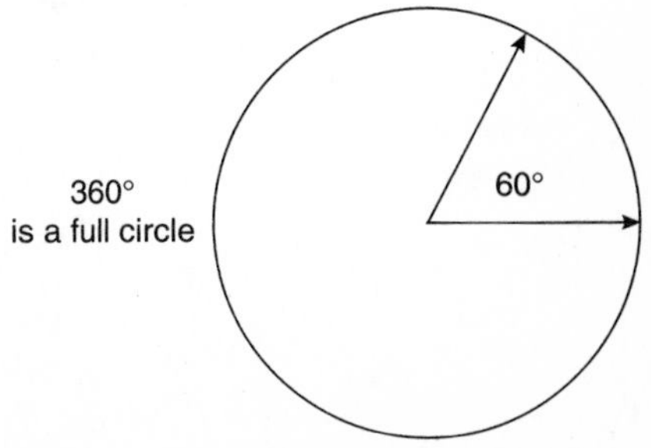

One complete revolution around a point is 360°. One-fourth of a revolution is 90°. A 90° angle is called a **right angle,** an angle size often used in construction. In a drawing, you can recognize a right angle because of the small square drawn in the vertex.

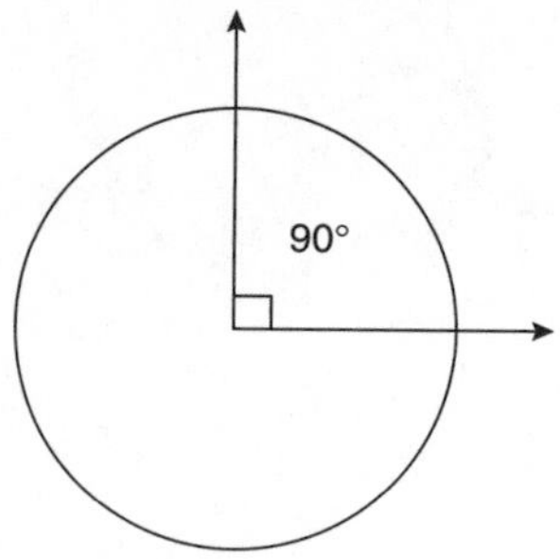

Lines can be related in the following ways.

parallel lines
(lines running in the same direction)

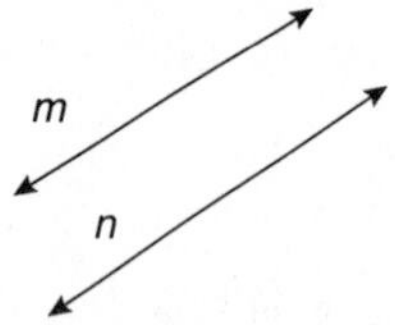

m* || *n* means line *m **is parallel to line *n*.**

intersecting lines
(lines crossing at one point)

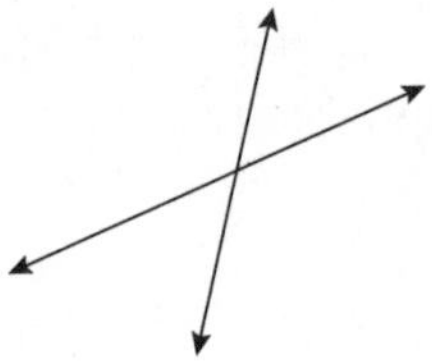

perpendicular lines
(lines intersecting at right angles)

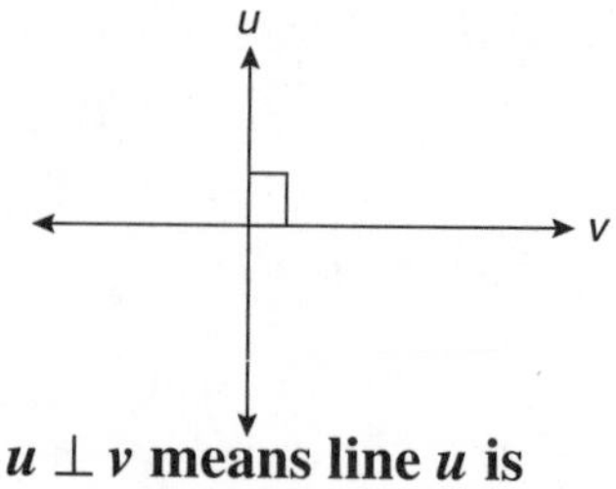

u* ⊥ *v **means line *u* is perpendicular to line *v*.**

Points, lines, and angles are the components you use to draw geometric figures. These figures are drawn on a flat surface called a **plane.** Some of the figures you will see on the GED Mathematics Test are called **polygons,** closed geometric figures with straight sides. Generally polygons are named according to the number of sides they contain.

A **triangle** is a polygon with three sides and three angles. ΔABC is shown at the right. An important property of triangles is that the **sum of the three angles of any triangle is 180°.** In ΔABC,

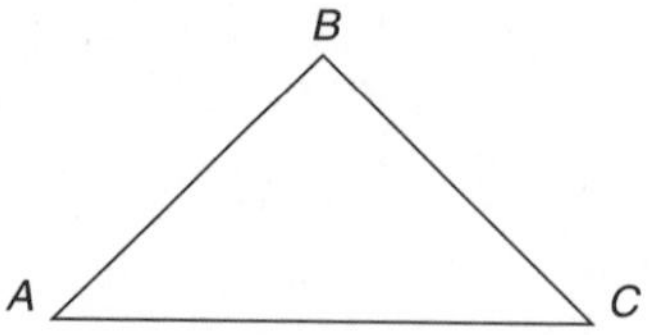

$$\angle A + \angle B + \angle C = 180°$$

There are several important types of triangles. Figure 1 is an **equilateral triangle;** the three sides are equal and the three angles are also equal (each being 60°). Figure 2 is an **isosceles triangle;** two sides are equal, as are the two angles opposite the equal sides. Figure 3 is a **right triangle,** a triangle with a right angle.

Figure 1

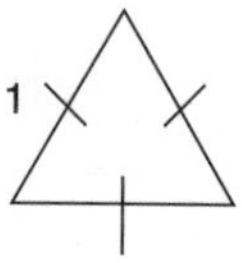

Figure 2

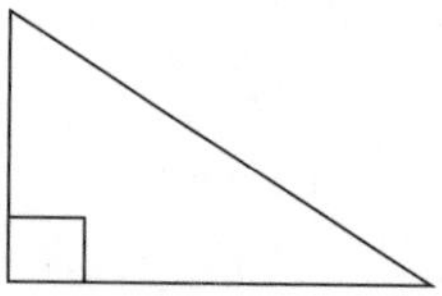

Figure 3

A **quadrilateral** is a polygon with four sides and four angles. There are several quadrilaterals that are familiar figures.

A **parallelogram** is a quadrilateral with opposite sides parallel and equal and four angles. Opposite angles are equal.

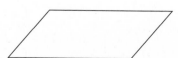

A **rectangle** is a quadrilateral with opposite sides parallel and equal and four right angles.

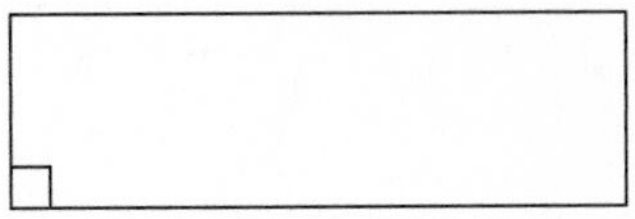

A **square** is a quadrilateral with all four sides equal, opposite sides parallel, and four right angles.

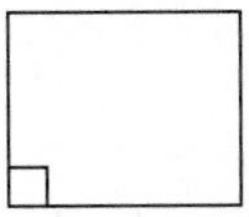

A **trapezoid** is a quadrilateral with four sides, of which only one pair of sides is parallel.

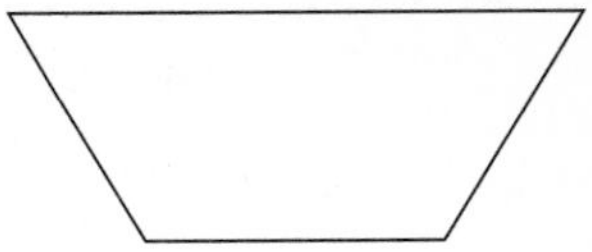

Polygons may have more than four sides. A **pentagon** has five sides and five angles, an **octagon** has eight sides and eight angles, and so on.

Another plane figure is the circle. A **circle** is a set of points all the same distance from a center point. The distance from the center to the circle is called the **radius.** A radius can be drawn from any point on the circle to the center. A **diameter** is a straight line that goes through the center of the circle and has its endpoints on the circle. A diameter is twice as long as a radius.

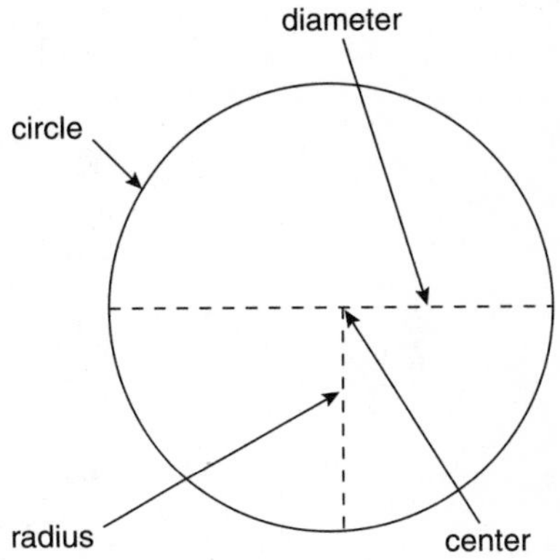

Some geometric figures are not flat; they are three-dimensional figures called **solids.** Four common solids can be found on the GED Mathematics Test.

A **rectangular solid,** also called a rectangular box, is a three-dimensional figure whose **faces** are rectangles. The faces are the sides, bottom, and top of the box. All corners are right angles. A box is described by its length, width, and height.

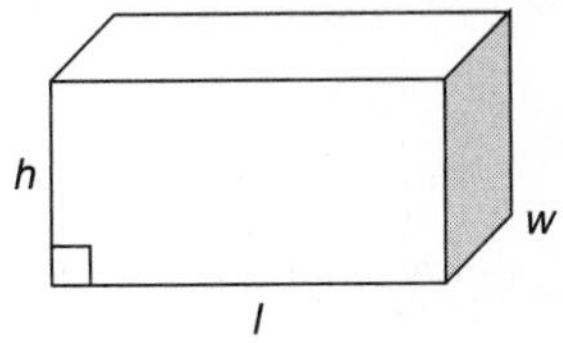

A **cube** is a solid whose faces are squares. All corners are right angles. The lengths of all edges are equal.

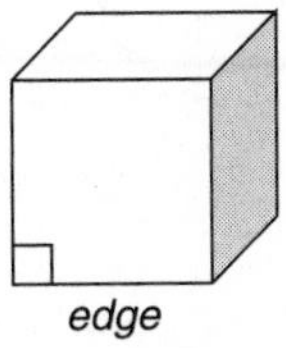

A **cylinder** is a solid figure. The top and bottom bases of the cylinder are circles. The sides of the cylinder are perpendicular to the bases. A cylinder is described by its radius and height.

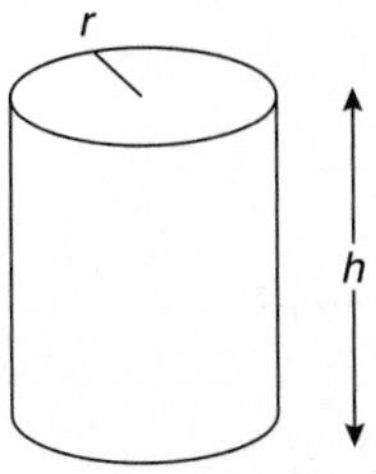

A **sphere** is a geometric figure shaped like a ball. A sphere is described by the diameter of the circle cut through the center of the sphere. The distance around the circle is the circumference of the sphere.

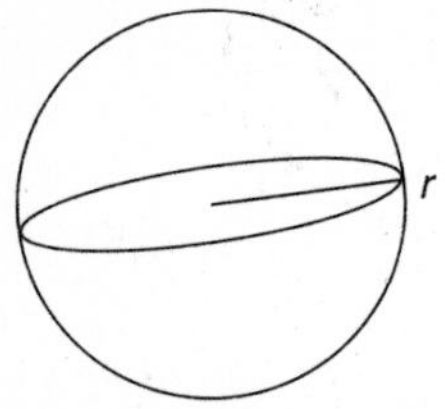

EXERCISE 1

Geometry Figures and Shapes

Directions: Match the geometry vocabulary to the following descriptions.

1. ______ Location in space
2. ______ Unit of measure for angles
3. ______ Point of intersection of the sides of an angle
4. ______ A flat surface
5. ______ Degrees in a full circle
6. ______ Lines running across
7. ______ A polygon with four equal sides
8. ______ Sum of the angles of a triangle
9. ______ Triangle with two sides equal
10. ______ Lines running in the same direction, not intersecting
11. ______ A figure shaped like a soda can
12. ______ Distance from the center to the circle
13. ______ Side of a rectangular solid
14. ______ Measure of a right angle
15. ______ Lines running up and down
16. ______ Lines intersecting at right angles
17. ______ Triangle with all sides equal
18. ______ A quadrilateral with only one pair of parallel sides
19. ______ A polygon with eight sides
20. ______ The study of figures and shapes

A. cylinder
B. degree
C. equilateral
D. face
E. geometry
F. horizontal
G. isosceles
H. octagon
I. parallel
J. perpendicular
K. plane
L. point
M. radius
N. square
O. trapezoid
P. vertex
Q. vertical
R. 90°
S. 180°
T. 360°

Answers are on page 940.

Measurement of Figures

$a^2+b^2=c^2$

You see geometric figures everywhere. The cover of this book is a rectangle, and the top of a card table is a square. The sail on a sailboat is a triangle, and a clock face is a circle. Dice are cubes, a gift box is a rectangular solid, and a can of corn is a cylinder. You often have to measure the size of these and other geometric figures. In the following sections you will review three types of measures and the formulas you can use to find the measures of geometric figures. Remember to refer to formula page 922 as you study the next few pages.

Perimeter

Perimeter is the distance around a figure. Measuring for a fence around a yard, putting a baseboard around a room, or setting up a baseball diamond are uses of perimeter. You will find formulas for perimeter on the formula page of the GED Mathematics Test.

Tip

Keep in mind that the perimeter of a figure is the linear measure of the distance all the way around the figure, so you can add all the sides of the figure.

Example 1 Find the perimeter of this square.

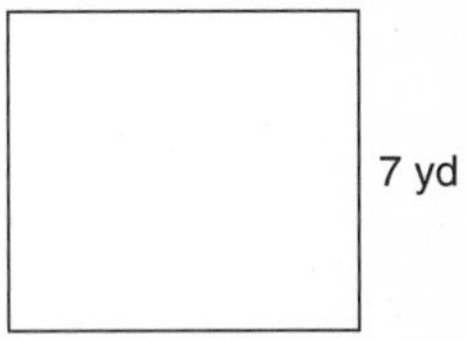

From the formula page you see that for a square Perimeter = 4 × side.

Perimeter = 4 × 7 = **28 yards**

Example 2 Find the perimeter of this rectangle.

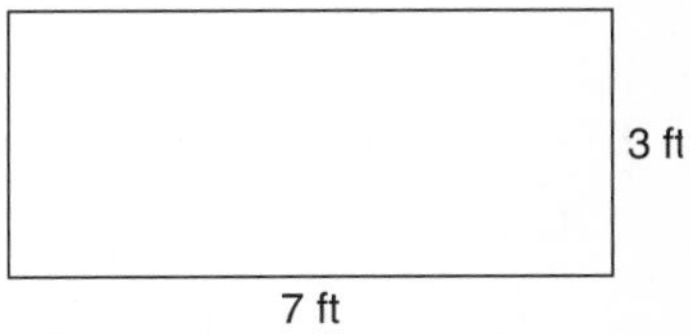

From the formula page you see that for a rectangle
Perimeter = 2 × length + 2 × width.

Perimeter = 2 × 7 + 2 × 3 = 14 + 6 = **20 feet**

Example 3 Find the perimeter of this triangle.

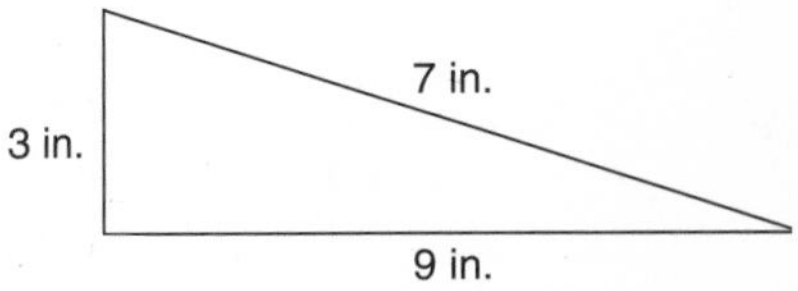

From the formula page you see that for a triangle
Perimeter = $side_1$ + $side_2$ + $side_3$.

Perimeter = 3 + 7 + 9 = **19 inches**

Tip

The circumference of a circle is the perimeter of (or distance around) a circle. The ratio of the circumference of a circle to the diameter of a circle is a constant number called π (pi). π = approximately 3.14. This number is used in the formulas associated with circles. You may also use $\frac{22}{7}$ for π when it is convenient to use a fraction instead of a decimal value.

Example 4 Find the circumference of this circle.

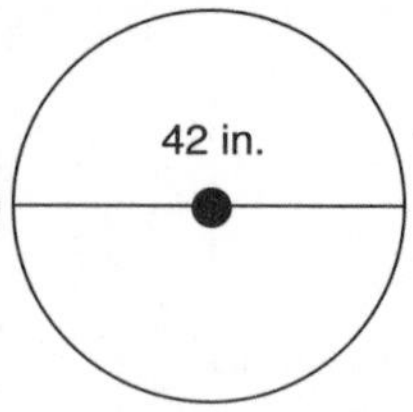

From the formula page you see that for a circle Circumference = $\pi \times$ diameter. (π is about 3.14 or $\frac{22}{7}$)

Circumference = $\frac{22}{7} \times 42 =$ **132 inches**

EXERCISE 2

Perimeter

Directions: Solve each problem. Use the formula page as needed.

1. A baseball diamond is a square with distances between the bases as shown. How far will the batter run if he hits a home run?

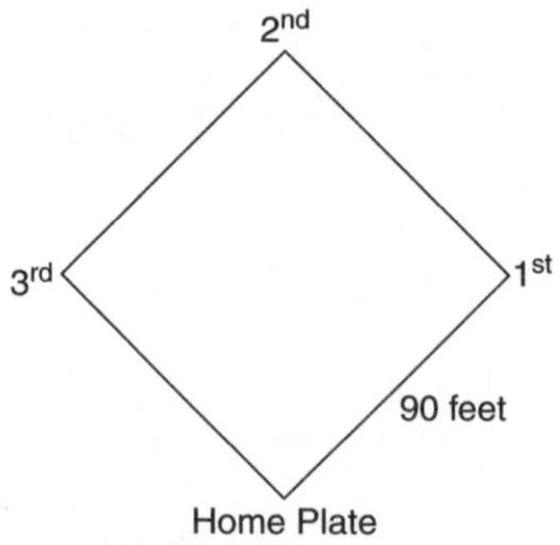

2. Find, in feet, the amount of framing needed to frame a picture $8\frac{1}{2}$ inches by 11 inches.

3. How much binding is needed around a triangular sail for the toy sailboat shown at the right?

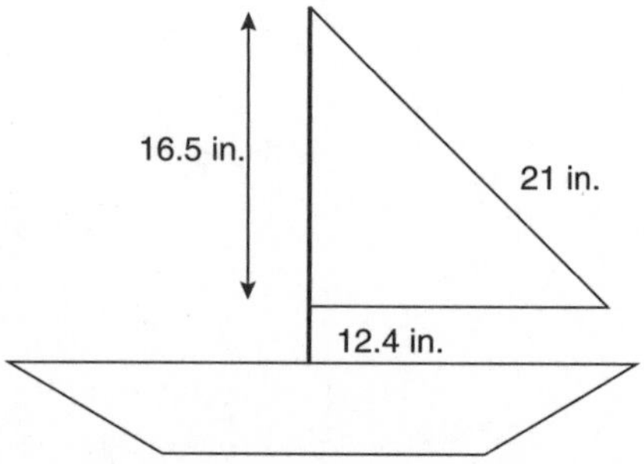

4. A farmer wants to fence a rectangular pasture 400 *yards* by 224 *yards*. The cost of fencing is $15.75 per eight-*foot* section. What will his cost be?

5. To jog 6 miles, how many times must you jog around a city block that is $\frac{1}{4}$ mile long by $\frac{1}{8}$ mile wide?

6. Find the perimeter of the figure at the right.

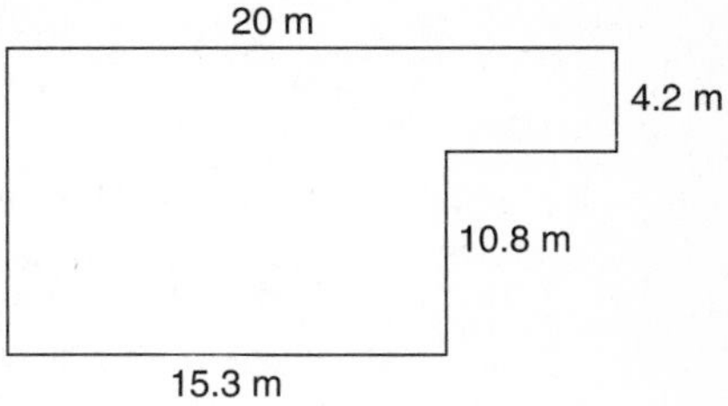

7. How many feet of fencing are needed to fence the yard at the right? (Hint: Do not put fencing around the house.)

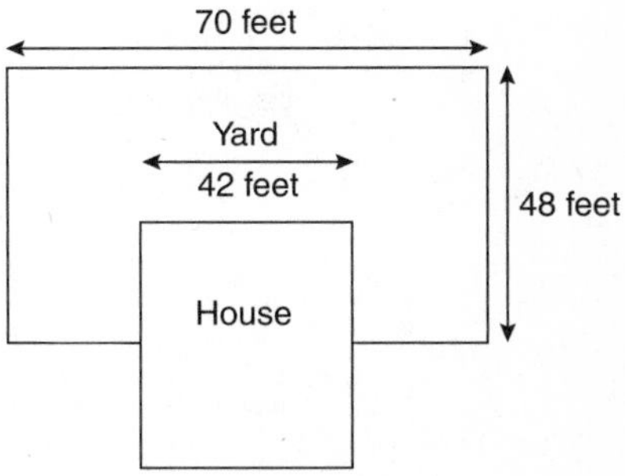

8. Find the perimeter of the ice-skating rink with the given dimensions. (Hint: Think of the rink as made up of 2 half-circles at the top and bottom of the rectangle.)

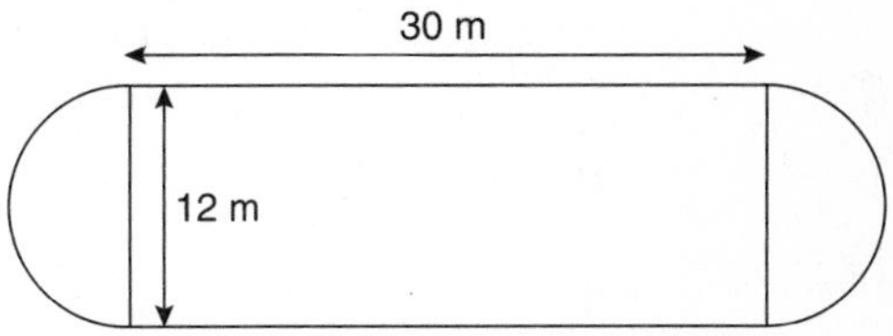

Answers are on page 940.

Area

$a^2+b^2=c^2$

Area is the amount of surface over a certain region. It can be used to describe the size of farmland, floor space, or a tabletop. Area is measured in **square units** such as **square inches** or **square feet.** Imagine a square that has one-inch sides. This is a square inch.

When you are asked to find the area in square inches, you are actually finding the number of squares one inch by one inch that could fit on the surface you are measuring. For example, the rectangle to the right contains 8 square inches.

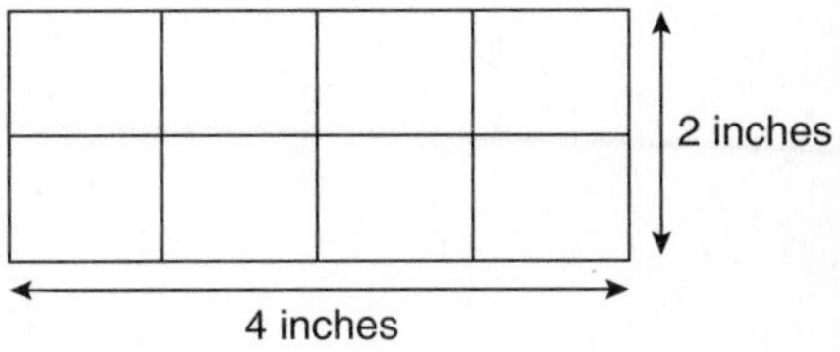

Remember that the formula page of the GED Test will provide the formulas for the area of the square, the rectangle, the triangle, the parallelogram, the trapezoid, and circle.

Tip

Answers in area problems are given in square units, such as square inches or square meters.

The **area of a square** = side^2. The area equals the side times the side. Given a square with a side of 7 inches, the area equals 7 in. × 7 in. = 49 square inches.

The **area of a rectangle** = length × width. The area equals the length times the width.

Example 1 How much surface area is the rectangular top of a desk 3 feet by 5 feet?

From the formula page for a rectangle
Area = length times width.
3 ft × 5 ft = **15 square feet, or 15 ft^2**

The **area of a triangle** = $\frac{1}{2}$ × base × height.

To find the area of a triangle, multiply the base by the height and find $\frac{1}{2}$ of that amount.

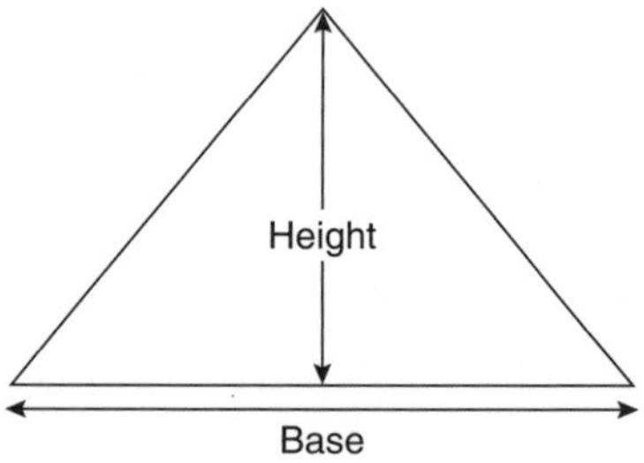

Example 2 Find the area of a triangle with a base of 6 inches and height of 9 inches.

From the formula page for a triangle

Area = $\frac{1}{2}$ × base × height.

$\frac{1}{2} \times 6 \times 9 = \frac{1}{2} \times 54 =$ **27 square inches, or 27 in.^{2}**

The **area of a circle** = π × radius^2, where π is approximately 3.14 or $\frac{22}{7}$.

Example 3 Find the area of a circle whose diameter is 12 inches.

First find the radius by dividing the diameter 12 by 2. 12 ÷ 2 = 6

From the formula page for a circle

Area = π × radius^2.

$3.14 \times 6^2 = 3.14 \times 36 =$ **113.04 sq in.**

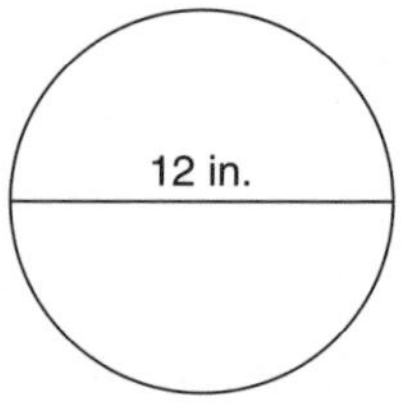

EXERCISE 3

Area

Directions: Solve each problem. For questions 1–3, find the area of the figures.

1.

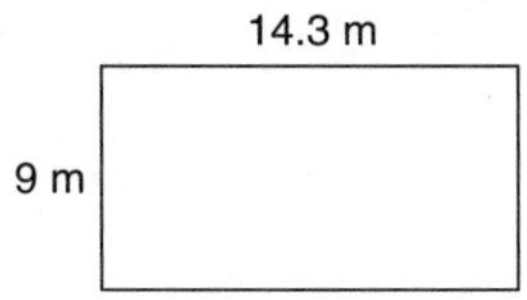

2.

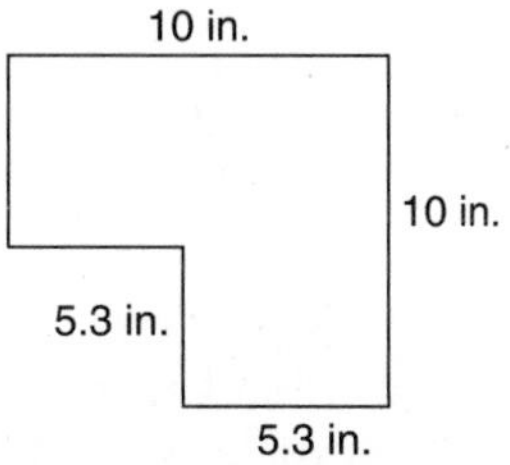

(This shape combines a square and a rectangle.)

3.

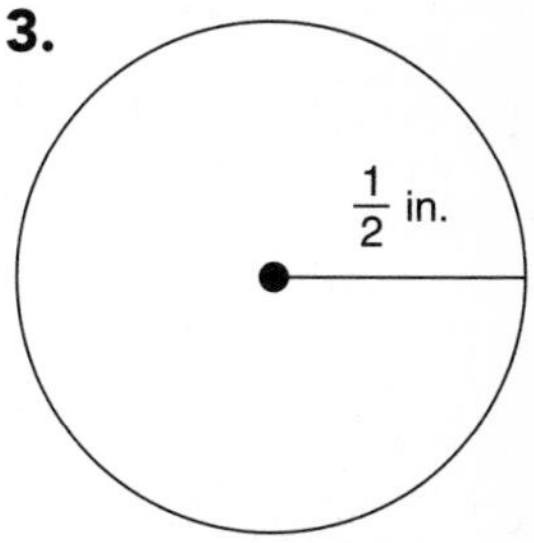

(Use $\frac{22}{7}$ for π.)

4. How many square yards of carpet are needed for a room 30 feet by 15 feet? (1 sq yd = 9 sq ft)

5. At $1.75 per square foot, find the rental cost for an office 20 feet by 15 feet.

6. How many square feet is the largest circular rug that can be put on the floor of a room 10 feet by 12 feet?

Questions 7–10 are based on the following information and diagram.

The diagram below shows the backyard at the Singer house. In the yard are an 18-foot diameter swimming pool, an 8-foot square garden, and a 10-foot by 20-foot patio deck. The rest of the yard is covered with grass.

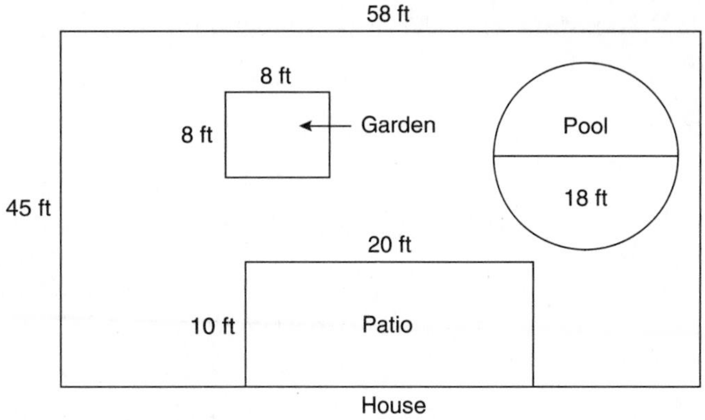

7. How large is the patio?

8. What percentage (to the nearest 1 percent) of the yard is covered by the pool?

9. How many square yards (to the nearest hundredth) of outdoor carpeting are needed to cover the patio?

10. To the nearest whole number, how many times larger is the pool than the garden?

Answers are on page 940.

Volume

$a^2+b^2=c^2$

Volume is the amount of space contained in a solid, three-dimensional figure. Examples of solids are shown below.

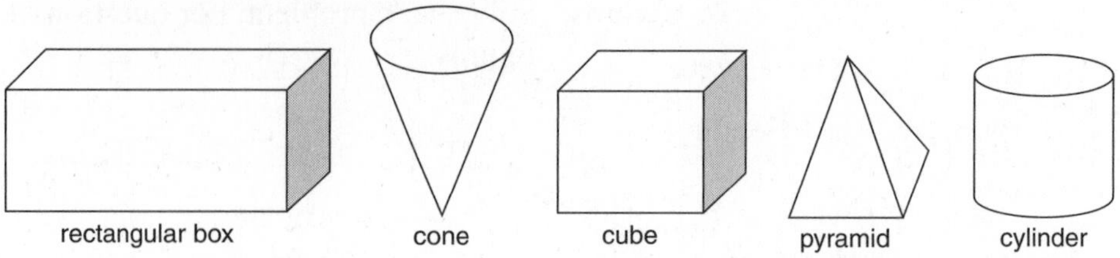

Volume is measured in **cubic units,** such as cubic feet, cubic inches, or cubic yards. For example, a cubic inch is a cube with edges each one inch long.

The formula page of the GED Mathematics Test gives formulas for the volume of a rectangular container, a cone, a cube, a square pyramid, and a cylinder. Look at each of these formulas.

The **volume of a cube** = edge^3. A die and a square box are examples of cubes. Each edge of the cube has the same length. Thus, the volume of a cube is equal to the edge cubed, or edge times edge times edge.

Example 1 Find the volume of the cube at the right.

Volume = edge^3 $2^3 = 2 \times 2 \times 2 =$ **8 cu in.**

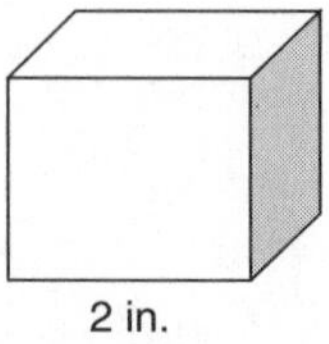

The **volume of a rectangular container** is length × width × height.

Example 2 What is the volume of the container at the right?

Volume = length × width × height

$18 \times 15 \times 6 =$ **1620 cm^3**

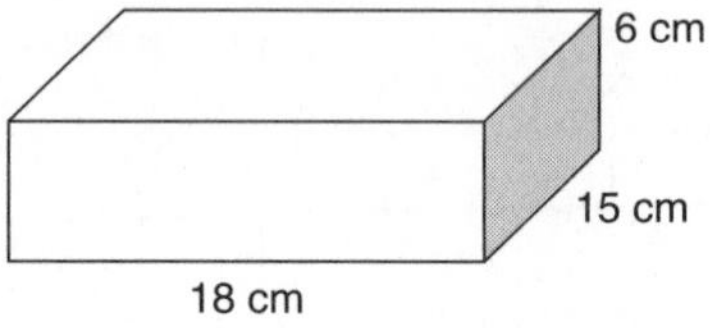

The **volume of a cylinder** = $\pi \times$ (radius of the base)$^2 \times$ height of the cylinder. π is approximately equal to 3.14.

Example 3 Find the volume of the container at the right.

Volume = $\pi \times$ radius$^2 \times$ height

$3.14\,(3)^2(5) =$ **141.3 cu in.**

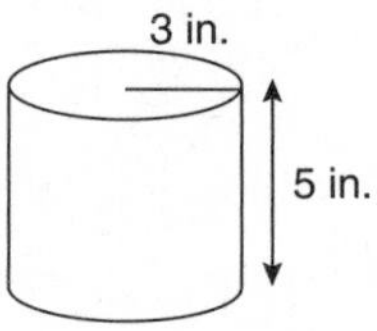

The **volume of a square pyramid** = $\frac{1}{3} \times (\text{base edge})^2 \times \text{height}$.

Example 4 Find the volume of the pyramid at the right.

Volume = $\frac{1}{3} \times \text{edge}^2 \times \text{height}$

$\frac{1}{3} \times 4^2 \times 6 =$ **32 cu in.**

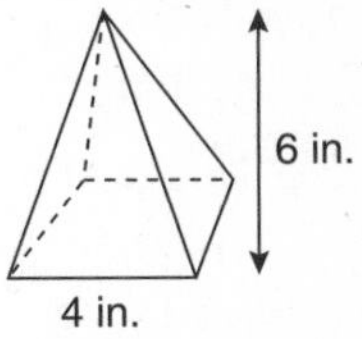

The **volume of a cone** = $\frac{1}{3} \times \pi \times \text{radius}^2 \times \text{height}$. π is approximately equal to 3.14.

Example 5 Find the volume of the cone at the right.

Volume = $\frac{1}{3} \times \pi \times \text{radius}^2 \times \text{height}$

$\frac{1}{3} \times 3.14 \times 2^2 \times 9 =$ **37.68 cu in.**

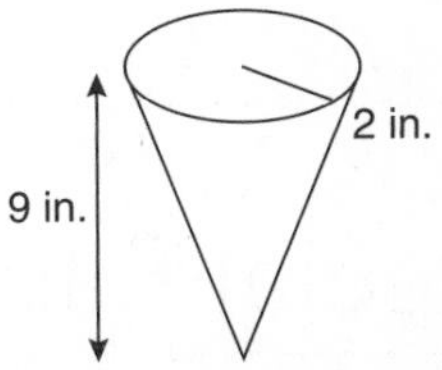

Tip

On the GED Mathematics Test you may be asked to find the perimeter, circumference, area, or volume of a figure. However, you may not be told directly which measurement you are to find. Keep in mind that the perimeter is what goes around a figure, the area (measured in square units) is what covers the surface of a figure, and the volume (measured in cubic units) is the capacity of an object.

EXERCISE 4

Volume

Directions: Solve each problem.

1. Find the volume of a freezer chest that is 6 feet long, 4 feet deep, and 3 feet wide.
2. How many gallons of water will fill a fish tank that is 18 inches by 12 inches by 48 inches? (There are 231 cubic inches per gallon.) Round your answer to the nearest gallon.
3. How much topsoil is needed to cover a garden 25 feet by 40 feet to a depth of 6 inches?
4. The highway department stores sand in a cone-shaped structure as shown. How many cubic yards of sand can be stored in the storage building with a diameter of 45 feet and height of 15 feet? (There are 27 cu ft in one cu yd.)

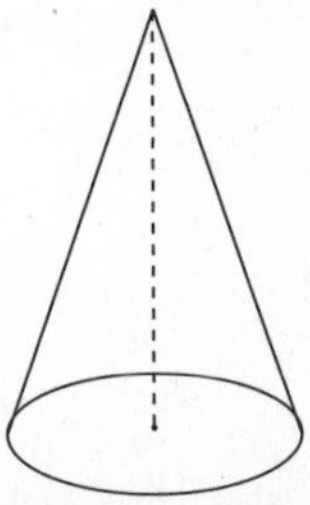

5. A crystal in the shape of a square pyramid is used as a paperweight. What is the volume of the crystal if the edge of the base is 4 centimeters and the crystal is 9 centimeters tall?

6. The farmer's silo has the dimensions shown at the right. What is the volume of the silo? (Use $\frac{22}{7}$ for π.)

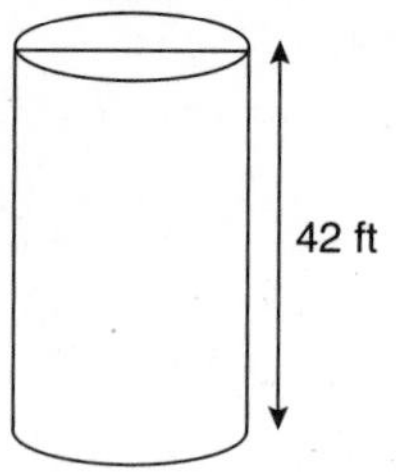

Answers are on page 941.

Special Pairs of Angles

There are special angular relationships that can be used to find the measure of angles whose measure is not known. On the GED Mathematics Test you will be asked to use your understanding of these relationships. Look at some rules that apply to certain pairs of angles.

Complementary angles are two angles whose sum is 90°. That means the two angles together make a right angle. A 60° angle and a 30° angle are **complement**s of each other because their sum is 90°.

Example 1 What is the complement of a 53° angle?

Solution: 90° – 53° = 37°

A **37° angle** is the complement of a 53° angle.

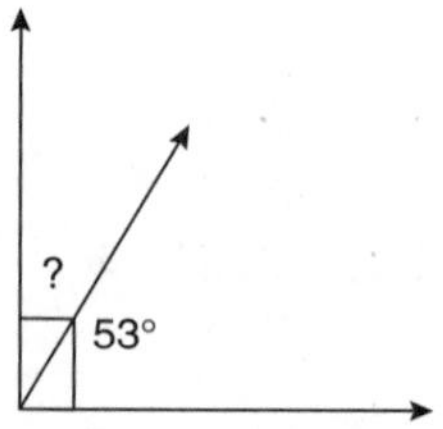

Supplementary angles are two angles whose sum is 180°. When the two angles are placed side by side, their sides form a straight line. A 110° angle is the **supplement** of a 70° angle because their sum is 180°.

Example 2 What is the supplement of a 30° angle?

Solution: = 180° – 30° = 150°

A **150° angle** is supplementary to a 30° angle.

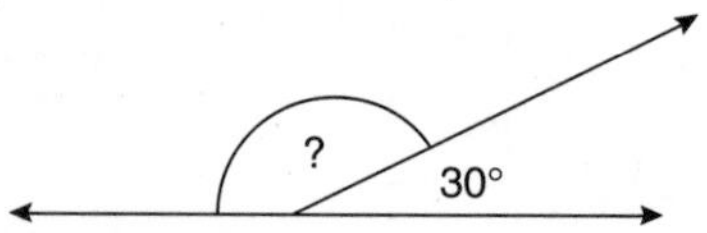

Vertical angles are formed when two lines intersect. The pair of angles opposite each other are equal. In the picture at the right, ∠*ABC* and ∠*DBE* are vertical angles. Therefore, ∠*ABC* = ∠*DBE*. In addition, ∠*ABD* and ∠*CBE* are vertical angles, so ∠*ABD* = ∠*CBE*. Sometimes, as in Example 3, you may be given a pair of intersecting lines and the measurement of one angle. From that one angle, you can find the measure of the other angles.

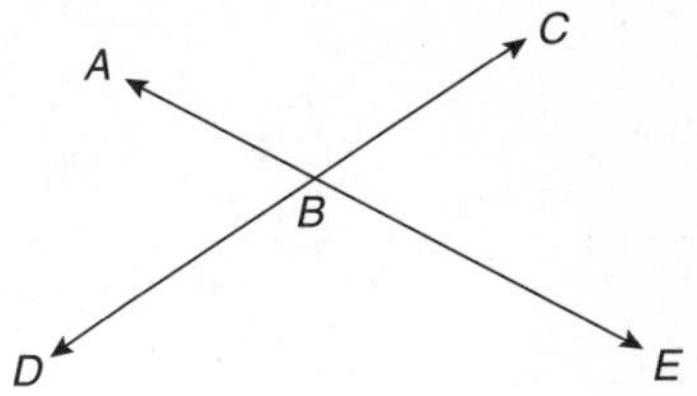

Example 3 Find the measure of ∠*HFJ*.

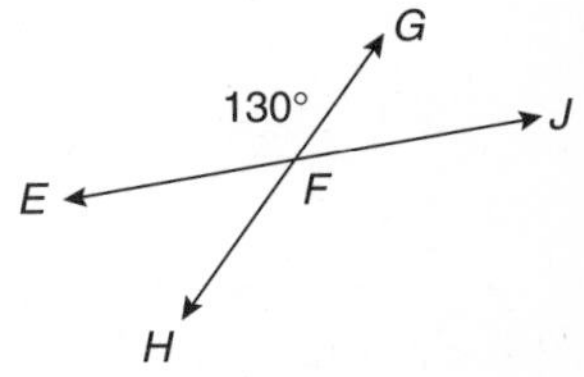

Solution: ∠*EFG* and ∠*HFJ* are vertical angles. Therefore, they are equal.
∠*HFJ* = **130°**

Example 4 Find the measure of ∠*GFJ*.

Solution: Notice that ∠*GFJ* is supplementary to ∠*EFG*. Together, they are on a straight line that equals 180°.

180° – 130° = 50°, so ∠*GFJ* = **50°.**

Corresponding angles are formed when you have angles placed in the same relative position in a figure. When parallel lines are cut by a third line called a **transversal,** corresponding angles are formed.

For example, in the picture at the right, angles *a* and *e* are corresponding because they are above lines *l* and *m*, respectively, and they are to the left of the transversal *t*. Other pairs of corresponding angles are *c* and *g*, *b* and *f*, and *d* and *h*. Corresponding angles are equal. So ∠*a* = ∠*e*, ∠c = ∠*g*, ∠*b* = ∠*f*, and ∠*d* = ∠*h*.

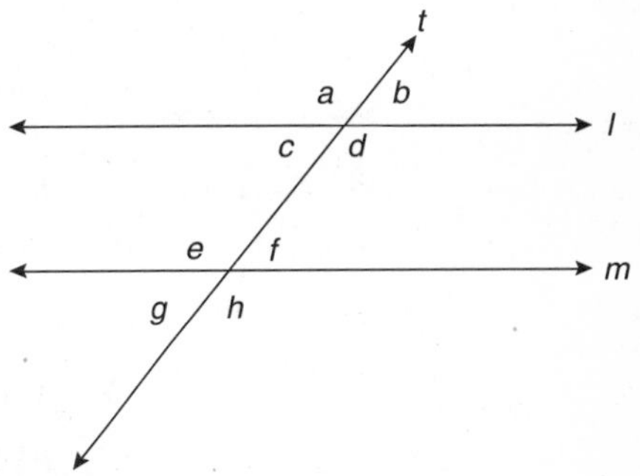

Example 5 In the drawing above, if ∠*a* = 100°, find the measure of ∠*h*.

Solution: ∠*a* = ∠*e* because they are corresponding angles. So ∠*e* = 100°. Then ∠*e* = ∠*h* because they are vertical angles. Therefore, ∠*h* = **100°.**

Sometimes, angles are merely parts of a picture in a problem. Knowing these angle relationships (complementary, supplementary, vertical, and corresponding) can help you solve the problem if you look for a pair of angles formed by intersecting lines.

Example 6 Find the measure of the angle indicated.

The angle formed by the ladder and the ground is a supplementary angle with the 45° angle. To find the missing angle, subtract 45° from 180°.

Solution: 180° – 45° = **135°**

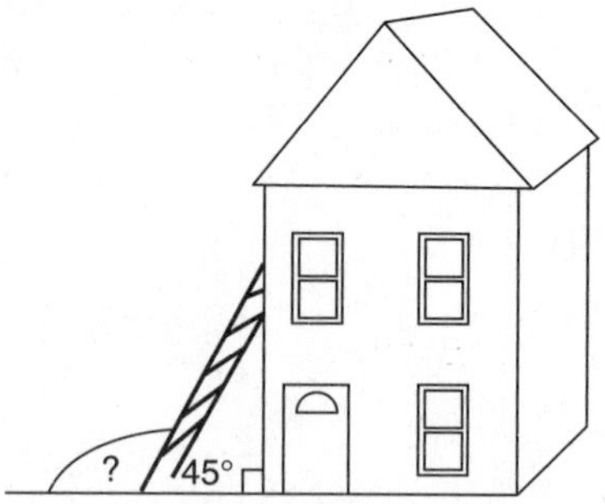

EXERCISE 5

Pairs of Angles

Directions: Solve each problem.

Use the picture at the right to answer questions 1–6.

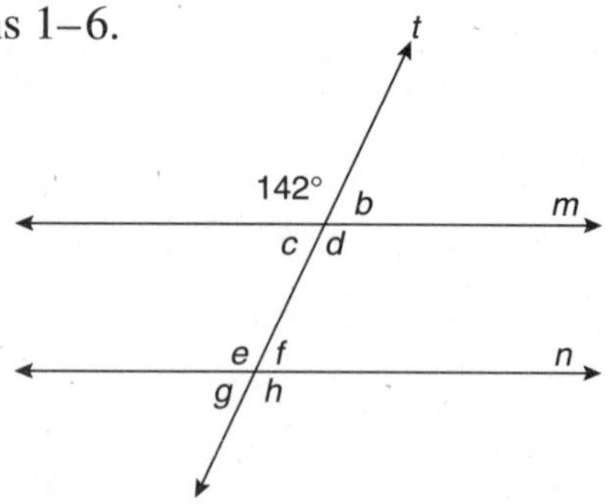

1. Find the measure of $\angle b$.
2. Find the measure of $\angle f$.
3. Find the measure of $\angle g$.
4. Find the measure of $\angle c$.
5. Find the measure of $\angle d$.
6. Find the measure of $\angle e$.

7. Two pieces of a puzzle fit together to form a right angle. If one piece has an angle of 52°, what is the angle of the complementary piece?
8. A carpenter is putting an oak chair rail around a dining room wall. He wants to make sure it fits nicely and looks straight. What is the measure of the angle that will supplement 75° to make a straight, snug fit?

Answers are on page 941.

Problem Solving Using Triangular Relationships

Triangles are the basis of land measurement. Surveyors use triangles to measure a small plot of ground, an entire state or county, or a large body of water. Triangles are used in science, navigation, and building construction. Carpenters use right triangles when no T squares or carpenter's squares are available. Astronomers use triangles to find out how far stars are from Earth. There are also important uses for triangles in maps, scale drawings, and architectural plans.

On the GED Mathematics Test you will find measurement problems concerning triangles. Remember that the three angles of every triangle add up to 180°. Use this fact to find the measure of the third angle of a triangle when the measure of the first two angles is known, as in the following example.

Example Find $\angle C$ in the triangle at the right.

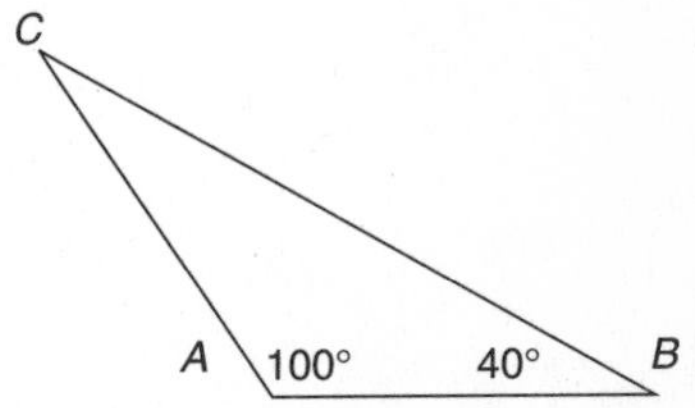

STEP 1 Add the two known angles.
$40° + 100° = 140°$

STEP 2 Then subtract the sum from 180°.
$180° - 140° = 40°$

$\angle C = 40°$

Tip

- When you see a three-sided figure in a drawing, look for a special triangular relationship.
- If all three sides of a triangle are equal, then all three angles are equal. If two sides of a triangle are equal, then the two angles opposite those sides are equal.
- The angle opposite the longest side is the largest angle, and the angle opposite the shortest side is the smallest angle.

EXERCISE 6

Angles in Triangles

Directions: Find the measurement of the missing angle in each of the following triangles.

1. ΔABC is an equilateral triangle. What is the measure of $\angle C$?
2. ΔRST is an isosceles triangle. Because two sides are equal, the two base angles are equal. If the two equal angles are each 65°, what is the measure of the third angle?
3. Find $\angle B$.

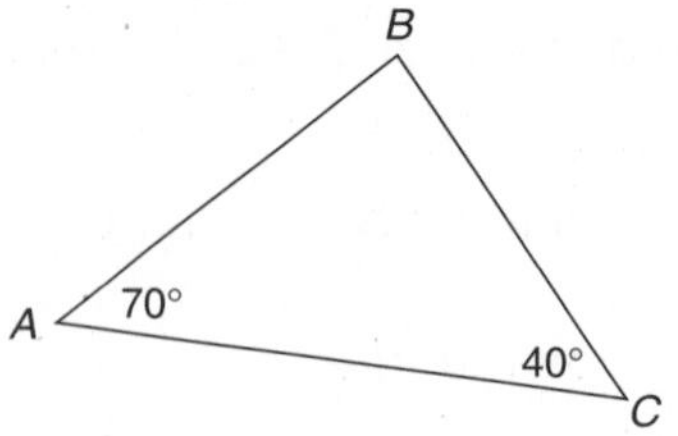

4. Find $\angle Q$.

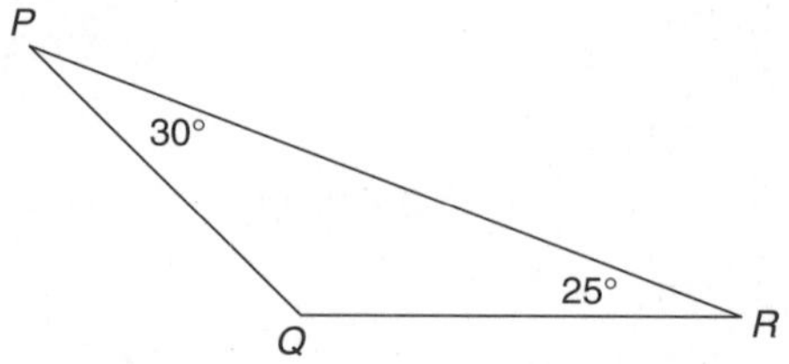

5. A right triangle contains a 60° angle. What is the measure of the third angle?

Answers are on page 941.

The Pythagorean Theorem

$a^2+b^2=c^2$

Although the **Pythagorean theorem** was developed by the Greek mathematician Pythagoras in about 500 B.C., it is still used today. Since the rule applies only to right triangles, the triangle has to include a 90° angle. In a right triangle, the side opposite the right angle is called the **hypotenuse,** and the other two sides are called the **legs** of the triangle.

THE PYTHAGOREAN THEOREM

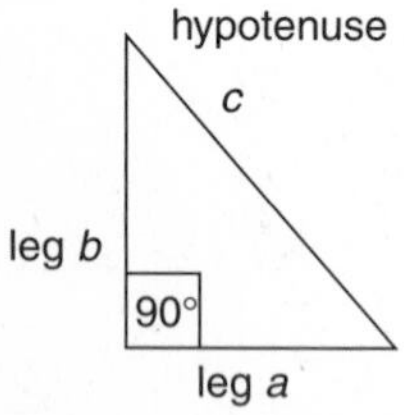

The Pythagorean theorem states that in a right triangle, the square of the hypotenuse equals the sum of the squares of the legs. According to the diagram, the Pythagorean theorem is written as $a^2 + b^2 = c^2$. In the right triangle, the legs are a and b and the hypotenuse is c.

Tip

To use the rule effectively, you need to be familiar with the use of squares and square roots. Review powers and square roots on page 711.

Example 1 Find the length of the hypotenuse of a right triangle with legs 6 inches and 8 inches.

STEP 1 Draw a right triangle and label its sides.

STEP 2 Using the Pythagorean theorem, substitute the numbers for legs *a* and *b* in the formula. $a^2 + b^2 = c^2$
$8^2 + 6^2 = c^2$

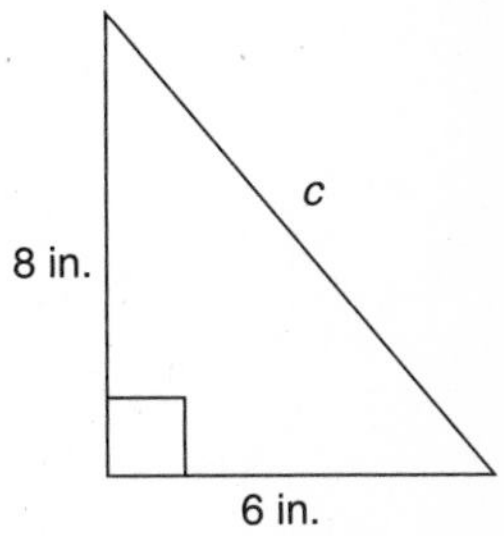

STEP 3 Square the numbers. $64 + 36 = c^2$

STEP 4 Add the numbers when looking for the hypotenuse. $100 = c^2$

STEP 5 Take the square root to find *c*. $c = \sqrt{100} = \mathbf{10\ in.}$

Example 2 asks you to find the length of a leg when the hypotenuse and one leg are given. You still use the Pythagorean theorem. However, to find a leg rather than the hypotenuse, you subtract instead of add before taking the square root.

Example 2 The hypotenuse of a right triangle is 13 feet. If one leg is 12 feet, what is the length of the other leg?

STEP 1 Draw a right triangle and label its sides.

STEP 2 Using the Pythagorean theorem, substitute the numbers for leg *b* and hypotenuse *c* in the formula. $a^2 + b^2 = c^2$
$a^2 + 12^2 = 13^2$

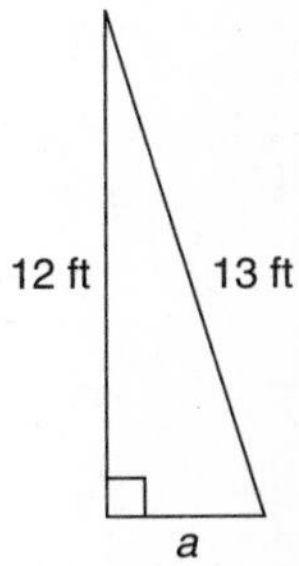

STEP 3 Square the numbers. $a^2 + 144 = 169$

STEP 4 Subtract the numbers when looking for a leg. $a^2 = 169 - 144 = 25$

STEP 5 Take the square root to find *a*. $a = \sqrt{25} = \mathbf{5\ ft}$

To solve the next problem, you first have to recognize a right-triangle relationship in a familiar figure.

Example 3 A painter is concerned about setting up his equipment too near the street. He leans a 50-foot ladder against the top of a 48-foot building. How far is the bottom of the ladder from the foot of the building?

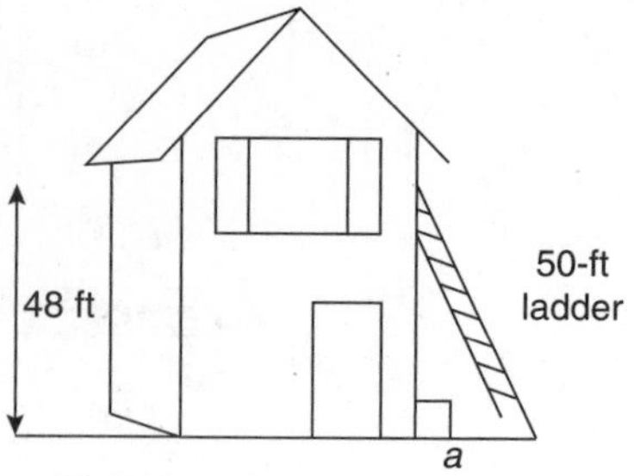

STEP 1 Look at the sketch and notice that the building makes a right angle with the ground. The leaning ladder completes a triangle.

STEP 2 Using the Pythagorean theorem, substitute the numbers for leg b and hypotenuse c in the formula.
$a^2 + b^2 = c^2$
$a^2 + 48^2 = 50^2$

STEP 3 Square the numbers. $a^2 + 2304 = 2500$

STEP 4 Subtract the numbers when looking for a leg. $a^2 = 2500 - 2304 = 196$

STEP 5 Take the square root to find a. $a = \sqrt{196} = \mathbf{14\ ft}$

Tip

Always make a sketch when working a geometry problem. If the sketch is a right triangle, consider using the Pythagorean theorem.

SOLVING PYTHAGOREAN THEOREM PROBLEMS

1. Sketch the information in the problem and label the parts.
2. Note the triangular shape; identify the right angle and the hypotenuse.
3. Substitute the values into the formula $a^2 + b^2 = c^2$.
4. Square the values.
5. Add if you are looking for the hypotenuse, or subtract if you are looking for a leg.
6. Take the square root.

EXERCISE 7

The Pythagorean Theorem

Directions: Solve each problem.

In problems 1–3, find the length of the missing side in the right triangle whose legs are a and b and whose hypotenuse is c.

1. $a = 9$, $b = 12$

2. $b = 4$, $c = 5$

3. $a = 10$, $b = 24$

4. The screen on Alberto's TV has the measurements shown. Find the measure of the diagonal for Alberto's TV.

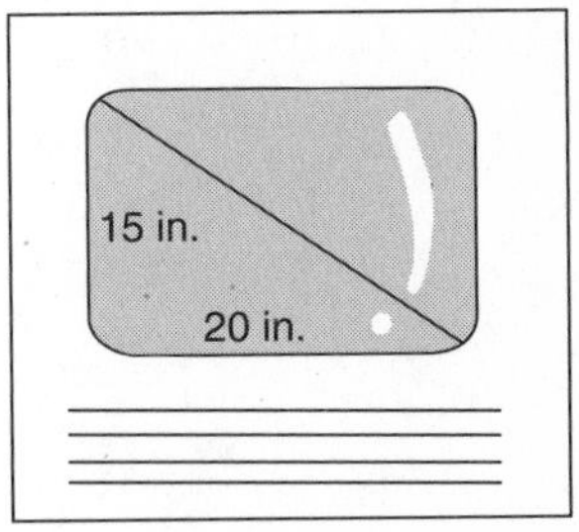

5. Can 20 inches, 21 inches, and 29 inches be the sides of a right triangle?

6. At summer camp, the swimming course runs across a small lake. To determine the length of the course, the camp counselors measure the two "dry" legs of a right triangle. What is the length in meters of the swimming course l in the figure below?

(1) 75
(2) 90
(3) 100
(4) 120
(5) 144

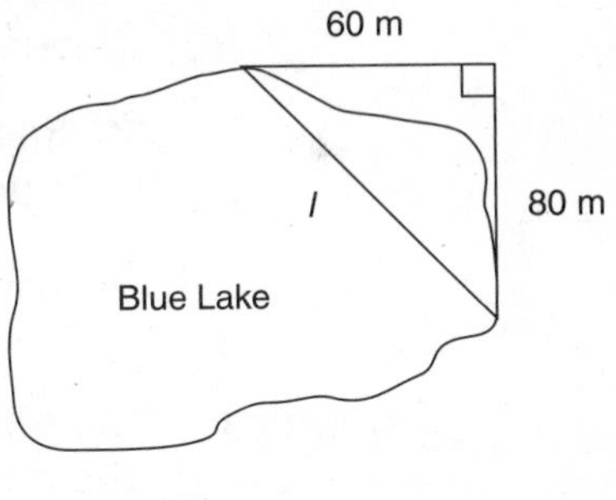

7. A television antenna is 24 feet tall and is held in place by *three* guy wires (braces) fastened at the top of the antenna and to hooks 7 feet from the base of the tower. If the antenna is installed on a flat roof, how many feet of guy wire are used?

(1) 40 **(2)** 50 **(3)** 60 **(4)** 65 **(5)** 75

8. A ladder that is 13 feet long is placed against a house. The foot of the ladder is 5 feet from the base of the house. How many feet above the ground does the ladder touch the building?

(1) 10 **(2)** 12 **(3)** 15 **(4)** 16 **(5)** 20

Answers are on page 941.

Similar Triangles

Similar triangles are figures that have the same shape. We often use similar figures to find hard-to-measure lengths, such as the distance across a lake or the height of a building. **Similar triangles** are two triangles whose **corresponding angles** are equal and whose **corresponding sides** are in proportion.

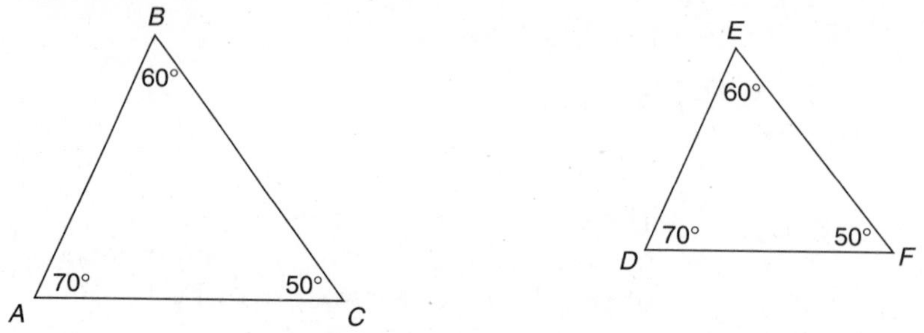

Look at ΔABC and ΔDEF. They are similar triangles because they have the same shape. You see that corresponding angles are equal. $\angle A = \angle D$, $\angle B = \angle E$, and $\angle C = \angle F$. Although the two triangles are not the same size, their sides are in proportion. You write this relationship as $\frac{\text{side } AB}{\text{side } DE} = \frac{\text{side } BC}{\text{side } EF} = \frac{\text{side } AC}{\text{side } DF}$.

SOLVING SIMILAR TRIANGLE PROBLEMS

1. Look for two triangles that have the same shape. Be sure the triangles are similar. Corresponding angles must be equal.
2. Redraw the triangles if necessary to show the corresponding sides and angles.
3. Set up and solve a proportion to find the missing length.

Example 1 On a sunny day, the village inspector used similar triangles to find the height of a flagpole without climbing it. She found that her 6-foot-tall coworker cast a 10-foot shadow at the same time the flagpole cast a 40-foot shadow. How tall is the flagpole?

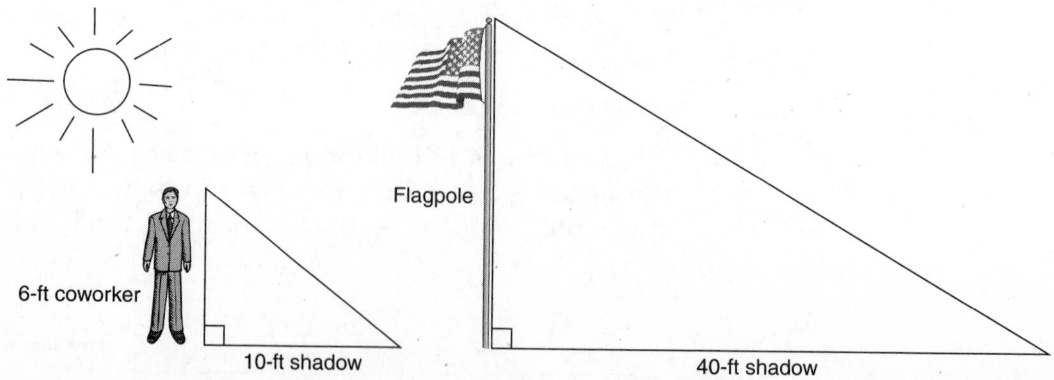

STEP 1 Notice that the coworker and the flagpole are at right angles to the ground. Set up a proportion. $\frac{\text{flagpole}}{\text{coworker}} = \frac{\text{flagpole shadow}}{\text{coworker shadow}}$

STEP 2 Fill in the numbers from the problem. Let *f* stand for flagpole. $\frac{f}{6} = \frac{40}{10}$

STEP 3 Solve the proportion for *f* by cross multiplying and then dividing.

$$f = \frac{6 \times 40}{10} = \frac{240}{10} = \mathbf{24\ ft}$$

Another type of problem involving similar triangles is a surveying problem.

<u>**Example 2**</u> The figure below shows a method of measuring the width of a river. If measurements are taken along the riverbank as shown, how wide is the river?

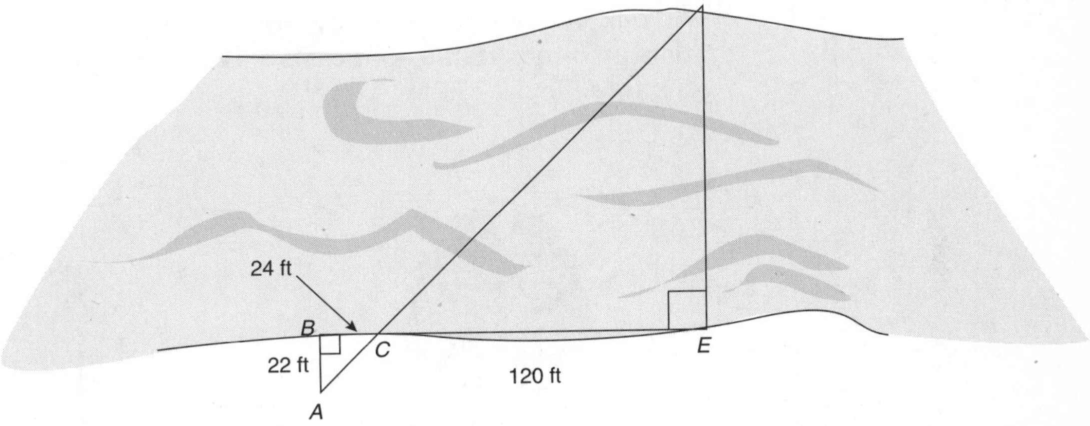

STEP 1 Look to see if there are two similar triangles. $\angle B = \angle E$ because they are both right angles, and both angles at point *C* are the same because they are vertical angles. Since two pairs of angles are the same, the triangles must be similar.

STEP 2 Redraw the small triangle by turning it in the same direction as the large triangle. Label the sides.

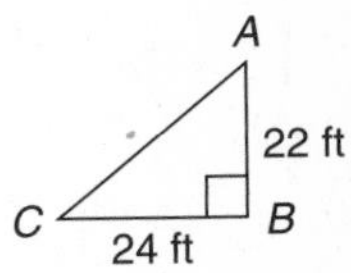

STEP 3 Set up a proportion with the sides of the triangles.

$$\frac{\text{side } AB}{\text{side } DE} = \frac{\text{side } CB}{\text{side } CE}$$

STEP 4 Fill in the values known.

$$\frac{22}{DE} = \frac{24}{120}$$

STEP 5 Solve for side *DE* by cross multiplying and dividing.

$$DE = \frac{120 \times 22}{24} = \frac{2640}{24} = \mathbf{110\ ft}$$

Tip

Always look for similar triangles when you are comparing two triangles.

EXERCISE 8

Similar Triangles

Directions: Solve each problem.

1. ΔABC is similar to ΔDEF. Find the length of DF.

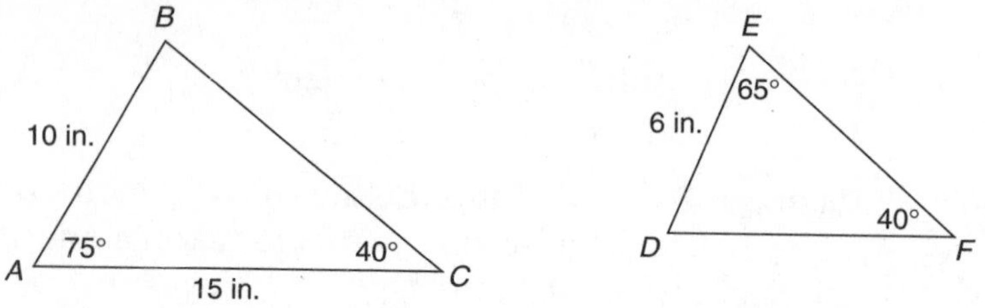

2. An oak tree along a parkway casts an 18-foot shadow at the same time an 8-foot traffic light casts a 12-foot shadow. Find the height of the tree.

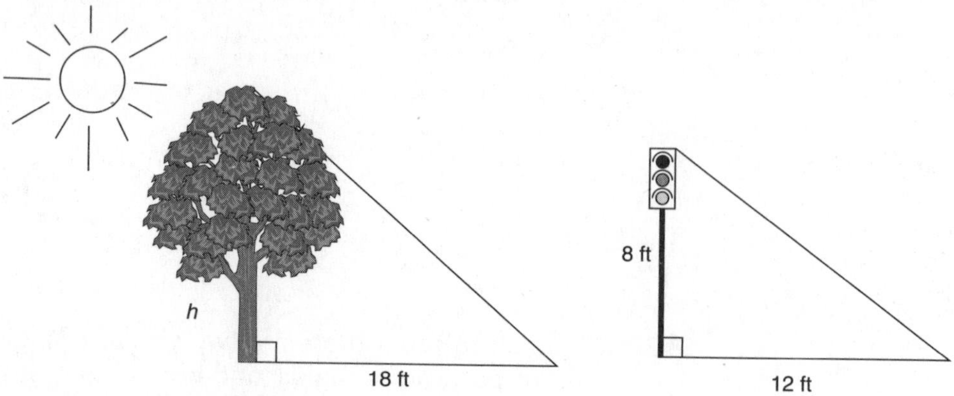

3. Suppose we need to find the distance *d* across a pond but are unable to swim to the other side and measure the distance directly. We can still find the distance. Find a marker on one side of the pond. On the other side of the pond, place a stake in the ground directly across from the marker. Measure a given distance *c* on a line perpendicular to the line determined by the marker and the stake. Then form two triangles as in the sketch below.

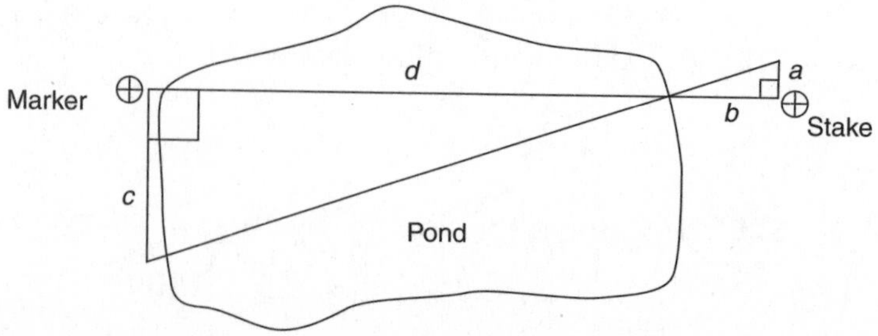

(a) With these measures, what would you do first to determine the distance, *d*?

(b) Find the distance across the pond if $a = 2$ feet, $b = 6$ feet, and $c = 50$ feet.

4. To find the height of a tower, Melissa held a yardstick perpendicular to the ground. She measured the shadow cast by the tower and the shadow cast by the yardstick. The tower's shadow was 42 feet, and the yardstick's shadow was 4 feet. How tall is the tower?

Answers are on page 942.

Trigonometric Ratios

$a^2+b^2=c^2$

Trigonometry is the branch of mathematics dealing with measurements in triangles. It is a system of computation based on the fact that the sides of the right triangle can be expressed as distinct ratios to the angles. Mathematicians have found and calculated these ratios for all to use. Trigonometry enables you to measure inaccessible distances as well as to solve problems in mechanics, electricity, and construction.

Remember that beside the right angle in a right triangle, there are two acute complementary angles (angles less than 90°). To avoid confusion when looking at the acute angles in the right triangle, the legs of the triangle are named in *relation to the angle under consideration.* Each angle is said to have an **adjacent side** (next to the angle) and an **opposite side** (opposite the angle). In the right triangle shown below when you consider $\angle A$, the adjacent side is AC, and the opposite side is BC. On the other hand, when you consider $\angle B$, the adjacent side is BC, and the opposite side is AC.

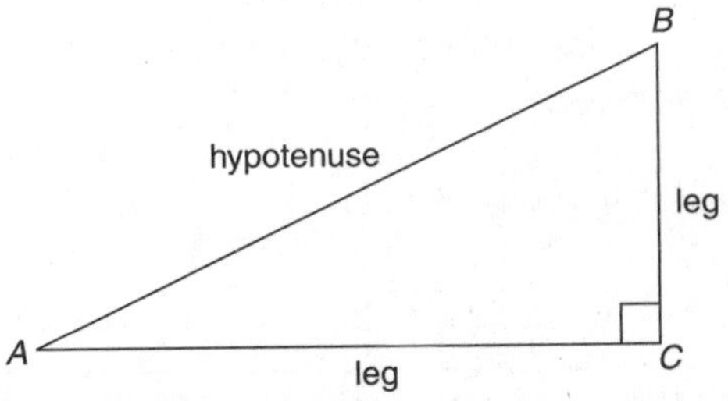

Acute Angle	Side Adjacent	Side Opposite
$\angle A$	AC	BC
$\angle B$	BC	AC

Tip

- It is important to know that *adjacent* and *opposite* depend entirely on the acute angle being considered. Obviously, the adjacent side to one of the angles will be the opposite side to the other angle.
- Note that the hypotenuse is never considered to be either adjacent or opposite. The hypotenuse is always the side directly across from the right angle.

All problems involving the legs and the hypotenuse of a right triangle can readily be solved by using **trigonometric ratios.** The formulas for these ratios can be found on formula page 922.

The **tangent ratio** of an angle is the ratio of the side opposite to the side adjacent. The tangent ratio is called the tangent of the angle or **tan angle.** The tangent of angle A can be written $\tan A = \frac{\text{opposite}}{\text{adjacent}}$.

The **sine ratio** of an angle is the ratio of the side opposite to the hypotenuse. The sine ratio is called the sine of the angle or **sin angle.** The sine of angle A can be written $\sin A = \frac{\text{opposite}}{\text{hypotenuse}}$.

The **cosine ratio** of an angle is the ratio of the side adjacent to the hypotenuse. The cosine ratio is called the cosine of the angle or **cos angle.** The cosine of angle A can be written $\cos A = \frac{\text{adjacent}}{\text{hypotenuse}}$.

Example 1 Find the tangent, sine, and cosine of angle A and angle B in the triangle shown at the right. (Use your calculator to find the decimal answers.)

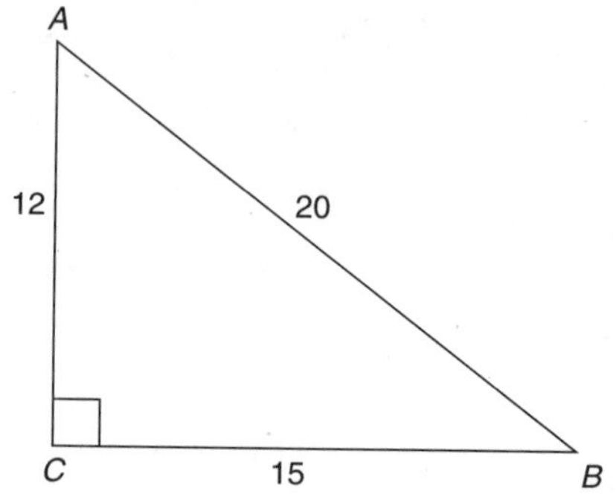

Solution: First, fill in the chart below with the values for the adjacent side, opposite side, and hypotenuse for each angle. Then using the ratios for tan, sin, and cos and your calculator, divide to find the answers.

Angle	Adj	Opp	Hyp	Tan	Sin	Cos
$\angle A$	12	15	20	$\frac{15}{12} = 1.25$	$\frac{15}{20} = .75$	$\frac{12}{20} = .6$
$\angle B$	15	12	20	$\frac{12}{15} = .8$	$\frac{12}{20} = .6$	$\frac{15}{20} = .75$

You will notice that the tan, sin, and cos for angle A and the tan, sin, and cos for angle B are reciprocals of each other.

Look at the two right triangles shown at right.

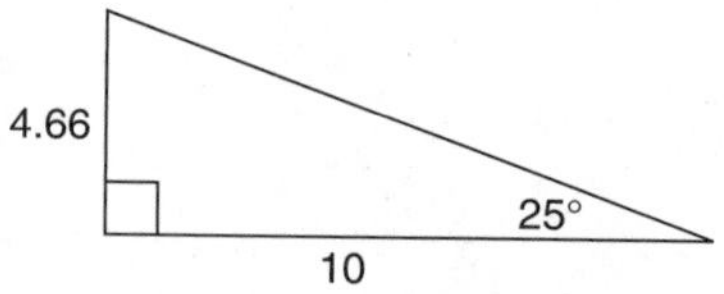

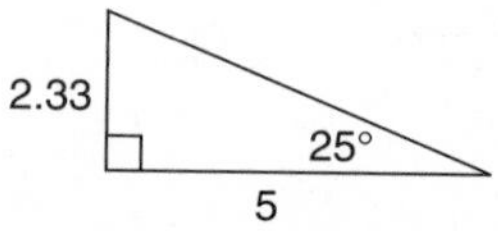

The two triangles are similar but not equal in size. Consider the tangent of the 25° angles in both triangles.

In the large triangle, $\tan 25° = \frac{4.66}{10} = 0.466$.

In the small triangle, $\tan 25° = \frac{2.33}{5} = 0.466$.

As you see, the tan 25° is always 0.466. Every angle has a definite value for the tangent, sine, and cosine. These values can be found in trigonometry tables or in scientific calculators.

On the calculator there are keys for *tan, sin,* and *cos.* To find the decimal value for the tan, sin, or cos, enter the value of the angle and then enter the appropriate key. For instance, to find the sin 45°, enter *45* and then enter *sin.* The answer displayed is 0.707106781, which is approximately 0.707.

<u>**Example 2**</u> Find the value of tan 12°.

Solution: Using your calculator, find tan 12° = 0.212556561, which is approximately **0.213.**

<u>**Example 3**</u> Find the height of the triangle at the right.

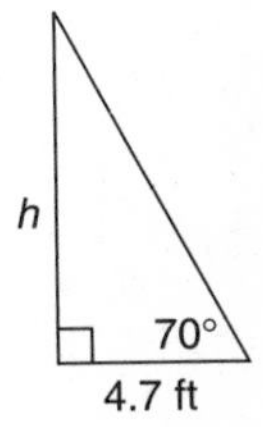

Solution: Set up the ratio for the tangent because you have the measure of the angle (70°) and the side adjacent (4.7), and you need to find the side opposite. Then solve the equation for *h*, by first finding tan 70° = 2.75.

$$\tan 70° = \frac{h}{4.7}$$

$$2.75 = \frac{h}{4.7}$$

$$4.7 \times 2.75 = \frac{h}{\cancel{4.7}} \times \cancel{4.7}$$

$$12.925 = h$$

The height of the triangle is **12.925 ft.**

EXERCISE 9

Trigonometric Ratios

Directions: Solve the following problems. Use formula page 922 for the trigonometry ratios and your calculator as needed.

1. Use the figure at the right to fill in the chart below.

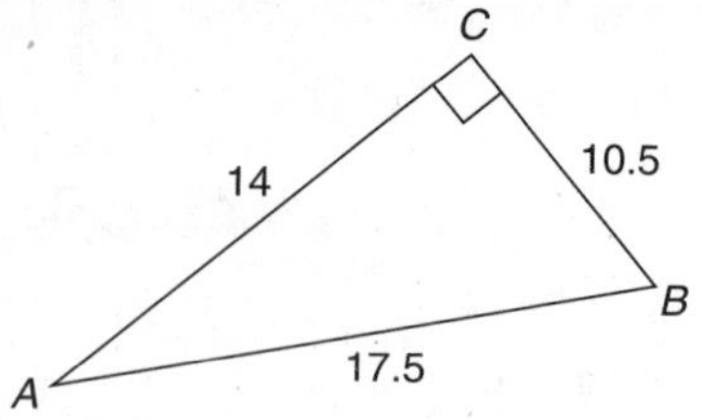

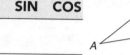

Angle	ADJ	OPP	HYP	TAN	SIN	COS
∠A						
∠B						

2. A ladder is placed against a building as shown at the right. Find the height, h, of the building.

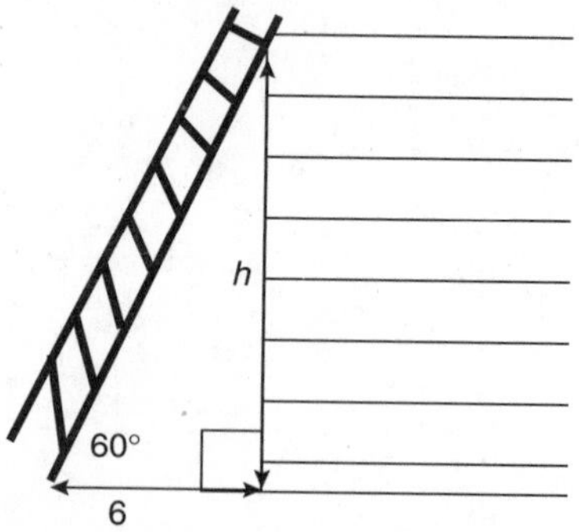

3. In an isosceles right triangle, find the tangent value of each of the two equal angles.

4. Which equation below can you use to find the length of the diagonal of the sheet of typing paper shown?

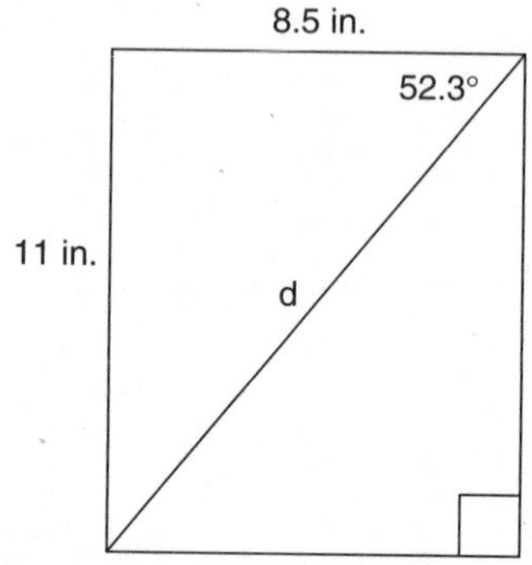

(1) $\sin 52.3° = \frac{11}{d}$

(2) $\sin 52.3° = \frac{d}{11}$

(3) $\tan 52.3° = \frac{8.5}{d}$

(4) $\tan 52.3° = \frac{11}{8.5} d$

(5) $\cos 52.3° = \frac{11}{d}$

Answers are on page 942.

EXERCISE 10

Geometry Review

$a^2+b^2=c^2$

Directions: Solve each problem. Refer to formula page 922 and use your calculator when necessary.

1. How many feet of weather stripping are needed to frame two windows with the dimensions indicated?

(1) 12
(2) 15
(3) 33
(4) 396
(5) 4752

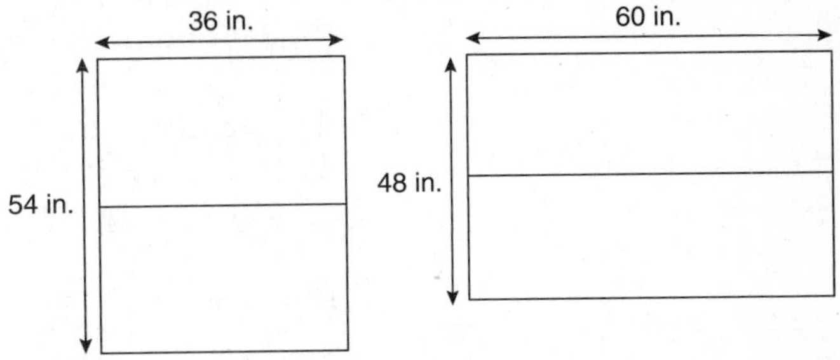

2. The Fantastic Food Company is redesigning its bran flakes box as shown. Find the capacity of the new box in cubic inches.

(1) 22
(2) 92
(3) 115
(4) 230
(5) 460

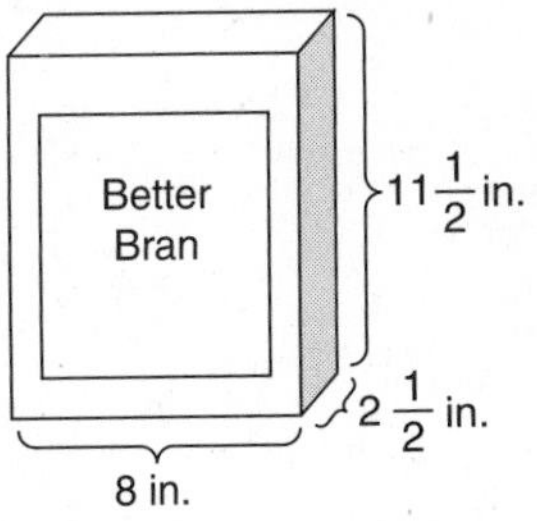

3. Fantastic Foods is also redesigning its soup can. Which of the following may be used to find the capacity of the new soup can?

(1) $(3.14)(1.5)^2(4)$
(2) $(3.14)(3)(4)$
(3) $(3.14)(1.5)^2$
(4) $(3.14)(3)^2$
(5) Not enough information is given.

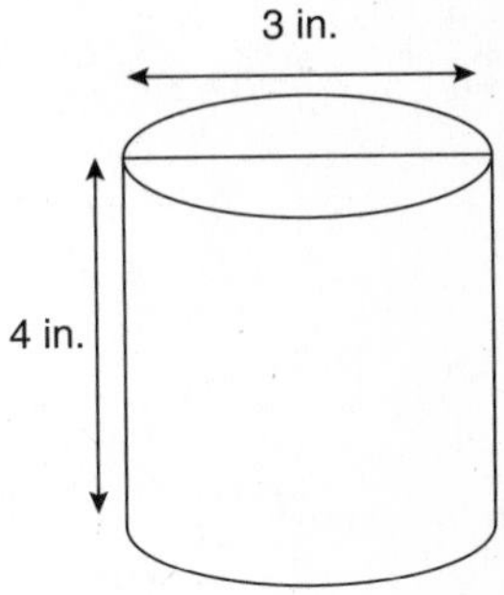

4. The diagonal of a rectangle is 17 inches. If the length of the rectangle is 15 inches, what is the width of the rectangle in inches?

(1) 4 **(2)** 8 **(3)** 16 **(4)** 32 **(5)** 64

5. A local radio station broadcasts over a 21-mile radius. How many square miles does this cover? (Use $\frac{22}{7}$ for π.)

(1) 66 **(2)** 441 **(3)** 1386 **(4)** 1764 **(5)** 5542

6. Ramon needs to carpet a room. Carpeting costs $16.99 per square yard. Disregarding waste, how much will it cost to carpet the room in the diagram?

   (1) $ 271.84
   (2) $ 815.52
   (3) $1703.42
   (4) $2446.56
   (5) Not enough information is given.

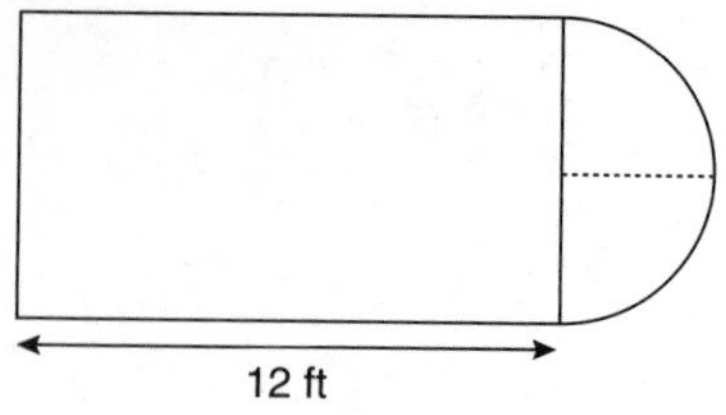

7. Liz planted a triangular flower bed with the dimensions shown below. What is the area, in square feet, of the garden?

   (1) 37
   (2) 45
   (3) 60
   (4) 120
   (5) 150

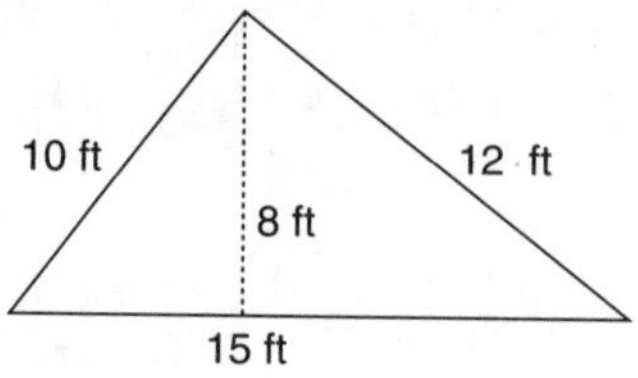

8. An observer on the shore sees a ship anchored off the coast. To find the distance to the ship, she makes the measurements shown in the figure. How far is it from the shoreline to the ship? (Note that *d* represents the distance from ship to shore.)

   (1) 65 m
   (2) 210 m
   (3) 400 m
   (4) 500 m
   (5) 10,000 m

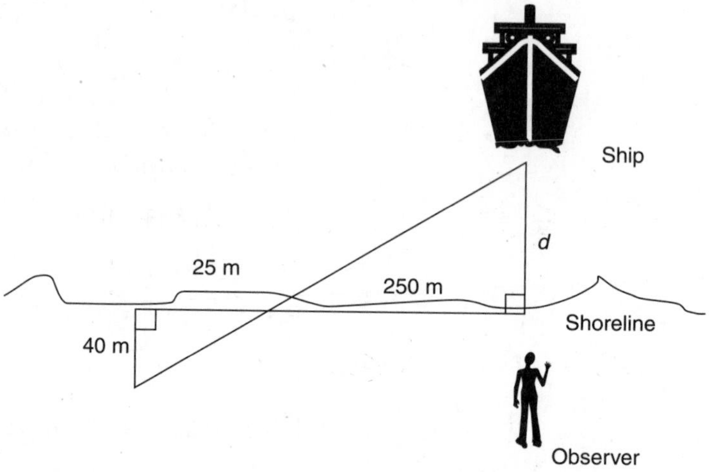

9. A right triangle contains a 60° angle. What is the measure of the third angle?

   (1) 30° (2) 120° (3) 150° (4) 210° (5) Not enough information is given.

10. How much larger is the supplement of a 57° angle than the complement of a 75° angle?

   (1) 18° (2) 105° (3) 108° (4) 123° (5) 228°

11. A circular pond has a circumference of 628 feet. What is the distance in feet from the center to the edge of the pond?

(1) 100 **(2)** 157 **(3)** 200 **(4)** 314 **(5)** 628

Use the information below to answer questions 12–14.

Maggie was curious about the height of a radio tower near her house. On a sunny day, her brother Murphy stood next to the tower. Both Murphy and the tower cast a shadow. The figure at right represents Murphy and the tower.

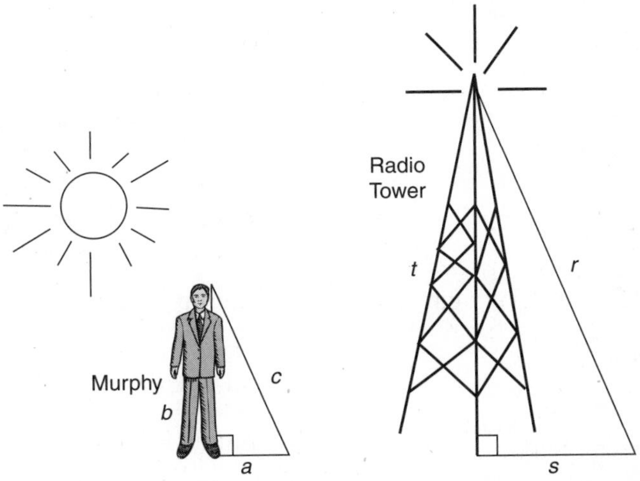

12. Which expression below correctly represents the height of the tower, *t*?

(1) $t = \frac{s \times b}{a}$ **(2)** $t = a + b + c$ **(3)** $t = s - r$ **(4)** $t = \frac{a \times b}{s}$ **(5)** $t = s \times a$

13. If Murphy is 5 feet tall and casts a 12-foot shadow while the tower casts a 42-foot shadow, how many feet tall is the tower?

(1) $17\frac{1}{2}$ **(2)** 20 **(3)** 30 **(4)** 35 **(5)** 60

14. If Murphy is 6 feet tall and casts an 8-foot shadow, what is the distance from the top of his head to the tip of his shadow?

(1) 7 feet **(2)** 10 feet **(3)** 14 feet **(4)** 50 feet **(5)** 100 feet

15. A delivery truck has a cargo area that is 8 feet by 8 feet by 12 feet. Approximately how many square boxes 2 feet on a side can be loaded into the cargo area?

(1) 48 **(2)** 96 **(3)** 160 **(4)** 768 **(5)** Not enough information is given.

Go to **www.GEDMath.com** for additional practice and instruction!

16. Using the triangle at the right, find the tangent, sine, and cosine of angle *B*.

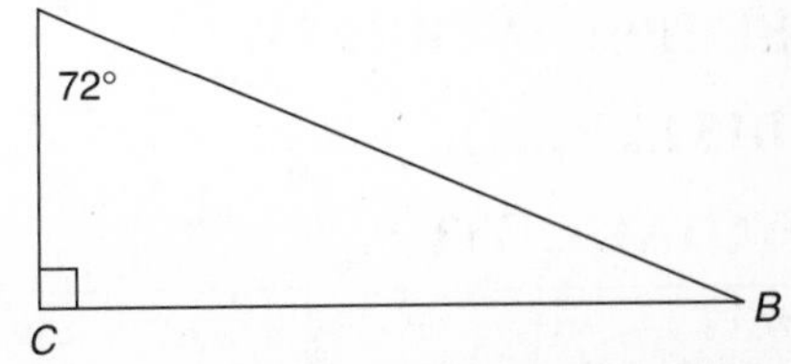

Answers are on page 942.

FORMULAS

AREA of a:	
square	Area = side^2
rectangle	Area = length × width
parallelogram	Area = base × height
triangle	Area = $\frac{1}{2}$ × base × height
trapezoid	Area = $\frac{1}{2} \times (\text{base}_1 + \text{base}_2) \times \text{height}$
circle	Area = $\pi \times \text{radius}^2$; π is approximately equal to 3.14.
PERIMETER of a:	
square	Perimeter = 4 × side
rectangle	Perimeter = 2 × length + 2 × width
triangle	Perimeter = $\text{side}_1 + \text{side}_2 + \text{side}_3$
CIRCUMFERENCE of a circle	Circumference = π × diameter; π is approximately equal to 3.14.
VOLUME of a:	
cube	Volume = edge^3
rectangular solid	Volume = length × width × height
square pyramid	Volume = $\frac{1}{3} \times (\text{base edge})^2 \times \text{height}$
cylinder	Volume = $\pi \times \text{radius}^2 \times \text{height}$; π is approximately equal to 3.14.
cone	Volume = $\frac{1}{3} \times \pi \times \text{radius}^2 \times \text{height}$; π is approximately equal to 3.14.
COORDINATE GEOMETRY	distance between points = $\sqrt{(x_2 - x_1)^2 + (y_2 - y_1)^2}$; (x_1, y_1) and (x_2, y_2) are two points in a plane. slope of a line = $\frac{y_2 - y_1}{x_2 - x_1}$; (x_1, y_1) and (x_2, y_2) are two points on the line.
PYTHAGOREAN RELATIONSHIP	$a^2 + b^2 = c^2$; a and b are legs and c the hypotenuse of a right triangle.
TRIGONOMETRIC RATIOS	$\sin = \frac{\text{opposite}}{\text{hypotenuse}}$ $\cos = \frac{\text{adjacent}}{\text{hypotenuse}}$ $\tan = \frac{\text{opposite}}{\text{adjacent}}$
MEASURES OF CENTRAL TENDENCY	**mean** = $\frac{x_1 + x_2 + \ldots + x_n}{n}$, where the xs are the values for which a mean is desired, and n is the total number of values for x. **median** = the middle value of an odd number of *ordered* scores, and halfway between the two middle values of an even number of *ordered* scores.
SIMPLE INTEREST	interest = principal × rate × time
DISTANCE	distance = rate × time
TOTAL COST	total cost = (number of units) × (price per unit)

CALCULATOR DIRECTIONS

To prepare the calculator for use the ***first*** time, press the (ON) (upper-rightmost) key. "DEG" will appear at the top-center of the screen and "0." at the right. This indicates the calculator is in the proper format for all your calculations.

To prepare the calculator for ***another*** question, press the (ON) or the red (AC) key. This clears any entries made previously.

To do any arithmetic, enter the expression as it is written. Press (=) (equals sign) when finished.

EXAMPLE A: 8 – 3 + 9

First press (ON) or (AC).
Enter the following:

(8) (–) (3) (+) (9) (=)

The correct answer is 14.

If an expression in parentheses is to be multiplied by a number, press (×) (multiplication sign) between the number and the parenthesis sign.

EXAMPLE B: 6(8 + 5)

First press (ON) or (AC).
Enter the following:

(6) (×) (() (8) (+) (5) ()) (=)

The correct answer is 78.

To find the square root of a number

- enter the number;
- press the (SHIFT) (upper-leftmost) key ("SHIFT" appears at the top-left of the screen);
- press (x^2) (third from the left on top row) to access its second function: square root.

<u>**DO NOT**</u> press (SHIFT) and (x^2) at the same time.

EXAMPLE C: $\sqrt{64}$

First press (ON) or (AC).
Enter the following:

(6) (4) (SHIFT) (x^2)

The correct answer is 8.

To enter a negative number such as –8,

- enter the number without the negative sign (enter 8);
- press the "change sign" ((+/–)) key (which is directly above the (7) key.

All arithmetic can be done with positive and/or negative numbers.

EXAMPLE D: –8 – –5

First press (ON) or (AC).
Enter the following:

(8) (+/–) (–) (5) (+/–) (=)

The correct answer is –3.

MATHEMATICS
Answer Key

CHAPTER 1

WHOLE NUMBERS AND OPERATIONS

Exercise 1: Whole Number Operations (Page 702)

1. 89

$$\begin{array}{r} 25 \\ \underline{+\,64} \\ 89 \end{array}$$

2. 471

$$\begin{array}{r} 425 \\ \underline{+\,46} \\ 471 \end{array}$$

3. 11,733

$$\begin{array}{r} 7348 \\ \underline{+\,4385} \\ 11{,}733 \end{array}$$

4. 614

$$\begin{array}{r} 578 \\ \underline{+\,36} \\ 614 \end{array}$$

5. 845

$$\begin{array}{r} 356 \\ 12 \\ \underline{+\,477} \\ 845 \end{array}$$

6. 234,634

$$\begin{array}{r} 228{,}347 \\ \underline{+\,6{,}287} \\ 234{,}634 \end{array}$$

7. 212

$$\begin{array}{r} 574 \\ \underline{-\,362} \\ 212 \end{array}$$

8. 2158

$$\begin{array}{r} 4383 \\ \underline{-\,2225} \\ 2158 \end{array}$$

9. 311,451

$$\begin{array}{r} 348{,}000 \\ \underline{-\,36{,}549} \\ 311{,}451 \end{array}$$

10. 2216

$$\begin{array}{r} 2860 \\ \underline{-\,644} \\ 2216 \end{array}$$

11. 613

$$\begin{array}{r} 712 \\ \underline{-\,99} \\ 613 \end{array}$$

12. 4121

$$\begin{array}{r} 5000 \\ \underline{-\,879} \\ 4121 \end{array}$$

13. 129

$$\begin{array}{r} 43 \\ \underline{\times\,3} \\ 129 \end{array}$$

14. 8265

$$\begin{array}{r} 87 \\ \underline{\times\,95} \\ 435 \\ \underline{7830} \\ 8265 \end{array}$$

15. 12,596

$$\begin{array}{r} 268 \\ \underline{\times\,47} \\ 1876 \\ \underline{10720} \\ 12596 \end{array}$$

16. 120,000

$$\begin{array}{r} 4000 \\ \underline{\times\,30} \\ 120000 \end{array}$$

17. 16,512

$$\begin{array}{r} 258 \\ \underline{\times\,64} \\ 1032 \\ \underline{15480} \\ 16512 \end{array}$$

18. 67,680

$$\begin{array}{r} 4230 \\ \underline{\times 16} \\ 25380 \\ \underline{42300} \\ 67680 \end{array}$$

19. 41

$$\begin{array}{r} 41 \\ 7\overline{)287} \end{array}$$

20. 627

$$\begin{array}{r} 627 \\ 9\overline{)5643} \end{array}$$

21. 270

$$\begin{array}{r} 270 \\ 15\overline{)4050} \end{array}$$

22. 903

$$\begin{array}{r} 903 \\ 6\overline{)5418} \end{array}$$

23. 20

$$\begin{array}{r} 20 \\ 60\overline{)1200} \end{array}$$

24. 465 r8

$$\begin{array}{r} 465\ r8 \\ 16\overline{)7448} \end{array}$$

Exercise 2: Problem Solving (page 706)

1. **(5)** 50,076
   Question: What will the mileage on the odometer read at the end of the trip?
   Information: 49,752 beginning reading, 162 miles each way.
   Operation: Addition
   Setup and Estimation:
   $49800 + 150 + 150 = 50{,}100$
   Calculation:
   $49{,}752 + 162 + 162 = 50{,}076$
   Reasonable answer? Yes, because the new reading is about 300 miles more than the original reading.
2. **(2)** $3,000,000
   Question: How much was each person's share?
   Information: 4 people, $12,000,000 ticket.
   Operation: Divide
   Setup and Estimation: $4\overline{)12000000}$ = 3000000
   Calculation: 3,000,000 is the same answer.
   Reasonable answer? Yes, because 4×3 million = 12 million.
3. **(4)** 180,000
   Question: How many square miles larger is Canada than the U.S.?
   Information: 3,675,633 U.S., 3,851,809 Canada.
   Operation: Subtract
   Setup and Estimation:
   $3{,}850{,}000 - 3{,}670{,}000 = 180{,}000$
   Calculation:
   $3{,}851{,}809 - 3{,}675{,}633 = 176{,}176$
   Reasonable answer? Yes, the estimate is very close to the exact answer.
4. **(3)** $18,333
   Question: What was the total cost for 97 TVs at the lowest price?
   Information: $189 lowest price, 97 TVs.
   Operation: Multiply
   Setup and Estimation: $200 \times 100 = 20{,}000$
   Calculation: $189 \times 97 = 18{,}333$
   Reasonable answer? Yes, the number is close to the estimate.
5. **(2)** $832
   Question: How much should she put aside for the tax payment each month?
   Information: $2,496 quarterly, 3 months
   Operation: Divide
   Setup and Estimation: $2400 \div 3 = 800$
   Calculation: $2496 \div 3 = \$832$
   Reasonable answer? Yes, the amount is less than a thousand per month.
6. **(3)** $1575
   Question: How much does he have left each month after paying the rent?
   Information: $2000 income per month, $425 monthly rent
   Operation: Subtract
   Setup and Estimation: $2000 - 400 = 1600$
   Calculation: $\$2000 - 425 = \$1575$
   Reasonable answer? Yes, more than half the monthly income is left.
7. **(5)** $12,500
   Question: What is the total cost of the bonus program?
   Information: $500 per employee, 25 employees.
   Operation: Multiply
   Setup and Estimation: $500 \times 30 = 15{,}000$
   Calculation: $\$500 \times 25 = \$12{,}500$
   Reasonable answer? Yes, this is about $1000 for every two employees.

CHAPTER 2

NUMBER SENSE

Exercise 1: Powers and Roots (page 714)

1.	64	$8 \times 8 = 64$
2.	729	$9 \times 9 \times 9 = 729$
3.	1	$1 \times 1 \times 1 \times 1 \times 1 \times 1 \times 1 = 1$
4.	16	$2 \times 2 \times 2 \times 2 = 16$
5.	1	A number to zero power is 1.
6.	1000	$10 \times 10 \times 10 = 1000$
7.	0	$0 \times 0 = 0$
8.	27	$3 \times 3 \times 3 = 27$
9.	144	$12 \times 12 = 144$
10.	625	$5 \times 5 \times 5 \times 5 = 625$
11.	9	$81 = 9^2$
12.	3	$9 = 3^2$
13.	1	$1 = 1^2$

14. 7.1 or $5\sqrt{2}$ — $\sqrt{50}$ is a little larger than the $\sqrt{49} = 7$, so 7.1 is a good estimate.
$\sqrt{50} = \sqrt{25 \times 2} = 5\sqrt{2}$

15. 5.7 or $4\sqrt{2}$ — $\sqrt{32}$ is a little less than the $\sqrt{36} = 6$, so 5.7 is a good estimate.
$\sqrt{32} = \sqrt{16 \times 2} = 4\sqrt{2}$

16. 12 — $144 = 12^2$

17. 5.3 or $2\sqrt{7}$ — $\sqrt{28}$ is a little more than $\sqrt{25} = 5$, so 5.3 is a good estimate.
$\sqrt{28} = \sqrt{4 \times 7} = 2\sqrt{7}$

18. 20 — $400 = 20^2$

19. 0 — $0 = 0^2$

20. 3.5 or $2\sqrt{3}$ — $\sqrt{12}$ is a little more than $\sqrt{9} = 3$, so 3.5 is a good estimate.
$\sqrt{12} = \sqrt{4 \times 3} = 2\sqrt{3}$

Exercise 2: Order of Operations (page 716)

1. 32 — $5 + 9 \times 3 = 5 + 27 = 32$

2. 65 — $(4 + 9) \times 5 = 13 \times 5 = 65$

3. 7 — $12 - 3 - 2 = 9 - 2 = 7$

4. 34 — $2 + 6 \times 4 + 8 = 2 + 24 + 8 = 26 + 8 = 34$

5. 1 — $12 - (7 + 4) = 12 - 11 = 1$

6. 9 — $12 - 7 + 4 = 5 + 4 = 9$

7. 5 — $\frac{6+9}{3} = \frac{15}{3} = 5$

8. 11 — $\frac{6}{3} + 9 = 2 + 9 = 11$

9. 48 — $8 \times 3 + 6 \times 4 = 24 + 24 = 48$

10. 20 — $4 \times (8 - 3) = 4 \times 5 = 20$

11. 29 — $4 \times 8 - 3 = 32 - 3 = 29$

12. 40 — $30 + 5 \times 2 = 30 + 10 = 40$

13. 0 — $7 - 5 + 3 - 5 = 2 + 3 - 5 = 5 - 5 = 0$

14. 8 — $6 + 21 \div 3 - 5 = 6 + 7 - 5 = 13 - 5 = 8$

15. 20 — $15 - 3 + 2^3 = 15 - 3 + 8 = 12 + 8 = 20$

16. 256 — $4(5 + 3)^2 = 4(8)^2 = 4(64) = 256$

Exercise 3: Arithmetic Expressions (page 718)

1. (2) $75 + 15 \times 55$
15 hrs @ \$55 + \$75 = $15 \times 55 + 75$

2. (4) $12 \times .45 + 8 \times .50$
One dozen = 12
12 at .45 plus 8 at .50

3. (1) $5.00 - (3.98 + .31 - .75)$
Add price + tax and subtract the coupon; then subtract that amount from \$5.

4. (3) $\frac{5+7+3+9}{4}$
To find the average, find the total and then divide by 4.

Exercise 4: Word Problems (page 719)

1. (4) \$61,920 — $\$5160 \times 12 = \$61,920$

2. (2) 6 — $395 \div 72 = 5$ r35

3. (3) 830 — $5500 \div 500 = 11$
$9130 \div 11 = 830$

4. (5) Not enough information is given. Information not given: amount used for expenses

5. (5) Edison
Lincoln = 1686 – 1420 = 266
Mead = 1982 – 1650 = 332
Sandburg = 2234 – 1847 = 387
Austin = 1648 – 1296 = 352
Edison = 1846 – 1318 = 528

6. (1) 1865
$266 + 332 + 387 + 352 + 528 = 1865$

7. (1) 373 — $1865 \div 5 = 373$

8. (3) $1298 - (350 + 375 + 417)$

9. (3) $\frac{19700 - (3150 + 500)}{60}$

10. (4) $4800 + 25 \times 43$

Exercise 5: Evaluating Formulas (page 723)

1. 144 sq in.
Area of a square = side^2 = 12^2 = 144 sq in.

2. 48 in.
Perimeter of a square = 4 × side = 4 × 12 = 48 in.

3. 125 cu in.
Volume of a cube = edge^3 = 5^3 = 125 cu in.

4. 76 mi
Distance = rate × time = 38 × 2 = 76

5. 54 sq cm
Area of a triangle= $\frac{1}{2}$ × base × height = $\frac{1}{2} \times 12 \times 9 = 54$

6. \$149.85
Total cost = (number of units) × (price per unit) = 3 × \$49.95 = \$149.85

7. 1130.4 cu in.
Volume of a cylinder = π × radius^2 × height = $3.14 \times 6^2 \times 10 = 1130.4$ cu in.

CHAPTER 3

DECIMAL NUMBERS AND OPERATIONS

Exercise 1: Reading and Writing Decimals (page 726)

1. **(2)** .05
2. **(1)** 6.2
3. **(4)** 100.025
4. **(2)** 1032
5. **(3)** 430.006
6. .7
7. 6.032
8. .0065

Exercise 2: Comparing Decimals (page 728)

1. **(a)** .05 **(b)** 4.1 **(c)** .7 **(d)** .51 **(e)** 1.033
2. **(a)** 2.15, 2.105, 1.95 **(b)** .0503, .005, .0035 **(c)** 6.607, 6.4, 6.07, 6
3. 14.003 lb, 14.03 lb, 14.3 lb, 14.3033 lb
4. 4.67 lb, 4.067 lb, 4.0067 lb

Exercise 3: Rounding Decimals (page 730)

1. .188
2. $1827
3. $1.70
4. $1.36
5. 3.14
6. 99°

Exercise 4: Scientific Notation (page 733)

1. 8.2×10^{-3}
2. 5.0×10^{2}
3. 3.82×10^{4}
4. 5.8×10^{-1}
5. 1624
6. .312
7. 8.24
8. 7130

Exercise 5: Adding and Subtracting Decimals (page 735)

1. 15.04

12.4
+2.64
15.04

2. 17.91

5.9
2.46
6
3.07
+ .48
17.91

3. 37.8

43.0
– 5.2
37.8

4. 78.3

85.2
– 6.9
78.3

5. 968.749

237.42
96.4
298.674
186.21
+ 150.045
968.749

6. $347.56

42.87
5.93
20
17.48
38.40
124.68

472.24
–124.68
347.56

7. 2877.8 mi

28054.1
–25176.3
2877.8

8. (1) $2.55

4.75
1.95
+ .75
7.45

10.00
– 7.45
2.55

9. (2) 1.4

104.2
–102.8
1.4

10. (2) 46.25

46.75
– .50
46.25

11. $51.45
17.50 + 4.95 + 6 + 16.25 + 6.75 = 51.45

12. $215.11
160 + 51.45 + 3.66 = 215.11

Exercise 6: Multiplying Decimals (page 738)

1. .513

$$\begin{array}{r} 0.342 \\ \underline{\times 1.5} \\ 1710 \\ \underline{3420} \\ .5130 \end{array}$$

2. .01564

$$\begin{array}{r} 46 \\ \underline{\times .00034} \\ 184 \\ \underline{1380} \\ .01564 \end{array}$$

3. .0510

$$\begin{array}{r} .85 \\ \underline{\times .06} \\ .0510 \end{array}$$

4. .5525

$$\begin{array}{r} 6.50 \\ \underline{\times .085} \\ 3250 \\ \underline{52000} \\ .55250 \end{array}$$

5. \$8.96

$$\begin{array}{r} \$128 \\ \underline{\times .07} \\ 8.96 \end{array}$$

6. \$21.735 or \$21.74

$$\begin{array}{r} \$72.45 \\ \underline{\times .3} \\ 21.735 \end{array}$$

7. (3) 7.85×12

8. (3) $(3.5 \times 1.69) + (2 \times 3.30)$

Exercise 7: Dividing Decimals (page 741)

1. 120.1 $\quad .05\overline{)6.005}$ = 120.1

2. .004 $\quad 3\overline{).012}$ = .004

3. 70 $\quad .04\overline{)2.80}$ = 70

4. 700 $\quad .08\overline{)56.00}$ = 700

5. 1.9 $\quad 2.5\overline{)4.75}$ = 1.9

6. 6.09 $\quad 4\overline{)24.36}$ = 6.09

7. 16 $\quad 1.25\overline{)20.00}$ = 16

Exercise 8: Multiplying and Dividing Decimals by Multiples of 10 (page 742)

1. 3.8 **2.** 4720 **3.** 9.72

4. .0617 **5.** 4.5612 **6.** .057

7. \$34 **8.** \$250 **9.** 5 days

$1.5 \times 10 = 15$

$75 \div 15 = 5$

Exercise 9: Estimating (page 743)

1. Estimate: $5 + 12 + 75 + 10 + 8 = 110$
Exact: $4.8 + 12.3 + 74.5 + 10 + 8.1 = 109.7$

2. Estimate: $25 + 3 = 28$, $50 - 28 = 22$
Exact: $24.75 + 2.50 = 27.25$, $50 - 27.25 = 22.75$

3. Estimate: $13 \times 10 = 130$
Exact: $12.95 \times 10 = 129.50$

4. Estimate: $36 \div 2 = 18$
Exact: $36 \div 1.75 = 20.57$ Answer = 20 streamers

Exercise 10: Decimal Word Problems (page 744)

1. (2) 3
Estimate: $12 \div 3 = 4$
Exact: $12 \div 3.2 = 3.7$
Only 3 complete shelves.

2. (5) \$2677.29
Estimate: \$400 + 500 + 400 + 600 + 700 = \$2600
Exact: \$425 + 485.75 + 399.87 + 642.15 + 724.52 = 2677.29

3. (2) 17.8
Estimate: $2500 \div 125 = 20$
Exact: $2492 \div 140 + 17.8$

4. (3) 8.6408
Estimate: $3 \times 3 = 9$
Exact: $3.086 \times 2.8 = 8.6408$

5. (2) \$339.02
Estimate: gross pay = 300 + 100 = 400,
deductions = 30 + 80 = 110,
net pay = 400 –110 = 290
Exact: gross pay = 338 + 114.03 = 452.03,
deductions = 31.64 + 81.37 = 113.01,
net pay = 452.03 – 113.01 = 339.02

6. (2) \$7.68
Estimate: $300 \div 40 = 7.5$
Exact: $307.20 \div 40 = 7.68$

7. (4) \$20,099
Estimate: $3500 + 50 \times 300 = 3500 + 15000 = 18500$
Exact: $3500 + 48 \times 345.81 = 20{,}098.88 \approx 20{,}099$

8. (3) \$.08
Estimate: $1.00 \div 12 = .08$
Exact: $.99 \div 12 = .0825 \approx .08$

9. **(2)** 24.7
Estimate: $9000 - 7000 = 2000$, $2000 \div 60 = 33.33$
Exact: $8747.6 - 7353.2 = 1394.4$
$1394.4 \div 56.4 = 24.72 \approx 24.7$

10. **(3)** \$5.49
Estimate: $7 + 1 + 6 + 10 + 6 + 4 + 5 = 39$, and 39 is close to 42, so $42 \div 7 = 6$
Exact: $7.25 + .80 + 5.75 + 10 + 6 + 3.70 + 4.90 = 5.485 \approx 5.49$

CHAPTER 4

FRACTIONS AND OPERATIONS

Exercise 1: Types of Fractions (page 748)

1. C like fractions
2. E mixed numbers
3. B improper fractions
4. A proper fractions
5. D unlike fractions

Exercise 2: Raising and Reducing Fractions (page 752)

1. 9 **2.** 15 **3.** 6 **4.** 9 **5.** 24
6. 12 **7.** 3 **8.** 3 **9.** 4 **10.** 1
11. 2 **12.** 5 **13.** $\frac{3}{4}$ **14.** $\frac{3}{4}$ **15.** $\frac{1}{3}$
16. $\frac{1}{3}$ **17.** $\frac{5}{6}$ **18.** $\frac{2}{3}$

Exercise 3: Changing Between Fractions and Decimals (page 756)

1. $\frac{5}{100} = \frac{1}{20}$
2. $\frac{450}{1000} = \frac{9}{20}$
3. $\frac{7}{100}$
4. $\frac{32}{100} = \frac{8}{25}$
5. $\frac{5}{1000} = \frac{1}{200}$
6. $3\frac{1}{10}$
7. $.37\frac{1}{2}$ — $8\overline{)3.00} = .37\frac{4}{8}$
8. .2 — $5\overline{)1.0} = .2$
9. $.44\frac{4}{9}$ — $9\overline{)4.00} = .44\frac{4}{9}$
10. 1.25 — $4\overline{)5.00} = 1.25$
11. $.83\frac{1}{3}$ — $6\overline{)5.00} = .83\frac{2}{6}$

Exercise 4: Changing Improper Fractions and Mixed Numbers (page 757)

1. $\frac{14}{9}$ **2.** $\frac{49}{4}$ **3.** $\frac{17}{5}$ **4.** $\frac{33}{8}$ **5.** $\frac{5}{2}$
6. $\frac{20}{3}$ **7.** $1\frac{1}{3}$ **8.** $2\frac{3}{7}$ **9.** 1 **10.** $1\frac{1}{8}$
11. $3\frac{2}{5}$ **12.** $1\frac{1}{2}$

Exercise 5: Comparing Numbers (page 761)

1. $\frac{7}{8}$ **2.** $\frac{2}{3}$ **3.** $\frac{3}{4}$
4. $<$ **5.** $>$ **6.** $>$
7. $<$ **8.** $<$ **9.** $<$
10. $>$ **11.** $=$ **12.** $=$
13. $<$ **14.** $>$ **15.** $=$

Exercise 6: Adding and Subtracting Fractions (page 765)

1. $\frac{4}{5}$ — $\frac{1}{10} + \frac{7}{10} = \frac{8}{10} = \frac{4}{5}$
2. $\frac{11}{12}$ — $\frac{2}{3} + \frac{1}{4} = \frac{8}{12} + \frac{3}{12} = \frac{11}{12}$
3. $\frac{11}{24}$ — $\frac{3}{8} + \frac{1}{12} = \frac{9}{24} + \frac{2}{24} = \frac{11}{24}$
4. 1 — $\frac{5}{6} + \frac{1}{6} = \frac{6}{6} = 1$
5. $7\frac{3}{4}$ — $1\frac{5}{12} + 6\frac{4}{12} = 7\frac{9}{12} = 7\frac{3}{4}$
6. $7\frac{17}{35}$ — $4\frac{1}{5} + 3\frac{2}{7} = 4\frac{7}{35} + 3\frac{10}{35} = 7\frac{17}{35}$
7. $9\frac{1}{3}$ — $4\frac{2}{9} + 5\frac{1}{9} = 9\frac{3}{9} = 9\frac{1}{3}$
8. $10\frac{1}{24}$
$3\frac{7}{8} + 2\frac{5}{6} + 3\frac{1}{3} = 3\frac{21}{24} + 2\frac{20}{24} + 3\frac{8}{24} = 8\frac{49}{24} = 10\frac{1}{24}$
9. $\frac{3}{5}$ — $\frac{9}{10} - \frac{3}{10} = \frac{6}{10} = \frac{3}{5}$
10. $\frac{1}{8}$ — $\frac{5}{8} - \frac{1}{2} = \frac{5}{8} - \frac{4}{8} = \frac{1}{8}$
11. $\frac{3}{10}$ — $\frac{4}{5} - \frac{1}{2} = \frac{8}{10} - \frac{5}{10} = \frac{3}{10}$
12. $\frac{3}{8}$ — $\frac{11}{16} - \frac{5}{16} = \frac{6}{16} = \frac{3}{8}$
13. $2\frac{1}{8}$ — $4\frac{3}{4} - 2\frac{5}{8} = 4\frac{6}{8} - 2\frac{5}{8} = 2\frac{1}{8}$
14. $13\frac{2}{3}$
$25\frac{1}{6} - 11\frac{1}{2} = 25\frac{1}{6} - 11\frac{3}{6} = 24\frac{7}{6} - 11\frac{3}{6} = 13\frac{4}{6} = 13\frac{2}{3}$
15. $5\frac{1}{3}$ — $10 - 4\frac{2}{3} = 9\frac{3}{3} - 4\frac{2}{3} = 5\frac{1}{3}$
16. $19\frac{1}{5}$ — $20 - \frac{4}{5} = 19\frac{5}{5} - \frac{4}{5} = 19\frac{1}{5}$

Exercise 7: Multiplying Fractions (page 767)

1. $\frac{1}{6}$ — $\frac{6}{15} \times \frac{5}{12} = \frac{30}{180} = \frac{1}{6}$
2. $\frac{3}{70}$ — $\frac{3}{8} \times \frac{2}{15} \times \frac{6}{7} = \frac{36}{840} = \frac{3}{70}$
3. $32\frac{2}{3}$ — $8\frac{1}{6} \times 4 = \frac{49}{6} \times \frac{4}{1} = \frac{196}{6} = \frac{98}{3} = 32\frac{2}{3}$
4. $\frac{1}{12}$ — $\frac{5}{9} \times \frac{2}{5} \times \frac{3}{8} = \frac{30}{360} = \frac{1}{12}$
5. $5\frac{5}{6}$ — $2\frac{1}{2} \times 2\frac{1}{3} = \frac{5}{2} \times \frac{7}{3} = \frac{35}{6} = 5\frac{5}{6}$
6. $2\frac{5}{14}$ — $2\frac{3}{4} \times \frac{6}{7} = \frac{11}{4} \times \frac{6}{7} = \frac{66}{28} = \frac{33}{14} = 2\frac{5}{14}$
7. $6\frac{1}{2}$ — $1\frac{3}{10} \times 5 = \frac{13}{10} \times \frac{5}{1} = \frac{65}{10} = 6\frac{5}{10} = 6\frac{1}{2}$
8. $4\frac{1}{2}$ — $3\frac{3}{8} \times 1\frac{3}{9} = \frac{27}{8} \times \frac{12}{9} = \frac{324}{72} = 4\frac{36}{72} = 4\frac{1}{2}$

Exercise 8: Dividing Fractions (page 769)

1. $\frac{3}{5}$ — $\frac{4}{10} \div \frac{2}{3} = \frac{4}{10} \times \frac{3}{2} = \frac{12}{20} = \frac{3}{5}$
2. $2\frac{1}{2}$ — $\frac{3}{7} \div \frac{6}{35} = \frac{3}{7} \times \frac{35}{6} = \frac{105}{42} = 2\frac{1}{2}$
3. $\frac{1}{8}$ — $1\frac{3}{8} \div 11 = \frac{11}{8} \times \frac{1}{11} = \frac{11}{88} = \frac{1}{8}$
4. $\frac{1}{10}$ — $\frac{2}{5} \div 4 = \frac{2}{5} \times \frac{1}{4} = \frac{2}{20} = \frac{1}{10}$
5. $2\frac{4}{9}$ — $3\frac{2}{3} \div 1\frac{1}{2} = \frac{11}{3} \div \frac{3}{2} = \frac{11}{3} \times \frac{2}{3} = \frac{22}{9} = 2\frac{4}{9}$
6. $3\frac{3}{5}$ — $9 \div 2\frac{1}{2} = \frac{9}{1} \div \frac{5}{2} = \frac{9}{1} \times \frac{2}{5} = \frac{18}{5} = 3\frac{3}{5}$

Exercise 9: Item Sets (page 770)

1. (3) $47.04
   6 × .98 = 5.88, 8 × 5.88 = 47.04
2. (3) 6 — $6 - 5\frac{1}{4} = \frac{3}{4}$
   $\frac{3}{4} \times 8 = 6$
3. (1) $52.56 — 8 × 13.95 = 111.60
   47.04 + 12 = 59.04
   111.60 – 59.04 = 52.56
4. (2) $\frac{3}{8}$ mi — $\frac{7}{8} - \frac{1}{2} = \frac{7}{8} - \frac{4}{8} = \frac{3}{8}$
5. (3) $\frac{7}{8}$ mi — $\frac{3}{4} - \frac{1}{4} = \frac{2}{4}$
   $\frac{2}{4} + \frac{3}{8} = \frac{7}{8}$
6. (5) Not enough information is given.
7. (3) $19.08 — $1\frac{1}{2} \times 12.72 = 19.08$
8. (5) Not enough information is given.
   The chart is for the second week in April, not the third.
9. (3) $(12.72 \times 40) + (1\frac{1}{2} \times 12.72 \times 3\frac{1}{4})$

Exercise 10: Fraction Review (page 773)

1. (1) $5\frac{1}{4}$ ft — $8 - 2\frac{3}{4} = 5\frac{1}{4}$
2. (4) 51¢ — 6 × .085 = .51
3. (2) $2\frac{1}{2}$ mi — $\frac{1}{2} + \frac{5}{8} + 1\frac{3}{8} = 2\frac{1}{2}$
4. (4) 20 — $30 \div 1\frac{1}{2} = 20$
5. (5) Not enough information is given.
   The weight of the cartons is not included.
6. (2) $5\frac{3}{4}$ in. — $10\frac{1}{2} - 2(2\frac{3}{8}) = 5\frac{3}{4}$
7. (4) $760 — $285 + \frac{2}{3}(285) + 2(\frac{1}{2})(285) = 760$
8. (3) $[10\frac{1}{2} - (10\frac{1}{2} \times \frac{1}{6})] \div \frac{1}{4}$
9. (1) $1\frac{1}{8}$ ft — $6 - 3(1\frac{5}{8}) = 1\frac{1}{8}$
10. (2) 24,000 — $\frac{3}{4} \times \frac{2}{3} \times 48000 = 24000$

CHAPTER 5

NUMBER RELATIONSHIPS

Exercise 1: Number Line (page 777)

1. $-1 < 1\frac{1}{2}$ or $1\frac{1}{2} > -1$
2. $-4 < -1\frac{1}{2}$ or $-1\frac{1}{2} > -4$
3. $-2 < 0$ or $0 > -2$
4. $-3 < 1$ or $1 > -3$

Exercise 2: Signed Numbers (page 778)

1. –12 **2.** –15 **3.** –3 **4.** +75 **5.** +4.5
6. < **7.** < **8.** < **9.** > **10.** <
11. > **12.** 9 **13.** $\frac{1}{2}$ **14.** $2\frac{3}{4}$ **15.** 3

Exercise 3: Combining Signed Numbers (page 780)

1. 15 **2.** –2 **3.** –1 **4.** –17
5. –5 **6.** –33 **7.** –96 **8.** –3
9. 35 **10.** –19 **11.** 3.8 **12.** –7.7

Exercise 4: Eliminating Double Signs (page 781)

1. –4 **2.** 1 **3.** –5
4. 22 **5.** –19 **6.** $158

Exercise 5: Multiplying and Dividing Signed Numbers (page 783)

1. 40 **2.** –144 **3.** –30 **4.** –88 **5.** 225
6. 36 **7.** –84 **8.** 0 **9.** –5 **10.** 3
11. $-\frac{1}{2}$ **12.** 5 **13.** $-7\frac{1}{2}$ **14.** –$2214

Exercise 6: Using Signed Numbers in Problem Solving (page 783)

1. (2) 20°
2. (4) 575 + 125 + 46 – (98 + 26 + 38 + 310 + 50)
3. (3) +376
4. (4) 4
5. 1032 burned (–1032)

CHAPTER 6
STATISTICS AND DATA ANALYSIS

Exercise 1: Ratio and Rate (page 786)

1. $\frac{1}{4}$ 2. $\frac{1}{4}$ 3. $\frac{3}{2}$ 4. $\frac{3}{4}$

5. $\frac{11}{1}$ 6. $\frac{20}{1}$ 7. $\frac{8}{1}$ 8. $\frac{7}{1}$

Exercise 2: Applications of Ratio (page 788)

1. $\frac{3}{5}$ $\frac{\$120 \text{ supplies}}{\$200 \text{ total}} = \frac{3}{5}$
2. 5 $\$200 \div \$40 = 5$
3. $\frac{24}{5}$ $\frac{\$120 \text{ supplies}}{\$25} = \frac{24}{5}$
4. $\frac{1}{4}$ $\frac{\$1{,}700{,}000 \text{ liabilities}}{\$6{,}800{,}000 \text{ assets}} = \frac{1}{4}$
5. $\frac{1}{3}$ $\frac{250 \text{ female}}{750 \text{ members}} = \frac{1}{3}$
6. \$2.43 $\$729 \div 300 = \$2.43$
7. 175 lbs $250 - 75 = 175$
8. \$2.09 $\$365 \div 175 = 2.0857 \approx \$2.09$

Exercise 3: Solving Proportions (page 790)

1. 4 $m = \frac{2 \times 10}{5} = \frac{20}{5} = 4$
2. 1 $x = \frac{3 \times 7}{21} = \frac{21}{21} = 1$
3. $6\frac{2}{3}$ $y = \frac{5 \times 20}{15} = \frac{100}{15} = 6\frac{2}{3}$
4. 8 $z = \frac{4 \times 12}{6} = \frac{48}{6} = 8$
5. 15 $n = \frac{30 \times 12}{24} = \frac{360}{24} = 15$

Exercise 4: Application of Proportion (page 791)

1. (2) $\frac{128 \times 20}{8}$
2. (2) 42 $\frac{2 \text{ managers}}{9 \text{ salesclerks}} = \frac{N \text{ managers}}{189 \text{ salesclerks}}$

   $N = \frac{2 \times 189}{9} = 42$
3. (5) 18 $2\frac{1}{4} \div \frac{1}{8} = 18$
4. (3) 420 $\frac{2 \text{ pancakes}}{120 \text{ calories}} = \frac{7 \text{ pancakes}}{N \text{ calories}}$

   $N = \frac{7 \times 120}{2} = 420$
5. (3) 15 inches $\frac{6}{4} = \frac{?}{10}$

   $? = \frac{6 \times 10}{4} = 15$

CHAPTER 7
PERCENTS

Exercise 1: Interchanging Percents, Fractions, and Decimals (page 796)

1.	87%	$\frac{87}{100}$	.87
2.	40%	$\frac{40}{100} = \frac{2}{5}$	.40
3.	2%	$\frac{2}{100} = \frac{1}{50}$	.02
4.	$16\frac{2}{3}\%$	$\frac{50}{3} \times \frac{1}{100} = \frac{1}{6}$	$.16\frac{2}{3}$
5.	$7\frac{1}{2}\%$	$7\frac{1}{2} \times \frac{1}{100} =$	$.07\frac{1}{2}$
		$\frac{15}{2} \times \frac{1}{100} = \frac{3}{40}$	or .075
6.	9%	$\frac{9}{100}$	.09
7.	300%	$\frac{300}{100} = 3$	3.00
8.	125%	$\frac{125}{100} = \frac{5}{4}$	1.25
9.	.5%	$\frac{5}{10} \times \frac{1}{100} = \frac{1}{200}$	.005
10.	9.9%	$9\frac{9}{10} \times \frac{1}{100} = \frac{99}{1000}$	.099
11.	$\frac{1}{2}\%$	$\frac{1}{2} \times \frac{1}{100} = \frac{1}{200}$	$.5 \times .01 = .005$
12.	75%	$\frac{75}{100} = \frac{3}{4}$	.75
13.	$\frac{1}{4}\%$	$\frac{1}{4} \times \frac{1}{100} = \frac{1}{400}$	$.25 \times .01 = .0025$
14.	5%	$\frac{5}{100} = \frac{1}{20}$	.05
15.	50%	$\frac{1}{2}$	.50

16. 60% $3 \div 5 = .6 = 60\%$
17. 95% $.95 \div .01 = 95$
18. $33\frac{1}{3}\%$ $1 \div 3 = .33\frac{1}{3} = 33\frac{1}{3}\%$
19. .25% $.0025 \div .01 = .25$
20. 37.5% $3 \div 8 = .375 = 37.5\%$
21. 450% $4.5 \div .01 = 450$
22. 90% $9 \div 10 = .90 = 90\%$
23. 62.5% $.625 \div .01 = 62.5$
24. 225% $2.25 \div .01 = 225$
25. 40% $.4 \div .01 = 40$

Exercise 2: Percent Problems (page 800)

1. 1.2 — $.04 \times 30 = 1.2$
2. 200 — $\frac{14}{N} = \frac{7}{100}$; $N = \frac{14 \times 100}{7} = 200$
3. 25% — $\frac{14}{56} = \frac{N}{100}$; $N = \frac{14 \times 100}{56} = 25$
4. 90 — $45 \times 2.00 = 90$
5. 400 — $\frac{10}{N} = \frac{2.5}{100}$; $N = \frac{10 \times 100}{2.5} = 400$
6. 35% — $\frac{210}{600} = \frac{N}{100}$; $N = \frac{210 \times 100}{600} = 35$
7. .31 — $62 \times .005 = .31$
8. 112.5 — $\frac{18}{N} = \frac{16}{100}$; $N = \frac{18 \times 100}{16} = 112.5$
9. 9% — $\frac{30.60}{340} = \frac{N}{100}$; $N = \frac{30.60 \times 100}{340} = 9$
10. 400% — $\frac{20}{5} = \frac{N}{100}$; $N = \frac{20 \times 100}{5} = 400$

Exercise 3: Percent Word Problems (page 802)

1. 80% — $\frac{32}{40} = \frac{N}{100}$; $N = \frac{32 \times 100}{40} = 80$
2. $12,000 — $\frac{1800}{N} = \frac{15}{100}$; $N = \frac{1800 \times 100}{15} = 12000$
3. $23.98 — $.80 \times 3 \times 9.99 = 23.98$
4. 24% — $\frac{120}{500} = \frac{N}{100}$; $N = \frac{120 \times 100}{500} = 24$
5. $252 — $.12 \times 2100 = 252$
6. 20% — $\frac{420}{2100} = \frac{N}{100}$; $N = \frac{420 \times 100}{2100} = 20$
7. $26,460 — $12 \times 1.05 \times 2100 = 26460$

Exercise 4: Interest Problems (page 806)

1. **(2)** $540
   90 days is $\frac{1}{4}$ of a year, so
   $i = prt = 18000 \times .12 \times \frac{1}{4} = 540.$
2. **(3)** $31,968.75
   $p + prt = 31000 + 31000 \times .125 \times \frac{1}{4} = \$31{,}968.75$
3. **(2)** $\frac{480 \times 100}{6000}$
   $\frac{480}{6000} = \frac{N}{100}$
   $N = \frac{480 \times 100}{6000}$
4. **(4)** $4,500
   $\frac{360}{N} = \frac{8}{100}$
   $N = \frac{360 \times 100}{8} = 4500$
5. **(3)** $12,600
   $15{,}000 + 65{,}000 + 5{,}000 - 25{,}000 = 60{,}000$
   $i = prt = 60{,}000 \times .105 \times 2 = 12600$
6. **(1)** $1200
   $60000 \times .09 - 60000 \times .07 = 1200$

Exercise 5: Percent Review (page 807)

1. **(5)** $160.45
   $1.07(14.95 + 135) = 160.45$
2. **(3)** $15.90 – .20(15.90)
3. **(4)** $22,712
   $\$18{,}800 + 3 \times .08 \times (18800 - 2500) = 22712$
4. **(4)** $40,000
   $\frac{1200}{N} = \frac{3}{100}$
   $N = \frac{1200 \times 100}{3} = 40000$
5. **(4)** $91,680
   $\$96{,}000 - .045(96000) = 91680$
6. **(4)** 25
   $\frac{6000}{24000} = \frac{N}{100}$
   $N = \frac{6000 \times 100}{24000} = 25$
7. **(2)** $\frac{1}{10}$
   $\frac{2400}{24000} = \frac{1}{10}$
8. **(3)** 15
   $\frac{1200 + 2400}{24000} = \frac{N}{100}$
   $N = \frac{3600 \times 100}{24000} = 15$
9. **(5)** $1680
   $1.12 \times 1500 = 1680$
10. **(5)** Not enough information is given.
11. **(1)** $\frac{24000 \times 100}{67}$
    $\frac{24000}{N} = \frac{67}{100}$
    $N = \frac{24000 \times 100}{67}$

CHAPTER 8

PROBABILITY

Exercise 1: Probability (page 810)

1. $\frac{1}{52}$

2. 25% $\frac{13}{52} = \frac{1}{4} = 25\%$

3. $\frac{1}{13}$ $\frac{4}{52} = \frac{1}{13}$

4. 0

5. **(5)** $\frac{5}{6}$

6. **(4)** $33\frac{1}{3}\%$ $\frac{2}{6} = \frac{1}{3} = 33\frac{1}{3}\%$

7. **(5)** 50% $\frac{3}{6} = \frac{1}{2} = 50\%$

8. **(1)** 0

9. **(5)** $66\frac{2}{3}\%$ $\frac{4}{6} = \frac{2}{3} = 66\frac{2}{3}\%$

10. **(5)** 100%

11. **(2)** $\frac{1}{12}$

12. **(2)** $\frac{1}{10}$

13. **(3)** $\frac{1}{2}$

14. **(4)** $\frac{3}{4}$ $960 - 240 = 720$ not broken

$\frac{720}{960} = \frac{3}{4}$

Exercise 2: Dependent Probability (page 813)

1. $\frac{1}{13}$ $\frac{4}{52} = \frac{1}{13}$

2. $\frac{1}{17}$ $\frac{3}{51} = \frac{1}{17}$

3. $\frac{4}{51}$

4. $\frac{4}{17}$ $\frac{12}{51} = \frac{4}{17}$

5. $\frac{3}{10}$

6. $\frac{2}{3}$ $\frac{6}{9} = \frac{2}{3}$

7. $\frac{1}{8}$

8. $\frac{2}{9}$

9. $\frac{1}{4}$ $\frac{2}{8} = \frac{1}{4}$

10. $\frac{1}{7}$

CHAPTER 9

DATA ANALYSIS

Exercise 1: Measures of Central Tendency (page 818)

1. $3713.14

$$\frac{4300 + 5600 + 1875 + 4250 + 2876 + 4108 + 2983}{7} = 3713.14$$

2. 43.5 is the opponents' average score
60 is the Three Lakes' average score
$(37 + 63 + 42 + 24 + 44 + 51) \div 6 = 43.5$
$(48 + 45 + 53 + 72 + 68 + 74) \div 6 = 60$

3. 60.5
Arranging the scores in order: 45, 48, 53, 68, 72, 74
The middle is between 53 and 68. $68 - 53 = 15$ and $15 \div 2 = 7.5$. $53 + 7.5 = 60.5$

4. 29 points
$74 - 45 = 29$

5. 5 W
There are 5 W to only 1 L.

6. $83.38
$\$109.88 - 26.50 = \$83.38$

7. Mean = $55.57
Median = $50.55
Mean = $(34.81 + 50.55 + 26.50 + 49.50 + 109.88 + 54.56 + 63.19) \div 7 = 55.57$
Median: 50.55 is the middle value because there are three stocks less expensive and three stocks more expensive.

8. Cisco Systems (50.55) is the mode because it had the highest volume.

9. Total investment would be $13,638. The average price per share would be $68.19.
$100 \times 109.88 + 100 \times 26.50 = 13638$
$13638 \div 200 = 68.19$

10. $50.50
$(49.50 + 49.50 + 2.25 + 49.50 + 2.25 - 1.50) \div 3 = 50.50$

Exercise 2: Charts, Tables, and Schedules (page 822)

1. 10,061 $32{,}440 - 22{,}379 = 10{,}061$

2. **(1)** $\frac{1}{8}$ $\frac{30000}{270000} = \frac{1}{9}$

The closest answer to this estimate is $\frac{1}{8}$.

3. **(4)** 76% $\frac{188315}{248791} = \frac{N}{100}$

$N = \frac{188315 \times 100}{248791} = 75.6 \approx 76$

4. (4) Asian/Pacific Islander
Asian/Pacific Islander % change = 50%

5. (3) 350.8 $(10504 - 6996) \div 10 = 350.8$

6. The pattern shows that each successive number increases by the next odd number. For instance, from 1 to 4, the increase is 3 and then from 4 to 9, the increase is 5, and then from 9 to 16, the increase is 7, and so on.

7. $\frac{1}{125}$ $\frac{5 \text{ square root}}{625 \text{ square}} = \frac{1}{125}$

8. 576 $8^2 \times 3^2 = 64 \times 9 = 576$

9. 9 $\sqrt{9} \times \sqrt{9} = 3 \times 3 = 9$

10. 5.66 $\sqrt{8} + \sqrt{8} = 2.83 + 2.83 = 5.66$

11. 20% Sports = 3 × 4 minutes = 12 minutes

$$\frac{12}{60} = \frac{N}{100}$$

$$N = \frac{12 \times 100}{60} = 20$$

12. $\frac{3}{20}$

weather and traffic = 3 × 3 minutes = 9 minutes

$$\frac{9}{60} = \frac{3}{20}$$

Exercise 3: Circle Graphs (page 827)

1. $91,300
$.55(92000 + 156000 + 250000) \div 3 = 91300$

2. $4320 $.12 \times 36{,}000 = 4320$

3. $810 $(.27 \times 36000) \div 12 = 810$

4. Not enough information is given.

5. $\frac{29}{100}$ 29% is 29 per hundred

6. $\frac{1}{20}$ $5\% = \frac{5}{100} = \frac{1}{20}$

7. $1080
$(9\% - 6\%) \times 36000 = 3\% \times 36000 = .03 \times 36000 = 1080$

8. $720
$(12\% - 10\%) \times 36000 = 2\% \times 36000 = .02 \times 36000 = 720$

Exercise 4: Bar Graphs (page 829)

1. $24,000

2. $28,000
$(20{,}000 + 28{,}000 + 29{,}000 + 35{,}000) \div 4 = 28{,}000$

3. 2001

4. $2000 $31000 - 29000 = 2000$

5. $29,000
$(24{,}000 + 28{,}000 + 31{,}000 + 33{,}000) \div 4 = 29{,}000$

6. $\frac{5}{6}$ $\frac{20000}{24000} = \frac{5}{6}$

7. (1) Expenses rose faster than income from 1998 to 2001.

Exercise 5: Line Graphs (page 831)

1. sales in 1999 and 2001

2. millions of dollars

3. months

4. six million dollars

5. $9,000,000

6. higher

Exercise 6: Mixed Graph Practice (page 832)

1. $\frac{3}{100}$ 3% means 3 per hundred.

2. $900 $(\$18{,}000 \times .60) \div 12 = 900$

3. $2520 $.07 \times 36{,}000 = 2520$

4. $40,000 $\frac{24000}{N} = \frac{60}{100}$

$$N = \frac{24000 \times 100}{60} = 40000$$

5. $25,200 $.63 \times 40000 = 25{,}200$

6. 200 ft $1450 - 1250 = 200$

7. 1557 ft $1450 + 107 = 1557$

8. 3 $1250 \div 450 = 2.8 \approx 3$

9. 31% $\frac{450}{1450} = \frac{N}{100}$

$$N = \frac{450 \times 100}{1450} = 31.03$$

10. 940 ft

$(450 + 550 + 1000 + 1250 + 1450) \div 5 = 940$

11. 1000 ft
The middle value is the Eiffel Tower at 1000 ft

12. 111 floors
$1450 \div 13 = 111.53$
Round the answer to 111 because there cannot be .53 floors.

13. 7500 $3000 + 4500 = 7500$

14. April and July

15. $90,250
$4000 \times 8.50 + 4500 \times 12.50 = 90250$

16. attendance increases

17. attendance declines

18. $6083\frac{1}{3}$

$(500 + 1000 + 1500 + 2000 + 3000 + 4500 + 5000 + 6500 + 4000 + 4500 + 3000 + 1000) \div 6 = 6083\frac{1}{3}$

CHAPTER 10
ALGEBRA

Exercise 1: Terms (page 836)

1. 8 and n
2. $8x$, $7y$, and -6
3. $2x^2$ and $-\frac{3}{x}$
4. $8ab$ and 12

Exercise 2: Evaluating Algebraic Expressions (page 837)

1. 4
   $12 - 4n = 12 - 4 \times 2 = 12 - 8 = 4$
2. 3
   $3y + 9 = 3 \times (-2) + 9 = -6 + 9 = 3$
3. 12
   $x^2 - 3x + 2 = 5^2 - 3 \times 5 + 2 = 25 - 15 + 2 = 12$
4. 150 miles
   $d = rt = 60 \times 2.5 = 150$
5. 44 inches
   $P = 2(l + w) = 2(15 + 7) = 2 \times 22 = 44$

Exercise 3: Equations (page 838)

1. 5 plus 7 times a number is 19.
2. 9 times a number is 27.
3. A number less 5 is 23.
4. 10 divided by a number less 5 is 0.
5. A number divided by 8 is 9.

Exercise 4: Eyeballing (page 839)

1. 2	2. 5	3. 13	4. 2
5. 10	6. 5	7. 3	8. 4

Exercise 5: One-Step Equations (page 841)

1. 9
   $x + 6 = 15$
   $x + 6 - 6 = 15 - 6$
   $x = 9$
2. 3
   $2x = 6$
   $x = \frac{6}{2} = 3$
3. 15
   $5x = 75$
   $x = \frac{75}{5} = 15$
4. 15
   $x - 3 = 12$
   $x = 12 + 3 = 15$
5. 36
   $\frac{x}{3} = 12$
   $x = 12 \times 3 = 36$
6. 8
   $x - 8 = 0$
   $x = 0 + 8 = 8$
7. 64
   $\frac{x}{4} = 16$
   $x = 16 \times 4 = 64$
8. 28
   $\frac{1}{2}x = 14$
   $x = 14 \times 2 = 28$

Exercise 6: Translating English to Algebra (page 843)

1. $x - 5$
2. $14x$
3. $\frac{x - y}{3}$
4. $x^2 + y^2$
5. $\frac{3}{4}y$
6. $7 + 2x$
7. $x^2 + 12$
8. $\frac{x^3}{4}$
9. $\frac{5x}{2x}$
10. $\frac{x}{2} + 3$

Exercise 7: Translating Sentences to Equations (page 844)

1. $\frac{x}{4} = 18$
2. $x - 2 = 40$
3. $3x + 1 = 25$
4. $9 + \frac{x}{2} = 13$
5. $6x = 35$
6. $x - y = 8$
7. $2x + 18 = 22$
8. $\frac{x}{4} = 18$
9. $2x - 3 = 5x + 9$
10. (3) $x - 48 = 75$
11. (1) $x - 5 = 19$
12. (4) $\frac{x}{7} = 5$
13. (3) $25 + 32h = 84$
14. (1) $x + 6 = \frac{7}{6}x$

Exercise 8: Solving One-Step Algebra Word Problems (page 846)

1. 15 — $x - 7 = 8$
2. 16 — $52 \div 3.25 = x$
3. \$2500 — $\frac{3}{4}x = 1875$
4. \$192 — $x - 120 = 72$
5. 12 feet — $x - 5\frac{1}{2} = 6\frac{1}{2}$
6. 158 lbs — $x + 14 = 172$
7. 36 years old — $x + 12 = 48$
8. \$18,000 — $.09x = 1620$

Exercise 9: Combining Like Terms (page 847)

1. $15x$
2. $5x^2 + 7x + 9$
3. $3y$
4. $3a$
5. $9x + 9y$
6. $x + y$
7. $7x^2 + 5x$
8. $12a^2 + 5a$
9. $13x - 3$
10. $6x + 9xy - 3y$

Exercise 10: Simplifying Grouping Symbols (page 848)

1. $15x + 10$
2. $28x - 32$
3. $18x - 7$
4. $-2x + 2$
5. $6x + 12 - 9y$
6. $-30x + 72$
7. $-11x - 18$
8. $2x - 2y$
9. $5x - 2$

Exercise 11: Solving Multistep Equations (page 850)

1. $x = 2$

$3x + 9 = 15$
$3x = 15 - 9 = 6$
$x = \frac{6}{3} = 2$

2. $x = 14$

$2x - 26 = 2$
$2x = 2 + 26 = 28$
$x = \frac{28}{2} = 14$

3. $x = 4$

$8(x - 4) = 0$
$8x - 32 = 0$
$8x = 32$
$x = \frac{32}{8} = 4$

4. $x = 1$

$2(5x - 11) + 12x = 0$
$10x - 22 + 12x = 0$
$22x - 22 = 0$
$22x = 22$
$x = \frac{22}{22} = 1$

5. $x = 21$

$\frac{4x}{3} - 14 = 14$
$\frac{4x}{3} = 28$
$4x = 84$
$x = \frac{84}{4} = 21$

6. $x = 15$

$\frac{x}{3} + 4 = 9$
$\frac{x}{3} = 5$
$x = 15$

Exercise 12: Setting Up and Solving Multistep Equations (page 851)

1. **(4)** $3(x + 32) = 180$
2. **(2)** \$28

$3(x + 32) = 180$
$3x + 96 = 180$
$3x = 84$
$x = \frac{84}{3} = 28$

3. **(4)** $2x + 24 = 56$
4. **(1)** 16

$2x + 24 = 56$
$2x = 56 - 24 = 32$
$x = \frac{32}{2} = 16$

5. **(1)** $x + 2x + 38 = 8324$
6. **(5)** 5524

$x + 2x + 38 = 8324$
$3x + 38 = 8324$
$3x = 8324 - 38 = 8286$
$x = \frac{8286}{3} = 2762$
$2x = 2(2762) = 5524$

Exercise 13: One-Step Inequalities (page 853)

1. **(a)** $x \neq 18$
2. **(b)** $x \leq 25$
3. **(a)** $x \geq 16$
4. **(b)** $x \leq 10$
5. $x > -2$
6. $x < 2$
7. $x < -7$
8. $x > -36$
9. $x \geq 4$
10. $x < -2$
11. $x \leq 7$
12. $x < 4$

Exercise 14: Ordered Pairs (page 856)

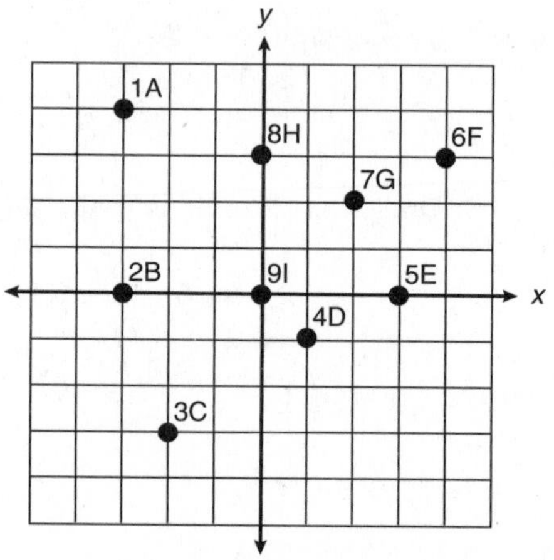

Exercise 15: Distance Between Two Points (page 858)

1. 3 units
2. 4 units
3. 5 units
   $d = \sqrt{(x_2 - x_1)^2 + (y_2 - y_1)^2}$
   $d = \sqrt{(4 - 0)^2 + (3 - 0)^2}$
   $d = \sqrt{16 + 9} = \sqrt{25} = 5$
4. 3.2 units
   $d = \sqrt{(x_2 - x_1)^2 + (y_2 - y_1)^2}$
   $d = \sqrt{(2 - 1)^2 + (2 - -1)^2}$
   $d = \sqrt{1 + 9} = \sqrt{10} = 3.16 = 3.2$
5. 6.4 units
   $d = \sqrt{(x_2 - x_1)^2 + (y_2 - y_1)^2}$
   $d = \sqrt{(-3 - 1)^2 + (4 - -1)^2}$
   $d = \sqrt{16 + 25} = \sqrt{41} = 6.4$
6. 3 units
7. 4.2 units
   $d = \sqrt{(x_2 - x_1)^2 + (y_2 - y_1)^2}$
   $d = \sqrt{(0 - 3)^2 + (3 - 0)^2}$
   $d = \sqrt{9 + 9} = \sqrt{18} = 4.2$
8. 1.4
   $d = \sqrt{(x_2 - x_1)^2 + (y_2 - y_1)^2}$
   $d = \sqrt{(0 - 1)^2 + (0 - -1)^2}$
   $d = \sqrt{1 + 1} = \sqrt{2} = 1.4$

Exercise 16: Intercepts (page 860)

1. x-intercept (4, 0)
   $0 = x - 4$
   $4 = x$
   y-intercept (0, –4)
   $y = 0 - 4$
   $y = -4$
2. x-intercept (3, 0)
   $0 = 2x - 6$
   $6 = 2x$
   $3 = x$
   y-intercept (0, –6)
   $y = (2)0 - 6$
   $y = -6$
3. x-intercept (–5, 0)
   $0 = x + 5$
   $-5 = x$
   y-intercept (0, 5)
   $y = 0 + 5$
   $y = 5$

Exercise 17: The Slope of a Line (page 862)

1. slope $= \frac{\text{change in y}}{\text{change in x}} = \frac{4 - 0}{3 - 0} = \frac{4}{3}$
2. slope $= \frac{-1 - 0}{-5 - 6} = \frac{-1}{-11} = \frac{1}{11}$
3. slope $= \frac{3 - 3}{-9 - 9} = \frac{0}{-18} = 0$
4. slope $= \frac{-2 - -1}{-1 - -2} = \frac{-1}{1} = -1$
5. slope $= \frac{2 - 0}{-1 - 3} = \frac{2}{-4} = -\frac{1}{2}$
6. slope $= \frac{3 - 0}{3 - -3} = \frac{3}{6} = \frac{1}{2}$
7. slope = 0 (horizontal line)
8. no slope (vertical line)

Exercise 18: Multiplying Algebraic Expressions (page 864)

1. $24x^3$
2. $-28x^2y$
3. $-18a^3b^2$
4. $-15x^3y^3$
5. $2x^3 + 2x$
6. $6y^3 - 12y^2 - 21y$
7. $x^2 + 7x + 10$
8. $x^2 - 5x + 4$

Exercise 19: The Greatest Common Factor (page 866)

1. $7y^2(3y - 2)$
2. $4a^2(25a^2 - 4)$
3. $11p^4(11p - 3)$
4. $4(2x^2 - 1)$
5. $9x^2y^2(x + 4y)$
6. $5x^2(2x^3 - x + 2)$
7. $x^2(4x^2 + 25x - 20)$
8. $9x(x^2 - 1)$
9. $x(3x + 1)$
10. $6xy(y + 2x)$

Exercise 20: Factoring by Grouping (page 867)

1. $x(x + 4) + 3(x + 4) = (x + 4)(x + 3)$
2. $x(x - 2) + 5(x - 2) = (x - 2)(x + 5)$
3. $2y(4y + 3z) + 3z(4y + 3z) = (4y + 3z)(2y + 3z)$
4. $2y^2(x - 4) + 1(x - 4) = (x - 4)(2y^2 + 1)$

Exercise 21: Factoring to Reverse FOIL (page 869)

1. $(x - 8)(x + 1)$
2. $(x - 4)(x - 1)$
3. $(x + 5)(x - 3)$
4. $(x - 4)(x + 4)$
5. $(x - 4)(x - 2)$
6. $(x - 10)(x + 10)$

Exercise 22: Algebra Review (page 869)

1. **(2)** $1500 - 240x$
2. **(5)** $\frac{1}{3}x + 70 = \frac{1}{2}x$
3. **(3)** 9
   $x + x + 6 + 2x = 42$
   $4x + 6 = 42$
   $4x = 36$
   $x = 9$
4. **(1)** 8 yards per second
   $d = rt$
   $200 = 25t$
   $t = 200 \div 25 = 8$
5. **(3)** 156
   $h = 100t - 16t^2$
   $h = 100 \times 3 - 16 \times 3^2 = 300 - 144 = 156$

6. 81 $\frac{72+78+85+2\times85}{5}=\frac{405}{5}=81$

7. 88 $\frac{68+76+80+2D}{5}=80$

$\frac{224+2D}{5}=80$

$224+2D=80\times5=400$

$2D=400-224=176$

$D=176\div2=88$

8. $x-5=10$

9. $\frac{10}{x}=5$

10. $x+5=10$ or $5+x=10$

11. $5+x=10$ or $x+5=10$

12. $5-x=10$

13. $\frac{x}{10}=5$

14. $5x=10$

15. 11

16. 3

17. 36

18. 9

19. $x<1$

20. $x<-10$

21. **(1)** −3

22. **(3)** 20

$55x=45(x+2)=45x+90$

$55x-45x=10x=90$

$x=9$

$x+2=11$

$9+11=20$

23. **(3)** $24x=672$

24. **(4)** $32

$x+2x=48,\ 3x=48,\ x=16,\ 2x=32$

25. **(5)** Not enough information is given.

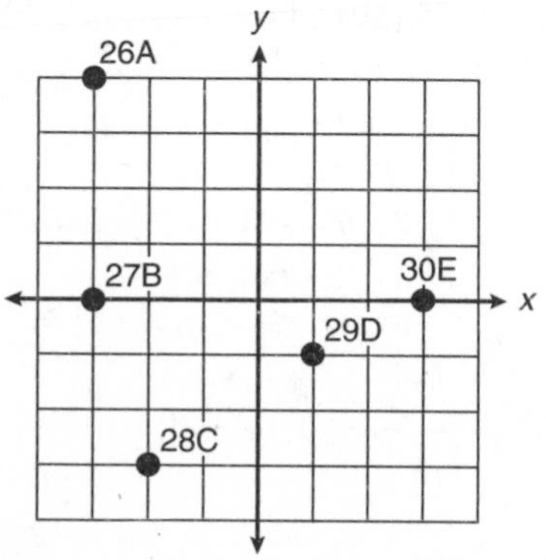

31. 4 units

32. 5 units

$d=\sqrt{(2--2)^2+(4-1)^2}=\sqrt{16+9}=\sqrt{25}=5$

33. $\frac{4-1}{2--2}=\frac{3}{4}$

34. slope = 0 because the line is horizontal.

35. $63x^3$

36. $-10x^2y$

37. $8y^3-6y^2-12y$

38. $x^2+3x-18$

39. $2y^2(6y-7)$

40. $5x^2y^2(x+5y)$

41. $(x-2)(x-8)$

42. $(x-9)(x+9)$

CHAPTER 11
MEASUREMENT

Exercise 1: Conversions (page 875)

1. 15 ft — $5\text{ yards}\times\frac{3\text{ ft}}{1\text{ yd}}=15\text{ ft}$

2. 2.5 lb — $40\text{ oz}\times\frac{1\text{ lb}}{16\text{ oz}}=2.5\text{ lbs}$

3. 4 days — $96\text{ hrs}\times\frac{1\text{ day}}{24\text{ hrs}}=4\text{ days}$

4. 5 gal — $20\text{ qts}\times\frac{1\text{ gal}}{4\text{ qt}}=5\text{ gal}$

5. 64 oz — $2\text{ qts}\times\frac{32\text{ oz}}{1\text{ qt}}=64\text{ oz}$

6. 2880 min — $2\text{ days}\times\frac{24\text{ hrs}}{1\text{ day}}\times\frac{60\text{ min}}{1\text{ hr}}=2880\text{ min}$

7. 1.5 qt — $3\text{ pts}\times\frac{1\text{ qt}}{2\text{ pts}}=1.5\text{ qt}$

8. 2.7 mi — $14110\text{ ft}\times\frac{1\text{ mi}}{5280\text{ ft}}=2.7\text{ mi}$

9. $.37

There are 64 ounces in a half gallon, so there are eight 8-ounce glasses of milk in a half gallon. Then $2.96 ÷ 8 = .37

10. 704 shrubs

$2\times5280\text{ ft}=10560\text{ ft},\ 10560\div15=704$

Exercise 2: Basic Operations with Measurements (page 878)

1. 6 ft 7 in.

9 feet 4 inches =	8 feet 16 inches
	− 2 feet 9 inches
	6 feet 7 inches

2. 4 hours 20 minutes

1 hour 20 minutes
+ 3 hours
4 hours 20 minutes

3. 121 pounds 12 ounces

130 pounds =	129 pounds 16 ounces
	− 8 pounds 4 ounces
	121 pounds 12 ounces

4. 37.1 inches
   5.3 inches × 7 = 37.1 inches
5. 7 feet 6 inches

$$\begin{array}{r} \text{7 feet 6 inches} \\ 3\overline{)\text{22 feet 6 inches}} \\ \underline{\text{21 feet}} \\ \text{1 foot} = \underline{\text{12 inches}} \\ \text{18 inches} \end{array}$$

6. 40 minutes
   5 hours 20 minutes = 320 minutes
   320 minutes ÷ 8 = 40 minutes
7. 7 ounces
   1 pound 4 ounces = 20 ounces
   20 ounces − 13 ounces = 7 ounces
8. 1 foot 8 inches
   6 foot 8 inches ÷ 4 = 80 inches ÷ 4 = 20 inches = 1 foot 8 inches
9. **(3)** $3.25
   45 × 4 inches = 180 inches
   $180 \text{ inches} \times \frac{1 \text{ yard}}{36 \text{ inches}} = 5 \text{ yards}$
   5 × $.65 = $3.25
10. **(4)** 19($365)
    1 pound 3 ounces = 19 ounces
    19 × $365 = $6935
11. **(4)** $193.50
    $2\frac{1}{2} + 3 + 4\frac{3}{4} + 7\frac{1}{4} + 4 = 21\frac{1}{2}$ hours
    $21\frac{1}{2} \times \$9 = \$193.50$

Exercise 3: The Metric System (page 880)

1. gram
2. .001 or $\frac{1}{1000}$
3. liter
4. 25
5. less
6. shorter
7. more
8. 75
9. meter
10. 10

Exercise 4: Metric Measurement (page 883)

1. 50,000 cm
   500. meters = 50000 centimeters
2. 7.423 grams
   7423. milligrams = 7.423 grams
   3 places
3. 503 millimeters
   50.3 centimeters = 503 millimeters
   one place
4. 27 grams
   .027 kilograms = 27 grams
   three places
5. 1,047 liters
   1 kiloliter = 1000 liters
   1000 + 47 = 1047 liters
6. 6.42 meters
   642. centimeters = 6.42 meters
   2 places
7. 17.15 meters
   400 cm + 1285 cm + 30 cm = 1715 cm = 17.15 m
8. 5.999 grams
   857 milligrams × 7 = 5999 milligrams = 5.999 grams
9. 1 kilometer
   1000 meters = 1 kilometer
10. U.S.
    80 km = 80 × .621 mi = 49.68 mi
    55 mph > 49.68 mph
11. **(2)** .75 × $6.40
12. **(3)** 91 .91 × 100 = 91

Exercise 5: Money Problems (page 885)

1. $101.33
   (49.95 + 2 × 14.95 + 3 × 4.95) × 1.07 = 101.329 = 101.33
2. **(3)** $200
   2 × $138 = $276
   2 × 2000 ÷ 50 × 5.95 = $476
   $476 – $276 = $200
3. **(2)** $51.48
   78 ÷ 3 × $1.98 = $51.48
4. **(3)** Friendly Flakes
   Better Bran = $2.79 ÷ 25 oz = $.1116/oz
   Wheatos = $2.49 ÷ 12 oz = $.21/oz
   Friendly Flakes = $3.19 ÷ 29 oz = $.11/oz
   Sugar Snaps= $2.39 ÷ 20 oz = $.1195/oz
5. **(2)** $.12
   36 ÷ 2 = 18
   $8.64 ÷ 18 – $6.48 ÷ 18 = .12
6. **(4)** .34 + 3(.28)

Exercise 6: Time Problems (page 888)

1. **(2)** 3
   $\$.75 \div \$.05 \times 12 \text{ minutes} \div \frac{60 \text{ minutes}}{1 \text{ hour}} = 3 \text{ hours}$
2. **(3)** $4\frac{1}{2} \times 12 \times 5 \times 4$
3. **(1)** 362.5 miles
   8:30 A.M. to 3:45 P.M. = $7\frac{1}{4}$ hours
   $7\frac{1}{4}$ hours × 50 mph = 362.5 miles
4. **(4)** 2
   On 5/21 he worked $1\frac{1}{2}$ hours overtime, and on 5/24 he worked $\frac{1}{2}$ hour overtime for a total of 2 hours overtime.

5. **(3)** $550
$40 \times \$12.85 + 2 \times \$18 = \$550$
6. **(3)** $375.50
3% + 25% + 7% = 35% deductions
$\$550 - .35(\$550) = \$375.50$
7. **(2)** $960 \times \frac{1}{3}$
$\frac{20 \text{ minutes}}{60 \text{ minutes}} = \frac{1}{3}$
$d = rt = 960 \text{ mph} \times \frac{1}{3} \text{ hr} = 320 \text{ miles}$
8. **(5)** $75 \div 2\frac{1}{2}$

Exercise 7: Scales and Meters (page 892)

1. **(4)** $2\frac{1}{2}$
$\frac{1 \text{ inch}}{180 \text{ miles}} = \frac{N \text{ inches}}{450 \text{ miles}}$
$N = \frac{1 \times 450}{180} = 2\frac{1}{2}$
2. **(3)** 1 in. = 200 mi
$2000 \text{ mi} \div 10 \text{ in.} = 200$ miles per inch
3. **(1)** $113.63
$(4752 \text{ kWh} - 3843 \text{ kWh}) \times \$.125 = \$113.63$
4. **(4)** $77.89
$(173 \times \$.3065 + \$2.00 + \$19.16) \times 1.05 =$
$\$77.893725 = \$77.89$

CHAPTER 12
GEOMETRY

Exercise 1: Geometry Figures and Shapes (page 896)

1. L. point
2. B. degree
3. P. vertex
4. K. plane
5. T. 360°
6. F. horizontal
7. N. square
8. S. 180°
9. G. isosceles
10. I. parallel
11. A. cylinder
12. M. radius
13. D. face
14. R. 90°
15. Q. vertical
16. J. perpendicular
17. C. equilateral
18. O. trapezoid
19. H. octagon
20. E. geometry

Exercise 2: Perimeter (page 898)

1. 360 feet $4 \times 90 \text{ feet} = 360 \text{ feet}$
2. $3\frac{1}{4}$ feet
Perimeter of a rectangle = $2 \times \text{length} + 2 \times \text{width} =$
$2 \times 8\frac{1}{2} \text{ inches} + 2 \times 11 \text{ inches} = 39 \text{ inches}$
$39 \text{ inches} \times \frac{1 \text{ ft}}{12 \text{ in}} = 3\frac{1}{4} \text{ feet}$
3. 49.9 inches
Perimeter of a triangle = $\text{side}_1 + \text{side}_2 + \text{side}_3 =$
$16.5 + 21 + 12.4 = 49.9$ inches
4. $7371.00
$(2 \times 400 \text{ yd} + 2 \times 224 \text{ yd}) \times 3 \text{ ft/yd} \times$
$1 \text{ section/8 ft} \times \$15.75\text{/section} = \$7371$
5. 8 times
$6 \text{ miles} \div (2 \times \frac{1}{4} + 2 \times \frac{1}{8}) = 8$
6. 70 m
$20 + 4.2 + 4.7 + 10.8 + 15.3 + 15 = 70$
7. 194 feet
$70 + 2 \times 48 + 70 - 42 = 194$
8. 97.68 m
$2 \times 30 + \pi \times 12 = 97.68$

Exercise 3: Area (page 901)

1. 128.7 sq m
Area of a rectangle = length × width =
14.3m × 9m = 128.7 sq m
2. 75.09 sq in.
Area of rectangle = length × width = $10 \times 4.7 =$
47
Area of square = $\text{side}^2 = 5.3^2 = 28.09$
$47 + 28.09 = 75.09$
3. $\frac{11}{14}$ sq in.
Area of a circle = $\pi \times \text{radius}^2 = \frac{22}{7} \times (\frac{1}{2})^2 = \frac{11}{14}$
4. 50 sq yd
Area of a rectangle = length × width = $15 \times 30 =$
450 sq ft
450 sq ft ÷ 9 sq ft/sq yd = 50 sq yd
5. $525
20 ft × 15 ft × $1.75/sq ft = $525
6. 78.5 sq ft
The diameter of the largest circle that will fit is 10 feet. So the radius is 5 feet. Using the formula for the area of a circle, $\pi \times \text{radius}^2 = 3.14 \times 5^2 =$
78.5
7. 200 sq ft
$20 \times 10 = 200$ sq ft
8. 10%
area of pool = $3.14 \times 9^2 = 254.34$
area of yard = $58 \times 45 = 2610$
$\frac{254.34}{2610} = \frac{N\%}{100\%}$
$N = \frac{254.34 \times 100}{2610} = 9.7 \approx 10$
9. 22.22 sq yd
area of patio = 200 sq ft
200 sq ft ÷ 9 sq ft/sq yd = 22.22 sq yd

10. 4
Area of pool = 254.34 sq ft
Area of garden = $8 \times 8 = 64$
$254.34 \div 64 = 3.97 \approx 4$

Exercise 4: Volume (page 903)

1. 72 cu ft
Volume of a rectangular container =
length × width × height = $6 \times 4 \times 3 = 72$ cu ft

2. 45 gal
Volume of tank = $18 \times 12 \times 48 = 10368$ cu in.
10368 cu in. ÷ 231 cu in./gal = $44.88 \approx 45$

3. 500 cu ft
Volume = $25 \times 40 \times .5 = 500$ cu ft

4. 294.375 cu yd
Volume of a cone = $\frac{1}{3} \times \pi \times$ radius$^2 \times$ height = $\frac{1}{3} \times$
$3.14 \times 22.5^2 \times 15 = 7948.125$
7948.125 cu ft ÷ 27 cu ft/cu yd = 294.375

5. 48 cu cm
Volume of a square pyramid = $\frac{1}{3} \times$ edge$^2 \times$ height =
$\frac{1}{3} \times 4^2 \times 9 = 48$

6. 25,872 cu ft
Volume of a cylinder = $\pi \times$ radius$^2 \times$ height =
$\frac{22}{7} \times 14^2 \times 42 = 25872$

Exercise 5: Pairs of Angles (page 906)

1. 38°
$\angle b$ and 142° are supplementary angles, so
180°–142° = 38°.

2. 38°
$\angle f$ and $\angle b$ are corresponding angles, so they are equal and both equal to 38°.

3. 38°
$\angle g$ and $\angle f$ are vertical angles, so they are equal and both equal to 38°.

4. 38°
$\angle g$ and $\angle c$ are corresponding angles, so they are equal and both equal to 38°.

5. 142°
$\angle d$ is vertical to 142° and, therefore, equal to 142°.

6. 142°
$\angle e$ corresponds to 142°, so it is equal to 142°.

7. 38°
If two angles combine to form a right angle, they are complementary and must add up to 90°, so 90° – 52° = 38°.

8. 105°
If two angles combine to form a straight line, they are supplementary and must add up to 180°.
180° – 75° = 105°

Exercise 6: Angles in Triangles (page 908)

1. 60°
The three equal angles of an equilateral triangle add up to 180°, so each must be 60°.

2. 50°
65° + 65° = 130° so 180° – 130° = 50°

3. 70° 180° – 70° – 40° = 70°

4. 125° 180° – 30° – 25° = 125°

5. 30° 180° – 90° – 60° = 30°

Exercise 7: The Pythagorean Theorem (page 911)

1. 15
$a^2 + b^2 = c^2$
$9^2 + 12^2 = c^2$
$81 + 144 = 225$
$c = \sqrt{225} = 15$

2. 3
$a^2 + b^2 = c^2$
$a^2 + 4^2 = 5^2$
$a^2 + 16 = 25$
$a = \sqrt{9} = 3$

3. 26
$a^2 + b^2 = c^2$
$10^2 + 24^2 = c^2$
$100 + 576 = 676$
$c = \sqrt{676} = 26$

4. 25
$a^2 + b^2 = c^2$
$15^2 + 20^2 = c^2$
$225 + 400 = 625$
$c = \sqrt{625} = 25$

5. yes
$20^2 + 21^2 = 29^2$
$400 + 441 = 841$

6. **(3)** 100
$a^2 + b^2 = c^2$
$60^2 + 80^2 = c^2$
$3600 + 6400 = 10000$
$c = \sqrt{10000} = 100$

7. (5) 75

$a^2 + b^2 = c^2$

$7^2 + 24^2 = c^2$

$49 + 576 = 625$

$c = \sqrt{625} = 25$

3 wires $\times$ 25 = 75

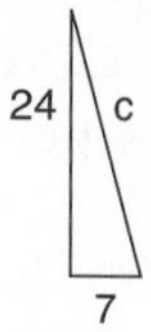

8. (2) 12

$a^2 + b^2 = c^2$

$a^2 + 5^2 = 13^2$

$a^2 + 25 = 169$

$a = \sqrt{144} = 12$

Exercise 8: Similar Triangles (page 914)

1. 9 in.

$\frac{10}{15} = \frac{6}{DF}$

$DF = \frac{6 \times 15}{10} = 9$

2. 12 ft

$\frac{h}{18} = \frac{8}{12}$

$h = \frac{8 \times 18}{12} = 12$

3. (a) Find the land measures and set up a proportion.

(b) 150 ft

$\frac{2}{6} = \frac{50}{d}$

$d = \frac{6 \times 50}{2} = 150$

4. 31.5 ft

$\frac{h}{42} = \frac{3}{4}$

$h = \frac{3 \times 42}{4} = 31.5$

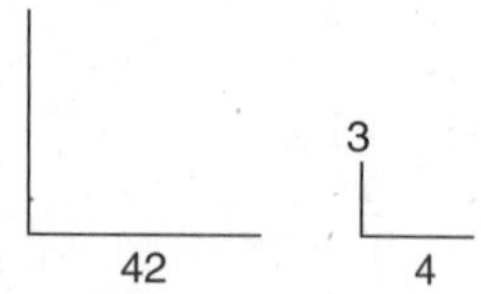

Exercise 9: Trigonometric Ratios (page 918)

1.

Ang	Adj	Opp	Hyp	Tan	Sin	Cos
$\angle A$	14	10.5	17.5	$\frac{10.5}{14}$	$\frac{10.5}{17.5}$	$\frac{14}{17.5}$
$\angle B$	10.5	14	17.5	$\frac{14}{10.5}$	$\frac{14}{17.5}$	$\frac{10.5}{17.5}$

2. 10.4 ft

$\tan 60° = \frac{h}{6}$

$h = 6 \times \tan 60° = 6 \times 1.73 = 10.39 \approx 10.4$

3. 1

In an isosceles right triangle, one angle is 90° and the other two equal angles are 45° each.

$\tan 45° = 1$

4. (1) $\sin 52.3° = \frac{11}{d}$

sin of an angle = $\frac{\text{side opposite}}{\text{hypotenuse}}$

Exercise 10: Geometry Review (page 919)

1. (3) 33 $\quad \frac{2(36 + 54 + 48 + 60)}{12} = 33$

2. (4) 230

Volume of rectangular container = length $\times$ width $\times$ height = $11\frac{1}{2} \times 2\frac{1}{2} \times 8 = 230$

3. (1) $(3.14)(1.5)^2(4)$

4. (2) 8

$a^2 + b^2 = c^2$

$a^2 + 15^2 = 17^2$

$a^2 + 225 = 289$

$a^2 = 64$

$a = 8$

5. (3) 1386

Area of a circle = $\pi \times \text{radius}^2 = \frac{22}{7} \times 21^2 = 1386$

6. (5) Not enough information is given.

7. (3) 60 sq ft

Area of a triangle = $\frac{1}{2} \times$ base $\times$ height = $\frac{1}{2} \times 15 \times 8 = 60$

8. (3) 400 m

$\frac{d}{250} = \frac{40}{25}$

$d = \frac{40 \times 250}{25} = 400$

9. (1) 30°

A right triangle has a 90° angle which added to the 60° angle equals 150°. So 180° – 150° = 30°.

10. (3) 108°

Supplement = 180° – 57° = 123°

Complement = 90° – 75° = 15°

123° – 15° = 108°

11. (1) 100

Circumference of a circle = $\pi \times$ diameter

$628 = 3.14 \times d$

$d = 628 \div 3.14 = 200$

radius = $200 \div 2 = 100$

12. (1) $t = \frac{s \times b}{a}$

13. (1) $17\frac{1}{2}$

$\frac{t}{42} = \frac{5}{12}$

$t = \frac{5 \times 42}{12} = 17\frac{1}{2}$

14. (2) 10 feet

Use the Pythagorean theorem.

$6^2 + 8^2 = d^2$

$36 + 64 = 100$

$d = \sqrt{100} = 10$

15. (2) 96

Volume of truck = $8 \times 8 \times 12 = 768$ cu ft

Volume of box = $2 \times 2 \times 2 = 8$ cu ft

$768 \div 8 = 96$

16. $\angle B = 18°$

$\tan 18° = .32$

$\sin 18° = .31$

$\cos 18° = .95$

Posttests

How do I use the Posttests?

You have been moving closer to your goal—passing the actual GED Tests—by completing the instructional material in the five test areas: Language Arts, Writing; Social Studies; Science; Language Arts, Reading; and Mathematics. Now it's time to measure your readiness for the GED Tests. These tests are similar to the actual GED Tests in terms of content areas, format, level of thinking skills, and percentages found on the real tests. After you have completed the Posttests, you will be better able to determine whether you are ready to take the GED Test and, if not, what areas you need to review. Evaluation Charts are included to help you judge your performance. We recommend the following approach to the Posttests.

1. Take only one Posttest at a time. Try to finish the test within the allotted time so that you can see how you will do on the actual GED Tests. If you are not done within that time period, mark where you were when the time was up and finish the test. You need to finish the entire Posttest so that you can make use of the Evaluation Charts.

Time Allowed for Each Test	
Language Arts, Writing	
Part I: Editing	75 minutes
Part II: Essay	45 minutes
Social Studies	80 minutes
Science	80 minutes
Language Arts, Reading	65 minutes
Mathematics	
Booklet One	45 minutes
Booklet Two	45 minutes

2. Check the answers in the Answer Keys and fill in the Evaluation Charts. The charts follow each test. Be sure to read the explanations for all of the questions that you missed.

3. Refer to the review pages given in the Evaluation Charts if you still need work in certain areas.

4. Although these are Posttests, you should give them your best effort. If an item seems difficult, mark it and come back later. Always answer every question—even if you have to make an "educated guess." Sometimes you may know more than you think. Also, blanks count as wrong answers on the actual GED Tests, so it's always wise to answer every question as best you can.

Good luck on the Posttests and on the GED!

POSTTEST

Language Arts, Writing

Part I: Editing

The following items are based on documents of several paragraphs marked by letters. Each paragraph contains numbered sentences. Most sentences contain errors, but a few may be correct as written. Read the documents, and then answer the questions based on them. For each item, choose the answer that would result in the best rewriting of the sentence or sentences. The best answer must be consistent with the meaning and tone of the rest of the document.

Answer each of the 50 questions as carefully as possible, choosing the best of five answer choices and blackening in the grid. If you find a question too difficult, do not waste time on it. Work ahead and come back to it later when you can think it through carefully.

When you have finished the test, check your answers using the Evaluation Chart on page 961. Use the chart to determine whether or not you are ready to take the final Practice Test, or, if not, in what areas you need more work.

Language Arts, Writing Posttest Answer Grid

1	①	②	③	④	⑤	18	①	②	③	④	⑤	35	①	②	③	④	⑤
2	①	②	③	④	⑤	19	①	②	③	④	⑤	36	①	②	③	④	⑤
3	①	②	③	④	⑤	20	①	②	③	④	⑤	37	①	②	③	④	⑤
4	①	②	③	④	⑤	21	①	②	③	④	⑤	38	①	②	③	④	⑤
5	①	②	③	④	⑤	22	①	②	③	④	⑤	39	①	②	③	④	⑤
6	①	②	③	④	⑤	23	①	②	③	④	⑤	40	①	②	③	④	⑤
7	①	②	③	④	⑤	24	①	②	③	④	⑤	41	①	②	③	④	⑤
8	①	②	③	④	⑤	25	①	②	③	④	⑤	42	①	②	③	④	⑤
9	①	②	③	④	⑤	26	①	②	③	④	⑤	43	①	②	③	④	⑤
10	①	②	③	④	⑤	27	①	②	③	④	⑤	44	①	②	③	④	⑤
11	①	②	③	④	⑤	28	①	②	③	④	⑤	45	①	②	③	④	⑤
12	①	②	③	④	⑤	29	①	②	③	④	⑤	46	①	②	③	④	⑤
13	①	②	③	④	⑤	30	①	②	③	④	⑤	47	①	②	③	④	⑤
14	①	②	③	④	⑤	31	①	②	③	④	⑤	48	①	②	③	④	⑤
15	①	②	③	④	⑤	32	①	②	③	④	⑤	49	①	②	③	④	⑤
16	①	②	③	④	⑤	33	①	②	③	④	⑤	50	①	②	③	④	⑤
17	①	②	③	④	⑤	34	①	②	③	④	⑤						

POSTTEST

Questions 1–10 refer to the following document.

National Parks

(A)

(1) The first national park in the United States and in the world was created in 1872. **(2)** Yellowstone in Wyoming was the first of more than fifty national parks that has been established throughout the United States. **(3)** These parks, which have become very popular with individuals from all over the world, preserve some of the most diverse beauty in nature.

(B)

(4) There are three national parks that are the most visited, and these three parks are the Grand Canyon in Arizona, Yosemite in California, and Great Smoky Mountains in Tennessee and North Carolina. **(5)** Each year hundreds of thousands of visitors hike, camp, or simply drive through these parks, enjoying the beauty found there. **(6)** For instance, the Grand Canyon, the most well known of all U.S. parks, is an astounding example of erosion, displaying multicolored rock layers along its canyon walls. **(7)** In addition to its waterfalls, granite peaks, and alpine lakes, Yosemite impresses visitors that are more than 2,000 years old with its ancient trees. **(8)** Great Smoky Mountains National Park is known for its diverse animals and plants, ancient mountains, and in the fall the colors are very striking.

(C)

(9) Because of the existence of these parks, it is possible to see an active volcano glowing red lava occasionally cracks through the shiny black lava crust to seep out in a fantastic show of light. **(10)** Alternatively, we might see miles and miles of a river of tall grasses, inhabited by thousands of birds, reptiles, and orchids. **(11)** Still another site has preserved the remains of ancient cliff dwellings, mysteriously abandoned to the dessert by their inhabitants long ago.

(D)

(12) Whatever choice appeals, our national parks work to protect these pleasures for us. **(13)** In turn, you must work to protect our national parks. **(14)** Perhaps the simple pleasure of sitting for a time under a large tree by a clear stream of splashing water is enough appeal for most of us.

Source: *The Complete Guide to America's National Parks.* 10th Ed. Fodor's Travel Publications, Inc. 1998. © National Park Foundation

1. Sentence 2: **Yellowstone in Wyoming was the first of more than fifty national parks <u>that has been established</u> throughout the United States.**

Which is the best way to write the underlined portion of the text? If the original is the best way, choose option (1).

(1) that has been established
(2) which had been established
(3) which have been established
(4) that have been established
(5) which will be established

2. Sentence 4: **There are three national parks that are the most visited, and these three parks are the Grand Canyon in Arizona, Yosemite in California, and Great Smoky Mountains in Tennessee and North Carolina.**

If you rewrote sentence 4 beginning with

Three of the most visited national parks

the next word would be

(1) are
(2) because
(3) often
(4) have
(5) yet

POSTTEST

3. Sentence 7: **In addition to its waterfalls, granite peaks, and alpine lakes, Yosemite impresses visitors that are more than 2000 years old with its ancient trees.**

Which is the best way to write the underlined portion of the text? If the original is the best way, choose option (1).

(1) that are more than 2,000 years old with its ancient trees.
(2) , and it has ancient trees for 2,000 years.
(3) with its ancient trees that are more than 2,000 years old.
(4) despite more than 2,000 years of ancient trees.
(5) who are more than 2,000 years old, with its ancient trees.

4. Sentence 8: **Great Smoky Mountains National Park is known for its diverse animals and plants, ancient mountains, and in the fall the colors are very striking.**

Which is the best way to write the underlined portion of the text? If the original is the best way, choose option (1).

(1) in the fall the colors are very striking.
(2) fall colors are very striking.
(3) during fall, colorful and striking.
(4) because of striking fall colors.
(5) striking fall colors.

5. **Which sentence below would be the most effective at the beginning of paragraph C?**

(1) The national parks strive to protect the beauty and wonders of nature.
(2) National parks are not expensive to visit.
(3) Volcanoes are very spectacular to see from a distance.
(4) Some national parks are extremely crowded during summer.
(5) Camping has become extremely popular in national parks.

6. Sentence 9: **Because of the existence of these parks, it is possible to see an active volcano, glowing red lava occasionally cracks through the shiny black lava crust to seep out in a fantastic show of light.**

Which is the best way to write the underlined portion of the text? If the original is the best way, choose option (1).

(1) volcano, glowing
(2) volcano, but glowing
(3) volcano, so glowing
(4) volcano although glowing
(5) volcano, where glowing

7. Sentence 10: **Alternatively, we might see miles and miles of a river of tall grasses, inhabited by thousands of birds, reptiles, and orchids.**

What correction should be made to sentence 10?

(1) change see to sea
(2) change river to River
(3) insert a comma after tall
(4) remove the comma after birds
(5) no correction is necessary

8. Sentence 11: **Still another site has preserved the remains of ancient cliff dwellings, mysteriously abandoned to the dessert by their inhabitants long ago.**

What correction should be made to sentence 11?

(1) change site to sight
(2) insert a comma after site
(3) change dessert to desert
(4) change their to there
(5) change inhabitants to inhabitant's

POSTTEST

9. Sentence 13: **In turn, you must work to protect our national parks.**

What correction should be made to sentence 13?

(1) change you to we
(2) insert a comma after you
(3) replace to protect with for protecting
(4) change our to are
(5) no correction is necessary

10. What revision would make paragraph D more effective?

(1) move sentence 14 to follow sentence 12
(2) move sentence 14 to the beginning of paragraph D
(3) remove sentence 14
(4) remove sentence 13
(5) no revision is necessary

Questions 11–20 refer to the following document.

Driving Skills and Strategies

(A)

(1) The development of good driving strategies are not only desirable but also necessary. **(2)** Automobiles continue to be the major form of transportation in the country. **(3)** The increasing congestion of roads has become more and more of an issue and aspect of life today. **(4)** People drive more than ever before and should be prepared to handle a variety of situations drivers may encounter.

(B)

(5) Some strategies are important for driving in general. **(6)** For example, you should always be aware of weather conditions, and adjust your speed and equipment accordingly. **(7)** Don't allow the gas tank to run down to low, and stop every two to three hours to stretch and prevent fatigue when driving long distances. **(8)** Reduce the possibility of encountering road rage by being attentive and to have respect of other drivers. **(9)** Don't drive after dark if your night vision is poor. **(10)** A seatbelt is one thing you should always remember to wear. **(11)** Other skills are specific to particular situations. **(12)** When driving in mountains, for example, use a lower gear when going up or down steep grades will reduce stress on the brakes and engine. **(13)** When going downhill tap the brakes repeatedly rather than applying full pressure. **(14)** The method of tapping the brakes helped avoid overheating and brake failure.

(C)

(15) The test of a driver doesnt stop once a license is issued. **(16)** Our driving skills are tested all the time we are on the road driving. **(17)** Using good skills and good strategies may indeed be a life-or-death requirement.

11. Sentence 1: **The development of good driving strategies are not only desirable but also necessary.**

Which is the best way to write the underlined portion of the text? If the original is the best way, choose option (1).

(1) strategies are not
(2) strategies were not
(3) strategies being not
(4) strategies is not
(5) strategies should not

12. Sentence 3: **The increasing congestion of roads has become more and more of an issue and aspect of life today.**

The most effective revision of sentence 3 would include which group of words?

(1) have become more and more
(2) congestion after life today
(3) increasing roads more
(4) without more road congestion
(5) because of life today

POSTTEST

13. Sentence 7: **Don't allow the gas tank to run down to low, and stop every two to three hours to stretch and prevent fatigue when driving long distances.**

What correction should be made to sentence 7?

(1) change Don't to Do Not
(2) replace to low with too low
(3) insert a comma after stretch
(4) change fatigue to Fatigue
(5) change distances to distance

14. Sentence 8: **Reduce the possibility of encountering road rage by being attentive and to have respect of other drivers.**

Which is the best way to write the underlined portion of the text? If the original is the best way, choose option (1).

(1) and to have respect
(2) , and with respect
(3) but to have respect
(4) and be respect
(5) and acting respectful

15. Sentence 10: **A seatbelt is one thing you should always remember to wear.**

The most effective revision of sentence 10 would begin with which group of words?

(1) One thing to that
(2) After you wear one
(3) Always remember to
(4) For the purpose of wearing
(5) One of the things to wear

16. **What revision should be made to sentence 11 to make the document "Driving Skills and Strategies" more effective?**

(1) move sentence 11 to follow sentence 13
(2) begin a new paragraph with sentence 11
(3) remove sentence 11
(4) move sentence 11 to follow sentence 15
(5) move sentence 11 to follow sentence 17

17. Sentence 12: **When driving in mountains, for example, use a lower gear when going up or down steep grades will reduce stress on the brakes and engine.**

Which is the best way to write the underlined portion of the text? If the original is the best way, choose option (1).

(1) use a lower gear
(2) using a lower gear
(3) used a lower gear
(4) you use a lower gear
(5) then use a lower gear

18. Sentence 13: **When going downhill tap the brakes repeatedly rather than applying full pressure.**

What correction should be made to sentence 13?

(1) insert a comma after hill
(2) change brakes to breaks
(3) insert a comma after brakes
(4) change than to then
(5) change applying to apply

19. Sentence 14: **The method of tapping the brakes helped avoid overheating and brake failure.**

What correction should be made to sentence 14?

(1) replace tapping with hitting
(2) change helped to helps
(3) insert to after helped
(4) change avoid to avoiding
(5) insert a comma after overheating

20. Sentence 15: **The test of a driver doesnt stop once a license is issued.**

What correction should be made to sentence 15?

(1) change test to testing
(2) insert a comma after driver
(3) change doesnt to doesn't
(4) change license to License
(5) no correction is necessary

POSTTEST

Questions 21–30 refer to the following document.

Human Resources Manager
Smithson and Company
3519 Main St.
New York City, New York

Dear Ms. Reynolds:

(A)

(1) In response to your job, listing at the Monroe Career Center, I would like to apply for the position of retail sales manager. **(2)** My educational background and work experience have provided me with the appropriate qualifications advertised by your company expected for the job.

(B)

(3) Currently, two courses in marketing and retailing are courses I have been taking as I am presently registered at Urban College. **(4)** This semester I am enrolled in Retail Merchandising and Customer Service, last semester I successfully completed courses in retailing and retail merchandise management. **(5)** As you can see, my education and experience have given me thorough preparation for a retail sales manager position. **(6)** Furthermore, I have gained several year's of valuable work experience from my employment at Kenton's Department Store. **(7)** For one year, I worked in the position of sales clerk. **(8)** After one year, I was promoted to the position of assistant department manager.

(C)

(9) I am an enthusiastic and responsible worker, and I found the prospect of a career in retail sales exciting. **(10)** I would never be happy in an accounting job, which does not involve much people contact. **(11)** Enclosed is my resume and several letters of recommendation which will attest to my qualifications.

(D)

(12) Your company has a reputation for being an excellent organization for which to work, so I am very pleased to learn that an opportunity for employment exists. **(13)** Thank you very much for considering my application for this position. **(14)** One thing I will be looking forward to will be hearing some communication with regards to my application.

21. Sentence 1: **In response to your job, listing at the Monroe Career Center, I would like to apply for the position of retail sales manager.**

What correction should be made to sentence 1?

(1) change <u>your</u> to <u>you're</u>
(2) remove the comma after <u>job</u>
(3) change <u>would</u> to <u>will</u>
(4) insert a comma after <u>apply</u>
(5) no correction is necessary

22. Sentence 10: **I would never be happy in an accounting job, which does not involve much people contact.**

What revision should be made to sentence 10 to improve paragraph C?

(1) move sentence 10 to follow sentence 11
(2) begin a new paragraph with sentence 10
(3) move sentence 10 to the beginning of paragraph C
(4) remove sentence 10
(5) no revision is necessary

POSTTEST

23. Sentence 3: **Currently, two courses in marketing and retailing are courses I have been taking as I am presently registered at Urban College.**

If you rewrote sentence 3 beginning with

Currently, I am registered at Urban College

the next words would be

(1) , where I
(2) presently I
(3) courses are
(4) as courses
(5) but I have

24. Sentence 4: **This semester I am enrolled in Retail Merchandising and Customer Service, last semester I successfully completed courses in retailing and retail merchandise management.**

Which is the best way to write the underlined portion of the text? If the original is the best way, choose option (1).

(1) *Service,* last
(2) *Service,* since last
(3) *Service,* just last
(4) *Service* and, last
(5) *Service.* Last

25. Sentence 5: **As you can see, my education and experience have given me thorough preparation for a retail sales manager position.**

What revision should be made to sentence 5 to improve paragraph B?

(1) move sentence 5 to follow sentence 3
(2) move sentence 5 to follow sentence 6
(3) move sentence 5 to follow sentence 8
(4) remove sentence 5
(5) no revision is necessary

26. Sentence 6: **Furthermore, I have gained several year's of valuable work experience from my employment at Kenton's Department Store.**

What correction should be made to sentence 6?

(1) change year's to years
(2) insert a comma after experience
(3) replace from with during
(4) change Store to store
(5) no correction is necessary

27. Sentence 9: **I am an enthusiastic and responsible worker, and I found the prospect of a career in retail sales exciting.**

What correction should be made to sentence 9?

(1) change am to was
(2) insert a comma after enthusiastic
(3) remove the comma after worker
(4) change found to find
(5) change exciting to excited

28. Sentence 2: **My educational background and work experience have provided me with the appropriate qualifications advertised by your company expected for the job.**

Which is the best way to write the underlined portion of the text? If the original is the best way, choose option (1).

(1) advertised by your company expected for the job.
(2) and that your company advertised for the job.
(3) advertised after your company's expectations.
(4) and job expectation outside your company.
(5) expected for the job your company advertised.

POSTTEST

29. Sentence 11: **Enclosed is my resume and several letters of recommendation which will attest to my qualifications.**

What correction should be made to sentence 11?

(1) change is to are
(2) insert a comma after resume
(3) change letters to letter's
(4) insert a comma after recommendation
(5) change will to did

30. Sentence 14: **One thing I will be looking forward to will be hearing some communication with regards to my application.**

The most effective revision of sentence 14 would include which group of words?

(1) regarding my recent
(2) because of the thing
(3) in communication beyond
(4) looking for my application
(5) hearing from you

Questions 31–41 refer to the following document.

Language

(A)

(1) Although more people speak Chinese than any other language. **(2)** That frequency of use is primarily because of the immensity of the Chinese population. **(3)** It has been recognized that throughout the world, the language used most commonly by different people is English. **(4)** English had served as the language of communication for international business and government relations.

(B)

(5) As a result, the majority of people who use English are speaking English as a second language. **(6)** There is actually fewer people speaking English who have English as a native language than there are people speaking English who have a different native language. **(7)** For example, a Malaysian businessman and a japanese businessman may very well conduct business in English.

(C)

(8) How hard is English to learn? **(9)** The easiest time in life to learn any language is between birth and approximately the age of fourteen. **(10)** This is also a time of life when nutrition is very important. **(11)** Children have an innate ability to learn language they have the time to do so. **(12)** While some adults have greater language abilities than others, in general, the difficulty of learning English or any other language depends on the language with which someone begins. **(13)** Languages are grouped into families, so the closer the relation of the first language to English, the easier English will be to learn.

(D)

(14) If English is your native language, how long will they take to learn? **(15)** The English language is a language that consists of more than 750,000 words with additional words continually added to it all the time. **(16)** Truly mastering language is a life-long process.

31. Sentences 1 and 2: **Although more people speak Chinese than any other language. That frequency of use is primarily because of the immensity of the Chinese population.**

Which is the best way to write the underlined portion of the text? If the original is the best way, choose option (1).

(1) language. That
(2) language and
(3) language which
(4) language, but
(5) language, that

POSTTEST

32. Sentence 3: **It has been recognized that throughout the world, the language used most commonly by different people is English.**

If you rewrote sentence 3 beginning with

Throughout the world

the next words would be

(1) common people
(2) by different
(3) English is
(4) English people
(5) language recognizes

33. Sentence 4: **English <u>had served</u> as the language of communication for international business and government relations.**

Which is the best way to write the underlined portion of the text? If the original is the best way, choose option (1).

(1) had served
(2) having served
(3) has been served
(4) serves
(5) would serve

34. What revision would improve the text, "Language"?

(1) move sentence 5 to follow sentence 8
(2) remove sentence 5
(3) combine paragraphs A and B into one paragraph
(4) begin a new paragraph with sentence 6
(5) remove sentence 16

35. Sentence 6: **<u>There is</u> actually fewer people speaking English who have English as a native language than there are people speaking English who have a different native language.**

Which is the best way to write the underlined portion of the text? If the original is the best way, choose option (1).

(1) There is
(2) There are
(3) There were
(4) There was
(5) There can be

36. Sentence 7: **For example, a Malaysian businessman and a japanese businessman may very well conduct business in English.**

What correction should be made to sentence 7?

(1) remove the comma after <u>example</u>
(2) change <u>Malaysian</u> to <u>malaysian</u>
(3) change <u>japanese</u> to <u>Japanese</u>
(4) insert a comma after <u>may</u>
(5) no correction is necessary

37. Sentence 10: **This is also a time of life when nutrition is very important.**

What revision should be made to sentence 10 to improve paragraph C?

(1) move sentence 10 to follow sentence 11
(2) begin a new paragraph with sentence 10
(3) move sentence 10 to follow sentence 12
(4) move sentence 10 to follow sentence 13
(5) remove sentence 10

POSTTEST

38. Sentence 11: **Children have an innate ability to learn language they have the time to do so.**

Which is the best way to write the underlined portion of the text? If the original is the best way, choose option (1).

(1) they have the time
(2) as well as the time
(3) , they have the time
(4) they spend the time
(5) but have the time

39. Sentence 12: **While some adults have greater language abilities than others, in general, the difficulty of learning English or any other language depends on the language with which someone begins.**

Which is the best way to write the underlined portion of the text? If the original is the best way, choose option (1).

(1) depends on
(2) depend on
(3) depending on
(4) dependent on
(5) depended on

40. Sentence 14: **If English is your native language, how long will they take to learn?**

What correction should be made to sentence 14?

(1) replace If with When
(2) remove the comma after language
(3) insert a comma after long
(4) replace they with it
(5) no correction is necessary

41. Sentence 15: **The English language is a language that consists of more than 750,000 words, with additional words continually added to it all the time.**

The most effective revision of sentence 15 would begin with which group of words?

(1) However, more than
(2) Adding to the time
(3) Any language which
(4) Too many words added
(5) English consists of

POSTTEST

Questions 42–50 refer to the following document.

Bugs

(A)

(1) Many bugs such as spiders, ladybugs, or lacewings are helpful because they eat other insects that harm crops and plants. **(2)** Some bugs pollinate flowers and crops like bees and wasps. **(3)** Other bugs such as butterflies or dragonflies were beneficial because they add beauty to gardens and outdoor displays. **(4)** However, some bugs are truly pests that need to be controlled or prevented from multiplying.

(B)

(5) In the event of bugs being inside our homes, we are faced by a real nuisance. **(6)** Within our homes, Indian meal moths and beetles can infest supplies after being carried into the house in pet food, food, or seed. **(7)** Indian moths or miller moths feed on dried fruit and chocolate. **(8)** The moths spin cocoons and may spread throughout the house. **(9)** The house can also be infested by red flour beetles. **(10)** These beetles may appear in dry cereal, crackers, and pet food.

(C)

(11) To avoid problems, check foods, especially flours and cereals, for any signs of insects after you've purchased the food and are putting them away. **(12)** Store the food in airtight containers, and clean the containers regularly. **(13)** Vacuum up any spilled food immediately. **(14)** If you do find an infestation, seal up the affected food and remove it from you're home. **(15)** The examination of the other various foods that might be in your pantry is necessary as a check for any signs of problems.

(D)

(16) With a little effort, we can control some insect problems. **(17)** That plague us. **(18)** With a little education, we can learn what to do about those insects that create the problems.

Source: Homework: Fighting Insects in the Kitchen. *Chicago Tribune,* April 2, 2000.

POSTTEST

42. Sentence 2: **Some bugs <u>pollinate flowers and crops like bees and wasps</u>.**

Which is the best way to write the underlined portion of the text? If the original is the best way, choose option (1).

(1) pollinate flowers and crops like bees and wasps.
(2) pollinating flowers and crops like bees and wasps.
(3) like bees and wasps pollinate flowers and crops.
(4) pollinate like bees and wasps in flowers and crops.
(5) pollinate flowers with bees and wasps by crops.

43. Sentence 3: **Other bugs such as butterflies or dragonflies <u>were beneficial because they</u> add beauty to gardens and outdoor displays.**

Which is the best way to write the underlined portion of the text? If the original is the best way, choose option (1).

(1) were beneficial because they
(2) are beneficial because they
(3) were beneficial because it
(4) are benefited because they
(5) being beneficial because they

44. Sentence 4: **However, some bugs are truly pests that need to be controlled or prevented from multiplying.**

What revision should be made to sentence 4 to improve paragraph A?

(1) remove sentence 4
(2) move sentence 4 to follow sentence 1
(3) move sentence 4 to follow sentence 2
(4) begin paragraph A with sentence 4
(5) no revision is necessary

45. Sentence 5: **In the event of bugs being inside our homes, we are faced by a real nuisance.**

The most effective revision of sentence 5 would include which group of words?

(1) can be a real
(2) our homes being
(3) but we are
(4) without any bugs
(5) will not face

46. Sentence 9: **The house can also be infested by red flour beetles.**

The most effective revision of sentence 9 would begin with which group of words?

(1) Although infested by
(2) The red house
(3) While no flour beetles
(4) Just like beetles
(5) Red flour beetles

POSTTEST

47. Sentence 11: **To avoid problems, check foods, especially flours and cereals, for any signs of insects after you've purchased the food and <u>are putting them</u> away.**

Which is the best way to write the underlined portion of the text? If the original is the best way, choose option (1).

(1) are putting them
(2) were putting them
(3) put them
(4) are putting it
(5) are putting him

48. Sentence 14: **If you do find an infestation, seal up the affected food and remove it from you're home.**

What correction should be made to sentence 14?

(1) remove the comma after <u>infestation</u>
(2) insert a comma after <u>food</u>
(3) replace <u>it</u> with <u>them</u>
(4) change <u>you're</u> to <u>your</u>
(5) no correction is necessary

49. Sentence 15: **The examination of the other various foods that might be in your pantry is necessary as a check for any signs of problems.**

If you rewrote sentence 15 beginning with

Examine the other food

the next word would be

(1) in
(2) without
(3) check
(4) among
(5) problems

50. Sentences 16 and 17: **With a little effort, we can control some insect <u>problems. That</u> plague us.**

Which is the best way to write the underlined portion of the text? If the original is the best way, choose option (1).

(1) problems. That
(2) problems that
(3) problems and
(4) problems, they
(5) problems might

POSTTEST

Part II: The Essay

Directions: This part of the test is designed to find out how well you write. The test has one question that asks you to present an opinion and explain your ideas. Your essay should be long enough to develop the topic adequately. In preparing your essay, you should take the following steps:

1. Read the directions and topic carefully.
2. Think about your ideas and plan your essay before you write.
3. Use scratch paper to make notes of your ideas.
4. Write your essay in ink on two other pages of paper.
5. After finishing your writing, read your paper carefully and make appropriate changes.

TOPIC

If you could live anywhere in the world, where would you choose to live?

In your essay, identify the place where you would most like to live. Explain the reasons for your selection.

Information on evaluating your essay is on page 962.

POSTTEST

Language Arts, Writing Answer Key

PART I: EDITING

1. **(4)** The pronoun *that* refers to *parks* and requires the verb *have* for correct subject and verb agreement.

2. **(1)** To reduce wordiness, improve the sentence with this revision: *Three of the most visited national parks are the Grand Canyon in Arizona, Yosemite in California, and Great Smoky Mountains in Tennessee and North Carolina.*

3. **(3)** The sentence must be restructured so that the trees are 2000 years old rather than the visitors.

4. **(5)** Changing the last item in the series to *striking fall colors* makes the sentence have a parallel structure.

5. **(1)** Adding a topic sentence helps provide a focus for the paragraph which gives examples of beauty and diversity in nature.

6. **(5)** The sentence contains a comma splice that is best corrected by using subordination to make one clause dependent upon the other.

7. **(5)** No correction is necessary.

8. **(3)** The spelling for the word needed in the sentence is *desert*.

9. **(1)** The pronoun *you* is not consistent with the rest of the sentence and passage.

10. **(2)** Sentence 14 introduces an example of a pleasurable choice, and the other sentences in paragraph D continue the idea.

11. **(4)** The subject of the sentence *development* requires the verb *is* for appropriate subject and verb agreement and tense.

12. **(1)** Reducing wordiness will improve the sentence: *Roads have become more and more congested today.*

13. **(2)** Use the word *too* rather than *to* so that the spelling is consistent with the meaning.

14. **(5)** The phrase *and acting respectful* matches the phrase *being attentive* to provide a parallel structure in the sentence.

15. **(3)** Omit vague words with an improved revision: *Always remember to wear a seatbelt.*

16. **(2)** A new idea about particular situations is introduced with sentence 11, which also serves as a topic sentence.

17. **(2)** This phrase must be revised so that a subject is provided for the verb *will reduce* and the sentence is complete.

18. **(1)** Placing a comma after the introductory phrase *when going downhill* helps the reader comprehend the meaning more easily.

19. **(2)** The verb must be in the present tense to be consistent with the passage and to state a fact.

20. **(3)** An apostrophe is needed where a letter has been omitted in a contraction.

21. **(2)** Remove the comma after *job* to avoid confusing the meaning.

22. **(4)** Sentence 10 is irrelevant to the main idea of the paragraph.

23. **(1)** An improved version of the sentence would omit repetitious wording with this revision: *Currently, I am registered at Urban College where I have been taking two courses in marketing and retailing.*

24. **(5)** Correct the comma splice by separating these two sentences.

25. **(3)** Sentence 5 effectively closes paragraph B by stating the main idea of the paragraph.

26. **(1)** The noun *years* is plural and not possessive, so no apostrophe is needed.

27. **(4)** Keep the verb tense in the sentence and paragraph consistent by changing *found* to the present tense.

28. (5) The sentence must be structured so that the qualifications are *expected for the job* and not *advertised by the company.*

29. (1) The verb *are* must be used to agree with the subject of the sentence *my resume and several letters of recommendation.*

30. (5) Improve the sentence by reducing wordiness with this revision: *I look forward to hearing from you.*

31. (5) Sentence 1 is a fragment that can be corrected by attaching it to sentence 2.

32. (3) Reduce wordiness and avoid the passive voice with this revision: *Throughout the world, English is the language most commonly used.*

33. (4) Change the verb to the present tense *serves* to be consistent with the document because the information is presented as a fact.

34. (3) Paragraphs A and B should be combined into one paragraph because all of the sentences support the idea that English is a very popular language.

35. (2) The verb *are* agrees with the subject *people* and is consistent with the tense in the rest of the sentence.

36. (3) Capitalize nationalities.

37. (5) Sentence 10 is irrelevant to the paragraph's main idea of language learning.

38. (2) Correct the run-on sentence by subordinating the second sentence so that it is dependent on the first sentence.

39. (1) No correction is necessary.

40. (4) The pronoun *it* should be used to refer correctly to the antecedent *English.*

41. (5) An improved version of this sentence avoids unnecessary wordiness: *English consists of more than 750,000 words with new words added all the time.*

42. (3) The modifying phrase must be placed so that *like bees and wasps* clearly describes *bugs* rather than *crops.*

43. (2) The verb must be present tense to be consistent with the rest of the paragraph.

44. (5) No revision is necessary.

45. (1) Improve the sentence by avoiding the passive voice and reducing wordiness: *Bugs can be a real nuisance inside our homes.*

46. (5) Use the active voice rather than the passive voice for an improved sentence: *Red flour beetles can also infest the house.*

47. (4) The pronoun *it* should replace the pronoun *them* because the antecedent is *food.*

48. (4) Change the spelling of *you're* to *your* because the meaning requires the possessive pronoun.

49. (1) The wordiness of the sentence can be improved with this revision: *Examine the other food in your pantry for any signs of problems.*

50. (2) Correct the fragment by attaching *That plague us* to the preceding independent sentence.

Evaluation Chart

Use the answer key on pages 959–960 to check your answers to the Posttest. Then find the item number of each question you missed and circle it on the chart below to determine the writing content areas in which you need more practice. Pay particular attention to areas where you missed half or more of the questions. The page numbers for the content areas are listed on the chart below. For those questions that you missed, review the skill pages indicated.

CONTENT AREA	ITEM NUMBER	REVIEW PAGES
Nouns	26	69–73, 102–104
Verbs	19, 27, 33, 43	73–86, 102–104
Subject/Verb Agreement	1, 11, 29, 35	87–91, 102–104
Pronoun Use	9, 40, 47	91–95, 102–104
Sentence Fragments	17, 31, 50	105–108, 131–134
Run-ons, Comma Splices, Sentence Combining	2, 6, 24, 38	108–115, 131–134
Independent/Dependent Clauses, Effective Sentence Structure	12, 15, 23, 30, 32, 41, 45, 46, 49	116–125, 131–134
Dangling or Misplaced Modifiers	3, 22, 42	126–128, 131–134
Parallel Structure	4, 14	129–134
Capitalization, Punctuation	18, 20, 21, 36	135–144, 150–152
Spelling	8, 13, 48	147–149, 150–152
Paragraph Composition	5, 25	153–157, 165–168
Text Division	34, 16	157–160, 165–168
Paragraph Unity and Coherence	10, 28, 37	160–165, 165–168
No Correction	7, 39, 44	135–144, 147–149, 165–168

POSTTEST

Part II: The Essay

If possible, give your essay to an instructor to evaluate. That person's opinion of your writing will be useful in deciding what further work you need to do to write a good essay.

If, however, you are unable to show your work to someone else, you can try to evaluate your own essay. Use the five questions in the Essay Evaluation Checklist to help evaluate your writing. The more questions that you can answer with a strong *yes,* the better your chances are for achieving a passing or high score.

Essay Evaluation Checklist

YES	NO	
		1. Does the essay answer the question asked?
		2. Does the main point of the essay stand out clearly?
		3. Does each paragraph contain specific examples and details that develop and explain the main point?
		4. Are the ideas organized clearly into paragraphs and complete sentences?
		5. Is the essay easy to read, or do problems in grammar, usage, punctuation, spelling, or word choice interfere?

Important Note

On the actual GED Language Arts, Writing Test, you will be given one score, which is a composite of your scores from Part I and Part II of the test. This score is determined by grading your essay holistically, giving it a score, then combining this score with your score from Part I in a proportion determined by the GED Testing Service.

Because you are not able to score your essay holistically, it is not possible for you to determine a valid composite score for your performance on this Language Arts, Writing Test. Instead, it is best to look at your performance on each part of the test separately. In this way, you will be able to determine whether you need additional work in one part of the test or the other. Remember that you must take both parts of the Language Arts, Writing Test for your score to count.

POSTTEST

Social Studies

This Social Studies Posttest will give you an opportunity to evaluate your readiness for the actual GED Social Studies Test. This test contains 50 questions. Some of the questions are based on short reading passages, and some of them require you to interpret a graph, chart or table, map, or an editorial cartoon.

You should take approximately 70 minutes to complete this test. At the end of 70 minutes, stop and mark your place. Then finish the test. This will give you an idea of whether or not you can finish the actual GED Test in the time allotted. Try to answer as many questions as you can. Blanks will count as wrong answers, so make a reasonable guess for the answers to questions of which you are not sure.

Use the Answer Key on pages 984–987 to check your answers to the Social Studies Posttest. Then find the item number of each question you missed and circle it on the Evaluation Chart on page 988 to determine the skills and content areas in which you need more practice. Pay particular attention to areas where you missed half or more of the questions. The page numbers for the content areas and the critical thinking skills are listed on the chart. The numbers in **boldface** are questions based on graphics. For those questions that you missed, review the pages indicated.

Social Studies Posttest Answer Grid

1	①	②	③	④	⑤	18	①	②	③	④	⑤	35	①	②	③	④	⑤
2	①	②	③	④	⑤	19	①	②	③	④	⑤	36	①	②	③	④	⑤
3	①	②	③	④	⑤	20	①	②	③	④	⑤	37	①	②	③	④	⑤
4	①	②	③	④	⑤	21	①	②	③	④	⑤	38	①	②	③	④	⑤
5	①	②	③	④	⑤	22	①	②	③	④	⑤	39	①	②	③	④	⑤
6	①	②	③	④	⑤	23	①	②	③	④	⑤	40	①	②	③	④	⑤
7	①	②	③	④	⑤	24	①	②	③	④	⑤	41	①	②	③	④	⑤
8	①	②	③	④	⑤	25	①	②	③	④	⑤	42	①	②	③	④	⑤
9	①	②	③	④	⑤	26	①	②	③	④	⑤	43	①	②	③	④	⑤
10	①	②	③	④	⑤	27	①	②	③	④	⑤	44	①	②	③	④	⑤
11	①	②	③	④	⑤	28	①	②	③	④	⑤	45	①	②	③	④	⑤
12	①	②	③	④	⑤	29	①	②	③	④	⑤	46	①	②	③	④	⑤
13	①	②	③	④	⑤	30	①	②	③	④	⑤	47	①	②	③	④	⑤
14	①	②	③	④	⑤	31	①	②	③	④	⑤	48	①	②	③	④	⑤
15	①	②	③	④	⑤	32	①	②	③	④	⑤	49	①	②	③	④	⑤
16	①	②	③	④	⑤	33	①	②	③	④	⑤	50	①	②	③	④	⑤
17	①	②	③	④	⑤	34	①	②	③	④	⑤						

POSTTEST

Questions 1 and 2 are based on the following cartoon.

Reprinted with permission from *The Detroit News*

1. What does a balanced budget mean in terms of government revenue?

(1) Goverment generates more revenue than it spends.
(2) Goverment revenue equals its spending.
(3) Government receives less revenue than it spends.
(4) Government revenues will stay the same.
(5) Government revenues will decrease.

2. Which of the following is a correct interpretation of this cartoon?

(1) The budget will not be balanced if the economy "crashes."
(2) The budget is balanced because the economy is stable.
(3) The budget is balanced because the economy is weak.
(4) The budget will remain balanced under all economic conditions.
(5) The budget will not be balanced if the economy is strong.

Questions 3 and 4 are based on the following excerpt.

WE, THEREFORE, the Representatives of the UNITED STATES of AMERICA in General Congress, Assembled, appealing to the Supreme Judge of the world for the rectitude of our intentions, do, in the Name, and by Authority of the good People of these Colonies, solemnly publish and declare, That these United Colonies are, and of Right ought to be, FREE AND INDEPENDENT STATES . . .

3. This statement was proclaimed by members of which group?

(1) Constitutional Convention
(2) Boston Tea Party participants
(3) Articles of Confederation writers
(4) Second Continental Congress
(5) First House of Representatives

4. Which of the following statements supports the author's opinion?

(1) All people should be free from government control.
(2) The United States should be free from outside control.
(3) Wealthy countries have the right to control weaker countries.
(4) The people shall have the right to vote for their leaders.
(5) The United States needs a strong federal government.

POSTTEST

Question 5 is based on the following graph.

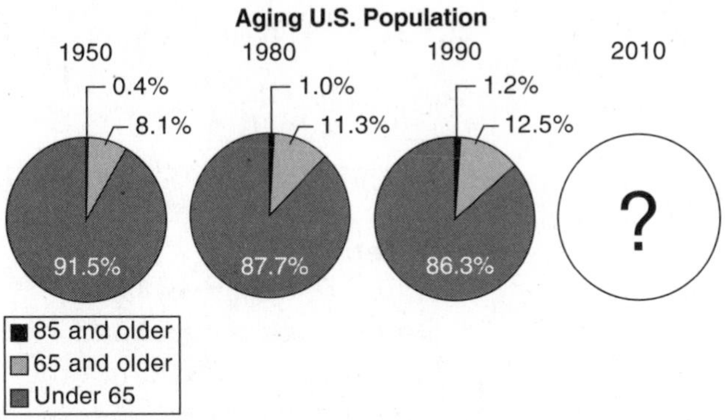

Source: Bureau of the Census, U.S. Department of Commerce

5. Which adult population statistical prediction for 2010 would be likely, given the information in the circle graphs?

(1) 1 percent over 85 years of age and 31 percent 65 and older
(2) 2 percent over 85 years of age and 30 percent 65 and older
(3) 0.5 percent over 85 years of age and 12 percent 65 and older
(4) 2 percent over 85 years of age and 10 percent 65 and older
(5) 2 percent over 85 years of age and 15 percent 65 and older

6. Liberals believe that the problems of the country should be solved by a strong federal government. They support funding social programs, limiting military spending, and negotiating as the basis for American foreign policy. Which one of the following federal programs would liberals in America be likely to oppose?

(1) guaranteed government loans to college students
(2) a national health insurance program
(3) stricter pollution laws
(4) the Star Wars space defense system
(5) job training for the disabled

Question 7 is based on the following graph.

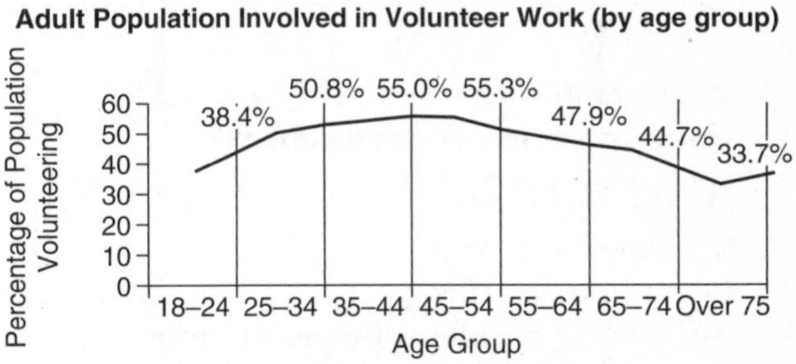

Source: Statistical Abstract of the United States

7. Based on the information in the graph, which of the following people is most likely to be involved in a community volunteer program?

(1) twenty-two-year-old college graduate
(2) self-employed thirty-five-year-old saleswoman
(3) eighteen-year-old high school senior
(4) retired fifty-three-year-old high school teacher
(5) thirty-year-old mother of one child

POSTTEST

Questions 8 and 9 refer to the following chart.

Constitutional Powers: Three Branches of Government

LEGISLATIVE	EXECUTIVE	JUDICIAL
• Passes bills into laws • Lays and collects taxes • Regulates commerce among states and with other foreign nations • Coins money; establishes values and standards • Declares war • Raises and supports armies • Provides for a militia	• Serves as Commander-in-Chief of Army, Navy, and militia • Makes treaties with other nations with Senate consent • Appoints ambassadors, judges of the Supreme Court, and Cabinet officers • Enforces laws of Congress	• Settles controversies among states and citizens • Determines the constitutionality of laws • Determines original and appellate jurisdiction of the Supreme Court • Interprets the laws • Determines the constitutionality of the President's actions

8. Which is *not* a power held by any of the three branches of government?

(1) printing money
(2) collecting taxes
(3) raising an army
(4) settling problems between states
(5) establishing child care centers

9. Considering the powers of the legislative branch, evaluate and select the reason that the writers of the Constitution of the United States might have given the power to declare war to Congress and not to the executive branch.

(1) Congress best represents the people and should finalize the decision to declare war.
(2) The president shouldn't be involved in any affair regarding military decisions.
(3) Congress should make all decisions involving problems between the states.
(4) The president's being the Supreme commander of the armed forces creates a conflict of interest.
(5) The president of the United States has enough information to declare war.

POSTTEST

Questions 10 and 11 refer to the following passage.

Archaeologists study past societies through the analysis of artifacts found buried at old dwelling sites. These artifacts could include weapons, tools, pottery, or personal items. Anthropologists study human remains and fossils to determine the physical nature and possible behaviors of ancient people. Scientists study remains throughout the world to try to understand past cultures. In some cases, as in Egypt, an artifact like the Rosetta Stone provides enough information to help archaeologists decipher written language that tells of ancient lifestyles. Because of the Rosetta Stone, we can read the hieroglyphics of ancient Egypt and understand this extinct civilization.

10. Which of the following discoveries was most likely made by an anthropologist?

(1) artifacts from the Titanic, which sank on its maiden voyage
(2) skeletal remains from the Yucatán Peninsula in Mexico
(3) farming tools used by the Hopi Indians in New Mexico
(4) spears and shields used by the Vikings in Northern Scotland
(5) murals in caves drawn by the Anasazi Indians in Arizona

11. Based on the passage, which of the following could be selected as the most accurate artifact representing the United States in the late 20th century?

(1) electric light bulb
(2) printing press
(3) computer
(4) telephone
(5) steam engine

POSTTEST

Question 12 is based on the following graph.

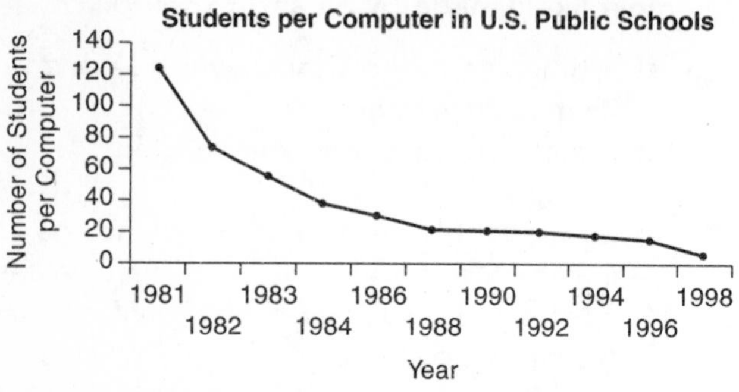

Source: National Center for Education Statistics, U.S. Dept. of Education; National Education Association

12. Which of the following statements best supports the data provided in the line graph?

(1) More students are wealthier and can afford the newest technology.
(2) Fewer students are sharing computers in the public schools.
(3) The United States has prioritized spending on computers with tax dollars.
(4) Schools have used more budgeted income for buying computers.
(5) More students have computers in their classrooms because of corporate donations.

Questions 13 through 16 are based on the following amendments to the Constitution of the United States.

(16)
The Congress shall have power to lay and collect taxes on incomes, from whatever source derived, without apportionment among the several states, and without regard to any census or enumeration.

(19)
The right of citizens of the United States to vote shall not be denied or abridged by the United States or by any state on account of sex.

(24)
The right of citizens of the United States to vote in any primary or other election for President or Vice President, for electors for President or Vice President, or for Senator or Representative in Congress, shall not be denied or abridged by the United States or any state by reason of failure to pay any poll tax or other tax.

(25)
In case of the removal of the President from office or of his death or resignation, the Vice President shall become President.

13. Which of the following statements is best supported by the text?

(1) Congress can only issue new tax laws after each census.
(2) The American people vote on income tax laws every four years.
(3) Almost half of the money in the federal budget comes from personal income tax.
(4) The House of Representatives and the Senate have the power to collect taxes.
(5) Tax laws in the United States can never be changed.

POSTTEST

14. What is another name for Amendment 19, ratified in 1920?

(1) Lame Duck Amendment
(2) Woman Suffrage Amendment
(3) Prohibition of Liquor Amendment
(4) Income Tax Amendment
(5) Rights of Accused Person Amendment

15. What conclusion can be drawn from a reading of Amendment 24?

(1) Individual states should have the right to issue poll taxes.
(2) No state can take away a person's right to vote because of failure to pay a poll tax.
(3) Congress has the power to create a special tax for voters who are new citizens of the United States.
(4) All citizens had to pay a poll tax after the creation of this amendment.
(5) A poll tax was created to finance national campaign expenses.

16. Which of the following facts supports the main idea in Amendment 25?

(1) Lyndon Johnson became president after John Kennedy's assassination.
(2) Franklin D. Roosevelt served more than two terms as president.
(3) Richard Nixon nominated Gerald Ford to office.
(4) Bill Clinton was impeached in 1999.
(5) Grover Cleveland was elected president for a second term.

Questions 17 and 18 refer to the following graph.

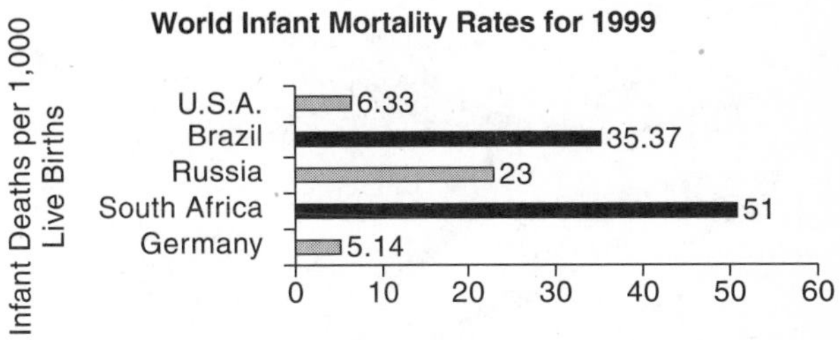

National Center for Health Statistics, U.S. Department of Health and Human Services

17. Which country had the lowest infant mortality rate in 1999?

(1) U.S.A.
(2) Brazil
(3) Russia
(4) South Africa
(5) Germany

18. Based on the information in this bar graph, what conclusion can you draw?

(1) Southern hemisphere countries (Brazil and South Africa) had higher infant mortality rates.
(2) Northern hemisphere countries (U.S.A., Russia, and Germany) had higher infant mortality rates.
(3) Countries with advanced technology had lower infant mortality rates.
(4) Countries with higher populations had greater infant mortality rates.
(5) Countries with smaller populations had greater infant mortality rates.

POSTTEST

Questions 19 and 20 refer to the following map.

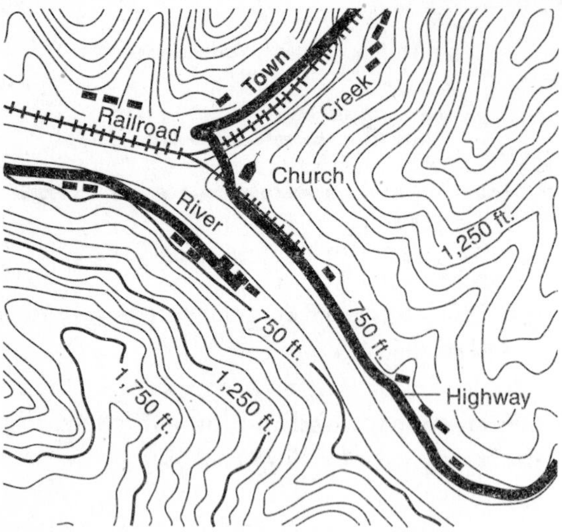

plains—extensive areas with little or no change in elevation
hills—elevations of 500 to 1,000 ft. that have sides sloping up to flat or rounded tops
plateaus—elevations of less than 500 ft. with sides that rise sharply to broad rounded tops
trenches—steep-sided valleys usually associated with plateaus
mountains—elevations of over 1,000 ft., usually with steep rocky inclines on all sides and a pointed or rounded top

19. Based on the land elevations indicated on the map, what is the dominant topographical feature in this area?

(1) plateaus
(2) plains
(3) hills
(4) mountains
(5) river valley

20. The topography shown on this map would most likely apply to which of the following?

(1) the plains of Ohio
(2) the swamp region of Mississippi
(3) the rolling hills of Kentucky
(4) the mountains of West Virginia
(5) the cornfields of Iowa

Question 21 is based on the following passage.

Vice President Andrew Johnson succeeded Lincoln as president after Lincoln's assassination. Johnson was from Tennessee and was the only Southern senator not to join the Confederacy when war broke out. Lincoln had trusted him totally, but many in Congress did not. In spite of Johnson's refusal to join the Confederacy, his every action appeared to be suspiciously pro-South to them.

21. Which of the following actions by Andrew Johnson does *not* support these congressmen's opinion of him?

(1) his issue of a proclamation forgiving most Confederates
(2) his demand that Confederate states ratify the Thirteenth Amendment abolishing slavery
(3) his veto of the civil rights bill that guaranteed rights to freed slaves
(4) his veto of the Freedman's Bureau bill that had been approved without the input of the southern states
(5) his opposition to the Fourteenth Amendment that toughened the stand of Congress against former Confederate loyalists

22. How does a presidential primary election differ from a general election?

(1) A presidential primary is usually of local interest only.
(2) A person does not have to be a registered voter to vote in a primary.
(3) A primary election does not determine who will be the president of the United States.
(4) A primary election determines the number of electoral college votes a particular candidate gets.
(5) A primary election must have only two opposing candidates on the ballot.

POSTTEST

Questions 23–24 are based on the following chart.

Average After-Tax Income in 1977 and 1999

Income Group	1977 Average Income	1999 Average Income
Lowest fifth	$ 10,000	$ 8,800
Second fifth	$ 22,100	$ 20,000
Middle fifth	$ 32,400	$ 31,400
Fourth fifth	$ 42,600	$ 41,500
Highest fifth	$ 74,000	$102,300
Top one percent	$234,700	$515,600

Source: Center on Budget and Policy Priorities (CBPP)

23. The Center on Budget and Policy Priorities (CBPP) breaks the U.S. population into fifths based on the after-tax household income level. Which conclusion can be drawn based on the facts in this chart comparing 1999 to 1977 average income?

(1) The highest-fifth income group demonstrated the greatest increase in earnings.
(2) Only two income groups demonstrated a decline in earnings.
(3) The middle-fifth income group demonstrated more of an increase than the lowest-fifth in earnings.
(4) The top one percent income group's earnings increased more than that of the other income groups.
(5) All income groups increased their average incomes in 1999.

24. Which of the following statements is best supported by the information in the chart?

(1) The government takes the same percentage of taxes every year.
(2) There are more people earning over $500,000 than under $8,000.
(3) The CBPP does not consider after-tax household incomes in this report.
(4) The government takes more taxes from those whose income is in the top one percent.
(5) The gap between the top one percent and the lowest-fifth is substantial and increasing.

POSTTEST

Questions 25–27 are based on the map below.

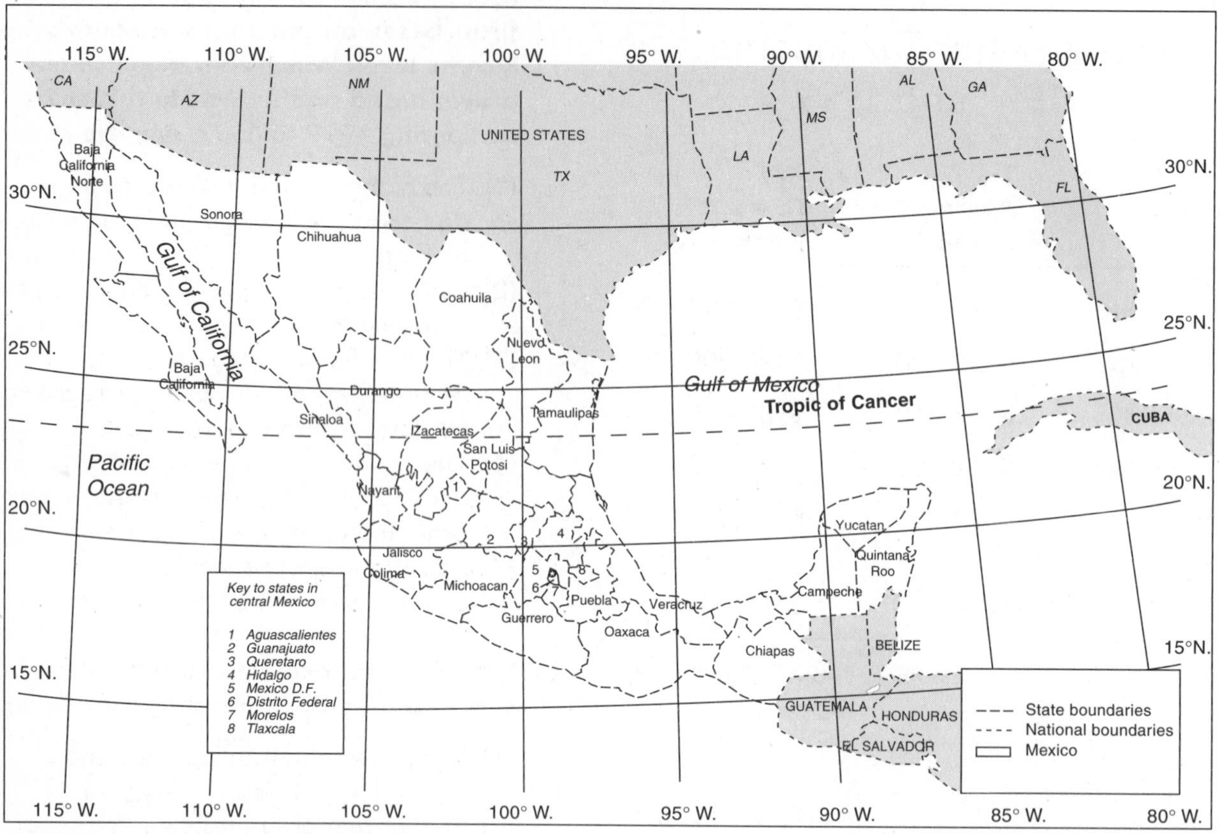

25. Durango, Mexico, is located at 25 degrees north and 105 degrees west. A pilot traveling from Durango to the country of Guatemala would have to follow which instructions as he leaves Durango and travels?

(1) 15 degrees north and 90 degrees west
(2) 10 degrees north and 15 degrees east
(3) 10 degrees south and 90 degrees west
(4) 10 degrees north and 15 degrees west
(5) 10 degrees south and 15 degrees east

26. How would this map be most useful?

(1) identifying political boundaries
(2) developing a highway map
(3) identifying topographical formations
(4) recognizing historical landmarks
(5) identifying population centers

27. Looking from west to east on the map, one hour is added for every 15 degrees. If it is 9:00 P.M. in eastern Arizona, what time would it be on the eastern coast of Florida?

(1) 7:00 P.M.
(2) 8:00 P.M.
(3) 9:00 P.M.
(4) 10:00 P.M.
(5) 11:00 P.M.

POSTTEST

Questions 28 and 29 are based on the graph below.

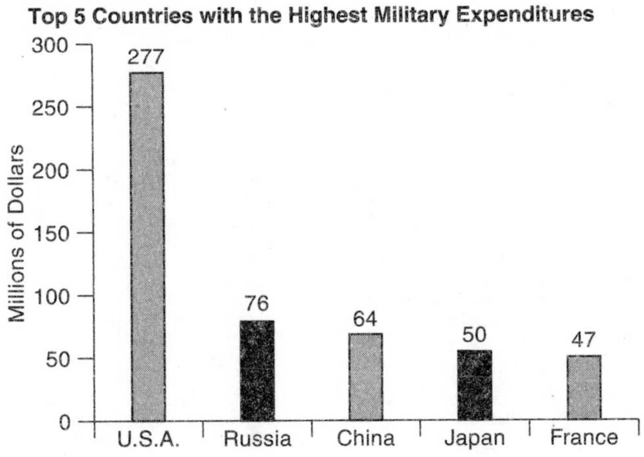

Source: U.S. Dept. of Defense

28. What conclusion can be drawn from the bar graph?

(1) The United States spends over three times as much in military expenditures as Russia.
(2) The countries of central Europe spend over $200 million on maintaining an army.
(3) The United States is the most advanced in its military technology.
(4) Japan and Russia spend the same amount of money on military expenditures.
(5) The United States spends the least amount on military expenditures.

29. What could be the best explanation to support the decision of the United States regarding its military expenditures?

(1) Americans are concerned about being taken over by another country.
(2) Americans are very wealthy and can afford the expenditures.
(3) The United States recruits high school and college students to join its armed forces.
(4) The United States considers itself a world-wide "watch dog" for underprotected countries.
(5) If the United States spends $277 million on defense, no wars will be declared.

30. In recent years, the top two manufacturers of soft drinks, Coca-Cola and PepsiCo, each sought to purchase the number three and four soft drink producers, Dr. Pepper and Seven-Up. However, the Federal Trade Commission prevented the takeover. Why do you think the FTC refused the companies' attempts?

The takeovers would

(1) reduce the quality and variety of the product offered
(2) create a monopoly, concentrating merchandising power in the hands of a single company
(3) interfere with free competition in the soft drink industry among its four largest manufacturers
(4) drive the prices up, forcing consumers to buy fewer soft drinks
(5) force the other smaller, independent bottlers to merge with one of the two giants

POSTTEST

Questions 31–33 are based on the following definitions.

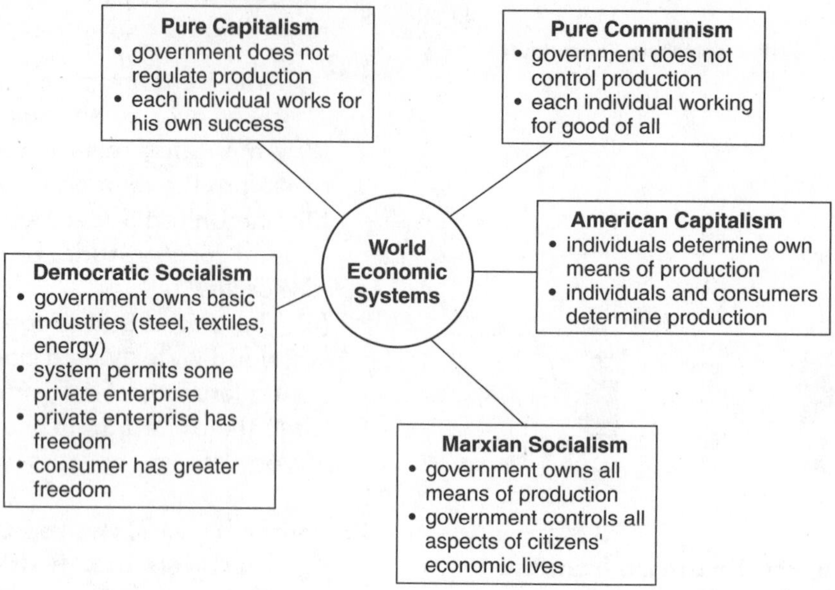
Pure Capitalism
• government does not regulate production
• each individual works for his own success
Pure Communism
• government does not control production
• each individual working for good of all
World Economic Systems
American Capitalism
• individuals determine own means of production
• individuals and consumers determine production
Democratic Socialism
• government owns basic industries (steel, textiles, energy)
• system permits some private enterprise
• private enterprise has freedom
• consumer has greater freedom
Marxian Socialism
• government owns all means of production
• government controls all aspects of citizens' economic lives

31. Using the diagram above, under which economic system would decisions about the production and distribution of goods be determined by a central authority?

(1) pure communism
(2) Marxian socialism
(3) democratic socialism
(4) American capitalism
(5) pure capitalism

32. Biologist Charles Darwin believed that the species that was best able to adapt would continue to exist—survival of the fittest. Under which of the following situations would his theory apply?

(1) Franklin Roosevelt's New Deal and government-funded work programs
(2) Teddy Roosevelt's progressivism and regulation of big business activities
(3) Herbert Hoover's conservatism and noninterference in the affairs of business
(4) Dwight Eisenhower's policies of moderation in defense spending
(5) Lyndon Johnson's Great Society and generous spending for social programs

33. An economic system is designed to meet the needs of the people by establishing production priorities and allocating the limited resources. In which one of the following economic systems would there be the most coordinated use of production facilities while still permitting individual consumer choice?

(1) pure communism
(2) Marxian socialism
(3) democratic socialism
(4) American capitalism
(5) pure capitalism

POSTTEST

Questions 34 and 35 refer to the following map.

Electoral Votes by State

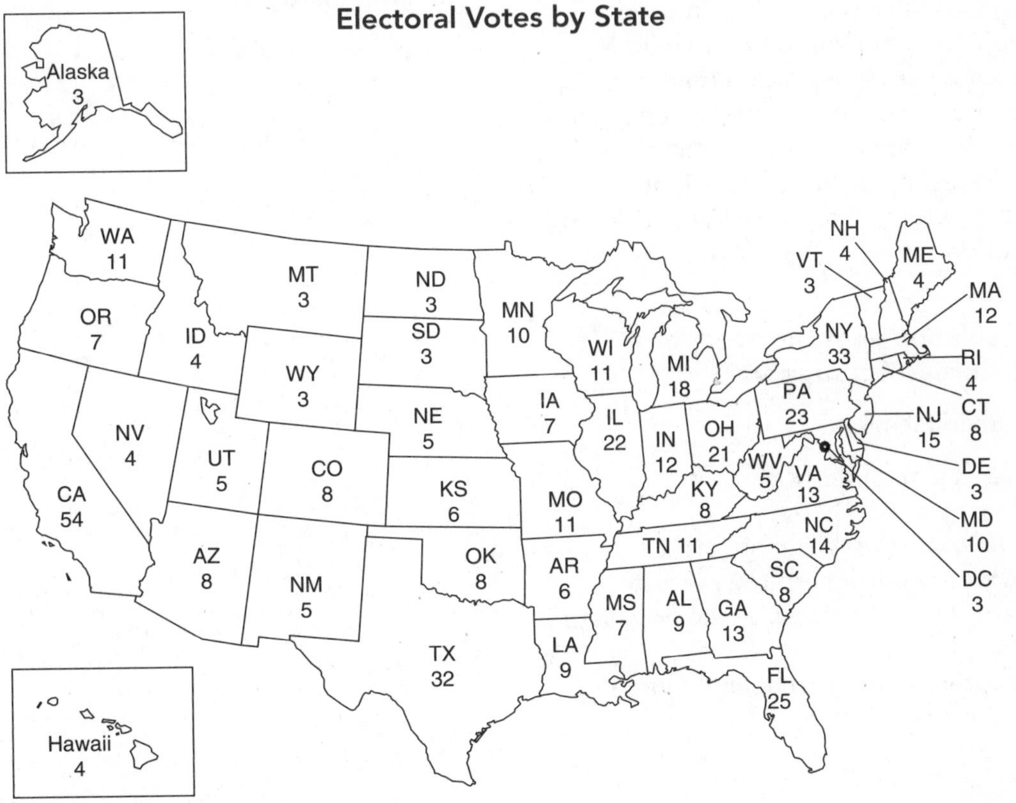

34. Which of the following statements is supported by the information in the map?

(1) Texas has more representatives than any other state.
(2) All the states in the Northeast (such as New York and Pennsylvania) have more representatives than states in the Southeast (such as Georgia and Louisiana).
(3) Hawaii has the fewest number of representatives.
(4) Western states (such as Nevada and California) have gained representatives over the years.
(5) There are 435 members in the House of Representatives.

35. A candidate for president needs 270 electoral votes to be elected. Which group of states would have the largest number of electoral votes?

(1) Nebraska, North Carolina, California
(2) Texas, Ohio, Minnesota
(3) Pennsylvania, Tennessee, Oregon
(4) Wisconsin, Mississippi, Connecticut
(5) Florida, Virginia, New York

POSTTEST

Question 36 is based on the following excerpt.

In 1679 the Habeas Corpus Act in England made it illegal for a person to be retained in prison without a trial. It also ruled that an individual could not be imprisoned twice for the same crime. The writers of the Constitution of the United States also included the rights granted in the Habeas Corpus Act in Article I of the Constitution.

36. What resolution does the need for a Habeas Corpus Act support?

Every individual must

(1) serve as a member of a jury if summoned
(2) pay an excessive bail if arrested
(3) be protected from arbitrary arrest
(4) accept decisions made by the appellate court
(5) be protected from cruel and unusual punishment if arrested

Questions 37 and 38 are based upon the following letter.

U.S. DEPARTMENT OF COMMERCE
BUREAU OF THE CENSUS
WASHINGTON, DC 20233-2000
OFFICE OF THE DIRECTOR

United States Census 2000

March 13, 2000

To all households:

This is your official form for the United States Census 2000. It is used to count every person living in this house or apartment – people of all ages, citizens and non-citizens.

Your answers are important. First, the number of representatives each state has in Congress depends on the number of people living in the state.

The second reason may be more important to you and your community. The amount of government money your neighborhood receives depends on your answers. That money gets used for schools, employment services, housing assistance, roads, services for children and the elderly, and many other local needs.

Your privacy is protected by law (Title 13 of the United States Code), which also requires that you answer these questions. That law ensures that your information is only used for statistical purposes and that no unauthorized person can see your form or find out what you tell us – no other government agency, no court of law, NO ONE.

Please be as accurate and complete as you can in filling out your census form, and return it in the enclosed postage-paid envelope. Thank you.

Sincerely,

Kenneth Prewitt

Kenneth Prewitt
Director
Bureau of the Census

Enclosures

D-16A(L)

Source: U.S. Census Bureau

37. Based on the information in this letter from the Census Bureau what conclusion can you can draw?

(1) Inaccurate responses are customary and permitted by the government.
(2) Senior citizens are exempt from completing and submitting their census form.
(3) Some Americans fail to complete and submit their census forms.
(4) The census is taken every year in the United States.
(5) The official census form is issued by the state government.

POSTTEST

38. Which of the following arguments would best persuade an individual to accurately fill out his census form?

(1) The census helps the government allocate revenue for community needs for all Americans.
(2) The Census provides valuable statistics for Internal Revenue Service Employees.
(3) The census provides numerous benefits only for citizens of the United States.
(4) The census offers employment services for single-family homeowners.
(5) The census presents lawyers with significant documentation for public use.

39. In 1972 eighteen-year-olds were given the right to vote. This occurrence is an example of which of the following methods to effect changes in our system of government?

(1) a United States Court decision
(2) a law enacted by both houses of Congress
(3) an amendment to the United States Constitution
(4) an executive order from the President of the United States
(5) a consensus of the legislatures in the fifty states

Question 40 is based on the following excerpt.

Ellis Island is a symbol of America's immigrant heritage. For more than six decades—1892 to 1954—the immigrant depot processed the greatest tide of incoming humanity in the nation's history. Some twelve million people landed here; today their descendents account for almost 40% of the country's population. Opened on January 1, 1892, Ellis Island ushered in a new era of immigration with each newcomer's eligibility to land now determined by federal law. The government established a special bureau to process the record numbers that were arriving at the end of the 19th century. Fleeing hardships such as poverty, religious persecution, or political unrest in their homelands, they journeyed to the United States in search of freedom and opportunity. More than 70% landed in New York, the country's largest port. First and second class passengers were processed on board ship, but third or steerage class were ferried to Ellis Island where they underwent medical and legal examinations in the main building.

—Excerpted from "Ellis Island," National Monument New York, U.S. Department of the Interior National Park Service by Brian Feeney

Library of Congress

40. Which of the following is a clear implication of the passage?

(1) All immigrants were detained at Ellis Island.
(2) Ellis Island was the gateway to America for many immigrants.
(3) Most of the immigrants that arrived at Ellis Island were from the Middle East.
(4) The government did not need to open an immigration center on Ellis Island.
(5) All passengers underwent legal examinations on Ellis Island.

POSTTEST

41. The United States has put quotas (limits) on the number of automobiles that foreign countries can export to America. Which of the following is a belief that helps to justify the quotas?

(1) American manufacturers must be protected from unfair competition.
(2) Exporting automobiles should not cost more than exporting other products.
(3) Foreign manufacturers deserve to meet their own business needs.
(4) The dollar amount of trade between other car-manufacturing countries is too low.
(5) There should be no demand for foreign cars by American consumers.

42. The fact that the U.S. Constitution can be amended is the basis for what belief of the Founding Fathers?

(1) They made legislative mistakes in the original writing.
(2) They acknowledged their lack of writing skills in framing the constitution.
(3) They accounted for any further changes in values and needs of the American people.
(4) They included this power as required by the Supreme Court.
(5) They considered all possible circumstances in the original Constitution.

Question 43 is based on the following cartoon.

"Great news! The shareholders have approved your heart bypass!"

Bruce Beattie, Copley News Service

43. What is the main idea of the cartoon?

(1) Corporate shareholders influence health care expenditures in America.
(2) Only elderly patients have HMOs in the United States.
(3) Doctors are benefiting financially from corporate health care.
(4) Americans in general are concerned about the cost of health care.
(5) Corporate health care managers are not covering major health problems.

POSTTEST

Questions 44-46 are based on the following cartoon.

Rube Goldberg reprinted by permission of United Feature Syndicate, Inc.

44. What would the reader infer to be the main idea of this cartoon?

Television

(1) portrays an accurate picture of a presidential candidate
(2) enhances characteristics that may not be important for the presidency
(3) allows voters to fairly judge a candidate's character
(4) attracts more viewers of a particular gender
(5) predicts how a candidate will perform in office

45. Since 1952, politicians have relied on television to educate the American public. Which argument could be best used by a campaign manager to support the need for extra funds for televised broadcasts?

American viewers are

(1) easily influenced by what they see on television
(2) rarely persuaded by the debates on television
(3) always entertained by the commercials during television broadcasts
(4) only interested in speaking with the candidates directly
(5) only concerned with watching sporting events in the Fall

46. Americans viewed the first presidential debate between candidates in 1960. Fifty-seven percent of the people voting in this election felt that viewing the debates affected their choice of candidate. Radio listeners, on the other hand, were not as confident with the outcome of the debate. What qualities of a candidate would be highlighted in a television broadcast but not as well in a radio broadcast?

(1) sense of humor
(2) awareness of foreign policy
(3) intelligence and verbal expression
(4) confidence and poise
(5) ability to secure party support

POSTTEST

Question 47 is based on the following map.

Modern Middle East

47. What conclusion can you draw about the distribution of oil-producing areas in the Middle East?

(1) The distribution of crude oil is not uniform throughout the Middle East.
(2) The amount of oil available is dependent upon the size of the country.
(3) The major oil-producing areas are all located on the coast of the Black Sea.
(4) The Middle East produces more oil than the United States.
(5) The amount of oil produced is not determined by the size of the country.

POSTTEST

Question 48 is based on the following excerpt.

. . . millions of other women were experiencing their own unique odysseys at home as a result of the gender climate changes brought on by the demand for men in fighting jobs. In fact, there were 350,000 women in uniform and estimated 6.5 million at work in war-related jobs on the home front. Harder to measure but equally important were the contributions of the women who stayed home, raised the children, taught school, clerked in schools and banks, kept the fabric of society together. At night they went to bed wondering if their sons or husbands were safe in those far-off places where they were fighting for their lives every day. All these experiences—for the women in uniform, for those assembling airplanes or ships, for the women who kept families and communities together—shaped that generation of women as much as combat shaped the men of their time. . . .

—Excerpted from "Women in Uniform and Out" in *The Greatest Generation* by Tom Brokaw

48. The following quotations are also from Tom Brokaw's book, *The Greatest Generation.* Which does not support the author's opinion as stated in the passage?

(1) "A full-blown spirit of patriotism was in every heart." Marion Rivers Nittel
(2) "You had to do your part." Alison Ely Campbell
(3) "Everyone should learn the meaning of that famous little four-letter word—Work." Bob Bush
(4) "The one time the Nation got together was WWII. We stood as one. We spoke as one. We clenched our fists as one." Daniel Inouye
(5) "We were trained so well I didn't believe anything could kill us." Leonard Lovell

POSTTEST

Question 49 is based on the following map.

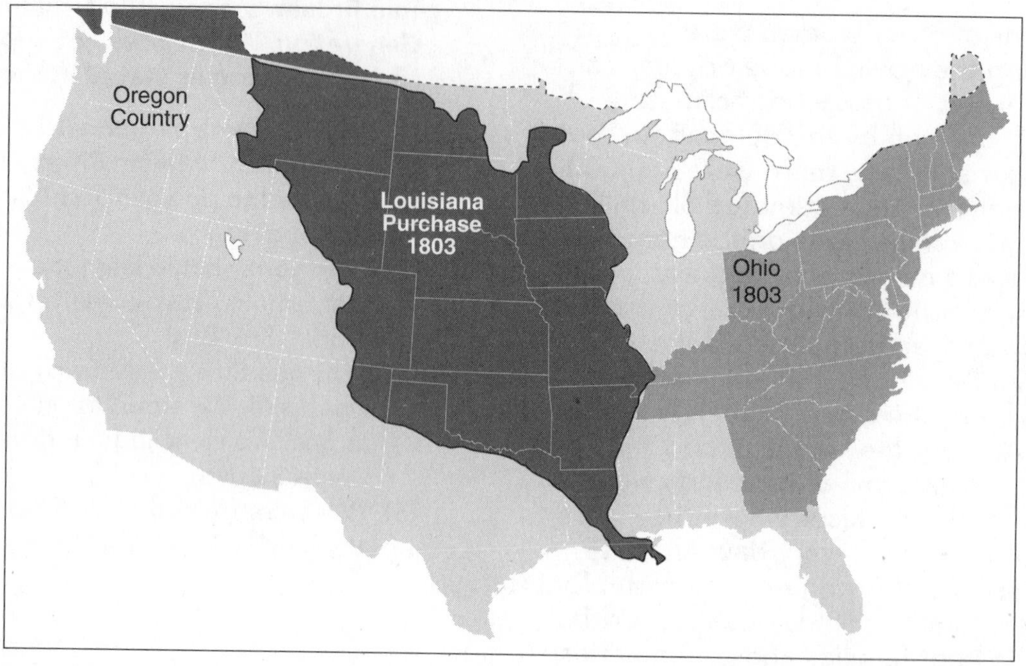

In 1803, France agreed to sell over 800,000 square miles of Louisiana territory to the United States for $15 million. The purchase of the Louisiana Territory increased the national debt of the United States, but it also doubled the size of the nation.

49. Which of the following statements best helps to explain the decision of the United States to purchase the Louisiana Territory and is supported by the information provided?

(1) The Louisiana Territory was inexpensive, and the United States needed to spend its budget surplus.
(2) The United States wanted to expand its territory westward in order to increase the size of the nation.
(3) Americans needed to purchase the Louisiana Territory in order to preserve its culture and traditions.
(4) The United States wanted to expand its territory westward in order to improve relations with the local Native American tribes.
(5) The purchase of the Louisiana Territory was essential for the United States to gain access to the Atlantic Ocean.

POSTTEST

Question 50 is based on the following pictures.

© The Granger Collection, New York

© The Granger Collection, New York

50. What argument would the presidents of the Union Pacific and the Central Pacific railroads have used to justify expenses incurred throughout the creation of the transcontinental railroad?

The transcontinental railroad would allow for

(1) affordable travel for all Americans
(2) improved relations with Native Americans
(3) industrial growth throughout the United States
(4) increased job security for all railroad employees
(5) pleasant working conditions for immigrant railroad laborers

POSTTEST

Social Studies Answer Key

1. **Comprehension (2)** To balance any financial account is to ensure that your spending does not exceed what you earn.

2. **Comprehension (1)** By representing the budget as a boat that is positioned over a wave, the cartoonist is making a statement about the changeable nature of the economy. The budget could be said to be in a stable position that is only temporary. The cartoonist wants to alert people to the fact that the economy is very changeable and that the budget needs to be carefully watched as the economy changes.

3. **Comprehension (4)** The Second Continental Congress, made up of representatives from the original thirteen colonies, is giving a declaration of its intention to decree independence from England. After that time, a convention of representatives was gathered to create a constitution that the new independent government could use as an outline in the formation of the laws of this new country. The House of Representatives was not created until after the Constitution called for the three separate branches of government.

4. **Evaluation (2)** In declaring the colonies separate from England, the representatives are declaring themselves to be a new nation. This new nation was to be governed by those that live in the nation and have a personal investment in how the new nation is governed.

5. **Application (5)** The change for both groups seems to be a slow increase. This would mean that an increase to 2 percent for those over 85 years of age is likely as well as an increase for the age group of 65 years and older. It would seem more likely that the increase for the 65 and older age group might be more realistically 15 percent, given growth in the past. It is not likely that the statistics for the 65 and older age group would jump up to 30 percent.

6. **Application (4)** If liberals are for limited military sepending, then the Star Wars defense program would not be something they would financially support.

7. **Analysis (4)** The graph states that it would be most likely that the 53-year-old would volunteer more. The graph gives no information about occupation or financial situation with regard to volunteerism.

8. **Comprehension (5)** The information does not indicate that child care is under the authority of any of these branches of the government. The legislative branch covers the printing of money and raising an army (choices 1 and 3). The executive branch collects taxes (choice 2). The judicial branch settles the problems between states (choice 4).

9. **Evaluation (1)** Because the people of a state elect the members of Congress (House of Representatives and the Senate), this branch can best determine the sentiments of the people of this nation and would represent their opinions about declaring war better than a single president.

10. **Analysis (2)** The information in the paragraph mentions that the anthropologist studies human skeletal remains while the archaeologist studies the artifacts. In this case the remains on the Yucatán Peninsula would be the discovery that would involve the anthropologist.

11. **Analysis (3)** The computer would be the best choice for the late 20th century United States. The other artifacts are from a much earlier time period in U.S. history.

12. **Analysis (2)** The graph tells us that there are fewer people per computer in the public schools than there were in the past. It does not indicate why the ratio has changed. There is no information regarding finances or technology.

13. **Analysis (4)** The amendments listed do not address the census and tax laws. Amendment 16 states that Congress has the power to lay and collect taxes on income.

14. **Comprehension (2)** The women's suffrage movement was created by women interested in having equal say in the running of the government. Suffragettes fought to have the right to vote for elected officials, which up to this time had been denied them.

15. **Analysis (2)** The ability to vote and to participate in the government of the United States is deemed a right granted to every citizen. The right to vote is not dependent on current financial status.

16. **Analysis (1)** The automatic change in leadership ensures that the United States is never without an active president and military leader.

17. **Comprehension (5)** The mortality rate for Germany is 5.14. This mortality rate is lower than the other nations listed including the United States.

18. **Analysis (1)** This is the only logical conclusion that can be inferred from the information presented in the graph. While some of the other choices may be true, you cannot determine this from looking at the graph.

19. **Comprehension (4)** The contour lines in the map show a substantial difference in elevation. The terms as defined indicate that the landforms would be designated as mountains and not hills. Many contour lines would also indicate that the area does not contain plains or plateaus.

20. **Application (4)** Plains, swamps, and cornfields are flat landform areas. This map shows enough change of elevation that these landforms are more accurately designated as mountains and not hills.

21. **Evaluation (2)** By demanding that the Confederate states ratify the Thirteenth Amendment, President Johnson is showing what is considered to be a strong pro-North attitude. The other responses support a pro-South attitude.

22. **Comprehension (3)** The president of the United States is determined only by a general election. The primary election determines what candidate a political party chooses to run in the general election.

23. **Analysis (4)** The chart shows that the income of the top one-percent increased more than $280,000. The lowest fifth, second fifth, and the middle fifth all had a decrease in income from 1977 to 1999. The fourth fifth had a decrease of $2,500.

24. **Analysis (5)** The chart does not give any information about taxes with respect to these groups. The chart also does not give us information concerning how many people are involved in each of the groups. This chart does highlight the difference in the range of incomes from highest to lowest and demonstrates that the lower groups are earning less while the higher income groups continue to earn much more.

25. **Application (5)** Since Guatemala is south and east of the starting point in central Mexico, only choice 5 gives directions for travel both south and east.

26. **Application (1)** This map clearly indicates political regions in Mexico as well as southern states in the United States and Central American country borders.

27. **Application (5)** Florida is 30 degrees east of Arizona. This means that there are two time zones between the two areas; therefore, it would be two hours later in Florida.

28. **Analysis (1)** The United States spends 277 million dollars in military expenditures, and this is clearly more than three times the 76 million that Russia spends on its military.

29. Analysis (1) In spending so much money on its military, the United States demonstrates a priority on its defense. It can be assumed that to place such an importance on defense, there must be a fear that such a defense might be needed against invasion.

30. Analysis (3) The takeovers would allow the top two soft drink companies to be in control of the third and fourth soda producers. This would greatly limit the competition in the soft drink industry.

31. Application (2) Marxian socialism gives the control of all means of production to the government. The other economic systems allow for individual businesses to compete in product development and marketing.

32. Application (3) Under the theory that the strongest survive, governments would not create the social support systems mentioned in choices 1 and 5. Moderation in spending (choice 4) also limits the ability to create a very strong military. If there is a belief in noninterference in business, then the stronger business will be successful. This is possibly at the cost of smaller businesses, which is in keeping with the philosophy expressed by Darwin.

33. Application (3) Democratic socialism controls the main resource industries, while allowing some private enterprise. The consumer has greater freedom under this economic system than other socialist systems.

34. Analysis (2) In spite of the continued popularity of relocating in the South for business, climate, or retirement, a large percentage of the population is still concentrated in the Northeast.

35. Application (1) Nebraska, North Carolina and California together would have the most electoral votes at 73. The next highest group of states would be Florida, Virginia and New York with 71 electoral votes.

36. Analysis (3) Any citizen accused of a crime gets an opportunity to face the accuser and be informed of the crime for which he/she is accused before being held by police.

37. Analysis (3) The government has attempted to create awareness in the need for accurate reporting of the census. Information is given to all the households concerning the need to identify the population in all areas so that federal funds are dispensed fairly.

38. Evaluation (1) Studies show that more people respond to a statistical survey if they can see an advantage for themselves or a benefit for their community. This document clearly indicates that correct reporting of an individual area will entitle the area to greater funds for schools, roads, and social service groups. The benefits are for all residents, not just the citizens of the United States.

39. Analysis (3) Constitutional changes throughout the years have allowed women to vote. Later changes allowed those who are eighteen years old and, therefore, eligible to serve in the armed forces a vote, thereby giving them a voice in their country's government.

40. Comprehension (2) Ellis Island was the gateway to the United States for many immigrants, but it was only one of several ports of entry. Not all immigrants had to be processed on the island; those passengers in first or second class were processed on board the ship. Those processed on Ellis Island came from a great variety of foreign lands.

41. Evaluation (1) The government has a responsibility first to the industries that support the economy of our own nation. In many cases, foreign automobile manufacturers have built plants in the United States. By building the foreign cars here and using American laborers, foreign companies have decreased the concern that the selling of foreign cars in the United States competes too much with American corporations.

42. **Evaluation (3)** The creators of the Constitution realized they could not foresee all the possible situations that might challenge their new democratic country. They created a system that would allow for these adjustments but required that changes would oblige a large percentage of the representative government to agree to the Constitutional amendments.

43. **Analysis (1)** HMOs have been accused of placing the monetary benefits of health care above the medical needs of the patient. Since the HMOs are at the mercy of their stockholders to show profits, expenditures may be limited to allow for greater profits.

44. **Comprehension (2)** Television gives the voters a chance to see the candidates in a presidential election as well as hear their views on the issues. Candidates are aware that many voters are swayed by appearance and personality traits that are accentuated by television. A candidate might hire a professional to assist in creating an image on the television that will make him or her more appealing to the viewers.

45. **Evaluation (1)** Since television has become an important source of information for the voting public, campaign managers are aware that it is important to budget enough money for quality advertising production and to buy effective broadcast time slots.

46. **Analysis (4)** The first television debate was between Richard M. Nixon and John F. Kennedy. Political scholars often refer to this famous debate because it became a contest of public opinion of appearances. Kennedy, who was a younger, more physically attractive candidate, appeared calm and confident. Nixon, who perspired under the harsh lights, appeared nervous and, therefore, slightly dishonest. The main lesson learned by those who are seeking public office was that the value of appearances might equal the opinions on the issues of any candidate.

47. **Analysis (1)** The deposits of oil are determined by processes of nature and are not impacted by political borders. The deposits are not given any production values and cannot be compared to deposits found elsewhere.

48. **Evaluation (5)** All the other responses were similar in their support of teamwork and a cooperative united American spirit that kept the country together while the United States sent troops to fight overseas in World War II.

49. **Evaluation (2)** Expansion of territory has always tempted nations. At this time, the United States was expanding in population and many people wanted to venture out into the new frontier to farm and build ranches. This led to conflicts with the native tribes, but the United States was willing to go to war over its interests in expanding territory and resources.

50. **Evaluation (3)** Businesses in the West were unsatisfied with transporting raw materials and products by shipping around the southern tip of South America or through Panama. A railway system that connected the two sides of the nation was an eventual necessity for a country with a growing economy. It wasn't until much later that railways were used as a form of travel for enjoyment.

Evaluation Chart

Use the answer key on pages 984–987 to check your answers to the Posttest. Then find the item number of each question you missed and circle it on the chart below to determine the Social Studies content areas in which you need more practice. Pay particular attention to areas where you missed half or more of the questions. Numbers in boldface indicate questions based on graphics. The page numbers for the content areas are listed on the chart below. For those questions that you missed, review the skill pages indicated.

SKILL AREA/ CONTENT AREA	COMPREHENSION (pages 217–230)	APPLICATION (pages 231–236)	ANALYSIS (pages 237–262)	EVALUATION (pages 271–274)
World History (pages 297–326)	**17**	**31, 32, 33**	10, 11, **18,**	
U.S. History (pages 327–366)	3, **14,** 40, **44**		**13, 15, 16,** 37, **46**	4, 21, 38, 48, **49, 50**
Civics and Government (pages 367–398)	**8,** 22	6, **35**	**7, 34,** 36, 39	**9,** 42, **45**
Economics (pages 399–426)	**1, 2**		**12, 23, 24, 28, 29,** 30, **43**	41
Geography (pages 427–443)	**19**	**5, 20, 25, 26, 27**	**47**	

POSTTEST

Science

The Science Posttest consists of 50 multiple-choice questions. The questions are based on graphs, maps, tables, diagrams, editorial cartoons, and reading passages. Answer each question as carefully as possible, choosing the best of five answer choices and blackening in the grid. If you find a question too difficult, do not waste time on it. Work ahead and come back to it later when you can think it through carefully.

You should take approximately 80 minutes to complete this test. At the end of 80 minutes, stop and mark your place. Then finish the test. This will give you an idea of whether or not you can finish the real GED Test in the time allotted. Try to answer as many questions as you can. A blank will count as a wrong answer, so make a reasonable guess for answers to questions of which you are not sure.

When you are finished with the test, check your answers and turn to the Evaluation Chart on page 1014. Use the chart to evaluate whether or not you are ready to take the actual GED Test and, if not, in what areas you need more work.

Science Posttest Answer Grid

1	①	②	③	④	⑤	18	①	②	③	④	⑤	35	①	②	③	④	⑤
2	①	②	③	④	⑤	19	①	②	③	④	⑤	36	①	②	③	④	⑤
3	①	②	③	④	⑤	20	①	②	③	④	⑤	37	①	②	③	④	⑤
4	①	②	③	④	⑤	21	①	②	③	④	⑤	38	①	②	③	④	⑤
5	①	②	③	④	⑤	22	①	②	③	④	⑤	39	①	②	③	④	⑤
6	①	②	③	④	⑤	23	①	②	③	④	⑤	40	①	②	③	④	⑤
7	①	②	③	④	⑤	24	①	②	③	④	⑤	41	①	②	③	④	⑤
8	①	②	③	④	⑤	25	①	②	③	④	⑤	42	①	②	③	④	⑤
9	①	②	③	④	⑤	26	①	②	③	④	⑤	43	①	②	③	④	⑤
10	①	②	③	④	⑤	27	①	②	③	④	⑤	44	①	②	③	④	⑤
11	①	②	③	④	⑤	28	①	②	③	④	⑤	45	①	②	③	④	⑤
12	①	②	③	④	⑤	29	①	②	③	④	⑤	46	①	②	③	④	⑤
13	①	②	③	④	⑤	30	①	②	③	④	⑤	47	①	②	③	④	⑤
14	①	②	③	④	⑤	31	①	②	③	④	⑤	48	①	②	③	④	⑤
15	①	②	③	④	⑤	32	①	②	③	④	⑤	49	①	②	③	④	⑤
16	①	②	③	④	⑤	33	①	②	③	④	⑤	50	①	②	③	④	⑤
17	①	②	③	④	⑤	34	①	②	③	④	⑤						

POSTTEST

Choose the *best* answer to each question that follows.

Question 1 refers to the following cartoon.

Malcom Mayes/artizans.com

1. Which of the following environmental concerns does not support the main idea of this cartoon that people are observing unusual weather patterns?

(1) an increase in carbon dioxide in the air
(2) cutting down the rain forest
(3) forest fires in western states
(4) overharvesting of seafood species
(5) burning of fossil fuels around the world

2. As many as twenty-five persons can benefit from a single organ and tissue donor. Thousands of people are in need of an organ or tissue transplant, and anyone, regardless of age, race, or gender can be a donor. Organs that can't be placed are often used for research on a variety of diseases and conditions. Which of the following body parts is a tissue that could be used in a transplant?

(1) heart
(2) kidney
(3) cornea
(4) pancreas
(5) lungs

Questions 3 and 4 refer to the following diagram.

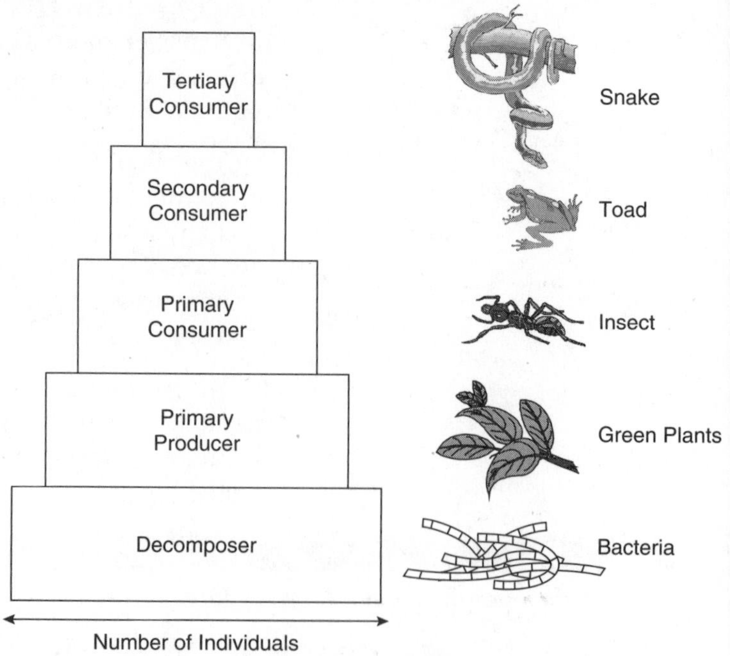

3. The illustration proves the well-known fact that which of the following forms the largest group in the animal world?

(1) amphibians
(2) insects
(3) mammals
(4) birds
(5) reptiles

4. How would the South American boa constrictor, which eats amphibians, be categorized in this ecosystem?

(1) decomposer
(2) primary producer
(3) primary consumer
(4) secondary consumer
(5) tertiary consumer

POSTTEST

Question 5 is based on the following passage.

Cathie remembers feeling exceptionally exhausted and irritable every January. After years of struggling with this "winter depression," Cathie went to talk to a physician about her health concerns. She was diagnosed as having *Seasonal Affective Disorder*, or SAD. Millions of Americans are also affected by this disease, which causes anxiety, fatigue, and food cravings. SAD is associated with lower intensity and abbreviated periods of sunshine. The dark, gloomy hours of winter along with the shortened days cause this disorder to be the most severe from November through March. People who suffer from Seasonal Affective Disorder claim to find relief with exercise and bright-light therapies.

5. Based on the passage, where in the United States would a physician encounter the *most* cases of SAD?

(1) southern Florida
(2) northern Minnesota
(3) eastern Virginia
(4) western Iowa
(5) southwestern Arizona

Question 6 is based on the following passage.

Fat can be defined loosely as a source for energy storage in the human body. The human anatomy is designed to carry food reserves to ensure the body's survival when food becomes scarce. However, in our slim-conscious society, many people go to great lengths to keep fat from accumulating on their bodies, sometimes with harmful effects.

Fat is more efficient in storing energy than carbohydrates for several reasons. First, fat is a highly concentrated energy source. Second, fat weighs less than the same energy amount of carbohydrates. Third, fat is much more efficient to carry as an energy source because it does not hold water as do carbohydrates. For example, an average 70-kilogram human male normally has about 11 kilograms of fat in his body. This fat represents enough stored energy to keep him alive for a month without eating. The same amount of energy stored as starch would double his body weight.

6. Which view does the passage support?

(1) Being obese is healthier than being underweight.
(2) Reserves of fat serve no purpose in the human body.
(3) Excessive dieting can be detrimental to one's health.
(4) Fats lead to high levels of cholesterol.
(5) One heavy meal each day suffices for usual intake.

POSTTEST

Question 7 refers to the following information.

soil conservationist	assists government agencies, industries, and private individuals in the area of soil and water conservation, insect control, and land use
hydrologist	studies the surface of the earth and underground waters
meteorologist	works with the atmosphere
astronomer	studies objects and matter *beyond* Earth's atmosphere
tectonophysicist	studies the structural features of the Earth

7. There are many careers in the area of earth science. In which of the careers above would you study seismic waves and the epicenters of earthquakes?

(1) soil conservationist
(2) tectonophysicist
(3) meteorologist
(4) astronomer
(5) hydrologist

Questions 8 and 9 are based on the following passage.

Although most animals and some plants detect and respond to sound vibrations, the precise sensitivity that we call *hearing* is rare in the living world. It is highly developed only in birds and mammals, and the same operational system applies in all vertebrate auditory systems. Sound waves cause a liquid within the organism's auditory apparatus to vibrate. These vibrations are picked up by receptors that transmit signals to nerve cells. These cells then communicate the sound to the brain. Humans can hear *vibrational frequencies* of 20 to 20,000 cycles per second; cats respond to frequencies of up to 50,000 cycles per second; and porpoises and bats pick up frequencies of 100,000 cycles per second.

8. Which statement does the passage support?

(1) Humans have the best hearing of all animals.
(2) Cats and porpoises are adapted to hearing low frequencies.
(3) Ears are damaged by high frequencies.
(4) Some frequencies are beyond the human hearing range.
(5) Invertebrates have better "hearing" systems than vertebrates.

9. If subjected to sound frequencies of 25,000 to 100,000 cycles per second, which of the following would be *least* affected?

(1) a porpoise
(2) a house cat
(3) a cheetah
(4) a bat
(5) a human being

POSTTEST

Question 10 is based on the following picture.

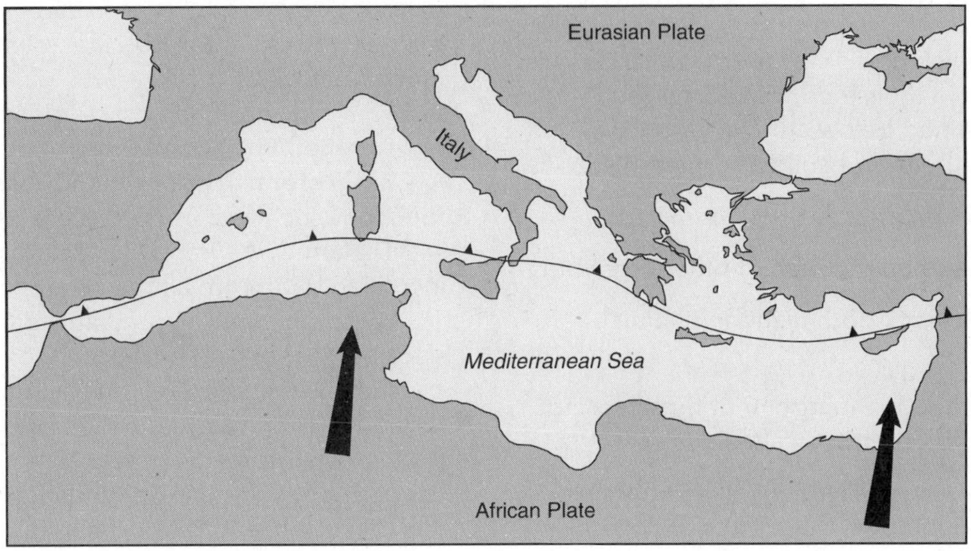

10. Which of the following hypotheses is possible if the African plate continues to push toward the Eurasian plate?

(1) Italy will become less mountainous.
(2) The Mediterranean Sea will decrease in size.
(3) The Alps will not be affected.
(4) A volcano will definitely erupt in Italy.
(5) The Mediterranean Sea will increase in depth.

POSTTEST

Question 11 is based on the following information.

One way in which organisms are classified is by how they obtain their food for energy use. Listed and defined below are five categories that describe the food habits of organisms.

herbivore—feeds directly on plant matter

carnivore—feeds on the flesh of other organisms

omnivore—includes both plant and animal matter in its diet

parasite—obtains its nourishment by attaching itself to another organism, called a *host*

decomposer—usually lives in soil and obtains food by breaking down the wastes and remains of other organisms

11. Based on the information above, what would be the relationship between a flea and its canine or feline victim?

(1) prey-predator
(2) organism-decomposer
(3) parasite-host
(4) herbivore-carnivore
(5) omnivore-carnivore

Question 12 is based on the following information.

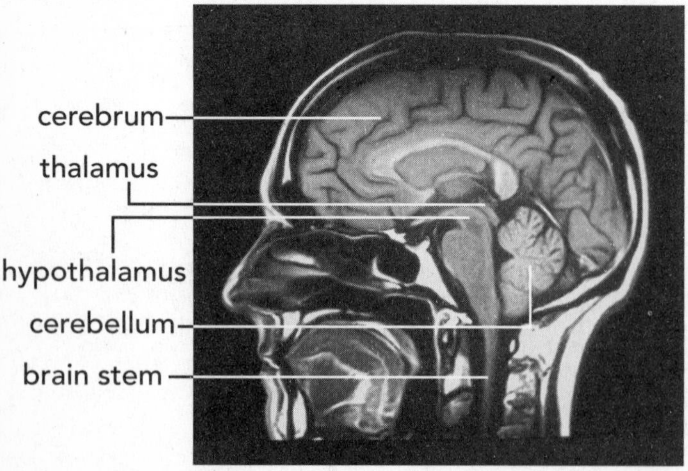

© UHB Trust/Stone

Though the brain represents less than 2 percent of your body weight, it uses 25 percent of the oxygen you breathe and 70 percent of your glucose supply.

The brain has five basic regions:

Cerebellum. Coordinates body movement.

Brain stem. Responsible for basic life functions such as blood pressure and breathing.

Thalamus. A Grand Central relay station for incoming data from all the senses except smell.

Hypothalamus. A regulator of hunger, thirst, sleep, sexuality, and emotions.

Cerebrum. Our gray matter, home to thought, vision, language memory, emotions. It's divided into hemispheres. If you're right-handed, odds are the right hemisphere is where you make sense of music, images, space, emotions. Your left hemisphere is apt to focus on math, language, speech. In left-handed people, tasks are usually reversed.

The brain works via the communication of nerve cells along complicated circuit patterns that register on encephalograms as brain waves, including the relaxed "alpha waves" so beloved by meditators.

12. What conclusion can you draw from the information provided about the brain?

(1) An injury to the brain stem may result in sensory dysfunction.
(2) Eating disorders do not involve testing on any regions of the brain.
(3) All regions of the brain are essential for normal human function.
(4) The brain uses a higher percentage of oxygen than any other organ.
(5) The cerebrum is the most essential region of the brain.

POSTTEST

Question 13 is based on the following information.

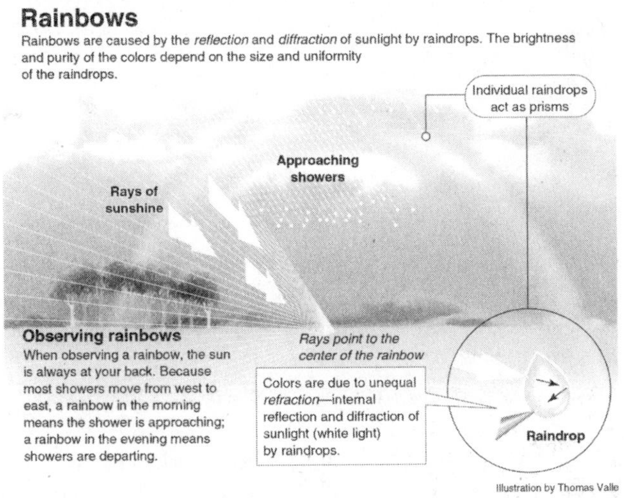
Rainbows
Rainbows are caused by the *reflection* and *diffraction* of sunlight by raindrops. The brightness and purity of the colors depend on the size and uniformity of the raindrops.
Individual raindrops act as prisms
Approaching showers
Rays of sunshine
Observing rainbows
When observing a rainbow, the sun is always at your back. Because most showers move from west to east, a rainbow in the morning means the shower is approaching; a rainbow in the evening means showers are departing.
Rays point to the center of the rainbow
Colors are due to unequal *refraction*—internal reflection and diffraction of sunlight (white light) by raindrops.
Raindrop
Illustration by Thomas Valle

Source: *Chicago Tribune* June 13, 2000.
Courtesy, Thomas Valle

13. According to the information provided, what conclusion can be drawn about rainbows?

(1) All rainbows are equal in color intensity and dimension.
(2) The absorption and retention of light make up the first stage in the creation of a rainbow.
(3) A rainbow usually occurs when the sun is setting.
(4) A rainbow always occurs at the end of a powerful storm.
(5) Refraction, reflection, and diffraction of light are essential in the formation of a rainbow.

Question 14 is based on the following diagram.

Pea Plants

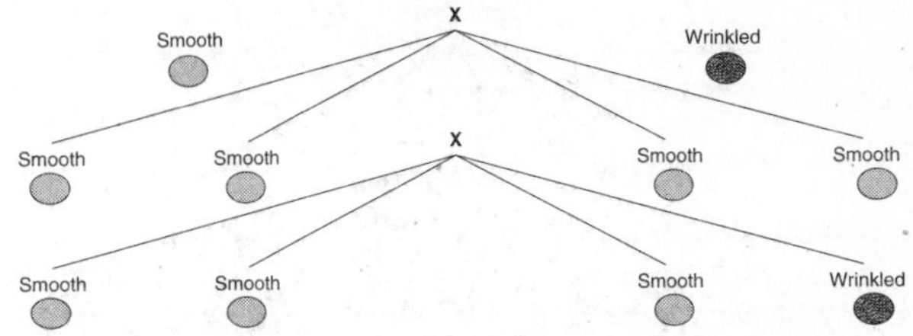
Smooth
X
Wrinkled
Smooth
Smooth
X
Smooth
Smooth
Smooth
Smooth
Smooth
Wrinkled

14. Based on the information above, what would a geneticist say about the example of the pea plants?

(1) It has no relationship to human transmission of traits.
(2) It is true only in the plant world.
(3) It helps show transmission of traits from parents to offspring.
(4) It is too dated to have application in today's world.
(5) It is based purely on chance.

POSTTEST

Question 15 is based on the following information.

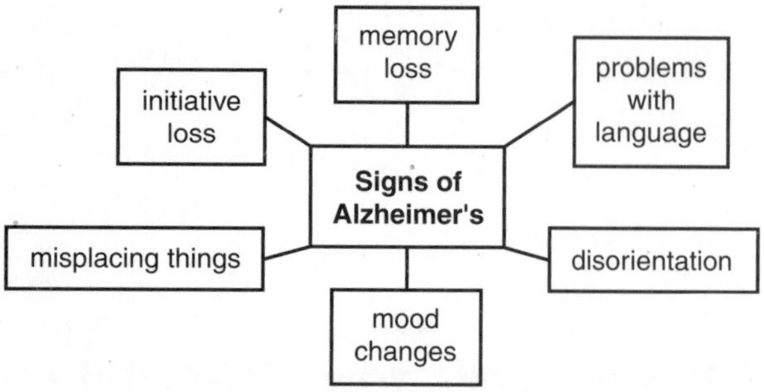

15. Alzheimer's disease is a degenerative brain disorder that affects more than four million Americans. Neuroscientists have many theories about the causes of Alzheimer's and are searching for clues as to causes of the neuronal destruction of the brain in this disease. Which of the following factors would *not* contribute to a loss of brain function?

(1) stroke
(2) head trauma
(3) clogged arteries
(4) aging
(5) arthritis

Question 16 is based on the diagram and the information below.

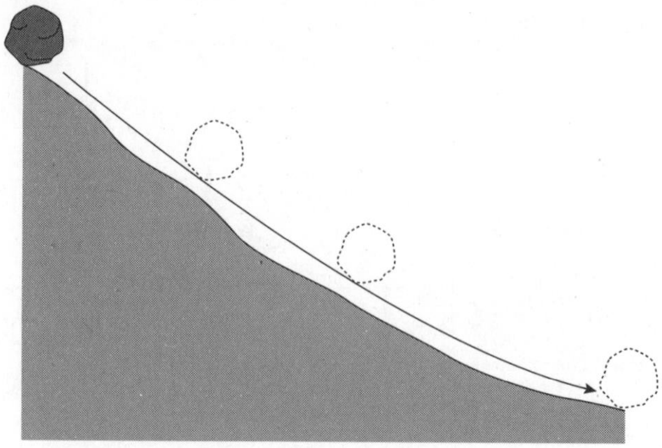

Mechanical energy is classified in two ways: energy waiting to be used and energy causing action. When an object is at rest at a place from which it can move, it is said to have *potential energy*. One example is the rock illustrated in the diagram; the higher the rock sits on the hill, the greater the potential energy. Other examples are an idling car, a ball in one's hand, or a cocked pistol.

Kinetic energy is the energy of motion. Once an object is upset from its position and set into motion, the potential energy is converted to kinetic energy. Examples are depressing the accelerator of a car, throwing a ball, or firing a pistol.

16. In the diagram, what is the rock in the resting position at the top of the hill said to have?

(1) mechanical force
(2) mechanical advantage
(3) no energy
(4) kinetic energy
(5) potential energy

POSTTEST

Question 17 is based on the following information.

Food	How Much We Eat/ Person/Year	
	1970	Today
Eggs	309	237
Red meat (pounds)	132	110
Whole milk (gallons)	26	9
Cheese (pounds)	11	27
Fruits (pounds)	101	124
Grains (pounds)	135	189
Nonfat/1% milk (gallons)	2	6
Poultry (pounds)	34	63
Seafood (pounds)	12	15
Vegetables (pounds)	271	320
Yogurt (pounds)	1	4
Fats and oils (pounds)	55	67
Soft drinks (gallons)	24	52
Sugars (pounds)	123	150

Source: U.S. Department of Agriculture, *Hope Health Letter,* April 1999

17. What assumption can be made about the eating habits over the years?

More people are

(1) becoming vegetarians
(2) consuming whole milk dairy products
(3) trying to eat healthier foods
(4) eating more beef than chicken
(5) eliminating soft drinks from their diets

Questions 18 and 19 are based on the following passage.

The orderly pattern of the atoms in a crystal influences many properties apart from its external appearance. One of these properties is cleavage. *Cleavage* refers to the ability of a crystal to split in a certain direction along its surface. The direction of the cleavage is always parallel to a possible crystal face. Cleavage planes are dependent on the atomic structure, and they pass between sheets of atoms in well-defined directions.

How easily a mineral cleaves and the effect of the cleavage vary from one mineral to another. A crystal whose cleavage results in exceptionally smooth surfaces is said to show *eminent cleavage;* other types of cleavages are classified as *distinct* or *poor.* All crystalline gemstones undergo cleavage before they can be mounted in a setting. This cutting process may also be easy or difficult. A diamond cleaves easily despite its great hardness and may be cut into many different forms.

18. According to the passage, what can we conclude about cleavage?

(1) All crystals demonstrate good cleavage.
(2) Some crystals with poor cleavage may not be used for gemstones.
(3) Eminent cleavage is inherent in all crystals of the quartz family.
(4) Cleavage of diamonds is a random property and differs from stone to stone.
(5) Cleavage improvement depends on the location of mineral excavation.

19. Based on the knowledge that cleavage is characteristic of crystals, which of the following gems would not have this property?

(1) ruby
(2) emerald
(3) pearl
(4) diamond
(5) sapphire

POSTTEST

Question 20 is based on the following chart.

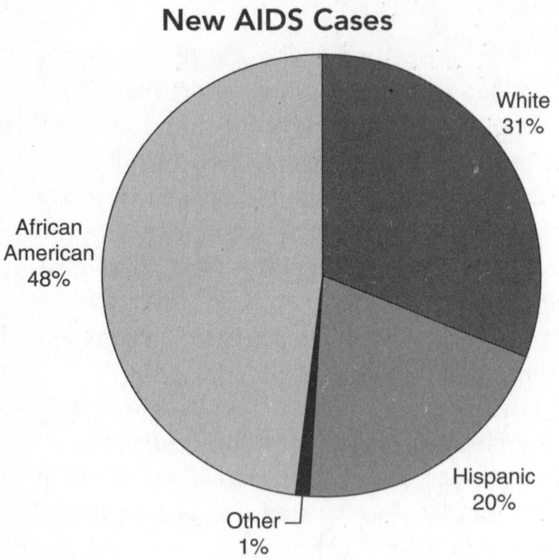

Source: Centers for Disease Control.

20. According to statistics from the Centers for Disease Control, the number of deaths by AIDS has dropped; however, the slowing decline concerns experts. Considering the data about new AIDS cases provided in the circle graph, what conclusion can be drawn about the AIDS epidemic in 2000?

(1) All races are equally affected by the AIDS epidemic.
(2) AIDS medications are powerful and extremely successful.
(3) Many people are still misinformed about the severity of AIDS.
(4) More children and teenagers are affected by AIDS than adults.
(5) Most people are not concerned about AIDS.

Questions 21 and 22 are based on the following passage.

Off the coast of Chile and Peru, ocean currents and winds cause a rising of cold, nutrient-laden water. This enrichment of the ocean's surface layer results in an abundant plankton crop, which in turn supports large fish and seabird populations.

El Niño is the name for a set of oceanographic conditions that occurs every five to eight years, causing disturbances in Earth's biological and weather systems. El Niño (Spanish for "Christ child") gets its name from the fact that it usually happens around Christmas.

El Niño occurs when trade winds that drive the currents weaken and fail. In the ocean, the supply of nutrients is cut off, and rather sterile warm water kills off the plankton. The fish and seabirds starve.

Dramatic changes also take place in the world's weather. As the trade winds subside, the wind patterns around the globe are disrupted. For example, the normally cool European continent may experience prolonged periods of torrid temperatures as its normal wind patterns change. El Niño's effects may be felt for as long as two years at a time.

21. According to the passage, El Niño occurs with failed trade winds. Thus, a conclusion that can be drawn is that a resumption of trade winds off the coast of South America is likely to result in what phenomena?

(1) a major anchovy and tuna migration
(2) an end to El Niño conditions
(3) an increase in weather disruptions
(4) a continuation in high European temperatures
(5) a condition known as *El Aguaje*

22. A spokesman states, "El Niño will have no effect on world food prices." Why is the speaker probably in error?

(1) Food consumption goes up during El Niño.
(2) Food production increases because of El Niño.
(3) New food sources are constantly being found.
(4) Loss of fish and variable weather conditions reduce food availability.
(5) The Northern Hemisphere makes up the Southern Hemisphere's food losses.

POSTTEST

Question 23 is based on the following chart.

Evaluation of the Water Quality in United States Watersheds, 2000

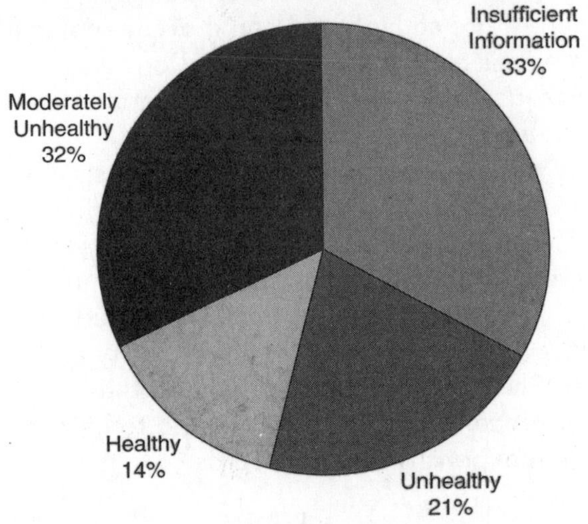

Source: U.S. Environmental Protection Agency *2000 World Almanac*

23. A *watershed* is an area of land that catches precipitation and drains to rivers and lakes. Which of the following conclusions can be drawn about the quality of water in the watersheds of the United States in 2000?

(1) The EPA (Environmental Protection Agency) need not be concerned.
(2) More than 75% of the water in the watersheds is dangerously polluted.
(3) Contaminated water in watersheds is a serious problem around the world.
(4) Over 50% of the water in watersheds may pose a health risk.
(5) It is very difficult to analyze water in watersheds.

Question 24 is based on the following passage.

A plant stem's two main functions are to support the leaves and to transport materials between roots and leaves. As a stem develops, it possesses three types of permanent tissues: *surface tissue, ground tissue,* and *vascular tissue.* The surface and ground tissues support and give structure to the plant. The vascular tissues are the transport systems of the plant. The vascular tissues usually exist in one of three patterns and are known as the *phloem* and *xylem.*

Both the xylem and phloem are made up of several different types of cells that make up transport tubes for needed nutrients. In general, xylem nutrients (sap) travel from the roots to the rest of the plant. Phloem sap is derived from photosynthesizing leaves and from there is carried throughout the plant.

24. What would we be able to study by injecting a nutrient dye into the root of a plant?

(1) phloem sap transport
(2) all vascular tissues
(3) xylem sap transport
(4) pith and cortex cells
(5) total plant photosynthesis

POSTTEST

Question 25 is based on the following table.

Wind Chill Index (and its Effect on Skin)

Wind Speed MPH	Degrees in Fahrenheit 35	30	25	15	10	5	0
5	33	27	21	12	7	0	–5
10	22	16	10	–3	–9	–15	–22
15	16	9	2	–11	–18	–25	–31
20	12	4	–3	–17	–24	–31	–39
25	8	1	–7	–22	–29	–36	–44
30	6	–2	–10	–25	–33	–41	–49
35	4	–4	–12	–27	–35	–43	–52
40	3	–5	–13	–29	–37	–45	–53
45	2	–6	–14	–30	–38	–46	–54

Source: National Weather Source, NOAA, U.S. Department of Commerce *World Almanac 2000*

25. Temperature and wind combine to cause heat loss. Hypothermia occurs when the body temperature falls more than 4°F below normal. Death can occur if hypothermia persists for over three hours. According to the table above, in which of the following temperature and wind combinations would the body temperature be the lowest and a person most at risk for developing hypothermia?

(1) windspeed of 5 mph and a temperature of 5°F
(2) windspeed of 10 mph and a temperature of 15°F
(3) windspeed of 25 mph and a temperature of 35°F
(4) windspeed of 30 mph and a temperature of 15°F
(5) windspeed of 35 mph and a temperature of 30°F

Question 26 is based on the following passage.

Nuclear scientists have determined that a fourth state of matter exists: *plasma*. The state of plasma is reached when matter acquires a temperature so high that some of the molecules and atoms are broken down into ions and electrons. Stellar and interstellar matter mostly occur as forms of plasma.

On Earth, plasma exists in the ionosphere, in flames, and in chemical and nuclear explosions. Matter in a controlled thermonuclear reactor also exists in a plasma state. Plasma is most like a gas. However, it differs from un-ionized gas in that it is a good conductor of electricity and heat. Scientists hope to understand the occurrence of plasma in nature and to harness it as an inexpensive energy source.

26. Based on the passage, how can the cost of developing thermonuclear power with plasma be defended?

(1) It is applicable to all technologies.
(2) A plasma power source can be used without special equipment.
(3) It can provide an inexpensive power source.
(4) It is almost perfected already.
(5) Current nuclear power is too dangerous.

POSTTEST

Questions 27 and 28 are based on the following illustration.

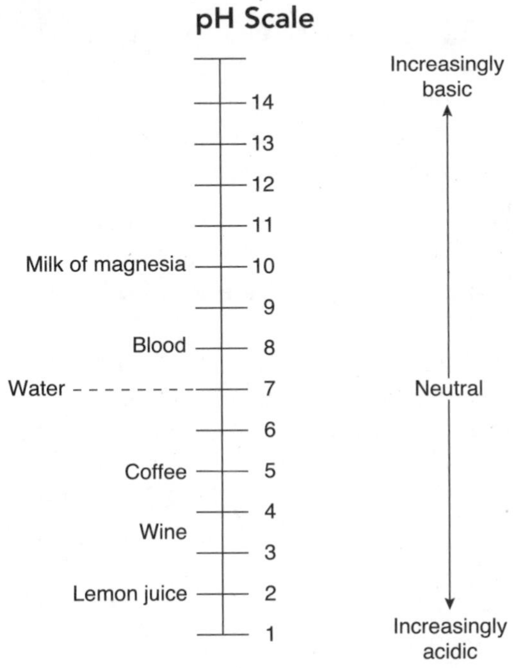

27. According to the scale above, how would a substance that registers 2.5 on the pH scale be categorized?

(1) base
(2) neutral substance
(3) alkali
(4) acid
(5) hydroxide

28. According to the scale, how would a substance that registers 7 on the pH scale be categorized?

(1) base
(2) neutral substance
(3) alkali
(4) acid
(5) hydroxide

Question 29 is based on the following information.

© Sally A. Morgan/Ecoscene/CORBIS

29. According to the Costa Rica Rainforests Outward Bound School, the rain forests of the world are disappearing at a rate of eighty acres per minute, day and night. In December 2000, 53,694,993 acres of rain forest were destroyed. Which of the following facts about rain forests illustrates the negative effect of their destruction on the environment?

(1) The soil of the rain forest is low in nutrients, so farmers cannot reuse the same land every year.
(2) Ranchers clear and use the land for pastures for their cattle because land is inexpensive.
(3) Trees from the rain forest are used to supply the growing population with lumber for homes and furniture.
(4) The release of carbon dioxide into the air during the burning of the rain forests adds to the greenhouse effect.
(5) Almost half of the tropical rain forest deforestation occurs in South America.

POSTTEST

Question 30 is based on the following passage.

Although water is the most common hydrogen-oxygen compound, hydrogen and oxygen form another compound called *hydrogen peroxide,* H_2O_2. Hydrogen peroxide was first obtained by treating barium peroxide with an acid. Very small quantities of hydrogen peroxide are present in dew, rain, and snow because of the action of ultraviolet light on oxygen and water vapor.

Hydrogen peroxide has many different applications, depending upon its concentration. A 3 percent solution is used in the home as a mild antiseptic and germicide. A 30 percent solution is used in industry as a bleaching agent because of the permanency of the whiteness it produces. Concentrations of 90 percent are used as oxidizing agents in rockets and high explosives.

30. According to the information in the passage, what can we predict that adding water to an industrial-strength hydrogen peroxide solution will result in?

(1) an explosion
(2) a new substance
(3) an antiseptic
(4) a rocket fuel
(5) a bleaching agent

Question 31 is based on the following information.

Most common symptoms of Lupus

Lupus is difficult to diagnose because symptoms come and go with the disease. Here's how frequently various symptoms occur.

Symptom	Percentage of patients who experience it
Achy joints	95 percent
Fever over 100 degrees	90 percent
Arthritis (swollen joints)	90 percent
Prolonged or extreme fatigue	81 percent
Skin rashes	74 percent
Anemia	71 percent
Kidney involvement	50 percent
Chest pain on deep breathing	45 percent
Butterfly-shaped rash across cheeks and nose	42 percent
Sun or light sensitivity	30 percent
Hair loss	27 percent
Abnormal blood clotting problems	20 percent
Raynaud's phenomenon (fingers turn white or blue in cold)	17 percent
Seizures	15 percent
Mouth or nose ulcers	12 percent

Source: Lupus Foundation of America, *Daily Herald,* December 20, 1999

POSTTEST

31. ***Systemic lupus erythematosus,* or lupus, affects a few million people in the United States. Most of these people are young women. Lupus is a chronic, autoimmune disease that affects connective tissue in any part of the body. An attack can damage organs and the nervous system. What conclusion can be drawn about lupus?**

(1) Lupus is easy for a physician to diagnose.
(2) Most victims of lupus are middle-aged women.
(3) Lupus can affect almost every system of the body.
(4) It is uncommon to have skin problems with lupus.
(5) Hormones most likely are unrelated to the lupus disease.

Question 32 is based on the following definitions and illustration.

reflection—angular return of a light wave
refraction—apparent bending of light waves through different media
diffraction—bending of light waves near an obstacle
interference—altering of brightness of light waves
polarization—restriction of light waves to one plane

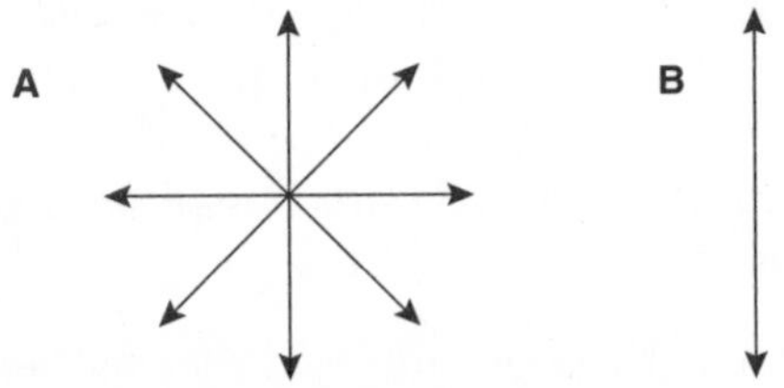

32. A certain type of lens changes the direction of light rays from A to B. What property does this illustrate?

(1) deflection
(2) diffraction
(3) reflection
(4) refraction
(5) polarization

33. Tissue engineering is the ability to grow cells in a laboratory. These cells are collected from an animal, a donor organ, or a patient's body and grown in liquid nutrients that allow them to divide and multiply. This science explores the possibility of replacing or repairing human body parts. How is the term *engineering* as used in this process applied?

By the use of

(1) science and mathematics to produce a material
(2) biology, medicine, and engineering to produce a material
(3) mathematics and engineering to produce a material
(4) history, mathematics, and biology to produce a material
(5) chemistry, mathematics, and engineering to produce a material

POSTTEST

Question 34 is based on the following information.

RICE (rest, ice, compression, and elevation) Routine for First Aid	
Rest	Rest the injured part of your body to reduce further swelling and bleeding. Avoid moving the injured part.
Ice	Apply an ice pack to the injured area for twenty to thirty minutes every two to three hours for the first forty-eight hours after an injury. This will help relieve pain and minimize bruising and swelling.
Compression	Wear a compressed bandage for at least two days to help reduce bleeding and swelling.
Elevation	Raise the injured part of your body (above your heart when possible) to help reduce swelling.

Source: American Medical Association

34. The *RICE* routine for first aid would be helpful for which of the following soft-tissue injuries?

(1) broken leg
(2) strained muscle
(3) dislocated shoulder
(4) detached retina
(5) herniated disk

Question 35 is based on the following passage.

Quasars are recent additions to our body of knowledge about the physical universe. *Quasars* (quasi-stellar objects) are astronomical objects that are starlike in appearance and emit nonthermal radiation, usually more ultraviolet and infrared radiation than stars.

Quasars were first discovered in the early 1960s when telescopes picked up mysterious radio-wave emission sources that, at the time, could not be explained. Since then, thousands of radio-emitting and radio-quiet quasars have been located.

One interesting feature of quasars is that their energy output can change by great amounts in a short period of time. To date, scientists have not been able to account for these energy changes.

35. What belief does the information in the passage support?

(1) We really know nothing about our physical universe.
(2) Scientists hold the key to all knowledge about outer space.
(3) Scientists are baffled by new discoveries in outer space.
(4) We often make significant discoveries by accident.
(5) We will someday know everything about our physical universe.

Questions 36 and 37 are based on the following passage.

Chemists have determined that elements with atomic numbers greater than 92 are all radioactive. In general, their half-lives are much shorter than the age of the universe. This means that they no longer exist in nature and have all been artificially produced by scientists in nuclear reactions.

POSTTEST

Elements 93 through 105 in the periodic table have been created and named, and scientists have claimed discovery of elements 106 and 107. The *transuranium elements,* as they are called, become less stable as the atomic number and mass increase. For example, element number 93, neptunium, has a half-life of two million years, while element number 104, kurchatovium, has a half-life of seventy seconds.

The transuranium elements are the heaviest elements that exist and are readily fissionable when subjected to nuclear bombardment. Chemists studying these elements and the periodic table predict that stable elements may be found around atomic numbers 114 or 126.

36. According to the passage, what can we predict about the half-life of element number 105?

It is

(1) measured in days or weeks
(2) less than seventy seconds
(3) incalculable (not capable of being determined)
(4) greater than the other transuranium elements
(5) greater than two million years

37. Based on the information in the passage, which of the following relationships appears to be true for those elements 93 through 105?

(1) The greater the atomic number, the higher the half-life.
(2) The greater the atomic number, the lower the half-life.
(3) The greater the radioactivity, the greater the half-life.
(4) The greater the half-life, the greater the radioactivity.
(5) The greater the atomic number, the greater the element stability.

Question 38 is based on the following picture.

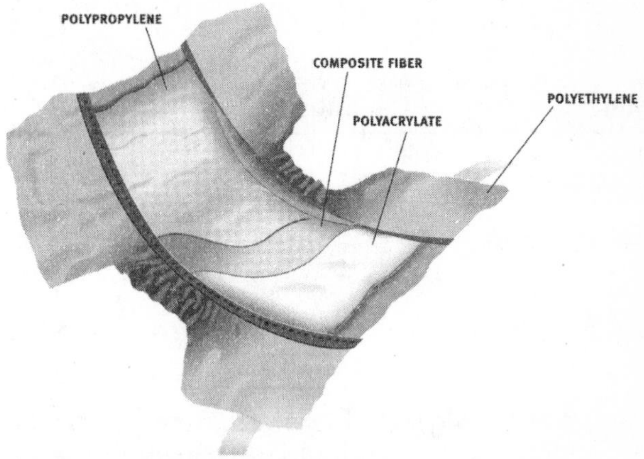

MOST MATERIALS used in a disposable diaper are synthetic. Polypropylene, used in winter athletic underwear, makes up the inner layer; it is soft and stays dry, drawing fluid away from the skin. At the core is the polyacrylate superabsorbent powder, combined with fluffy cellulose. A layer of fiber (cellulose or synthetic) fights gravity by distributing fluid over the entire surface of the powder instead of letting it pool in one spot. The outermost layer is mostly microporous polyethylene; it keeps in fluid but lets out vapor. Adhesives hold it all together: elasticized hydrophobic polypropylene cuffs around the thighs contain leaks; Velcro or sticky tabs hold the diaper on the baby.

Source: *Scientific American,* December 2000

38. A disposable diaper is made of both synthetic and natural polymers. Which one of the following is a supporting detail useful to promote the use of disposable diapers?

Diapers

(1) may have allergens in the fiber area
(2) add to the landfills in the United States
(3) allow babies to be changed less often
(4) do not allow air to circulate around babies
(5) are superabsorbent so babies may toilet-train later

POSTTEST

Questions 39 and 40 are based on the following chart.

Minerals

Mineral	Source	Deficiency Condition
Macrominerals		
Calcium (Ca)	Canned fish, milk, dairy products	Rickets in children; osteomalacia and osteoporosis in adults
Chlorine (Cl)	Meats, salt-processed foods, table salt	—
Magnesium (Mg)	Seafoods, cereal grains, nuts, dark green vegetables, cocoa	Heart failure due to spasms
Phosphorus (P)	Animal proteins	—
Potassium (K)	Orange juice, bananas, dried fruits, potatoes	Poor nerve function; irregular heartbeat; sudden death during fasting
Sodium (Na)	Meats, salt-processed foods, table salt	Headache, weakness, thirst, poor memory, appetite loss
Sulfur (S)	Proteins	—
Trace minerals		
Chromium (Cr)	Liver, animal and plant tissue	Loss of insulin efficiency with age
Cobalt (Co)	Liver, animal proteins	Anemia
Copper (Cu)	Liver, kidney, egg yolk, whole grains	—
Fluorine (F)	Seafoods, fluoridated drinking water	Dental decay
Iodine (I)	Seafoods, iodized salts	Goiter
Iron (Fe)	Liver, meats, green leafy vegetables, whole grains	Anemia; tiredness and apathy
Manganese (Mn)	Liver, kidney, wheat germ, legumes, nuts, tea	Weight loss, dermatitis
Molybdenum (Mo)	Liver, kidney, whole grains, legumes, leafy vegetables	—
Nickel (Ni)	Seafoods, grains, seeds, beans, vegetables	Cirrhosis of liver, kidney failure, stress
Selenium (Se)	Liver, organ meats, grains, vegetables	Kashan disease (a heart disease found in China)
Zinc (Zn)	Liver, shellfish, meats, wheat germ, legumes	Anemia, stunted growth

Source: *ChemCom: Chemistry in the Community*

POSTTEST

39. Bob discovered that he had high blood pressure, which was the result of years of poor eating habits. Bob's company physician gave him a healthy diet to follow that would help to lower his blood pressure naturally and economically but not create a mineral deficiency. Which of the following statements is irrelevant to Bob's understanding of his new, healthy diet?

(1) Low-fat dairy products, green leafy vegetables, and tofu are good sources of calcium.
(2) Lean red meat, whole-grain cereals, and beans are valuable sources of iron.
(3) A daily vitamin and mineral supplement is more important than a well-balanced diet.
(4) Whole-wheat breads fortified with iron and calcium are better choices than white breads.
(5) The restriction of sodium-rich foods is essential in reducing the risk of heart disease.

40. What conclusion was Bob able to draw about minerals after reading this chart provided by his physician?

(1) Minerals are more important to the body than vitamins.
(2) A vegetarian diet may be deficient in minerals.
(3) Minerals found in healthy foods help the body to function properly.
(4) Adults need minerals in their diet more than do children.
(5) Multivitamins are necessary in order to provide the body with minerals.

Questions 41 and 42 are based on the following passage.

Cancer is one of the leading causes of death in our society. *Cancer* is a disease in which a cell in the body loses its sensitivity to factors which regulate cell growth and division. The cell begins to multiply without restriction, creating a growing mass called a *tumor,* which interferes with the structure and functioning of the organ in which it is located.

Frequently, cancer cells become *metastatic,* meaning that they travel, settling in a number of places and giving rise to secondary tumors. Much of medical research is devoted to finding ways of preventing, controlling, and curing cancer.

41. Because of the metastatic trait of cancer cells, how can we judge a cancer treatment to be effective?

(1) if the entire body has been proven free of tumors over a period of time
(2) if the highest possible levels of treatment have been used
(3) if the original-source tumor has been identified
(4) if no new cancer cells are found in two weeks
(5) if the complete tumor is removed

42. When would it be correct to reject any proposed cure for cancer?

(1) if it was not able to alter the ability of cancer cells to metastasize
(2) if it was based on research that was with a variety of human volunteer subjects
(3) if it was based on research for a period of time, with frequent checks and controls
(4) if it was based on surgery, radiation therapy, and/or chemotherapy
(5) if it was based on lifestyle elements of diet, exercise, and attitudes

POSTTEST

Question 43 is based on the following definitions.

Plants can *propagate*, or reproduce themselves, by one of five different methods. Listed and described below are five parts of plants out of which new plants are known to grow.

bud—a protuberance of a plant that can be cut off and planted, resulting in a new plant

runner—a horizontal plant offshoot that runs above or below ground and that can develop root systems to start new plants

bulb—an underground fleshy bud that multiplies and whose leaves store food; bulbs can be separated to grow a new plant

seed—a grain or ripened ovule of a mature plant that, when planted in moist soil, sprouts a new plant

stem cutting—a section of a plant that, when placed in a moist environment, develops roots and grows into a new plant

43. New peonies, perennial plants that produce showy flowers, can be propagated from the parent plant by dividing *corms* that grow underground. This reproductive form described most closely resembles which of the following?

(1) bud
(2) runner
(3) bulb
(4) seed
(5) stem cutting

Question 44 is based on the following chart.

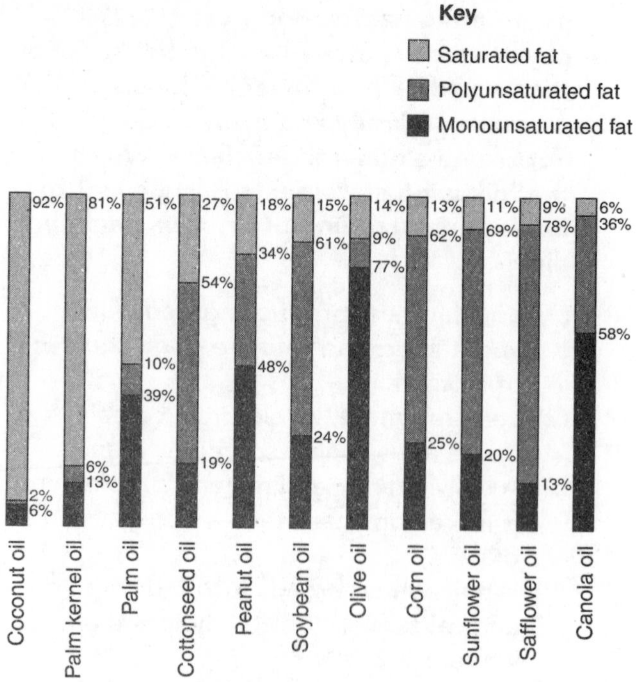

Source: *American Medical Association*

44. Roy's doctor recommended that he watch his blood cholesterol level because his of reading of over 200 milligrams per deciliter (mg/dl). Although Roy's cholesterol was not excessively high, his doctor advised him to improve his eating and exercise habits because of a genetic disposition to heart disease. Which of the oils below would be the best choice for Roy if he wanted to reduce his intake of saturated fats?

(1) coconut oil
(2) canola oil
(3) peanut oil
(4) soybean oil
(5) palm oil

POSTTEST

Question 45 is based on the following picture.

45. Stuart Wilkinson, the engineer of "Chew-Chew" said, "we stole the idea of eating food from the biological world, but we are marrying that idea to useful robotic capabilities." Which of the following would not be an application of Stuart Wilkinson's theory?

(1) a leaf mulcher that feeds on foliage
(2) a trash compactor that feeds on garbage
(3) a lawn mower that feeds on grass clippings
(4) a garden cultivator that feeds on soil
(5) a recycling truck that feeds on petroleum

Question 46 is based on the following chart.

How much sleep do we need?	
Toddlers	11 hours of sleep every night, plus a two-hour nap during the day
Preschoolers	11 to 12 hours of sleep a night
School-age children	10 hours
Teens	$9\frac{1}{4}$ hours of sleep every night (most get less than $8\frac{1}{2}$)
Adults	About 8 hours of sleep every night. To determine exactly how much sleep you need, on a night you feel fairly rested, sleep until you wake up on your own. Feel rested? The length of time you slept is how much sleep you need.

If you get one hour less sleep than you need each night for eight nights in a row, your brain will need sleep as desperately as if you had stayed up all night.

Source: William Dement, sleep researcher, Stanford University, *Hope Health Letter,* April 2000

46. Parents complain that their teenagers could sleep all day if they let them. According to this chart on sleep, how many hours does the average teenager need per week in order to be mentally alert in school?

(1) seventy-seven hours
(2) sixty-four hours
(3) fifty-six hours
(4) forty-five hours
(5) thirty-five hours

POSTTEST

Question 47 is based on the following chart.

Water Use in the United States

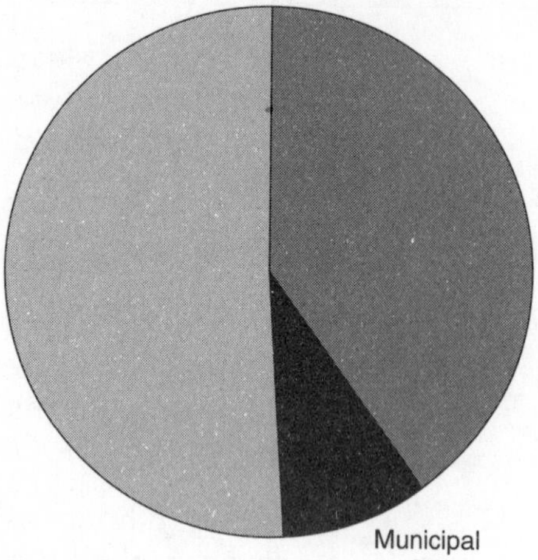

Source: *ChemCom: Chemistry in the Community*

47. Ninety-seven percent of the world's water supply is difficult, if not impossible, to obtain or to use because it is in the oceans or in the form of glaciers and ice caps. Scientists are exploring methods of conserving and protecting the rest of Earth's water supply for the growing population. According to the information provided, which of the following activities most directly affects the water supply?

(1) drinking and cooking
(2) irrigating field crops
(3) flushing toilets and bathing
(4) growing all types of food
(5) producing energy and manufacturing

Question 48 is based on the following passage.

The science of producing and transmitting sound waves in materials has become widespread with many practical applications. *Ultrasonics* was first developed during World War II as a method of detecting enemy submarines. Today ultrasonics has many applications. When the waves used are of a low amplitude, ultrasonics can be used to map the ocean's depths, detect flaws in materials, locate cancers in the human body, and scan fetuses for deformities.

Higher-amplitude waves are used in cleaning, manufacturing materials, and determining fatigue tests for metals. The destruction of bacteria and the use of tightly focused ultrasound as a surgical knife are biological applications of high-amplitude waves.

48. According to the passage, what is a low amplitude ultrasonic scanning of the human body able to do?

(1) give a clear picture of interior body details
(2) remove cancerous materials without radiation
(3) remove bacteria painlessly
(4) serve as an antiviral agent in infectious cases
(5) aid the body's immune system

POSTTEST

Question 49 is based on the following picture.

© T.J. Florian / Rainbow

49. Along with energy obtained from fossil fuels, nuclear sources, and water, environmentalists are encouraging the use of energy from wind. The turbines in the picture are formed like the wings of an aircraft, allowing for maximum wind force. Which of the following concerns of environmentalists and consumers would *not* demonstrate the need for obtaining energy from the wind?

(1) global fuel shortages
(2) increase in air pollution
(3) rising consumer expenses
(4) limitless supply of energy
(5) hazardous leaks and explosions

Question 50 is based on the following passage.

Insectivorous (insect-eating) plants are among the most fascinating members of the plant kingdom. They combine the characteristics of a plant with those of an animal. These plants have highly specialized leaves that capture and digest insects. The proteins of the digested insect supply the plant with nitrogen, which is usually unavailable in the poor soils in which these plants grow.

The Venus's-flytrap of North and South Carolina is an example of an insectivorous plant. The leaves of this plant are hinged along the middle and swing upward and inward. An insect landing on the leaf triggers a sensitive motor mechanism that closes the leaf blades. The captured insect is then slowly digested by enzymes secreted by cells in the leaves.

50. According to the passage, what is the probable effect of growing insectivorous plants in richer soils?

(1) Plants grow to a much larger size.
(2) Plants are unable to take larger insects.
(3) Plants are able to obtain nitrogen from sources other than insects.
(4) Plants bloom in more frequent cycles.
(5) Plants grow with deeper roots.

Science Answer Key

1. **Comprehension (4)** Although the overharvesting of seafood species is an environmental concern, it is not a cause or result of unusual weather patterns.

2. **Application (3)** The cornea is considered a tissue that could be donated to restore eyesight. The other choices are organs.

3. **Evaluation (2)** The illustration proves that of the animals listed, insects form the largest group.

4. **Application (5)** A boa constrictor is a snake that eats amphibians. The chart shows snakes that eat toads (a kind of amphibian) would be classified as tertiary consumers.

5. **Application (2)** Most of the cases would be found in the northern states, where the winters are the longest.

6. **Evaluation (3)** The passage supports the view that excessive dieting can be dangerous to one's health, and many people are very concerned about their body fat.

7. **Application (2)** A tectonophysicist studies the earth's structure, and that would include the study of earthquakes.

8. **Evaluation (4)** The passage supports the statement that some frequencies are beyond the human hearing range, which extends to only 20,000 cycles per second (thus making higher frequency levels inaudible).

9. **Application (5)** Human beings would be least affected because they are not capable of hearing frequencies of 25,000 cycles per second and more.

10. **Analysis (2)** The possible hypothesis is that the Mediterranean Sea will become smaller because of the subduction of the African plate beneath the crust of Eurasia.

11. **Application (3)** The flea lives on the dog's or cat's blood; therefore, the relationship would be described as parasite-host.

12. **Analysis (3)** According to the data provided, the conclusion is that all regions of the brain are vital.

13. **Analysis (5)** In order for a rainbow to occur, there must be refraction, reflection, and diffraction of light through water molecules.

14. **Evaluation (3)** By studying heredity in pea plants, geneticists have learned how plants and animals transmit traits to their offspring.

15. **Application (5)** Arthritis is an inflammation of the joints and would not affect the function of the brain.

16. **Comprehension (5)** The rock is not in motion, so it has potential energy.

17. **Analysis (3)** According to the chart, more people are trying to eat less fat and more fruits, vegetables, and grains, so the assumption is that people are trying to eat healthier.

18. **Analysis (2)** A conclusion from the passage is that a crystal must have good cleavage in order to be cut into a gemstone.

19. **Application (3)** Although considered by many to be a great gemstone, a pearl is not a crystal and would not have the property of cleavage.

20. **Analysis (3)** The data on the circle graph prove that many people are still contracting AIDS; therefore, it can be assumed that all people need to be educated on the severity of the disease.

21. **Analysis (2)** A resumption of the trade winds would reverse the condition that caused El Niño.

22. **Evaluation (4)** The speaker is in error because El Niño *does* affect fishing and agricultural harvests, leading to reduced food supplies.

23. **Analysis (4)** Pollution seriously affected 21% of the water and moderately affected another 32%. This means that over 50% was affected at some level.

24. **Application (3)** The dye would be absorbed by the xylem at the root level and would be distributed throughout the plant.

25. **Application (4)** The wind chill would be most severe at –25 degrees Fahrenheit.

26. **Evaluation (3)** The cost can be defended because the passage states that scientists hope to harness plasma as an inexpensive energy source.

27. **Application (4)** An acid registers below 7 on the pH scale.

28. **Application (2)** The number 7 represents neutrality on the pH scale.

29. **Analysis (4)** This is the only choice that indicates an environmental effect.

30. **Comprehension (3)** We can predict that diluting an industrial hydrogen peroxide solution with water will reduce it to a concentration suitable for use as an antiseptic.

31. **Analysis (3)** According to the chart, we can conclude that lupus attacks all of the body systems.

32. **Application (5)** Polarization of light rays is the restriction of reflected rays to one plane.

33. **Comprehension (2)** Tissue engineering involves the knowledge of life processes (biology), disease (medicine), and science and mathematical principles (engineering).

34. **Application (2)** A strained muscle is the only soft-tissue injury listed.

35. **Evaluation (4)** According to the passage, quasars were discovered when astronomers picked up mysterious wave emissions from planetary objects. This fact supports the belief that the discovery of quasars was an accident.

36. **Comprehension (2)** The passage says that element 104 has a half-life of seventy seconds. The half-life decreases as the atomic number increases; therefore, we can predict that element 105 has a shorter half-life.

37. **Evaluation (2)** According to the information in the passage, the true relationship is that the transuranium elements become less stable as their atomic numbers increase. This means that the greater the atomic number, the lower the half-life.

38. **Analysis (3)** Because of the combination of polymers, a baby does not feel the wetness of the diaper and the diaper holds more liquid. Thus, a baby does not feel uncomfortable and would not need to be changed as often.

39. **Evaluation (3)** Healthy foods provide important minerals and vitamins naturally and economically and are a better choice for changing eating habits.

40. **Analysis (3)** Information in the chart leads to the conclusion that if Bob eats the right foods, he will get all of the minerals needed. Choice (5) is not a valid conclusion because a multivitamin isn't necessary if a person eats a balanced diet.

41. **Evaluation (1)** Since cancer can spread so widely, only long-term scans of the body that indicate an absence of cancer can indicate that the cancer has been cured.

42. **Evaluation (1)** A cure for cancer would likely include preventing cancer from metastasizing or spreading to other sites in the body.

43. **Application (3)** A *corm* is similar to a bulb, which grows underground and stores food for the plants usage. Corms and bulbs multiply and can be divided to start new plants.

44. **Application (2)** Canola oil is the best choice for Roy because it has the lowest amount of saturated fats of all the oils listed.

45. **Application (5)** A recycling truck that feeds on petroleum would not be an example of eating food to fuel a robot.

46. **Comprehension (2)** According to the chart, a teenager needs about nine hours of sleep per day, or sixty-three hours in seven days.

47. **Application (5)** According to the circle graph, industry uses more than half (51%) of the water supply.

48. **Comprehension (1)** The passage states that low-amplitude ultrasonics can be used to pinpoint the location of potential deformities in the unborn.

49. **Application (4)** All of the choices listed are concerns except for choice (4), which is a positive attribute of energy from wind.

50. **Analysis (3)** From the information given, the only choice that can be made is that plants may become less dependent on insects for nitrogen.

SCIENCE POSTTEST

Evaluation Chart

Use the answer key on pages 1012–1014 to check your answers to the Posttest. Then find the item number of each question you missed and circle it on the chart below to determine the Science content areas in which you need more practice. Pay particular attention to areas where you missed half or more of the questions. The page numbers for the content areas are listed on the chart below. For those questions that you missed, review the skill pages indicated.

SKILL AREA/ CONTENT AREA	COMPREHENSION (pages 217–230)	APPLICATION (pages 231–236)	ANALYSIS (pages 237–262)	EVALUATION (pages 271–274)
Life Sciences (Biology) (pages 459–496)	33, 46	2, 4, 5, 9, 11, 15, 24, 34, 43, 44, 45, 47	12, 17, 20, 31, 40, 50	3, 6, 8, 14, 39, 41, 42
Earth & Space Science (pages 497–532)	1	7, 25, 49	10, 21, 23, 29	22, 35
Physical Sciences (Chemistry and Physics) (pages 533–577)	16, 30, 36, 48	19, 27, 28, 32	13, 18, 38	26, 37

Language Arts, Reading

The Language Arts, Reading Posttest will give you the opportunity to evaluate your readiness for the actual GED Language Arts, Reading Test. This test contains 40 questions based on seven excerpts from **fiction** (novels and short stories), **poems, drama,** and several types of **nonfiction prose** (*informational texts* such as newspaper or magazine articles, or speeches; commentaries about *visual texts; literary nonfiction* such as essays, biographies, diaries, letters, or reviews; or *business documents*).

You should take approximately 65 minutes to complete this test. At the end of 65 minutes, stop and mark your place. Then finish the test. This will give you an idea of whether or not you can finish the actual GED Test in the time allotted. Try to answer as many questions as you can. A blank will count as a wrong answer, so make a reasonable guess for answers to questions of which you are not sure.

When you are finished with the test, check your answers and turn to the Evaluation Chart on page 1030. Use the chart to evaluate whether or not you are ready to take the actual GED Test and, if not, in what areas you need more work.

Language Arts, Reading Posttest Answer Grid

1	①	②	③	④	⑤	15	①	②	③	④	⑤	28	①	②	③	④	⑤
2	①	②	③	④	⑤	16	①	②	③	④	⑤	29	①	②	③	④	⑤
3	①	②	③	④	⑤	17	①	②	③	④	⑤	30	①	②	③	④	⑤
4	①	②	③	④	⑤	18	①	②	③	④	⑤	31	①	②	③	④	⑤
5	①	②	③	④	⑤	19	①	②	③	④	⑤	32	①	②	③	④	⑤
6	①	②	③	④	⑤	20	①	②	③	④	⑤	33	①	②	③	④	⑤
7	①	②	③	④	⑤	21	①	②	③	④	⑤	34	①	②	③	④	⑤
8	①	②	③	④	⑤	22	①	②	③	④	⑤	35	①	②	③	④	⑤
9	①	②	③	④	⑤	23	①	②	③	④	⑤	36	①	②	③	④	⑤
10	①	②	③	④	⑤	24	①	②	③	④	⑤	37	①	②	③	④	⑤
11	①	②	③	④	⑤	25	①	②	③	④	⑤	38	①	②	③	④	⑤
12	①	②	③	④	⑤	26	①	②	③	④	⑤	39	①	②	③	④	⑤
13	①	②	③	④	⑤	27	①	②	③	④	⑤	40	①	②	③	④	⑤
14	①	②	③	④	⑤												

POSTTEST

Questions 1–6 are based on the following excerpt.

In this drama based on the famous Scopes Trial of 1925, Henry Drummond, a lawyer, takes on the case of high school science teacher Bertram Cates. Cates defied Tennessee law at the time by teaching scientist Charles Darwin's Theory of Evolution.

WHAT FREEDOM IS THE LAWYER DEFENDING?

Drummond *(Sighing)* Someday I'm going to get me an *easy* case. An open-and-shut case. I've got a friend up in Chicago. Big lawyer. Lord how the money rolls in! You know why? He never takes a case unless it's a sure thing. Like a jockey who won't go in a race unless he can ride the favorite.

Cates You sure picked the long shot this time, Mr. Drummond.

Drummond Sometimes I think the law is like a horse race. Sometimes it seems to me I ride like fury, just to end up back where I started. Might as well be on a merry-go-round, or a rocking horse . . . or . . . [*He half-closes his eyes. His voice is far away, his lips barely move*] Golden Dancer . . .

Cates What did you say?

Drummond That was the name of my first long shot. Golden Dancer. She was in the big side window of the general store in Wakeman, Ohio. I used to stand out in the street and say to myself, "If I had Golden Dancer I'd have everything in the world that I wanted." [*He cocks an eyebrow*] I was seven years old and a very fine judge of rocking horses. [*He looks off again, into the distance*] Golden Dancer had a bright red mane, blue eyes, and she was gold all over, with purple spots. When the sun hit her stirrups, she was a dazzling sight to see. But she was a week's wages for my father. So Golden Dancer and I always had a plate glass window between us. [*Reaching back for the memory*] But—let's see, it wasn't Christmas; must've been my birthday—I woke up in the morning and there was Golden Dancer at the foot of my bed! Ma had skimped on the groceries, and my father'd worked nights for a month. [*Re-living the moment*] I jumped into the saddle and started to rock—[*Almost a whisper*] And it *broke*! It was split in two! The wood was rotten, the whole thing was put together with spit and sealing wax! All shine and no substance! [Turning to Cates] Bert, whenever you see something bright, shining, perfect-seeming—all gold, with purple spots—look behind the paint! And if it's a lie—show it up for what it really is!

—Excerpted from *Inherit the Wind* by Jerome Lawrence and Robert E. Lee

1. What is meant by the defense lawyer Drummond when he says (lines 7–9), "Like a jockey who won't go in a race unless he can ride the favorite"?

(1) He is referring to a lawyer who never takes a case unless he is certain he can win.
(2) He is talking about a jury that decides based on public opinion.
(3) He is discussing the teaching practices of a most popular high school teacher.
(4) He is advising a radio man about the placement of a microphone in the courtroom.
(5) He is giving advice to a would-be candidate for president of the United States.

POSTTEST

2. If Drummond were to advise new parents about raising their first child, what would he likely say?

(1) Sacrifice at all costs in order to give the child what he or she needs.
(2) Consult the law regarding appropriate discipline for a child.
(3) Never buy a child toys that could cause severe personal injury.
(4) Use your judgment and be careful in your selection of children's items.
(5) Don't let your child talk you into frivolous, unnecessary expenses.

3. When Drummond states (lines 15–17), "Might as well be on a merry-go-round, or a rocking horse," what two things is he comparing?

(1) birth and death
(2) love and marriage
(3) success and failure
(4) a carnival and the beach
(5) the law and a horse race

4. When Drummond tells Cates about the Golden Dancer incident, what tone is evident in the paragraph?

(1) joy at getting the greatest birthday present
(2) thankfulness for the wisdom of his parents
(3) anger at the poor quality of the rocking horse
(4) nostalgia at the warmth of his favorite memory
(5) sadness at the end of his childhood days

5. Cates had refused to teach only creationism (the theory according to the Bible that God created the world out of nothing) and taught the theory of evolution (the theory that animals and plants changed over time in the universe). At the end of the speech about Golden Dancer, Drummond says, "And if it's a lie—show it up for what it really is!" What connection can you make between Cates's action and Drummond's statement?

(1) Drummond is foolishly encouraging Cates to challenge the state law.
(2) Drummond is supporting Cates in taking a risk to teach science.
(3) Drummond is telling Cates that school boards decide curriculum.
(4) Drummond is showing Cates scientific and religious differences.
(5) Drummond is challenging the state loyalty oath Cates must take.

6. Although this particular passage does not include dialogue by prosecutor Matthew Harrison Brady, we know from history that a man upon whom his character is based ran unsuccessfully for President three times. Why would a man with a national reputation prosecute a teacher in a small town so aggressively?

(1) He had nothing better to do as a defeated presidential candidate.
(2) He personally had proved the theory of creationism over evolutionism.
(3) He hoped that victory in this famous trial would help his campaign.
(4) He was probably paying back a political favor to the town mayor.
(5) He was listening to his wife who desperately wanted to be first lady.

POSTTEST

Questions 7–12 are based on the following passage.

WHY AREN'T THE GRAPES SWEET?

One man, one family driven from the land; this rusty car creaking along the highway to the west. I lost my land, a single tractor took my land. I am alone and I am bewildered. And in the night one family camps in a ditch and another family pulls in and the tents come out. The two men squat on their hams and the women and children listen. Here is the node, you who hate change and fear revolution. Keep these two squatting men apart; make them hate, fear, suspect each other. Here is the anlage* of the thing you fear. This is the zygote.* For here "I lost my land" is changed; a cell is split and from its splitting grows the thing you hate—"We lost *our* land." The danger is here, for two men are not as lonely and perplexed as one. And from this first "we" there grows a still more dangerous thing: "I have a little food" plus "I have none." If from this problem the sum is "We have a little food," the thing is on its way, the movement has direction. Only a little multiplication now, and this land, this tractor are ours. The two men squatting in a ditch, the little fire, the side-meat stewing in a single pot, the silent, stone-eyed women; behind the children listening with their souls to words their minds do not understand. The night draws down. The baby has a cold. Here, take this blanket. It's wool. It was my mother's blanket—take it for the baby. This is the thing to bomb. This is the beginning—from "I" to "we." If you who own the things people must have could understand this, you might preserve yourself. If you could separate causes from results, if you could know that Paine, Marx, Jefferson, Lenin, were results, not causes, you might survive. But that you cannot know. For the quality of owning freezes you forever into "I," and cuts you off forever from the "we."

—Excerpted from *The Grapes of Wrath*
by John Steinbeck

**anlage* means foundation

**zygote* means a cell formed from two reproductive cells

7. What is the most likely occupation of the narrator of the passage?

(1) mechanic
(2) landlord
(3) tenant farmer
(4) grandmother
(5) fugitive

8. According to this passage, if the *one man, one family* identified in lines 1 and 2 were to win the lottery and buy a vast estate, what would the man be unable to do?

(1) provide adequately for his family
(2) share a common bond with humanity
(3) take his family on a camping trip
(4) continue on the journey westward
(5) return to the land he knew

9. What effect is produced by the use of short, simple sentences in lines 30–33?

The sentences emphasize the idea that

(1) the narrator is practically illiterate
(2) life is every man for himself in most cases
(3) a beginning stems from simple, concrete things
(4) a basic structure for life is easily found
(5) simple language is most effective for survival

POSTTEST

10. What meaning is suggested by "stone-eyed" in the phrase "stone-eyed women" (line 27)?

The women's eyes

(1) reveal no feeling
(2) seem very bright
(3) look very bored
(4) appear quite round
(5) show much concern

11. What is the overall purpose of this passage?

To present a theme of conflict between

(1) various age groups
(2) man and nature
(3) man and the supernatural
(4) man and woman
(5) socio-economic classes

12. Paine, Marx, Jefferson, and Lenin all wrote about human rights and revolution. What connection exists between those writers and this passage?

Both the writers and the passage

(1) have a humorous tone
(2) call for peace at any price
(3) suggest religious changes
(4) discuss social issues
(5) identify scientific problems

Questions 13–18 are based on the following poem.

WHAT DOES LIGHT REPRESENT TO THE SPEAKER?

The Truly Great

1 I think continually of those who were truly great.
Who, from the womb, remembered the soul's history
Through corridors of light where the hours are suns,
Endless and singing. Whose lovely ambition
Was that their lips, still touched with fire,
Should tell of the spirit clothed from head to foot in song.
The desires falling across their bodies like blossoms.

What is precious is never to forget
The essential delight of the blood drawn from ageless springs
Breaking through rocks in worlds before our earth.
Never to deny its pleasure in the simple morning light
Nor its grave evening demand for love.
Never to allow gradually the traffic to smother
With noise and fog the flowering of the spirit.

Near the snow, near the sun, in the highest fields
See how these names are fêted* by the waving grass,
And by the streamers of white cloud,
And whispers of wind in the listening sky;
Who wore at their hearts the fire's center.
Born of the sun they traveled a short while towards the sun,
And left the vivid air signed with their honor.

—by Stephen Spender

**fêted* means celebrated

13. What kinds of people are described in lines 3–10 as among those who were truly great?

(1) poets
(2) warriors
(3) firefighters
(4) technicians
(5) doctors

POSTTEST

14. If the speaker of this poem were in charge of giving out a government grant, which project would have the greatest chance for funding?

(1) a scientific research project investigating genetic makeup of segmented worms
(2) a museum showcasing individuals who have inspired the spirit of humanity
(3) a private industry seeking to develop more energy-efficient airplane engines
(4) a non-profit organization planning to clean up sites contaminated by nuclear waste
(5) a project to analyze social relationships of primates and their offspring

15. What belief about great people is suggested by the speaker in lines 25–30?

(1) They are celebrated by nature.
(2) They are buried by stereotyping.
(3) They are replaced by others.
(4) They are inspired by music.
(5) They are saddened by fate.

16. What is the purpose of using the phrase *"traveled a short while towards the sun"* (lines 32–33)?

It reinforces the idea that these individuals

(1) visited many countries throughout the world
(2) lived only for a short span of time
(3) explored much of space in satellite ships
(4) achieved some inspiring acts during their lives
(5) moved to climates with more sunshine

17. What is the overall purpose of the poem?

(1) to educate about nature
(2) to question the forms of art
(3) to condemn events in history
(4) to discourage modern progress
(5) to commemorate great poets

18. The poet wrote the poem during a time period that has been described as an age of disillusionment. In what way does this poem relate to those times?

The poem

(1) mirrors the dark disillusionment of the age
(2) ridicules those who are discouraged
(3) reminds us to celebrate inspiration and spirit
(4) predicts great changes and disasters in the world
(5) serves as an attack on corrupt politics

Questions 19–24 are based on the following passage.

WHO IS THE ADVENTURER AND HOW DOES HE HAPPEN TO COME UPON THE GREEN DOOR? WHAT ROLE DOES THE "FANTASTIC AFRICAN" PLAY IN GETTING THE ADVENTURER TO THE DOOR?

Passage One

He drew up the other chair. The tea brightened the girl's eyes and brought back some of her color. She began to eat with a sort of dainty ferocity like some starved wild animal. She seemed to regard the young man's presence and the aid he had rendered her as a natural thing—not as though she undervalued the conventions; but as one whose great stress gave her the right to put aside the artificial for the human. But gradually, with the return of strength and comfort, came also a sense of the little conventions that belong; and she began to tell him her little story. It was one of a thousand such as the city yawns at every day—the shop girl's story of insufficient wages, further reduced by "fines" that go to swell the store's profits, of time lost through illness; and then of lost positions, lost hope, and—the knock of the adventurer upon the green door.

POSTTEST

Passage Two

Wondering, he [Rudolf] descended to the sidewalk. The fantastic African was still there. Rudolf confronted him with his two cards in his hand.

"Will you tell me why you gave me these cards and what they mean?" he asked.

In a broad, good-natured grin the negro exhibited a splendid advertisement of his master's profession.

"Dar it is, boss," he said, pointing down the street. "But I `spect you is a little late for de fust act."

Looking the way he pointed Rudolf saw above the entrance to a theatre the blazing electric sign of its new play, "The Green Door."

Passage Three

"All the same, I believe it was the hand of Fate that doped out the way for me to find her."

Which conclusion, under the circumstances, certainly admits Rudolf Steiner to the ranks of the true followers of Romance and Adventure.

—Excerpted from "The Green Door" by O. Henry [pen name of William Sydney Porter]

19. In Passage One, what are the implications of the line, "It was one of a thousand such as the city yawns at every day"?

(1) There are many such tales of crime and punishment.
(2) There are many men who follow romance and adventure.
(3) There are many underpaid young women without hope.
(4) There are many aspiring but starving artists and actors.
(5) There are many who follow city political conventions.

20. If Rudolf were a businessman on his way to his office today and he encountered a homeless person asking for assistance, what would be Rudolf's likely response?

(1) Get a job like everyone else.
(2) Sorry, I'm late for work.
(3) Your life is up to Fate.
(4) The city has services to help you.
(5) Tell me how I can help you.

21. In Passage Two, Rudolf encounters the negro distributing cards. The effect of the author's style does *not* apply to which of the following?

(1) a contrast in characterization between Rudolf and the negro
(2) the similar characterizations of the shop girl, Rudolf, and the negro
(3) the contrast in language of Rudolf and the down-to-earth negro
(4) a plot detail explaining how Rudolf was led to the green door
(5) an explanation of the connection between the title and the plot

22. What is the effect of the author's use of figurative language in this line from Passage One: "She began to eat with a sort of dainty ferocity like some starved wild animal"?

(1) It creates a poetic effect, which makes the reader feel as if the selection is not really fiction.
(2) It creates confusion for the reader in making a comparison of a starving girl to a wild animal.
(3) It makes the main character Rudolf appear "larger than life" in his great generosity.
(4) It sets the stage for a later comparison between the shop girl and the negro who uses colorful language.
(5) It creates a vivid mental image, which also encourages the reader to have sympathy for the shop girl's plight.

POSTTEST

23. The author O. Henry usually ends his short stories with the use of irony (a twist of events). The character Rudolf Steiner believes that he came to assist the shop girl through "the hand of Fate." How is this an example of irony?

(1) Rudolf was led to the girl through circumstances and not Fate (chance).
(2) Rudolf sees the girl's address printed on the back of the doctor's card.
(3) Rudolf is not really a true follower of Romance and Adventure.
(4) Rudolf is looking for a piano tuner and goes to the door by mistake.
(5) Rudolf picks the door where the girl lives even though all the doors are green.

24. The collection of short stories in which "The Green Door" is included, *41 Stories by O. Henry,* is organized by five content headings. A clue in Passage One tells the reader where the story is logically grouped. On this basis, under which heading should the story appear?

(1) The Big City
(2) Con Men and Hoboes
(3) The Wild West and the Tame West
(4) Our Neighbors to the South: Domestic
(5) Our Neighbors to the South: Foreign

Questions 25–30 are based on this passage from a novel translated from the Spanish.

DO YOU BELIEVE THAT IN THE HEART OF EVERY PERSON—REGARDLESS OF OCCUPATION—BEATS A POET?

Neruda tightened his grip around the postman's elbow and led him firmly to the lamppost where his bicycle was parked.

"And you think you can think just standing there? If you want to be a poet, you have to be able to think while you walk . . . You are now going to walk along the beach to the bay and as you observe the movement of the sea, you are going to invent metaphors."

"Give me an example!"

"Listen to this poem: 'Here on the Island, the sea, so much sea. It spills over from time to time. It says yes, then no, then no. It cannot be still. My name is sea, it repeats, striking a stone but not convincing it. Then with the seven green tongues, of seven green tigers, of seven green seas, it caresses it, kisses it, wets it, and pounds on its chest, repeating its own name.'"

He paused with an air of satisfaction. "What do you think?"

"It's weird."

"Weird? You certainly are a severe critic."

"No, sir. The *poem* wasn't weird. What was weird was the way I felt when you recited it."

"My dear Mario, please try to express yourself more clearly. I simply cannot spend the whole morning in your delightful company."

"How can I explain it to you? When you recited that poem, the words went from over there to over here."

"Like the sea, then!"

"Yeah, they moved just like the sea."

"That's the rhythm."

"And I felt weird because with all that movement, I got dizzy."

"You got dizzy?"

"Of course. I was like a boat tossing upon your words."

The poet's eyelids rose slowly.

"Like a boat tossing upon my words."

"Uh-huh."

"You know what you just did, Mario?"

"No, what?"

"You just invented a metaphor."

"But it doesn't count, 'cause it just came out by accident."

"All images are accidents, my son."

Mario placed his hand over his heart in an attempt to control the wild palpitations. He was sure his chest would burst open right there. But he pulled himself together, and with one impertinent finger shaking just inches away from his emeritus client's nose, said, "Do you think that everything in the world, I mean *everything,*

POSTTEST

like the wind, the ocean, trees, mountains, fire, animals, houses, deserts, the rain . . ."

". . . Do you think the whole world is a metaphor for something?"

—Excerpted from *The Postman* by Antonio Skarmeta
(*Il Postino* translated by Katherine Silver)

25. When the poet Neruda says to the postman, "And you think you can think just standing there," what is implied about the postman?

(1) He has parked his bicycle illegally.
(2) He cannot do two things at the same time.
(3) He must think by being active.
(4) He cannot write while standing up.
(5) He cannot talk and write at the same time.

26. If the poet Neruda were to compose a new poem and recite it to the postman, can you predict Mario's reaction?

(1) He would feel the poem itself was weird.
(2) He would feel his reaction to the poem was weird.
(3) He would be moved to write a poem of his own.
(4) He would be in awe of the poet's creativity.
(5) He would feel inspired to change his occupation.

27. When Mario felt the rhythm of the poem, what did he compare himself to?

(1) a sea captain steering a vessel
(2) a young man peddling down a hill
(3) the wind rustling through the trees
(4) a teacher talking to a misbehaving student
(5) a boat "tossing" upon the poet's words

28. When the postman asks, ". . . the wind, the ocean, trees, mountains, fire, animals, houses, deserts, the rain . . . Do you think the whole world is a metaphor for something?" What does the poet imply?

That a metaphor may be

(1) majestic sights such as trees and mountains
(2) only "living" things such as animals or deserts
(3) powerful elements of nature such as the ocean or fire
(4) any mental or physical image whatsoever
(5) only man-made structures such as houses

29. How is the overall perspective (point of view) of the passage achieved?

(1) first person narration by the postman Mario
(2) dialogue plus third person narration by the author
(3) first person narration by the poet Neruda
(4) third person narration by an observer of Mario and Neruda
(5) third person narration by the seas which come "alive"

30. Reflecting on the passage as a whole, what is the poet Neruda teaching the postman and the reader?

(1) Poetry is really all around us in life.
(2) Metaphors cannot be invented.
(3) Images are not just accidents.
(4) Poets need a quiet atmosphere.
(5) Most poetry is about the sea and sky.

POSTTEST

Questions 31–35 are based on the following excerpt.

WHY DO ROADS REPRESENT FREEDOM?

Nothing speaks America like The Road—symbol of freedom and the pioneer spirit, celebration of democracy and individuality. Long before the automobile, Americans, obsessed with what lay beyond the horizon, blazed trails across the landscape, built railroad tracks through the western wilderness. When the motorcar rolled onto the scene, they embraced it as a pleasure machine that freed them to rediscover the country under their own steam.

But if the automobile revved the nation's restless frontier spirit, it caused a road crisis out of which came in mid-century the most ambitious and costly—129 billion dollars—public-works project in U.S. history: the Interstate Highway System (otherwise known as the Dwight D. Eisenhower System of Interstate and Defense Highways). Marked by uniform red-white-and-blue numbered shields, the 42,742-mile network makes up less than 2 percent of the country's roads, yet it carries more than 21 percent of the traffic. It's America's circulatory system, the modern Main Street.

Early in this century, the country boasted some 2 million miles of local thoroughfares, of which only about 140 miles were paved. Laid largely for the purpose of getting rural folks to town more easily, roads often dead-ended at a state or county line, leaving ongoing travelers to the vagaries of rustic byways.

The first national highway, begun in 1912, linked New York City and San Francisco—the route later traced by Interstate 80. No joy ride, the Lincoln Highway spurred federal highway advocates. Planning for the network began in the late 1930s, when public interest was piqued by the hype over Germany's fast, efficient Autobahns. On a more fantastic scale, General Motors' "Futurama" exhibit at the 1939 World's Fair wowed visitors with its vision of an America streamlined by superhighways. "Imagine the *possibilities*" was the seductive message. Behind it were the road industries, hoping to profit from the dream of a national expressway system.

—Excerpted from *America's Main Streets* by Alison Kahn

31. According to the passage, what was one road problem drivers encountered early in the century?

(1) gasoline shortages
(2) few paved roads
(3) heavy traffic
(4) construction delays
(5) poor lighting

32. The passage points out that although interstates are fewer in number than regular roads, they are heavily used.

Which of the choices below demonstrates this same relationship?

(1) grains of sand on a beach
(2) drops of water in an ocean
(3) snowflakes in a snowstorm
(4) vowels in the English language
(5) staples in a metal stapler

33. What is emphasized by the comparison of the Interstate Highway System to the circulatory system (lines 24–25)?

(1) size and productivity
(2) speed and safety
(3) importance and cost
(4) importance and function
(5) complexity and productivity

POSTTEST

34. What is suggested about the Lincoln Highway in lines 36–38?

The highway

(1) was extremely congested by vehicles
(2) was used for essential transport
(3) was very costly because of high tolls
(4) was constructed for urban travel
(5) was difficult to travel upon

35. This excerpt from *America's Main Streets* has been published accompanied by several quotations. The quotation by Walt Whitman in *Song of the Road* states: "O public road . . . you express me better than I express myself."

What connection can be drawn between this quotation and the excerpt?

(1) Both identify the road as a symbol of individuality.
(2) Both emphasize the number of highways.
(3) Both contain a factual and somber tone.
(4) Both state complaints about the interstates.
(5) Both treat highway development sarcastically.

Questions 36–40 are based on the following document.

WHAT EXPECTATIONS ARE EXPLAINED?

Eldvorak Medical Center
Patient Rights and Responsibilities

Your rights and responsibilities as a patient are important for you to know. Eldvorak Medical Center is committed to a policy of providing the highest quality care possible. As a patient, you are entitled to respectful and considerate care that is age appropriate and that is respectful of human dignity. In turn, we request that you accept your responsibilities as a patient.

A Patient's Rights
You have the right to feel safe and be treated with care. A plan for your care should be explained to you before you sign any document of consent, and you should have the right to participate in any decision making about that care. If you wish to refuse treatment, it is your right to do so unless it is against the law. As a patient, you are entitled to privacy and confidentiality. For example, only you and those people who are taking care of you have the right to read your medical records unless you give written permission to others. Also, you have the right to examine your medical bill and to receive an explanation of it. You have the right to have visitors during visiting hours, phone calls, and mail provided that you are not too sick. If you wish to formulate an advance directive such as a Living Will or Durable Healthcare Power of Attorney, you have the right to do so and can obtain help through Patient Services.

A Patient's Responsibilities
Your responsibilities include informing the hospital about anything pertaining to your health care such as previous illness or currently used medications. This is necessary so that we can give you the best possible care. It is your responsibility to ask questions when you do not understand something and to let the hospital know if you do not understand English or if you have problems hearing, seeing, or speaking. You are also responsible for treating other patients respectfully and respecting hospital staff, property, and policies. You are expected to pay your bill on time, or to contact the billing office if payment is a problem. If you have any questions regarding your rights and responsibilities, do not hesitate to discuss them with your doctor, nurse, or patient representative.

POSTTEST

36. According to the document on page 1025, who would have access to a patient's medical records without written permission?

(1) an insurance agent
(2) a visiting cousin
(3) an attending nurse
(4) a current employer
(5) a spiritual adviser

37. From the document, you could predict that if the hospital were to hire a new employee, which commitment would the hospital want that employee to demonstrate?

(1) cleanliness
(2) economy
(3) teamwork
(4) human dignity
(5) punctuality

38. Which is an example of unacceptable behavior on the part of a patient?

(1) requesting to read your medical records(analysis)
(2) receiving a visitor during hours
(3) asking a question of a technician
(4) reviewing the medical charges
(5) treating another patient disrespectfully

39. Which of the lines below best illustrates the tone of respectfulness that the hospital tries to convey?

(1) Your responsibilities include informing the hospital . . .
(2) In turn, we request that you accept your responsibilities . . .
(3) You are expected to pay your bill on time, or to contact . . .
(4) It is your responsibility to ask questions if . . .
(5) This is necessary so that we can give you . . .

40. How is the document organized?

(1) a general policy statement of specific considerations
(2) an argument in defense of various hospital hiring policies
(3) an advertisement to publicize specialized services
(4) a statement of warning citing consequences
(5) a presentation of research survey results

POSTTEST

Language Arts, Reading Answer Key

Inherit the Wind

1. **Comprehension (1)** The clue is the expression "ride the favorite" associated with winning. Just before this, Drummond had talked about a lawyer in Chicago who "never takes a case unless it's a sure thing."

2. **Application (4)** Drummond was not saying that parents should never sacrifice for their children, but his own parents had sacrificed unnecessarily to buy an expensive rocking horse toy that broke the first time he rode it. He is advocating the use of caution in looking below the surface of something that appears "bright, shining, perfect-seeming—all gold."

3. **Analysis (5)** Drummond is comparing the law and a race horse. He said at the beginning of this paragraph, "Sometimes I think the law *is* like a race horse."

4. **Analysis (3)** As a child, Drummond imagines the rocking horse having "everything in the world!" As an adult, he seems very angry as he talks about the rocking horse splitting in two, about its being "all shine, and no substance," about the need to "look behind the paint," and ultimately about its being "a lie." The extent to which his parents had to sacrifice in order to buy him the toy must also have made him angry.

5. **Synthesis (2)** The connection is that a "lie" would be teaching without the honesty of presenting an alternative theory. Drummond is supporting Cates in his challenge of the Tennessee law which allowed only the teaching of creationism and did not allow the teaching of an alternative, scientific view of evolution. Drummond is not saying that one theory should be taught over the other, but he is supporting Cates's right to academic freedom and is encouraging him to take a risk to teach according to his view of the curriculum.

6. **Synthesis (3)** It is reasonable to assume that if Brady ran unsuccessfully for president *three* times, he really, really wanted to be president. While the case may have been about one teacher in a small town, the case took on big implications of freedom of speech regarding the teacher's right to teach. One can assume that Brady would think all the publicity surrounding freedom of speech and creationism versus evolution (or religion versus science) would give him additional national exposure and help his campaign.

The Grapes of Wrath

7. **Comprehension (3)** From lines 1 to 4, it is clear that the man has lost his land. A reference to farming is clear from the word "*tractor.*"

8. **Application (2)** Wealth would enable a man to provide for his family, go camping, travel west, or return to a place he'd been before. However, the last line of the passage specifies that "*the quality of owning*" isolates an individual so that he no longer shares in the "*we*" of human experience.

9. **Analysis (3)** The simple structure of the sentences illustrates the basics of life, showing simple ideas, simple things, basic needs. The narrator states that from this beginning, more develops.

10. **Analysis (1)** The eyes of the women are compared to stones: flat, hard, unreflecting. They do not show much emotion or warmth.

11. **Synthesis (5)** The passage contrasts the men and family who have nothing with the owners, showing a difference between the haves and have-nots. A theme of social class conflict is portrayed.

12. **Synthesis (4)** Human rights and revolution are social issues. The passage from Steinbeck also contains an examination of social issues with its discussion of human problems, relationships, and movements.

"The Truly Great"

13. Comprehension (1) When the speaker identifies those "*Whose lovely ambition /Was that their lips, still touched with fire,/should tell of the spirit,*" (lines 8–10), he is speaking of poets.

14. Application (2) Although any of the projects might be worthwhile, the poem is a tribute honoring those who serve to inspire humanity's spirits. As a result, the speaker would most likely fund a museum showcasing such individuals.

15. Analysis (1) In lines 27–30, the poem states that the names of these honored individuals are "*feted by the waving grass/ And by the streams of white cloud,/And whispers of wind. . .*" suggesting that even nature celebrates these people.

16. Analysis (4) The sun represents a symbol of enlightenment and inspiration. The words "*traveled a short while*" suggest living. The phrase reinforces the idea that certain individuals performed some inspiring acts during their lives.

17. Synthesis (5) The poem links poets with positive images and words, such as "*sun,*" "*lovely ambition,*" "*essential delight,*" and suggests that even nature celebrates poets. The purpose of the poem is to honor and commemorate great poets.

18. Synthesis (3) The images and tone of the poem are uplifting. The poem does not reflect dark disillusionment or foster ridicule. No specific disasters or corrupt politics are cited. We are called upon to remember inspiration and spirit and honor those who help us to do so.

"The Green Door"

19. Comprehension (3) The passage describes a young man's coming to the aid of a starving shop girl who is weak from lack of nutrition; we can presume that she eats poorly because of "insufficient wages," "illness," and "lost positions." The line "It was one of a thousand such . . . " indicates that there are many other shop girls in the same situation. There is no evidence for the statements in the other choices.

20. Application (5) Since Rudolf showed himself to be one who personally helped a starving shop girl, we would expect his response to be one of personal involvement rather than refusing (choice 1), making an excuse (choice 2), acting helpless (choice 3), or putting it off on someone else (choice 4).

21. Analysis (2) The characters of the shop girl, the seemingly well-off Rudolf, and the negro [spelling according to the pre-1920 short story] are not at all similar. All other statements are true.

22. Analysis (5) The author's use of the simile "like some starved wild animal" creates a vivid mental picture but also tells the reader how desperate the shop girl is. This desperateness invokes the reader's sympathy. There is no support for the other choices.

23. Synthesis (5) The irony is that he could have gone to *any* of the doors, but because of Fate (or Chance) he knocks on the door of the young, desperate girl. As the true Adventurer, Rudolf Steiner follows the path of Fate, as directed more than once by the cards given to him by the negro. It is also ironic that the electric sign of the new play is also the title, "The Green Door." Choices 1, 2, and 3 are not correct statements. Regarding choice 4, elsewhere in the story Rudolf only *says* to the girl that he was looking for a piano tuner; he does this because she must not know the truth as to how he found her.

24. Synthesis (1) The clue in Passage One that this is a collection of city stories is the line, "*It was one of a thousand such as the city yawns at every day—the shop girl's story . . . .*" There is no evidence for the other choices.

The Postman

25. Comprehension (3) The poet is emphasizing that thinking (and, therefore, writing poetry) is an active rather than a passive process. The postman must *work* at thinking. The other choices are not direct statements about the process of thinking.

26. Application (2) In the passage, when Neruda recited his poem, the postman Mario said, "The *poem* wasn't weird. What was weird was the way *I* felt when you recited it." We can assume that the postman would feel the same if the poet were to compose a new poem and recite to the postman. This eliminates the other choices.

27. Analysis (5) Mario really *felt* the rhythm of the poem and said, "I got dizzy." He went on to say, "I was like a boat tossing upon your words." This negates the other choices.

28. Analysis (4) In mentioning both living and non-living elements of nature plus man-made things such as houses, the poet implies that a metaphor may be any mental or physical image whatsoever. The other choices do not preclude the use of metaphors, but those choices are all exclusive. The correct choice is inclusive.

29. Synthesis (2) The author tells the story in the third person ("Neruda tightened *his* grip . . . " and "Mario placed *his* hand over his heart . . . "), and the author uses dialogue to quote Mario and Neruda. Choices 1 and 3 are incorrect because both the postman Mario's and the poet Neruda's comments are in quotes; if this were first person narration by either of them, their comments would not be in quotes. Choice 4 is incorrect because there is no other observer. Choice 5 is incorrect because while the seas are described with "seven green tongues" within the poem recited, the seas are not narrating the story.

30. Synthesis (1) The poet Neruda is teaching the postman that poetry is really all around us in life. Choice 2 is incorrect because Neruda tells Mario, "You just invented a metaphor." Choice 3 is incorrect because Neruda says, "All images are accidents, my son." Choice 4 is not necessarily true because some poets need a quiet atmosphere and others do not. Choice 5 is not necessarily accurate because poetry can be about any subject, and it would be difficult to say *most* poetry is about the sea and sky. (There is no simple way to review all poetry for all time to determine the subject matter of most poems.)

America's Main Streets

31. Comprehension (2) In lines 26–28, the passage states that only 140 of two million miles were paved.

32. Application (4) The vowels in the English language are like the interstates compared to regular roads because there are fewer vowels than other letters, but the vowels are used heavily.

33. Analysis (4) The circulatory system is important to the life of a human being, and the interstate system is important to the life of the country. Both the interstate system and the circulatory system share similar functions of moving and transporting material.

34. Analysis (5) The Lincoln Highway is described as "*No joy ride.*" Early road construction could not easily address problems of geography and climate. Lincoln Highway "*spurred federal highway advocates,*" indicating that the difficulty of using the highway prompted a call for more and better highway construction.

35. Synthesis (1) The quotation states "*you express me,*" and lines 1 and 2 of the passage recognize the "Road" as a symbol of individuality.

Eldvorak Medical Center

36. Comprehension (3) The patient's nurse would be one of the people taking care of him, so as specified in lines 19–23, that nurse would have access to the records.

37. Application (4) Although any of these characteristics might be appreciated in an employee, the dominant emphasis of the document is on respect for human dignity. This quality, therefore, would be especially necessary in an employee.

38. Analysis (5) Making fun of another patient would show disrespect. According to lines 44–45, a patient's responsibilities include showing respect toward other patients.

39. Analysis (2) This statement is the most respectful because rather than telling an individual what responsibilities he or she should observe, it *asks*, as indicated with the polite word, "*requests,*" that an individual observe them.

40. Synthesis (1) The document gives hospital policy, including items of information in two areas: rights and responsibilities. It does not argue, advertise, or warn. No survey results are included.

LANGUAGE ARTS, READING POSTTEST

Evaluation Chart

Use the answer key on pages 1027–1030 to check your answers to the Posttest. Then find the item number of each question you missed and circle it on the chart below to determine the reading content areas in which you need more practice. Pay particular attention to areas where you missed half or more of the questions. The page numbers for the content areas are listed on the chart below. For those questions that you missed, review the skill pages indicated.

	COMPREHENSION (pages 217–230)	**APPLICATION (pages 231–236)**	**ANALYSIS (pages 237–262)**	**SYNTHESIS (pages 263–270)**
Fiction (pages 589–614)	7, 19, 25	8, 20, 26	9, 10, 21, 22, 27, 28	11, 12, 23, 24, 29, 30
Poetry (pages 615–636)	13	14	15, 16	17, 18
Drama (pages 637–654)	1	2	3, 4	5, 6
Nonfiction Prose (pages 655–684)	31, 36	32, 37	33, 34, 38, 39	35, 40

POSTTEST

Mathematics

This Posttest will give you the opportunity to evaluate your readiness for the actual GED Mathematics Test. The Mathematics Posttest, like the GED Test, consists of two parts: Part I (calculator allowed) has 25 questions, and Part II (no calculator allowed) has 25 questions. Part I and Part II have a combined score of 50 points. Each part should take approximately 45 minutes, for a total test time of 90 minutes. Remember to use the calculator only during Part I. You may use the formula page throughout both Parts I and II.

When you take this Posttest, keep track of your time on each part. At the end of 45 minutes, if you have not completed Part I, mark your place and then finish the test. Do the same with Part II. This will give you an idea of whether you can finish the real GED Test in the time allotted. Try to answer as many questions as you can. A blank will count as a wrong answer, so make a reasonable guess for answers to questions of which you are not sure.

When you are finished with the test, check your answers and turn to the Evaluation Chart on page 1050. Use the chart to evaluate whether you are ready to take the final Practice Test and, if not, in what areas you need more work.

POSTTEST

Part I

Mathematics Posttest Answer Grid

1 (1) (2) (3) (4) (5)

2 (1) (2) (3) (4) (5)

3 (1) (2) (3) (4) (5)

4

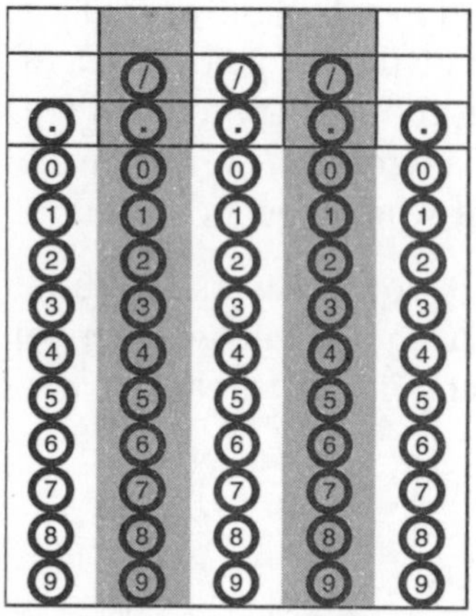

5

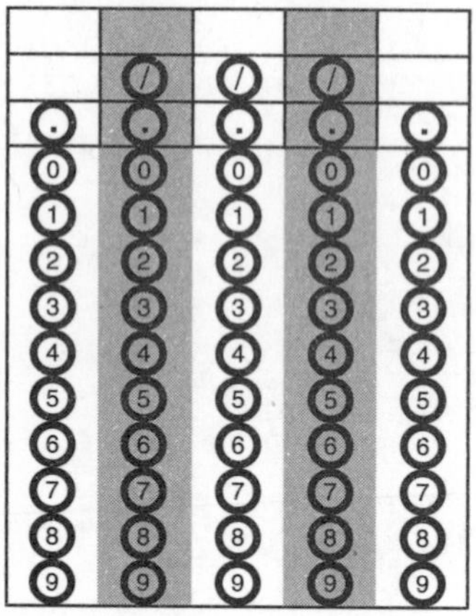

6 (1) (2) (3) (4) (5)

7 (1) (2) (3) (4) (5)

8 (1) (2) (3) (4) (5)

9 (1) (2) (3) (4) (5)

10 (1) (2) (3) (4) (5)

11 (1) (2) (3) (4) (5)

12

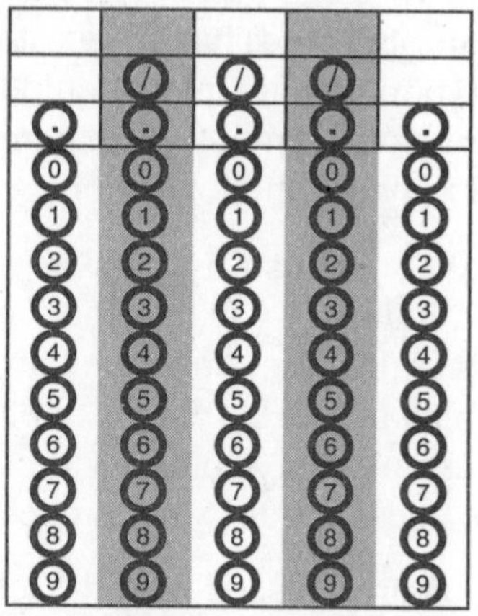

13

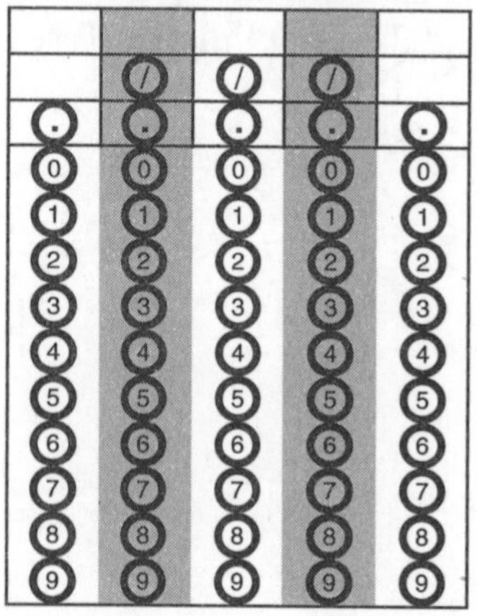

14 (1) (2) (3) (4) (5)

15 (1) (2) (3) (4) (5)

16 (1) (2) (3) (4) (5)

17

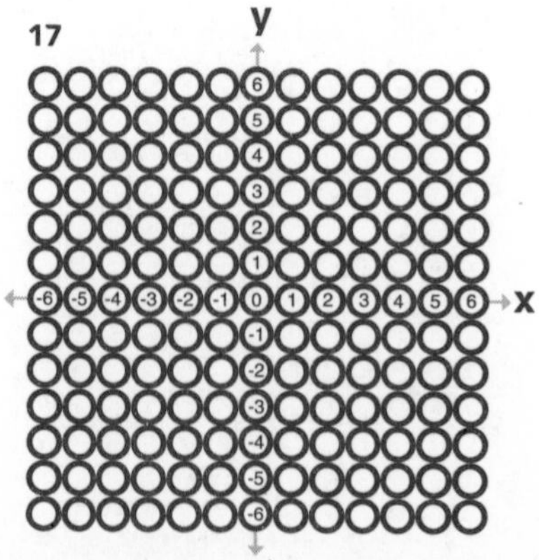

18 (1) (2) (3) (4) (5)

19 (1) (2) (3) (4) (5)

20 (1) (2) (3) (4) (5)

21

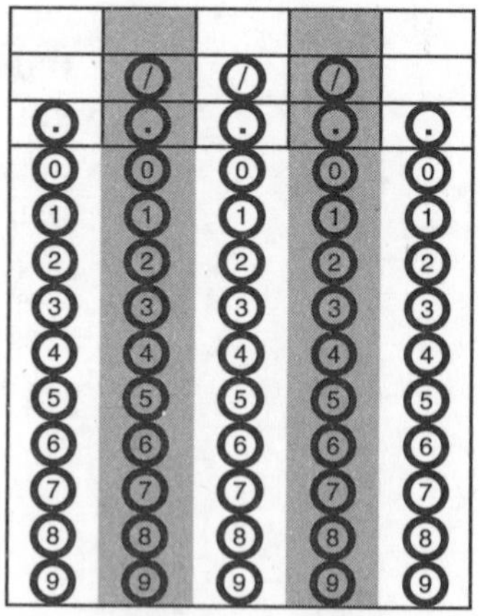

22

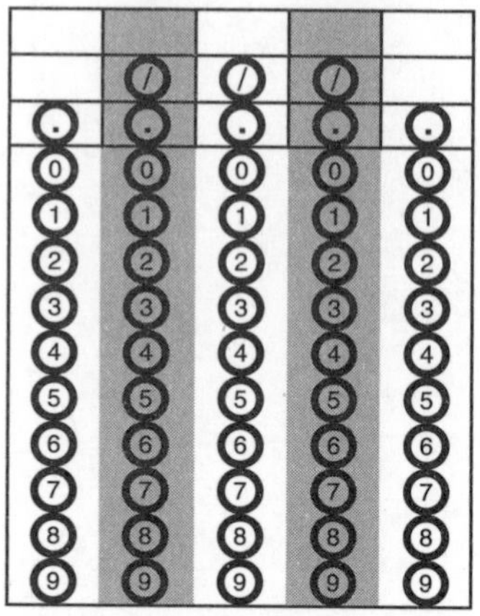

23 (1) (2) (3) (4) (5)

24 (1) (2) (3) (4) (5)

25 (1) (2) (3) (4) (5)

FORMULAS

AREA of a:	
square	Area = side^2
rectangle	Area = length × width
parallelogram	Area = base × height
triangle	Area = $\frac{1}{2}$ × base × height
trapezoid	Area = $\frac{1}{2} \times (\text{base}_1 + \text{base}_2) \times$ height
circle	Area = $\pi \times \text{radius}^2$; π is approximately equal to 3.14.
PERIMETER of a:	
square	Perimeter = 4 × side
rectangle	Perimeter = 2 × length + 2 × width
triangle	Perimeter = $\text{side}_1 + \text{side}_2 + \text{side}_3$
CIRCUMFERENCE of a circle	Circumference = π × diameter; π is approximately equal to 3.14.
VOLUME of a:	
cube	Volume = edge^3
rectangular solid	Volume = length × width × height
square pyramid	Volume = $\frac{1}{3} \times (\text{base edge})^2 \times$ height
cylinder	Volume = $\pi \times \text{radius}^2 \times$ height; π is approximately equal to 3.14.
cone	Volume = $\frac{1}{3} \times \pi \times \text{radius}^2 \times$ height; π is approximately equal to 3.14.
COORDINATE GEOMETRY	distance between points = $\sqrt{(x_2 - x_1)^2 + (y_2 - y_1)^2}$; (x_1, y_1) and (x_2, y_2) are two points in a plane. slope of a line = $\frac{y_2 - y_1}{x_2 - x_1}$; (x_1, y_1) and (x_2, y_2) are two points on the line.
PYTHAGOREAN RELATIONSHIP	$a^2 + b^2 = c^2$; a and b are legs and c the hypotenuse of a right triangle.
MEASURES OF CENTRAL TENDENCY	**mean** = $\frac{x_1 + x_2 + \ldots + x_n}{n}$, where the xs are the values for which a mean is desired, and n is the total number of values for x. **median** = the middle value of an odd number of *ordered* scores, and halfway between the two middle values of an even number of *ordered* scores.
SIMPLE INTEREST	interest = principal × rate × time
DISTANCE	distance = rate × time
TOTAL COST	total cost = (number of units) × (price per unit)

POSTTEST

Part I

Directions: Solve each problem. You may use your calculator and the formula page as needed.

Questions 1–3 refer to the following information.

To help decide how much to charge for its services, Custom Computers management compiled the following employee data.

Number of Employees	19	18	8	5
Weekly Wages Each Employee Earned	$360	$400	$480	$600

1. Which expression below represents the average wages the company pays per employee each week?

(1) $\frac{360 + 400 + 480 + 600}{4}$

(2) $\frac{19(360) + 18(400) + 8(480) + 5(600)}{19 + 18 + 8 + 5}$

(3) $\frac{19(360) \times 18(400) \times 8(480) \times 5(600)}{19 + 18 + 8 + 5}$

(4) $(19 + 18 + 8 + 5)(360 + 400 + 480 + 600)$

(5) $4(360 + 400 + 480 + 600)$

2. What percent of the employees earn more than $400 per week?

(1) 2.6%
(2) 13%
(3) 26%
(4) 31%
(5) 50%

3. If Custom Computers gives a 4% raise to all employees, how much will this add to the weekly payroll?

(1) $ 83.52
(2) $ 835.20
(3) $ 8,352
(4) $20,880
(5) $21,715.20

4. Valentina purchased $3\frac{1}{2}$ yards of nylon as shown on the sales slip. Including tax, how much change should she get back from a $20 bill?

QTY.	PRICE	AMOUNT
$3\frac{1}{2}$ yd	$2.40/yd	
	5% Tax	
	Total	

Mark your answer in the circles in the grid on your answer sheet.

5. Ahmed borrowed $450 from his credit union to buy a copier. If the interest rate is 9.9% and he takes the loan for a year, what will be his monthly payment to the nearest penny to repay the loan plus interest?

Mark your answer in the circles in the grid on your answer sheet.

POSTTEST

Questions 6 and 7 refer to the following information.

Juan worked as a waiter on Saturday nights to supplement his income. He kept a list of the tips he received for 8 weeks and the number of hours he worked each Saturday night.

Week	1	2	3	4	5	6	7	8
Tips	$98	$75.25	$84	$92	$60	$86.50	$90.60	$77
Hours	6	6	5	6	4	6	6	5

6. What was the median amount of Juan's weekly tips?

(1) $ 60
(2) $ 85.25
(3) $ 92
(4) $ 84
(5) $663

7. In addition to his tips, Juan's employer paid him $3 per hour. How much did he actually earn per hour, including his wages and his tips during week 3?

(1) $15.00
(2) $16.80
(3) $19.80
(4) $87
(5) $99

8. Temperatures in degrees Celsius (C) may be changed to degrees Fahrenheit (F) by using the formula $F = 1.8C + 32°$. Find the temperature in degrees Fahrenheit when C equals 25°.

(1) 45°
(2) 57°
(3) 58.8°
(4) 77°
(5) 102.6°

9. How many full gallons of regular lead-free gas can Josie buy for $20?

GAS PUMP	
Regular Lead-free	1.69^9
Premium Lead-free	1.89^9

(1) 10
(2) 11
(3) 12
(4) 13
(5) 14

10. Wesley willed his estate to Margaret, Betty Jo, and Johnny. He gave Margaret $20,000. Betty Jo got $2\frac{1}{2}$ times as much as Margaret. Johnny got $3\frac{1}{2}$ times as much as Margaret. What was the total value of the estate?

(1) $ 26,000
(2) $ 50,000
(3) $ 70,000
(4) $120,000
(5) $140,000

POSTTEST

11. The weekly investment report shows each company's stocks with its high bid, low bid, closing bid prices, and the net change from last week's closing bid. What is the average net change for all five companies listed?

COMPANY	HIGH	LOW	CLOSE	CHANGE
U.S. Investments	23.16	22.91	23.61	+.38
Global Growth	15.13	14.77	15.13	+.14
Select Services	22.01	21.94	21.97	–.09
United Funds	14.56	14.29	14.56	+.09
American Mutual	17.36	16.94	17.26	+.08

(1) .02
(2) .06
(3) .6
(4) .12
(5) 1.2

12. If 24-karat gold is pure gold and 12-karat gold is 50% gold, how many karats is 75% gold?

Mark your answer in the circles in the grid on your answer sheet.

13. If 27 out of 30 people passed a driving test, what percent failed?

Mark your answer in the circles in the grid on your answer sheet.

14. The 10 finalists in the local beauty pageant include 3 blonds, 4 brunettes, 1 redhead, and 2 black-haired women. What is the probability that the winner will be a brunette?

(1) $\frac{1}{9}$
(2) $\frac{1}{10}$
(3) $\frac{2}{5}$
(4) $\frac{4}{9}$
(5) $\frac{2}{3}$

15. In the equation $x^2 + 7x = 0$, which value of x makes the equation true?

(1) only –7
(2) only 7
(3) only 0
(4) 0 or –7
(5) 0 or 7

POSTTEST

Question 16 refers to the following information.

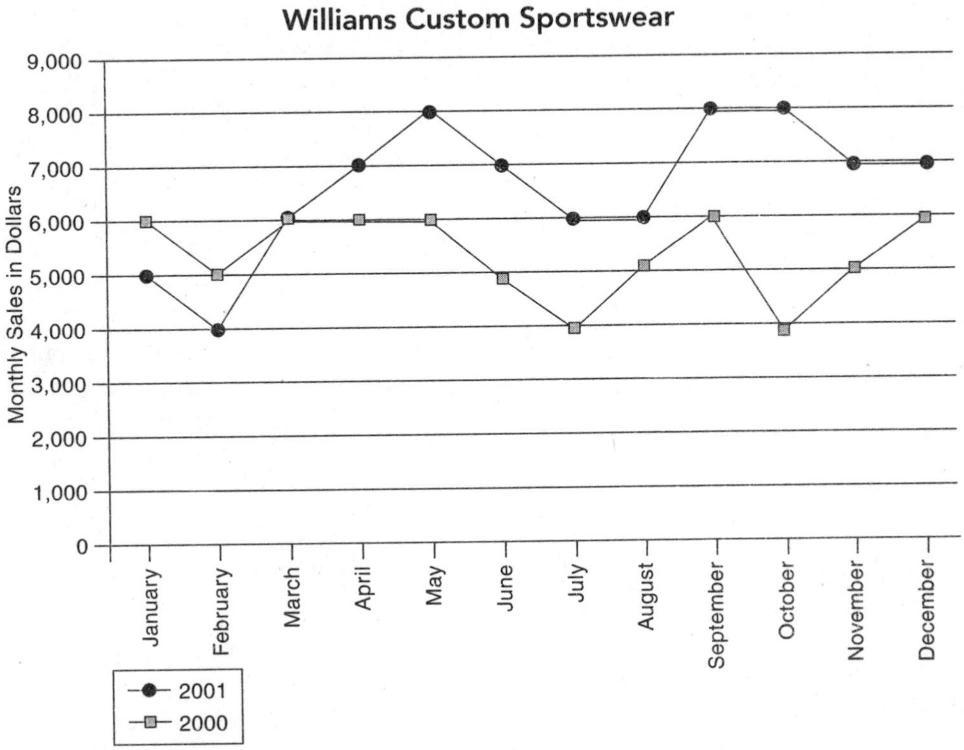

16. Which statement best describes the graph?

(1) Average sales were higher in 2001.
(2) Average monthly sales were about the same in both years.
(3) Average monthly sales doubled in 2001.
(4) Average sales were higher in 2000.
(5) Sales were always higher in the summer than in the rest of the year.

17. Show the location of the point that satisfies the equation $y = 2x + 3$ when $x = -1$.

Mark your answer on the coordinate plane grid on your answer sheet.

POSTTEST

Questions 18 and 19 refer to the following information.

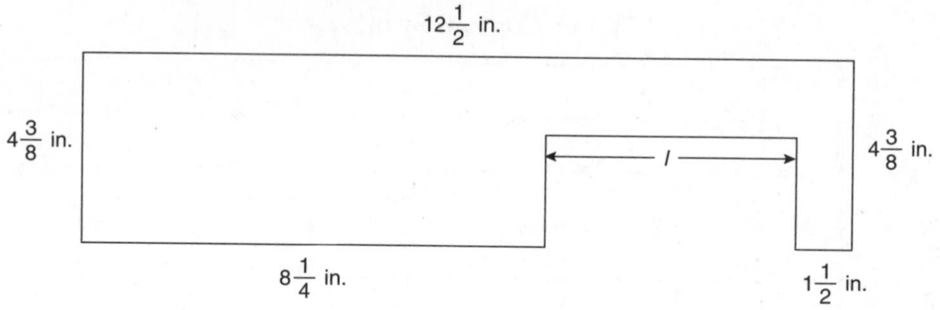

18. Find the missing length (l) in inches.

(1) $2\frac{3}{4}$
(2) $3\frac{1}{4}$
(3) $4\frac{1}{4}$
(4) $9\frac{3}{4}$
(5) Not enough information is given.

19. How many inches of molding would be needed to frame the figure above?

(1) $16\frac{7}{8}$
(2) $26\frac{5}{8}$
(3) $33\frac{3}{4}$
(4) 37
(5) Not enough information is given.

20. On a scale drawing $\frac{1}{2}$ inch = 10 miles. If the length of a road on this scale is 4 inches, which of the following could be used to find the length of the road?

(1) $10 \times 4 \times \frac{1}{2}$
(2) $10 \times 4 \times 2$
(3) $2(10 + 4)$
(4) $(10 + 4) \div 2$
(5) $(10 + 4) \div \frac{1}{2}$

21. Find the height of the 32-inch TV screen shown below. Round your answer to the nearest tenth of an inch.

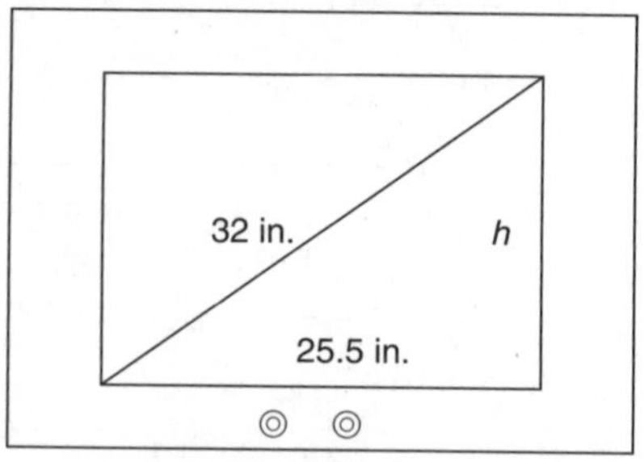

Mark your answer in the circles in the grid on your answer sheet.

POSTTEST

22. Find the difference between the volume of the cylinder and the volume of the rectangular box below. Round your answer to the nearest cubic inch.

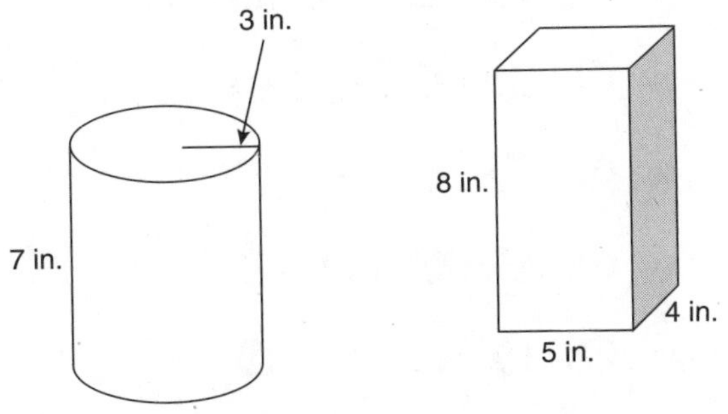

Mark your answer in the circles in the grid on your answer sheet.

23. If the cube and rectangular box have the same volume, which equation can you use to find the height (h) of the box?

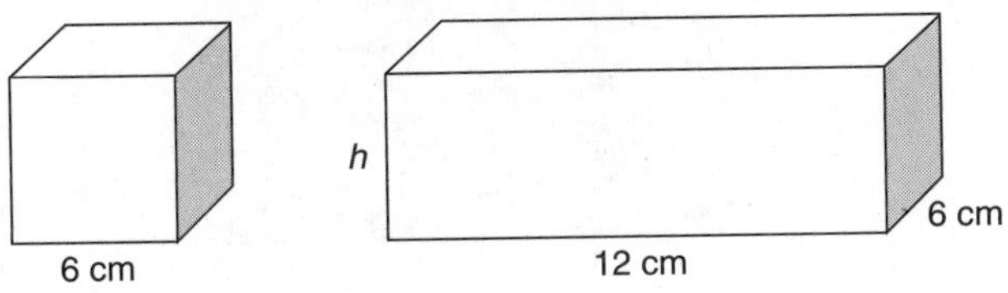

(1) $6^3 = 6 \times 12 \times h$
(2) $6^2 = 6 \times 12 \times h$
(3) $6^3 = 6 + 12 + h$
(4) $6 = (6 + 12)h$
(5) $h = 6 \times 6 \times 12$

24. If a ream of paper (500 sheets) is 2.125 inches thick, how thick is one sheet of paper? Give your answer in scientific notation.

(1) 1.0625×10^3
(2) 42.5×10^3
(3) 4.25×10^3
(4) 4.25×10^{-3}
(5) 4.25×10^{-2}

25. The balance on a \$6000 loan is reduced by each monthly payment. If the payment is \$250 per month, the formula for figuring the balance is: balance = 6000 – 250m, where m is the number of months. Which of the following is the graph of that formula?

(1)
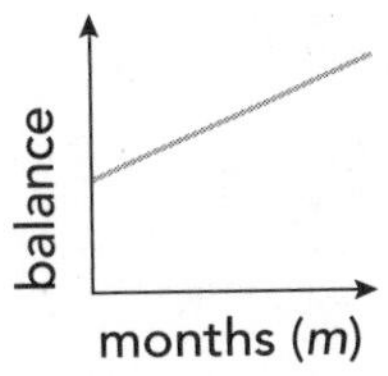

(2)
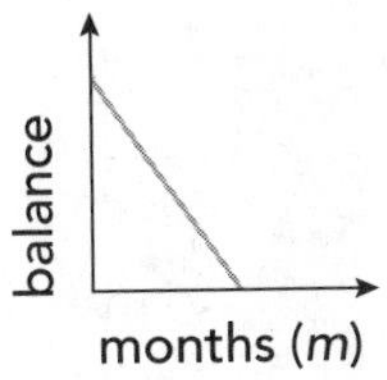

(3)
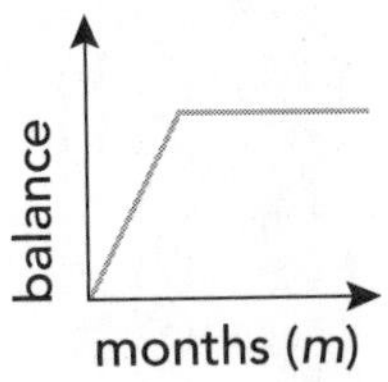

(4)
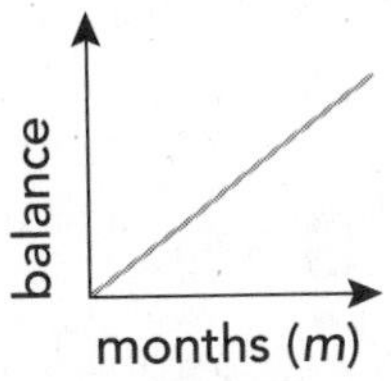

(5)
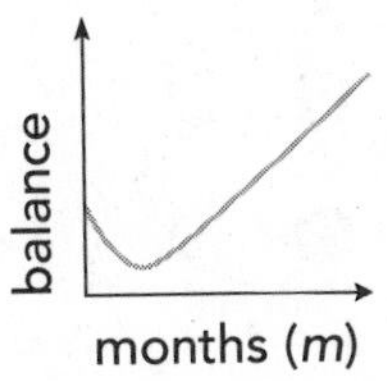

POSTTEST

Part II

Mathematics Posttest Answer Grid

26 ① ② ③ ④ ⑤

27 ① ② ③ ④ ⑤

28 ① ② ③ ④ ⑤

29 ① ② ③ ④ ⑤

30 ① ② ③ ④ ⑤

31

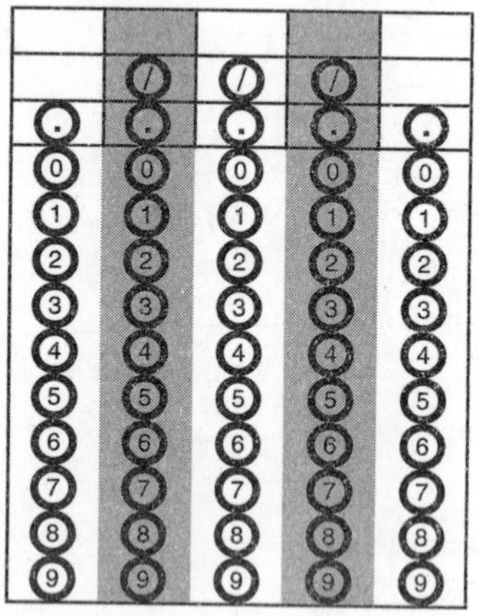

32 ① ② ③ ④ ⑤

33 ① ② ③ ④ ⑤

34 ① ② ③ ④ ⑤

35 ① ② ③ ④ ⑤

36 ① ② ③ ④ ⑤

37

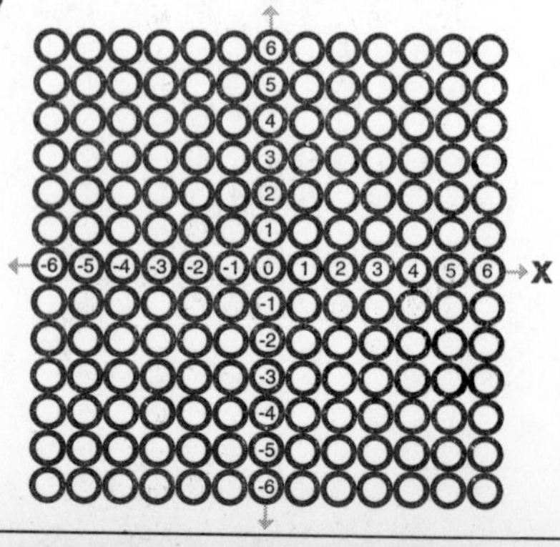

38 ① ② ③ ④ ⑤

39 ① ② ③ ④ ⑤

40 ① ② ③ ④ ⑤

41 ① ② ③ ④ ⑤

42 ① ② ③ ④ ⑤

43

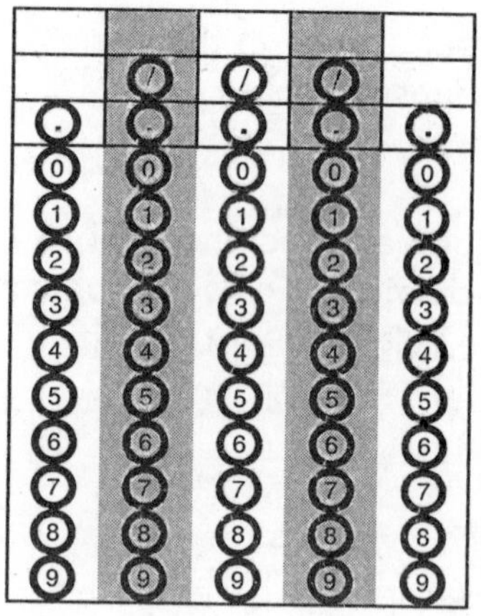

44 ① ② ③ ④ ⑤

45 ① ② ③ ④ ⑤

46 ① ② ③ ④ ⑤

47 ① ② ③ ④ ⑤

48 ① ② ③ ④ ⑤

49 ① ② ③ ④ ⑤

50 ① ② ③ ④ ⑤

POSTTEST

Part II

Directions: Solve each problem. Do *not* use a calculator. Use the formula page as needed.

26. A store had received a supply of 8 dozen calculators and sold them for $9.99 each. If the store sold all but 2 dozen of the calculators, approximately how much money did it make?

(1) $ 72
(2) $ 100
(3) $ 172
(4) $ 720
(5) $1000

27. If it takes 4.5 gallons of paint to paint 3 rooms, how many whole gallons of paint will you have to buy to paint 7 rooms?

(1) 9
(2) 10
(3) 11
(4) 12
(5) 13

28. Arrange the following numbers in order from the *smallest* value to the *greatest:*

1^5, 2^3, 4^1, and 6

(1) 6, 4^1, 1^5, 2^3
(2) 1^5, 4^1, 6, 2^3
(3) 1^5, 2^3, 4^1, 6
(4) 6, 4^1, 2^3, 1^5
(5) 2^3, 4^1, 6, 1^5

29. Many calculators express very large or very small numbers in scientific notation. If the number 4.32×10^4 appears in the display of a calculator, what is the value of this number?

(1) .0432
(2) 4.0032
(3) 432
(4) 43,200
(5) 4,320,000

Questions 30 and 31 refer to the following information.

An adult education class of 30 students had the following characteristics.

Adult Student Marital Status

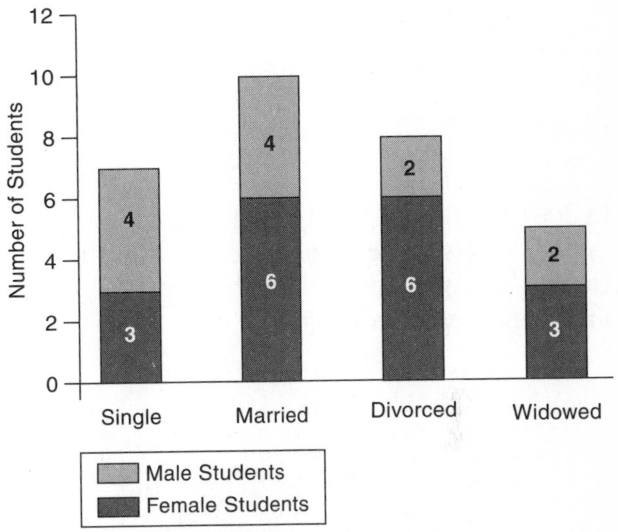

30. What is the probability that a student selected at random from this class is married?

(1) $\frac{1}{3}$
(2) $\frac{1}{5}$
(3) $\frac{2}{3}$
(4) $\frac{2}{15}$
(5) $\frac{1}{2}$

31. What percent of the widowed students are female?

Mark your answer in the circles in the grid on your answer sheet.

POSTTEST

32. The force of gravity is 6 times greater on the earth than it is on the moon. What is the weight of a 150-pound man on the moon?

(1) 25 pounds
(2) 144 pounds
(3) 156 pounds
(4) 900 pounds
(5) Not enough information is given.

Questions 33–35 refer to the following information.

In 2001 the Barnes family total income was $45,000. This circle graph describes how the Barnes family distributed their income to cover their expenses and savings.

Barnes Family Budget 2001

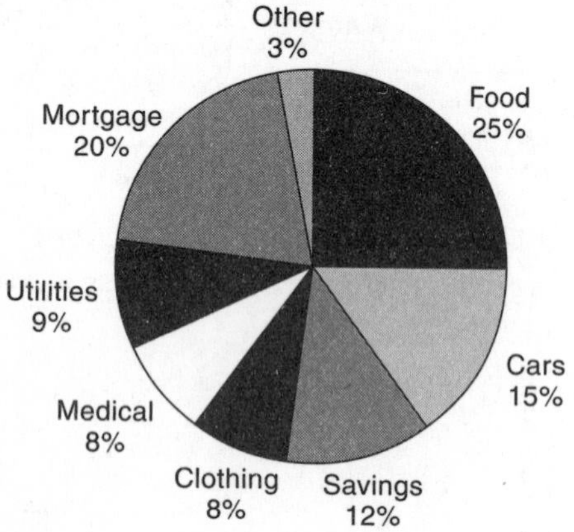

33. Housing costs include home mortgage payments and utilities. How much were the housing costs in 2001 for the Barnes family?

(1) $ 1,551
(2) $ 4,050
(3) $ 9,000
(4) $13,050
(5) $15,517

34. If the money is spent equally, how much is allocated to each person in the Barnes family for clothing in 2001?

(1) $ 900
(2) $1200
(3) $1800
(4) $3600
(5) Not enough information is given.

35. If the Barnes family income rose 10% in 2002 and the family followed the same budget, how much money would be put into savings in 2002?

(1) $ 450
(2) $ 540
(3) $4500
(4) $5400
(5) $5940

POSTTEST

36. In the expression $x + 2 > 13$, which of the following could be the value of x?

(1) 2
(2) 9
(3) 11
(4) 13
(5) Not enough information is given.

37. In the figure below find the coordinates of the midpoint of the line segment.

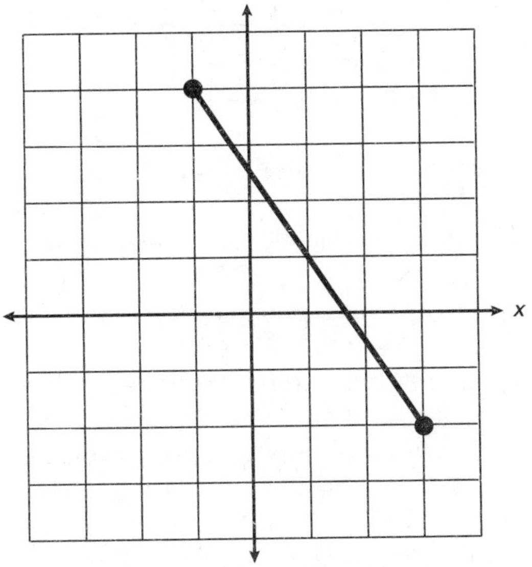

Mark your answer on the coordinate plane grid on your answer sheet.

38. How many inches long is the radius of the largest circle that can fit inside a rectangle 18 inches long and 12 inches wide?

(1) 3
(2) 6
(3) 9
(4) 12
(5) 18

39. Jane got a good deal on her new coat. She bought her coat on sale as shown and then used her coupon to further reduce the price. Which expression below shows how much she paid for the coat originally selling for $126?

COAT SALE TAKE 25% OFF the original price.	COUPON Take an additional 10% off already reduced prices.

(1) (.75)(.90)(126)
(2) (.25)(.10)(126)
(3) .25(126) – .10(126)
(4) 126 – .25(.10)
(5) 126 – .25(126) – .10(126)

40. Find the measure of $\angle x$ in the triangle below.

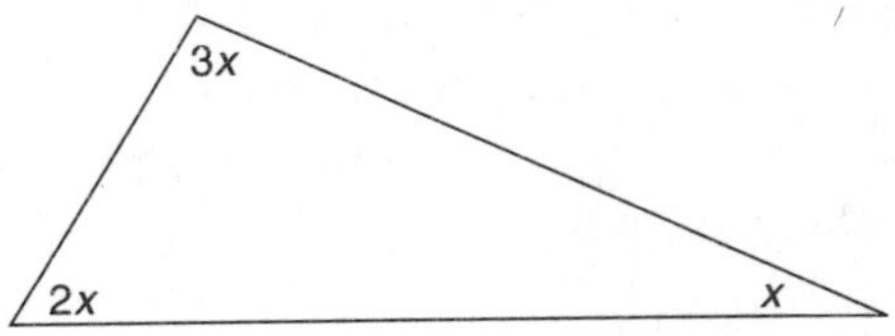

(1) 15°
(2) 30°
(3) 45°
(4) 60°
(5) 75°

41. An 84-cm wire is cut into three pieces. The second piece is 4 cm longer than the first piece and the third piece is twice as long as the second piece. Find the length of the shortest piece.

(1) 18
(2) 22
(3) 28
(4) 32
(5) 36

POSTTEST

42. Which expression below represents the cost of one roll of paper towels if the price is 3 rolls for $t and you get a 75¢ rebate?

(1) $\frac{t}{3} - .75$
(2) $3t + .75$
(3) $3t - .75$
(4) $\frac{t}{3} + .75$
(5) $\frac{t - .75}{3}$

43. On the Illinois state tax form, numbers are to be rounded to the nearest dollar. If Heather earned $8265.53 at her part-time job, what number would she enter on the form for earnings?

Mark your answer in the circles in the grid on your answer sheet.

44. Together two computers cost $2700 per year to rent. If one costs twice as much as the other, what is the monthly cost of the most expensive one?

(1) $ 75
(2) $ 150
(3) $ 225
(4) $ 900
(5) $1800

45. Which statement best describes the relationship between lines *M* and *N*?

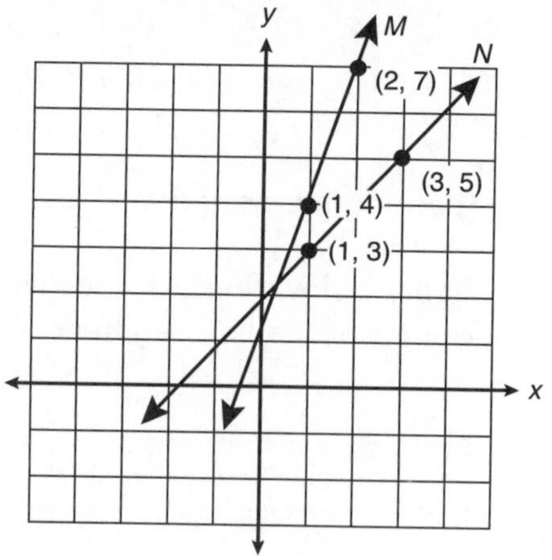

(1) Line *M* and line *N* both have positive slopes.
(2) Line *M* and line *N* both have negative slopes.
(3) Line *M* has a positive slope, and line *N* has a negative slope.
(4) Line *M* has a negative slope, and line *N* has a positive slope.
(5) There is not enough information to calculate the slopes of line *N* and line *M*.

46. A driver drove 50 miles in 50 minutes. How many miles per hour was he driving?

(1) 25
(2) 45
(3) 50
(4) 60
(5) Not enough information is given.

POSTTEST

47. The sketch below shows two pieces of baseboard joined together to make a strong, tight fit. If one board is cut to a 75° angle, what is the measure of the angle with the question mark?

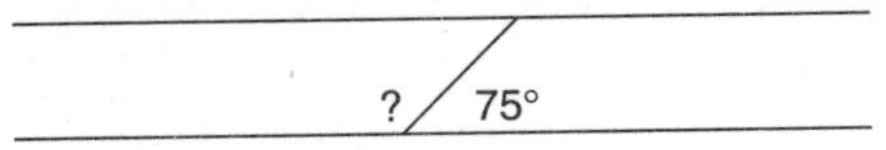

(1) 15°
(2) 45°
(3) 60°
(4) 105°
(5) 285°

48. How many square inches larger is the area of ΔABC than ΔCDE shown in the figure?

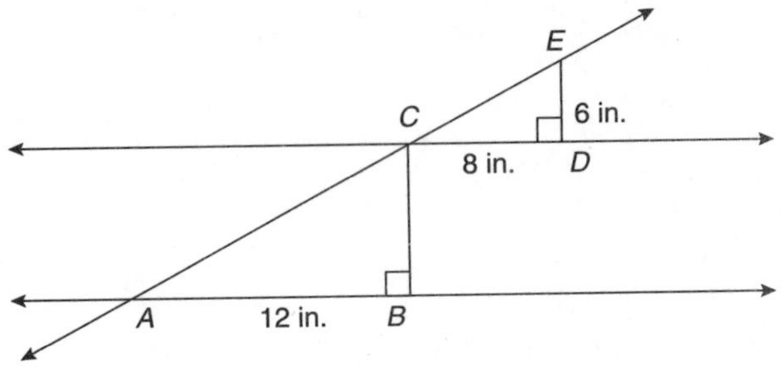

(1) 9
(2) 24
(3) 30
(4) 54
(5) 78

49. What is the area of the parallelogram shown in the diagram?

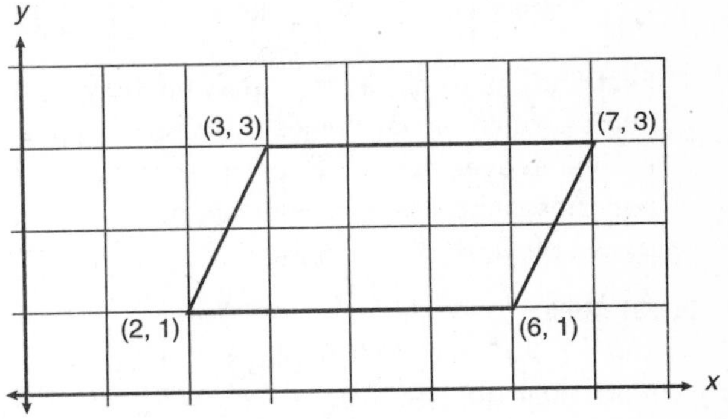

(1) 8 sq units
(2) 12 sq units
(3) 18 sq units
(4) 42 sq units
(5) Not enough information is given.

50. Two cars leave town at the same time. One travels west at 56 mph, and the other travels south at 42 mph. After one hour, how far apart are the cars?

(1) 10 miles
(2) 14 miles
(3) 70 miles
(4) 98 miles
(5) 196 miles

Answers are on page 1046.

POSTTEST

Mathematics Answer Key

Part I

1. (2) $\frac{19(360) + 18(400) + 8(480) + 5(600)}{19 + 18 + 8 + 5}$

First find the total wages paid by multiplying the number of employees times the weekly wages each employee earned for each category. Then add those amounts. Finally divide by the sum of the employees.

2. (3) 26%

There are 13 out of 50 employees that make more than $400 per week.

To find the percent, set up a proportion.

$\frac{13}{50} = \frac{N\%}{100\%}$

Solve for $N = \frac{13 \times 100}{50} = \frac{1300}{50} = 26.$

3. (2) $835.20

$19(360) + 18(400) + 8(480) + 5(600) = 20880$

$20880 \times 4\% = 20880 \times .04 = 835.20$

4. 11.18

$3\frac{1}{2} \times \$2.40 = \$8.40$

$8.40 \times .05 = +\ .42$

8.82

$\$20.00 - 8.82 = \$11.18$

5. 41.21

$\$450 \times 9.9\% = 450 \times .099 = \$44.55$

$450 + 44.55 = 494.55$

$494.55 \div 12 = \$41.21$ 25 = $41.21

6. (2) $85.25

Put the numbers in order and select the middle value.

60, 75.25, 77, 84, 86.50, 90.60, 92, 98

$(84 + 86.50) \div 2 = 85.25$

7. (3) $19.80

$5 \times 3 = 15$ and $15 + 84 = 99$

$\$99 \div 5 = \$19.80$

8. (4) 77°

$F = 1.8C + 32 = 1.8 \times 25 + 32 = 45 + 32 = 77$

9. (2) 11

$20 \div 1.699 = 11.77$

10. (5) $140,000

Margaret	= $ 20,000
Betty Jo = $2\frac{1}{2} \times 20,000$	= $ 50,000
Johnny = $3\frac{1}{2} \times 20,000$	= $ 70,000
Total	= $140,000

11. (4) .12

$\frac{.38 + .14 - .09 + .09 + .08}{5} = \frac{.60}{5} = .12$

12. 18

$\frac{12}{N} = \frac{50}{75}$

$N = \frac{12 \times 75}{50} = 18$

13. 10

$30 - 27 = 3$ failed

$\frac{3}{30} = \frac{N}{100}$ $N = \frac{3 \times 100}{30} = 10$

14. (3) $\frac{2}{5}$

$\frac{4 \text{ brunettes}}{3 + 4 + 1 + 2 \text{ women}} = \frac{4}{10} = \frac{2}{5}$

15. (4) 0 or –7

If $x = -7$, then $(-7)^2 + 7(-7) = 0.$

$49 - 49 = 0$

If $x = 0$, then $0^2 + 7(0) = 0.$

$0 + 0 = 0$

Either $x = 0$ or $x = -7$ make the equation true.

16. (1) Average sales were higher in 2001.

17.

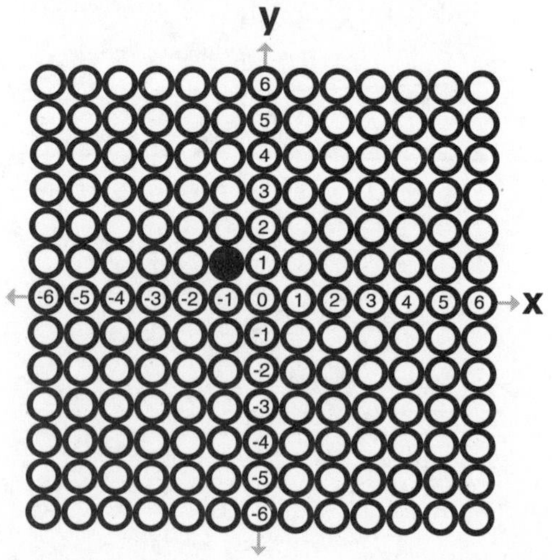

18. (1) $2\frac{3}{4}$

$8\frac{1}{4} + 1\frac{1}{2} = 9\frac{3}{4}$

$12\frac{1}{2} - 9\frac{3}{4} = 2\frac{3}{4}$

19. (5) Not enough information is given.

You cannot determine the two lengths where the figure indents.

20. (2) $10 \times 4 \times 2$

Since there are two half-inches in a whole inch, you would multiply 4×2 to get 8 half-inches and then times 10 miles.

21. 19.3 in.

Use the Pythagorean relationship.

$a^2 + b^2 = c^2$

$25.5^2 + h^2 = 32^2$

$650.25 + h^2 = 1024$

$h^2 = 373.75$

$h = \sqrt{373.75} = 19.3$

22. 38

Volume of a cylinder =

$\pi \times \text{radius}^2 \times \text{height} =$

$3.14 \times 3^2 \times 7 = 197.82$ cu in.

Volume of a rectangular box =

length × width × height =

$5 \times 4 \times 8 = 160$ cu in.

$197.82 - 160 = 37.82 = 38$ cu in.

23. (1) $6^3 = 6 \times 12 \times h$

Volume of a cube = edge^3 = 6^3

Volume of a rectangular box =

length × width × height = $6 \times 12 \times h$

So $6^3 = 6 \times 12 \times h$

24. (4) 4.25×10^{-3}

$2.125 \div 500 = .00425 = 4.25 \times 10^{-3}$

25. (2) As payments are made on the balance each month, the balance is reduced.

Part II

26. (4) $720

8 dozen – 2 dozen = 6 dozen = $6 \times 12 = 72$

Round $9.99 to $10, then 72 × $10 = $720.

27. (3) 11 gallons

$\frac{4.5 \text{ gal}}{3 \text{ rooms}} = \frac{N \text{ gal}}{7 \text{ rooms}}$

$N = \frac{4.5 \times 7}{3} = 10.5$

You must buy 11 gallons.

28. (2) $1^5, 4^1, 6, 2^3$

$1^5 = 1,\ 4^1 = 4,\ 6 = 6,\ 2^3 = 8$

29. (4) 43,200

$4.32 \times 10^4 = 43200$

Move the decimal point 4 places to the right.

30. (1) $\frac{1}{3}$

$\frac{10 \text{ married}}{30 \text{ total}} = \frac{1}{3}$

31. 60

$\frac{3}{5} = .60 = 60\%$

32. (1) 25 pounds

$\frac{150}{6} = 25$

33. (4) $13,050

20% + 9% = 29% = .29

$45,000 × .29 = $13,050

34. (5) Not enough information is given.

You don't know how many people are in the family.

35. (5) $5940

New income =

100% of $45,000 + 10% of $45,000 =

110% of $45,000 = 1.10 × 45000 = $49,500

Savings is 12% of $49,500 =

.12 × $49500 = $5940

36. (4) 13

$x + 2 > 13$

When $x = 13$, then $13 + 2 = 15$, and 15 is greater than 13.

37.

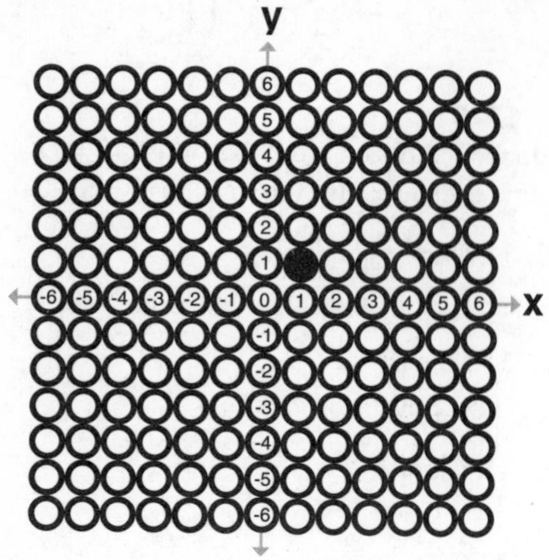

38. (2) 6

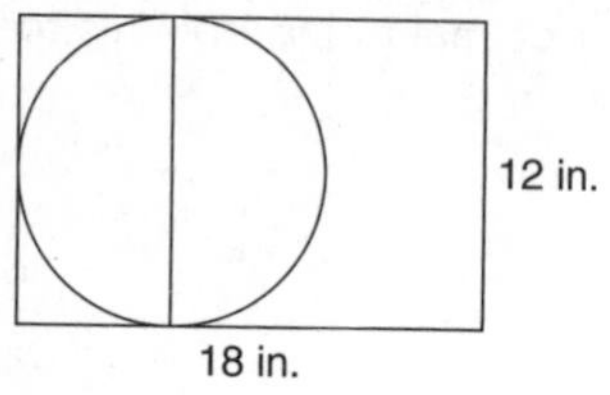

The diameter of the circle must be 12. So the radius is half of that, or 6.

39. (1) (.75)(.90)(126)

100% – 25% = 75% =.75

100% – 10 % = 90% = .90

For coat sale, pay 75% of $126.

Using coupon, pay 90% of the 75% of $126 = (.75)(.90)(126).

40. (2) 30°

$x + 2x + 3x = 180°$

$6x = 180°$

$x = 30°$

41. (1) 18

Let x = shortest piece

$x + 4$ = second piece

$2(x + 4)$ = third piece

$x + x + 4 + 2(x + 4) = 84$

$2x + 4 + 2x + 8 = 84$

$4x + 12 = 84$

$4x = 72$

$x = 18$

42. (1) $\frac{t}{3}$ – .75

$\frac{t}{3}$ = cost of one roll

Then subtract the 75¢ rebate.

43. $8266

In $8265.53, the 53 cents is greater than 50 cents, so round up to the nearest dollar.

44. (2) $150

x = least expensive computer

$2x$ = most expensive computer

$x + 2x = \$2700$

$3x = 2700$

$x = 900$

$2x = 1800$

Divide by 12 to calculate monthly cost.

$1800 ÷ 12 = $150

45. (1) Line *M* and line *N* both have positive slopes.

Use the slope of a line formula $\frac{y_2 - y_1}{x_2 - x_1}$.

Slope of line $M = \frac{7-4}{2-1} = \frac{3}{1} = 3$

Slope of line $N = \frac{5-3}{3-1} = \frac{2}{2} = 1$

Both slopes are positive numbers.

46. (4) 60

$\frac{50 \text{ miles}}{50 \text{ minutes}} = \frac{N \text{ miles}}{60 \text{ minutes}}$

$N = \frac{50 \times 60}{50} = 60$

60 miles in 60 minutes is 60 mph.

47. (4) 105°

The two angles must add up to 180°.

180° – 75° = 105°

48. (3) 30

Area $\Delta CDE = \frac{1}{2} \times 6 \times 8 = 24$ sq in.

Since ΔABC is similar to ΔCDE, the sides are in proportion.

$\frac{12}{8} = \frac{CB}{6}$

$CB = \frac{6 \times 12}{8} = \frac{72}{8} = 9$

Area $\Delta ABC = \frac{1}{2} \times 9 \times 12 = 54$ sq in.

$\Delta ABC - \Delta CDE = 54 - 24 = 30$

49. (1) 8 sq units

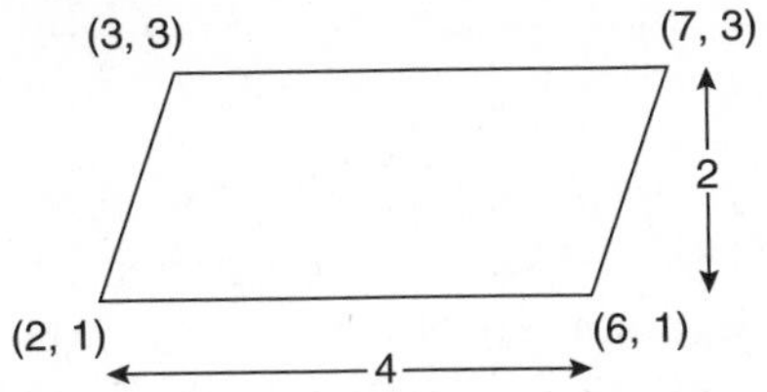

Area of a parallelogram = base × height = 4 × 2 = 8 sq units

50. (5) 70 miles

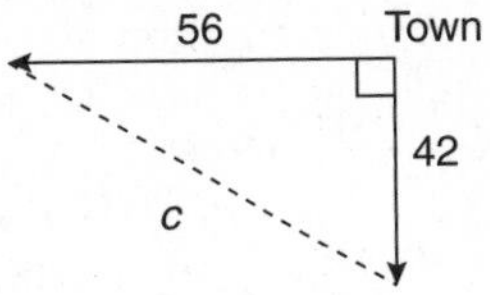

Use the Pythagorean relationship.

$a^2 + b^2 = c^2$

$56^2 + 42^2 = c^2$

$3136 + 1764 = c^2$

$4900 = c^2$

$c = \sqrt{4900} = 70$

MATHEMATICS POSTTEST

Evaluation Chart

After you use the answer key to check your answers to the Posttest, use the evaluation chart to determine the mathematics skills and content areas in which you need more practice. Circle the number of each question you miss. Pay particular attention to areas where you missed half or more of the questions.

SKILL and CONTENT AREA	ITEM NUMBER	REVIEW PAGES
Number Operations and Number Sense	Part I 1, 2, 3, 4, 5, 9, 10	699–774, 793–808
	Part II 26, 27, 28, 29, 32, 43	
Data Analysis, Statistics, and Probability	Part I 6, 7, 11, 12, 13, 14, 25	785–792, 809–834
	Part II 30, 31, 33, 34, 35, 39	
Measurement and Geometry	Part I 18, 19, 21, 22	873–921
	Part II 37, 38, 40, 47, 48, 49, 50	
Algebra, Functions, and Patterns	Part I 8, 15, 16, 17, 20, 23, 24	835–872
	Part II 36, 41, 42, 44, 45, 46	

Practice Tests

How do I use the Practice Tests?

Realizing that practice makes perfect, we've added Practice Tests as final indicators of your readiness for the actual GED Test. These tests are just like the Posttests in terms of format, level of difficulty, and percentages found on the real test. After you have completed the Practice Tests, you will be better able to determine whether you are ready to take the GED Test and, if not, what areas you need to review. As with the Posttests, Evaluation Charts are included to help you judge your performance. We recommend the following approach to the Practice Tests.

1. **Take only one Practice Test at a time.** Try to finish the test within the allotted time so that you can see how you will do on the actual GED Tests. If you are not done within that time period, mark where you were when the time was up and finish the test. You need to finish the entire Practice Test so that you can make use of the Evaluation Charts.

Time Allowed for Each Test	
Language Arts, Writing	
Part I: Editing	75 minutes
Part II: Essay	45 minutes
Social Studies	80 minutes
Science	80 minutes
Language Arts, Reading	65 minutes
Mathematics	
Booklet One	45 minutes
Booklet Two	45 minutes

2. **Check the answers in the Answer Keys and fill in the Evaluation Charts.** The charts follow each test. Be sure to read the explanations for all of the questions that you missed.

3. **Refer to the review pages given in the Evaluation Charts** if you still need work in certain areas.

4. **Although these are Practice Tests, you should give them your best effort.** If an item seems difficult, mark it and come back later. Always answer every question—even if you have to make an "educated guess." Sometimes you may know more than you think. Also, blanks count as wrong answers on the actual GED Tests, so it's always wise to answer every question as best you can.

Good luck on the Practice Tests and on the GED!

PRACTICE TEST

Language Arts, Writing

Part I: Editing

The following items are based on documents of several paragraphs marked by letters. Each paragraph contains numbered sentences. Most sentences contain errors, but a few may be correct as written. Read the documents and then answer the questions based on them. For each item, choose the answer that would result in the best rewriting of the sentence or sentences. The best answer must be consistent with the meaning and tone of the rest of the document.

Answer each of the 50 questions as carefully as possible, choosing the best of five answer choices and blackening in the grid. If you find a question too difficult, do not waste time on it. Work ahead and come back to it later when you can think it through carefully.

When you have finished the test, check your answers using the Evaluation Chart on page 1069. Use the chart to determine whether or not you are ready to take the actual GED Test and, if not, in what areas you need more work.

Language Arts, Writing Practice Test Answer Grid

1	①	②	③	④	⑤	18	①	②	③	④	⑤	35	①	②	③	④	⑤
2	①	②	③	④	⑤	19	①	②	③	④	⑤	36	①	②	③	④	⑤
3	①	②	③	④	⑤	20	①	②	③	④	⑤	37	①	②	③	④	⑤
4	①	②	③	④	⑤	21	①	②	③	④	⑤	38	①	②	③	④	⑤
5	①	②	③	④	⑤	22	①	②	③	④	⑤	39	①	②	③	④	⑤
6	①	②	③	④	⑤	23	①	②	③	④	⑤	40	①	②	③	④	⑤
7	①	②	③	④	⑤	24	①	②	③	④	⑤	41	①	②	③	④	⑤
8	①	②	③	④	⑤	25	①	②	③	④	⑤	42	①	②	③	④	⑤
9	①	②	③	④	⑤	26	①	②	③	④	⑤	43	①	②	③	④	⑤
10	①	②	③	④	⑤	27	①	②	③	④	⑤	44	①	②	③	④	⑤
11	①	②	③	④	⑤	28	①	②	③	④	⑤	45	①	②	③	④	⑤
12	①	②	③	④	⑤	29	①	②	③	④	⑤	46	①	②	③	④	⑤
13	①	②	③	④	⑤	30	①	②	③	④	⑤	47	①	②	③	④	⑤
14	①	②	③	④	⑤	31	①	②	③	④	⑤	48	①	②	③	④	⑤
15	①	②	③	④	⑤	32	①	②	③	④	⑤	49	①	②	③	④	⑤
16	①	②	③	④	⑤	33	①	②	③	④	⑤	50	①	②	③	④	⑤
17	①	②	③	④	⑤	34	①	②	③	④	⑤						

PRACTICE TEST

Choose the *best* answer to each question that follows.

Questions 1–9 refer to the following document.

Allergies

(A)

(1) More people than ever report suffering from seasonal allergies and millions more suffer all year. **(2)** Although no cure is currently available, some simple practices within the home can help. **(3)** The library is a helpful place to find information about allergies.

(B)

(4) The impact and effect of allergens can be reduced by implementing certain housekeeping practices. **(5)** Work to control and decrease dust in your home. **(6)** Clean hard furniture to avoid circulating dust with a damp cloth into the air. **(7)** Blinds, shades, fans, and draperies also needs attention. **(8)** Be especially attentive to cleaning in the bedroom. **(9)** Remember that you probably spend at least eight hours of every day there, so wash bed linens and blankets weakly in hot water temperatures of at least 130 degrees. **(10)** Don't hang sheets outside to dry because pollens and molds may gather on it.

(C)

(11) Kill mold and mildew in the kitchen and bathrooms by using a disinfectant weekly in those rooms. **(12)** Have a regular plan that you follow for cleaning in each of the rooms in your home.

(D)

(13) It is believed by various people that some type of relief from allergies may occur by establishing these practices. **(14)** Most importantly, however, remember to take medication as prescribed by your doctor and follow any advice you have been given. **(15)** You many not be able to prevent all allergic reactions, but by taking action, you may be able to help control them.

Source: "Cleaning house can reduce impact of allergens in the air." *Daily Herald.* Sunday, October 29, 2000.

1. Sentence 2: **Although no cure is currently <u>available, some</u> simple practices within the home can help.**

Which is the best way to write the underlined portion of the text? If the original is the best way, choose option (1).

(1) available, some
(2) available some
(3) available, but some
(4) available. Some
(5) available with some

2. Sentence 3: **The library is a helpful place to find information about allergies.**

What revision should be made to sentence 3?

(1) move sentence 3 to the beginning of paragraph A
(2) move sentence 3 to follow sentence 1
(3) move sentence 3 to follow sentence 8
(4) remove sentence 3
(5) no revision is necessary

3. Sentence 4: **The impact and effect of allergens can be reduced by implementing certain housekeeping practices.**

The most effective revision of sentence 4 would begin with which group of words?

(1) After reducing practices
(2) Certain housekeeping practices
(3) The practicing with several
(4) For certain allergens
(5) By the effect of

PRACTICE TEST

4. Sentence 6: **Clean hard furniture <u>to avoid circulating dust with a damp cloth</u> into the air.**

Which is the best way to write the underlined portion of the text? If the original is the best way, choose option (1).

(1) to avoid circulating dust with a damp cloth
(2) avoiding circulating dust with a damp cloth
(3) with a damp cloth to avoid circulating dust
(4) to circulate dust with a damp cloth
(5) and avoid circulating dust with a damp cloth

5. Sentence 7: **Blinds, shades, fans, and draperies <u>also needs</u> attention.**

Which is the best way to write the underlined portion of the text? If the original is the best way, choose option (1).

(1) also needs
(2) also needing
(3) have needed also
(4) also need
(5) also are needing

6. Sentence 9: **Remember that you probably spend at least eight hours of every day there, so wash bed linens and blankets weakly in hot water temperatures of at least 130 degrees.**

What correction should be made to sentence 9?

(1) change <u>there</u> to <u>they're</u>
(2) replace <u>so</u> with <u>for</u>
(3) insert a comma after <u>linens</u>
(4) change <u>weakly</u> to <u>weekly</u>
(5) change <u>degrees</u> to <u>Degrees</u>

7. Sentence 10: **Don't hang sheets outside to dry because pollens and molds <u>may gather on it</u>.**

Which is the best way to write the underlined portion of the text? If the original is the best way, choose option (1).

(1) may gather on it.
(2) will gather on it.
(3) gather on it.
(4) gathers on them.
(5) may gather on them.

8. Sentence 11: **Kill mold and mildew in the kitchen and bathrooms by using a disinfectant weekly in those rooms.**

Which revision would improve the text, "Allergies"?

(1) move sentence 11 to follow sentence 8
(2) remove sentence 11
(3) combine paragraphs B and C into one paragraph
(4) move sentence 11 to follow sentence 12
(5) remove sentence 15

9. Sentence 13: **It is believed by various people that some type of relief from allergies may occur by establishing these practices.**

If you rewrote sentence 13 beginning with

Establishing these practices

the next words should be

(1) may offer
(2) believes types of
(3) allergies occur
(4) are a variety
(5) by believing

PRACTICE TEST

Questions 10–18 refer to the following document.

Holidays

(A)

(1) Whether the day is identified by a turkey, a Santa Claus, or a red heart, a holiday commemorates a special time for celebration. **(2)** Indeed, holidays can certainly provide some wonderful experiences that can long be remembered. **(3)** However, sometimes expectations of holiday celebrations exceeding reality, causing a general feeling of disappointment.

(B)

(4) As preparations for holiday celebrations begin well in advance of the actual day, very often, our expectations rise. **(5)** All around us, we see decorations displayed, we hear people talk about plans, foods, and activities. **(6)** Media may inundate us with ads, shows, articles, and music. **(7)** The creation of some false impressions may be created in our minds by stereotypes of family gatherings and friendships. **(8)** As a result, the perfect holiday exists more in our minds then in our homes.

(C)

(9) To have an enjoyable, if not perfect, holiday, a couple of suggestions can help. **(10)** First of all it is extremely valuable to maintain a sense of humor. **(11)** Secondly, we should prepare ourselves to enjoy the day for what it brings. **(12)** If you let go of the image of the ideal, we'll relax and have a better time. **(13)** There is no set way in which anyone has to celebrate a holiday. **(14)** Humor can relieve awkward moments or tensions and smooth ruffled feelings. **(15)** A quiet day can sometimes be as welcome as one filled with activity. **(16)** Avoid a clash between reality and expectations and have a happy holiday.

10. Sentence 3: **However, sometimes expectations of holiday celebrations <u>exceeding reality</u>, causing a general feeling of disappointment.**

Which is the best way to write the underlined portion of the text? If the original is the best way, choose option (1).

(1) exceeding reality
(2) exceed reality
(3) exceeds reality
(4) in exceeding reality
(5) excessive reality

11. Sentence 5: **All around us, we see decorations <u>displayed, we</u> hear people talk about plans, foods, and activities.**

Which is the best way to write the underlined portion of the text? If the original is the best way, choose option (1).

(1) displayed, we
(2) displayed we
(3) displayed, hearing
(4) displayed, but we
(5) displayed and

12. Sentence 7: **The creation of some false impressions may be created in our minds by stereotypes of family gatherings and friendships.**

The most effective revision of sentence 7 would include which group of words?

(1) may create some
(2) stereotyping minds of
(3) since family gatherings
(4) despite the false
(5) being false to

PRACTICE TEST

13. Sentence 8: **As a result, the perfect holiday exists more in our minds then in our homes.**

What correction should be made to sentence 8?

(1) insert a comma after As
(2) change exists to existed
(3) change minds to minds'
(4) change then to than
(5) insert a comma after then

14. Sentence 10: **First of all it is extremely valuable to maintain a sense of humor.**

What correction should be made to sentence 10?

(1) insert a comma after all
(2) change is to are
(3) change to maintain to too maintain
(4) replace a with the
(5) no correction is necessary

15. Sentence 12: **If you let go of the image of the ideal, we'll relax and have a better time.**

What correction should be made to sentence 12?

(1) replace you with we
(2) change let to let's
(3) remove the comma after ideal
(4) replace we'll with we'd
(5) no correction is necessary

16. Sentence 13: **There is no set way in which anyone has to celebrate a holiday.**

If you rewrote sentence 13 beginning with

No one

the next word should be

(1) holiday
(2) there
(3) does
(4) celebrate
(5) has

17. Sentence 14: **Humor can relieve awkward moments or tensions and smooth ruffled feelings.**

What revision should be made to sentence 14?

(1) move sentence 14 to follow sentence 9
(2) move sentence 14 to follow sentence 10
(3) begin a new paragraph with sentence 14
(4) remove sentence 14
(5) no revision is necessary

18. Sentence 15: **A quiet day can sometimes be as welcome as one filled with activity.**

What correction should be made to sentence 15?

(1) change quiet to quite
(2) insert a comma after day
(3) change be to been
(4) replace with with by
(5) no correction is necessary

PRACTICE TEST

Questions 19–26 refer to the following document.

Director of Customer Service
Packemin Airlines
100 W. Sorree Drive
Dallas, TX

Dear Mr. Wescott:

(A)

(1) For many years, I have been pleased with your airlines service. **(2)** However, last week when I was booked on a direct flight from Dallas to Pittsburgh, a combination of errors, problems, and I received some poor service, caused me severe inconvenience. **(3)** As a result, I believe I am entitled to some compensation from your company. **(4)** I am sure that you will agree to the validity of my complaint, and I will be waiting to hear from you.

(B)

(5) The first problem began at the gate when I was told that mechanical problems had grounded the plane. **(6)** Your representative assured me that I would be booked on another flight leaving in four hours. **(7)** However, that flight flew first to Denver and would require a change of planes to fly on to Pittsburgh. **(8)** Reluctantly, I agreed to the change, and flew to Denver.

(C)

(9) When I arrived in Denver, however, I was told that the connecting flight had been cancelled. **(10)** Your service representative suggested that if I agreed to fly to Los Angeles, your company would then fly me first-class on another plane to Pittsburgh. **(11)** Having little other choice, I waited another five hours, then boarded the plane to Los Angeles.

(D)

(12) When I arrived in Los Angeles, however, your service representative tells me that because of a strike, no planes were flying until further notice. **(13)** After spending the rest of the night on an airport bench, limited service was restored. **(14)** I was put in an economy class seat on an indirect flight to Pittsburgh with a stop over in Seattle. **(15)** Once I reached Seattle, however, all passengers and me were told that weather conditions in Pittsburgh had prompted the cancellation of all flights to that area.

(E)

(16) Exhausted and defeated, I managed to fly home to Dallas where I was told that the location of my luggage was completely unknown because of mechanical failure of equipment, strike, weather, and computer error. **(17)** Attached is copies of my boarding passes.

19. Sentence 1: **For many years, I have been pleased with your airlines service.**

What correction should be made to sentence 1?

(1) change years to year's
(2) change have been to will be
(3) insert a comma after pleased
(4) change your to you're
(5) change airlines to airline's

20. Sentence 8: **Reluctantly, I agreed to the change, and flew to Denver.**

What correction should be made to sentence 8?

(1) remove the comma after change
(2) replace and with but
(3) change flew to flying
(4) change Denver to denver
(5) no correction is necessary

PRACTICE TEST

21. Sentence 4: **I am sure that you will agree to the validity of my complaint, and I will be waiting to hear from you.**

What revision should be made to sentence 4?

(1) begin a new paragraph with sentence 4
(2) move sentence 4 to follow sentence 2
(3) remove sentence 4
(4) move sentence 4 to follow sentence 15
(5) move sentence 4 to follow sentence 17

22. Sentence 2: **However, last week when I was booked on a direct flight from Dallas to Pittsburgh, a combination of errors, problems, and I received some poor service, caused me severe inconvenience.**

Which is the best way to write the underlined portion of the text? If the original is the best way, choose option (1).

(1) I received some poor service
(2) I received, some poor service
(3) that poor service I received
(4) after receiving poor service
(5) poor service

23. Sentence 12: **When I arrived in Los Angeles, however, your service representative tells me that because of a strike, no planes were flying until further notice.**

What correction should be made to sentence 8?

(1) remove the comma after Los Angeles
(2) change tells to told
(3) replace because of with due to
(4) change strike to Strike
(5) change were to are

24. Sentence 13: **After spending the rest of the night on an airport bench, limited service was restored.**

Which is the best way to write the underlined portion of the text? If the original is the best way, choose option (1).

(1) bench, limited
(2) bench, some limited
(3) bench that limited
(4) bench, I learned limited
(5) bench, finally limited

25. Sentence 15: **Once I reached Seattle, however, all passengers and me were told that weather conditions in Pittsburgh had prompted the cancellation of all flights to that area.**

Which is the best way to write the underlined portion of the text? If the original is the best way, choose option (1).

(1) all passengers and me were
(2) everybody there were
(3) all passengers and I were
(4) airline representatives
(5) I was

26. Sentence 17: **Attached is copies of my boarding passes.**

Which is the best way to write the underlined portion of the text? If the original is the best way, choose option (1).

(1) Attached is
(2) Attached are
(3) Attaching to
(4) Attached were
(5) Attached being

PRACTICE TEST

Questions 27–34 refer to the following document.

Great Fortune

(A)

(1) If you suddenly obtained a fortune next friday, what would you do with it? **(2)** You could spend it, give it away, or hoard it for awhile. **(3)** Often millionaires done a combination of all three of these options. **(4)** Two examples of millionaires who have lived lavishly but also donated large sums of money are John D. Rockefeller and Alfred Nobel. **(5)** Rockefeller, a multimillionaire from his organization of the Standard Oil Company. **(6)** He became fabulously wealthy and leaves his family a fortune. **(7)** He also donated millions of dollars to libraries education, museums, and medical research. **(8)** On the other hand, Alfred Nobel, who made his fortune from dynamite and explosives, never married. **(9)** At his death, he established a foundation to award Nobel Prizes in the five areas of chemistry, physics, medicine, literature, and peace. **(10)** Each year the Nobel foundation may award a gold medal and a cash prize to individuals or organizations who have made an outstanding contribution in one of the five areas.

(B)

(11) It is obviously a fact that the management of a multimillion-dollar fortune allows many different kinds of choices. **(12)** Not all people wish to confront those choices or be that rich. **(13)** There are various other people, though, who dream of little else beyond that. **(14)** However much your fortune may be, though, you will still need to spend it, give it away, or hoard it for awhile.

27. Sentence 1: **If you suddenly obtained a fortune next friday, what would you do with it?**

What correction should be made to sentence 1?

(1) insert had after suddenly
(2) replace next with on
(3) change friday to Friday
(4) remove the comma after friday
(5) replace would with will

28. Sentence 3: **Often millionaires done a combination of all three of these options.**

Which is the best way to write the underlined portion of the text? If the original is the best way, choose option (1).

(1) done
(2) doing
(3) has done
(4) have done
(5) should doing

29. What revision would make the text more effective?

Begin a new paragraph

(1) with sentence 2
(2) with sentence 4
(3) with sentence 6
(4) with sentence 7
(5) with sentence 9

30. Sentence 5: **Rockefeller, a multimillionaire from his organization of the Standard Oil Company.**

Which is the best way to write the underlined portion of the text? If the original is the best way, choose option (1).

(1) Rockefeller, a
(2) Rockefeller, being a
(3) Rockefeller who was a
(4) Rockefeller became a
(5) Rockefeller that became a

PRACTICE TEST

31. Sentence 6: **He became fabulously wealthy and <u>leaves his</u> family a fortune.**

Which is the best way to write the underlined portion of the text? If the original is the best way, choose option (1).

(1) leaves his
(2) leaving his
(3) left his
(4) has left his
(5) leaves their

32. Sentence 7: **He also donated millions of dollars to libraries education, museums, and medical research.**

What correction should be made to sentence 7?

(1) replace <u>also</u> with <u>additionally</u>
(2) change <u>dollars</u> to <u>dollar's</u>
(3) insert a comma after <u>libraries</u>
(4) insert a comma after <u>and</u>
(5) change <u>medical</u> to <u>Medical</u>

33. Sentence 11: **It is obviously a fact that the management of a multimillion-dollar fortune allows many different kinds of choices.**

The most effective revision of sentence 11 would begin with which group of words?

(1) Because of the facts
(2) A fortune in gold
(3) One fact about management
(4) There is a difference
(5) Many choices exist

34. Sentence 13: **There are various other people, though, who dream of little else beyond that.**

The most effective revision of sentence 13 would begin with which group of words?

(1) Else other people
(2) Various dreams of
(3) Some people, however,
(4) Though dreams of
(5) other people, therefore,

PRACTICE TEST

Questions 35–43 refer to the following document.

Crime Protection

(A)

(1) In ancient Rome, it was generally accepted that only thieves and murderers went out after dark. **(2)** Good citizens make sure that they were home by then. **(3)** Today, however, people work at night, shop at night, attend school at night, and travel almost anywhere. **(4)** Changes have come about in our habits while crime has also changed. **(5)** Nevertheless, crime is still a factor in our world, and we need to take a few precautions to protect our homes and ourselves.

(B)

(6) First, lights and possibly a radio or TV should be set on timers. **(7)** The picking up of mail and daily newspapers by a neighbor is a second action to take. **(8)** Thirdly, arrange to have the grass cut or draperies opened and closed regularly the home should appear occupied.

(C)

(9) Some everyday precautions can help us avoid being crime victims. **(10)** Keep doorways to entrances well lighted, and dark, isolated areas are places to avoid. **(11)** When returning to a parked car, the car keys should be ready. **(12)** Check the car quickly to be certain no one is hiding in the back. **(13)** Finally, look around and be alert.

(D)

(14) A little common sense and a few basic precautions goes a long way toward keeping ourselves safe.

35. Sentence 2: **Good citizens make sure that they were home by then.**

What correction should be made to sentence 2?

(1) change <u>make</u> to <u>made</u>
(2) change <u>they</u> to <u>you</u>
(3) change <u>were</u> to <u>are</u>
(4) replace <u>by</u> with <u>before</u>
(5) no correction is necessary

36. Sentence 4: **Changes have come about in our habits while crime has also changed.**

The most effective revision of sentence 4 would include which group of words?

(1) have changed
(2) has not changed
(3) crime habits
(4) will change our
(5) neither crime nor

37. Sentence 5: **Nevertheless, crime is still a factor in our world, and we need to take a few precautions to protect our homes and ourselves.**

What correction should be made to sentence 5?

(1) remove the comma after <u>Nevertheless</u>
(2) change <u>world</u> to <u>World</u>
(3) replace <u>and</u> with <u>but</u>
(4) change <u>homes</u> to <u>homes'</u>
(5) no correction is necessary

PRACTICE TEST

38. What sentence below would be most effective at the beginning of paragraph B?

(1) The effects of crime cause many problems and many expenses.
(2) Although people are disturbed by crime occurring in our society, we haven't found a way to completely eliminate it.
(3) Before leaving home, you need to make preparations for any pets you have.
(4) Some basic actions can help prevent problems when a trip means that a home will be unoccupied for a while.
(5) In other parts of the world, crime is also a problem for the people living there.

39. Sentence 7: **The picking up of mail and daily newspapers by a neighbor is a second action to take.**

If you rewrote sentence 7 beginning with

Secondly, ask a trusted neighbor

the next word should be

(1) acting
(2) take
(3) by
(4) of
(5) to

40. Sentence 8: **Thirdly, arrange to have the grass cut or draperies opened and closed <u>regularly the home should appear</u> occupied.**

Which is the best way to write the underlined portion of the text? If the original is the best way, choose option (1).

(1) regularly the home should appear
(2) regularly, so the home appears
(3) regularly, the home should appear
(4) regularly, but the home should appear
(5) regularly and, the home should appear

41. Sentence 10: **Keep doorways to entrances well lighted, and <u>dark, isolated areas are places to avoid</u>.**

Which is the best way to write the underlined portion of the text? If the original is the best way, choose option (1).

(1) dark, isolated areas are places to avoid
(2) avoiding dark, isolated areas
(3) avoiding places that are dark, isolated
(4) places to avoid are isolated areas
(5) avoid dark, isolated areas

42. Sentence 11: **When returning to a parked car, <u>the car keys should be</u> ready.**

Which is the best way to write the underlined portion of the text? If the original is the best way, choose option (1).

(1) the car keys should be
(2) the keys to the car should be
(3) the keys should be in hand and
(4) have the car keys
(5) having the car keys

43. Sentence 14: **A little common sense and a few basic precautions goes a long way toward keeping ourselves safe.**

What correction should be made to sentence 14?

(1) insert a comma after <u>sense</u>
(2) change <u>goes</u> to <u>go</u>
(3) change <u>goes</u> to <u>went</u>
(4) change <u>safe</u> to <u>safely</u>
(5) no correction is necessary

PRACTICE TEST

Questions 44–50 refer to the following document.

Microwave Ovens

(A)

(1) Many people own and operate microwave ovens but are not really aware of exactly how a microwave oven cooks their food. **(2)** A magnetron tube in the oven converts electrical energy to microwave energy and directs that energy to a fanlike stirrer. **(3)** The stirrer evenly channels into the oven the short radio waves they penetrate food and cause the molecules in the food to vibrate. **(4)** This vibration, or friction, creates the heat that cooks the food. **(5)** Glass, paper, and most types of china are used in microwave cooking because the microwaves can pass through these containers, but the microwaves do not pass through metal. **(6)** The microwaves penetrate the food to a depth of about one inch. **(7)** The interior of the food receives the heat which spreads as the cooking process continues on. **(8)** When the microwaves stop, the friction action continues, slows, and it stops.

(B)

(9) Most microwave ovens have settings such as warm, defrost, simmer, medium high, and high so that a person can choose the speed at which their food cooks. **(10)** The amount of time that is necessary for food to cook is dependent on the amount of food someone is cooking. **(11)** One hot dog may cook in one minute while four hot dogs take about two minutes. **(12)** Microwave ovens vary in features and size, but owners can safely and effectively use this household appliance by following instructions carefully.

44. Sentence 3: **The stirrer evenly channels into the oven the short radio waves they penetrate food and cause the molecules in the food to vibrate.**

Which is the best way to write the underlined portion of the text? If the original is the best way, choose option (1).

(1) waves they
(2) waves and, they
(3) waves that
(4) waves, they
(5) waves these

45. Sentence 4: **This vibration, or friction, creates the heat that cooks the food.**

Which is the best way to write the underlined portion of the text? If the original is the best way, choose option (1).

(1) friction, creates
(2) friction create
(3) friction that creates
(4) friction have created
(5) friction are creating

46. Sentence 7: **The interior of the food receives the heat which spreads as the cooking process continues on.**

If you rewrote sentence 7 beginning with

As cooking continues,

the next word should be

(1) spreading
(2) on food
(3) which spreads
(4) the heat
(5) process is

PRACTICE TEST

47. Sentence 8: **When the microwaves stop, the friction action continues, slows, and it stops.**

Which is the best way to write the underlined portion of the text? If the original is the best way, choose option (1).

(1) and it stops.
(2) and stopped.
(3) and they stop.
(4) and stopping.
(5) and stops.

48. What sentence below would be most effective at the beginning of paragraph B?

(1) Any person using a microwave oven needs to know some basic information to operate it.
(2) Technology has been responsible for the invention and use of many home products we use today.
(3) Cooking in a traditional oven is a different process from cooking in a microwave.
(4) The cost of microwave ovens has decreased even as the quality of the product has increased.
(5) Many people do not really like to cook food in microwave ovens.

49. Sentence 9: **Most microwave ovens have settings such as warm, defrost, simmer, medium high, and high so that a person can choose the speed at which their food cooks.**

Which is the best way to write the underlined portion of the text? If the original is the best way, choose option (1).

(1) their food cooks.
(2) the food cooks.
(3) their food will cook.
(4) their food cooked.
(5) your food cooks.

50. Sentence 10: **The amount of time that is necessary for food to cook is dependent on the amount of food someone is cooking.**

The most effective revision of sentence 10 would begin with which group of words?

(1) Although the amount
(2) Being necessary in cooking
(3) The time needed
(4) Depending on time
(5) The right amount

PRACTICE TEST

Part II: The Essay

Directions: This part of the test is designed to find out how well you write. The test has one question that asks you to present an opinion and explain your ideas. Your essay should be long enough to develop the topic adequately. In preparing your essay, you should take the following steps:

1. Read the directions and topic carefully.
2. Think about your ideas and plan your essay before you write.
3. Use scratch paper to make notes of your ideas.
4. Write your essay in ink on two other pages of paper.
5. After finishing your writing, read your paper carefully and make appropriate changes.

TOPIC

Has technology greatly affected your life, or is your life largely unaffected by technology?

In your essay, state your opinion and give examples supporting it.

Information on evaluating your essay is on page 1070.

Language Arts, Writing Answer Key

PART I: EDITING

1. **(1)** No correction is necessary.
2. **(4)** The sentence is irrelevant to the paragraph topic about home practices affecting allergies.
3. **(2)** The active voice is an improvement over the passive voice: *Certain housekeeping practices can reduce the effects of allergens.*
4. **(3)** Structure the sentence so that the modifying phrase *with a damp cloth* follows *furniture* and provides clear meaning.
5. **(4)** The verb *need* agrees with the subject *Blinds, shades, fans, and draperies.*
6. **(4)** Change the spelling of *weakly* to *weekly* to obtain the meaning needed for the sentence to make sense.
7. **(5)** Use the pronoun *them* to refer to sheets.
8. **(3)** Paragraph C, which continues support for the main idea about using housekeeping practices to reduce allergens, should be combined with paragraph B.
9. **(1)** The wordiness of the sentence is improved with this revision: *Establishing these practices may offer some relief from allergies.*
10. **(2)** The sentence needs an appropriate verb to avoid being a fragment.
11. **(5)** Correct the comma splice by using *and* to join the two verbs *see* and *hear.*
12. **(1)** Using the active rather than passive voice improves the sentence: *Stereotypes of family gatherings and friendships may create some false impressions.*
13. **(4)** Change the spelling of *then* to *than* to obtain the appropriate meaning for the sentence.
14. **(1)** Use a comma after an introductory part to a sentence.
15. **(1)** To be consistent with the rest of the sentence and paragraph, use *we.*
16. **(5)** Reduce wordiness and create a more effective sentence with this revision: *No one has to celebrate a holiday in any set way.*
17. **(2)** Sentence 14 provides additional explanation for sentence 10.
18. **(5)** No correction is necessary.
19. **(5)** The possessive noun *airlines* needs an apostrophe and should be changed to *airline's.*
20. **(1)** No comma is needed because there are not two complete sentences.
21. **(5)** Sentence 4 serves to conclude the letter.
22. **(5)** Make the sentence parallel by using *poor service* to fit with *errors* and *problems.*
23. **(2)** The verb *tells* should be changed to the past tense *told* to remain consistent with the sentence and the rest of the letter.
24. **(4)** A subject must be added to the independent clause so that *service* does not spend the night on a bench.
25. **(5)** A subject pronoun and an appropriate verb are needed.
26. **(2)** The verb *are* is needed to agree with the subject *copies.*
27. **(3)** Days of the week should be capitalized.
28. **(4)** The verb that appropriately matches the subject *millionaires* is *have done.*
29. **(2)** Sentence 4 begins a paragraph of information about two examples of millionaires.
30. **(4)** Correct the fragment by adding an appropriate verb.
31. **(3)** Use the past-tense verb *left* to remain consistent with the rest of the sentence and paragraph.
32. **(3)** Use commas to set off the items in a series.

33. (5) Improve the wordiness of the sentence with this revision: *Many choices exist when managing a multimillion-dollar fortune.*

34. (3) Avoid vague wordiness with this revision: *Some people, however, dream of little else.*

35. (1) Change the verb *make* to the past tense to be consistent with the meaning of the sentence and paragraph.

36. (1) A more succinct and effective revision would be the following: *Our habits have changed, and so has crime.*

37. (5) No correction is necessary.

38. (4) The paragraph identifies actions people can take to protect their homes when residents are away.

39. (5) Reduce wordiness in the original sentence with this revision: *Secondly, ask a trusted neighbor to pick up mail and daily newspapers.*

40. (2) Correct the run-on by using the best coordinating conjunction.

41. (5) The underlined part of the sentence should be made parallel to the first part.

42. (4) Correct the dangling modifier so that the understood subject *you* instead of *keys* returns to a parked car.

43. (2) *A little common sense and a few basic precautions* is the subject of the sentence and requires the verb *go* for correct agreement.

44. (3) The run-on sentence can be corrected by subordinating the second sentence so that it is dependent on the first.

45. (1) No correction is necessary.

46. (4) The sentence can be revised to be more easily understood and less wordy with this version: *As cooking continues, the heat spreads to the interior of the food.*

47. (5) The series of actions in the sentence should be parallel.

48. (1) An appropriate topic sentence for the paragraph identifies the main idea of basic information needed for a person using a microwave.

49. (2) The pronoun *their* is plural, but the antecedent *a person* is singular.

50. (3) A shorter, more effective version of the sentence would read this way: *The time needed to cook the food depends on the amount of food cooked.*

Evaluation Chart

Use the Answer Key on pages 1067–1068 to check your answers to the Practice Test. Then find the item number of each question you missed and circle it on the chart below to determine the writing content areas in which you need more practice. Pay particular attention to areas where you missed half or more of the questions. The page numbers for the content areas are listed below on the chart. For those questions that you missed, review the skill pages indicated.

CONTENT AREA	ITEM NUMBER	REVIEW PAGES
Nouns	19	69–73, 102–104
Verbs	23, 31, 35	73–86, 102–104
Subject/Verb Agreement	5, 26, 28, 43	87–91, 102–104
Pronoun Use	7, 15, 25, 49	91–95, 102–104
Sentence Fragments	10, 30	105–108, 131–134
Run-ons, Comma Splices, Sentence Combining	11, 40, 44	108–115, 131–134
Independent/Dependent Clauses, Effective Sentence Structure	3, 9, 12, 16, 33, 34, 36, 39, 46, 50	116–125, 131–134
Dangling or Misplaced Modifiers	4, 24, 42	126–128, 131–134
Parallel Structure	20, 41, 47	129–134
Capitalization, Punctuation	14, 22, 27, 32	135–144, 150–152
Spelling	6, 13	147–149, 150–152
Paragraph Composition	38, 48	153–157, 165–168
Text Division	8, 29	157–160, 165–168
Paragraph Unity and Coherence	2, 17, 21	160–165, 165–168
No Correction	1, 18, 37, 45	135–144, 116–125, 165–168

PRACTICE TEST

Part II: The Essay

If possible, give your essay to an instructor to evaluate. That person's opinion of your writing will be useful in deciding what further work you need to do to write a good essay.

If, however, you are unable to show your work to someone else, you can try to evaluate your own essay. Use the five questions in the Essay Evaluation Checklist to help evaluate your writing. The more questions that you can answer with a strong *yes,* the better your chances are for achieving a passing or high score.

Essay Evaluation Checklist

YES	NO	
		1. Does the essay answer the question asked?
		2. Does the main point of the essay stand out clearly?
		3. Does each paragraph contain specific examples and details that develop and explain the main point?
		4. Are the ideas organized clearly into paragraphs and complete sentences?
		5. Is the essay easy to read, or do problems in grammar, usage, punctuation, spelling, or word choice interfere?

Important Note

On the actual GED Language Arts, Writing Test, you will be given one score, which is a composite of your scores from Part I and Part II of the test. This score is determined by grading your essay holistically, giving it a score, then combining this score with your score from Part I in a proportion determined by the GED Testing Service.

Because you are not able to score your essay holistically, it is not possible for you to determine a valid composite score for your performance on this Language Arts, Writing Test. Instead, it is best to look at your performance on each part of the test separately. In this way, you will be able to determine whether you need additional work in one part of the test or the other. Remember that you must take both parts of the Language Arts, Writing Test for your score to count.

PRACTICE TEST

Social Studies

This Social Studies Practice Test will give you an opportunity to evaluate your readiness for the actual GED Social Studies Test. This test contains 50 questions. Some of the questions are based on short reading passages, and some of them require you to interpret a graph, chart or table, map, or an editorial cartoon.

You should take approximately 70 minutes to complete this test. At the end of 70 minutes, stop and mark your place. Then finish the test. This will give you an idea of whether or not you can finish the actual GED Test in the time allotted. Try to answer as many questions as you can. A blank will count as a wrong answer, so make a reasonable guess for the answers to questions of which you are not sure.

Use the Answer Key on pages 1089–1091 to check your answers to the Social Studies Practice Test. Then find the item number of each question you missed and circle it on the Evaluation Chart on page 1092 to determine the skills and content areas in which you need more practice. Pay particular attention to areas where you missed half or more of the questions. The page numbers for the content areas and the critical thinking skills are listed on the chart. The numbers in **boldface** are questions based on graphics. For those questions that you missed, review the pages indicated.

Social Studies Practice Test Answer Grid

1	①	②	③	④	⑤	18	①	②	③	④	⑤	35	①	②	③	④	⑤
2	①	②	③	④	⑤	19	①	②	③	④	⑤	36	①	②	③	④	⑤
3	①	②	③	④	⑤	20	①	②	③	④	⑤	37	①	②	③	④	⑤
4	①	②	③	④	⑤	21	①	②	③	④	⑤	38	①	②	③	④	⑤
5	①	②	③	④	⑤	22	①	②	③	④	⑤	39	①	②	③	④	⑤
6	①	②	③	④	⑤	23	①	②	③	④	⑤	40	①	②	③	④	⑤
7	①	②	③	④	⑤	24	①	②	③	④	⑤	41	①	②	③	④	⑤
8	①	②	③	④	⑤	25	①	②	③	④	⑤	42	①	②	③	④	⑤
9	①	②	③	④	⑤	26	①	②	③	④	⑤	43	①	②	③	④	⑤
10	①	②	③	④	⑤	27	①	②	③	④	⑤	44	①	②	③	④	⑤
11	①	②	③	④	⑤	28	①	②	③	④	⑤	45	①	②	③	④	⑤
12	①	②	③	④	⑤	29	①	②	③	④	⑤	46	①	②	③	④	⑤
13	①	②	③	④	⑤	30	①	②	③	④	⑤	47	①	②	③	④	⑤
14	①	②	③	④	⑤	31	①	②	③	④	⑤	48	①	②	③	④	⑤
15	①	②	③	④	⑤	32	①	②	③	④	⑤	49	①	②	③	④	⑤
16	①	②	③	④	⑤	33	①	②	③	④	⑤	50	①	②	③	④	⑤
17	①	②	③	④	⑤	34	①	②	③	④	⑤						

PRACTICE TEST

Questions 1 and 2 refer to the following diagram.

Any new business faces many challenges and obstacles. The following diagram illustrates the five major barriers to new businesses entering into economic competition:

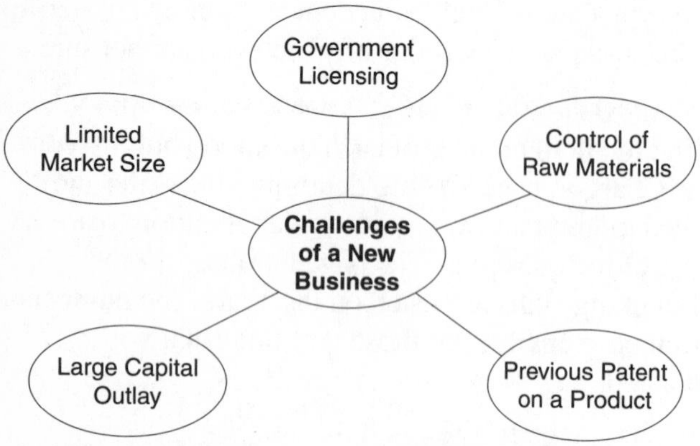

1. Which obstacle listed below would confront a new business that needs private funding and bank loans?

(1) control of raw materials
(2) limited market size
(3) government licensing
(4) large capital outlay
(5) previous patent on a product

2. A new restaurant in town wanted to begin serving alcoholic drinks with dinner to attract a broader clientele. But the owners discovered that the city issued only a certain number of liquor permits, and none would be available until an existing business gave up its permit. This situation describes which barrier to competition?

(1) patent on a product
(2) government licensing
(3) control of raw materials
(4) limited market size
(5) large capital outlay

Question 3 refers to the following purpose statement.

UNITED NATIONS

The purposes of the United Nations are as follows:

- to maintain peace and security
- to develop friendly relations among nations
- to achieve international cooperation in solving economic, social, cultural and humanitarian problems and in promoting respect for human rights and fundamental freedoms
- to be a center for harmonizing the actions of nations in attaining these common ends.

3. Which of the following statements would likely be inconsistent with the convictions of the delegates that created and approved the charter of the United Nations?

(1) Each country is to be honored equally with all the others.
(2) Countries must settle disagreements peacefully.
(3) Countries should attempt to stop wars from occurring.
(4) Countries must work together to maintain world peace.
(5) Countries should not have defense treaties with other nations.

PRACTICE TEST

Questions 4 through 6 refer to the following cartoon.

4. According to the cartoon, how was the agreement between the PLO and Israel reached?

(1) It was established by a long and lasting peace.
(2) It was made through a solid friendship.
(3) It was forged by a skillful negotiator.
(4) It was built on an unstable foundation.
(5) It was guaranteed to last for years.

5. In this cartoon, how did the U.S. president most likely feel?

(1) confused as to the next steps toward peace
(2) relieved over peace between the PLO and Israel
(3) concerned over his reelection campaign
(4) anxious about the peace agreement
(5) happy over a new style of architecture

6. What perspective does the United States appear to have in this cartoon?

(1) an uninterested and uninvolved bystander
(2) a mediator between adversarial countries
(3) a politician biased toward organized governments
(4) an activist promoting revolution
(5) an insecure statesman seeking world approval

Questions 7–9 are based on the following passage.

The first mail deliveries to the American West went by steamship to Panama, crossed to the Pacific by rail, and then traveled again by ship to San Francisco. The process took at least a month, and letters arrived in huge, unsorted bundles.

Official overland delivery began in 1858, with John Butterfield's stagecoach company bringing the mail over a 2,800-mile route in only 24 days. The short-lived Pony Express further reduced the time to ten days. But the effort had its dangers. The ad for riders read, "Wanted: Young, skinny, wiry fellows not over 18. Must be expert riders, willing to risk death daily. Orphans preferred."

The completion of the transcontinental railroad in 1869 changed mail delivery to the West forever. Letters and packages arrived in cities and small towns alike, quickly and presorted.

7. Which of the following was the major obstacle to efficient mail delivery in the early days of the American West?

(1) lack of willing riders
(2) unreliability of stagecoaches
(3) distance to be covered
(4) post office red tape
(5) sorting process

8. California residents requested improved overland mail delivery in 1856. They took this action because they placed a high value on which of the following?

(1) support of the government
(2) communication with friends and family
(3) employment of orphans
(4) the hardships of frontier life
(5) railroad travel

9. The major change in mail service to the West is comparable to which of the following?

(1) the gradual settlement of the Midwestern states
(2) the increase in postal rates between the 1960s and 1990s
(3) the development of small telephone companies because of the breakup of the AT&T monopoly
(4) the growing competition among personal computer companies
(5) the improvement of international telephone communication because of the laying of the transatlantic cable

Question 10 is based on the following passage.

The Monroe Doctrine demanded that Europe stay out of the affairs of the Americas. President Theodore Roosevelt used the doctrine to support a position on imperialism that he called the Roosevelt Corollary. It stated that the United States had a right to move into areas of the Americas needing our civilizing power.

10. In which incident would Roosevelt have used the corollary to defend his actions?

(1) Roosevelt's approval of England's colonization of India and Egypt
(2) the United Nations' participation in a conference to end French-German rivalry in Morocco
(3) Roosevelt's support for the Open Door policy for trade with China
(4) Roosevelt's negotiating an informal understanding between the United States and Japan to end unwanted immigration
(5) the aiding of Panamanian rebels against the Colombian government.

Questions 11–13 are based on the following information.

The president of the United States is often advised by members of his Cabinet, most of whom are heads or secretaries of one of fourteen executive government departments. The executive departments help regulate and serve many aspects of American life. For example, funeral services for ex-military personnel are provided by the National Cemetery System, an agency administered by the Department of Veterans Affairs. The general services provided by five of the executive departments are as follows:

Department of Agriculture—responsible for improving farms and farm income and reducing poverty, hunger, and malnutrition

Department of Commerce—responsible for encouraging international trade and economic growth and preventing unfair trade

Department of the Interior—responsible for the conservation of public lands and natural resources, including wildlife and historic places

Department of State—responsible for formulating and carrying out foreign policy and protecting American overseas interests

Department of Transportation—responsible for the planning and safety of highways, mass transit, railroads, aviation, and waterways

11. An agency builds merchant ships for the federal government and provides aid to private shipbuilders. Which Cabinet member heads this agency's department?

(1) secretary of commerce
(2) secretary of agriculture
(3) secretary of the interior
(4) secretary of state
(5) secretary of transportation

PRACTICE TEST

12. An agency helps the establishment and development of businesses owned by minorities. Which Cabinet member heads this agency's department?

(1) secretary of commerce
(2) secretary of agriculture
(3) secretary of the interior
(4) secretary of state
(5) secretary of transportation

13. An agency administers the standardization, grading, and classifying of over 600 farm products. Which Cabinet member heads this agency's department?

(1) secretary of commerce
(2) secretary of agriculture
(3) secretary of the interior
(4) secretary of state
(5) secretary of transportation

Question 14 is based on the following time line.

Chinese Dynasties

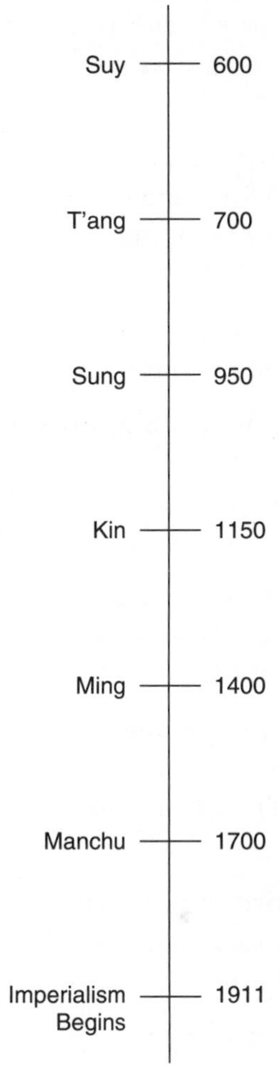

14. What information can be determined from the time line of Chinese Dynasties?

(1) The Ming Dynasty was the longest of the six.
(2) The Manchu Dynasty currently rules.
(3) There have been only six Chinese dynasties in history.
(4) The name of each dynasty includes three or four letters.
(5) Chinese law required a change of dynasty after 250 years.

PRACTICE TEST

Questions 15–17 are based on the following information.

Lobbyists work to affect foreign policy and to influence domestic issues. There are five general types of lobbyists:

economic lobby groups—representatives of American businesses and industries who attempt to influence domestic and international policy in their favor

ethnic lobby groups—associations based on common national or cultural background

foreign-government lobby groups—representatives of foreign countries who attempt to influence legislation in favor of their own nation's business and national interests

public-interest lobby groups—representatives working to protect the welfare of most or all of the American public

single-issue lobby groups—representatives working to promote legislation that affects only one issue, usually not related to economics

15. A group works to promote laws that protect the environment. This is an example of a(n)

(1) economic lobby
(2) ethnic lobby
(3) foreign-government lobby
(4) public-interest lobby
(5) single-issue lobby

16. A group works to promote legislation that outlaws abortions. This is an example of a(n)

(1) economic lobby
(2) ethnic lobby
(3) foreign-government lobby
(4) public-interest lobby
(5) single-issue lobby

17. A group works to promote legislation that allows offshore oil exploration and drilling. This is an example of a(n)

(1) economic lobby
(2) ethnic lobby
(3) foreign-government lobby
(4) public-interest lobby
(5) single-issue lobby

18. The term *melting pot* was coined by Israel Zangwell in 1907 to express the idea that immigrants from many countries came to America to form one nation. Zangwell had a vision of people sharing their traditions to become one united people. Fifty years later, Jesse Jackson said that the United States was more like a vegetable soup. Which vision about the United States did Jackson express?

(1) Many types of people live together but do not give up their distinct identities.
(2) All Americans physically look alike and act very much alike.
(3) Americans give up traditions to live together in peace.
(4) Americans are no longer more concerned with food than with cultural ideas.
(5) People from other cultures are no longer accepted as true Americans.

Questions 19 through 22 refer to the following chart.

1st Amendment Guarantees freedom of religion, speech, press, assembly, and petition
2nd Amendment Guarantees the right to bear arms
3rd Amendment Restricts the manner in which the federal government may house troops in the homes of citizens

PRACTICE TEST

4th Amendment
Protects individuals against unreasonable searches and seizures

5th Amendment
Provides that a person can be tried for a serious federal crime only if he or she has been accused of that crime by a grand jury; protects individuals against self-incrimination and against being tried twice for the same crime; prohibits unfair, arbitrary actions by the federal government; prohibits the federal government from taking private property for public use without paying a fair price for the property taken

6th Amendment
Guarantees persons accused of crime the right to a speedy and fair trial

7th Amendment
Guarantees the right to a jury trial in cases of civil suits heard in federal courts

8th Amendment
Protects against cruel and unusual punishment

9th Amendment
Establishes that the people have rights beyond those stated in the Constitution

10th Amendment
Establishes that all powers not guaranteed to the federal government and not prohibited to the states are held by each state

19. Without the promise of a Bill of Rights, several states would probably not have ratified the Constitution. Which of the following was the main argument in support of the Bill of Rights?

(1) guarantee of individual freedoms
(2) protection of the government from American citizens
(3) promise of the end of the Revolutionary War
(4) guarantee of more federal involvement in state affairs
(5) designation of more power to the executive department

20. In 1963, Martin Luther King, Jr., led a freedom march of more than 200,000 people in Washington, D.C. Which amendment covered their right to express their views?

(1) 3rd Amendment
(2) 4th Amendment
(3) 8th Amendment
(4) 1st Amendment
(5) 5th Amendment

21. From your reading of the 7th Amendment, what assumption can you make about the American judicial system before the writing of the Bill of Rights?

(1) The courts were always unfair and unpopular.
(2) A trial did not always include a jury of one's peers.
(3) Only wealthy citizens were allowed to have a trial by jury.
(4) Citizens were often executed without a trial.
(5) A jury was necessary only in federal court trials.

22. Bill Clinton's first nomination for attorney general, Zoë Baird, was rejected because she once had hired undocumented workers as household help without paying taxes on their wages. Congress later approved the appointment of Janet Reno, the first woman to hold this important position. These events support which of the following conclusions about the American people?

(1) They did not want a woman as attorney general.
(2) They wanted the attorney general to obey the laws.
(3) They did not trust the president's judgment.
(4) They did not believe in discriminating against undocumented workers.
(5) They preferred Zoë Baird to Janet Reno.

PRACTICE TEST

Questions 23 and 24 are based on the following chart.

Rulers of England

Elizabeth II
1952–

George VI
1936–1952

Edward VIII
1936*

George V
1910–1936

Edward
1901–1910

Victoria
1837–1901

William IV
1830–1837

George IV
1820–1830

George III
1760–1820

George II
1727–1760

George I
1714–1727

* abdicated (gave up throne)

23. The rulers of England had similar names. What might be the explanation for this?

(1) By law they must name their heirs the same.
(2) The royal name maintains the people's confidence in the ruling monarchy.
(3) Rulers had limited names from which to choose.
(4) Religious tradition required names from the family.
(5) This affords easier recognition by a working class.

24. Which of the following conclusions can you draw from this chart?

(1) All rulers have been of the Catholic religion.
(2) All rulers have been in power for the same length of time.
(3) All rulers in England have not been men.
(4) All rulers have been successful leaders.
(5) All rulers have served until their deaths.

25. *La Linea* is the Hispanic name for the 1,950-mile southern border of the United States. It draws thousands of jobless migrants from Mexico's interior. To them, *La Linea* represents much more than a national boundary. The crossing of the muddy waters of the Tijuana River and Rio Grande River by these families is similar to which of the following?

(1) the crossing of the Atlantic by Columbus
(2) the crossing of the Atlantic by enslaved Africans
(3) the crossing of the Atlantic or Pacific by Irish, Polish, and Chinese-Americans
(4) the crossing of the Delaware River by Washington's troops
(5) the crossing of the English Channel by American soldiers

PRACTICE TEST

Questions 26 and 27 refer to the following geologic time line.

- **Precambrian Era**
- Earth forms
- Molten land surfaces cool
- Atmosphere develops
- Oceans and weather begin
- Single cell life begins
- Land masses take shape
- **Paleozoic Era**
- Fish evolve
- Insects, plants, and reptiles evolve
- Continents collide together and create supercontinent pangaea
- **Mesozoic Era**
- Continents separate
- Appalachian Mountains form
- Dinosaurs evolve
- Rocky Mountains form
- **Cenozoic Era**
- Mammals evolve
- Cascade Mountains form
- **Today**

26. What might be the best explanation for having four eras?

(1) A new era starts every time a species evolves.
(2) Geologic eras are divided by large scale changes of land.
(3) Geologic time has been equally divided.
(4) Eras are based on a mathematical equation.
(5) Scientists have named eras at random.

27. What statement could be true based on the information provided in the time line?

(1) Changes took place over time in both living things and land form features.
(2) Dinosaurs became extinct when the Rocky Mountains formed.
(3) Humans could hunt dinosaurs for food.
(4) Fish were the first life forms.
(5) The Cascade Mountains must be older than the Appalachian Mountains.

28. Acid rain is a toxic by-product of coal and oil-burning industries, power plants, and automobile exhaust. Because of the natural water cycle, acid rain can travel as far as 2,500 miles from its source. This information supports which of the following conclusions?

(1) Acid rain cannot be considered a localized pollution problem.
(2) Acid rain is a natural phenomenon.
(3) The effects of acid rain can easily be confined to industrial areas.
(4) Acid rain is limited to cities.
(5) Rural areas are free from the effects of acid rain.

29. As cities grew in the twentieth century, so did their social problems. Overcrowding, traffic jams, crime, pollution and unemployment became commonplace. Faced with decaying downtowns and "white flight" to the suburbs, city planners began to incorporate social programs in their plans for economic and physical urban renewal. Efforts to rehabilitate low-income, inner-city neighborhoods are based on which of the following assumptions?

(1) Downtown areas are not worth saving.
(2) Suburbanites cannot be tempted back into the cities.
(3) Low-income families won't be willing to move to the suburbs.
(4) Government intervention can correct and prevent social problems.
(5) Low-income neighborhoods won't cost much to improve.

PRACTICE TEST

Question 30 is based on the following graph.

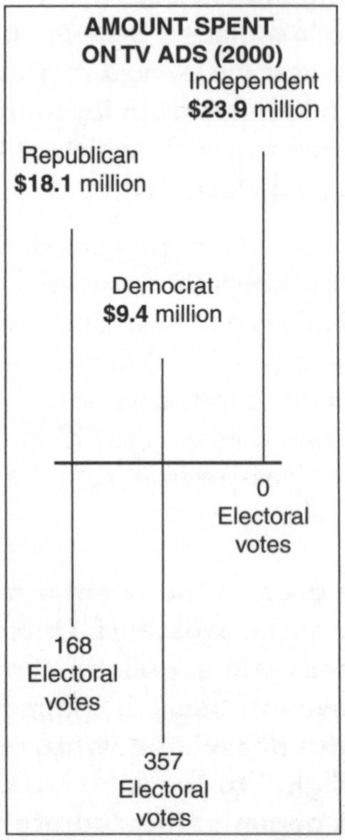

30. What is the main idea of this graph?

(1) The more a candidate spends on ads, the better the chances of getting elected.
(2) Presidential candidates spend too much on their campaign ads.
(3) The Democratic party is opposed to spending excessively on political campaigns.
(4) Spending a lot on political ads does not guarantee election.
(5) Political ads have no effect on an election.

Questions 31 and 32 refer to the following map and caption.

In 1872, the U.S. government began to set aside and conserve natural and unusually scenic areas as national parks. The most recent parks were established in Alaska and Nevada between 1980 and 1986. The map shows the general location of America's national parks.

31. According to the map, where are the majority of national parks located?

(1) in the Northeast (Maine, New York, Massachusetts)
(2) in the Southwest (Texas, New Mexico, Arizona)
(3) in the West (California, Oregon, Nevada)
(4) in Alaska and Hawaii
(5) in most of the states

32. Which of the following best accounts for the locations of many of the national parks?

(1) These areas were still undeveloped for residential or agricultural use.
(2) These areas couldn't be used for anything else.
(3) These areas were difficult to reach.
(4) These areas were rich in natural resources such as oil, gold, and timber.
(5) These areas could be bought cheaply by the government.

PRACTICE TEST

Questions 33 and 34 are based on the following political cartoon.

Steve Lindstrom, Duluth News Tribune. 5886 Alborn-Brookston Rd. Alborn, MN 55702

33. Which of the following best summarizes the main idea expressed in the cartoon?

The United States should

(1) increase its national debt and reduce the budget surplus
(2) eliminate the budget surplus
(3) continue spending because of a stable economy
(4) increase federal spending despite the national debt
(5) watch federal spending because of serious national debt

34. What is meant by the captain of the Titanic's exclamation, "Resume Federal overspending—it's just a little ice cube."

(1) The budget surplus is small and insignificant.
(2) The government should resume spending money.
(3) The budget surplus isn't a concern to the taxpayers.
(4) The government needs to put an end to the budget surplus.
(5) The taxpayers need to watch overspending.

PRACTICE TEST

Question 35 is based on the following passage.

The Bubonic Plague of the mid-fourteenth century was the most devastating natural disaster in European history. We now know that this plague was caused by rats that were infected by bacteria-carrying fleas. The rats carried the disease as they were unknowingly transported with cargo ships through trade routes. A third of the entire population of Europe is thought to have been killed by this plague.

35. What caused the Bubonic Plague?

(1) poor sanitation in crowded European cities
(2) a disease carried by sailors through trade routes
(3) a highly contagious virus spread by human contact
(4) rats that carried the disease through crowded cities
(5) fleas on rats that carried the deadly bacteria through trade routes

Questions 36 and 37 are based on the following excerpt.

Brown *vs.* Topeka Board of Education

On May 17, 1954, the Supreme Court ruled in a unanimous decision that separate but equal facilities were unconstitutional because they violated the children's 14th Amendment rights by separating them solely on the classification of color of their skin. An excerpt from this Supreme Court decision delivered by Chief Justice Warren reads as follows:

"Segregated schools are not equal and cannot be made equal, and hence they are deprived of the equal protection of the laws."

36. Which of the following is not a value expressed in this court's opinion?

(1) equality for all races
(2) equality of gender in all schools
(3) equality for all ages and abilities
(4) equality of teaching materials
(5) equality in schools protected by the law

37. What assumption can be made based on this excerpt from the Supreme Court's decision in *Brown vs. Topeka Board of Education*?

(1) Many children could not afford to attend school.
(2) Segregated schools were against the law after this ruling.
(3) All schools were segregated until this ruling.
(4) Segregated schools were acceptable in some states.
(5) Individuals of all races can now teach school.

PRACTICE TEST

38. A monarchy that had been under native rule since 1795, the Hawaiian Islands began to attract American missionaries during the late nineteenth century. In addition to the opportunity to bring religion to natives, Hawaii offered new agricultural and military resources. Despite anti-imperialist objections, Hawaii became an American territory in 1898. Which of the following assumptions prompted the first missionaries to go to the Hawaiian islands?

(1) The native monarchy would fail.
(2) Americans would soon develop a taste for tropical fruit.
(3) Native Hawaiians would wish Hawaii to become the fiftieth American state.
(4) Native Hawaiians would welcome the opportunity to become Christians.
(5) The American government would welcome new sites for military bases.

39. One factor in the law of supply and demand is the ratio of sellers to buyers. The more sellers of a product, the greater the choices a buyer has. This principle of supply and demand has a special effect on the real estate market. When there have been more houses on the market for a long period than there have been buyers, which of the following is likely to happen?

(1) A buyer will offer more than the seller's asking price.
(2) A seller will refuse to consider an offer lower than the asking price.
(3) A seller will accept an offer lower than the asking price.
(4) More people will put up their homes for sale.
(5) Potential buyers will wait until house prices go down.

Question 40 is based on the following picture and caption.

Library of Congress

Chinese immigrants brought unique customs to the United States. Though their traditional dress and neighborhoods made them feel at home, they also helped isolate the Chinese community from other Americans. Chinese isolation did not increase American tolerance for their cultural differences.

40. Which of the following statements provides the best support for the opinion stated in this caption?

(1) Immigrants are usually openly accepted by native-born Americans into American lifestyles.
(2) Immigrants should give up all of their wealth in order to gain permission to live in the United States.
(3) Immigrants are never really welcomed by the more established ethnic groups in the United States.
(4) Immigrants must give up all of their customs in order to become true Americans.
(5) Immigrants contribute to the diversity of a nation but experience delays in acculturation.

Question 41 is based on the following map.

Civil War Battle Sites

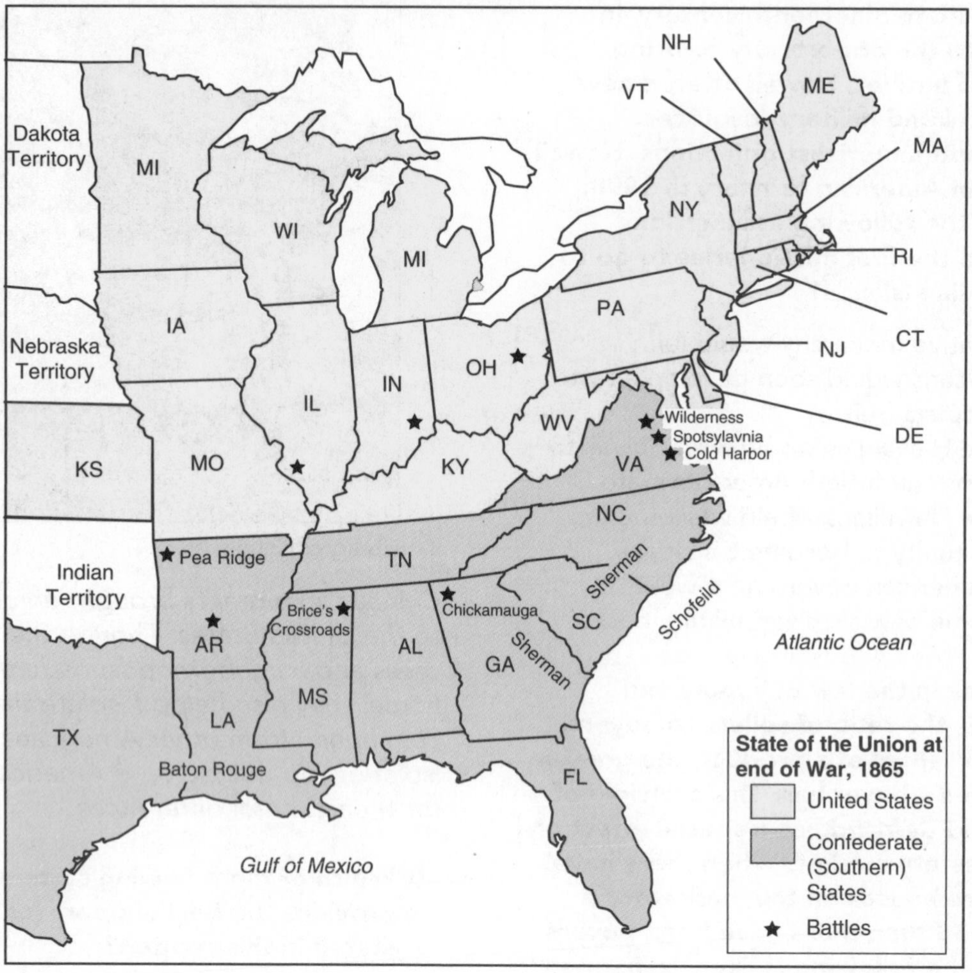

41. What do you infer to be the main idea of the map?

(1) All battles were fought in the Southern states.

(2) A battle was fought in every state in the Union.

(3) Most battles were fought in the Southern states.

(4) Many battles were fought near Lake Superior.

(5) No battles were fought in the North.

PRACTICE TEST

Questions 42 and 43 are based on the following passage.

THE OATH OF AMERICAN CITIZENSHIP
(Taken when naturalized)

"I hereby declare, on oath, that I absolutely and entirely renounce and abjure all allegiance and fidelity to any foreign prince, potentate, state or sovereignty of whom or which I have heretofore been a subject or citizen; that I will support and defend the Constitution and laws of the United States of America against all enemies, foreign and domestic; that I will bear true faith and allegiance to the same; that I will bear arms on behalf of the United States when required by law; that I will perform noncombatant service in the Armed Forces of the United States when required by the law; that I will perform work of national importance under civilian direction when required by the law; and that I take this obligation freely without any mental reservation or purpose of evasion; so help me God. In acknowledgement whereof I have hereunto affixed my signature."

42. Which of the following is the best restatement of the following sentence from the Oath of American Citizenship? "I absolutely and entirely renounce and abjure all allegiance and fidelity to any foreign prince, potentate, state, or sovereignty of whom or which I have heretofore been a subject or citizen"

(1) I will give up my previous allegiance to any other country.
(2) I will continue to declare allegiance to my native country.
(3) I am an American, yet I will still be faithful to my country's king.
(4) I promise to tell the truth whenever possible.
(5) I will only support the United States in times of peace.

43. Which of the following is not a consequence of becoming an American citizen?

(1) I will support the Constitution of the United States.
(2) I will bear arms for this country when required by law.
(3) I will perform required noncombatant service in the Armed Forces.
(4) I will renounce my citizenship in any other country.
(5) I will become either a Republican or Democrat.

44. In 1974, 1986, and again in 1999, the U.S. Congress established committees to investigate alleged wrongdoings by the president and his staff. What is this congressional action an example of?

(1) amending the Constitution
(2) overriding a veto
(3) passing a bill
(4) applying checks and balances
(5) approving a treaty

PRACTICE TEST

Questions 45 and 46 apply to the following excerpt.

Alcohol as a Drug

Alcohol is a drug that affects your overall driving ability. Alcohol slows your reaction time so that it takes you longer to act in an emergency. It affects your vision. Alcohol may make you overconfident and unable to concentrate (think) well. Drivers who drink may make more mistakes.

Alcohol affects your driving even if you are below the level of legal intoxication. Drinking even a small amount of alcohol increases your chances of having an accident. Do not drink and drive.

Blood Alcohol Concentration (BAC)

BAC is a measurement of the amount of alcohol in your system based on a test of your breath, blood or urine. It is illegal to drive if your BAC is .10 percent (1/10th of one percent) or greater. However, you can be convicted of DUI if your BAC is less than .10 percent and your driving ability is impaired. Your BAC can be affected by:

- the amount you drink. Twelve ounces of beer, five ounces of wine or one and one-half ounces of "hard" liquor contain the same amount of alcohol.

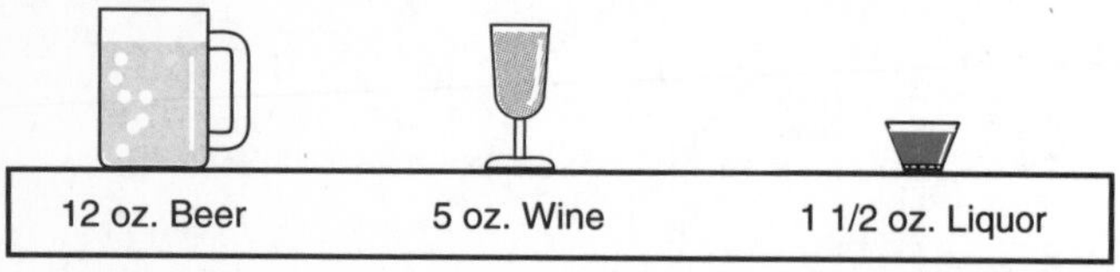

- time. Time is the only way to remove the effects of alcohol. Food, coffee and showers do not speed up the elimination of alcohol from your body.
- your body weight or size. Usually, heavier people have more blood and body fluids to dilute the alcohol.
- Other things affect your reaction to alcohol. These include food eaten, your tolerance of alcohol and any drugs you may have taken.

—Excerpted from Illinois 2000 Rules of the Road

45. Driving under the influence of alcohol is a very serious offense. Alcohol is the number one killer on American roadways. According to this passage, which of the following results are not precipitated by alcohol consumption?

(1) diminished vision
(2) heightened concentration
(3) weakened response time
(4) disguised overconfidence
(5) delayed reaction time

46. If you had to offset the effects of having too much alcohol, which strategy would be most effective?

(1) drinking three glasses of water to dilute the alcohol
(2) taking several aspirin and drinking fruit juice
(3) drinking four cups of regular coffee
(4) eating crackers to absorb the alcohol
(5) stopping drinking and waiting several hours

PRACTICE TEST

Question 47 is based on the following chart.

Comparison of Size and Population of Continents, 1900–1999

CONTINENT	AREA (1,000 sq. miles)	POPULATION 1950	1980	1999
North America	9,400	221,000	372,000	476,000
South America	6,900	111,000	242,000	343,000
Europe	3,800	392,000	484,000	727,000
Asia	17,400	1,411,000	2,601,000	3,641,000
Africa	11,700	229,000	470,000	778,000
Australia	3,300	12,000	23,000	30,000
Antarctica	5,400		UNINHABITED	

47. From studying this chart, what conclusion can you draw?

(1) The larger the area in square miles, the higher the population.
(2) The population of each continent increases at the same rate.
(3) The area of a continent doesn't always determine population.
(4) Between 1950 and 1980 all continents had an increase in population.
(5) The area in square miles of each continent changes with population.

Question 48 is based on the following cartoon.

US PURCHASES ALASKA FOR $7 MILLION

THE TWO PETER FUNKS.

RUSSIAN STRANGER—"*I say, little boy, do you want to trade? I've got a fine lot of bears, seals, icebergs and Esquimaux—They're no use to me, I'll swop 'em all for those boats you've got.*"
[Billy, like other foolish boys, jumps at the idea.]

In the cartoon, Secretary Seward is shown being tricked into buying "worthless" Alaska.

48. Which of the following is a fact provided in the information about the purchase of Alaska?

(1) The United States paid too much money for the purchase of Alaska.
(2) Congress unanimously approved the decision to purchase Alaska.
(3) The Russian government was forced to sell Alaska to the United States.
(4) Secretary Seward experienced criticism over his desire to purchase Alaska.
(5) The Territory of Alaska was beautiful and bountiful.

PRACTICE TEST

Questions 49 and 50 refer to the following graph.

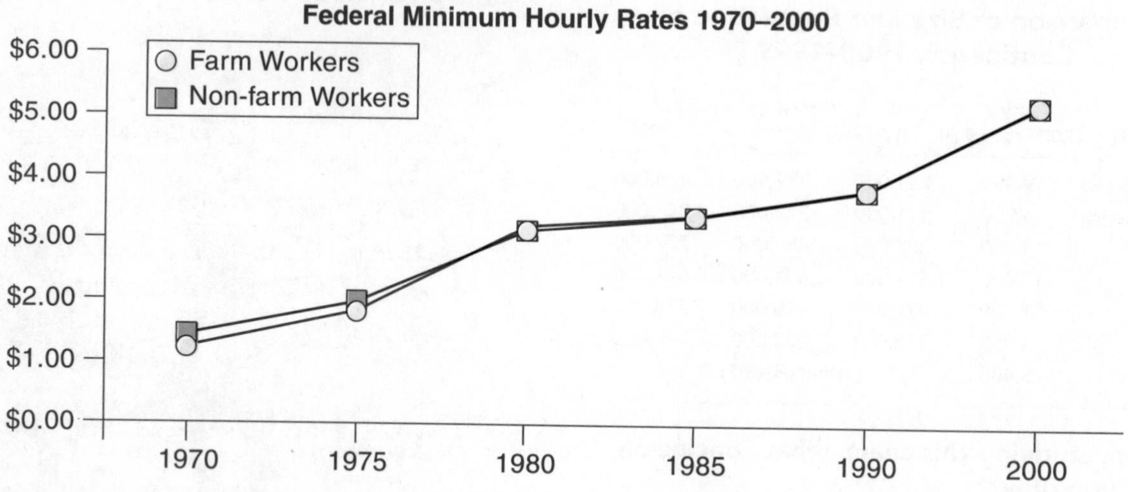

49. What conclusion is supported by the information in the line graph?

(1) The minimum wage more than doubled between the 1970s and the 1990s.
(2) Wages for farm workers always lag behind wages for non-farm workers.
(3) The minimum wage in the seventies was too low.
(4) The minimum wage will never increase above $5.15.
(5) More people than ever before are earning the minimum wage.

50. Which of the following is the most probable cause of the increase in the minimum wage?

(1) the increase in the number of women in the workforce
(2) the increase in the total national debt
(3) a recognition of the importance of unskilled workers
(4) an attempt to decrease unemployment
(5) a continued rise in the cost of living

PRACTICE TEST

Social Studies Answer Key

1. **Comprehension (4)** If the new business was having financial difficulties in starting up, business managers might seek private funding to supply the large capital outlay.

2. **Application (2)** The license to serve alcohol is issued by the local government.

3. **Evaluation (5)** One of the main goals for the United Nations is to prevent war. Treaties establish a mutual trust among countries for security.

4. **Analysis (4)** The cartoonist has the peace agreement founded on a house of cards. This would indicate that the peace settlement is not on a secure foothold and might collapse at any time.

5. **Evaluation (4)** By qualifying the handshake with the word *gently* the cartoonist draws our attention to the fact that the peace is being established on unsecured ground. This would make anyone who has an interest in long-term peace slightly anxious.

6. **Evaluation (2)** Very often larger and more powerful nations that have voiced an interest in world peace are called in to help the peace negotiations along. The United States often finds itself active in assisting in the peace process for other countries.

7. **Comprehension (3)** The stagecoach and Pony Express were both attempts to solve the larger problem of the vast distance that needed to be covered by mail carriers.

8. **Evaluation (2)** The mail is a form of communication. Those out west wanted a greater reliability and efficiency in communicating with the eastern sections of the United States.

9. **Application (5)** The improvement of communication with a direct connection over great distances through the transcontinental railway is a direct comparison with the new technology of the transatlantic cable.

10. **Application (5)** The Monroe Doctrine specifies the area of the Americas. While Panama and Colombia are part of Central and South America, the other choices involve areas other than the Americas.

11. **Application (5)** The Department of Transportation is responsible for transportation on waterways.

12. **Application (1)** The Department of Commerce, which is responsible for protecting against unfair trade, would assist a minority business.

13. **Application (2)** The Department of Agriculture is in charge of farm policy and standardization.

14. **Comprehension (1)** At 300 years, the Ming Dynasty lasted the longest of these Chinese dynasties listed.

15. **Analysis (4)** The environment is a public interest that affects the quality of life for all Americans.

16. **Analysis (5)** The abortion issue is considered a single-item issue because this group is concerned with a single law.

17. **Analysis (1)** Offshore exploration and drilling are economic concerns that could affect specific businesses.

18. **Application (1)** In vegetable soup the individual member ingredients do not lose their individual flavors. The combination of these unique flavors adds to the variety available in the soup. Jesse Jackson was encouraging the individual cultures to remain distinct and cooperate instead of melting into a generic single culture (choice 2) or fighting with each other (choice 3).

19. **Analysis (1)** Many of the early Americans came to this country to escape persecution. The Constitution needed to create a plan for this country that protected the citizens from the same kind of injustices that they had felt in their homelands.

20. **Application (4)** The right to free speech and assembly is in the first amendment of the Bill of Rights.

21. **Analysis (2)** A jury of one's peers is a cornerstone of the U.S. judicial system.

22. **Evaluation (2)** Since Zoë Baird had broken the law in the past, the American people determined that she was untrustworthy. Since another woman was confirmed, the issue was not about gender.

23. **Comprehension (2)** The custom of naming children after the parents or relatives is out of respect or honor to the person. The English royalty also found that the level of confidence of the English people was higher when it was easy to recognize that the monarch was of the royal family by birth.

24. **Analysis (3)** Two of the rulers of England on the chart were women, Queen Victoria and Queen Elizabeth. No other information is made available about the monarchy of England.

25. **Application (3)** Since the people of Mexico cross *La Linea* to attempt to become part of the American Dream, it relates to the crossing of an ocean by other immigrants on their way to America. Columbus (choice 1) was interested in creating a shorter trade route to the Indies, and Africans were abducted to use as an enslaved workforce (choice 2). Choices 4 and 5 are incidents of water crossing during battle.

26. **Evaluation (2)** The Eras are not divided equally or through a mathematical equation. A new era begins when the surface condition on the Earth changes drastically. This change of the surface condition might lead to an evolutionary change in a species.

27. **Analysis (1)** Choices 2 and 3 are incorrect because dinosaurs were not in existence with humans and were not affected by the development of the Rockies. Choice 4 is incorrect because single-cell life was the first to appear on the planet. Choice 5 is incorrect because the Appalachians are older than the Cascades.

28. **Evaluation (1)** Since acid rain travels so far from its source, it cannot be considered a local problem. People are unable to control the water cycle, so it is impossible to confine the problem to a specific area.

29. **Analysis (4)** The city government can have a great impact on the renovation of its neighborhoods. Specific planning to eliminate trouble areas and set up social programs can also improve the conditions that plague a city. Many of these plans are long range and costly, but plans are considered worth the cost if they improve the quality of life for the city and suburban residents.

30. **Analysis (4)** The chart shows that the candidate that spent the most money received no electoral votes. The other choices are not validated by the information in the chart.

31. **Comprehension (2)** The southwestern areas like Arizona (which contains the Grand Canyon) have more areas of national parks indicated by black dots.

32. **Analysis (1)** Since the southwestern areas like Arizona (where the Grand Canyon is located) have vast areas of natural beauty with no residents or farms on a majority of the land, it was easier for the United States government to establish national parks in this region.

33. **Analysis (4)** The caption leads us to believe that the threat of a large national debt is unseen and, therefore, not a concern.

34. **Comprehension (2)** By resuming federal spending, the government is not showing any concern for the possible problems of a large national debt. The concerns do not include any actions by the taxpayers.

35. **Comprehension (5)** Although poor sanitation did cause the population of rats to grow, and the disease did spread by human contact and along trade routes, the source of the Plague has been determined to be fleas that were carried by rats.

36. **Evaluation (4)** Teaching materials would not be a value concern. The right to an equal education does not stipulate what materials the school would choose to employ.

37. **Analysis (2)** Segregated schools were ruled unconstitutional because they were not equal.

38. **Analysis (4)** The missionaries assumed the Hawaiians would want the missionaries to bring religion to them. The other choices would not have been reasons that the missionaries would have traveled to the islands.

39. **Analysis (3)** If there were competition among sellers for a limited number of buyers, a home seller would have to consider an offer that is below the original asking price. Choices (1) and (2) refer to times when there are many homebuyers and few houses available.

40. **Evaluation (5)** Each large wave of incoming immigrants from foreign lands has had to experience a certain degree of prejudice and mistrust from earlier immigrants. These immigrants have had to blend into American culture to compete for jobs. Many cultural groups are torn between keeping their traditions and culture alive and melting into the American culture.

41. **Comprehension (3)** While some battles were fought in the North, most battles were fought on Southern soil.

42. **Comprehension (1)** To become a citizen of the United States, a person must break allegiance with his or her previous country and swear loyalty to America.

43. **Analysis (5)** Becoming a citizen does not require anyone to declare a political party.

44. **Analysis (4)** Investigating the president for alleged wrongdoings is part of the checks and balances system that allows the judicial branch to check the executive branch. This process does not change the Constitution or have any effect on vetoing or passing a bill.

45. **Comprehension (2)** Alcohol has the opposite effect on concentration. Drinking impairs judgment and prevents the ability to focus attention.

46. **Application (5)** The only successful method of combating the effects of alcohol is to wait until the body systems have filtered the blood through the liver and kidneys. There is no way to reduce effects, increase absorption rates, or counteract the alcohol.

47. **Analysis (3)** As in the case of Europe, the population is not limited to the size of the continent in square miles. Between 1900 and 1950 Europe had a drop in its population, mainly from disease, war, and emigration. Many of the continents had much higher gains in population as compared to the other continents, as in the example of the Asian continent.

48. **Analysis (4)** The caption indicates that the cartoonist thought Secretary Seward should have been criticized for being "duped" into the purchase of the frozen wastelands of Alaska.

49. **Evaluation (1)** The graph does not guarantee that farm workers will always lag behind non-farm workers who earn minimum wage. There is no information about the value of minimum wage in the past or the increase for minimum wage in the future. No information is given in the chart about the number of American workers who earn minimum wage.

50. **Analysis (5)** Minimum wage has been increased in the past to allow for the increases in the cost of living because of inflation or other economic changes. The increase is not an attempt to decrease unemployment, but rather to safeguard the salaries of low-income groups.

SOCIAL STUDIES PRACTICE TEST

Evaluation Chart

Use the Answer Key on pages 1089–1091 to check your answers to the Practice Test. Then find the item number of each question you missed and circle it on the chart below to determine the Social Studies content areas in which you need more practice. Pay particular attention to areas where you missed half or more of the questions. Numbers in boldface indicate questions based on graphics. The page numbers for the content areas are listed below on the chart. For those questions that you missed, review the skill pages indicated.

SKILL AREA/ CONTENT AREA	**COMPREHENSION (pages 217–230)**	**APPLICATION (pages 231–236)**	**ANALYSIS (pages 237–262)**	**EVALUATION (pages 271–274)**
World History (pages 297–326)	**14, 23,** 35	25	**24, 27**	**26**
U.S. History (pages 327–366)	7, **41**	9, 10, 18	**4,** 37, 38, **48**	**5, 6,** 8, 36, **40**
Civics and Government (pages 367–398)	42, 45	11, 12, 13, **20,** 46	15, 16, 17, **19, 21,** 29, **30,** 43, 44	3, **22**
Economics (pages 399–426)	**1, 33**	**2**	**34,** 39, **50**	**49**
Geography (pages 427–443)	**31**		**32, 47**	28

Science

The Science Practice Test consists of 50 multiple-choice questions. The questions are based on graphs, maps, tables, diagrams, editorial cartoons, and reading passages. Answer each question as carefully as possible, choosing the best of five answer choices and blackening in the grid. If you find a question too difficult, do not waste time on it. Work ahead and come back to it later when you can think it through carefully.

You should take approximately 80 minutes to complete this test. At the end of 80 minutes, stop and mark your place. Then finish the test. This will give you an idea of whether you can finish the real GED Test in the time allotted. Try to answer as many questions as you can. A blank will count as a wrong answer, so make a reasonable guess for answers to questions of which you are not sure.

When you are finished with the test, check your answers and turn to the Evaluation Chart on page 1116. Use the chart to evaluate whether or not you are ready to take the actual GED Test and, if not, in what areas you need more work.

Science Practice Test Answer Grid

1	①	②	③	④	⑤	18	①	②	③	④	⑤	35	①	②	③	④	⑤
2	①	②	③	④	⑤	19	①	②	③	④	⑤	36	①	②	③	④	⑤
3	①	②	③	④	⑤	20	①	②	③	④	⑤	37	①	②	③	④	⑤
4	①	②	③	④	⑤	21	①	②	③	④	⑤	38	①	②	③	④	⑤
5	①	②	③	④	⑤	22	①	②	③	④	⑤	39	①	②	③	④	⑤
6	①	②	③	④	⑤	23	①	②	③	④	⑤	40	①	②	③	④	⑤
7	①	②	③	④	⑤	24	①	②	③	④	⑤	41	①	②	③	④	⑤
8	①	②	③	④	⑤	25	①	②	③	④	⑤	42	①	②	③	④	⑤
9	①	②	③	④	⑤	26	①	②	③	④	⑤	43	①	②	③	④	⑤
10	①	②	③	④	⑤	27	①	②	③	④	⑤	44	①	②	③	④	⑤
11	①	②	③	④	⑤	28	①	②	③	④	⑤	45	①	②	③	④	⑤
12	①	②	③	④	⑤	29	①	②	③	④	⑤	46	①	②	③	④	⑤
13	①	②	③	④	⑤	30	①	②	③	④	⑤	47	①	②	③	④	⑤
14	①	②	③	④	⑤	31	①	②	③	④	⑤	48	①	②	③	④	⑤
15	①	②	③	④	⑤	32	①	②	③	④	⑤	49	①	②	③	④	⑤
16	①	②	③	④	⑤	33	①	②	③	④	⑤	50	①	②	③	④	⑤
17	①	②	③	④	⑤	34	①	②	③	④	⑤						

PRACTICE TEST

Choose the *best* answer to each question that follows.

Question 1 is based on the following chart.

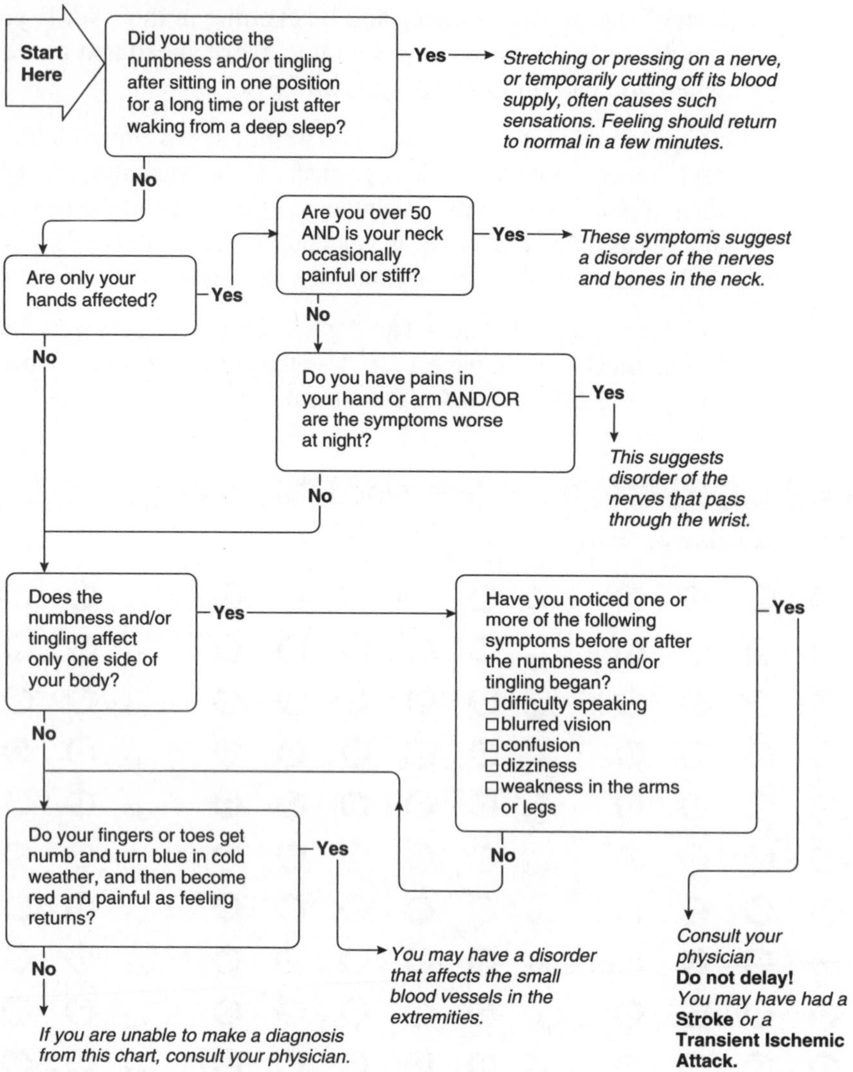

Source: *American Medical Association 1994 Family Medical Guide*

1. Debbie consulted the chart on numbness and/or tingling after she experienced weakness in her right arm and leg for three hours after grocery shopping. She also felt slightly nauseated and light-headed. According to this chart, what could be a possible diagnosis to be determined by her doctor?

Debbie may have sustained

(1) a disorder of the nerves that passes through the wrist
(2) a temporary loss of blood supply
(3) a disorder that affects the small blood vessels in the extremities
(4) a disturbance of blood supply to the brain (stroke)
(5) a chronic fatigue disorder

PRACTICE TEST

2. According to meteorologist Tom Skilling, when a golf ball flies through the air, it must push aside the air in its path. This motion uses energy that would otherwise carry the ball forward. A golf ball flying through more dense air will transfer the energy imparted to it by the golf club more rapidly than if it were flying through less dense air, which will cause it to fall sooner. When would a golfer who wants his ball to travel the greatest distance hope to play golf?

(1) late in the afternoon
(2) on a humid day
(3) early in the evening
(4) in the fall season
(5) on a hot, dry day

Question 3 refers to the following drawing.

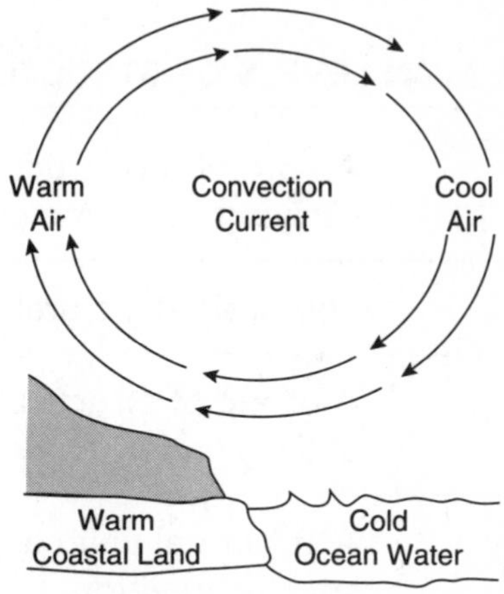

3. In normal nighttime conditions, the wind next to Earth's surface blows toward the water from the land. From this fact, what can you deduce about nighttime conditions?

(1) Ocean currents are not as strong as during the day.
(2) Ocean temperature changes more quickly than land temperature.
(3) The sun is not warming either the land or the ocean.
(4) The temperature of the land is higher than that of the ocean.
(5) The temperature of the land is lower than that of the ocean.

PRACTICE TEST

Questions 4 and 5 refer to the following chart.

FIVE COMMON LEVELS OF STRUCTURAL ORGANIZATION	
organelle	An organized structure found in a cell's cytoplasm. Each organelle takes part in carrying out some cellular function.
cell	The basic structural and functional unit of life.
tissue	A group of structurally similar cells that are organized to perform the same activity.
organ	A structural unit composed of several tissues that work together to perform a specific function.
organ system	An association of several organs that work together to perform one or more functions.

4. When Derek reached forty-three years of age, his pancreas no longer produced sufficient insulin, a hormone that controls sugar levels in the blood. As a result, Derek was diagnosed as having diabetes, a condition that can often be controlled through proper diet. Because it is made up of several types of specialized tissues, how is the pancreas best classified?

(1) organelle
(2) cell
(3) tissue
(4) organ
(5) organ system

5. As soon as you put food in your mouth, saliva begins breaking the food down into a form your cells can use. This process is further carried out in your stomach and small intestine. Your mouth, stomach, and small intestine work together to complete the digestive process. What is this known as?

(1) organelle
(2) cell
(3) tissue
(4) organ
(5) organ system

PRACTICE TEST

Questions 6 and 7 are based on the following passage.

What does an aluminum rowboat have in common with a helium-filled balloon? Both the rowboat and balloon exhibit **buoyancy**—the tendency of an object to float in liquid or to rise in gas.

The rowboat and balloon each have two forces acting on them: a downward gravitational force (equal to the object's weight) and an upward buoyancy force. The buoyancy force is equal to the weight of liquid or gas that the object displaces (takes the place of).

A rowboat floats in water because the upward buoyancy force exactly balances the downward gravitational force. A 500-pound rowboat sinks just to the point where it displaces 500 pounds of water.

A rock sinks in water because the gravitational force is greater than the buoyancy force.

A helium-filled balloon rises in air because it displaces a volume of air that weighs more than the weight of the helium, gas-filled balloon. In other words, the upward buoyancy force is greater than the downward gravitational force.

6. Which of the following objects is not designed to employ the buoyancy principle?

(1) submarine
(2) life preserver
(3) hot-air balloon
(4) kite
(5) canoe

7. When Tally swims, she notices that if she takes a deep breath, she floats. If she exhales all the air in her lungs, she sinks. Which of the following is the best explanation of Tally's discovery?

After exhaling, but not before, Tally displaces an amount of water that

(1) weighs less than her body
(2) weighs more than her body
(3) is equal to her body weight
(4) has more volume than her body volume
(5) has less volume than her body volume

Question 8 is based on the following diagram.

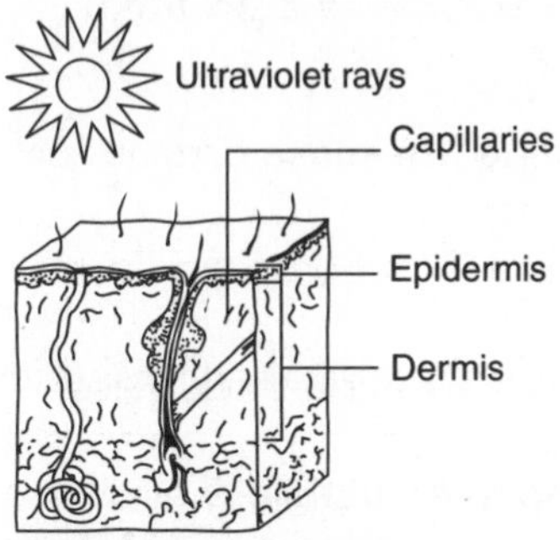

The sun and your skin
The sun's ultraviolet rays can penetrate the semitransparent epidermis and reach the underlying dermis. Blood vessels dilate and let more blood flow near the surface, making the skin look red. Burned skin also looks red.

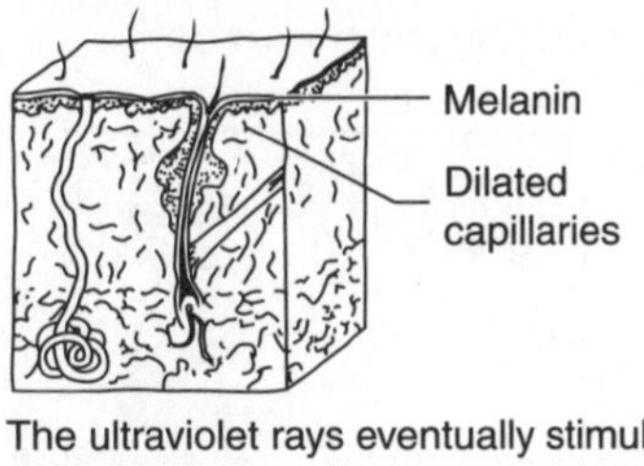

The ultraviolet rays eventually stimulate certain cells to produce more melanin, a skin pigment that protects the underlying tissues. The melanin moves upward toward the epidermis, darkening it.

Source: 1994 American Medical Association *Family Medical Guide*

8. Which of the following facts are true *only* for a suntan and *not* a sunburn?

A suntan

(1) is caused by ultraviolet rays from the sun
(2) emerges after the cells produce more melanin
(3) encourages premature aging of the skin
(4) occurs between 10:00 A.M. and 2:00 P.M.
(5) is precipitated by blood flowing near the surface of the skin

PRACTICE TEST

9. Which of the following is the best evidence that light travels at a greater speed than sound?

(1) Humans have separate sense organs for vision and hearing.
(2) Light travels through outer space, but sound doesn't.
(3) Light passes easily through thick glass, but sound doesn't.
(4) Lightning is seen before thunder is heard.
(5) The frequency of visible light is much greater than that of sound.

Question 10 refers to the following cartoon.

10. With which of the following opinions would the cartoonist most likely agree?

(1) Most new cars should not have to use premium gasoline to run *efficiently.*
(2) Sport utility vehicles are the best cars to drive even though they have poor gas mileage.
(3) Americans feel that they have little control over the price of gasoline.
(4) The consumer controls the retail prices of most production in the United States.
(5) Most people are angry and determined to resist the increases in gas prices.

Question 11 refers to the following information.

EFFECTS OF STRESS

Brain	behavioral and emotional problems
Heart	disturbance of rate and rhythm
Lungs	asthma conditions possibly more serious
Digestive Tract	indigestion, ulcers
Skin	outbreaks of skin problems
Hair	hair loss

11. What conclusion can you draw from this chart about the effects of stress on the body?

(1) An occasional period of stress affects the lungs of most people.
(2) People who are bald have high amounts of stress in their lives.
(3) Those who suffer heart attacks have probably experienced very stressful situations.
(4) Only the main organs of the body are affected by stress.
(5) Physical and mental stress affects the entire human body.

12. Many people feel that while it is acceptable to raise animals such as cows for slaughter, it is not acceptable to kill more intelligent animals such as whales or chimpanzees. What value concerning intelligence is reflected by this position?

(1) Food production for human consumption is more important than animal rights.
(2) Humans should have a higher regard for those animals of higher intelligence.
(3) Animals should not be harmed when used for medical research.
(4) The only justification for killing an animal is for use as a source of food.
(5) Animals that are only physically similar to people should be treated differently.

Question 13 is based on the following drawing and passage.

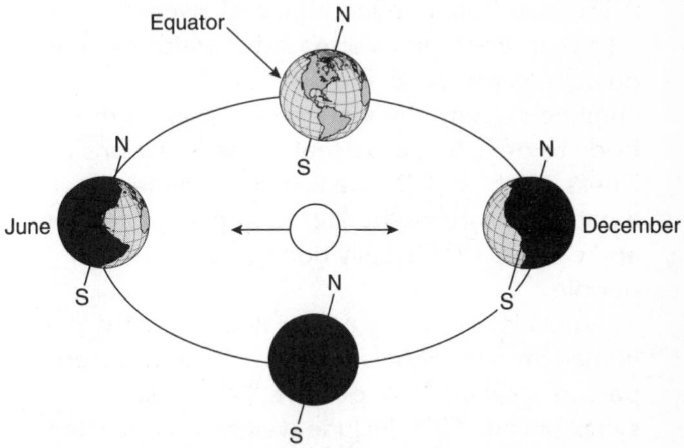

Earth's rotation axis is tilted with respect to the direction of the Sun's rays. This tilt remains constant as Earth rotates on its axis and as it moves around the Sun. The tilt leads to two important consequences for Earth:

Summer occurs in the hemisphere that is tilted toward the Sun while winter occurs in the hemisphere that is tilted away from the Sun.

The hemisphere that is tilted toward the Sun has longer days and shorter nights than the hemisphere that is tilted away from the Sun.

13. Where would a town be located that will most nearly have twelve hours of daylight and twelve hours of darkness during the month of December?

(1) close to the North Pole
(2) close to the South Pole
(3) halfway between the equator and North Pole
(4) halfway between the equator and the South Pole
(5) close to the equator

PRACTICE TEST

Questions 14 and 15 are based on the following passage.

AIDS (acquired immunodeficiency syndrome) is a serious, contagious disease for which there is no cure as yet. AIDS is a disease of the human immune system, the system that enables the body to destroy germs that cause infections and illness. With an AIDS-weakened immune system, a patient may develop life threatening infections and cancers that usually don't affect healthy people.

AIDS is caused by a virus known as HIV, the human immunodeficiency virus. Once infected, a person is called "HIV positive." The first symptoms of AIDS include weight loss, swollen lymph nodes, body weakness, persistent cough, and chronic yeast infections of the mouth or genital areas. Other symptoms include pneumonia and a type of cancer characterized by the presence of purplish spots.

An HIV-positive person may show no symptoms of AIDS for years after he or she becomes infected. Furthermore, without showing symptoms, that person may be unaware that he or she is infected. However, *an HIV-positive person is infectious and can transmit the HIV virus to other people.* The HIV virus is spread from the blood of an infected person to the blood of an uninfected one. Because blood cells are present in sexual fluids, the HIV virus can spread from one person to another during sexual activity.

AIDS is spread in one of three main ways:

- by having unsafe sex with an infected person
- by sharing a needle with an infected drug user
- from an infected mother to the fetus during pregnancy, or to the baby during delivery or breast feeding

AIDS is preventable, and people can protect themselves from AIDS by engaging only in safe sex or abstinence and by staying away from intravenous drugs.

14. Which of the following would a child with AIDS or an immunodeficiency *not* need to be protected from?

A child with

(1) chickenpox
(2) mumps
(3) measles
(4) appendicitis
(5) scarlet fever

15. An increase in the number of reported HIV-positive people is occurring in the United States. Which of the following is the *least* likely cause of the growth?

(1) an increasing awareness by doctors of the symptoms of AIDS
(2) an increasing effort to educate U.S. citizens about the AIDS problem
(3) an increase in the spread of the AIDS disease
(4) an increase in testing to determine who has the HIV virus
(5) an increase of HIV-positive people into the United States from foreign countries

Question 16 is based on the following drawing.

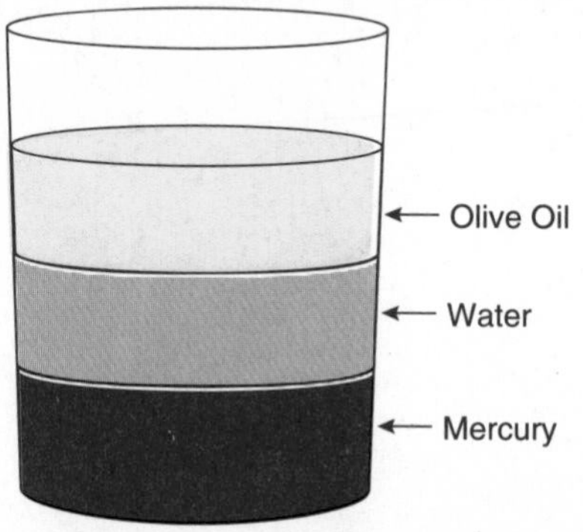

16. What can you can infer from the drawing above about the density of water?

(1) It is lesser than the density of olive oil.
(2) It is greater than the density of mercury.
(3) It is greater than the density of ice.
(4) It is greater than the density of olive oil.
(5) It is equal to the density of olive oil.

PRACTICE TEST

Questions 17 and 18 refer to the following drawing.

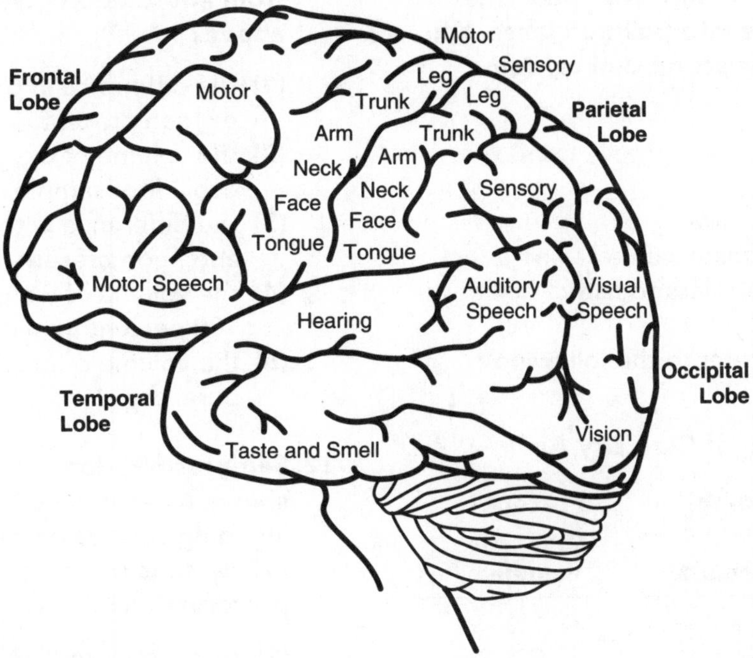

17. Wayne has suffered a severe injury to his occipital lobe. Which of the following conditions could he experience?

(1) deafness
(2) emphysema
(3) blindness
(4) paralysis of legs
(5) severe stuttering

18. Which facts below represent the best evidence that brain size is not the main cause for differences in intelligence?

A. The brain of an adult is larger than that of a baby.
B. The brain of a human being is larger than that of a cat.
C. The brains of all adult humans are about the same size.
D. The brain of an elephant is larger than that of a human being.

(1) A and B
(2) A and D
(3) B and C
(4) B and D
(5) C and D

PRACTICE TEST

19. To fight the effects of acid rain, scientists in many countries dump large quantities of calcium carbonate into polluted lakes. You can infer from this action that calcium carbonate is

(1) an acid
(2) a base
(3) a neutral substance
(4) a powdered substance
(5) a substance harmless to fish

Questions 20 and 21 refer to the following table.

Composition of Pure Dry Air

Gas	Symbol or Formula	Percent by Volume
Nitrogen	N_2	78.1%
Oxygen	O_2	20.9%
Argon	Ar	0.9%
Carbon dioxide	CO_2	0.03%
Neon	Ne	very small amounts
Helium	He	
Krypton	Kr	
Xenon	Ze	
Hydrogen	H_2	
Nitrous Oxide	N_2O	
Methane	CH_4	

20. While conducting an experiment, a scientist wished to remove a trace, or small amount, of gas from pure, dry air. Which gas would she remove in order to provide the least significant change?

(1) argon
(2) nitrogen
(3) oxygen
(4) methane
(5) carbon dioxide

21. Which of the following can be determined from information given in the table above?

(1) the difference in percent of helium and oxygen present in pure, dry air
(2) the volume of oxygen present in a one cubic foot sample of pure, dry air
(3) the difference in the percent of argon and neon present in pure, dry air
(4) the volume of water vapor present in 100 percent humid air
(5) the volume of propane gas present in pure, dry air

22. Self-preservation is a natural reaction shown by an animal for the purpose of avoiding serious harm. Which of the following is the best example of self-preservation?

(1) a goose swimming near a cygnet (young swan)
(2) a salmon swimming back to the place of its birth to lay eggs
(3) a bee spreading pollen as it flies from flower to flower
(4) a dog barking when it sees its owner
(5) a mouse running when it sees a cat

PRACTICE TEST

Questions 23 and 24 refer to the following diagram.

Series Circuit

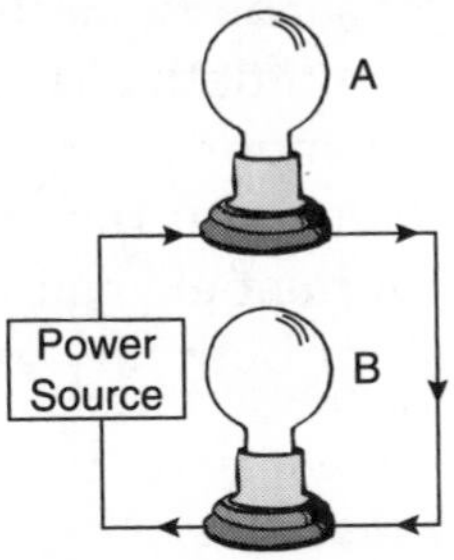

If bulb A burns out, bulb B also goes out.

Parallel Circuit

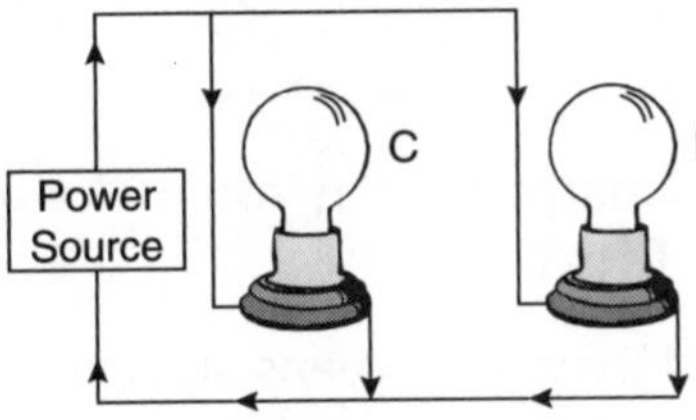

If bulb C burns out, bulb D stays lit.

23. Four wall sockets are wired in series with an emergency shutoff switch. If the shutoff switch is opened, what happens to the wall sockets?

(1) Only the socket closest to the switch goes out.
(2) All four wall sockets go out.
(3) All four wall sockets stay on.
(4) Two wall sockets go out, one on each side of the switch.
(5) Only the socket farthest from the switch goes out.

24. What is most likely the main advantage of buying a string of holiday tree lights that are wired in a parallel circuit rather than in a series circuit?

(1) Parallel circuits cost less to make.
(2) Different-colored lights can be used in parallel circuits.
(3) Parallel circuits use less electricity.
(4) Burned-out bulbs are found more easily in parallel circuits.
(5) Bulbs are closer together in parallel circuits.

Question 25 refers to the following diagram.

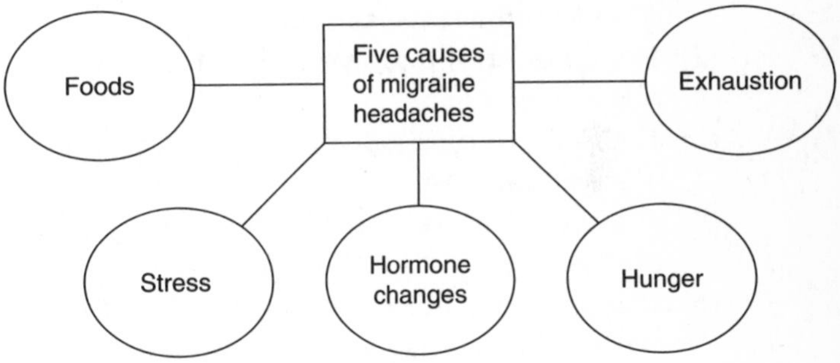

25. Which of the choices below would probably *not* trigger a migraine headache?

(1) eating cheese and chocolate
(2) waiting for the birth of a baby
(3) working an extra shift
(4) taking a walk around the block
(5) cutting calorie intake

PRACTICE TEST

Questions 26 and 27 refer to the following passage.

Temperature and pressure affect the amount of gas that can be dissolved in a liquid. An increase in temperature decreases the amount of dissolved gas. An increase in pressure increases the amount of dissolved gas.

26. Soda pop has a fizz because of dissolved carbon dioxide gas. If a cold bottle of soda is left open on a kitchen counter, which of the following will occur?

(1) The amount of dissolved carbon dioxide gas will remain the same.
(2) The amount of dissolved carbon dioxide gas will increase.
(3) The amount of dissolved carbon dioxide gas will decrease.
(4) The temperature of the soda will be greater than that of the room.
(5) The pressure that the soda exerts on the bottle will increase.

27. In a stream, fish tend to swim in shaded areas along the riverbank or in regions of deep water. What is the most likely reason for this?

The water in these places

(1) has the largest possible amount of hydrogen gas
(2) has the least amount of dissolved carbon dioxide gas
(3) has the greatest amount of dissolved carbon dioxide gas
(4) has the least amount of dissolved oxygen gas
(5) has the greatest amount of dissolved oxygen gas

Question 28 is based on the following information.

Almost every eight seconds another baby boomer celebrates a fiftieth birthday. Experts claim that fifty is an important medical milestone in a person's life. The following list includes a few important elements for a thorough checkup for both fifty-year-old men and women:

- blood pressure test
- eye exam
- cholesterol test
- skin exam
- colonoscopy

28. What assumption can you make about turning fifty?

(1) Most insurance plans stop covering preventative procedures.
(2) All people experience serious health problems.
(3) The human body works less efficiently.
(4) Good life-style habits are no longer important.
(5) Everyone's body systems will break down in the same way.

PRACTICE TEST

Question 29 is based on the following cartoon.

29. Considering the message of the artist's cartoon, which of the statements below would the artist most likely make?

(1) People should know that a hamburger made with lean beef on a whole wheat bun provides the body with niacin.
(2) Parents need to be concerned about microbial pathogens in food, which cause millions of cases of human illness per year.
(3) All people are advised to limit their portions of red meat to a total of about three ounces per day.
(4) Americans have the right to choose convenient high-fat fast foods over healthy meals prepared at home.
(5) An average teenage boy should consume about 800 calories more per day than an average woman.

Question 30 is based on the drawing below.

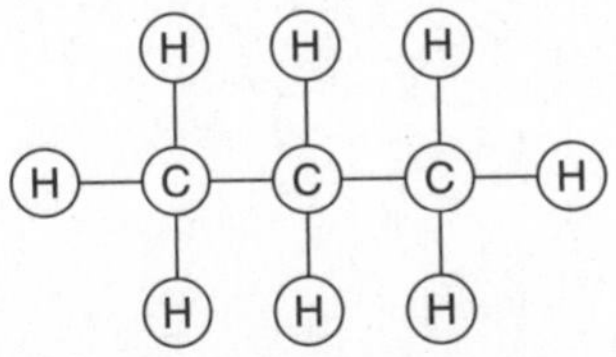

30. The drawing shows the molecular structure of propane. Each *H* stands for one hydrogen atom, and each *C* stands for one carbon atom. How would the formula for a propane molecule be written?

(1) 3C8H
(2) $3C_8H$
(3) C_3H_8
(4) C_8H_3
(5) C_8H_8

Question 31 is based in the following information.

People of all ages can have high blood pressure. High blood pressure can increase the risk of heart attack and stroke. Doctors recommend having a blood pressure reading taken at least twice a year. A blood pressure reading will always be two numbers: one written over the other. The upper number, *systolic pressure,* represents the amount of pressure in the blood vessels when the heart beats and pushes blood through the circulatory system. The lower number, *diastolic pressure,* represents the pressure in the blood vessels between beats, when the heart is resting. The guidelines for blood pressure are as follows:

normal blood pressure—below 130/85
high normal blood pressure—between 130/85 and 139/89
high blood pressure—140/90 or higher

31. If high blood pressure runs in the family, physicians recommend making changes in lifestyle, weight, and diet. Which of the following changes would probably not help lower blood pressure?

(1) starting an exercise program
(2) cutting back on salt in the diet
(3) quitting cigarette smoking
(4) reducing stress in the workplace
(5) moving to a different climate

PRACTICE TEST

Question 32 is based on the following graph.

Main Substances in Sea Water (by weight)

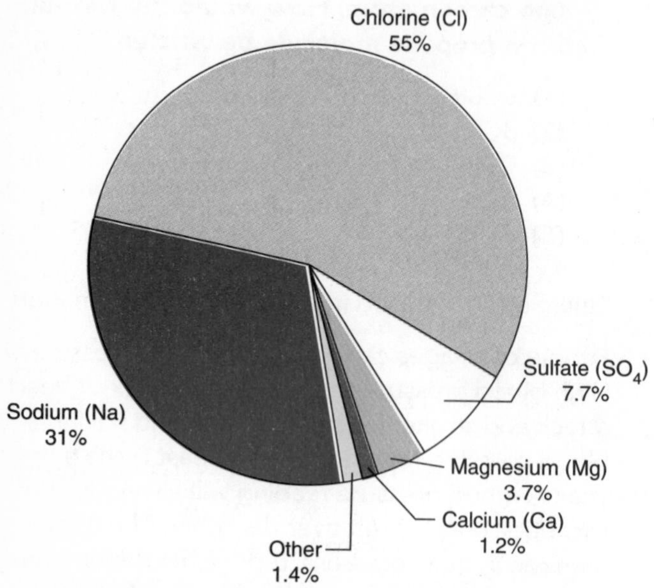

32. From information given on the graph, you can deduce that the main substance dissolved in sea water is which of the following compounds?

(1) magnesium oxide (MgO)
(2) sulfuric acid (H_2SO_4)
(3) calcium chloride ($CaCl_2$)
(4) potassium chloride (KCl)
(5) sodium chloride (NaCl)

Question 33 is based on the following chart.

Weight Guidlines											
Height	21	22	23	24	25	26	27	28	29	30	31	BMI
5'	107	112	118	123	128	133	138	143	148	153	158	Weight (pounds)
5'1"	111	116	122	127	132	137	143	148	153	158	164	
5'2"	115	120	126	131	136	142	147	153	158	164	169	
5'3"	118	124	130	135	141	146	152	158	163	169	175	
5'4"	122	128	134	140	145	151	157	163	169	174	180	
5'5"	126	132	138	144	150	156	162	168	174	180	186	
5'6"	130	136	142	148	155	161	167	173	179	186	192	
5'7"	134	140	146	153	159	166	172	178	185	191	198	
5'8"	138	144	151	158	164	171	177	184	190	197	203	
5'9"	142	149	155	162	169	176	182	189	196	203	209	
5'10"	146	153	160	167	174	181	188	195	202	209	216	
5'11"	150	157	165	172	179	186	193	200	208	215	222	
6'	154	162	169	177	184	191	199	206	213	221	228	
6'1"	159	166	174	182	189	197	204	212	219	227	234	
Source: National Center for Health Statistics					Overweight					Obese		

Note: Body Mass Indexes are not accurate for young children, pregnant or breast-feeding women, the frail, elderly, or very muscular people.

Source: National Center for Health Statistics

33. BMI stands for *body mass index*. According to guidelines set by the National Heart, Lung, and Blood Institute, if you have a BMI of 30 or over you are considered to be obese. Fifty-five percent of American adults have a BMI of 25 or above. Which of the following people should not be concerned about BMI?

(1) Chloe, a hearing impaired two-year-old child
(2) Roger, a middle-aged man with arthritis
(3) Paulette, an elderly woman with high blood pressure
(4) Alex, a young adult with diabetes
(5) Ryan, a teenager with heart disease

PRACTICE TEST

34. Which of the following facts is the *best evidence* that helium gas is lighter than air?

(1) Helium will not burn when exposed to flame in the presence of oxygen.
(2) By volume, helium makes up only 0.0005 percent of air.
(3) Helium atoms do not combine with other air atoms.
(4) Helium-filled balloons rise in air more easily than other balloons.
(5) Helium has the lowest boiling point of all known elements.

35. *Triclosan* is an active ingredient in antibacterial products. It is an agent that damages the cell walls of bacteria by slowing their ability to multiply. Although antibacterial products significantly eliminate many germs, the Food and Drug Administration has concerns that overuse of these products could lead to new strains of resistant bacteria. Which of the following conclusions can be drawn from the information provided on antibacterial products?

(1) All antibacterial products are more dangerous than helpful to people.
(2) The FDA is not concerned with consumer usage of antibacterial products.
(3) Products created to fight "super bugs" could actually help create them.
(4) Triclosan should be eliminated from antibacterial hand soap.
(5) Only day care providers and hospital employees need antibacterial products.

Question 36 is refers to the following chart.

Speed of Animals

ANIMAL	MPH (miles per hour)
cheetah	70
zebra	40
cat (domestic)	30
squirrel	12
chicken	9

Source: *Natural History Magazine*

36. Speed is a measurement of movement. Velocity is always measured in terms of a unit of distance divided by a unit of time. The cheetah, which can run at 70 MPH, is the fastest mammal; and the Peregrine falcon, which can fly at 220 MPH, is the fastest bird. What is the possible velocity that a gazelle can achieve if the animal's speed is similar to that of a cheetah?

(1) 220 miles per hour
(2) 95 miles per hour
(3) 70 miles per hour
(4) 65 miles per hour
(5) 45 miles per hour

PRACTICE TEST

Questions 37 and 38 are based on the following passage.

In recent years, scientists have discovered that Earth's temperature is slowly increasing. In fact, scientists believe that today's average temperature is several degrees higher than the average at the beginning of the Industrial Revolution in the late 1700s. This warming is thought to be caused by a phenomenon known as the *greenhouse effect*.

In a greenhouse, sunlight passes through a glass roof and provides energy to the plants growing inside. The glass prevents heat in the greenhouse from escaping. Similarly, sunlight passes through our atmosphere and warms Earth's surface. Much of the surface heat is prevented from escaping because of absorption by greenhouse gases in the atmosphere. As long as the average level of greenhouse gases does not increase, Earth's temperature stays in a comfortable range.

Two main greenhouse gases are carbon dioxide and carbon monoxide. Since the Industrial Revolution, humans have increased the amount of atmospheric carbon dioxide by burning fossil fuels (wood, coal, and oil) both for the production of electricity and for home heating. By driving cars, humans have increased the amount of atmospheric carbon monoxide, present in car exhaust.

Scientists point out that further increases in Earth's average temperature could result in the melting of the polar ice caps and in the changing of weather patterns worldwide.

37. Which of the following does *not* contribute to the greenhouse effect?

(1) a forest fire out of control
(2) a bus that runs on diesel fuel
(3) soil bacteria that release carbon dioxide gas
(4) a gas-powered lawn mower
(5) a hydroelectric power plant

38. Some scientists predict that if something is not done to stop the increase in atmospheric greenhouse gases, the average temperature of Earth may increase 6°F to 10°F in the next fifty years. Which of the following actions would be *most effective* toward helping solve the problem of the greenhouse effect?

(1) reducing human dependence on all types of fossil fuels
(2) raising the gas tax on foreign and domestic cars
(3) restricting the use of fireplaces to wintertime only
(4) developing efficient electric cars to replace gasoline-powered cars
(5) recording changes in Earth's average temperature for the next fifty years

PRACTICE TEST

Questions 39 and 40 are based on the following drawing.

Refraction of White Light by a Glass Prism

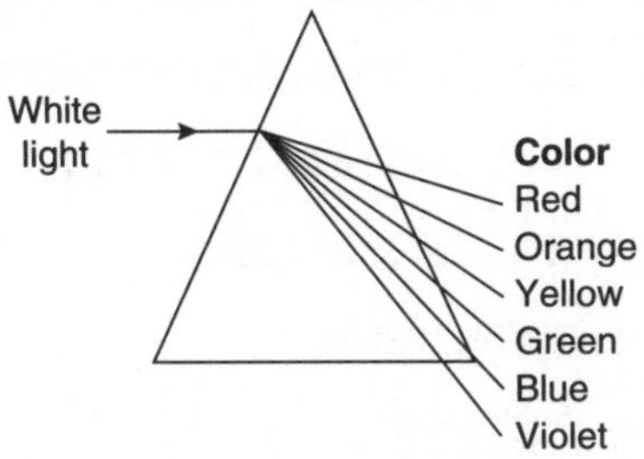

39. What does the *refraction* of white light through a glass prism show?

(1) White light travels in a straight line as it passes through a glass prism.
(2) White light consists of several types of colored light.
(3) White light cannot pass through glass without separation into color components.
(4) Glass absorbs white light but allows colored light to pass through.
(5) Red light refracts more than violet light when passing through a glass prism.

40. What is the *best* evidence that sunlight is a form of white light (light that looks white but consists of many colors)?

(1) a clear blue sky
(2) a full moon
(3) a color television
(4) a rainbow
(5) a color photograph

Question 41 is based on the following pictures.

Healthy Bone

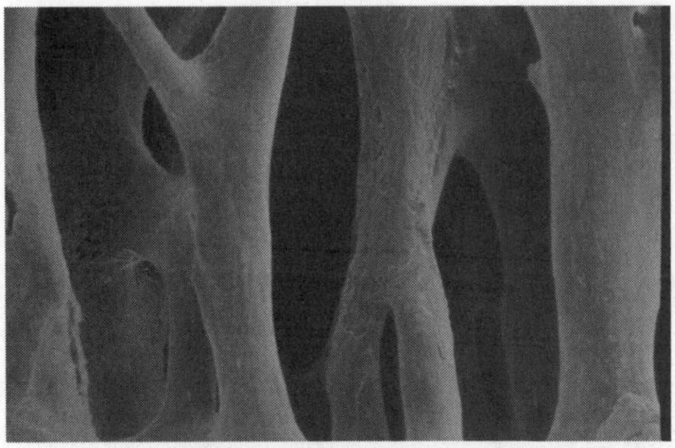

Bone with Osteoporosis

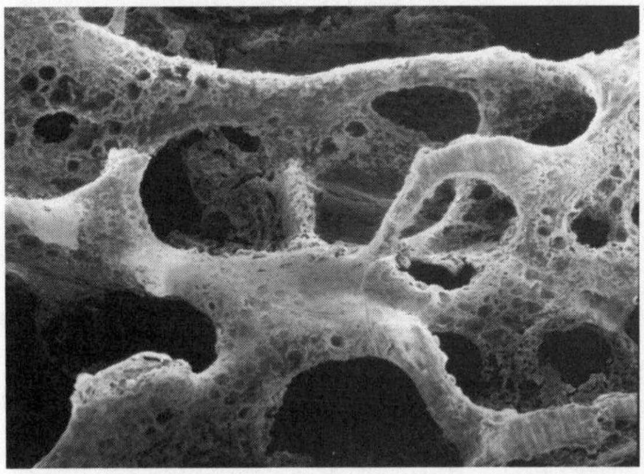

Both photographs © Professor P. Motta/Department of Anatomy/University "La Sapienza," Rome/SPL/Photo Researchers

41. Each year in the United States over one million senior citizens encounter a bone fracture due to osteoporosis. Which of the following is *not* a fact about strong bones and osteoporosis?

(1) Exercising helps to keep bones strong throughout one's life.
(2) Drinking milk and eating calcium rich foods in the teenage years may help to prevent osteoporosis.
(3) Consuming alcohol and smoking can increase the risk of osteoporosis.
(4) Women are at a greater risk than men for developing osteoporosis.
(5) Doctors should warn underweight patients about risks of developing osteoporosis.

PRACTICE TEST

Question 42 is based on the drawing below.

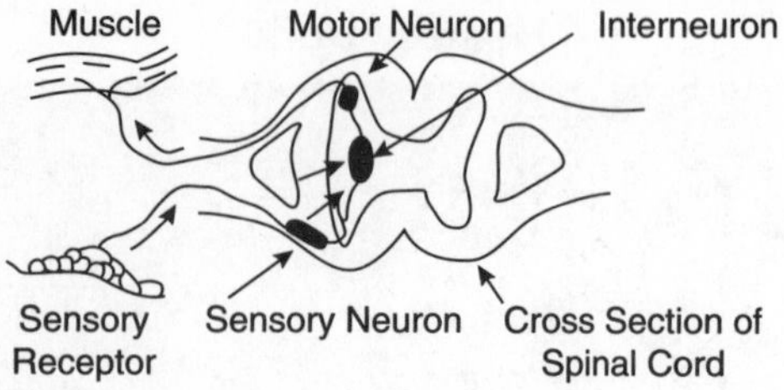

42. A reflex reaction, such as pulling your hand back from a hot grill, does not immediately involve the brain. The nerve impulse that controls the reaction takes place in a simple reflex arc as shown above. In a simple reflex arc, where does an interneuron transmit the nerve impulse?

(1) at the sensory receptor
(2) to a motor neuron
(3) to the brain
(4) to an interneuron
(5) to the muscles that react

Question 43 is based on the following passage.

"Women seem to be more talented than men in experiencing and developing their emotions," claims Michael E. Thase, M.D., a professor of psychiatry and depression expert. Thase says women have "a greater capacity to feel," and they are more commonly involved in issues that relate to relationships and family problems. While men may worry about their jobs, they tend to distract themselves from their feelings. Women tend to brood rather than deny their feelings.

—Excerpted from "Get Inside Your Head" in *USA Weekend*, January 23,1999

43. Based on the passage, which of the disorders below would probably affect more men than women?

(1) generalized anxiety disorder
(2) social phobias
(3) oppositional defiance disorder
(4) premenstrual syndrome
(5) depression

Questions 44 and 45 refer to the graph below.

Percent of Carbohydrates in Selected Foods

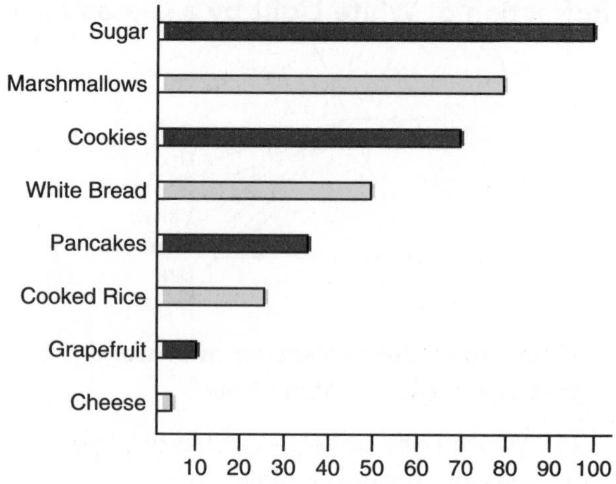

44. If Sue had to reduce carbohydrates in her diet, which of the following foods should she eliminate?

(1) wild rice
(2) chocolate chip cookies
(3) oranges
(4) Swiss cheese
(5) waffles

45. Which statement is *best* supported by information given in the graph?

(1) Cooking increases the carbohydrate content of food.
(2) Sugar is not a form of carbohydrate.
(3) The carbohydrate content of food increases as sugar content increases.
(4) A food that does not contain sugar has zero carbohydrate content.
(5) All foods contain some amount of natural sugar.

PRACTICE TEST

Questions 46 and 47 are based on the following passage.

Naturalistic gardening is becoming increasingly popular in the United States. There are numerous reasons for this rise to prominence. First, gardening in harmony with Nature is partly founded in the new environmental ethic that has developed in the last 30 years. Reacting against the pervasive use of chemicals in the landscape and the incessant howl of lawnmowers, people have sought an alternative to the manicured carpet of lawn that was mandated by a century-old unspoken social compact. The answer for many has become the American Prairie.

This recent conversion to landscaping with prairie plants, which were almost universally considered "weeds" until only a decade ago, also possesses a strong utilitarian component. A prairie landscape requires only a fraction of the maintenance devoted to more traditional lawns and gardens. Long-term costs are, therefore, lower. Fertilizers are seldom necessary for success with prairie natives. Pesticides are discouraged, as they can harm the birds, bees and butterflies that the prairie is so adept at supporting, and watering is not a requirement to keep the prairie green. The deep-rooted prairie plants obtain moisture from the lower reaches of the soil profile, with some plants having roots ten to fifteen feet deep. Others simply enter a temporary dormancy during dry periods, waiting to resume growth with the advent of the next rain.

—Excerpted from *Whence This Prairie in My Yard? A Short History of Prairie Landscaping in the US* by Neil Diboll

46. Which of the following statements from *From Whence This Prairie in My Yard?* does not support the fact that a prairie is a self-regenerating system?

(1) Naturalistic gardening is becoming increasingly popular in the United States.
(2) As the prairie matures, many plants may seed and expand wildly.
(3) Once the seeds are planted, the meadow will begin to develop and evolve.
(4) Once established, a prairie will outlive the person who plants it.
(5) A prairie's direction and evolution are largely ceded to natural forces.

47. The author of this passage, Neil Diboll, would most likely agree with which of the following opinions?

(1) Prairie restoration should not be used as alternative suburban landscaping.
(2) Master landscapers have beautifully manicured lawns and gardens.
(3) People who plant prairie grasses are purchasing expensive "weeds."
(4) Rodents, snakes, and bugs need to be eliminated from gardens.
(5) People need to re-examine the use of toxic chemicals in their gardens.

PRACTICE TEST

48. Albert Einstein developed the principles necessary for laser in 1916 in his paper on quantum theory. Light amplification by stimulated emission of radiation, or LASER surgery, is becoming more common in many areas of medicine. For example, a person suffering from a vision defect can consider undergoing laser eye surgery. A patient may choose laser surgery as a safer and less invasive type of procedure. Which of the details below supports this opinion?

Laser surgery

(1) can be performed more quickly and cuts back on hospital stays for patients
(2) is less expensive and is covered by most managed care insurance plans
(3) is an option for plastic surgery, angioplasty, or gallstone and kidney stone surgery
(4) can precisely focus energy on a specific area and minimize damage to surrounding tissue
(5) is performed routinely in most hospitals across the United States

Question 49 is refers to the following cartoon.

Ann Cleaves/Palasadian-Post

49. What was the assumption of the artist of this cartoon?

(1) El Niño was the cause of most mishaps and problems in the United States.
(2) Many people incorrectly blamed El Niño for unexplainable situations.
(3) All unusual weather patterns were blamed on El Niño.
(4) El Niño did not have an impact on the lives of Americans.
(5) Abnormal warmth in Alaska and Canada was the effect of El Niño.

Question 50 is based on the following passage.

Astronomy enthusiasts are able to explore the universe over the Internet. There are numerous websites developed for people to learn the latest in astronomy research and to climb aboard a spacecraft and orbit the planets. There are even websites available for individuals to log on for telescope time in order to observe stars, nebulae, and galaxies. Millions of viewers logged on to observe the crash of Comet Shoemaker-Levy 9 into Jupiter in 1994, and even more viewers watched the Mars landing in 1997.

50. What conclusion can be drawn from this astronomy passage?

(1) Computers will lure people away from viewing the universe through telescopes.
(2) Not many people are interested in NASA and its space programs.
(3) Technology is empowering more people to learn about their universe.
(4) Only computer specialists are able to understand the use of astronomy web sites.
(5) Computer web sites for astronomy are expensive and difficult to develop.

Science Answer Key

1. **Application (4)** Considering all of Debbie's symptoms, she could suspect that she suffered a stroke; however, her doctor should make the diagnosis.

2. **Application (2)** When the lighter molecules of water, humidity, are added to dry air, the air will become less dense. Thus, playing golf on a humid day would enable the ball to travel through the air more easily.

3. **Comprehension (5)** In normal nighttime conditions, the land is colder than the ocean. As a result, the air over the ocean rises, which causes a breeze to flow from the land.

4. **Comprehension (4)** Because the pancreas is a structural unit containing several types of tissue, it is best classified as an organ.

5. **Comprehension (5)** The question describes the digestive process, which involves several organs working together to perform a specific function.

6. **Application (4)** A kite rises in air because of the pressure of the wind against its surface, not because of buoyancy.

7. **Evaluation (1)** After exhaling, Tally sinks, which means that her weight is greater than the buoyancy force. Therefore, the weight of the water she displaces is less than her body weight.

8. **Analysis (2)** This is the only fact that is true only for a suntan.

9. **Evaluation (4)** An electrical discharge in a cloud causes both thunder and lightning. You see the lightning before you hear the thunder because light travels faster than sound.

10. **Analysis (3)** The consumer in the cartoon appears as if he is not going to fight the increase in fuel costs.

11. **Analysis (5)** The chart illustrates that stress can affect all areas of the body as well as trigger emotional and behavioral problems.

12. **Evaluation (2)** Many people feel that more-intelligent species should be preserved from slaughter, possibly because of their value in research on intelligence.

13. **Application (5)** A town that is located just south of the equator will have twelve hours of daylight and twelve hours of darkness during December.

14. **Application (4)** Appendicitis is the only illness named that isn't contagious.

15. **Evaluation (2)** Increasing efforts to educate citizens about AIDS can only help in the worldwide effort to conquer the disease.

16. **Comprehension (4)** When liquids don't freely mix, the one with the greater density sinks to the bottom. The liquid with the least density floats on top.

17. **Application (3)** According to the diagram, the occipital lobe controls vision.

18. **Evaluation (5)** These are the only choices that suggest that brain size is not a determining factor in differences in intelligence.

19. **Application (2)** A base neutralizes an acid. Choice (1) would increase acidity. Choice (3) is incorrect because a neutral substance such as water would have no effect. Choices (4) and (5) can't be inferred from the action of the scientists.

20. **Application (4)** A scientist would choose to remove methane, for its percent by volume is the smallest amount of all gases listed; therefore, it would most likely provide an inconsequential change.

21. **Analysis (2)** The volume of oxygen is the only gas measurable in pure, dry air, according to this chart.

22. **Application (5)** A mouse running when it sees a cat is the only choice that represents a natural reaction intended to avoid harm.

23. **Application (2)** Since the switch and wall sockets are wired in series, if one goes out, they all go out. Opening the switch breaks the circuit, and all the sockets go out.

24. **Analysis (4)** If the bulbs are wired in a parallel circuit, the burned-out bulb does not affect the other good bulbs, making the burned-out one easy to find.

25. **Application (4)** All of the other choices could trigger a migraine headache according to the diagram. A walk around the block should be relaxing.

26. **Application (3)** The amount of carbon dioxide gas will decrease as the temperature of the pop increases. The soda will then taste flat.

27. **Analysis (5)** Cold water has a greater amount of dissolved oxygen gas than warm water, which explains why fish tend to swim in shaded areas or in deep water, where the temperature is lower.

28. **Analysis (3)** After fifty the body begins to work less efficiently in all people.

29. **Application (2)** All of the choices above are true; however, choice (2) supports the author's message that the mother is concerned about food poisoning because she is wearing rubber gloves and a mask.

30. **Comprehension (3)** The correct way to show three carbon atoms and eight hydrogen atoms is with the formula C_3H_8.

31. **Application (5)** A change in temperature is not one of the changes recommended by a physician to lower blood pressure.

32. **Analysis (5)** The two major substances in sea water are chlorine(Cl) and sodium(Na). The compound sodium chloride (NaCl) is most often called table salt.

33. **Application (1)** The note by the passage states that BMIs are not accurate for young children. All of the other people should watch their weight because of health issues.

34. **Evaluation (4)** This is the only choice which involves a relationship between the relative weights of air and helium gas.

35. **Analysis (3)** The passage only indicates that overuse of the products could lead to new strains of bacteria. Scientists have labeled these strains "super bugs."

36. **Application (3)** If the speed of a gazelle is similar to that of a cheetah, the gazelle must be able to run approximately 70 mph.

37. **Application (5)** A hydroelectric plant converts the energy of flowing water to electricity. No greenhouse gases are emitted in the process.

38. **Evaluation (1)** Reducing our dependence on all types of fossil fuels would reduce the atmospheric greenhouse gases released.

39. **Comprehension (2)** Each color component of white light refracts (changes direction) a different amount as it enters and leaves a prism. This is how a prism separates white light into its color components.

40. **Evaluation (4)** A rainbow forms because suspended raindrops act as tiny prisms and cause sunlight to separate into its color components.

41. **Analysis (5)** This choice is an opinion rather than a fact; however, people that are underweight can run a risk of osteoporosis. All of the other answers are facts about osteoporosis.

42. **Analysis (2)** The interneuron receives the nerve impulse from the sensory neuron and transmits the impulse to the motor neuron.

43. **Application (3)** Oppositional defiance disorder affects more men than women.

44. **Application (2)** According to the graph, a cookie has a higher percentage of carbohydrates than the other items.

45. Evaluation (3) The graph indicates that as the sugar content increases the carbohydrate content increases.

46. Analysis (1) Although choice (1) is true, it does not support the fact that a prairie is a self-regenerating system.

47. Evaluation (5) A person interested in prairie restoration would most likely discourage the use of pesticides and fertilizers.

48. Analysis (4) The fact that laser surgery focuses energy on a specific area and causes less damage supports the opinion that it is safer and less invasive.

49. Analysis (2) El Niño affected weather patterns in the United States, but it was incorrectly thought to be responsible for unrelated incidents.

50. Analysis (3) Although choice (1) may occur someday, the passage does not indicate that situation could take place. Choices (2) and (4) are not true since the passage stated that millions of people logged on to the sites.

Evaluation Chart

Use the Answer Key on pages 1113–1115 to check your answers to the Practice Test. Then find the item number of each question you missed and circle it on the chart below to determine the Science content areas in which you need more practice. Pay particular attention to areas where you missed half or more of the questions. The page numbers for the content areas are listed below on the chart. For those questions that you missed, review the skill pages indicated.

SKILL AREA/ CONTENT AREA	COMPREHENSION (pages 217–230)	APPLICATION (pages 231–236)	ANALYSIS (pages 237–262)	EVALUATION (pages 271–274)
Life Sciences (Biology) (pages 459–496)	4, 5 29, 31, 33, 36,	1, 14, 17, 22, 25, 42, 48 43, 44	11, 28, 35, 41,	12, 15, 18, 45
Earth & Space Science (pages 497–532)	3	2, 13, 37	8, 10, 46, 49, 50	38, 47
Physical Sciences (Chemistry and Physics) (pages 533–577)	16, 30, 39	6, 19, 20, 23, 26	21, 24, 27, 32	7, 9, 34, 40

PRACTICE TEST

Language Arts, Reading

The Language Arts, Reading Practice Test will give you the opportunity to evaluate your readiness for the actual GED Language Arts, Reading Test. This test contains 40 questions based on seven excerpts from **fiction** (novels and short stories), **poems, drama,** and several types of **nonfiction prose** (*informational texts* such as newspaper or magazine articles, or speeches; commentaries about *visual texts; literary nonfiction* such as essays, biographies, diaries, letters, or reviews; or *business documents*).

You should take approximately 65 minutes to complete this test. At the end of 65 minutes, stop and mark your place. Then finish the test. This will give you an idea of whether or not you can finish the actual GED Test in the time allotted. Try to answer as many questions as you can. A blank will count as a wrong answer, so make a reasonable guess for answers to questions of which you are not sure.

When you are finished with the test, check your answers and turn to the Evaluation Chart on page 1132. Use the chart to evaluate whether or not you are ready to take the actual GED Test and, if not, in what areas you need more work.

Language Arts, Reading Practice Test Answer Grid

1	①	②	③	④	⑤	15	①	②	③	④	⑤	28	①	②	③	④	⑤
2	①	②	③	④	⑤	16	①	②	③	④	⑤	29	①	②	③	④	⑤
3	①	②	③	④	⑤	17	①	②	③	④	⑤	30	①	②	③	④	⑤
4	①	②	③	④	⑤	18	①	②	③	④	⑤	31	①	②	③	④	⑤
5	①	②	③	④	⑤	19	①	②	③	④	⑤	32	①	②	③	④	⑤
6	①	②	③	④	⑤	20	①	②	③	④	⑤	33	①	②	③	④	⑤
7	①	②	③	④	⑤	21	①	②	③	④	⑤	34	①	②	③	④	⑤
8	①	②	③	④	⑤	22	①	②	③	④	⑤	35	①	②	③	④	⑤
9	①	②	③	④	⑤	23	①	②	③	④	⑤	36	①	②	③	④	⑤
10	①	②	③	④	⑤	24	①	②	③	④	⑤	37	①	②	③	④	⑤
11	①	②	③	④	⑤	25	①	②	③	④	⑤	38	①	②	③	④	⑤
12	①	②	③	④	⑤	26	①	②	③	④	⑤	39	①	②	③	④	⑤
13	①	②	③	④	⑤	27	①	②	③	④	⑤	40	①	②	③	④	⑤
14	①	②	③	④	⑤												

PRACTICE TEST

Questions 1–6 are based on the following passage.

IS THE NARRATOR TRULY SUPERIOR TO THE KING AND HIS PEOPLE?

. . . With a common impulse the multitide rose slowly up and stared into the sky. I followed their eyes, as sure as guns, there was my eclipse beginning! The life went boiling through my veins; I was a new man! The rim of black spread slowly into the sun's disk, my heart beat higher and higher, and still the assemblage and the priest stared into the sky, motionless. I knew that this gaze would be turned upon me, next. When it was I was ready. I was in one of the most grand attitudes ever struck, with my arm stretched up pointing to the sun. It was a noble effect. You could see the shudder sweep the mass like a wave. Two shouts rang out, one close upon the heels of the other:

"Apply the torch!"

"I forbid it!"

The one was from Merlin, the other from the king.

Merlin started from his place to apply the torch himself, I judged. I said: "Stay where you are. If any man moves—even the king—before I give him leave, I will blast him with thunder, I will consume him with lightnings!" The multitude sank meekly into their seats, as I was just expecting they would. Merlin hesitated a moment or two, and I was on pins and needles during that little while. Then he sat down, and I took a good breath; for I knew I was master of the situation now. The king said:

"Be merciful, fair sir, and essay* no further in this perilous matter, lest disaster follow. It was reported to us that your powers could not attain unto their full strength until the morrow; but-"

"You Majesty thinks the report may have been a lie?"

"It *was* a lie."

That made an immense effect; up went appealing hands everywhere, and the king was assailed with a storm of supplications that I might be bought off at any price, and the calamity stayed. The king was eager to comply. He said:

"Name any terms, reverend sir, even to the halving of my kingdom; but banish this calamity, spare the sun!"

My fortune was made, I would have taken him up in a minute, but *I* couldn't stop an eclipse; the thing was out of the question. So I asked time to consider.

**essay* means try

—Excerpted from *A Connecticut Yankee in King Arthur's Court* by Mark Twain

1. What is about to happen to the narrator?

He is about to be

(1) announced to the king
(2) put into prison
(3) burned at the stake
(4) married to the princess
(5) exposed as an actor

2. Which one of the following events would the narrator have been *least* likely to use in saving himself?

(1) a sudden thunderstorm
(2) a rumbling earthquake
(3) an approaching tornado
(4) a migration of birds
(5) a falling comet in the sky

PRACTICE TEST

3. Which word best describes the portrayal of the king and his people?

(1) gullible
(2) vicious
(3) friendly
(4) sophisticated
(5) enthusiastic

4. Based on the passage, what is the best way to describe the relationship between Merlin and the narrator?

(1) polite
(2) indifferent
(3) supportive
(4) cheerful
(5) antagonistic

5. What is the overall tone of the passage?

(1) gloomy
(2) serious
(3) bitter
(4) inspirational
(5) humorous

6. In many of his writings, Mark Twain attacked belief in superstition.

What connection can be made between this practice and the passage below?

(1) The attitude of the narrator makes him vulnerable.
(2) The beliefs of the king and people make them look foolish.
(3) The image of an eclipse compares to darkness in superstition.
(4) The dialogue contrasts with superstitious beliefs.
(5) The characterization reveals various personality traits.

Questions 7–12 are based on the following poem.

WHAT DOES THE SPEAKER WISH?

My Heart Leaps Up

My heart leaps up when I behold
A rainbow in the sky;
So was it when my life began;
So is it now I am a man;
So be it when I shall grow old,
Or let me die!
The Child is father of the Man;
And I could wish my days to be
Bound each to each by natural piety.

—by William Wordsworth

7. In line 3, *"So was it when my life began;"* what does the word "it" mean?

(1) thrill over thunderstorms
(2) joy at seeing a rainbow
(3) disbelief of promises
(4) dismay at the unattainable
(5) disillusionment with life

8. Which would be the most effective substitution for "rainbow" in the poem?

(1) star
(2) skyscraper
(3) pyramid
(4) celebrity
(5) statue

9. What is the tone of the speaker as revealed in line 4?

(1) confused
(2) proud
(3) surprised
(4) indifferent
(5) determined

PRACTICE TEST

10. What idea is suggested by the line "The Child is father of the Man" (line 7)?

(1) Children often control their parents.
(2) Unnatural results come from disorder.
(3) Fathers must be responsive to children.
(4) Experiences in childhood shape adults.
(5) Youth sometimes knows much wisdom.

11. The overall purpose of the poem is to direct attention to which of the following?

(1) the wonders of nature
(2) the life span of man
(3) the changes from pollution
(4) the passing of childhood
(5) the past to the future

12. A major conflict in literature involves man against nature. How does that conflict relate to this poem?

The conflict

(1) reinforces the mood
(2) appears in the imagery
(3) contrasts with the theme
(4) illustrates the speaker's attitude
(5) shapes the poet's style

Questions 13–18 are based on the following play excerpt.

IS MORTIMER A ROMANTIC MAN?

Act One

MORTIMER See that statute* there. That's a horundinida carnina.

MARTHA Oh, no, dear—that's Emma B. Stout ascending to heaven.

MORTIMER No, no,—standing on Mrs. Stout's left ear. That bird—that's a red-crested swallow. I've only seen one of those before in my life.

ABBY (crosses *around above table and pushes chair* R. into table). I don't know how you can be thinking about a bird now–what with Elaine and the engagement and everything.

MORTIMER It's a vanishing species. (*He turns away from window.*) Thoreau was very fond of them. (*As he crosses to desk to look through various drawers and papers.*) By the way, I left a large envelope around here last week. It was one of the chapters of my book on Thoreau. Have you seen it?

MARTHA (*pushing armchair into table*). Well, if you left it here it must be here somewhere.

ABBY (*crossing to* D. L. *of* MORTIMER). When are you going to be married? What are your plans? There must be something more you can tell us about Elaine.

MORTIMER Elaine? Oh, yes, Elaine thought it was brilliant. (*He crosses to sideboard, looks through cupboards and drawers.*)

MARTHA What was, dear?

MORTIMER My chapter on Thoreau. (*He finds a bundle of papers (script) in R. drawer and takes them to table and looks through them.*)

ABBY (*at* C.). Well, when Elaine comes back I think we ought to have a little celebration. We must drink to your happiness. Martha, isn't there some of that Lady Baltimore cake left?

PRACTICE TEST

(*During last few speeches* MARTHA *has picked up pail from sideboard and her cape, hat and gloves from table in U. L. corner.*)

MARTHA (*crossing* D. L.). Oh, yes!

ABBY And I'll open a bottle of wine.

MARTHA (*as she exits to kitchen*). Oh, and to think it happened in this room!

MORTIMER (*has finished looking through papers, is gazing around room*). Now where could I have put that?

ABBY Well, with your fiancée sitting beside you tonight, I do hope that play will be something you can enjoy for once. It may be something romantic. What's the name of it?

MORTIMER "Murder Will Out."

ABBY Oh dear! (*She disappears into kitchen as* MORTIMER *goes on talking.*)

*Mortimer means *statue*

—Excerpted from *Arsenic and Old Lace* by Joseph Kesselring

13. What is Martha referring to when she says, "Oh, and to think it happened in this room!"(lines 62–63)?

(1) the proposal of marriage
(2) the sighting of a statue
(3) a plan for a celebration
(4) the writing of a book
(5) a speech of Thoreau's

14. Which of the following gifts would Abby most likely encourage Mortimer to give Elaine?

(1) a statue of a bird
(2) a bouquet of red roses
(3) a book on Thoreau
(4) a murder mystery
(5) a pair of gloves

15. Which of the following best describes Abby's feeling about Mortimer's marriage?

(1) uncomfortable
(2) embarrassed
(3) excited
(4) amused
(5) fearful

16. What can we conclude that Mortimer's occupation might be?

(1) librarian
(2) biology teacher
(3) actor
(4) writer
(5) sculptor

17. Which of the following words best describes the overall tone of this passage?

(1) thoughtful
(2) angry
(3) determined
(4) bored
(5) light-hearted

18. Later in the play, Mortimer discovers that Martha and Abby have been poisoning old men and burying them in the basement so that the men will not be lonely anymore.

From this information and the passage given, what is the most likely purpose of the play?

(1) to provoke serious thought about crime
(2) to entertain with irreverent humor
(3) to probe into historical events
(4) to examine the nature of truth seriously
(5) to provide a philosophical view of marriage

PRACTICE TEST

Questions 19–24 are based on the following passage.

As you read this passage from a 1971 novel, think about the main character Chance and how he interacted with the few people in his world.

WHAT POSITIVE CHARACTERISTICS AND LIMITATIONS DID THE AUTHOR GIVE TO CHANCE?

Chance walked though the rooms, which seemed empty; the heavily curtained windows barely admitted the daylight. Slowly he looked at the large pieces of furniture shrouded in old linen covers, and at the veiled mirrors. The words that the Old Man had spoken to him the first time had wormed their way into his memory like firm roots. Chance was an orphan, and it was the Old Man himself who had sheltered him in the house ever since Chance was a child. Chance's mother had died when he was born. No one, not even the Old Man, would tell him who his father was. While some could learn to read and write, Chance would never be able to manage this. Nor would he ever be able to understand much of what others were saying to him or around him. Chance was to work in the garden, where he would care for plants and grasses and trees which grew there peacefully. He would be as one of them: quiet, openhearted in the sunshine and heavy when it rained. His name was Chance because he had been born by chance. He had no family. Although his mother had been very pretty, her mind had been as damaged as his; the soft soil of his brain, the ground from which all his thoughts shot up, had been ruined forever. Therefore, he could not look for a place in the life led by people outside the house or the garden gate. Chance must limit his life to his quarters and to the garden; he must not enter other parts of the household or walk out into the street. His food would always be brought to his room by Louise, who would be the only person to see Chance and talk to him. No one else was allowed to enter Chance's room. Only the Old Man himself might walk and sit in the garden. Chance would do exactly what he was told or else he would be sent to a special home for the insane where, the Old Man said, he would be locked in a cell and forgotten.

Chance did what he was told. So did black Louise.

—Excerpted from *Being There* by Jerzy Kosinski

19. "It was the Old Man himself who had sheltered him in the house since Chance was a child." What does this suggest about their relationship?

The Old Man was Chance's

(1) guardian
(2) father
(3) landlord
(4) brother
(5) gardener

20. What would most likely happen to Chance if he were to venture outside the house?

(1) He would be locked up in a cell and forgotten.
(2) He would end up in a special home for the insane.
(3) He would develop a successful gardening business.
(4) He would not understand the world around him.
(5) He would search for his long-lost relatives.

PRACTICE TEST

21. Which of the following paragraph details does *not* support the conclusion that Chance is very limited in his abilities?

(1) While some could learn to read and write, Chance would never be able to manage this.
(2) Nor would he ever be able to understand much of what others were saying . . . around him.
(3) Chance was to work in the garden, where he would care for plants and grasses and trees. . .
(4) . . . her mind had been as damaged as his; the soft soil of his brain. . . had been ruined forever.
(5) . . . he must not enter other parts of the household or walk out into the street.

22. From details in the passage, what type of person may Chance be compared to?

(1) an insane adult
(2) an unhappy teenager
(3) a controlling master
(4) an ungrateful son
(5) an obedient child

23. What is the overall purpose of the passage from this novel?

(1) compare and contrast the characters of the Old Man and Chance
(2) provide a background description of Chance and his life
(3) explain the heredity (similar disabilities) of Chance's mother
(4) promote the health benefits of peaceful gardening
(5) point out the problems of raising orphans in one's home

24. Later in the novel the reader learns that the Old Man dies, that Chance packs his suitcase, and leaves through the gate for the first time. Chance is struck by a limousine carrying the wife of a dying rich man. From then on, he comes to have power and influence. From what the reader knows already about Chance, what is the reader's probable reaction to the change in Chance's lifestyle and stature?

(1) jealousy
(2) hostility
(3) amusement
(4) surprise
(5) indifference

PRACTICE TEST

Questions 25–30 are based on the following passage.

As you read excerpts from this 1996 novel, you enter the world of a special group of friends who call themselves the "Ya-Ya Sisterhood."

IN THESE TWO PASSAGES, HOW DOES IT FEEL FOR THE NARRATOR (AND OTHERS) TO FEEL *OUTSIDE* HER MOTHER'S INNER CIRCLE?

Passage One

Mama and the Ya-Yas were always using different plays on my mother's name. If Teensy walked into a party that lacked pizzazz, she might announce, "This party needs to be *Vivi-fied.*" Sometimes they declared things to be "Re-Vivi-fication projects," like the time Mama and Necie redesigned the uniforms of my Girl Scout troop.

When I was young, I thought my mother was so internationally well known that the English language had invented words just for her. As a child, I would turn to the skinny "V" section of Webster's and study the many words that referred to Mama. There was "vivid," which meant "full of life; bright; intense." And "vivify," which meant "to give life or to make more lively." There were "vivace," "viva," "vivacious," "vivacity," "vivarium," and "viva voce." Mama was the source of all these words. She was also the reason for the phrase *"Vive le roi"* (which she told us meant "Long live Vivi the Queen!"). All these definitions had to do with life, like Mama herself.

Passage Two

It was not until I was in second or third grade that my friend M'lain Chauvin told me that Mama had nothing to do with those words in the dictionary. We got into a fight about it and Sister Henry Ruth intervened. When the nun confirmed M'lain's claim, I was heartbroken at first. It changed my whole perception of reality. It began the unraveling of unquestioned belief that the world revolved around Mama. But along with my disappointment came a profound relief, although I could not admit it at the time.

I thought my mother was a star for so many years that when I found out she wasn't, I was stupefied. Had she once been a star and her bright burning had dimmed? Maybe because she had us? Or had Mama never been a star to begin with? Somewhere guilt developed whenever I seemed to eclipse Mama in any little way. Even winning a spelling bee made me worry, because I never trusted that I could shine without obliterating her.

I did not understand then that my mother lived in a world that could not or would not acknowledge her radiance, her *pull* on the earth—at least not as much as she needed. So she made up her own solar system with the other Ya-Yas and lived in its orbit as fully as she could.

My father was not included in this orbit, not really. All the Ya-Ya husbands existed in a separate universe from the Ya-Yas and us kids.

—Excerpted from *Divine Secrets of the Ya-Ya Sisterhood* by Rebecca Wells

25. Which of the following is *not* evidence of Mama's persona (appearance or role) as a "star"?

(1) The English language had invented words just for her.
(2) She was the reason for the phrase, "Long live Vivi, the Queen!"
(3) Sometimes they declared things to be "Re-Vivi-fication projects."
(4) It began the unraveling of the unquestioned belief that the world revolved around Mama.
(5) So she made up her own solar system with the other Ya-Yas.

PRACTICE TEST

26. If the details about Mama in this passage were in a science book, in what section would you most likely find them?

(1) atomic structure (chemistry)
(2) genetics and heredity (biology)
(3) reflection and refraction (physics)
(4) geologic time (geology)
(5) stars and solar systems (astronomy)

27. The narrator's experiences in her youth "changed [her] whole perception of reality." This reality may be described as all of these feelings *except* for which of the following?

(1) disappointment
(2) relief
(3) sorrow
(4) pride
(5) astonishment

28. The author uses details to describe the narrator's actions and feelings when she was in the second or third grade. What effect does this have on the reader?

(1) to establish sympathy for the narrator
(2) to create greater admiration for Mama
(3) to enhance the importance of the narrator's father
(4) to develop understanding for Sister Henry Ruth
(5) to explain rivalry between "Aunts" Teensy and Necie

29. From which point of view is the story told?

(1) the Ya-Ya member, Necie
(2) the husband of a Ya-Ya
(3) the daughter of a Ya-Ya
(4) Vivi, one of the Ya-Yas
(5) M'lain Chauvin, a friend

30. What is the overall purpose of the passages from this novel?

(1) to give an English language lesson on "V" words
(2) to explore a daughter's feelings about her mother
(3) to explain how a human "star" can rise and fall
(4) to compare and contrast personalities of the Ya-Yas
(5) to examine the relationship between the narrator's parents

PRACTICE TEST

Questions 31–35 are based on the following passage.

HOW CAN BEING A MORE EFFECTIVE LISTENER HELP TO REDUCE STRESS? HOW MIGHT THE RELATIONSHIPS YOU HAVE WITH PERSONS AT WORK OR AT HOME IMPROVE IF YOUR LISTENING SKILLS IMPROVED?

Take a moment to reflect on your own listening skills at work. Do you really listen to your colleagues? Do you let them finish their thoughts before you take your turn? Do you sometimes finish sentences for other people? In meetings are you patient and responsive—or are you impatient and reactive? Do you allow words from others to sink in, or do you assume you know what the person is trying to say, so you jump in? Simply asking yourself these and related questions can be enormously helpful. Most people I've asked (I'm in this category too), admit that, at least some of the time, their listening skills could use a little improvement.

There are a variety of reasons why effective listening is an excellent stress-reducing technique. First of all, people who listen well are highly respected and sought after. Truly great listeners are so rare that when you are around one, it feels good, it makes you feel special. Since effective listeners are loved by the people they work with (and the people they live with), they avoid many of the common stressful aspects of work—backstabbing, resentment, sabotage, and ill feelings. Good listeners are easy to be around, so quite naturally, you want to reach out and help them. Therefore, when you become a better listener, there will probably be plenty of people in your corner to offer assistance. People tend to be loyal to good listeners because they feel acknowledged and respected.

Effective listening helps you to understand what people are saying the first time they say it, thus allowing you to avoid a great number of mistakes and misinterpretations which, as you know, can be very stressful. If you ask people what frustrates them and makes them angry, many will tell you that "not being listened to" is right near the top of their lists. So, being more attentive to what others are saying also helps you avoid many, if not most, interpersonal conflicts. Finally, effective listening is an enormous time-saver because it helps you eliminate sloppy mistakes. Instructions as well as concerns from others become crystal clear, thus helping fend off unnecessary, time-consuming errors.

—Excerpted from "Use Effective Listening as a Stress-Reducing Tool" in *Don't Sweat the Small Stuff at Work* by Richard Carlson, Ph.D.

31. According to the author, which of the following is not a stressful aspect of work?

(1) backstabbing
(2) resentment
(3) sabotage
(4) ill feelings
(5) overtime pay

32. According to the author, if a person were to use effective listening techniques at a meeting of a homeowners' association, what is likely to be the result?

(1) Neighbors would *not* notice the difference.
(2) Neighbors would compete just to speak.
(3) Neighbors would elect the person as president.
(4) Neighbors would feel better around the person.
(5) Neighbors would organize a block party.

PRACTICE TEST

33. What is the topic sentence (main idea) of the second paragraph of the passage?

(1) There are a variety of reasons why effective listening is an excellent stress-reducing technique.
(2) First of all, people who listen well are highly respected and sought after.
(3) Truly great listeners are so rare that when you are around one, it feels good. . .
(4) Good listeners are easy to be around, so, quite naturally, you want to reach out and help them.
(5) People tend to be loyal to good listeners because they feel acknowledged and respected.

34. What is the overall tone (attitude) that the author conveys in the essay?

(1) sarcastic and bitter
(2) optimistic and positive
(3) amazed and wondering
(4) pessimistic and defeating
(5) indifferent and cool

35. In the introduction to the book in which the essay is included, the author says, "You can surrender to the fact that work is inherently stressful and there's nothing you can do about it, or . . . ." From what the reader has learned from the essay passage included, select the words which most likely finished the author's statement.

(1) You can learn to be more assertive and aggressive so that others do not take unfair advantage of you.
(2) You can begin to walk a slightly different path and learn to respond in new, more peaceful ways to the demands of work.
(3) You can take a seminar in avoiding the political aspects of the day-to-day work environment.
(4) You can learn that the world of work does not encourage loyalty or mutual respect.
(5) You can learn to be silent and tune out the unreasonable demands of your boss or co-workers.

Questions 36–40 are based on the following article.

WHAT HAS MADE UP THE ESSENTIAL ELEMENTS OF FILM COMEDY IN THE PAST? HOW IS FILM COMEDY DIFFERENT IN THE PRESENT? WHO DO YOU THINK ARE THE FUNNIEST ACTORS AND ACTRESSES, BOTH PAST AND PRESENT?

Passage One

There are no lasting formulas to comedy, but I've found a few theories over the years. Comedy is like bass fishing. Everyone is an expert, the fish is smarter than all of them, and the flashiest, shiniest lures never work. Always, the audience will make its own discoveries. The mere whiff of someone working overtime, straining for a laugh, is the biggest laugh killer of all.

With a tip of the hat to manic geniuses like the Marx Brothers and Jim Carrey, who manage to make their intricate and bizarre humor look spontaneous, the great moments of comedy tend to be stolen moments. The joke you never expected. Director Ernst Lubitsch was an early master of this, building elegantly hilarious jokes, one on top of the other, until his audience was charmed and satisfied. In "Ninotchka" (1939), a sterling example of the "Lubitsch touch," watch what comedic mileage he gets out of a hat. Greta Garbo portrays an unbending Russian envoy who has come to Paris to supervise the sale of some jewels for the benefit of the socialist republic. Upon arriving at her needlessly upscale hotel, she is already in a bad mood. She sees a window display featuring a flamboyant [elaborate] hat. The chapeau strikes her as a frivolous display of capitalism, and she comments darkly to her Bolshevik [communist] accomplices: "How can such a civilization survive which permits their women to put such things on their heads? *It won't be long now, comrades.*"

Continues on page 1128

PRACTICE TEST

Passage Two

Today Lubitsch would do it not unlike modern film-comedy masters like James L. Brooks, Mike Nichols, or Woody Allen. If only for the sparkling exchanges of dialogue that mark their work, each of them has long been in the big-screen comedy hall of fame. But the timeless images of their films often come not in the banter but in the devastating dialogue-free moments like Jane Craig's (Holly Hunter) daily cathartic [tension releasing] cry in "Broadcast News."

—Excerpted from Newsweek Extra 2000: A New Millenium: "A Century at the Movies," Summer 1998

36. The author of the article states that "the great moments of comedy tend to be stolen moments." what is he saying about the best of comedy?

(1) It is mysterious.
(2) It is enjoyable.
(3) It is hilarious.
(4) It is touching.
(5) It is unexpected.

37. How would early master director Ernst Lubitsch direct a modern film-comedy?

He would probably

(1) mix comedy and tragedy for a new type of comedy
(2) follow the comedic pattern of current master directors
(3) include a great deal of dialogue among characters
(4) focus on a great deal of slapstick (physical) dimensions
(5) use a great deal of outrageous costumes and props

38. Whch of the following comparisons is *not* made when the author discusses theories of comedy?

(1) the expert bass fisherman, fish, and lures and comedy
(2) Ernst Lubitsch's and modern comedy directors' techniques
(3) sparkling dialogue and hall of fame quality of comedy
(4) great moments of comedy and spontaneous humor
(5) the Marx Brothers' and Mike Nichols's types of comedy

39. What is the effect of the author's use of the supporting detail in the example in which Greta Garbo goes to Paris to sell jewels for the socialist republic and focuses on a flamboyant hat?

(1) The hat becomes a symbol of socialism in Russia.
(2) The hat creates great sympathy for the theme of capitalism.
(3) The hat reveals a very dark side of the Russian envoy's character.
(4) The hat allows for the building of one joke on top of another.
(5) The hat explains the film narrator's third-person point of view.

40. Later in the *Newsweek* article on comedy, the author writes, "In the quest for fast-moving global entertainment, these days studios often trim these quiet moments. Move things along! The audience is ahead of you!" In light of the previous passages quoted, what is the probable result?

(1) displeasure by the audience in not wanting to move too quickly
(2) great film success as measured by box office receipts
(3) savings to the studios in making shorter films that cost less
(4) recognized genius by those who write critical film reviews
(5) improvement of acting techniques of comedic film stars

Language Arts, Reading Answer Key

A Connecticut Yankee in King Arthur's Court

1. **Comprehension (3)** In the passage, Merlin shouts "Apply the torch!" The other choices are not supported in the passage.
2. **Application (4)** The migration of birds is the least likely event to be used because it is the least threatening.
3. **Analysis (1)** The king and his people really believe that the narrator is controlling the eclipse.
4. **Analysis (5)** Merlin urges that the narrator be burned when he shouts "*Apply the torch!*" Also, Merlin is the last one to obey the narrator, and the narrator expects some trouble from Merlin, indicating that their relationship is antagonistic.
5. **Synthesis (5)** The tone is humorous because of the situation and action. The word choice such as "*The multitude sank meekly into their seats*" and "*Name any terms, reverend sir, . . . spare the sun!*" adds to the humor.
6. **Synthesis (2)** The king and people appear foolish because of their immediate readiness to believe the narrator capable of destroying the sun. In this way, Twain attacks superstitious belief as a cause of foolish behavior and contrasts it to rational thought.

"My Heart Leaps Up"

7. **Comprehension (2)** The pronoun "*it*" refers to the concept of joy at seeing a rainbow that the speaker experienced.
8. **Application (1)** A star would be the most effective substitution because, like a rainbow, it is a natural object unlike the other choices.
9. **Analysis (5)** The speaker is determined, as shown in the phrase "*So be it*" and also by the use of an exclamation mark as emphasis.
10. **Analysis (4)** The experience of childhood guides and produces, or "*fathers,*" a man. Therefore, the child becomes the father of the man.
11. **Synthesis (1)** The image of nature, "*a rainbow in the sky*", and the speaker's response "*My heart leaps up*" affirm the value of nature. The tie to nature is also recognized in the words "*wish my days to be/Bound each to each by natural piety.*" The combination of these directs the reader to the wonders of nature.
12. **Synthesis (3)** The conflict of man against nature contrasts to the theme of harmony with nature found in this poem.

"Arsenic and Old Lace"

13. **Comprehension (1)** References to the engagement of Mortimer and Elaine are made repeatedly throughout lines 13 to 57.
14. **Application (2)** Abby would encourage a romantic gift such as roses because she appears to be somewhat sentimental. She wants to celebrate the engagement with a toast, and she hopes the play will be something to enjoy, which she describes in lines 70–71 as "*It may be something romantic.*"
15. **Analysis (3)** Abby expresses her excitement and interest by asking Mortimer several questions about Elaine and the engagement. Abby also proposes having a celebration.
16. **Analysis (4)** Mortimer's occupation must be writer because in lines 24 to 28, he says that he is looking for a large envelope that contains "*one of the chapters of* **my** book on Thoreau." Further support is evident in lines 38–39 when he states that "*Elaine thought it* (meaning his chapter) *was brilliant.*"
17. **Synthesis (5)** The tone of the passage is light-hearted because the language "*That's a horundinida carnina,*" and the dialogue, "*that's Emma B. Stout ascending to heaven,*" create an expectation of fun.

18. Synthesis (2) The light-hearted tone of the play, the characterization, and the treatment of the situation provide humor and entertainment. Irreverent humor pokes fun at what we normally take seriously.

Being There

19. Comprehension (1) The text states that the Old Man "had sheltered him since Chance was a child." That leads to the interpretation of "guardian." The text states that Chance was an orphan, so the Old Man cannot be his father (choice 2), and there is no reference to a brother (choice 4). There is no reference to paying rent, so the Old Man cannot be the landlord (choice 3). Chance works in the garden, so the Old Man cannot be his gardener (choice 5).

20. Application (4) The text tells us that this one house is all Chance has ever known since childhood and that Chance does not understand most of what is said to him or around him. If he were to venture outside the gate, he probably wouldn't understand the world around him. In civilized society, we do not lock up (choice 1) those of lower ability, nor do we put them in institutions for the insane (choice 2). With his lower ability, he probably could not develop on his own a successful gardening business (choice 3). Since he is an orphan, he would have limited success in looking for relatives (choice 5), and we have no evidence that he is interested in doing so.

21. Analysis (3) Choice 3 states that Chance is to care for plants, trees, and grasses; gardening itself is no indication that anyone, including Chance, has very limited capabilities. Choices 1, 2, 4, and 5 are all statements supported by the text.

22. Analysis (5) Chance is most like an obedient child because all his life he has always done "exactly as he was told" by the Old Man. He has never questioned that he could never venture outside the garden or speak to anyone else. There is no support for the other choices, especially that of an unhappy teenager (choice 2) who is likely to rebel.

23. Synthesis (2) Most of the supporting details describe Chance and his life since childhood, which form the overall purpose of the passage. Choices 1 and 3 minimally describe the Old Man and Chance's mother, but these characters are not the central focus. There is no explanation of health benefits of gardening (choice 4) or problems of raising orphans (choice 5).

24. Synthesis (4) The reader has come to know that Chance is a man of limited ability, little knowledge of the world, and sheltered experience; therefore, the reader should have a reaction of surprise that he adopts a new lifestyle that includes influence and power. There is no reason for the reader to react with jealousy, hostility, amusement, or indifference.

Divine Secrets of the Ya-Ya Sisterhood

25. Comprehension (4) This is the option that uses the phrase *unraveling of unquestioned belief that the world revolved around Mama.* A star attracts a great deal of attention and expects others to be drawn to her. Choices 1, 2, 3, and 5 all contain clues of special attention or "star" status: invented words, queen, projects, and her own solar system.

26. Application (5) The details that lead to the astronomy section are references to "star," "pull on the earth," "orbit," "solar system," and "separate universe." There are no details as references to the other sciences—chemistry, biology, physics, or geology (choices 1, 2, 3, and 4).

27. Analysis (4) The narrator uses the words *disappointment* (choice 1), *relief* (choice 2), *heartbroken* (a word that is associated with *sorrow* in choice 3), and *stupefied* (a synonym for *astonishment* in choice 5). The only choice for which there is no evidence is pride.

28. Analysis (1) The author's details have the effect of causing the reader to feel sympathy for the narrator because she has a mother who must be the center of attention and a father who seems to be fairly uninvolved. Choices 2, 3, 4, and 5 are not true statements.

29. Synthesis (3) The point of view from which the story is told is that of the daughter of a Ya-Ya. There are many references to "Mama" and to "my mother." The daughter is not named in these passages.

30. Synthesis (2) The overall purpose of the passages from the novel is to explore a daughter's feelings about her mother both in the past and in the present. The narrator mentions developing guilt if she were to "eclipse Mama in any little way," even "winning a spelling bee." The intent of the passages is not to be a lexicon of words (choice 1). The passages do not give much attention to explaining how a human "star" can rise and fall (choice 3) or to comparing and contrasting personalities of the Ya-Yas (choice 4). The narrator's father is mentioned in only one line, so there is no examining of the relationship between the narrator's parents (choice 5).

Use Effective Listening as a Stress-Reducing Tool

31. Comprehension (5) The author identifies the most stressful aspects of work as the actions in choices 1 through 4 but does not mention *overtime pay*. One might argue that working overtime causes stress, but the author did not mention that; in any event it would be the *working* and not the *pay* that would be stressful.

32. Application (4) Effective listening should lead to better relationships, so a person's neighbors would most likely feel better around such a person. Choice 1 is false because neighbors *would* notice the difference in more effective listening. Choice 2 is false because effective listening should not generate competition. Choices 3 and 5 are not necessarily true because we cannot guarantee those actions.

33. Analysis (1) The first sentence is the main idea of the paragraph; all other sentences provide supporting details that help to explain why effective listening helps to reduce stress.

34. Synthesis (2) The author gives many examples in which the reader can improve listening skills and thereby avoid mistakes and interpersonal conflicts. By his explaining how people can improve, the author conveys an optimistic and positive attitude.

35. Synthesis (2) The author teaches the reader to reduce stress by more effective listening. Reducing stress leaves one more at peace despite the demands of work. The author would not favor being *aggressive* (choice 1), *avoiding* political aspects of work environment (choice 3), encouraging lack of *loyalty or mutual respect* (Choice 4), or being *silent* so as to *tune out* others (choice 5).

A Century at the Movies

36. Comprehension (5) In Passage One, the next line after the sentence with "stolen moments" is "The joke you never expected." Also, further support for this view is found in the first paragraph: "Always, the audience will make its own discoveries." Certainly, comedy can be described in the ways indicated by the other choices; however, those do not explain "stolen moments."

37. Application (2) In Passage Two, the author states, "Today Lubitsch would do it *not unlike* modern film-comedy masters like James L. Brooks, Mike Nichols, or Woody Allen."

38. Analysis (3) In Passage Two, the author states, "But the timeless images of their films often come not in the banter but in the devastating *dialogue-free* moments . . . " This is the only false comparison.

39. Analysis (4) In Passage One, the author states, "Director Ernst Lubitsch was an early master of this, building elegantly hilarious jokes, *one on top of the other,* until his audience was charmed and satisfied." The hat allows for the building of jokes.

40. Synthesis (1) We can expect that the audience would be displeased at being rushed because of these author's comments: "the audience will make its own discoveries," ". . . stolen moments. The joke you never expected," and "dialogue-free moments."

Evaluation Chart

Use the Answer Key on pages 1129–1131 to check your answers to the Practice Test. Then find the item number of each question you missed and circle it on the chart below to determine the reading content areas in which you need more practice. Pay particular attention to areas where you missed half or more of the questions. The page numbers for the content areas are listed below on the chart. For those questions that you missed, review the skill pages indicated.

	COMPREHENSION (pages 217–230)	**APPLICATION (pages 231–236)**	**ANALYSIS (pages 237–262)**	**SYNTHESIS (pages 263–270)**
Fiction (pages 589–614)	1, 19, 25	2, 20, 26	3, 4, 21, 22, 27, 28	5, 6, 23, 24, 29, 30
Poetry (pages 615–636)	7	8	9, 10	11, 12
Drama (pages 637–654)	13	14	15, 16	17, 18
Nonfiction Prose (pages 655–684)	31, 36	32, 37	33, 38, 39	34, 35, 40

PRACTICE TEST

Mathematics

The Mathematics Practice Test will give you the opportunity to evaluate your readiness for the actual GED Mathematics Test. The Practice Test, like the GED Test, consists of two parts: Part I (calculator allowed) has 25 questions, and Part II (no calculator allowed) has 25 questions. Part I and Part II have a combined score of 50 points. Each part should take approximately 45 minutes, for a total test time of 90 minutes.

Remember to use the calculator only during Part I. The official GED calculator is the Casio *fx*-260 solar calculator. You should practice using that specific calculator. Remember, too, that you may use the formula page throughout both Parts I and II.

When you take this Practice Test, keep track of your time on each part. At the end of 45 minutes, if you have not completed Part I, mark your place and then finish the test. Do the same with Part II. This will give you an idea of whether you can finish the real GED Test in the time allotted. Try to answer as many questions as you can. A blank will count as a wrong answer, so make a reasonable guess for answers to questions of which you are not sure.

When you finish the test, check your answers and turn to the Evaluation Chart on page 1150. Use the chart to evaluate whether you are ready to take the actual GED Test and, if not, in what areas you need more work.

PRACTICE TEST

Part I

Mathematics Practice Test Answer Grid

1 ① ② ③ ④ ⑤

2 ① ② ③ ④ ⑤

3 ① ② ③ ④ ⑤

4
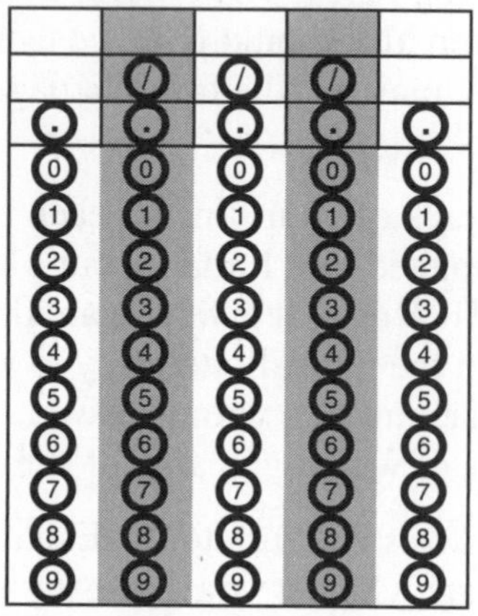

5
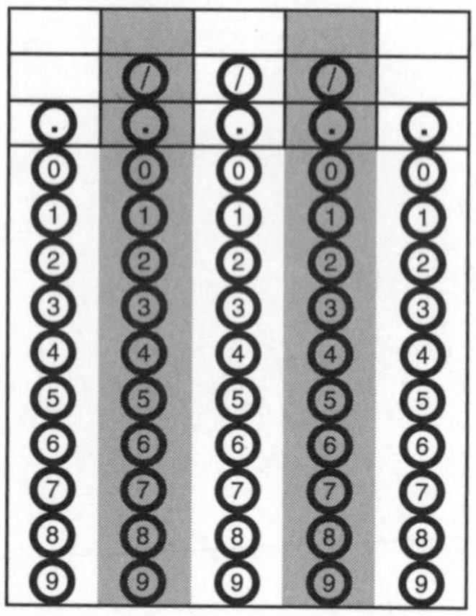

6 ① ② ③ ④ ⑤

7 ① ② ③ ④ ⑤

8 ① ② ③ ④ ⑤

9 ① ② ③ ④ ⑤

10 ① ② ③ ④ ⑤

11 ① ② ③ ④ ⑤

12
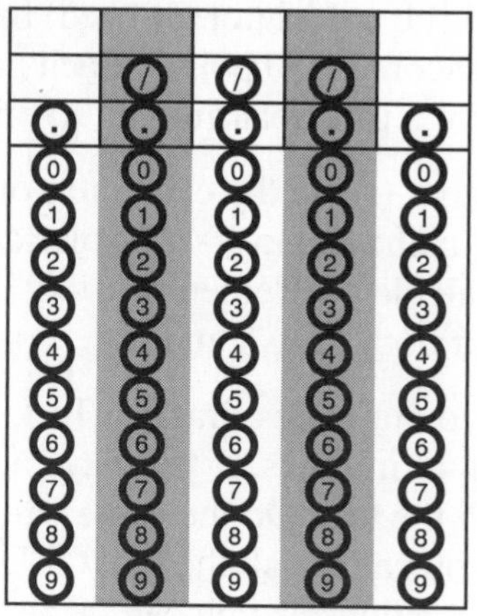

13
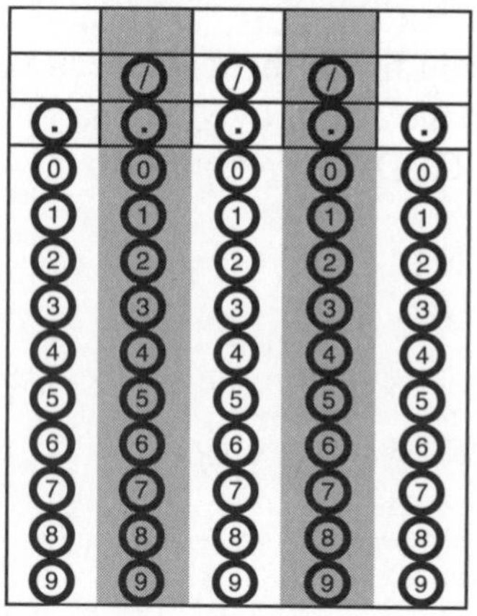

14 ① ② ③ ④ ⑤

15 ① ② ③ ④ ⑤

16 ① ② ③ ④ ⑤

17
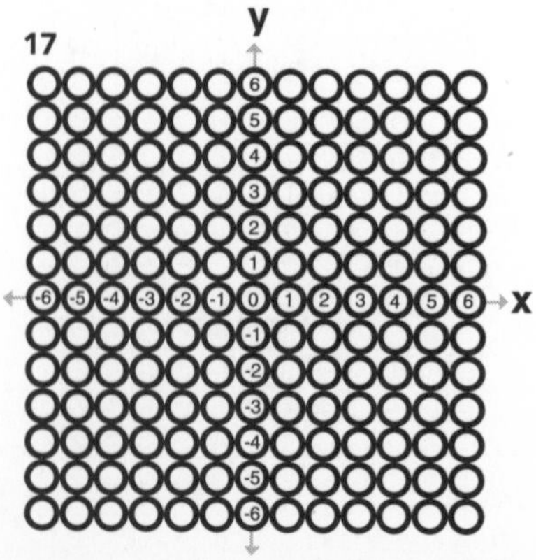

18 ① ② ③ ④ ⑤

19 ① ② ③ ④ ⑤

20 ① ② ③ ④ ⑤

21
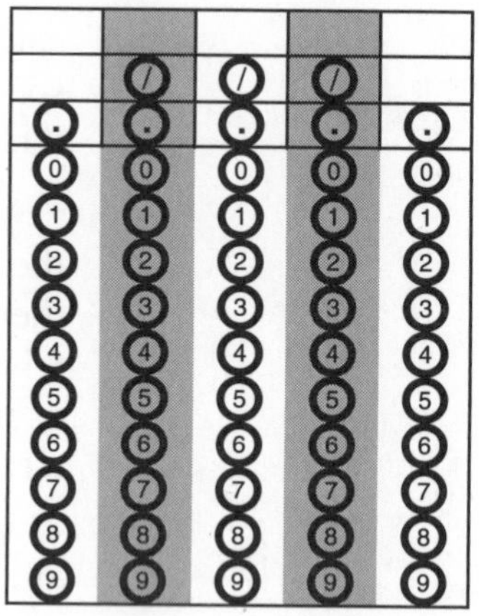

22
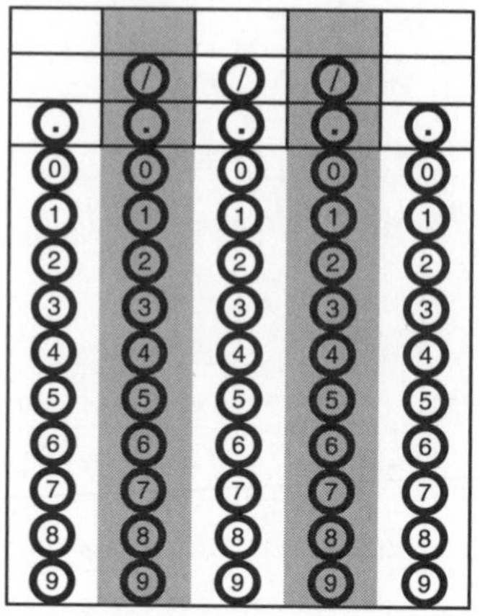

23 ① ② ③ ④ ⑤

24 ① ② ③ ④ ⑤

25 ① ② ③ ④ ⑤

FORMULAS

AREA of a:	
square	Area = side^2
rectangle	Area = length × width
parallelogram	Area = base × height
triangle	Area = $\frac{1}{2}$ × base × height
trapezoid	Area = $\frac{1}{2} \times (\text{base}_1 + \text{base}_2) \times$ height
circle	Area = $\pi \times \text{radius}^2$; π is approximately equal to 3.14.
PERIMETER of a:	
square	Perimeter = 4 × side
rectangle	Perimeter = 2 × length + 2 × width
triangle	Perimeter = $\text{side}_1 + \text{side}_2 + \text{side}_3$
CIRCUMFERENCE of a circle	Circumference = π × diameter; π is approximately equal to 3.14.
VOLUME of a:	
cube	Volume = edge^3
rectangular solid	Volume = length × width × height
square pyramid	Volume = $\frac{1}{3} \times (\text{base edge})^2 \times$ height
cylinder	Volume = $\pi \times \text{radius}^2 \times$ height; π is approximately equal to 3.14.
cone	Volume = $\frac{1}{3} \times \pi \times \text{radius}^2 \times$ height; π is approximately equal to 3.14.
COORDINATE GEOMETRY	distance between points = $\sqrt{(x_2 - x_1)^2 + (y_2 - y_1)^2}$; (x_1, y_1) and (x_2, y_2) are two points in a plane. slope of a line = $\frac{y_2 - y_1}{x_2 - x_1}$; (x_1, y_1) and (x_2, y_2) are two points on the line.
PYTHAGOREAN RELATIONSHIP	$a^2 + b^2 = c^2$; a and b are legs and c the hypotenuse of a right triangle.
MEASURES OF CENTRAL TENDENCY	**mean** = $\frac{x_1 + x_2 + \ldots + x_n}{n}$, where the xs are the values for which a mean is desired, and n is the total number of values for x. **median** = the middle value of an odd number of *ordered* scores, and halfway between the two middle values of an even number of *ordered* scores.
SIMPLE INTEREST	interest = principal × rate × time
DISTANCE	distance = rate × time
TOTAL COST	total cost = (number of units) × (price per unit)

PRACTICE TEST

Part I

Directions: Solve each problem. You may use your calculator and the formula page as needed.

Questions 1 and 2 refer to the following information.

Consumer Credit Company

DATE	REFERENCE NUMBER	DESCRIPTION	CREDITS	CHARGES
9/2	S2X9	Payment Thank You	156.45	
9/8	M3X7	American Retail Co.		78.56
9/10	DN43	State Services, Inc.		12.84
		Total Credits and Charges	156.45	91.40
Previous Balance 276.45	– Payments/ Credits –156.45	+ Finance Charge +1.80	+ Current Purchases +91.40	= New Balance 213.20
Past Due 0	+ Late Fee 0	+ Minimum Payment 21.32	+ Finance Charge 1.80	= Payment Due 23.10

1. Which numerical expression below describes the new balance?

(1) 276.45 – 156.45
(2) 276.45 + 91.40
(3) 156.45 – 91.40
(4) 156.45 + 91.40 + 1.80
(5) 276.45 – 156.45 + 1.80 + 91.40

2. The finance charge is calculated on the previous balance less the payment. If the finance charge is $1.80, by what monthly rate of percent is the finance charge calculated?

(1) .6%
(2) 1.5%
(3) 6%
(4) 15%
(5) 18%

3. Select the expression that is not equivalent to the other expressions.

(1) $6x - 3$
(2) $4x - 10x - 3$
(3) $10x - 3 - 4x$
(4) $3(2x - 1)$
(5) $x - 3 + 5x$

4. Assuming no waste, how many boards each $1\frac{1}{2}$ feet long can be cut from a board that is 12 feet long?

Mark your answer in the circles in the grid on your answer sheet.

5. At a cost of $.90 per foot, what is the price of a board that is 78 inches long?

Mark your answer in the circles in the grid on your answer sheet.

PRACTICE TEST

6. The payroll sheet below gives you the information to find Jason's net pay (take-home pay). Net pay (*n*) is calculated using gross pay (*g*) less any deductions (*d*): $n = g - d$. Gross pay is equal to hours worked times the hourly rate of pay. Deductions such as state tax, federal tax, and social security (FICA) are based on percents of the gross pay. Other deductions such as union dues may be set amounts. Use the information below to find Jason's net pay.

NAME	HOURS	PAY RATE	FICA AT 7%	STATE TAX 3%	FEDERAL TAX 15%	UNION DUES	NET PAY
Jason	40	$12				$4.80	

(1) $120
(2) $124.80
(3) $355.20
(4) $360
(5) $480

7. The choices below list the price of an 8-ounce package of fish sticks at five different stores. Which is least expensive per package?

(1) buy one at $3.80 and get one free
(2) $1.89 each
(3) 5 for $9
(4) buy 3 at $6.88 and get one extra for free
(5) $5.19 for 3

Questions 8 and 9 refer to the following information.

The Martins bought a house that cost $80,000. They made a down payment of $12,000. They will have to pay $420 a month in mortgage payments and $700 a year in real estate taxes.

8. The down payment was what percent of the total cost of the house?

(1) 9
(2) 10
(3) 12
(4) 15
(5) 20

9. Which expression represents the Martins' yearly mortgage payments and real estate taxes?

(1) $\frac{\$420}{12}$
(2) $\frac{\$700}{12}$
(3) 12($420)
(4) 12($700)
(5) 12($420) + $700

PRACTICE TEST

10. The sales tax rate in Cook County is 8.5%, and the sales tax rate in DuPage County is 7.5%. How much money would you save by buying a \$198 item in DuPage County rather than in Cook County?

(1) \$ 1.98
(2) \$ 3.11
(3) \$14.85
(4) \$16.83
(5) \$19.80

11. Home plate in softball has the dimensions shown below. How many square inches does the surface of the plate cover?

(1) 45.5
(2) 66
(3) 72.25
(4) 208.25
(5) 280.5

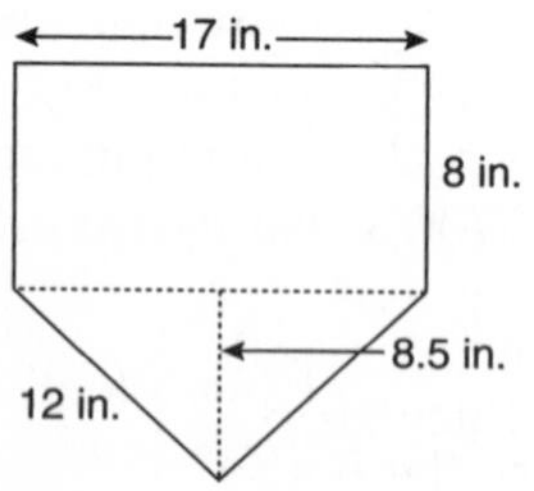

12. Before she goes camping, La Verne has to buy a tent pole to replace the one lost on her last outing. If the area of the front of the tent is 22 square feet and the base of the tent has the dimensions indicated below, how tall must the pole be?

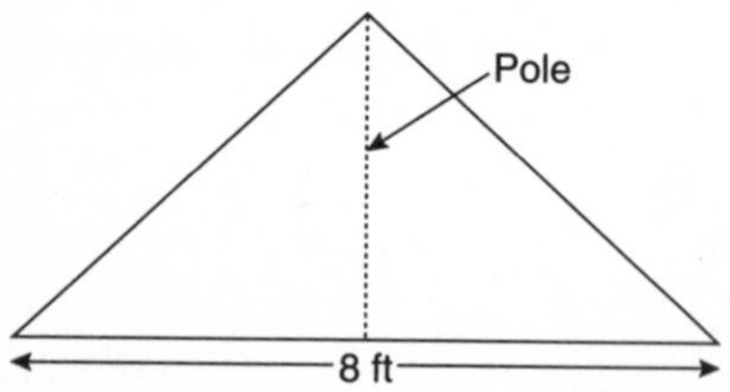

Mark your answer in the circles in the grid on your answer sheet.

Questions 13–15 refer to the following information.

Age of 42 U.S. Presidents at Inauguration

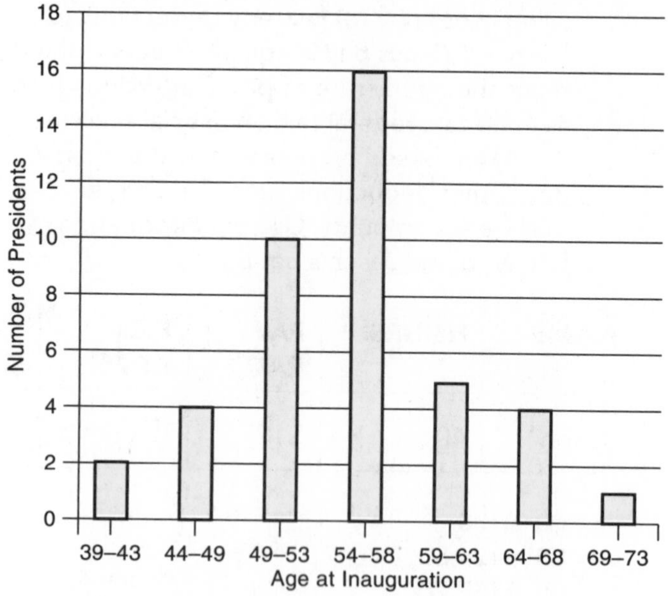

13. What fraction of the presidents was in the 44–53 age groups at inauguration?

Mark your answer in the circles in the grid on your answer sheet.

14. In what age group does the median age for the president at inauguration fall?

(1) 44–49
(2) 49–53
(3) 54–58
(4) 59–63
(5) 64–68

15. Which statement below does *not* describe the information presented in the bar graph?

(1) About $\frac{1}{7}$ of the presidents were ≤ 49 years of age at inauguration.
(2) About $\frac{1}{4}$ of the presidents were ≥ 59 years of age at inauguration.
(3) About half the presidents were in the 54–58 age group at inauguration.
(4) The president is more likely to be ≤ 59 years of age at inauguration.
(5) Forty-two presidents were between the ages of 38 and 74 at inauguration.

PRACTICE TEST

16. Using the information below, find the difference in cost between using Company A and Company B to rent a car for a 500-mile trip over 3 days.

Car Rental Company	Daily Rate	Mileage Rate
A	\$42/day	10¢ per mile
B	\$31/day	21¢ per mile

(1) \$11
(2) \$22
(3) \$27.50
(4) \$33
(5) \$65

17. From the following list of ordered pairs select the y-intercept and show its location on the coordinate plane grid. (3, 0), (4, –2), (0, –3), and (–1, 4).

Mark your answer on the coordinate plane grid on your answer sheet.

18. What percent of the yard shown below is covered by the swimming pool? Round your answer to the nearest whole percent.

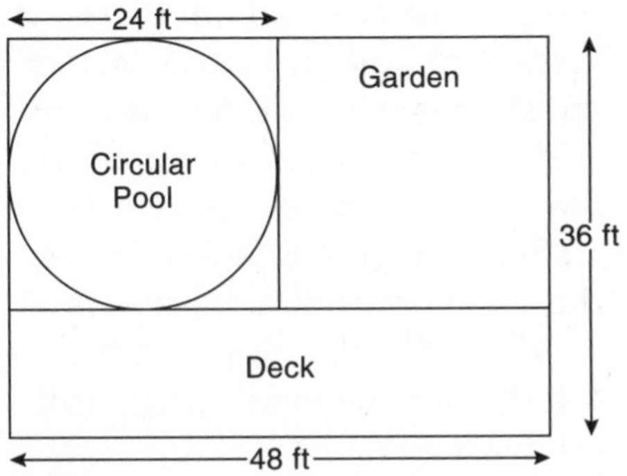

(1) 5%
(2) 21%
(3) 26%
(4) 33%
(5) 50%

19. Find the distance between points A and B.

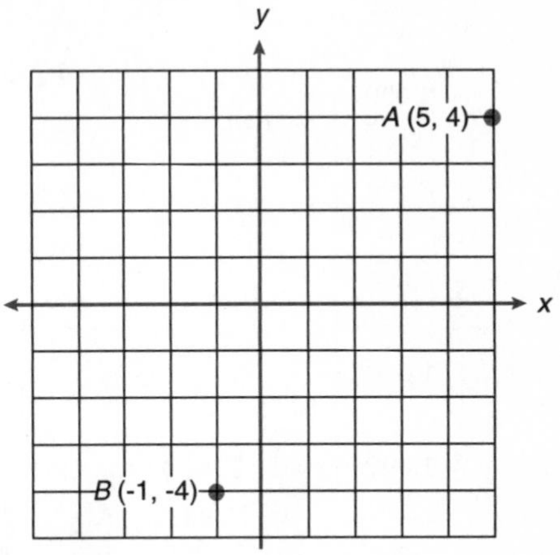

(1) 4 units
(2) 6 units
(3) 8 units
(4) 10 units
(5) 12 units

Questions 20 and 21 refer to the following information.

Jaime keeps his savings in a shoebox. He began with \$500 he received as a present. Each year he added \$250 to the box. His total savings (y) after (x) years are given by the equation $y = 500 + 250x$.

20. How much money did Jaime have at the end of 20 years?

(1) \$ 500
(2) \$ 750
(3) \$ 5,000
(4) \$ 5,500
(5) \$15,000

21. If Jaime had invested the original amount in a certificate of deposit at a simple interest rate of 5.5% annually for 20 years, how much would the certificate alone be worth at the end of the 20 years?

Mark your answer in the circles in the grid on your answer sheet.

PRACTICE TEST

Questions 22–24 refer to the following information.

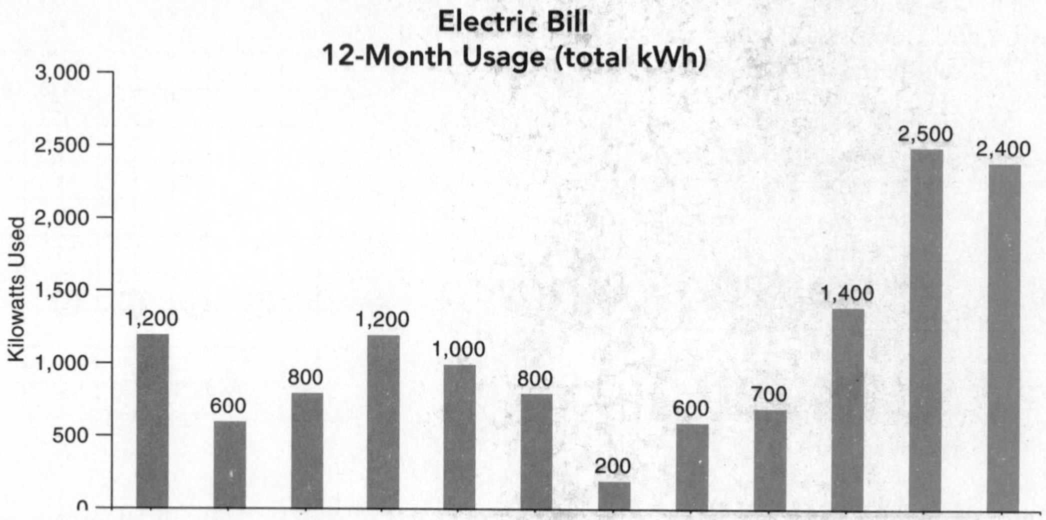

Meter Information for August 1–31

Dates	Meter #	Load Type	Previous Reading	Current Reading	Difference
8/1–8/31	999888888	General	60255	62655	2400

22. What is the average kWh used per day during the month of August? Round your answer to the nearest tenth of a kilowatt.

Mark your answer in the circles in the grid on your answer sheet.

23. What is the median monthly amount of kilowatt usage during the 12 months? Round your answer to the nearest whole number.

(1) 500
(2) 800
(3) 900
(4) 1117
(5) 1350

24. If the customer charge is $.08987 per kilowatt used and there is a 3.5% tax, what is the total amount due for the month of August? Round your answers to the nearest penny.

(1) $ 7.55
(2) $ 75.49
(3) $215.69
(4) $223.24
(5) $291.18

25. A shipment of glassware is rejected if more than 1.5% of the glasses are defective. If 42 broken glasses are found in a shipment of 3000 glasses, which statement below is true?

(1) 1.2% of the glasses are defective, and the shipment should *not* be rejected.
(2) 1.4% of the glasses are defective, and the shipment should *not* be rejected.
(3) 1.5% of the glasses are defective, and the shipment should be rejected.
(4) 1.6% of the glasses are defective, and the shipment should be rejected.
(5) 71.4% of the glasses are defective, and the shipment should be rejected.

PRACTICE TEST

Part II

Mathematics Practice Test Answer Grid

26 ① ② ③ ④ ⑤

27 ① ② ③ ④ ⑤

28 ① ② ③ ④ ⑤

29 ① ② ③ ④ ⑤

30 ① ② ③ ④ ⑤

31

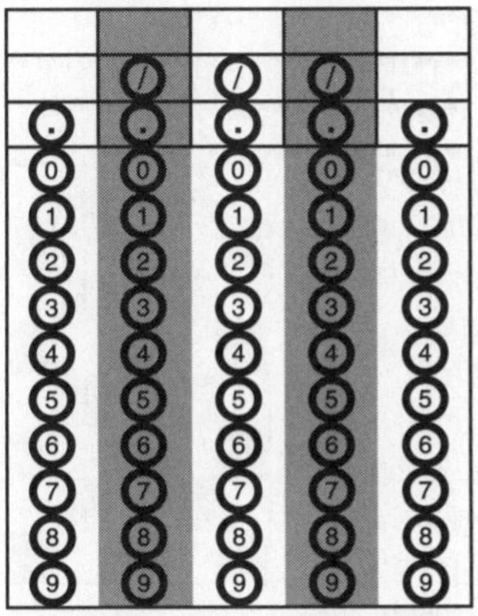

32 ① ② ③ ④ ⑤

33 ① ② ③ ④ ⑤

34 ① ② ③ ④ ⑤

35 ① ② ③ ④ ⑤

36 ① ② ③ ④ ⑤

37

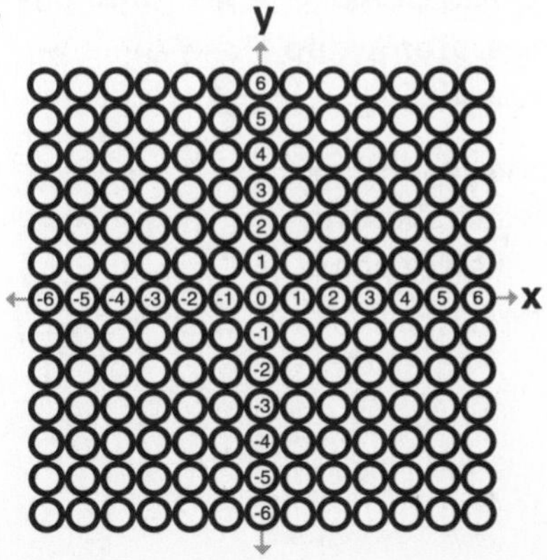

38 ① ② ③ ④ ⑤

39 ① ② ③ ④ ⑤

40 ① ② ③ ④ ⑤

41 ① ② ③ ④ ⑤

42 ① ② ③ ④ ⑤

43

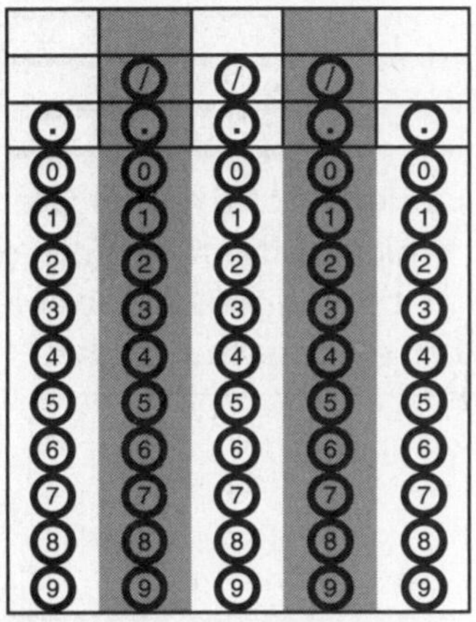

44 ① ② ③ ④ ⑤

45 ① ② ③ ④ ⑤

46 ① ② ③ ④ ⑤

47 ① ② ③ ④ ⑤

48 ① ② ③ ④ ⑤

49 ① ② ③ ④ ⑤

50 ① ② ③ ④ ⑤

PRACTICE TEST

Part II

Directions: Solve each problem. Do *not* use a calculator. Use the formula page as needed.

26. Compact discs are on sale at Super Sounds for \$13.98 each. Which of the following is closest to the price of five discs?

(1) \$60
(2) \$65
(3) \$70
(4) \$75
(5) \$80

27. Below is a sketch of a rectangular vegetable garden. Which of the following expressions represents the number of feet of fencing required to enclose the garden?

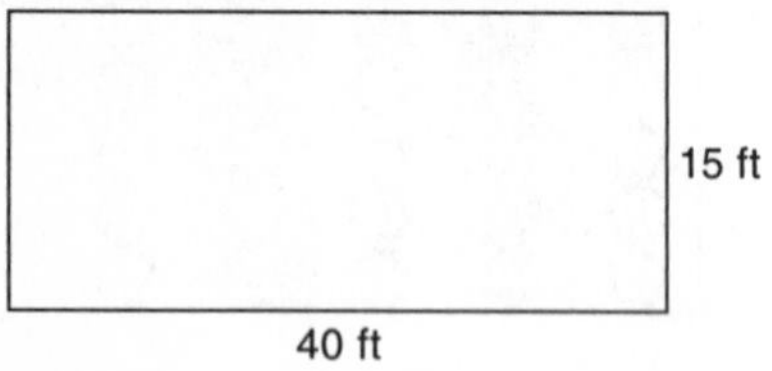

(1) 40×15
(2) $40 + 15$
(3) $2(40) + 15$
(4) $(40 + 15)^2$
(5) $2(40) + 2(15)$

28. What is the ratio of the width to the height of the door at the right?

(1) 2:3
(2) 1:2
(3) 1:3
(4) 2:7
(5) 1:8

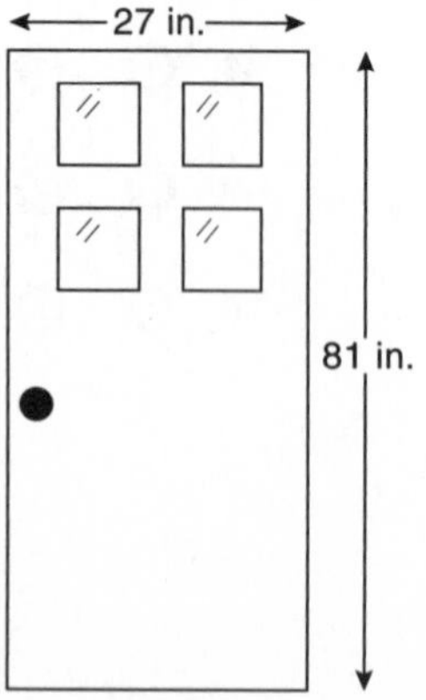

29. Arrange the packages pictured below in order from *lightest* to *heaviest*.

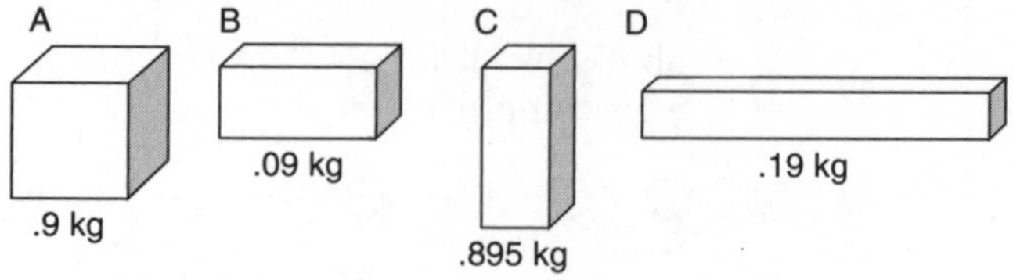

(1) A, D, C, B
(2) D, B, C, A
(3) B, D, C, A
(4) A, B, D, C
(5) B, A, C, D

30. A checkerboard is shown at the right. If the edge of each small square is 2.5 cm, which numerical expression below describes the surface area of the checkerboard?

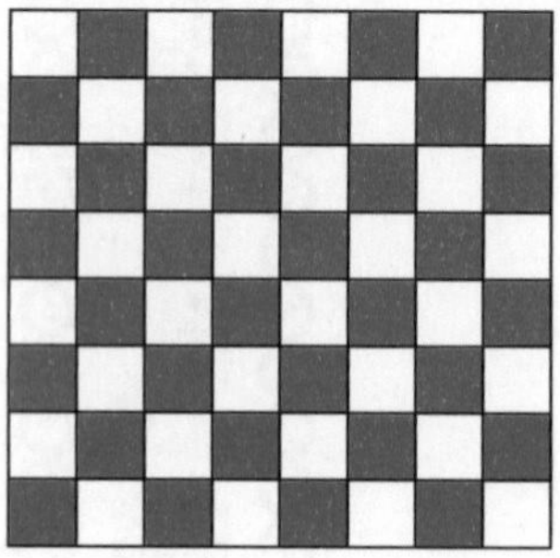

(1) 8×2.5
(2) $8^2 \times (2.5)^2$
(3) $8\,(2.5)^2$
(4) $8^2 \times 2.5$
(5) $8^2 + 2.5^2$

31. A refrigerator is measured in cubic feet. How many cubic feet of space does the refrigerator at the right occupy?

Mark your answer in the circles in the grid on your answer sheet.

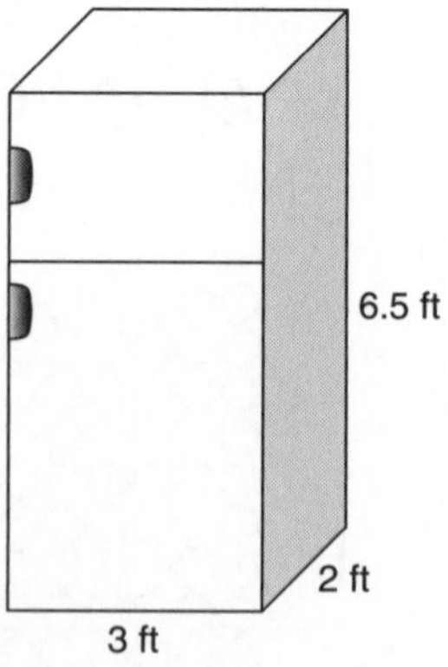

PRACTICE TEST

Questions 32 and 33 refer to the following information.

The restaurant tab below shows the order served at one table. The customers left a 15% tip on the subtotal.

Casey's Café

Qty	Food Order	Amt
1	Steak Diane	14.95
1	Shrimp Scampi	15.95
2	Chablis @ 4.50	9.00
2	Coffee @ 1.25	2.50
1	Orange Sherbet	2.70
1	Apple pie	3.50
	SUBTOTAL	48.60
	7% TAX	3.40
	TOTAL	

32. How much did the customers pay for the tip, rounded to the nearest dollar?

(1) \$4
(2) \$5
(3) \$6
(4) \$7
(5) \$8

33. Which numerical expression below *cannot* be used to find the total bill including tip?

(1) 1.22(48.60)
(2) 48.60 + .07(48.60) + .15(48.60)
(3) 48.60 + .22(48.60)
(4) 48.60(1 + .07 + .15)
(5) .07(48.60) + .15(48.60)

Questions 34 and 35 refer to the following information.

The graph below shows the percent of the U.S. population living in each of the four major areas in the continental United States in the year 2000. The population of the United States was about 280,000,000.

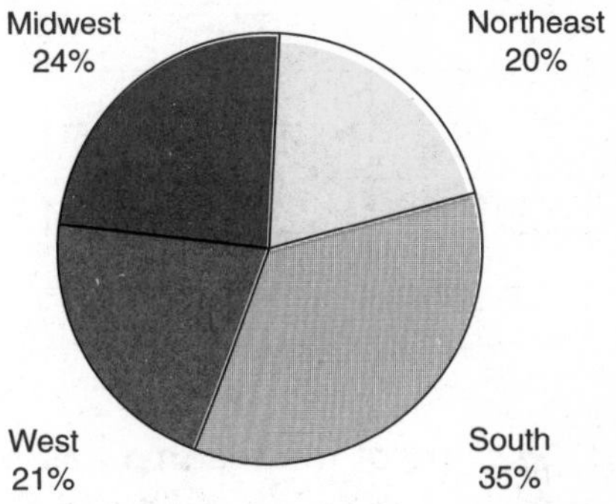

34. Approximately how many people lived in the Northeast?

(1) 280,000
(2) 28 million
(3) 560,000
(4) 56 million
(5) Not enough information is given.

35. If the U.S. population grows overall by 1% per year, what was the 2001 population statistic in scientific notation?

(1) 28.28×10^7
(2) 2.828×10
(3) 2828×10
(4) 2.828×10^8
(5) $28.28 \times 10{,}000$

PRACTICE TEST

Questions 36 and 37 refer to the information on the graph below.

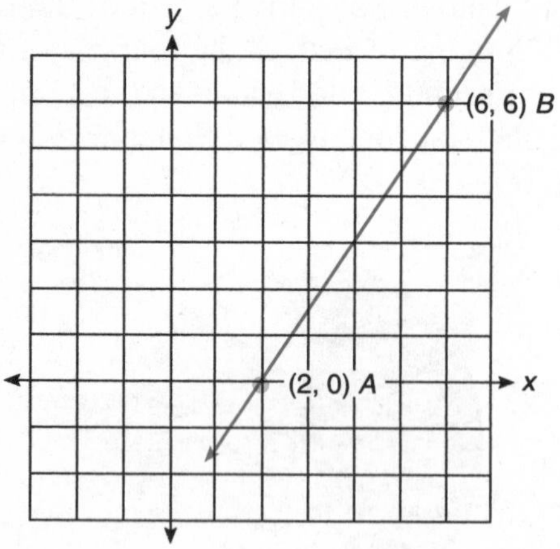

36. Find the slope of the line that passes through the two points indicated on the graph.

(1) $\frac{2}{3}$
(2) $\frac{3}{2}$
(3) $\frac{3}{4}$
(4) $\frac{4}{3}$
(5) $\frac{-2}{3}$

37. Plot the point that represents the midpoint between *A* and *B*.

Mark your answer on the coordinate plane grid on your answer sheet.

Questions 38 and 39 refer to the following information.

A community college conducted a survey of businesses in its district to determine the number of employees who had used its computer-training center. The college mailed the survey to 100 small businesses, 100 medium-sized businesses, and 100 large businesses. The rate of response is important in deciding how reliable survey results are. Here are the data on the response to this survey.

Company	Response	No Response	Total
SMALL	79	21	100
MEDIUM-SIZED	40	60	100
LARGE	25	75	100

38. What was the overall percent of No Response for all companies?

(1) 21%
(2) 48%
(3) 52%
(4) 156%
(5) Not enough information is given.

39. Which statement below best describes how No Response is related to the size of the business?

(1) The smaller the company, the more likely it is to make no response.
(2) The larger the company, the less likely it is to respond.
(3) The large companies responded better than the medium and small companies.
(4) All companies have similar rates of response.
(5) The rate of response was highest among large companies.

PRACTICE TEST

Questions 40 and 41 refer to the following plan for a swimming pool.

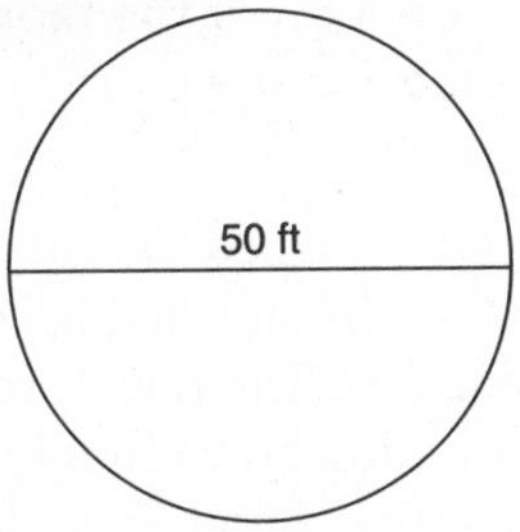

40. Which of the following is closest, in feet, to the distance around the pool?

(1) 1.57
(2) 15.7
(3) 157
(4) 314
(5) 1963

41. How many cubic feet of water will the pool hold if the entire pool has a depth of 5 feet?

(1) 392.5
(2) 785
(3) 1,570
(4) 9,812.5
(5) 39,250

42. If $12a - 5 = 4a + 11$, then $a =$

(1) 2
(2) 3
(3) 5
(4) 8
(5) 12

43. Each of the four members of the Rodriguez family bought a ticket for the music festival. A total of 360 tickets was sold. If one ticket holder will win the grand prize, what is the probability that the winner will be someone in the Rodriguez family?

Mark your answer in the circles in the grid on your answer sheet.

44. Antonio is a brick mason. Let x stand for the hourly wage he pays his apprentice. Antonio makes \$5 more than three times the wage of his apprentice. Which of the following expresses Antonio's hourly wage?

(1) $3x + 5$
(2) $3(x + 5)$
(3) $3x + 3$
(4) $x + 5$
(5) $3x$

45. Which graph below best describes the relationship between a number and the square of the number?

(1)
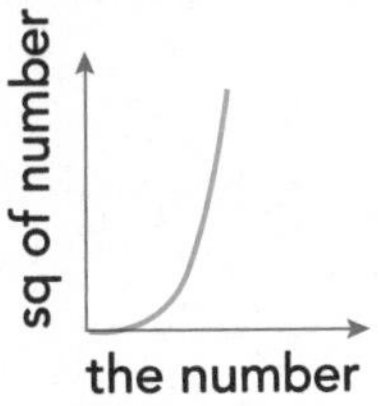

(2)
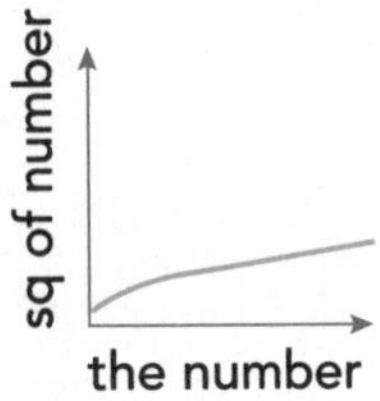

(3)
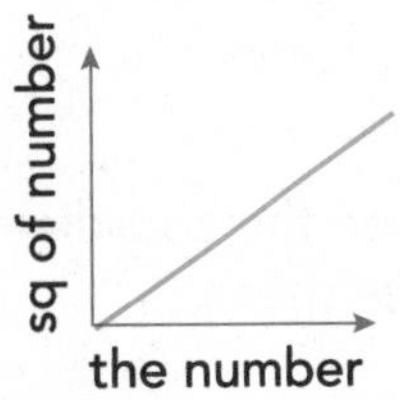

(4)
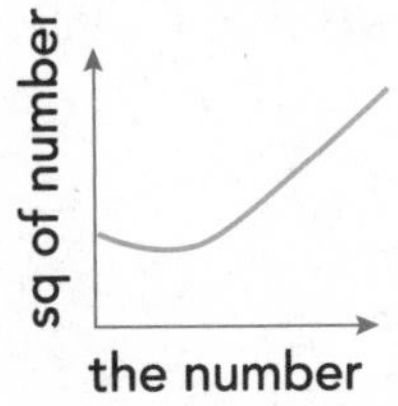

(5)
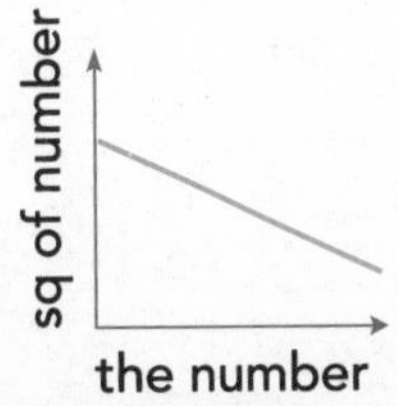

PRACTICE TEST

46. Kenyatta drove for three hours at an average speed of 55 mph and then for another two hours at *x* mph. If the total distance she drove was 245 miles, which of the following equations will give you the speed she drove for the last two hours?

(1) $5 \times (55 + x) = 245$

(2) $3(55) + 2x = 245$

(3) $(55 + x) \times (3 + 2) = 245$

(4) $\frac{55 + x}{5} = 245$

(5) $55 + x + 3 + 2 = 245$

47. In the figure below, $QR = 120$. What is the length of PQ?

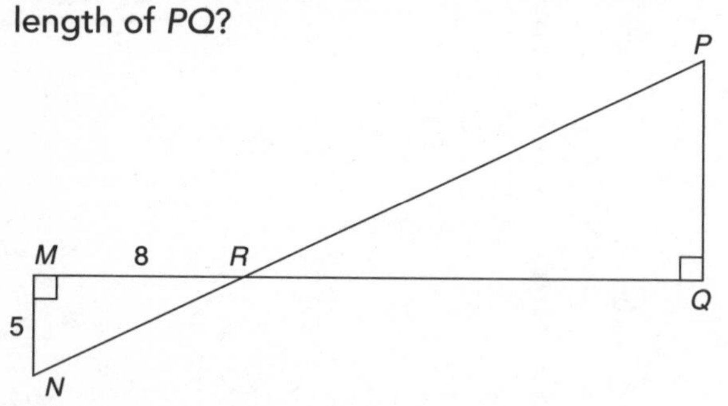

(1) 15
(2) 24
(3) 64
(4) 75
(5) 100

48. Which of the following expresses the relationship among the sides of the figure?

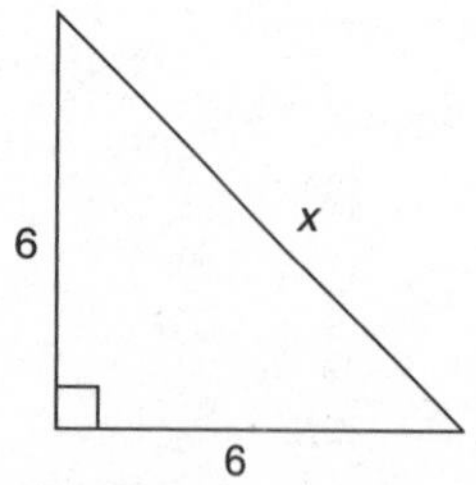

(1) $x = 6 + 6$

(2) $x = 2(6)$

(3) $x^2 = 2(6) + 2(6)$

(4) $x = \frac{6 + 6}{2}$

(5) $x^2 = 6^2 + 6^2$

49. A family spends $115 per week on groceries. If the family income is $575 per week, what fraction of the family income is *not* spent on groceries?

(1) $\frac{1}{4}$

(2) $\frac{3}{4}$

(3) $\frac{1}{5}$

(4) $\frac{4}{5}$

(5) Not enough information is given.

50. From the sketch of the basketball court free-throw zone shown below, select the expression that represents the area of the zone.

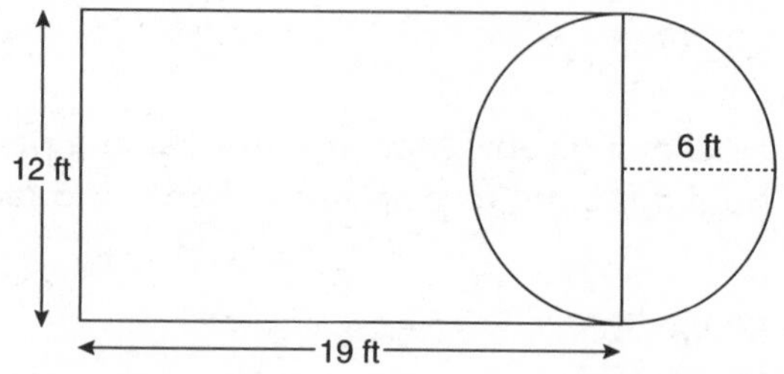

(1) $12 \times 19 \times 6$
(2) $12 \times 19 \times \pi \times 6^2$
(3) $12 \times 19 + .5 \times \pi \times 6^2$
(4) $12 \times 19 + \pi \times 12$
(5) $12 \times 19 + \pi \times 6^2$

Answers are on page 1147.

PRACTICE TEST

Mathematics Answer Key

Part I

1. **(5) 276.45 – 156.45 + 1.80 + 91.40**
new balance = previous balance – payments/credits + finance charge + current purchases

2. **(2) 1.5%**
276.45 – 156.45 = $120
$\frac{1.80}{120} = \frac{N\%}{100\%}$
$N = \frac{1.80 \times 100}{120} = \frac{180}{120} = 1.5$

3. **(2) 4x – 10x –3**
$6x - 3$
$4x - 10x - 3 = -6x - 3$
$10x - 3 - 4x = 6x - 3$
$3(2x - 1) = 6x - 3$
$x - 3 + 5x = 6x - 3$

4. **8**
$12 \div 1\frac{1}{2} = \frac{12}{1} \div \frac{3}{2} = \frac{\cancel{12}^{4}}{1} \times \frac{2}{\cancel{3}_{1}} = 8$

5. **5.85**
78 ÷ 12 = 6.5
.90 × 6.5 = $5.85

6. **(3) $355.20**
12 × 40 = 480
.07 × 480 = 33.60
.03 × 480 = 14.40
.15 × 480 = 72.00
+ 4.80
$124.80
$480 – $124.80 = $355.20

7. **(4) buy 3 at $6.88 and get an extra one for free**
3.80 ÷ 2 = $1.90
one for $1.89
9 ÷ 5 = $1.80
6.88 ÷ 4 = $1.72
5.19 ÷ 3 = $1.73

8. **(4) 15**
$\frac{12000}{80000} = \frac{N\%}{100\%}$
$N = \frac{12000 \times 100}{80000} = 15$

9. **(5) 12($420) + $700**
12 months times $420 plus taxes

10. **(1) $1.98**
8.5% – 7.5% = 1% = .01
.01 × 198 = 1.98

11. **(4) 208.25 sq in.**
Area of rectangle = length × width
= 17 × 8 = 136 sq in.
Area of triangle = $\frac{1}{2}$ × base × height
$= \frac{1}{2} \times 17 \times 8.5 = \frac{144.5}{2}$ sq in.
= 72.25 sq in.
136 + 72.25 = 208.25 sq in.

12. **5.5**
Area of a triangle = $\frac{1}{2}$ × base × height
$22 = \frac{1}{2} \times 8 \times h$
$44 = 8h$
$5.5 = h$

13. **$\frac{1}{3}$**
$\frac{14}{42} = \frac{1}{3}$

14. **(3) 54–58**
The median is age group 54–58, which means that 21 presidents were ≥ 54–58 years old and 21 were ≤ 54–58 years old at inauguration.

15. **(3) About half the presidents were in the 54–58 age group at inauguration.**
This is the one statement that does not describe the graph because 16 out of 42 is more nearly one-third than one-half.

16. **(2) $22**
Company A = 3 × 42 + 500 × .10 = 176
Company B = 3 × 31 + 500 × .21 = 198
198 – 176 = 22

17. (0, –3)

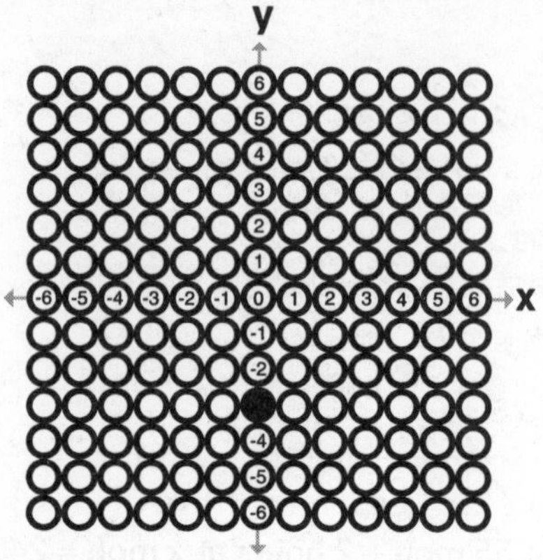

18. (3) 26%

Area of rectangular yard = length × width =

$36 \times 48 = 1728$

Area of pool = $\pi \times \text{radius}^2 = 3.14 \times 12^2 = 452.16$

$\frac{452.16}{1728} = \frac{N\%}{100\%}$

$N = \frac{452.16 \times 100}{1728} = 26.16667 \approx 26$

19. (4) 10 units

Distance between two points

$d = \sqrt{(x_2 - x_1)^2 + (y_2 - y_1)^2}$

$d = \sqrt{(5 - (-1))^2 + (4 - (-4))^2}$

$d = \sqrt{6^2 + 8^2} = \sqrt{100} = 10$

20. (4) $5500

$y = 500 + 250x = 500 + 250(20) = 5500$

21. 1050

Interest = principal × rate × time

$I = 500 \times 5.5\% \times 20$

$I = 500 \times .055 \times 20 = 550$

Total value = 500 + 550 = 1050

22. 77.4

62655 – 60255 = 2400

2400 ÷ 31 = 77.4

23. (3) 900

200, 600, 600, 700, 800, 800, ▲ 1000, 1200, 1200, 1400, 2400, 2500

The median is in the middle between 800 and 1000.

$\frac{800 + 1000}{2} = \frac{1800}{2} = 900$

24. (4) $223.24

$$\begin{array}{rr} 2400 \times .08987 = & 215.688 \\ 215.688 \times .035 = & +\ \ 7.54908 \\ \hline & 223.23708 \end{array}$$

This rounds to 223.24.

25. (2) 1.4% of the glasses are defective and the shipment should *not* be rejected.

$\frac{42}{3000} = \frac{N\%}{100\%}$

$N = \frac{42 \times 100}{3000} = 1.4$

Part II

26. (3) $70

$13.98 rounds to $14

5 × $14 = $70

27. (5) 2(40) + 2(15)

Perimeter of rectangle = 2(length) + 2(width)

2(40) + 2(15)

28. (3) 1:3

$\frac{27}{81} = \frac{1}{3}$

29. (3) B, D, C, A

B .09 kg = .090 kg (lightest)

D .19 kg = .190 kg

C .895 kg = .895 kg

A .9 kg = .900 kg (heaviest)

30. (2) $8^2 \times (2.5)^2$

8 × 8 checkerboard = 64 squares

2.5 × 2.5 = area of each square

$8^2 \times (2.5)^2$ = total area

31. 39

Volume of rectangular solid =

length × width × height =

3 × 2 × 6.5 = 39

32. (4) $7

48.60 × .15 = $7.29

33. (5) .07(48.60) + .15(48.60)

Choice (5) does not add the tip and the tax to the 48.60 subtotal.

34. (4) 56 million

280,000,000 × .20 = 56,000,000

35. (4) 2.828×10^8

$280{,}000{,}000 \times .01 = 2{,}800{,}000.00$
$280{,}000{,}000 + 2{,}800{,}000 = 282{,}800{,}000 =$
2.828×10^8

36. (2) $\frac{3}{2}$

Slope of a line $= \frac{y_2 - y_1}{x_2 - x_1} = \frac{6-0}{6-2} = \frac{6}{4} = \frac{3}{2}$

37. .(4, 3)

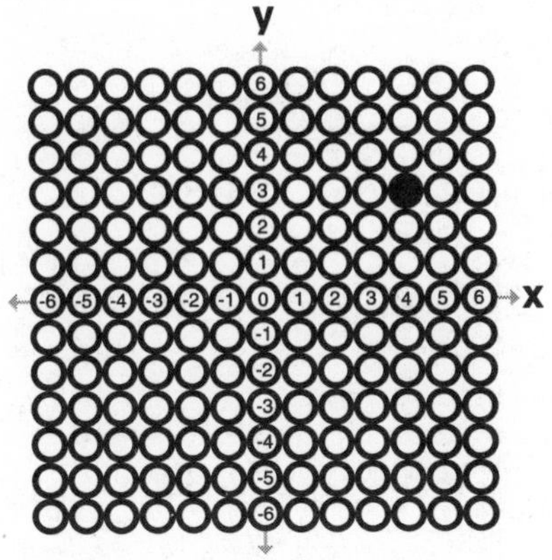

38. (3) 52%

$21 + 60 + 75 = 156$
$100 + 100 + 100 = 300$

$\frac{156}{300} = \frac{N\%}{100\%}$

$N = \frac{156 \times 100}{300} = 52$

39. (2) The larger the company, the less likely it is to respond.

Only 25% of the large companies responded.

40. (3) 157

Circumference of a circle = $\pi \times$ diameter =
$3.14 \times 50 = 157.00$

41. (4) 9812.5

Volume of a cylinder = $\pi \times \text{radius}^2 \times$ height =
$3.14 \times 25^2 \times 5 =$
$3.14 \times 625 \times 5 = 9812.5$ cu ft

42. (1) 2

$12a - 5 = 4a + 11$
$8a = 16$
$a = 2$

43. $\frac{1}{90}$

$\frac{4}{360} = \frac{1}{90}$

44. (1) $3x + 5$

45. (1) The larger the number is, the greater its square will be.

46. (2) $3(55) + 2x = 245$

3 hours at 55 mph + 2 hours at x mph = 245 miles

47. (4) 75

Triangle *PQR* is similar to triangle *NMR*.

$\frac{5}{8} = \frac{PQ}{120}$

$PQ = \frac{5 \times 120}{8} = 75$

48. (5) $x^2 = 6^2 + 6^2$

The sides of a right triangle are related by the Pythagorean relationship $a^2 + b^2 = c^2$.
So $6^2 + 6^2 = x^2$.

49. (4) $\frac{4}{5}$

$575 - 115 = 460$

$\frac{460}{575} = \frac{4}{5}$

50. (3) $12 \times 19 + .5 \times \pi \times 6^2$

Area of a rectangle = length $\times$ width = 12×19
area of a circle = $\pi \times \text{radius}^2 = \pi \times 6^2$
half of circle = $.5 \times \pi \times 6^2$
rectangle + half circle = $12 \times 19 + .5 \times \pi \times 6^2$

Evaluation Chart

After you use the answer key to check your answers to the Practice Test, use the evaluation chart to determine the mathematics skill and content areas in which you need more practice. Circle the number of each question you missed. Pay particular attention to areas where you missed half or more of the questions.

SKILL and CONTENT AREAS	ITEM NUMBER	REVIEW PAGES
Number Operations and Number Sense	Part I 1, 2, 4, 10, 24, 25	699–774, 793–808
	Part II 26, 29, 30, 32, 49	
Data Analysis, Statistics, and Probability	Part I 7, 8, 9, 13, 14, 15, 22, 23	785–792, 809–834
	Part II 28, 34, 35, 38, 39, 43, 45	
Measurement and Geometry	Part I 5, 11, 12, 17, 18, 19	873–921
	Part II 27, 31, 36, 37, 40, 41, 47, 48	
Algebra, Functions, and Patterns	Part I 3, 6, 16, 20, 21	835–872
	Part II 33, 42, 44, 46, 50	

Index

Q

R

S

T